Philosophy of Education

# BLACKWELL PHILOSOPHY ANTHOLOGIES

Each volume in this outstanding series provides an authoritative and comprehensive collection of the essential primary readings from philosophy's main fields of study. Designed to complement the *Blackwell Companions to Philosophy* series, each volume represents an unparalleled resource in its own right, and will provide the ideal platform for course use.

# Philosophy of Education
## An Anthology

Edited by

*Randall Curren*

**Blackwell**
Publishing

BLACKWELL PUBLISHING
350 Main Street, Malden, MA 02148-5020, USA
9600 Garsington Road, Oxford OX4 2DQ, UK
550 Swanston Street, Carlton, Victoria 3053, Australia

The right of Randall Curren to be identified as the Author of the Editorial Material in this Work has been asserted in accordance with the UK Copyright, Designs, and Patents Act 1988.

First published 2007 by Blackwell Publishing Ltd

11   2017

*Library of Congress Cataloging-in-Publication Data*

Philosophy of education : an anthology / edited by Randall Curren.
       p. cm. — (Blackwell philosophy anthologies)
   Includes bibliographical references and index.
   ISBN 978-1-4051-3022-6 (hardback : alk. paper)
   ISBN 978-1-4051-3023-3 (pbk. : alk. paper)
   1. Education—Philosophy. I. Curren, Randall R.

   LB17.P484 2006
   370′.1—dc22

                                                        2006019407

A catalogue record for this title is available from the British Library.

Set in 9/11pt Ehrhardt
by Graphicraft Limited, Hong Kong
Printed and bound in Singapore
by C.O.S. Printers Pte Ltd

The publisher's policy is to use permanent paper from mills that operate a sustainable forestry policy, and which has been manufactured from pulp processed using acid-free and elementary chlorine-free practices. Furthermore, the publisher ensures that the text paper and cover board used have met acceptable environmental accreditation standards.

For further information on
Blackwell Publishing, visit our website:
www.blackwellpublishing.com

# Contents

Contents

# Part V   Curriculum and the Content of Schooling

# Preface

The aim of this volume is to provide a representative sampling of the most philosophically compelling and essential readings on the fundamental philosophical questions of educational practice and policy. Its focus and organization are thus topical, rather than historical, theoretical, or person-centered. It attempts to provide a reasonably balanced and comprehensive introduction to the most basic and important topics in philosophy of education, but it does not attempt to provide a similarly comprehensive overview of the field's history, or contending theories, or influential figures. Many readers coming to philosophy of education for the first time will not have antecedent interests in historical texts, the theoretical movements that have shaped and colored educational thought, or 'who's who' in this field. Whether they are students of philosophy, students of education, philosophers, educators, or members of the general public who are interested in educational matters, they *will* expect to encounter thoughtful and thought-provoking explorations of basic aspects of education and current public debates about education. That is a reasonable expectation, and the readings presented here aim to satisfy that expectation and in so doing provide the best all-round introduction to the field available in one volume.

Those who require a more extensive understanding of philosophy of education and its history are encouraged to consult the editor's companion to this anthology, *A Companion to the Philosophy of Education*, in the Blackwell Companions reference series. Its 45 chapters provide a comprehensive survey of the field's history, contemporary approaches, topics pertaining to teaching and learning, the politics and ethics of schooling, and higher education. The two volumes have been designed to supplement each other and provide together the most comprehensive resource available for teaching and learning philosophy of education. Instructors who wish to combine readings in this anthology with related readings from the *Companion* will find there are many ways to do so.

The historical readings in this anthology are concentrated in the first two sections in Part I, and instructors will generally find that it is useful to begin with these. In other respects, the order of topics can easily be varied and various topics might be dropped to suit different purposes and course plans. Instructors who wish to supplement the historical readings in this volume with further readings in the classics will find some suggestions on how to do so in the "Note to Instructors on the Classics" on pp. xvi–xx.

This collection took shape under the guidance of Nick Bellorini and with many helpful suggestions from numerous anonymous readers and colleagues who reviewed and commented on working drafts of the table of contents. I'm grateful for their generous efforts. They include Jonathan Adler, Sigal Ben-Porath, Larry Blum, Jon Bradley, Harry Brighouse, Aine Donovan, Catherine Elgin, Paul Farber, Walter Feinberg, Charles Howell, Ingrid Lunt, Gary Matthews, Michael Matthews, David McCabe, Laura Purdy, Harvey Siegel, Jan Steutel, and Susan Verducci. I am especially grateful to Doret De Ruyter, Meira Levinson, and Emily Robertson for their very extensive and helpful suggestions. I would also like to acknowledge the assistance of George Martin and Bernie Todd Smith, my student interns through the summers of 2004 and 2005, who helped me research, obtain, and evaluate scores of potential selections. My students Cecelia Rios Aguilar, Elizabeth Hallmark, and Laura Waterstripe worked through the 2004 draft version of the contents with me and proved to be very astute readers and critics. All who use this volume will be very much in their debt. Finally, I must thank Kelvin Matthews, Gillian Kane, and Valery Rose for their fine work and good cheer in shepherding this work through production.

# Acknowledgements

The editor and publisher gratefully acknowledge the permission granted to reproduce the copyright material in this book:

1: Plato, *Republic*, Books VI and VII, pp. 1125–42, from *Plato: Complete Works*, ed. John M. Cooper, trans. Grube and Reeve (Indianapolis, IN: Hackett, 1997). Reprinted by permission of Hackett Publishing Company Inc. All rights reserved.

2: Plato, *Laws*, pp. 72–5; 643a–645c, from *Plato: The Laws*, ed. and trans. Trevor J. Saunders (London: Penguin Classics, 1970). © Trevor J. Saunders 1970. Reprinted with permission of Penguin Books UK Ltd.

3: Isocrates, *Antidosis*, pp. 249–61, from *Isocrates I*, trans. David Mirhady and Yun Lee Too (Austin, TX: University of Texas Press, 2000). © 2000. Reproduced by permission of the University of Texas Press.

4: John Locke, *Of the Conduct of the Understanding*, pp. 167–71, 172–82, from *John Locke: Some Thoughts Concerning Education and Of the Conduct of the Understanding*, ed. Ruth W. Grant and Nathan Tarcov (Indianapolis, IN: Hackett, 1996). Reprinted by permission of Hackett Publishing Company Inc. All rights reserved.

5: Jean-Jacques Rousseau, pp. 37–42, 481–2, from *"Emile," or On Education*, trans. Allan Bloom (New York: Basic Books/HarperCollins, 1979). Reprinted with permission of the Perseus Books Group.

6: John Dewey, "The Democratic Conception of Education," pp. 81, 83, 86–99, from *Democracy and Education* (New York: Free Press/Macmillan, 1966). © 1916, renewed 1944 by John Dewey. Reprinted with permission of Scribner, an imprint of Simon & Schuster Adult Publishing Group.

7: R. S. Peters, "Education as Initiation," pp. 87–111, from Reginald D. Achambault (ed.), *Philosophical Analysis and Education* (New York: The Humanities Press, 1965). Reprinted with permission of Taylor & Francis.

8: Paulo Freire, pp. 57–74, from *Pedagogy of the Oppressed*, trans. Myra Bergman Ramos (New York: The Seabury Press, 1970). © Paulo Freire 1970, 1993. Reprinted with the kind permission of Continuum USA and Penguin Books UK.

9: Aristotle, *Politics*, pp. 2116–17, 2121–7, 1334a12, from Jonathan Barnes (ed.), *The Complete Works of Aristotle*, trans. Benjamin Jowett (Princeton, NJ: Princeton University Press, 1984). © 1984 by the Jowett Copyright Trustees. Reprinted by permission of Princeton University Press.

10: Jean-Jacques Rousseau, Book III, pp. 184–6, 187–8, 189, 190–1, 192–3, 194–6, 488, from

*"Emile," or On Education*, trans. Allan Bloom (New York: Basic Books/HarperCollins, 1979). Reprinted with permission of the Perseus Books Group.

*11*: John Dewey, "Labor and Leisure," pp. 250–60, from *Democracy and Education* (New York: Free Press/Macmillan, 1966). © 1916, renewed in 1944 by John Dewey. Reprinted with permission of Scribner, an imprint of Simon & Schuster Adult Publishing Group.

*12*: Amartya Sen, chs. 2 and 12, pp. 38–43, 47–9, 292–7, 302, 351, from *Development as Freedom* (Oxford: Oxford University Press, 1999). Reprinted with permission of Oxford University Press.

*13*: Otfried Höffe, "The Liberal Studies in a Global World: A Self-examination," pp. 213–27, from *Theory and Research in Education* 1(2) (2003). © Sage Publications 2003. Reprinted with permission of Sage Publications Ltd.

*14*: Joel Feinberg, "The Child's Right to an Open Future," pp. 124–9, 131–8, 140–1, 142–53, *Freedom & Fulfillment: Philosophical Essays* (Princeton, NJ: Princeton University Press 1980). © 1992 Princeton University Press. Reprinted with permission of Princeton University Press.

*15*: Eamonn Callan, chs. 2 and 3, pp. 34–6, 39–41, 42, 60–9, from *Creating Citizens: Political Education and Liberal Democracy* (Oxford: Clarendon Press, 1997). Reprinted with permission of Oxford University Press.

*16*: Susan Moller Okin, "Mistresses of their Own Destiny: Group Rights, Gender, and Realistic Rights of Exit," pp. 205–30, from *Ethics* 112 (January 2002). © 2002 The University of Chicago. Reprinted by permission of the University of Chicago Press.

*17*: John Stuart Mill, pp. 103–7, from Elizabeth Rapaport (ed.), *On Liberty* (Indianapolis, IN: Hackett, 1978). Reprinted by permission of Hackett Publishing Company Inc. All rights reserved.

*18*: Amy Gutmann, "Democracy and Democratic Education," pp. 1–9, from *Studies in Philosophy and Education* 12 (1993). Reprinted with permission of Springer Verlag.

*19*: Charles L. Howell, "Justice, Inequality, and Home Schooling," pp. 1–9, from *Home School Researcher* 15(3) (2003). © National Home Education Research Institute 2003. Reprinted with permission of National Home Education Research Institute and the author.

*20*: Kenneth A. Strike, "Is Teaching a Profession: How Would We Know?," pp. 91–6, 99, 100–1, 102–4, 105–6, 108–9, 110–17, from *Journal of Personnel Evaluation in Education* 4 (1990). Reprinted with permission of Springer Verlag.

*21*: Hannah Arendt, "The Crisis in Education," pp. 176, 178–9, 180–4, 185–6, 188–90, 196, from *Between Past and Future* (London: Faber & Faber, 1961). © 1954, 1956, 1957, 1958, 1960, 1961 by Hannah Arendt. Reproduced by permission of Pollinger Limited and the proprietor.

*22*: Milton Friedman, "The Role of Government in Education," pp. 85–96, 97–8, from *Capitalism and Freedom* (Chicago, IL: University of Chicago Press, 1962). Reprinted by permission of the University of Chicago Press.

*23*: Colin Crouch, "The Case of Education," pp. 26–35, 50–7, from *Commercialization or Citizenship: Education Policy and the Future of Public Services* (London: Fabian Society, 2003). Reprinted with permission of the Fabian Society.

*24*: Harry Brighouse, "Channel One, the Anti-Commercial Principle, and the Discontinuous Ethos," pp. 528–49, from *Educational Policy* 19(3) (July 2005). Reprinted by permission of Sage Publications Inc.

*25*: Thomas F. Green, "The System in Motion," pp. 90–100, from *Predicting the Behavior of the Educational System*, reprint of original 1980 Syracuse University Press edition (Troy, NY: Educator's International Press, 1997). © 1980, 1997 Thomas F. Green. Reprinted with the kind permission of the author.

*26*: Amy Gutmann, "Distributing Primary Schooling," pp. 128–39, from *Democratic Education* (Princeton, NJ: Princeton University Press, 1987). © 1987 by Princeton University Press. 1999 paperback edition. Reprinted by permission of Princeton University Press.

*27*: Christopher Jencks, "Whom Must We Treat Equally for Educational Opportunity to be Equal?," pp. 518–33, from *Ethics* 98 (April 1988). Reprinted by permission of the University of Chicago Press.

*28*: K. Anthony Appiah, "Culture, Subculture, Multiculturalism: Educational Options," pp. 71–89, from Robert K. Fullinwider (ed.), *Public Education*

## Acknowledgements

*in a Multicultural Society* (Cambridge: Cambridge University Press, 1996). © 1996 Cambridge University Press. Reprinted by permission of the publisher and author.

*29*: Lawrence Blum, "The Promise of Racial Integration in a Multicultural Age," pp. 383–403, 408–11, 412–21, 423–4, from Stephen Macedo and Yael Tamir (eds.), *Nomos XLIII: Moral and Political Education* (New York: New York University Press, 2002). Reprinted by permission of the publisher.

*30*: Meira Levinson and Sanford Levinson, "'Getting Religion': Religion, Diversity, and Community in Public and Private Schools," pp. 110–18, 123–4, 305–6, from Alan Wolfe (ed.), *School Choice: The Moral Debate* (Princeton, NJ: Princeton University Press, 2003). © 2003 Princeton University Press. Reprinted with permission of Princeton University Press.

*31*: G. E. Zuriff, "The Myths of Learning Disabilities," pp. 395–405, from *Public Affairs Quarterly* 10(4) (October 1996). Reprinted with permission of Public Affairs Quarterly.

*32*: Lorella Terzi, "A Capability Perspective on Impairment, Disability, and Special Needs," pp. 197–223, from *Theory and Research in Education* 3(2) (2005). © Sage Publications 2005. Reprinted with permission of Sage Publications Ltd.

*33*: Laura Purdy, "Educating Gifted Children," pp. 192–9, from Randall Curren (ed.), *Philosophy of Education 1999* (Urbana, IL: Philosophy of Education Society, 2000).

*34*: Joel Kupperman, "Perfectionism and Educational Policy," pp. 111–19, from *Public Affairs Quarterly* 1 (January 1987). Reprinted with permission of Public Affairs Quarterly.

*35*: Philip W. Jackson, "Real Teaching," pp. 75–8, 79–83, 84, 86–97, from *The Practice of Teaching* (New York: Teachers College Press, 1986). © 1986 by Teachers College, Columbia University. All rights reserved. Reprinted with permission of the publisher.

*36*: Israel Scheffler, "Philosophies-of and the Curriculum," pp. 212–14, 214–18, from James F. Doyle (ed.), *Educational Judgments: Papers in Philosophy of Education* (London: Routledge & Kegan Paul, 1973). © Israel Scheffler. Reprinted with the kind permission of the author.

*37*: David T. Hansen, "Understanding Students," pp. 171–85, from *Journal of Curriculum and Supervision* 14(2) (Winter 1999). Reproduced by permission of ASCD (Association for Supervision and Curriculum Development), Alexandria.

*38*: Terence H. McLaughlin, "Beyond the Reflective Teacher," pp. 9–18, 19–25, from *Educational Philosophy and Theory* 31(1) (1999). Reprinted by permission of Blackwell Publishing Ltd and the author.

*39*: John Dewey, "Social Control," pp. 51–60, from *Experience and Education* (New York: Touchstone, 1997). © 1938 by Kappa Delta Pi. Reprinted with the kind permission of Kappa Delta Pi, International Honor Society in Education.

*40*: Nel Noddings, "Moral Education," pp. 175–82, 210–11, from *Caring: A Feminine Approach to Ethics and Moral Education* (Berkeley, CA: University of California Press, 1984). © 2003 The Regents of the University of California. Permission via Copyright Clearance Center.

*41*: Elizabeth Chamberlain and Barbara Houston, "School Sexual Harassment Policies: The Need for Both Justice and Care," pp. 146–66, from Michael Katz, Nel Noddings and Kenneth A. Strike (eds.), *Justice and Caring: The Search for Common Ground in Education* (New York: Teachers College Press, 1999). © 1999 by Teachers College, Columbia University. All rights reserved. Reprinted with permission of the publisher.

*42*: Jean-Jacques Rousseau, Books II and III, pp. 125, 132–3, 140–1, 157–8, 167, 168–70, 171, 172–7, from *"Emile," or On Education*, trans. Allan Bloom (New York: Basic Books/HarperCollins, 1979). Reprinted by permission of the Perseus Books Group.

*43*: D. C. Phillips, "The Good, the Bad, and the Ugly: The Many Faces of Constructivism," pp. 5–12, from *Educational Researcher* 24(7) (1995). © 1995 by the American Educational Research Association. Reproduced with permission of the publisher.

*44*: Richard E. Grandy, "Constructivisms and Objectivity: Disentangling Metaphysics from Pedagogy," pp. 113–23, from Michael R. Matthews (ed.), *Constructivism in Science Education* (Dordrecht: Kluwer Academic Publishers, 1998). © 1998 Kluwer Academic Publishers. Reprinted with permission of Springer Verlag.

*45*: Catherine Z. Elgin, "Education and the Advancement of Understanding," pp. 131–40, from David Steiner (ed.), *Proceedings of the 20th World Congress of Philosophy*, vol. 3 (Charlottesville, VA: Philosophy Documentation Center, 1999). Reprinted with permission of the publisher.

*46*: John Locke, *Some Thoughts Concerning Education*, section 81, p. 58, from Ruth W. Grant and Nathan Tarcov (eds.), *"Some Thoughts Concerning Education" and "Of the Conduct of the Understanding"* (Indianapolis, IN: Hackett, 1996). Reprinted with permission of Hackett Publishing Company Inc. All rights reserved.

*47*: Jean-Jacques Rousseau, pp. 89–91, from *"Emile," or On Education*, trans. Allan Bloom (New York: Basic Books/HarperCollins, 1979), Book II. Reprinted with permission of the Perseus Books Group.

*48*: Matthew Lipman, "Education for Critical Thinking," pp. 210–15, 218–30, from *Thinking in Education*, 2nd edn. (Cambridge: Cambridge University Press, 2003). © 2003 Matthew Lipman, published by Cambridge University Press. Reprinted with permission of the publisher and the author.

*49*: Harvey Siegel, "The Reasons Conception," pp. 32–47, 149–54, from *Educating Reason* (New York: Routledge, 1988). © 1988 Harvey Siegel. Reprinted with the kind permission of the author.

*50*: Emily Robertson, "The Value of Reason: Why Not a Sardine Can Opener?," pp. 1–14, from Randall Curren (ed.), *Philosophy of Education 1999* (Urbana, IL: Philosophy of Education Society, 2000). © 2000 Philosophy of Education Society.

*51*: Robert Paul Wolff, "A Discourse on Grading," pp. 58–68, from *The Ideal of the University* (Boston, MA: Beacon Press, 1969). © 1969 Robert Paul Wolff.

*52*: Randall Curren, "Coercion and the Ethics of Grading and Testing," pp. 425–41, from *Educational Theory* 45(4) (Fall 1995). © 1995 Board of Trustees, University of Illinois. Reprinted with permission of Blackwell Publishing Ltd.

*53*: Stephen P. Norris, Jacqueline P. Leighton, and Linda M. Phillips, "What is at Stake in Knowing the Content and Capabilities of Children's Minds? A Case for Basing High Stakes Tests on Cognitive Models," pp. 283–307, from *Theory and Research in Education* 2(3) (2004). © 2004 Sage Publications. Reprinted by permission of Sage Publications Ltd.

*54*: Robert K. Fullinwider, "Moral Conventions and Moral Lessons," pp. 321–38, from *Social Theory and Practice* 15(3) (Fall 1989). © 1989 *Social Theory and Practice*. Reprinted with permission of *Social Theory and Practice*.

*55*: Randall Curren, pp. 201–12, 253–4, from *Aristotle on the Necessity of Public Education* (Lanham, MD: Rowman & Littlefield, 2000). © 2000 Rowman & Littlefield Publishers, Inc. Reprinted with permission of Rowman & Littlefield Publishing Corporation.

*56*: J. David Velleman, "Motivation by Ideal," pp. 90–2, 93–103, from *Philosophical Explorations* V(2) (May 2002). Reprinted with permission of Taylor & Francis; www.tandf.co.uk.

*57*: Harry Brighouse, "Should We Teach Patriotic History?," pp. 157–75, from Kevin McDonough and Walter Feinberg (eds.), *Education and Citizenship in Liberal-Democratic Societies* (Oxford: Oxford University Press, 2003). © 2003 Harry Brighouse. Reprinted with the kind permission of the author.

*58*: Robert T. Pennock, "Should Creationism be Taught in the Public Schools?," pp. 111–18, 119–33, from *Science & Education* 11 (2002). © 2002 Kluwer Academic Publishers. Reprinted with permission of Springer Verlag.

*59*: Michael J. Reiss, "Conflicting Philosophies of School Sex Education," pp. 371–82, from *Journal of Moral Education* 24(4) (1995). © 1995 The Norham Foundation. Reprinted with permission of Taylor & Francis and the author.

*60*: Maxine Greene, "The Artistic–Aesthetic Curriculum," pp. 177–85, 227–30, from *Variations on a Blue Guitar* (New York: Teachers College Press, 2001). © 2001 Teachers College, Columbia University. All rights reserved. Reprinted with permission of the publisher.

Every effort has been made to trace copyright holders and to obtain their permission for the use of copyright material. The publisher apologizes for any errors or omissions in the above list and would be grateful if notified of any corrections that should be incorporated in future reprints or editions of this book.

# A Note to Instructors on the Classics

The historical selections included in this anthology comprise only about twenty percent of the whole, but they have been carefully chosen to provide a substantial introduction to the most important figures – Plato, Rousseau, and Dewey – and works from secondary figures – Isocrates, Aristotle, Locke, and Mill – that are important points of reference for contemporary debates. Where English translations are required, widely available translations of the highest quality have been used. Instructors who prefer to supplement the selections in this anthology with further readings in the classics should have no difficulty finding compatible and affordable full-text editions. Some suggestions follow for those who would like to know more about the content which various selections might add to their courses.

The Plato selections in this anthology are drawn from *Plato: Complete Works*, edited by John Cooper (Cooper, 1997). Many of the excellent translations in this volume are also available separately in inexpensive paper-bound editions, including those most likely to be used in philosophy of education courses:

Plato's brief dialogues *Apology* and *Crito* might be used in their entirety to introduce Socrates, his interesting denial that he is a teacher, and his commitments to respecting the rational element in human nature and honoring the results of careful, principled reasoning. Socrates denies that he has the

knowledge of virtue that a true teacher of it would need to have, and a third brief dialogue, *Euthyphro*, helps make it clear that he thinks that it is impious to claim such (god-like) knowledge, yet pious or respectful of what is divine to cultivate the thinking and reasoning part of ourselves and others. These three dialogues are available together in a slim volume, *The Trial and Death of Socrates* (Plato, 2001). For further background, see David Reeve's chapter "The Socratic Movement" in the *Companion to the Philosophy of Education* (Curren, 2006), and chapter 1 of Curren (2000).

The brief but complex dialogue *Meno* provides another interesting and much used starting-point for discussing the nature of teaching. It addresses the question of whether virtue can be taught, but its interest lies even more in its opening lessons about (Socratic) inquiry into the nature of a thing, its memorable illustration of how to teach geometry through questioning (an apparently different form of Socratic questioning or teaching), its "paradox of inquiry" and mysterious suggestion that all learning may be a form of recollection, and its closing repudiation of Socrates' own doctrine that virtue is a form of knowledge. The first part of the dialogue (70–80c) appears to depict the historical Socrates, and the second part (80d–100) seems to confront the limitations of Socratic inquiry and the awkward triad of propositions: (1) Socrates denied he had knowledge of virtue; (2) Socrates asserted that having knowledge of virtue is essential to possessing virtue; (3) Socrates was in fact virtuous. This dialogue is available separately (Plato, 1980) or with the *Euthyphro, Apology,* and *Crito* (Plato, 2002).

The dialogue *Protagoras* (Plato, 1992a) poses the same general question as *Meno,* and it too seems to be an exercise in attempting to overcome an important limitation of Socratic thought, namely its neglect of the non-rational dimension of virtue or human goodness. The bulk of the dialogue is a lengthy debate between Socrates and the sophist Protagoras and, although Socrates is portrayed as winning the debate, it is clear that Plato is moving toward conceptions of virtue and moral education that combine elements of the views of both. There is some merit in allowing students to read the vivid depiction of moral education in the "Great Speech" of Protagoras (317e–328d), even if it is not possible to read the entire dialogue.

Included in this anthology are selections from Plato's *Republic* and *Laws,* his two great works of moral, political, and educational philosophy. Although the latter is less widely read and lacks the abundant literary brilliance of the former, its theory of education is developed in greater detail and framed in a way that reveals more about the way Plato thinks the citizens of actual cities should be educated and governed. The *Republic* is a more captivating work, but also more easily misread. Contrary to the expectations of many readers, it says little about how the ideal society it imagines would be governed, let alone how an actual society would be governed.

Our selection from the *Republic* (no. 1) includes the end of Book VI and the first half of Book VII (504–525c), encompassing the account of the nature of knowledge and its highest object, the Form of the Good; the Line; the Cave and the idea that the fundamental task of education is to "turn the *psyche,*" or the student's *desire,* toward the love and pursuit of wisdom; philosopher kings and queens and their education; higher education as a pursuit of understanding facilitated by the abstract sciences. Those who want to read more of the *Republic,* but not the bulk of it, might continue on in Book VII to section 535 for the full account of the curriculum of higher learning. For the account of the education that would precede this higher learning, Books II–IV could be added. These pose, and answer in the affirmative, the question of whether it is inherently advantageous to be a just or virtuous person. In developing and defending this answer, Plato

describes a social division of labor, a parallel psychic division of labor, and the kind of education needed to establish virtue and the corresponding psychic harmony essential to happiness. Book V concerns the importance of civic unity and stability (the ancient Greek world being one in which internal conflict and constitutional instability were rampant), and the idea that raising children in common would promote unity and stability. This might be read as background to contemporary debates about the competing claims of parents and public authorities to control the aspects of children's schooling that matter to civic harmony. Book X (595–608b) returns to the topic of poetry, discussed earlier in Books II and III in connection with the supervision of storytellers and the kinds of stories children should and should not hear. Homer was known as "The Educator of the Greeks," and Plato was concerned that the curriculum this implies did not consistently portray virtue as inherently advantageous and the gods as good (377d ff.). Book X moves beyond the matter of regulating culture and the curriculum, and argues that art and narrative are severely limited in their capacity to educate. This closing book of the *Republic* has given rise to much debate through the ages, and might be read in connection with Maxine Greene's lecture "The Artistic–Aesthetic Curriculum" (no. 60), and the chapters on "Romanticism" and "Aesthetics and the Educative Powers of Art" in the *Companion* (Curren, 2006).

Our selection from Book I of the *Laws* (no. 2) is a brief but philosophically rich description of the nature of education. It appears in the midst of a lengthy discussion of the alleged educational value of drinking parties (supervised, of course), the role of practice in the development of the virtues, and the fundamental educational aims of a just society. Books I and II could be read in their entirety, or with some deletions, for a better understanding of all this. For the account of constitutional rule, legislation imposed through rational, informed, and voluntary compliance, and the relationships between law and education, one could continue with the following excerpts: Book III: 698e–693b (competing titles to authority); Book IV, 712c to the end (the constitution and the role of education in a just rule of law); Book V, up to 734c (the moral foundations of law and education); Book VI, 765d–66b (the Minister of Education); Book VII, 793b–98e, 804d–5b, 810c–12a (where the *Laws* itself – a work of *philosophy* – is identified as the model for what children should read), Book IX up to 854a, 857c (philosophical legislation justified), 859a, and 861d–4c. For an overview of the educational ideas in the *Laws* and additional references, see chapter 2 of Curren, (2000).

Those who wish to pursue further study in the educational thought and practice of Isocrates will find the full text of *Antidosis*, which is excerpted here (no. 3), in David Mirhady and Yun Lee Too's *Isocrates I* (Mirhady and Too, 2000). This volume also contains Isocrates' speech *Against the Sophist*, in which he critiques his pedagogical rivals. A second volume, *Isocrates II* (Papillon, 2004), contains a third important statement of Isocrates' educational ideas, entitled *Panathenaicus*. Both volumes contain informative introductions and further references.

The educational thought of Aristotle is represented by a selection (no. 9) from his *Politics*, which includes a brief excerpt from Book VII and most of Book VIII, and less directly by a selection on the moral and intellectual virtues (no. 55), which includes exegesis of material from Books II and VI of Aristotle's *Nicomachean Ethics*. The translation of the *Politics* is taken from volume 2 of *The Complete Works of Aristotle*, edited by Jonathan Barnes (Barnes, 1984), but is also available in an inexpensive paper bound edition (Aristotle, 1996). The whole of Books VII and VIII might be used, to place the extracts from them within Aristotle's description of the best possible society, which is not an ideal city governed by a "god among men" (such as the city of Plato's *Republic*), but a "second best city" (an attempt to improve upon the city of Plato's *Laws*). However, it is difficult to acquire much understanding of Aristotle's political theory and his conception of the political dimensions of education – its role as the primary tool of statesmanship – without reading a good deal more. Perhaps most important would be: Book I, 1–2 (the nature of a political community and the threefold sense in which it is natural for human beings to live in cities); Book II, 2–4 (a critique of the common rearing of children in the *Republic*); Book III, 6–18 (the theory of constitutions, legitimate and illegitimate; the supremacy of law; the importance of a large middle class and a "mixed" constitution in which citizens of all classes have constitutional means to protect their interests); Book IV, 1 (the best constitution for most states). Aristotle describes his *Politics* and *Nicomachean Ethics* as both parts of "political science," and the two are ideally read together and in full. The most salient selections from the latter (*NE*) would be: Book II, 1–6 and 9 (moral virtue and how it is acquired); Book VI, 1–2, 5–8, and 11–13 (intellectual virtue,

practical wisdom, the unity of the virtues); Book V, 1–2 (the educative aspect of law, justice and sharing in rule); Books VIII–IX (friendship, friendship and justice, political friendship); Book X, 6–8 (the happiest and second happiest kinds of lives); Book X, 9 (legislation and how people become good, or why you need to understand legislative science just to run a household – an advertisement for his lectures on politics to follow). The translation of the *Nicomachean Ethics* appearing in the *Complete Works* is recommended and is available separately in updated form (Aristotle, 1998). For more on Aristotle's philosophy of education, see Curren (2000) and chapter 1 of the *Companion*.

Two selections from the educational writings of John Locke are included here. One (no. 46) is a brief section on reasoning with children, drawn from *Some Thoughts Concerning Education* (1693), and the other (no. 4) is a more substantial extract from *Of the Conduct of the Understanding* (1706). Both were written as practical guides, the one concerning the upbringing and home schooling of an English gentleman, and the other concerning the means by which such a gentleman may pursue a kind of higher learning for liberty. They are reprinted together in an edition edited by Ruth Grant and Nathan Tarcov (Locke, 1996), and are explained at some length by the latter in the "Enlightenment Liberalism" chapter of the *Companion*. The usefulness of adding further sections from the *Thoughts* would be in developing any or all of four themes: (1) Locke's rejection of coercive and punitive methods; (2) the views he and Rousseau hold in common, such as the idea that spoiling children corrupts their judgment and undermines their freedom; (3) the *practical* thrust of his educational thought, which sets it (and Enlightenment educational models generally) apart from the Renaissance humanism that preceded it and the German Romanticism that followed it (see "Humanism" and "Romanticism" in the *Companion*); (4) Locke's endorsement of home schooling, and its rejection by advocates of democratic or common schooling (see Pangle and Pangle, 1993).

Apart from possible further selections from either or both of the *Thoughts* and *Conduct*, the most useful supplement to the readings included here would be an introduction to Locke's political philosophy, which endorses a natural right of self-governance, popular sovereignty exercised through a social contract, and rights of religious liberty and rebellion. A good choice for a short selection would be chapter 7 of Locke's *Second Treatise of Government*

(Locke, 1980), entitled "Of Paternal Power." The purpose of this chapter is to refute a theory of the authority of kings that interprets it as analogous to the authority of fathers over children, but it can be read for its account of parental educational duties and the freedom that must be accorded all persons as they grow up and develop a mature capacity for rational judgment. Read with this purpose in mind, it is particularly relevant to debates concerning educational authority and the educational responsibilities of adults to children, and it is sufficient to read sections 54–9, 63–5, 67, and 69. Another good choice would be to read Locke's brief *Letter Concerning Toleration* (Locke, 1983), which remains a powerful statement of the grounds for religious and civil liberties. It would provide useful background for contemporary debates concerning schooling, religion, culture, and the right to "exit" or make a different life for oneself.

Although the *Conduct* was written as a kind of practical appendix to Locke's monumental *Essay Concerning Human Understanding* (Locke, 1975), the details of the latter are not essential to understanding the former. What matters is his general rejection of the doctrine of innate ideas (*Essay*, Book I), his general thesis that all ideas are derived from experience (Book II), and his conception of knowledge as an intuition (a clear and distinct mental perception) of a "relation of ideas" or relationship between one idea and another (Book IV). It is this conception of knowledge that is apt to confuse readers who come to Locke's *Conduct* having been taught that Locke is an *empiricist*, whereas Descartes was something altogether different, namely a *rationalist*. What distinguishes the two is their *theories of ideas*, not their conception of the nature and criterion of *knowledge*, which is the same (and indistinguishable from Rousseau's). For an account of the educational influence of Locke's empiricist theory of ideas, see chapter 16, "Theories of Teaching and Learning," in the *Companion*.

Four selections from Rousseau's great educational work *Emile* (1762) are included in this anthology: the opening (no. 5); a selection from Book III on the practical arts and their value, which is closely tied to his theory of the professions, the inversion of value in society, and the origins of inequality (no. 10); a selection from Books II and III on curiosity, the exercise of the senses and reason, learning about the world and morals through inquiry, and the perils of pride or comparative self-love (no. 42); and a brief selection from Book II on why Locke

is (allegedly) wrong to recommend reasoning with children (no. 47). *Emile* is a massive and highly redundant work, so extensive editing is required to produce selections that do not unnecessarily tax the reader. I have relied on the unabridged translation of Allan Bloom (Rousseau, 1979) and taken pains to preserve more of the philosophical content than one typically finds in selections from *Emile* prepared for students.

In order to follow the thread of Rousseau's developmental ideas and get a fuller picture of his debts to Stoicism, one would need to add the following pages from Books I and II: pp. 47–54, 59, 62–3, 65–9, 77–100, 107–8 (using the page numbers in Rousseau, 1979). There is an especially important illustration of natural moral learning at p. 98. Those who wish to pursue at greater length the (Stoic) idea, that what is moral or in accordance with nature can be learned through the study of nature itself, will want to consider using readings from the "confession of faith" in Book IV, using at least some of pp. 272–86, 295–6, 305–7, and 313–14. The arguments in this section aim to reconcile faith and reason by using the argument from design and other arguments to establish the basic tenets of *natural religion*, a widely theorized common core of Christianity that could be intuitively known and so needn't be taught through an official state religion (see the Editor's Prologue to chapter 6 of the *Companion*). The discovery of natural religion for oneself is intended as the culmination of a natural education, and there are important political ramifications of this evident in Rousseau's work *On the Social Contract* (Rousseau, 1988) – see, especially, Book II, chapter 7 ("On the Legislator") and Book IV, chapter 8 ("On Civil Religion"). Rousseau describes *Emile* and *On the Social Contract* as closely related works, and they are both centrally concerned with the difficulties inherent in creating societies of citizens who are both free and civic-minded. Another of Rousseau's statements on civic education, which is often neglected, is chapter 4 ("Education") of *The Government of Poland* (Rousseau, 1985). Finally, many instructors will want to add a substantial selection from Book V of *Emile*, on the very different education of Sophie, or women, which Rousseau envisions.

For background, exposition, and analysis of Rousseau's educational theory, see Patrick Riley's contribution to chapter 7 of the *Companion*, and chapters 9 (the education of men, women, and citizens) and 10 (on the education of Sophie) of his *Cambridge Companion to Rousseau* (Riley, 2001).

Our brief selection from the works of John Stuart Mill (no. 17) is drawn from *On Liberty* (Mill, 1978). Those who are interested in giving their students a more expansive grounding in classical liberalism, or Mill's vision of social progress through free experimentation in ways of living, might consider using further material from *On Liberty*. For background, references, and further ideas, see Wendy Donner's essay on Mill's philosophy of education in chapter 6 of the *Companion*.

Most of two key chapters from John Dewey's book *Democracy and Education* (1916) are included in this collection (nos. 6 and 11). Instructors familiar with this work may want to supplement these with more from the same book, but many will find it more satisfactory to have their students read all of Dewey's compact and very accessible book *Experience and Education* (published 1938; Dewey, 1997), from which our third selection from his works (no. 39) is drawn. The latter is the only concise, comprehensive statement of Dewey's educational philosophy, and it provides a useful retrospective assessment of the progressive education movement Dewey did so much to inspire. Another option would be to use either or both of two short early works by Dewey, *The School and Society* (1899) and *The Child and the Curriculum* (1902), which are reprinted together in Jackson (1991). For an overview of Dewey's educational philosophy and further references, see chapter 7 of the *Companion*.

Further background and starting points for exploring and teaching the classics of philosophy of education may be found in the *Companion*, as well as in Curren (1998) and Rorty (1998).

## References

Aristotle 1996: *The Politics and the Constitution of Athens*, trans. B. Jowett and J. Barnes (Cambridge: Cambridge University Press).

Aristotle 1998: *The Nicomachean Ethics*, trans. D. Ross, J. L. Ackrill, and J. O. Urmson (Oxford: Oxford University Press).

Barnes, J. (ed.) 1984: *The Complete Works of Aristotle* (Princeton, NJ: Princeton University Press).

Cooper, J. (ed.) 1997: *Plato: Complete Works* (Indianapolis, IN: Hackett).

Curren, R. 1998: "Education, History of Philosophy of," *Routledge Encyclopedia of Philosophy*, ed. E. Craig (London: Routledge), vol. 3, pp. 222–31.

Curren, R. 2000: *Aristotle on the Necessity of Public Education* (Lanham, MD: Rowman & Littlefield).

Curren, R. (ed.) 2006: *A Companion to the Philosophy of Education* (Oxford: Blackwell).

Dewey, J. 1916: *Democracy and Education* (New York: The Free Press).

Dewey, J. 1997: *Experience and Education* (New York: Touchstone).

Jackson, P. (ed.) 1991: *The School and Society and the Child and the Curriculum* (Chicago, IL: University of Chicago Press).

Locke, J. 1975: *An Essay Concerning Human Understanding* (Oxford: Clarendon Press).

Locke, J. 1980: *Second Treatise of Government* (Indianapolis, IN: Hackett).

Locke, J. 1983: *A Letter Concerning Toleration* (Indianapolis, IN: Hackett).

Locke, J. 1996: *Some Thoughts Concerning Education and Of the Conduct of the Understanding* (Indianapolis, IN: Hackett).

Mill, J. S. 1978: *On Liberty* (Indianapolis, IN: Hackett).

Mirhady, D. and Y. L. Too. 2000: *Isocrates I* (Austin: University of Texas Press).

Pangle, L. S. and T. L. Pangle. 1993: *The Learning of Liberty* (Lawrence: University Press of Kansas).

Papillon, T. 2004: *Isocrates II* (Austin, TX: University of Texas Press).

Plato 1975: *Laws*, trans. T. Saunders (London: Penguin).

Plato 1980: *Meno*, 2nd edn., trans. G. M. A. Grube (Indianapolis, IN: Hackett).

Plato 1992a: *Protagoras*, trans. S. Lombardo and K. Bell (Indianapolis, IN: Hackett).

Plato 1992b: *Republic*, 2nd edn., trans. G. M. A. Grube and C. D. C. Reeve (Indianapolis, IN: Hackett).

Plato 2001: *The Trial and Death of Socrates*, 3rd edn., trans. G. M. A. Grube (Indianapolis, IN: Hackett).

Plato 2002: *Five Dialogues*, 2nd edn., trans. G. M. A. Grube (Indianapolis, IN: Hackett).

Riley, P. 2001: *The Cambridge Companion to Rousseau* (Cambridge: Cambridge University Press).

Rorty, A. 1998: *Philosophers on Education: New Historical Perspectives* (London: Routledge).

Rousseau, J.-J. 1979: *"Emile," or On Education*, trans. A. Bloom (New York: Basic Books).

Rousseau, J.-J. 1985: *The Government of Poland*, trans. W. Kendall (Indianapolis, IN: Hackett).

Rousseau, J.-J. 1988: *On the Social Contract*, trans. D. A. Cress (Indianapolis, IN: Hackett).

# General Introduction

Any book that presumes to present a whole field of study to an audience must begin from some conception of the nature, boundaries, and organization of that field. Without this, it would be greatly impaired in communicating the field's object and purpose, its central questions, and its means of addressing those questions. What, then, is philosophy of education? What is its object of investigation? What purposes does it bring to its investigations? We could answer that its object of study is education in all of its disparate manifestations, and that its purposes are to both understand and guide education. This would be reasonable, as far as it goes, but it would not yet *define* philosophy of education, because it would not distinguish it from educational studies generally. The boundaries of the two fields are not the same. Although philosophy of education seems to fall within educational studies, it is distinguishable from the rest of educational studies by the fact that it also falls within philosophy.

What does it mean, then, for philosophy of education to be the kind of study of education that is *philosophical*?

One answer implicit in the field's history is that work in philosophy of education is philosophical because it develops or applies *a philosophy of education*, or system of "beliefs about life and schooling" (Broudy, 1979, p. 3). This was the dominant view during the early and mid-twentieth century, when philosophy of education was often presented as a field of contending philosophies such as *pragmatism*, *realism*, and *existentialism* (Brubacher, 1942; Henry, 1955), and it has not entirely disappeared. It is not a good answer to our question about what makes philosophy of education philosophical, however, because there is a lot of work in philosophy of education that doesn't develop or rely on a general philosophy of education. The development or application of a philosophy of education might be a *sufficient condition* for a piece of work on education to be philosophical, but it is not a *necessary condition*.

Another reason this answer fails to tell us what makes work in philosophy of education philosophical is that it does not tell us what makes *a philosophy of education* philosophical. We are looking for the boundary of a part of educational studies, the philosophical part, and the answer given is more or less that the philosophical part is the one consisting of philosophies. This is inaccurate, as we have just seen, but it is also unhelpfully circular, because it doesn't tell us enough about what a philosophy of education *is*.

A third consideration, which further undermines this answer, is that the idea of a systematic philosophy of education became more problematic in the course of the twentieth century as nonphilosophical forms of educational research became better established. Philosophy can not claim to create through its own methods all that is useful in understanding and guiding education, so even when it takes the lead in attempting to synthesize a comprehensive theory or philosophy of education, it must do so with vigilant regard to its own limitations and the need to draw on the results of other forms of research and analysis. It is most plausible to think of philosophy of education not as the whole of educational theory, but as contributing in various ways to an enterprise that must ultimately be a joint product of the different kinds of research that would be necessary to fully understand and adequately guide educational practices (Hirst, 1983). This tells us something important about philosophy of education, but not what we wanted to know. Conceiving of the field as engaged in diverse contributions to educational theory would provide us with one possible basis for organizing it or categorizing the different kinds of work belonging to philosophy of education (Curren, 1998), but it does not in itself tell us what makes those kinds of work philosophical.

Another possible answer might be that work on education must use, apply, or discuss the work of leading philosophers in order to qualify as philosophical. However, although references to philosophers noted for their work in philosophy at large or in *other* sub-fields of philosophy do abound in philosophy of education, this isn't a necessary requirement. Neither is it necessary to adopt the standpoint and analytical resources of any of those other sub-fields of philosophy, such as ethics, epistemology, or philosophy of science (cf. Soltis, 1981). Applying other people's theories or analyses is not *necessary* to making one's own work philosophical. It can be helpful – sometimes marvelously so – but it's not essential to doing philosophical work. Both of these answers are like the first in also being unhelpful, because they fail to engage the basic question at issue of what distinguishes philosophical investigations from other kinds of investigations.

So what *is* it that makes philosophy of education *philosophical*? We can answer this in an abstract way through a description of the general character of the questions posed and the general character of the methods used to address those questions. If the purposes of philosophy of education are to *understand* and *guide* education, as I've suggested, then its questions are both theoretical and practical, and it can be said to engage in analysis that is sometimes descriptive, sometimes normative or action-guiding, and sometimes both. This is still too general, but

we can make it less so by adding that philosophical questions and analyses lie beyond the reach of scientific methods, and aim for the most reasonable and illuminating conclusions achievable without such methods. They get below the surface of things, often by struggling with puzzles that arise from common beliefs and practices, and they aim to produce a satisfyingly deep and general account that makes sense of what was initially puzzling, troubling, or simply taken for granted. Applied to practices, the point is often not simply to arrive at a better and deeper understanding, but also to determine what is and is not justified.

This characterization of philosophical inquiry might be refined, but there is admittedly no guarantee that doing so would allow us to identify a sharp dividing line between what is philosophical and what is not. There may not be any sharp dividing line. A great deal of good philosophical work is not *conspicuously* philosophical, especially in areas of practical philosophy where the questions addressed are specific to narrowly defined contexts. Questions such as "What is knowledge?," "What is education?," and "What is law?" are conspicuously philosophical, because they are highly general and abstract, and they do not fall neatly within the province of any scientific methods of investigation. The question "What is the meaning of a proper name?" is less general, but still obviously philosophical. More specific still is the question "What is the meaning of a grade?" or "What kind of judgment does a grade express?" Although grades are much less pervasive and basic than proper names, they are still rather pervasive (within certain historical, cultural, and institutional limits), and the question of what they mean is a rather basic question about them. What grades mean is also something of a mystery, and it is a mystery one would need to solve in order to explain and justify some aspects of how grades are assigned. The tangle of semantic and ethical matters that comes into view makes the question "What is the meaning of a grade?" a significantly philosophical one, though less conspicuously philosophical than the very abstract questions with which we began. Much the same is true of questions about the proper role of student evaluation in schools, the scope of educators' professional authority, and whether knowledge or understanding is the more appropriate goal for science education. They, too, can be answered more or less philosophically, or in ways that are more or less sensitive to the conceptual and normative complexities that become evident as soon as one probes a bit below the surface. These latter sorts of questions demand knowledge and attention to the details of specific institutional practices and their contexts, and in grappling with such questions philosophy of education shades into educational theory and policy studies, just as political philosophy shades into political theory, and philosophy of law shades into legal theory. There are likely to be deep normative and conceptual questions in the vicinity, but the context and facts will matter a great deal as well, and the degree and form of attention to each in a given piece of work will be a complex function of purpose, context, audience, and personal interest and style. An effective analysis will be sensitive to the relevant facts and carefully reasoned, but its philosophical sophistication may be revealed, not by what it says, but by how artfully it steers clear of complexity that is not required by the task at hand. Philosophical essays that "finesse" the deeper and more intractable issues in this way may be unusually successful in defending substantial conclusions about educational practice or policy – about what should be done – while not appearing very philosophical at all.

An important implication of this brief exploration of what makes philosophy of education philosophical is that learning how to think and write philosophically about education is very much a matter of learning how to analyze things effectively for yourself, borrowing from others or not, as you see fit, in trying to make sense of the topic or problem you are struggling with. To make progress with this you need good models of analysis to *critique*, *emulate*, and *improve upon*, and you need to ground your responses to these models in *careful, analytical reading*. This is one reason why philosophy anthologies, whether for the whole of philosophy, or for a specific sub-field, are usually arranged topically, and not as a gallery of important theories or philosophers. It also explains why an anthology of this size provides more than enough material for a course in philosophy of education: the readings that follow are not *information* to be remembered and recited, but a stimulus to think philosophically about education for yourself. Getting the most out of them is not like getting the most out of the morning newspaper. It's more like getting the most out of a fitness center or gym.

What remains to be explained is the organizational plan by which these readings are arranged. Philosophy of education begins with aspects of education that are basic, controversial, or both, and the organization of this anthology is designed with that in mind. The book's five parts correspond to five normatively basic aspects of education itself, or *five basic questions* about the conduct of education: What are its aims? What authority does it rest on? What responsibilities does it entail? How, or in what manner, should it be carried out? What should its content be? There is a unity to this list rooted in the idea of *governance* and the proposition that education involves, or is a special form of, governance.

I begin with the observation that the term "education" refers in its primary sense to more-or-less systematic practices of supervising and guiding the activities of persons in ways intended to promote valuable forms of learning and development. These activities, the activities of learning, typically include attending to explanations, lectures, or demonstrations, and in those moments teachers are not only facilitating learning, or creating and managing opportunities for learning, but are also *teaching*. Teaching is a central feature of education, but it is not the whole or the essence of education. The same is true of other prominent features of education. We could agree that education involves the transmission of culture and the communication of care (or valuing of students and what is learned), and it might even be true that both are always present in some sense when students are being educated. It would nevertheless remain true that education, considered as an institutionalized human practice, is essentially, if only in part, a form of governance.

The value of considering education in this light is that it directs our attention to the set of philosophically basic questions about education listed above – questions that are related to the philosophically basic aspects of governance. It does *not* reflect or imply any thought that the supervision of students, or the authority of teachers, is a more important feature of education than teaching, or care, or culture. The pivotal idea is simply that *as* a form of governance, education requires justification, and it entails responsibilities, aims, a manner of going about its business, and substance or a communicated content. These are the philosophically or normatively fundamental aspects of governance, and it is no coincidence that the subject-matter constituting the field of philosophy of education can be organized into categories corresponding to them: the authority to educate (justification), the adequate and equitable provision of education (responsibilities), the aims of education and associated ideas about its nature (aims), pedagogy, the learning it aims to induce, and educational ethics (manner), and curriculum (substance or content). Within these categories we encounter an array of specific debates that arise from relationships between the five basic questions and the variety of answers that may be given in response to each. Some of the debates hinge on philosophically sensitive ideas that are strongly related to governance itself, such as justice, equality, and non-discrimination. Some involve ethical ideas, such as virtue, autonomy, and care, which are invoked in answering some or all of the five basic questions. Finally, some involve philosophically sensitive ideas, such as knowledge, capability, and rationality, which are introduced by the answers themselves.

It is not uncommon for an article or book chapter in philosophy of education to address more than one of these five basic questions, and to do so in a way that discusses connections between them. That is to be expected, but it complicates the editor's task and results in some overlap between the various sections. A notable consequence of this for the present volume is that curricular matters are not as shortchanged as it may appear. In addition to the selections in Part V, the following selections in I–IV are also substantially concerned with the content of what is taught and learned: Plato (no. 1; knowledge and the abstract sciences); Peters (no. 7; initiation into ways of knowing); Freire (no. 8; curriculum and the "banking" model of schooling); Aristotle (no. 9; liberal studies); Höffe (no. 13; liberal studies); Brighouse (no. 24; television in schools); Appiah (no. 28; multicultural curricula); Purdy (no. 33; enrichment); Kupperman (no. 34; intellectual and artistic excellence); Rousseau (no. 42; the curriculum of discovery); Elgin (no. 45; learning science); Lipman (no. 48; critical thinking). Other connections

between readings in the various sections and parts will be evident in the index and in the introductions to the five major parts.

A related, concluding observation is that on this account of the divisions of philosophy of education, an ethical framework that addressed all five aspects of governance might provide a unifying, guiding perspective on education. Now and then in the readings that follow the discerning reader will find hints of this associated with the idea of an ethic of respect for persons as rational or self-determining agents. One could imagine the pieces fitting together in something like the following way: guided by such an ethic, the primary aim and responsibility of educators would be to promote good judgment and effective self-determination, and to do so equitably, or displaying equal respect within their sphere of educational authority. The scope of the educational authority they possess, the manner in which they exercise that authority, and the content of the education they provide would in turn be limited and shaped by the character of this responsibility. They would endeavor to cultivate the intellectual and moral virtues essential to good judgment, to nurture capabilities that would provide the basis of lives worth living, and to enable each student to understand the circumstances of her own life and the possibilities that lie before her. While promoting prudent and effective self-determination in such ways, educators would teach in a manner respectful of their students and the goods inherent in the subjects they teach. This is barely an outline, and not the only one suggested by the readings that follow. I leave it as an exercise for the reader to investigate how far it, or some alternative starting point, might take us toward a systematic philosophy of education.

## References

Broudy, H. 1979: "Philosophy of Education between the Yearbooks," *Philosophy of Education since Mid-century*, ed. J. Soltis (New York: Teachers College Press), pp. 2–16.

Brubacher, J. (ed.) 1942: *Philosophies of Education: The Forty-first Yearbook of the National Society for the Study of Education*, Part I (Chicago, IL: University of Chicago Press).

Curren, R. 1998: "Education, Philosophy of." *Routledge Encyclopedia of Philosophy*, ed. E. Craig (London: Routledge), vol. 3, pp. 231–40.

Henry, N. (ed.) 1955: *Modern Philosophies of Education: The Fifty-fourth Yearbook of the National Society for the Study of Education* (Chicago, IL: University of Chicago Press).

Hirst, P. 1983: "Educational Theory." *Educational Theory and its Foundation Disciplines*, ed. P. Hirst (London: Routledge & Kegan Paul), pp. 3–29.

Soltis, J. 1981: *Philosophy and Education: Eightieth Yearbook of the National Society for the Study of Education* (Chicago, IL: University of Chicago Press).

# PART I

# The Nature and Aims of Education

# Introduction to Part I

Most questions about education will lead one, sooner or later, to ask about the *nature* of education and whether there are certain *aims* that are somehow inherent in its nature or for some reason necessary or desirable. This makes questions and theories about the nature and aims of education a good place to begin in learning to think philosophically about education, though they are also a good place to end. Wherever one starts, one will be drawn back to them in attempting to address other educational questions in a deep and systematic way.

In beginning to think about such basic matters as what education really is and why one should care about it, one is likely to have in mind the kinds of schools one has grown up with and spent time in. This is a natural and useful frame of reference, as it is both familiar and fundamental to many of the educational facts of life we must contend with. Nevertheless, schooling as we know it is only one of the forms that education might take, and we need not consider schooling to be the whole of education. To think about what is and is not essential to education, we can use our imagination and experiment in thought with unfamiliar possibilities, but it can also be useful to adopt a more historically and culturally extended frame of reference. The readings in this part provide a starting point for doing that. They are more heavily historical than the readings in Parts II–V, and they provide not only a historical

introduction to the field of philosophy of education, but also an introduction to conceptions of education grounded in cultural and educational experiences very different from our own. The selections from Paulo Freire, Amartya Sen and Otfried Höffe add contemporary perspectives from outside the English-speaking world, including two from developing countries outside of Europe (Brazil and India).

The general topic of the nature and aims of education is divided here into three sub-topics, beginning with the general question "What is Education?" The more specific idea of a *liberal education* will then be taken up in connection with questions about how education and work are related. The third sub-topic, "Autonomy and Exit Rights," concerns the historically important and recently prominent idea that the promotion or facilitation of individual autonomy, or the ability to "exit" a life course in favor of one that might be better, should be one of the chief aims of education.

## What is Education?

Philosophy of education as we know it began in ancient Greece as an integral facet of the philosophy of Socrates (*c.*470–399 BC) and others who called themselves philosophers, but whom we (following Socrates and his followers) call sophists and orators.

Most important among the latter was the orator Isocrates (436–338 BC), who established a thriving school of rhetoric about four years after Plato opened his Academy. The sophists, orators, and philosophers all developed approaches to higher education, and defended those approaches against the competing claims of their competitors. This was one important starting point for philosophy of education. Socrates' student, Plato (c.427–347 BC), developed critiques of the instruction provided by sophists and orators, most notably in a pair of dialogues, *Protagoras* and *Gorgias* (named after two well-known sophists). Isocrates offered defenses of his own methods as well as critiques of his rivals, most substantially in *Antidosis*, *Against the Sophists*, and *Panathenaicus*. Although Isocrates has never been considered a serious philosophical rival to Plato or Aristotle (384–322 BC), he established himself through his teaching and educational philosophy as the "father of Classical Humanism" and a principal architect of the form that higher education would take for many hundreds of years.

Philosophical attention to primary education was not associated with the pedagogical claims of philosophy itself, on the other hand, but with the democratization of Athens, the invention of group lessons that made education accessible to larger numbers of Athenians, and the decline of Athens in the aftermath of the Peloponnesian Wars. With education made accessible to a wider spectrum of Athenians, the question of whether *aretê* (virtue, goodness, or excellence) can be taught, or only inherited, was in the air. Public education was almost nonexistent in the world of Plato and Aristotle, but against the backdrop of Athens's decline both of these philosophers argued that public education is essential to a just and well-run society. Both regarded teaching and practice as important sources of *aretê*.

Because Socrates did not write anything himself, we only know how he philosophized and what he thought through the writings of his student Plato. Plato's philosophical writings take the form of dialogues, and Socrates is a dominating presence in many of them. Classicists group Plato's dialogues into the early or Socratic dialogues (in which Socrates is apparently depicted much as he actually was), the transitional dialogues (in which we see Socrates much as he was, but also the beginnings of Plato's own attempts to identify and overcome problems in Socratic thought), the middle dialogues (in which Socrates appears essentially as a mouthpiece for

Plato's "perfected" version of Socratic philosophy), and the late dialogues (in which Socrates may not even appear, and where some important ideas characteristic of the middle dialogues are abandoned). Our first reading, "Turning the *Psyche*," is drawn from Plato's *Republic*, a middle dialogue that is widely regarded as his greatest work.

The *Republic* is a work in ten "books," a book or papyrus roll being about the length of a modern chapter, but with an endpoint determined not by theoretical or narrative closure, but by where the paper runs out. We pick up toward the end of Book VI, with the introduction of the "Form of the Good" (the nature of goodness, conceived as an abstract entity). Socrates describes this as the highest object of knowledge or understanding, and one that must be known by those who govern a society (in the Greek context, a *polis* or city-state), if they are to be capable guardians of justice and the common good. Book VII opens with one of the most striking and memorable images in all of philosophy, the allegory of the cave, which depicts the effect of education on the human *psyche* (mind, soul, or that which animates the body). We are told that education is not, as some think, a putting of knowledge into the mind like "putting sight into blind eyes," but the art of turning the student in the right direction. This implies first, that a *desire* to learn or *love* of learning must be awakened, and second that the desiring intellect must be directed toward "higher things" that are truly knowable. We are also told that what is knowable is not visible and changing ("becoming") things, but things like mathematical objects that have natures that are the same through and through and are unchanging ("being"). The reading ends with a description of mathematics as the first step in the course of higher learning leading toward the dialectical or philosophical inquiry through which one may approach the Forms and achieve understanding.

Our second reading, "Knowing How to Rule and be Ruled as Justice Demands" (no. 2) is drawn from *The Laws*, which Plato worked on through the last ten years of his life. We meet in it, not Socrates and philosophical youths such as Glaucon and Adeimantus (his interlocutors through most of the *Republic*), but an elderly "Athenian Stranger" and peers from Crete and Sparta, the two cities in Plato's world noted for having a semblance of public education – although limited to military training, unfortunately. At the point where the selection begins in Book I, the Athenian has been persuading Clinias (the Cretan) and Megillus (the Spartan) that proper systems of law and public education would aim at peace and the whole of virtue, not war and courage alone. Out of respect for what is best in human nature, they would cultivate the ethical virtues, but would aim beyond those to the cultivation or fullest expression of the rational element in human nature. Courage involves doing what is right or required by reason in the face of danger, and it is taught through guided practice in facing danger. Why, then, should moderation, or the disposition to do what is right in the face of intoxicating pleasures, not similarly be taught through guided practice in handling pleasure? If it should, then what could be a better place to do so than drinking parties? The selection begins with the general notion that practice is fundamental to learning, and goes on to define education, properly understood, as a "training which produces a keen desire to become a perfect citizen who knows how to rule and be ruled as justice demands." This requires a complex form of self-governance, and Plato continues by exploring the ideas of self-governance, rational self-control, and freedom through a remarkable image: a human being is like "a puppet of the gods" pulled about by strings, free only to the extent that education and the law enable him or her to act rationally. The question of whether we can be free while caused to do what we do is only one of several philosophical puzzles posed by this image and the surrounding discussion. The idea that freedom is not a gift of nature or providence, but a product of education, has far-reaching implications.

Our selection from Isocrates, "An Educated Person Can Speak Well and Persuade" (no. 3), is an extract from his fictional forensic speech, "Antidosis," in which he defends himself against an invented *sycophant*, or habitual litigant, Lysimachus. The charges he imagines are similar to those actually brought against Socrates, that he corrupted the youth of Athens and taught them to argue unscrupulously. This fictional context allows Isocrates to defend his own character and teaching against a common image of rhetoric as an unprincipled form of verbal self-advancement. Much as Plato in the *Gorgias* defends philosophy as the true political art devoted to the common good of Athens, Isocrates describes the art of rhetoric he teaches as philosophy in the service of the polis. But while Plato imagines a political art resting on systematic knowledge of what is good for human beings, much as medical practice would rest on medical science, Isocrates denies that

human beings can acquire such knowledge. Plato envisions *practical wisdom* as an educational attainment grounded in systematic knowledge (*epistêmê*), whereas Isocrates envisions it as an educational attainment grounded in the study of speech (*logos*) or speaking well and persuasively. "We use the same arguments by which we persuade others in our own deliberations," he says, and "we regard as sound advisors those who debate with themselves most skillfully about public affairs." Speech and the ability to persuade one another are what separate us from animals and give rise to cities, laws, and "nearly all our inventions." What better form of education could there be than practice in analyzing, critiquing, and constructing speeches of enduring value?

Our next selection, "The Exercise of Reason" (no. 4), is drawn from the opening sections of John Locke's *Of the Conduct of the Understanding* (1706), a work intended as a handbook of self-education for those in English society who have already received a basic education, probably at a boarding school occupied with the study of Latin and Greek, but preferably at home with a tutor. Locke begins from the idea that it is a fundamental right of human beings that they should be able to think for themselves and govern themselves by their own reason. The judicious use of one's understanding is indeed not just a right, according to Locke, but a "fundamental duty which every man owes himself" (*Conduct*, §41). The *Conduct* opens with the assertion that we act from our beliefs, and are thus free only to the extent that our beliefs are the product not of prejudice, reverence, or habit, but of our own careful thinking. The education that Locke prescribes is thus an education for liberty, and at the same time a preparation to make the best use of our mental faculties. Those faculties need to be freed from prejudice and exercised, and we need to acquire a sufficient breadth of experience in order to think effectively about all that concerns us. We need to learn to overcome confusion and prejudice by making sure we are reasoning with clear and determinate ("determined") ideas, not mere words, and we need practice in reasoning through things carefully and completely. The aim of education is thus not to "know everything," but to enable us to "think and reason right" in what concerns us in our lives and as citizens.

The opening pages of Jean-Jacques Rousseau's *Emile* (1762) are extracted here under the title "The Education of Nature" (no. 5). They present an argument for an education "from nature" that aims to produce a "natural man." Rousseau asserts that education has three sources: nature, men, and things. An education from nature is simply "the internal development of our faculties and our organs," and it is beyond our control, he says. He also asserts that a sound education requires that all three forms of education coincide, which is possible only if the art of education adopts nature's own goal and sequence of stages (defined largely by forms of motivation, leading from the pleasant, to the useful, to the rationally desirable). A "natural education" to produce a "natural man" is thus the proper course, and this seems to mean an education that allows a child's faculties to fully and freely "ripen," perhaps with some stage-setting of the learning environment to ensure that needed experiences occur.

What may seem surprising is that Rousseau also praises the system of Spartan education attributed to Lycurgus, which he was acquainted with through Plutarch's *Lives*. The latter writes that:

> The training of the Spartans lasted into the years of full maturity. No man was allowed to live as he pleased, but in their city, as in a military encampment, they always had a prescribed regimen and employment in public service, considering that they belonged entirely to their country and not to themselves, watching over the boys, if no other duty was laid upon them, and either teaching them some useful thing, or learning it themselves from their elders. (*Lyc.* XXIV.1–2)

Lycurgus thereby "denatured" man, and that is a good thing, says Rousseau, because it made Spartans into citizens devoted to the common good. It seems, then, that Rousseau praises both "natural" education to be a man "for oneself" and "denaturing" education to be a citizen "for others." How can these be reconciled by letting a "natural" education run its course? How can the exercise of individual freedom and rights be reconciled with submission to the corresponding duties and common good of one's political community? What kind of society and political system would this require? Why does Rousseau regard attempts to combine natural and denaturing education in the circumstances of existing societies as contradictory and unworkable? Rousseau's answers to these questions will require a much fuller account of the trajectory of a natural education, the kind of "man" it will yield, and the social and political worlds he will inhabit.

The reconciliation of "individual" and "social" aims of education is also a central theme of our sixth selection, "The Democratic Conception of Education," from John Dewey's book *Democracy and Education* (1916). As Dewey understands democracy, it is not just a form of government, but primarily a mode of social life that is unique in providing an adequate setting for human flourishing: "a freeing of individual capacity in a progressive growth directed to social aims." Education is itself just such a promotion of "growth." Dewey thus conceives of democracy itself as educative in a way that reconciles the good of the individual and the good of society. Democratic education will also embody this reconciliation; it will promote individual "growth," while preparing individuals to cooperate in a form of social life that is itself growth-promoting. This reconciliation rests on the possibility of a specific (democratic) form of social life, and much of the selection is a comparative study of the failings of three alternatives: the society of Plato's *Republic*, nineteenth-century conceptions of education in accordance with nature, and the nationalistic form of state-funded education created in nineteenth-century Germany. Writing during World War I, and against the backdrop of the Industrial Revolution and the emergence of public school systems, Dewey concludes by observing that democratic schools should be designed to compensate for differences of opportunity, overcome the social class divisions that hinder cooperation in solving society's problems, promote international cooperation, and encourage the idea that national sovereignty is provisional. Dewey is thinking beyond a world of lawlessly contending nations and national school systems to something more cosmopolitan.

R. S. Peters's article "Education as Initiation" (no. 7) provides its own comparative study of some prominent ways of thinking about the nature and aims of education, but it is unlike any of the previous selections in having an analytical focus on the language of education and educational "aims." Peters argues that education "can have no ends beyond itself," but that the word "education" implies certain standards: an educated person is made better, develops cognitively, comes to care about what is valuable, and acts as a voluntary and comprehending agent in the course of being *initiated* in a meaningful way into public traditions and forms of knowledge. The teacher must show students respect and create a sense of union in a common enterprise. In developing this view, Peters also considers and critiques sociological and economic perspectives on education, which impute extrinsic functions or ends to it, and the child-centered "ideology" of growth of potentialities from within, associated with the Progressive Education Movement. Peters acknowledges that this "ideology" of growth captures important truths about the *manner* of education, but he notes that it was never fully endorsed by Rousseau, Dewey or any other major thinker, and he argues that it ignores the role of "intentional transmission of worthwhile content."

A final view of the nature and aims of education is provided by chapter 2 of Paulo Freire's *Pedagogy of the Oppressed* (1968), included here under the title "Banking v. Problem-solving Models of Education" (no. 8). We see in it a language and moral ideal of human freedom not unlike Locke's and that of the Enlightenment generally: he says that the "vocation" of men is not to be "automatons" who are merely means to others' ends, but to be "beings for themselves." His theory of the function of school systems in Latin America, and in capitalist societies generally, is that they are intended to preserve for the minority a "profitable situation," by *oppressing*, or exerting "overwhelming control" over, the majority. According to this theory, schools in capitalist societies do not merely fail to live up to the moral ideal of human liberation, but actively work against it. They do so, Freire argues, through a "banking model" of education that communicates a mythologized and static view of the world and trains students in passive, unthinking acceptance of their subordinate position. What a true and genuinely liberating education would do is replace this with a socially leveling form of classroom dialogue, reflection, and problem solving, focused on transforming the students' place in the world. Such an education would be *humanizing* in the sense that it would promote *praxis*, or action in the world expressive of the actor's humanity.

## Liberal Education and the Relationship between Education and Work

Most people today would agree that one of the purposes of schools is to prepare young people for the world of work, perhaps in part by teaching them to work hard. Indeed, one can scarcely imagine a system of universal and compulsory schooling that would not include preparation for the world of work among its acknowledged functions. But schooling was not always universal and compulsory, and education was not always understood to be preparation for work. This is evident in the origins of our word "school," which derives from the Greek *scholē*, meaning "leisure." The "old education" of Athens was a preparation not for work but for *leisure*. The knightly warriors who received it spent their daytime leisure in athletic contests and their night-time leisure at drinking parties where they entertained each other with music and recitations. Their schooling in *gymnastikē* (athletics) and *musikē* (music, poetry, and narratives – the "Arts of the Muses") was thus a preparation for their leisure. Leisure was not equated with mere *amusement*, however. It was contrasted with *productive labor* in such a way that public service – even military service – was considered a use of leisure, or time free from the necessity of satisfying material needs. Leisure represented the opportunity to flourish as a human being or to pursue what is intrinsically, not just instrumentally, good. It is in leisure, the Greeks believed, that we can do what is fully *humanizing* or expressive of our best potentialities.

Our first reading on this topic, "Liberal v. 'Mechanical' Education" (no. 9) is drawn from Books VII and VIII of Aristotle's *Politics*. Aristotle argues that the "excellences of leisure" should be the concern of both individuals and states, and that this requires care that the body and desiring element in the *psyche* are formed with a view to the flourishing of citizens' rational capacities. He advocates public education that is "the same for all" as a basis for cultivating the moral and intellectual excellences essential to human flourishing and happiness (*eudaimonia*). Education should not only include "necessary" practical arts, but much more what is "liberal" or conducive to spending one's leisure in activities that express what is best in human nature. Aristotle discusses the study of music at length, emphasizing its capacity to shape character and judgment, yet noting that even it becomes illiberal or "mechanical" if it is pursued in order to entertain others with displays of virtuosity (making it an activity pursued not for itself as an intrinsic good, but for an extrinsic end), and is pursued so intensively that it interferes with the development and exercise of the highest virtues. He understands those highest virtues to be practical wisdom (*phronēsis*) and contemplative wisdom (*sophia*), making wisdom the ultimate, intrinsic goal of a liberal education. He notes elsewhere that to be educated is to be able to form a sound judgment of an investigation or exposition, a person of "universal education" being one who is able to do this in all or nearly all domains of knowledge.

Aristotle is not specific about what counts as "necessary" practical arts, but he probably has in mind what is necessary to meeting one's material needs and exercising the human excellences. He clearly distinguishes between material *needs* and unnecessary *luxuries*, which do not make people happy, but distract them from what does. In the context of his time, the arts he would have considered necessary to meeting's one material needs would probably be those of a landowner of moderate means who needs to read, write, draw, and use arithmetic to prudently manage his farm, while others do the manual labor. What is truly "necessary" preparation for productive employment is an interesting question, especially in a dynamic global economy where little is certain and most people make a living by selling their labor to others.

The Greek view of leisure as a cultural value was questioned during the Reformation and Enlightenment, and ideas about education followed suit. A disdain for idleness and learning for learning's sake (i.e., as an inherently worthwhile and rewarding activity) is evident in Locke's writings. In Rousseau we encounter something that goes far beyond this: a theory of the origins of *inequality* that places much of the blame on the history of progress in the arts and sciences. In the story of the "Fall of Man," the ejection of Adam and Eve from the Garden of Eden is associated with pride, the "root of all evil," and man's defiance in tasting the fruit of the Tree of Knowledge. Knowledge is a dangerous thing in this story, and the "fallen" state of man, his alleged lost innocence, and the perils of knowledge, have been recurrent themes in European thought. They are developed in Rousseau's *Emile* and other works through the idea that the advancement of the arts and sciences has caused an "inversion of value" in modern societies. Labor has value to the extent that it satisfies essential human needs, he asserts, but the advancement of specialized learning has fueled the emergence of occupations that command rewards and prestige far in excess of their capacity to satisfy any such needs. In response, Rousseau holds that a proper education, even of a "gentleman," should not only include a trade, but should enable the learner to grasp the true value of work. Our reading on these themes, "Learning the Value of Work" (no. 10), is drawn from Book III of *Emile*. Work is "an indispensable duty," and everyone must learn a trade not only to be able to use it, but to "conquer the prejudices that despise a trade," writes Rousseau.

In "Education for Labor and Leisure," John Dewey (no. 11) discusses Aristotle's distinction between liberal and mechanical education, and the social division of labor it assumes. In Book VII of his *Politics*, Aristotle describes the best state he thought possible, which was a kind of ideal aristocracy in which *all* citizens are enabled by public education to become fully virtuous and live the happy lives that he believed only virtuous people could have. Yet he supposed this would only be possible through the labor of a multitude of non-citizens. Dewey observes that we need to do more to overcome this bifurcated vision of society and education than merely acknowledge "the dignity of labor." "The revolution is still incomplete," he says, because it is still widely assumed that liberal education and a useful education are distinct types and are appropriate to children born to different social classes. We need to imagine one form of education for all children, writes Dewey, a form of education that is at the same time both liberal and useful. He argues that this becomes easier as the substance of work changes and becomes more intellectually demanding, and it will be easier still when the "evils of the existing economic situation" are eliminated and democratic social control replaces autocracy in the workplace. Whatever the nature of their labor, everyone in a democratized workplace will need to exercise "social intelligence" at work, just as they will in their role as citizens.

The views of Aristotle, Rousseau, and Dewey all suggest some acceptance of preparation for productive employment as a part of education, whether in the form of elementary "practical arts" (reading, writing, drawing, and arithmetic), a specific trade (the boy, Emile, will learn carpentry), or a strengthening of widely applicable practical and social "intelligence." The extent to which investments in education actually pay off in productivity gains and improved living standards is another matter, and one of more than a little interest to public policy. In "Education and Standards of Living" (no. 12), Amartya Sen takes aim at the so-called "Lee Thesis," the doctrine that the denial of diverse freedoms, civil liberties, and social services such as public education and universal health care, stimulates rapid economic development. Sen regards access to education not as a "luxury" that must wait until prosperity has arrived, but as an "instrumental freedom" that expands individuals' *capabilities* or substantial freedom "to live the kinds of lives that people have reason to value." It does this by enabling people to *function* in ways they otherwise could not, and in doing this it both stimulates economic development and raises living standards in ways that are independent of income levels. This *capability perspective* is built on the proposition that freedom is both the proper *aim* of development and a primary *means* to it. This selection closes with a comparison between this perspective and the narrower perspective on education and economic development provided by *human capital theory*.

Every age needs its own reminders of the value of a liberal education and why it is shortsighted and self-defeating to focus too much on the vocational and monetary rewards of education. Otfried Höffe's lecture, "The Liberal Studies in a Global World" (no. 13), offers a series of observations about the contributions to human well-being that the humanities can make in an age of globalization struggling with the specter of a "clash of cultures." An Aristotle scholar and one of Germany's leading philosophers, Höffe presented this lecture (translated from his original German) in the United States a year after the terrorist attacks of September 11, 2001. His concern about the international situation and its potential to unfold as a tragedy is evident in many of his remarks, including most obviously his observations about the important truths that can be learned from the tragedies of Aeschylus and Sophocles. The foreignness of his idiom and the distance between his perspective and that of many Americans only reinforce his points about the need for an enlargement of our perception and regard for other cultures, for a sense of history, and for the cultural tools to critique ideologies and fully grasp the dynamic of human conflict and its resolution.

## Autonomy and Exit Rights

We have encountered already in our selections from Plato, Locke, Freire, and Sen, the idea that education makes those who are educated *freer*. Plato and Locke understand freedom in this context to be a *capacity* to govern oneself rationally or well, making freedom an educational goal closely associated with *phronêsis* (sound judgment, prudence, or practical wisdom), which for two millennia was widely considered to be the ultimate aim of education. Freire and Sen are concerned both with the capacity to govern oneself – a capacity impaired by oppression, deprivation, and mis-education or no education – but also the educational contributions

to having substantial freedom in the world or meaningful *options* for how to live one's life. Related to both of these conceptions of the educational promotion of freedom is a recent strand of work in philosophy of education that identifies *autonomy* as an important educational goal related to children's prospective rights of self-determination as well as their future good or interest in living satisfying lives. Much of the debate revolves around the compatibility of autonomy promotion with the rights of parents to live *their* lives as they choose, and with the public interest in promoting good citizenship. A second line of inquiry considers the nature and presuppositions of the idea of autonomy itself. What is meant by "autonomy" is not always well defined, but it is generally understood to include an acquired ability to evaluate in some way the values one has grown up with, to formulate at least one alternative conception of how one might live one's life (one "exit" option), and to act in pursuit of the alternative one prefers.

Joel Feinberg's 1980 article "The Child's Right to an Open Future" (no. 14) provides an unusually clear discussion of the idea of respect for children's future autonomy, and illustrates what is at stake with an extended discussion of a pair of court cases pertaining to the exemption of Amish communities from the otherwise universal minimum education requirements in the states of Kansas (*State v. Garber*) and Wisconsin (*Wisconsin v. Yoder*). Feinberg does not contest the decision approving an exemption in *Yoder*, but he argues on moral principle – appealing to children's rights of self-determination and their future well-being – that education should send children "out into the world with as many open opportunities as possible," equipped to choose "whichever sort of life best fits [their] native endowment and natural disposition." Parts 3 and 4 of the article address and attempt to resolve the apparently paradoxical character of promoting autonomy and the child's good: will not a child's education, whatever its content, actually *narrow* the range of life options a child will have by the time she is an adult? Will not a child's education also inevitably shape what she will find satisfying as an adult, making what is good for her largely a *function of* her education, and not an independent goal that could *guide* her education?

Feinberg defends autonomy as a *right* of self-determination and as a *capacity* that aids people in living fulfilling lives. By contrast, Eamonn Callan develops a political defense of education that promotes autonomy. He argues that political virtue presupposes autonomy; that education should promote the virtues of citizenship on which liberal democracy depends, but only if this does not "make our lives bad"; that this does not make our lives bad, because autonomy is compatible with living a good life; that education should therefore promote autonomy as a virtue of citizenship. In the sections of his book *Creating Citizens* (no. 15), which are extracted here as "Justice, Autonomy, and the Good," Callan's argument is developed through a vivid exploration of the idea that *integrity* is essential to a good life. Callan argues that although autonomy is incompatible with a *simple* kind of integrity, it is not incompatible with integrity generally. Integrity requires reasonableness, he argues, and in a pluralistic society reasonableness entails reflection on the conflicting judgments of reasonable others; it entails autonomy or "reasoned self-rule" in just the way that citizenship in such a society does.

Callan develops his analysis in dialogue with John Rawls's influential book, *Political Liberalism*, published in 1993. Rawls begins from a "political conception of the person," according to which people have two moral powers – a sense of justice and a conception of the good – as well as powers of reason. He argues that a reasonable citizen is committed to *reciprocity*, or finding and agreeing upon fair terms of cooperation, and to accepting the *burdens of judgment* as conditions on "the use of public reason in directing the legitimate exercise of political power in a constitutional regime" (Rawls, 1993: 54). The burdens of judgment are factors that give rise to differences of judgment among reasonable people, and acknowledging them when faced with beliefs and judgments different from one's own is fundamental to respectful engagement with others in the enterprise of public reason. Callan's

basic argument is that accepting these burdens of judgment, and being educated to accept them, will compel us to recognize that there is less to be said *against* other people's views of the good – and *for* our own – than we thought. We will be compelled to see that our own (more or less systematic or "comprehensive") conception of how to live may be questioned, and to see other kinds of lives as possible for us. In other words, an effective education for the virtues of citizenship in a pluralistic democracy would yield "substantial ethical autonomy."

Is autonomy, considered as a universal right to meaningful self-determination, a mere cultural preference with no more standing than a cultural preference that only boys be educated and women be subordinate to their husbands? Should religious organizations and their schools be exempt, as they are in the United States, from the otherwise universal provisions of federal anti-discrimination law governing gender discrimination? In her reading "'Mistresses of their Own Destiny': Group Rights, Gender, and Realistic Rights of Exit" (no. 16), Susan Moller Okin examines three arguments for tolerating religious and other cultural practices that are held to be beneficial to those who share the cultures but which are autonomy-limiting and discriminatory. Such arguments typically point to the benefits to individuals of enabling cultural groups to survive and flourish, and to the fact that such groups are voluntary associations that people are at liberty to withdraw from or "exit" if they so desire. Okin observes that such "exit rights" must be meaningful, however, and not limited by gender discrimination or educational practices designed to make an exit unthinkable. She argues that there are substantial elements of patriarchy in the cultures in question, and that the right to exit is inadequate "as a palliative for oppression."

## References

Plutarch, 1914: *Lycurgus*, in *Plutarch's Lives*, vol. 1, trans. Bernadotte Perrin (Cambridge, MA: Harvard University Press).

Rawls, J. 1993: *Political Liberalism* (New York: Columbia University Press).

# What is Education?

# 1

# Turning the *Psyche*

# Plato

**Book VI**

[You've] often heard it said that the form of the good is the most important thing to learn about and that it's by their relation to it that just things and the others become useful and beneficial. You know very well now that I am going to say this, and, besides, that we have no adequate knowledge of it. And you also know that, if we don't know it, even the fullest possible knowledge of other things is of no benefit to us, any more than if we acquire any possession without the good of it. Or do you think that it is any advantage to have every kind of possession without the good of it? Or to know everything except the good, thereby knowing nothing fine or good?

No, by god, I don't.

Furthermore, you certainly know that the majority believe that pleasure is the good, while the more sophisticated believe that it is knowledge.

Indeed I do.

And you know that those who believe this can't tell us what sort of knowledge it is, however, but in the end are forced to say that it is knowledge of the good.

And that's ridiculous.

Of course it is. They blame us for not knowing the good and then turn around and talk to us as if we did know it. They say that it is knowledge of the good – as if we understood what they're speaking about when they utter the word "good."

That's completely true.

What about those who define the good as pleasure? Are they any less full of confusion than the others? Aren't even they forced to admit that there are bad pleasures?

Most definitely.

So, I think, they have to agree that the same things are both good and bad. Isn't that true?

Of course.

It's clear, then, isn't it, why there are many large controversies about this?

How could it be otherwise?

And isn't this also clear? In the case of just and beautiful things, many people are content with what are believed to be so, even if they aren't really so, and they act, acquire, and form their own beliefs on that basis. Nobody is satisfied to acquire things that are merely believed to be good, however, but everyone wants the things that really *are* good and disdains mere belief here.

Editor's title. Previously published as *Republic* in *Plato: Complete Works*, ed. John M. Cooper, trans. Grube and Reeve (Indianapolis, IN: Hackett, 1997), pp. 1125–42, Books VI and VII, Sections 504e–525c. Reprinted by permission of Hackett Publishing Company Inc. All rights reserved.

That's right.

Every soul pursues the good and does whatever it does for its sake. It divines that the good is something but it is perplexed and cannot adequately grasp what it is or acquire the sort of stable beliefs it has about other things, and so it misses the benefit, if any, that even those other things may give. Will we allow the best people in the city, to whom we entrust everything, to be so in the dark about something of this kind and of this importance?

That's the last thing we'd do.

I don't suppose, at least, that just and fine things will have acquired much of a guardian in someone who doesn't even know in what way they are good. And I divine that no one will have adequate knowledge of them until he knows this.

You've divined well.

But won't our constitution be perfectly ordered, if a guardian who knows these things is in charge of it?

Necessarily. But, Socrates, you must also tell us whether you consider the good to be knowledge or pleasure or something else altogether.

What a man! It's been clear for some time that other people's opinions about these matters wouldn't satisfy you.

Well, Socrates, it doesn't seem right to me for you to be willing to state other people's convictions but not your own, especially when you've spent so much time occupied with these matters.

What? Do you think it's right to talk about things one doesn't know as if one does know them?

Not as if one knows them, he said, but one ought to be willing to state one's opinions as such.

What? Haven't you noticed that opinions without knowledge are shameful and ugly things? The best of them are blind – or do you think that those who express a true opinion without understanding are any different from blind people who happen to travel the right road?

They're no different.

Do you want to look at shameful, blind, and crooked things, then, when you might hear illuminating and fine ones from other people?

By god, Socrates, Glaucon said, don't desert us with the end almost in sight. We'll be satisfied if you discuss the good as you discussed justice, moderation, and the rest.

That, my friend, I said, would satisfy me too, but I'm afraid that I won't be up to it and that I'll disgrace myself and look ridiculous by trying. So let's abandon the quest for what the good itself is for the time being, for even to arrive at my own view about it is too big a topic for the discussion we are now started on. But I am willing to tell you about what is apparently an offspring of the good and most like it. Is that agreeable to you, or would you rather we let the whole matter drop?

It is. The story about the father remains a debt you'll pay another time.

I wish that I could pay the debt in full, and you receive it instead of just the interest. So here, then, is this child and offspring of the good. But be careful that I don't somehow deceive you unintentionally by giving you an illegitimate account of the child.[1]

We'll be as careful as possible, so speak on.

I will when we've come to an agreement and recalled some things that we've already said both here and many other times.

Which ones?

We say that there are many beautiful things and many good things, and so on for each kind, and in this way we distinguish them in words.

We do.

And beauty itself and good itself and all the things that we thereby set down as many, reversing ourselves, we set down according to a single form of each, believing that there is but one, and call it "the being" of each.

That's true.

And we say that the many beautiful things and the rest are visible but not intelligible, while the forms are intelligible but not visible.

That's completely true.

With what part of ourselves do we see visible things?

With our sight.

And so audible things are heard by hearing, and with our other senses we perceive all the other perceptible things.

That's right.

Have you considered how lavish the maker of our senses was in making the power to see and be seen?

I can't say I have.

Well, consider it this way. Do hearing and sound need another kind of thing in order for the former to hear and the latter to be heard, a third thing in whose absence the one won't hear or the other be heard?

No, they need nothing else.

And if there are any others that need such a thing, there can't be many of them. Can you think of one?

I can't.

You don't realize that sight and the visible have such a need?

How so?

Sight may be present in the eyes, and the one who has it may try to use it, and colors may be present in things, but unless a third kind of thing is present, which is naturally adapted for this very purpose, you know that sight will see nothing, and the colors will remain unseen.

What kind of thing do you mean?

I mean what you call light.

You're right.

Then it isn't an insignificant kind of link that connects the sense of sight and the power to be seen – it is a more valuable link than any other linked things have got, if indeed light is something valuable.

And, of course, it's very valuable.

Which of the gods in heaven would you name as the cause and controller of this, the one whose light causes our sight to see in the best way and the visible things to be seen?

The same one you and others would name. Obviously, the answer to your question is the sun.

And isn't sight by nature related to that god in this way?

Which way?

Sight isn't the sun, neither sight itself nor that in which it comes to be, namely, the eye.

No, it certainly isn't.

But I think that it is the most sunlike of the senses.

Very much so.

And it receives from the sun the power it has, just like an influx from an overflowing treasury.

Certainly.

The sun is not sight, but isn't it the cause of sight itself and seen by it?

That's right.

Let's say, then, that this is what I called the offspring of the good, which the good begot as its analogue. What the good itself is in the intelligible realm, in relation to understanding and intelligible things, the sun is in the visible realm, in relation to sight and visible things.

How? Explain a bit more.

You know that, when we turn our eyes to things whose colors are no longer in the light of day but in the gloom of night, the eyes are dimmed and seem nearly blind, as if clear vision were no longer in them.

Of course.

Yet whenever one turns them on things illuminated by the sun, they see clearly, and vision appears in those very same eyes?

Indeed.

Well, understand the soul in the same way: When it focuses on something illuminated by truth and what is, it understands, knows, and apparently possesses understanding, but when it focuses on what is mixed with obscurity, on what comes to be and passes away, it opines and is dimmed, changes its opinions this way and that, and seems bereft of understanding.

It does seem that way.

So that what gives truth to the things known and the power to know to the knower is the form of the good. And though it is the cause of knowledge and truth, it is also an object of knowledge. Both knowledge and truth are beautiful things, but the good is other and more beautiful than they. In the visible realm, light and sight are rightly considered sunlike, but it is wrong to think that they are the sun, so here it is right to think of knowledge and truth as goodlike but wrong to think that either of them is the good – for the good is yet more prized.

This is an inconceivably beautiful thing you're talking about, if it provides both knowledge and truth and is superior to them in beauty. You surely don't think that a thing like that could be pleasure.

Hush! Let's examine its image in more detail as follows.

How?

You'll be willing to say, I think, that the sun not only provides visible things with the power to be seen but also with coming to be, growth, and nourishment, although it is not itself coming to be.

How could it be?

Therefore, you should also say that not only do the objects of knowledge owe their being known to the good, but their being is also due to it, although the good is not being, but superior to it in rank and power.

And Glaucon comically said: By Apollo, what a daemonic superiority!

It's your own fault; you forced me to tell you my opinion about it.

And I don't want you to stop either. So continue to explain its similarity to the sun, if you've omitted anything.

I'm certainly omitting a lot.

Well, don't, not even the smallest thing.

I think I'll have to omit a fair bit, but, as far as is possible at the moment, I won't omit anything voluntarily.

Don't.

Understand, then, that, as we said, there are these two things, one sovereign of the intelligible kind and place, the other of the visible (I don't say "of heaven" so as not to seem to you to be playing the sophist with the name).[2] In any case, you have two kinds of thing, visible and intelligible.

Right.

It is like a line divided into two unequal sections.[3] Then divide each section – namely, that of the visible and that of the intelligible – in the same ratio as the line. In terms now of relative clarity and opacity, one subsection of the visible consists of images. And by images I mean, first, shadows, then reflections in water and in all close-packed, smooth, and shiny materials, and everything of that sort, if you understand.

I do.

In the other subsection of the visible, put the originals of these images, namely, the animals around us, all the plants, and the whole class of manu-factured things.

Consider them put.

Would you be willing to say that, as regards truth and untruth, the division is in this proportion: As the opinable is to the knowable, so the likeness is to the thing that it is like?

Certainly.

Consider now how the section of the intelligible is to be divided.

How?

As follows: In one subsection, the soul, using as images the things that were imitated before, is forced to investigate from hypotheses, proceeding not to a first principle but to a conclusion. In the other subsection, however, it makes its way to a first principle that is *not* a hypothesis, proceeding from a hypothesis but without the images used in the previous subsection, using forms themselves and making its investigation through them.

I don't yet fully understand what you mean.

Let's try again. You'll understand it more easily after the following preamble. I think you know that students of geometry, calculation, and the like hypo-thesize the odd and the even, the various figures, the three kinds of angles, and other things akin to these in each of their investigations, as if they knew them. They make these their hypotheses and don't think it necessary to give any account of them, either to themselves or to others, as if they were clear to everyone. And going from these first principles through the remaining steps, they arrive in full agreement.

I certainly know that much.

Then you also know that, although they use visible figures and make claims about them, their thought isn't directed to them but to those other things that they are like. They make their claims for the sake of square itself and the diagonal itself, not the diagonal they draw, and similarly with the others. These figures that they make and draw, of which shadows and reflections in water are images, they now in turn use as images, in seeking to see those others themselves that one cannot see except by means of thought.

That's true.

This, then, is the kind of thing that, on the one hand, I said is intelligible, and, on the other, is such that the soul is forced to use hypotheses in the investigation of it, not travelling up to a first prin-ciple, since it cannot reach beyond its hypotheses, but using as images those very things of which images were made in the section below, and which, by comparison to their images, were thought to be clear and to be valued as such.

I understand that you mean what happens in geometry and related sciences.

Then also understand that, by the other sub-section of the intelligible, I mean that which reason itself grasps by the power of dialectic. It does not consider these hypotheses as first principles but truly as hypotheses – but as stepping stones to take off from, enabling it to reach the unhypothetical first principle of everything. Having grasped this prin-ciple, it reverses itself and, keeping hold of what follows from it, comes down to a conclusion with-out making use of anything visible at all, but only of forms themselves, moving on from forms to forms, and ending in forms.

I understand, if not yet adequately (for in my opinion you're speaking of an enormous task), that you want to distinguish the intelligible part of that which is, the part studied by the science of dialectic, as clearer than the part studied by the so-called sciences, for which their hypotheses are first prin-ciples. And although those who study the objects of these sciences are forced to do so by means of thought rather than sense perception, still, because they do not go back to a genuine first principle, but proceed from hypotheses, you don't think that they understand them, even though, given such a principle, they are intelligible. And you seem to me to call the state of the geometers thought but not understanding, thought being intermediate between opinion and understanding.

Your exposition is most adequate. Thus there are four such conditions in the soul, corresponding to the four subsections of our line: Understanding for the highest, thought for the second, belief for the third, and imaging for the last. Arrange them in a ratio, and consider that each shares in clarity to the degree that the subsection it is set over shares in truth.

I understand, agree, and arrange them as you say.

## Book VII

Next, I said, compare the effect of education and of the lack of it on our nature to an experience like this: Imagine human beings living in an underground, cavelike dwelling, with an entrance a long way up, which is both open to the light and as wide as the cave itself. They've been there since childhood, fixed in the same place, with their necks and legs fettered, able to see only in front of them, because their bonds prevent them from turning their heads around. Light is provided by a fire burning far above and behind them. Also behind them, but on higher ground, there is a path stretching between them and the fire. Imagine that along this path a low wall has been built, like the screen in front of puppeteers above which they show their puppets.

I'm imagining it.

Then also imagine that there are people along the wall, carrying all kinds of artifacts that project above it – statues of people and other animals, made out of stone, wood, and every material. And, as you'd expect, some of the carriers are talking, and some are silent.

It's a strange image you're describing, and strange prisoners.

They're like us. Do you suppose, first of all, that these prisoners see anything of themselves and one another besides the shadows that the fire casts on the wall in front of them?

How could they, if they have to keep their heads motionless throughout life?

What about the things being carried along the wall? Isn't the same true of them?

Of course.

And if they could talk to one another, don't you think they'd suppose that the names they used applied to the things they see passing before them?[4]

They'd have to.

And what if their prison also had an echo from the wall facing them? Don't you think they'd believe that the shadows passing in front of them were talking whenever one of the carriers passing along the wall was doing so?

I certainly do.

Then the prisoners would in every way believe that the truth is nothing other than the shadows of those artifacts.

They must surely believe that.

Consider, then, what being released from their bonds and cured of their ignorance would naturally be like, if something like this came to pass.[5] When one of them was freed and suddenly compelled to stand up, turn his head, walk, and look up toward the light, he'd be pained and dazzled and unable to see the things whose shadows he'd seen before. What do you think he'd say, if we told him that what he'd seen before was inconsequential, but that now – because he is a bit closer to the things that are and is turned towards things that are more – he sees more correctly? Or, to put it another way, if we pointed to each of the things passing by, asked him what each of them is, and compelled him to answer, don't you think he'd be at a loss and that he'd believe that the things he saw earlier were truer than the ones he was now being shown?

Much truer.

And if someone compelled him to look at the light itself, wouldn't his eyes hurt, and wouldn't he turn around and flee towards the things he's able to see, believing that they're really clearer than the ones he's being shown?

He would.

And if someone dragged him away from there by force, up the rough, steep path, and didn't let him go until he had dragged him into the sunlight, wouldn't he be pained and irritated at being treated that way? And when he came into the light, with the sun filling his eyes, wouldn't he be unable to see a single one of the things now said to be true?

He would be unable to see them, at least at first.

I suppose, then, that he'd need time to get adjusted before he could see things in the world above. At first, he'd see shadows most easily, then images of men and other things in water, then the things themselves. Of these, he'd be able to study the things in the sky and the sky itself more easily at night, looking at the light of the stars and the moon, than during the day, looking at the sun and the light of the sun.

Of course.

Finally, I suppose, he'd be able to see the sun, not images of it in water or some alien place, but the sun itself, in its own place, and be able to study it.

Necessarily so.

And at this point he would infer and conclude that the sun provides the seasons and the years, governs everything in the visible world, and is in some way the cause of all the things that he used to see.

It's clear that would be his next step.

What about when he reminds himself of his first dwelling place, his fellow prisoners, and what passed for wisdom there? Don't you think that he'd count himself happy for the change and pity the others?

Certainly.

And if there had been any honors, praises, or prizes among them for the one who was sharpest at identifying the shadows as they passed by and who best remembered which usually came earlier, which later, and which simultaneously, and who could thus best divine the future, do you think that our man would desire these rewards or envy those among the prisoners who were honored and held power? Instead, wouldn't he feel, with Homer, that he'd much prefer to "work the earth as a serf to another, one without possessions,"[6] and go through any sufferings, rather than share their opinions and live as they do?

I suppose he would rather suffer anything than live like that.

Consider this too. If this man went down into the cave again and sat down in his same seat, wouldn't his eyes – coming suddenly out of the sun like that – be filled with darkness?

They certainly would.

And before his eyes had recovered – and the adjustment would not be quick – while his vision was still dim, if he had to compete again with the perpetual prisoners in recognizing the shadows, wouldn't he invite ridicule? Wouldn't it be said of him that he'd returned from his upward journey with his eyesight ruined and that it isn't worthwhile even to try to travel upward? And, as for anyone who tried to free them and lead them upward, if they could somehow get their hands on him, wouldn't they kill him?

They certainly would.

This whole image, Glaucon, must be fitted together with what we said before. The visible realm should be likened to the prison dwelling, and the light of the fire inside it to the power of the sun. And if you interpret the upward journey and the study of things above as the upward journey of the soul to the intelligible realm, you'll grasp what I hope to convey, since that is what you wanted to hear about. Whether it's true or not, only the god knows. But this is how I see it: In the knowable realm, the form of the good is the last thing to be seen, and it is reached only with difficulty. Once one has seen it, however, one must conclude that it is the cause of all that is correct and beautiful in anything, that it produces both light and its source in the visible realm, and that in the intelligible realm it controls and provides truth and understanding, so that anyone who is to act sensibly in private or public must see it.

I have the same thought, at least as far as I'm able.

Come, then, share with me this thought also: It isn't surprising that the ones who get to this point are unwilling to occupy themselves with human affairs and that their souls are always pressing upwards, eager to spend their time above, for, after all, this is surely what we'd expect, if indeed things fit the image I described before.

It is.

What about what happens when someone turns from divine study to the evils of human life? Do you think it's surprising, since his sight is still dim, and he hasn't yet become accustomed to the darkness around him, that he behaves awkwardly and appears completely ridiculous if he's compelled, either in the courts or elsewhere, to contend about the shadows of justice or the statues of which they are the shadows and to dispute about the way these things are understood by people who have never seen justice itself?

That's not surprising at all.

No, it isn't. But anyone with any understanding would remember that the eyes may be confused in two ways and from two causes, namely, when they've come from the light into the darkness *and* when they've come from the darkness into the light. Realizing that the same applies to the soul, when someone sees a soul disturbed and unable to see something, he won't laugh mindlessly, but he'll take into consideration whether it has come from a brighter life and is dimmed through not having yet become accustomed to the dark or whether it has come from greater ignorance into greater light and is dazzled by the increased brilliance. Then he'll declare the first soul happy in its experience and life, and he'll pity the latter – but even if he chose to make fun of it, at least he'd be less ridiculous than if he laughed at a soul that has come from the light above.

What you say is very reasonable.

If that's true, then here's what we must think about these matters: Education isn't what some people declare it to be, namely, putting knowledge into souls that lack it, like putting sight into blind eyes.

They do say that.

But our present discussion, on the other hand, shows that the power to learn is present in everyone's soul and that the instrument with which each learns is like an eye that cannot be turned around from darkness to light without turning the whole body. This instrument cannot be turned around from that which is coming into being without turning the whole soul until it is able to study that which is and the brightest thing that is, namely, the one we call the good. Isn't that right?

Yes.

Then education is the craft concerned with doing this very thing, this turning around, and with how the soul can most easily and effectively be made to do it. It isn't the craft of putting sight into the soul. Education takes for granted that sight is there but that it isn't turned the right way or looking where it ought to look, and it tries to redirect it appropriately.

So it seems.

Now, it looks as though the other so-called virtues of the soul are akin to those of the body, for they really aren't there beforehand but are added later by habit and practice. However, the virtue of reason seems to belong above all to something more divine, which never loses its power but is either useful and beneficial or useless and harmful, depending on the way it is turned. Or have you never noticed this about people who are said to be vicious but clever, how keen the vision of their little souls is and how sharply it distinguishes the things it is turned towards? This shows that its sight isn't inferior but rather is forced to serve evil ends, so that the sharper it sees, the more evil it accomplishes.

Absolutely.

However, if a nature of this sort had been hammered at from childhood and freed from the bonds of kinship with becoming, which have been fastened to it by feasting, greed, and other such pleasures and which, like leaden weights, pull its vision downwards – if, being rid of these, it turned to look at true things, then I say that the same soul of the same person would see these most sharply, just as it now does the things it is presently turned towards.

Probably so.

And what about the uneducated who have no experience of truth? Isn't it likely – indeed, doesn't it follow necessarily from what was said before – that they will never adequately govern a city? But neither would those who've been allowed to spend their whole lives being educated. The former would fail because they don't have a single goal at which all their actions, public and private, inevitably aim; the latter would fail because they'd refuse to act, thinking that they had settled while still alive in the faraway Isles of the Blessed.

That's true.

It is our task as founders, then, to compel the best natures to reach the study we said before is the most important, namely, to make the ascent and see the good. But when they've made it and looked sufficiently, we mustn't allow them to do what they're allowed to do today.

What's that?

To stay there and refuse to go down again to the prisoners in the cave and share their labors and honors, whether they are of less worth or of greater.

Then are we to do them an injustice by making them live a worse life when they could live a better one?

You are forgetting again that it isn't the law's concern to make any one class in the city outstandingly happy but to contrive to spread happiness throughout the city by bringing the citizens into harmony with each other through persuasion or compulsion and by making them share with each other the benefits that each class can confer on the community.[7] The law produces such people in the city, not in order to allow them to turn in whatever direction they want, but to make use of them to bind the city together.

That's true, I had forgotten.

Observe, then, Glaucon, that we won't be doing an injustice to those who've become philosophers in our city and that what we'll say to them, when we compel them to guard and care for the others, will be just. We'll say: "When people like you come to be in other cities, they're justified in not sharing in their city's labors, for they've grown there spontaneously, against the will of the constitution. And what grows of its own accord and owes no debt for its upbringing has justice on its side when it isn't keen to pay anyone for that upbringing. But we've made you kings in our city and leaders of the swarm, as it were, both for yourselves and for the rest of the city. You're better and more completely educated than the others and are better able to share in both types of life. Therefore each of you in turn must go down to live in the common dwelling place of the others and grow accustomed to seeing in the dark. When you are used to it, you'll see vastly better than the people there. And because you've seen the truth about fine, just, and good things, you'll know each image for what it is and also that of which it is the image. Thus, for you and for us, the city will be governed, not like the majority of cities nowadays, by people who fight over shadows and struggle against one another in order to rule – as if that were a great good – but by people who are awake rather than dreaming, for the truth is surely this: A city whose prospective rulers are least eager to rule must of necessity be most free from civil war, whereas a city with the opposite kind of rulers is governed in the opposite way."

Absolutely.

Then do you think that those we've nurtured will disobey us and refuse to share the labors of the city, each in turn, while living the greater part of their time with one another in the pure realm?

It isn't possible, for we'll be giving just orders to just people. Each of them will certainly go to rule as to something compulsory, however, which is exactly the opposite of what's done by those who now rule in each city. This is how it is. If you can find a way of life that's better than ruling for the prospective rulers, your well-governed city will become a possibility, for only in it will the truly rich rule – not those who are rich in gold but those who are rich in the wealth that the happy must have, namely, a good and rational life. But if beggars hungry for private goods go into public life, thinking that the good is there for the seizing, then the well-governed city is impossible, for then ruling is something fought over, and this civil and domestic war destroys these people and the rest of the city as well.

That's very true.

Can you name any life that despises political rule besides that of the true philosopher?

No, by god, I can't.

But surely it is those who are not lovers of ruling who must rule, for if they don't, the lovers of it, who are rivals, will fight over it.

Of course.

Then who will you compel to become guardians of the city, if not those who have the best understanding of what matters for good government and who have other honors than political ones, and a better, life as well?

No one.

Do you want us to consider now how such people will come to be in our city and how – just as some are said to have gone up from Hades to the gods – we'll lead them up to the light?

Of course I do.

This isn't, it seems, a matter of tossing a coin, but of turning a soul from a day that is a kind of night to the true day – the ascent to what is, which we say is true philosophy.

Indeed.

Then mustn't we try to discover the subjects that have the power to bring this about?

Of course.

So what subject is it, Glaucon, that draws the soul from the realm of becoming to the realm of what is? And it occurs to me as I'm speaking that we said, didn't we, that it is necessary for the prospective rulers to be athletes in war when they're young?

Yes, we did.

Then the subject we're looking for must also have this characteristic in addition to the former one.

Which one?

It mustn't be useless to warlike men.

If it's at all possible, it mustn't.

Now, prior to this, we educated them in music and poetry and physical training.

We did.

And physical training is concerned with what comes into being and dies, for it oversees the growth and decay of the body.

Apparently.

So it couldn't be the subject we're looking for.

No, it couldn't.

Then, could it be the music and poetry we described before?

But that, if you remember, is just the counterpart of physical training. It educated the guardians through habits. Its harmonies gave them a certain harmoniousness, not knowledge; its rhythms gave them a certain rhythmical quality; and its stories, whether fictional or nearer the truth, cultivated other habits akin to these. But as for the subject you're looking for now, there's nothing like that in music and poetry.

Your reminder is exactly to the point; there's really nothing like that in music and poetry. But, Glaucon, what is there that does have this? The crafts all seem to be base or mechanical.

How could they be otherwise? But apart from music and poetry, physical training, and the crafts, what subject is left?

Well, if we can't find anything apart from these, let's consider one of the subjects that touches all of them.

What sort of thing?

For example, that common thing that every craft, every type of thought, and every science uses and that is among the first compulsory subjects for everyone.

What's that?

That inconsequential matter of distinguishing the one, the two, and the three. In short, I mean number and calculation, for isn't it true that every craft and science must have a share in that?

They certainly must.

Then so must warfare.

Absolutely.

In the tragedies, at any rate, Palamedes is always showing up Agamemnon as a totally ridiculous general. Haven't you noticed? He says that, by inventing numbers, he established how many troops there were in the Trojan army and counted their ships and everything else – implying that they were uncounted before and that Agamemnon (if indeed he didn't know how to count) didn't even know how many feet he had? What kind of general do you think that made him?

A very strange one, if that's true.

Then won't we set down this subject as compulsory for a warrior, so that he is able to count and calculate?

More compulsory than anything. If, that is, he's to understand anything about setting his troops in order or if he's even to be properly human.

Then do you notice the same thing about this subject that I do?

What's that?

That this turns out to be one of the subjects we were looking for that naturally lead to understanding. But no one uses it correctly, namely, as something that is really fitted in every way to draw one towards being.

What do you mean?

I'll try to make my view clear as follows: I'll distinguish for myself the things that do or don't lead in the direction we mentioned, and you must study them along with me and either agree or disagree, and that way we may come to know more clearly whether things are indeed as I divine.

Point them out.

I'll point out, then, if you can grasp it, that some sense perceptions *don't* summon the understanding to look into them, because the judgment of sense perception is itself adequate, while others encourage it in every way to look into them, because sense perception seems to produce no sound result.

You're obviously referring to things appearing in the distance and to *trompe l'oeil* paintings.

You're not quite getting my meaning.

Then what do you mean?

The ones that don't summon the understanding are all those that don't go off into opposite perceptions at the same time. But the ones that do go off in that way I call *summoners* – whenever sense perception doesn't declare one thing any more than its opposite, no matter whether the object striking the senses is near at hand or far away. You'll understand my meaning better if I put it this way: These, we say, are three fingers – the smallest, the second, and the middle finger.

That's right.

Assume that I'm talking about them as being seen from close by. Now, this is my question about them.

What?

It's apparent that each of them is equally a finger, and it makes no difference in this regard whether the finger is seen to be in the middle or at either end, whether it is dark or pale, thick or thin, or anything else of that sort, for in all these cases, an ordinary soul isn't compelled to ask the understanding what a finger is, since sight doesn't suggest to it that a finger is at the same time the opposite of a finger.

No, it doesn't.

Therefore, it isn't likely that anything of that sort would summon or awaken the understanding.

No, it isn't.

But what about the bigness and smallness of fingers? Does sight perceive them adequately? Does it make no difference to it whether the finger is in the middle or at the end? And is it the same with the sense of touch, as regards the thick and the thin, the hard and the soft? And do the other senses reveal such things clearly and adequately? Doesn't each of them rather do the following: The sense set over the hard is, in the first place, of necessity also set over the soft, and it reports to the soul that the same thing is perceived by it to be both hard and soft?

That's right.

And isn't it necessary that in such cases the soul is puzzled as to what this sense means by the hard, if it indicates that the same thing is also soft, or what it means by the light and the heavy, if it indicates that the heavy is light, or the light, heavy?

Yes, indeed, these are strange reports for the soul to receive, and they do demand to be looked into.

Then it's likely that in such cases the soul, summoning calculation and understanding, first tries to determine whether each of the things announced to it is one or two.

Of course.

If it's evidently two, won't each be evidently distinct and one?

Yes.

Then, if each is one, and both two, the soul will understand that the two are separate, for it wouldn't understand the inseparable to be two, but rather one.

That's right.

Sight, however, saw the big and small, not as separate, but as mixed up together. Isn't that so?

Yes.

And in order to get clear about all this, understanding was compelled to see the big and the small, not as mixed up together, but as separate – the opposite way from sight.

True.

And isn't it from these cases that it first occurs to us to ask what the big is and what the small is?

Absolutely.

And, because of this, we called the one the intelligible and the other the visible.

That's right.

This, then, is what I was trying to express before, when I said that some things summon thought, while others don't. Those that strike the relevant sense at the same time as their opposites I call summoners, those that don't do this do not awaken understanding.

Now I understand, and I think you're right.

Well, then, to which of them do number and the one belong?

I don't know.

Reason it out from what was said before. If the one is adequately seen itself by itself or is so perceived by any of the other senses, then, as we were saying in the case of fingers, it wouldn't draw the soul towards being. But if something opposite to it is always seen at the same time, so that nothing is apparently any more one than the opposite of

one, then something would be needed to judge the matter. The soul would then be puzzled, would look for an answer, would stir up its understanding, and would ask what the one itself is. And so this would be among the subjects that lead the soul and turn it around towards the study of that which is.

But surely the sight of the one does possess this characteristic to a remarkable degree, for we see the same thing to be both one and an unlimited number at the same time.

Then, if this is true of the one, won't it also be true of all numbers?

Of course.

Now, calculation and arithmetic are wholly concerned with numbers.

That's right.

Then evidently they lead us towards truth.

Supernaturally so.

Then they belong, it seems, to the subjects we're seeking. They are compulsory for warriors because of their orderly ranks and for philosophers because they have to learn to rise up out of becoming and grasp being, if they are ever to become rational.

That's right.

And our guardian must be both a warrior and a philosopher.

Certainly.

Then it would be appropriate, Glaucon, to legislate this subject for those who are going to share in the highest offices in the city and to persuade them to turn to calculation and take it up, not as laymen do, but staying with it until they reach the study of the natures of the numbers by means of understanding itself, nor like tradesmen and retailers, for the sake of buying and selling, but for the sake of war and for ease in turning the soul around, away from becoming and towards truth and being.

Well put.

## Notes

1. Throughout, Socrates is punning on the word *tokos*, which means either a child or the interest on capital.
2. The play may be on the similarity of sound between *ouranou* ("of heaven") and *horatou* ("of the visible"). More likely, Socrates is referring to the fact that *ouranou* seems to contain the word *nou*, the genitive case of *nous* ("understanding"), and relative of *noētou* ("of the intelligible"). If he said that the sun was sovereign of heaven, he might be taken to suggest in sophistical fashion that it was sovereign of the intelligible and that there was no real difference between the good and the sun.

3. The line is illustrated below:

Understanding (*noēsis*)

Thought (*dianoia*)

Belief (*pistis*)
Imagination (*eikasia*)

4. Reading *parionta autous nomizein onomazein* in b5.
5. Reading *hoia tis an eiē phusei, ei* in c5.
6. *Odyssey* xi. 489–90.
7. See 420b–421c, 462a–466c.

# 2

# Knowing How to Rule and be Ruled as Justice Demands

## Plato

[W]e ought to take the preliminary step of defining education and its potentialities, because we have ventured on a discussion which is intended to lead us to the god of wine, and we are agreed that education is as it were the route we have to take.

CLINIAS: Certainly let's do that, if you like.

ATHENIAN: I am going to explain how one should describe education: see if you approve of my account.

CLINIAS: Your explanation, then, please.

ATHENIAN: It is this: I insist that a man who intends to be good at a particular occupation must practice it from childhood: both at work and at play he must be surrounded by the special 'tools of the trade'. For instance, the man who intends to be a good farmer must play at farming, and the man who is to be a good builder must spend his playtime building toy houses; and in each case the teacher must provide miniature tools that copy the real thing. In particular, in this elementary stage they must learn the essential elementary skills. For example, the carpenter must learn in his play how to handle a rule and plumb-line, and the soldier must learn to ride a horse (either by actually doing it, in play, or by some similar activity). We should

try to use the children's games to channel their pleasures and desires towards the activities in which they will have to engage when they are adult. To sum up, we say that the correct way to bring up and educate a child is to use his playtime to imbue his soul with the greatest possible liking for the occupation in which he will have to be absolutely perfect when he grows up. Now, as I suggested, consider the argument so far: do you approve of my account?

CLINIAS: Of course.

ATHENIAN: But let's not leave our description of education in the air. When we abuse or commend the upbringing of individual people and say that one of us is educated and the other uneducated, we sometimes use this latter term of men who have in fact had a thorough education – one directed towards petty trade or the merchant-shipping business, or something like that. But I take it that for the purpose of the present discussion we are not going to treat this sort of thing as 'education'; what we have in mind is education from childhood in *virtue*, a training which produces a keen desire to become a perfect citizen who knows how to rule and be ruled as justice demands. I suppose we should want to mark

Editor's title. Previously published in *Plato: The Laws*, ed. and trans. Trevor J. Saunders (London: Penguin Classics, 1970), pp. 72–5; 643a–645c. © Trevor J. Saunders 1970. Reprinted with permission of Penguin Books UK Ltd.

off this sort of training from others and reserve the title 'education' for it alone. A training directed to acquiring money or a robust physique, or even to some intellectual facility not guided by reason and justice, we should want to call coarse and illiberal, and say that it had no claim whatever to be called education. Still, let's not quibble over a name; let's stick to the proposition we agreed on just now: as a rule, men with a correct education become good, and nowhere in the world should education be despised, for when combined with great virtue, it is an asset of incalculable value. If it ever becomes corrupt, but can be put right again, this is a lifelong task which everyone should undertake to the limit of his strength.

CLINIAS:   True. We agree with your description.

ATHENIAN:   Here is a further point on which we agreed some time ago: those who can control themselves are good, those who cannot are bad.

CLINIAS:   Perfectly correct.

ATHENIAN:   Let's take up this point again and consider even more closely just what we mean. Perhaps you'll let me try to clarify the issue by means of an illustration.

CLINIAS:   By all means.

ATHENIAN:   Are we to assume, then, that each of us is a single individual?

CLINIAS:   Yes.

ATHENIAN:   But that he possesses within himself a pair of witless and mutually antagonistic advisers, which we call pleasure and pain?

CLINIAS:   That is so.

ATHENIAN:   In addition to these two, he has opinions about the future, whose general name is 'expectations'. Specifically, the anticipation of pain is called 'fear', and the anticipation of the opposite is called 'confidence'. Over and against all these we have 'calculation', by which we judge the relative merits of pleasure and pain, and when this is expressed as a public decision of a state, it receives the title 'law'.

CLINIAS:   I can scarcely follow you; but assume I do, and carry on with what comes next.

MEGILLUS:   Yes, I'm in the same difficulty.

ATHENIAN:   I suggest we look at the problem in this way: let's imagine that each of us living beings is a puppet of the gods. Whether we have been constructed to serve as their plaything, or for some serious reason, is something beyond our ken, but what we certainly do know is this: we have these emotions in us, which act like cords or strings and tug us about; they work in opposition, and tug against each other to make us perform actions that are opposed correspondingly; back and forth we go across the boundary line where vice and virtue meet. One of these dragging forces, according to our argument, demands our constant obedience, and this is the one we have to hang on to, come what may; the pull of the other cords we must resist. This cord, which is golden and holy, transmits the power of 'calculation', a power which in a state is called the public law; being golden, it is pliant, while the others, whose composition resembles a variety of other substances, are tough and inflexible. The force exerted by law is excellent, and one should always co-operate with it, because although 'calculation' is a noble thing, it is gentle, not violent, and its efforts need assistants, so that the gold in us may prevail over the other substances. If we do give our help, the moral point of this fable, in which we appear as puppets, will have been well and truly made; the meaning of the terms 'self-superior' and 'self-inferior' will somehow become clearer, and the duties of state and individual will be better appreciated. The latter must digest the truth about these forces that pull him, and act on it in his life; the state must get an account of it either from one of the gods or from the human expert we've mentioned, and incorporate it in the form of a law to govern both its internal affairs and its relations with other states. A further result will be a clearer distinction between virtue and vice; the light cast on that problem will perhaps in turn help to clarify the subject of education and the various other practices, particularly the business of drinking parties. It may well be thought that this is a triviality on which a great deal too much has been said, but equally it may turn out that the topic really does deserve this extended discussion.

# 3

# An Educated Person Can Speak Well and Persuade

## Isocrates

[240] You will learn even more clearly from what I am about to say how far I am from corrupting the youth. If I were doing this, it is not Lysimachus or those of his ilk who would be upset on their behalf, but instead you would see the fathers and the relations of the students all upset, bringing charges, and seeking to punish me. [241] Instead, they bring me their sons, pay my fees, and rejoice when they see them spending the day with me, while the sykophants slander us and give us trouble. Who would be happier than these to see many of the citizens corrupted and depraved? They know that among people like that they have power, but they are ruined by gentlemen of intelligence, when they are caught. [242] Thus it makes sense for them to seek to root out all such activities which they think will make people better and less tolerant of their evils and sykophancies. But it is right for you to do just the opposite, and treat those activities to which they are most hostile as the finest of all.

[243] Something extraordinary has happened to me. I will be honest even if some say I change positions too easily. A little before, I said that many gentlemen (*kaloi kagathoi*) were deceived about philosophy and were highly critical of it. Now I have assumed that the arguments I made are so clear and apparent to everyone that I do not think anyone is unaware of its power, or condemns me for corrupting my students, or feels as I accused them of feeling a little while ago. [244] If I must speak the truth and say what is in my mind, I think all who envy me want to be able to think and speak well themselves, but they neglect these things, some through laziness, others because they downplay their own natural ability, and still others for various other reasons (and there are many). [245] But toward those who apply themselves diligently and wish to acquire the things they themselves desire, they are irritated and jealous, they are upset, and they go through the same sort of experience as lovers. What more fitting explanation could one offer for their behavior than this? [246] They praise and envy those who can speak well, but they fault young people who wish to achieve this honor, although there is no one who would not pray to the gods to be able to speak well himself, and if not himself, then his children and relatives. [247] They claim that those who accomplish this through labor and philosophy – which they want to get for themselves from the gods[1] – are neglecting their duty. Sometimes they pretend

to mock them as being deceived and cheated, but then when they feel like it, they change and speak of them as able to profit from their expertise. [248] When some danger befalls the city, they listen to their advisers who are best at speaking on public matters and they do whatever such men advise. Yet they think they should slander those who take the trouble to present themselves to be useful to the city at such times. They find fault with the ignorance of the Thebans and of other enemies, but they continually criticize those who seek to do everything they can to escape this disease.

[249] This is a sign not only of their confusion, but also of their disrespect for the gods. They regard Persuasion (*Peithō*) as a god, and they see Athens sacrificing to her every year, but they claim that those who wish to share in the power that the goddess has are being corrupted by desire for something evil. [250] Worst of all, although they assume the soul is more important than the body, despite knowing this, they welcome those who engage in gymnastics more than those who engage in philosophy. Surely it is irrational to praise those who engage in a lesser activity rather than a higher activity. Everyone knows that Athens never accomplished the remarkable deeds for which it is renowned through physical training, but that it became the most blessed and greatest of all the Hellenic city states through man's intellect.

[251] Someone younger than I without the anxieties of this occasion might bring together many more of their contradictions. For instance, on the same subject one could say that if some people inherited a vast sum of money from their ancestors and did not serve the city's interests but instead abused their fellow citizens and dishonored their wives and children, would anyone dare to blame those who were responsible for the wealth and not demand that the offenders themselves be punished? [252] What if others who have learned armed combat do not use their knowledge against the enemy but cause an uprising and kill many fellow citizens, or receive the best possible training in boxing and the pankration,[2] but then instead of entering athletic contests, they hit everyone they meet? Who would not praise their teachers and then put to death those who made bad use of what they learned?

[253] Thus we should have the same understanding of speaking (*hoi logoi*) as we do of other matters, and not judge similar cases in the opposite way, or show hostility toward this facility, which of all human capabilities is responsible for the greatest goods. For in our other facilities, as I said earlier,[3] we do not differ from other living beings, and in fact we are inferior to many in speed, strength, and other resources. [254] But since we have the ability to persuade one another and to make clear to ourselves what we want, not only do we avoid living like animals, but we have come together, built cities, made laws, and invented arts (*technē*). Speech (*logos*) is responsible for nearly all our inventions. [255] It legislated in matters of justice and injustice and beauty and baseness, and without these laws, we could not live with one another. By it we refute the bad and praise the good; through it, we educate the ignorant and recognize the intelligent. We regard speaking well to be the clearest sign of a good mind, which it requires, and truthful, lawful, and just speech we consider the image (*eidolon*) of a good and faithful soul. [256] With speech we fight over contentious matters, and we investigate the unknown. We use the same arguments by which we persuade others in our own deliberations; we call those able to speak in a crowd "rhetorical" (*rhētorikoi*); we regard as sound advisers those who debate with themselves most skillfully about public affairs. [257] If one must summarize the power of discourse, we will discover that nothing done prudently occurs without speech (*logos*), that speech is the leader of all thoughts and actions, and that the most intelligent people use it most of all.

Because Lysimachus perceived none of this, he dared to prosecute those who had their hearts set on an activity responsible for so many important benefits. [258] Why should we be surprised at him, when even some of those who are experts in argumentation bring similar charges against beneficial public speeches as those brought by the basest men? They are not ignorant of the speeches' power, or of the speed with which they benefit those who employ them, but they expect that by slandering their discourse they will increase the honor of their own profession. [259] Perhaps, I could speak much more bitterly about them than they do about me, but I do not think I should either be like those who are destroyed by envy or blame those who do no harm to their pupils but are also less able to benefit others. Still, I shall say a few things about them, primarily because they have done so about me, but also so that you may better understand their power and may treat each of us fairly, [260] in addition to making clear that although I am concerned with political discourse (*hoi politikoi logoi*), which they say is quarrelsome, I am much gentler than they are.

If they always disparage me, I am not inclined to do the same but will speak the truth about them. [261] I think the leaders in eristic and those who teach astrology, geometry, and other branches of learning do not harm but rather benefit their students, less than they promise but more than others think. [262] Most men regard such studies as babbling and hairsplitting, since none of them is useful in personal or public life. Students do not remember them for very long because they do not have a bearing on our lives, or help with our activities, but are in every respect nonessential. [263] On this matter my view is not the same nor is it so different: I think that those who consider this education irrelevant to public affairs are correct, and those who praise it also utter the truth. I have stated contradictory views on this issue because by their nature these subjects are not at all like the other ones we teach. [264] Other subjects naturally help us when we gain an understanding of them. But these do not benefit us even if we become specialists in them (unless we choose to earn our living from them), but they do benefit us when we learn them. [265] When we spend time in the detail and precision of astrology and geometry, we are forced to put our minds to matters that are hard to learn, and moreover, we get used to working persistently hard at[4] what has been said and demonstrated to us, and we cannot let our minds wander. When we are exercised and sharpened in these matters, we are able to receive and learn more important and significant material more quickly and easily. [266] I don't think we should call what does not at present benefit our ability to speak or act "philosophy." Instead, I call such activity a "mental gymnastics" and a "preparation for philosophy" – a more mature subject than what children learn in schools but for the most part similar. [267] When children have worked hard at grammar, music, and the rest of education, they have not yet made progress in speaking better or in deliberating on public affairs, although they have become better prepared to learn the greater and more serious subjects. [268] I would advise the young to spend some time in these subjects but not to allow their natures to become withered up by them or stranded in the discourses of the older sophists,[5] of whom one said the number of elements is infinite;[6] Empedocles, that it is four, among which are strife and love;[7] Ion, that it is not more than three;[8] Alcmaeon, that it is only two;[9] Parmenides and Melissus, that it is one;[10] and Gorgias, [that it is] nothing at all.[11] [269] I think that such quibblings resemble wonder-workings,

which provide no benefit but attract crowds of the ignorant. Those wishing to do something useful must rid all their activities of pointless discourse and irrelevant action.

[270] I have presented a sufficient account and advice on these matters. Concerning wisdom (*sophia*) and philosophy (*philosophia*), it would not be fitting for someone pleading about other issues to speak about these terms, since they have nothing to do with all other activities, but since I am on trial for just such matters and am claiming that what some people call "philosophy" is not really that at all, it is appropriate for me to define it and to show you what it is, when rightly understood.

[271] I understand it quite simply. Since human nature cannot attain knowledge that would enable us to know what we must say or do, after this I think that the wise (*sophoi*) are those who have the ability to reach the best opinions (*doxai*) most of the time, and philosophers are those who spend time acquiring such an intelligence as quickly as possible. [272] I can reveal which activities have such power, but I hesitate to do so because they are so very unexpected and so far removed from other people's ideas. I fear that as soon as you hear them you will fill the whole courtroom with shouting and protest. But despite these feelings, I shall try to discuss them. I am embarrassed if I appear to some to be afraid of betraying the truth because of my old age and the short life I have left. [273] I ask that you do not decide ahead of time that I am so mad that being in peril I would choose to utter words contrary to your view, unless I considered them consistent with what I have already said and thought that I had true and evident proofs of them.

[274] I think that an art that can produce self-control (*sōphrosynē*) and justice (*dikaiosynē*) in those who are by nature badly disposed to virtue (*aretē*) has never existed and does not now exist, and that those who previously made promises to this effect will cease speaking and stop uttering nonsense before such an education (*paideia*) is discovered. [275] In my view, people improve and become worthier if they are interested in speaking well, have a passion for being able to persuade their audience, and also desire advantage (*pleonexia*) – not what foolish people think it is but that which truly has this power. [276] I think I can quickly show that this is so.

In the first place, someone who chooses to speak and write speeches worthy of praise and honor will not possibly select topics that are unjust or insignificant or that deal with private arguments but those public issues which are important and noble and promote human welfare. If he does not discover any such topics, he will accomplish nothing. [277] Then from the evidence relevant to his topic, he will select the most appropriate and advantageous. Someone who is accustomed to examine and evaluate such topics will have this same facility not only for the speech at hand but also for other affairs. As a result, those who are philosophical and ambitious in their devotion to speaking (*logoi*) will at the same time speak well and think intelligently. [278] Moreover, anyone who wishes to persuade others will not neglect virtue but will devote even more attention to ensuring that he achieves a most honorable reputation among his fellow citizens. Who could fail to know that speeches seem truer when spoken by those of good name than by the disreputable, and that arguments acquire more authority when they come from one's life than from mere words. The more ardently someone wants to persuade his audience, the more he will strive to be a gentleman (*kalos kagathos*) and to have a good reputation among the citizens.

[279] Let none of you think that everyone else knows how it supports the cause of persuasion if one can please the jury, and that philosophers alone are ignorant of the power of goodwill. They know this far more acutely than others. [280] In addition, they know that plausibility (*to eikos*), and inference, and all forms of proof contribute only that part of the speech in which each of them is uttered, whereas the reputation of being a gentleman not only makes the speech more persuasive but also makes the actions of one who has such a reputation more honorable. Intelligent men must covet this more than anything else.

[281] This brings me to the subject of advantage (*pleonexia*), which is the most problematic of the issues I have mentioned. If someone assumes that people gain advantages by stealing, misrepresenting, or doing something evil, he is under the wrong impression. No one is more disadvantaged in his entire life than such men; no one lives in greater poverty or in greater disrepute; and no one is more thoroughly wretched. [282] You should now realize that those who are most righteous and most devoted in service to the gods receive and will continue to receive more advantages from the gods, just as those who are most devoted to the interests of their family and fellow citizens and have the best reputation among them will gain more advantages from other human beings. [283] This is the truth, but it is,

furthermore, helpful to speak in this way on the subject, since Athens is in such a state of confusion and chaos that some people no longer use words naturally but transfer them from the finest deeds to the basest activities.[12] [284] They call buffoons and those who can mock and imitate others "talented" (*euphyeis*), when this term rightly applies to those who are most virtuous by nature.[13] And they think that those who rely on a wicked nature and evil deeds to gain a little profit while acquiring an evil reputation are at an advantage, not those who are most righteous and just, who profit from good and not evil. [285] And they declare that those who neglect the necessities of life and admire the logical tricks of the ancient sophists do "philosophy," having disregarded those who learn and practice what allows them to manage well their own homes and the city's commonwealth[14] – for which one must work hard, engage in philosophy, and do everything necessary.

Because you accept the arguments of those who slander this kind of education (*paideia*), you have been driving the young away from such activities. [286] You have led the most promising of them to spend their youth in drink, social gatherings, amusements, and games, while neglecting the serious business of self-improvement, and those with baser natures to pass the day in the sort of undisciplined behavior that no honest slave would have previously dared.[15] [287] Some of them chill wine in the Nine Fountains;[16] others drink in the taverns, while others play dice in the gambling dens; and many hang out in the schools for flute girls.[17] And none of those who claim to be concerned about these youths has ever brought those who encourage such behavior before this jury of yours. Instead, they harass me, although if anything, I deserve thanks for turning my students away from such activities.

[288] The race of sykophants is so hostile to everyone that far from reproaching those who spend twenty or thirty minas to obtain women who will consume the rest of their household, instead they rejoice at their lavishness; but if someone spends anything on his own education (*paideia*), the sykophants say they are being corrupted. Who could bring a more unjust charge than this against my pupils? [289] Although they are in the prime of their lives, they disregarded the pleasures that most men of the same age desire, and although they had the option of taking life easy and spending nothing, they chose to pay out money and work. As soon as they left childhood, they knew what many older people do not, [290] that in order to supervise this age correctly and

properly and to start life in a favorable way, a person must tend to himself before attending to his affairs, must not hurry or seek to rule others before finding someone to oversee his intellect, must not rejoice in or pride himself on other good things as much as on those that the soul produces as a result of education. Surely one should not blame but rather praise those who use such logic, and regard them as the best and most prudent of their contemporaries.

[291] I am amazed that those who congratulate naturally able speakers for the fine talent they have been endowed with nonetheless still find fault with those who wish to become like these and accuse them of desiring an unjust and bad education. Does anything that is noble turn out shameful or wicked if one works to attain it? We will not find any such thing, and everywhere else we praise those who can acquire some benefit by their own effort, more than those who inherit it from their ancestors. [292] This is reasonable. It is better in all other matters and especially in speaking to gain repute not by good luck but by practice. Those who become skilled speakers by nature and luck do not aspire for what is best but are accustomed to use words as they come. On the other hand, those who acquire this ability by means of philosophy and reasoning do not speak thoughtlessly and are less careless in their affairs.

[293] As a result, it is appropriate for everyone, especially you jurors, to want many to become skilled speakers through education. For you excel and are superior to others not because of your attention to military matters, or because you have the best constitution, or are the most effective guardians of the laws your ancestors left to you, but because of that feature which makes human nature superior to that of other living creatures and the Greek race superior to the barbarians, [294] namely, a superior education in intellect and speech. Accordingly, it would be a most terrible outcome if you vote to condemn those who wish to surpass their contemporaries in the very things in which you surpass everyone else, and pile misfortune on those who obtain the kind of education in which you are the leaders. [295] You must not ignore the fact that our city is thought to be the teacher of all those who are skilled in speaking and teaching.[18] And this is reasonable, for people see that the city makes available the greatest rewards for those who have this ability and provides the greatest number and variety of opportunities for exercising them for those who choose to compete and wish to engage in such activities. [296] Furthermore, everyone here acquires

experience, which most of all produces the ability to speak. In addition, they think that our common dialect, and its moderation,[19] our flexibility, and our love of language contribute significantly to our culture of discourse (*hē tōn logōn paideia*). Hence, they are right to think that all who have skill at speaking are students of Athens.

[297] Be careful to avoid becoming utterly ridiculous by condemning as something trifling this reputation that you have among the Greeks more than I have among you. You will clearly be convicting yourselves of the same injustice, [298] and you will have acted just as if the Spartans should attempt to punish those who practice military arts, or the Thessalians thought to punish those who practiced horsemanship.[20] You must guard against this so as not to make such a mistake about yourselves, or to make the speeches of the city's accusers more credible than those of its encomiasts.

[299] I think that you are not unaware that some of the Greeks are hostile to you, and that others are as fond of you as they can be and lay their hopes of salvation in you. The latter say that Athens is the only city (*polis*), that the others are villages (*kōmai*), and that Athens rightly should be called the capital (*astu*) of Greece because of its size and the resources we provide to others, and especially for the character of the inhabitants. [300] They say none are more gentle, more sociable, or better suited to someone who would spend his whole life here. People use such warm terms that they do not hesitate to declare that punishment by an Athenian man is more pleasant than favorable treatment through the savagery of others. Others dismiss this praise; they describe the bitterness and wickedness of the sykophants and accuse the whole city of being unsociable and cruel. [301] It is up to the jurors who are sensible to destroy those who are responsible for such words, because they heap a great shame on Athens, and to honor those who contribute some part to the praise it receives, even more than the athletes who win in the prize competitions. [302] These men acquire a much finer and more fitting reputation for the city than athletes.[21] We have many rivals in athletic competition, but in education, all would judge us winners. Even those with slight ability to reason should make clear that they honor men who excel in those activities for which Athens is highly regarded, and they are not jealous but agree with the other Greeks about them.

[303] None of these things ever concerned you, but you have failed to perceive your interests to

such a degree that you prefer to listen to those who slander you than to those who praise you, and you think that those who cause many to hate Athens are more democratic than those who dispose their associates to think well of the city. [304] If you are sensible, you will stop this confusion. You will not, as you do now, either treat philosophy harshly or dismiss it, but you will accept that the cultivation of the soul is the best and most worthwhile activity. You will encourage young men with adequate wealth and leisure to pursue education and this kind of training. [305] You will value those who are willing to work hard and prepare themselves for service to the city. You will hate those who live dissolutely and think of nothing other than how they can extravagantly enjoy their inheritance, and you will regard them as traitors, both of Athens and of their ancestors' reputations. If they see you treating either of these groups in this manner, the youth will gradually despise easy living and will be willing to attend to themselves and to philosophy.

[306] Recall the beauty of the magnificent achievements of our city and our ancestors. Reflect on them yourselves and consider who the man was who drove out the tyrants, restored the people, and established the democracy, who his ancestors were, and what kind of education he received;[22] what sort of person defeated the barbarians at the battle of Marathon and gained glory from this feat for our city;[23] [307] and who after him freed the Greeks and led our forefathers to the leadership and power they obtained. After he understood the natural advantages of Piraeus, he built a wall around the city with the Spartans objecting.[24] And after him, who filled the Acropolis with silver and gold and made private households teem with great prosperity and wealth?[25] [308] If you look at each of these individuals, you will find that they did not accomplish these things living like sykophants, or negligently, or like the multitude, but rather they excelled and were pre-eminent not only in birth and reputation but also in their ability to think and speak. In this way they became responsible for all these benefits.

[309] So it is only reasonable that with these examples in mind you should examine this case in the interests of the people, that in their private disputes, they may obtain justice and have their due share of other public privileges, and you should cherish, honor, and cultivate those who are superior by nature and education as well as those who desire to be such. You know that leadership in noble and important enterprises, the ability to save our city from danger, and the protection of democracy are in the hands of such men, not sykophants.

## Notes

1. I.e., without working for it.
2. Lit. "a complete contest"; an exercise involving both boxing and wrestling.
3. Sections 253–257 are cited verbatim from 3.5–9.
4. The majority of manuscripts read "we get used to speaking (*legein*) and working on . . ."
5. "The older sophists" are the Presocratics and not the great political leaders, like Solon, Cleisthenes, and Themistocles, mentioned in 232–235. By using "sophist" in connection with these thinkers, Isocrates is attempting to give the noun a more positive connotation than it often has at this time.
6. The reference is to Anaxagoras of Clazomenae (*c*.500–428). In his work *On Nature*, he declared that all things were infinite with respect to their number and size.
7. Empedocles of Acragas (*c*.495–435) wrote a poem in two books entitled *On Nature* in which he taught that there were four elements, fire, water, earth, and air, which came together through love and were divided by strife.
8. Ion of Chios (fifth century) is credited with the idea that everything is made up of three things. Some of them are always at war, but when they come together, they produce offspring.
9. Alcmeon of Croton (fifth century) proposed that human affairs generally occur in opposing pairs; health was a balance – or not – of these opposites.
10. In his poem *Truth*, Parmenides of Elea wrote of what *is* as being all together, one and continuous. He is said to have come with Zeno to Athens, where he met the young Socrates. Melissus, the pupil of Parmenides, wrote a work entitled *On Nature or on What Exists*. Paraphrases are preserved in the Pseudo-Aristotelian *On Melissus, Xenophanes, and Gorgias*.
11. Gorgias, introduced as the successful but also irresponsible teacher of rhetoric at section 155, now appears a nihilist. This aspect of his thinking is represented by his work *On Not Being*; cf. 10.3.
12. Isocrates may have in mind Thuc. 3.82. Aristotle (*Topics* 112a32) treats the misassignments of words as a form of verbal attack.
13. Cf. 7.49. Note that at 7.74 Isocrates says that he will cite less extensive passages from his prior works.

14. Protagoras had claimed to teach *euboulia*, i.e., good management of one's household (*oikos*) and the city (*polis*); see Plato, *Protagoras* 318e–319a.
15. Cf. 7.48 on the pastimes of contemporary youth.
16. The Nine Fountains were most likely situated between the Acropolis and the Pnyx; see Thuc. 2.15.5.
17. See Plato, *Symposium* 212c–d, for the association of flute girls with a dissipated lifestyle. Flute girls may have also doubled as prostitutes for young men.
18. For the motif of Athens as the teacher of Greece, see Thuc. 2.41.1, 7.63, and Plut., *Moralia* 784b; cf. Plut., *Lycurgus* 30, for Sparta as the teacher of Greece.
19. Cf. 4.50; on the historical consistency of the Attic language, see Herod. 1.57–58.

20. Isocrates here invokes three cultural stereotypes – Athenians as intellectuals, Spartans as militarists, and Thessalians as equestrians – all of which serve to affirm the superiority of Athens for pursuing intellectual, over the physical, arts.
21. For similar comparisons of intellectuals with athletes, see, e.g., Xenophanes 2 and Plato, *Apology* 36d.
22. Cleisthenes; see above, 232.
23. Miltiades, who is not previously named.
24. Themistocles; see above, 233. For his construction of the long walls around Piraeus, see Thuc. 1.93.
25. Pericles; see above, 234. Pericles moved the treasury of the Delian League from Delos to Athens; cf. Thuc. 2.13.

# 4

# The Exercise of Reason

## John Locke

§1. *Introduction*   The last resort a man has recourse to in the conduct of himself is his understanding; for though we distinguish the faculties of the mind, and give the supreme command to the will as to an agent, yet the truth is, the man which is the agent determines himself to this or that voluntary action upon some precedent knowledge, or appearance of knowledge, in the understanding. No man ever sets himself about anything but upon some view or other which serves him for a reason for what he does: and whatsoever faculties he employs, the understanding, with such light as it has, well or ill informed, constantly leads; and by that light, true or false, all his operative powers are directed. The will itself, how absolute and uncontrollable soever it may be thought, never fails in its obedience to the dictates of the understanding. Temples have their sacred images, and we see what influence they have always had over a great part of mankind. But in truth the ideas and images in men's minds are the invisible powers that constantly govern them, and to these they all universally pay a ready submission. It is therefore of the highest concernment that great care should be taken of the understanding, to conduct it right in the search of knowledge and in the judgments it makes.

The logic now in use has so long possessed the chair, as the only art taught in the Schools for the direction of the mind in the study of the arts and sciences, that it would perhaps be thought an affectation of novelty to suspect that rules that have served the learned world these two or three thousand years, and which, without any complaint of defects, the learned have rested in, are not sufficient to guide the understanding.[1] And I should not doubt but this attempt would be censured as vanity or presumption, did not the great Lord Verulam's authority justify it;[2] who, not servilely thinking learning could not be advanced beyond what it was, because for many ages it had not been, did not rest in the lazy approbation and applause of what was, because it was, but enlarged his mind to what might be. In his preface to his *Novum Organum*,[3] concerning logic he pronounces thus: *Qui summas dialecticae partes tribuerunt atque inde fidissima scientiis praesidia comparari putarunt, verissime et optime viderunt intellectum humanum sibi permissum merito suspectum esse debere. Verum infirmior omnino est malo medicina; nec ipsa mali expers.*

Editor's title. Previously published as *Of the Conduct of the Understanding*, in Ruth W. Grant and Nathan Tarcov (eds.), *John Locke: Some Thoughts Concerning Education and Of the Conduct of the Understanding* (Indianapolis, IN: Hackett, 1996), pp. 167–71, 172–82. Reprinted by permission of Hackett Publishing Company Inc. All rights reserved.

*Siquidem dialectica quae recepta est, licet ad civilia et artes quae in sermone et opinione positae sunt rectissime adhibeatur, naturae tamen subtilitatem longo intervallo non attingit; et prensando quod non capit, ad errores potius stabiliendos et quasi figendos quam ad viam veritati aperiendam valuit.*

'They,' says he, 'who attributed so much to logic, perceived very well and truly, that it was not safe to trust the understanding to itself, without the guard of any rules. But the remedy reached not the evil; but became a part of it: for the logic which took place, though it might do well enough in civil affairs and the arts which consisted in talk and opinion, yet comes very far short of subtlety in the real performances of nature, and, catching at what it cannot reach, has served to confirm and establish errors, rather than to open a way to truth.' And therefore a little after he says, 'That it is absolutely necessary that a better and perfecter use and employment of the mind and understanding should be introduced.' *Necessario requiritur ut melior et perfectior mentis et intellectus humani usus et adoperatio introducatur.*

§2. *Parts*[4]   There is, it is visible, great variety in men's understandings, and their natural constitutions put so wide a difference between some men in this respect, that art and industry would never be able to master; and their very natures seem to want a foundation to raise on it that which other men easily attain unto. Amongst men of equal education there is great inequality of parts. And the woods of America, as well as the schools of Athens, produce men of several abilities in the same kind. Though this be so, yet I imagine most men come very short of what they might attain unto in their several degrees by a neglect of their understandings. A few rules of logic are thought sufficient in this case for those who pretend to the highest improvement; whereas I think there are a great many natural defects in the understanding capable of amendment, which are overlooked and wholly neglected. And it is easy to perceive that men are guilty of a great many faults in the exercise and improvement of this faculty of the mind, which hinder them in their progress and keep them in ignorance and error all their lives. Some of them I shall take notice of, and endeavor to point out proper remedies for in the following discourse.

§3. *Reasoning*   Besides the want of determined ideas, and of sagacity and exercise in finding out and laying in order intermediate ideas, there are three miscarriages that men are guilty of in reference to their reason, whereby this faculty is hindered in them

from that service it might do and was designed for. And he that reflects upon the actions and discourses of mankind, will find their defects in this kind very frequent and very observable.

1. The first is of those who seldom reason at all, but do and think according to the example of others, whether parents, neighbors, ministers, or who else they are pleased to make choice of to have an implicit faith in, for the saving of themselves the pains and trouble of thinking and examining for themselves.

2. The second is of those who put passion in the place of reason, and, being resolved that shall govern their actions and arguments, neither use their own nor hearken to other people's reason, any farther than it suits their humor, interest, or party; and these one may observe commonly content themselves with words which have no distinct ideas to them, though, in other matters, that they come with an unbiased indifference to, they want not abilities to talk and hear reason, where they have no secret inclination that hinders them from being tractable[5] to it.

3. The third sort is of those who readily and sincerely follow reason, but, for want of having that which one may call *large, sound, round-about sense*, have not a full view of all that relates to the question and may be of moment to decide it. We are all short sighted, and very often see but one side of a matter; our views are not extended to all that has a connection with it. From this defect I think no man is free. We see but in part, and we know but in part, and therefore it is no wonder we conclude not right from our partial views. This might instruct the proudest esteemer of his own parts, how useful it is to talk and consult with others, even such as come short of him in capacity, quickness and penetration: for since no one sees all, and we generally have different prospects of the same thing, according to our different, as I may say, positions to it, it is not incongruous to think nor beneath any man to try, whether another may not have notions of things which have escaped him, and which his reason would make use of if they came into his mind. The faculty of reasoning seldom or never deceives those who trust to it; its consequences from what it builds on are evident and certain, but that which it oftenest, if not only, misleads us in is that the principles from which we conclude, the grounds upon which we bottom our reasoning, are but a part, something is left out which should go into the reckoning to make it just and exact. Here we may imagine a vast and

almost infinite advantage that angels and separate spirits may have over us; who, in their several degrees of elevation above us, may be endowed with more comprehensive faculties, and some of them perhaps have perfect and exact views of all finite beings that come under their consideration, can, as it were, in the twinkling of an eye, collect together all their scattered and almost boundless relations. A mind so furnished, what reason has it to acquiesce in the certainty of its conclusions!

In this we may see the reason why some men of study and thought, that reason right and are lovers of truth, do make no great advances in their discoveries of it. Error and truth are uncertainly blended in their minds; their decisions are lame and defective, and they are very often mistaken in their judgments: the reason whereof is, they converse but with one sort of men, they read but one sort of books, they will not come in the hearing but of one sort of notions; the truth is, they canton out to themselves a little Goshen[6] in the intellectual world, where light shines, and, as they conclude, day blesses them; but the rest of that vast firmament[7] they give up to night and darkness, and so avoid coming near it. They have a pretty traffick with known correspondents in some little creek; within that they confine themselves, and are dexterous managers enough of the wares and products of that corner with which they content themselves, but will not venture out into the great ocean of knowledge, to survey the riches that nature has stored other parts with, no less genuine, no less solid, no less useful, than what has fallen to their lot in the admired plenty and sufficiency of their own little spot, which to them contains whatsoever is good in the universe. Those who live thus mued up within their own contracted territories, and will not look abroad beyond the boundaries that chance, conceit, or laziness has set to their enquiries, but live separate from the notions, discourses and attainments of the rest of mankind, may not amiss be represented by the inhabitants of the Marian islands; who, being separated by a large tract of sea from all communion with the habitable parts of the earth, thought themselves the only people of the world. And though the straitness of the conveniences of life amongst them had never reached so far as to the use of fire, until the Spaniards, not many years since, in their voyages from Acapulco to Manilia brought it amongst them; yet in the want and ignorance of almost all things, they looked upon themselves, even after that the Spaniards had brought amongst them the notice of variety of nations abounding in sciences, arts and conveniences of life, of which they knew nothing, they looked upon themselves, I say, as the happiest and wisest people of the universe. But for all that, nobody, I think, will imagine them deep naturalists, or solid metaphysicians; nobody will deem the quickest sighted amongst them to have very enlarged views in ethics or politics, nor can anyone allow the most capable amongst them to be advanced so far in his understanding as to have any other knowledge but of the few little things of his and the neighboring islands within his commerce, but far enough from that comprehensive enlargement of mind which adorns a soul devoted to truth, assisted with letters, and a free consideration of the several views and sentiments of thinking men of all sides. Let not men therefore that would have a sight of, what everyone pretends to be desirous to have a sight of, truth in its full extent, narrow and blind their own prospect. Let not men think there is no truth but in the sciences that they study, or the books that they read. To prejudge other men's notions before we have looked into them is not to show their darkness, but to put out our own eyes. *Try all things, hold fast that which is good*,[8] is a divine rule coining from the Father of Light and Truth; and it is hard to know what other way men can come at truth, to lay hold of it, if they do not dig and search for it as for gold and hid treasure; but he that does so must have much earth and rubbish before he gets the pure metal; sand, and pebbles, and dross usually lie blended with it, but the gold is nevertheless gold, and will enrich the man that employs his pains to seek and separate it. Neither is there any danger he should be deceived by the mixture. Every man carries about him a touchstone, if he will make use of it, to distinguish substantial gold from superficial glitterings, truth from appearances. And indeed the use and benefit of this touchstone, which is natural reason, is spoiled and lost only by assumed prejudices, overweening presumption, and narrowing our minds. The want of exercising it in the full extent of things intelligible, is that which weakens and extinguishes this noble faculty in us. [ . . . ]

It will possibly be objected, Who is sufficient for all this? I answer, more than can be imagined. Everyone knows what his proper business is, and what, according to the character he makes of himself, the world may justly expect of him; and to answer that, he will find he will have time and opportunity enough to furnish himself, if he will not deprive himself by a narrowness of spirit of those helps that are at hand. I do not say to be a good geographer that a man should visit every mountain, river, promontory and creek upon the face of the earth, view the buildings, and survey the land everywhere, as if he were going to make a purchase. But yet everyone must allow that he shall know a country better that makes often sallies into it, and traverses it up and down, than he that like a mill horse goes still round in the same track, or keeps within the narrow bounds of a field or two that delight him. He that will enquire out the best books in every science, and inform himself of the most material authors of the several sects of philosophy and religion, will not find it an infinite work to acquaint himself with the sentiments of mankind concerning the most weighty and comprehensive subjects. Let him exercise the freedom of his reason and understanding in such a latitude as this, and his mind will be strengthened, his capacity enlarged, his faculties improved; and the light, which the remote and scattered parts of truth will give to one another, will so assist his judgment, that he will seldom be widely out, or miss giving proof of a clear head and a comprehensive knowledge. At least, this is the only way I know to give the understanding its due improvement to the full extent of its capacity, and to distinguish the two most different things I know in the world, a logical chicaner from a man of reason. Only, he that would thus give the mind its flight, and send abroad his enquiries into all parts after truth, must be sure to settle in his head determined ideas of all that he employs his thoughts about, and never fail to judge himself, and judge unbiasedly of all that he receives from others, either in their writings or discourses. Reverence or prejudice must not be suffered to give beauty or deformity to any of their opinions.

§4. *Of Practice and Habits* We are born with faculties and powers capable almost of anything, such at least as would carry us farther than can easily be imagined: but it is only the exercise of those powers which gives us ability and skill in anything, and leads us towards perfection.

A middle-aged ploughman will scarce ever be brought to the carriage and language of a gentleman, though his body be as well proportioned, and his joints as supple, and his natural parts not any way inferior. The legs of a dancing master and the fingers of a musician fall as it were naturally, without thought or pains, into regular and admirable motions. Bid them change their parts, and they will in vain endeavor to produce like motions in the members not used to them, and it will require length

of time and long practice to attain but some degrees of a like ability. What incredible and astonishing actions do we find rope dancers and tumblers bring their bodies to; not but that sundry in almost all manual arts are as wonderful; but I name those which the world takes notice of for such, because on that very account they give money to see them. All these admired motions beyond the reach, and almost the conception, of unpracticed spectators are nothing but the mere effects of use and industry in men, whose bodies have nothing peculiar in them from those of the amazed lookers on.

As it is in the body, so it is in the mind; practice makes it what it is, and most even of those excellences which are looked on as natural endowments will be found, when examined into more narrowly, to be the product of exercise, and to be raised to that pitch only by repeated actions. Some men are remarked for pleasantness in raillery; others for apologues and apposite diverting stories. This is apt to be taken for the effect of pure nature, and that the rather, because it is not got by rules, and those who excel in either of them never purposely set themselves to the study of it as an art to be learned. But yet it is true that at first some lucky hit, which took with somebody and gained him commendation, encouraged him to try again, inclined his thoughts and endeavors that way, until at last he insensibly got a facility in it without perceiving how; and that is attributed wholly to nature which was much more the effect of use and practice. I do not deny that natural disposition may often give the first rise to it; but that never carries a man far without use and exercise, and it is practice alone that brings the powers of the mind as well as those of the body to their perfection. [ . . . ]

To what purpose all this, but to show that the difference, so observable in men's understandings and parts, does not arise so much from their natural faculties as acquired habits. He would be laughed at that should go about to make a fine dancer out of a country hedger, at past fifty. And he will not have much better success, who shall endeavor at that age to make a man reason well, or speak handsomely, who has never been used to it, though you should lay before him a collection of all the best precepts of logic or oratory. Nobody is made anything by hearing of rules, or laying them up in his memory; practice must settle the habit of doing without reflecting on the rule, and you may as well hope to make a good painter or musician extempore by a lecture and instruction in the arts of music and painting, as a coherent thinker or strict reasoner by a set of rules, showing him wherein right reasoning consists.

This being so, that defects and weakness in men's understandings, as well as other faculties, come from want of a right use of their own minds, I am apt to think the fault is generally mislaid upon nature, and there is often a complaint of want of parts, when the fault lies in want of a due improvement of them. We see men frequently dexterous and sharp enough in making a bargain, who, if you reason with them about matters of religion, appear perfectly stupid.

§5. *Ideas*   I will not here, in what relates to the right conduct and improvement of the understanding, repeat again the getting clear and determined ideas, and the employing our thoughts rather about them than about sounds put for them, nor of settling the signification of words which we use with ourselves in the search of truth or with others in discoursing about it. Those hindrances of our understandings in the pursuit of knowledge, I have sufficiently enlarged upon in another place; so that nothing more needs here to be said of those matters.[9]

§6. *Principles*   There is another fault that stops or misleads men in their knowledge, which I have also spoken something of, but yet is necessary to mention here again, that we may examine it to the bottom and see the root it springs from, and that is a custom of taking up with principles that are not self-evident and very often not so much as true. It is not unusual to see men rest their opinions upon foundations that have no more certainty and solidity than the propositions built on them and embraced for their sake. Such foundations are these and the like, viz. the founders or leaders of my party are good men, and therefore their tenets are true; it is the opinion of a sect that is erroneous, therefore it is false; it has been long received in the world, therefore it is true; or it is new, and therefore false.

These, and many the like, which are by no means the measures of truths and falsehood, the generality of men make the standards by which they accustom their understanding to judge. And thus they, falling into a habit of determining truth and falsehood by such wrong measures, it is no wonder they should embrace error for certainty, and be very positive in things they have no ground for.

. . . True or false, solid or sandy, the mind must have some foundation to rest itself upon, and, as I have remarked in another place, it no sooner entertains any proposition, but it presently hastens to some hypothesis to bottom it on; until then it is unquiet and unsettled. So much do our own very tempers dispose us to a right use of our understandings, if we would follow as we should the inclinations of our nature.

In some matters of concernment, especially those of religion, men are not permitted to be always wavering and uncertain, they must embrace and profess some tenets or other; and it would be a shame, nay, a contradiction too heavy for anyone's mind to lie constantly under, for him to pretend seriously to be persuaded of the truth of any religion, and yet not to be able to give any reason of his belief, or to say anything for his preference of this to any other opinion. And therefore they must make use of some principles or other, and those can be no other than such as they have and can manage; and to say they are not in earnest persuaded by them, and do not rest upon those they make use of, is contrary to experience, and to allege that they are not misled when we complain they are.

If this be so, it will be urged, why then do they not make use of sure and unquestionable principles,[10] rather than rest on such grounds as may deceive them, and will, as is visible, serve to support error as well as truth?

To this I answer, the reason why they do not make use of better and surer principles, is because they cannot; but this inability proceeds not from want of natural parts (for those few whose case that is are to be excused) but for want of use and exercise. Few men are from their youth accustomed to strict reasoning, and to trace the dependence of any truth in a long train of consequences to its remote principles, and to observe its connection; and he that by frequent practice has not been used to this employment of his understanding, it is no more wonder that he should not, when he is grown into years, be able to bring his mind to it, than that he should not be on a sudden able to grave or design, dance on the ropes, or write a good hand, who has never practiced either of them.

Nay, the most of men are so wholly strangers to this, that they do not so much as perceive their want of it. They dispatch the ordinary business of their callings by rote, as we say, as they have learned it, and, if at any time they miss success, they impute it to anything rather than want of thought or skill; that they conclude (because they know no better) they have in perfection. . . . Thus being content with this short and very imperfect use of his understanding, he never troubles himself to seek out methods of improving his mind, and lives all his life without any notion of close reasoning in a continued connection of a long train of consequences from sure foundations, such as is requisite for the making out and clearing most of the speculative truths most men own to believe and are most concerned in. Not to mention here what I shall have occasion to insist on by and by more fully, viz. that in many cases it is not one series of consequences will serve the turn, but many different and opposite deductions must be examined and laid together, before a man can come to make a right judgment of the point in question. What then can be expected from men that neither see the want of any such kind of reasoning as this, nor, if they do, know they how to set about it, or could perform it? You may as well set a countryman who scarce knows the figures, and never cast up a sum of three particulars, to state a merchant's long account, and find the true balance of it.

What then should be done in the case? I answer, we should always remember what I said above, that the faculties of our souls are improved and made useful to us just after the same manner as our bodies are. Would you have a man write or paint, dance or fence well, or perform any other manual operation dexterously and with ease, let him have ever so much vigor and activity, suppleness and address naturally, yet nobody expects this from him unless he has been used to it, and has employed time and pains in fashioning and forming his hand or outward parts to these motions. Just so it is in the mind; would you have a man reason well, you must use him to it betimes, exercise his mind in observing the connection of ideas and following them in train. Nothing does this better than mathematics, which therefore I think should be taught all those who have the time and opportunity, not so much to make them mathematicians as to make them reasonable creatures; for though we all call ourselves so, because we are born to it if we please, yet we may truly say nature gives us but the seeds of it; we are born to be, if we please, rational creatures, but it is use and exercise only that makes us so, and we are indeed so no farther than industry and application has carried us. And therefore, in ways of reasoning which men have not been used to, he that will observe the conclusions they take up must be satisfied they are not at all rational.

. . .

He that has to do with young scholars, especially in mathematics, may perceive how their minds open by degrees, and how it is exercise alone that opens them. Sometimes they will stick a long time at a part of a demonstration, not for want of will and application, but really for want of perceiving the connection of two ideas that, to one whose understanding is more exercised, is as visible as anything can be. The same would be with a grown man beginning to study mathematics; the understanding, for want of use, often sticks in very plain way, and he himself that is so puzzled, when he comes to see the connection, wonders what it was he stuck at in a case so plain.

§7. *Mathematics*    I have mentioned mathematics as a way to settle in the mind a habit of reasoning closely and in train; not that I think it necessary that all men should be deep mathematicians, but that having got the way of reasoning, which that study necessarily brings the mind to, they might be able to transfer it to other parts of knowledge as they shall have occasion. For, in all sorts of reasoning, every single argument should be managed as a mathematical demonstration, the connection and dependence of ideas should be followed until the mind is brought to the source on which it bottoms and observes the coherence all along, though, in proofs of probability, one such train is not enough to settle the judgment as in demonstrative knowledge.

Where a truth is made out by one demonstration, there needs no farther enquiry, but in probabilities where there wants demonstration to establish the truth beyond doubt, there it is not enough to trace one argument to its source, and observe its strength and weakness, but all the arguments, after having been so examined on both sides, must be laid in balance one against another, and upon the whole the understanding determine its assent.

This is a way of reasoning the understanding should be accustomed to, which is so different from what the illiterate are used to, that even learned men oftentimes seem to have very little or no notion of it. Nor is it to be wondered, since the way of disputing in the Schools leads them quite away from it, by insisting on one topical argument,* by the success of which the truth or falsehood of the question is to be determined and victory adjudged

---

* [Editor's note: Locke refers here to the disputations practiced in the universities of his time and arguments that relied on a single general principle or "topic."]

to the opponent or defendant; which is all one as if one should balance an account by one sum charged and discharged, when there are a hundred others to be taken into consideration.

This therefore it would be well if men's minds were accustomed to, and that early, that they might not erect their opinions upon one single view, when so many other are requisite to make up the account, and must come into the reckoning before a man can form a right judgment. This would enlarge their minds, and give a due freedom to their understandings, that they might not be led into error by presumption, laziness or precipitancy; for I think nobody can approve such a conduct of the understanding as should mislead it from truth, though it be ever so much in fashion to make use of it.

To this perhaps it will be objected, that to manage the understanding, as I propose, would require every man to be a scholar, and to be furnished with all the materials of knowledge, and exercised in all the ways of reasoning. To which I answer, that it is a shame for those that have time and the means to attain knowledge, to want any helps or assistance for the improvement of their understandings that are to be got, and to such I would be thought here chiefly to speak. Those methinks, who by the industry and parts of their ancestors have been set free from a constant drudgery to their backs and their bellies, should bestow some of their spare time on their heads, and open their minds by some trials and essays in all the sorts and matters of reasoning. I have before mentioned mathematics, wherein algebra gives new helps and views to the understanding. If I propose these, it is not, as I said, to make every man a thorough mathematician, or a deep algebraist; but yet I think the study of them is of infinite use even to grown men; first, by experimentally convincing them that, to make anyone reason well, it is not enough to have parts wherewith he is satisfied and that serve him well enough in his ordinary course. A man in those studies will see that, however good he may think his understanding, yet in many things, and those very visible, it may fail him. This would take off that presumption that most men have of themselves in this part; and they would not be so apt to think

their minds wanted no helps to enlarge them, that there could be nothing added to the acuteness and penetration of their understandings.

Secondly, the study of mathematics would show them the necessity there is, in reasoning, to separate all the distinct ideas, and see the habitudes that all those concerned in the present enquiry have to one another, and to lay by those which relate not to the proposition in hand and wholly to leave them out of the reckoning. This is that which in other subjects, besides quantity, is what is absolutely requisite to just reasoning, though in them it is not so easily observed nor so carefully practiced. In those parts of knowledge where it is thought demonstration has nothing to do, men reason as it were in the lump: and, if, upon a summary and confused view or upon a partial consideration, they can raise the appearance of a probability, they usually rest content; especially if it be in a dispute where every little straw is laid hold on, and everything that can but be drawn in any way to give color to the argument is advanced with ostentation. But that mind is not in a posture to find the truth, that does not distinctly take all the parts asunder, and, omitting what is not at all to the point, draw a conclusion from the result of all the particulars which any way influence it. There is another no less useful habit to be got by an application to mathematical demonstrations, and that is, of using the mind to a long train of consequences; but, having mentioned that already, I shall not again here repeat it.

As to men whose fortunes and time is narrower, what may suffice them is not of that vast extent as may be imagined, and so comes not within the objection.

Nobody is under an obligation to know everything. Knowledge and science in general is the business only of those who are at ease and leisure. Those who have particular callings ought to understand them; and it is no unreasonable proposal, nor impossible to be compassed, that they should think and reason right about what is their daily employment. This one cannot think them incapable of, without levelling them with the brutes, and charging them with a stupidity below the rank of rational creatures.

**Notes**

1.  The logic Locke refers to was central to the educational program of the ecclesiastical Schools throughout the Middle Ages and was derived from Aristotle's philosophy. Locke criticizes the logic associated with

the Schools throughout this work and offers his own approach as an alternative to it. See, for example, section 7. Mathematics.

2. Locke refers here to Francis Bacon (1561–1626), who was made Baron Verulam in 1618.

3. The passage is actually to be found in the preface to Bacon's *Instauratio Magna*, an unfinished work of which the *Novum Organum* was originally meant to be a part.

4. Talents, or abilities.

5. Locke's original reads "untractable."

6. The fertile land assigned to the Israelites in Egypt; Gen. 45:10.

7. Locke uses the Latin word, *Expansum*, here.

8. I Thess. 5:21. From a 1611 English version of I Thess. 5:19–22; "Quench not the spirit: Despise not prophecyings: Prove all things; hold fast that which is good. Abstaine from all appearance of evill."

9. *Essay* II xxix; III ix, x, xi.

10. The word "rather" appears before "make" in this phrase in the original text.

# 5

# The Education of Nature

## Jean-Jacques Rousseau

### *Emile*: Book I

Everything is good as it leaves the hands of the Author of things; everything degenerates in the hands of man. He forces one soil to nourish the products of another, one tree to bear the fruit of another. He mixes and confuses the climates, the elements, the seasons. He mutilates his dog, his horse, his slave. He turns everything upside down; he disfigures everything; he loves deformity, monsters. He wants nothing as nature made it, not even man; for him, man must be trained like a school horse; man must be fashioned in keeping with his fancy like a tree in his garden.

Were he not to do this, however, everything would go even worse, and our species does not admit of being formed halfway. In the present state of things a man abandoned to himself in the midst of other men from birth would be the most disfigured of all. Prejudices, authority, necessity, example, all the social institutions in which we find ourselves submerged would stifle nature in him and put nothing in its place. Nature there would be like a shrub that chance had caused to be born in the middle of a path and that the passers-by soon cause to perish by bumping into it from all sides and bending it in every direction.

It is to you that I address myself, tender and foresighted mother, who are capable of keeping the nascent shrub away from the highway and securing it from the impact of human opinions! Cultivate and water the young plant before it dies. Its fruits will one day be your delights. Form an enclosure around your child's soul at an early date. Someone else can draw its circumference, but you alone must build the fence.

Plants are shaped by cultivation, and men by education. If man were born big and strong, his size and strength would be useless to him until he had learned to make use of them. They would be detrimental to him in that they would keep others from thinking of aiding him.* And, abandoned to himself, he would die of want before knowing his needs. And childhood is taken to be a pitiable state! It is not seen that the human race would have perished if man had not begun as a child.

We are born weak, we need strength; we are born totally unprovided, we need aid; we are born

Editor's title. Previously published as *"Emile," or On Education*, trans. Allan Bloom (New York: Basic Books/HarperCollins, 1979), pp. 37–42, 481–2. Reprinted with permission of the Perseus Books Group.

* Similar to them on the outside and deprived of speech as well as of the ideas it expresses, he would not be in a condition to make them understand the need he had of their help, and nothing in him would manifest this need to them. [Original footnote]

43

stupid, we need judgment. Everything we do not have at our birth and which we need when we are grown is given us by education.

This education comes to us from nature or from men or from things. The internal development of our faculties and our organs is the education of nature. The use that we are taught to make of this development is the education of men. And what we acquire from our own experience about the objects which affect us is the education of things.

Each of us is thus formed by three kinds of masters. The disciple in whom their various lessons are at odds with one another is badly raised and will never be in agreement with himself. He alone in whom they all coincide at the same points and tend to the same ends reaches his goal and lives consistently. He alone is well raised.

Now, of these three different educations, the one coming from nature is in no way in our control; that coming from things is in our control only in certain respects; that coming from men is the only one of which we are truly the masters. Even of it we are the masters only by hypothesis. For who can hope entirely to direct the speeches and the deeds of all those surrounding a child?

Therefore, when education becomes an art, it is almost impossible for it to succeed, since the conjunction of the elements necessary to its success is in no one's control. All that one can do by dint of care is to come more or less close to the goal, but to reach it requires luck.

What is that goal? It is the very same as that of nature. This has just been proved. Since the conjunction of the three educations is necessary to their perfection, the two others must be directed toward the one over which we have no power. But perhaps this word *nature* has too vague a sense. An attempt must be made here to settle on its meaning.

Nature, we are told, is only habit. What does that mean? Are there not habits contracted only by force which never do stifle nature? Such, for example, is the habit of the plants whose vertical direction is interfered with. The plant, set free, keeps the inclination it was forced to take. But the sap has not as a result changed its original direction; and if the plant continues to grow, its new growth resumes the vertical direction. The case is the same for men's inclinations. So long as one remains in the same condition, the inclinations which result from habit and are the least natural to us can be kept; but as soon as the situation changes, habit ceases and

the natural returns. Education is certainly only habit. Now are there not people who forget and lose their education? Others who keep it? Where does this difference come from? If the name *nature* were limited to habits conformable to nature, we would spare ourselves this garble.

We are born with the use of our senses, and from our birth we are affected in various ways by the objects surrounding us. As soon as we have, so to speak, consciousness of our sensations, we are disposed to seek or avoid the objects which produce them, at first according to whether they are pleasant or unpleasant to us, then according to the conformity or lack of it that we find between us and these objects, and finally according to the judgments we make about them on the basis of the idea of happiness or of perfection given us by reason. These dispositions are extended and strengthened as we become more capable of using our senses and more enlightened; but constrained by our habits, they are more or less corrupted by our opinions. Before this corruption they are what I call in us *nature*.

It is, then, to these original dispositions that everything must be related; and that could be done if our three educations were only different from one another. But what is to be done when they are opposed? When, instead of raising a man for himself, one wants to raise him for others? Then their harmony is impossible. Forced to combat nature or the social institutions, one must choose between making a man or a citizen, for one cannot make both at the same time.

Every particular society, when it is narrow and unified, is estranged from the all-encompassing society. Every patriot is harsh to foreigners. They are only men. They are nothing in his eyes. This is a drawback, inevitable but not compelling. The essential thing is to be good to the people with whom one lives. Abroad, the Spartan was ambitious, avaricious, iniquitous. But disinterestedness, equity, and concord reigned within his walls. Distrust those cosmopolitans who go to great length in their books to discover duties they do not deign to fulfill around them. A philosopher loves the Tartars so as to be spared having to love his neighbors.

Natural man is entirely for himself. He is numerical unity, the absolute whole which is relative only to itself or its kind. Civil man is only a fractional unity dependent on the denominator; his value is determined by his relation to the whole, which is the social body. Good social institutions are those that best know how to denature man, to take his absolute existence from him in order to give him a relative one and transport the *I* into the common unity, with the result that each individual believes himself no longer one but a part of the unity and no longer feels except within the whole. A citizen of Rome was neither Caius nor Lucius; he was a Roman. He even loved the country exclusive of himself. Regulus claimed he was Carthaginian on the grounds that he had become the property of his masters. In his status of foreigner he refused to sit in the Roman senate; a Carthaginian had to order him to do so. He was indignant that they wanted to save his life. He conquered and returned triumphant to die by torture. This has little relation, it seems to me, to the men we know.[1]

The Lacedaemonian Pedaretus runs for the council of three hundred. He is defeated. He goes home delighted that there were three hundred men worthier than he to be found in Sparta. I take this display to be sincere, and there is reason to believe that it was. This is the citizen.[2]

A Spartan woman had five sons in the army and was awaiting news of the battle. A Helot arrives; trembling, she asks him for news. "Your five sons were killed." "Base slave, did I ask you that?" "We won the victory." The mother runs to the temple and gives thanks to the gods. This is the female citizen.[3]

He who in the civil order wants to preserve the primacy of the sentiments of nature does not know what he wants. Always in contradiction with himself, always floating between his inclinations and his duties, he will never be either man or citizen. He will be good neither for himself nor for others. He will be one of these men of our days: a Frenchman, an Englishman, a bourgeois.[4] He will be nothing.

To be something, to be oneself and always one, a man must act as he speaks; he must always be decisive in making his choice, make it in a lofty style, and always stick to it. I am waiting to be shown this marvel so as to know whether he is a man or a citizen, or how he goes about being both at the same time.

From these necessarily opposed objects come two contrary forms of instruction – the one, public and common; the other, individual and domestic.

Do you want to get an idea of public education? Read Plato's *Republic*. It is not at all a political work, as think those who judge books only by their titles. It is the most beautiful educational treatise ever written.

When one wishes to refer to the land of chimeras, mention is made of Plato's institutions. If Lycurgus had set his down only in writing, I would find them far more chimerical. Plato only purified the heart of man; Lycurgus denatured it.[5]

Public instruction no longer exists and can no longer exist, because where there is no longer fatherland, there can no longer be citizens. These two words, *fatherland* and *citizen*, should be effaced from modern languages. I know well the reason why this is so, but I do not want to tell it. It has nothing to do with my subject.[6]

I do not envisage as a public education those laughable establishments called *colleges*.*[7] Nor do I count the education of society, because this education, tending to two contrary ends, fails to attain either. It is fit only for making double men, always appearing to relate everything to others and never relating anything except to themselves alone. Now since these displays are common to everyone, no one is taken in by them. They are so much wasted effort.

From these contradictions is born the one we constantly experience within ourselves. Swept along in contrary routes by nature and by men, forced to divide ourselves between these different impulses, we follow a composite impulse which leads us to neither one goal nor the other. Thus, in conflict and floating during the whole course of our life, we end it without having been able to put ourselves in harmony with ourselves and without having been good either for ourselves or for others.

There remains, finally, domestic education or the education of nature. But what will a man raised uniquely for himself become for others? If perchance the double object we set for ourselves could be joined in a single one by removing the contradictions of man, a great obstacle to his happiness would be removed. In order to judge of this, he would have to be seen wholly formed: his inclinations would have to have been observed, his progress seen, his development followed. In a word, the natural man

---

* There are in the academy of Geneva and the University of Paris professors whom I like very much and believe to be very capable of instructing the young well, if they were not forced to follow the established practice. I exhort one among them to publish the project of reform which he has conceived. Perhaps, when it is seen that the ill is not without remedy, there will be a temptation to cure it. [Original footnote]

would have to be known. I believe that one will have made a few steps in these researches when one has read this writing.

To form this rare man, what do we have to do? Very much, doubtless. What must be done is to prevent anything from being done. When it is only a question of going against the wind, one tacks. But if the sea is heavy and one wants to stand still, one must cast anchor. Take care, young pilot, for fear that your cable run or your anchor drag and that the vessel drift without your noticing.

In the social order where all positions are determined, each man ought to be raised for his. If an individual formed for his position leaves it, he is no longer fit for anything. Education is useful only insofar as fortune is in agreement with the parents' vocation. In any other case it is harmful to the student, if only by virtue of the prejudices it gives him. In Egypt where the son was obliged to embrace the station of his father, education at least had a sure goal. But among us where only the ranks remain and the men who compose them change constantly, no one knows whether in raising his son for his rank he is not working against him.

In the natural order, since men are all equal, their common calling is man's estate and whoever is well raised for that calling cannot fail to fulfill those callings related to it. Let my student be destined for the sword, the church, the bar. I do not care. Prior to the calling of his parents is nature's call to human life. Living is the job I want to teach him. On leaving my hands, he will, I admit, be neither magistrate nor soldier nor priest. He will, in the first place, be a man. All that a man should be, he will in case of need know how to be as well as anyone; and fortune may try as it may to make him change place, he will always be in his own place.

## Notes

1. Livy *Roman History*, Summary of XVIII; Cicero *Offices* III 26–27; Horace *Odes* III 5.
2. Plutarch *Lycurgus* XXV; *Sayings of Spartans* 231B, *Sayings of Kings* 191F.
3. Plutarch *Agesilaus* XXIX; *Sayings of Spartan Women* 241C.
4. Rousseau is the first writer to use the word *bourgeois* in the modern sense popularized by Marx. It is defined in opposition to *citizen*, and the understanding connected with the term is central to all later political thought. Cf. *Social Contract* I6 note. However, Rousseau does frequently use it in its more ordinary meaning of *middle-class* as opposed to *peasant*, *poor*, or *noble*. Of course, these two senses are closely related.
5. Rousseau bases himself particularly on Plutarch's *Lycurgus*.
6. Cf. *Social Contract* IV 8.
7. Public schools, almost exclusively under clerical supervision and with clerics as teachers. Rousseau's first draft of the note was somewhat different; in particular "forced to follow the established practice . . ." was originally "forced to follow rules which they did not make . . ." This change indicates the problem and clarifies the last sentence of the preceding paragraph. Rousseau's book contains the new rules intended to take the place of the old ones which are the true source of the modern corruption. The first of these new rules is that man is naturally good.

# 6

# The Democratic Conception in Education

## John Dewey

To say that education is a social function, securing direction and development in the immature through their participation in the life of the group to which they belong, is to say in effect that education will vary with the quality of life which prevails in a group. Particularly is it true that a society which not only changes but which has the ideal of such change as will improve it, will have different standards and methods of education from one which aims simply at the perpetuation of its own customs. . . .

Any education given by a group tends to socialize its members, but the quality and value of the socialization depends upon the habits and aims of the group.

Hence, once more, the need of a measure for the worth of any given mode of social life. In seeking this measure, we have to avoid two extremes. We cannot set up, out of our heads, something we regard as an ideal society. We must base our conception upon societies which actually exist, in order to have any assurance that our ideal is a practicable one. But, as we have just seen, the ideal cannot simply repeat the traits which are actually found. The problem is to extract the desirable traits of forms of community life which actually exist, and employ them to criticize undesirable features and suggest improvement. Now in any social group whatever, even in a gang of thieves, we find some interest held in common, and we find a certain amount of interaction and cooperative intercourse with other groups. From these two traits we derive our standard. How numerous and varied are the interests which are consciously shared? How full and free is the interplay with other forms of association? If we apply these considerations to, say, a criminal band, we find that the ties which consciously hold the members together are few in number, reducible almost to a common interest in plunder; and that they are of such a nature as to isolate the group from other groups with respect to give and take of the values of life. Hence, the education such a society gives is partial and distorted. If we take, on the other hand, the kind of family life which illustrates the standard, we find that there are material, intellectual, æsthetic interests in which all participate and that the progress of one member has worth for the experience of other members – it is readily communicable – and

Previously published in John Dewey, *Democracy and Education* (New York: Free Press/Macmillan, 1966), pp. 81, 83, 86–99. © 1916, renewed 1944 by John Dewey. Reprinted with permission of Scribner, an imprint of Simon & Schuster Adult Publishing Group.

that the family is not an isolated whole, but enters intimately into relationships with business groups, with schools, with all the agencies of culture, as well as with other similar groups, and that it plays a due part in the political organization and in return receives support from it. In short, there are many interests consciously communicated and shared; and there are varied and free points of contact with other modes of association.

[ . . . ]

**The Democratic Ideal.** The two elements in our criterion both point to democracy. The first signifies not only more numerous and more varied points of shared common interest, but greater reliance upon the recognition of mutual interests as a factor in social control. The second means not only freer interaction between social groups (once isolated so far as intention could keep up a separation) but change in social habit – its continuous readjustment through meeting the new situations produced by varied intercourse. And these two traits are precisely what characterize the democratically constituted society.

Upon the educational side, we note first that the realization of a form of social life in which interests are mutually interpenetrating, and where progress, or readjustment, is an important consideration, makes a democratic community more interested than other communities have cause to be in deliberate and systematic education. The devotion of democracy to education is a familiar fact. The superficial explanation is that a government resting upon popular suffrage cannot be successful unless those who elect and who obey their governors are educated. Since a democratic society repudiates the principle of external authority, it must find a substitute in voluntary disposition and interest; these can be created only by education. But there is a deeper explanation. A democracy is more than a form of government; it is primarily a mode of associated living, of conjoint communicated experience. The extension in space of the number of individuals who participate in an interest so that each has to refer his own action to that of others, and to consider the action of others to give point and direction to his own, is equivalent to the breaking down of those barriers of class, race, and national territory which kept men from perceiving the full import of their activity. These more numerous and more varied points of contact denote a greater diversity of stimuli to which an individual has to respond; they consequently put a premium on variation in his

action. They secure a liberation of powers which remain suppressed as long as the incitations to action are partial, as they must be in a group which in its exclusiveness shuts out many interests.

The widening of the area of shared concerns, and the liberation of a greater diversity of personal capacities which characterize a democracy, are not of course the product of deliberation and conscious effort. On the contrary, they were caused by the development of modes of manufacture and commerce, travel, migration, and intercommunication which flowed from the command of science over natural energy. But after greater individualization on one hand, and a broader community of interest on the other have come into existence, it is a matter of deliberate effort to sustain and extend them. Obviously a society to which stratification into separate classes would be fatal, must see to it that intellectual opportunities are accessible to all on equable and easy terms. A society marked off into classes need be specially attentive only to the education of its ruling elements. A society which is mobile, which is full of channels for the distribution of a change occurring anywhere, must see to it that its members are educated to personal initiative and adaptability. Otherwise, they will be overwhelmed by the changes in which they are caught and whose significance or connections they do not perceive. The result will be a confusion in which a few will appropriate to themselves the results of the blind and externally directed activities of others.

**The Platonic Educational Philosophy.** Subsequent chapters will be devoted to making explicit the implications of the democratic ideas in education. In the remaining portions of this chapter, we shall consider the educational theories which have been evolved in three epochs when the social import of education was especially conspicuous. The first one to be considered is that of Plato. No one could better express than did he the fact that a society is stably organized when each individual is doing that for which he has aptitude by nature in such a way as to be useful to others (or to contribute to the whole to which he belongs); and that it is the business of education to discover these aptitudes and progressively to train them for social use. Much which has been said so far is borrowed from what Plato first consciously taught the world. But conditions which he could not intellectually control led him to restrict these ideas in their application. He never got any conception of the indefinite plurality of activities which may characterize an individual and a social group, and consequently limited his view to a limited number of *classes* of capacities and of social arrangements.

Plato's starting point is that the organization of society depends ultimately upon knowledge of the end of existence. If we do not know its end, we shall be at the mercy of accident and caprice. Unless we know the end, the good, we shall have no criterion for rationally deciding what the possibilities are which should be promoted, nor how social arrangements are to be ordered. We shall have no conception of the proper limits and distribution of activities – what he called justice – as a trait of both individual and social organization. But how is the knowledge of the final and permanent good to be achieved? In dealing with this question we come upon the seemingly insuperable obstacle that such knowledge is not possible save in a just and harmonious social order. Everywhere else the mind is distracted and misled by false valuations and false perspectives. A disorganized and factional society sets up a number of different models and standards. Under such conditions it is impossible for the individual to attain consistency of mind. Only a complete whole is fully self-consistent. A society which rests upon the supremacy of some factor over another irrespective of its rational or proportionate claims, inevitably leads thought astray. It puts a premium on certain things and slurs over others, and creates a mind whose seeming unity is forced and distorted. Education proceeds ultimately from the patterns furnished by institutions, customs, and laws. Only in a just state will these be such as to give the right education; and only those who have rightly trained minds will be able to recognize the end, and ordering principle of things. We seem to be caught in a hopeless circle. However, Plato suggested a way out. A few men, philosophers or lovers of wisdom – or truth – may by study learn at least in outline the proper patterns of true existence. If a powerful ruler should form a state after these patterns, then its regulations could be preserved. An education could be given which would sift individuals, discovering what they were good for, and supplying a method of assigning each to the work in life for which his nature fits him. Each doing his own part, and never transgressing, the order and unity of the whole would be maintained.

It would be impossible to find in any scheme of philosophic thought a more adequate recognition on one hand of the educational significance of social arrangements and, on the other, of the dependence of those arrangements upon the means used to educate the young. It would be impossible to find a deeper sense of the function of education in discovering and developing personal capacities, and training them so that they would connect with the activities of others. Yet the society in which the theory was propounded was so undemocratic that Plato could not work out a solution for the problem whose terms he clearly saw.

While he affirmed with emphasis that the place of the individual in society should not be determined by birth or wealth or any conventional status, but by his own nature as discovered in the process of education, he had no perception of the uniqueness of individuals. For him they fall by nature into classes, and into a very small number of classes at that. Consequently the testing and sifting function of education only shows to which one of three classes an individual belongs. There being no recognition that each individual constitutes his own class, there could be no recognition of the infinite diversity of active tendencies and combinations of tendencies of which an individual is capable. There were only three types of faculties or powers in the individual's constitution. Hence education would soon reach a static limit in each class, for only diversity makes change and progress.

In some individuals, appetites naturally dominate; they are assigned to the laboring and trading class, which expresses and supplies human wants. Others reveal, upon education, that over and above appetites, they have a generous, outgoing, assertively courageous disposition. They become the citizen-subjects of the state; its defenders in war; its internal guardians in peace. But their limit is fixed by their lack of reason, which is a capacity to grasp the universal. Those who possess this are capable of the highest kind of education, and become in time the legislators of the state – for laws are the universals which control the particulars of experience. Thus it is not true that in intent, Plato subordinated the individual to the social whole. But it is true that lacking the perception of the uniqueness of every individual, his incommensurability with others, and consequently not recognizing that a society might change and yet be stable, his doctrine of limited powers and classes came in net effect to the idea of the subordination of individuality.

We cannot better Plato's conviction that an individual is happy and society well organized when each individual engages in those activities for which he has a natural equipment, nor his conviction that it is the primary office of education to discover this equipment to its possessor and train him for its effective use. But progress in knowledge has made us aware of the superficiality of Plato's lumping of individuals and their original powers into a few sharply marked-off classes; it has taught us that original capacities are indefinitely numerous and variable. It is but the other side of this fact to say that in the degree in which society has become democratic, social organization means utilization of the specific and variable qualities of individuals, not stratification by classes. Although his educational philosophy was revolutionary, it was none the less in bondage to static ideals. He thought that change or alteration was evidence of lawless flux; that true reality was unchangeable. Hence while he would radically change the existing state of society, his aim was to construct a state in which change would subsequently have no place. The final end of life is fixed; given a state framed with this end in view, not even minor details are to be altered. Though they might not be inherently important, yet if permitted they would inure the minds of men to the idea of change, and hence be dissolving and anarchic. The breakdown of his philosophy is made apparent in the fact that he could not trust to gradual improvements in education to bring about a better society which should then improve education, and so on indefinitely. Correct education could not come into existence until an ideal state existed, and after that education would be devoted simply to its conservation. For the existence of this state he was obliged to trust to some happy accident by which philosophic wisdom should happen to coincide with possession of ruling power in the state.

**The "Individualistic" Ideal of the Eighteenth Century.** In the eighteenth-century philosophy we find ourselves in a very different circle of ideas. "Nature" still means something antithetical to existing social organization; Plato exercised a great influence upon Rousseau. But the voice of nature now speaks for the diversity of individual talent and for the need of free development of individuality in all its variety. Education in accord with nature furnishes the goal and the method of instruction and discipline. Moreover, the native or original endowment was conceived, in extreme cases, as nonsocial or even as antisocial. Social arrangements were thought of as mere external expedients by which these nonsocial individuals might secure a greater amount of private happiness for themselves.

Nevertheless, these statements convey only an inadequate idea of the true significance of the movement. In reality its chief interest was in progress and in social progress. The seeming antisocial philosophy was a somewhat transparent mask for an impetus toward a wider and freer society – toward cosmopolitanism. The positive ideal was humanity. In membership in humanity, as distinct from a state, man's capacities would be liberated; while in existing political organizations his powers were hampered and distorted to meet the requirements and selfish interests of the rulers of the state. The doctrine of extreme individualism was but the counterpart, the obverse, of ideals of the indefinite perfectibility of man and of a social organization having a scope as wide as humanity. The emancipated individual was to become the organ and agent of a comprehensive and progressive society.

The heralds of this gospel were acutely conscious of the evils of the social estate in which they found themselves. They attributed these evils to the limitations imposed upon the free powers of man. Such limitation was both distorting and corrupting. Their impassioned devotion to emancipation of life from external restrictions which operated to the exclusive advantage of the class to whom a past feudal system consigned power, found intellectual formulation in a worship of nature. To give "nature" full swing was to replace an artificial, corrupt, and inequitable social order by a new and better kingdom of humanity. Unrestrained faith in Nature as both a model and a working power was strengthened by the advances of natural science. Inquiry freed from prejudice and artificial restraints of church and state had revealed that the world is a scene of law. The Newtonian solar system, which expressed the reign of natural law, was a scene of wonderful harmony, where every force balanced with every other. Natural law would accomplish the same result in human relations, if men would only get rid of the artificial man-imposed coercive restrictions.

Education in accord with nature was thought to be the first step in insuring this more social society. It was plainly seen that economic and political limitations were ultimately dependent upon limitations of thought and feeling. The first step in freeing men from external chains was to emancipate them from the internal chains of false beliefs and ideals. What was called social life, existing institutions, were too false and corrupt to be intrusted with this work. How could it be expected to undertake it when the undertaking meant its own destruction? "Nature" must then be the power to which the enterprise was to be left. Even the extreme sensationalistic theory of knowledge which was current derived itself from this conception. To insist that mind is originally passive and empty was one way of glorifying the possibilities of education. If the mind was a wax tablet to be written upon by objects, there were no limits to the possibility of education by means of the natural environment. And since the natural world of objects is a scene of harmonious "truth," this education would infallibly produce minds filled with the truth.

**Education as National and as Social.** As soon as the first enthusiasm for freedom waned, the weakness of the theory upon the constructive side became obvious. Merely to leave everything to nature was, after all, but to negate the very idea of education; it was to trust to the accidents of circumstance. Not only was some method required but also some positive organ, some administrative agency for carrying on the process of instruction. The "complete and harmonious development of all powers," having as its social counterpart an enlightened and progressive humanity, required definite organization for its realization. Private individuals here and there could proclaim the gospel; they could not execute the work. A Pestalozzi could try experiments and exhort philanthropically inclined persons having wealth and power to follow his example. But even Pestalozzi saw that any effective pursuit of the new educational ideal required the support of the state. The realization of the new education destined to produce a new society was, after all, dependent upon the activities of existing states. The movement for the democratic idea inevitably became a movement for publicly conducted and administered schools.

So far as Europe was concerned, the historic situation identified the movement for a state-supported education with the nationalistic movement in political life – a fact of incalculable significance for subsequent movements. Under the influence of German thought in particular, education became a civic function and the civic function was identified with the realization of the ideal of the national state. The "state" was substituted for humanity; cosmopolitanism gave way to nationalism. To form the citizen, not the "man," became the aim of education.[1] The historic situation to which reference is made is the after-effects of the Napoleonic conquests, especially in Germany. The German states felt (and

subsequent events demonstrate the correctness of the belief) that systematic attention to education was the best means of recovering and maintaining their political integrity and power. Externally they were weak and divided. Under the leadership of Prussian statesmen they made this condition a stimulus to the development of an extensive and thoroughly grounded system of public education.

This change in practice necessarily brought about a change in theory. The individualistic theory receded into the background. The state furnished not only the instrumentalities of public education but also its goal. When the actual practice was such that the school system, from the elementary grades through the university faculties, supplied the patriotic citizen and soldier and the future state official and administrator and furnished the means for military, industrial, and political defense and expansion, it was impossible for theory not to emphasize the aim of social efficiency. And with the immense importance attached to the nationalistic state, surrounded by other competing and more or less hostile states, it was equally impossible to interpret social efficiency in terms of a vague cosmopolitan humanitarianism. Since the maintenance of a particular national sovereignty required subordination of individuals to the superior interests of the state both in military defense and in struggles for international supremacy in commerce, social efficiency was understood to imply a like subordination. The educational process was taken to be one of disciplinary training rather than of personal development. Since, however, the ideal of culture as complete development of personality persisted, educational philosophy attempted a reconciliation of the two ideas. The reconciliation took the form of the conception of the "organic" character of the state. The individual in his isolation is nothing; only in and through an absorption of the aims and meaning of organized institutions does he attain true personality. What appears to be his subordination to political authority and the demand for sacrifice of himself to the commands of his superiors is in reality but making his own the objective reason manifested in the state – the only way in which he can become truly rational. The notion of development which we have seen to be characteristic of institutional idealism (as in the Hegelian philosophy) was just such a deliberate effort to combine the two ideas of complete realization of personality and thoroughgoing "disciplinary" subordination to existing institutions.

The extent of the transformation of educational philosophy which occurred in Germany in the generation occupied by the struggle against Napoleon for national independence, may be gathered from Kant, who well expresses the earlier individual-cosmopolitan ideal. In his treatise on Pedagogics, consisting of lectures given in the later years of the eighteenth century, he defines education as the process by which man becomes man. Mankind begins its history submerged in nature – not as Man who is a creature of reason, while nature furnishes only instinct and appetite. Nature offers simply the germs which education is to develop and perfect. The peculiarity of truly human life is that man has to create himself by his own voluntary efforts; he has to make himself a truly moral, rational, and free being. This creative effort is carried on by the educational activities of slow generations. Its acceleration depends upon men consciously striving to educate their successors not for the existing state of affairs but so as to make possible a future better humanity. But there is the great difficulty. Each generation is inclined to educate its young so as to get along in the present world instead of with a view to the proper end of education: the promotion of the best possible realization of humanity as humanity. Parents educate their children so that they may get on; princes educate their subjects as instruments of their own purposes.

Who, then, shall conduct education so that humanity may improve? We must depend upon the efforts of enlightened men in their private capacity. "All culture begins with private men and spreads outward from them. Simply through the efforts of persons of enlarged inclinations, who are capable of grasping the ideal of a future better condition, is the gradual approximation of human nature to its end possible. . . . Rulers are simply interested in such training as will make their subjects better tools for their own intentions." Even the subsidy by rulers of privately conducted schools must be carefully safeguarded. For the rulers' interest in the welfare of their own nation instead of in what is best for humanity, will make them, if they give money for the schools, wish to draw their plans. We have in this view an express statement of the points characteristic of the eighteenth century individualistic cosmopolitanism. The full development of private personality is identified with the aims of humanity as a whole and with the idea of progress. In addition we have an explicit fear of the hampering influence of a state-conducted and state-regulated education upon the attainment of these ideas. But in less than two decades after this time, Kant's philosophic successors, Fichte and Hegel, elaborated the idea that the chief function of the state is educational; that in particular the regeneration of Germany is to be accomplished by an education carried on in the interests of the state, and that the private individual is of necessity an egoistic, irrational being, enslaved to his appetites and to circumstances unless he submits voluntarily to the educative discipline of state institutions and laws. In this spirit, Germany was the first country to undertake a public, universal, and compulsory system of education extending from the primary school through the university, and to submit to jealous state regulation and supervision all private educational enterprises.

Two results should stand out from this brief historical survey. The first is that such terms as the individual and the social conceptions of education are quite meaningless taken at large, or apart from their context. Plato had the ideal of an education which should equate individual realization and social coherency and stability. His situation forced his ideal into the notion of a society organized in stratified classes, losing the individual in the class. The eighteenth century educational philosophy was highly individualistic in form, but this form was inspired by a noble and generous social ideal: that of a society organized to include humanity, and providing for the indefinite perfectibility of mankind. The idealistic philosophy of Germany in the early nineteenth century endeavored again to equate the ideals of a free and complete development of cultured personality with social discipline and political subordination. It made the national state an intermediary between the realization of private personality on one side and of humanity on the other. Consequently, it is equally possible to state its animating principle with equal truth either in the classic terms of "harmonious development of all the powers of personality" or in the more recent terminology of "social efficiency." All this re-enforces the statement which opens this chapter: The conception of education as a social process and function has no definite meaning until we define the kind of society we have in mind.

These considerations pave the way for our second conclusion. One of the fundamental problems of education in and for a democratic society is set by the conflict of a nationalistic and a wider social aim. The earlier cosmopolitan and "humanitarian" conception suffered both from vagueness and from lack of definite organs of execution and agencies of administration. In Europe, in the Continental states particularly, the new idea of the importance of education for human welfare and progress was captured by national interests and harnessed to do a work whose social aim was definitely narrow and exclusive. The social aim of education and its national aim were identified, and the result was a marked obscuring of the meaning of a social aim.

This confusion corresponds to the existing situation of human intercourse. On the one hand, science, commerce, and art transcend national boundaries. They are largely international in quality and method. They involve interdependencies and cooperation among the peoples inhabiting different countries. At the same time, the idea of national sovereignty has never been as accentuated in politics as it is at the present time. Each nation lives in a state of suppressed hostility and incipient war with its neighbors. Each is supposed to be the supreme judge of its own interests, and it is assumed as matter of course that each has interests which are exclusively its own. To question this is to question the very idea of national sovereignty which is assumed to be basic to political practice and political science. This contradiction (for it is nothing less) between the wider sphere of associated and mutually helpful social life and the narrower sphere of exclusive and hence potentially hostile pursuits and purposes, exacts of educational theory a clearer conception of the meaning of "social" as a function and test of education than has yet been attained.

Is it possible for an educational system to be conducted by a national state and yet the full social ends of the educative process not be restricted, constrained, and corrupted? Internally, the question has to face the tendencies, due to present economic conditions, which split society into classes some of which are made merely tools for the higher culture of others. Externally, the question is concerned with the reconciliation of national loyalty, of patriotism, with superior devotion to the things which unite men in common ends, irrespective of national political boundaries. Neither phase of the problem can be worked out by merely negative means. It is not enough to see to it that education is not actively used as an instrument to make easier the exploitation of one class by another. School facilities must be secured of such amplitude and efficiency as will in fact and not simply in name discount the effects of economic inequalities, and secure to all the wards

of the nation equality of equipment for their future careers. Accomplishment of this end demands not only adequate administrative provision of school facilities, and such supplementation of family resources as will enable youth to take advantage of them, but also such modification of traditional ideals of culture, traditional subjects of study and traditional methods of teaching and discipline as will retain all the youth under educational influences until they are equipped to be masters of their own economic and social careers. The ideal may seem remote of execution, but the democratic ideal of education is a farcical yet tragic delusion except as the ideal more and more dominates our public system of education.

The same principle has application on the side of the considerations which concern the relations of one nation to another. It is not enough to teach the horrors of war and to avoid everything which would stimulate international jealousy and animosity. The emphasis must be put upon whatever binds people together in cooperative human pursuits and results, apart from geographical limitations. The secondary and provisional character of national sovereignty in respect to the fuller, freer, and more fruitful association and intercourse of all human beings with one another must be instilled as a working disposition of mind. If these applications seem to be remote from a consideration of the philosophy of education, the impression shows that the meaning of the idea of education previously developed has not been adequately grasped. This conclusion is bound up with the very idea of education as a freeing of individual capacity in a progressive growth directed to social aims. Otherwise a democratic criterion of education can only be inconsistently applied.

**Summary.** Since education is a social process, and there are many kinds of societies, a criterion for educational criticism and construction implies a *particular* social ideal. The two points selected by which to measure the worth of a form of social life are the extent in which the interests of a group are shared by all its members, and the fullness and freedom with which it interacts with other groups. An undesirable society, in other words, is one which internally and externally sets up barriers to free intercourse and communication of experience. A society which makes provision for participation in its good of all its members on equal terms and which secures flexible readjustment of its institutions through interaction of the different forms of associated life is in so far democratic. Such a society must have a type of education which gives individuals a personal interest in social relationships and control, and the habits of mind which secure social changes without introducing disorder.

Three typical historic philosophies of education were considered from this point of view. The Platonic was found to have an ideal formally quite similar to that stated, but which was compromised in its working out by making a class rather than an individual the social unit. The so-called individualism of the eighteenth-century enlightenment was found to involve the notion of a society as broad as humanity, of whose progress the individual was to be the organ. But it lacked any agency for securing the development of its ideal as was evidenced in its falling back upon Nature. The institutional idealistic philosophies of the nineteenth century supplied this lack by making the national state the agency, but in so doing narrowed the conception of the social aim to those who were members of the same political unit, and reintroduced the idea of the subordination of the individual to the institution.

## Note

1.  There is a much neglected strain in Rousseau tending intellectually in this direction. He opposed the existing state of affairs on the ground that it formed *neither* the citizen nor the man. Under existing conditions, he preferred to try for the latter rather than for the former. But there are many sayings of his which point to the formation of the citizen as ideally the higher, and which indicate that his own endeavor, as embodied in the *Émile*, was simply the best makeshift the corruption of the times permitted him to sketch.

# 7

# Education as Initiation[1]

## R. S. Peters

### Introductory

A novel feature of the 1960s is the extent to which education has become a subject for public debate and theoretical speculation. Previously it had been something that was prized or taken for granted by those few who had it, but not widely discussed. Of course there were plenty of school-day reminiscences; but these were indicative more of narcissistic self-absorption than of a passionate interest in education.

All this is now changed. Some politicians whose noses quiver at the scent of any sort of under-privilege, have found in education a quarry that they think they may more safely run to earth than the ferocious old foxes of private ownership and disparity of income. Others, with nervous eyes on the technical achievements of the U.S.A. and U.S.S.R., gladly listen to economists who assure them that education is a commodity in which it is profitable for a community to invest. Sociologists assure teachers that they have a role of acting as a socialising agency in the community.

Teachers tend to be either bitter or gratified at this growing grasp of the obvious. Here are they, quiet men working at the job at which they have always worked – underpaid, unappreciated, under-staffed. And now all this. Confronted with such a welter of chatter by people, many of whom have no inside experience of the object of their theorising, it would be human, in one sense, for the teacher to turn a deaf ear. But in another sense it would not be human. For one of the distinguishing features of man is that he alone of all creatures has a variable conceptual framework which determines the aspects under which he acts. A man can conceive of his task as a teacher in many different ways. To shut his ears arbitrarily to such different accounts is to limit his view of the world – to take refuge in a kind of monadic myopia.

It may well be, however, that some of the descriptions given of what he is doing *qua* teacher seriously misrepresent what is distinctive of his calling by the generality of the description or by assimilating it to something else. Suppose, to take a parallel case, kissing were to be described as a movement of the lips that has the function of stimulating the organism. The generality of this description would omit some essential features of kissing; furthermore, by describing it as a mere bodily movement it would

Originally published in Reginald D. Achambault (ed.), *Philosophical Analysis and Education* (New York: The Humanities Press, 1965), pp. 87–111. Reprinted with permission of Taylor & Francis.

be assimilated to salivation or to a knee-jerk which is, I think, dangerously misleading. Indeed I often think that a conceptual scheme such as that employed by behaviourists is not simply intellectually mistaken; it is also morally dangerous. For such men may habitually come to think of their fellows in such attenuated terms which they regard as scientifically sterile. Luckily most behaviourists to date have been humane men who have talked like kings in their laboratories but have preserved the common touch of ordinary discourse when they emerge. But succeeding generations may be more consistent.

Teachers may be afflicted by a similar conceptual blight if they think too much in terms of their socialising role, or pay too much attention to the notion that education is a commodity in which the nation should invest, or to the suggestion that their main concern should be for the mental health of children. Education is different from social work, psychiatry, and real estate. Everything is what it is and not some other thing. In all the hubbub about plant, supply of teachers, shortage of provision, streaming, and selection, too little attention is being paid to what it is that so many are deemed to be without. Education has become rather like the Kingdom of Heaven in former times. It is both within us and amongst us, yet it also lies ahead. The elect possess it, and hope to gather in those who are not yet saved. But what on earth it is is seldom made clear.

## 'Education' and Extrinsic Ends

To get clearer about the concept of 'education', then, is an urgent necessity at the present time. Such conceptual clarification is preeminently the task of a philosopher of education. But is a philosopher who embarks on such a task committed to the suspect conviction shared by Socrates that there is some 'essence' of education which conceptual analysis can explicate? In suggesting that teachers may be affected by a conceptual blight if they pay too much attention to economists, sociologists and psychologists, have I already put my foot on the primrose path that leads to essentialism?

Frankly I do not much mind if I have. What would be objectionable would be to suppose that certain characteristics could be regarded as essential irrespective of context and of the questions under discussion. In the context of the planning of resources it may be unobjectionable to think of education as something in which a community can invest; in the context of a theory of social cohesion education may be harmlessly described as a socialising process. But if one is considering it from the point of view of the teacher's task in the classroom these descriptions are both too general and too embedded in a dangerous dimension; for they encourage a conformist or instrumental way of looking at education.

Perhaps one of the reasons why these economic and sociological descriptions of education can be misleading, if taken out of context, is that they are made from the point of view of a spectator pointing to the 'function' or effects of education in a social or economic system. They are not descriptions of it from the point of view of someone engaged in the enterprise. In a similar way one might say that the function of the medical art is to provide employment for the makers of medicine bottles or to increase the population. But this is not what the doctor conceives of himself as doing *qua* doctor, and it would be regrettable if he came to view what he should be doing *qua* doctor in terms of such remoter effects of his art. Furthermore a description of what he is doing in terms of these effects does little to distinguish his art from that of the chemist. What is essential to education must involve an aspect under which things are done which is both intentional and reasonably specific. Things like increasing the suicide rate or providing employment for printers should not be built into the concept of 'education'.

There are, of course, some intentional and specific activities falling under moral education and sex education which are forms of socialisation in an obvious sense. The teacher has to decide on the extent to which he is to concentrate more on these types of education than on the development of other forms of awareness – e.g. scientific, mathematical. Such decisions about the content of education are usually decisions about priorities. Also, as I shall argue later, all education can be regarded as a form of 'socialisation' in so far as it involves initiation into public traditions which are articulated in language and forms of thought. But this description is too general in that it fails to mark out the difference between education and other forms of socialisation. In the context in which the sociologist is speaking it may be quite clear what specific aspect of the teacher's role is being picked out. But the fact is that when these notions get noised abroad they are not always understood in the specific sense in which the sociologist may be using them. The teacher who hears that he is an agent of socialisation may come to think of himself as a sort of social worker striving in a very *general* sort of way to help children to fit into society. He may get the impression that the teacher's task is not to educate children, in the sense in which I will later define it, but to concentrate on helping them to get on with others and to settle down contentedly to a simple job, healthy hobbies, and a happy home life. It may well be the case that for some children, whose plight in our status-ridden society is spotlighted by the Newsom Report *Half Our Future*,[2] there is not much more that can be done. But so little is known about the conditions which are necessary for that cognitive development which education requires that it would be rash and dangerous to come to such a conclusion too soon. Such research as has been done[3] suggests that a great number of children, because of their early schooling and home life, are grossly deprived in this respect. It would be disastrous to say too soon that a large percentage of children are not capable of education before a serious and sustained attempt has been made to provide the necessary conditions without which talk of education is a pious hope. My fear is that teachers will be led by too undiscriminating talk of their socialising role to conceive of their task in terms of 'gentling the masses'. Clearer and more specific concepts both of 'education' and of 'socialisation' should help to avert this danger.

The other danger, which is encouraged more perhaps by the way in which economists rather than sociologists speak of 'education' lies in the widespread tendency to assimilate it to some sort of instrumental process. It is actually easy to see how such an assimilation can be encouraged by rather cavalier handling of the concept. To bring this out I must now make the first of three conceptual points about 'education' which are necessary for the explication of its essence.

'Education'[4] relates to some sorts of processes in which a desirable state of mind develops. It would be as much of a logical contradiction to say that a person had been educated and yet the change was in no way desirable as it would be to say that he had been reformed and yet had made no change for the better. Education, of course, is different from reform in that it does not suggest that a man has been lifted out of a state of turpitude into which he has lapsed. But it is similar in that it implies some change for the better. Furthermore education is usually thought of as intentional. We put ourselves or others in the relevant situations, knowing what we are doing. I know that Rousseau claimed that

'education comes to us from nature, from men, and from things'. There is this derivative sense of 'education' in which almost anything can be regarded as part of it – visiting a brothel, perhaps. But the central uses of the term are confined to situations where we deliberately put ourselves or others in the way of something that is thought to be conducive to valuable states of mind.

Given, then, that 'education' implies the intentional bringing about of a desirable state of mind, it is only too easy to assimilate it to the most familiar cases of bringing about what is desirable. First of all, there are cases where something is done of a neutral sort for the sake of something else that is thought to be worth-while. Buses are boarded in order to listen to a concert; stamps are licked in order to communicate with a friend. So education, from the point of view of those being educated, often appears as something which has to be gone through, in order that some desirable outcome will ensue, like a well-paid job or a position of prestige in the community. If, on the other hand, it is viewed from the point of view of the teacher, a second type of model crops up – that of the useful arts where neutral materials are fashioned into something that is valuable. Just as clay is made into pots or rubber into golf-balls, so minds are moulded into some desirable end-product, or topped up with something desirable like beer-mugs. When education is viewed in either of these two ways the question 'What is the use of it?' has pointed application – especially if a lot of money has to be spent on it.

There is, however, a fundamental confusion involved in these ways of thinking. This is due to applying these banal ways of conceiving of the promotion of what is valuable to education itself rather than to the processes or activities involved in it. Obviously enough activities which can form part of the content of education can be viewed as being either instrumentally or intrinsically valuable. It is possible to think of science or of carpentry, for instance, as being both valuable in themselves and valuable as means to increasing production or the provision of houses. Thus it is reasonable to ask what the purpose of instructing or of training someone in such activities might be. But it is as absurd to ask what the aim of education is as it is to ask what the aim of morality is, if what is required is something extrinsic to education. The only answer that can be given is to point to something intrinsic to education that is regarded as valuable such as the training of intellect or character. For to call something 'educational' is to intimate that the processes and activities themselves contribute to or involve something that is worth-while. Talk about 'the aims of education' depends to a large extent on a misunderstanding about the sort of concept that 'education' is.

To enlarge upon this point which is crucial for my thesis: 'Education' is not a concept that marks out any particular type of process such as training, or activity such as lecturing; rather it suggests criteria to which processes such as training must conform. One of these is that something of value should be passed on. Thus we may be educating someone while we are training him; but we need not be. For we may be training him in the art of torture. The demand, however, that there should be something of value in what is being transmitted cannot be construed as meaning that education itself should lead on to or produce something of value. This is like saying, to revert to my previous parallel, that reform must lead up to a man being better. The point is that making a man better is not an aim extrinsic to reform; it is a criterion which anything must satisfy which is to be called 'reform'. In the same way a necessary feature of education is often extracted as an extrinsic end. People thus think that education must be for the sake of something extrinsic that is worth-while, whereas the truth is that being worth-while is part of what is meant by calling it 'education'. The instrumental and moulding models of education provide a caricature of this necessary feature of desirability by conceiving of what is worth-while as an end brought about by the process or as a pattern imposed on the child's mind.

Confirmation of this thesis about 'education' can be obtained by a brief examination of the concept of 'aim'. This term has its natural home in the context of activities like shooting and throwing. 'Aiming' is associated with the concentration of attention on some object which must be hit or pierced. When the term is used more figuratively it has the same suggestion of the concentration on something within the field of an activity. It is odd to use it, like the term 'purpose' or 'motive', to suggest some end extrinsic to the activity. We ask people what they are aiming at when they seem rather confused about their purposes, or when they seem to be threshing around in rather an aimless way, or when they are drawing up their plan of campaign and have to formulate what they intend in a coherent way. Asking a person what he is aiming at is a way of getting him to concentrate or clear his mind about

what he is trying to do. It is obvious enough, therefore, why the term 'aim' is used so frequently in the context of education. For this is a sphere where people engage with great seriousness in activities without always being very clear about what they are trying to achieve. To ask questions about the aims of education is therefore a way of getting people to get clear about and focus their attention on what is worthwhile achieving. It is not to ask for the production of ends extrinsic to education.

Of course moral policies cannot be derived from definitions. A man who has been brought to see these conceptual points about 'the aims of education' could reasonably reply 'Well, I am against education then. I prefer to train people in science simply in order to increase productivity in the community, or to get them well-paid jobs. I cannot see any point in teaching science unless it can be shown to be obviously useful in these ways'. This is an arguable position. But it should not masquerade as a view about the aims of *education*.

## 'Education' and 'Growth'

Historically speaking, when the utilitarian or the moulding models of education have been challenged, others were substituted which likened education to a natural process in which the individual develops or 'grows' like a plant towards something that is presumed to be desirable. Gradually, a positive child-centred ideology emerged which was passionately embraced by those in revolt against traditional methods still prevalent in the schools.

The word 'ideology' is used advisedly to draw attention to a loose assembly of beliefs whose origin in an indeterminate matrix of psychological preoccupation is more obvious than their validity. The ideology of the 'progressive' child-centred educator, who believes in 'growth', cannot be attributed to any one central thinker. He or, more likely, she, tends to believe that education consists in the development from within of potentialities rather than 'moulding' from without, that the curriculum should arise from the needs and interests of the child rather than from the demands of the teacher, that self-expression is more important than the discipline of 'subject-matter', that children should not be coerced or punished, that children should be allowed to 'learn from experience' rather than be told things. The difficulty is to pin down such views to any one important educational theorist.

Froebel certainly stressed the importance of study-ing the child at his various stages and adapting what was provided to the child's interests and stage of development. But he believed very definitely in structuring the environment along desirable lines (witness his 'gifts') and his conception of education was dominated by the mystical demand that in the individual that unity should be experienced which permeated the whole of Nature. Dewey, with whose name concepts such as 'growth' and 'experience' are closely associated, had to write a book[5] in order to disclaim responsibility for some of the doctrines and practices of the Progressive Education Move-ment and to rectify misunderstandings of his more moderate position. Even Rousseau himself, so some interpreters argue, did not believe that education con-sisted purely in aiding the enfoldment of 'natural' propensities, but in guiding the boy, stage by stage, towards 'moral freedom', self-reliance and self-control, and a love of truth and justice.

It would require the erudition of a historian of educational thought and practice to trace the develop-ment of the child-centred, Progressive ideology in England and the U.S.A. This would be beyond the scope of this paper and the competence of its author. But what emerged as associated with this ideology was a model of the educational situation in which the teacher was regarded as one who has studied the laws of development, and who has to provide appropriate conditions by arranging the 'environment' so that the child can 'realise himself' to the full or 'grow' without becoming stunted or arrested. This model avoids the illiberal and instru-mental intimations of the other models; but, like Icarus, it cannot remain for long romantically aloft once the glare of philosophical analysis is turned upon it. For concepts such as 'self-realisation' and 'growth' presuppose standards of value which determine both the sort of 'self' which is worth realising and the direction of growth. Human beings are not like flowers in having a predetermined end which serves as a final cause of their development. 'Growing' or 'realising oneself' implies doing things which are thought to be worth-while rather than others. The standards by reference to which they are judged to be worth-while are grasped by men and handed on from generation to generation. The moulding model of the educator at least brings out this inescapable fact that the teacher has to choose what is worth-while encouraging in children; but it does so, as I have already argued, by using too brutal a metaphor.[6]

In spite, however, of the lack of determinate-ness about standards which unanalysed uplift about 'growth' and 'self-realisation' often encourages, such caricatures of an educational situation are morally important in another way; for they suggest another dimension in which value-judgments can enter into education, which relate to the *manner* rather than to the matter of education. They emphasise the place of *procedural* principles. By this I mean that they stress the importance of letting individuals choose for themselves, learn by experience, and direct their own lives. The importance of such principles, which all stress the self-direction of the individual, was often overlooked by traditional teachers. They represent value judgments not so much about the matter of what is taught, nor about some illusory 'end' for which things are taught, but about the manner in which children are to be treated. This is salutary not simply from a general moral stand-point but more specifically because it picks out one sort of way in which values can be conceived of as being intrinsic to education, rather than as extrinsic ends. Indeed I have argued elsewhere that much of the controversy about 'aims' of education is in reality concerned with disagreements about such principles of procedure.[7] The problem for those who emphasise 'growth' is to do this in a way which does justice to the fact that no educator can be indifferent to the way in which an individual grows. Dewey's treatment of the case of the burglar who might grow in stature as a burglar is one of the most unsatisfactory passages in his argument.[8]

Conceptually speaking, however, the 'growth' model of education, like the instrumental or mould-ing model, is a caricature; though like all effective caricatures, it distorts a face by emphasising some of its salient features. For just as the instrumental and moulding models erect the necessary moral feature of 'education' into an extrinsic end, so also the growth model converts a necessary feature of educational processes into a procedural prin-ciple. Evidence of this is provided by the tendency of its adherents to stress the connection between 'education' and 'educere' rather than 'educare', thereby moulding the concept towards 'leading out' rather than 'stamping in'. This emerges as a persuasive definition of 'education' which intim-ates that nothing is to be counted as 'education' in which such procedural principles to do with 'leading out' are ignored. The rationale underly-ing this transition from a conceptual point about 'education' to specific moral principles needs further elucidation, which is my second main conceptual point about 'education'.

It comes about as follows: although 'education' picks out no specific processes it does imply criteria which processes involved must satisfy in addition to the demand that something valuable must be passed on. It implies, first of all, that the individual who is educated shall come to care about the valuable things involved, that he shall want to achieve the relevant standards. We would not call a man 'educated' who knew about science but cared nothing for truth or who regarded it merely as a means to getting hot water and hot dogs. Furthermore it implies that he is initiated into the content of the activity or forms of knowledge in a meaningful way, so that he knows what he is doing. A man might be conditioned to avoid dogs or induced to do something by hypnotic suggestion. But we could not describe this as 'education' if he did not know what he was learning while he learnt it. Some forms of drill might also be ruled out on these grounds, if the individual was made to repeat mindlessly a series of narrowly conceived stereotyped acts. For something to count as education a minimum of comprehension must be involved. This is quite compatible with children being told to do things in the early stages. For they do, in an embryonic way, know what they are meant to be doing and understand the standards which they are expected to attain. Furthermore there is a minimal sense in which they act as voluntary agents; for they can rebel and refuse to do what is required of them. These conditions do not apply to what has been induced by hypnosis, drugs, or brutal forms of brain-washing.

Those who believe in such authoritarian methods of education assume that, though children may not care about these performances in the early stages, once they get started on them they will eventually come to care. They will thus emerge as educated men. Growth-theorists, on the other hand, grasping that being educated implies interest in and care for what is worth-while, assumed that this could only develop if the worth-while things are always presented in a way which attracts the child. On psychological grounds they held that coercion and command are ineffective methods for getting children to care about what is worth-while. Furthermore they had moral scruples about treating children in this way, which emerged as procedural principles demanding that children should be allowed to learn by experience and choose for themselves. Their concept of 'education' was moulded by their consciences.

In brief my second conceptual point is that to be 'educated' implies (a) caring about what is worthwhile and (b) being brought to care about it and to possess the relevant knowledge or skill in a way that involves at least a minimum of understanding and voluntariness. This point has been blown up by 'growth' theorists into a persuasive definition of 'education' in which 'education' is equated with the observance of procedural principles to do with self-determination. The main defect of their view, however, is not that they were induced by psychological speculation and moral demands to puff up conceptual points about 'education' into procedural principles. Rather it is that they evaded the other feature stressed by traditional teachers that education involves the intentional transmission of worth-while content.

Plato's image of education as turning the eye of the soul outwards towards the light is, in these respects at least, much more apposite than either of the two models so far considered. For though he was convinced that there are truths to be grasped and standards to be achieved, which are public objects of desire, he claimed that coercing people into seeing them or trying to imprint them on wax-like minds was both psychologically unsound and morally base. Plato emphasised, quite rightly, what growth theorists evaded, the necessity for objective standards being written into the content of education. But he was not unmindful of the procedural principles stressed by 'growth' theorists.

## 'Education' and Cognition

The emphasis on 'seeing' and 'grasping' for oneself which is to be found both in Plato and in the 'growth' theorists suggests a third conceptual point about 'education' in addition to those already made about the value of what is passed on and the manner in which it is to be assimilated. This concerns the cognitive aspect of the content of education.

We often say of a man that he is highly trained, but not educated. What lies behind this condemnation? It is not that the man has mastered a skill of which we disapprove. For we could say this of a doctor or even of a philosopher who had mastered certain ploys or moves in argument; and we might very much approve of their expertise. It is not that he goes through the moves like a mindless robot. For he may be passionately committed to the skill in question and may exercise it with intelligence and determination. It is rather that he has a very limited conception of what he is doing. He does not see its connection with anything else, its place in a coherent pattern of life. It is, for him, an activity which is cognitively adrift. The slogans of the educationalist such as 'education is of the whole man' bear witness not simply to a protest against too much specialised training, but also to the conceptual connection between 'education' and seeing what is being done in a perspective that is not too limited. We talk about a person as being trained as a philosopher, scientist, or cook, when we wish to draw attention to his acquired competence in a specific discipline of thought or art which has its own intrinsic standards; we do not use the phrase 'education as a philosopher, scientist, or cook'. We can, however, ask the further question whether such people are educated *men*. To ask this question is at least to probe the limitations of their professional vision.

Confirmation of this conceptual connection between 'education' and cognitive perspective is provided by considering what we say about less specialised matters. We talk more naturally of 'educating the emotions', than we do of training them. This is surely because the distinct emotions are differentiated by their cognitive core, by the different beliefs that go with them. The fundamental difference, for instance, between what is meant by 'anger' as distinct from 'jealousy' can only be brought out by reference to the different sorts of beliefs that the individual has about the people and situations with which he is confronted. A man who is jealous must think that someone else has something to which he is entitled; what comes over him when he is subject to a fit of jealousy is intimately connected with this belief. But a man who is angry need have no belief as specific as this; he may just regard someone as frustrating one of his purposes. If, therefore, we are contemplating bringing about changes in people's emotional attitudes or reactions, our main task consists in trying to get them to see the world differently in relation to themselves. The eye of the jealous man must be made less jaundiced by altering his concept of what he has a right to, or by getting him to see the actions of others in another light. We speak of 'education' because of the work that has to be done on his beliefs.

If, on the other hand, we speak, as we sometimes do, of *training* the emotions, the implications are different. We think of standard situations such as those of the fighter pilot or the gentleman in the drawing room. Such moral heroes have to acquire by training or by drill a pattern of habits which will not be disrupted in emergencies; they will not be paralysed by fear or overcome by grief or jealousy in a public place. 'Training' suggests the acquisition of appropriate habits of response in a limited situation. It lacks the wider cognitive implications of 'education'. We talk naturally of 'the training of character' when we wish to ensure reliability of response in accordance with a code; for 'character' is exhibited in the things which people can decide to do and can manifest itself in a very rigid and unadaptive form of behaviour.[9] But when we speak of 'moral education' we immediately envisage addressing ourselves to the matter of what people believe, and to questions of justification and questions of fact connected with such beliefs. To make my point even more sharply: 'sex education' is given by doctors, schoolmasters, and others who are capable of working information and value judgments about sexual matters into a complicated system of beliefs about the functioning of the body, personal relationships, and social institutions. If these oracles proceeded to try a bit of 'sex-training' with their pupils no class-room could contain their activities.

I have often wondered what converted physical training into physical education. No doubt, historically speaking, this came about, as do most changes in educational institutions, through pressures of a militant group requiring fuller recognition. But the underlying rationale of the change was surely the conviction on the part of some that exercising the body must not be seen merely as a skilful and disciplined business related to a specific end such as physical fitness; rather it is to be seen as related to and contributing to other worth-while things in life. To be asked to imagine that one is a leaf is to be given an unusual way of conceiving of what one is doing in the gym. But at least it conveys the impression that one is not just being trained in circumscribed skills.

This connection between 'education' and cognitive content explains why it is that some activities rather than others seem so obviously to be of educational importance. Few skills have a wide-ranging cognitive content. There is very little to know about riding bicycles, swimming, or golf. It is largely a matter of 'knowing how' rather than of 'knowing that',[10] of knack rather than of understanding. Furthermore what there is to know throws very little light on much else. In history, science, or literature, on the other hand, there is an immense amount to know, and, if it is properly assimilated, it constantly throws light on, widens, and deepens one's view of countless other things. Similarly games are of limited educational value. For, even if a game requires great skill and has considerable cognitive content internal to it (e.g., bridge), part of what is meant by calling it a 'game' is that it is set apart from the main business of living, complete in itself, and limited to particular times and places.[11] Games can be conceived of as being of educational import- ance only in so far as they provide opportunities for acquiring knowledge, qualities of mind and character, and skills that have application in a wider area of life. Hence their accepted importance for moral education. That *many* games have these features in a pre-eminent degree is a myth perpetuated by schoolmasters who convert esoteric enthusiasms into educational panaceas.

It might be objected that in drawing attention to the cognitive content implied by 'education' I am in danger of degrading it to the level of mere instruc- tion. To suggest this would be to misunderstand the main lines of the analysis which is being proposed. My thesis is not that 'education' refers to any special sort of process which might be equated with instruction, training, or drill; rather that it encapsulates three basic criteria which such processes must satisfy. Neither instruction alone, nor train- ing alone, could properly be so described. For both training and instruction might be in futile things like opium-taking, thus failing to satisfy the first cri- terion of being worth-while. Furthermore instruc- tion might consist in presenting inert ideas which are incomprehensible to children, whilst training might approximate to mindless drill, thus failing to satisfy the second criterion of 'education' already picked out.

Those, however, who have been hostile to mere instruction with its suggestion of 'inert ideas' have been too prone to conceive of education as if it were merely a matter of acquiring skills. This is, perhaps, because the tendency of American pragmatism and behaviourism is to assimilate thinking to doing, to regard it as 'surrogate behaviour'. But an 'educated' man is distinguished not so much by what he does as by what he 'sees' or 'grasps'. If he does something very well, in which he has been trained, he must see this in perspective, as related to other things. It is difficult to conceive of a training that would result in an 'educated' man in which a modicum of instruction has no place. For being educated involves 'knowing that' as well as 'knowing how'.

It might also be objected that I am equating the concept of 'education' with that of 'liberal education'. This is not my intention. The demand that education should be 'liberal' has usually been put forward as a protest against confining what goes on to the service of some extrinsic end such as the production of material goods or the promotion of health or empire. The mind, it is argued, should be allowed to pursue its own bent untrammelled by such restrictions. Allegiance should be given only to standards such as those connected with truth which are intrinsic to the mind's functioning. This interpretation of 'liberal', raises different issues about education which are more relevant to the first point I made about it when I stressed its necessary connection with the promotion of what is desirable. There is, however, another interpretation of 'liberal' which is closer to the point I have just been mak- ing about cognitive perspective. This is the plea that education should not be confined to specialist training. The individual, it is argued, should be trained in more than one form of knowledge. This requires more than what is written into the con- cept of 'education'. For whereas an 'educated' man can be trained in one sphere – e.g. science, and yet be sufficiently cognizant of other ways of looking at the world, so that he can grasp the historical perspective, social significance, or stylistic merit of his work and of much else besides, 'liberal' educa- tion requires that he should also be *trained*, to some degree at least, in such other ways of thinking. This is a much stronger requirement than that which is implied by anything that I have said about 'education', though it is obviously a development of what is intimated by it.

But I must digress no further on this point. The discussion has been sufficient, I think, to exhibit the importance both of training and of instruction in education and to safeguard my thesis against the misinterpretation that I am equating education with either of these processes.

## Education as Initiation

I now propose to put forward a more positive account of education which is constructed, in a truly dialectic manner, out of considerations brought forward in criticism of the discarded models, and which is consistent with the three criteria of 'education' that I have made explicit. Of course this account will not itself present yet another model; for to produce such a model would be to sin against the glimmerings of light that may have so far flickered over my treatment of the concept of 'education'. For, I have claimed, 'education' marks out no particular type of transaction between teachers and learners; it states criteria to which such transactions have to conform.

'Education' involves essentially processes which intentionally transmit what is valuable in an intelligible and voluntary manner and which create in the learner a desire to achieve it, this being seen to have its place along with other things in life. Terms like 'training' and 'instruction' – perhaps even 'teaching' – are too specific. Education can occur without these specific transactions and they can take place in ways which fail to satisfy all the criteria implied by 'education'. The term 'initiation', on the other hand, is general enough to cover these different types of transaction if it is also stipulated that initiation must be into worth-while activities and modes of conduct.

No man is born with a mind; for the development of mind marks a series of individual and racial achievements. A child is born with an awareness not as yet differentiated into beliefs, wants, and feelings. All such specific modes of consciousness, which are internally related to types of object in a public world, develop later *pari passu* with the pointing out of paradigm objects. Gradually the child comes to want things which there are means of obtaining instead of threshing round beset by unruly and unrealistic wishes; he comes to fear things that may hurt him, and to believe that things will come to pass which have come to pass. He learns to name objects, to locate his experience in a spatio-temporal framework, and to impose causal and means-to-end categories to make sense of events and actions. He creates pools of predictability by making promises and stating his intentions. In the beginning it was not at all like this. Such an embryonic mind is the product of initiation into public traditions enshrined in a public language, which it took our remote ancestors centuries to develop.

With the mastery of basic skills the door is opened to a vaster and more variegated inheritance. Further differentiation develops as the boy becomes initiated more deeply into distinctive forms of knowledge such as science, history, mathematics, religious and aesthetic appreciation, and into the practical types of knowledge involved in moral, prudential, and technical forms of thought and action. Such differentiations are alien to the mind

of a child and primitive man – indeed to that of a pre-seventeenth-century man. To have a mind is not to enjoy a private picture-show or to exercise some inner diaphanous organ; it is to have an awareness differentiated in accordance with the canons implicit in all these inherited traditions. 'Education' marks out the processes by means of which the individual is initiated into them.

Why do I start off my positive account of 'education' with this selective thumb-nail sketch of the social history of mind? Partly because I want to establish the notion of initiation in the centre of my account, and partly because I want to draw attention to the enormous importance of the *impersonal content and procedures* which are enshrined in public traditions. Initiation is always into some body of knowledge and mode of conduct which it takes time and determination to master. This association with activities which have what I called 'cognitive content' satisfies the third of the three essential criteria of education that I dwelt on in my earlier discussion of inadequate models. But there are additional points to stress about the importance in education of impersonal content and procedures.

There have been many like Dewey who have attacked the notion that education consists in the transmission of a body of knowledge. Stress is placed instead on critical thinking, individual experimentation and problem-solving. I have witnessed lessons in American schools where this view was slavishly applied: the teacher used poems purely to encourage 'critical thinking'; history was used, as it were, to provide riders for problem-solving. The notion that poetry should be listened to, or that one has to be, to a certain extent, a historian in order to understand a historical problem, was an alien one. The emphasis on 'critical thinking' was salutary enough, perhaps, when bodies of knowledge were handed on without any attempt being made to hand on also the public procedures by means of which they had been accumulated, criticised, and revised. But it is equally absurd to foster an abstract skill called 'critical thinking' without handing on anything concrete to be critical about. For there are as many brands of 'critical thinking' as there are disciplines, and in the various disciplines such as history, science, and philosophy, there is a great deal to be known before the peculiar nature of the problem is grasped.

It is of course important that people should be initiated gradually into the procedures defining a discipline as well as into mastery of the established content, that people should learn to think historic-ally for instance, not just know some history. But the only way to learn to think historically is to probe the past with someone who has mastered this form of thought. The procedures of a discipline can only be mastered by an exploration of its established con-tent under the guidance of one who has already been initiated. Whitehead said that a merely well-informed man is the most useless bore on God's earth. I do not entirely agree. I always find encyclopaedias interesting. Equally boring, in my view, are those for whom being critical is a substitute for being well informed about anything. To parody Kant: content without criticism is blind, but criticism without content is empty.

The further point needs also to be made that the critical procedures by means of which established content is assessed, revised, and adapted to new dis-coveries, have public criteria written into them that stand as impersonal standards to which both teacher and learner must give their allegiance. The trouble with the models of education that I considered is that they fail to do justice to this essential inter-subjectivity of education which D. H. Lawrence referred to as 'the holy ground'. To liken education to therapy, to conceive of it as imposing a pattern on another person or as fixing the environment so that he 'grows', fails to do justice to the shared imper-sonality both of the content that is handed on and of the criteria by reference to which it is criticized and revised. The teacher is not a detached operator who is bringing about some kind of result in another person which is external to him. His task is to try to get others on the inside of a public form of life that he shares and considers to be worth-while. In science it is truth that matters, not what any indi-vidual believes to be true; in morals it is justice, not the pronouncements of any individual.

At the culminating stages of education there is little distinction between teacher and taught; they are both participating in the shared experience of exploring a common world. The teacher is simply more familiar with its contours and more skilled in handling the tools for laying bare its mysteries and appraising its nuances. Occasionally in a tutorial this exploration takes the form of a dialogue. But more usually it is a group experience. The great teachers are those who can conduct such a shared exploration in accordance with rigorous canons, and convey, at the same time, the contagion of a shared enterprise in which all are united by a common zeal. That is why humour is such a valuable aid to teachers;

for if people can laugh together they step out of the shadows of self-reference cast by age, sex, and position. This creation of a shared experience can act as a catalyst which releases a class to unite in their common enterprise. This feeling of fraternity is part of the emotional underpinning for an enterprise conducted according to impersonal principles.

There has been too much loose talk about the dimension of the personal in teaching. Indeed one often fears that 'the enjoyment of good personal relationships' with pupils is in danger of becoming a substitute for teaching them something. What is required of the teacher, in addition to the feeling of fraternity already mentioned, is respect for persons, not intimate relations with his pupils. In a teaching situation love must be of a type that is appropriate to the special type of relationship in which the teacher is placed, to his concept of them as pupils rather than as sons or brothers. The teacher must always remember that he is dealing with others who are distinctive centres of consciousness, with peculiar idiosyncratic purposes and feelings that criss-cross their institutional roles. Each one is bound up with and takes pride of some sort in his own achieve-ments; each one mirrors the world from a distinctive point of view. In the early stages of education the emphasis on individual differences must be more marked; for the enterprise is to present the basic skills, which are necessary for later explorations, in the manner which is most appropriate to minds comparatively unformed by public traditions. Hence the relevance of activity methods and of the model of individual growth; hence the appositeness of the slogan 'We teach children, not subjects'; hence the need for teachers to understand what psychologists have discovered about individual differences and child development. Such a 'child-centred' approach is as appropriate in dealing with the backward or difficult adolescent as it is at the infant stage. For the crucial difference is not one of age, but of the development of motivation and of cognitive struc-ture, and of degrees of initiation into public and differentiated modes of thought.

At the other end of the enterprise of education, however, in universities, adult education classes, and the later stages of secondary education, the emphasis is more on the canons implicit in the forms of thought than on individual avenues of initiation. Respect for persons, enlivened by fratern-ity, here provides the warmth in which the teacher can perform his cardinal function of exhibiting the form of thought into which he is trying to initiate others. It is one thing to understand the canons of any discipline or mode of conduct; it is quite another to apply them with skill and judgment in particular circumstances. Judgment, said Quintilian, is the final flower of much experience. But such experience has to be acquired in the company of a man who already has judgment; it cannot be learnt from books or formal lectures alone. Oakeshott has written so tellingly on this aspect of the personal element in education that it would be otiose for me to labour this point any further.[12] Need I add that the notion of 'initiation' is a peculiarly apt description of this essential feature of education which consists in experienced persons turning the eye of others outwards to what is essentially independent of persons?

'Initiation' is an apt description, too, of that other aspect of education stressed by the 'growth' theorists, the requirement that those who are being educated should want to do or master the worth-while things which are handed on to them. This must be done in such a way that the coercion of the old formal instructor is not replaced by the cajol-ing of the progressive child-watcher. I am inclined to think that the value of command and direction is underestimated by modern educational theory, especially perhaps with less intelligent children. At least it indicates clearly what the educator con-siders to be worth-while and is certainly preferable to bribery and the production of irrelevant incent-ives. At least it may awaken some rebellion in the child and generate a jet of desire in him to do what he thinks worth-while, if he can find an avenue. Where everything is only to be done if it can be seen by the child to relate to what he wants, the coinage of wanting becomes debased because there is too little with which he may contrast it.

This brings me to my final and perhaps most fundamental point about 'education'. I have remarked before that 'education' implies standards, not necessarily aims. It consists in initiating others into activities, modes of conduct and thought which have standards written into them by reference to which it is possible to act, think, and feel with varying degrees of skill, relevance and taste. If teachers are not convinced of this they should be otherwise employed. They may be a bit hazy about why these things are more valuable than others. This is not surprising; for the problem of justification in general is a very difficult problem with which moral philosophers since Socrates have been con-stantly wrestling. The relative weight to be given to

these valuable things also presents acute problems; hence the importance of having a system which per-mits options. But *that* these things are valuable no dedicated teacher would dispute.

Now the teacher, having himself been initiated, is on the inside of these activities and modes of thought and conduct. He understands vividly, per-haps, that some created objects are beautiful and others not; he can recognise the elegance of a proof, or a paragraph, the cogency of an argument, the clarity of an exposition, the wit of a remark, the neatness of a plot and the justice and wisdom of a decision. He has perhaps a love of truth, a passion for justice, and a hatred of what is tasteless. To ask him what the aim or point of this form of life is, into which he has himself been initiated, seems an otiose question. For, like Socrates, he senses that really to understand what is good is, *ipso facto*, to be committed to its pursuit. How can a man who really understands what a cogent argument is, or a wise and just decision, settle for one that is slipshod, slovenly, or haphazard? This sort of question, he senses, can only be asked by barbarians outside the gates. Of course he realises that science, mathematics, and even history *can* be viewed in an instrumental way. They contribute to hospitals being built and staffed, wars being won, the cultivation of the land, and to communication across the face of the earth. And then what, he asks? What are men going to do, how are they going to think, what are they going to appreciate when their necessary appetites are satisfied? Are these hard men indifferent to all that constitutes being civilised?

Children, to a large extent, are. They start off in the position of the barbarian outside the gates. The problem is to get them inside the citadel of civilisation so that they will understand and love what they see when they get there. It is no use con-cealing the fact that the activities and modes of thought and conduct which define a civilised form of life are difficult to master. That is why the edu-cator has such an uphill task in which there are no short cuts. The insistence, which one confronts in American schools, that children should be happy, ignores this brutal fact. People can be happy lying in the sun; but happiness such as this is not the con-cern of the educator. Most of our thinking about 'welfare' is bedevilled by the confusion of being happy with living a worth-while life.

It may well be asked: if this is what is meant by 'education', how many people are capable of it? This is not a philosophical question; for though a philosopher might concern himself with the general conditions necessary for the application of a concept, it is an empirical question to determine to what extent such conditions are actually realized. To take a parallel: a philosopher might map out what it means to be moral and what general conditions must be satisfied for the concept to have application – e.g. the possession of a central nervous system, the ability to feel sympathy for others. But it is not his business, *qua* philosopher, to speculate about how many people there may be in whom such conditions are satisfied.

It is clear, however, from this analysis of 'education' that there are necessary conditions to do with cognitive structure and motivation. Although it is not a philosopher's task to speculate about the empirical facts in this matter, it is not out of place for him to note that very little is known about them. As has been remarked before, such evidence as there is suggests that a great deal depends on early conditions in the home and school. Since a large proportion of the population in Great Britain suffers from an environment which militates against such motivation and cognitive development it would be unwise as well as unfair to conclude too soon that education can only be for the 'elite'.

Many educators, seeing both the indignity and the inefficacy of the traditional attempts to coerce children into doing difficult things for which they had no inclination, preached the doctrine of 'interest'. If these difficult things could be ingeniously harnessed to what children want, then, they said, the task and not the man will exert the discipline. Skill, judgment, and discrimination can be erected on a foundation of existing wants. There is much in this technique. In the Youth Service, for instance, we used a predictable interest in sex to develop manners, skill in dancing, and taste in clothes and personal adornment. The hope was that eventually the girls would come to value manners and skill in dancing for their own sake and not purely as a means to getting a boy, and would develop outwards from this solid centre. One technique of initiation is therefore to lure people inside the citadel by using their existing interests in the hope that, once inside, they will develop other interests which previously were never dreamed of. The danger of this technique is that, if used to the exclusion of others, it reinforces the instrumental attitude. It encourages people to think that things are only worth doing well if they are patently relevant to some extrinsic end.

This is, of course, a very limited conception of initiation. For it neglects the fluidity of wants. What people in fact want or are interested in is, to a large extent, a product of their previous initiation. The job of the educator is not simply to build on existing wants but to present what is worth wanting in such a way that it creates new wants and stimulates new interests. If teachers do not do this others will – advertisers, for instance, and other members of 'the peer group'. There are interesting studies emerging recently from the U.S.A. suggesting a connection between permissive methods in education and group conformity.[13] If teachers do not hold up standards of achievement to children in a way that gets them working, others will lure them along less exacting paths. Whitehead has much that it is wise to say here on the stage of 'romance' in education. Any method which can create interest in what is worth-while should not be debarred – even talk and chalk, if employed by a man who is good at it.[14] But the stage of romance must be followed by the stage of precision. The crunch of standards must come with all that it entails in blood, sweat, and tears. The 'playway' may open up a vista of a Promised Land; but of itself it may provide little of the precision, skill and judgment which may be necessary for getting there. The pupil has gradually to get the grammar of the activity into his guts so that he can eventually win through to the stage of autonomy. But he cannot do this unless he has mastered the moves made by his predecessors which are enshrined in living traditions. *How* he can come best to this is an empirical question; but talk of encouraging 'creativeness' is mischievous unless children are also equipped with competence; talk of 'problem-solving' is cant unless children are knowledgeable enough to recognize a real problem when they see one. The only way into mastering what Oakeshott calls the 'language' of any form of thought or activity is by first being initiated into its 'literature'.[15] This is an arduous business.

As a matter of fact there is evidence to suggest that the teacher may not have to rely purely on specific interests, or on the admiration which children have for him and their desire to please him, to provide incentives for precision. For there may well be a generalized interest in achievement and competence for its own sake.[16] To master some difficult task, to get things right, to do what is right, is a very powerful source of motivation. It can grip young children as well as absorbed adults. Perhaps it was one of the driving forces of the Puritan movement which once galvanised England into activity. It can, of course, degenerate into compulsiveness; it can be harnessed to things that are both futile and wicked. But when harnessed to things that are also worthwhile, it is not to be despised. There is much to be said for the generalized Puritan virtues of enterprise, orderliness, thoroughness, and perseverance – especially in education.

Education, then, can have no ends beyond itself. Its value derives from principles and standards implicit in it. To be educated is not to have arrived at a destination; it is to travel with a different view. What is required is not feverish preparation for something that lies ahead, but to work with precision, passion and taste at worth-while things that lie to hand. These worth-while things cannot be forced on reluctant minds, neither are they flowers towards which the seeds of mentality develop in the sun of the teacher's smile. They are acquired by contact with those who have already acquired them and who have patience, zeal, and competence enough to initiate others into them.

'There is a quality of life which lies always beyond the mere fact of life'.[17] The great teacher is he who can convey this sense of quality to another, so that it haunts his every endeavour and makes him sweat and yearn to fix what he thinks and feels in a fitting form. For life has no one purpose; man imprints his purposes upon it. It presents few tidy problems; mainly predicaments that have to be endured or enjoyed. It is education that provides that touch of eternity under the aspect of which endurance can pass into dignified, wry acceptance, and animal enjoyment into a quality of living.

## Notes

1. Another version of this paper was given as an Inaugural Lecture to the Chair of the Philosophy of Education at the University of London Institute of Education, delivered in December 1963.
2. *Half Our Future*, a report of the Central Advisory Council for Education (London: H. M. Stationery Office, 1963).
3. See, for instance, B. Bernstein, 'Social Class and Linguistic Development: A Theory of Social Learning' in *Education, Economy, and Society*, ed. Halsey, Floud, and Anderson (New York: Free Press, 1961).
4. 'Education' is actually both what Ryle calls a 'task' term and an 'achievement' term (see G. Ryle, *The Concept of Mind* [London: Hutchinson, 1949] pp. 149–153). The complications introduced by this cannot be dealt with in a paper of this nature and do not affect the main lines of the analysis.
5. J. Dewey, *Experience and Education* (New York: Macmillan, 1938).
6. For further comments on both 'moulding' and 'growth' metaphors see I. Scheffler, *The Language of Education* (Springfield, Illinois: Thomas, 1960), Chapter 3.
7. R. S. Peters, *Authority, Responsibility, and Education* (London: Allen & Unwin, 2nd edition, 1963), Chapter 7.
8. J. Dewey, *Experience and Education* (London: Constable, 1961), pp. 37–38.
9. For further complications in the concept of 'character' see R. S. Peters, 'Moral Education and the Psychology of Character' in *Philosophy*, January 1962.
10. See G. Ryle, *The Concept of Mind* (London: Hutchinson, 1949), Chapter 2.
11. See J. Huizinga, *Homo Ludens* (London: Kegan Paul, 1949), Chapter 1.
12. See M. Oakeshott, 'Political Education' in *Rationalism in Politics* (London: Methuen, 1962).
13. See, for example, F. Kerlinger, 'The Implications of the Permissiveness Doctrine in American Education' in H. Burns and C. Brauner (eds.), *Philosophy and Education* (New York: Ronald Press, 1962).
14. A. N. Whitehead, *The Aims of Education* (London: Williams & Norgate, 1962), Chapter 2.
15. See M. Oakeshott, 'The Teaching of Politics in a University' in *Rationalism in Politics* (London: Methuen, 1962).
16. See D. McClelland, *The Achievement Motive* (New York: Appleton-Century, 1953), and other more recent publications, as well as R. White, 'Competence and the Psycho-sexual Stages of Development' in M. R. Jones (ed.), *Nebraska Symposium on Motivation* (Lincoln: University of Nebraska Press, 1960).
17. A. N. Whitehead, *Religion in the Making* (Cambridge University Press, 1926), p. 80.

# 8

# Banking *v.* Problem-solving Models of Education

## Paulo Freire

A careful analysis of the teacher-student relationship at any level, inside or outside the school, reveals its fundamentally *narrative* character. This relationship involves a narrating Subject (the teacher) and patient, listening objects (the students). The contents, whether values or empirical dimensions of reality, tend in the process of being narrated to become lifeless and petrified. Education is suffering from narration sickness.

The teacher talks about reality as if it were motionless, static, compartmentalized, and predictable. Or else he expounds on a topic completely alien to the existential experience of the students. His task is to "fill" the students with the contents of his narration – contents which are detached from reality, disconnected from the totality that engendered them and could give them significance. Words are emptied of their concreteness and become a hollow, alienated, and alienating verbosity.

The outstanding characteristic of this narrative education, then, is the sonority of words, not their transforming power. "Four times four is sixteen; the capital of Pará is Belém." The student records, memorizes, and repeats these phrases without perceiving what four times four really means, or realizing the true significance of "capital" in the affirmation "the capital of Pará is Belém," that is, what Belém means for Pará and what Pará means for Brazil.

Narration (with the teacher as narrator) leads the students to memorize mechanically the narrated content. Worse yet, it turns them into "containers," into "receptacles" to be "filled" by the teacher. The more completely he fills the receptacles, the better a teacher he is. The more meekly the receptacles permit themselves to be filled, the better students they are.

Education thus becomes an act of depositing, in which the students are the depositories and the teacher is the depositor. Instead of communicating, the teacher issues communiqués and makes deposits which the students patiently receive, memorize, and repeat. This is the "banking" concept of education, in which the scope of action allowed to the students extends only as far as receiving, filing, and storing the deposits. They do, it is true, have the opportunity to become collectors or cataloguers of the things they store. But in the last analysis, it is men themselves who are filed away through the lack of creativity, transformation, and knowledge in this (at best) misguided system. For apart from inquiry, apart from the praxis,

Originally published in *Pedagogy of the Oppressed*, trans. Myra Bergman Ramos (New York: The Seabury Press, 1970), pp. 57–74. © Paulo Freire 1970, 1993. Reprinted by the kind permission of Continuum USA and Penguin Books UK.

men cannot be truly human. Knowledge emerges only through invention and re-invention, through the restless, impatient, continuing, hopeful inquiry men pursue in the world, with the world, and with each other.

In the banking concept of education, knowledge is a gift bestowed by those who consider themselves knowledgeable upon those whom they consider to know nothing. Projecting an absolute ignorance onto others, a characteristic of the ideology of oppression, negates education and knowledge as processes of inquiry. The teacher presents himself to his students as their necessary opposite; by considering their ignorance absolute, he justifies his own existence. The students, alienated like the slave in the Hegelian dialectic, accept their ignorance as justifying the teacher's existence – but, unlike the slave, they never discover that they educate the teacher.

The *raison d'être* of libertarian education, on the other hand, lies in its drive towards reconciliation. Education must begin with the solution of the teacher-student contradiction, by reconciling the poles of the contradiction so that both are simultaneously teachers *and* students.

This solution is not (nor can it be) found in the banking concept. On the contrary, banking education maintains and even stimulates the contradiction through the following attitudes and practices, which mirror oppressive society as a whole:

(a)  the teacher teaches and the students are taught;
(b)  the teacher knows everything and the students know nothing;
(c)  the teacher thinks and the students are thought about;
(d)  the teacher talks and the students listen – meekly;
(e)  the teacher disciplines and the students are disciplined;
(f)  the teacher chooses and enforces his choice, and the students comply;
(g)  the teacher acts and the students have the illusion of acting through the action of the teacher;
(h)  the teacher chooses the program content, and the students (who were not consulted) adapt to it;
(i)  the teacher confuses the authority of knowledge with his own professional authority, which he sets in opposition to the freedom of the students;
(j)  the teacher is the Subject of the learning process, while the pupils are mere objects.

It is not surprising that the banking concept of education regards men as adaptable, manageable beings. The more students work at storing the deposits entrusted to them, the less they develop the critical consciousness which would result from their intervention in the world as transformers of that world. The more completely they accept the passive role imposed on them, the more they tend simply to adapt to the world as it is and to the fragmented view of reality deposited in them.

The capability of banking education to minimize or annul the students' creative power and to stimulate their credulity serves the interests of the oppressors, who care neither to have the world revealed nor to see it transformed. The oppressors use their "humanitarianism" to preserve a profitable situation. Thus they react almost instinctively against any experiment in education which stimulates the critical faculties and is not content with a partial view of reality but always seeks out the ties which link one point to another and one problem to another.

Indeed, the interests of the oppressors lie in "changing the consciousness of the oppressed, not the situation which oppresses them";[1] for the more the oppressed can be led to adapt to that situation, the more easily they can be dominated. To achieve this end, the oppressors use the banking concept of education in conjunction with a paternalistic social action apparatus, within which the oppressed receive the euphemistic title of "welfare recipients." They are treated as individual cases, as marginal men who deviate from the general configuration of a "good, organized, and just" society. The oppressed are regarded as the pathology of the healthy society, which must therefore adjust these "incompetent and lazy" folk to its own patterns by changing their mentality. These marginals need to be "integrated," "incorporated" into the healthy society that they have "forsaken."

The truth is, however, that the oppressed are not "marginals," are not men living "outside" society. They have always been "inside" – inside the structure which made them "beings for others." The solution is not to "integrate" them into the structure of oppression, but to transform that structure so that they can become "beings for themselves." Such transformation, of course, would undermine the oppressors' purposes; hence their utilization of the banking concept of education to avoid the threat of student *conscientização*.[2]

The banking approach to adult education, for example, will never propose to students that they critically consider reality. It will deal instead with such vital questions as whether Roger gave green grass to the goat, and insist upon the importance of learning that, on the contrary, *R*oger gave green grass to the *r*abbit. The "humanism" of the banking approach masks the effort to turn men into automatons – the very negation of their ontological vocation to be more fully human.

Those who use the banking approach, knowingly or unknowingly (for there are innumerable well-intentioned bank-clerk teachers who do not realize that they are serving only to dehumanize), fail to perceive that the deposits themselves contain contradictions about reality. But, sooner or later, these contradictions may lead formerly passive students to turn against their domestication and the attempt to domesticate reality. They may discover through existential experience that their present way of life is irreconcilable with their vocation to become fully human. They may perceive through their relations with reality that reality is really a *process*, undergoing constant transformation. If men are searchers and their ontological vocation is humanization, sooner or later they may perceive the contradiction in which banking education seeks to maintain them, and then engage themselves in the struggle for their liberation.

But the humanist, revolutionary educator cannot wait for this possibility to materialize. From the outset, his efforts must coincide with those of the students to engage in critical thinking and the quest for mutual humanization. His efforts must be imbued with a profound trust in men and their creative power. To achieve this, he must be a partner of the students in his relations with them.

The banking concept does not admit to such partnership – and necessarily so. To resolve the teacher-student contradiction, to exchange the role of depositor, prescriber, domesticator, for the role of student among students would be to undermine the power of oppression and serve the cause of liberation.

Implicit in the banking concept is the assumption of a dichotomy between man and the world: man is merely *in* the world, not *with* the world or with others; man is spectator, not re-creator.

In this view, man is not a conscious being (*corpo consciente*); he is rather the possessor of *a* consciousness: an empty "mind" passively open to the reception of deposits of reality from the world outside. For example, my desk, my books, my coffee cup, all the objects before me – as bits of the world which surrounds me – would be "inside" me, exactly as I am inside my study right now. This view makes no distinction between being accessible to consciousness and entering consciousness. The distinction, however, is essential: the objects which surround me are simply accessible to my consciousness, not located within it. I am aware of them, but they are not inside me.

It follows logically from the banking notion of consciousness that the educator's role is to regulate the way the world "enters into" the students. His task is to organize a process which already occurs spontaneously, to "fill" the students by making deposits of information which he considers to constitute true knowledge.[3] And since men "receive" the world as passive entities, education should make them more passive still, and adapt them to the world. The educated man is the adapted man, because he is better "fit" for the world. Translated into practice, this concept is well suited to the purposes of the oppressors, whose tranquility rests on how well men fit the world the oppressors have created, and how little they question it.

The more completely the majority adapt to the purposes which the dominant minority prescribe for them (thereby depriving them of the right to their own purposes), the more easily the minority can continue to prescribe. The theory and practice of banking education serve this end quite efficiently. Verbalistic lessons, reading requirements,[4] the methods for evaluating "knowledge," the distance between the teacher and the taught, the criteria for promotion: everything in this ready-to-wear approach serves to obviate thinking.

The bank-clerk educator does not realize that there is no true security in his hypertrophied role, that one must seek to live *with* others in solidarity. One cannot impose oneself, nor even merely co-exist with one's students. Solidarity requires true communication, and the concept by which such an educator is guided fears and proscribes communication.

Yet only through communication can human life hold meaning. The teacher's thinking is authenticated only by the authenticity of the students' thinking. The teacher cannot think for his students, nor can he impose his thought on them. Authentic thinking, thinking that is concerned about *reality*, does not take place in ivory tower isolation, but only in communication. If it is true that thought has meaning only when generated by action upon the world, the subordination of students to teachers becomes impossible.

Because banking education begins with a false understanding of men as objects, it cannot promote the development of what Fromm calls "biophily," but instead produces its opposite: "necrophily."

> While life is characterized by growth in a structured, functional manner, the necrophilous person loves all that does not grow, all that is mechanical. The necrophilous person is driven by the desire to transform the organic into the inorganic, to approach life mechanically, as if all living persons were things. . . . Memory, rather than experience; having, rather than being, is what counts. The necrophilous person can relate to an object – a flower or a person – only if he possesses it; hence a threat to his possession is a threat to himself; if he loses possession he loses contact with the world. . . . He loves control, and in the act of controlling he kills life.[5]

Oppression – overwhelming control – is necrophilic; it is nourished by love of death, not life. The banking concept of education, which serves the interests of oppression, is also necrophilic. Based on a mechanistic, static, naturalistic, spatialized view of consciousness, it transforms students into receiving objects. It attempts to control thinking and action, leads men to adjust to the world, and inhibits their creative power.

When their efforts to act responsibly are frustrated, when they find themselves unable to use their faculties, men suffer. "This suffering due to impotence is rooted in the very fact that the human equilibrium has been disturbed."[6] But the inability to act which causes men's anguish also causes them to reject their impotence, by attempting

> . . . to restore [their] capacity to act. But can [they], and how? One way is to submit to and identify with a person or group having power. By this symbolic participation in another person's life, [men have] the illusion of acting, when in reality [they] only submit to and become a part of those who act.[7]

Populist manifestations perhaps best exemplify this type of behavior by the oppressed, who, by identifying with charismatic leaders, come to feel that they themselves are active and effective. The rebellion they express as they emerge in the historical process is motivated by that desire to act effectively. The dominant elites consider the remedy to be more domination and repression, carried out in the name of freedom, order, and social peace (that is, the peace of the elites). Thus they can condemn – logically, from their point of view – "the violence of a strike by workers and [can] call upon the state in the same breath to use violence in putting down the strike."[8]

Education as the exercise of domination stimulates the credulity of students, with the ideological intent (often not perceived by educators) of indoctrinating them to adapt to the world of oppression. This accusation is not made in the naïve hope that the dominant elites will thereby simply abandon the practice. Its objective is to call the attention of true humanists to the fact that they cannot use banking educational methods in the pursuit of liberation, for they would only negate that very pursuit. Nor may a revolutionary society inherit these methods from an oppressor society. The revolutionary society which practices banking education is either misguided or mistrusting of men. In either event, it is threatened by the specter of reaction.

Unfortunately, those who espouse the cause of liberation are themselves surrounded and influenced by the climate which generates the banking concept, and often do not perceive its true significance or its dehumanizing power. Paradoxically, then, they utilize this same instrument of alienation in what they consider an effort to liberate. Indeed, some "revolutionaries" brand as "innocents," "dreamers," or even "reactionaries" those who would challenge this educational practice. But one does not liberate men by alienating them. Authentic liberation – the process of humanization – is not another deposit to be made in men. Liberation is a praxis: the action and reflection of men upon their world in order to transform it. Those truly committed to the cause of liberation can accept neither the mechanistic concept of consciousness as an empty vessel to be filled, nor the use of banking methods of domination (propaganda, slogans – deposits) in the name of liberation.

Those truly committed to liberation must reject the banking concept in its entirety, adopting instead a concept of men as conscious beings, and consciousness as consciousness intent upon the world.

They must abandon the educational goal of deposit-making and replace it with the posing of the problems of men in their relations with the world. "Problem-posing" education, responding to the essence of consciousness – *intentionality* – rejects communiqués and embodies communication. It epitomizes the special characteristic of consciousness: being *conscious of*, not only as intent on objects but as turned in upon itself in a Jasperian "split" – consciousness as consciousness *of* consciousness.

Liberating education consists in acts of cognition, not transferrals of information. It is a learning situation in which the cognizable object (far from being the end of the cognitive act) intermediates the cognitive actors – teacher on the one hand and students on the other. Accordingly, the practice of problem-posing education entails at the outset that the teacher-student contradiction be resolved. Dialogical relations – indispensable to the capacity of cognitive actors to cooperate in perceiving the same cognizable object – are otherwise impossible.

Indeed, problem-posing education, which breaks with the vertical patterns characteristic of banking education, can fulfill its function as the practice of freedom only if it can overcome the above contradiction. Through dialogue, the teacher-of-the-students and the students-of-the-teacher cease to exist and a new term emerges: teacher-student with students-teachers. The teacher is no longer merely the-one-who-teaches, but one who is himself taught in dialogue with the students, who in turn while being taught also teach. They become jointly responsible for a process in which all grow. In this process, arguments based on "authority" are no longer valid; in order to function, authority must be *on the side of* freedom, not *against* it. Here, no one teaches another, nor is anyone self-taught. Men teach each other, mediated by the world, by the cognizable objects which in banking education are "owned" by the teacher.

The banking concept (with its tendency to dichotomize everything) distinguishes two stages in the action of the educator. During the first, he cognizes a cognizable object while he prepares his lessons in his study or his laboratory; during the second, he expounds to his students about that object. The students are not called upon to know, but to memorize the contents narrated by the teacher. Nor do the students practice any act of cognition, since the object towards which that act should be directed is the property of the teacher rather than a medium evoking the critical reflection of both teacher and students. Hence in the name of the "preservation of culture and knowledge" we have a system which achieves neither true knowledge nor true culture.

The problem-posing method does not dichotomize the activity of the teacher-student: he is not "cognitive" at one point and "narrative" at another. He is always "cognitive," whether preparing a project or engaging in dialogue with the students. He does not regard cognizable objects as his private property, but as the object of reflection by himself and the students. In this way, the problem-posing educator constantly re-forms his reflections in the reflection of the students. The students – no longer docile listeners – are now critical co-investigators in dialogue with the teacher. The teacher presents the material to the students for their consideration, and re-considers his earlier considerations as the students express their own. The role of the problem-posing educator is to create, together with the students, the conditions under which knowledge at the level of the *doxa* is superseded by true knowledge, at the level of the *logos*.

Whereas banking education anesthetizes and inhibits creative power, problem-posing education involves a constant unveiling of reality. The former attempts to maintain the *submersion* of consciousness; the latter strives for the *emergence* of consciousness and *critical intervention* in reality.

Students, as they are increasingly posed with problems relating to themselves in the world and with the world, will feel increasingly challenged and obliged to respond to that challenge. Because they apprehend the challenge as interrelated to other problems within a total context, not as a theoretical question, the resulting comprehension tends to be increasingly critical and thus constantly less alienated. Their response to the challenge evokes new challenges, followed by new understandings; and gradually the students come to regard themselves as committed.

Education as the practice of freedom – as opposed to education as the practice of domination – denies that man is abstract, isolated, independent, and unattached to the world; it also denies that the world exists as a reality apart from men. Authentic reflection considers neither abstract man nor the world without men, but men in their relations with the world. In these relations consciousness and world are simultaneous: consciousness neither precedes the world nor follows it.

La conscience et le monde sont dormés d'un même coup: extérieur par essence à la conscience, le monde est, par essence relatif à elle.[9]

In one of our culture circles in Chile, the group was discussing (based on a codification) the anthropological concept of culture. In the midst of the discussion, a peasant who by banking standards was completely ignorant said: "Now I see that without man there is no world." When the educator responded: "Let's say, for the sake of argument, that all the men on earth were to die, but that the earth itself remained, together with trees, birds, animals, rivers, seas, the stars . . . wouldn't all this be a world?" "Oh no," the peasant replied emphatically. "There would be no one to say: 'This is a world'."

The peasant wished to express the idea that there would be lacking the consciousness of the world which necessarily implies the world of consciousness. *I* cannot exist without a *not-I*. In turn, the *not-I* depends on that existence. The world which brings consciousness into existence becomes the world *of* that consciousness. Hence, the previously cited affirmation of Sartre: "*La conscience et le monde sont dormés d'un même coup.*"

As men, simultaneously reflecting on themselves and on the world, increase the scope of their perception, they begin to direct their observations towards previously inconspicuous phenomena:

> In perception properly so-called, as an explicit awareness [*Gewahren*], I am turned towards the object, to the paper, for instance. I apprehend it as being this here and now. The apprehension is a singling out, every object having a background in experience. Around and about the paper lie books, pencils, ink-well, and so forth, and these in a certain sense are also "perceived", perceptually there, in the "field of intuition"; but whilst I was turned towards the paper there was no turning in their direction, nor any apprehending of them, not even in a secondary sense. They appeared and yet were not singled out, were not posited on their own account. Every perception of a thing has such a zone of background intuitions or background awareness, if "intuiting" already includes the state of being turned towards, and this also is a "conscious experience", or more briefly a "consciousness of" all indeed that in point of fact lies in the co-perceived objective background.[10]

That which had existed objectively but had not been perceived in its deeper implications (if indeed it was perceived at all) begins to "stand out," assuming the character of a problem and therefore of challenge. Thus, men begin to single out elements from their "background awarenesses" and to reflect upon them. These elements are now objects of men's consideration, and, as such, objects of their action and cognition.

In problem-posing education, men develop their power to perceive critically *the way they exist* in the world *with which* and *in which* they find themselves; they come to see the world not as a static reality, but as a reality in process, in transformation. Although the dialectical relations of men with the world exist independently of how these relations are perceived (or whether or not they are perceived at all), it is also true that the form of action men adopt is to a large extent a function of how they perceive themselves in the world. Hence, the teacher-student and the students-teachers reflect simultaneously on themselves and the world without dichotomizing this reflection from action, and thus establish an authentic form of thought and action.

Once again, the two educational concepts and practices under analysis come into conflict. Banking education (for obvious reasons) attempts, by mythicizing reality, to conceal certain facts which explain the way men exist in the world; problem-posing education sets itself the task of demythologizing. Banking education resists dialogue; problem-posing education regards dialogue as indispensable to the act of cognition which unveils reality. Banking education treats students as objects of assistance; problem-posing education makes them critical thinkers. Banking education inhibits creativity and domesticates (although it cannot completely destroy) the *intentionality* of consciousness by isolating consciousness from the world, thereby denying men their ontological and historical vocation of becoming more fully human. Problem-posing education bases itself on creativity and stimulates true reflection and action upon reality, thereby responding to the vocation of men as beings who are authentic only when engaged in inquiry and creative transformation. In sum: banking theory and practice, as immobilizing and fixating forces, fail to acknowledge men as historical beings; problem-posing theory and practice take man's historicity as their starting point.

Problem-posing education affirms men as beings in the process of *becoming* – as unfinished, uncompleted beings in and with a likewise unfinished reality. Indeed, in contrast to other animals who are unfinished, but not historical, men know themselves to be unfinished; they are aware of their incompletion. In this incompletion and this awareness lie the very roots of education as an exclusively human manifestation. The unfinished character of men and the transformational character of reality necessitate that education be an ongoing activity.

Education is thus constantly remade in the praxis. In order to *be*, it must *become*. Its "duration" (in the Bergsonian meaning of the word) is found in the interplay of the opposites *permanence* and *change*. The banking method emphasizes permanence and becomes reactionary; problem-posing education – which accepts neither a "well-behaved" present nor a predetermined future – roots itself in the dynamic present and becomes revolutionary.

Problem-posing education is revolutionary futurity. Hence it is prophetic (and, as such, hopeful). Hence, it corresponds to the historical nature of man. Hence, it affirms men as beings who transcend themselves, who move forward and look ahead, for whom immobility represents a fatal threat, for whom looking at the past must only be a means of understanding more clearly what and who they are so that they can more wisely build the future. Hence, it identifies with the movement which engages men as beings aware of their incompletion – an historical movement which has its point of departure, its Subjects and its objective.

The point of departure of the movement lies in men themselves. But since men do not exist apart from the world, apart from reality, the movement must begin with the men-world relationship. Accordingly, the point of departure must always be with men in the "here and now," which constitutes the situation within which they are submerged, from which they emerge, and in which they intervene. Only by starting from this situation – which determines their perception of it – can they begin to move. To do this authentically they must perceive their state not as fated and unalterable, but merely as limiting – and therefore challenging.

Whereas the banking method directly or indirectly reinforces men's fatalistic perception of their situation, the problem-posing method presents this very situation to them as a problem. As the situation becomes the object of their cognition, the naïve or magical perception which produced their fatalism gives way to perception which is able to perceive itself even as it perceives reality, and can thus be critically objective about that reality.

A deepened consciousness of their situation leads men to apprehend that situation as an historical reality susceptible of transformation. Resignation gives way to the drive for transformation and inquiry, over which men feel themselves to be in control. If men, as historical beings necessarily engaged with other men in a movement of inquiry, did not control that movement, it would be (and is) a violation of men's humanity. Any situation in which some men prevent others from engaging in the process of inquiry is one of violence. The means used are not important; to alienate men from their own decision-making is to change them into objects.

This movement of inquiry must be directed towards humanization – man's historical vocation. The pursuit of full humanity, however, cannot be carried out in isolation or individualism, but only in fellowship and solidarity; therefore it cannot unfold in the antagonistic relations between oppressors and oppressed. No one can be authentically human while he prevents others from being so. Attempting *to be more* human, individualistically, leads to *having more*, egotistically: a form of dehumanization. Not that it is not fundamental *to have* in order *to be* human. Precisely because it *is* necessary, some men's *having* must not be allowed to constitute an obstacle to others' *having*, must not consolidate the power of the former to crush the latter.

Problem-posing education, as a humanist and liberating praxis, posits as fundamental that men subjected to domination must fight for their emancipation. To that end, it enables teachers and students to become Subjects of the educational process by overcoming authoritarianism and an alienating intellectualism; it also enables men to overcome their false perception of reality. The world – no longer something to be described with deceptive words – becomes the object of that transforming action by men which results in their humanization.

Problem-posing education does not and cannot serve the interests of the oppressor. No oppressive order could permit the oppressed to begin to question: Why? While only a revolutionary society can carry out this education in systematic terms, the revolutionary leaders need not take full power before they can employ the method. In the revolutionary process, the leaders cannot utilize the banking method as an interim measure, justified on grounds of expediency, with the intention of *later* behaving in a genuinely revolutionary fashion. They must be revolutionary – that is to say, dialogical – from the outset.

# Notes

1.  Simone de Beauvoir, *La Pensée de Droite, Aujord'hui* (Paris); ST, *El Pensamiento político de la Derecha* (Buenos Aires, 1963), p. 34.
2.  The term '*conscientização*' refers to learning to perceive social, political, and economic contradictions, and to take action against the oppressive elements of reality.
3.  This concept corresponds to what Sartre calls the "digestive" or "nutritive" concept of education, in which knowledge is "fed" by the teacher to the students to "fill them out." See Jean-Paul Sartre, "Une idée fundamentale de la phénomenologie de Husserl: L'intentionalité," *Situations I* (Paris, 1947).
4.  For example, some professors specify in their reading lists that a book should be read from pages 10 to 15 – and do this to "help" their students!
5.  Eric Fromm, *The Heart of Man* (New York, 1966), p. 41.
6.  Ibid., p. 31.
7.  Ibid.
8.  Reinhold Niebuhr, *Moral Man and Immoral Society* (New York, 1960), p. 130.
9.  Sartre, op. cit., p. 32.
10. Edmund Husserl, *Ideas – General Introduction to Pure Phenomenology* (London, 1969), pp. 105–6.

# Liberal Education and the Relationship between Education and Work

# 9

# Liberal *v.* Mechanical Education

## Aristotle

### Book VII

. . .

15. Since the end of individuals and of states is the same, the end of the best man and of the best constitution must also be the same; it is therefore evident that there ought to exist in both of them the excellences of leisure; for peace, as has been often repeated, is the end of war, and leisure of toil. But leisure and cultivation may be promoted not only by those excellences which are practised in leisure, but also by some of those which are useful to business. For many necessaries of life have to be supplied before we can have leisure. Therefore a city must be temperate and brave, and able to endure: for truly, as the proverb says, 'There is no leisure for slaves,' and those who cannot face danger like men are the slaves of any invader. Courage and endurance are required for business and philosophy for leisure, temperance and justice for both, and more especially in times of peace and leisure, for war compels men to be just and temperate, whereas the enjoyment of good fortune and the leisure which comes with peace tend to make them insolent. Those then who seem to be the best-off and to be in the possession of every good, have special need of justice and temperance – for example, those (if such there be, as the poets say) who dwell in the Islands of the Blest; they above all will need philosophy and temperance and justice, and all the more the more leisure they have, living in the midst of abundance. There is no difficulty in seeing why the state that would be happy and good ought to have these excellences. If it is disgraceful in men not to be able to use the goods of life, it is peculiarly disgraceful not to be able to use them in time of leisure – to show excellent qualities in action and war, and when they have peace and leisure to be no better than slaves. That is why we should not practise excellence after the manner of the Lacedaemonians. For they, while agreeing with other men in their conception of the highest goods, differ from the rest of mankind in thinking that they are to be obtained by the practice of a single excellence. And since these goods and the enjoyment of them are greater than the enjoyment derived from the excellences . . . and that for its own sake, is evident from what has been said; we must now consider how and by what means it is to be attained.

Editor's title. Previously published as *Politics*, from Jonathan Barnes (ed.), *The Complete Works of Aristotle*, Books VII and VIII, trans. Benjamin Jowett (Princeton, NJ: Princeton University Press, 1984), pp. 2116–17, 2121–7, 1334a12. © 1984 by the Jowett Copyright Trustees. Reprinted by permission of Princeton University Press.

We have already determined that nature and habit and reason are required, and, of these, the proper nature of the citizens has also been defined by us. But we have still to consider whether the training of early life is to be that of reason or habit, for these two must accord, and when in accord they will then form the best of harmonies. Reason may be mistaken and fail in attaining the highest ideal of life, and there may be a like influence of habit. Thus much is clear in the first place, that, as in all other things, birth implies an antecedent beginning, and that there are beginnings whose end is relative to a further end. Now, in men reason and mind are the end towards which nature strives, so that the birth and training in custom of the citizens ought to be ordered with a view to them. In the second place, as the soul and body are two, we see also that there are two parts of the soul, the rational and the irrational, and two corresponding states – reason and appetite. And as the body is prior in order of generation to the soul, so the irrational is prior to the rational. The proof is that anger and wishing and desire are implanted in children from their very birth, but reason and understanding are developed as they grow older. For this reason, the care of the body ought to precede that of the soul, and the training of the appetitive part should follow: none the less our care of it must be for the sake of the reason, and our care of the body for the sake of the soul.

[ . . . ]

## Book VIII

1. No one will doubt that the legislator should direct his attention above all to the education of youth; for the neglect of education does harm to the constitution. The citizen should be moulded to suit the form of government under which he lives. For each government has a peculiar character which originally formed and which continues to preserve it. The character of democracy creates democracy, and the character of oligarchy creates oligarchy; and always the better the character, the better the government.

Again, for the exercise of any faculty or art a previous training and habituation are required; clearly therefore for the practice of excellence. And since the whole city has one end, it is manifest that education should be one and the same for all, and that it should be public, and not private – not as at present, when everyone looks after his own children

separately, and gives them separate instruction of the sort which he thinks best; the training in things which are of common interest should be the same for all. Neither must we suppose that anyone of the citizens belongs to himself, for they all belong to the state, and are each of them a part of the state, and the care of each part is inseparable from the care of the whole. In this particular as in some others the Lacedaemonians are to be praised, for they take the greatest pains about their children, and make education the business of the state.

2. That education should be regulated by law and should be an affair of state is not to be denied, but what should be the character of this public education, and how young persons should be educated, are questions which remain to be considered. As things are, there is disagreement about the subjects. For men are by no means agreed about the things to be taught, whether we look to excellence or the best life. Neither is it clear whether education is more concerned with intellectual or with moral excellence. The existing practice is perplexing; no one knows on what principle we should proceed – should the useful in life, or should excellence, or should the higher knowledge, be the aim of our training? – all three opinions have been entertained. Again, about the means there is no agreement; for different persons, starting with different ideas about the nature of excellence, naturally disagree about the practice of it. There can be no doubt that children should be taught those useful things which are really necessary, but not all useful things; for occupations are divided into liberal and illiberal; and to young children should be imparted only such kinds of knowledge as will be useful to them without making mechanics of them. And any occupation, art, or science, which makes the body or soul or mind of the freeman less fit for the practice or exercise of excellence, is mechanical; wherefore we call those arts mechanical which tend to deform the body, and likewise all paid employments, for they absorb and degrade the mind. There are also some liberal arts quite proper for a freeman to acquire, but only in a certain degree, and if he attends to them too closely, in order to attain perfection in them, the same harmful effects will follow. The object also which a man sets before him makes a great difference; if he does or learns anything for his own sake or for the sake of his friends, or with a view to excellence, the action will not appear illiberal; but if done for the sake of others, the very same action will be thought menial

and servile. The received subjects of instruction, as I have already remarked, are partly of a liberal and partly of an illiberal character.

3. The customary branches of education are in number four; they are – reading and writing, gymnastic exercises, and music, to which is sometimes added drawing. Of these, reading and writing and drawing are regarded as useful for the purposes of life in a variety of ways, and gymnastic exercises are thought to infuse courage. Concerning music a doubt may be raised – in our own day most men cultivate it for the sake of pleasure, but originally it was included in education, because nature herself, as has been often said, requires that we should be able, not only to work well, but to use leisure well; for, as I must repeat once again, the first principle of all action is leisure. Both are required, but leisure is better than occupation and is its end; and therefore the question must be asked, what ought we to do when at leisure? Clearly we ought not to be playing, for then play would be the end of life. But if this is inconceivable, and play is needed more amid serious occupations than at other times (for he who is hard at work has need of relaxation, and play gives relaxation, whereas occupation is always accompanied with exertion and effort), we should introduce amusements only at suitable times, and they should be our medicines, for the emotion which they create in the soul is a relaxation, and from the pleasure we obtain rest. But leisure of itself gives pleasure and happiness and enjoyment of life, which are experienced, not by the busy man, but by those who have leisure. For he who is occupied has in view some end which he has not attained; but happiness is an end, since all men deem it to be accompanied with pleasure and not with pain. This pleasure, however, is regarded differently by different persons, and varies according to the habit of individuals; the pleasure of the best man is the best, and springs from the noblest sources. It is clear then that there are branches of learning and education which we must study merely with a view to leisure spent in intellectual activity, and these are to be valued for their own sake; whereas those kinds of knowledge which are useful in business are to be deemed necessary, and exist for the sake of other things. And therefore our fathers admitted music into education, not on the ground either of its necessity or utility, for it is not necessary, nor indeed useful in the same manner as reading and writing, which are useful in money-making, in the management of a household,

in the acquisition of knowledge and in political life, nor like drawing, useful for a more correct judgement of the works of artists, nor again like gymnastic, which gives health and strength; for neither of these is to be gained from music. There remains, then, the use of music for intellectual enjoyment in leisure; which is in fact evidently the reason of its introduction, this being one of the ways in which it is thought that a freeman should pass his leisure; as Homer says –

But he who alone should be called to the pleasant feast,

and afterwards he speaks of others whom he describes as inviting

The bard who would delight them all.

And in another place Odysseus says there is no better way of passing life than when men's hearts are merry and

The banqueters in the hall, sitting in order, hear the voice of the minstrel.

It is evident, then, that there is a sort of education in which parents should train their sons, not as being useful or necessary, but because it is liberal or noble. Whether this is of one kind only, or of more than one, and if so, what they are, and how they are to be imparted, must hereafter be determined. Thus much we are already in a position to say; for the ancients bear witness to us – their opinion may be gathered from the fact that music is one of the received and traditional branches of education. Further, it is clear that children should be instructed in some useful things – for example, in reading and writings – not only for their usefulness, but also because many other sorts of knowledge are acquired through them. With a like view they may be taught drawing, not to prevent their making mistakes in their own purchases, or in order that they may not be imposed upon in the buying or selling of articles, but perhaps rather because it makes them judges of the beauty of the human form. To be always seeking after the useful does not become free and exalted souls. Now it is clear that in education practice must be used before theory, and the body be trained before the mind; and therefore boys should be handed over to the trainer, who creates in them the proper habit of body, and to the wrestling-master, who teaches them their exercises.

4. Of those states which in our own day seem to take the greatest care of children, some aim at producing in them an athletic habit, but they only injure their bodies and stunt their growth. Although the Lacedaemonians have not fallen into this mistake, yet they brutalize their children by laborious exercises which they think will make them courageous. But in truth, as we have often repeated, education should not be exclusively, or principally, directed to this end. And even if we suppose the Lacedaemonians to be right in their end, they do not attain it. For among barbarians and among animals courage is found associated, not with the greatest ferocity, but with a gentle and lion-like temper. There are many races who are ready enough to kill and eat men, such as the Achaeans and Heniochi, who both live about the Black Sea; and there are other mainland tribes, as bad or worse, who all live by plunder, but have no courage. It is notorious that the Lacedaemonians themselves, while they alone were assiduous in their laborious drill, were superior to others, but now they are beaten both in war and gymnastic exercises. For their ancient superiority did not depend on their mode of training their youth, but only on the circumstance that they trained them when their only rivals did not. Hence we may infer that what is noble, not what is brutal, should have the first place; no wolf or other wild animal will face a really noble danger; such dangers are for the brave man. And parents who devote their children to gymnastics while they neglect their necessary education, in reality make them mechanics; for they make them useful to the art of statesmanship in one quality only, and even in this the argument proves them to be inferior to others. We should judge the Lacedaemonians not from what they have been, but from what they are; for now they have rivals who compete with their education; formerly they had none.

It is an admitted principle that gymnastic exercises should be employed in education, and that for children they should be of a lighter kind, avoiding severe diet or painful toil, lest the growth of the body be impaired. The evil of excessive training in early years is strikingly proved by the example of the Olympic victors; for not more than two or three of them have gained a prize both as boys and as men; their early training and severe gymnastic exercises exhausted their constitutions. When boyhood is over, three years should be spent in other studies; the period of life which follows may then be devoted to hard exercise and strict diet. Men ought not to labour at the same time with their minds and with their bodies; for the two kinds of labour are opposed to one another; the labour of the body impedes the mind, and the labour of the mind the body.

5. Concerning music there are some questions which we have already raised; these we may now resume and carry further; and our remarks will serve as a prelude to this or any other discussion of the subject. It is not easy to determine the nature of music, or why anyone should have a knowledge of it. Shall we say, for the sake of amusement and relaxation, like sleep or drinking, which are not good in themselves, but are pleasant, and at the same time 'make care to cease', as Euripides says? And for this end men also appoint music, and make use of all three alike – sleep, drinking, music – to which some add dancing. Or shall we argue that music conduces to excellence, on the ground that it can form our minds and habituate us to true pleasures as our bodies are made by gymnastic to be of a certain character? Or shall we say that it contributes to the enjoyment of leisure and mental cultivation, which is a third alternative? Now obviously youths are not to be instructed with a view to their amusement, for learning is no amusement, but is accompanied with pain. Neither is intellectual enjoyment suitable to boys of that age, for it is the end, and that which is imperfect cannot attain the end. But perhaps it may be said that boys learn music for the sake of the amusement which they will have when they are grown up. If so, why should they learn themselves, and not, like the Persian and Median kings, enjoy the pleasure and instruction which is derived from hearing others? (for surely persons who have made music the business and profession of their lives will be better performers than those who practise only long enough to learn). If they must learn music, on the same principle they should learn cookery, which is absurd. And even granting that music may form the character, the objection still holds: why should we learn ourselves? Why cannot we attain true pleasure and form a correct judgement from hearing others, as the Lacedaemonians do? – for they, without learning music, nevertheless can correctly judge, as they say, of good and bad melodies. Or again, if music should be used to promote cheerfulness and refined intellectual enjoyment, the objection still remains – why should we learn ourselves instead of enjoying the performances of others? We may illustrate what we are saying by our conception of

the gods; for in the poets Zeus does not himself sing or play on the lyre. Indeed we call professional performers artisans; no freeman would play or sing unless he were intoxicated or in jest. But these matters may be left for the present.

The first question is whether music is or is not to be a part of education. Of the three things mentioned in our discussion, which does it produce – education or amusement or intellectual enjoyment? – for it may be reckoned under all three, and seems to share in the nature of all of them. Amusement is for the sake of relaxation, and relaxation is of necessity sweet, for it is the remedy of pain caused by toil; and intellectual enjoyment is universally acknowledged to contain an element not only of the noble but of the pleasant, for happiness is made up of both. All men agree that music is one of the pleasantest things, whether with or without song; as Musaeus says,

Song is to mortals of all things the sweetest.

Hence and with good reason it is introduced into social gatherings and entertainments, because it makes the hearts of men glad: so that on this ground alone we may assume that the young ought to be trained in it. For innocent pleasures are not only in harmony with the end of life, but they also provide relaxation. And whereas men rarely attain the end, but often rest by the way and amuse themselves, not only with a view to a further end, but also for the pleasure's sake, it may be well at times to let them find a refreshment in music. It sometimes happens that men make amusement the end, for the end probably contains some element of pleasure, though not any ordinary pleasure; but they mistake the lower for the higher, and in seeking for the one find the other, since every pleasure has a likeness to the end of action. For the end is not desirable for the sake of any future good, nor do the pleasures which we have described exist for the sake of any future good but of the past, that is to say, they are the alleviation of past toils and pains. And we may infer this to be the reason why men seek happiness from these pleasures. But music is pursued, not only as an alleviation of past toil, but also as providing recreation. And who can say whether, having this use, it may not also have a nobler one? In addition to this common pleasure, felt and shared in by all (for the pleasure given by music is natural, and therefore adapted to all ages and characters), may it not have also some influence over the character and the soul? It must have such an influence if characters are affected by it. And that they are so affected is proved in many ways, and not least by the power which the songs of Olympus exercise; for beyond question they inspire enthusiasm, and enthusiasm is an emotion of the character of the soul. Besides, when men hear imitations, even apart from the rhythms and tunes themselves, their feelings move in sympathy. Since then music is a pleasure, and excellence consists in rejoicing and loving and hating rightly, there is clearly nothing which we are so much concerned to acquire and to cultivate as the power of forming right judgements, and of taking delight in good dispositions and noble actions. Rhythm and melody supply imitations of anger and gentleness, and also of courage and temperance, and of all the qualities contrary to these, and of the other qualities of character, which hardly fall short of the actual affections, as we know from our own experience, for in listening to such strains our souls undergo a change. The habit of feeling pleasure or pain at mere representations is not far removed from the same feeling about realities; for example, if any one delights in the sight of a statue for its beauty only, it necessarily follows that the sight of the original will be pleasant to him. The objects of no other sense, such as taste or touch, have any resemblance to moral qualities; in visible objects there is only a little, for there are figures which are of a moral character, but only to a slight extent, and all do not participate in the feeling about them. Again, figures and colours are not imitations, but signs, of character, indications which the body gives of states of feeling. The connexion of them with morals is slight, but in so far as there is any, young men should be taught to look, not at the works of Pauson, but at those of Polygnotus, or any other painter or sculptor who expresses character. On the other hand, even in mere melodies there is an imitation of character, for the musical modes differ essentially from one another, and those who hear them are differently affected by each. Some of them make men sad and grave, like the so-called Mixolydian, others enfeeble the mind, like the relaxed modes, another, again, produces a moderate and settled temper, which appears to be the peculiar effect of the Dorian; the Phrygian inspires enthusiasm. The whole subject has been well treated by philosophical writers on this branch of education, and they confirm their arguments by facts. The same principles apply to rhythms; some have a character of rest, others of motion, and of these latter again, some have a more vulgar, others a nobler movement. Enough has been said to show that music has a power of forming the character, and should therefore be introduced into the education of the young. The study is suited to the stage of youth, for young persons will not, if they can help, endure anything which is not sweetened by pleasure, and music has a natural sweetness. There seems to be in us a sort of affinity to musical modes and rhythms, which makes some philosophers say that the soul is a harmony, others, that it possesses harmony.

6. And now we have to determine the question which has been already raised, whether children should be themselves taught to sing and play or not. Clearly there is a considerable difference made in the character by the actual practice of the art. It is difficult, if not impossible, for those who do not perform to be good judges of the performance of others. Besides, children should have something to do, and the rattle of Archytas, which people give to their children in order to amuse them and prevent them from breaking anything in the house, was a capital invention, for a young thing cannot be quiet. The rattle is a toy suited to the infant mind, and education is a rattle or toy for children of a larger growth. We conclude then that they should be taught music in such a way as to become not only critics but performers.

The question what is or is not suitable for different ages may be easily answered; nor is there any difficulty in meeting the objection of those who say that the study of music is mechanical. We reply in the first place, that they who are to be judges must also be performers, and that they should begin to practise early, although when they are older they may be spared the execution; they must have learned to appreciate what is good and to delight in it, thanks to the knowledge which they acquired in their youth. As to the vulgarizing effect which music is supposed to exercise, this is a question which we shall have no difficulty in determining when we have considered to what extent freemen who are being trained to political excellence should pursue the art, what melodies and what rhythms they should be allowed to use, and what instruments should be employed in teaching them to play; for even the instrument makes a difference. The answer to the objection turns upon these distinctions; for it is quite possible that certain methods of teaching and learning music do really have a degrading effect. It is evident then that the learning of music ought not to impede the business of riper years, or to degrade the body or render it unfit for civil or military training, whether for bodily exercises at the time or for later studies.

The right measure will be attained if students of music stop short of the arts which are practised in professional contests, and do not seek to acquire those fantastic marvels of execution which are now the fashion in such contests, and from these have passed into education. Let the young practise even such music as we have prescribed, only until they are able to feel delight in noble melodies and rhythms, and not merely in that common part of music in which every slave or child and even some animals find pleasure.

# 10

# Learning the Value of Work

## Jean-Jacques Rousseau

### *Emile*: Book III

. . .

I hate books. They only teach one to talk about what one does not know. It is said that Hermes engraved the elements of the sciences on columns in order to shelter his discoveries from a flood. If he had left a good imprint of them in man's head, they would have been preserved by tradition. Well-prepared minds are the surest monuments on which to engrave human knowledge.

Is there no means of bringing together so many lessons scattered in so many books, of joining them in a common object which is easy to see and interesting to follow and can serve as a stimulant even at this age? If one can invent a situation where all man's natural needs are shown in a way a child's mind can sense, and where the means of providing for these needs emerge in order with equal ease, it is by the lively and naïve depiction of this state that the first exercise must be given to his imagination.

Ardent philosopher, I see your imagination kindling already. Do not put yourself out. This situation has been found; it has been described and, without prejudice to you, much better than you would describe it yourself – at least with more truth and simplicity. Since we absolutely must have books, there exists one which, to my taste, provides the most felicitous treatise on natural education. This book will be the first that my Emile will read. For a long time it will alone compose his whole library, and it will always hold a distinguished place there. It will be the text for which all our discussions on the natural sciences will serve only as a commentary. It will serve as a test of the condition of our judgment during our progress; and so long as our taste is not spoiled, its reading will always please us. What, then, is this marvelous book? Is it Aristotle? Is it Pliny? Is it Buffon? No. It is *Robinson Crusoe*.

Robinson Crusoe on his island, alone, deprived of the assistance of his kind and the instruments of all the arts, providing nevertheless for his subsistence, for his preservation, and even procuring for himself a kind of well-being – this is an object interesting for every age and one which can be made agreeable to children in countless ways. This is how

Editor's title. Previously published as *"Emile," or On Education*, trans. Allan Bloom (New York: Basic Books/ HarperCollins, 1979), Book III, pp. 184–6, 187–8, 189, 190–1, 192–3, 194–6, 488. Reprinted with permission of the Perseus Books Group.

we realize the desert island which served me at first as a comparison. This state, I agree, is not that of social man; very likely it is not going to be that of Emile. But it is on the basis of this very state that he ought to appraise all the others. The surest means of raising oneself above prejudices and ordering one's judgments about the true relations of things is to put oneself in the place of an isolated man and to judge everything as this man himself ought to judge of it with respect to his own utility.

This novel, disencumbered of all its rigmarole, beginning with Robinson's shipwreck near his island and ending with the arrival of the ship which comes to take him from it, will be both Emile's entertainment and instruction throughout the period which is dealt with here. I want it to make him dizzy; I want him constantly to be busy with his mansion, his goats, his plantations; I want him to learn in detail, not from books but from things, all that must be known in such a situation; I want him to think he is Robinson himself, to see himself dressed in skins, wearing a large cap, carrying a large saber and all the rest of the character's grotesque equipment, with the exception of the parasol, which he will not need. I want him to worry about the measures to take if this or that were lacking to him; to examine his hero's conduct; to investigate whether he omitted anything, whether there was nothing to do better; to note Robinson's failings attentively; and to profit from them so as not to fall into them himself in such a situation. For do not doubt that he is planning to go and set up a similar establishment. This is the true "castle in Spain" of this happy age when one knows no other happiness than the necessities and freedom.

What a resource this folly would be for a skillful man who knew how to engender it solely for the sake of taking advantage of it. The child, in a hurry to set up a storehouse for his island, will be more ardent for learning than is the master for teaching. He will want to know all that is useful, and he will want to know only that. You will not need to guide him; you will have only to restrain him. Now let us hurry to establish him on this island while he still limits his felicity to it; for the day is nearing when, if he still wants to live there, he will not want any longer to live there alone, and when Friday, who now hardly concerns him, will not for long be enough for him.

The practice of the natural arts, for which a single man suffices, leads to the investigation of the arts of industry, which need the conjunction of many hands. The former can be exercised by solitaries, by savages; but the others can be born only in society and make it necessary. So long as one knows only physical need, each man suffices unto himself. The introduction of the superfluous makes division and distribution of labor indispensable; although a man working alone earns only subsistence for one man, a hundred men working in harmony will earn enough to give subsistence to two hundred. Therefore, as soon as a part of mankind rests, it is necessary that the joint efforts of those who work make up for the idleness of those who do nothing.

Your greatest care ought to be to keep away from your pupil's mind all notions of social relations which are not within his reach. But when the chain of knowledge forces you to show him the mutual dependence of men, instead of showing it to him from the moral side, turn all his attention at first toward industry and mechanical arts which make men useful to one another. In taking him from workshop to workshop, never allow him to view any work without putting his hand to the job himself or to leave without knowing perfectly the reason for all that is done there, or at least all that he has observed. To achieve this, work yourself; everywhere provide the example for him. To make him a master, be everywhere an apprentice; and reckon that an hour of work will teach him more things than he would retain from a day of explanations.

There is a public esteem attached to the different arts in inverse proportion to their real utility. This esteem is calculated directly on the basis of their very uselessness, and this is the way it ought to be. The most useful arts are those which earn the least, because the number of workers is proportioned to men's needs, and work necessary to everybody must remain at a price the poor man can pay. On the other hand, these important fellows who are called artists instead of artisans, and who work solely for the idle and the rich, set an arbitrary price on their baubles. Since the merit of these vain works exists only in opinion, their very price constitutes a part of that merit, and they are esteemed in proportion to what they cost. The importance given them by the rich does not come from their use but from the fact that the poor cannot afford them. *Nolo habere bona nisi quibus populus inv`iderit.*

* Petronius. [Original footnote]¹

What will your pupils become if you let them adopt this stupid prejudice, if you encourage it yourself, if, for example, they see you enter a goldsmith's shop with more respect than a locksmith's? What judgment will they make of the true merit of arts and the veritable value of things, when they see that the price is set by whim everywhere in contradiction to the price based on real utility, and that the more a thing costs the less it is worth? The first moment you let these ideas into their heads, abandon the rest of their education. In spite of you, they will be raised like everyone else. You have wasted fourteen years of effort.

Emile, planning to furnish his island, will have other ways of seeing. Robinson Crusoe would have attached much more importance to a toolmaker's shop than Said's[2] gewgaws. The former would have appeared to him to be a very respectable man, and the other a little charlatan.

[ ... ]

It is by their palpable relation to his utility, his security, his preservation, and his well-being that he ought to appraise all the bodies of nature and all the works of men. Thus, iron ought to be much more valuable in his eyes than gold, and glass than diamonds. Similarly, he honors a shoemaker or a mason far more than a Lempereur, a Leblanc,[3] and all the jewelers of Europe. A pastry chef especially is a very important man in his eyes, and he would give the whole Academy of Sciences for the lowest candymaker of the rue des Lombards. The goldsmiths, the engravers, and the gilders are in his view nothing but loafers who play perfectly useless games. He does not treat even clock-making very seriously. The happy child enjoys time without being its slave. He profits from it and does not know its value. The calm of the passions, which makes the passage of time always uniform, takes the place for him of an instrument for measuring it at need.* In assuming he has a watch as well as in making him cry, I gave myself a common Emile, to be useful and to make myself understood; for, with respect to the true one, a child so different from others would not serve as an example for anything.

There is an order no less natural and still more judicious by which one considers the arts according to the relations of necessity which connect them, putting in the first rank the most independent and in the last those which depend on a greater number of others. This order, which provides important considerations about the order of society in general, is similar to the preceding one and subject to the same inversion in men's esteem. The result of this is that raw materials are used in crafts without honor and almost without profit, and that the more hands they pass through, the more labor increases in price and becomes honorable. I am not examining whether it is true that the skill is greater and merits more recompense in the detailed arts which give the final form to these materials than in the initial work which converts them to the use of men. But I do say that, with each thing, the art whose use is the most general and the most indispensable is incontestably the one which merits the most esteem; and the one to which other arts are less necessary also merits esteem ahead of the more subordinate ones, because it is freer and nearer independence. These are the true rules for appraising the arts and manufactures. Anything else is arbitrary and depends on opinion.

The first and most respectable of all the arts is agriculture; I would put ironworking in the second rank, woodworking in the third, and so on. The child who has not been seduced by vulgar prejudices will judge of them precisely thus. What important reflections on this point our Emile will draw from his *Robinson Crusoe*! What will he think on seeing that the arts are only perfected in being subdivided, in infinitely multiplying the instruments of all of them? He will say to himself, "All these people are stupidly ingenious. One would believe they are afraid that their arms and their fingers might be of some use, so many instruments do they invent to do without them. To practice a single art they are subjected to countless others. A city is needed for every worker. As for my companion and me, we put our genius in our adroitness. We make ourselves tools that we can take everywhere with us. All those people so proud of their talents in Paris would not know how to do anything on our island and would be our apprentices in their turn."

[ ... ]

The society of the arts consists in exchange of skills, that of commerce in exchange of things, that

* Time loses its measure for us when our passions want to adjust its course according to their taste. The wise man's watch is evenness of temper and peace of soul. He is always on time for himself, and he always knows what that time is. [Original footnote]

of banks in exchange of signs and money. All these ideas are connected, and the elementary notions are already grasped. We laid the foundations for all this at an early age with the help of Robert, the gardener. It only remains for us now to generalize these same ideas and extend them to more examples to make him understand the workings of trade taken by itself and presented to his senses by the details of natural history regarding the products peculiar to each country, by the details of arts and sciences regarding navigation, and finally, by the greater or lesser problems of transport according to distance, the situation of lands, seas, rivers, etc.

No society can exist without exchange, no exchange without a common measure, and no common measure without equality. Thus all society has as its first law some conventional equality, whether of men or of things.

[ . . . ]

To what an abundance of interesting objects can one thus turn a pupil's curiosity without ever abandoning the real material relations which are within his reach or allowing a single idea that he cannot conceive to spring up in his mind! The art of the master consists in never letting his pupil's observations dwell on minutiae which lead nowhere but in bringing him ever closer to the great relations he must know one day in order to judge well of the good and bad order of civil society. One must know how to match the conversations with which one entertains him to the turn of mind he has been given. A question which could not even stir the attention of another is going to torment Emile for six months.

We go to dine in an opulent home. We find the preparations for a feast – many people, many lackeys, many dishes, an elegant and fine table service. All this apparatus of pleasure and festivity has something intoxicating about it which goes to the head when one is not accustomed to it. I have a presentiment of the effect of all this on my young pupil. While the meal continues, while the courses follow one another, while much boisterous conversation reigns at the table, I lean toward his ear and say, "Through how many hands would you estimate that all you see on this table has passed before getting here?" What a crowd of ideas I awaken in his brain with these few words! Instantly, all the vapors of the delirium are dispelled. He dreams, he reflects, he calculates, he worries. While the philosophers, cheered by the wine, perhaps by the ladies next to them, prate and act like children, he is all alone philosophizing for himself in his corner. He questions me; I refuse to answer; I put him off to another time. He gets impatient; he forgets to eat and drink; he burns to get away from the table to discuss with me at his ease. What an object for his curiosity! What a text for his instruction! With a healthy judgment that nothing has been able to corrupt, what will he think of this luxury when he finds that every region of the world has been made to contribute; that perhaps twenty million hands have worked for a long time; that it has cost the lives of perhaps thousands of men, and all this to present to him with pomp at noon what he is going to deposit in his toilet at night?

Spy out with care the secret conclusions he draws in his heart from all his observations. If you have guarded him less well than I assume, he may be tempted to turn his reflections in another direction and to regard himself as an important person in the world, seeing so many efforts concerted to prepare his dinner. If you get a presentiment of this reasoning, you can easily forestall it before he makes it, or at least efface its impression immediately. Not yet knowing how to appropriate things other than by material enjoyment, he can judge of their suitability or lack of it for him only by means of relations accessible to his senses. The comparison of a simple, rustic dinner, prepared by exercise, seasoned by hunger, freedom, and joy, with his magnificent formal feast will suffice to make him feel that all the apparatus of the feast did not give him any real profit, and that since his stomach left the peasant's table as satisfied as it left the financier's, there was nothing more in the one than in the other that he could truly call his own.

[ . . . ]

What remains for us to do after having observed all that surrounds us? To convert to our use all that we can appropriate for ourselves and to profit from our curiosity for the advantage of our well-being. Up to now we have provided for instruments of every kind without knowing which we shall need. Perhaps useless to ourselves, ours will be able to serve other men; and perhaps, in our turn, we shall need theirs. Thus we would all be advantaged by these exchanges. But to make them, our mutual needs must be known. Each must know what others have which he can use and what he can offer them in return. Let us suppose ten men, each of whom has ten sorts of needs. Each must, for what he needs, apply himself to ten sorts of work; but, given the differences of genius and talent, one man will be less successful at one sort of work, another man at another. Although fit for diverse things, all will do the same ones and will be ill served. Let us form a society of these ten men and let each apply himself, for himself and for the nine others, to the kind of occupation which suits him best. Each will profit from the talents of the others as if he alone had them all. Each will perfect his own by continuous practice, and it will turn out that all ten, perfectly well provided for, will even have a surplus for others. That is the apparent principle of all our institutions. It is not part of my subject to examine its consequences here. I have done it in another writing.[4]

According to this principle, a man who wanted to regard himself as an isolated being, not depending at all on anything and sufficient unto himself, could only be miserable. It would even be impossible for him to subsist. For, finding the whole earth covered with thine and mine and having nothing belonging to him except his body, where would he get his necessities? By leaving the state of nature, we force our fellows to leave it, too. No one can remain in it in spite of the others, and it would really be leaving it to want to remain when it is impossible to live there, for the first law of nature is the care of preserving oneself.

Thus the ideas of social relations are formed little by little in a child's mind, even before he can really be an active member of society. Emile sees that, in order to have instruments for his use, he must in addition have instruments for the use of other men with which he can obtain in exchange the things which are necessary to him and are in their power. I easily bring him to feel the need for these exchanges and to put himself in a position to profit from them.

[ . . . ]

You trust in the present order of society without thinking that this order is subject to inevitable revolutions, and it is impossible for you to foresee or prevent the one which may affect your children. The noble become commoners, the rich become poor, the monarch becomes subject. Are the blows of fate so rare that you can count on being exempted from them? We are approaching a state of crisis and the age of revolutions.* Who can answer for what will

become of you then? All that men have made, men can destroy. The only ineffaceable characters are those printed by nature; and nature does not make princes, rich men, or great lords. What, then, will this satrap whom you have raised only for greatness do in lowliness? What will this publican who knows how to live only with gold do in poverty? What will this gaudy imbecile, who does not know how to make use of himself and puts his being only in what is alien to himself, do when he is deprived of everything? Happy is the man who knows how to leave the station which leaves him and to remain a man in spite of fate! That vanquished king who, full of rage, wants to be buried under the debris of his throne may be praised as much as one pleases; I despise him. I see that he exists only by his crown, and that he is nothing at all if he is not a king. But he who loses it and does without it is then above it. From the rank of king which a coward, a wicked man, or a madman can fill, he rises to the station of man, which so few men know how to fill. Then he triumphs over fortune; he braves it. He owes nothing except to himself; and when there remains nothing for him to show except himself, he is not nothing, he is something. Yes, I prefer a hundred times over the king of Syracuse becoming a schoolmaster at Corinth and the king of Macedonia becoming a clerk at Rome to an unfortunate Tarquin not knowing what to become if he does not reign, and to the heir and son of a king of kings,† the plaything of whoever dares to insult his distress, wandering from court to court, seeking help everywhere, and finding affronts everywhere for want of knowing how to do anything other than perform a trade which is no longer in his power.

A man and a citizen, whoever he may be, has no property to put into society other than himself. All his other property is in it in spite of him; and when a man is rich, either he does not enjoy his riches or the public enjoys them, too. In the first case, he robs from others that of which he deprives himself; and in the second, he gives them nothing. Thus the social debt remains with him in its entirety so long as he pays only with his property. "But my father, In earning it, served society . . ." So be it; he has paid his debt, but not yours. You owe others more

---

* I hold it to be impossible that the great monarchies of Europe still have long to last. All have shined, and every state which shines is on the decline. I have reasons more particular than this maxim for my opinion, but it is unseasonable to tell them, and everyone sees them only too well. [Original footnote]

† Vonones, son of Phrates, king of the Parthians. [Original footnote]

than if you were born without property, since you were favored at birth. It is not just that what one man has done for society should relieve another from what he owes it; for each, owing himself wholly, can pay only for himself and no father can transmit to his son the right to be useless to his fellows. This is, however, what he does, according to you, in transmitting to him his riches, which are the proof and the price of work. He who eats in idleness what he did not earn himself steals it. A man whom the state pays an income for doing nothing hardly differs in my eyes from a brigand who lives at the expense of passers-by. Outside of society isolated man, owing nothing to anyone, has a right to live as he pleases. But in society, where he necessarily lives at the expense of others, he owes them the price of his keep in work. This is without exception. To work is therefore in indispensable duty for social man. Rich or poor, powerful or weak, every idle citizen is a rascal.

Now, of all the occupations which can provide subsistence to man, that which brings him closest to the state of nature is manual labor. Of all conditions, the artisan's is the most independent of fortune and men. The artisan depends only on his work. He is as free as the farmer is slave. For the latter is dependent on his field, whose harvest is at another's discretion. The enemy, the prince, a powerful neighbor, or a lawsuit can take this field away from him. By means of this field he can be vexed in countless ways. But wherever they want to vex the artisan, his baggage is soon packed. He takes his hands and goes away. However, agriculture is man's first trade. It is the most decent, the most useful, and consequently the most noble he can practice. I do not say to Emile, "Learn agriculture." He knows it. He is familiar with all the kinds of rustic work. He began with them, he constantly returns to them. I say to him therefore, "Cultivate the inheritance of your fathers. But if you lose that inheritance, or if you have none, what is to be done? Learn a trade."

"A trade for my son! My son an artisan! Sir, are you in your right mind?" I am thinking clearly, more clearly than you, madame, who want to reduce him to never being able to be anything but a lord, a marquess, a prince, and perhaps one day less than nothing. I want to give him a rank which he cannot lose, a rank which does him honor at all times; and whatever you may say about it, he will have fewer equals with this title than with all those he will get from you.

The letter kills, and the spirit enlivens. The goal is less to learn a trade in order to know a trade than to conquer the prejudices that despise a trade. You will never be reduced to working to live. Well, too bad – too bad for you! But, that is not important; do not work out of necessity; work out of glory. Lower yourself to the artisan's station in order to be above your own. In order to subject fortune and things to yourself, begin by making yourself independent of them. To reign by opinion, begin by reigning over it.

## Notes

1. "I want only those good things which are envied by the people." Petronius, *Satyricon* 100. The context concerns love.
2. The identity of this person is unknown.
3. Parisian jewelers.
4. *Discourse on the Origins of Inequality*, as Rousseau himself indicated in a later note. Cf. particularly *O.C.* III, pp. 164, 173–8; R. Masters (ed.), *The Discourses*, pp. 141–2, 154–60, See also *Discourse on Political Economy* and Plato *Republic* 369B–373E.

# 11

# Education for Labor and Leisure

## John Dewey

**1. The Origin of the Opposition.** [ . . . ] Probably the most deep-seated antithesis which has shown itself in educational history is that between education in preparation for useful labor and education for a life of leisure. The bare terms "useful labor" and "leisure" confirm the statement already made that the segregation and conflict of values are not self-inclosed, but reflect a division within social life. Were the two functions of gaining a livelihood by work and enjoying in a cultivated way the opportunities of leisure, distributed equally among the different members of a community, it would not occur to any one that there was any conflict of educational agencies and aims involved. It would be self-evident that the question was how education could contribute most effectively to both. And while it might be found that some materials of instruction chiefly accomplished one result and other subject matter the other, it would be evident that care must be taken to secure as much overlapping as conditions permit; that is, the education which had leisure more directly in view should indirectly re-enforce as much as possible the efficiency and the enjoyment of work, while

that aiming at the latter should produce habits of emotion and intellect which would procure a worthy cultivation of leisure.

These general considerations are amply borne out by the historical development of educational philosophy. The separation of liberal education from professional and industrial education goes back to the time of the Greeks, and was formulated expressly on the basis of a division of classes into those who had to labor for a living and those who were relieved from this necessity. The conception that liberal education, adapted to men in the latter class, is intrinsically higher than the servile training given to the latter class reflected the fact that one class was free and the other servile in its social status. The latter class labored not only for its own subsistence, but also for the means which enabled the superior class to live without personally engaging in occupations taking almost all the time and not of a nature to engage or reward intelligence.

That a certain amount of labor must be engaged in goes without saying. Human beings have to live and it requires work to supply the resources of life. Even if we insist that the interests connected

Editor's title. Previously published in John Dewey, *Democracy and Education* (New York: Free Press/Macmillan, 1966), pp. 250–60. © 1916, renewed in 1944 by John Dewey. Reprinted with permission of Scribner, an imprint of Simon & Schuster Adult Publishing Group.

with getting a living are only material and hence intrinsically lower than those connected with enjoyment of time released from labor, and even if it were admitted that there is something engrossing and insubordinate in material interests which leads them to strive to usurp the place belonging to the higher ideal interests, this would not – barring the fact of socially divided classes – lead to neglect of the kind of education which trains men for the useful pursuits. It would rather lead to scrupulous care for them, so that men were trained to be efficient in them and yet to keep them in their place; education would see to it that we avoided the evil results which flow from their being allowed to flourish in obscure purlieus of neglect. Only when a division of these interests coincides with a division of an inferior and a superior social class will preparation for useful work be looked down upon with contempt as an unworthy thing: a fact which prepares one for the conclusion that the rigid identification of work with material interests, and leisure with ideal interests is itself a social product.

The educational formulations of the social situation made over two thousand years ago have been so influential and give such a clear and logical recognition of the implications of the division into laboring and leisure classes, that they deserve especial note. According to them, man occupies the highest place in the scheme of animate existence. In part, he shares the constitution and functions of plants and animals– nutritive, reproductive, motor or practical. The *distinctively* human function is reason existing for the sake of beholding the spectacle of the universe. Hence the truly human end is the fullest possible of this distinctive human prerogative. The life of observation, meditation, cogitation, and speculation pursued as an end in itself is the proper life of man. From reason moreover proceeds the proper control of the lower elements of human nature – the appetites and the active, motor, impulses. In themselves greedy, insubordinate, lovers of excess, aiming only at their own satiety, they observe moderation – the law of the mean – and serve desirable ends as they are subjected to the rule of reason.

Such is the situation as an affair of theoretical psychology and as most adequately stated by Aristotle. But this state of things is reflected in the constitution of classes of men and hence in the organization of society. Only in a comparatively small number is the function of reason capable of operating as a law of life. In the mass of people, vegetative and animal functions dominate. Their energy of intelligence is so feeble and inconstant that it is constantly overpowered by bodily appetite and passion. Such persons are not truly ends in themselves, for only reason constitutes a final end. Like plants, animals and physical tools, they are means, appliances, for the attaining of ends beyond themselves, although unlike them they have enough intelligence to exercise a certain discretion in the execution of the tasks committed to them. Thus by nature, and not merely by social convention, there are those who are slaves – that is, means for the ends of others.[1] The great body of artisans are in one important respect worse off than even slaves. Like the latter they are given up to the service of ends external to themselves; but since they do not enjoy the intimate association with the free superior class experienced by domestic slaves they remain on a lower plane of excellence. Moreover, women are classed with slaves and craftsmen as factors among the animate instrumentalities of production and reproduction of the means for a free or rational life.

Individually and collectively there is a gulf between merely living and living worthily. In order that one may live worthily he must first live, and so with collective society. The time and energy spent upon mere life, upon the gaining of subsistence, detracts from that available for activities that have an inherent rational meaning; they also unfit for the latter. Means are menial, the serviceable is servile. The true life is possible only in the degree in which the physical necessities are had without effort and without attention. Hence slaves, artisans, and women are employed in furnishing the means of subsistence in order that others, those adequately equipped with intelligence, may live the life of leisurely concern with things intrinsically worth while.

To these two modes of occupation, with their distinction of servile and free activities (or "arts") correspond two types of education: the base or mechanical and the liberal or intellectual. Some persons are trained by suitable practical exercises for capacity in *doing* things, for ability to use the mechanical tools involved in turning out physical commodities and rendering personal service. This training is a mere matter of habituation and technical skill; it operates through repetition and assiduity in application, not through awakening and nurturing thought. Liberal education aims to train intelligence for its proper office: to know. The less this knowledge has to do with practical affairs, with making or producing, the more adequately it engages intelligence. So consistently does Aristotle draw the line between menial and liberal education that he puts what are now called the "fine" arts, music, painting, sculpture, in the same class with menial arts so far as their practice is concerned. They involve physical agencies, assiduity of practice, and external results. In discussing, for example, education in music he raises the question how far the young should be practiced in the playing of instruments. His answer is that such practice and proficiency may be tolerated as conduce to appreciation; that is, to understanding and enjoyment of music when played by slaves or professionals. When professional power is aimed at, music sinks from the liberal to the professional level. One might then as well teach cooking, says Aristotle. Even a liberal concern with the works of fine art depends upon the existence of a hireling class of practitioners who have subordinated the development of their own personality to attaining skill in mechanical execution. The higher the activity the more purely mental is it; the less does it have to do with physical things or with the body. The more purely mental it is, the more independent or self-sufficing is it.

These last words remind us that Aristotle again makes a distinction of superior and inferior even within those living the life of reason. For there is a distinction in ends and in free action, according as one's life is merely accompanied by reason or as it makes reason its own medium. That is to say, the free citizen who devotes himself to the public life of his community, sharing in the management of its affairs and winning personal honor and distinction, lives a life accompanied by reason. But the thinker, the man who devotes himself to scientific inquiry and philosophic speculation, works, so to speak, *in* reason, not simply *by* it. Even the activity of the citizen in his civic relations, in other words, retains some of the taint of practice, of external or merely instrumental doing. This infection is shown by the fact that civic activity and civic excellence need the help of others; one cannot engage in public life all by himself. But all needs, all desires imply, in the philosophy of Aristotle, a material factor; they involve lack, privation; they are dependent upon something beyond themselves for completion. A purely intellectual life, however, one carries on by himself, in himself; such assistance as he may derive from others is accidental, rather than intrinsic. In *knowing*, in the life of theory, reason finds its own full manifestation; knowing for the sake of knowing irrespective of any application is alone independent, or self-sufficing. Hence only the education that

makes for power to know as an end in itself, without reference to the practice of even civic duties, is truly liberal or free.

**2. The Present Situation.** If the Aristotelian conception represented just Aristotle's personal view, it would be a more or less interesting historical curiosity. It could be dismissed as an illustration of the lack of sympathy or the amount of academic pedantry which may coexist with extraordinary intellectual gifts. But Aristotle simply described without confusion and without that insincerity always attendant upon mental confusion, the life that was before him. That the actual social situation has greatly changed since his day there is no need to say. But in spite of these changes, in spite of the abolition of legal serfdom, and the spread of democracy, with the extension of science and of general education (in books, newspapers, travel, and general intercourse as well as in schools), there remains enough of a cleavage of society into a learned and an unlearned class, a leisure and a laboring class, to make his point of view a most enlightening one from which to criticize the separation between culture and utility in present education. Behind the intellectual and abstract distinction as it figures in pedagogical discussion, there looms a social distinction between those whose pursuits involve a minimum of self-directive thought and æsthetic appreciation, and those who are concerned more directly with things of the intelligence and with the control of the activities of others.

Aristotle was certainly permanently right when he said that "any occupation or art or study deserves to be called mechanical if it renders the body or soul or intellect of free persons unfit for the exercise and practice of excellence." The force of the statement is almost infinitely increased when we hold, as we nominally do at present, that all persons, instead of a comparatively few, are free. For when the mass of men and all women were regarded as unfree by the very nature of their bodies and minds, there was neither intellectual confusion nor moral hypocrisy in giving them only the training which fitted them for mechanical skill, irrespective of its ulterior effect upon their capacity to share in a worthy life. He was permanently right also when he went on to say that "all mercenary employments as well as those which degrade the condition of the body are mechanical, since they deprive the intellect of leisure and dignity," – permanently right, that is, if gainful pursuits as matter of fact deprive the intellect of the conditions of its exercise and so of its dignity. If his statements are false, it is because they identify a phase of social custom with a natural necessity. But a different view of the relations of mind and matter, mind and body, intelligence and social service, is better than Aristotle's conception only if it helps render the old idea obsolete in fact – in the actual conduct of life and education.

Aristotle was permanently right in assuming the inferiority and subordination of mere skill in performance and mere accumulation of external products to understanding, sympathy of appreciation, and the free play of ideas. If there was an error, it lay in assuming the necessary separation of the two: in supposing that there is a natural divorce between efficiency in producing commodities and rendering service, and self-directive thought; between significant knowledge and practical achievement. We hardly better matters if we just correct his theoretical misapprehension, and tolerate the social state of affairs which generated and sanctioned his conception. We lose rather than gain in change from serfdom to free citzenship if the most prized result of the change is simply an increase in the mechanical efficiency of the human tools of production. So we lose rather than gain in coming to think of intelligence as an organ of control of nature through action, if we are content that an unintelligent, unfree state persists in those who engage directly in turning nature to use, and leave the intelligence which controls to be the exclusive possession of remote scientists and captains of industry. We are in a position honestly to criticize the division of life into separate functions and of society into separate classes only so far as we are free from responsibility for perpetuating the educational practices which train the many for pursuits involving mere skill in production, and the few for a knowledge that is an ornament and a cultural embellishment. In short, ability to transcend the Greek philosophy of life and education is not secured by a mere shifting about of the theoretical symbols meaning free, rational, and worthy. It is not secured by a change of sentiment regarding the dignity of labor, and the superiority of a life of service to that of an aloof self-sufficing independence. Important as these theoretical and emotional changes are, their importance consists in their being turned to account in the development of a truly democratic society, a society in which all share in useful service and all enjoy a worthy leisure. It is not a mere change in the concepts of culture – or a liberal mind – and social service which

requires an educational reorganization; but the educational transformation is needed to give full and explicit effect to the changes implied in social life. The increased political and economic emancipation of the "masses" has shown itself in education; it has effected the development of a common school system of education, public and free. It has destroyed the idea that learning is properly a monopoly of the few who are predestined by nature to govern social affairs. But the revolution is still incomplete. The idea still prevails that a truly cultural or liberal education cannot have anything in common, directly at least, with industrial affairs, and that the education which is fit for the masses must be a useful or practical education in a sense which opposes useful and practical to nurture of appreciation and liberation of thought.

As a consequence, our actual system is an inconsistent mixture. Certain studies and methods are retained on the supposition that they have the sanction of peculiar liberality, the chief content of the term liberal being uselessness for practical ends. This aspect is chiefly visible in what is termed the higher education – that of the college and of preparation for it. But is has filtered through into elementary education and largely controls its processes and aims. But, on the other hand, certain concessions have been made to the masses who must engage in getting a livelihood and to the increased rôle of economic activities in modern life. These consessions are exhibited in special schools and courses for the professions, for engineering, for manual training and commerce, in vocational and prevocational courses; and in the spirit in which certain elementary subjects, like the three R's, are taught. The result is a system in which both "cultural" and "utilitarian" subjects exist in an inorganic composite where the former are not by dominant purpose socially serviceable and the latter not liberative of imagination or thinking power.

In the inherited situation, there is a curious intermingling, in even the same study, of concession to usefulness and a survival of traits once exclusively attributed to preparation for leisure. The "utility" element is found in the motives assigned for the study, the "liberal" element in methods of teaching. The outcome of the mixture is perhaps less satisfactory than if either principle were adhered to in its purity. The motive popularly assigned for making the studies of the first four or five years consist almost entirely of reading, spelling, writing, and arithmetic, is, for example, that ability to read, write, and figure accurately is indispensable to getting ahead. These studies are treated as mere instruments for entering upon a gainful employment or of later progress in the pursuit of learning, according as pupils do not or do remain in school. This attitude is reflected in the emphasis put upon drill and practice for the sake of gaining automatic skill. If we turn to Greek schooling, we find that from the earliest years the acquisition of skill was subordinated as much as possible to acquisition of literary content possessed of æsthetic and moral significance. Not getting a tool for subsequent use but present subject matter was the emphasized thing. Nevertheless the isolation of these studies from practical application, their reduction to purely symbolic devices, represents a survival of the idea of a liberal training divorced from utility. A thorough adoption of the idea of utility would have led to instruction which tied up the studies to situations in which they were directly needed and where they were rendered immediately and not remotely helpful. It would be hard to find a subject in the curriculum within which there are not found evil results of a compromise between the two opposed ideals. Natural science is recommended on the ground of its practical utility, but is taught as a special accomplishment in removal from application. On the other hand, music and literature are theoretically justified on the ground of their culture value and are then taught with chief emphasis upon forming technical modes of skill.

If we had less compromise and resulting confusion, if we analyzed more carefully the respective meanings of culture and utility, we might find it easier to construct a course of study which should be useful and liberal at the same time. Only superstition makes us believe that the two are necessarily hostile so that a subject is illiberal because it is useful and cultural because it is useless. It will generally be found that instruction which, in aiming at utilitarian results, sacrifices the development of imagination, the refining of taste and the deepening of intellectual insight – surely cultural values – also in the same degree renders what is learned limited in its use. Not that it makes it wholly unavailable but that its applicability is restricted to routine activities carried on under the supervision of others. Narrow modes of skill cannot be made useful beyond themselves; any mode of skill which is achieved with deepening of knowledge and perfecting of judgment is readily put to use in new situations and is under personal control. It was not

the bare fact of social and economic utility which made certain activities seem servile to the Greeks but the fact that the activities directly connected with getting a livelihood were not, in their days, the expression of a trained intelligence nor carried on because of a personal appreciation of their meaning. So far as farming and the trades were rule-of-thumb occupations and so far as they were engaged in for results external to the minds of agricultural laborers and mechanics, they were illiberal – but only so far. The intellectual and social context has now changed. The elements in industry due to mere custom and routine have become subordinate in most economic callings to elements derived from scientific inquiry. The most important occupations of today represent and depend upon applied mathematics, physics, and chemistry. The area of the human world influenced by economic production and influencing consumption has been so indefinitely widened that geographical and political considerations of an almost infinitely wide scope enter in. It was natural for Plato to deprecate the learning of geometry and arithmetic for practical ends, because as matter of fact the practical uses to which they were put were few, lacking in content and mostly mercenary in quality. But as their social uses have increased and enlarged, their liberalizing or "intellectual" value and their practical value approach the same limit.

Doubtless the factor which chiefly prevents our full recognition and employment of this identification is the conditions under which so much work is still carried on. The invention of machines has extended the amount of leisure which is possible even while one is at work. It is a commonplace that the mastery of skill in the form of established habits frees the mind for a higher order of thinking. Something of the same kind is true of the introduction of mechanically automatic operations in industry. They may release the mind for thought upon other topics. But when we confine the education of those who work with their hands to a few years of schooling devoted for the most part to acquiring the use of rudimentary symbols at the expense of training in science, literature, and history, we fail to prepare the minds of workers to take advantage of this opportunity. More fundamental is the fact that the great majority of workers have no insight into the social aims of their pursuits and no direct personal interest in them. The results actually achieved are not the ends of *their* actions, but only of their employers. They do what they do, not freely and intelligently, but for the sake of the wage earned. It is this fact which makes the action illiberal, and which will make any education designed simply to give skill in such undertakings illiberal and immoral. The activity is not free because not freely participated in.

Nevertheless, there is already an opportunity for an education which, keeping in mind the larger features of work, will reconcile liberal nurture with training in social serviceableness, with ability to share efficiently and happily in occupations which are productive. And such an education will of itself tend to do away with the evils of the existing economic situation. In the degree in which men have an active concern in the ends that control their activity, their activity becomes free or voluntary and loses its externally enforced and servile quality, even though the physical aspect of behavior remain the same. In what is termed politics, democratic social organization makes provision for this direct participation in control: in the economic region, control remains external and autocratic. Hence the split between inner mental action and outer physical action of which the traditional distinction between the liberal and the utilitarian is the reflex. An education which should unify the disposition of the members of society would do much to unify society itself.

## Note

1. Aristotle does not hold that the class of actual slaves and of natural slaves necessarily coincide.

# 12

# Education and Standards of Living

## Amartya Sen

### Instrumental Freedoms

In presenting empirical studies in this work, I shall have the occasion to discuss a number of instrumental freedoms that contribute, directly or indirectly, to the overall freedom people have to live the way they would like to live. The diversities of the instruments involved are quite extensive. However; it may be convenient to identify five distinct types of freedom that may be particularly worth emphasizing in this instrumental perspective. This is by no means an exhaustive list, but it may help to focus on some particular policy issues that demand special attention at this time.

In particular, I shall consider the following types of instrumental freedoms: (1) *political freedoms*, (2) *economic facilities*, (3) *social opportunities*, (4) *transparency guarantees*, and (5) *protective security*. These instrumental freedoms tend to contribute to the general capability of a person to live more freely, but they also serve to complement one another. While development analysis must, on the one hand, be concerned with the objectives and aims that make these instrumental freedoms consequentially important, it must also take note of the empirical linkages that tie the distinct types of freedom *together*, strengthening their joint importance. Indeed, these connections are central to a fuller understanding of the instrumental role of freedom. The claim that freedom is not only the primary object of development but also its principal means relates particularly to these linkages.

Let me comment a little on each of these instrumental freedoms. *Political freedoms*, broadly conceived (including what are called civil rights), refer to the opportunities that people have to determine who should govern and on what principles, and also include the possibility to scrutinize and criticize authorities, to have freedom of political expression and an uncensored press, to enjoy the freedom to choose between different political parties, and so on. They include the political entitlements associated with democracies in the broadest sense (encompassing opportunities of political dialogue, dissent and critique as well as voting rights and participatory selection of legislators and executives).

*Economic facilities* refer to the opportunities that individuals respectively enjoy to utilize economic resources for the purpose of consumption, or production, or exchange. The economic entitlements

Editor's title. Previously published in *Development as Freedom* (Oxford: Oxford University Press, 1999), chs. 2 and 12, pp. 38–43, 47–9, 292–7, 302, 351. Reprinted with permission of Oxford University Press.

that a person has will depend on the resources owned or available for use as well as on conditions of exchange, such as relative prices and the working of the markets. Insofar as the process of economic development increases the income and wealth of a country, they are reflected in corresponding enhancement of economic entitlements of the population. It should be obvious that in the relation between national income and wealth, on the one hand, and the economic entitlements of individuals (or families), on the other, distributional considerations are important, in addition to aggregative ones. How the additional incomes generated are distributed will clearly make a difference.

The availability and access to finance can be a crucial influence on the economic entitlements that economic agents are practically able to secure. This applies all the way from large enterprises (in which hundreds of thousands of people may work) to tiny establishments that are run on micro credit. A credit crunch, for example, can severely affect the economic entitlements that rely on such credit.

*Social opportunities* refer to the arrangements that society makes for education, health care and so on, which influence the individual's substantive freedom to live better. These facilities are important not only for the conduct of private lives (such as living a healthy life and avoiding preventable morbidity and premature mortality), but also for more effective participation in economic and political activities. For example, illiteracy can be a major barrier to participation in economic activities that require production according to specification or demand strict quality control (as globalized trade increasingly does). Similarly, political participation may be hindered by the inability to read newspapers or to communicate in writing with others involved in political activities.

I turn now to the fourth category. In social interactions, individuals deal with one another on the basis of some presumption of what they are being offered and what they can expect to get. In this sense, the society operates on some basic presumption of trust. *Transparency guarantees* deal with the need for openness that people can expect: the freedom to deal with one another under guarantees of disclosure and lucidity. When that trust is seriously violated, the lives of many people – both direct parties and third parties – may be adversely affected by the lack of openness. Transparency guarantees (including the right to disclosure) can thus be an important category of instrumental freedom. These

guarantees have a clear instrumental role in preventing corruption, financial irresponsibility and underhand dealings.

Finally, no matter how well an economic system operates, some people can be typically on the verge of vulnerability and can actually succumb to great deprivation as a result of material changes that adversely affect their lives. *Protective security* is needed to provide a social safety net for preventing the affected population from being reduced to abject misery, and in some cases even starvation and death. The domain of protective security includes *fixed* institutional arrangements such as unemployment benefits and statutory income supplements to the indigent as well as ad hoc arrangements such as famine relief or emergency public employment to generate income for destitutes.

## Interconnections and Complementarity

These instrumental freedoms directly enhance the capabilities of people, but they also supplement one another, and can furthermore reinforce one another. These interlinkages are particularly important to seize in considering development policies.

The fact that the entitlement to economic transactions tends to be typically a great engine of economic growth has been widely accepted. But many other connections remain under-recognized, and they have to be seized more fully in policy analysis. Economic growth can help not only in raising private incomes but also in making it possible for the state to finance social insurance and active public intervention. Thus the contribution of economic growth has to be judged not merely by the increase in private incomes, but also by the expansion of social services (including, in many cases, social safety nets) that economic growth may make possible.[1]

Similarly, the creation of social opportunities, through such services as public education, health care, and the development of a free and energetic press, can contribute both to economic development and to significant reductions in mortality rates. Reduction of mortality rates, in turn, can help to reduce birth rates, reinforcing the influence of basic education – especially female literacy and schooling – on fertility behavior.

The pioneering example of enhancing economic growth through social opportunity, especially in basic education, is of course Japan. It is sometimes forgotten that Japan had a higher rate of literacy than

Europe had even at the time of the Meiji restoration in the mid-nineteenth century, when industrialization had not yet occurred there but had gone on for many decades in Europe. Japan's economic development was clearly much helped by the human resource development related to the social opportunities that were generated. The so-called East Asian miracle involving other countries in East Asia was, to a great extent, based on similar causal connections.[2]

This approach goes against – and to a great extent undermines – the belief that has been so dominant in many policy circles that "human development" (as the process of expanding education, health care and other conditions of human life is often called) is really a kind of luxury that only richer countries can afford. Perhaps the most important impact of the type of success that the East Asian economies, beginning with Japan, have had is the total undermining of that implicit prejudice. These economies went comparatively early for massive expansion of education, and later also of health care, and this they did, in many cases, *before* they broke the restraints of general poverty. And they have reaped as they have sown. Indeed, as Hiromitsu Ishi has pointed out, the priority to human resource development applies particularly to the early history of Japanese economic development, beginning with the Meiji era (1868–1911), and that focus has not intensified with economic affluence as Japan has grown richer and much more opulent.[3]

## Different Aspects of China-India Contrast

The central role of individual freedoms in the process of development makes it particularly important to examine their determinants. Substantial attention has to be paid to the social influences, including state actions, that help to determine the nature and reach of individual freedoms. Social arrangements may be decisively important in securing and expanding the freedom of the individual. Individual freedoms are influenced, on one side, by the social safeguarding of liberties, tolerance, and the possibility of exchange and transactions. They are also influenced, on the other side, by substantive public support in the provision of those facilities (such as basic health care or essential education) that are crucial for the formation and use of human capabilities. There is need to pay attention to both types of determinants of individual freedoms.

The contrast between India and China has some illustrative importance in this context. The governments of both China and India have been making efforts for some time now (China from 1979 and India from 1991) to move toward a more open, internationally active, market-oriented economy. While Indian efforts have slowly met with some success, the kind of massive results that China has seen has failed to occur in India. An important factor in this contrast lies in the fact that from the standpoint of social preparedness, China is a great deal ahead of India in being able to make use of the market economy.[4] While pre-reform China was deeply skeptical of markets, it was not skeptical of basic education and widely shared health care. When China turned to marketization in 1979, it already had a highly literate people, especially the young, with good schooling facilities across the bulk of the country. In this respect, China was not very far from the basic educational situation in South Korea or Taiwan, where too an educated population had played a major role in seizing the economic opportunities offered by a supportive market system. In contrast, India had a half-illiterate adult population when it turned to marketization in 1991, and the situation is not much improved today.

The health conditions in China were also much better than in India because of the social commitment of the pre-reform regime to health care as well as education. Oddly enough, that commitment, while totally unrelated to its helpful role in market-oriented economic growth, created social opportunities that could be brought into dynamic use after the country moved toward marketization. The social backwardness of India, with its elitist concentration on higher education and massive negligence of school education, and its substantial neglect of basic health care, left that country poorly prepared for a widely shared economic expansion. The contrast between India and China does, of course, have many other aspects (including the differences in their respective political systems, and the much greater variation *within* India of social opportunities such as literacy and health care); these issues will be addressed later. But the relevance of the radically different levels of social preparedness in China and India for widespread market-oriented development is worth noting even at this preliminary stage of the analysis.

It must, however, also be noted that there are real handicaps that China experiences compared with India because it lacks democratic freedoms. This is particularly so when it comes to flexibility of economic policy and the responsiveness of public action to social crisis and unforeseen disasters. The most prominent contrast lies perhaps in the fact that China has had what is almost certainly the largest recorded famine in history (when thirty million people died in the famine that followed the failure of the Great Leap Forward in 1958–61), whereas India has not had a famine since independence in 1947. When things go well, the protective power of democracy may be less missed, but dangers can lie round the corner (as indeed the recent experiences of some of the East Asian and Southeast Asian economies bring out). This issue too will have to be discussed more fully later on in this book.

[ . . . ]

Surprise may well be expressed about the possibility of financing support-led processes in poor countries, since resources are surely needed to expand public services, including health care and education. In fact, the need for resources is frequently presented as an argument for *postponing* socially important investments until a country is already richer. Where (as the famous rhetorical question goes) are the poor countries going to find the means for "supporting" these services? This is indeed a good question, but it also has a good answer, which lies very considerably in the economics of relative costs. The viability of this support-led process is dependent on the fact that the relevant social services (such as health care and basic education) are very *labor intensive*, and thus are relatively inexpensive in poor – and low-wage – economies. A poor economy may *have* less money to spend on health care and education, but it also *needs* less money to spend to provide the same services, which would cost much more in the richer countries. Relative prices and costs are important parameters in determining what a country can afford. Given an appropriate social commitment, the need to take note of the variability of relative costs is particularly important for social services in health and education.[5]

It is obvious that the growth-mediated process has an advantage over its support-led alternative; it may, ultimately, offer more, since there are more deprivations – *other than* premature mortality, or high morbidity, or illiteracy – that are very directly connected with the lowness of incomes (such as being inadequately clothed and sheltered). It is clearly better to have high income *as well as* high longevity (and other standard indicators of quality of life),

rather than only the latter. This is a point worth emphasizing, since there is some danger of being "overconvinced" by the statistics of life expectancy and other such basic indicators of quality of life.

For example, the fact that the Indian state of Kerala has achieved impressively high life expectancy, low fertility, high literacy and so on despite its low income level per head is certainly an achievement worth celebrating and learning from. And yet the question remains as to why Kerala has not been able to build on its successes in human development to raise its income levels as well, which would have made its success more complete; it can scarcely serve as a "model" case, as some have tried to claim. From a policy point of view, this requires a critical scrutiny of Kerala's economic policies regarding incentives and investments ("economic facilities," in general), despite its unusual success in raising life expectancy and the quality of life.[6] Support-led success does, in this sense, remain shorter in achievement than growth-mediated success, where the increase in economic opulence and the enhancement of quality of life tend to move together.

On the other hand, the success of the support-led process as a route does indicate that a country need not wait until it is much richer (through what may be a long period of economic growth) before embarking on rapid expansion of basic education and health care. The quality of life can be vastly raised, despite low incomes, through an adequate program of social services. The fact that education and health care are also productive in raising economic growth adds to the argument for putting major emphasis on these social arrangements in poor economies, *without* having to wait for "getting rich" *first*.[7] The support-led process is a recipe for rapid achievement of higher quality of life, and this has great policy importance, but there remains an excellent case for moving on from there to broader achievements that include economic growth as well as the raising of the standard features of quality of life.

[ . . . ]

## Human Capital and Human Capability

I must also briefly discuss another relation which invites a comment, to wit, the relation between the literature on "human capital" and the focus in this work on "human capability" as an expression of freedom. In contemporary economic analysis the emphasis has, to a considerable extent, shifted from seeing capital accumulation in primarily physical terms to viewing it as a process in which the productive quality of human beings is integrally involved. For example, through education, learning, and skill formation, people can become much more productive over time, and this contributes greatly to the process of economic expansion.[8] In recent studies of economic growth (often influenced by empirical readings of the experiences of Japan and the rest of East Asia as well as Europe and North America), there is a much greater emphasis on "human capital" than used to be the case not long ago.

How does this shift relate to the view of development – development as freedom – presented in this book? More particularly, what, we may ask, is the connection between "human capital" orientation and the emphasis on "human capability" with which this study has been much concerned? Both seem to place humanity at the center of attention, but do they have differences as well as some congruence? At the risk of some oversimplification, it can be said that the literature on human capital tends to concentrate on the agency of human beings in augmenting production possibilities. The perspective of human capability focuses, on the other hand, on the ability – the substantive freedom – of people to lead the lives they have reason to value and to enhance the real choices they have. The two perspectives cannot but be related, since both are concerned with the role of human beings, and in particular with the actual abilities that they achieve and acquire. But the yardstick of assessment concentrates on different achievements.

Given her personal characteristics, social background, economic circumstances and so on, a person has the ability to do (or be) certain things that she has reason to value. The reason for valuation can be *direct* (the functioning involved may directly enrich her life, such as being well-nourished or being healthy), or *indirect* (the functioning involved may contribute to further production, or command a price in the market). The human capital perspective can – in principle – be defined very broadly to cover both types of valuation, but it is typically defined – by convention – primarily in terms of indirect value: human qualities that can be employed as "capital" in *production* (in the way physical capital is). In this sense, the narrower view of the human capital approach fits into the more inclusive perspective of human capability, which can cover both direct and indirect consequences of human abilities.

Consider an example. If education makes a person more efficient in commodity production, then this is clearly an enhancement of human capital. This can add to the value of production in the economy and also to the income of the person who has been educated. But even with the same level of income, a person may benefit from education – in reading, communicating, arguing, in being able to choose in a more informed way, in being taken more seriously by others and so on. The benefits of education, thus, exceed its role as human capital in commodity production. The broader human-capability perspective would note – and value – these additional roles as well. The two perspectives are, thus, closely related but distinct.

The significant transformation that has occurred in recent years in giving greater recognition to the role of "human capital" is helpful for understanding the relevance of the capability perspective. If a person can become more productive in making commodities through better education, better health and so on, it is not unnatural to expect that she can, through these means, also directly achieve more – and have the freedom to achieve more – in leading her life.

The capability perspective involves, to some extent, a return to an integrated approach to economic and social development championed particularly by Adam Smith (both in the *Wealth of Nations* and in *The Theory of Moral Sentiments*). In analyzing the determination of production possibilities, Smith emphasized the role of education as well as division of labor, learning by doing and skill formation. But the development of human capability in leading a worthwhile life (as well as in being more productive) is quite central to Smith's analysis of "the wealth of nations."

Indeed, Adam Smith's belief in the power of education and learning was peculiarly strong. Regarding the debate that continues today on the respective roles of "nature" and "nurture," Smith was an uncompromising – and even a dogmatic – "nurturist." Indeed, this fitted in well with his massive confidence in the improvability of human capabilities:

> The difference of natural talents in different men is, in reality, much less than we are aware of; and the very different genius which appears to distinguish men of different professions, when grown up to maturity, is not upon many occasions so much the cause, as the effect of division of labour. The difference between

the most dissimilar characters, between a philosopher and a common street porter, for example, seems to arise not so much from nature, as from habit, custom, and education. When they came into the world, and for the first six or eight years of their existence, they were, perhaps, very much alike, and neither their parents nor play-fellows could perceive any remarkable difference.[9]

It is not my purpose here to examine whether Smith's emphatically nurturist views are right, but it is useful to see how closely he links *productive* abilities and *lifestyles* to education and training and presumes the improvability of each.[10] That connection is quite central to the reach of the capability perspective.[11]

There is, in fact, a crucial valuational difference between the human-capital focus and the concentration on human capabilities – a difference that relates to some extent to the distinction between means and ends. The acknowledgment of the role of human qualities in promoting and sustaining economic growth – momentous as it is – tells us nothing about *why* economic growth is sought in the first place. If, instead, the focus is, ultimately, on the expansion of human freedom to live the kind of lives that people have reason to value, then the role of economic growth in expanding these opportunities has to be integrated into that more foundational understanding of the process of development as the expansion of human capability to lead more worthwhile and more free lives.[12]

The distinction has a significant practical bearing on public policy. While economic prosperity helps people to have wider options and to lead more fulfilling lives, so do more education, better health care, finer medical attention, and other factors that causally influence the effective freedoms that people actually enjoy. These "social developments" must directly count as "developmental," since they help us to lead longer, freer and more fruitful lives, *in addition* to the role they have in promoting productivity or economic growth or individual incomes.[13] The use of the concept of "human capital," which concentrates only on one part of the picture (an important part, related to broadening the account of "productive resources"), is certainly an enriching move. But it does need supplementation. This is because human beings are not merely means of production, but also the end of the exercise.

Indeed, in arguing with David Hume, Adam Smith had the occasion to emphasize that to see human beings only in terms of their productive use is to slight the nature of humanity:

> it seems impossible that the approbation of virtue should be of the same kind with that by which we approve of a convenient or a well-contrived building, or that we should have no other reason for praising a man than that for which we commend a chest of drawers.[14]

Despite the usefulness of the concept of human capital, it is important to see human beings in a broader perspective (breaking the analogy with "a chest of drawers"). We must go *beyond* the notion of human capital, after acknowledging its relevance and reach. The broadening that is needed is additional and inclusive, rather than, in any sense, an *alternative* to the "human capital" perspective.

It is important to take note also of the instrumental role of capability expansion in bringing about *social* change (going well beyond *economic* change). Indeed, the role of human beings even as instruments of change can go much beyond economic production (to which the perspective of "human capital" standardly points), and include social and political development. For example, as was discussed earlier, expansion of female education may reduce gender inequality in intrafamily distribution and also help to reduce fertility rates as well as child mortality rates. Expansion of basic education may also improve the quality of public debates. These instrumental achievements may be ultimately quite important – taking us well beyond the production of conventionally defined commodities.

In looking for a fuller understanding of the role of human capabilities, we have to take note of:

(1) their *direct* relevance to the well-being and freedom of people;
(2) their *indirect* role through influencing *social* change; and
(3) their *indirect* role through influencing *economic* production.

The relevance of the capability perspective incorporates each of these contributions. In contrast, in the standard literature human capital is seen primarily in terms of the third of the three roles. There is a clear overlap of coverage, and it is indeed an important overlap. But there is also a strong need to go well beyond that rather limited and circumscribed role of human capital in understanding development as freedom.

# Notes

1. On this see Jean Drèze and Amartya Sen, *Hunger and Public Action* (Oxford: Clarendon Press, 1989).
2. On this see World Bank, *The East Asian Miracle: Economic Growth and Public Policy* (Oxford: Oxford University Press, 1993). See also Vito Tanzi et al., *Economic Policy and Equity* (1999).
3. See Hiromitsu Ishi, "Trends in the Allocation of Public Expenditure in Light of Human Resource Development – Overview in Japan," mimeographed, Asian Development Bank, Manila, 1995. See also Carol Gluck, *Japan's Modern Myths: Ideology in the Late Meiji Period* (Princeton, NJ: Princeton University Press, 1985).
4. On this see Jean Drèze and Amartya Sen, *India: Economic Development and Social Opportunity* (Delhi: Oxford University Press, 1995), and the Probe Team, *Public Report on Basic Education in India* (Delhi: Oxford University Press, 1999).
5. This issue is discussed in Drèze and Sen, *Hunger and Public Action* (1989).
6. I shall return to this question later on; see also Drèze and Sen, *India: Economic Development and Social Opportunity* (1995).
7. The need for supplementing and supporting market-friendly policies for economic growth with a rapid expansion of the social infrastructure (such as public health care and basic education) is discussed in some detail, in the context of the Indian economy, in my joint book with Jean Drèze, *India: Economic Development and Social Opportunity* (1995).
8. On this and related issues, see Robert J. Barro and Jong-Wha Lee, "Losers and Winners in Economic Growth," Working Paper 4341, National Bureau of Economic Research (1993); Xavier Sala-i-Martin, "Regional Cohesion: Evidence and Theories of Regional Growth and Convergence," Discussion Paper 1075, CEPR, London, 1994; Robert J. Barro and Xavier Sala-i-Martin, *Economic Growth* (New York: McGraw-Hill, 1995); Robert J. Barro, *Getting It Right: Markets and Choices in a Free Society* (Cambridge, MA: MIT Press, 1996).
9. Adam Smith, *An Inquiry into the Nature and Causes of the Wealth of Nations* (1776), republished, edited by R. H. Campbell and A. S. Skinner (Oxford: Clarendon Press, 1976), pp. 28–9.
10. See Emma Rothschild, "Condorcet and Adam Smith on Education and Instruction," in *Philosophers on Education*, ed. Amélie O. Rorty (London: Routledge, 1998).
11. See, for example, Felton Earls and Maya Carlson, "Toward Sustainable Development for the American Family," *Daedalus* 122 (1993), and "Promoting Human Capability as an Alternative to Early Crime," Harvard School of Public Health and Harvard Medical School, 1996.
12. I have tried to discuss this issue in "Development: Which Way Now?" *Economic Journal* 93 (1983), reprinted in *Resources, Values and Development* (Cambridge, MA: Harvard University Press, 1984; 1997), and also in *Commodities and Capabilities* (1985).
13. To a considerable extent the annual *Human Development Reports* of the United Nations Development Programme, published since 1990, have been motivated by the need to take a broader view of this kind. My friend Mahbub ul Haq, who died recently, played a major leadership role in this, of which I and his other friends are most proud.
14. Smith, *The Theory of Moral Sentiments* (1759; revised edition, 1790), republished, ed. D. D. Raphael and A. L. Macfie (Oxford: Clarendon Press, 1976), book 4, chapter 24, p. 188.

# 13

# The Liberal Studies in a Global World: A Self-examination

## Otfried Höffe

### Introduction

In many places, universities are obligated to follow political aims, which are becoming more and more economic: education and research are considered worthy of being supported if they promise to be marketable. Once again, the liberal studies, especially the humanities, have to justify themselves. Because, from a political perspective, they are fighting with their back against the wall, I do not want to present here a piece of philosophical research, but to bring together arguments on behalf of liberal studies that amount to the idea that they are indispensable to a global world.

### Five Grades of Knowledge

In his posthumous autobiography *Le Premier Homme* (*The First Man*), Albert Camus writes about his elementary school that it:

> offered them not only an escape from the 'poor, meager' family life. In Monsieur Bernard's class in any case it nourished a hunger in them that was even more

essential to the child than to the man, the hunger for discovery.   (1995: 166)

What Camus describes as personal experience, Aristotle – that thinker who, already before Thomas Aquinas, and outside of the Christian world, in the world of Islam, was named by al-Farabi 'the philosopher' – describes in anthropological terms. Aristotle describes Camus's hunger for discovery thus: *Pantes anthrôpoi tou eidenai oregontai physei*: 'all men by nature desire to know'; and this desire is not tied to any use it might have.

That the modern writer and the ancient philosopher agree on this point contains a message for the global world, which the liberal studies communicate. Despite the important differences of individuals, groups, cultures or epochs, one should not ignore the essential things in common: an innate desire for knowledge, independent of its utility.

Surprisingly, this idea is not found in those writings of Aristotle that one could call his anthropology, in the connection of his ethics and political philosophy, possibly completed by *De Anima*. Instead, it is found at the start of the allegedly obsolete *Metaphysics*. Non-philosophers expect to

Originally published in *Theory and Research in Education* 1(2) (2003): pp. 213–27. © Sage Publications 2003. Reprinted with permission of Sage Publications Ltd.

find in metaphysics a far-removed speculation on the supernatural, and philosophers like Horkheimer (1947, p. 4), to find a system which assigns 'all beings, including man and his ends' a place in the whole. Whoever reads Aristotle's *Metaphysics* itself is disappointed. Its start treats nature, not the supernatural. Its justification is based on experience, on that love (*agapêsis*) for perceptions, which goes through all the five senses and which social research easily confirms. Concerning the beginnings of the individual it is developmental psychology, and for the history of our species it is cultural anthropology, which show that man can and often really does seek a pure knowledge that is free of all needs and utility.

Aristotle's series of grades of knowledge is convincing even today. It starts with perception (*aisthêsis*), goes via memory (*mnêmê*) and experience (*empeiria*) to science (*epistêmê*) and ends up with that first science, theory, which includes not only first philosophy, but also theoretical physics, theoretical biology and theoretical psychology. In loose terms, the humanities cultivate five stages of knowledge or epistemic abilities (with additional sub- and co-forms) that, unlike Aristotle's series of stages, are more strongly intertwined. By 'knowledge' is meant not merely a propositional 'knowing-that', but also a 'knowhow'. The humanities look for (1) a cultivation of perception and (2) a cultivation of memory; (3) they care for a cultivation of judgement that culminates in enlightenment; (4) within the cultivation of memory, they look for anamnestic justice; (5) lastly, they contribute to debates about orientation and meaning. In all of these stages, creativity and originality, including the joy of discovery and of putting it together, play a large role.

Sometimes the humanities are engaged in purely methodological debates abstracting from all content. But I prefer considerations based on typical examples, thus saturating our thoughts with experience. From my first example, the two introductory chapters of Aristotle's *Metaphysics*, a whole bundle of arguments can be gained. They concern the natural desire for knowledge and discovery, for which reason the liberal arts are humanities in a first and literal sense; they are activities in which the *humane* of humans expresses itself.

The liberal arts' desire for knowledge begins with a grade, which the methodology of liberal arts often skips, i.e. a cultivation of perception. The liberal arts sensitize us in an emphatic sense: art sciences teach us to see colours, forms, and materials; music sciences

to hear melodies, rhythms, and composition; literary sciences and philosophy, to read texts.

Simple perceptions do not, of course, deal with that with which the literary sciences and philosophy are concerned, i.e. the reading of texts. Seeing, hearing, the feeling of materials and perhaps even smelling, pass over into judgements, i.e. into a decoding and interpreting, which is how, for example, the philosopher deals with it in the frontispiece of Bacon's *Instauratio magna* (*Great Instauration*). There, it will be recalled, a ship drives through the strait of Gibraltar with the two 'pillars of Hercules' and ventures out with full sails into the limitless ocean. The ship that is going out into the boundless ocean symbolises the free curiosity that frees itself from its chains – the strait – and gets involved in the adventure of a boundless desire for knowledge which is, though, in contrast to Aristotle, not epistemically gradated. The two pillars represent conflicting directions, i.e. rationalism and empiricism, which the ship with its middle way seeks to reconcile. Just as the ship needs equipment and a crew, natural science requires instruments and the cooperation of many researchers. Furthermore, just as the ship must defeat the dangers of the ocean, so research must defeat those natural dangers that threaten human beings. In so doing, it certainly avails itself of the forces of nature – in the frontispiece, the wind.

The frontispiece of Hobbes' *Leviathan*, another emblematic masterpiece, stimulates a similar decoding: on the upper half, a gigantic human figure rises behind a city and behind mountains with some villages on them. It is a symbol of the state, which is, according to Hobbes, an enormous, artificial human being. If one looks more closely, one sees that the body is composed of nothing other than tiny human beings: an image of the fact that the state or the sovereign is a representative of all citizens, who are in turn completely absorbed by the all-powerful state. The crowned ruler – whose facial features, by the way, are not unlike Hobbes' – carries both the symbol of state power, the sword, and the crosier, which stands for the power of decision in religious matters. Finally, the peacefulness of the landscape points to the task of the twofold powers, the responsibility to maintain peace.

Now, the humanities are also humanities in the second sense that they help to disclose (they discover or reconstruct lost sources) and preserve the riches of humanity. In preserving, they serve the second grade of knowledge, the cultivation of memory.

Once more, they do not, of course, preserve plain memory. For certain preconceptions often exist which, upon closer inspection, are not correct. Here the humanities correct false pre-conceptions. Whoever reads Aristotle's *Metaphysics* will reveal Horkheimer's assessment to perhaps be a great evaluation, but nevertheless clearly false. The humanities contribute to enlightenment, though not always in Kant's exact sense, i.e. 'the human being's emergence from his self-incurred immaturity' (8:35: 17). They nevertheless contribute to its little sister: instead of relying on foreign opinions, one reads the texts oneself and forms one's own opinion.

As a parenthetical aside, let me say that important texts are better read in the original. Moreover, mastering a first foreign language actively, and learning a second one passively, increases one's ability to communicate. It shows something that the global world cannot do without: a reciprocal recognition. Whoever studies other languages values other cultures as equal in principle, that is, as worthy of knowing them through their language. Everybody should actively learn one foreign language and a second one passively.

In any case, the humanities contribute to something that a global world cannot do without. They have the character of enlightenment, but can also be called formation or emancipation: the humanities help one to be free from the provincial, even parochial perspectives in which one grows up.

This enlightenment promises pleasant, political side-effects. For example, if in Muslim countries the humanities flourish, if they grab not only a narrow educational group, but larger parts of the population, then they free them from a close-minded fixation on their own culture; they promote the knowledge, then the openness to, and finally the tolerance for what is foreign. In particular, they remind Muslims of the fact that Mohammed speaks out, not primarily against Jews or Christians, but against polytheism and for a pure monotheism; they show them that Mohammed wrongly considers the Christian doctrine of the Trinity to be anti-monotheistic; they clarify that the amalgamation of religion and state and society is partly common ground of ancient oriental cultures and was partly learned from what was then Byzantium; they remind them of the enlightenment within the Muslim world that, from the time of al-Kindi, even Mu'taxilites, to Averroes, lasted more than three hundred years. Finally, they could even inspire that critical hermeneutic with regard to the Koran that Christendom has known for a long time, at least for that part that can separate what is genuinely religious from supplementary accumulations.

In any case, the humanities overcome egocentrism of cultures and epochs. Insofar as they open up a look at other cultures and other times, we learn to understand in three ways: (1) we understand others in their diversity, (2) we understand both others and ourselves in a lot of common elements, and (3) by contrast to others, we better understand ourselves. In contrast with the ancient world, for instance, the present comes into sharper focus. We practice thereby a special induction, not the generalization of many similar cases, but the art of finding out in an individual case both general and particular features. And from this art of waking texts up to life (or pieces of music, works of art, city structures), one learns such important cognitive abilities as analysing, establishing relationships, and judging, all of this in a clear and concise language.

Insofar as the humanities can be sufficiently inspired by philosophy, they are carried out by what Aristotle calls the *pan pepaideumenos*, a well-educated, even all-rounded person. Such a person is not a walking encyclopaedia. Instead, she has a methodical ability to judge, for example, what kind of accuracy is required in mathematics, what kind in rhetoric, and what kind in philosophical ethics and politics (*Nicomachean Ethics* I 1: 1094b, 11; see Höffe, 1996, esp. chs. II 1 and II 5).

It is together, and not in the particular disciplines, and still less in particular research projects, that the humanities achieve the comprehensive and methodologically fundamental remembrance of past cultures and ages that merits the name 'cultivation of memory'. They merit the name above all when the methodical memory occurs in as comprehensive a manner as possible, when it, in particular, exercises an impartiality that amounts to justice in memory. For example, this anamnestic justice hinders one from remembering his own culture mostly for its positive achievements while, concerning unloved neighbours, remembering primarily the negative achievements. (Only Germany loves the negative memories more than the positive ones.)

Of course, the humanities are not interested in all cultural data indiscriminately. The musical sciences, art sciences, literary sciences, and history of philosophy single out above all those sources – like, for instance, Aristotle's *Metaphysics* – that merit longer study. For this task, the ability to judge extends itself through the humanities' consciousness of quality. And the fact that not only al-Farabi and Thomas Aquinas are in agreement in appreciating Aristotle, but also hundreds of other Christian, Islamic, and Jewish thinkers, as well as specialists from the entire world, shows that this appreciation does not allow itself to be discredited as subjective arbitrariness. Exemplariness is able to achieve consensus, in particular when it is not defended dogmatically. A judgement of quality that claims 'Aristotle instead of Plato' or 'Kant instead of Aristotle' does not achieve consensus.

In Aristotle's *Metaphysics* as well as in other great books, but also in works of music, art, and architecture, we do not merely admire outstanding quality from a distance. It is more important that the content of the works make an impression on us, that it moves us existentially and, thanks to its art of representation, that it knows how to arouse us, whether it stimulates us to think for ourselves, or whether it excites or calms us down.

Great literature is not fast-food entertainment, but presents to us the human passions, for instance, letting the passions conflict with each other and letting the conflict either end in a catastrophe or be overcome in a constructive solution. With the existential dimension, we enter into the fifth grade of knowledge, that of debates about orientation and meaning. Literature that engages us in these debates may even persuade us to accept the conclusion of Rainer Maria Rilke's poem 'Archäischer Torso Apollo': 'You must change your life'. Because this message is not always readily apparent in the classical works, the humanities are once more in demand: they must for each generation and for each culture bring those works to discussion. Then Sainte-Beuves' assertion applies: '*Un vrai classique . . . c'est un auteur qui a enrichi l'esprit humain*', a true classical author is an author who enriches the human spirit, both collectively, for mankind, and particularly, for each individual. Thus, the humanities help us to nourishment that can hold for an entire lifetime. Put more modestly, they help us to provisions with which we can fill our backpack for a full life.

## Personal Examples

Here, I offer some personal examples. I began by touching on the introductory chapters of the *Metaphysics*, I added the two frontispieces, Kant's *Enlightenment* treatise, and a Rilke poem. I would like to continue presenting both philosophical and non-philosophical examples. In accordance with the comparative view, we next pack into the backpack not any individual work, but several works from different times and cultures. I confront an Icelandic Saga, the Wölsungen Saga, and a Greek tragedy, Aeschylus' *Oresteia*.

With these works we do not become acquainted merely with two cultures that are distant to us and to each other; we extend our understanding of 'existential meaning', which then does not only refer to personal life and, in the global world, to an order of all of humanity. The confrontation of the two works opens our eyes to the danger of the measureless passion that is accompanied by that readiness for violence, which is controlled by one of the most important and indispensable institutions in a global world, i.e. by the alternative to private justice: the public criminal court.

As long as there is no such institution, the blood feud has the character of law. After a murder or deep offence to one's honour, the family members or kin have a duty – analogous to law – to take revenge on the guilty or on one of his relatives for his act. The Wölsungen Saga shows how this principle leads to a conflagration of violence, to an escalation of retaliation and counterretaliation that only comes to rest in the final catastrophe. Aeschylus' *Oresteia* also begins with a series of great, bloody acts: Agamemnon, who sacrifices his daughter for the sake of the journey to Troy, is killed after his return by his unfaithful wife Clytemnestra and her lover Aegisthus, a deed which her son Orestes avenges, but a compassionless pursuit by the Erinyes, the Furies, follows. As in the Wölsungen Saga, the passions themselves are incapable of learning in the *Oresteia*. Nevertheless, the violence comes to an end, not on its own, but by the authoritative decision of Athena. The goddess of wisdom founds a new institution, the criminal court of Athens, the Areopagus. This has a pleasant result, a comprehensive flourishing of the community that is not merely economic, but cultural. A criminal court is justified not only by legal morals, justice, but also by an enlightened self-interest. Because of this insight, the Greeks are not completely incorrect when they, in the concept of wellbeing, or *eudaimonia*, combine enlightened self-interest with morality.

The *Oresteia* is certainly not a philosophical treatment of the justification of the criminal court. As a drama, it shows which passions lurk within men, e.g., ambition, lust for power, and even greed, passions which are present in the Wölsungen Saga and are found in many other dramas and epics and thus are not unique to certain cultures and ages. This message, to which the humanities open up one's eyes, shows to the global world (1) that a further human core is valid regardless of culture and time, (2) that, on its account, an answer that is valid independently of culture and age is to be sought, in this case the public court and (3) that the answer, in order not to be merely intellectually, but also emotionally, recognized, requires the appropriate experiences and learning processes. In another tragedy, *Agamemnon*, Aeschylus brings the necessary learning process to the formula *pathei mathos*: learn through suffering (verse 177, see also verse 250 f). With that formula, both literature and the humanities correct the intellectual misunderstanding that decisive learning is for human beings mostly intellectual.

Unfortunately, Aeschylus' formula also applies collectively; that is, it seems that even mankind as a whole is able to learn primarily only through suffering. For this reason, we quickly put another work of Kant's into our backpack, the classical treatment of a global order of justice and peace, *Toward Perpetual Peace*. Prudence includes the ability to learn for the sake of one's own wellbeing, but mankind is prudent only to a moderate degree. For, on the one hand, there had to be many wars, even two World Wars, within one and a half centuries, until mankind made certain starting points of the Kantian writing into a reality in the form of the United Nations. On the other hand, following the Nuremberg and Tokyo trials, mankind let the institution of the world criminal court go back to sleep with Rwanda and the former Yugoslavia; it had to re-establish the institution and, as is well known, on account of the lack of continuity the world criminal court is supported by only an overwhelming agreement of the governments of the world, but not one without exceptions.

Great literary works bar themselves from a simple interpretation. The competing of two basically different – even basic – laws, is inherent in the *Oresteia*: according to the older, matriarchal law and to the law of blood ties, represented by the Erinyes, the murder of the mother is an absolute taboo. According to the new law, the law of equality (possibly with patriarchal undertones), represented by Apollo, even a mother deserves severe punishment for her crime. In this situation of competing basic laws, Aeschylus first lets many judges in a new criminal court vote for, as well as against, Orestes.

Only then does Athena arise and follow the principle '*in dubio pro reo*', because Orestes is not clearly guilty, she acquits him.

The humanities, which open up the *Oresteia* for a global world, could show that world four things. It could point out that basic conflicts know neither simple diagnoses ('Orestes is guilty') nor simple therapies ('He should thus be punished'). Furthermore, it shows that basic conflicts, contra Huntington, are not merely between cultures, but also arise within them. Moreover, it makes it clear that such conflicts cannot be judged and decided by one of the disputing parties, but only by a third party. It reveals that all others must subordinate themselves to this third party, an (international) criminal court. Last, but not least, it shows that the principle '*in dubio pro reo*' must hold.

Another tragedy, Sophocles' *Antigone*, calls attention to the difficulty that hinders learning through the passions. First, and once again, two laws conflict with one another. The law of the older social form, that of the blood relationship, represented by Antigone, who wants to bury her brother, conflicts with the law of the newer social form, the polis – specifically, the law that, according to King Creon's edict, denies the brother a funeral because he rebelled against his homeland. In the unfolding of the tragedy a new conflict emerges that is no longer between human beings, but is instead within a person: with Antigone the task of burying her brother conflicts with the desire to live and marry Creon's son Haemon. Creon's governing office comes into conflict with his concern for his family, for Haemon threatens to kill himself if Antigone dies. These internal conflicts however, become clear to the protagonists rather late, as late as a certain right of the opposite side becomes evident. At the beginning of the tragedy Antigone and Creon appear with self-confidence, even self-righteousness. Antigone says, full of pride: 'I will bury him: well for me to die in doing that. I shall rest, a loved one with him whom I have loved, sinless in my crime' (verse 72). And Creon does not speak any less proudly: '[A]nd if any makes a friend of more account than his fatherland, that man hath no place in my regard' (verse 189 f.). While Creon appeals to no one less than Zeus (verse 304), Antigone appeals to 'the unwritten and unfailing statutes of heaven,' for 'their life is not of today or yesterday, but from all time' (verse 454 f.). Only at the end does she confess: 'Nay, then, if these things are pleasing to the gods, when I have suffered my doom, I shall come to know my sin' (verse 925 f.). And Creon owns up to 'folly' (verse 1269) and, earlier, to being 'troubled in soul' (verse 1095).

Regarding the insights that are revealed too late, Sophocles draws attention to two faults that make both protagonists guilty, even if one sees Creon as more culpable than Antigone: self-righteousness and blindness. Overcoming them constitutes a moral task that is, in the ethics that we are familiar with – from Aristotle to Kant, and utilitarianism to discourse ethics – never noticed, let alone solved. Ordinary language, this time more sophisticated than philosophy, has its own expression, but it is almost exclusively used with children: only he who has a completely moral standing overcomes self-righteousness and blindness. It consists of willingness to hear. In this sense, Creon must let himself be asked by a guard: 'Has it bitten you in the ear?' (verse 317). Haemon reproaches Creon: 'Thou wouldst speak, and then hear no reply?' (verse 757); and the blind seer, Teiresias laments: 'Self-will, we know, incurs the charge of folly' (verse 1018).

Both philosophical ethics and the global world should learn that there are conflicts that require self-assurance to become modest because they fit neither into the moralizing schema 'good versus evil', nor even into the schema 'good versus bad'. In order to appreciate this, one certainly must correct a deep, emotional uptightness and self-righteous blindness, be open to a complex conflict-situation, and be prepared to communicate and negotiate. Generally speaking, in addition to those insights in complex conflict-situations, one needs that cultivation of timeliness which is suggested by the willingness to hear. Only with their help will complex conflict-situations be detected and recognized before the course of the tragedy has already begun.

Greek tragedy can also help to overcome another narrow-minded perspective: the reduction of the *ergon tou anthropou* (Aristotle, *Nicomachean Ethics* I 6: 1097b, 27 f.), of the Logos that distinguishes human beings, to propositional language, to accounts that describe the world. Tragedy points to that other type of speech that, amid the countless oppressions, banishments, wars, and civil wars, unfortunately is quite relevant today: a language that bemoans cruel occurrences and which does not understand the course of the world that permits them. The language consists of calls of aches and pains, of laments and fears, of the crying out to God for help which nevertheless brings none; it even consists – one must put it paradoxically – of a Logos in which the Logos has been lost, of a 'language of silence', of an often conclusive silencing.

A further task of the humanities in a global world, associated with our third grade of knowledge, is the ability to counter cultural and generational prejudices. The corresponding potential of the humanities to criticize ideology does not lie merely in critical theory nor, moreover, in the moral critique from the Sophists to the European moralists to Nietzsche, although one or other of these author's texts belongs in our backpack, for instance, Seneca's *Moral Letters to Lucilius*, Montaigne's *Essays*, Pascal's *Pensées*, or Nietzsche's *Genealogy of Morals*. We can benefit from other examples of ideological critique: e.g. whether in philosophical history, social history, or art history, the medievalists contradict the dogged prejudice of the 'dark' Middle Ages that was already held by Petrarch more than 650 years ago. Instead of that, they present us with an age that is exciting in many ways, i.e. intellectually, socially, legally and in art, music and architecture.

The creative reader finds a further ideological critique in the catchword 'social justice'. The expression is highly regarded in political rhetoric. In Europe, at least, social justice is considered to be the natural guide of democratic policy, but the historian of ideas is sceptical of this. For the heretofore relevant distinctions of justice, go back to Aristotle. Within the context of special justice, Aristotle recognizes distributive justice and commutative justice, and he divides the latter category into (voluntary) justice in exchange and (involuntary, corrective) criminal justice. Social justice, on the other hand, is missing. Only more than two millennia later, in the middle of the 19th century, does the expression emerge. Moreover, it does not emerge in philosophy or in legal or political theory, but in Christian social ethics.

Neither the late birth nor the Christian context makes social justice illegitimate. The late birth, however, raises the question: which heretofore unknown area demands a new 'social justice'? The Christian context raises the question of whether this area is indeed seen from the standpoint of justice or whether viewpoints that are foreign to justice, such as pity, benevolence and charity, sneak in. For, within social morality, justice is responsible only for that basic part which men owe each other to recognize. This moment of moral indebtedness implies that one may *demand* justice, whereas one *asks* for pity, benevolence, and generosity; in the latter case, one is disappointed in the case of offence, whereas, in the former case, one is outraged. By virtue of the moment of reciprocity, justice is a matter of law and duty, of giving and getting. If a person stresses only rights, only what she can get, she has dismissed justice.

Menander's comedy *The Arbitration* contains another piece of ideological critique. Whoever took matrimonial love and loyalty to be an 'invention' of Christianity or of other main religions will learn better, and will find it more difficult to explain the aforementioned virtues as valid only in relation to culture. Having debuted around the year 300 BC in Athens, the comedy portrays Charisios, grieving in his marriage, not as an empowered avenger, but as someone who no longer enjoys life and is even melancholic. His wife Pamphile contradicts her father, who wants to return home, with words in which resonate the confession of a debt. 'A law exists for both husband and wife/ that says that he should always love the woman he chose/ and that she should do everything that pleases him' (verse 1075–7). One later hears echoes of the Christian matrimonial formula, 'Faithful in good days as in bad days', when, according to Charisios, his wife says: 'In order to share my life with myself, you are there . . . If a misfortune should come about, you may not shirk it' (verse 1219–22).

The humanities also have good arguments against the charge that was mentioned in the introduction, namely, that they are not sufficiently marketable or, more generally, supportable. First of all, it is the humanities that indicate which works prove themselves to be supportable in the long run. Leaving behind the realm of texts, there are works, such as the Egyptian pyramids, the Acropolis in Athens, the pagodas of East Asia, the Japanese Zen gardens, or the great parks throughout the world, that are neither created for short-term use nor for mere survival. They have lasted through the centuries and, generation after generation, bring a large gain economically speaking, i.e. through tourism. These works, however, must be disclosed, partly in the physical sense in which one excavates or restores them, and partly in the intellectual sense of art tours and museum catalogues.

The public has long known that the work of the humanities stands behind both tasks. At my home university, for example, it is the rich group of general-study lectures, mainly carried out by the humanities, that attracts hundreds of listeners evening after evening, including students and professors of all faculties and many from outside the university. It is similar in other places: in ecclesiastic and political academies, in the culture and feature section of newspapers, in museum catalogues, one needs the humanities in all five grades of knowledge: for seeing and hearing and learning to read; for research-led preservation of past ages; for the cultivation of analysis, judgement, and language; for anamnestic justice, including a 'buffering resistance', the ability not to style every current innovation as a revolutionary change. In the age of globalization, for example, we have to remember a number of much older globalizations: that philosophy and the sciences, as well as medicine and technology, have spread very rapidly since antiquity; that the same is true of many religions, consequently called 'world religions'; that as early as Hellenistic times something like a region of world trade – with world prices and even world trade centres like Alexandria – developed. In the age of traditional gold currency, i.e. in the years between 1887 and 1914, global trade between the developed countries occurred almost at the current level.

The humanities can encounter the political and economic pressure to justify themselves with two further arguments, namely, by pointing out two fortunate side effects of their potential for formation and critique. On the one hand, because of the decreased number of weekly work hours and the increased pension time for many Europeans, the portion of the way of life that is not centred on wages has increased substantially. Because the population is highly educated, the need for correspondingly highly qualified offerings has grown. The offerings that are procured by the humanities keep up with the offerings of so-called 'recreational' parks relatively easily, not merely qualitatively, but also quantitatively. Museums and expositions are often over-filled, cultural excursions are desired, and the call for senior universities sounds ever more strongly. On the other hand, the humanities have accomplished an amazing social-political feat in a small amount of time. They have acted according to the free market and made a virtue out of necessity, through which they, not insignificantly, freed themselves from the fluctuations of the job market: the argument applies first and foremost to Germany, but in a general manner perhaps to the USA, too.

Some years ago the traditional job market for many departments collapsed; for *Gymnasium* teachers – teachers at a level corresponding in the USA to advanced high school work and the first two years of college – there were hardly any open places. The humanities reacted to this situation in exactly that manner that the modern job market requires: flexibly and creatively. They established a course of study that is less than the doctorate, the *Magister Artium*, for which the combination of two majors, or one major with two minors, is characteristic, and for which the achievements that are demanded are precisely those which the current occupational world consistently demands in addition to flexibility and creativity: the ability to solve problems. Here also belong the ability to analyse difficult texts; the ability to relativize Euro-centric or Ameri-centric perspectives; the capacity to notice and recognize others in their diversity; furthermore, the ability to work on problems independently; to organize problems in comprehensive summaries; and to formulate all of this concisely. Lastly, one learns team spirit, the ability to communicate, and interdisciplinary thinking. The result is thus not surprising: the students of humanities are not only active in such classic vocational areas as publishing houses, newspapers, radio and television organizations, and further education, but are also found in the personnel and staff departments of businesses and, more and more, in corporate consulting.

As is well known, a role model for liberal studies, the natural scientist and philosopher Thales, absorbed by his observations of the heavens, is said to have fallen into a well as he wandered about, causing a Thracian maiden to laugh at him (Plato, *Theaetetus* 174a). A second anecdote, however, corrects the underlying claim that the humanities are unpractical for life. As Thales was being reproached for his poverty and, along with it, the uselessness of philosophy, he rented out all of the oil presses in his country because, on account of his astronomical knowledge, he predicted a rich olive harvest the following winter. He then loaned out the oil presses during harvest for a high price, thus making a healthy profit (Aristotle, *Politics* I 11).

I would like to offer a penultimate argument as a response to the political pressure on the humanities to justify themselves. It has to do with the discipline that is booming right now, the biological sciences. Radically new possibilities are now emerging, particularly in the application of the biological sciences to medicine, e.g. in stem cell research. Because its ethical valuation is not readily apparent, it demands a biomedical ethics. The latter is enjoying a boom that a minister of finance can only envy. Whereas he must reckon with

economic fluctuations, the need for medical ethics is always growing. Though the hot topics are always changing, the almost overwhelming leaps in progress raise new questions again and again. Because the questions have an existential import – indeed, what is at stake here is the beginning and end of human life, health, sickness, and life and death – the persistent boom cannot be thought away from any functioning democracy. Biomedical ethics requires, among other things, the discussion between the life sciences and the humanities.

At first only a small part appears to be in demand, namely, philosophical and theological ethics and jurisprudence. In fact, social history and cultural anthropology are demanded as well. Because the Western ethic of healing and helping goes back at least to Hippocratic medicine, classical philologists are also required. Insofar as in the age of globalization ethical guidelines must be authenticated interculturally, a look at other cultures is required, too. If the contribution of these sciences is to be fundamental, then they cannot be satisfied with ad hoc information. They need that thematic breadth and, above all, that deep breadth that is not subjected to the wind that fashionably turns in accordance with the current themes.

The reflections offered so far have made use of a proud group of arguments and are nevertheless still not enough. For, in a broader sense of the concept, they 'instrumentalize' the humanities, which are called 'liberal' studies on other grounds. Many of the arguments mentioned so far can be summarized in the first meaning of 'liberal', i.e. the political one. As opposed to a dogmatic and autocratic thought and to a fixation on one's own culture and age, the humanities promote, in accordance with their method, cultural openness and tolerance. A second meaning, that of Cicero, is found in the Latin phrase *artes liberales*, later translated into English as 'the liberal arts', with its use of 'liberal' as an adjective. This meaning rested originally on the distinction between freeman and slave, and it only applies within boundaries. It is right that the humanities are worthy of a free man, but not because they, in contrast to slaves, renounce manual labour. A third meaning might apply to general studies in a senior university: they are open to people free of obligation, which means without being paid for and without having to prepare oneself for a professional activity.

With a fourth meaning of 'liberal', which is in fact, however, the primary one, we go back to Aristotle's *Metaphysics*. 'Free' there applies to whoever does not let himself be torn down in the exchange of useful relations, who instead lives for his own sake (I 2: 982b, 25f.). Hence Aristotle closes the Thales anecdote with words that generally apply to the humanities: 'It would be easy for philosophers to become rich, if they only wanted to, but it does not appeal to them very much' (*Politics* I 11: 1259a, 17f.). The *Nicomachean Ethics* gives the reason why this is so in criticising the *chrêmatistês bios*, the life that is dedicated to wealth alone (I 3: 1009a, 5–7). Whoever exclusively seeks wealth misjudges the extent to which wealth has practical importance. He or she overlooks the fact that wealth has no value in itself, but serves other ends, for instance, bringing about a secure, pleasant life and indicating success. Whether individuals or society, whoever is looking for nothing other than wealth succumbs to a structural disappointment: he holds for a final

end what in truth functions only as an intermediate one.

Herein lies a further – perhaps even the most important – task of the humanities. They contribute once more to humanization, namely, to the insight that mankind is an end in itself. Whether in relation to individuals or in relation to society, they raise objections to a life that dehumanizes in the literal sense, a life that errs in the hunt for power, honour, and wealth, i.e. in serving the three aforementioned passions, imperiousness, ambition, and greed. The humanities have to do with works that directly or indirectly pose the question of meaning, as the Rilke poem does; they aid the discussion of this question. Above all, they open up the desire for knowledge to things for which it is worthy to be born, such essential things as philosophy and literature, music, the fine arts, and architecture.

## Acknowledgement

This article was translated into English by Robert Clewis.

## References

Aeschylus (1998) *Agamemnon*, translated by Howard Rubenstein (El Cajon).

Aeschylus (1999) *Oresteia*, translated by Ted Hughes (New York).

Aristotle (1968, 1963) *Metaphysica*, edited by W. Jaeger (Oxford: Clarendon Press); translated by Hugh Tredennick, 2 vols (London/Cambridge, MA: Harvard University Press).

Aristotle (1979, 1975) *Ethica Nicomachea*, edited by I. Bywater (Oxford: Clarendon Press); translated by W. D. Ross (Oxford: Oxford University Press).

Aristotle (1990, 1972) *Politica*, edited by W. D. Ross (Oxford: Clarendon Press); translated by Benjamin Jowett (Oxford: Clarendon Press).

Bacon, Francis (1980) *The Great Instauration* (Arlington Heights, IL: New Atlantis).

Camus, Albert (1994/95) *Le Premier Homme* (Paris: dt. Der erste Mensch, Reinbek).

Hobbes, T. (1991) *Leviathan or the Matter, Form and Power of a Commonwealth, Ecclesiastical and Civil (1651)* (Cambridge: Cambridge University Press).

Höffe, O. (1996) *Praktische Philosophie* (Berlin: Das Modell des Aristoteles).

Horkheimer, M. (1947) *Eclipse of Reason* (New York: Oxford University Press).

Kant, Immanuel (1996) 'An Answer to the Question: What is Enlightenment?', translated by Mary J. Gregor, *Practical Philosophy* (New York: Cambridge University Press).

Kant, Immanuel (1996) 'Toward Perpetual Peace. A Philosophical Project', in M. J. Gregor (ed.), *I. Kant: Practical Philosophy* (New York: Cambridge University Press), pp. 311–51.

Menander (1945) 'The Arbitration (Epitrepontes)', in *Two Plays of Menander*, translated by Gilbert Murray (New York).

Plato (1973) *Theaetetus*, translated by John McDowell (Oxford: Clarendon Press).

Rilke, R. M. (1966) 'Archäischer Torso Apollos', in *Werke in 3 Bänden*, 1, 313 (Frankfurt am Main).

Sophocles, *Antigone*, trans. R. C. Jebb (Cambridge: Cambridge University Press, 1900).

# Autonomy and Exit Rights

# 14

# The Child's Right to an Open Future

## Joel Feinberg

### 1

How do children's rights raise special philosophical problems? Not all rights of children, of course, do have a distinctive character. Many whole classes of rights are common to adults and children; many are exclusive possessions of adults; perhaps none at all are necessarily peculiar to children. In the common category are rights not to be mistreated directly, for example the right not to be punched in the nose or to be stolen from. When a stranger slaps a child and forcibly takes away his candy in order to eat it himself, he has interfered wrongfully with the child's bodily and property interests and violated his or her rights just as surely as if the aggressor had punched an adult and forcibly helped himself to her purse. Rights that are common to adults and children in this way we can call "A-C-rights".

Among the rights thought to belong only to adults ("A-rights") are the legal rights to vote, to imbibe, to stay out all night, and so on. An interesting subspecies of these are those autonomy-rights (protected liberties of choice) that could hardly apply to small children, the free exercise of one's

religion, for example, which presupposes that one has religious convictions or preferences in the first place. When parents choose to take their child to religious observances and to enroll him in a Sunday School, they are exercising *their* religious rights, not (or not yet) those of the child.

The rights which I shall call "C-rights", while not strictly peculiar to children, are generally characteristic of them, and possessed by adults only in unusual or abnormal circumstances. Two subclasses can be distinguished, and I mention the first only to dismiss it as not part of the subject matter of this essay, namely those rights that derive from the child's dependence upon others for the basic instrumental goods of life – food, shelter, protection. Dependency-rights are common to all children, but not exclusive to them, of course, since some of them belong also to handicapped adults who are incapable of supporting themselves and must therefore be "treated as children" for the whole of their lives.

Another class of C-rights, those I shall call "rights-in-trust," look like adult autonomy rights of class *A*, except that the child cannot very well exercise his free choice until later when he is more

Originally published in *Freedom & Fulfillment: Philosophical Essays* (Princeton, NJ: Princeton University Press, 1980), pp. 124–9, 131–8, 140–1, 142–53. © 1992 Princeton University Press. Reprinted with permission of Princeton University Press.

fully formed and capable. When sophisticated autonomy rights are attributed to children who are clearly not yet capable of exercising them, their names refer to rights that are to be *saved* for the child until he is an adult, but which can be violated "in advance," so to speak, before the child is even in a position to exercise them. The violating conduct guarantees *now* that when the child is an autonomous adult, certain key options will already be closed to him. His right while he is still a child is to have these future options kept open until he is a fully formed self-determining adult capable of deciding among them. These "anticipatory autonomy rights" in class *C* are the children's rights in which I am most interested, since they raise the most interesting philosophical questions. They are, in effect, autonomy rights in the shape they must assume when held "prematurely" by children.

Put very generally, rights-in-trust can be summed up as the single "right to an open future," but of course that vague formula simply describes the form of the particular rights in question and not their specific content. It is plausible to ascribe to children a right to an open future only in some, not all respects, and the simple formula leaves those respects unspecified. The advantage of the general formula, however, is that it removes temptation to refer to certain rights of children by names that also apply to rights of adults that are quite different animals.[1] The adults's right to exercise his religious beliefs, for example, is a class *A* right, but the right of the same name when applied to a small child is a right-in-trust, squarely in class *C*. One can avoid confusing the two by referring to the latter simply as part of the child's right to an open future (in respect to religious affiliation). In that general category it sits side by side with the right to walk freely down the public sidewalk as held by an infant of two months, still incapable of self-locomotion. One would violate that right in trust *now*, before it can even be exercised, by cutting off the child's legs. Some rights with general names are rather more difficult to classify, especially when attributed to older, only partly grown, children. Some of these appear to have one foot in class *A* and the other in the rights-in-trust subclass of the *C* category. For example, the right of free speech, interpreted as the freedom to express political opinions, when ascribed to a ten year old is perhaps mainly an actual *A*-right, but it is still partly a *C*-right-in-trust, at least in respect to those opinions which the child might one day come to form but which are presently beyond his ken.

People often speak of a child's "welfare" or his "interests." The interests protected by children's *A*-*C*-rights are those interests the child actually has *now*. Their advancement is, in a manner of speaking, a constituent of the child's good *qua* child right now. On the other hand the interests he might come to have as he grows up are the ones protected by his rights-in-trust of class *C*. While he is still a child these "future interests" include those that he will in fact come to have in the future and also those he will never acquire, depending on the directions of his growth.

It is a truism among philosophers that interests are not the same things as present desires with which they can, and often do, clash. Thus if the violation of a child's autonomy right-in-trust can not always be established by checking the child's *present* interests, *a fortiori* it cannot be established by determining the child's present *desires* or *preferences*.[2] It is the adult he is to become who must exercise the choice, more exactly, the adult he will become if his basic options are kept open and his growth kept "natural" or unforced. In any case, that adult does not exist yet, and perhaps he never will. But the child is *potentially* that adult, and it is that adult who is the person whose autonomy must be protected now (in advance).

When a mature adult has a conflict between getting what he wants now and having his options left open in the future, we are bound by our respect for his autonomy not to force his present choice in order to protect his future "liberty." His present autonomy takes precedence even over his probable future good, and he may use it as he will, even at the expense of the future self he will one day become. Children are different. Respect for the child's future autonomy, as an adult, often requires preventing his free choice now. Thus the future self does not have as much moral weight in our treatment of adults as it does with children. Perhaps it should weigh as much with adults pondering their *own* decisions as it does with adults governing their own children. In the self-regarding case, the future self exerts its weight in the form of a claim to prudence, but prudence cannot rightly be imposed from the outside on an autonomous adult.

## 2

Moral perplexity about children's *C*-rights-in-trust is most likely to arise when those rights appear to conflict with certain *A*-rights of their parents, and the courts must adjudicate the conflict. Typically the conflict is between the child's protected personal interests in growth and development (rather than his immediate health or welfare) and the parents' right to control their child's upbringing, or to determine their own general style of life, or to practice their own religion free of outside interference. Very often the interests of the general community as represented by the state are involved too, for example the concern that children not be a source of infection to others, that they grow up well enough informed to be responsible voting citizens, or that they not become criminal or hopeless dependents on state welfare support. Thus custody hearings, neglect proceedings against parents, and criminal trials for violating compulsory school attendance laws and child labor statutes often become three-cornered contests among the rights of children, parents, and the state as representative of the collective interests of the community.[3] Sometimes, however, the community's interests are only marginally involved in the case, and the stark conflict between parent and child comes most clearly to the fore. Among the more difficult cases of this kind are those that pose a conflict between the religious rights of parents and their children's rights to an open future.

Children are not legally capable of defending their own future interests against present infringement by their parents, so that task must be performed for them, usually by the state in its role of *parens patriae*. American courts have long held that the state has a "sovereign power of guardianship" over minors and other legally incompetent persons which confers upon it the right, or perhaps even the duty, to look after the interests of those who are incapable of protecting themselves. Mentally disordered adults, for example, who are so deranged as to be unable to seek treatment for themselves, are entitled, under the doctrine of *parens patriae*, to psychiatric care under the auspices of the state. Many "mentally ill" persons, however, are not cognitively deranged, and some of these do not wish to be confined and treated in mental hospitals. The government has no right to impose treatment on these persons, for the doctrine of *parens patriae* extends only to those unfortunates who are rendered literally incapable of deciding whether to seek medical treatment themselves; and even in these cases, the doctrine as liberally interpreted grants power to the state only to "decide for a man as we assume he would decide for himself if he were of sound mind."[4] When the courts must decide for *children*, however, as they presume the children themselves would (or will) when they are adults, their problems are vastly more difficult. As a general rule, the courts will not be so presumptuous as to speak now in the name of the future adult; but, on the other hand, there are sometimes ways of interferring with parents so as to postpone the making of serious and final commitments until the child grows to maturity and is legally capable of making them himself.

. . .

[A] close case, I think, but one where the interests of children do seem prior to the religious interests of their parents, was that in which the Kansas courts refused to permit an exemption for Amish communities from the requirement that all children be sent to state-accredited schools.[5] The Amish are descended from eighteenth century immigrants of strong Protestant conviction who settled in this country in order to organize self-sufficient farming communities along religious principles, free of interference from unsympathetic outsiders. There is perhaps no purer example of religious faith expressed in a whole way of life, of social organization infused and saturated with religious principle. The aim of Amish education is to prepare the young for a life of industry and piety by transmitting to them the unchanged farming and household methods of their ancestors and a thorough distrust of modern techniques and styles that can only make life more complicated, soften character, and corrupt with "worldliness". Accordingly, the Amish have always tried their best to insulate their communities from external influences, including the influence of state-operated schools. Their own schools teach only enough reading to make a lifetime of Bible study possible, only enough arithmetic to permit the keeping of budget books and records of simple commercial transactions. Four or five years of this, plus exercises in sociality, devotional instruction, inculcation of traditional virtues, and on-the-job training in simple crafts of field, shop, or kitchen are all that is required, in a formal way, to prepare children for the traditional Amish way of life to which their parents are bound by the most solemn commitments.

More than this, however, was required by law of any accredited private school in the state of Kansas. Education is compulsory until the age of sixteen, and must meet minimal curricular standards including courses in history, civics, literature, art, science, and mathematics more advanced than elementary arithmetic. Why not permit a limited exemption from these requirements out of respect for the constitutional right of the Amish to the free exercise of their religion and to the self-contained way of life that is inseparable from that exercise? The case for the exemption was a strong one. The Amish "sincerity" is beyond any question. The simple "unworldly" life that is part of their religion is *prima facie* inconsistent with modern education; and the virtues of simplicity and withdrawal are "important", that is, more than merely incidental or peripheral to the Amish religion. Moreover, the small size of the Amish sect would minimize the effect of an exemption on the general educational level in Kansas. Indeed, insofar as there is a *public* interest involved in this problem (in addition to the clash of private interests) it seems to weigh more heavily on the Amish side of the scale, for as Mill pointed out in *On Liberty*,[6] we all profit from the example of others' "experiments in living". They permit us to choose our own way of life more aware of the various alternatives that are open, thus facilitating our own reasoning about such choices and reducing the possibility of error in our selection. Living examples of radically different ways of life constantly before our eyes cannot help but benefit all of us, if only by suggesting different directions in case our majority ways lead to dead ends.

The case against the exemption for the Amish must rest entirely on the rights of Amish *children*, which the state as *parens patriae* is sworn to protect. An education that renders a child fit for only one way of life forecloses irrevocably his other options. He may become a pious Amish farmer, but it will be difficult to the point of practical impossibility for him to become an engineer, a physician, a research scientist, a lawyer, or a business executive. The chances are good that inherited propensities will be stymied in a large number of cases, and in nearly all cases, critical life-decisions will have been made irreversibly for a person well before he reaches the age of full discretion when he should be expected, in a free society, to make them himself. To be prepared for anything, including the worst, in this complex and uncertain world would seem to require as much knowledge as a child can absorb throughout his minority. These considerations have led many to speak of the American child's birth-right to as much education as may be available to him, a right no more "valid" than the religious rights of parents, but one which must be given reluctant priority in cases of unavoidable conflict.

Refusal to grant the exemption requested by the Amish only puts them in the same kind of position *vis-à-vis* their children as all other parents. They are permitted and indeed expected to make every reasonable effort to transmit by example and precept their own values to their children. This is in fact a privileged position for parents, given their special relations of intimacy and affection with their children, even when compared to the rival influences of neighbors and schools; but still, in the interest of eventual full maturity, self-fulfillment, and natural many-sided development of the children themselves, parents must take their chances with outside influences.

The legal setback to the Amish at the hands of the Kansas Supreme Court was only temporary, however, and six years later in the case of *Wisconsin v. Yoder*[7] they won a resounding victory in the Supreme Court of the United States. The Amish litigants in that case had been convicted of violating Wisconsin's compulsory school attendance law (which requires attendance until the age of sixteen) by refusing to send their children to public or accredited private school after they had graduated from the eighth grade. The U.S. Supreme Court upheld the Wisconsin Supreme Court's ruling that application of the compulsory school-attendance law to the Amish violated their rights under the Free Exercise of Religion Clause of the First Amendment.[8] The Court acknowledged that the case required a balancing of legitimate interests but concluded that the interest of the parents in determining the religious upbringing of their children outweighed the claim of the state in its role as *parens patriae* "to extend the benefit of secondary education to children regardless of the wishes of their parents."

Mr. Chief Justice Burger delivered the opinion of the Court which showed a commendable sensitivity to the parental interests and the ways they are threatened by secular public education:

> The concept of a life aloof from the world and its values is central to their faith . . . High school attendance with teachers who are not of the Amish faith, and may even be hostile to it, interposes a serious barrier to integration of the Amish child into the Amish religious community . . . Compulsory school attendance to the age of sixteen for Amish children carries with it a very real threat of undermining Amish community and religious practice as they exist today; they must either abandon belief and be assimilated into society at large, or be forced to migrate to some other and more tolerant region.[9]

Burger shows very little sensitivity, however, to the interests of the Amish child in choosing his own vocation in life. At one point he begs the question against anyone who suggests that some Amish children might freely and even wisely decide to enter the modern world if given the choice:

> The value of all education must be assessed in terms of its capacity to prepare the child for life. It is one thing to say that compulsory education for a year or two beyond the eighth grade may be necessary when its goal is the preparation of the child for life in modern society as the majority live, but it is quite another if the goal of education be viewed as the preparation of the child for life in the separated agrarian community that is the keystone of the Amish faith.[10]

But how *is* "the goal of education" to be viewed? That is the question that must be left open if the Court is to issue a truly neutral decision. To *assume* that "the goal" is preparation for modern commercial-industrial life is to beg the question in favor of the state, but equally, to assume that "the goal" is preparation for a "life aloof from the world" is to beg the question in favor of the parents. An impartial decision would assume only that education should equip the child with the knowledge and skills that will help him choose whichever sort of life best fits his native endowment and matured disposition. It should send him out into the adult world with as many open opportunities as possible, thus maximizing his chances for self-fulfillment.

More than eighty percent of the way through his opinion, the Chief Justice finally addresses the main issue:

> The state's case . . . appears to rest on the potential that exemption of Amish parents from the requirements of the compulsory education law might allow some parents to act contrary to the best interests of their children by foreclosing their opportunity to make an intelligent choice between the Amish way of life and that of the outside world.[11]

That is indeed the argument that Burger must rebut, and his attempt to do so is quite extraordinary:

> The same argument could, of course, be made with respect to all church schools short of college. [Burger forgets that church schools must satisfy certain minimal curricular standards if they are to be accredited by the state. The state of Wisconsin has not prohibited the Amish from establishing parochial schools that meet the same standards that other church schools do.]

Indeed it seems clear that if the State is empowered, as *parens patriae*, to "save" a child from himself or his Amish parents by requiring an additional two years of compulsory formal high school education, the State will in large measure influence if not determine, the religious future of the child. Even more markedly than in *Prince*, therefore, this case involves the fundamental interest of parents, as contrasted with that of the State, to guide the religious future and education of their children.[12]

Burger seems to employ here a version of the familiar argument that to prevent one party from determining an outcome is necessarily to determine a different outcome, or to exercise undue "influence" on the final outcome. So it has been argued in similar terms that to prevent one party's coercion of a second party's decision is itself to influence that decision coercively.[13] Often this sort of argument is directed at inactions as well as actions so that the would-be guarantor of impartiality is beaten from the start. Thus it is sometimes said that to abstain from coercion is to permit an outcome that could have been prevented and thus to exercise undue influence, or (in other contexts) that not to punish is to "condone." The upshot of these modes of reasoning is the conclusion that state neutrality is not merely difficult but impossible in principle, that by doing nothing, or permitting no other parties to do anything that will close a child's options before he is grown, the state in many cases itself closes some options.

There are two ways of replying to this argument of Burger's. The first is to claim that there is some reasonable conception of neutrality that is immune to his blanket dismissal, so that while there are severe practical difficulties that stand in the way, they are not insolvable in principle, and that in any event, even if perfect neutrality is unachievable in an imperfect world, there is hope that it can be approached or approximated to some degree. Ideally, the neutral state (in this "reasonable conception") would act to let *all* influences, or the largest and most random possible assortment of influences, work equally on the child, to open up all possibilities to him, without itself influencing him toward one or another of these. In that way, it can be hoped that the chief determining factor in the grown child's choice of a vocation and life-style will be his own governing values, talents, and propensities. The second reply to Burger is to ask, on the supposition that neutrality *is* impossible, why the Court should automatically favor the interests of the parents when they conflict with those of their children.

Despite these animadversions on Mr. Chief Justice Burger's reasoning, I do not wish to contend that the decision in *Yoder* was mistaken. The difference between a mere eight years of elementary education and a mere ten years of mostly elementary education seems so trivial in the technologically complex modern world, that it is hard to maintain that a child who has only the former is barred from many possible careers while the child who has only the latter is not. It is plausible therefore to argue that what is gained for the educable fourteen year old Amish child by guaranteeing him another two years of school is more than counterbalanced by the corrosive effect on the religious bonds of the Amish community. From the philosophical standpoint, however, even the sixteen-year-old educable youth whose parents legally withdraw him from school has suffered an invasion of his rights-in-trust.

I am more sympathetic to the separate concurring opinion in the *Yoder* case, written by Mr. Justice White and endorsed by Justices Brennan and Stuart, than to the official majority opinion written by the Chief Justice, and I should like to underline its emphasis. These justices join the majority only because the difference between eight and ten years is minor in terms of the children's interests but possibly crucial for the very survival of the Amish sect. (Secular influences on the children had been minimal during the first eight years since they attended a "nearby rural schoolhouse," with an overwhelming proportion of students of the Amish faith, none of whom played rock records, watched television, or the like.) Nevertheless, even though the facts of this case are not favorable for the State's position, the case is still a close one, and had the facts been somewhat different, these justices would have upheld the *C*-rights represented by the state whatever the cost to the Amish sect. "This would be a very different case for me," Mr. Justice White wrote, "if respondents' claim were that their religion forbade their children from attending any school at any time and from complying in any way with the educational standards set by the State."[14] In that hypothetical case, as in various intermediate ones where we can imagine that the respondents withdrew their children after two or four years of schooling, no amount of harm to the parents' interest in the religious upbringing of their children could overturn the children's rights-in-trust to an open future.

White gives eloquent answer to Burger's claim that compulsory education of Amish youth in large modern high schools is in effect a kind of indoctrination in secular values. Education can be compulsory, he argues, only because, or only when, it is neutral:

> the State is not concerned with the maintenance of an educational system as an end in itself; it is rather attempting to nurture and develop the human potential of its children, whether Amish or non-Amish: to expand their knowledge, broaden their sensibilities, kindle their imagination, foster a spirit of free inquiry, and increase their human understanding and tolerance. It is possible that most Amish children will wish to continue living the rural life of their parents, in which case their training at home will adequately equip them for their future role. Others, however, may wish to become nuclear physicists, ballet dancers, computer programmers, or historians, and for these occupations, formal training will be necessary . . . A State has a legitimate interest not only in seeking to develop the latent talents of its children but also in seeking to prepare them for the life style that they may later choose, or at least to provide them with an option other than the life they have led in the past.[15]

The corrective emphasis of the White concurring opinion then is on the danger of using *Yoder* uncritically as a precedent for finding against Children's *C*-rights when they are clearly in conflict with the supervisory rights of their parents. [ . . . ]

## 3

The coherence of the above account of the child's right to an open future is threatened by a number of philosophical riddles. The existence of such a right, as we have seen, sets limits to the ways in which parents may raise their own children, and even imposes duties on the state, in its role as *parens patriae*, to enforce those limits. The full statement of the grounds for these protective duties will invoke the interrelated ideals of autonomy (or self-determination) and self-fulfillment, and these concepts are notoriously likely to generate philosophical confusion. Moreover, both friends and enemies of the child's right to an open future are likely to use the obscure and emotionally charged epithet "paternalism," the one side accusingly, the other apologetically, a practice that can only detract further from conceptual clarity.

The pejorative term "paternalism" is commonly applied to acts of authorities or rule-makers which are thought to treat adults as if they were children, for example orders prohibiting some sort of pre-dominately self-regarding behavior, when they are issued for the subject's "own good" quite apart from his own considered preferences in the matter, or actions that deliberately impose some pattern on the subject's life without his consent or even against his wishes, but once more, like bitter medicine, "for his own good." How is it possible then for parents to be "paternalistic" in a similarly derogatory sense, toward their own children? The term can be applied pejoratively in this way only because there is a series of stages in a child's growth between total helplessness and incapacity at the beginning and near self-sufficiency at the threshhold of adulthood. Blameable "paternalism" must consist in treating the child at a given stage as if he were at some earlier, less developed, stage. But "paternalism" in the upbringing of children, in some sense, is inevitable and therefore wholly proper, whether imposed by the state in the child's interest or by the parents themselves, and that is because there will be some respects at least in which even an older child cannot know his own interest, some respects in which he must be protected from his own immature and uninformed judgment. Moreoever, since children are not born with a precisely determined character structure, they must be socialized by measures of discipline if they are to become fit members of the adult community, and this must be done even if it is against the wishes of the pre-socialized children themselves. As Kenneth Henley puts its: "We cannot always await their consent to the sometimes painful steps of growing up."[16]

It is characteristic of parents, of course, not only to protect children from their own folly, but also to protect them from external dangers generally, including the dangers posed by other persons. [ . . . ]

Typically the state must shoulder a greater burden of justification for its interferences with parents for the sake of their children than that which is borne by parents in justification of *their* interferences with children for the children's own sake. That is because state action by its very nature tends to be cumbersome, and heavy-handed, and because it constitutes a threat to such well-established parental rights as the right to supervise the upbringing of one's own children and the right to the free exercise of one's own religion (which unavoidably influences the developing attitudes and convictions of the children). But although the burden on the state is characteristically heavier than that shouldered by

parents for their own interventions, it is essentially of the same general kind, requiring the same sorts of reasons. In either case, the justification appeals (to speak roughly at first) to the eventual *autonomy* and to *the good* of the child.

The word "autonomy," which plays such an essential role in the discussion of children's rights, has at least two relevant senses. It can refer either to the *capacity* to govern oneself, which of course is a matter of degree, or (on the analogy to a political state) to the *sovereign authority* to govern oneself, which is absolute within one's own moral boundaries (one's "territory," "realm," "sphere," or "business"). Note that there are two parallel senses of the term "independent," the first of which refers to self-sufficiency, the *de facto* capacity to support oneself, direct one's own life, and be finally responsible for one's own decisions, and the second of which, applied mainly to political states, refers to *de jure* sovereignty and the right of self-determination. In a nutshell, one sense of "autonomy" (and also of "independence") refers to the capacity and the other to the right of self-determination. When the state justifies its interference with parental liberty by reference to the eventual autonomy of the protected child, it argues that the mature adult that the child will become, like all free citizens, has a *right of self-determination*, and that that right is violated in advance if certain crucial and irrevocable decisions determining the course of his life are made by anyone else before he has the *capacity of self-determination* himself.

The child's own good is not necessarily promoted by the policy of protecting his budding right of self-determination. There is no unanimity among philosophers, of course, about that in which a human being's own good consists, but a majority view that seems to me highly plausible would identify a person's good ultimately with his *self-fulfillment* – a notion that is not identical with that of autonomy or the right of self-determination. Self-fulfillment is variously interpreted, but it surely involves as necessary elements the development of one's chief aptitudes into genuine talents in a life that gives them scope, an unfolding of all basic tendencies and inclinations, both those that are common to the species and those that are peculiar to the individual, and an active realization of the universal human propensities to plan, design and make order.[17] Self-fulfillment, so construed, is not the same as achievement and not to be confused with pleasure or contentment, though achievement is often highly fulfilling, and fulfillment is usually highly gratifying.

One standard way of deriving the right of self-determination is to base it solidly on the good of self-fulfillment. A given normal adult is much more likely to know his own interests, talents, and natural dispositions (the stuff of which his good is composed) than is any other party, and much more capable therefore of directing his own affairs to the end of his own good than is a government official, or a parent at an earlier stage who might preempt his choices for him. The individual's advantages in this regard are so great that for all practical purposes we can hold that recognition and enforcement of the right of self-determination (autonomy) is a causally necessary condition for the achievement of self-fulfillment (the individual's own good). This is the view of John Stuart Mill who argued in *On Liberty* that the attempt even of a genuinely benevolent state to impose upon an adult an external conception of his own good is almost certain to be self-defeating, and that an adult's own good is "best provided for by allowing him to take his own means of pursuing it."[18] Promotion of human well-being and the prevention of harms are primary in Mill's system, so that even so basic a right as that of self-determination must be derived from its conducibility to them. In those rare cases where we can know that free exercise of a person's autonomy will be against his own interests, as for example when he freely negotiates his own slavery in exchange for some other good, there we are justified in interfering with his liberty in order to protect him from harm.

The second standard interpretation of the right of self-determination holds that it is entirely *underivative*, as morally basic as the good of self-fulfillment itself. There is no necessity, on this view, that free exercise of a person's autonomy will promote his own good, but even where self-determination is likely, on objective evidence, to lead to the person's own harm, others do not have a right to intervene coercively "for his own good." By and large, a person will be better able to achieve his own good by making his own decisions, but even where the opposite is true, others may not intervene, for autonomy is even more important a thing than personal well-being. The life that a person threatens by his own rashness is after all *his* life; it *belongs* to him and to no one else. For that reason alone, he must be the one to decide – for better or worse – what is to be done with it in that private realm where the interests of others are not directly involved.[19]

A compromising way of regarding the adult's right of autonomy is to think of it as neither derivative from nor more basic than its possessor's own good (self-fulfillment), but rather as coordinate with it. In the more plausible versions of this third view,[20] a person's own good, in the vast majority of cases, will be most reliably furthered if he is allowed to make his own choices in self-regarding matters, but where that coincidence of values does not hold, one must simply do one's best to balance autonomy against personal well-being, and decide between them intuitively, since neither has automatic priority over the other. In any case, the two distinct ideals of sovereign autonomy (self-determination) and personal well-being (self-fulfillment) are both likely to enter, indeed to dominate, the discussion of the grounding of the child's right to an open future. That right (or class of rights) must be held in trust *either* out of respect for the sovereign independence of the emerging adult (and derivatively in large part for his own good) or for the sake of the life-long well-being of the person who is still a child (a well-being from which the need of self-government "by and large" can be derived), or from both. In such ways the good (self-fulfillment) and the right (self-determination) of the child enter the justificatory discussion. And both can breed paradox from the start, unless handled with care.

The paradoxes I have in mind both have the form, *prima facie*, of vicious circles. Consider first the self-determination circle. If we have any coherent conception of the fully self-determined adult, he is a person who has determined both his own life-circumstances and his own character. The former consists of his career-type (doctor, lawyer, merchant, chief), his life-style (swinger, hermit, jogger, scholar), and his religious affiliation and attitude (piety, hypocrisy, indifference, total absorption), among other things. The latter is that set of habitual traits that we create by our own actions and cultivated feelings in given types of circumstances, our characteristic habits of response to life's basic kinds of situations. Aristotle analyzed these as deeply rooted *dispositions* to act or feel in certain ways in certain kinds of circumstances, and since his time it has become a philosophical truism that we are, in large part, the products of our own making, since each time we act or feel in a given way in a given kind of circumstance, we strengthen the disposition to act or feel in that (brave or cowardly, kind or cruel, warm or cold) way in similar circumstances in the future. Now, whatever policy is adopted by a child's parents, and whatever laws are passed and enforced by the state, the child's options in respect to life circumstances and character will be substantially narrowed well before he is an adult. He will have to be socialized and educated, and these processes will inevitably influence the development of his own values, tastes, and standards, which will in turn determine in part how he acts, feels, and chooses. That in turn will reenforce his tendencies to act, feel, and choose in similar ways in the future, until his character is set. If the parents and the state try to evade the responsibility for character and career formation by an early policy of drift, that will have consequences on the child too, for which they shall have to answer. And in any case, simply by living their own lives as they choose, the parents will be forming an environment around the child that will tend to shape his budding loyalties and habits, and they will be providing in their own selves ready models for emulation.[21] This inevitable narrowing of options can yet be done without violation of the child's *C-right* of self-determination provided it is somehow in accordance with the child's actual or presumptive, explicit or tacit *consent*. But we can hardly ask the child's actual explicit consent to our formative decisions because at the point when these processes start – where the "twig begins to be bent" – he is not developed enough to give his consent. But neither has he values and preferences of his own for the parents to consult and treat as clues to what his disposition to give or withhold consent would be. At the early stage the parents cannot even ask in any helpful way what the child *will* be like, apart from the parental policies under consideration, when he *does* have relevant preferences, values, and the capacity to consent. That outcome will depend on the character the child will have then, which in part depends, in turn, on how his parents raise him now. They are now shaping the him who is to decide later and whose presumptive later decision cannot be divined. As Henley puts it: "Whether a certain sort of life would please a child often depends upon how he has been socialized, and so we cannot decide to socialize him for that life by asking whether that kind of life would please him."[22]

The paradox of self-determination can be put even more forcefully as an infinite regress. If the grown-up offspring is to determine his own life, and be at least in large part the product of his own "self-determination," he must already have a self fully formed and capable of doing the determining.

But he cannot very well have determined *that* self on his own, because he would have to have been already a formed self to do that, and so on, *ad infinitum*. The vicious circle is avoided only by positing an infinite series of prior selves, each the product of an earlier self.[23]

The paradoxes of self-fulfillment present much the same sort of appearance as the paradoxes of self-determination and can be expressed in quite parallel language. These arise, however, not when we ask what a child will come to prefer, choose, or consent to later in the exercise of his matured autonomy, but rather, simply, what would be good for him, his presumptive choice notwithstanding. To answer this question we must seek to learn his governing propensities, his skills and aptitudes, his highest "potential". We must gauge how his nature is "wound up" and in what direction he is faced, in order to determine what would fulfill his most basic tendencies. We stumble into the vicious circle when we note that if a person's own good is to be understood as self-fulfillment, we cannot fully know the small child's long term future good until its "nature" is fully formed, but equally we cannot determine how best to shape its nature until we know what will be for its own good. We cannot just leave the child's entire future open for him to decide later according to his settled adult values, because he must begin to acquire those values now in childhood, and he will in fact acquire his governing dispositions now, whatever we do. And in closing his future options in some ways now by our educating, our socializing, our choice of influential environments, we cannot be guided entirely by what accords with the child's own future character, because that character will in large part be a product of the self we are molding now. In a nutshell: the parents help create some of the interests whose fulfillment will constitute the child's own good. They cannot aim at an independent conception of the child's own good in deciding how to do this, because to some extent, the child's own good (self-fulfillment) depends on which interests the parents decide to create. The circle is thus closed.

**4**

Closed, but not closed tight. The plausible-sounding propositions that seem to lock us into paradox in reality are only approximate generalizations, merely partial truths whose soft spots make viable escape-hatches. The "paradoxes" stem from a failure to appreciate how various judgments used in their formulation are only partly true, and how certain central distinctions are matters of degree. It is an overstatement, for example, that there is any early stage at which a child's character is *wholly* unformed and his talents and temperament *entirely* plastic, without latent bias or limit, and another that there can be *no* "self-determination" unless the self that does the determining is already *fully* formed. Moreover, it is a distortion to represent the distinction between child and adult in the rigid manner presupposed by the "paradoxes."

There is no sharp line between the two stages of human life; they are really only useful abstractions from a continuous process of development every phase of which differs only in degree from that preceding it. Many or most of a child's *C*-rights-in-trust have already become *A*-rights by the time he is ten or twelve. Any "mere child" beyond the stage of infancy is only a child in some respects, and already an adult in others. Such dividing lines as the eighteenth or twenty first birthday are simply approximations (plausible guesses) for the point where *all* the natural rights-in-trust have become actual *A*-rights. In the continuous development of the relative-adult out of the relative-child there is no point before which the child himself has no part in his own shaping, and after which he is the sole responsible maker of his own character and life plan. The extent of the child's role in his own shaping is again a process of constant and continuous growth already begun at birth, as indeed is the "size" of his self, that is the degree to which it is already formed and fixed.

Right from the beginning the newborn infant has a kind of rudimentary character consisting of temperamental proclivities and a genetically fixed potential for the acquisition of various talents and skills. The standard sort of loving upbringing and a human social environment in the earliest years will be like water added to dehydrated food, filling it out and actualizing its stored-in tendencies. Then the child's earliest models for imitation will make an ineluctable mark on him. He will learn one language rather than another, for instance, and learn it with a particular accent and inflection. His own adult linguistic style will be in the making virtually from the beginning. For the first year or two he will have no settled dispositions of action and feeling of the kind Aristotle called virtues and vices (excellences and defects of character), but

as Aristotle said, he is born with the capacity to acquire such dispositions, and the process is underway very early as his basic habits of response are formed and reenforced.

At a time so early that the questions of how to socialize and educate the child have not even arisen yet, the twig will be bent in a certain definite direction. From then on, the parents in promoting the child's eventual autonomy and well-being will have to respect that initial bias from heredity and early environment. Thus from the beginning the child must – inevitably *will* – have some "input" in its own shaping, the extent of which will grow continuously even as the child's character itself does. I think that we can avoid, or at least weaken, the paradoxes if we remember that the child can contribute towards the making of his own self and circumstances in ever-increasing degree. Always the self that contributes to the making of the new self is itself the product both of outside influences and an earlier self that was not quite as fully formed. That earlier self, in turn, was the product both of outside influences and a still earlier self that was still less fully formed and fixed, and so on, all the way back to infancy. At every subsequent stage the immature child plays an ever-greater role in the creation of his own life, until at the arbitrarily fixed point of full maturity or adulthood, he is at last fully and properly in charge of himself, sovereign within his terrain, his more or less finished character the product of a complicated interaction of external influences and ever-increasing contributions from his own earlier self. At least that is how growth proceeds when parents and other authorities raise a child with maximal regard for the autonomy of the adult he will one day be. That is the most sense that we can make of the ideal of the "self-made person," but it is an intelligible idea, I think, with no paradox in it.

Similarly, the parents who raise their child in such a way as to promote his self-fulfillment most effectively will at every stage try to strengthen the basic tendencies of the child as manifested at that stage. They will give him opportunities to develop his strongest talents, for instance, after having enjoyed opportunities to discover by various experiments just what those talents are. And they will steer the child toward the type of career that requires the kind of temperament the child already has rather than a temperament that is alien to him by his very nature. There can be no self-fulfillment for a child prone to sedentary activity by his native body type and endowed with fine motor control over his sensitive fingers if he is inescapably led into a job calling for a large muscled, energetic person with high gross motor control but no patience for small painstaking tasks, or vice versa. The child will even have very basic tendencies toward various kinds of attitudes from an early stage, at least insofar as they grow naturally out of his inherited temperamental propensities. He may be the naturally gregarious, outgoing sort, or the kind of person who will naturally come to treasure his privacy and to keep his own counsels; he may appreciate order and structure more or less than spontaneity and freedom; he may be inclined, *ceteris paribus*, to respect or to challenge authority. Such attitudes grow from basic dispositions of temperament and are the germ in turn of

fundamental convictions and styles of life that the child will still be working out and trying to understand and justify when he is an adult. The discerning parent will see all of these things ever more clearly as the child grows older, and insofar as he steers the child at all, it will be in the child's own preferred directions. At the very least he will not try to turn him upstream and make him struggle against his own deepest currents. Then if the child's future is left open as much as possible for his own finished self to determine, the fortunate adult that emerges will already have achieved, without paradox, a certain amount of self-fulfillment, a consequence in large part of his own already autonomous choices in promotion of his own natural preferences.

## Notes

1. John Locke preferred the more uniform usage according to which all human rights are *A-C* rights. In his usage, from which I here depart, we are all *born* with certain rights which we possess throughout our lives, from infancy through senectitude. Some of these rights, however, children cannot exercise, though they continue to possess them until they acquire the requisite capability. "Thus we are born free as we are born rational; not that we have actually the exercise of either; age that brings one, brings with it the other too" (*Second Treatise of Government*, Section 61). It would be a mistake to elevate this terminological difference into a philosophical quarrel. Obviously Locke can say everything in his terminology that I can in mine and *vice versa*. He was concerned to emphasize the similarity in the moral status of children and adults, whereas this paper focuses on the differences. I have no objection if people talk about *A*-rights as if they are actually possessed by small infants (e.g. the right to vote as one pleases) provided it is clearly understood that they are "possessed" in the sense that they are held in trust for the autonomous adults the children will (probably) become one day, and they are subject to violation now in a way that is *sui generis*.
2. *Pace* William O. Douglas in his dissenting opinion in *Wisconsin v. Yoder*, 406 U.S. 205 (1972).
3. For an illuminating analysis of these three sided conflicts see Stuart J. Baskin, "State Intrusion into Family Affairs: Justifications and Limitations," 26 *Stanford Law Review* 1383 (1974).
4. Note on "Civil Restraint. Mental Illness, and the Right to Treatment," 77 *Yale Law Journal* 87 (1967).
5. *State v. Garber*, 197 Kan. 567 (1966).
6. J. S. Mill, *On Liberty*, Chap. 3, paragraph 2, 3.
7. *Wisconsin v. Yoder, et al.* 406 U.S. 205 (1972).
8. As made applicable to the states by the Fourteenth Amendment.
9. *Wisconsin v. Yoder, op. cit.*, pp. 209, 216.
10. Ibid., p. 213.
11. Ibid., p. 230.
12. Ibid.
13. Consider also the commonly heard argument that state policies that keep religious observances and practices out of the public schools have the effect of "establishing" one religion in preference to all the others, namely the "religion of secular humanism." The conclusion then presented is not that the state should try nevertheless to be as neutral as it can, but rather that since neutrality is absolutely impossible whichever policy is adopted, the state might as well permit Christian observances.
14. Ibid., p. 236.
15. Ibid., pp. 237–8.
16. Kenneth Henley, "The Authority to Educate," in *Having Children: Philosophical and Legal Reflections on Parenthood*, ed. Onora O'Neill and William Ruddick (New York: Oxford University Press, 1978), p. 255. Henley's excellent article is strongly recommended.
17. For a further analysis of self-fulfillment, see my "Absurd Self-fulfillment: An Essay on the Merciful Perversity of the Gods," in *Time and Cause: Essays Presented to Richard Taylor*, ed. Peter van Inwagen (Dortrecht: Reidel, 1979).
18. John Stuart Mill, *On Liberty*, Chapter V, paragraph 11.
19. This second interpretation of autonomy rights is defended in my essay "Legal Paternalism," *Canadian Journal of Philosophy*, vol. 1 (1971), pp. 105–24, and also in my "Freedom and Behavioral Control" in *The Encyclopedia of Bioethics*, ed. Warren T. Reich (New York: The Free Press, 1978).

20. See, for example, Jonathan Glover, *Causing Death and Saving Lives* (New York: Penguin Books, 1977), pp. 74–85.

21. Henley (see note 16 above) makes this point especially well in his discussion of the parents' religious rights: "In the early years of the child's socialization, he will be surrounded by the religious life of his parents; since the parents have a right to live such religious lives, and on the assumption that children will normally be raised by their parents, parental influence on the child's religious life is both legitimate and unavoidable. But at such an early stage it can hardly be said that coercion is involved; the child simply lives in the midst of a religious way of life and comes to share in it. But surely the assertion that the child is born with religious liberty must entail that parents are under at least moral constraints not to *force* their religious beliefs upon the child once he is capable of forming his own views . . ." (op. cit., pp. 260–1).

22. Henley, ibid., p. 256.

23. Cf. John Wisdom's not altogether playful argument that moral responsibility presupposes that we have *always* existed, in his *Problems of Mind and Matter* (Cambridge: Cambridge University Press, 1934), pp. 110–34.

# 15

# Justice, Autonomy, and the Good

## Eamonn Callan

### How Burdensome are the Burdens of Judgement?

I have argued that Rawls's political conception of the person severely erodes the distinction between public and non-public spheres and that the values embodied in that conception are necessary to the political education that Rawlsian political liberalism supports. To the extent that there is erosion, political education must mould and constrain the identity of citizens beyond the public sphere.

But how substantial should we expect the moulding and constraining to be? The idea we need to focus on here is the burdens of judgement. The burdens are a more subversive idea than Rawls's anodyne discussion of them would suggest. But to see this clearly, we need to keep a grip on the sense in which people must accept them in order to be reasonable. Presented as an abstract catalogue of causes of error and disagreement, the burdens of judgement are platitudinous, and their implications for the background culture of liberal politics appear slight. But nominal assent to a list of abstractions is not enough; the relevant acceptance must rather be an active and taxing psycho-

logical disposition, pervasively colouring the beliefs we form and the choices we make. A merely nominal assent, however widely shared, could not create the kind of mutual forbearance and respect in social cooperation that Rawls sees as the necessary manifestations of a shared reasonableness. After all, it is one thing to grant the truism that the concepts employed in framing our comprehensive doctrines are subject to hard cases or that we always select from an array of values that admit reasonable alternatives; it is quite another, when the doctrine I ardently uphold entails a particular resolution of a hard case or a certain choice from the range of available values, to acknowledge that opposing views are equally reasonable, and that the political significance of the doctrine I cherish must be curtailed by deference to the reasonableness of beliefs I vehemently reject.

If an active rather than a merely nominal acceptance of the burdens of judgement is a necessary end of the political education that Rawlsian political liberalism supports, how might such an acceptance be encouraged in children and adolescents among whom it has yet to develop? Imagine a child growing up in a home where a particular

Editor's title. Originally published in *Creating Citizens: Political Education and Liberal Democracy* (Oxford: Clarendon Press, 1997), Chapters 2 and 3, pp. 34–6, 39–41, 42, 60–9. Reprinted with permission of Oxford University Press.

comprehensive doctrine is affirmed that entails strong views on matters of both ethical and political controversy, such as homosexuality, economic inequality, abortion, and the like. These views might or might not be taught with respect for the child's growing powers of reason, but even if they were, active acceptance of the burdens of judgement is hardly the inevitable outcome. For the most part, parents will naturally reason with the child inside the framework of the comprehensive doctrines they favour. The desire to perpetuate their own deepest values in the lives of their children is fundamental to the project of parenthood as most people understand it, and so we should expect some tendency to soften the hardness of hard cases and to overlook the selectivity among values that any doctrine will embody. The family is no doubt the first and most important school of justice. Rawls knows that as well as anyone else (Rawls 1971: 462–7). But there may yet be some aspects of justice for which the family is generally an unsuitable educational vehicle. [ . . . ] But even in advance of that argument, it is surely obvious that acceptance of those particular burdens of judgement that stem from pluralism in conceptions of the good and the right is an end of political education for which many families will be ill-suited.

The natural partiality of the family as an instrument of moral education may make it a powerful ally for political liberalism by securing the survival across generations of strongly held convictions that compose an overlapping consensus of doctrines in support of a liberal constitution. Yet the same partiality is also a threat to political liberalism so far as doctrines learned in the family press outside the boundaries of a reasonable pluralism. That outcome is avoided only so far as future citizens learn at some stage to accept the burdens of judgement in other institutional settings, and the school is an obvious candidate for that role. If acceptance has to be the complex and onerous psychological disposition I have specified, the hardness of hard cases must be brought out by investigating specific ethical questions from multiple perspectives once the child or adolescent can learn to understand something of the variety of reasonable views from the inside; the effects of contingencies of social position and experience on disparities among such views must be imaginatively explored; and the various ways in which reasonable ethical doctrines select and order values must also be appreciated as these give shape to conflicting ways of life.

Now the educational task I have just described, although it is intended to address only the development of the sense of justice in tandem with the powers of reason, will profoundly affect the development of a conception of the good as well. That is inevitable once the burdens of judgement are applied to comprehensive and partially comprehensive doctrines. Indeed, Rawls explicitly notes that these burdens apply to the rational – that aspect of reason which corresponds to our capacity for a conception of the good – as well as to the reasonable (Rawls 1993: 56); and from the standpoint of education, the cultivation of the two moral powers cannot be parcelled out into separate, mutually insulated processes of learning. The attempt to understand the reasonableness of convictions that may be in deep conflict with doctrines learned in the family cannot be carried through without inviting the disturbing question that these convictions might be the framework of a better way of life, or at least one that is just as good. That question is unavoidable because to understand the reasonableness of beliefs that initially seem wrong or even repellent I must imaginatively entertain the perspective those very beliefs furnish, and from that perspective my own way of life will look worse, or at least no better, than what that perspective affirms. Although many who undergo this kind of education might eventually answer the question in a way that reaffirms commitments instilled within the family, these have a new psychological context that makes it implausible to say that the 'same' conception of the good is affirmed before and after we have come to accept the burdens of judgement.[1] One obvious difference is that the original commitments are now ratified on the basis of independent reflection rather than sheer deference to the dictates of the family or community into which one is born. Stephen Macedo has observed that the public virtues of liberalism 'have a private life' (Macedo 1990: 265). That is obviously true of comprehensive liberalism, and it looks as if political liberalism is no exception to the rule.

[ . . . ]

## Back to Comprehensive Liberalism

But what is left now of the contrast between political and comprehensive liberalism in their relation to pluralism? Rawls wants to say there is a large difference, and that the difference is brought into relief in the practice of civic education:

The liberalisms of Kant and Mill may lead to requirements designed to foster the values of autonomy and individuality as ideals to govern much if not all of life. But political liberalism has a different aim and requires far less. It will ask that children's education include such things as knowledge of their constitutional and civic rights. . . . Moreover, their education should also prepare them to be fully cooperating members of society and enable them to be self-supporting; it should also encourage the political virtues so that they want to honor the fair terms of cooperation with the rest of society.   (Rawls 1993: 199)

But the contrast Rawls draws is bogus because the political virtues that implement the fair terms of cooperation bring autonomy through the back door of political liberalism. That becomes obvious once we reflect on the educational task of securing active acceptance of the burdens of judgement. Future citizens must be taught to think in particular ways about doctrines that properly lie outside the scope of public reason: they must become critically attuned to the wide range of reasonable political disagreement within the society they inhabit and to the troubling gap between reasonable agreement and the whole moral truth. This will require serious imaginative engagement with rival views about good and evil, right and wrong, and this in turn means that these views must be confronted in their own terms, without the peremptory dismissal they might receive according to whatever doctrine a child learns in the family. The moral authority of the family and the various associations in which the child grows up must be questioned to the extent that the society contains reasonable alternatives to whatever that authority prescribes. All this looks like a pretty familiar depiction of central elements in an education for autonomy because the psychological attributes that constitute an active acceptance of the burdens of reason, such as the ability and inclination to subject received ethical ideas to critical scrutiny, also constitute a recognizable ideal of ethical autonomy.[2]

Rawls is ready to concede that the accidental effect, though not the intention, of the education that political liberalism demands might sometimes be acceptance of a comprehensive ideal such as autonomy by children whose families adhere to other moral doctrines: 'The unavoidable consequences of reasonable requirements for children's education may have to be accepted, often with regret' (Rawls 1993: 200). But the distinction between educational intentions and unintended effects marks no distance

between comprehensive and Rawls's political liberalism. Learning to accept the burdens of judgement in the sense necessary to political liberalism is conceptually inseparable from what we ordinarily understand as the process of learning to be ethically (and not just politically) autonomous. Rawls cannot coherently say that coming to accept the burdens of judgement is an unintended effect of the education his theory implies. And since coming to accept the burdens means attaining a substantial ethical autonomy, he cannot regard the achievement of autonomy as a merely accidental consequence of the pursuit of humbler educational goals.

The upshot of all this is that Rawlsian political liberalism is really a kind of closet comprehensive liberalism. My argument has been an attempt to pull it out of the closet. To agree with Rawls is to accept a pervasive and powerful constraint (the burdens of judgement) on how we should think about the various convictions and practices that proliferate in the background culture of liberal politics and how we should form our own convictions and make our own choices in that setting. That constraint enjoins us to be ethically autonomous to a substantial degree and, given the requirement of reciprocity, to respect the autonomy of others when we cooperate politically with them.

[ . . . ]

Suppose for the moment that the political argument for autonomy is sound so far as it goes. That would leave us with a more manageable ethical question about the overall value of autonomy than we would otherwise have. The success of the political argument would mean that the justification of educational practices that encourage autonomy in future citizens does not require us to show that it is necessary to the good life, even under the general social conditions of modern liberal democracies. All that needs to be shown is that autonomy does not make our lives bad. For only if it had that consequence would we have grounds to think that the general liabilities of autonomy might outweigh its substantial political benefits as a necessary ingredient of the virtue of justice.

The claim that autonomy makes our lives bad might be pressed from many different perspectives. The most interesting general objections will identify some widely prized goods and try to show that the growth of autonomy is at odds with their realization. Recent communitarian objections to liberal conceptions of autonomy have taken this form, and these certainly deserve a careful response. [ . . . ]

## Simple Integrity

Someone has simple integrity when three conditions hold. First, the roles with which the individual identifies circumscribe her pursuit of the good closely and locate that good within the shared practices of her community. Second, the responsibilities her roles entail are harmonized, so that there is ordinarily no or at most modest friction between them. Third, the individual identifies wholeheartedly with the role or configuration of roles that structures her life, and she lives in close fidelity to its requirements. That is not just to say that her commitment is characterized by a high degree of assurance; truly wholehearted commitment is also untainted by hypocrisy, self-deception, or evasion.

Membership of a particular religion is a role that commonly entails acceptance of the ideal of simple integrity, even if the ideal is only roughly approximated in the lives of most ordinary believers. The role gives a steady focus to one's pursuit of the good inside a community of like-minded people. Faith imposes the necessary harmony on the domain of responsibilities because its demands are accorded a paramount status in deliberation, and a coherent interpretation is provided of the significance of other attachments. The condition of wholehearted-ness is affirmed in that the individual must be genuinely devoted to God or her gods if the demands of faith are to be met. So when a distinguished philosopher of religion, who also happens to be a Presbyterian minister, suggests that Christians must bring Jesus along on their honeymoon, especially on their honeymoon, he is not joking (Adams 1986: 188–9). Those of us who do not share his faith may smile, but that is only because we share the liberal assumption that all roles, whether it be as lover of this person or worshipper of that god, are discrete spheres of engagement among which the autonomous agent freely moves – or aimlessly flits. But some will say that our assumption merely betrays the prejudice of those who have forgotten the value of simple integrity.

Consider how the value of simple integrity might be used to argue against an education that would conduce to autonomy. The child who is born into a conservative religious family need not have made any independent choice to be a member of her particular religion for membership to be the supreme commitment that determines her good. By the time she is capable of choice, her religion already constitutes what MacIntyre calls 'the given

starting-point' for pursuit of the good (MacIntyre 1981: 204–5). And if part of the value membership provides is simple integrity, there is reason to argue that induction into her role as one of the faithful should not have to pull against the appeal of rival values. To subject her faith to that crisis would be to endanger the wholehearted commitment upon which simple integrity depends. Notice that to accept this conclusion one need not take a favourable view of whatever metaphysical pretensions the child's faith might entail. The argument only asks of us to accept the centrality of simple integrity to the good life and that virtue's dependence on a particular kind of social and educational setting.

## Integrity and Pluralism

I approach the question of the value of simple integrity indirectly by looking at an example of a life in which it is instantiated; then I compare it with a life in which is has been lost.

My example of simple integrity is Jacob of Josefov, the protagonist of Isaac Bashevis Singer's novel *The Slave* (Singer 1980a). Jacob's story takes place in seventeenth-century Poland in the years immediately after a Cossack invasion. Jacob's family was slaughtered, and he has been sold into slavery far from his native village. There he tries to maintain his faith despite total isolation from his fellow Jews, recurring doubt about the goodness of God, and his love for Wanda, a gentile who shows him great kindness during his enslavement. Although Jacob is ransomed by the Jews of Josefov, he secretly returns to the village of his captivity after a dream that Wanda is pregnant. The Torah requires this, since he cannot allow his child to grow up among idolators. Jacob and Wanda flee together and begin a new life in a remote village. Wanda has converted and is now Sarah, Jacob's pious wife. But her original identity must be kept secret, since the penalty for conversion under Polish law is death. Sarah dies in childbirth, although not before the fact of her conversion is disclosed. So Jacob must run away with his newborn child, isolated once again from his people. But at another level, Jacob continues to belong to his people, and his sense of belonging is powerful even as he flees. Recalling the words of his biblical namesake upon his deathbed, Jacob sees his own tragedy as but another enactment of a story that is part of the history of God's inscrutable dealings with his chosen people:

His name was Jacob also; he too had lost a beloved wife, the daughter of an idolator, among strangers; Sarah too was buried by the way and had left him a son. Like the Biblical Jacob, he was crossing the river, bearing only a staff, pursued by another Esau. Everything remained the same: the ancient love, the ancient grief. Perhaps four thousand years would again pass; somewhere, at another river, another Jacob would walk mourning another Rachel.   (Singer 1980a: 258–9)

The emotional resonance of this passage, and indeed the novel as a whole depends on its evocation of a mode of life in which individual experience is invested with the significance of an immemorial narrative, and thereby rescued from the pointlessness of brute suffering. Jacob is the very antithesis to the ethically disinherited children described by MacIntyre, cast adrift by an upbringing that leaves them 'unscripted, anxious stutterers in their actions as in their words' because they have not been initiated into a world of narratively structured roles (MacIntyre 1981: 201). In Jacob's case, his role as one of the chosen people is the supreme commitment of his life, and all his experience is enmeshed with the story of Jews who accepted the burdens of that role before him and those who will accept them after he dies – his biblical namesake as well as the Jacob who will mourn another Rachel four thousand years hence. Despite his status as an outcast, his love and grief are not the emotions of a solitary man but 'the ancient love, the ancient grief' of all who have contended with suffering and evil while submitting to the authority of God.

So Jacob very obviously meets the first two conditions of simple integrity. His understanding of the good is fixed by the shared understandings of his community, and the roles in terms of which he defines his good entail no conflicting responsibilities because one role is absolutely sovereign. Jacob also evinces the wholeheartedness that simple integrity demands. One might be inclined to deny or at least qualify that claim because of the religious doubts which beset him throughout much of the novel. But there are different ways in which engagement with a particular role may be subject to doubt, and not all of these can be aptly viewed as a dilution of simple integrity. Although Jacob is sometimes racked with doubt, his honest and considered view is that this is merely the work of Satan. Thus he never identifies with his own doubts, never allows them to become part of the fabric of his commitments and beliefs. Doubt is a potent force in his life, but it is understood as an utterly

alien thing, at odds with that true self who will follow wherever God leads. This purely episodic doubt is very different from misgivings that come to qualify a belief in the propriety of a particular role commitment. The man who arrives at the considered view that his doubts about the existence of God are well-grounded can no longer find his true self unambivalently in religious practice, unlike Jacob who 'can forget the fool within, with his fruitless questions' (Singer 1980a: 104).

If we insisted that immunity to even episodic doubt were necessary to the wholeheartedness of simple integrity, we would have an absurdly demanding condition of that virtue. But it does seem reasonable to say that simple integrity is destroyed when doubt about our commitments becomes a settled qualification to them. When that happens in the case of religious conviction, for example, one can no longer be confident that the self who worships (or tries to) rather than the self who doubts is not 'the fool within'. There is no longer a sharply delineated true self, pitted against the menacing forces of doubt; instead the self is simply a site for inconclusive warfare between faith and its enemies. There may be room for integrity here, but it could not be simple integrity.

My foil for Jacob of Josefov is his creator. The story of Isaac Bashevis Singer exhibits a very different pattern to the life of Jacob, despite obvious common ground. Singer was born into a devout Jewish family in Poland, and the doubts that assailed Jacob afflicted Singer at a very early age. But for Singer there could be no final victory over doubt. His brother introduced him to secular literature and modern science, and although these did not give him a creed he could live with, they further alienated him from the faith of his parents. That faith remained a thing to be admired, but from a distance that Singer himself could not traverse. The young man whom he describes in his autobiographical *Love and Exile* lives a life so chaotic that it borders on comedy. He is a philanderer with ascetic leanings, whose reading ranges from the Cabala to contemporary novels, and whose restless imagination seems the only fixed point in his identity. By the time the book ends, Singer's career as a writer in America is under way; but as an exile from his homeland and the traditions of his forbears, there can be none of the moral poise of Jacob of Josefov as he flees his community. *Love and Exile* closes with Singer's poignant declaration that he is 'lost in America, lost forever' (Singer 1984: 352).

The vocation of the artist does give shape to the story of this avowedly lost soul. But this is not a role with established conventions that closely circumscribe one's pursuit of the good and place one in a community with shared moral understandings. So even if Singer's commitment to his art were passionate and unambivalent, this would provide only a faint parallel to Jacob's integrity. The twentieth-century novel is a place where voices talk about everything in every possible way, as Salman Rushdie has said (Rushdie 1991: 428). That is certainly true of Singer's fiction and the mercurial self to whom it gives expression. For although he can sympathetically portray the virtues of Jacob of Josefov, he can also celebrate the implacable scepticism and contempt for tradition of a man who is Jacob's spiritual opposite (Singer 1980b). The world of Singer's imagination is shot through with moral ambiguity, and although good and evil are his abiding preoccupation he does not pretend to see them with the precision and certainty of Jacob.

Perhaps the deepest contrast between Jacob and Singer is revealed when we think of their lives in terms of MacIntyre's metaphor of the good life as a quest (MacIntyre 1981: 203). That metaphor has been taken by some to indicate a creeping liberalism in MacIntyre's thought (J. White and P. White 1986: 157–8; Macedo 1990: 327), as if what he had in mind were an open-ended search for life's meaning on the model that Singer's memoir might illustrate. But the quest MacIntyre envisages is informed from its beginning by some partly determinate sense of the ultimate end of human life, and progress in the quest is measured by the gradual realization of that end, as well as an unfolding understanding of its personal significance. Jacob's story is just such a quest. His task is to follow wherever God leads because he is God's 'slave'. His death as a man who maintained simple integrity against the temptations of the world is the consummation of his long journey. On the other hand, when Singer confronts his future as a man who is 'lost forever' I take him to mean that insofar as his life can be construed as an ethical quest it is an irrevocable failure. People who cannot understand their lives in relation to a paramount good higher than whatever else the world has to offer – the *telos* of human life, as MacIntyre would have it – can have no clear and constant sense of when they are moving towards or away from the good; and when that loss of direction is felt with grief or regret it will be natural to describe one's predicament, as Singer does, through images of disorientation or abandonment.

A life of integrity must exhibit some inner consistency or unity. We might compare such a life to a work of art that dissolves into absurdity in the absence of some overarching unity that makes it more than the sum of its parts. A musical composition cannot be just an assemblage of notes or phrases, a poem is not merely a rubble of words and images; and a life of integrity must be more than a random series of actions and experiences. Simple integrity may be seen as ensuring the necessary unity of a good or meaningful life. One might say that good lives express who we are, and then it might be tempting to add that without simple integrity there is nothing sufficiently determinate to express. Comparing lives with respect to unity, like comparing works of art along that dimension, may often be idle. But we are on very safe ground in saying that there is a lot more cohesion in Jacob's life than in Singer's, and that Singer's life seems perilously close to disintegration. And even if our own lives are rather more like Singer's than Jacob's, we may be inclined to contemplate the gap between us and Jacob with some of Singer's feeling at the end of *Love and Exile*: we too are lost in America, so to speak.

But these thoughts cannot amount to a credible argument for saying that simple integrity is the only integrity. A life can certainly descend into absurdity when riven by conflict between radically disparate roles or the kind of anomie which threatens to overwhelm Singer in his youth. Yet the sheer singleness of purpose of those with simple integrity is not the only alternative to absurdity. The analogy between the unity of a good life and the unity of a work of art is indeed a revealing one. But the trouble with equating integrity with simple integrity is that the equation does not take that analogy seriously enough.

Suppose a critic compares one of the great, sprawling novels of the nineteenth-century, *War and Peace* perhaps, with some clever little novella that belabours a single theme, and she deprecates Tolstoy's masterpiece for its comparative lack of unity. That would be a gross mistake. One might be tempted to object that there are other criteria of aesthetic excellence than unity – complexity or the like – and that *War and Peace* is peerless by these other standards. But that would be to concede too much to the critic because it would suggest that so far as unity goes she is right when surely she is wrong. What she does not understand is that the spacious structure of an epic novel can accommodate many diverse themes, weave together different and contrasting stories, without lapsing into absurdity, and at its best may achieve a depth which is itself a precious kind of unity. 'Depth involves discerning an underlying unity among apparently complex and unrelated phenomena' (Kekes 1990: 440). Of course, the unity of aesthetic depth can also be achieved by a narrow focusing of purpose. There is Kafka as well as Tolstoy, Racine as well as Shakespeare. But if the unity of a work of art is to be our model for that unity of a life to which we might rationally aspire, there seems no reason to suppose that a richly variegated life such as Singer's, which combines many diverse ideals and affinities into an intricate whole, might not achieve the kind of unity worth having.

Moreover, comparing Jacob and Singer with respect to the integration of their lives is only indirectly relevant to the real possibilities of integrity that each life affords. In an important recent article, Cheshire Calhoun proposes that standing for one's own best judgement about how to live, rather than the integration of the self, is the core of integrity (Calhoun 1995). This seems right. The religious doubts that torment Jacob in the wake of the Cossack massacres are part of the evidence for his integrity. His doubts are part of his struggle to form his best judgement about how to live in a particular deliberative setting. Singer contrasts Jacob's spiritual travails with the complacency and self-deception of those Jews who resumed their lives as if nothing important had happened. The faith that survives Jacob's ordeal of doubt is truly wholehearted, in the sense I stipulated above, not only by virtue of its ultimate assurance but also because it does not depend on the evasion of disturbing possibilities that others lacked the courage to face (Singer 1980a: 101–6). If the integration of a life were the key to integrity, then Jacob's self-satisfied fellow Jews would be the paragons of that virtue, and his wrenching doubts would be a stain on his integrity rather than its exemplary expression. A life of integrity requires an inner consistency or unity *only* to whatever extent standing for one's best judgement does.

But the human world that Singer so artfully creates in *The Slave* is not our world of pluralism. It is a world of sharp moral polarities of the kind we might find in an ancient folk tale, devoid of all gradation and ambiguity. Beyond the borders of Jacob's faith and the quest it enjoins, Singer depicts a nightmare of unremitting evil and ugliness, populated by bestial peasants and dissolute nobles. The moral contrasts that frame Singer's narrative are part of what persuades us to see Jacob as a man of simple integrity: someone struggling to form his best judgement about how to live in *this* world could not but choose as Jacob did, or so we are invited to think. But then the charm of simple integrity begins to seem like so much idle nostalgia. For our moral world is replete with gradations and complexities, a world in which reasonable people reach very different conclusions about the good and the right, and yet all must find some basis for a decent society in which they might live together. Reading a novel set in premodern Poland relieves us of worries about the voting habits that Jacob of Josefov might have if he lived among us. But someone who regards all gentiles as little more than benighted idolaters is perhaps unlikely to exhibit the civility we would want.

The process of forming one's best judgement about how to live depends on careful assessment of the reasons available in a given social setting for living one way rather than another. That is why I cannot form my own best judgement without a keen, albeit critical regard for the best judgement of those who share the milieu within which I must choose (Calhoun 1995: 259–60). But reasonable pluralism means that the best judgement of many will be both very different from mine and yet defensible, and to pretend otherwise where reasonable pluralism holds is sheer bad faith.

This is the truth in Bernard Williams's much quoted observation that for us there is no route back from reflectiveness (Williams 1985: 163–4). As an empirical generalization, Williams's claim is false. Many if not most of us are still sufficiently unreflective that the question of whether to go back or not does not even arise, and we often raise our children so as to pre-empt the question for them too. Powerful forces in contemporary societies – from the revival of ancient tribalisms to the atomizing tendencies of a global economy – may further erode the social space for individual and collective thoughtfulness in our lives (Barber 1995). But Williams's observation can be read as expressing an important ethical truth: so long as reasonable pluralism obtains, the attempt to formulate one's best judgement about how to live must proceed in light of due reflection on the conflicting judgements of reasonable others, who may understand something important we ourselves have yet failed to grasp. We cannot change that predicament simply by silencing them or pretending that their thoughts are irrelevant to our integrity. Therefore, an education that seeks to arrest the development of autonomy so as to protect the growth of simple integrity runs the risk of being self-defeating. Such an education might well succeed in instilling the moral assurance that simple integrity entails, but only at the cost of entrenching a complacency or close-mindedness that is destructive of real integrity, simple or otherwise.

Unlike Jacob, Singer came to occupy a milieu of reasonable pluralism, initially through reading secular literature, and the result was that a life of simple integrity was no longer possible for him. To be sure, even the individual who fits the pattern of Singer must impose some order upon his life, sorting through the ambivalences and hesitations that respect for the best judgement of others will tend to elicit, and this cannot be done by harmonizing all possible values into some optimum composite. Yet if one lives in consciousness of the variety of good lives, it is natural to want to encompass many values in one's life, and so instead of the tight cohesion of a life of simple integrity one ends up with a pattern rather more messy and unsteady, but perhaps richly fulfilling for all that, and just as expressive in its own way of respect for an ethical order that is not reducible to the projections of individual desire.[3]

Paradoxically, those who live with an openness to the diversity of good lives will also be conscious of the losses which their openness exacts. If simple integrity is itself within the category of such lives, its loss may be felt with the pathos of Singer at the end of *Love and Exile*. But on reflection one may decide that the gains offset the loss or that what is lost is not a real option anyhow. Giving up on the good life as a linear quest may occasion a painful feeling of disorientation. But it may also yield a powerful sense of liberation.

## Autonomy and the Good: A Modest Convergence

I have argued that autonomy is an ideal unscathed by a battery of communitarian objections that suggest its realization would alienate us from the good.[4] But my modest thesis is only that the autonomy required by the development of justice need not make our lives bad; I do not say the autonomy intrinsic to justice is needed to make our lives good. The relation between autonomy and integrity that I sketched in [the previous section] might appear to support the more ambitious thesis that autonomy

is essential to our good under pluralism. If forming my own best judgement about how to live requires me to reflect autonomously on the judgements that others make and on the criticisms they might level against mine, then how can a good life be possible at all if I shirk the requirement?

The range of things that make our lives good are many and various. Plausible monistic theories of the good, such as the subtler forms of utilitarianism, cannot deny this. They only acquire some credibility by accepting the diversity of goods, and then telling a story about how the diversity disguises a unity that is revealed by the right theory (Becker 1992). Now the quality of anyone's judgement about how to live could hardly be more than one important element in the goodness of her life. If we could trade-off some autonomy to ensure that our children turned out well and did not die before us, I suspect that almost all of us would do so without thinking that might be a poor bargain. To say this is not to go back on my claim that under pluralism autonomy is deeply implicated in the virtue of integrity. But the value of maximal integrity may sometimes be an unreliable guide to what would make our lives good or better, all things considered, given the great variety of things that affect our well-being.

There is a difference between forming my best judgement about how to live and arriving at the judgement that is merely good enough, so to speak. The fact that some of the more philosophically inclined among us may say that only the best judgement will suffice does not mean that our cerebral idiosyncrasies reveal the final truth about the good life for anyone, much less everyone. Some significant degree of autonomous development might be necessary to our well-being, even if it is not quite the radical and wide-ranging autonomy associated with the virtue of justice. That is likely for a couple of reasons that have already been touched on. A good life could not be devoid of integrity, although it might fall well short of maximal integrity, and a good life could hardly be lived in utter disregard of the conditions of responsible choice. Given the connection between integrity and responsible choice on the one hand and autonomy on the other, a life that spurns autonomy altogether and is yet good seems scarcely imaginable. [ . . . ]

The point to be emphasized here is that the ambitious thesis about the convergence between autonomy and the good is simply irrelevant to what I want to say about the proper ends of political education. The core of my argument is the thesis that the development of the virtue of justice under pluralism implies the growth of autonomy to a notably sophisticated level. We would have strong reason to reject an education that encourages that process if the autonomy at issue made our lives bad as a rule. Some communitarian arguments suggest that autonomy does make our lives bad, but these have turned out to be entirely unconvincing. Therefore, we have no grounds to revise the conception of civic education that Rawls's political conception of the person would warrant. The proposal that the very substantial degree of autonomy justice demands of us is also essential to our well-being is beside the point and probably false.

## Notes

1. I assume here that we have ruled out the kind of integrity-destroying compartmentalization that I discussed earlier as a way of preserving doctrines learned in the non-public sphere from doubts provoked by the burdens of judgement.

2. The subversive impetus of the educational task to which Rawls is implicitly committed is easy to underestimate if we think of the autonomy that is relevant merely as a particular capacity. The claim that autonomy is a capacity (or repertoire of capacities) is familiar in contemporary philosophical literature (e.g. G. Dworkin 1988; Meyers 1989). By itself, the acquisition of new capacities does not necessarily affect the learner's basic values at all, however complex the capacities might be. People acquire the ability to do calculus or speak a foreign language, and what they learn has not the slightest effect on their prior ethical loyalties. But the accession of autonomy in the sense that matters here is an alteration of character rather than a mere expansion to a repertoire of capacities. 'Autonomy' signifies not merely the ability to subject received ideas to critical scrutiny; it also refers to the motivational and affective propensities that guide the exercise of the ability in securing a self-directed life. Rawls's argument compels us to construe its latent commitment to autonomy as a matter of character rather than bare capacity because we fall short of active acceptance of the burdens of judgement in the absence of the motivational and affective propensities that would support the exercise of the capacity for criticism. The difference between capacity and character is educationally as well as politically important. For it suggests that an education directed towards autonomy in the sense that sustains civic virtue will attempt to elicit the desire to think autonomously, nourish a proper pride in independent judgement and a disdain for both thoughtless conformity and nonconformity, all the while refining the deliberative capacities that desire and emotion will inform. All this makes the educational task a lot more controversial than it might otherwise be.

3. The aspiration towards objectivity or truth that is relevant here might be expressed through the kind of ethical cognitivism that P. F. Strawson has expounded: 'One cannot read Pascal or Flaubert, Nietzsche or Goethe, Shakespeare or Tolstoy, without encountering these profound truths. It is certainly possible, in a cooly analytic frame of mind, to mock the whole idea of the profound truth; but we are guilty of mildly bad faith if we do. For in most of us the ethical imagination succumbs again and again to *these* pictures of man, and it is precisely as truth that we wish to characterize them while they hold us captive' (Strawson 1974: 28–9). Notice that it is crucial to the kind of experience Strawson here describes that 'the profound truth' is encountered not as a mere object of desire. Finding such 'truth' in Tolstoy, say, is not like discovering a new flavour of ice-cream one likes. The 'truth' is rather something that holds us captive, that elicits an assent at least phenomenologically the same as we experience in the shock of insight in less epistemologically controversial areas of our lives. What is intimated in such experiences is an understanding of value quite different from crass subjectivism. But since 'the profound truth' may point in directions at odds with the roles we currently occupy and the shared values of our community, it is an understanding of value which does not lend itself to a comfortably communitarian reading either.

4. [Editor's note: Only the objection pertaining to integrity could be included in this selection.]

## References

Adams, R. M. (1986) 'The Problem of Total Devotion', in Audi and Wainwright (1986), 169–94.

Audi, R., and Wainwright, W. J. (eds.) (1986) *Rationality, Religious Belief, and Moral Commitment* (Ithaca, NY).

Barber, B. R. (1995) *Jihad vs. McWorld* (New York).

Becker, L. C. (1992) 'Good Lives: Prolegomena', *Social Philosophy and Policy*, 9: 15–37.

Calhoun, C. (1995) 'Standing for Something', *Journal of Philosophy*, 92: 235–60.

Cooper, D. E. (ed.) (1986) *Education, Values and Mind: Essays for R. S. Peters* (London).

Dworkin, G. (1988) *The Theory and Practice of Autonomy* (Cambridge).

Kekes, J. (1990) 'Moral Depth', *Philosophy*, 65: 439–53.

Macedo, S. (1990) *Liberal Virtues: Citizenship, Virtue and Community in Liberal Constitutionalism* (Oxford).

MacIntyre, A. (1981) *After Virtue* (Notre Dame, IN).

Meyers, D. T. (1989) *Self, Society, and Personal Choice* (New York).

Rawls, J. (1971) *A Theory of Justice* (Cambridge, Mass.).

Rawls, J. (1993) *Political Liberalism* (New York).

Rushdie, S. (1991) *Imaginary Homelands: Essays and Criticism, 1981–1991* (London).

Singer, I. B. (1980a) *The Slave* (New York).

Singer, I. B. (1980b) 'The Blasphemer', in *A Friend of Kafka and Other Stories* (New York).

Singer, I. B. (1984) *Love and Exile* (New York).

Strawson, P. F. (1974) *Freedom and Resentment and Other Essays* (London).

White, P. and White, J. (1986) 'Education, Liberalism and the Human Good', in Cooper (1986), 149–71.

Williams, B. (1985) *Ethics and the Limits of Philosophy* (Cambridge, MA).

# 16

# "Mistresses of their Own Destiny": Group Rights, Gender, and Realistic Rights of Exit*

## Susan Moller Okin

Many recent arguments for rights or exemptions for religious or other cultural groups that may not themselves be liberal are based on liberal premises – whether the central liberal value be individual autonomy or tolerance for diversity of ways of life.[1] Any consistent defense of group rights or exemptions that is based on liberal premises has to ensure that at least one individual right – the right to exit one's group of origin – trumps any group right. What this entails will be explored later, but for several reasons, the claim itself seems prima facie incontrovertible. Not to be able to leave the group in which one has been raised for an alternative mode of life is a serious violation of the kind of freedom that is basic to liberalism. Indeed, advocates of the rights of groups that do not espouse or practice liberal principles with regard to their own members frequently justify these rights provisionally: any group to which such rights are accorded must (at least) allow its members the right of exit. It seems, moreover, that any liberal defender of the rights of groups should recognize that individuals must be not only formally free but substantively and more or less equally free to leave their religions or cultures of origin; they must have realistic rights of exit.

Given this, it is surprising that so little attention has been paid in the literature about multicultural group rights to the fact that persons in different subgroups within most cultural and religious groups have very different chances of being able to exit from them successfully. As I shall argue here, in many cultural or religious groups on whose behalf liberal theorists have argued for special rights or exemptions, women are far less likely than men to be able to exercise the right of exit. They need not even be formally discriminated against in the public sphere, though they often are, for this to be so. For sex discrimination of various kinds is more likely than other forms of discrimination to occur out of public view, within the domestic sphere. Wherever it occurs, the unequal treatment of girls and women can mean, as I shall show, that by the time they reach young adulthood in many cultures and religions, they are effectively far less able to exit their respective groups of origin than are men. Any liberal group rights theorist – especially any who is concerned to defend the claims of illiberal groups to rights or exemptions – should be concerned about this inequality. For some individuals not to be able to choose an alternative mode of life, when

Previously published in *Ethics* 112 (January 2002): pp. 205–30. © 2002 The University of Chicago. Reprinted by permission of the University of Chicago Press.

others in the group are far more likely to be able to do so, is a serious violation of the equality of persons that is basic to liberalism.

My argument has three main parts. First, I show, looking at three examples, that liberal defenders of group rights tend not to take gender inequality as seriously as other forms of morally arbitrary inequality (such as that of race or caste, for example) when considering group rights and the limitations that should be placed on them by anyone starting from liberal premises. Second, I specify and discuss a number of reasons that contribute to women's being, in many cultural contexts, significantly less able than men to chart their own courses of life – outside of their community of origin if they should so choose. I then return to the three theorists discussed earlier, looking at their arguments for why religious or cultural groups – whether liberal or illiberal in their internal practices – must permit their members the right to exit the group. Each of the three calls on the right of exit at least in part to lessen the effect of illiberal or oppressive internal group practices. I show, drawing on the second section, that the option of exit is, in the great majority of cases concerning group rights, considerably less likely to be available to female than to male members of the group.

I conclude that the theories I examine thus contain several problematic elements. If girls and women are treated unequally in various important ways within their cultural groups, it cannot but affect their capacities to exercise the right of exit that is of crucial importance to each theory. Moreover, women's having an unequal capacity to exit leads to another significant inequality, for it cannot but affect their potential to influence the directions taken by the group. Thus they have less chance of being able to change the group's norms and practices – including being able to remedy their status and to achieve gender equality within the group. To call on the right of exit as a palliative for oppression is unsatisfactory for another reason, too, for in many circumstances, oppressed persons, in particular women, are not only less able to exit but have many reasons not to *want* to exit their culture of origin; the very idea of doing so may be unthinkable. Rather, they want, and should have the right, to be treated fairly within it. Thus, I conclude, the right of exit, while no doubt important, does not have the clout it is often thought to have in arguments defending the rights of illiberal groups within liberal contexts. Instead, it is inherently problematic. Those most

likely to need it are those least likely to be able to employ it. Neither may they see it as a desirable or even an imaginable option.

## Gender and other Forms of Inequality in Group Rights Theories

As I have argued elsewhere, tensions exist between the feminist project of achieving equality between the sexes and the multicultural project of recognizing minority religious or other cultural groups by granting them special group rights.[2] Both the neglect of significant groups, whose interests may differ, within groups and the lack of attention to the private sphere have resulted in a widespread failure to recognize that, in cases where groups with more patriarchal beliefs and practices exist as minorities within contexts that are generally less patriarchal, women may well be harmed rather than benefited by special group rights. But until recently, inequalities between the sexes within groups received scant attention from those arguing for group rights. Even those – such as Will Kymlicka – who explicitly deny rights to cultural or religious groups that overtly discriminate against women are insufficiently attentive to private sphere discrimination, which often has serious impacts on women's well-being and life opportunities.[3] Not surprisingly, though, liberals who defend the right of illiberal, overtly discriminatory groups to regulate the lives of their members pose greater problems from a feminist point of view.

Ayelet Shachar has recently published very important work addressing these problems.[4] She has critiqued accommodations of cultural or religious groups that include differential membership status for women or give them unequal rights in marriage and divorce. In doing so, she has shed considerable light, as almost no other theorist has, on "the troubling fact that some categories of 'at-risk' group members are being asked to shoulder a disproportionate share of the costs of multiculturalism."[5] Shachar's and my diagnoses of the problem overlap, although her treatment of many of the cases and issues is both more detailed and more comprehensive. We also arrive at similar conclusions about how to address the tension between women's equality and multicultural group rights; in particular, we both insist that any legitimate liberal model of multiculturalism "take into account . . . the voices of less powerful group members" – notably, women.[6] Somewhat unaccountably, then, Shachar distances herself from my position, which she labels the "re-universalized citizenship" response and presents as "requir[ing] that women make a choice of penalties between their rights as citizens and their group identities."[7]

Notwithstanding this misconception, Shachar's feminist analysis of the issues is excellent, and it is no coincidence that she is one of the very few theorists concerned with group rights who takes exception to the exit solution – addressing in particular the problem of women being offered exit rights as a response if and when they object to their treatment within their cultural group. As she says, the "troubling doctrine of 'implied consent' assumes that those who have not used the exit option have implicitly agreed to their own subordination."[8]

More generally, in the context of arguments for group rights, as I have suggested, the right of exit is cited as helping to legitimate the illiberal treatment of some or all group members. More generally, discrimination against women and girls is, at best, overlooked or mentioned briefly, only to be passed over. Not infrequently, it is given special status in a negative sense – by being perceived as somehow not really discrimination or at least absolved from the scrutiny that is given to other types of discrimination. It is, of course, in one sense not surprising that gender inequality is less or differently scrutinized, even often ignored, by liberals arguing for group rights. For, as I have argued, since virtually all cultures are to some degree patriarchal, it is exceedingly difficult to reconcile the claim that women be treated equally with the practices of many religions and other cultural groups, including many of those claiming special rights. But gender inequality is nonetheless a problem that any liberal theorist needs to understand and address since, despite the common tendency to forget the fact, women are more than half of those individuals who constitute the world's population, and any theory based on the liberty or well-being of individuals cannot afford to ignore them or to pay relatively little attention to discrimination against them. First, then, let us look at three examples in which discrimination between the sexes is treated less seriously than other forms of discrimination.

The first is Joseph Raz's essay, "Multiculturalism: A Liberal Perspective." Raz argues for the recognition of multicultural group rights, though he does not specify clearly just which rights he would defend. He claims generally that "multiculturalism requires a political society to recognize the equal standing of all the stable and viable cultural communities existing in that society."[9] His argument is based on the fact of "value pluralism" in contemporary societies and, in line with his general emphasis on autonomy, on the rights of individuals to freedom and well-being or prosperity – for which he claims that "full and unimpeded membership in a respected and flourishing cultural group" is a prerequisite.[10] While arguing for such rights, Raz does not think that all cultural groups merit them. One dimension on which cultures can be judged for this purpose is "obvious," he says. "Some cultures repress groups of either their own members or of outsiders. Slave cultures, racially discriminatory cultures, and homophobic cultures are obvious examples." He states: "Such cultures may be supported only to the degree that it is possible to neutralize their oppressive aspects, or compensate for them" (e.g., by permitting exit, which I shall discuss below).[11]

It is striking that Raz does not include sexist or patriarchal cultures in his list. Rather, he discusses them separately. Having already mentioned the "treatment of women" as one of those reasons, along with "decadence, . . . vulgarity, [and] lack of sense of humour," that make cultures in general tend to disapprove of each other, he seems already to have given it a different, less serious, valance.[12] He reintroduces it in order to illustrate the point that what is not oppressive in one context may become oppressive in another – more multicultural – one. He first says: "Set aside the various cultures which repressed women." (A feminist reader may wonder why he uses the past tense here and may also wonder how many, and which, cultures this set-aside retains.) He continues: "Probably all cultures known to us, even those which did not repress women, distinguished between men and women in that a large array of social relationships, occupations, leisure activities, educational and cultural opportunities, and the like were gender-specific." But provided such separation "does not carry with it the implication of an inferior status" and neither men's nor women's "full development and self-expression" are stunted, "there is nothing wrong with such gender-sensitive cultures so long as they succeed in socializing the young to a willing acceptance of their ways." (Again, given the first two conditions, and that gender specificity and separation are typically coupled with claims of female inferiority, one wonders which cultures he has in mind.) However, Raz goes on to say that, if transplanted to a different cultural context in which "gender determination of opportunities" is a rarity, "the transplanted group is transformed into an oppressive one." What results in this transformation? Precisely, he says, the culture's failure to continue to be able to socialize "all its young to accept its ways and reject the ideas prevalent in the general culture." The latter's "prevailing notions of gender non-discrimination and the debate about feminism is [sic] bound to filter across the cultural barriers," affecting the minority culture's members' perceptions of their own practices, which many will come to understand "as consigning women to an inferior status." The new setting can not only, according to Raz, "lead to a change in the meaning of some of its practices"; it can "make them oppressive."[13]

This is a strange and unconvincing story, not only because the pervasively "gender-sensitive" but acceptably egalitarian societies Raz invents bear little relation to the real world. If the practices of such hypothetical cultures did not imply female inferiority, and if indeed, as he specifies, they "provided the opportunities available to either men or women . . . adequate for their full development and self-expression," then why and how would the feminism and the prevailing nondiscrimination of the new context cause them to be understood so differently? If they were not previously oppressive, how could the move to a new cultural context "make them oppressive"?[14] Raz's own definition of 'oppression' is an objective one: he says that it is "a result of a structural feature of [a] culture which systematically frustrates the ability of people, or groups of people, to fulfill or give expression to an important aspect of their nature within that society."[15] But according to the story he tells about gender and culture, the key to what makes the previously non-oppressive practices oppressive depends on the subjective perceptions of its members: the young women are now unable to be successfully socialized to accept them. Would it not be truer to Raz's own definition to acknowledge that so long as the culture existed in relative isolation, its socializing techniques prevented its people – most importantly, its young women – from perceiving the oppressiveness of oppressive practices? For if such practices come to be seen as systematically frustrating the fulfillment of an important aspect of their nature in the new setting, how could it be that they did not do so in the old? Perhaps Raz might respond that the women's "nature" has been significantly changed by their move to a new cultural

setting. If so, however, Raz gives no account of why we should expect greater human plasticity in the case of gender than in other, seemingly similar, cases. As we saw, he is unwilling to extend the advantages of group recognition to slave cultures, racially discriminatory cultures, and homophobic cultures. Yet such cultures, too, not infrequently succeed in successfully socializing their oppressed members into not recognizing their oppression.[16] But Raz does not even raise the possibility that slave-holding, racist, and homophobic cultures are not oppressive until they come to be perceived as such by their oppressed members. Women and their treatment, it seems, are different. The fact that women are successfully socialized into their various degrees of inferior status in virtually all of the world's cultures means, Raz implies, that they are less oppressed.

The second example I shall discuss of lesser scrutiny's being given to sex discrimination than to another form of discrimination (racial) occurs at a fairly pivotal point in William Galston's defense of group rights in "Two Concepts of Liberalism." Galston tests his theory of "the Diversity State" which, as he has argued, should cede considerable liberty to minority cultural groups, including religious groups, that do not respect the value of individual autonomy, though they must meet certain other conditions. He tests it by considering two cases.[17] While I think the two cases are extremely similar, Galston does not. In the first, Bob Jones University sought to keep its tax-exempt status while forbidding its students, on religious grounds, from dating interracially. Galston thinks, as I do, that the Supreme Court decided correctly in denying this request. His reasoning is that the free exercise of religion protected by the First Amendment – though it may in many conflictual cases require the nonprohibition of "conduct judged obnoxious by public principles" – does not properly extend to "associations conducting their internal affairs in a manner contrary to core public purposes," which include the government's "fundamental, overriding interest in eradicating racial discrimination."[18] In the second case, a fundamentalist religious school in Dayton, Ohio, terminated the employment of a (married) pregnant teacher because of its religious belief that mothers with young children should not engage in paid work outside their homes. The Ohio Civil Rights Commission ordered full reinstatement with back pay, but its decision was reversed by a court. The Supreme Court, which Galston says "ducked the issue" of religious freedom, heard the case and reversed again, stating that "we have no doubt that the elimination of prohibited sex discrimination is a sufficiently important state interest to bring the case within the ambit of the cited authorities" and that "even religious schools cannot claim to be wholly free from some state regulation."[19] However, Galston voices disagreement with the Court in this case, unlike the other, saying: "I believe a reasonable case can be made in this instance for giving priority to free exercise claims."[20] Strangely, while he acknowledges that "the teacher unquestionably experienced serious injury through loss of employment on religious grounds,"[21] Galston does not even mention sex discrimination in the context of this case. He presents the Civil Rights Commission's finding that the school had impermissibly "discriminated on the basis of religion," without mentioning the Supreme Court's reference to sex discrimination.[22]

But surely the Dayton case is no less an example of sex discrimination than the Bob Jones case is one of racial discrimination. After all, if the young teacher involved had been a man about to become a father, the school would have had no objection to his continued employment. Moreover, its policy in the actual case seems unrelated to the expected child's well-being, since leaving the mother unemployed could have undermined an intention on the part of the parents-to-be to have the father take care of the baby. As Galston says, the reason for the school's ending her contract was so that it could not only preach but also practice its "distinctive religious views" (by which he means, but does not say, its sex-discriminatory views about the roles of parents), and to disallow this would have "forced [the religious community] to conform to majoritarian beliefs and practices concerning gender."[23]

How and why is this different from the Bob Jones University case? There, the religious institution was not, and should not have been, according to Galston, permitted to enforce racial discrimination. Here, the religious institution was not, but should have been, according to Galston, allowed to practice sex discrimination. Implicit in his analysis, clearly, is the belief that it is less offensive for a religion to enforce its views about sex roles than its views about race relations on its dissenting members, but he does not explain what justifies this belief. His stated reasoning on the matter is unconvincing. He argues that since the religious community was not coextensive with the political community, the Dayton teacher had the secure and available right

of exit, since she had outside of the religious community "a wide array of other employment options."[24] There are two major problems with this reasoning. First, the Bob Jones students who wanted to date interracially also had plenty of exit options if they were prepared to go outside of the particular religious community. They could have opted for a nonracist religious college, of which there were surely many, or for a secular one. Yet Galston does not apply this reasoning to their case. Second, by forcing exit in the one case and not the other, he radically reduces the opportunities for change within the religion in the one case and not the other. Let us speculate that both the students at Bob Jones who wanted to date interracially and the teacher in Dayton who wanted to share the care of their baby with her husband, though in general religious fundamentalists, objected, respectively, to the racism and the sexism of their religion. Perhaps both aimed, by their choices, to try to initiate change within it. Galston's analysis and solution would give only the former any chance of effecting change from within.

Here, we are reminded that important aspects of exit rights reach far beyond the interests of the particular individuals involved. If the existence of such rights is held to justify oppression or the silencing of dissent within a group, on the ground that dissenters or those who consider themselves oppressed can leave, this is likely to reinforce conservative tendencies within the group. For it clearly tends to disempower potential reformers and thus to empower those who are likely to want to preserve the group's hierarchy and prevent its beliefs and practices from changing. On the one hand, as Albert Hirschman famously argued, having the meaningful and substantive opportunity of exit is likely to enhance one's ability to exert influence on both the general direction and specific decisions taken by one's group, since one – and those like oneself – can, whether overtly or, more often, implicitly, plausibly threaten to leave.[25] On the other hand, having only the purely formal right of exit, without any real capacity to exercise it, tends to eviscerate such capacity for influence. But being subject to *involuntary* exit, in order to practice one's dissent, as the Dayton teacher was, is even worse than merely having the formal right of exit, since it utterly eliminates one's potential influence. These aspects of exit rights are clearly relevant in any analysis of group rights that is concerned with the kinds of intragroup inequalities often faced by women.

My final example of gender inequality's being taken less than fully seriously comes from Chandran Kukathas's arguments that any truly tolerant liberal society should leave alone religious or cultural groups to live by their own ways. (He argues that even worse forms of treatment of children than of women should be permitted, as I shall also discuss.) Though not an advocate of positive group rights, Kukathas is the most extreme defender of tolerance for the internal practices – even extremely coercive and harmful ones – of diverse groups within liberal contexts. His position seems to have hardened over time, so that by 1997, he claimed that the tolerant liberal state was justified in interfering with almost no illiberal practices of groups within it. However, since he does not retract the positions somewhat more restrictive of group practices that he took in a 1992 article, it seems reasonable to consider them alongside his more recent statements. In the earlier article, Kukathas set certain limits on the practices of cultural or religious groups that should be protected against interference by the wider society. He writes: "In recognizing the right of exit, they would also have to abide by liberal norms forbidding slavery [including 'voluntary slavery'] and physical coercion. More generally, they would be bound by liberal prohibitions on 'cruel, inhuman or degrading treatment.' "[26] It is unclear just how Kukathas thinks such norms can justifiably be enforced. Does he mean, given his initial reference to the right of exit, simply that members who object to such treatment must have the right to leave the group? Or does he mean that the liberal state can intervene so as to curtail any such group practices? He seems to mean the former only, since the passage concludes with the statement that "cultural groups that persisted in violating such norms would therefore disappear as their dissident members exercised their enforceable claims against the community."[27] However, this is often neither a viable nor a desired option for persons treated badly by their groups; it is a particularly unfeasible route to offer to dissenting (but helpless) children; and it is, as we shall see, an option often far less available to a group's female than to its male members.

Moreover, in his more recent article, Kukathas takes a more extreme position, arguing that a whole range of practices that "could count as intolerable" by liberal standards should be tolerated by liberal states. Some of the most extreme such practices affect children of both sexes, whose parents or group Kukathas thinks should be permitted to limit their

socialization so as to restrict their opportunities to prepare for life outside their group of origin, to subject them to high-risk initiation rites, and even to deny them conventional medical care in life-threatening situations. A number of the other practices he argues groups should be allowed to practice seriously affect girls and women. They include "denying them the right to hold property, or limiting their access to education, or 'forcing' them into unequal marriages," as well as mandatory "operations (performed with or without the fully informed consent of the subject) which are physically harmful . . . [including] clitoridectomy."[28] It is not at all easy to reconcile Kukathas's position regarding these to-be-tolerated, though seemingly intolerable, practices with the minimal restrictions he argued in his earlier article could rightly be placed on groups. If slavery – even voluntary slavery – and physical coercion are beyond the pale, then how can forcing women into unequal marriages (in which they can become quasi slaves, including sexual slaves, of their husbands) be sanctioned? If physical coercion and cruel, inhuman, or degrading treatment are ruled out, then how can clitoridectomy (which Kukathas agrees with Amy Gutmann in calling a form of torture) be tolerated?[29] Again, a double standard seems to be operating, as with the other theorists I have discussed, though here it is even more antifeminist as well as dismissive of the rights of children in some cultural groups to life and physical integrity.

## Cultural Factors Affecting Women's Realistic Rights of Exit

Clearly, defenders of cultural group rights or exemptions are often relatively insensitive to issues of gender and sometimes explicitly differentiate sex inequality from other forms of morally arbitrary inequality such as racial discrimination. Not surprisingly, as we shall see, this tendency to neglect issues of gender or treat them less than seriously continues into their discussions relevant to, or their conclusions about, the issue of exit rights. However, because of the general tendency of most cultures to try to control the lives of girls and women more than those of boys and men, women's capacities to exit their cultures of origin are usually considerably more restricted than men's.[30] There are at least three major reasons this is so, which are often closely linked. I shall focus on education, practices concerning marriage and divorce, and socialization for gender roles and gender hierarchy.

In many of the world's cultures, girls receive far less education than boys. This is especially likely to be so in poorer countries, where education is not freely provided and many families cannot afford much education, and in cultural contexts where girls, but not boys, are expected to play a major role in taking care of younger siblings and performing other domestic work.[31] However, it is also the case in a few much more affluent societies, mostly Muslim ones. Factors affecting girls' educational deprivation include specific religious or other cultural beliefs that women's only significant role in life is to bear and rear children and marital practices in which girls are married very young and/or become part of their husbands' families once married. The education of daughters, in such cases, may be considered a luxury, or even a waste of their parents' money. When only some children can stay in school, often boys are given preference. The World Bank's figures on adult illiteracy by sex and by country reveal some of the results of such practices. Illiteracy rates are much higher for women in many countries, especially poorer countries.[32] The rates of female to male illiteracy in the world's two most populous countries, China and India, in which the prevalent culture or cultures are still in their various ways highly patriarchal, are 27 percent: 10 percent and 62 percent: 35 percent, respectively. Clearly, many factors, including poverty, affect women's lesser chances of becoming educated. However, cultural factors are clearly significant, since among both the poorest and the richest countries, those with highly patriarchal traditions and cultural heritages have some of the highest discrepancies between female and male literacy.

It is not only the *lack* of education that can disproportionately affect girls' future potential to exit their cultural groups of origin; what is imparted to them in the course of their education can also have far-ranging effects.[33] In the United States, fundamentalist Christians, as in the case of *Mozert v. Hawkins*, have claimed the right, even in the public schools, to shelter their children from any alternatives but enculturation into strict gender roles, claiming this as in accordance with religious truth.[34] But for the exceptional case of *Wisconsin v. Yoder*, the courts have not allowed religious exemptions within public schooling. However, according to James Dwyer, approximately 1.5 million children in the United States are in private fundamentalist

Christian schools and about 2.6 million are in Catholic schools. In both cases, but especially in the former (since there is great variation among Catholic schools, though all are ultimately accountable to a male-only hierarchy), the message often given to girls is that they are less than fully equal to boys and that their proper role in life is to care for their families and to obey their husbands. Dwyer relates that teachers in some fundamentalist schools "openly tell their students that a woman must submit to a subordinate, obedient role in the home; if she does not, 'the doors are wide open to Satan.'"[35] That the belief in hierarchical marriage extends further than fundamentalist fringes was confirmed in June of 1998 by a vote of the leadership of the largest Protestant denomination in the United States, the Southern Baptist Convention, that wives should "graciously submit to the servant leadership of their husbands." Dwyer argues strongly and persuasively that it is a violation of children's rights to subject them to this and other forms of indoctrination. But a number of liberal defenders of group rights, even though they claim that illiberal groups should be required to allow their members to exit, think that parents should be free to thus define and restrict their children's education.

Other cultural practices that can radically affect a woman's capacity to exit her culture of origin are early or involuntarily arranged marriage and other practices that result in significant inequalities in marriage, including lesser rights to exit from a bad marriage. In many cultural groups, girls are married early (sometimes even as children, though cohabitation does not usually begin until after puberty), and marriages are often arranged for them, regardless of their preferences about either the timing or the husband.[36] Commonly cited reasons for these practices are to ensure the wife's virginity at the time of marriage, to accustom her to her husband's family while she is still malleable, and, of course, to enable parents to have a very large say, if not the only say, in whom their children can marry. The frequent results of early marriage for girls include interruption of their education, very long years of childbearing with accompanying depletion of their health, and age differences between themselves and their husbands that augment the latter's already often significant power over them.[37] But in addition to this, of course, arranged and early marriages preempt young women's choices about the kinds of lives they might want to lead, including the choice to exit their cultural group. Once married within it, especially since such marriages are unequal in many ways, a woman is far more encumbered by its requirements of her than a man is, has far less power than her husband (and often his family, especially his mother) to make decisions about her life, and, in most cases, has little room to maneuver her destiny.[38] Uma Narayan's moving essay "Contesting Cultures" and the powerful short stories of Chitra Banerjee Divakaruni pay testimony to the burdens often borne by women expected to submit to arranged marriages and, once within them, to their husbands and their husbands' families.[39] In many of the cultures with these marriage customs, divorce is also much more difficult for a woman to attain than for her husband, and she often has far less chance of gaining custody of their children, though she has usually altered her life far more than he has for the sake of the marriage. These factors, too, of course, restrain her options of exiting an unhappy or abusive relationship, let alone changing the course of her life or her cultural membership.

The overall socialization that girls undergo and the expectations placed on them in many cultures also tend to undermine their self-esteem – a necessary quality for persons to plan their own lives and pursue such plans, including, if they wish, choosing a different mode of life from that into which they were born. Even in our prevalent North American culture, where most young women's opportunities are relatively expansive, eating disorders show up in far more women than men as a symptom of self-esteem problems in a society obsessed with female beauty that is focused on thinness. In many other cultures, the more extreme and pervasive inequality between the sexes surely cannot fail to damage many women's self-esteem. One of the young Indian brides interviewed in a recent *New York Times* article explained that no woman in her family had ever called her husband by his first name, since "for a wife, your husband is God."[40] And Martha Nussbaum has recently spoken and written of women in South Asia's SEWA (Self-Employed Women's Association) who are so accustomed to modesty and humility that their first training in the program consists of learning to stand up, look someone in the eye, and say their names. Without a cultural context that allows one to develop a sound sense of self, it is difficult to imagine a woman being able even to conceive of exit as an option.[41]

Such cultural practices concerning girls and women affect the relationship between gender, group rights, and the realistic capacity for exit in the context of a number of liberal states. In multicultural liberal states where group rights exist, sexist biases within the various cultures can seriously affect girls' and young women's access to education, choices about and status within marriage, and socialization for subordinate status. In the case of India, the existence of "communalism," in particular, the rights of the country's various religious groups to rule their members entirely in the realm of personal law – which regulates such crucial matters as marriage, divorce, child custody, and inheritance – is clearly detrimental to women's status, including their opportunities to be educated.[42] Many aspects of the religious-group rights system in India, and the custom of arranged marriage, certainly make it even more difficult for women than it is for men to exercise the right to exit the religious group into which they were born, should they want to do so or even be able to conceive of doing so.

In the context of liberal states whose majority cultures are less patriarchal than those of most immigrant groups and other indigenous ethnic or religious groups that are actual or potential claimants of group rights, such rights would be likely to affect adversely the education and the marriages of girls, as well as other important aspects of their lives relevant to this discussion. In many of the cultural groups that now form significant minorities in the United States, Canada, and Europe, families place their daughters under significantly greater constraints than their sons. A recent study by Laurie Olsen of first-generation immigrant adolescents in an urban California high school focuses particularly on the experiences of the young women. Olsen shows that, even in the absence of group rights, tight controls are often exerted on them. The young women are expected, far more than the young men, to perpetuate their parents' cultures; they are expected to negotiate their way between these cultures and that of the surrounding United States, often at considerable cost to themselves. Like the boys, they go through the traumas of being different and of having to learn English as fast as possible. Like the boys, too, they often experience racism and exclusionary treatment from the majority culture. But unlike the boys, they carry the added burdens of both the patriarchal attitudes of their own cultures and the expectation that they are responsible for the preservation of these cultures. As Olsen writes, though the girls from the various cultures "handle the dilemmas differently . . . each hears the clock ticking in terms of cultural expectations about marriage, having children, and assuming female roles." The young women with whom she spoke were unsure if or when their parents would expect or arrange their marriages, require their help in assuming responsibility for siblings or other family members, or send them back to their homelands to begin a process of traditional marriage.[43] But clearly, the girls – unlike their brothers – are very rarely allowed to decide how to combine the surrounding majority culture with their own culture of origin or to choose between the two. They are expected to maintain and to reproduce in their own marriages and children their original cultural identity. To this end, their parents frequently restrict or dictate their mode of dress, their participation in extracurricular and social activities, and their choices of further education, future employment, time of marriage and, in some cultural groups, not only the ethnicity of their husband but their actual husband. Many spoke of marriage within their cultures as "a state of isolation and constriction," and they feared they might be assigned to husbands who would control them strictly or even abuse them.[44] Olsen found that it was largely in order to prevent such power imbalances in marriage that the young women wanted to further their educations and gain employment skills, though they often had few realistic plans for accomplishing these goals.

For those who want to become "American," the constraints can be harsh, and Olsen was told by some that they often lie to their parents, risking severe penalties if found out. But many, not surprisingly, are extremely attached to their cultures and religions, as well as to their families. They chafe against and are sometimes severely distressed by the restrictions placed on their lives but are very far from considering the option of leaving their cultural or religious group. The words of a seventeen-and-a-half-year-old Indian student from Fiji capture the dilemma such young women face. Suddenly faced with a coerced marriage that would not allow her to graduate from high school, she said: "I don't know what to do now. My dreams and plans are all messed up. . . . I am tormented." But when a teacher suggested that she need not, perhaps, go through with the marriage, she responded indignantly: "In our religion, we have to think of our parents first. It would kill them if I ran away or disobeyed them. . . . For me, I couldn't marry someone who wasn't a Muslim. I will do it the Muslim way. And I would never go against my parents!"[45] A young woman like this has a formal right of exit, since as a resident of the United States, she could legally change her religion. So also could she appeal to the law against her parents in order to prevent the unwanted marriage. But clearly neither of these options is thinkable to her, for, given the manner in which she has been raised, by doing either, she would lose much of what she most values in life. As we shall see, theorists who look to exit rights in order to counterbalance or mitigate discrimination or oppression within groups do not often seem to consider the depth of acquired cultural attachments, which can render the exit option not merely undesirable but unthinkable.[46] As Ayelet Shachar writes, in the context of women oppressed within groups whose traditions are "accommodated" by multicultural states, the "right of exit 'solution' . . . throws on the already beleaguered individual the responsibility to either miraculously transform the legal-institutional conditions that keep her vulnerable or find the resources to leave her whole world behind."[47]

## Rights of Exit and Realistic Rights of Exit for Women

All liberal defenders of group rights, as I have mentioned, insist that such rights cannot be justified unless individuals have the right to exit their cultures or religions of origin. Those who reject the centrality of individual freedom or autonomy in favor of toleration and who are more concerned that the state not interfere with the internal lives of groups than that groups not restrict their own members' beliefs or behavior nevertheless express the view that individuals must have the right of exit.[48] Disagreement does not begin until the question arises as to what such a right requires, and here, as we shall see, views diverge widely. Let us now turn back to the theorists discussed above – Raz, Galston, and Kukathas – in order to examine what they say about the right of exit in light of their own treatment of gender inequality and the points I have just made about its strong links with many cultures and religions. Specifically, I shall bring to bear on their arguments both the fact that various cultural practices concerning women are liable to effectively nullify or severely restrict their rights of exit and the point that even a realistic right of exit is by no means always a satisfactory solution to the forms of culturally reinforced discrimination women often experience.

Raz raises the issue of the individual's right of exit from his or her cultural group explicitly in the context of groups that oppress at least some of their own members. "Such cultures," he says, "may be supported only to the degree that it is possible to neutralize their oppressive aspects, or compensate for them (for example, by providing convenient exit from the oppressive community to members of the discriminated-against group)."[49] Later, he reinforces this connection between the likelihood of repression and the individual's right of exit:

> Moreover, the opportunity to exit from a group is a vital protection for those members of it who are repressed by its culture. Given that most cultures known to us are repressive to a lesser or greater degree, the opportunity of exit is of vital importance as a counter to the worry that multiculturalism encourages repressive cultures to perpetuate their ways. . . . [While] groups should be encouraged to change their repressive practices . . . this is a very slow process. Opportunities of exit should be encouraged as a safeguard, however imperfect, for members who cannot develop and find adequate avenues for self-expression within their native culture.[50]

While Raz is clearly aware of some of the difficulties of leaving one's cultural group, he does not specify what conditions he thinks must obtain to ensure that opportunities of exit as a "viable option" are available.[51] As we have seen, however, for girls and women especially, formal rights of exit are a less than satisfactory palliative for oppression for several reasons. First, as I pointed out above and as Raz himself implies in his example, girls are often successfully socialized into the acceptance of practices that they would be likely to come to regard as oppressive if they were living in a less sexist cultural context. Second, as we have seen, many cultures are far more inclined to shortchange girls than boys educationally. But having an education that prepares one for alternative modes of life is surely an essential prerequisite for a realistic or substantive right of exit. Third, in many cultural or religious groups, families control their daughters' times of marriage and choices of husbands far more than they do their sons'. Once a young woman is married within a culture, especially if she bears children early (as is often expected of her to prove her fertility and ensure the continuation of the male line) and especially if the terms of marriage and divorce are biased against her (as is also often the case), her capacity to exit even her marriage,

let alone her cultural group, is severely restricted. Further, the right of exit from one's cultural group is, surely, often not at all desired as the sole option to such modes of female deprivation or oppression. As accounts such as Olsen's make clear, young women, not surprisingly, often value their cultural and familial ties extremely highly, even though they suffer from and chafe against their oppressive aspects. An adolescent girl faced with the choice of either giving up her education and marrying against her will or leaving her family and her culture of origin may find this choice very far from a convenient opportunity to exit. It may well be such an unbearable choice as to be, in practice, no choice at all.

Galston raises issues pertinent to exit early in his discussion of group rights, in the context of Justice Douglas's dissent in *Yoder*. He quotes Douglas on the right of students to be "masters of their own destiny" and also his ensuing statement that "if a child is harnessed to the Amish way of life by those in authority over him and if his education is truncated, his entire life may be stunted and deformed."[52] While Galston disagrees with Douglas's position, he acknowledges that there is "obviously something to Douglas's distinction between the interests and standing of parents and those of their children." He continues by arguing that anyone who wishes (as Galston does) to deny Jehovah's Witnesses or Christian Scientists the right to let their children die for lack of conventional medical treatment yet allow the Amish to deny their children an education adequate for other ways of life "must either find some principled basis for distinguishing these cases or treat them similarly."[53] While distinguishing himself from liberals primarily focused on individual autonomy, and claiming that "properly understood, liberalism is about the protection of diversity, not the valorization of choice," he aims to show that "respect for diversity, and especially group diversity, does not improperly disregard individual autonomy claims."[54] As we saw earlier, however, Galston recognizes that there can be significant tension between individual autonomy and commitment to a wide diversity of ways of life. Since "many cultures or groups do not place a high value on choice and (to say the least) do not encourage their members to exercise it" and since membership in such a group may be among "the deepest sources of . . . identity," throwing state power behind the promotion of individual autonomy can "weaken or undermine" such groups.[55]

Given this, however, Galston is adamant that individuals should retain the right of exit: the liberal state "must defend . . . the personal liberty not to be coerced into, or trapped within, ways of life" and "accordingly, . . . must safeguard the ability of individuals to shift allegiances and cross boundaries."[56] As well as ensuring that groups protect human life, protect and promote the "normal development of basic capacities," and develop "social rationality (the kind of understanding needed to participate in the society, economy, and polity)" in their members, the liberal "Diversity State" Galston favors must "enforce strong prohibitions" against coerced entrance into and exit from such groups.[57] He concludes that "in circumstances of genuine pluralism, individual freedom is adequately protected by secure rights of exit coupled with the existence of a wider society open to individuals wishing to leave their groups of origin."[58]

However, Galston's defense of illiberal groups that do not value autonomy, and his position on the Dayton case in particular, are incompatible with any kind of realistic or meaningful right of exit, especially for women. Neither is the right of exit sufficient to justify the kinds of restrictions on individuals that his theory permits. He himself acknowledges that his position is "hardly unproblematic." On the one hand, there are "entrance problems," since people are born into groups that they do not choose for themselves. On the other hand, there are "exit problems, especially if 'exit' is understood substantively as well as formally." And thus Galston acknowledges, in conclusion, that a "meaningful" right of exit seems to require a number of conditions: the awareness of alternatives to one's current way of life, the ability to assess these alternatives if one wishes, freedom from brainwashing and from other forms of coercion, and the ability to participate effectively in at least some other ways of life. As he says, this protection of a meaningful right of exit "brings us back some distance toward policies more typically associated with autonomy concerns."[59]

Undoubtedly, Galston's conditions for the existence of a meaningful right of exit bring us back very far toward autonomy-based policies.[60] Moreover, the issue of sex-role indoctrination can illustrate well just how far. If parents are permitted to educate their children in sheltered settings in which they are taught, by example, doctrine, and the content of their curriculum, that it is the will of an omnipotent and punitive God that women's proper role in life is to

be an obedient wife and a full-time mother, how can the girls be said to be "aware of . . . alternatives" in any meaningful way, to be able to "assess these alternatives" (or even to think it desirable to do so), or to be able to "participate effectively" in other roles or ways of life? As I briefly indicated above, many fundamentalist religious schools and other institutions of cultural groups do socialize their children into the inevitability of sex roles and sex hierarchy and the godlessness of any departure from them. By thus limiting their autonomy, most especially in the case of girls, they clearly do not meet the specific requirements Galston sets out for meaningful exit, without which his argument loses its claim to being liberal. Also, as I pointed out earlier, the right of exit is insufficient to justify illiberal practices, especially if it is the kind of involuntary exit to which Galston does not object in the case of the Dayton woman who wanted to continue teaching after the birth of her child. For this kind of forced exit especially prevents those within the group who might want to liberalize it from the inside from having any chance of doing so. Even the bare availability of exit for such practical dissenters, though, is insufficient to gain them what others may take for granted: the choice between exerting a fair share of influence within their cultural group and exiting from it if they should find any of its beliefs or practices unduly constraining. Rights of exit provide no help to women or members of other oppressed groups who are deeply attached to their cultures but not to their oppressive aspects. It is likely to be far preferable, from their point of view, to have the wider society address the discrimination they suffer from, just as it would for its other citizens.

Kukathas, who, as we saw earlier, defends the right of religious or cultural groups to be left alone even to the point of allowing children to die preventable deaths, paradoxically also claims that the members of such groups have "the inalienable right to leave – to renounce membership of – the community."[61] Later, in the context of addressing the problem of various injustices that might occur within groups, he adds: "What is crucially important here . . . is the extent to which the individual does enjoy a *substantial* freedom to leave."[62] The right of exit is of considerable importance in Kukathas's argument for three reasons. First, an important basis for his argument against positive group rights is his liberal attachment to individual rights, and not being captive in a group one wishes to leave seems fundamental among such rights. Second, like both

Raz and Galston, he thinks that the right of exit mitigates the harm of group injustice or oppression. Third, unlike these other theorists, he notes that "the nature of his community is transformed" by the individual's freedom to leave, "particularly if the formal right comes with substantive opportunities."[63] Thus, implicitly, at least, he acknowledges the important relationship between exit and voice.

In several ways, however, Kukathas both recognizes the limitations of and significantly dilutes the exit rights on which he insists. First, he acknowledges (but fails to respond to) the point that the exit option is "insufficient to ensure any kind of freedom from oppression since it is precisely the most vulnerable members of such communities who would find exit most difficult and costly."[64] This is a valid and important point, which, as we have seen, is particularly pertinent to women and children in many cultural contexts. It badly needs a response. But instead, apparently discounting this point, he claims that if persons or subgroups who seem to be being treated unjustly by their group do not leave it, this mitigates the injustice: "If an individual continues to live in a community and according to ways that (in the judgment of the wider society) treat her unjustly, even though she is free to leave, then our concern about the injustice diminishes."[65] This, however, is one of the passages in which he stresses that the freedom to leave must be "substantial" – must have "considerable substantive bite" – and that certain conditions must hold for this to be so. However, the only condition he mentions, which he regards as the most important, is the existence of a wider liberal society that is open to those wishing to leave their groups. For freedom of exit to be "credible," he says, there must exist in such a society "a considerable degree of individual independence."[66] But while Kukathas is clearly aware that substantial freedom to leave depends in part in having somewhere to go, he largely ignores another important prerequisite: that one must have the capacity to get there. Given many of the group practices Kukathas claims must be permitted by a tolerant society, it is impossible to see how some members – a child who has been allowed to die, for example – could leave; and it is hard to see how others could leave without enormous difficulty, including persons of both sexes deprived of the education required for alternative modes of life and girls and women who had, in addition, no access to property, had undergone clitoridectomy, or had been forced into unequal marriages (especially if at an early age, without access to contraception, or with little or no possibility of initiating divorce). It is perhaps not surprising that Kukathas does not elaborate what capacities individuals must have in order to have a "substantial" right of exit, since such requirements would run into serious conflict with many of the group practices he thinks should be permitted.

## Conclusion

As I have argued elsewhere, in the case of groups that have emigrated from cultures which are more patriarchal to a more liberal majority culture, as well as in other multicultural states, rights to maintain cultural practices that discriminate against women are frequently among those sought after by group leaders.[67] Raz, Galston, and Kukathas seem prepared to concede such rights to minority groups, whether immigrant or not. Each tries to mitigate the rights or exemptions by specifying that individuals must have the right of exit, but in no case is the argument convincing. Raz, to be sure, would rather the wider society successfully discourage the repressive practices of groups but sees the right of exit as a safeguard while this lengthy process takes place. However, he neither specifies what having a realistic right of exit would entail nor considers the substantial obstacles that are likely to impede women's exit from such groups. Galston clearly does not put overt sex discrimination in the same serious category as overt racial discrimination, the elimination of which he does think overrides group rights. It is fine with him, apparently, if girls in Christian schools learn from who is and who is not allowed to teach them, as well as from what they are directly taught in class, that it is divinely ordained that the mothers of young children should not be employed outside of the home. But this runs directly contrary to his stated requirements for a person's having a "meaningful right of exit." And Kukathas thinks that groups should be allowed, within tolerant liberal states, to continue even practices that harm or restrict women (as well as children) seriously, as he has recently made clear. He, too, states that persons must have "substantial" rights of exit from such groups, but the only condition he specifies is the existence of a wider liberal society that is willing to take them in. He takes no account of the extent to which many of the practices he advocates permitting groups to practice would make some of their members' exercise of their exit options extremely difficult or even impossible.

In proposing that the right to exit one's cultural or religious group of origin somehow makes the repressive practices of some such groups more tolerable to liberals, the three theorists whose arguments I have discussed seem insufficiently aware of the impossible position in which this is bound to put some persons. To be sure, Kukathas mentions, though he does not respond to, the objection that often the most repressed are the least able to exit. Neither Raz nor Galston even mentions this relevant fact. And none of the three takes seriously enough the problem that, even if it were feasible or even possible in a practical sense, exit may not be an option at all desirable, or even thinkable, to those most in need of it. But this is not infrequently the case, which partly explains why women put up with some of the practices they do. Only by neglecting such pertinent facts could one argue, in the name of tolerance or in the name of individual freedom and well-being, for group rights that might give no recourse at all to a seventeen-year-old girl forced to choose between not finishing high school in order to marry a virtual stranger and losing her ties with not only her family but also her religion. What kind of a choice is one between total submission and total alienation from the person she understands herself to be? Is this a choice that a group within a liberal state should place some of its members in the position of having to make? The liberal state, I conclude, should not only not give special rights or exemptions to cultural and religious groups that discriminate against or oppress women. It should also enforce individual rights against such groups when the opportunity arises and encourage all groups within its borders to cease such practices.[68] Not to do so, from the point of view of a liberal who takes women's, children's, and other potentially vulnerable persons' rights seriously, is to let toleration for diversity run amok.

## Notes

\* Justice William Douglas wrote: "If a parent keep his child out of school beyond the grade school, then the child will be forever barred from entry into the new and amazing world of diversity that we have today. The child may decide that that is the preferred course, or he may rebel. It is the student's judgment, not his parents', that is to be essential if we are to give full meaning to the Bill of Rights and of the right of students to be masters of their own destiny. If he is harnessed to the Amish way of life by those in authority over him and if his education is truncated, his entire life may be stunted and deformed" (*Wisconsin v. Yoder*, 406 U.S. 205, 245–6 [1972], Justice Douglas dissenting). Converting the phrase into "mistresses of their own destiny" has an unavoidable irony, since there is no apparent way of making it apply specifically to young women without using a word that both has sexual connotations and makes reference to them in relation to men.

1. The autonomy-based argument I focus on here is that of Joseph Raz in "Multiculturalism: A Liberal Perspective," in *Ethics in the Public Domain* (Oxford: Clarendon, 1994), pp. 170–91; those based on tolerance for diversity are that of William Galston in "Two Concepts of Liberalism," *Ethics* 105 (April 1995): 516–34; and that of Chandran Kukathas in "Are there Any Cultural Rights?" *Political Theory* 20 (February 1992): 105–39, and "Cultural Toleration," in *Nomos XXXIX: Ethnicity and Group Rights*, ed. Ian Shapiro and Will Kymlicka (New York: New York University Press, 1997), pp. 69–104.

2. Susan Moller Okin, "Is Multiculturalism Bad for Women?" *Boston Review* 22 (1997): 25–8, and "Feminism and Multiculturalism: Some Tensions," *Ethics* 108 (1998): 661–84. The former, with comments by twelve scholars and a response by me, was subsequently published as Joshua Cohen, Martha Nussbaum, and Matthew Howard (eds.), *Is Multiculturalism Bad for Women?* (Princeton, NJ: Princeton University Press, 1999).

3. Will Kymlicka, *Liberalism, Community, and Culture* (Oxford: Clarendon, 1989), and *Multicultural Citizenship: A Liberal Theory of Minority Rights* (Oxford: Oxford University Press, 1995).

4. Ayelet Shachar: "Group Identity and Women's Rights in Family Law: The Perils of Multicultural Accommodation," *Journal of Political Philosophy* 6 (1998): 285–305; "The Paradox of Multicultural Vulnerability: Identity Groups, the State and Individual Rights," in *Multicultural Questions*, ed. Christian Joppke and Steven Lukes (Oxford: Oxford University Press, 1999); and "On Citizenship and Multicultural Vulnerability," *Political Theory* 28 (February 2000): 64–89.

5. Shachar, "On Citizenship and Multicultural Vulnerability," p. 65.

6. Ibid., p. 81; cf. Okin, "Feminism and Multiculturalism: Some Tensions," pp. 683–84.

7. Shachar, "On Citizenship and Multicultural Vulnerability," p. 86, n. 48.

8. Ibid., pp. 79–80, quotation from p. 80. See also Shachar, "The Paradox of Multicultural Vulnerability," p. 100.

9. Raz, "Multiculuralism: A Liberal Perspective," p. 174. This requirement is rather vague. What would it mean, e.g., to give a group whose membership numbered in the hundreds "equal standing" with one whose membership numbered in the tens of millions?

10. For his arguments about autonomy, see Joseph Raz, *The Morality of Freedom* (Oxford: Clarendon, 1986), esp. chap. 14. The quotations are from Raz, "Multiculturalism: A Liberal Perspective," pp. 171, 174.

11. Raz, "Multiculturalism: A Liberal Perspective," p. 184.

12. Ibid., p. 179.

13. Ibid., p. 186.

14. I do not mean here to deny that a new social context cannot make some of a cultural group's practices worse for women. This has clearly been the case for immigrant women in polygynous marriages now living in France. As some said when interviewed, what was a barely tolerable institution in their North African countries of origin is an unbearable imposition in the French context. However, the main reason for this was clearly the change in living conditions: whereas in Africa, each wife had her own hut and some privacy, living in a French apartment designed for a nuclear family made polygynous marriage in practice much worse. It was clearly by no means principally a change in the women's perception of the practice. "News Section," *International Herald Tribune* (February 2, 1996).

15. Raz, "Multiculturalism: A Liberal Perspective," p. 184.

16. See, e.g., Elinor Burkett, "God Created Me to Be a Slave," *New York Times Magazine* (October 12, 1997): 56–60.

17. Galston also mentions the Civil War Amendments and Brown v. Board of Education of Topeka, 347 U.S. 483 (1954). He says of the amendments and the earlier race cases, but not of the more recent gender case, that they "have significantly reshaped our understanding" (p. 531).

18. Galston, "Two Concepts of Liberalism", p. 532. The second quotation is from Bob Jones University v. United States, 461 U.S. 574, 604 (1983).

19. Galston, ibid., p. 533. The other quotations are from Ohio Civil Rights Commission v. Dayton Schools, 477 U.S. 619, 628 (1986).

20. Galston, ibid., p. 533.

21. Ibid., p. 532.

22. Ibid.

23. Ibid., p. 533.

24. Ibid.

25. See Albert O. Hirschman, *Exit, Voice, and Loyalty: Responses to Declines in Firms, Organizations, and States* (Cambridge, MA: Harvard University Press, 1970).

26. Kukathas, "Are there Any Cultural Rights?" p. 128.

27. Ibid.

28. Kukathas, "Cultural Toleration," p. 70.

29. Ibid., p. 88, citing Amy Gutmann, "The Challenge of Multiculturalism in Political Ethics," *Philosophy & Public Affairs* (1993): 171–206, p. 195.

30. For more detail on cultural controls on women, see Okin, "Feminism and Multiculturalism: Some Tensions," esp. pp. 667–70, and references, esp. n. 17; also see Cohen, Nussbaum, and Howard (eds.), passim.

31. In many cases, the costs and unavailability of education have risen due to the structural adjustment policies enforced on indebted countries since the 1970s by the World Bank and the International Monetary Fund. It is well documented that this and other cuts in social spending have had considerably worse impacts on women and girls in these countries than on men and boys. See, e.g., Haleh Afshar and Carolynne Dennis (eds.), *Women and Adjustment Policies in the Third World* (New York: St. Martin's, 1992); Mariarosa Dalla Costa and Giovanna F. Dalla Costa (eds.), *Paying the Price: Women and the Politics of International Economic Strategy* (London: Zed, 1995).

32. Of the forty poorest countries for which data are available for 1995, the illiteracy rates for women are nontrivially higher – in most cases much higher – than those of men in all but three. In eighteen cases – India, Pakistan, and sixteen African countries – the illiteracy rates for women are between 150 percent and 200 percent of men's, and in four others – Tanzania, Zambia, Cambodia, and China – they are more than twice as high. In the lower-middle- and middle-income economies, the discrepancies between the sexes are still high. In only seven out of the twenty-six such countries with data available are the figures equal or almost so. In ten, the rate of women's illiteracy is between 150 percent and 200 percent of men's; in four, it is between twice and three times as high; and in another three, it is three times as high or more. Of the last seven countries, four are predominantly Muslim. In the upper-middle and high-income countries, where illiteracy is in general much lower, for obvious reasons, there are still wide discrepancies between the sexes in a few countries where it is high, most notably Saudi Arabia, Malaysia, and Gabon, but much less discrepancy in others where it is also quite high, including the most affluent Muslim countries, Kuwait and United Arab Emirates. *Human Development Report* (Oxford: Oxford University Press, for the World Bank, 1997), pp. 220–1.

33. For a more general discussion of the importance of education for substantive rights of exit, see Rob Reich, *Bridging Liberalism and Multiculturalism in American Education* (Chicago: University of Chicago Press, 2002).

34. Mozert v. Hawkins County Bd. of Education, 827 F.2d 1058 (6th Cir. 1987).

35. James G. Dwyer, *Religious Schools v. Children's Rights* (Ithaca, NY: Cornell University Press, 1998), p. 26.

36. In a recent *New York Times* story about Indians in the United States who practice arranged marriage, it was fairly evident that the men involved had more choice about the marriages being arranged for them,

about the marital partners, and about the timing. One twenty-year-old woman, a student at Barnard – who had obviously put much effort into her education – clearly did not want to terminate her education as she was being required to do by her parents, but she saw herself as having no choice. She said: "I wish it didn't have to be this way, but I can't really do anything about it" (Celia Dugger, "In India, an Arranged Marriage of Two Worlds," *New York Times* (July 20, 1998).

37. Neera Kuckreja Sohoni, *The Burden of Girlhood: A Global Inquiry into the Status of Girls* (Oakland, CA: Third Party, 1995), chap. 3.

38. Another anecdote in Dugger's *New York Times* story is about a young, though fully adult, married woman who has to wear what her mother-in-law decrees, even while at home, and to await her mother-in-law's permission to resume her education. See Shachar, "On Citizenship and Multicultural Vulnerability," pp. 73–7, for discussion of how and why women are often given the role of bearers of their cultures.

39. Uma Narayan, "Contesting Cultures," in her *Dislocating Cultures: Identities, Traditions, and Third World Feminisms* (New York: Routledge, 1997), pp. 3–39; Chitra Banerjee Divakaruni, *Arranged Marriage* (New York: Doubleday, 1995). See also Chitra Banerjee Divakaruni, *The Mistress of Spices* (New York: Doubleday, 1997).

40. Dugger.

41. Martha Nussbaum, *Women and Human Development: The Capabilities Approach* (Cambridge: Cambridge University Press, 2000), p. 268.

42. Obviously, communalism in India – given the country's history of violent religious conflict, has important virtues, but these do not include the promotion of women's equality in most Indian states, with a few exceptions, such as Kerala, where women's status is notably higher than average. On the effects of religious group rights on women, see Kirti Singh, "Obstacles to Women's Rights in India," in *Human Rights of Women: National and International Perspectives*, ed. Rebecca J. Cook (Philadelphia: University of Pennsylvania Press, 1994), pp. 375–96, esp. pp. 378–89.

43. Laurie Olsen, *Made in America: Immigrant Students in Our Public Schools* (New York: New Press, 1997), p. 124.

44. Ibid., p. 134.

45. Ibid., pp. 136, 138.

46. Jeffrey Spinner-Halev points out that Olsen's respondents almost all say that they will raise their own daughters less restrictively, concluding that "their experiences and views [are] testimony to the tremendous power of liberal public culture" ("Feminism, Multiculturalism, Oppression, and the State," *Ethics* 112 [October 2001]: 84–113, p. 90). However, in saying that this proves "liberalism . . . victorious" (p. 90),

he does not take sufficient account of the troublesome fact that, to the extent that multiculturalism helps these young women's parents and their traditional culture to prevail over their own preferences now, they themselves will lead radically unfree lives (they are, as he acknowledges, "caught in lives that they will not like" [p. 89]) although they are residents or citizens of a liberal state.

47. Shachar, "On Citizenship and Multicultural Vulnerability," p. 80.

48. See, e.g., Galston, "Two Concepts of Liberalism," pp. 553–4.

49. Raz, "Multiculturalism: A Liberal Perspective," p. 184.

50. Ibid., p. 187.

51. Ibid., p. 190.

52. Wisconsin v. Yoder, 406 U.S. 205, 245–6 (1972), quoted in Galston "Two Concepts of Liberalism," p. 517.

53. Galston, "Two Concepts of Liberalism," pp. 517–18.

54. Ibid., pp. 523, 518.

55. Ibid., pp. 521–2.

56. Ibid., p. 522.

57. Ibid., pp. 525, 528.

58. Ibid., p. 533.

59. Ibid., p. 534.

60. See Kimberly A. Yuracko, "Enforcing Liberalism: Liberal Responses to Illiberal Groups," in *Handbook of Global Legal Policy*, ed. Stuart S. Nagel (New York: Dekker, 2000), pp. 485–509, for an insightful discussion of the relationship between toleration-based and autonomy-based arguments for group rights.

61. Kukathas, "Are there Any Cultural Rights?" p. 117.

62. Ibid., p. 133.

63. Ibid., p. 128.

64. Kukathas, "Cultural Toleration," p. 87. He responds to the charge that the extent of tolerance of group practices he advocates would make society into a "mosaic of tyrannies" by citing examples of the persecution of groups by the wider society and claiming that "islands of tyranny in a sea of indifference" are to be preferred to more centralized tyranny. Most of his examples, however, have little or nothing to do with the control of groups in order to protect their members; one such example is the twentieth-century persecution of Jews.

65. Kukathas, "Are there Any Cultural Rights?" p. 133.

66. Ibid., p. 134.

67. Okin, "Is Multiculturalism Bad for Women?," passim; Bhikhu Parekh, "Minority Practices and Principles of Toleration," *International Migration Review* 30 (April 1996): 251–84.

68. These guidelines should, of course, apply equally to old groups as to newly arrived ones. For example, religious groups such as the Catholic Church and Orthodox Judaism should be denied tax-exempt status as long as they discriminate against women.

# Educational Authority

# Introduction to Part II

The education of children is an enterprise predicated on some *authority* or right to determine within limits the aims to be achieved, the content to be taught, and the manner in which the enterprise is to be carried out. This authority is, in the first place, a right to limit the freedom of children pursuant to certain goals and subject to certain constraints, but in recent practice it also encompasses the right of governments to appropriate resources and limit the liberty of others, in ways necessary to fulfill the educational responsibilities associated with the possession of authority. The proper *division* of educational authority among parents, states, professional educators, commercial and other private entities, and children themselves as they mature is a matter much debated. Joel Feinberg's article in Part I (no. 14) provided a preview of the issues from a children's rights perspective, and the selections that follow provide a basis for examining them from other perspectives. Running through all of these selections are questions about the foundations and scope of public educational authority. The first section, "The Boundaries of Educational Authority," collects together diverse views on the basis of educators' authority and the division of authority between state, home, and professionals. The second section, "The Commercialization of Schooling," focuses on the division of authority between public authorities and commercial enterprises, the linkages between this

and parental choice, and the erosion of the boundary between education and commercial influence within public schools themselves.

## The Boundaries of Educational Authority

"Education and the limits of state authority" (no. 17) is drawn from John Stuart Mill's *On Liberty* (1859), a classic of nineteenth-century liberal thought. Mill frames his discussion of education as an instance of misplaced ideas about parental liberty, but it is often cited for its resistance to government involvement in determining the content of education. Mill posits a "sacred" parental duty to provide a good education, and he affirms the existence of a legitimate state authority to "require and compel" the fulfillment of that duty up to an appropriate standard. However, on the question of whether the state should *provide* education itself on more than a small scale, he argues it should not. How will the various contending "sects and parties" agree on what is to be taught? And if they could agree, would the resulting education not constitute a "mere contrivance for molding people to be exactly like one another?" Mill advocates public examinations to enforce educational standards, and financial assistance to those who cannot afford school fees. Mill attempts to strike the right balance between parental and state authority over education, by requiring parents to satisfy the educational needs of the child and society, while allowing parents to retain authority over many aspects of education. One can ask whether this is the right balance, and whether there is not some interest of the child or society that warrants more expansive state authority over education, perhaps through a system of public schools.

In her reading "Democracy and Democratic Education" (no. 18), Amy Gutmann defends a democratic ideal of *conscious social reproduction*, which aims to preserve the foundations of democracy itself. What could be a more compelling basis for democratic authority over education than the need to promote the civic virtues essential to a democratic political culture? Gutmann writes that: "Education should prepare citizens for consciously *reproducing* (not replicating) their society," and "we should therefore support a set of educational practices to which citizens, acting collectively, have consciously agreed, provided that those also prepare future citizens for participating intelligently in the political processes that shape their society." Gutmann does not rule out the privatization of state-run schools on principle, but she regards it as "an unpromising path to democratic education."

Home schooling, once strictly regulated and very rare in the United States, is now widespread and barely regulated at all in many states (see Reich, 2002, chapter 6). Do Gutmann's arguments (or Callan's, Feinberg's, or Okin's) provide a basis for prohibiting or discouraging home schooling? Is there any just basis on which governments can claim the authority to deny parents the liberty to educate their children at home, so long as they satisfy reasonable standards of educational adequacy? How feasible would it be to enforce such standards? In "Justice, Inequality, and Home Schooling" (no. 19), Charles L. Howell considers and rejects three arguments for prohibiting or discouraging homeschooling. The first alleges that withdrawing children into homeschooling erodes social cohesion. The second alleges that it undercuts public authority over the formation of citizens (Gutmann's *conscious social reproduction*). The third, which Howell devotes by far the most attention to, alleges that home schooling exacerbates *inequality*. He acknowledges that there is something to this argument, since inequality *has* been exacerbated by the flight of educated and affluent Americans from urban school districts. Howell examines whether a strong form of *equality of*

*opportunity* is a requirement of justice that governments should honor – and can only honor by limiting or prohibiting home schooling. He concludes that the underlying rationale for full equality of opportunity is conceptually and morally problematic, and that homeschooling is not inconsistent with weaker forms of educational equality.

In describing the division of educational authority involved in her concept of democratic education, Gutmann refers to the authority of *professional educators*. The idea, which has broad currency, is that democratic communities will define the purposes and make policy, but will *delegate* authority over the details and daily operations of schools to professionals whose qualifications are established through approved processes of certification, competitive selection, and periodic review. In his reading "Is Teaching a Profession: How Would We Know?" (no. 20), Kenneth A. Strike addresses in detail the attribution of professional status to teachers and the implications of that status for the division of authority among teachers and democratic communities. Claims to professional status typically rest on the possession of esoteric knowledge, and such knowledge forms not only the basis of professional judgment, but also the only sound basis for judging or assessing the performance of members of the profession. It follows that professions are self-regulating through peer evaluation, and to that extent are not directly subject to democratic control. If teaching is a profession, then, it cannot properly be held accountable through measures of student outcomes. *Is* teaching a profession? If it is a profession, what is the nature of its esoteric knowledge base? Strike explores the possible answers to the latter question, and raises important further questions along the way. Do teachers have the authority or right to "compel students to learn things because teachers know that those things are good?" Are teachers best thought of as experts in *pedagogy* or as practitioners of an *intellectual discipline*? To what extent is a teacher's exercise of professional authority an exercise of *academic freedom*?

Educational authority *over students* is the subject of Hannah Arendt's "The Crisis of Education" (no. 21) from her 1954 book *Between Past and Future*. Written over half a century ago in reaction to a "crisis" in American education associated with the Progressive Education Movement (cf. Peters' remarks in Part I), this chapter remains a compelling statement of the underlying logic of educational authority over children and a teacher's authority in her classroom. Classical liberal theory suggested the view that adults have basic educational responsibilities to children, and a *derivative* authority to restrict the liberty of children to the extent, and only to the extent, necessary to fulfill those responsibilities (Locke, 1980, chapter 7). Arendt does not reject this, but she emphasizes another responsibility that educators have: a responsibility for the future course of the world in which students will act for good or ill. Is the lesson of twentieth century authoritarianism that teachers should treat students as *peers* (cf. reading no. 8 in Part I), or that they should use the authority they have to safeguard the future against the worst elements in human nature? Her critique of the concept of pedagogy as a "science of teaching" divorced from specific content resonates with Strike's analysis of the knowledge base for teacher professionalism.

## The Commercialization of Schooling

Milton Friedman's chapter "The Role of Government in Education" (no. 22) is drawn from his 1962 book *Capitalism and Freedom*. In it he challenges "the administration of schools as a government function," and calls for the sale of public or government-operated school facilities to private enterprises. Most justified, in his view, would be a system of both public and private schools, in which parents choosing private schools would receive "vouchers" toward the cost of those schools. Friedman concedes that citizenship education has "neighborhood effects" (benefits beyond those enjoyed by students and their families) that warrant government action to require and fund education, but he argues there is no clear basis for direct government administration of schools. Apart from continuing to operate a limited number of schools in areas where they are particularly needed, the government's role should be limited to ensuring that minimum content standards are met. The American public school movement was founded largely on the idea that children from different backgrounds should mingle and develop bonds conducive to democratic citizenship and social stability (see Pangle and Pangle, 1993, and the readings by Appiah, Blum, and Levinson and Levinson in Part III), but Friedman suggests the need for this is not clear and it "conflicts with the preservation of freedom itself." He means by this both freedom of thought and parental choice of schools, and he argues that choice would create

a more efficient and diverse system of schools; a market system in which teacher salaries reflect merit, instead of a bureaucratic and mediocre system in which teachers have colluded to link salaries to credentials and seniority.

Writing four decades later, in "Commercialization or Citizenship: The Case of Education" (no. 23), Colin Crouch addresses the two ways in which markets and private firms have been introduced into the compulsory school system in the UK: through the introduction of non-commercial market analogues or choice mechanisms, and through contracting out of educational services to commercial enterprises. These changes have been introduced in the interest of creating markets and bringing greater efficiency to the provision of schooling. But to what extent is this consistent with regarding education as a right of citizenship? Crouch offers an analysis of the tensions between the model of schooling as a publicly administered right of citizenship and schooling as a service distributed through price and market mechanisms, and he provides an assessment of the dynamic that results from trying to combine the two. Are the innovations actually creating the efficiencies and quality promised by markets? Do they promise improvements in the quality of education for the poor and underserved? Or are they likely to exacerbate inequalities of educational and social opportunity? Are they creating true markets and greater public accountability, or a class of privileged insider commercial enterprises whose "customer" is not the student or student's family, but the government entities that determine which firms receive long-term contracts? As the boundaries between commercial and educational activities break down, will the content of schooling become more, or less, adequate to the needs of students and society?

This last question is the focus of Harry Brighouse's reading "Channel One, the Anti-Commercial Principle, and the Discontinuous Ethos" (no. 24). Brighouse describes Channel One television broadcasts in public schools in the USA as "the most celebrated and notorious" of the deals through which private corporations are increasingly allowed to "market themselves" inside schools and influence the content of schooling. These deals have become more common as public funding for schools has eroded, raising questions about the extent to which public *responsibility* is being abdicated and public *authority* over educational content is being compromised. Are school officials doing anything wrong in making these deals? Is it an abuse of their authority to sell "access" to captive student audiences? Can an education that encourages consumption and debt transmit the virtues of thrift and prudence on which a competitive economy is built? How well can a school prepare students for democratic citizenship, if it allows them to be bombarded with the message that they are first and foremost *consumers*? Might a growing corporate presence in schools undermine their function as *public spaces* for conducting the public's business of preparing citizens?

Brighouse argues that the growing presence of commercial messages in schools is "a symptom of a deeply mistaken attitude on the part of administrators as to what schools should be doing." His argument hinges not on considerations of civic education, as some do, but on the principle that "the ethos of schools should be discontinuous with the mainstream culture," which is "deeply

materialistic" and one-dimensional. He holds that the endorsement of commercialism by a school "devalues" it in the eyes of nearly everyone involved, and limits its ability to provide students with alternative conceptions of worthwhile pursuits and fulfilling lives. In the interest of creating an autonomy facilitating, discontinuous ethos, there should be no television watching in schools at all, and school districts should make efforts to expose students to different ways of life, in part by ensuring that "school populations are composed of children from diverse backgrounds." This concluding thought suggests that the goal of autonomy facilitation generates an argument for a system of *common schools* analogous to a central argument in Friedman's chapter, raising the question of whether a *regulated* market system might serve as well as a public system in creating an approximation to schools with student populations representative of the diversity that exists in society.

## References

Locke, J. 1980: *Second Treatise of Government* (Indianapolis, IN: Hackett).

Pangle, L. S. and T. L. Pangle 1993: *The Learning of Liberty* (Lawrence: University Press of Kansas).

Reich, R. 2002: *Bridging Liberalism and Multiculturalism in American Education* (Chicago, IL: Chicago University Press).

# The Boundaries of
# Educational Authority

# 17

# Education and the Limits of State Authority

## John Stuart Mill

I have already observed that, owing to the absence of any recognized general principles, liberty is often granted where it should be withheld, as well as withheld where it should be granted; and one of the cases in which, in the modern European world, the sentiment of liberty is the strongest is a case where, in my view, it is altogether misplaced. A person should be free to do as he likes in his own concerns, but he ought not to be free to do as he likes in acting for another, under the pretext that the affairs of the other are his own affairs. The State, while it respects the liberty of each in what specially regards himself, is bound to maintain a vigilant control over his exercise of any power which it allows him to possess over others. This obligation is almost entirely disregarded in the case of the family relations – a case, in its direct influence on human happiness, more important than all others taken together. The almost despotic power of husbands over wives needs not be enlarged upon here, because nothing more is needed for the complete removal of the evil than that wives should have the same rights and should receive the protection of law in the same manner as all other persons; and because, on this subject, the defenders of established

injustice do not avail themselves of the plea of liberty but stand forth openly as the champions of power. It is in the case of children that misapplied notions of liberty are a real obstacle to the fulfillment by the State of its duties. One would almost think that a man's children were supposed to be literally, and not metaphorically, a part of himself, so jealous is opinion of the smallest interference of law with his absolute and exclusive control over them, more jealous than of almost any interference with his own freedom of action: so much less do the generality of mankind value liberty than power. Consider, for example, the case of education. Is it not almost a self-evident axiom that the State should require and compel the education, up to a certain standard, of every human being who is born its citizen? Yet who is there that is not afraid to recognize and assert this truth? Hardly anyone, indeed, will deny that it is one of the most sacred duties of the parents (or, as law and usage now stand, the father), after summoning a human being into the world, to give to that being an education fitting him to perform his part well in life toward others and toward himself. But while this is unanimously declared to be the father's duty, scarcely anybody,

Editor's title. Previously published in Elizabeth Rapaport (ed.), *On Liberty* (Indianapolis, IN: Hackett, 1978), pp. 103–7. Reprinted by permission of Hackett Publishing Co. Inc. All rights reserved.

in this country, will bear to hear of obliging him to perform it. Instead of his being required to make any exertion or sacrifice for securing education to his child, it is left to his choice to accept it or not when it is provided gratis! It still remains unrecognized that to bring a child into existence without a fair prospect of being able, not only to provide food for its body, but instruction and training for its mind is a moral crime, both against the unfortunate offspring and against society; and that if the parent does not fulfill this obligation, the State ought to see it fulfilled at the charge, as far as possible, of the parent.

Were the duty of enforcing universal education once admitted there would be an end to the difficulties about what the State should teach, and how it should teach, which now convert the subject into a mere battlefield for sects and parties, causing the time and labor which should have been spent in educating to be wasted in quarreling about education. If the government would make up its mind to require for every child a good education, it might save itself the trouble of providing one. It might leave to parents to obtain the education where and how they pleased, and content itself with helping to pay the school fees of the poorer classes of children, and defraying the entire school expenses of those who have no one else to pay for them. The objections which are urged with reason against State education do not apply to the enforcement of education by the State, but to the State's taking upon itself to direct that education; which is a totally different thing. That the whole or any large part of the education of the people should be in State hands, I go as far as anyone in deprecating. All that has been said of the importance of individuality of character, and diversity in opinions and modes of conduct, involves, as of the same unspeakable importance, diversity of education. A general State education is a mere contrivance for molding people to be exactly like one another; and as the mold in which it casts them is that which pleases the predominant power in the government – whether this be a monarch, a priesthood, an aristocracy, or the majority of the existing generation – in proportion as it is efficient and successful, it establishes a despotism over the mind, leading by natural tendency to one over the body. An education established and controlled by the State should only exist, if it exist at all, as one among many competing experiments, carried on for the purpose of example and stimulus to keep the others up to a certain standard of excellence. Unless, indeed, when society in general is in so backward a state that it could not or would not provide for itself any proper institutions of education unless the government undertook the task, then, indeed, the government may, as the less of two great evils, take upon itself the business of schools and universities, as it may that of joint stock companies when private enterprise in a shape fitted for undertaking great works of industry does not exist in the country. But in general, if the country contains a sufficient number of persons qualified to provide education under government auspices, the same persons would be able and willing to give an equally good education on the voluntary principle, under the assurance of remuneration afforded by a law rendering education compulsory, combined with State aid to those unable to defray the expense.

The instrument for enforcing the law could be no other than public examinations, extending to all children and beginning at an early age. An age might be fixed at which every child must be examined, to ascertain if he (or she) is able to read. If a child proves unable, the father, unless he has some sufficient ground of excuse, might be subjected to a moderate fine, to be worked out, if necessary, by his labor, and the child might be put to school at his expense. Once in every year the examination should be renewed, with a gradually extending range of subjects, so as to make the universal acquisition and, what is more, retention of a certain minimum of general knowledge virtually compulsory. Beyond that minimum there should be voluntary examinations on all subjects, at which all who come up to a certain standard of proficiency might claim a certificate. To prevent the State from exercising, through these arrangements, an improper influence over opinion, the knowledge required for passing an examination (beyond the merely instrumental parts of knowledge, such as, languages and their use) should, even in the higher classes of examinations, be confined to facts and positive science exclusively. The examinations on religion, politics, or other disputed topics should not turn on the truth or falsehood of opinions, but on the matter of fact that such and such an opinion is held, on such grounds, by such authors, or schools, or churches. Under this system, the rising generation would be no worse off in regard to all disputed truths than they are at present; they would be brought up either churchmen or dissenters as they now are, the State merely taking care that they should be instructed churchmen, or instructed dissenters. There would be nothing to hinder them from being taught religion, if their parents chose, at the same schools where they were taught other things. All attempts by the State to bias the conclusions of its citizens on disputed subjects are evil; but it may very properly offer to ascertain and certify that a person possesses the knowledge requisite to make his conclusions on any given subject worth attending to. A student of philosophy would be the better for being able to stand an examination both in Locke and in Kant, whichever of the two he takes up with, or even if with neither: and there is no reasonable objection to examining an atheist in the evidences of Christianity, provided he is not required to profess a belief in them. The examinations, however, in the higher branches of knowledge should, I conceive, be entirely voluntary. It would be giving too dangerous a power to governments were they allowed to exclude anyone from professions, even from the profession of teacher, for alleged deficiency of qualifications; and I think, with Wilhelm von Humboldt, that degrees or other public certificates of scientific or professional acquirements should be given to all who present themselves for examination and stand the test, but that such certificates should confer no advantage over competitors other than the weight which may be attached to their testimony by public opinion.

It is not in the matter of education only that misplaced notions of liberty prevent moral obligations on the part of parents from being recognized, and legal obligations from being imposed, where there are the strongest grounds for the former always, and in many cases for the latter also. The fact itself, of causing the existence of a human being, is one of the most responsible actions in the range of human life. To undertake this responsibility – to bestow a life which may be either a curse or a blessing – unless the being on whom it is to be bestowed will have at least the ordinary chances of a desirable existence, is a crime against that being. And in a country, either overpeopled or threatened with being so, to produce children, beyond a very small number, with the effect of reducing the reward of labor by their competition is a serious offense against all who live by the remuneration of their labor. The laws which, in many countries on the Continent, forbid marriage unless the parties can show that they have the means of supporting a family do not exceed the legitimate powers of the State; and whether such laws be expedient or not (a question mainly dependent on local circumstances and feelings), they are not objectionable as violations of liberty. Such laws are interferences of the State to prohibit a mischievous act – an act injurious to others, which ought to be a subject of reprobation and social stigma, even when it is not deemed expedient to superadd legal punishment. Yet the current ideas of liberty, which bend so easily to real infringements of the freedom of the individual in things which concern only himself, would repel the attempt to put any restraint upon his inclinations when the consequence of their indulgence is a life or lives of wretchedness and depravity to the offspring, with manifold evils to those sufficiently within reach to be in any way affected by their actions. When we compare the strange respect of mankind for liberty with their strange want of respect for it, we might imagine that a man had an indispensable right to do harm to others, and no right at all to please himself without giving pain to anyone.

# 18

# Democracy and Democratic Education

## Amy Gutmann

In the 17th century, when John Locke wrote *Some Thoughts Concerning Education*, education was closely identified with governance. The identification is no longer apparent in ordinary language, nor in contemporary political or educational philosophy. We need to revive the identification in order to understand the relationship between education and democracy (or any other political system). Education entails governance – whether of the young by the old, the ignorant by the knowledgeable, the foolish by the wise, or the relatively powerless by the powerful. And politics is the means by which educational authority establishes and asserts itself in all but the simplest human societies.

The most defensible conception of democratic education is democratic in both its end and its means. The end of democratic education is to create democratic citizens, people who are willing and able to govern their own lives and share in governing their society. And the means of educational governance are a complex balancing of parental, professional, and public authority, a combination consistent with the political ideals of representative democracy, which support the basic liberties of all adult members of a society.

We must also understand democratic education by the ends and means it opposes. In its commitment to critical deliberation, democratic education rejects inculcating blind allegiance to any political system and to any conception of the good life. In its commitment to pluralistic authority, democratic education opposes claims to exclusive (or ultimate) educational authority by parents, professionals, philosopher-kings, or self-appointed vanguards who shield themselves from public accountability.

The most profound problem that education poses for any pluralistic society with democratic aspirations is how to reconcile individual freedom and civic virtue. Children cannot be educated to maximize both individual freedom and civic virtue. Yet reasonable people value and intermittently demand both. We value freedom of speech and press, but want (other) people to refrain from false and socially harmful expression. We value freedom of religion and association, yet we want governments to shape our social environment so people are likely to believe in good (or at least socially benign) religions and philosophies of life rather than repugnant ones. We value the freedom to choose our marital partners and re-choose them, yet we also prize stable families

Previously published in *Studies in Philosophy and Education* 12 (1993): pp. 1–9. Reprinted with permission of Springer Verlag.

(for, among other reasons, their greater contribution to social welfare). We value living and working where we like, and we also value friendly and familiar places to live and work. We are proud to support the extension of our freedoms to other people, but we also fear that opening up our borders and our markets will erode our own way of life and standard of living.

These tensions between individual freedom and civic virtue pose a challenge for education in every pluralistic society. The challenge is simultaneously philosophical and political. How can we resolve these tensions philosophically in light of the political disagreement that exists among reasonable people on the relative value of individual freedom and civic virtue? Some people seem willing to settle for freedom for themselves and civic virtue for other citizens and children, but this solution obviously won't work. Far from obvious, however, is how any society can justly resolve its internal disagreements.

Should priority be given to one value over the other? If so, which one? Philosophers of what I call the "family state" give priority to teaching those civic virtues that bind citizens together in mutual pursuit of a comprehensive common good.[1] These communitarian philosophers appear untroubled by the fact that societies united by a comprehensive common good have been without exception repressive and discriminatory. The common good of the New England Puritans of seventeenth-century Salem commanded them to hunt witches; the common good of the Moral Majority in the United States today commands them not to tolerate homosexuals. Philosophers of the family state want us to live in Salem, but not believe in witches. Yet the protection of individual freedom is all that stands between intolerant movements like the Moral Majority in the United States and the contemporary equivalent of witch hunting.

In reaction to the repressive implications of the family state and in defense of the priority of individual freedom, many philosophers of what one might call the "state of individuals" argue that education must remain neutral among conceptions of the good life. "We have no right," Bruce Ackerman says, "to look upon future citizens as if we were master gardeners who can tell the difference between a pernicious weed and a beautiful flower. A system of liberal education provides children with a sense of the very different lives that could be theirs."[2] But this radically individualistic conception of education is politically troubling in its own way. It fails to justify imposing a politics of "liberal neutrality"[3] among conceptions of the good life on citizens who (reasonably) value civic virtue as well as individual freedom.

Communitarian philosophers of the family state assert their commitment to civic virtue and liberal philosophers of the state of individuals assert their commitment to individual freedom at the expense of denying the legitimacy of the other value. The practical consequence of their thinking is that basic individual freedoms are sacrificed to communal virtue or individual freedom is expanded so far as to forego the virtues essential to creating and maintaining a good society.

This resistance to recognizing the legitimacy of education for *both* individual freedom and civic virtue stems from formulating our educational options as a dichotomy. Either we must educate children so that they are free to choose among the widest range of lives because freedom of choice is the paramount good, or we must educate children so that they will choose *the* life that is best because a rightly-ordered soul is the paramount good. Let children define their own identity or let society define it for them. Give children liberty or give them virtue. This is a morally false choice. Cultivating character and intellect through education constrains children's future choices, but it does not uniquely determine them. There need be nothing illegitimate about such constraints (consistent with moral autonomy), although some constraints (epitomized by political and religious indoctrination) surely are illegitimate.

We stand at a philosophical and political impasse unless we can defend an alternative to communitarian solidarity – which insists that children be educated to accept the singularly correct and comprehensive conception of the good life – and liberal neutrality – which insists that education not predispose children toward *any* conception of the good life. Both philosophies of education denigrate citizenship, although in radically different ways, by taking serious moral disagreements off the political (and educational) agenda. At the same time, they disserve the genuine values – of individual freedom and civic virtue – that they claim to champion.

The ideal of democratic education denies the validity of this dichotomy between individual freedom and civic virtue, which dominates the current debate between philosophers of the state of individuals and the family state. Individual freedom of choice is most valuable in a society that also cultivates many of the civic virtues typically defended by communitarians, among them, veracity, self-discipline, diligence, compassion, and loyalty. These civic virtues are bound to bias (and often legitimately *intended* to bias) citizens towards some ways of life and away from others. And the civic virtues essential to a democracy include the "strength of mind, individuality, [and] independence" that liberals, following the l8th-century philosopher of education Noah Webster, typically call upon education to cultivate in future citizens.[4]

We can make some progress in this controversy between communitarians and liberals (or, more accurately, individualists) if we develop a more democratic ideal of education. Education should prepare citizens for consciously *reproducing* (not replicating) their society. We should therefore support a set of educational practices to which citizens, acting collectively, have consciously agreed, provided that those practices also prepare future citizens for participating intelligently in the political processes that shape their society. The ideal of democratic education – *conscious social reproduction* – both supports democratic decisionmaking and constrains what democracies are permitted to do in education. Democracies must act so as to secure the conditions for future democratic deliberations.

For a society to reproduce itself *consciously*, it must be *nonrepressive*. It must not restrict rational consideration of different ways of life. Instead it must cultivate the kind of character and the kind of intellect that enables people to choose rationally (one might say "autonomously") among different ways of life. The democratic principle of nonrepression prevents the state, and any group within it, from using education unnecessarily to restrict rational deliberation of differing conceptions of good lives and societies. It also requires the state to cultivate the capacity for rational deliberation. Nonrepression is therefore not a principle of purely negative freedom. It secures freedom from interference only to the extent that it forbids using education to restrict rational deliberation or consideration of different ways of life. Nonrepression is compatible with (indeed it requires) the use of education to teach those civic virtues – such as veracity, nonviolence, toleration and mutual respect – that serve as foundations for rational deliberation of differing ways of life. These civic virtues are to be taught both by example and by argument. If citizens are to live up to the democratic ideal of

sharing political sovereignty, they must learn not just to *behave* in accordance with democratic values but also to *understand* them (and therefore to *think* critically about them).

Nonrepression is not neutral among conceptions of the good life, nor is its strongest defense based on an ideal of political neutrality. The ideal of democratic education itself generates the principled defense of nonrepression, and the principle of nonrepression then sets practical limits on popular authority. Because *conscious* social reproduction is the ideal of democratic education, majorities as well as minorities must be prevented from using education to stifle rational deliberation of competing conceptions of the good.

For a *society* rather than some segment of it to reproduce itself, it must be *nondiscriminatory*. *Everyone* must be educated nonrepressively. Nondiscrimination extends the logic of nonrepression, since states and families can be selectively repressive by excluding entire groups of children from schooling or by denying them an education conducive to rational deliberation. Repression commonly takes the more passive form of discrimination in education against ethnic and racial minorities, girls, and other disfavored groups in society. The effect of educational discrimination is often to repress, at least temporarily, the capacity and sometimes even the desire of disfavored groups to participate in politics or to assert their own preferences in private life. Discrimination in education is therefore a cause as well as an effect of political disadvantage, as highlighted by the history of educational discrimination against African-Americans in the United States.

In its most general application to education, the principle of nondiscrimination prevents the state, and all groups within it, from denying anyone an educational good on grounds irrelevant to the legitimate social purpose of that good. Applied to the education necessary to prepare children for future citizenship, the nondiscrimination principle becomes a principle of nonexclusion. No educable child – regardless of race, religion, ethnicity, sex, parental interest (or disinterest) – may be excluded from an education adequate to participate in democratic politics.

A pluralistic democratic society can neither resolve nor avoid the problem of discrimination in education by "privatizing" schools. Proponents of privatization in the United States have suggested that governments offer parents "educational vouchers" worth up to a specified sum when spent on schooling of their choice for their children. Some European countries distribute public monies to established religious groups to run their own schools on their own terms. Unconstrained (i.e., truly privatized) voucher plans risk increasing racial, religious, and ethnic segregation, and decreasing educational opportunity for disadvantaged children whose parents are unlikely to find them a good school. The alternative of delegating education to religious and ethnic groups has been a recipe for perpetuating rather than ameliorating existing religious and ethnic hostilities. But the most fundamental problem with privatization plans concerns not their consequences (although they are bad enough) but their implicit denial of governmental responsibility for nondiscrimination and nonrepression in education. Regardless of whether schools are operated by public or private authorities, democratic governments retain ultimate (although by no means exclusive) responsibility for nondiscrimination and nonrepression in education just as they retain responsibility for public safety even if they decide to "privatize" their police forces. Although the operation of schools and police forces can be privatized, responsibility for fulfillment of their public purposes cannot be.[5] Given the all-too-human temptation of public officials to pass both bucks together, privatization remains an unpromising path to democratic education.

For a society to be *reproductive*, it must institute practices of democratic *deliberation and decision-making* for its adult citizens, and for children to the extent necessary for cultivating their capacities of democratic deliberation. To shape their society, citizens and their representatives engage in collective deliberations and decisionmaking at different levels of government. They need not replicate their current practices, and they must not do so in the many instances where those practices are repressive or discriminatory. (The aims of democratic education will not be fully realized, for example, until American citizens can share in self-determination not only in government but also in their daily work. Or until Soviet citizens are free to campaign and vote in multi-party elections.) Reproduction never requires replication. Nonrepression and nondiscrimination often do not permit it.

Democratic reproduction also places special demands on education, to cultivate deliberative capacities and social responsibility in students. Education entails authority, but *democratic* educational authorities must prepare children for self-governance

while they are being governed. Democratic schools are so-called not because they treat students as the intellectual or political equals of their teachers, but because they teach students self-governance. John Dewey's Laboratory School at the University of Chicago, which distributed decisionmaking authority and responsibility even to the youngest students, aimed at being a "miniature community, an embryonic democratic society,"[6] not by putting the most important curricular and hiring decisions up to majority vote but by allowing students to practice their political skills and to assume significant responsibilities in the school, skills and responsibilities that were appropriate to their level of intellectual and social development.

Studies amply demonstrate that conventional civics and history courses in American schools have little impact on students' political knowledge, political interest, sense of political efficacy, political trust, or civic tolerance.[7] Both the means and the ends of these conventional courses are misconceived. History and civics courses should teach lessons in democratic deliberation, lessons similar to the one that Diane Ravitch observed being taught in a public high school in Brooklyn, New York. The students were asked to discuss whether it was right for the United States to drop the atomic bomb on Hiroshima:

> The lesson was taught in a Socratic manner. Bruckner did not lecture. He asked questions and kept up a rapid-fire dialogue among the students. "Why?" "How do you know?" "What does this mean?" . . . By the time the class was finished, the students had covered a great deal of material about American foreign and domestic politics during World War II; they had argued heatedly: most of them had tried out different points of view, seeing the problem from different angles.[8]

The most relevant result of such courses from the perspective of democratic education is not an increase in political knowledge, cultural literacy (in the narrow sense), or even political trust or efficacy, but an increase in the willingness and ability of students to *reason and argue about politics, collectively and critically, respectful of their reasonable differences*, a willingness and ability that is distinctively democratic.

If this understanding of democratic education is correct, then the ideal of democratic education lies at the core of a commitment to democracy. The ideal of democracy is often said to be collective self-determination. But there is no "collective self" to be determined. There are just so many individual selves that must find a fair way of sharing the goods (and bads) of a society together. It would be dangerous, as liberal critics of communitarianism charge, to assume that any state – even a democratic one – *constitutes* the collective self of a society, and that its policies in turn define the best interests of its citizens.

But we do not need this dangerous metaphysical assumption to defend a democratic ideal, an ideal of citizens sharing in deliberatively determining the future shape of their society. The democratic society that citizens determine is not a self that defines their best interests. There remain independent standards for defining the best interests of individuals and reasons for thinking that individuals, rather than collectivities, are generally the best judges of their own interests. To avoid the misleading metaphysical connotations of the concept of collective self-determination, we may better identify the democratic ideal as conscious social reproduction, the same ideal that guides democratic education.

The convergence of democratic ideals is of course not a coincidence. Democratic education supplies the foundations upon which a democratic society can cede civil and political freedoms to its adult citizens without placing their welfare or its very survival at great risk. In the absence of democratic education, risks – even great risks – will still be worth taking for the sake of respecting the rights of citizens to be free from the political repression that all but inevitably accompanies an authoritarian state. But our passion for democracy should not blind us to the risks involved in democratizing countries whose educational and political systems have perpetuated religious intolerance, ethnic hatred, and blind obedience to authority. Democratic government depends on democratic education for its full moral and political strength.

The dependency is reciprocal. Without democratic government, the best education to which a society could aspire might be similar to that practised for thirteen centuries in Imperial China, where a centralized state supported schools and designed a thorough system of examinations that determined access on highly meritocratic grounds to all state offices. When working at its best, the Chinese educational system stimulated considerable social

mobility,[9] but the nondemocratic state usurped control of what rightly belongs to citizens: political decisions concerning (among other important things) how future citizens are educated outside the home. When it usurps democratic authority, the state also eliminates the strongest, political rationale for democratic education: teaching the virtues of democratic deliberation for the sake of future citizenship. Democratic education therefore follows at the same time as it reinforces a more general political commitment to democracy.

Democratic citizens learn how to govern by first being fairly governed as children. After they have been governed, they must have a right to govern themselves (without repression or discrimination). This is a democratic understanding of politics and education: being governed and governing in turn, where governing includes the nurturing of children by parents, their formal instruction by professionals, the structuring of public education by public officials accountable to citizens, and the shaping of economy and culture by both private and public authorities.

Recent defenses of democracy, most notably by the philosophers Richard Rorty and Michael Walzer, have taken the form of a priority principle: democracy has priority over philosophy.[10] What citizens decide is right takes precedence over what philosophers demonstrate to be right. The case for democratic education and democracy more generally does not entail giving priority to democracy over philosophy. The priority principle misleads us about both philosophy and democracy, and unnecessarily weakens the case for democracy. If the wisest philosophers, like Socrates, are distinguished not just by knowing what they do not know but also by publicly admitting the limits of their knowledge, then far from subordinating itself to democracy, philosophy is the source of democracy's strongest moral defense. Philosophy defends democracy when it discovers that the best life and the best society to which we can aspire must be among those that we can recognize and claim as our own. Philosophers cannot simply give citizens a good society, anymore than parents can give their children a good life. One reason for this inherent limit on the power of philosophers (and parents) is that a good life must be one that people live from the inside, by accepting and identifying it as their own. Another reason is that any credible standard for a good life will leave room for discretionary choices on the part of the people who are living those lives. Philosophers, like parents who would tell people precisely how to live their lives, are morally pretentious. Democratic education embraces this insight of liberal neutrality, but it rejects the view that individual freedom is therefore the only legitimate end of education and democracy.

Returning to the question with which we began: should a society try to teach freedom or virtue? The ideal of democratic education commits a society to teaching virtue, what might best be called *democratic* virtue, the character that is necessary for a flourishing constitutional democracy. The virtues of democratic character include veracity, self-discipline, nonviolence, toleration, mutual respect for reasonable differences of opinion, the ability to deliberate, to think critically about one's life and one's society, and therefore to participate in conscious social reproduction. Democratic education thereby cultivates both personal and political autonomy, the capacity of all educable citizens to deliberate, both individually and collectively, among a wide range of personal and political lives. Within the constraints of nonrepression and nondiscrimination, a democratic society leaves citizens free to shape their personal and political lives in a plurality of images that they can legitimately identify with their informed, moral choices.

The pedagogical demands of democratic education are therefore great. Schools, for example, must cultivate both moral character (the virtues of veracity, nonviolence, tolerance, etc.) and the capacity for moral reasoning (logic, critical understanding, etc.) in future citizens. Nothing less will do. People adept at logical reasoning who lack moral character are sophists of the worst sort: they rationalize their self-interest, by cleverly using moral arguments to serve whatever ends they happen to choose for themselves. They do not take morality seriously nor are they able to distinguish between the obvious moral demands and the agonizing dilemmas of life. But neither can we find democratic citizens among people who possess sturdy moral character without a developed capacity for reasoning. Such people are ruled only by habit and authority, and are incapable of constituting a society of sovereign citizens. Education in character and in moral reasoning are therefore both necessary, neither sufficient, for creating democratic citizens. Under the best of circumstances, democratic education is demanding. In societies beset by some combination of disintegrating or authoritarian families, nihilism or ideological fundamentalism, drug or alcohol epidemics, authoritarian workplaces, unemployment, and manipulated or commercialized mass media, democratic educators and policymakers face a much more formidable task.

The distinctive features of democratic theory are its simultaneous refusal to dissolve the tensions between individual freedom and civic virtue in a potent philosophical solution (of communitarian solidarity or liberal neutrality) and its insistence on finding a principled way of living with the tensions, in keeping with the democratic ideal of conscious social reproduction. Living with tensions is never easy, nor is it without its sacrifices. But for any pluralistic society, whose citizens value both individual freedom and civic virtue, communitarian solidarity and liberal neutrality – the alternatives to democracy that promise an escape from moral tensions – are far worse.

## Notes

1. My discussions of the family state and most other matters in this essay are more fully developed in *Democratic Education* (Princeton, NJ: Princeton University Press, 1987).
2. Bruce Ackerman, *Social Justice in the Liberal State* (New York: Yale University Press, 1980) p. 139.
3. Because neutrality has become such a philosophically popular defense of liberalism these days, it bears mentioning that the neutrality defense is conspicuously absent from the classical liberal tradition. Neither John Locke, John Stuart Mill, Immanuel Kant, nor any other major classical liberal philosopher invokes neutrality as a defense of religious liberty or any other individual right. The critique of liberal neutrality, far from being a critique of classical liberalism, spares liberalism from a damaging misinterpretation. My defense of democratic education is consistent with certain contemporary contractarian understandings of liberalism. Insofar as democratic education requires a defense of nonrepression and nondiscrimination, it is a *liberal* democratic conception.
4. Noah Webster, 'On the Education of Youth in America' [1790], in Frederick Rudolph (ed.), *Essays on Education in the Early Republic* (Cambridge, MA: Harvard University Press, 1965).
5. The best review and balanced critique of the recent privatization movement in the United States is

John D. Donahue, *The Privatization Decision: Public Ends, Private Means* (New York: Basic Books, 1989).

6. John Dewey, 'The School and Society', in *'The Child and the Curriculum' and 'The School and Society'* [1900, 1915] (Chicago: University of Chicago Press, 1956), p. 18.

7. See, for example, M. Kent Jennings, Kenneth P. Langton, and Richard G. Niemi, 'Effects of High School Civics Curriculum,' in M. Kent Jennings and Richard G. Niemi, *The Political Character of Adolescence: The Influence of Families and Schools* (Princeton, NJ: Princeton University Press, 1974), pp. 191–2. Jennings, Lee H. Ehman, and Niemi also find that only a small minority of high-school history and civics teachers take as one of their major goals to challenge their students to think critically about history or politics. 'Social Studies Teachers and Their Pupils,' in *The Political Character of Adolescence*, p. 226.

8. Diane Ravitch, *The Schools We Deserve: Reflections on the Educational Crises of Our Times* (New York: Basic Books, 1985), p. 228.

9. See Ping-Ti Ho, *The Ladder of Success in Imperial China: Aspects of Social Mobility, 1368–1911* (New York: Columbia University Press, 1962), esp. pp. 257–62.

10. See Richard Rorty, 'The Priority of Democracy to Philosophy', in Merrill D. Peterson and Robert C. Vaughan (eds.), *The Virginia Statute for Religious Freedom: Its Evolution and Consequences in American History* (New York: Cambridge University Press, 1990); and Michael Walzer, 'Philosophy and Democracy,' *Political Theory* 9 (August 1981), pp. 384–94.

# 19

# Justice, Inequality, and Home Schooling

## Charles L. Howell

A number of critics of home schooling have suggested that the withdrawal of children from schools reflects and reinforces a broader societal trend. In the past half century, the most educated and affluent citizens have withdrawn en masse first from cities to suburbs, then from public into private spaces, and most recently into electronic networks and controlled-access communities. This position will be referred to as the *privatization argument*. In this article, the implications of the privatization argument for home schooling are explored through philosophical analysis.

Why is it that critics believe that privatization in general and home schooling in particular should be deplored and resisted? Three distinct reasons for concern appear in the literature. The first is that through withdrawal into private pursuits, we are losing our public cohesion, our ability and willingness to work together for common benefit, and that the erosion of that capacity is producing a society that is poorer, meaner, and on balance worse for all its members (Lubienski, 2000). A second is that withdrawal undercuts public authority over the formation of future citizens, which Gutmann (1987). Callan (1997), Curren (2000), and others suggest democratic societies need to sustain themselves. The

third is that the trend toward withdrawal exacerbates inequality, allowing the privileged sectors of the society to capitalize on their advantages and to deny similar opportunities to others (Apple, 2000).

In Section II, I examine the basis for each of these concerns. The first two, it turns out, are ineffectual. One depends on an assumption about the effects of home schooling that has not been confirmed by empirical study. The other depends on a definition of democracy that home schoolers probably do not accept. Only the third generates a compelling objection to home schooling, and then only if one accepts as a requirement of justice a version of equal opportunity, which I shall call *strong equality*. In Section III, I examine the rationale for strong equality and how it would apply to home schooling. In Section IV, I consider two arguments advocates of home schooling might give for not accepting strong equality as a condition of justice.

The aim of this inquiry is to present more clearly than has been done in the past what is at issue in the debate about home schooling and privatization. Philosophical analysis cannot settle factual questions. It cannot determine the effects of home schooling or the proper balance between parental and civic obligations. What it can do is trace the logic

Previously published in *Home School Researcher* 15(3) (2003): pp. 1–9. © 2003 National Home Education Research Institute. Reprinted with permission of National Home Education Research Institute and the author.

that leads people from factual claims to conclusions about how we ought to live and how children ought to be educated. Parties to the debate must then decide whether the factual premises are credible and whether the conclusions conflict with their experience, prior knowledge, or strongly held moral principles. This approach will not resolve the dispute over home schooling, but it is to be hoped that it will cut through some of the hyperbole and circumlocution that have plagued the debate and help parties see why their reasons do not count as reasons for others.

## Three Versions of the Argument: A Preliminary Assessment

Of the three versions of the privatization argument, cohesion depends most directly on an empirical claim, namely that home schoolers withdraw from public life and undercut possibilities for cooperation with fellow citizens. It is not impossible that this claim could turn out to be true. Granted, researchers have found that home schoolers join support groups, engage in political action, and participate in church and other voluntary activities (Stevens, 2001). There may be others, however, who do not do so, and their isolation might offset the engagement of activists and thus vindicate the critique.

The problem is that evidence of isolation effects has not yet been produced, while evidence of engagement abounds. Moreover, even if such isolation effects are found, there is a further complication. Public school attendance does not guarantee social cohesion. As Coleman et al. (1966) showed, communities vary enormously in social capital, or capacity for cooperative social interaction; schools can foster cooperation, but they cannot be expected to eliminate these differences. On the contrary, Annette Lareau's (2000) study of home–school interaction suggests that schools' efforts to promote parental involvement have very little effect on the extent and intensity of social interconnections in a community. The cohesion critique requires evidence that rebuts this research as well as the findings on home schoolers' sociability. In the present state of knowledge on these matters, it is highly speculative.

The second version of the privatization argument – maintenance of democracy – is not so obviously dependent on an empirical claim. Because many factors affect a state's political character, empirical tests of the sustainability of different types of regimes are extremely difficult to conduct. The argument must therefore be understood as conceptual. From the idea of democracy, we deduce the conditions for sustaining it. Thus, when Gutmann (1987) asks who, in a democratic society, should have authority over the education of future citizens, the answer is understood to be self-evident.

The problem with this approach is that the concept of democracy is malleable, and different versions have different conditions for maintenance. The accounts of Madison, Dahl (1956), and Mansfield (1978) all allow for, and indeed require, considerable dispersal of power, which seems compatible with home schoolers' efforts to control the education of their children. The accounts of Dewey (1927) and Gutmann and Thompson (1996) are less tolerant of the exercise of private power, and therefore less hospitable to home schooling. Critics of home schooling can thus point to several accounts of democracy that support their position, but so can its defenders. The critics must then go on to show that their version of democracy is to be preferred to others. The grounds of debate shift, and the focus of critique is no longer home schooling, but rather a conception of democracy that critics regard as untenable. Until widespread agreement on these matters is achieved, democratic sustainability will not generate a very compelling objection to home schooling.

The third version of the privatization argument, inequality, is more promising than the others for two reasons. First, proponents of home schooling have long argued that children get a better education at home than in school; the difference in quality is likely to exacerbate inequality. Second, one well-known source of educational inequality is the influence of a student's home background (Fishkin, 1981; Vallentyne, 1989). To some extent, this influence may be counteracted by school attendance; if so, then withdrawing a child from school would make home influence stronger and thus accentuate inequality.

Again, there are difficulties. Home schoolers do seek to provide educational advantages for their children, but not all of these advantages are of the same kind, nor is it clear by what standard they are to be compared with public schools. How, for example, are the ideals favored by Evangelical Christian denominations, and inculcated by some home-schooling parents, to be measured against the intellectual independence cultivated by unschoolers or the conventional academic skills on which schools typically focus?

Suppose we do agree on a standard of comparison – standardized test scores or some other measure of performance. It must still be shown that (a) home-schooled students do indeed have an advantage, and (b) this advantage exacerbates rather than ameliorates inequality. This is by no means a trivial exercise.

In the case of (a), much recent research suggests that home schooling may indeed increase academic achievement. These studies, however, are by no means conclusive; all are to some degree subject to self-selection effects. Now suppose these effects can be eliminated, and an academic advantage for home schoolers is conclusively demonstrated. This result would not, in itself, show that home schooling increases inequality. A common measure of educational inequality is the degree to which children's achievement reflects their parents' income and level of education. If, as recent studies suggest, the home school advantage is relatively insensitive to these characteristics, then the effect of home schooling on inequality depends on who decides to home school. Condition (b) is satisfied only when more affluent families home school, because only then is the achievement gap between rich and poor widened. When poor families home school, inequality is ameliorated. If that is the case, then the equality argument implies that more poor families should home school their children. This is clearly not the result for which critics are aiming.

A more general problem with the inequality argument is that public schools themselves are grossly unequal. Schools in property-rich districts with high proportions of educated and affluent families consistently outperform schools in poorer districts with less advantaged populations. Within schools, families seek advantages for their children by enrolling them in a variety of specialized programs, ranging from International Baccalaureate to second-language immersion programs, and by supporting their participation in extracurricular activities that require investments of money and time beyond the capacity of poor families. Home schoolers, in short, could cause a great deal of inequality without doing worse than schools do.

This difficulty would be eliminated, however, if critics evaluated home schooling not in relation to public schools as they are now, but in relation to schools that have undergone egalitarian reform.

Suppose, for example, public schools were to move in the direction Jonathan Kozol (1991) advocates: all children getting roughly the same education, with supplementary resources directed on the basis of need. William Duncombe (1999) has suggested that such an arrangement could equalize average outcomes on the level of school districts, and consequently also for different social classes and racial groups. If this result were achieved, the influence of home would be eliminated; a child's future well-being would no longer depend on the family into which she is born. A number of social theorists have argued that only this pattern of outcomes yields real equality of opportunity. Let us refer to this standard as *strong equality*, to distinguish it from other, weaker interpretations of equal opportunity that merely ban discrimination without equalizing life chances.

As grounds for a critique of home schooling, strong equality is ideal because it can be achieved only in schools. Only through central control can a uniform plan of instruction be administered and adjusted in the right way to produce equal outcomes. Home schooling would disrupt the pattern of outcomes, allowing parents to influence the quality of education their children received and thus preventing society as a whole from ensuring that accidents of birth do not skew life prospects. This line of argument avoids the complications of cohesion and maintenance of democracy. The empirical evidence of family influence and inequality is all in its favor.

Ironically, the present inequality of public schools strengthens rather than weakens this argument. The inequality is caused, in large measure, by the very practices to which critics object. Urban schools declined when affluent and well-educated families moved out to the suburbs. Poor children receive a less challenging education in part because ambitious parents channel their children into specialized programs. Within individual classrooms, activist middle-class parents are able to tailor their children's school experience to provide what Lareau (2000) calls "home advantage" (p. 176). These are precisely the practices with which Apple and others take issue. To point out that such factors make strong equality difficult to achieve reinforces their argument.

Strong equality, in short, generates a clearer and more consistent critique of home schooling than other versions of the privatization argument. It is indeed true that home schooling would tend to thwart the aims of schools if they were redesigned to eliminate family advantage. But are the premises of strong equality plausible? Can a compelling claim be made that this is indeed a principle of justice?

In Section III, I present the most promising argument in defense of strong equality. This section examines the reasoning that leads egalitarian critics from premises that are accepted widely, even by home schoolers themselves, to conclusions that home schooling advocates are bound to find deeply troubling. In Section IV, I explore lines of resistance to this argument. This section explains how home schoolers, and also parents who seek to promote their children's future well-being in a variety of other ways, could accept the claim that they are sustaining and possibly increasing inequality, yet at the same time have reason to believe that they are not acting unjustly.

## Strong Equality: Rationale and Educational Implications

Strong equality is advanced as a principle of distributive justice – a rule for distributing resources fairly. Theories of distributive justice nearly always require equality within some domain. Even libertarian theories, which allow extensive inequality, usually emphasize that everyone has the same right to enjoy the property she owns and everyone is entitled to police protection and the administration of justice (Nozick, 1974). As one leading egalitarian points out, the question for social theorists is not whether justice requires equality, but rather within what domain it is required (Dworkin, 1985). Outside the domain of equality, inequality in various forms is allowed.

Strong equality holds that inequality is permissible only if it is caused by acts or circumstances for which a person can be held responsible. The underlying idea is that a just social policy would not allow people's well-being to depend on factors beyond their control. Kymlicka (1990) characterizes this approach as "ambition sensitive" and "endowment insensitive." A person's ambition (choices and effort) may legitimately affect her well-being, but her endowment (effects of chance and of other people's effort and choices) should not do so. Rawls (1971) makes a similar point by suggesting that outcomes should be affected by morally relevant factors (i.e., a person's character, choices, willingness to make an effort), but not by factors that are not morally relevant (such as skin color, national origin, or socioeconomic background). He called this principle "fair equality of opportunity," distinguishing it from "formal equality of opportunity," which focuses solely on non-discrimination, ignoring other factors that might unfairly affect a person's chance

of success (Rawls, 1971, pp. 73–4). Dworkin (1981), Bernard Williams (1972), Arneson (1989), Cohen (1989), and Roemer (1995) all propose variations on this basic theme that a just social order ought to rectify inequalities that arise from factors beyond a person's control. For convenience, let us refer to this principle as the *responsibility thesis*.

In egalitarian hands, the responsibility thesis is a powerful tool. It provides a succinct argument for redistributing resources, and it exploits the reasoning of those who defend inequality on the grounds that economic outcomes reflect people's *life choices*. According to market theory, the rich become rich because they prepare themselves to offer what society most values; the poor remain poor because they decline to do so. To transfer resources from rich to poor is wrong, since the poor could have gotten resources for themselves if they had been willing to do useful work. People deserve the outcomes that are due to their choices and effort.

But, as egalitarians point out, the corollary of that argument is just as compelling. People whose choices and effort are similar deserve equal outcomes, and thus the effects of other factors should be equalized. So, if two people are equally willing to contribute and expend equal effort, and through luck, opportunity, education, or family background one ends up on the street and the other in an executive suite, then the life choices argument seems to imply that their circumstances ought to be equalized. So, at any rate, argue the proponents of strong equality.

Education, by Kymlicka's (1990) definition, is an endowment, an item outside the agent's control that affects her well-being and should therefore be equalized. How good an education a child gets is determined not by her but by adults – parents, political leaders, school officials. True, as students grow older, ambition and effort do make a difference, opening up opportunities for some and foreclosing them for others. But as Rawls (1971) observes, families strongly influence children's "willingness to make an effort" (p. 74). Children's choices reflect adult expectations and guidance, and thus they cannot be held fully responsible for the consequences. As Kozol (1991) maintains, no child ever chooses a second-rate education, even though in certain circumstances some may act as if that is all they want or expect.

Education, then, is an endowment. The responsibility thesis will therefore require that its effects – educational outcomes – be equalized. The principle of strong equality thus demands what Underwood (1995) calls "vertical equity" (p. 493) – not just simple equality, with everyone treated the same, but resources allocated on the basis of need, as Kozol (1991) has advocated. But how do we determine what count as needs and resources? To avoid terminological disputes, let us designate whatever diminishes educational outcomes as a need and whatever enhances them as a resource. In some cases this may generate counterintuitive classifications, but the resulting formula accurately represents what the responsibility thesis requires.

Would home schooling necessarily disrupt the resource/need system of allocation? If we adopt the traditional view of resources as public expenditure, probably not. Nearly all home school families spend much less per child than even poorly equipped public schools. But, as educational research since the 1970s has demonstrated, monetary resources are not the only input that matters. Educational outcomes are also affected by adult expectations, parents' educational level, the climate of school and home life, and a host of other factors that don't show up on a balance sheet. Shirley Brice Heath (1996) has shown that even the speech patterns of families and communities affect educational outcomes, by either teaching or not teaching children the discursive patterns valued by schools and the larger society.

If children's life chances are to be equalized, then factors of this kind must be taken into account and the inequalities they generate removed by compensatory programs. Clearly, home schooling would obstruct such an effort, first because the effects of differences in home environment and parental influence are magnified, and second because the equalizing effects of school are eliminated. In effect, home schooling directs massive resources (parental attention and care and the cultural opportunities of the home and community) to precisely those children with the fewest needs (because of family solidarity, parents' educational background, and parents' involvement in their education).

From the premise of strong equality, it clearly follows that home schooling is wrong, and the critics' position is vindicated. But what action is to be taken on the basis of that conclusion? Would egalitarian critics forbid home schooling?

Clearly not Apple (2000). His criticism of home schoolers is circumspect. He does not doubt the sincerity of their concern for their children. What worries him is not so much the direct effect of home schooling on the gap between the educational haves and have-nots, as its ideological impact. He anticipates that arguments for home schooling will indirectly support other forms of privatization and ultimately help to justify deepening inequality. Apple's underlying message, in short, takes the form of political criticism, not policy proposals designed to make things difficult for home schoolers.

Kozol (1991), too, shrinks from the broader implications of the responsibility thesis, and seems unwilling to try to block the unearned advantages enjoyed by children of ambitious and successful families. His version of the needs-resources formula applies only to public funding. What families spend on their own children – summer camps, music lessons, home computers, and the like – is their own business. Their attempts to advance their children's life prospects may be regrettable, callous, and myopic, but so long as they do not impinge on the allocation of public resources, they are not properly a target for state action.

This cautious stance, however, is more likely an expression of prudence than of principle. The state could redistribute educational advantages, even those generated by the private actions of families, and if strong equality is [required as a matter of justice] then it ought to do so. If, for example, wealthy parents improve their children's educational outcomes by providing home computers, music lessons, or summer camp, then the state could do the same for less fortunate children.

No doubt this would be expensive. Replicating all of the advantages that wealthy parents provide for their children could exhaust public resources at their current levels. There are, however, ways to avoid this result. A more steeply progressive tax system would curb discretionary spending in upper income brackets, reducing the need for compensatory programs. Or, in a more focused strategy, excise taxes could be imposed on specific items used by the wealthy to provide educational advantages for their children: for example, musical instruments, instructional services, home Internet connections, and computers for non-business use. The taxes would both discourage purchase of these items and generate funds to support public provision for families that can't afford them. Home schooling itself could also be taxed; or it could be discouraged through regulation, book-keeping requirements, and expansion of amenities offered only to students in public schools.

It might be argued that these measures violate constitutional protections. A number of state and federal courts have held that families have a constitutional right to provide for the education of their children; such a right may only be limited in further-ance of a compelling state interest. This constitu-tional principle, however, is not properly speaking an argument against the egalitarian position. Strong equality is advanced not as a recommendation for public policy within a pre-existing constitutional framework, but rather as a prescription for a just society and a just constitutional order. If strong equality really is a principle of justice and the United States Constitution prevents its realization, so much the worse for the Constitution. Justice would require that it be amended or abrogated.

Strong equality, then, is a straightforward prin-ciple with a clear rationale, and could easily be applied to an educational system. If it is indeed a principle of justice, then parental efforts on behalf of their children, including home schooling, are a source of injustice and should be blocked or dis-couraged by state action. This is not the only pos-sible formulation of the privatization argument: As we have already seen, critics also view privatization as a threat to public cohesion and the democratic political order. Strong equality, however, appears to be the most cogent interpretation of the privatiza-tion argument as it applies to home schooling.

No doubt advocates of home schooling will resist this conclusion. If so, they must reject the principle of strong equality on which it is based. But can they offer principled reasons for doing so? Like many others in this society, most defenders of home schooling probably subscribe to some version of the responsibility thesis: that a person deserves what she works for and is responsible for the consequences of her choices. Can anyone who believes this con-sistently reject the rest of the egalitarian argument? This is the issue explored in the next section.

## Arguments Against Strong Equality

Home schoolers and their allies have many differ-ent reasons for rejecting the policies outlined in the last section. Some believe home schooling is justified by Biblical precepts, some see parental control over the education of children as a natural right, and still others believe that the structure of school inhibits learning.

However important these beliefs are to home schoolers, though, they do not answer the present objection, because critics do not generally share them. What is needed is a response that shows why the critics' conclusion is wrong without relying

on premises they are unlikely to accept. In this section I introduce and evaluate two arguments of this type. Both address the policy implications of strong equality, and both rely on premises that are widely accepted both by home schoolers and by public school advocates. Only one, however, turns out to offer a secure defense of home schooling.

The first argument depends on a widely held view about agency and paternalism. Nearly every person is or is in the process of becoming a moral agent, capable of deciding what she values and what will enhance her well-being. Recognizing this capacity requires that we honor each person's autonomy – her right to act on her own behalf and in accordance with her own beliefs and desires. Only in special cases is that right abridged: notably, when the sub-ject lacks the capacity to act for her own good. In such cases, a person or institution may act pater-nalistically on behalf of the subject, temporarily limiting her scope of action to further her long-term well being.

The standard example of paternalism is the treat-ment of children. Because they cannot anticipate the demands of adult life, we must guide their actions and often override their choices. The family and school both play this role. Their justification for doing so is that control is necessary to secure the child's future well being.

Public schools typically acknowledge this require-ment, though they may not always satisfy it. The slogans of educational reform in the past decade – "inclusive education," "success for all," "equity and excellence" – all speak to the need to advance every child's interests. But, advocates of home schooling will ask, would egalitarian schools behave in this way?

Strong equality dictates that differences in family background are to be evened out, and schools are the primary means for doing so. To this end, resources (allocable items that improve outcomes) are distributed in proportion to need (any condition that diminishes outcomes). What would this mean for advanced students? By definition they have no unmet needs, no condition that causes substandard achievement. Thus they should be allocated no resources beyond those that are provided to every student. They should receive no differentiated instruction, no special attention from teachers, and no programs adapted to their capacities and inter-ests. Even if these accommodations cost nothing and consumed none of the teacher's time, they would be undesirable because they make equal outcomes more difficult to achieve.

Thus far, the advanced students do not appear to suffer any harm. They are treated the same as everyone else. There is, however, one crucial difference. For much of the school day, they aren't learning. Teaching, curriculum, and learning materials are all geared to the level of the students who make less effort and do not enjoy family advantage. Under this regime, if it is skillfully managed, slower students will progress steadily, but advantaged students, who start off knowing more, will learn less, and will spend much of their time not learning at all. In fact, home schoolers argue, they would make more progress working independently outside school. Egalitarians typically do not dispute this claim. Thus they must concede that the school regime they favor violates the duty of paternalism: It overrides some students' choices in ways that do not further their interests.

For critics of home schooling, this is a highly unfavorable conclusion. The duty of paternalism is widely accepted as an absolute requirement of just social institutions and a bedrock principle governing the treatment of children. If, as it appears, strong equality requires systematic violation of this norm, then it cannot be a principle of justice.

That is not to say moral principles never conflict. Moral abhorrence of torture, for example, often conflicts with soldiers' sense of obligation to comrades in wartime. But conflicts between valid moral principles are incidental; the conflict between strong equality and paternalism is not incidental, but deeply rooted in the structure of the two principles. In such cases, one of the principles must be wrong. Either strong equality is not a principle of justice, or it is acceptable to control children in ways that do not further their long-term interests. Some would regard this as a decisive refutation of the egalitarian position.

What could Apple (2000), and others of like belief, say to this argument? One response would be to point out that if justice demands strong equality, then subjecting intellectually advanced children to an unchallenging routine does serve their interests, because it is in everyone's interest to live in a just society. Parents and students who complain about this routine simply fail to understand justice. This rebuttal, however, will convince only those who already accept strong equality. It is ill-suited to the defense of a controversial social ideal in a pluralistic society.

But egalitarians could also argue that a child's interests are heterogeneous, and schools can satisfy the paternalism requirement by advancing some of these interests even if it does not advance others. An egalitarian school that fails to promote academic progress for advantaged children can still confer other benefits such as group skills, interracial understanding, and democratic dispositions. The problem here is that academic skills are measurable and their benefits clearly established, while benefits in other areas are difficult to define and evaluate. If egalitarians could clearly define and measure the value of the attitudinal changes they favor, and if it could be shown that schools do bring about changes of this type, they could overcome the paternalism objection.

Paternalism, then, provides only a relatively weak defense of home schooling against the egalitarian critique. Let us now turn to a more ambitious argument, one that challenges core assumptions of the responsibility thesis.

As Kymlicka's (1990) characterization implies, strong equality depends on a clean distinction between two kinds of factors, those that reflect an agent's choice and effort and those that lie beyond her control. The logical structure of the responsibility thesis requires that these two sets of items be clearly distinguishable. The economist Marc Fleurbaey (1995) refers to this requirement as the separability constraint. If the two kinds of factors are not cleanly separable, then either social policy will deny individual responsibility, erasing the results of people's initiative, or it will allow unearned advantage.

Thus far, the line between the two domains has appeared clear enough. The debate about home schooling focuses on childhood, and we have assumed that all the conditions of childhood are unearned and must be equalized. But are they?

Granted, the family advantages some children enjoy do not reflect their own effort or choices. But they do reflect initiative on the part of their parents. Why, then, should social policy try to even them out? Egalitarians could argue that their policies would deny benefits of parental initiative to children, not to parents, and thus neither parents nor children would be deprived of what they deserve. But that is true only if children's well-being does not affect the well-being of parents. Any parent who has ever worried over a child's health or rejoiced in her safety knows that is false. When the state tries to undercut family advantage, parents are deprived of pleasures and satisfactions they have planned and worked for – precisely the opposite of what the responsibility thesis prescribed.

The difficulty for the critics in compounded when we recognize that strong equality would rule out not only benefit to a child from a parent's initiative, but more generally benefit to any person from anyone else's choices and effort. The responsibility thesis holds that I am entitled only to the benefits to me of my choices, not those of others. If you and I cooperate, the benefit to me of your choice and effort and to you of mine must be distributed equally over the whole society; you and I get only as much benefit as we would have obtained by acting alone, which defeats the whole aim of cooperation. If, on the other hand, the responsibility thesis is slightly relaxed, joint responsibility is allowed, and individuals are entitled to benefits of cooperation, then strong equality turns out not to conflict with home schooling after all.

Egalitarians could try to avoid this predicament by drawing the line in a different place: not between benefits to oneself and another, but between opportunities and outcomes. Helping your own child would be acceptable if opportunities remained equal. Promoting her well-being, or your own or anyone else's, would be permitted just so long as the beneficiary didn't obtain opportunities that others lack. But this distinction, too, quickly blurs when we look at real-life examples. The benefits that matter most in our lives – education, health, skills and knowledge of various kinds – are valuable precisely because of what they allow us to do in the future. Their value lies in the opportunities that they generate. To deny parents the opportunity to provide these benefits would be to forbid them to enhance their children's well-being, or for that matter anyone else's or even their own, in any but the most trivial ways.

The separability argument is unlikely to convince egalitarian critics that home schooling is not wrong, unjust, and immoral. It does, however, defeat the responsibility thesis, by showing that it fails in its central aim of holding people responsible for their choices while immunizing them against factors beyond their control. It does so without introducing any new premise that is not widely accepted both by critics and by advocates of public education. Unlike the paternalism argument, it does not depend on empirical assumptions that new evidence might show to be false. Instead, it capitalizes on a basic internal flaw of the egalitarian argument: the assumption that choice, effort, and well-being can be defined in purely individual terms. Unfortunately for egalitarians, it cannot, and so the responsibility thesis collapses under its own weight, and the defense of home schooling against the most plausible version of the privatization argument is secure.

## Conclusion

Most people think that it is not wrong to keep children out of school if they can be decently educated at home. Since research clearly shows that most home-schooled children are indeed educated decently, and many better than decently, the critics face an uphill battle. They must start from uncontroversial premises and build up an argument, in small steps no one can object to, leading to a controversial conclusion. This strategy is not a peculiarity of egalitarians or educational critics; it is the standard mode of moral argument, and often the only practicable way to convince people with words that something is right or wrong when they do not see it that way based on their experience.

As the different versions of the privatization argument demonstrate, the strategy is not always successful. If key factual premises are unsupported by research or experience, then, the argument can be set aside pending new evidence, as in the case of cohesion. If an argument depends on moral premises not shared by those it aims to persuade, it can be dismissed summarily, as democratic maintenance was dismissed. But if, as in the case of strong equality, a valid argument starts from plausible premises and leads to a conclusion that is deeply disturbing, then it deserves scrutiny. Parties to the home schooling debate ignore such a challenge at their peril. If the argument is valid, one can reject its conclusion only if one is prepared to renounce the premises.

Those sympathetic to home schooling are not likely to accept the critics' conclusion that home schooling is wrong. Nor, as evidence of the benefits of home schooling accumulates, are they likely to argue that children who are home schooled do not thereby receive an advantage. What are they to say, then, to those who assert that this advantage, like other advantages parents bestow on their children, is unearned? Must they give up the belief that people deserve what they work for, and do not deserve that for which they do not work? Must the responsibility thesis be abandoned?

The analysis presented here suggests that what must be sacrificed is not the notion of desert based on choice and effort, but rather the assumption that "choice" means individual choice and "effort" must be unilateral, not coordinated with efforts by others. Our most beneficial projects are cooperative projects, undertaken in voluntary association with others who share our aims and values. Families' efforts to promote their children's well-being are a conspicuous example of such a cooperative project, not least because they would be fruitless if the child didn't cooperate. Home-schooled children deserve the benefits of this enterprise in the same way anyone else deserves the benefits of cooperative effort. That these benefits are enjoyed unequally throughout the population reflects the heterogeneity of families and children, not injustice.

Small-scale cooperation and voluntary action are by definition not public. It is easy to see how any increase in activity of this type could be viewed as privatization. This article has explored several reasons for criticism of privatization, of which the

one most relevant to home schooling is that it supports and maintains inequality. Home schooling, like other forms of voluntary cooperation, cannot avoid generating and maintaining inequality. Anyone who supports home schooling should be prepared to explain why the forms of inequality that it generates are not wrong, even though children ordinarily are not fully capable of choosing how they are educated. Anyone who opposes home schooling for egalitarian reasons should be prepared to explain why individual choice and effort are morally superior to coordinated choice and effort, as they must be if we are to conclude that people deserve the benefits of one but not the other.

# References

Apple, Michael (2000) The cultural politics of home schooling. *Peabody Journal of Education*, 75(1–2): 256–71.

Arneson, Richard (1989) Equality and equal opportunity for welfare. *Philosophical Studies*, 56: 77–93.

Callan, Eamonn (1997) *Creating Citizens: Political Education and Liberal Democracy* (Oxford: Clarendon Press).

Cohen, G. A. (1989) On the currency of egalitarian justice. *Ethics*, 99(4): 906–44.

Coleman, J. S., Cambell, E. Q., Hobson, C. J., MacPartland, J., Mood, A. M., Weinfeld, F., and York, R. (1996) *Equality of Educational Opportunity* (Washington, DC: U.S. Dept. of Health, Education, and Welfare, Office of Education).

Curren, Randall (2000) *Aristotle on the Necessity of Public Education* (Lanham, MD: Rowman & Littlefield).

Dahl, Robert A. (1956) *A Preface to Democratic Theory* (Chicago: University of Chicago Press).

Dewey, John (1927) *The Public and its Problems* (New York: Holt).

Duncombe, William (1999) Financing a sound basic education in New York: Comments on Fiscal Policy Institute Proposal. Notes distributed January 21, 1999 at the Center for Policy Research, Maxwell School, Syracuse University, New York.

Dworkin, Ronald (1981) What is equality? Part 2: Equality of resources. *Philosophy and Public Affairs*, 10(4): 283–345.

Dworkin, Ronald (1985) Why liberals should care about equality. In Ronald Dworkin (ed.), *A Matter of Principle* (Cambridge: Harvard University Press), pp. 205–13.

Fishkin, James (1981) *Justice, Equal Opportunity, and the Family* (New Haven, CT: Yale University Press).

Fleurbaey, Marc (1995) Equal opportunity or equal social outcome? *Economics and Philosophy*, 11(1): 25–55.

Gutmann, Amy (1987) *Democratic Education* (Princeton, NJ: Princeton University Press).

Gutmann, Amy, and Thompson, Dennis (1996) *Democracy and Disagreement* (Cambridge, MA: Harvard University Press).

Heath, Shirley Brice (1996) *Ways with Words: Language, Life, and Work in Communities and Classrooms* (Cambridge: Cambridge University Press).

Kozol, Jonathan (1991) *Savage Inequalities* (New York: HarperCollins).

Kymlicka, Will (1990) *Contemporary Political Philosophy* (New York: Oxford University Press).

Lareau, Annette (2000) *Home Advantage: Social Class and Parental Intervention in Elementary Education* (Lanham, MD: Rowman & Littlefield).

Lubienski, Chris (2000) Whither the common good? A critique of home schooling. *Peabody Journal of Education*, 75(1–2): 207–32.

Mansfield, Harvey (1978) *The Spirit of Liberalism* (Cambridge, MA: Harvard University Press).

Nozick, Robert (1974) *Anarchy, State and Utopia* (New York: Basic Books).

Rawls, John (1971) *A Theory of Justice* (Cambridge, MA: Harvard University Press).

Roemer, John (1995) Equality and responsibility. *Boston Review*. Available online at http://bostonreview.mit.edu/dreader/series/equality.html. (retrieved 9/6/02.)

Stevens, Mitchell (2001) *Kingdom of Children: Culture and Controversy in the Homeschooling Movement* (Princeton, NJ: Princeton University Press).

Underwood, Julie K. (1995) School finance reform as vertical equity. *University of Michigan Law Review*, 28: 493–519.

Vallentyne, Pater (1989) Equal opportunity and the family. *Public Affairs Quarterly*, 3(1): 27–45.

Williams, Bernard (1972) The idea of equality. In Peter Laslett and W. G. Runciman (eds.), *Philosophy, Politics and Society* (Oxford: Blackwell), pp. 110–13.

# 20

# Is Teaching a Profession:
# How Would We Know?

## Kenneth A. Strike

Is teaching a profession? This is an unprofitable formulation of the question. The concept of a profession is an ideal type (Haller and Strike, 1986). An ideal type will consist of a set of characteristics that specifies what constitutes a pure case (Hoy and Miskel, 1987). Among the characteristics that are often supposed to define professions are the possession of an esoteric knowledge base, a long and substantial amount of training required for entrance, the existence of a professional association that can speak authoritatively for the occupation, a code of ethics, significant professional autonomy, and a strong orientation toward service and client welfare. Such characteristics will be fully exemplified only by a few paradigm cases. The usual paradigm cases of professions are fee-for-services occupations such as medicine and law. Most cases of professions will lack some of these characteristics or possess them in lesser degree than these paradigm cases. These will be "quasi-professions." Teaching will be a quasi-profession since it will have some characteristics of a profession, but will have them to a lesser extent than the paradigm cases of professions. What do we gain by trying to decide if teaching *really* qualifies as a profession? Why not focus instead on a description of the characteristics that the occupation does have or should have?

One response might be that if it is believed that teaching is a profession, we will act differently. The status of the occupation will be enhanced. We may pay teachers better. We may find recruitment easier. We may have different policies about teacher education, teacher certification, or the management of schools (Howsam, 1980). We may organize teacher evaluation better. Policies and politics often turn on words and symbols.

But if policy turns on what we decide about whether teaching is a profession, why not formulate a conception of what a profession is to fit the requirements of policy? In this article I pursue this approach. Here I want to ask whether the occupation of teaching has or could have those characteristics, often associated with the professions, that justify certain authority relations. I am especially concerned about deciding whether teaching has characteristics that warrant autonomy and self-governance. Thus I will not seek to decide whether teaching is a profession in any general way. I will instead consider whether teaching is a profession in that it has characteristics that warrant significant autonomy and self-governance.

Previously published in *Journal of Personnel Evaluation in Education* 4 (1990), pp. 91–6, 99, 100–1, 102–4, 105–6, 108–9, 110–17. Reprinted with permission of Springer Verlag.

I shall hold that treating teaching as a self-governing profession involves the erosion of democratic authority over schooling. If so, the arguments for teaching being a profession must justify this erosion. Often the reason given for holding that professions are entitled to significant self-governance and autonomy is that professional practice is grounded in a knowledge base that is esoteric, a product of long academic preparation, and thus not readily available to lay persons or public officials. This being the case, decisions must be made by professionals who, in virtue of superior expertise, are in a position to make competent decisions. My analysis will focus on this argument.

## Professionalism and Democracy

I begin with two assumptions. The first is that central to the idea of a profession is the relationship between a guild and an esoteric body of knowledge (Kimball, 1988). The relationship involves authority and legitimacy. The guild claims authority over the work of its members. It will seek to set standards for competent practice, set educational standards, determine membership, judge malpractice, and gain autonomy from interference in practice by the non-initiated. This authority is legitimated by the possession of an esoteric knowledge base that grounds the practice of the members of the guild. The standard argument is that, because practice is grounded in an esoteric knowledge base, only initiates into the profession are able to make and execute the judgments on which competent practice depends. Thus, if clients are to be protected from incompetent practice, significant authority over practice must be ceded to the profession.

The second assumption is that professionalism is a form of governance and accountability. As a form of accountability professionalism is in competition with other forms of accountability, especially free choice and democratic control. Free choice protects consumers of a service by allowing them to choose those whom they believe will provide the desired quality of service. It subjects practice to market discipline. Professionalism competes with consumer sovereignty in that professional licensing restricts market availability. In cases where collective choice is appropriate, the practice of some occupation can be regulated by democratic authority. Practitioners may work for a public agency (schools or hospitals, for example) to which they are accountable. Here

professionalism competes with democracy in that the self-regulation and autonomy of professionals diminishes legislative and administrative control over the service professionals provide.

For teaching, it is the competition between professionalism and democracy that is of interest. Most teachers work in public agencies. While teachers work directly for administrators, and while they may work within organizations that are bureaucratically organized, administrative and bureaucratic authority derive from legislative authority. School boards are legislatures. Educational law and policy are made by state legislatures or by those who are responsible to them. Thus, the aspirations of teachers to organize as a self-regulating profession is competitive with this "democratic/bureaucratic" authority.

Professions' claim to authority over their work is justified by expertise. The appeal is to Plato's principle, "Those who know should rule." Values other than expertise are more central to democracy. Democratic forms of government are justified by appeal to such ideas as equal rights and the consent of the governed. Democratic and professional forms of authority can be mixed in institutions. In our society such mixtures are common. Moreover, no form of professionalism that seeks to dispense with democratic sovereignty is likely to succeed. In a democracy, professions will be legitimated by democratic bodies and ultimately accountable to them. Such autonomy and self-governance as they attain must be within a democratic framework.[1] Nevertheless, the professionalization of an occupation requires that democratic authority be kept at arm's length. Otherwise the notion that the profession is autonomous and self-regulating is mere fiction.

Two things follow. First, the principles that justify democratic authority and professionalism are different and competitive. Second, insofar as professionals control their work, their work will not be controlled democratically. The practical result is that, to the degree that teachers actually function as professionals, their decisions and their work will be beyond the immediate reach of legislators, administrators, and school boards.

These initial assumptions about professionalism suggest what is at stake in the attempt to professionalize teaching. Democracy and its associated values are at stake. Professionalization is not fundamentally a matter of training or recruiting better educated teachers or of respecting them and their judgment. It is fundamentally a matter of creating institutions that alter the authority relations between legislative and administrative power and that of the guild. When we are done professionalizing teaching, the guild will have more to say about how children are educated, and legislators and administrators will have less. A successful argument for the professionalization of teaching must show that such diminishment of democratic authority is justified.

The standard argument appeals to considerations of utility. Professional forms of accountability, when they are appropriate, are held to be superior to democratic forms because they yield better decisions and a higher quality of practice, and thus serve and protect the public interest or the interests of clients best. The incapacity of democratic forms of accountability to succeed in those areas where professionalism is appropriate is linked to the fact that the public, consumers, or members of legislatures are not initiates into the knowledge base. It is the lengthy training in this knowledge base that assures us that the judgment of professionals will be sound and that professionals will be attuned to the standards of professional practice and the needs of clients.

Note three things about this argument form.

First, it assumes that the imperative for democratic forms of accountability can be overcome by considerations of utility. Improvement of practice and gains in protection of the public interest must be sufficient reasons to prefer professional forms of accountability. This assumption is not self-evident. It may be far from self-evident to those for whom democracy is justified by considerations where the appeal to utility is not central (as is characteristic of rights based or social contract theories (Rawls, 1974; Locke, 1960). However, in our society, professions are legitimated and regulated by democratic bodies. Professionalism need not be an abrogation of the ultimate sovereignty of the people. The issue must therefore be posed as one concerning the optimal mix of democratic and professional forms of accountability.

Second, a crucial element in the argument for professionalization must be that a knowledge base with suitable characteristics actually exists. It is fundamentally the existence of a suitable knowledge base that legitimates the control of a profession over its work.

Finally, the knowledge base must play several roles in the practice of the members of the guild. Initiation into the knowledge base must account for both judgment and skill. But it also must account for the loyalty of the professional to the standards of practice of the profession and to the welfare of the client. There are other requirements as well. These are the topic for the next section of this article.

## Requirements for a Knowledge Base

In what follows I shall sketch several standards for a suitable knowledge base for a profession of teaching. These criteria are:

1   Something must be known.
2   The knowledge base must ground practice.
3   The knowledge base must be esoteric.
4   The knowledge base must be the basis of evaluation of practice.
5   The knowledge base must ground a profession of teaching.
6   The knowledge base must provide the basis for loyalty to professional standards and client welfare.
7   The knowledge base must help specify what the work of teachers is and be the basis of a division of labor between the authority of the guild and democratic/bureaucratic authority.
8   The knowledge base must suggest how the kind of teaching done by professionals differs from other forms of teaching in the society.

I shall discuss each of these in turn. Presumably there are two main candidates for a knowledge base (or some combination or integration of them), pedagogical knowledge and subject matter knowledge. Initially, I shall emphasize pedagogical knowledge. Moreover, I shall emphasize pedagogical knowledge that might be held to be quite separable from content knowledge. I readily grant that teachers cannot teach what they do not know, and that, where what is taught is esoteric, the teacher of it must possess esoteric knowledge. At the same time, I believe that a profession of teaching would be quite different depending on whether it was primarily grounded in a kind of technical pedagogical knowledge or whether it was grounded in subject matter. I shall conclude with some reflections on what a profession of teaching would be like if the knowledge base were predominately subject-matter knowledge.

Before proceeding, we must differentiate claims about the knowledge base from claims about the capacity of teachers. To assert that there is not an adequate knowledge base for a profession of teaching is not to denigrate the intellectual capacity or wisdom of teachers. It is to say something about the state of educational research. Likewise to say that there is an adequate knowledge base for teaching is not to praise the capacities of teachers. It is to say that there are things they must know if they are to be competent practitioners.

Consider now the eight criteria listed above.

## Something must be known

A thought experiment: imagine two choices. You may have one of the great physicians of antiquity, Hippocrates or Galen perhaps, as your personal physician, or you may have a mediocre graduate of an undistinguished modern medical school. One or the other will perform an appendectomy on you. We will allow the ancient to speak English, but whomever you choose must operate using the technology and knowledge of his period. Whom would you choose? Preferring anesthetics, antibiotics, accurate anatomy, and the technology of modern medicine, I should choose the mediocre graduate of the undistinguished medical school.

You may have one of the great teachers of antiquity, Socrates or Aristotle perhaps, to teach your children, or you may have your child taught by the mediocre graduate of an undistinguished modern teachers college. We will again let the ancient speak English. Whom would you choose? I should choose Aristotle.

One might argue that Aristotle would have some subject matter deficiencies. His views on astronomy are perhaps somewhat quaint. Nevertheless, putting aside subject matter for the moment, it is not obvious that much has happened in the last two millennia that would make the mediocre graduate of the undistinguished school of education a better teacher than Aristotle. In medicine, advances in medical knowledge have made the undistinguished modern practitioner a better practitioner than any ancient could have been. Can we say anything similar for advances in pedagogy?

Do we know anything about pedagogy? Of course. Do we know enough to ground a profession? The answer is less obvious. Consider a case that little is known about pedagogy. We may grant that there are numerous pieces of good research and that there are numerous sophisticated theories about teaching. There is also a good deal of worthwhile common knowledge. But the fundamental question about whether anything is known is whether the

numerous empirical and theoretical issues raised by this body of content are adequately resolved. For any intellectual profession, there will be, at any given time, a number of open issues. But where there is a strong knowledge base, there will also be a large background of claims where agreement is widespread, and there is likely to be some consensus on how outstanding issues are to be resolved.

The kind of resolution required must be both rational and social. It is necessary but not sufficient to consider some claim as part of a knowledge base that someone has provided an adequate rational defense of it. This defense must also have produced a reasonable degree of professional consensus. Otherwise, it is not possible for the profession to have standards of practice that are both reasonable and enforceable. On the other hand, professional agreement apart from adequate evidence is not a sufficient basis for a profession. Apart from an adequate evidential basis for the standards of practice of a profession, the formulation and enforcement of such standards amount to a kind of *coup d'etat*. Thus the knowledge base of a profession must be legitimated both epistemologically and socially.

Given this, it is unclear how much is known about the practice of teaching. There are many hypotheses about teaching that are as yet unresolved by research. It is unclear that there are many agreed-upon claims. But the matter is far worse than this. Educational research shows little agreement at the level of research programs (Shulman, 1986a). Consider that those who find the product process research tradition limited, often do so for theoretical reasons rather than methodological or empirical ones. They find the results platitudinous, not directed to the right questions, or not oriented to the most significant learning outcomes (Phillips, 1988). Thus, research on teaching not only has a large number of unresolved empirical issues, but exhibits considerable disagreement about what would constitute an adequate account of teaching. Many issues are not only unresolved but, apart from some theoretical unity, unresolvable.

Is enough known? Some things are known. Do they add up to a knowledge base for a profession? How much is required? Such questions are matters of judgment. One can say, however, that if the purpose of the knowledge base is to legitimate a high level of self-governance, then it seems that the knowledge base must be adequate to ground most of the routine practices of teaching, and it must be able to provide an approach to adjudicating outstanding matters of controversy about practice. A knowledge base for a profession must play a variety of social roles. It must show why the judgment of professionals is to be preferred to that of nonprofessionals about a wide range of practices. It must be able to resolve disputes about practice. A large list of things known about teaching that does not do this will not suffice. Given this, the claim that we possess an adequate base of pedagogical knowledge is doubtful.

[ . . . ]

## The knowledge base must ground practice

To hold that practice is grounded in a knowledge base is to assert that the possession of this knowledge base significantly enables practice. Put more simply, if practice is grounded in a knowledge base, teachers should routinely perform better because they possess it, and should routinely not be able to perform adequately apart from it.

[ . . . ]

No one need hold that possession of the knowledge base is sufficient for competent teaching. Experience and practice may be necessary to acquire the judgment necessary to successfully transform the knowledge base into practice. It is more interesting to ask whether possession of the knowledge base is necessary for competence. Here the response is fraught with potential paradox.[2]

Suppose that possession of the knowledge base is required for competent practice. What are we to say of current practitioners? We must either hold that they are not competent, or that they already possess the knowledge base. Neither response is especially palatable. Much of the case in favor of professionalization has been made by arguing that teacher education requires substantial upgrading. Moreover, it would be surprising if current teachers were found to be well versed in the kinds of things that are often held to constitute the knowledge base. Finally, if the knowledge base is defined by what current practitioners know, that is likely to degrade its character considerably. It is doubtful, for example, that many teachers are current in educational research. Shall we conclude that such research is not part of the knowledge base? Such a claim would make the suggestion that teaching is grounded in an *esoteric* knowledge base laughable.

Shall we conclude that current teachers are incompetent? Such a claim is not likely to justify transferring power over the work of teaching to its current practitioners. Moreover, en mass, current

teachers are not incompetent. Is their competence to be explained by their possession of a knowledge base? Is their relative degree of competence to be explained by their relative possession of a knowledge base? Is the difference between the majority of competent teachers and those who are incompetent to be explained by the relative possession of some knowledge base?

Those who claim that teaching is a profession must answer this list of rhetorical questions in the affirmative. Otherwise, they must find a way to reconcile the claim that teaching is grounded in an esoteric knowledge base with the fact that people routinely practice competently without possessing it. Yet to answer such questions affirmatively immediately generates others. What is this knowledge base? How did teachers come by it? (This is especially interesting if one assumes that it was not explicitly taught during a period of professional training.) How does it function to inform teacher behavior? Answers to such questions seem required if there is a body of pedagogical knowledge the possession of which substantially enhances competence.

[ . . . ]

## The knowledge base must be esoteric

I know of no reasons to suppose that useful knowledge must be esoteric. It is possible that there is much known about teaching that is common sense, or, if not, is sufficiently straightforward that little or no theoretical training is required to master it.

The requirement that the knowledge base for teaching be esoteric is a political requirement for a profession of teaching. Granting autonomy requires that the judgments necessary for competent teaching and evaluation be beyond the ken of the uninitiated. This is the principal reason that other forms of accountability are held to be inefficient. Judgments so grounded are the product of extensive training, training that the uninitiated are unlikely to have. Thus, only those who have devoted substantial time to mastering the knowledge base can make competent decisions about practice.

What kinds of characteristics might a knowledge base have that would make it the product of extensive training? Consider three possibilities. One is that it might be extensive. It might consist of assertions, none of which are overly esoteric in themselves, that are sufficiently numerous that only those who are willing to devote years to their acquisition might master them. A second possibility is that the knowledge base might consist largely of theory whose assertions are sufficiently complex and difficult that long study is required for their comprehension. A final possibility is that the knowledge base might consist of skills that are acquired by practice under the eye of a trained practitioner (Tom, 1984). Various combinations are possible.

Professions are characterized by a mix of knowledge types in which the second is dominant. Occupations that are characterized by long lists of nonesoteric claims are susceptible to "manualization." That is, it is possible to provide the uninitiated with a "cookbook" that would allow the novice to practice and judge practice with only a modest investment of time. Much computer work, data entry or word processing is of this sort.

Teaching is "manualized" if teaching skills can be reduced to numerous teaching behaviors that can be captured on an evaluation form where such behaviors can be noted and checked off by the non-expert. Thus a knowledge base that is extensive, but is not sophisticated, will not liberate teachers from administrative scrutiny. Indeed, it is likely to be an instrument of increased monitoring.

The acquisition of some skills requires a long period of training even though the theoretical knowledge associated with them is minimal. Many crafts are of this character. It may take long practice under the instruction of a practiced eye to become a capable craftsperson. Such crafts have much in common with professions. They require extensive training. Moreover, it is difficult for the uninitiated to exercise competent judgment about the excellencies exhibited in a craft. Such crafts differ from paradigm cases of professions in that they do not require the extensive theoretical training that professions require. As a consequence, they may lack as intimate an association with higher education.

Thus the kind of knowledge that seems most central to professions is cognitive knowledge that is esoteric in the sense that extensive training and instruction is required for its comprehension and for the development of the judgment that is grounded in this knowledge. It is not the numerousity of the claims of the knowledge base that is crucial. It is the sophistication.

To summarize, a knowledge base consisting of complex sophisticated theory is required to justify the view that only initiates are in a postion to make the kinds of judgments on which competent practice and evaluation depend and to associate the acquisition of this knowledge base with extensive university-based education.

### The knowledge base must be the basis of evaluation of practice

One assumption required to justify the autonomy of professionals is that performance cannot be fully appraised except by another professional. If practice is grounded in an esoteric knowledge base, only a person who possessed this knowledge base could judge the adequacy of the practice of another practitioner. Consequently, if teaching is a profession, evaluation must be rooted in the knowledge base.

Conversely, if teaching can be evaluated adequately by those who do not possess the knowledge base, that provides reason to suppose that teaching is not a profession. Those who hold that teaching is a profession thus should also hold that teaching cannot adequately be evaluated merely by looking at student achievement or by the use of rating forms that can be completed by nonexperts.

Consider how outcomes are connected to practice in a profession. Competence does not guarantee good outcomes. Competent lawyers lose cases, and competent physicians lose patients. The question of whether practice is competent is not a matter of the outcomes produced, but whether the practice in question is consistent with professional standards. Since one point of competent practice is to make certain outcomes more likely, the conception of competence cannot be divorced from outcomes. Moreover, while the connection between competence and practice is not so direct as to legitimate evaluative judgments made solely on the basis of outcomes, patterns of outcomes are relevant. If two physicians engaged in similar practices produce dramatically and inexplicably different outcomes, that is at least reason for concern. At the same time, it is unlikely to be grounds for a judgment that one physician is incompetent or less competent than another apart from some peer judgment of practice. If peers cannot provide an account of the failings of the practice that appeal to professional standards justified by appeal to the knowledge base, a judgment of incompetence is not likely to be supported.

If practice is rooted in an esoteric knowledge base, lay persons are deeply disadvantaged in judging practice. It is not just that they may not know that a given practice is justified. They may even be unaware of what the practice is. Even the description of a practice requires some grasp of the knowledge base. But, more important, the evaluation of a practice often turns on whether the professional has reasonable grounds for the practice. For teacher evaluation this means that an inspection of teacher's reasoning about practice is a central part of judging practice. Of course, only experts can judge the reasoning of other professionals.

It follows that peer evaluation is central in a profession. This means not only that professionals should be central in the appraisal of other professionals but that professionals must be central in setting standards and in professional socialization. Presumably only professionals are in a position to decide appropriate standards. Moreover, the socialization of professionals normally requires considerable modeling of competent practice and feedback on the extent to which the novice's attempts comport with professional standards.

Therefore, if teaching is a profession, evaluation must be grounded in an esoteric knowledge base. It follows that the knowledge base must be capable of supporting evaluation.

There are several tests that might be applied to see if indeed this relationship obtains. First, non-initiates should be found to be severely handicapped in the evaluation of teachers. Their judgments should be routinely unreliable. Second, professional teachers should exhibit a reasonable degree of agreement concerning the competence of other teachers. They should agree not only on whether some practice is competent, but on the reasons for it. Widespread and systematic disagreement suggests the lack of an agreed-upon knowledge base.

To summarize, if teaching is a profession a certain relation between the knowledge base and evaluation should obtain such that only professionals can adequately judge the practice of other professionals. The knowledge base should be of such a character as to support this relationship.

[ . . . ]

*The knowledge base must support loyalty to professional standards and client welfare*

Professionals are supposed to conform their practice to professional standards and to be guided by client welfare without need of constant external monitoring. This is supposed to result from initiation into the knowledge base. Thus there must be something about this knowledge base that promotes loyalty to

professional standards and to client welfare. What might this be?

A simple answer is that instruction in the knowledge base includes explicit instruction in professional ethics, perhaps emphasizing a code of ethics. While I do believe that instruction in professional ethics is appropriate and useful (see Strike, 1986; Soltis, 1986), I do not believe that direct classroom instruction in professional ethics is the central thing. Instead, the first thing about the ethics of any profession is that the values that guide practice should be internal to the concepts that regulate practice and should be acquired via the acquisition of these concepts. For example, justice is internal to law. One does not understand law unless one understands how its concepts and its practices are linked to justice. Likewise, one does not understand medicine apart from a concept of health. Students should be expected to acquire an appreciation of these concepts via mastery of the knowledge base of their profession, not in a course in professional ethics. Explicit instruction in professional ethics may be useful in increasing awareness of the moral commitments that inhere in other parts of the curriculum and in increasing sophistication in dealing with hard cases, but it should not be the mainstay of the ethical component of professional socialization.

Thus, the ethical concepts and values that regulate the practice of teaching should be internal to the knowledge base of teaching. Students should acquire them as they acquire the knowledge base. If so, then the knowledge base should have a connection to a set of goods and ethical standards that are internal to the practice of teaching, and one should be able to analyze the various parts of the curriculum in a way that displays what these goods and moral principles are.

This view suggests that the knowledge base for a profession cannot be merely "technical" if by that one means instrumental. If pedagogical knowledge is merely technical, then all of the goals of education and all of the ethical standards that regulate the practice of teaching are external to the technology of instruction. If so, then the ethics of teaching will be external to the knowledge base and will need to be taught as a special and distinct subject. Conversely, if the ethics of teaching is internal to the practice and the knowledge base of teaching, then it will not be possible to rigorously distinguish between those goals that teaching attempts to promote, the ethical principles that govern practice, and the techniques of teaching.

*The knowledge base must help specify what the work of teachers is and be the basis of a division of labor between the authority of the guild and democratic/bureaucratic authority*

The framing of the argument about professionalization in public agencies indicates that one problem to be solved in conceiving a profession of teaching is to work out a division of labor about who gets to decide what. As noted, in our society it is a given of policy that public schools are ultimately going to be under democratic control. Yet if teaching is to be a profession, some kinds of decisions must be ceded to a profession of teaching. How, then, shall we understand the division of labor between teachers, democratic authority, and administrators?

[ . . . ]

Our political system gives considerable weight to the principle that people are entitled to their own conception of their own good. It is not within the power of the state to decide what people shall live their lives for so long as they pursue their ends in ways that respect the rights of others (Ackermann, 1980; Dworkin, 1984). Moreover, when collective decisions about ends seem appropriate, our society has held that such decisions should be made democratically. The alternative is that our lives should be governed by philosopher kings, people whose wisdom about what is good for us entitles them to rule our lives. The question of whether teachers have expertise about and pursuantly some right to make decisions about the ends of education thus becomes a matter of great interest. If teachers claim expert knowledge about the goods people should realize in their lives, teacher professionalization is brought into conflict with a central principle of democratic polity. Teachers may claim some right to compel students to learn certain things because teachers know that these things are good. Such arguments make teachers candidates for the role of philosopher king. They should be regarded with great suspicion in a free society.

Suppose the knowledge teachers possess is merely technical. It consists solely in conceptions of how information and skills could be effectively transmitted, but involves no claims about the worth of what was transmitted. It is purely instrumental knowledge. Would the problem be solved? The general features of the solution suggested are that there be a division of labor between democratic authority and teacher authority such that educational policy (now conceived as the determination of what ends should be pursued in education) is to be made democrat-

ically, whereas the implementation of policy should rest with teachers. Is such a view tenable?

There are reasons to suppose that it is not. Consider what it would mean for curriculum decisions. Teachers would not be entitled to an independently achieved conception of the worth of what they teach. This they must discover in the judgment of the school board. However, once they had discovered the ends to be served they could make professional decisions about the curriculum that best served these ends. This picture does not come to terms with the extent to which the goods promoted by the practice of many disciplines and other intellectual practices are internal to those practices. They are connected to the practice in such a way that to disassociate the practice from these goods is to distort it. (This point is more fully developed later.)

This example suggests that the division of labor between democratic and professional authority that links it to a distinction between the determination of ends and the determination of means is too simple. If teachers are experts about subject matter as well as pedagogy, they will be experts about certain kinds of goods. Attempting to "contain" teacher expertise to the purely instrumental will require either that the knowledge base of teaching be construed as entirely pedagogical (and even here there will be difficulties) or that a knowledge of content be construed so as to exclude a grasp of the goods that are internal to the practice of disciplines. This, I shall shortly argue, is to require teachers to distort their subjects and to teach without integrity.

In summary, if teaching is a profession, the task of working out a division of labor between the professional authority of teachers over their own work and democratic authority requires both a view of the nature of the knowledge base and of the political interests involved. This in turn requires a knowledge base that will support a coherent division of labor.

[ . . . ]

## Final Thoughts: An Alternative Vision of Teachers as Professionals

I conclude with an alternative vision of professionalism, one that takes subject matter seriously as central to the knowledge base. This vision depends on the notion that what teachers do most centrally is to represent the learned disciplines and other similar activities[3] to their students. They teach disciplines such as mathematics, literature, and science.

They teach music, art, and sports. Even at the most elementary levels they transmit fundamental skills and values that are prerequisite to this task. Of course they do more than this. Nevertheless, I want to suggest that we can best express reasons for granting teachers the status of professionals and reasons for certain kinds of professional autonomy by seeing teachers as representatives of those activities which in their fullest development constitute the practice of learned disciplines.

The practice of disciplines requires several forms of independence. By independence, I mean independence from political authority even when it is democratic. Properly understood, this kind of independence can be seen as the basis of a form of professional autonomy. Truth is not democratic. Consequently, disciplines require forms of independence that protect the process of inquiry from external political interference. What is believed to be true in a discipline should be believed because the belief has met appropriate standards of evidence. Therefore, it is inappropriate to subject a discipline's judgments about what is true to democratic decision. Nor should the goods and excellences internal to the practice of disciplines be subject to political control. To do so is to violate the integrity of the discipline. Suppose that a given school board was to decide that poetry should be taught primarily as a form of vocational education. They reasoned that students who mastered the skills of producing sentimental rhymes might find lucrative employment writing greeting cards or song jingles. Teachers should emphasize the potential of poetic careers to their students and devalue such goods as the beauty of the language, its capacity to express emotion, or its potential to illuminate human experience. Why is this offensive? Consider that those goods that are internal to disciplines are so because they are essential to the character of that discipline. Consequently, to teach them in a way that is not true to these internal goods is to misrepresent the discipline, to distort it, and to deny something essential to its character. Teachers who do so undermine the integrity of their discipline. In effect, they lie to their students. If disciplinary practice is to have integrity, the goods internal to such practices and the excellences required to realize these goods cannot be subject to political control.

To connect these forms of independence to teaching, it is essential that teaching be seen as a way of practicing a discipline. Epistemological adequacy and a respect for the integrity of the goods internal to the practice of a discipline are central to appropriate forms of pedagogy. Consequently, the kinds of independence required to practice a discipline are also required to teach it. The epistemology of a discipline is central to teaching it with integrity. Such teaching attempts above all to teach the process of inquiry, to represent the forms that valid arguments take in the discipline, and to help students grasp the discipline not just as a batch of conclusions, but as a human activity, a "form of life" (Wittgenstein, 1953). This means that good teaching deals with arguments, explanations, dialogue, and debate (Green, 1971). The form of these activities is at heart a question of epistemology.

Similarly, it is central to good pedagogy that the teaching of a discipline expresses its internal goods and excellences in such a way that students can identify them and begin to participate in them. A teacher of poetry needs to show poetry as a medium of aesthetic experience. A good science teacher demonstrates that science is the pursuit of understanding of a certain sort. Often, these are not things said; they are things shown.

Thus it is essential to good pedagogy that teaching conform to a discipline's argument forms and express its values. The force of this argument is to see teaching as a special way of engaging in the practice of an intellectual discipline.[4] These comments are not primarily comments about what makes instruction effective although they do have something to do with effectiveness. They are comments about what gives teaching integrity. Teaching is a form of truth telling and of expression, not just a way to promote learning. The twin virtues of integrity and effectiveness have dual vices. The first of these is lack of integrity in representing disciplines. The second is pedagogical ineptness. It is primarily the first of these, integrity in representing the discipline to others, that is the basis of the independence teachers must have from democratic authority. Teachers must have the freedom to follow the argument where it leads, to consider and weigh evidence, and to express the goods internal to the practice they represent. If they lack this freedom, we compel them to subject their disciplines to inappropriate political authority. If we think that such independence is a trivial matter, we have a mistaken view of teaching.

On this view teachers are professionals because they are ambassadors to children from the intellectual disciplines. Their primary professional associations (as a matter of logic, not description) are communities of scholars (not unions!) organized around the practice of such disciplines where "practice" is understood to include teaching. If they are to have the status of professionals it will be because scholarship and inquiry, including their representation to the young, are held in high esteem. If they are to have autonomy it is because pedagogical forms are rooted in the practice of the disciple, and disciplines require independence if they are to play their social roles properly.[5]

This is, of course, not the common view. Indeed, it is a vision of education that I believe we have in large measure lost. I suspect there are at least two notable reasons. First, we increasingly see education primarily as human capital formation. To the extent that we see it solely in this way, we will not attend to either its epistemological forms or to these goods that make learning of intrinsic worth. Such matters are only accidentally required for human capital formation when they are required at all. Second, we see teaching as a kind of technology instead of a representation of the life of the mind to the young. Moreover, we seem often to understand the development of this technology in a way that divorces it from the character of disciplinary activity and links it instead to the psychology of learning. The technology of teaching thereby becomes disassociated from the epistemology of disciplines and from representing their internal goods. And it becomes disassociated from those concepts required to understand what teaching with integrity means.

Such views have their costs for teachers. Their status cannot be grounded in the status of the practice of learned disciplines, and their independence cannot be rooted in the kinds of independence required by the practice of disciplines. Scholarship is valued only as a means to external goods. Teachers are not ambassadors of a way of life of profundity and intrinsic worth. They are shopkeepers of instrumental cognitive wares. If they are to be respected as professionals, they must, therefore, represent their shopkeeping as an esoteric technology, one grounded not primarily in the worth of what they teach and their mastery of it, but in the esoteric character of the technology of instruction. Having uprooted teachers from their role of emissaries of the life of the mind, we seek to make them into engineers of a technology of learning.

The strategy is unlikely to succeed. I suspect this not primarily because I am suspicious about the existence of this technology (although I am certainly suspicious), but because I do not believe that a society that attaches only instrumental value to learning is very likely to value its teachers. Where the life

of the mind is valued, teachers who see themselves as its emissaries will be valued for that reason. If teachers buy into a strategy to enhance their status that does not attempt to enhance the status of the kinds of practices they represent, their successes are likely to be fleeting. If they pursue strategies that implicitly denigrate the life of the mind and represent all knowledge, including their own, as merely instrumental, their strategy will reinforce attitudes which will ultimately diminish their status further. Perhaps the most successful path toward teacher professionalization, teacher freedom, and teacher status is for teachers to work to enhance the status of those human activities that they represent and to view their teaching as a special way of practicing those activities themselves.

This conception of teaching as a profession has several implications for teacher evaluation. First, it makes subject matter competence (or competence in the practice) a central concern of evaluation, but with an emphasis on that special way of understanding subject matter required to communicate it to novices or the young. Second, it focuses particular attention on teachers' ability to understand the "epistemological position" of the learner, since understanding how the learner will understand and appraise an idea is crucial to representing it adequately. Third, since teachers qua experts in representing a given practice to the young are likely to be the repository of the expertise required to judge whether a practice is being represented with integrity, this view requires a central role for teachers in evaluation. Finally, in Scriven's (1988) sense, this view is duty-based in that it emphasizes an appraisal of those activities that are conceptually essential to teaching instead of focusing on identifying indicators of good teaching.

This view of a profession of teaching has two assets and four liabilities. The first asset is that this view has a conception of a knowledge base that is likely to be able to meet the eight standards described above. Lest the reader's courage fail, I do not plan to argue this point. Instead I invite the reader to perform a thought experiment. Suppose that a teacher of physics is a physicist whose practice of physics is its teaching. The teaching of physics is grounded in the knowledge base of physics. If this is granted, then it is reasonably clear that physics teaching is grounded in an esoteric knowledge base. I would submit that this knowledge base will meet most of the eight conditions sketched above. (I discuss the weak links below.)

The second asset of this view is that it lessens the tension between professionalism and democratic authority. It does this by linking professional autonomy and professional control to a view of liberty that is already widely accepted and understood in our society. Here professional autonomy is closely associated with academic freedom. I understand academic freedom to hold that the intellectual professions are to be free from political interference with respect to the conduct of their intellectual pursuits. Governments may not decide what is deemed to be true or what counts as a valid argument. Governments may not assert what goods are internal to these practices. If a profession of teaching is to be understood as I have suggested, the autonomy of teachers will turn out to be justified on much the same grounds. If so, we have come to understand the professional autonomy of teachers in a way that links it to a tradition of accommodation to the judgment of professionals that is already well established in our society.

The liabilities are four. First, this view suggests that there is not a profession of teaching per se. Instead teachers are members of as many professions as there are intellectual practices. While this is true, I do not suppose that it is particularly disastrous. Teachers will find themselves bound together across specializations by numerous ties. Most important will be those ties rooted in commonalities across practices. Science teachers will find some unity in the interconnections between sciences. The same can be said of other groups of teachers. There will be some things that teachers share in common because our intellectual life has some features in common. But there will also be professionally relevant divisions rooted in differences in the characteristics of intellectual practices. Math teachers are likely to find that they have more in common with one another than with physical education or art teachers. Organizationally, it follows that the crucial professional associations for most teachers will be those of the like-minded associations of science teachers and English teachers, rather than generic teachers' associations.

The second liability is that this view of a profession of teaching will tend to "deprofessionalize" teachers to the extent that they are not grounded in some intellectual practice. What are we to say, for example, of the professional status of the kindergarten teacher or of elementary teachers generally? One thing to be said is that we must not lose sight of how important such teachers are in establishing the prerequisites for initiating students into the intellectual practices. Thus, one should not disassociate elementary teachers from the intellectual practices too quickly.

The third liability of this view is that it is not child-centered or student-centered. Its standards are those of the practices applied to instruction. It requires of teachers that they care about their disciplines. It does not clearly require of teachers that they care for children (Noddings, 1984, p. 188). Similarly, it does not have much to say about the need for teachers to be able to understand students with special needs, characteristics, or problems. If my conception of teachers as professionals excludes such concerns, that would be a notable liability.

The fourth liability is that this view may seem to have the philosopher king problem. Teachers are supposed to have autonomy over those goods that are internal to their various intellectual practices. Does this not mean that teachers have professional authority over the aims of education? I think that it does not. The authority over ends that this view gives teachers is that authority required to practice their disciplines with integrity. It does not involve the authority to insist that their discipline be taught or taken. That a given discipline be taught continues to be a political decision. That it be taken by anyone in particular is to be determined either by consideration of the public interest or by individual choice. The teacher's right is to say, "If my discipline is to be taught, this is what constitutes teaching it with integrity."

These "liabilities" should be put in proper context. It should be carefully noted that describing a conception of teachers as professionals is not the same thing as fully characterizing the role of teacher. For example, that teachers are not care givers qua professionals does not mean that care giving is not a central and valuable part of their role. Also we must recall that here I have been concerned to explicate a conception of teachers as professionals that is intended to allow us to understand the forms of professional autonomy and self-governance that are appropriate to teaching. Other conceptions of what it means to be a professional are possible and, in different contexts, desirable. They may well include the care giver role or other aspects of the role more centrally. Thus in a more robust view of teachers as professionals it may be perfectly reasonable to see care giving as central to the professional responsibilities of teachers. But this article deals with those aspects of the role that entitle teachers to autonomy and self-governance in virtue of possessing an esoteric knowledge base. That teachers ought to be care givers and ought to be highly valued as such is simply true. That care giving is grounded in esoteric knowledge is less obvious. Finally, we may need to resist the temptation to treat teachers' professional standing as the basis of their status or social worth. Why not value teachers for what they do? Should we not esteem teachers because they faithfully care for our children and represent valued activities to them with integrity? Perhaps the need to contest the term "professional" speaks most clearly to the failure to value people in our society for morally appropriate reasons.

A final concern: Perhaps the reader is alarmed that my view disassociates the practice of teaching from the efficiency of teaching. Is not the point of teaching to promote learning? Now, I surely do not want to be represented as unconcerned about the effectiveness of teaching, and my suggestion that the teacher's primary concern should be the integrity of teaching should not be understood to license a cavalier disregard for outcomes. How then is teaching with integrity linked to effective teaching? I have two suggestions. First, part of what counts

as effective teaching is internal to teaching with integrity. Insofar as competent teaching is linked to providing comprehensible reasons or to exhibiting the goods internal to a practice, teaching with integrity will be teaching effectively. But, no doubt, effective teaching will depend on much else as well. Nothing I have said suggests that teachers may not be concerned for this "much else" whatever it turns out to be. However, insofar as this much else is conceived as a technology of teaching that is independent of the content of teaching, I have much doubt as to whether it can be the basis of a profession.[6] Second, I wonder if emphasizing effectiveness in one's teaching is a bit like aiming at happiness. It is a good way to miss. Happiness is often a byproduct of commitment to achieving something else. Those who aim at happiness find that its direct pursuit breeds attitudes, character traits, and habits that undermine happiness. Perhaps, too, those who emphasize teaching with integrity will show their students what is important about learning in a way that those who emphasize effectiveness will not. Perhaps effective teaching, like happiness, is a consequence of being concerned with something of intrinsic worth and with one's integrity in pursuing something of worth.

## Notes

1. The unionization of teaching has resulted in a view about the relations between democratic sovereignty and union power. The assumption that has guided the debate is that there is a tension between democratic authority and collective bargaining in the public sector. Democratic sovereignty is eroded when legislative bodies make policy via negotiation with special interest groups. The compromise that has been worked out in many jurisdictions (see *Norwalk v. Connecticut*) is that public sector unions will be limited to bargaining about wages, fringe benefits, and working conditions, but may not otherwise make policy a subject of collective bargaining. One might approach the question of the political meaning of teacher professionalization by asking about how professionalization would alter this division of labor. Two possibilities seem likely. First, insofar as professionalization requires negotiation of power sharing at the district level this division of labor must be modified (see Hobart and Mortola, 1988, pp. 10–13). Where this division of labor is required by state law or judicial decisions, legislative enablement is required. Second, teachers unions will need to deal with a difficult role conflict. As unions, their first duty is to look to the interests of their members. As professional societies, unions must first be concerned for professional

standards and client welfare. Whether unions could manage this role conflict is an open question.

2. The issue in what follows is not whether such knowledge as individual teachers may possess accounts in part for their ability to teach. I see no reason to deny that some teachers know things that make them better teachers. The issue is whether there is public knowledge, knowledge that meets the social standards for a professional knowledge base, that accounts for differences in teacher competence.

3. The choice of "disciplines" instead of "subject matter" is deliberate. Its point is to emphasize that what is being taught is a human activity, not just a product. I also wish the notion understood broadly so as to include any human activity sustained by a developed cognitive tradition. The arts and sports are included. The concept that is central to my argument is Alisdair MacIntyre's (1981) notion of a practice. MacIntyre defines a practice as "any coherent and complex form of socially established cooperative human activity through which goods internal to that form of activity are realized in the course of trying to achieve those standards of excellence which are appropriate to, and partially definitive of, that form of activity, with the result that human powers to achieve excellence, and

human conceptions of the ends and goods involved, are systematically extended" (p. 175).

4. The concept required to understand how teaching a discipline is a way of practicing it is epistemological relativism. Epistemological relativism (see Stout, 1988) is the view that the evidence for a particular claim is relative to the concepts the learner brings to the appraisal of that claim. When two experts discuss some disciplinary issue, they practice their discipline in a way that assumes a set of shared disciplinary concepts that is relevant to appraising the issue. When an expert addresses a disciplinary matter with a novice, the expert must explain or argue in ways that appeal to, extend, and modify the novice's current concepts. Shared disciplinary concepts cannot be assumed. In both cases, the discipline is being practiced because the activities being engaged in are the characteristic activities of the discipline such as explaining, arguing, seeking to understand, or investigating. These activities are dominated by the substance of the discipline and by its epistemology. At the same time, the way of engaging in these activities will be very different, depending on whether the expert is dealing with another expert or with a novice or a child. Given this, my, view of a profession might be thought to be quite congenial to the view argued by Lee Shulman (1986b). I believe that this is, in large measure, the case.

5. It may be worth noting that many of those whom we revere as great teachers are not so revered because they were especially effective pedagogues. Socrates may serve as an example. Why do we regard him as a great teacher? Possibly because he had something worth teaching, but I suspect that this misses the point. I would suppose that his greatness as a teacher consists in the fact that Socratic method exhibits the excellences of reasoned inquiry and because its process is determined by the nature of reasoned inquiry (see Plato, 1949). To see Socratic method as a kind of technology of efficient teaching is to dramatically misunderstand it. My preference for Aristotle as my preferred teacher expresses my preference for his views of the method of inquiry, not for his pedagogical technique.

6. Professor William Carlsen has suggested that "Putting aside subject matter to focus on teaching is like putting aside medicine to focus on bedside manner." I think this is an apt illustration of the role of "technical" pedagogical knowledge in a profession of teaching. Professor Carlsen has been of sufficient help in this article that, were it not unprofessional, I would blame some of it on him. It will be sufficient, however, to note his assistance and to thank him for it. The responsibility for my views, sadly, cannot be shared.

## References

Ackerman, B. (1980) *Social Justice in the Liberal State* (New Haven, CT: Yale University Press).

Dworkin, R. (1984) Liberalism. In M. J. Sandel (ed.), *Liberalism and its Critics* (New York: New York University Press).

Green, T. F. (1971) *The Activities of Teaching* (New York: McGraw-Hill).

Haller, E. J. and Strike, K. A. (1986) *An Introduction to Educational Administration* (New York: Longman).

Hobart, T. Y. and Mortola, E. J. (1988) *The New York Report: A Blueprint for Learning and Teaching*.

Howsam, R. B. (1980) The workplace: Does it hamper professionalization of pedagogy? *Phi Delta Kappan* 62, 93–6.

Hoy, W. K. and Miskel, C. G. (1987) *Educational Administration: Theory, Research, and Practice*, 3rd edn (New York: Random House).

Kimball, B. A. (1988) The problem of teachers' authority in light of the structural analysis of professions. *Educational Theory* 38: 1–9.

Locke, J. (1960) *Two Treatises of Government* (New York: Cambridge University Press).

MacIntyre, A. (1981) *After Virtue* (Notre Dame, IN: University of Notre Dame Press).

Noddings, N. (1984) *Caring: A Feminine Approach to Ethics and Moral Education* (Berkeley, CA: University of California Press).

*Norwalk v. Board of Education*, 138 Conn. 269, 83 A2d 482 (1951).

Phillips, D. C. (1988) On teacher knowledge: A skeptical dialogue. *Educational Theory* 38: 457–66.

Plato (1949) *Meno* (New York: Bobbs-Merrill).

Rawls, J. (1974) *A Theory of Justice* (Cambridge, MA: Harvard University Press).

Scriven, M. (1988) Duty-based teacher evaluation. *Journal of Personnel Evaluation in Education* 1: 319–34.

Shulman, L. S. (1986a) Paradigms and research programs in the study of teaching: A contemporary perspective. In M. C. Wittrock (ed.), *Handbook of Research on Teaching*, 3rd edn (New York: Macmillan).

Shulman, L. S. (1986b) Those who understand: Knowledge growth in teaching. *Educational Researcher* 15: 4–14.

Soltis, J. F. (1986) Teaching professional ethics. *Journal of Teacher Education* 37: 2–4.

Stout, J. (1988) *Ethics after Babel* (Boston, MA: Beacon Press).

Strike, K. A. (1986) The ethics of teaching. *Phi Delta Kappan* 70: 156–8.

Tom, A. (1984) *Teaching as a Moral Craft* (New York: Longman).

Wittgenstein, L. (1953) *Philosophical Investigations* (Oxford: Basil Blackwell).

# 21

# The Crisis in Education

# Hannah Arendt

## I

[ ... ]

The extraordinary enthusiasm for what is new, which is shown in almost every aspect of American daily life, and the concomitant trust in an "indefinite perfectibility" – which Tocqueville noted as the credo of the common "uninstructed man" and which as such antedates by almost a hundred years the development in other countries of the West – would presumably have resulted in any case in greater attention paid and greater significance ascribed to the newcomers by birth, that is, the children, whom, when they had outgrown their childhood and were about to enter the community of adults as young people, the Greeks simply called οἱ νέοι, the new ones. There is the additional fact, however, a fact that has become decisive for the meaning of education, that this pathos of the new, though it is considerably older than the eighteenth century, only developed conceptually and politically in that century. From this source there was derived at the start an educational ideal, tinged with Rousseau-ism and in fact directly influenced by Rousseau, in which education became an instrument of politics, and political activity itself was conceived of as a form of education.

[ ... ]

Now in respect to education itself the illusion arising from the pathos of the new has produced its most serious consequences only in our own century. It has first of all made it possible for that complex of modern educational theories which originated in Middle Europe and consists of an astounding hodgepodge of sense and nonsense to accomplish, under the banner of progressive education, a most radical revolution in the whole system of education. What in Europe has remained an experiment, tested out here and there in single schools and isolated educational institutions and then gradually extending its influences in certain quarters, in America about twenty-five years ago completely overthrew, as though from one day to the next, all traditions and all the established methods of teaching and learning. I shall not go into details, and I leave out of account private schools and especially the Roman Catholic parochial school system. The significant fact is that for the sake of certain

Previously published in *Between Past and Future* (London: Faber & Faber, 1961), pp. 176, 178–9, 180–4, 185–6, 188–90, 196. © 1954, 1956, 1957, 1958, 1960, 1961 by Hannah Arendt. Reproduced by permission of Pollinger Limited and the proprietor.

theories, good or bad, all the rules of sound human reason were thrust aside. Such a procedure is always of great and pernicious significance, especially in a country that relies so extensively on common sense in its political life. Whenever in political questions sound human reason fails or gives up the attempt to supply answers we are faced by a crisis; for this kind of reason is really that common sense by virtue of which we and our five individual senses are fitted into a single world common to us all and by the aid of which we move about in it. The disappearance of common sense in the present day is the surest sign of the present-day crisis. In every crisis a piece of the world, something common to us all, is destroyed. The failure of common sense, like a divining rod, points to the place where such a cave-in has occurred.

In any case the answer to the question of why Johnny can't read or to the more general question of why the scholastic standards of the average American school lag so very far behind the average standards in actually all the countries of Europe is not, unfortunately, simply that this country is young and has not yet caught up with the standards of the Old World but, on the contrary, that this country in this particular field is the most "advanced" and most modern in the world. And this is true in a double sense: nowhere have the education problems of a mass society become so acute, and nowhere else have the most modern theories in the realm of pedagogy been so uncritically and slavishly accepted. Thus the crisis in American education, on the one hand, announces the bankruptcy of progressive education and, on the other, presents a problem of immense difficulty because it has arisen under the conditions and in response to the demands of a mass society.

[ . . . ]

[W]hat makes the educational crisis in America so especially acute is the political temper of the country, which of itself struggles to equalize or to erase as far as possible the difference between young and old, between the gifted and the ungifted, finally between children and adults, particularly between pupils and teachers. It is obvious that such an equalization can actually be accomplished only at the cost of the teacher's authority and at the expense of the gifted among the students. However, it is equally obvious, at least to anyone who has ever come in contact with the American educational system, that this difficulty, rooted in the political attitude of the country, also has great advantages, not simply

of a human kind but educationally speaking as well; in any case these general factors cannot explain the crisis in which we presently find ourselves nor justify the measures through which that crisis has been precipitated.

## II

These ruinous measures can be schematically traced back to three basic assumptions, all of which are only too familiar. The *first* is that there exist a child's world and a society formed among children that are autonomous and must insofar as possible be left to them to govern. Adults are only there to help with this government. The authority that tells the individual child what to do and what not to do rests with the child group itself – and this produces, among other consequences, a situation in which the adult stands helpless before the individual child and out of contact with him. He can only tell him to do what he likes and then prevent the worst from happening. The real and normal relations between children and adults, arising from the fact that people of all ages are always simultaneously together in the world, are thus broken off. And so it is of the essence of this first basic assumption that it takes into account only the group and not the individual child.

As for the child in the group, he is of course rather worse off than before. For the authority of a group, even a child group, is always considerably stronger and more tyrannical than the severest authority of an individual person can ever be. If one looks at it from the standpoint of the individual child, his chances to rebel or to do anything on his own hook are practically nil; he no longer finds himself in a very unequal contest with a person who has, to be sure, absolute superiority over him but in contest with whom he can nevertheless count on the solidarity of other children, that is, of his own kind; rather he is in the position, hopeless by definition, of a minority of one confronted by the absolute majority of all the others. There are very few grown people who can endure such a situation, even when it is not supported by external means of compulsion; children are simply and utterly incapable of it.

Therefore by being emancipated from the authority of adults the child has not been freed but has been subjected to a much more terrifying and truly tyrannical authority, the tyranny of the majority. In any case the result is that the children have been so to speak banished from the world of grown-ups. They are either thrown back upon themselves or handed over to the tyranny of their own group, against which, because of its numerical superiority, they cannot rebel, with which, because they are children, they cannot reason, and out of which they cannot flee to any other world because the world of adults is barred to them. The reaction of the children to this pressure tends to be either conformism or juvenile delinquency, and is frequently a mixture of both.

The *second* basic assumption which has come into question in the present crisis has to do with teaching. Under the influence of modern psychology and the tenets of pragmatism, pedagogy has developed into a science of teaching in general in such a way as to be wholly emancipated from the actual material to be taught. A teacher, so it was thought, is a man who can simply teach anything; his training is in teaching, not in the mastery of any particular subject. This attitude, as we shall presently see, is naturally very closely connected with a basic assumption about learning. Moreover, it has resulted in recent decades in a most serious neglect of the training of teachers in their own subjects, especially in the public high schools. Since the teacher does not need to know his own subject, it not infrequently happens that he is just one hour ahead of his class in knowledge. This in turn means not only that the students are actually left to their own resources but that the most legitimate source of the teacher's authority as the person who, turn it whatever way one will, still knows more and can do more than oneself is no longer effective. Thus the non-authoritarian teacher, who would like to abstain from all methods of compulsion because he is able to rely on his own authority, can no longer exist.

But this pernicious role that pedagogy and the teachers' colleges are playing in the present crisis was only possible because of a modern theory about learning. This was, quite simply, the logical application of the *third* basic assumption in our context, an assumption which the modern world has held for centuries and which found its systematic conceptual expression in pragmatism. This basic assumption is that you can know and understand only what you have done yourself, and its application to education is as primitive as it is obvious: to substitute, insofar as possible, doing for learning. The reason that no importance was attached to the teacher's mastering his own subject was the wish to compel him to the exercise of the continuous activity of learning so that he would not, as they said, pass on "dead

knowledge" but, instead, would constantly demonstrate how it is produced. The conscious intention was not to teach knowledge but to inculcate a skill, and the result was a kind of transformation of institutes for learning into vocational institutions which have been as successful in teaching how to drive a car or how to use a typewriter or, even more important for the "art" of living, how to get along with other people and to be popular, as they have been unable to make the children acquire the normal prerequisites of a standard curriculum.

However, this description is at fault, not only because it obviously exaggerates in order to drive home a point, but because it fails to take into account how in this process special importance was attached to obliterating as far as possible the distinction between play and work – in favor of the former. Play was looked upon as the liveliest and most appropriate way for the child to behave in the world, as the only form of activity that evolves spontaneously from his existence as a child. Only what can be learned through play does justice to this liveliness. The child's characteristic activity, so it was thought, lies in play; learning in the old sense, by forcing a child into an attitude of passivity, compelled him to give up his own playful initiative.

The close connection between these two things – the substitution of doing for learning and of playing for working – is directly illustrated by the teaching of languages: the child is to learn by speaking, that is by doing, not by studying grammar and syntax; in other words he is to learn a foreign language in the same way that as an infant he learned his own language: as though at play and in the uninterrupted continuity of simple existence. Quite apart from the question of whether this is possible or not – it is possible, to a limited degree, only when one can keep the child all day long in the foreign-speaking environment – it is perfectly clear that this procedure consciously attempts to keep the older child as far as possible at the infant level. The very thing that should prepare the child for the world of adults, the gradually acquired habit of work and of not-playing, is done away with in favor of the autonomy of the world of childhood.

Whatever may be the connection between doing and knowing, or whatever the validity of the pragmatic formula, its application to education, that is, to the way the child learns, tends to make absolute the world of childhood in just the same way that we noted in the case of the first basic assumption. Here, too, under the pretext of respecting the child's independence, he is debarred from the world of grown-ups and artificially kept in his own, so far as that can be called a world. This holding back of the child is artificial because it breaks off the natural relationship between grown-ups and children, which consists among other things in teaching and learning, and because at the same time it belies the fact that the child is a developing human being, that childhood is a temporary stage, a preparation for adulthood.

[ . . . ]

## III

[ . . . ]

Human parents have not only summoned their children into life through conception and birth, they have simultaneously introduced them into a world. In education they assume responsibility for both, for the life and development of the child and for the continuance of the world. These two responsibilities do not by any means coincide; they may indeed come into conflict with each other. The responsibility for the development of the child turns in a certain sense against the world: the child requires special protection and care so that nothing destructive may happen to him from the world. But the world, too, needs protection to keep it from being overrun and destroyed by the onslaught of the new that bursts upon it with each new generation.

[ . . . ]

Normally the child is first introduced to the world in school. Now school is by no means the world and must not pretend to be; it is rather the institution that we interpose between the private domain of home and the world in order to make the transition from the family to the world possible at all. Attendance there is required not by the family but by the state, that is by the public world, and so, in relation to the child, school in a sense represents the world, although it is not yet actually the world. At this stage of education adults, to be sure, once more assume a responsibility for the child, but by now it is not so much responsibility for the vital welfare of a growing thing as for what we generally call the free development of characteristic qualities and talents. This, from the general and essential point of view, is the uniqueness that distinguishes every human being from every other, the quality by virtue of which he is not only a stranger in the world but something that has never been here before.

Insofar as the child is not yet acquainted with the world, he must be gradually introduced to it; insofar as he is new, care must be taken that this new thing comes to fruition in relation to the world as it is. In any case, however, the educators here stand in relation to the young as representatives of a world for which they must assume responsibility although they themselves did not make it, and even though they may, secretly or openly, wish it were other than it is. This responsibility is not arbitrarily imposed upon educators; it is implicit in the fact that the young are introduced by adults into a continuously changing world. Anyone who refuses to assume joint responsibility for the world should not have children and must not be allowed to take part in educating them.

In education this responsibility for the world takes the form of authority. The authority of the educator and the qualifications of the teacher are not the same thing. Although a measure of qualification is indispensable for authority, the highest possible qualification can never by itself beget authority. The teacher's qualification consists in knowing the world and being able to instruct others about it, but his authority rests on his assumption of responsibility for that world. Vis-à-vis the child it is as though he were a representative of all adult inhabitants, pointing out the details and saying to the child: This is our world.

Now we all know how things stand today in respect to authority. Whatever one's attitude toward this problem may be, it is obvious that in public and political life authority either plays no role at all – for the violence and terror exercised by the totalitarian countries have, of course, nothing to do with authority – or at most plays a highly contested role. This, however, simply means, in essence, that people do not wish to require of anyone or to entrust to anyone the assumption of responsibility for everything else, for wherever true authority existed it was joined with responsibility for the course of things in the world. If we remove authority from political and public life, it may mean that from now on an equal responsibility for the course of the world is to be required of everyone. But it may also mean that the claims of the world and the requirements of order in it are being consciously or unconsciously repudiated; all responsibility for the world is being rejected, the responsibility for giving orders no less than for obeying them. There is no doubt that in the modern loss of authority both intentions play a part and have often been simultaneously and inextricably at work together.

In education, on the contrary, there can be no such ambiguity in regard to the present-day loss of authority. Children cannot throw off educational authority, as though they were in a position of oppression by an adult majority – though even this absurdity of treating children as an oppressed minority in need of liberation has actually been tried out in modern educational practice. Authority has been discarded by the adults, and this can mean only one thing: that the adults refuse to assume responsibility for the world into which they have brought the children.

[ ... ]

What concerns us all [ ... ] is the relation between grown-ups and children in general or, putting it in even more general and exact terms, our attitude toward the fact of natality: the fact that we have all come into the world by being born and that this world is constantly renewed through birth. Education is the point at which we decide whether we love the world enough to assume responsibility for it and by the same token save it from that ruin which, except for renewal, except for the coming of the new and young, would be inevitable. And education, too, is where we decide whether we love our children enough not to expel them from our world and leave them to their own devices, nor to strike from their hands their chance of undertaking something new, something unforeseen by us, but to prepare them in advance for the task of renewing a common world.

# The Commercialization
# of Schooling

# 22

# The Role of Government in Education

## Milton Friedman

Formal schooling is today paid for and almost entirely administered by government bodies or non-profit institutions. This situation has developed gradually and is now taken so much for granted that little explicit attention is any longer directed to the reasons for the special treatment of schooling even in countries that are predominantly free enterprise in organization and philosophy. The result has been an indiscriminate extension of governmental responsibility.

In terms of the principles developed in chapter 2, governmental intervention into education can be rationalized on two grounds. The first is the existence of substantial "neighborhood effects," i.e., circumstances under which the action of one individual imposes significant costs on other individuals for which it is not feasible to make him compensate them, or yields significant gains to other individuals for which it is not feasible to make them compensate him – circumstances that make voluntary exchange impossible. The second is the paternalistic concern for children and other irresponsible individuals. Neighborhood effects and paternalism have very different implications for (1) general education for citizenship, and (2) specialized vocational education. The grounds for governmental intervention are widely different in these two areas and justify very different types of action.

One further preliminary remark: it is important to distinguish between "schooling" and "education." Not all schooling is education nor all education, schooling. The proper subject of concern is education. The activities of government are mostly limited to schooling.

## General Education for Citizenship

A stable and democratic society is impossible without a minimum degree of literacy and knowledge on the part of most citizens and without widespread acceptance of some common set of values. Education can contribute to both. In consequence, the gain from the education of a child accrues not only to the child or to his parents but also to other members of the society. The education of my child contributes to your welfare by promoting a stable and democratic society. It is not feasible to identify the particular individuals (or families) benefited and so to charge

Previously published in *Capitalism and Freedom* (Chicago, IL: University of Chicago Press, 1962), pp. 85–96, 97–8. Reprinted by permission of the University of Chicago Press.

for the services rendered. There is therefore a significant "neighborhood effect."

What kind of governmental action is justified by this particular neighborhood effect? The most obvious is to require that each child receive a minimum amount of schooling of a specified kind. Such a requirement could be imposed upon the parents without further government action, just as owners of buildings, and frequently of automobiles, are required to adhere to specified standards to protect the safety of others. There is, however, a difference between the two cases. Individuals who cannot pay the costs of meeting the standards required for buildings or automobiles can generally divest themselves of the property by selling it. The requirement can thus generally be enforced without government subsidy. The separation of a child from a parent who cannot pay for the minimum required schooling is clearly inconsistent with our reliance on the family as the basic social unit and our belief in the freedom of the individual. Moreover, it would be very likely to detract from his education for citizenship in a free society.

If the financial burden imposed by such a schooling requirement could readily be met by the great bulk of the families in a community, it might still be both feasible and desirable to require the parents to meet the cost directly. Extreme cases could be handled by special subsidy provisions for needy families. There are many areas in the United States today where these conditions are satisfied. In these areas, it would be highly desirable to impose the costs directly on the parents. This would eliminate the governmental machinery now required to collect tax funds from all residents during the whole of their lives and then pay it back mostly to the same people during the period when their children are in school. It would reduce the likelihood that governments would also administer schools, a matter discussed further below. It would increase the likelihood that the subsidy component of school expenditures would decline as the need for such subsidies declined with increasing general levels of income. If, as now, the government pays for all or most schooling, a rise in income simply leads to a still larger circular flow of funds through the tax mechanism, and an expansion in the role of the government. Finally, but by no means least, imposing the costs on the parents would tend to equalize the social and private costs of having children and so promote a better distribution of families by size.[1]

Differences among families in resources and in number of children, plus the imposition of a standard of schooling involving very sizable costs, make such a policy hardly feasible in many parts of the United States. Both in such areas, and in areas where such a policy would be feasible, government has instead assumed the financial costs of providing schooling. It has paid, not only for the minimum amount of schooling required of all, but also for additional schooling at higher levels available to youngsters but not required of them. One argument for both steps is the "neighborhood effects" discussed above. The costs are paid because this is the only feasible means of enforcing the required minimum. Additional schooling is financed because other people benefit from the schooling of those of greater ability and interest, since this is a way of providing better social and political leadership. The gain from these measures must be balanced against the costs, and there can be much honest difference of judgment about how extensive a subsidy is justified. Most of us, however, would probably conclude that the gains are sufficiently important to justify some government subsidy.

These grounds justify government subsidy of only certain kinds of schooling. To anticipate, they do not justify subsidizing purely vocational training which increases the economic productivity of the student but does not train him for either citizenship or leadership. It is extremely difficult to draw a sharp line between the two types of schooling. Most general schooling adds to the economic value of the student – indeed it is only in modern times and in a few countries that literacy has ceased to have a marketable value. And much vocational training broadens the student's outlook. Yet the distinction is meaningful. Subsidizing the training of veterinarians, beauticians, dentists, and a host of other specialists, as is widely done in the United States in governmentally supported educational institutions, cannot be justified on the same grounds as subsidizing elementary schools or, at a higher level, liberal arts colleges. Whether it can be justified on quite different grounds will be discussed later in this chapter.

The qualitative argument from "neighborhood effects" does not, of course, determine the specific kinds of schooling that should be subsidized or by how much they should be subsidized. The social gain presumably is greatest for the lowest levels of schooling, where there is the nearest approach to unanimity about content, and declines continuously as the level of schooling rises. Even this statement cannot be taken completely for granted. Many governments subsidized universities long before they subsidized lower schools. What forms of education have the greatest social advantage and how much of the community's limited resources should be spent on them must be decided by the judgment of the community expressed through its accepted political channels. The aim of this analysis is not to decide these questions for the community but rather to clarify the issues involved in making a choice, in particular whether it is appropriate to make the choice on a communal rather than individual basis.

As we have seen, both the imposition of a minimum required level of schooling and the financing of this schooling by the state can be justified by the "neighborhood effects" of schooling. A third step, namely the actual administration of educational institutions by the government, the "nationalization," as it were, of the bulk of the "education industry" is much more difficult to justify on these, or, so far as I can see, any other, grounds. The desirability of such nationalization has seldom been faced explicitly. Governments have, in the main, financed schooling by paying directly the costs of running educational institutions. Thus this step seemed required by the decision to subsidize schooling. Yet the two steps could readily be separated. Governments could require a minimum level of schooling financed by giving parents vouchers redeemable for a specified maximum sum per child per year if spent on "approved" educational services. Parents would then be free to spend this sum and any additional sum they themselves provided on purchasing educational services from an "approved" institution of their own choice. The educational services could be rendered by private enterprises operated for profit, or by non-profit institutions. The role of the government would be limited to insuring that the schools met certain minimum standards, such as the inclusion of a minimum common content in their programs, much as it now inspects restaurants to insure that they maintain minimum sanitary standards. An excellent example of a program of this sort is the United States educational program for veterans after World War II. Each veteran who qualified was given a maximum sum per year that could be spent at any institution of his choice, provided it met certain minimum standards. A more limited example is the provision in Britain whereby local authorities pay the fees of some students attend-

ing non-state schools. Another is the arrangement in France whereby the state pays part of the costs for students attending non-state schools.

One argument for nationalizing schools resting on a "neighborhood effect" is that it might otherwise be impossible to provide the common core of values deemed requisite for social stability. The imposition of minimum standards on privately conducted schools, as suggested above, might not be enough to achieve this result. The issue can be illustrated concretely in terms of schools run by different religious groups. Such schools, it can be argued, will instil sets of values that are inconsistent with one another and with those instilled in non-sectarian schools; in this way, they convert education into a divisive rather than a unifying force.

Carried to its extreme, this argument would call not only for governmentally administered schools, but also for compulsory attendance at such schools. Existing arrangements in the United States and most other Western countries are a halfway house. Governmentally administered schools are available but not compulsory. However, the link between the financing of schooling and its administration places other schools at a disadvantage: they get the benefit of little or none of the governmental funds spent on schooling – a situation that has been the source of much political dispute, particularly in France and at present in the United States. The elimination of this disadvantage might, it is feared, greatly strengthen the parochial schools and so render the problem of achieving a common core of values even more difficult.

Persuasive as this argument is, it is by no means clear that it is valid or that denationalizing schooling would have the effects suggested. On grounds of principle, it conflicts with the preservation of freedom itself. Drawing a line between providing for the common social values required for a stable society, on the one hand, and indoctrination inhibiting freedom of thought and belief, on the other is another of those vague boundaries that is easier to mention than to define.

In terms of effects, denationalizing schooling would widen the range of choice available to parents. If, as at present, parents can send their children to public schools without special payment, very few can or will send them to other schools unless they too are subsidized. Parochial schools are at a disadvantage in not getting any of the public funds devoted to schooling, but they have the compensating advantage of being run by institutions that are willing to subsidize them and can raise funds to do so. There are few other sources of subsidies for private schools. If present public expenditures on schooling were made available to parents regardless of where they send their children, a wide variety of schools would spring up to meet the demand. Parents could express their views about schools directly by withdrawing their children from one school and sending them to another, to a much greater extent than is now possible. In general, they can now take this step only at considerable cost – by sending their children to a private school or by changing their residence. For the rest, they can express their views only through cumbrous political channels. Perhaps a somewhat greater degree of freedom to choose schools could be made available in a governmentally administered system, but it would be difficult to carry this freedom very far in view of the obligation to provide every child with a place. Here, as in other fields, competitive enterprise is likely to be far more efficient in meeting consumer demand than either nationalized enterprises or enterprises run to serve other purposes. The final result may therefore be that parochial schools would decline rather than grow in importance.

A related factor working in the same direction is the understandable reluctance of parents who send their children to parochial schools to increase taxes to finance higher public school expenditures. As a result, those areas where parochial schools are important have great difficulty raising funds for public schools. Insofar as quality is related to expenditure, as to some extent it undoubtedly is, public schools tend to be of lower quality in such areas and hence parochial schools are relatively more attractive.

Another special case of the argument that governmentally conducted schools are necessary for education to be a unifying force is that private schools would tend to exacerbate class distinctions. Given greater freedom about where to send their children, parents of a kind would flock together and so prevent a healthy intermingling of children from decidedly different backgrounds. Whether or not this argument is valid in principle, it is not at all clear that the stated results would follow. Under present arrangements, stratification of residential areas effectively restricts the intermingling of children from decidedly different backgrounds. In addition, parents are not now prevented from sending their children to private schools. Only a highly limited class can or does do so, parochial schools aside, thus producing further stratification.

Indeed, this argument seems to me to point in almost the diametrically opposite direction – toward the denationalizing of schools. Ask yourself in what respect the inhabitant of a low income neighborhood, let alone of a Negro neighborhood in a large city, is most disadvantaged. If he attaches enough importance to, say, a new automobile, he can, by dint of saving, accumulate enough money to buy the same car as a resident of a high-income suburb. To do so, he need not move to that suburb. On the contrary, he can get the money partly by economizing on his living quarters. And this goes equally for clothes, or furniture, or books, or what not. But let a poor family in a slum have a gifted child and let it set such high value on his or her schooling that it is willing to scrimp and save for the purpose. Unless it can get special treatment, or scholarship assistance, at one of the very few private schools, the family is in a very difficult position. The "good" public schools are in the high income neighborhoods. The family might be willing to spend something in addition to what it pays in taxes to get better schooling for its child. But it can hardly afford simultaneously to move to the expensive neighborhood.

Our views in these respects are, I believe, still dominated by the small town which had but one school for the poor and rich residents alike. Under such circumstances, public schools may well have equalized opportunities. With the growth of urban and suburban areas, the situation has changed drastically. Our present school system, far from equalizing opportunity, very likely does the opposite. It makes it all the harder for the exceptional few – and it is they who are the hope of the future – to rise above the poverty of their initial state.

Another argument for nationalizing schooling is "technical monopoly." In small communities and rural areas, the number of children may be too small to justify more than one school of reasonable size, so that competition cannot be relied on to protect the interests of parents and children. As in other cases of technical monopoly, the alternatives are unrestricted private monopoly, state-controlled private monopoly, and public operation – a choice among evils. This argument, though clearly valid and significant, has been greatly weakened in recent decades by improvements in transportation and increasing concentration of the population in urban communities.

The arrangement that perhaps comes closest to being justified by these considerations – at least for primary and secondary education – is a combination of public and private schools. Parents who choose to send their children to private schools would be paid a sum equal to the estimated cost of educating a child in a public school, provided that at least this sum was spent on education in an approved school. This arrangement would meet the valid features of the "technical monopoly" argument. It would meet the just complaints of parents that if they send their children to private non-subsidized schools they are required to pay twice for education – once in the form of general taxes and once directly. It would permit competition to develop. The development and improvement of all schools would thus be stimulated. The injection of competition would do much to promote a healthy variety of schools. It would do much, also, to introduce flexibility into school systems. Not least of its benefits would be to make the salaries of school teachers responsive to market forces. It would thereby give public authorities an independent standard against which to judge salary scales and promote a more rapid adjustment to changes in conditions of demand and supply.

It is widely urged that the great need in schooling is more money to build more facilities and to pay higher salaries to teachers in order to attract better teachers. This seems a false diagnosis. The amount of money spent on schooling has been rising at an extraordinarily high rate, far faster than our total income. Teachers' salaries have been rising far faster than returns in comparable occupations. The problem is not primarily that we are spending too little money – though we may be – but that we are getting so little per dollar spent. Perhaps the amounts of money spent on magnificent structures and luxurious grounds at many schools are properly classified as expenditures on schooling. It is hard to accept them equally as expenditures on education. And this is equally clear with respect to courses in basket weaving, social dancing, and the numerous other special subjects that do such credit to the ingenuity of educators. I hasten to add that there can be no conceivable objection to parents' spending their own money on such frills if they wish. That is their business. The objection is to using money raised by taxation imposed on parents and non-parents alike for such purposes. Wherein are the "neighborhood effects" that justify such use of tax money?

A major reason for this kind of use of public money is the present system of combining the administration of schools with their financing. The parent who would prefer to see money used for better teachers and texts rather than coaches and corridors has no way of expressing this preference except by persuading a majority to change the mixture for all. This is a special case of the general principle that a market permits each to satisfy his own taste – effective proportional representation; whereas the political process imposes conformity. In addition, the parent who would like to spend some extra money on his child's education is greatly limited. He cannot add something to the amount now being spent to school his child and transfer his child to a correspondingly more costly school. If he does transfer his child, he must pay the whole cost and not simply the additional cost. He can only spend extra money easily on extra-curricular activities – dancing lessons, music lessons, etc. Since the private outlets for spending more money on schooling are so blocked, the pressure to spend more on the education of children manifests itself in ever higher public expenditures on items ever more tenuously related to the basic justification for governmental intervention into schooling.

As this analysis implies, the adoption of the suggested arrangements might well mean smaller governmental expenditures on schooling, yet higher total expenditures. It would enable parents to buy what they want more efficiently and thereby lead them to spend more than they now do directly and indirectly through taxation. It would prevent parents from being frustrated in spending more money on schooling by both the present need for conformity in how the money is spent and by the understandable reluctance on the part of persons not currently having children in school, and especially those who will not in the future have them in school, to impose higher taxes on themselves for purposes often far removed from education as they understand the term.[2]

With respect to teachers' salaries, the major problem is not that they are too low on the average – they may well be too high on the average – but that they are too uniform and rigid. Poor teachers are grossly overpaid and good teachers grossly underpaid. Salary schedules tend to be uniform and determined far more by seniority, degrees received, and teaching certificates acquired than by merit. This, too, is largely a result of the present system of governmental administration of schools and becomes more serious as the unit over which governmental control is exercised becomes larger. Indeed, this very fact is a major reason why professional educational organizations so strongly favor broadening the unit – from the local school district to the state, from the state to the federal government. In any bureaucratic, essentially civil-service organization, standard salary scales are almost inevitable; it is next to impossible to simulate competition capable of providing wide differences in salaries according to merit. The educators, which means the teachers themselves, come to exercise primary control. The parent or local community comes to exercise little control. In any area, whether it be carpentry or plumbing or teaching, the majority of workers favor standard salary scales and oppose merit differentials, for the obvious reason that the specially talented are always few. This is a special case of the general tendency for people to seek to collude to fix prices, whether through unions or industrial monopolies. But collusive agreements will generally be destroyed by competition unless the government enforces them, or at least renders them considerable support.

If one were to seek deliberately to devise a system of recruiting and paying teachers calculated to repel the imaginative and daring and self-confident and to attract the dull and mediocre and uninspiring, he could hardly do better than imitate the system of requiring teaching certificates and enforcing standard salary structures that has developed in the larger city and state-wide systems. It is perhaps surprising that the level of ability in elementary and secondary school teaching is as high as it is under these circumstances. The alternative system would resolve these problems and permit competition to be effective in rewarding merit and attracting ability to teaching.

[ . . . ]

Although many administrative problems would arise in changing over from the present to the proposed system and in its administration, these seem neither insoluble nor unique. As in the denationalization of other activities, existing premises and equipment could be sold to private enterprises that wanted to enter the field. Thus, there would be no waste of capital in the transition. Since governmental units, at least in some areas, would continue to administer schools, the transition would be gradual and easy. The local administration of schooling in the United States and some other countries would similarly facilitate the transition, since it would encourage experimentation on a small scale. Difficulties would doubtless arise in determining eligibility for grants from a particular governmental unit, but this is identical with the existing problem of determining which unit is obligated to provide schooling facilities for a particular child. Differences in size of grants would make one area more attractive than another just as differences in the quality of schooling now have the same effect. The only additional complication is a possibly greater opportunity for abuse because of the greater freedom to decide where to educate children. Supposed difficulty of administration is a standard defense of the status quo against any proposed change; in this particular case, it is an even weaker defense than usual because existing arrangements must master not only the major problems raised by the proposed arrangements but also the additional problems raised by the administration of schools as a governmental function.

## Notes

1. It is by no means so fantastic as may appear that such a step would noticeably affect the size of families. For example, one explanation of the lower birth rate among higher than among lower socio-economic groups may well be that children are relatively more expensive to the former, thanks in considerable measure to the higher standards of schooling they maintain, the costs of which they bear.

2. A striking example of the same effect in another field is the British National Health Service. In a careful and penetrating study, D. S. Lees establishes rather conclusively that, "Far from being extravagant, expenditure on NHS has been less than consumers would probably have chosen to spend in a free market. The record of hospital building in particular has been deplorable." "Health Through Choice," *Hobart Paper 14* (London: Institute of Economic Affairs, 1961), p. 58.

# 23

# Commercialization or Citizenship: The Case of Education

## Colin Crouch

School-level education has been a policy field where the contradictions between citizenship and commercialisation approaches have been particularly clear in government policy. The concept of citizenship entitlement is highly developed in education. Partly because so much of its provision is compulsory, partly because in a democracy all political parties are required to advocate opportunities for social mobility, there is an almost universal expectation that education should be available as a right, not needing to be purchased in the market – though in practice in the UK and some other countries this ideal has always been heavily compromised by the existence of fee-paying schools to which many wealthy people send their children.

The strong element of compulsion exists because, if having their children educated was voluntary, many parents would fail to do so. This would create problems of social order and might weaken the eventual economic capacity of these children. It is therefore difficult to apply one fundamental attribute of the market, freedom of consumer choice. It would be even more difficult to apply the other fundamental attribute: the payment of prices which reflect the production costs of the good or service offered. If this were applied, even fewer parents

would have their children educated, or they would buy very cheap and inadequate schooling. In principle compulsory consumption could be combined with all other attributes of the market: parents could be left free to choose from a range of private school suppliers, and to pay fees. There would however be severe political objections to enforced payment of private consumption. Education presents particularly difficult problems for a full application of market logic – which would mean treating it like any other good, offered for sale according to supply and demand – without distorting and degrading the service provided.

Markets and private firms therefore hover on the margins of the compulsory education system, in two main forms: the introduction of market analogues without privatisation into the school admissions system; and the contracting out of educational services, including increasingly the teaching of subjects in schools, to firms. Both will be explored below.

### Making Markets in Education

For parents and their children, the choice of school which a child will attend is the most market-like

Editor's title. Previously published in *Commercialization or Citizenship: Education Policy and the Future of Public Services* (London: Fabian Society, 2003), pp. 26–35, 50–7. Reprinted by permission of the Fabian Society.

aspect of the education system. Governments eager to introduce elements of the market have therefore concentrated attention on extending parents' freedom of choice in this field. However, for the reasons outlined above, they have had to do this without use of the price mechanism. This limits heavily the degree of marketisation that can be introduced, as it eliminates two fundamental roles of price within a true market: as a unitary indicator which is considered to summarise all relevant qualities of an item of the good in question, enabling it to be compared with rivals and facilitating choice; and as a rationing device for distribution. Governments have found solutions to these deficiencies. However, the result has been, not a happy compromise creating something new between citizenship and markets, but a dysfunctional stalemate. The problem of the absence of price as a quality indicator can in principle be tackled by constructing analogues to guide customers, and doing this has been a major element of policy. The main solution found by the Conservative Government and continued by Labour has been the introduction of official tests of pupils' performance, administered at ages seven, eleven, fourteen and sixteen. The results of these are published and used to rank and compare schools. Parents are encouraged to use them as indicators of quality when choosing schools for their children. At the same time, schools' performances in the annual GCSE and A Level GCE examinations are calculated, ranked and widely published in the press. All this facilitates a market-like process, but it has two principal defects which may distort educational provision.

First, partial indicators encourage schools to maximise performance on those items reflected in the indicators alone. If success in certain examinations is measured and published, the rational school will concentrate on those at the expense of other activities. There have been many examples of this, leading to demands that government adjust the indicators used so that they cover all relevant areas, and government has been responsive to these pleas. But there are two limitations to this strategy. First, if indicators multiply, they become too complex, and people find them difficult to appraise. As Onora O'Neill observed in the third of her 2002 BBC Reith Lectures, as targets become more and more technical and complex, and are changed with increasing frequency, the 'public' ceases to be able to understand them at all.[1] The new accountability is not to the public at all, but just to the political

centre. Second, as she also observed, the vast volume of work involved in record keeping and target-making means that the attention of professionals is increasingly focused on these, giving them less time for genuine engagement with the real public, their clients.

A second and highly contentious issue has been the use of pupils' performance as a judgement on school quality, when it is well known that children's academic achievements depend heavily on their social background. The Labour Government initiated a system of baseline testing to reflect this: children are tested on entry to a school; subsequent test performances can then be compared with their initial achievements to assess the value added by the school. The White Paper that eventually became the Education Act 2002 announced that indicators based on these baseline results will eventually be published alongside – but not instead of – the raw data. But many parents may be more interested in the raw data. They want to know both what the school achieves and the quality of its raw material, for in this way they can select schools with suitable fellow pupils for their children. The indicator system sends signals which can be used to reinforce social segregation. In any case, as Brighouse has pointed out, general school measures tell parents very little about the particular balance of characteristics that they seek for their child.[2]

Test scores have not been the only forms of quality signal developed by governments to make markets for school choice. Further indicators are provided by the reports of Ofsted, the Office for Standards in Education, introduced by the Conservatives to give more impetus to change and higher public prominence to school inspection than the school visits of HM Inspectorate of Schools. Ofsted grades schools into various categories, including the highly negative ones of 'having serious weaknesses', or 'requiring special measures' to improve them.

A further technique has been the development of different types of school. In some parts of the country the old 1944 system of a distinction between grammar schools and residual schools was never abolished, and New Labour has no objection to this situation continuing. The Conservative Education Reform Act 1988 had provided for the establishment of Grant Maintained Schools (GMS). To encourage schools to become GMSs the Government introduced certain inducements, such as generous capital and other grants which were not available to

LEA schools. GMSs were permitted to select up to 15 per cent of their pupils from outside their catchment areas, using whatever criteria they liked. GMS status therefore served as a signal to parents that this was a school in favoured financial circumstances and to some extent able to recruit pupils of its choice – a strong market signal.

In practice the implications of this policy were limited: not many GMSs were introduced; their distribution through the country was very uneven. Their contribution to increased choice and to a market in schools was therefore small, arbitrary and sometimes negative. Further extensions of this experiment were stopped by the Labour Government of 1997, which also changed the status of existing GMSs to that of foundation schools; for many purposes, including the crucial question of admissions, they were brought back under LEA responsibility.

However, at secondary level Labour also embarked on an alternative policy of its own for inserting new forms of school within the state system but possessing attractive qualities which would mark them out from ordinary schools. The 2001 White Paper proposed a major expansion of the existing experimental policy of 'specialist schools'. These seek to develop expertise in certain particular kinds of education – such as technology, arts, sports, business studies. To help them fulfil their particular mission, they will be able to select up to 10 per cent of their pupils based on ability within their chosen specialisms. The Government intends that 40 per cent of all secondary schools in England should be 'specialist' by 2005, with a further group in the category of 'working towards' specialist status. (The Government has now said that ultimately it wants all schools to have some kind of specialism.) In addition to LEAs, voluntary bodies, religious organisations and private firms can apply for the right to establish them. In addition to their limited selection right, specialist schools will have the right to pay teachers more than other schools. Schools which have been successful specialist schools for five years will have the chance to become advanced specialist schools, receiving more funding than those around them but also having some responsibilities to develop materials and training and provide services for these others.

The Government argues that specialist schools do not mark a return to selection, because a diversity of specialisms will be recognised, not just general academic ability, and no school is prohibited from working towards specialist status. It is in fact more concerned to make markets than intensify selection, the emphasis of the arguments of the White Paper being on expanding diversity in order to increase choice. However, since superior funding and privileges are to be a mark of specialist schools, it is clear that they are being marked out as more desirable, and not just diverse.

The White Paper introduced a further distinction among schools in its concept of the 'successful' school, formal criteria for defining which will be devised. Under certain conditions 'successful' schools might be permitted: to pay higher salaries to their teachers; to be exempted for teaching parts of the National Curriculum; and to expand their size irrespective of local admissions and school size policies.

The Conservative Education Reform Act 1988, which introduced the tests and the Ofsted model, concomitantly gave parents increased rights to choose individual schools within their local authority, rather than being allocated to their neighbouring school. Schools were then given incentives to attract parents, as they were rewarded financially if they could compete successfully with their neighbours in recruiting pupils. Labour retained all these policies and, as we have seen above, is strengthening some of the mechanisms which divert pupils numbers and resources to certain schools.

Together all these policies over the 1988 to 2001 period have put in place a powerful market analogue whereby customers (parents) are equipped with information to find the most successful schools, and providers (schools) have strong incentives to attract customers. This might seem to be a highly desirable situation, but it has a number of negative consequences. If, as the 2001 White Paper implies, all that is happening is that diversity is being expanded so that customers with different tastes can find providers to match, there would be little to worry about, apart from a large number of minor frictions when supply and demand for particular school characteristics did not match in certain areas. In reality however it is not a question of a wide diversity, but a ranking of 'good' and 'bad' schools. Test and examination results, Ofsted reports, the eventual designations of 'successful' schools all point in the same direction. In theory specialist schools will cover a wider range of attributes, but many of them will be 'specialising' in those areas of the curriculum which deliver the high test scores. Clearly, demand for these will exceed supply. In a true market the price of 'good' schools would rise to bring demand and supply into equilibrium. But this second, controversial role of price as a means of rationing is ruled out by the citizenship principles of the national education system.

The market approach therefore has to operate without substantive prices. In doing this however it does not produce a compromise, but continues to violate citizenship principles. As 'good' or popular schools use their additional resources to expand, 'poor' schools, starved of both pupils and resources, will necessarily decline, and will either eventually close or be left with a residuum of children whose parents do not care. Alternatively, poor schools, shaken out of their complacency as the spiral of decline envelops them, will make determined attempts to improve. In doing this they have an uphill task, as resources and pupils continue to haemorrhage from them.

If nearly all pupils end up in the successful schools while the poor schools decline, there are further negative components. It is a long, slow process. Schools cannot expand quickly, and during that period whole cohorts of children will pass through helplessly declining schools. It is also possible for schools to grow too big to continue with their current regimes; a successful school might be undermined by its very expansion. Further, in many parts of the country the closure of some schools and the removal of pupils to a different one imposes high transport costs on children, which government is already reluctant to meet.

But more insidious than these problems is a perverse analogue of a school fee which emerges when elements of the market are introduced into a theoretically non-selective system. If the supply of places in 'good' schools cannot rise to meet demand, there is competition among parents. This competition is resolved in ways which cannot be reconciled with the citizenship model. Schools' achievements are determined by two factors: the initial cultural capital that pupils bring with them (the quality of the raw materials) and the quality of the education which the school provides (the school's added value). While parents are 'customers', their children are the raw materials which are fashioned by the school to produce the end product. The customers thus make their own contribution to their children's schools' performance, and hence

to the schools' ability to acquire resources. Schools therefore have an incentive to admit children from parents likely to contribute strong social capital and to reject those who lack cultural capital. Children's educational potential therefore serves as a curious analogue of a school fee within the new price analogue system; the higher the ability of a child, the better chances its parents have of acquiring the school place they wanted; and the higher the subsequent 'profits' of the school. If this process proceeds unchecked, inequalities of achievement between schools which attract the 'best' pupils because of their own past record, and those which are unable to do so, will spiral. The quality of education of those in unfavoured schools will deteriorate. Any role which schools might play as channels of social mobility will be completely undermined.

The citizenship approach to these problems first limits schools' ability to choose their pupils in order to reduce the onset of the spiral of inequality; and second and more important takes direct action of various kinds to improve education quality in poor schools. The market and citizenship approaches are here mutually incompatible. The former works by using parental choice to encourage inequalities between schools to accumulate, and then redistributes resources from poor to successful schools. The citizenship approach tries to limit the destabilising effects on schools of parental choice, redistributes resources to poor schools, and takes many direct action measures to improve their performance.

Contradictory though they are, the Labour Government seeks to honour simultaneously the citizenship model and the new marketisation strategy. Since 1997 it has undertaken many measures for directly improving poor schools, and *Schools – Achieving Success* set out further strong and imaginative new policies for doing the same. The 2002 Green Paper proposed a number of measures for recognising vocational forms of education alongside academic ones – though in doing so it threatened even more complex indicators and measures of performance. But the 2001 White Paper had sustained and even reinforced all elements of the market analogue approach which constantly undermine the efforts of these schools to improve by encouraging parents with strong cultural capital to avoid them. Additional resources will be steered towards both successful schools and those experiencing particular difficulties; both specialist schools and those in areas of deprivation will be able to offer higher pay to help them recruit the best teachers. Every help offered to schools with problems is counteracted by an equivalent help offered to the privileged. There is little to prevent many of the former becoming residual schools for children unable to find a place in either a specialist school of some kind or a residentially favoured comprehensive; and somewhere in the middle there will be schools excluded from both contradictory redistributive flows. The solution held out by the White Paper for resolving these dilemmas was to increase the number of specialist schools and aspirants to that status, in order to ensure that they are not just a small elite. But the more that this is done, the more extreme is the ghetto to which the residual schools are consigned.

In many policy areas, in particular those concerned with the distribution of income, it has been made clear that New Labour's concept of egalitarianism means trying to move the lowest percentiles of the population closer to the median, while remaining unconcerned that the distance between the median and the top percentiles is increasing. The schools policy of the 2001 White Paper is a perfect example of this philosophy: it is concerned to ensure that the lowest percentiles achieve higher standards than they do at present, while creating mechanisms for ensuring that the upper percentiles move even further ahead. As a policy for increasing the all-round educational performance of the national workforce, this is entirely coherent. However, as a policy for securing equality of opportunity it cannot escape its internal contradictions. To the extent that competition for good jobs is a zero-sum game, the mechanisms of parental and school choice analysed above ensure that improving further the quality of schools available to those with most cultural capital wipes out any compensatory measures taken to help poor schools.

[ . . . ]

[Omitted here are sections that detail the commercialization of the Local Education Authorities themselves, through privatization of some and the imposition of commercial criteria of operation on others, and the way this has undermined public oversight. The author argues that, together with the difficulties inherent in creating markets in the education sector, this creates the potential for abuse or corruption as the central government becomes entangled in intense lobbying relationships with a small number of players who are competing for long-term contracts.]

## Contract-winning as the New Core Education Business

Non-market approaches to private sector involvement are very dominant in the new policies for commercialisation of citizenship services. Because the Government is not sure how to commercialise these areas, it wants information from insiders. Because it is desperate to maximise this new role of the private sector, it wants to make its offers to private firms as attractive as possible. It is therefore eagerly vulnerable to intensive lobbying by firms who see major opportunities of soft profits.

The Labour Government itself has sometimes been tough with contractors, for example imposing penalty clauses in contracts if they fail to deliver improved standards in schools which they take over. It could perhaps give greater guidance to local government staff on how to drive hard bargains in contract negotiations with private sector firms. To date all responsibility for educating LEAs in private-public partnerships seems to have been delegated to the firms themselves, who are unlikely to include this among their lessons.

The overall approach is courting the worst of two worlds, with both marketisation and citizenship losing out, not this time because of a clash between them, but because both clash with the practice of insider lobbying and preferred bidders. This approach runs all the risks of service deterioration of commercialisation discussed above, without the advantages – keen pricing, genuine choice for ultimate consumers – which the true market can often bring. It carries all the disadvantages of state involvement in commercial transactions – the formation of privileged circles of suppliers – without the restraining hand of the public service ethos which has been discarded in favour of a commercial one. Although the whole exercise is being carried out using the rhetoric of free-market economics, in reality it returns us to the world of relations between government and monopoly-holding 'court favourites' against which Adam Smith and others developed their initial formulations of that economics.

Government contracts within the commercialising welfare state are very attractive. As we have already noted, they are necessarily long-term – as much as 25 to 30 years in the case of buildings, such as schools. It would in fact be very difficult for, say, an LEA to contract out management of its school admissions services to a different firm every year or two, as the learning curves involved in getting to know the district and its schools would impose considerable inefficiencies. This process makes it very difficult to deal with dissatisfaction with the quality of a service being offered. Also, during a seven-year period a contractor can expect to develop very close relations with personnel in the contracting authority, making it a highly privileged insider when the contract eventually comes up for renewal.

Furthermore, in its eagerness to commercialise, the government has heavily subsidised most of these developments. For example, government invested £1.8 million in the New Models projects, most of which money went to private firms, though most of the work for the experiments was carried out by LEAs. The information flow within the projects is entirely unidirectional. The firm learns everything it wants about how the LEAs work and about their finances; they are told nothing equivalent about how the firm operates. It is then in a good position to bid to take over selected parts of the LEAs' work. The firms are in effect being subsidised in their attempts to secure profit-making contracts.

The character of the firms which have entered the new market is instructive. A number have emerged specifically around it. Their founders have usually been former teachers or LEA staff who saw the chances of higher incomes by going private at a time when the Government has been cutting expenditure on administration within public service, but subsidising higher spending on it if the same services are provided privately. These firms draw almost entirely on existing LEA staff for the personnel with which they will replace such staff if they win a contract.

Other participants in the market are firms which have lengthy histories in other economic sectors, and which have developed education service branches in response to government encouragement: for example, Arthur Andersen and PriceWaterhouseCoopers, both accountancy and management consultancy specialists; Group 4, security services and private prisons specialists; W. S. Atkins, an earlier spin-off of commercialised local government building and other services. Serco, experienced in missile warning systems, private prisons and young offenders' institutions, acquired QAA, a school inspection firm, in late 2000. Amey Roadstone, primarily a highways construction corporation, has linked up with Nord-Anglia, a specialist education firm.[3] These companies all have prior widespread experience of and success in how to win government contracts of various kinds. They have highly developed lobbying resources in Whitehall and Westminster and extensive contacts within government. It is these attributes which have given them their past success in winning government contracts, and which have encouraged them to enter the new sector of commercialised public education services, the substantive business of which is quite new to them. This is arguably the only added value which they bring to the education system. It is the value of the Whitehall insider, a value which is relevant to the delivery of education only because Government has decided to contract out; it is therefore not a quality which constitutes a reason for contracting-out in the first place or which delivers anything to the ultimate consumer of the services.

The risks inherent in this system of privileged contract insiders will multiply as the model spreads out to individual schools. As LEAs are weakened so that they cannot authoritatively monitor what is going on in schools' contracting activities, there are virtually no checks on how contract relations will be managed between highly skilled corporate lobbyists and voluntary governing bodies.

At the heart of the problem is the fact that these new education markets are being fashioned by government in response to firms' requests that they be created. It is not the case that an unsatisfied demand exists to which firms are responding; the demand is shaped to suit what the suppliers want to do, not what consumers want to receive. We must again remember that it is government, not the citizen-consumer, who is the customer in the commercialised welfare state.

[The previous discussion to which this refers is encapsulated in the following passage from Chapter 1:

> The citizen has a link, through the electoral and political system, to government (national or local). Government has a link, through the law of contract, with the privatized supplier. But the citizen has no link, neither of market nor of citizenship, to the supplier; . . . services users are not technically customers. And following privatization they can no longer raise questions of service delivery with government, because it has contracted such delivery away. (p. 21)]

## Conclusions: Democracy, Authority, Citizenship

If a service is an attribute of citizenship, it is managed through concepts of rights, participation and democratic authority. Fundamental to the historical operation of the British education system was the role of elected councillors wielding political authority; LEAs administered an area's schools under the formal authority of councillors. Parents could in principle make representations to councillors about the quality of services or problems they had with their children's schools; and LEA staff were able to take firm action on such issues as individual schools' admissions practices because they acted as public authorities.

In practice the system did not always work like that; unless parents knew how to exercise pressure, the local political system could easily slip into lethargy, and this may have been particularly likely to occur in one-party dominated areas with low educational expectations – a situation that characterised many Labour towns and cities. And unless there was dynamic professional leadership, LEA staff could also be inactive. But these weaknesses are open to reform; the mechanisms exist, they only want energetic stimulation. The mechanisms themselves have to be stripped away as the public education service is redefined to become a commercial service like any other. So long as the special citizenship characteristics are recognised, commercial firms are at a disadvantage in rivalling LEAs as providers. This is especially the case when virtually all the staff deployed by the private firms are former LEA staff; all that distinguishes them from their colleagues remaining in the public sector is that they lack the latter's public authority. If however most of the special attributes of public service are defined away and its activities translated into commercial terms, the balance shifts radically the other way; being outside the public sector is, by a trick of definition, changed from being a disadvantage to an advantage.

Because the actual delivery of education in schools was until recently seen as the core business, initial commercialisation was concentrated on authority functions. This was paradoxical, as the normal situation is for privatised industries to be monitored by public regulatory authorities. In education it has been the other way round. When Ofsted was established in 1994, it differed from the existing HM Inspectorate of Schools in contracting out rather than maintaining its own staff. Initially over 80 per cent of inspection teams were provided by the staff of LEA advisory and inspection services. However, many individuals discovered that they could earn more money by setting up inspection consultancies. Today, about 75 per cent of school

inspections are contracted out to private firms, in an 'industry' which was already worth around £118 million in 1997.[4]

When a private firm is invited to take over an LEA's functions because the authority is deemed to have 'failed', the administration of education in that area ceases to be a matter for local democracy, and does not even become one for local consumers. Instead it becomes a contractual relationship between central government and a privileged provider. Even when services for a 'failing' authority are provided by another LEA, the principle of local democratic accountability is broken. Within the 'failed' area the new authority providing the services has the same status as a private contractor; it does the work as part of a market contract, not as an element of local democracy.

When an LEA enters a commercialisation arrangement voluntarily, the situation might seem different: the private firms are merely contractors, agents subject to the will of their principal, which remains the legally constituted local political authority. But the political context is one in which, as we have seen, central government clearly favours the agents over the principals. Further, the fact that the LEA staff on whom the political authority depends for information and advice have been put into the position of competitors with rather than watchdogs over contractors, combined with the long-term nature of the contracts, make difficult any effective control of agent by principal. The system is too new for us to judge how extensively chains of subcontracting will develop, but if they do the current situation on the privatised railways demonstrates clearly how attempts by public authorities to regulate become caught in the labyrinth of contract law and inter-firm deals.

Now, the Government rarely speaks of commercial firms alone. LEAs are also invited to consider hiving off their services to religious organisations, voluntary sector partners, or even to other LEAs who may be able to offer a more efficient service.[5] Schools, like hospitals, have increasingly come to depend on volunteer help to overcome the staff shortages caused by their inadequate budgets of the 1980s and 1990s. However, commercial firms have far stronger incentives to push their role and win contracts than do voluntary organisations, especially as the efforts which a firm makes to win a contract can be offset against taxation as an acceptable business expense. Far from encouraging a growth in the role of the voluntary sector, commercialisation is likely to drive out its existing contribution. This has already happened in the case of careers advice services privatised during the 1980s by the Conservatives. At first charitable organisations bid for and won some of the contracts to replace the public service here. Gradually most have dropped away, being replaced by profit-making firms.

The provision of services by one LEA to the population of another raises different issues. A providing LEA cannot act as a democratically responsible local authority in the territory of another. As the Government's provisions make clear, within that territory the new LEA takes the form of a company, operating a commercial contract; similarly when a school takes over a poorly performing neighbour. This becomes another way of redefining the public authority role of local government as no different from commercial activity. The same is true for voluntary bodies; they take on the legal form of private contractors if they take on public education contracts. Another example is Connexions, the body established in 2001 to take over all supervision of the national careers advice service for young people, and various special services to young people with certain problems. Its local branches, which provide services for groups of local authority areas, are established as limited liability companies rather than as normal public-service organisations. The local units already remarkably incorporate named private firms into their formal governance structure. As this model grows, the normal mode of delivering local education services becomes that of the privileged insider commercial firm; the firm becomes the only acceptable form of organisation; and public service becomes an anomaly within its own heartland.

## Notes

1. 'Called to Account', O. O'Neill, Lecture no. 3 in 'A Question of Trust', the BBC Reith Lectures (2002).
2. 'Against Privatizing Schools in the UK' by H. Brighouse, *London Review of Education* (2003).
3. *Times Educational Supplement*, 25 May 2001.
4. *Times Educational Supplement*, 19 December 1997.
5. Letter from Secretary of State to CEOs explaining her new 'brokerage' concept of LEAs, 6 July 2001.

# 24

# Channel One, the Anti-Commercial Principle, and the Discontinuous Ethos

## Harry Brighouse

Public schools in the United States and elsewhere are increasingly willing to deal with private corporations in a way that allows those corporations effectively to market themselves inside the school gates. Typically, the private corporation provides some good that the school cannot get from public funds or in return for which it would normally have to forgo some other good. The deals take a variety of forms. Both Coca-Cola and Pepsi frequently bargain with school districts for exclusive rights to place their dispensing machines on school properties. General Mills deploys a "boxtop" scheme, whereby schools receive money for sending in boxtops collected by children at home: The scheme is advertised prominently in the participating schools by the use of posters that, of course, incorporate advertisements for the General Mills cereals to be used. Teachers and schools act as agents for Scholastic Books catalogues in return for which they enjoy free books for their classrooms. The Scholastic catalogue markets books, some of which come with "free gifts" (bracelets, necklaces, soft toys), and sells some toys and noneducational software. Fundraising activities frequently involve selling brand-name candy. Computer hardware and software manufacturers both donate, or sell at a subsidized price, their wares to schools, sometimes on condition that they will

be the exclusive providers, sometimes not. In the latter case, the benefits they get are the prominent displays of their logos on their equipment and, in the case of the software manufacturers, the knowledge that children will become habituated to using their software rather than alternatives.

These deals are by no means restricted to the United States. As *Marketing Week* (UK) reports, in a surprisingly critical story,

> Since Tesco launched its Computers for Schools scheme in 1990, Walkers Crisps tied up with News International to market its FreeBooks for Schools on-pack promotion in 1998 and The Mirror and United Biscuits launched a free maths equipment deal 2 years ago, major education marketing exercises have been thin on the ground. Now Schools Plus aims to become the mother of all corporate funding schemes in primary and secondary schools across the country. The company is on the verge of signing up global giants such as Coca-Cola and Burger King to an initiative, which, it claims, could raise millions of pounds for impoverished schools. Brands which join the scheme will be included in a book containing vouchers worth up to £250, which can be refunded against participating sponsors' products. The books will be sold to parents for £10, of which £7 will go into school funds, with the remaining £3 going to Schools Plus to cover costs. (McCawley, 2001)

Previously published in *Educational Policy* 19(3) (July 2005): pp. 528–49. Reprinted by permission of Sage Publications Inc.

The most celebrated and notorious of these kinds or schemes in the United States is Channel One. Channel One provides schools with television and video equipment on the condition that the schools agree to have their students watch 12 to 13 minutes of Channel One programming a day. The schools get free access to something they would otherwise have to pay for, and this frees up resources for other uses such as hiring an extra teacher or paying for other facilities. Channel One makes a profit because its programming is sponsored with advertisements, which the children get to – or, to put it more accurately, *have to* – watch.

I am going to focus on Channel One, but it is really a proxy for all deals of this kind, in which some noneducational resource is marketed on the school premises or through the schools in return for some payment either in money or in kind. Channel One has become the focus for a broad coalition of forces that oppose, for very diverse reasons, commercial presences in the classroom and on the curriculum; Phyllis Schlafly's Eagle Forum joins forces with Ralph Nader's PIRGS to lobby against it.[1] Part of my purpose in this article is to offer a normative analysis that makes sense of such a right-left coalition and, I hope, suggests why these forces might reasonably cooperate on a somewhat broader agenda. Many authors are willing to condemn Channel One and other such deals, but more are loathe to condemn the school administrators who make the deals (see, e.g., Apple, 2000, pp. 42, 223–5). After all, it can be bad that some practice is permitted but, given that it is permitted, perfectly acceptable for people to take advantage of it. One might argue, for example, that elite private schools should be abolished yet maintain that, given the harm that private schools do to state schools, parents, who have a special duty of care to their own children, can sometimes justifiably send their child to a private school. (Swift [2003] argues precisely this.)

I am going to argue, to the contrary, that administrators who deal with Channel One do something wrong. The central aim of my article is to show that dealing with Channel One is a symptom of a deeply mistaken attitude on the part of administrators as to what schools should be doing. The Channel One "case" should not be celebrated by opponents of commercialization and the involvement of private corporations in public schooling. Rather, our attention should focus on the administrators who do the deals; it is their views about the appropriate school ethos that are at fault.

The article is organized as follows. First, I describe Channel One in more detail. Then I look at some evidence concerning its pedagogical value. In section 2, I introduce a simple case against making deals with Channel One. In section 3, I examine the most prominent cost-benefit analysis of Channel One and argue that it fails fully to account for the benefit of Channel One by, wrongly, discounting the value of the programming. Section 4 introduces an additional cost: In forcing children to watch commercials during instructional time, the school forfeits the right to the children's respectful co-operation. It does so because it violates the anti-commercial principle that I describe and defend in section 5. I argue that the anti-commercial principle should have considerable weight in guiding administrators' decisions about how to deal with commercial interests and that the fault lies substantially with administrators who accept the Channel One deal. But the anti-commercial principle is nested in a deeper principle that the ethos of schools should be discontinuous with the mainstream culture. Administrators' failure to give proper weight to the discontinuity principle is what underpins their mistaken view that Channel One constitutes an all-things-considered benefit. However, my argument deflates the significance of Channel One and the other deals for which it is serving as a proxy. It is just of a kind with many other things that go on in schools, most of which never hit the headlines or even the notice of parents, teachers, and administrators.

## Channel One

Channel One was established by Chris Whittle, the founder of Edison Corporation in 1989 and was sold in 1994 to its current owner, Primedia. It operates in some 12,000 schools in the United States, which are obliged to show the programming to at least 80% of their students on at least 90% of days of instruction. (I have taken the figure 12,000 from a good number of sources in recent years: Primedia currently claims daily broadcasts to "more than 8 million teens in over 350,000 classrooms across America."[2]) Eighty percent and 90% are rough figures because technically, the schools can reject any program – the shows are available in the morning to be pre-screened to administrators, who are allowed to reject that show on various grounds. The advertisements take up

2 minutes of the 12-minute broadcast, but other parts of the broadcasts are devoted to weather, sports, and entertainment.

A good cost-benefit analysis of the deal is hard to arrive at because it is hard to assign a monetary value to the programming. So it is worth looking at some of the features of the programming itself. Two twenty-somethings, one of each sex, present a three-part broadcast, punctuated by two commercial breaks. The first item is a brief report of an international or national news item. The first commercial break is followed by an "in-depth" report on some matter that is either important in world or national affairs or is supposedly important to teenagers. The following items were shown during the period I studied (August-October 2003): Seeds of Peace (concerning Palestinian and Israeli youth participating in a program designed to build trust across those boundaries), Free Trade, Battle for Tibet, Depression, Dealing with Alcoholism, and a lengthy account of the California recall process, including a long interview with then-Governor Gray Davis and the promise of future interviews with candidates. A short, frivolous piece follows the second set of commercials: Gregory Hines's death, some entertainment or sports "news" – what journalists call a "human interest story." The content of the contemporary programs is quite different from that described in earlier academic critiques and in the propaganda of some anti-Channel One activists. The broadcasts compare favorably, in terms of the depth of consideration and length of items, with many local commercial broadcasts, and such cable offerings as CNN's Headline News service. The advertisements are a mix of public service announcements and standard fare TV commercials for products oriented at young people. (For a lengthy analysis, see Hoynes, 1997, 1998.)

## Why Not Make the Deal?

Let us assume that the equipment provided, and the news provision, are worth having and that the schools could not afford to purchase alternatives (I shall review these assumptions later). Then, surely, the right thing for the school to do is to make the deal. It benefits and it can devote some of the resources released to needy students. No one is worse off. So why should schools refrain?

First, we might say that although there is no reason that they should not take the bargain if it

is offered, there are reasons to block the bargain's availability – because sometimes bargains that individually make each person (or school) better off, collectively make them worse off. Consider standard coordination problems: Each person gets a better view by standing on tiptoe, but if everyone does it, no one gets a better view at all, and they are all worse off because standing on tiptoe is tiring. Tax-incentive competition for corporate relocation between the states almost certainly has this character: All states would be better off if the competition were prohibited by federal regulation, but, given the competition, each state is better off competing. The plausible story about the Channel One case will not involve coordination – one school's having Channel One does not directly make another school worse off in a way that can be rectified by following suit. The fear is that public knowledge that corporations can promote themselves in schools in return for providing resources strengthens the political hand of budget-cut advocates. This works at district, state, and federal levels, thus making schools that do not participate in the bargain worse off than those that do and worse off than they would be without the activity. Public information about these bargains may even lead voters to inflate (in their minds) the amount that the corporations will give, thus decreasing public funding by more than the amount the corporations are providing.

This is a conjectural reason for prohibiting the deals. It does not, however, provide any reason for administrators of particular schools to resist them given their availability. It is not necessarily hypocritical to believe that some practice should be outlawed but simultaneously to engage in that practice given that it is permitted. Someone might favor a drastic increase in the gasoline tax and yet refrain from individually paying the amount of that tax to the government on the grounds that, if that tax were in place, she would have access to cheaper and more convenient public transport.

So what is wrong, if anything, with individual schools making the deals? Another argument says that, above, I have misdescribed the bargain. The school is better off, certainly, in that it has equipment it would otherwise afford only by reallocating funds from other valuable programs. But it is not a costless bargain. There is a clear way in which the students are worse off – they are forced to watch the commercials or the poor quality news or both, and that is either bad in itself or represents an opportunity cost. What I mean by saying that it is an opportunity cost is that even if watching the programming has *some* educational value, it has less than the activities that time might have been devoted to in the absence of the deal.

How could we evaluate this argument? First, we would have to know what the educational value is of watching the programming. As I said before, good evidence about this is sparse. There are few studies of the educational effects of watching Channel One. The most prominent (Knupfer and Hayes, 1994) was done in Channel One's infancy, and the programming (both commercial and news) described is clearly different from recent broadcasts. Knupfer and Hayes (1994) have suggested that children retain the information imparted by the advertising longer and more impressively than the news information and that the broadcasts do "not appear to be effective in increasing students' knowledge of current events" (p. 58). Some reports claim that children retain information only when teachers plan lessons to follow up on the broadcast.[3]

But is teaching about current events the purpose of showing TV news in school? Few people remember most current events for long. Knupfer and Hayes (1994) focused on this because it is reasonably possible to evaluate it. But what is more important – educationally – is whether students become enculturated to critical ways of thinking about and debating current events. Do they come to presume that politicians' arguments should be scrutinized carefully, that news is news and sports are trivia, that reasons and causes behind events bear investigation because they are not superficially apparent? News programs that differ very little in their capacity to produce knowledge of particular current events may nevertheless differ considerably in their tendency to produce these kinds of understandings.

## A Standard Cost–Benefit Analysis

We do not just need to know the effects of the programs. We need to know, also, the opportunities for education forgone by spending 12 minutes watching the show. How do we calculate these? The most elaborate attempt at a cost-benefit analysis for Channel One is by Max Sawicky and Alex Molnar (1998). Their analysis is couched in monetary terms – they estimate the benefit in terms of the financial value of the equipment and the financial cost of having the children watch the program and

compare them. Their analysis assumes that the net financial value of the programming is zero because an alternative product, CNN's Newsroom-World View, is freely available. But this assumption is legitimate only if the CNN product is educationally at least as valuable as Channel One, and they offer no evidence to that effect. Another approach might compare what is done with the 12 minutes with what might otherwise be done. Perhaps spending the time on mathematics education, or foreign language learning, would be better. A natural and common strategy in making these sorts of arguments is to pick some educationally superior activity and say that the students would be better off if they were doing that and so impugn the deal.

Sawicky and Molnar (1998) effectively adopted this strategy in their calculation of the costs of showing the broadcasts. They aggregate the total funding for the schools, divide it by the number of minutes in the school day, and then express the daily costs of showing the broadcast as 12 times that amount. This method effectively assumes that nothing educationally valuable is achieved and that, by contrast, alternatives would have been, on average, as educationally valuable as what is achieved in the rest of the school day.

This strategy is illegitimate. Sawicky and Molnar (1998) compared the activities pursued during Channel One time with activities that might otherwise be undertaken. The question about opportunity costs is what the actual opportunity cost is of watching the news programming – in other words, what else would the students actually be doing if Channel One were not available? Consider the classic case of an opportunity cost. You enter the movie theater, having paid your unrecoverable entrance fee, and find that the movie is boring. In choosing whether to leave, you do not compare the prospective enjoyment derived from staying with the enjoyment you might have derived from watching a much better alternative. You compare it with the enjoyment you would derive from whatever you would actually do with the time salvaged by leaving the theater.

Think about the lesson as a unit of analysis. Each minute is not, taken alone, educationally exactly as valuable as the next. A lecturer might follow an especially complex argument with a pause and preface it with a joke. She might then ask students about the argument or invite them to find a flaw in one of the premises or in the reasoning, even when there is no flaw in either that premise or the reasoning. The components work together: The educationally valuable part is having students follow the complex argument and internalize the reasoning; the other components enable that to happen. Even if the Channel One broadcast is in itself educationally valueless, teachers may use the broadcast time as a substitute for some other activity or non-activity that is also not intrinsically valuable in itself but that allows something else to happen. They may, on the other hand, simply substitute it for some other valueless activity that has no other purpose. In either of these cases, the activity has no opportunity cost.

One observation from the Knupfer and Hayes (1994) study is suggestive. They report that "the large majority of teachers did not view the program but did paperwork or prepared lessons while the broadcast aired" (p. 55). Using the television as a baby-sitter is a strategy familiar to parents and teachers alike. Suppose that teachers use this broadcast instead of a video, or some other activity, to give downtime to the students and to gain time to review the next part of the lesson or grade papers. If what students would actually be doing rather than watch the broadcast is something equally valueless, the broadcast is, in effect, costless.

## Is Watching Commercials a Distinctive Cost?

Still, there might be something particularly costly about the children watching commercials in school, compared with watching low-quality but noncommercial television broadcasts or video. The presence of commercials is what has excited so much public and political and academic attention. And whereas Knupfer and Hayes's (1994) subjects did not remember any more about the news events than the control group, they did recall the advertisements. In a chilling anecdote (the implications of which are supported by the quantitative study), they report the response to a broadcast of a student to whom Channel One was new:

> Even though he viewed the broadcast during the time of Desert Storm news, he replied excitedly, "I didn't know they made peanut butter Snickers!" and proceeded to tell all about the "really neat commercial" for the candy bars. (p. 54)

Why might it be problematic that children see commercials in school? They watch an enormous number of commercials at home and are assaulted by commercial messages on their way to and from school as well as every time they enter any public space, except perhaps in some tightly regulated gated communities. Perhaps most schoolchildren are saturated with commercials already: The additional showings in school probably have no further effects, in which case they constitute dead time, rather than a positive harm.[4]

But could the commercials have positively bad effects because they are shown in school? Students might take commercials more seriously because they are shown in school, because schools have a distinctive authority. Or students' attitudes toward the school might be different. It is harder for people who force children to watch advertisements to expect those children to take them seriously, as doing so undermines the authority they would otherwise have.

I cannot show that either of these effects occurs. But I shall argue that students should be critical of administrators who force them to watch commercials without very powerful justification, because doing so violates a central component of the mission of the school.

Before proceeding to the argument, note that advertisements have no legitimate educational purpose. They aim to bypass the rationality of the audience and focus their desires on the goods advertised. Focusing children's attention on a noneducational product is not a legitimate activity for a school; and the appeal to emotion to that end further taints the practice. Even the public service announcements Channel One carries are formally like standard commercial advertisements. They target emotions, bypassing reason (and skepticism), to produce certain behaviors. They, too, are noneducational in some significant sense. But the public service announcements at least aim to modify the child's behavior in a way that will enhance the child's ability to flourish. The commercial commercials lack even that purpose; they simply aim to alter the child's preferences for corporate profit without regard to the child's good. Consider the contrast with another compulsory activity: climbing ropes in gym lessons. A recalcitrant student who asks, "Why should I be forced to do this?" can be told some plausible story about the educational value of trying to climb ropes. By contrast, the recalcitrant student who is forced to watch commercials on TV can only be told a story about the payment received from agents fundamentally unconcerned with their educational interests. People who force, or encourage, children to watch commercials with this purpose in school time without some compelling justification forfeit the right to the child's respectful cooperation. This forfeit occurs even if for most of those children it is true that because their families and other institutions facilitate the watching of commercials to saturation levels, the marginal contribution of the school has no appreciable effect on their susceptibility to the commercial messages.[5]

Why doesn't free access to the valuable video and television equipment, which frees up resources to pursue other purposes, constitute a compelling justification for the deal? The released resources can be used, for example, to benefit the least advantaged children, thus serving a vital goal of educational justice. Couldn't this be used as an appropriate answer to the recalcitrant student?

In fact, the actual financial value of the benefits is very limited, if Sawicky and Molnar (1998) are right (which there is no reason to doubt). Let us assume for a moment, with them, that the programming has no value, and let us assume that the equipment has real value. Sawicky and Molnar calculate the equipment's value by dividing Primedia's figure of $200 million worth of hardware in 12,000 schools, then assuming that annual depreciation is about 10% of the initial cost and that the "real" rental cost is twice the cost of depreciation. Rounding up here and there, they calculate the real rental value at $4,000 per school per year. If high schools average 750 students, this is about $5.30 per student per year – it would pay for an extra book per student. The Sawicky and Molnar analysis even assumes, charitably and implausibly, that schools would rent equally good equipment, whereas in fact they would be more likely to rent older but adequate equipment. It is utterly implausible that the actual value of the equipment could justify forcing children to watch commercial messages.

## The Anti-commercial Principle

Why exactly does the school that forces children to watch commercials without some very powerful justification forfeit its right to their respect and cooperation? In this section, I shall elaborate and provide a partial defense of what I have called the *anti-commercial principle*, which, I think, provides the best account of what the school does wrong in this case. However, the argument for the anti-commercial principle has deeper implications for the ethos of the school and the way it relates to its students. These implications are such that we cannot find anything special about Channel One: It is simply one of many manifest symptoms of the failure of school management teams, and often teachers also, to understand what is required of the school. Some of these implications will be welcome to both right and left critics of Channel One. Others may be more sectarian.

The basic idea is that school endorsement of commercialism devalues the school in the eyes of the students, parents, teachers, and administrators themselves, and this is a high cost, which can only be overridden by major financial contributions of a kind that Channel One's loan of equipment does not come close to reaching. Suppose that the advertisements shown in school do not have the bad effects that advertisements generally have, and the content of the news programming is pedagogically sound (and superior to the quasi-commercial-free alternative provided by CNN),[6] and the technical equipment really is worth something to the school. Still, the violation of the anti-commercial principle is sufficient of a bad to outweigh those considerations.

Here is the argument. All students have a compelling interest in being able to become an autonomous, self-governing person. An autonomous person, in this context, is someone who can make, and act on, her own judgments about how to live her life in the light of a wide range of reasons and evidence. Different people have different constitutions that suit them better for some ways of life than for others. Developing their capacity for autonomy enables them better to find ways of life that they can feel at one with or, to put it more cognitively, endorse from the inside. This in turn – endorsement from the inside – is a precondition of a person flourishing in her way of life. If someone is raised into a way of life that she cannot, because of her constitution, endorse from inside, she has no opportunity for well-being unless she also has been equipped to identify and practice ways of life that she can endorse from the inside. Perhaps the clearest kind of example concerns our sexuality: Some people, at least, experience their sexuality as an immutable aspect of their personality, and those who are brought up in circumstances that make exploring and expressing their particular sexuality impossible are thereby deprived of opportunities for well-being in a central part of their lives. But it is generally the case that different people's constitutions suit them differently for lives with different contours and that orient them to different challenges: The importance of autonomy is that it is a key to uncovering which paths are best for our own persons.

Barriers to autonomy include lack of information, lack of ability to reason about alternatives, and lack of the self-respect needed to make, or trust, one's own judgments. Whether we are able to be autonomous depends, at least in part, in our inhabiting an autonomy-supporting milieu in which alternative ways of life, and perspectives on ways of life, are made available to us in a nonthreatening but challenging way.

Two obvious spaces outside the school provide children with access to alternatives: the home and the mainstream culture. I understand home to be constituted by the immediate family, the extended family to which that immediate family provides access, and the community in which the immediate family is set. This last should not be understood geographically; increasingly, our families inhabit communities constructed out of a diverse set of networks, few – or maybe none – of which are found in the immediate neighborhood. I understand the mainstream culture, by contrast, to be constituted by a variety of forces: the public political culture, sometimes referred to as "civil society"; the culture manifested in the most readily available broadcast and print media; the messages transmitted in public spaces, such as advertising hoardings; sporting and cultural activities that reach beyond the immediate circle of interested individuals.[7] The mainstream culture is complex, and some aspects compete, sometimes very sharply, with others; for example, the cultural values communicated by MTV conflict with those promoted by the political religious right. But for many children in much of the United States, the mainstream cultural environment is not so complex; it consists of the space and messages underwritten by the large corporations that produce profit-seeking popular culture (the major sports, the major forms of popular music and film and TV, the major brand name producers of clothing, electrical goods, and food, etc.). Increasingly, those aspects of mainstream culture not involved with corporate sponsors of this kind are not readily accessible to children "on their own"; children get access, instead, only if their families or their schools facilitate it. Increasingly, that is, they are not truly part of the mainstream culture for children but only of some home cultures.

For some children, the home and mainstream cultures will present a wide range of valuable opportunities, either because the two present a disjunctive set of valuable opportunities or because the home allows them to tap into valuable opportunities beyond the immediate home life that are not readily present to most children. For other children, the range will be less wide because the home, the culture, or the two in tandem fail to make a wide range available. But in contemporary modern societies, both the home and the mainstream culture contain tendencies that press against autonomy. Even the most liberal parents will often tilt their children's experiences and inclinations toward ways of life readily congruent with their own; and the mainstream culture, at least as presented through the media, is, as many religious parents complain, deeply materialistic and mono-dimensional. The child from a liberal atheist family, for example, is highly unlikely to encounter the articulation of a religious life in a way that makes it a feasible alternative for her through exposure to contemporary television, magazines, radio, or film. For her to encounter such a way of life in a way that makes it a feasible way of life for her to enter, she has to encounter it, usually, through the mingling she does with other children and other adults in her community and school. In the context of the contemporary United States, in which communities of practice can and do isolate themselves from one another, the best bet is the school. (For a full version of the argument for autonomy, see Brighouse, 2000, chapter 4; for more on the other interests of children, see Brighouse, 2002 and 2003. See also MacLeod, 2003 for a detailed defense of the endorsement constraint.)

So the school has the difficult task of facilitating autonomy of children whose home values are at odds with those of the mainstream culture and those whose home values are those of the mainstream culture. It cannot rely simply on the curriculum to achieve this. School composition is an important component. But, equally important, the task requires that the school have an ethos that is noticeably discontinuous with that of both the home and the mainstream culture. In practice, in the United States, the central threat to its ability to perform this task comes from the mainstream public culture for two reasons.[8] First, that is the culture to which the greatest number of families already tip their hats, and so it enjoys something close to hegemony outside the school. Second, unlike any particular home cultures, its proponents collectively deploy massive resources to influence children and have numerous points of entry into most of their lives. We can rely on the family, the peer group, or the mainstream culture to ensure that children are exposed to the delights of major league sports, popular music, the different sides of the cola wars, Hollywood movies, fast food, television, celebrity adulation, fashionable clothing, teen magazines, and commercials.

Unlike religious or political entrepreneurs, commercial entrepreneurs do not even believe that the values they promote are good values. The dissemination of these values is a foreseen side effect of the pursuit of profit. The entrepreneurs themselves are indifferent about what values are spread and what effects these have on whether people are able to make and act on good judgments about how to live well. But it is important for the school (and for everyone else) to note these effects: They are as important an influence on shaping children's lives as they would be if they were intended and desired by the entrepreneurs causing them.

Given the resources behind the mainstream culture's values, and the likelihood that they will be accessible to almost all children beyond the school gates, it is particularly important for the school to foster an ethos in which they are given short shrift. A school that gives proper weight to its students' prospective interest in autonomy will aim to offer up alternatives to the mainstream culture for serious consideration, in the knowledge that the narrow range of alternatives in the mainstream culture are readily available. It will aim to foster an ethos that is discontinuous with both that of the home culture and that of the mainstream culture.

There is no single recommended ethos for all schools for two reasons. First, what counts as discontinuous will depend on the context. Different cities, and different communities within cities, will draw on different aspects of the mainstream culture and will themselves contain different home cultures, from which the school has to distinguish itself. Having a staff drawn largely from Asian backgrounds might contribute to discontinuity in a largely African American and White community more than in a largely Asian American community, for example. Furthermore, even in a given context, there may be multiple ways of achieving discontinuity. In a White, working class community, a school might aspire to discontinuity by finding a prominent place for soccer, Latin, and Cordon Bleu cooking or, alternatively, by a heavy emphasis on classical music and exploring Islam.

Discontinuity need not be radical. In fact, radical discontinuity might be counterproductive. If the ethos of the school is sufficiently foreign to those of the students' homes and society, it may be simply incomprehensible to the students and therefore fail to present any alternatives as realistic at all. So there is every reason to compromise with the external and home cultures, exactly and only to the extent necessary for the students to be able to appreciate the alternatives presented in the school as realistic for them. But discontinuity is broadly desirable. And, in compromising with the external culture, the school should refrain from incorporating and endorsing it. The anti-commercial principle does not, in fact, impugn popular commercial culture at all; it simply says that because children have ample opportunities to take up the values it offers without it being endorsed by the school, the school should not endorse it. Rather, in endorsing it, the school does a wrong for two reasons. First, it risks reinforcing their appeal and so skewing children's choices toward the options commercial culture presents. Second, it incurs a serious opportunity cost in failing to present valuable alternatives to the options presented by the commercial culture.

What counts as an endorsement is a difficult matter and open to contest. Perhaps Channel One excites such attention because forcing children to watch advertisements on television is such an unambiguous case of endorsement. But the pervasive logos and the presence of poster advertisements on school walls also constitute endorsement. Arranging a field trip to a Hollywood movie, or showing one in the classroom, constitutes endorsement, just as arranging a field trip to a Shakespeare play or reading one in class would. The presence of Pizza Hut or Taco Bell in the lunchroom, or of Coke machines throughout the school corridors, similarly constitute endorsements, not only of the particular products involved but of the general practice of consuming fast food and soda. Making a field trip to a Six Flags recreation park the "prize" for a collective fund-raising effort constitutes endorsement; and when the school organizes children into sales squads, it endorses marketing of the candies, cookies, and paper goods being sold. When it procures corporate sponsors for a "charity run" under its name, it not only endorses those sponsors, but it also violates the taboo against trumpeting one's own good works and simultaneously educates children that immodesty is no vice. When it interrupts classroom time with frivolous public address system announcements (publicizing the availability of football T-shirts, for example), it expresses contempt for the learning that is supposed to be going on in the classroom. When it truncates classroom activities to make way for a pep rally, it endorses the values expressed in that rally, even if it formally makes attendance voluntary.

Other cases are more opaque. Schools are sometimes, absurdly, taken to be endorsing the behavior of characters in novels on the curriculum. It is not so absurd, though, to think that schools, or teachers, are, in teaching a book, endorsing it as a piece of literature. It is entirely appropriate for people to read Jackie Collins or Barbara Cartland as leisure time reading; but it would be inappropriate for a teacher to assign them in class, at least without making clear the teacher's view that they do not constitute high-quality literature. No such discussion or explanation is necessary when teaching Jane Austen, Fydor Dostoevsky, or Richard Wright. Teachers are well-positioned to clarify to attentive students whether, to what extent, and in precisely what ways the use of a particular teaching material constitutes endorsement of it. Teaching a course on the Bible as literature normally constitutes endorsement of it as an important work of literature, whereas reading excerpts from it in a class on the history of the Reformation does not; and neither case normally constitutes endorsement of it as an authoritative religious text.

Let me recap the argument. The obligation to facilitate a child's prospective autonomy requires that the school ethos be discontinuous with the mainstream culture. The requirement of discontinuity supports the anti-commercial principle. Commercialism in schools violates the anti-commercial principle and thus undermines the school's capacity to deliver on its mission. Channel One, then, just contributes to a general problem of ethos in schools, which is that schools are continuous with the commercial mainstream culture outside, rather than providing a space that is distinct from and provides an alternative to that commercial culture. This problem is perhaps worsened by the efforts of for-profit companies and the kinds of deals I have talked about; but it emanates from within the institutions. The reason why principals make prima facie extraordinarily bad deals with companies like Channel One is that they themselves do not question this culture. They misunderstand the school's mission and neglect its obligation to facilitate the prospective autonomy of the students.

## Discontinuity, Schools, and Religious Activists

I want to look, very briefly, at three features of school life that are notable in the light of the demand for discontinuity: academic learning, the relationship of teachers to the mainstream culture, and the place of television in the school. Then I shall look at the implications of the demand for discontinuity for a certain kind of argument for school choice and reflect on the prospects for engaging religious opponents of Channel One into an overlapping consensus favoring discontinuity.

The academic curriculum has an important place in school life for a number of reasons, but one of these reasons is grounded in the demand for autonomy facilitation. A great deal of academic learning will take place only in the school or rather, only if it is promoted by the school. Most of us have limited opportunities to learn foreign languages, algebra, our first language's grammar, physics, or geology outside the school. There are opportunities outside the school for all these kinds of learning, but they are not opportunities for us, usually, unless we have developed the requisite basic skills and some enthusiasm for the activity at school (or, for most of us more rarely, in the home). Academic learning is valuable for acquisition of jobs and higher education. But it is also important because it provides children with windows onto new worlds: One child might learn a lifelong love for the abstractions of mathematics; another might gain valued insight into the life of 19th-century Russia; a third might discover in herself a facility to compose amusing doggerel. Most families will be limited in the range of skills and enthusiasms they facilitate, and the mainstream culture is by its nature rather narrow in this respect.

Teachers themselves are not, and should not (all) be, hermits. They have lives outside the school and interact daily with both the external world and their students. Teachers also construct personas for the purpose of interactions with students – the situation is not a natural one, and the teacher is not necessarily "himself" in it. There is no single ideal relationship between this constructed persona and the mainstream culture. But that is the point here. Any school will have a student body that is diverse in the kinds of personalities it contains and the kinds of ways of living that are a realistic alternative for each child. Some students think it is "cool" for teachers to be imbued in the same mainstream culture that they participate in outside. Others will be struck by the intensity of their teacher's engagement with the medieval world, Russian literature, their Christian faith, or Paul Robeson's music. Take a child whose home culture is unquestioningly imbued in the materialist values of the mainstream culture. Suppose first that she finds these values unsatisfying. It could be as valuable for her to meet and know adults in a school setting who are open about living lives that are detached, or perhaps semi-detached, from that culture, as it is for a homosexual child raised in an aggressively heterosexual setting to see adults who are open and relaxed about their homosexuality. Suppose, now, that the child is comfortable with these values. Still, encounters with the semi-detached teacher might prompt her to reflect on her life and perhaps as a result of that reflection, come to embrace its values as her own, rather than to simply go along with them. The point here is that as well as a discontinuous ethos, a school should aim for a teaching staff that is diverse, not just by sex and race but also by values – not because it should reflect the values of the student body but because the teaching staff collectively should embody a range of values for the students to reflect on.

Finally, what place should the televisual equipment that Channel One provides for "free" have in the life of the school? Here is an outlandish suggestion: Someone might argue that the purported benefit (the value of the televisual equipment, which Sawicky and Molnar [1998], for example, concede as a benefit) is not a benefit at all – not because it is outweighed by the bads of the commercial programming but because children should not be watching television at all in school, not even high-quality television.

Why might someone make this argument? It does not rely on the austere view that television, even good television, is always bad. It could be supported instead by two observations. First, watching television (or videos or DVDs) in the way that most of the students will be familiar with is bad for them. They are passive watchers; they expect not to have to work, but to be entertained, when watching; they treat it as "time off." The more television children watch, the more they eat; the more television adults watch, the more they get into debt: Television watching appears to cause obesity and overspending.[9] So even if children gain a significant educational benefit from a particular show, either because it is pedagogically sound or

because seeing it helps to train their aesthetic judgments, this might be outweighed by the effects of, again, the school tacitly endorsing the activity that is generally bad for them. We can accept that TV watching is a fact of life, and even think that it can contribute to a flourishing life when pursued in moderation and appropriately, but simultaneously suspect that the way it will usually actually be used in schools will simply be continuous with the way it is pursued in the culture as a whole.

The version of discontinuity invoked by this objection might seem excessively demanding, but the opponent of Channel One who rejects it faces a dilemma. To impugn the use of commercials in school, we have to appeal to similar considerations: The school implicating itself in the commercialism of the commercials brings about some harm that the mere commercialism itself does not. Television is, in American culture, an unremittingly commercial medium. Just to bring this home, it is worth noticing that an hour of children's shows on PBS carries more minutes of commercial messages than an hour of children's broadcasts on a commercial channel in the UK does. If the problem with the commercials is the endorsement of them by the school, isn't the endorsement of TV watching itself an indirect endorsement of commercial watching?

On balance, the view outlined may be too strong. After all, if we know that our students watch, and will continue to watch, a great deal of television and if we have reason to suspect that doing so is harmful, we might well reason that we should watch television with them, showing them different, less passive ways of doing it. We could inform them about its effects and prepare them to use television rather than allowing it to use them. Perhaps it is fine, and even valuable, for children to watch television in schools. But the wise principal and teacher will look carefully at the way it is used and will try to ensure that its use does not endorse or reinforce the norms of the external culture but instead contributes vitally to the academic and ethos-related missions of the school.

I conjectured earlier that the argument I would make against Channel One, and commercialism generally, in schools might be to suggest why activists from the religious right can cooperate well with activists from the anti-corporate left on this issue. But the emphasis on discontinuity might suggest otherwise; after all, don't religious conservatives argue for radical school choice and expanded home schooling on the grounds that parents have a right to inculcate their children in their own ways of life? Such arguments strongly press against the discontinuity; they suggest, in fact, commitment to a radical version of continuity.

My reading of religious arguments for choice is a bit different. I suspect, although I cannot prove, that the energy of religious proponents of choice is triggered more by hostility to the continuity of the culture of public schooling with that of the mainstream culture, in which they feel materialist values are inculcated into their children by default, than by the mere fact of discontinuity with their home culture. Demands for continuity with the home, in other words, are an articulation of opposition to continuity with the mainstream culture, rather than being fundamental principles. Religious parents do feel that their values are treated with contempt in the mainstream culture and, in my view, their perception is accurate. But it is entirely possible to treat their values with respect in a school governed by a thoroughly discontinuous ethos. Indeed, in a school committed to facilitating the autonomy of all its children (including those from nonreligious homes), spiritual and religious values and commitments would be treated to serious consideration; more serious and open than many American public schools currently achieve. In particular, a school district committed to discontinuity will go to some lengths to ensure that its school populations are composed of children from diverse cultural backgrounds so that they can serve as resources to facilitate each other's autonomy and will therefore be concerned not to alienate religious parents into private and home schooling. Of course, if religious parents pressing these arguments are really just seeking assistance in indoctrinating their own children, adoption of a discontinuous ethos will not re-engage them with public schooling. I simply doubt that this ungenerous characterization of their motives is accurate.[10]

Some might see the commercialization of schools as a part of the increasing privatization of formerly public space, akin and connected to the increasing incidence of home schooling, the expansion of school choice, and the privatization of school management. That may be right, but it is worth noting that commercialization of the culture of childhood also involves a penetration of corporate interests into what was formerly considered private space. The marketer is trying to insert herself and her interests between parent and child; the use in marketing literature of the phrase "the nag factor" (documented in Schor, 2004, and Linn, 2004) and the general idea that communication with children is to be used to disrupt their relationships with their parents is indicative of this. School choice in general and home schooling in particular is partly a reaction against this wrongful intrusion of corporate (quasi-public) interests into private space.[11]

## Conclusion

My argument has been that schools are obliged by their mission to have an ethos that is substantially discontinuous with the character of the mainstream public culture. Principals who understood and implemented this obligation would recognize that Channel One, not only because of the commercials it contains but also because of the ethos of its news presentation, cuts against the achievement of such an ethos. They would be suspicious even of the equipment provided by Primedia in the bargain struck, regarding it as quite possibly not a valuable product at all, because they would suspect that TV and video use usually feeds into, rather than distances itself from, the outside culture. Certainly, Channel One executives themselves do something wrong when they propose the deal. But their attempt to do wrong would fall on stony ground if it were not for the fact that school principals who misunderstand their missions were present to collude in the wrongdoing.

I have refrained from saying that such bargains could *never* be justified. This exposes my position to two possible misunderstandings. First, it might be thought that I do not advocate prohibiting the deals (say at the state or federal level). It would obviously be difficult to frame such prohibitions legally, but I would, indeed, advocate appropriately designed legislation. I have not made an argument for prohibition for two reasons. I am more interested here in why administrators should not take the deals even though they are legal. This is an interesting ethical question and a matter of pressing practical importance for activists resisting such deals in their communities. Furthermore, even if the deals were prohibited, this would leave intact the feature that underlies the willingness of administrators to make the deals; their failure to give due weight to the anti-commercial principle and, more fundamentally, the requirement of discontinuity in their school ethos. Prohibiting the deal would be good, but the ethos would still need changing.

The second misunderstanding would be that if I think sufficiently lucrative deals could, in principle, be justified, I must not regard the anti-commercial principle as a true principle. But I do. Commercial bargains could be justified, despite their violation of the anti-commercial principle, because the anti-commercial principle is not the only principle governing schooling. Seriously underfunded schools serving disadvantaged children have an obligation to provide at least an adequate education to the children they serve. The presence of Channel One in the classroom makes this more difficult. But suppose that, instead of televisual equipment, Primedia provided a very large cash payment that enabled the school to enlarge its staff by 10%, thus enabling it to implement a significant number of small classes for particularly disadvantaged students. Then, the gain to the disadvantaged just might compensate for the overall loss that watching Channel One represents.

The problem, of course, is this: It is highly unlikely that commercial firms will provide the kind of money that would make the bargain a good one, especially to underfunded schools populated with low-income children. So, in our world, there is little prospect of the commercialized contract being justified.

The Channel One deal constitutes a particularly flagrant violation of the anti-commercial principle and the demand for discontinuity. The other deals described in the introduction to this article also commit the violation. But more insidious are the everyday presumptions in numerous public high schools that favor and reinforce the hegemony of materialist values and commercial popular culture. The liberal principle of autonomy facilitation impugns all these tendencies. Schools simply have no business preparing their students to become uncritical consumers of commercial culture; their job is to facilitate their students' autonomy.

## Notes

1. For both Nader's and Schlafley's testimony to the U.S. Senate concerning Channel One, see http://www.commercialalert.org/index.php/category_id/2/subcategory_id/67/article_id/157. (This was last accessed November 19, 2004.)
2. See the Primedia corporate Web site at http://www.primedia.com/divisions/educationandtraining/channelone. (This was last accessed on April 20, 2004.)
3. See "What's on Channel 1?" at www.corpwatch.org. I've been unable to find the academic study on which this claim is based and have a suspicion that it is based on a misinterpretation of a comment Knupfer and Hayes (1994) make on pp. 56–7 about a school in which teachers would follow up in a separate class that not all students were enrolled in.
4. Greenberg and Brand (1993) studied two otherwise similar schools, one of which adopted Channel One and the other did not. Students in the Channel One school were in fact more likely to cite the names of brands advertised on Channel One, were more likely to intend to buy those brands, and were generally more materialistic. Their study does not, however, control for the ethos of the schools (and the attitudes of administrators, which might be a common cause behind the ethos and the decision whether to adopt Channel One).
5. Thanks to Charles Read for the unnervingly familiar rope-climbing example.
6. I call this alternative quasi-commercial-free because, of course, it is itself a commercial for CNN (whereas Channel One is not a commercial for Channel One because realistically, children will not watch Channel

One beyond high school). This is not obvious to Sawicky and Molnar (1998), but it is so obvious to my gang that the first two people I talked to about this article immediately pointed it out before reading the current footnote. A friend of mine reports that in the early years of CNN, he visited a posh Chicago hotel from England and saw on his in-room TV constant ads for CNN. Thinking that it looked pretty good, he called the concierge to see if he could get CNN – and was told that the channel, which seemed to consist solely of ads for CNN, was indeed CNN.
7. For example, folk music and soccer are not part of the mainstream culture in the United States, but baseball and rap music are.
8. Poverty makes it especially difficult for children to consider a wide range of ways of life as if they were realistic possibilities. Schools, however, cannot do a great deal about the poverty their students endure, but they can do something to react to the cultural backgrounds of their students.
9. For the obesity claim, see Robinson (1999) and Anderson, Crespo, Bartlett, Cheskin, and Pratt (1998). For the spending claim, see Schor (1998, pp. 79–83) presenting her own research and that of Shrum, O'Guinn, Serenick, and Faber (1991) and O'Guinn and Shrum (1997). Schor (2004) presents a study demonstrating that "children who spend more time watching television and using other media become more involved in consumer culture" (p. 169) and that "high consumer involvement is a significant cause of depression, anxiety, and psychosomatic complaints" (p. 167) as well as "worse relationships with parents"

(p. 170). So watching television is an indirect but significant cause of these harms. I hope to think through the significance of Schor's pathbreaking study in subsequent work.

10. I provide a much more elaborate version of this argument in Brighouse (2005). See also Burtt (1994), Galston (1995), and Schrag (1998) for a series of much

more concessive arguments for deference toward religious parents. The argument of this article developed as an oblique response to these three articles, especially Schrag's, which first set me thinking about this cluster of problems.

11. I'm grateful to Michael Olneck for discussing this thought with me.

## References

Anderson, R. E., Crespo, C. J., Bartlett, S. J., Cheskin, L. J., and Pratt, M. (1998) Relationship of physical activity and television watching with body weight and level of fatness among children: Results from the Third National Health and Nutrition Examination Survey. *Journal of the American Medical Association, 279*: 938–42.

Apple, M. (2000) *Educating the "Right" Way* (London: RoutledgeFalmer).

Brighouse, H. (2000) *School Choice and Social Justice* (Oxford: Oxford University Press).

Brighouse, H. (2002) What rights (if any) do children have? In D. Archard and C. MacLeod (eds.), *The Moral and Political Status of Children* (Oxford: Oxford University Press), pp. 31–52.

Brighouse, H. (2003) How should children be heard? *Arizona Law Review, 45*(3), pp. 691–711.

Brighouse, H. (2005) Faith schools in the UK: An unenthusiastic defence of a slightly reformed status quo. In Roy Gardner (ed.), *Faith Schools: Consensus or Conflict?* (London: RoutledgeFalmer), pp. 83–9.

Burtt, S. (1994) Religious parents, secular schools. *Review of Politics, 56*: 51–70.

Galston, W. (1995) Two concepts of liberalism. *Ethics, 105*: 516–34.

Greenberg, B. S. and Brand, J. E. (1993) Channel One: But what about the advertising? *Educational Leadership, 51*(4): 56–8.

Hoynes, W. (1997, May/June) *News for a captive audience: An analysis of Channel One Extra!* Retrieved from http://www.fair.org/extra/9705/ch1-hoynes.html

Hoynes, W. (1998) News for a teen market: The lessons of Channel One. *Journal of Curriculum Supervision, 13*: 339–56.

Knupfer, N. N. and Hayes, P. (1994) The effects of Channel One broadcasts on students' knowledge of current events. In A. De Vaney (ed.), *Watching Channel One: The Convergence of Students, Technology, and Private Business* (Albany, NY: State University of New York Press), pp. 42–60.

Linn, S. (2004) *Consuming Kids: The Hostile Takeover of Childhood* (New York: New Press).

MacLeod, C. (2003) Agency, goodness, and endorsement: Why we can't be forced to flourish. *Imprints, 7*(4): 131–59.

McCawley, I. (2001, May 31) Misspent youth. *Marketing Week*, pp. 26–8.

O'Guinn, T. C. and Shrum, L. J. (1997) The role of television in the construction of consumer reality. *Journal of Consumer Research, 23*: 278–94.

Robinson, T. N. (1999) Reducing children's television viewing to prevent obesity. *Journal of the American Medical Association, 282*: 1561–7.

Sawicky, M. and Molnar, A. (1998) *The Hidden Costs of Channel One: Estimates for the 50 States*. Retrieved from http://www.asu.edu/educ/lepsl/CERU/Documents/cace-98-02/CACE-98-02.htm

Schor, J. (1998) *The Overspent American* (New York: Harper Perennial).

Schor, J. (2004) *Born to Buy* (New York: Scribner).

Schrag, F. (1998) Diversity, schooling, and the liberal state. *Studies in Philosophy and Education, 17*: 29–46.

Shrum, L. J., O'Guinn, T., Serenick, R. J., and Faber, R. J. (1991) Processes and effects in the construction of normative consumer beliefs: The role of television. In R. H. Holman and M. R. Solomon (eds.), *Advances in Consumer Research* (Provo, UT: Association for Consumer Research), pp. 755–63.

Swift, A. (2003) *How Not to be a Hypocrite: School Choice for the Morally Perplexed* (London: RoutledgeFalmer).

# PART III

# Educational Responsibilities

# Introduction to Part III

What educational responsibilities do adults have toward children? Answers to this question refer to the adults' *roles* as parents, as citizens of political communities that have collective responsibilities to children, as government officials who act on behalf of those communities, as school administrators, and as teachers. Answers are also shaped by the aims of education, by the educational methods and resources that exist or can be invented, and by the extent of the authority that can be legitimately invoked to appropriate the needed resources and make claims on others' time and efforts. The *ethical logic* of answers is shaped by conceptions of the rights of children, the duties of the adults in question, fundamental principles of political justice, the human excellences and other goods that may be achieved through education, and the comparative benefits and costs of alternative policies and approaches. Justice and the rights of children require certain forms of *nondiscrimination* or *equality*, and these and other considerations suggest notions of what is educationally *adequate*. We have seen already an argument from parental duties in the selection from Mill in Part II, and arguments from children's rights and principles of *equal opportunity*, nondiscrimination, and the promotion of liberty or autonomy in the selections from Okin in Part I and Gutmann, Howell, and Brighouse in Part II. In Part I we considered some of the aims against which the adequacy of education might be measured.

Part III begins with a general consideration of "Educational Adequacy and Equality," and then considers two clusters of debates about educational adequacy and equality arising from two categories of differences found in the populations of students served by schools: differences of culture, race, and religion (grouped under the heading "Diversity and Nondiscrimination"), and differences of ability (under the heading "Impairment, Disability, and Excellence").

## Educational Adequacy and Equality

It seems intuitively obvious that in a society in which vastly different social, personal, and economic rewards are distributed through positions of employment, *fairness* requires that those positions be equally open to all members of society. Opportunities must be *equal*, but in what sense equal? It is natural to begin with the idea that positions must be distributed on the basis of *bona fide* job qualifications alone. But it is also natural to ask whether fairness requires that the opportunity to *acquire* those job qualifications must itself be fairly or equally distributed, insofar as those qualifications are products

223

of education and other services and resources (such as prenatal and medical care, adequate nutrition, and transportation) whose distribution is subject to political choice. Limiting this to the educational contributions to job qualifications (and quality of life generally), the question is whether *distributive justice* in society at large requires *equal educational opportunity*. We have already seen some of the complexity involved in the concept of equal educational opportunity in Howell's paper in Part II, and we will continue here with some further perspectives on the matter.

We begin with a reading from chapter 6 of Thomas Green's book *Predicting the Behavior of the Educational System* (1980), included here under the title "The Law of Zero-correlation" (no. 25). Green's aim is to understand why the growth of access to secondary schooling during the twentieth century did not yield the equalization of social and economic fortunes that some people imagined it might. The nineteenth century leaders of public school movements in the United States and other countries presented universal secondary education as "The Great Equalizer" that would eliminate poverty. Labor unions and their members supported the creation of universal public systems in the belief that those systems would improve the situation of working people and enable their children to "get ahead." School systems grew steadily for roughly a century, but by the 1960s it became apparent that universal access to secondary education was not eliminating poverty or "equalizing" social and economic fortunes through gains in social mobility. By and large, it continued to be the case that those born to families that were better off had better prospects, and those born to families that were worse off had worse prospects. It was natural to expect that equal educational opportunity and fair employment practices would have begun to eliminate patterns suggesting *hereditary privilege*. So why did universal access to secondary schooling and rising rates of high school completion not have a more equalizing effect? Was educational opportunity still not equal enough? Was universal access to *tertiary* or college education now required to create equal educational opportunity? Or was the idea of everyone "getting ahead" through a system that aims at universal completion of some level of education somehow misconceived?

One answer to these questions, evident in the work of Paulo Freire (see reading no. 8) and other *critical theorists*, is that it was never the *function* of public school systems to promote equality, rather, quite the contrary, to *preserve* it. This is not a philosophical theory, but an empirical one that must be judged in the court of historical evidence. There is a philosophical objection to it, however, which is that its plausibility seems to rest in part on the suspect assumption that all social institutions do just what they are designed to do and have singular functions that explain their existence. Can't the interactions of people pursuing their individual ends yield patterns no one intends? Can't the existence of an institution sometimes be explained through the interactions of different kinds of participants who have different kinds of reasons for participating in it?

Green constructs an alternative analysis of the dynamic of an expanding school system in which individual families participate with the aim of "getting ahead" or gaining a *positional* or competitive advantage for their children.[1] The fundamental point is that high school diplomas and other *credentials* confer a competitive advantage only if not everyone has them. As the labor market becomes saturated with high school graduates, a high school diploma ceases to give its possessor an advantage. In Green's terms, the *correlation* between social and economic rewards and educational attainment at that level drops to *zero*. Attainment at that level loses currency, except as a step to attainment at higher levels – the higher levels of the educational system that are created to meet the demand for credentials that are still rare enough to confer competitive advantage. At the same time, the liabilities entailed by *not* finishing high school sharply increase as employers find they can pick and choose among applicants with more advanced credentials. If universal attainment of an educational credential is pursued to help those who are lagging behind, it is thus a near certainty that those in the group of "last entry" will not obtain the benefits of the credential enjoyed by those who preceded them. The upshot is that we need to find a different way to think about equal educational opportunity, one that is concerned with *intrinsic* rather than *positional* educational goods, or one that does not aim to universalize attainment at some level, but may instead be compensatory in some way.

Amy Gutmann offers a comparative assessment of three conceptions of equal educational opportunity, and defends an alternative conception of her own, in "Interpreting Equal Educational

Opportunity" (no. 26), a selection from her book *Democratic Education* (1987). The three distributive questions she addresses concern the amount of resources that should be devoted to education, the way those resources should be distributed among children, and the way the children themselves should be assigned to schools and distributed within schools. The *maximization* view holds that the appropriate goal is to "maximize the life chances" of all citizens. The *equalization* view holds that education should "raise the life chances of the least advantaged (as far as possible) up to those of the most advantaged." The *meritocracy* view holds that education should be distributed in proportion to ability and effort. Gutmann argues that all three of these views have problems that make them unacceptable, and she proposes and defends a *democratic* standard of equal educational opportunity. The democratic standard identifies a *threshold* of educational *adequacy* corresponding to the kinds and amount of education required for effective participation in the civic life of a democracy. Gutmann's defense of this democratic threshold is predicated on her conception of democratic *conscious social reproduction*, presented in this volume in her paper in Part II (see reading no. 18).

Christopher Jencks's reading "Whom Must We Treat Equally for Educational Opportunity to be Equal?" (no. 27) begins with a set of conceptions of equal educational opportunity similar to those surveyed by Gutmann, and considers how they would apply to a teacher's allocation of her time and attention to different children in her classroom. Should "Ms. Higgins" give everyone *equal* time and attention? Should she reward *effort* with extra time and attention? Should she aim to *compensate* students disadvantaged by their circumstances with extra time and attention? Should she aim to compensate students not only for circumstantial disadvantages, but also ones due to heritable factors? Or should she allocate her time and attention as rewards for demonstrated *achievement*? Jencks offers a detailed study in the quandaries and indeterminacies that bedevil the ethically conscientious practitioner who would resolve these questions. Is giving equal time and attention the ethically "safe" default option, as Jencks concludes? What about students with learning disabilities? Does Gutmann's framework suggest that teachers should instead allocate their time and attention with a view to enabling as many students as possible to learn what is most essential?

## Diversity and Nondiscrimination

In "Culture, Subculture, Multiculturalism: Educational Options" (no. 28), K. Anthony Appiah defends a kind of multiculturalism with respect to the cultural content of public education in a multicultural society. Multiculturalism "is meant to be an approach to education and to public culture that acknowledges the diversity of cultures and subcultures" in the United States and other large-scale societies, and does not aim to impose the ideas and values of a single dominant or official cultural tradition. Appiah argues that multiculturalism is justified, because the alternative is discriminatory and gives members of the official culture unfair advantages in public life through "preferred access to the best educations." He then considers what a multicultural education would consist of. An approach that he examines and rejects is "separatism," which would teach children the cultures of "their own group." What we need, he says, is a pluralistic multiculturalism "that leaves you not only knowing and loving what is good in the traditions of your subculture but also understanding and appreciating the traditions of others." This is egalitarian, since it eliminates unfair cultural advantage, and it is "the only way to build bridges of loyalty across the ethnicities that have so often divided us." Appiah argues that multiculturalism of this kind demonstrates *respect* for children of diverse cultures by showing respect for the products of their cultures, and in doing this it may also reduce the unreflective sense of cultural superiority of children affiliated with the dominant or official culture. If Appiah is right, a multicultural curriculum is required both as a matter of equity and as a matter of educational adequacy for all students.

In "The Promise of Racial Integration in a Multicultural Age" (no. 29), Lawrence Blum is concerned primarily with the racial diversity of a school's student population, and his purpose is to defend a form of racially integrated schooling that he calls "educational ethnoracial pluralism," an ideal that attaches "importance and value" to "recognizing ethnoracial group identity, culture, and distinctness." Blum revisits the reasoning in the landmark *Brown v. Board of Education of Topeka* decision in 1954, and surveys subsequent commentary on racial segregation. He argues that the benefits of desegregation have been more or less equated with equality of educational opportunity or the opportunity to "get ahead" economically and socially, with the result that the moral, civic, and personal benefits of racially integrated schooling have been widely overlooked. The benefits of these kinds are very substantial, but "mere ethnoracial co-presence" is not enough, Blum argues; schools and teachers must treat children of different races *as equals*. Blum discusses the benefits of integrated schooling at length, including reductions in racial prejudice, acceptance of the social and civic equality of members of all races, a developed ability to work together on shared enterprises, and a strengthening of civic attachment and a sense of shared fate. Such benefits suggest that whether or not equality of educational opportunity can be created through schools that are mono-racial by choice, racially integrated schools can provide an education that is more adequate for everyone in some important respects.

"'Getting Religion': Religion, Diversity, and Community in Public and Private Schools," by Meira Levinson (a philosopher and school teacher) and Sanford Levinson (her constitutional lawyer father), extends these discussions of diversity, non-discrimination, and educational adequacy into the realm of religion (reading no. 30). Citing both traditional arguments and contemporary research, they defend common schooling as an essential foundation for a political culture free of "endless conflict," and as "enabling students' development of autonomy through interaction with students who are different" (cf. the readings by Friedman and Brighouse in Part II). Religiously diverse school populations would promote mutual tolerance and respect, and would thus be educationally valuable in a society characterized by "considerable mutual suspicion" between members of different religions. The association between religion and beliefs about how to live would also make religious diversity particularly salient for autonomy promotion. Levinson and Levinson oppose vouchers and systems of choice that would facilitate religiously homogenous schooling, and they propose some new "religious-diversity-promotion policies" for public schools. These aim to make public schools more hospitable to the practice of diverse religions, through adjustments in school calendars, lunch menus, and foreign language offerings, and through making time and space for prayer during school hours. Such measures could be defended as responsible accommodations of diversity, as well as reasonable steps to provide all students with an education more adequate to their needs as citizens in a religiously diverse and divided society.

## Impairment, Disability, and Excellence

How do responsible educators and educational systems respond to variations in students' abilities and potential to achieve things of inherent worth and value to society? To what extent do educational adequacy and equity require the same education for all children, and to what extent do they require education tailored to children's particular needs and circumstances? Should extra help be provided to students who learn more slowly or with difficulty? What about students of generally "normal" ability, whose learning is impaired in specific, limited ways, or students whose non-cognitive impairments make them unable to attend school without special services or accommodations? What about students who are "gifted" or excel in intellectual and artistic endeavors? Does equity demand extra help or special services for all students who struggle to learn the basics, or only help for those with specific impairments? Does equity demand special accommodations for students who have learned more than their peers and would make little further progress without more advanced work, or does equity require that schools refrain from accommodations that would allow such students to get even farther ahead of their peers? Should the promotion of excellence in intrinsically worthwhile pursuits be a focus of educational concern? One step removed from these normative questions are debates about the very concepts of *disability* and *intelligence*, and the uses of instruments such as IQ tests in categorizing children as *learning disabled* or *gifted*. To what extent are disabilities physical, and to what extent are they arbitrary but convenient labels, artifacts of tests, or functions of social arrangements? In what ways do the answers to this question matter to what is educationally adequate and equitable? If labeling children as "gifted" promotes snobbery and elitism, should educators make no special efforts on behalf of those who demonstrate unusual academic promise?

We begin with the concept of specific *learning disabilities*, and the special entitlements associated with such disabilities under the 1975 Individuals with Disabilities Act (IDEA) and the 1990 Americans with Disabilities Act (ADA). These laws require "reasonable" accommodations for persons with disabilities, in education and elsewhere, and they treat defined cognitive impairments or learning disabilities as comparable to physical impairments. In his reading "The Myths of Learning Disabilities" (no. 31), G. E. Zuriff examines the concept of a specific learning disability, and offers critiques of the *discrepancy test* through which learning disabilities are usually diagnosed, and the ethical logic through which students classified as learning disabled are given priority over students who simply have trouble learning. In doing this, he identifies three "myths": (1) learning disabled (LD) children have known brain dysfunctions; (2) there is a qualitative difference between LD children and slow learners established by discrepancy tests; (3) LD is a well-defined disorder (or class of disorders). He concludes that there is no sound ethical basis for discriminating between LD students and other students with severe academic problems, and argues that they would all benefit from and should receive the same special education.

Lorella Terzi's reading "A Capability Perspective on Impairment, Disability, and Special Needs" (no. 32) examines the general concept of *disability* and outlines a theoretical framework for conceptualizing the nature of disability and educational justice for persons with disabilities. Terzi begins by placing the concept of disability within the World Health Organization's (WHO's) evolving definitions of *impairment*, *disability*, and *handicap*, and surveys the competing claims of two prominent models of disability. The *individual model of disability* understands disability and the disadvantage arising from it "as primarily an individual condition arising from natural causes," while the *social model of disability* maintains that disability is a "disadvantage or restriction of activity" arising from the character of social arrangements. If disability is a function of individual "abnormalities" rather than "social arrangements," does that diminish the responsibility of society and educators to enable people with impairments to live rewarding and productive lives? Terzi argues that the *individual* and *social* models are both flawed, and she defends Amartya Sen's and Martha Nussbaum's *capability approach* as an alternative framework that is sensitive to the interplay of individual and contextual factors, and is "well suited to assessing the relevance of impairment and disability in designing just and inclusive institutional and social arrangements." The capability approach suggests a "multidimensional and relational concept of impairment and disability," which Terzi goes on to elaborate. This yields an approach that "sets aside the debate over whether the causes of disability are natural or social, and promotes a direct concern with functionings and with providing the social bases of adequate capability to pursue valued ends" (see reading no. 12 in Part I). The reading concludes with a discussion of educational equality for children with impairments and *inclusive* versus separate and specialized school settings.

What about children who are not disabled but "different" in a different way – children whose academic abilities so far exceed the norm that they may not derive much benefit from being in an ordinary age-graded classroom with their chronological peers? Laura Purdy's reading, "Educating Gifted Children" (no. 33), offers a *consequentialist* defense of *acceleration* (or allowing selected children to begin school early or skip grades) as the primary means that should be used to accommodate the needs of students who learn more easily and quickly than others. Purdy's basic argument for some form of accommodation is that "children become bored or rebellious if they are not challenged," and the failure to challenge them to develop their abilities will likely result in less satisfying lives for them, and less talent and ability to solve problems for society. Her argument is thus from the likely *consequences* of failing to provide special opportunities for "gifted" children, and is not premised on any claim of *entitlement*. One of several factors in her comparative analysis of acceleration and *enrichment* programs is cost: enrichment programs supplement standard offerings, and thus require a diversion of resources from other possible uses, while acceleration should actually save resources, since it results in some students spending fewer years in school. Purdy is not insensitive to egalitarian concerns, but she argues that it is better to develop the potential of all children and pursue a more egalitarian society through institutional reforms and reductions in "the hugely unequal social rewards created by current social arrangements." If a "winner take all" society can be justified only through equal opportunity (if at all), and equalizing opportunity would unethically limit the development of the highest achieving students, does justice demand policies to *limit* economic and social inequality?

Is there a *non*-consequentialist case to be made for greater efforts to promote high achievement in the arts and sciences – high achievement by students who demonstrate the requisite aptitude and motivation? Joel Kupperman offers such a case, grounded in an Aristotelian conception of human flourishing and excellence, in "Perfectionism and Educational Policy" (no. 34). He describes his view as a kind of *limited perfectionism*, which holds that "in some cases in which we are to choose among social arrangements none of which morally wrongs anyone, we should give some weight . . . to 'the realization of human excellence in the various forms of culture.'" Kupperman imagines a thoroughly hedonistic society that lacks intellectual and artistic creativity and accomplishment ("Tepid New World"), and argues that it would be "less acceptable than a society which has vigorous cultural activities of a high quality." His limited perfectionism does not rule out all compensatory efforts to promote equal educational opportunity, but it does support efforts to recruit teachers who have had a "good liberal education" and can be "successful in stimulating exceptionally promising students to think." It also supports efforts to overturn the unique position of athletics in many American schools, as the one arena in which outstanding achievement can be recognized without provoking the charge of *elitism*. To what extent does this charge of elitism reflect *anti-intellectualism* in American society, its schools, and possibly the colleges of education through which many teachers are certified?

## Note

1. The term "positional" is not used by Green, but has become widely used since the publication of his book. See Hollis, 1982.

## Reference

Hollis, M. 1982: "Education as a Positional Good." *Journal of Philosophy of Education* 16(2): 235–44.

# Educational Adequacy
# and Equality

## 25

# The Law of Zero-correlation

## Thomas F. Green

### The Law of Zero Correlation

Let us imagine a society whose educational system has grown at a uniform rate over a period of one-hundred years. By this, I mean that there has been a uniform increase in the proportion of each successive age cohort attaining at the $n^{th}$ level of the system. Let us suppose, moreover, that that rate of increase is precisely 10 percent per decade over the one-hundred-year period. That pattern of growth will then be represented by the diagonal in figure 25.1. I shall refer to that diagonal as the uniform growth line.

It will be true, without restriction, that if there is a level within the system that everyone completes, then completing that level can have no bearing whatever upon any social differences that may subsequently arise within the population. There may remain differences in opportunity, income, and so forth arising from the way that that level is completed, but, under such circumstances, there can be no social differences whose source is traceable to completing that level. I shall refer to this proposition as the law of zero correlation. The law states

simply that there is a point in the growth of the system at which there is no longer any correlation between educational attainment and either the distribution of educationally relevant attributes in the population or the distribution of non-educational social goods ordinarily associated with educational attainment.

The law of zero correlation is a tautology. Its truth arises from the fact that for there to be a correlation between any two variables, say, between educational attainment and lifetime earnings, both of the variables must be distributed in the population.[1] Neither can be uniformly distributed if its occurrence is to be used in explaining variations in the other variable. When the law of zero-correlation is understood in this way, no doubts can arise about its truth.

The name, "law of zero correlation," however, should not be misunderstood. It is not as though we set out to discover the correlation between educational attainment and other social differences and discovered that the correlation was zero. The point is rather that to even *try* to discover the correlation under such conditions is no longer an intelligible

Editor's title. Previously published in *Predicting the Behavior of the Educational System*, reprint of original 1980 Syracuse University Press edition (Troy, NY: Educator's International Press, 1997), pp. 90–100. © 1980, 1997 Thomas F. Green. Reprinted with the kind permission of the author.

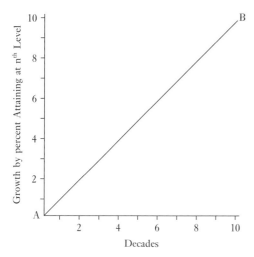

**Figure 25.1** Hypothetical uniform growth line

We may reason, however, that if Point B on the hypothetical growth line is a point of zero correlation, then so is point A, and for precisely the same reasons. When everyone attains the $n^{th}$ level of the system, there is no correlation between attainment at that level and subsequent possession of any particular social goods. But the same proposition will be true when *nobody* attains at the $n^{th}$ level.

We may now reason through a third step. Certified attainment at the $n^{th}$ level of the system is, of course, a second-order educational good distributed by the system. And so, at either A or B, it is impossible for the society to distribute non-educational social goods *on the basis of* the system's distribution of second-order educational goods. Yet, we know, as a matter of empirical fact and common knowledge, that the correlation between educational attainment, on the one hand, and the acquisition of non-educational social goods, on the other hand, rises at some point as the system grows from A to B. We know, therefore, that the direction of any line representing that correlation rises from A and descends ultimately to C on the horizontal axis.

We may summarize this set of inferences in a single observation. *The value of second-order educational benefits as a basis for allocating non-educational social goods is a curvilinear function of the proportion of each age-cohort that is successful in obtaining those goods.* We may represent this claim in figure 25.2.

With the growth of the system, therefore, its distributive behavior changes. As increasing numbers of each generation are successful in obtaining

task. At point B on the hypothetical growth line the question "What is the correlation between completing the $n^{th}$ level and securing some subsequent social benefit?" is no longer an askable question. It would be like asking for the correlation between having a heart and having a particular social status. The question is nonsensical.

With this qualification in mind, we may return to figure 25.1 and observe that point B in the hypothetical growth line is that point at which the growth of the system will reach zero correlation with respect to the $n^{th}$ level. Point B is the *point* of zero correlation. Let us now reinterpret the vertical axis in figure 25.1 to represent a scale of the strength of correlation through time between attainment at the $n^{th}$ level and the acquisition of non-educational social goods. We may then superimpose on the hypothetical growth line a curve representing this correlation at different points in the growth of the system.

We know by immediate inference from the tautological law of zero correlation that that curve will reach zero at a point on the horizontal axis opposite point B. Thus, we know the direction and terminus of a curve representing the declining strength of correlation between educational attainment at the $n^{th}$ level and whatever social goods are normally associated with education. We do not, however, know the full shape of that curve. We do not know its points of inflection nor the rate of its decline toward zero.

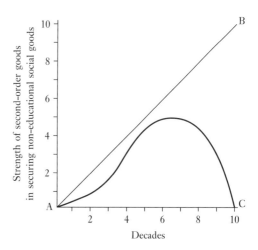

**Figure 25.2** Utility of second-order educational goods

higher and higher second-order goods from the system, the social value of those benefits at a specific level of the system will increase and then eventually decline. In a society where few have completed high school, high school completion is unlikely to be used as a screening prerequisite for job entry, job placement, or job security. The efficacy of such second-order benefits for the allocation of social goods will be fairly low. In a society where a great many of each generation have them, then their utility will be fairly high. In a society, however, where *every* youth receives such benefits of the system, the social value of having them will again decline and approach zero.

It can be doubted whether any society has reached a point of zero correlation at any level as high as, say, the twelfth level of the American system. There are societies that have not reached that point at a level as high as the third grade in the American system. The law of zero correlation, however, does not specify what will count as the $n^{th}$ level. It may be as high as college or as low as the first grade. But the important question is not whether or at what point it has been reached in this or that place, but *what, from a purely analytic point of view, can we expect to happen in any society as it approaches the point of zero correlation at some level of the system?*

## Corollaries of Zero Correlation

The utility of educational attainment, and of the second-order educational benefits associated with it, is a curvilinear function of the proportion of each age cohort successful in securing such goods. That is the principle implicit in the tautological law of zero correlation. This principle, however, does not stand alone. It has its corollaries.

### Transformation from attainment to achievement

The first of these is the *rule of transformation from educational attainment to educational achievement.* As we approach the point of zero correlation at the $n^{th}$ level of the system, then merely having a diploma or certificate at that level will no longer discriminate between individuals. It will become important to discriminate between diplomas, certificates, and programs. In a society where everyone earns a high school diploma, having one no longer bestows any particular advantages, but having one from this or that school or from this or that program

may still represent a mark of distinction and may, therefore, bestow considerable advantages. Thus, attention will shift from the level of attainment to the quality of achievement.

But why should this shift occur? Are there no other choices? We have seen already that the system is unlikely to grow very large unless there is a strong, positive, relation between the acquisition of educational goods and the acquisition of non-educational social goods. We have seen, moreover, that that relation is implemented through second-order educational benefits and that it requires some principle of legitimation.

We know, already, however, that these second-order educational benefits – certificates, diplomas, transcripts, and the like – play multiple roles within the system. First of all, they provide the practical medium of exchange between the units of the system without which it would not be a system at all. Viewed in that role, they are tokens of attainment. But we noted, further, that they provide the practical social link needed between the distribution of educational benefits by the system and the distribution of non-educational social goods by the society. Viewed in this role, they are surrogates of educational goods and have a mixed function. They are indicators of attainment, but, to a limited extent, also they are indicators of achievement. But such goods enter the system in a third way. By providing a means of exchange between units of the system, they may be accepted at par value, at inflated value, or at discounted value. In this function they are explicit indicators of achievement, and they help to define the status rank of units in the system.

As zero correlation is approached, the society loses its capacity to allocate social goods to accord with attainment. Therefore, the function of second-order goods as indicators of attainment will decline and their function as indicators of achievement will become relatively more important. In short, the status differentials of the system will become more prominent and of more practical importance for the social distribution of opportunities, status, and the like.

If the distributive mores of the system are to be preserved when zero correlation approaches then something must change. There are only two choices, and functionally they are the same. The first is to allocate non-educational social goods on the basis of attainment at the level of $n + 1$ or beyond where, presumably, the approach of zero correlation is more remote. Thus, we would expect the educational prerequisites for jobs to be upgraded and the system to press for higher levels of universal attainment. And in this proposal the interests of the incumbents of the system as employees, professionals, and technicians will match the interests of parents. Both will have an interest in expanding the system for higher rates of attainment at higher levels. The dynamics of intensification will be set in motion.

The second choice is to begin allocating social goods on the basis of different *ways* of attaining the $n^{th}$ level. This shift of attention from attainment to achievement is the functional equivalent of reducing the proportion of each age cohort securing a particular second-order educational good, and that is precisely, though not exclusively, what is accomplished, in another way, by the first of these choices. The tendency, in short, is to either press for levels of attainment beyond zero correlation or to find ways of replacing status differences associated with attainment by status differences associated with different kinds of schools and programs. This is the shift from attainment to achievement.

## Transforming utility

The second corollary of zero correlation is the *rule of transforming utility*. Let us recall that second-order educational goods appeared as the socially practical device permitting educational goods and non-educational social goods to be linked in their distribution. Their *justification or legitimation* in this function rests in their capacity to act as crude, but useful, surrogates of *educational* goods. Their value, therefore, is purely instrumental. There are no normative principles governing their instrumental use except those requiring them to be rationally adequate surrogates for educational goods.

Under conditions of zero correlation, however, second-order educational benefits have no instrumental value for the allocation of social goods outside the system. But, as we have seen, these goods act also as indicators of achievement within the system. They are used for the allocation of social goods by the society, but they are also used by the system for the allocation of access to the system, and this latter function is unaffected by the conditions of zero correlation. Thus, as we approach the point of zero correlation at the $n^{th}$ level, we must expect that the instrumental value of second-order benefits, as the tool for allocating social goods, will

become more and more problematic. Their remaining, and still secure, value will be their instrumental worth in securing access to subsequent levels of the system. In short, the chief instrumental worth of education is then merely to secure access to more education.[2] The chief value of a high school education is then that it permits access to the next level of the system. This is the meaning of the principle of transforming utility.

## Shifting benefits and liabilities

The third corollary of zero correlation may be expressed as the principle of shifting benefits and liabilities. As the social utility of second-order benefits declines for those who receive them, then the social liabilities suffered by any individual as a consequence of *not* securing them will increase. I state this principle as a corollary of zero correlation. It is of such importance, however, and its implications are so far-reaching that it might be viewed as a second and distinct law of systemic behavior. To secure anything approaching its full exposition we shall need to give this principle central attention for the remainder of this chapter and beyond.

To more fully grasp its significance, however, we need to return to figures 25.1 and 25.2. The diagonal in figure 25.1 was presented as a purely hypothetical account. In fact, however, it corresponds roughly to the experience in the United States from about 1900 to the present. In 1910 about 7 percent of the 17-year-old cohort completed high school. By 1940 it approached 50 percent and in 1965 it reached 76 percent. This means that in the United States we have been approaching the point of zero correlation at the 12th level of the system. It would be reasonable to expect this growth to level off. No matter what system we may choose to consider, its natural limit will fall short of its mathematical limit. In the United States, this growth curve levelled off at about 76 percent where it has remained since 1965. That this has happened at the 12th level in the American system is a fact of enormous significance, and especially so in view of the further fact that the period since 1965 has witnessed the most monumental effort in the history of American educational policy to continue its increase.

With these considerations in mind, let us re-examine the schema presented in figure 25.2. There, on purely conceptual grounds, I sketched the shape of a curvilinear function representing the social utility of second-order educational benefits corresponding to different points on a hypothetical path of uniform growth. If we examine that schema carefully, we shall see that the American system has reached a point in its expansion at the 12th level corresponding to an inflection point in the declining value of second-order educational benefits. In short, if the system expands further, the value of attainment, for those who secure it, will decline at that level *with increasing speed*. Can this conjecture be supported?

It presents a pair of puzzling questions. First of all, it is becoming more and more widely recognized that, *to those who possess it*, a high school diploma is less and less decisive in the scrap to secure the social goods of life. A higher level of attainment is required. Yet, if its efficacy is so slight, then why is there no apparent decline in the desire and effort to secure it? The immediate answer is that it is required for access to the next level of the system. The principle of transforming utility operates. Secondly, we would anticipate that in approaching the mathematical limit in the growth of the system at this level, each marginal gain will prove to be more difficult for the society to reach. And there seems to be no abatement in the continuing effort of the system to reach such a goal. Why then does the system appear to many as increasingly unsuccessful?

The answers to these questions are discoverable in the principle of shifting benefits and liabilities. That principle is that *as the social value of second-order benefits declines for those who receive them, the social liabilities suffered by any individual as a consequence of not securing them will increase.* As a first

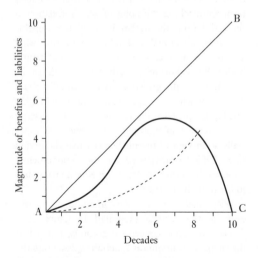

**Figure 25.3**  Shifting benefits and liabilities

step in rendering this principle precise, we may begin with its schematic formulation in figure 25.3.

This schema extends beyond what is contained in the principle itself. The principle deals only with the dynamics of the system at the upper end of the uniform growth line. It refers explicitly only to that point where the social utility (not the systemic utility) of second-order benefits declines *for those who receive them*. The representation in figure 25.3 *suggests* that this point is not reached until the growth of the system at the nth level passes 60 percent and that the downward slope of utility is not steep until slightly beyond that point.[3]

Such precision is more than we are warranted in concluding from the mere formulation of the principles so far set down. The principle of shifting benefits and liabilities explicitly warrants conjecture only about the *direction* of the liability curve at the upper end of the uniform growth line. The schematic shape of the lower end in figure 25.3 is based, however, upon the following considerations that are plausible enough on other grounds.

It seems, on the surface, unlikely that any society, in its allocation of social goods, will seriously limit the future of those who fail to secure a high school diploma when only 20 percent to 40 percent secure one. Surely in a society where less than 10 percent of each generation secures a high school diploma, nobody is likely to be either greatly advantaged in getting one or greatly disadvantaged by not getting one. Tenacity, guts, inventiveness, perhaps miserliness, and certainly long life, and just plain luck are likely to be much more significant than educational attainment. Thus, both the utility curve and the liability curve are schematically represented as fairly flat at the lower reaches of the uniform growth line, and this characterization seems justified even though it cannot be substantiated as a direct inference either from the law of zero correlation or from the principle of shifting benefits and liabilities.

There may seem to be a counter-argument. There have been societies where only a few are educated and where those few are greatly advantaged. However, if we think seriously about such examples, we shall recognize that such societies are usually characterized either by a caste system, a feudal system, or a strongly aristocratic tradition. In such cases, the educated few are greatly advantaged. But they are not advantaged *by* their education. They are advantaged *by* their birth. Is birth a matter of luck? It seems odd to say so, although in common parlance, people do speak of it as a matter of "good (or ill) fortune." In any case, the counter-argument cannot be sustained as a serious objection to the conjecture upon which we base the *schematic* shape of the utility and liability curves at the lower end of the uniform growth line.

## Implications of Shifting Benefits and Liabilities

The import of these conjectures can be gathered from two further observations on problems that have emerged on the American scene over the past two decades. To the best of my knowledge, the so-called drop-out problem was never viewed as a *social* problem in the United States until the mid-50s. By that time, curiously enough, the attainment rate at the 12th level of the American system had passed 60 percent. The drop-out problem in short comes into existence and intensifies as the number of drop-outs declines. It is now less talked about than it was in the mid-50s, but it is more intense as a problem. This peculiarity – that as we have fewer drop-outs the "drop-out problem" becomes more serious – is accounted for by the principle of shifting benefits and liabilities. Being a drop-out is nothing new, but the seriousness of being one is new. It began to be apparent in the United States when the growth of the system at the 12th level

passed the 60 percent point on the uniform growth curve. When there are lots of drop-outs, being one is no problem. When there are few, being one can be a disaster. The reason that we have a drop-out *problem* is not that we have too many drop-outs, but that we have too few. This is an uncharitable formulation, but, nonetheless, it expresses the point vividly.

Similar observations may be offered on the so-called problem of credentialism. Where only a few have finished high school, the society cannot use the completion of high school as a screen for either job entrance, advancement, or security. Credentialism can arise only in a society where lots of people have credentials. It becomes a problem, if it is a problem at all, as a consequence of the growth of the system. It is easy to see then that as any society approaches the point of zero correlation, as in the United States at the 12th level of the system, having a high school diploma is no big deal for those who have them, but not having one can be an unqualified disaster for those who do not. These points add weight to the conjectured shape of the liability curve in figure 25.3, both in its upper and lower sectors. They lend credibility to that schematic portrayal of the principle of shifting benefits and liabilities. These problems in the American system arise not because of the failure of the system, but because of its unparalleled success.

## Notes

1. It is vital to observe that this is a claim about educational attainment and not educational achievement.
2. One may note the similarity of this formulation of the rule of transforming utility to the remark of Dewey's that the only goal of education is more education. Dewey, however, had in mind an important point about the nature of *education*, how it contributes to the reconstruction of experience. The rule of transforming utility, however, says something about the nature of the educational *system*. It should not be confused with Dewey's point.

3. Note carefully: We have been considering what, from a purely analytic point of view is likely to happen as we *approach* the point of zero correlation. Zero correlation is a *terminus* in the growth of the system at a certain level. It is identified in recognizing that the law of zero correlation is a tautology. The point at which we begin to *approach* zero correlation on the utility curve must be determined empirically. Its meaning, however, is not determined empirically. These schema are intended to present the *meaning* of the systemic principles of behavior.

# 26

# Interpreting Equal Educational Opportunity

## Amy Gutmann

In its most liberal interpretation, the principle of equal educational opportunity offers a theoretically simple rule to solve all three distributional problems: The liberal state should devote as many resources to primary schooling as necessary, and distribute those resources, along with children themselves, in such a way as to maximize the life chances of all its future citizens.[1] Call this interpretation of equal educational opportunity *maximization*. A second, more common (and less consistently liberal) interpretation of equal educational opportunity requires the state to distribute educational resources so that the life chances of the least advantaged child are raised as far as possible toward those of the most advantaged. Call this interpretation *equalization*. A third, and perhaps the most common interpretation, requires the state to distribute educational resources in proportion to children's demonstrated natural ability and willingness to learn. Call this interpretation *meritocracy*.

Although each of these interpretations has been repeatedly offered in the literature on education as a distributive standard, none is plausible, once one draws out its practical implications. My aim in elaborating the implications of each interpretation in its pure form is not to belabor this critical point,

but to be constructive: to demonstrate the need for a more complex and credible standard, and (more importantly) to begin developing one. I shall develop a more democratic standard for distributing primary schooling after understanding the strengths and weaknesses of each interpretation.

### Maximization

Maximization requires the state to devote as many resources to education as needed to maximize children's life chances. "Our kind of society," John Gardner argues, "demands the maximum development of individual potentialities *at every level of ability* . . . [so] that each youngster may achieve the best that is in him. . . ."[2] If our kind of society is purely liberal, then Gardner's claim is correct. Maximization supports the fundamental liberal values of free choice and neutrality among different ways of life, and distributes the chance to benefit from these values as equally as possible among all citizens.[3] But if our kind of society is also democratic, then we must look more carefully and critically at maximization.

Editor's title. Previously published in *Democratic Education* (Princeton, NJ: Princeton University Press, 1987), pp. 128–39. © 1987 by Princeton University Press. 1999 paperback edition. Reprinted by permission of Princeton University Press.

The hidden weakness of maximization is what may be called the problem of the moral ransom. The rule offers us something morally valuable on the implicit condition that we give up everything else that we value. The state could spend an endless amount on education to increase the life chances of children. Yet its resources are limited, and police protection, public parks, baseball stadiums, and stereo systems are also valuable. The price of using education to maximize the life chances of children would be to forego these other goods.[4]

Someone sympathetic to maximization might try to avoid this criticism by adding a proviso that the state must devote as many resources to education as can maximize children's life chances *provided that the increase in life chances is not trivial*. Though reasonable, this proviso does not save maximization from the problem of the moral ransom. Even if the proviso establishes a theoretical limit to investment in education, there is still no practical limit to what we can now collectively spend to increase children's life chances substantially. Most parents are not willing to make such a sacrifice even for their own children. Perhaps parents should sacrifice even more than they now do for their children's education, but there is no good reason to obligate them to minimize the other, noneducational pursuits that they value in order to maximize their children's life chances. Nor is there good reason to obligate citizens collectively to invest so much in education as to maximize the life chances of the next generation.

A more promising defense argues that maximization requires many social commitments beyond improving schools, raising teachers' salaries, and funding more educational research and development. Maximization commits the state to providing children and their parents with many other opportunity goods, such as police protection, housing, and health care, without which education could not perform its function of maximizing life chances. Because most cultural goods – public parks and museums, perhaps even stadiums and stereos – are also educational, maximization commits the state to their provision as well. As the number of goods included in maximization increases, the price of its hidden ransom decreases. The reformulated offer, a dedicated liberal could argue, is one that we can but we ought not refuse.

The more inclusive maximization becomes, however, the less guidance it gives for making hard choices among the many valuable opportunity goods, all of which the state cannot possibly provide. There

is no limit in sight to the amount the state can spend on improving schools, teachers' salaries, the arts, or popular culture to expand children's choices later in life. Nor is there an apparent limit to the amount the state can spend on police protection, housing, or health care to increase their chances of living a longer life. If proponents make maximization into an inclusive good, analogous to the Aristotelian or the utilitarian conception of happiness, then they must be willing to accept less than the maximum of the many goods – such as better schools – that it includes. Only inclusive goods are plausibly worth maximizing, but they require acceptance of less than the maximum of the many valuable goods that they include. Should the state invest in school buildings or stadiums, or neither, leaving parents with more money to spend on travel? Maximization provides no answer.

There is no intuitively obvious answer with which all citizens could agree, nor has a way been found to derive a single correct answer from some self-evident philosophical principle (or set of principles). These are the conditions under which democratic determination of social priorities makes the most sense. Even if the maximization interpretation of equal educational opportunity is correct, it needs to be supplemented by a democratic standard: states should use fair democratic processes to determine how to expand the life chances of their future citizens.

But maximization is not correct. It relies on a general misconception: that a society should strive to maximize the goods that it values most. No exclusive earthly good – not even educational opportunity, broadly understood – is so valuable as to be worthy of maximization. If the state need not be committed to using education to maximize children's life chances, then democratic citizens should be free not only to set priorities among all the goods that expand educational opportunity, but also to choose between educational opportunity and all the other goods that it excludes.

## Equalization

One way of avoiding the many problems posed by maximization is to interpret equal educational opportunity less liberally and more literally. Since its explicit terms do not mention maximization, equal educational opportunity might be construed to demand only equalization: use education to raise the life chances of the least advantaged (as far as possible) up to those of the most advantaged. The scope of the equal opportunity principle is now significantly narrowed: it says nothing about how much a state should spend on education relative to other goods, or on the education of any particular child except in relation to what it provides for other children. This may already be an important, albeit implicit, liberal concession to democracy. The liberal silence concerning how to determine the distribution of education relative to other social goods leaves room for a democratic determination of priorities, even if it does not demand such a determination. I develop the implications of such a democratic principle by examining the case of school financing.

According to equalization, the educational attainment of children should not differ in any systematic and significant manner with their natural or environmentally determined characteristics.[5] Rightly distributed, education should be used to overcome all environmental and natural causes of differential educational attainment, since these causes of social inequalities are beyond people's control, and therefore "arbitrary from a moral perspective."[6] If "even the willingness to make an effort, to try, . . . is itself dependent upon happy family and social circumstances,"[7] then equal educational opportunity must aim also to equalize effort or the results of unequal effort.

One sympathetic critic of equalization takes it to be a proper moral ideal. In the absence of any competing moral demands, he argues, the state should try to eliminate all inequalities in life chances that result from morally arbitrary differences; the presence of other moral demands, however, renders the price too high. To equalize educational opportunity, the state would have to intrude so far into family life as to violate the equally important liberal ideal of family autonomy.[8] Liberals cannot simply reformulate the principle of family autonomy to permit as much intrusion as necessary to achieve equalization, because the necessary amount would eliminate one of the life chances that citizens value most – the freedom to educate their own children.

Intuitionism seems to be a plausible way of handling the problem of conflicting liberal ideals. Aware of the weakness of maximization, one can conceive of equalization as just one among several liberal ideals, none of which must be fully realized to satisfy the demands of liberal justice. Liberalism, so conceived, consists of "ideals without an ideal":

"How its principles are to be balanced remains an open question to be faced in particular cases as they present themselves."[9]

To be faced by whom? Because it offers no answer to the question of whose intuitions will do the balancing, intuitionism avoids rather than solves the political problem of balancing conflicting ideals. The American polity contains a variety of conflicting moral principles and conflicting moral intuitions. Invoking "American" intuitions, therefore, cannot resolve the conflict between equalizing educational opportunity and respecting family autonomy. Our intuitions on this issue differ, as recent controversies over school financing and busing suggest. How the principles should be balanced will depend upon whose intuitions should do the balancing. Because intuitions also differ over who should make the hard choices between the equalization of educational opportunity and family autonomy, intuitionism itself cannot resolve this moral and political problem.

One might doubt even the more limited claim that while equalization is in itself a worthy moral ideal, in practice it must be balanced against other equally worthy ideals, such as family autonomy. The intuitionist understanding of equalization makes a necessity out of a virtue. Even if equalization did not conflict with other liberal ideals, there is good reason to choose its incomplete rather than its complete realization. Completely realized, equalization requires the state to devote all its educational resources to educationally less able children until they reach either the same level of educational attainment as the more able or the highest level that they are capable of attaining.[10] Given limited educational resources and unlimited capacity for educational innovation, this time may never come, in which case the state would provide no educational resources to the more able.[11] This is an unacceptable consequence, because equality of life chances is not in itself a sufficiently important value to outweigh the value of enabling all children to develop their talents to some socially acceptable degree.

A thought experiment can help show why equalization takes equality too seriously. Suppose we know that every difference in the educational achievement of children is beyond their control and correctable by some expensive, but finite, amount of remedial education. Must we then create an educational system that eliminates all differences among children's educational attainments?

The answer is no, and not because equalization would be socially inefficient. There is good reason to accept many differences in educational attainment.[12] The good reason is that many differences in educational achievement can be eliminated only by eradicating the different intellectual, cultural, and emotional dispositions and attachments of children. Some children are more proficient at (and interested in) cultivating friendships and having fun than they are at learning what schools teach. Such variety among children makes their lives, as well as the lives of others, rich and interesting. Many children, moreover, will live more rewarding lives in an environment where competition is not universal but is partly limited by their predispositions for academic achievement, which (whether culturally or genetically created) are undeserved. A society fully charged with competition and so stripped of diversity would be a less desirable place for children, parents, and probably even teachers to live.

Not all variety, on the other hand, is valuable in a society where children who lack learning do not have a reasonable chance to participate in making democratic decisions. The democratic truth in equalization is that all children should learn enough to be able not just to live a minimally decent life, but also to participate effectively in the democratic processes by which individual choices are socially structured. *A democratic state, therefore, must take steps to avoid those inequalities that deprive children of educational attainment adequate to participate in the political processes.*

## Meritocracy

The democratic truth in equalization reveals the flaw in meritocracy. A meritocracy is dedicated to distributing all educational resources in proportion to natural ability and willingness to learn. In principle, therefore, meritocracy must provide those children with relatively few natural abilities and little inclination to learn with the fewest educational resources and the least educational attention, and those children with the greatest natural abilities and motivation with the most.

In practice, few meritocrats accept the full implications of the standard that they profess. They typically invoke the meritocratic interpretation of equal educational opportunity to argue not against providing an adequate education for all children, but for providing a better education for gifted children instead of concentrating resources on the "average" child and the slow learner. A meritocratic distribution of educational resources, they argue, would give educationally gifted children what they deserve and also give society what it needs: a greater pool of human capital to increase social productivity. The case for meritocracy seems strongest when so used, but the meritocratic standard still proves too much for all but the most ardent meritocrat to accept. In principle, meritocracy does not require – it may even preclude – educating less talented and less motivated children up to a socially basic level of literacy. Furthermore, nothing in the meritocratic interpretation of equal educational opportunity secures an education adequate for democratic citizenship to children who happen to have (whether by nature, nurture, or their own free will) little intellectual talent or motivation.

The democratic truth in equalization – that states must secure an education for all children adequate to participate in the democratic political processes – does not rule out a restricted form of meritocracy in which educational resources above the level that is adequate for citizenship are distributed in proportion to children's demonstrated intellectual ability and willingness to learn. Once all children are guaranteed enough education to participate in politics, a democrat might defend a limited meritocracy on grounds of just desserts: children who demonstrate greater intellectual ability and/or greater motivation deserve to be provided with more education than those who demonstrate less.

A more egalitarian democrat might reasonably challenge this claim: Why do more gifted or motivated children deserve more education if they have done little or nothing to deserve their greater intellectual gifts or motivation? "Because intellectual talent and motivation are fitting bases for deserving education even if they are not themselves deserved," the less egalitarian democrat might reply. "Courageous soldiers deserve Medals of Honor, even if they do not deserve their courage. Similarly, intellectually talented children and highly motivated children deserve more education, even if they do not deserve their greater talents and motivation."[13]

The meritocrat's response still is insufficient to support even a more restricted meritocracy, where education above the "threshold" level necessary for citizenship *must* be distributed, as a matter of justice, in proportion to intellectual merit. Rewarding dessert is a reasonable way to distribute educational resources above the threshold level, but surely not the only reasonable way. A good case can be made for the use of education above the minimum to compensate less gifted and less motivated children for their undeserved disadvantages. Another good case can be made for using educational resources above the threshold to develop new skills and interests in all children, which might be useful to society as well as satisfying to citizens in the future. Yet another case can be made for concentrating resources on those students who are both intellectually gifted and motivated, on grounds of social utility rather than of desert: the welfare of society as a whole is most likely to be advanced in this way.

Suppose I made each case fully, compared them, and concluded that the case for rewarding merit is, on balance, the best. Suppose also (for the sake of argument) that I am right. I still cannot conclude that my policy preference should dominate a democratic one, provided the democratic one does not violate the principled constraints on democracy. Being right is neither necessary nor sufficient grounds for commanding political authority, by either liberal or democratic standards.[14]

When reasonable alternatives are recognizable, meritocracy is put in its proper, democratic place. If democratic institutions allocate educational resources *above* the threshold level so as to reward intellectual desert, then a limited meritocracy is properly part of society's democratic standard for distributing education. The democratic interpretation of meritocracy does not hold that education above the threshold *must* be distributed according to desert (regardless of democratic preferences) but that it *may* be so distributed (depending on the results of fair democratic processes).

## The Democratic Standard Stated

The standard of democratic distribution developed so far can be formulated more precisely as two principles. Call the first the *democratic authorization principle*. It recognizes the mistake in maximization by granting authority to democratic institutions to determine the priority of education relative to other social goods. Call the second the *democratic threshold principle*. It avoids the mistakes in both equalization and meritocracy by specifying that inequalities in the distribution of educational goods can be justified if, but only if, they do not deprive any child of the ability to participate effectively in the democratic process (which determines, among other things, the

priority of education relative to other social goods). The democratic threshold principle thus places limits on the legitimate discretion of democratic decisionmaking established by the authorization principle. The threshold principle establishes a realm of what one might call nondiscretionary democratic authority. It does so by imposing a moral requirement that democratic institutions allocate sufficient resources to education to provide all children with an ability adequate to participate in the democratic process. Democratic institutions still retain the discretionary authority to decide how much more education to provide above the threshold established by the second principle.[15]

Although education above the threshold may be democratically distributed according to meritocratic principles, education below the threshold must not be. Democratic decisionmaking may still be the most effective way to determine the threshold. Whether it is will depend partly on an empirical assessment of how we can best guarantee all children an adequate education, and partly on a normative assessment of what adequacy entails. Since educational adequacy is relative and dependent on the particular social context, the best way of determining what adequacy practically entails may be a democratic decisionmaking process that follows upon public debate and deliberation. But to say that the threshold requirements are more likely to be satisfied by democratic institutions than by nondemocratic institutions is not to say that democratic institutions have moral discretion in deciding whether to provide an adequate level of education for all citizens.

The distinction between the nondiscretionary and discretionary realms of democratic authority is already incorporated in the rationales for some present educational policies. In passing Public Law 94–142 (the "Education for All Handicapped Children Act"), Congress mandated an "appropriate" rather than an optimal level of education for handicapped children, leaving states and local school districts free to provide more (but not less) if they wish. The educational provisions of some state constitutions suggest a threshold requirement. The New Jersey Supreme Court has interpreted Article IV of its state constitution to require the state to guarantee "that educational opportunity which is needed in the contemporary setting to equip a child for his role as a citizen. . . ."[16] In many states, so-called "Foundation Programs" (which guarantee a level of state funding to local school districts) invoke the ideal of providing an adequate educational foundation for school-age children in all school districts. In practice (and perhaps even in political intent), however, most Foundation Programs are funded at levels so low as to leave property-poor districts with far fewer resources than they would need to reach any reasonable estimate of the democratic threshold. Although many of our schools fall far short of satisfying the demands of the threshold, implementing the two-part democratic standard does not require a revolution in our way of thinking about education. Rather, it requires more self-conscious use of that standard in arguing about educational policy, and it requires more work in figuring out how to translate that standard into effective educational reform.

A democratic critic might ask: can a standard dictate a threshold and still remain democratic in any meaningful sense? This question arises again in discussing school finance; it cannot be answered in the abstract. But some reasons may be suggested here for remaining hopeful that the answer is yes. The answer would be no if nondemocratic institutions were more reliable than democratic ones in implementing the threshold and if the threshold were so high as to leave no room for democratic support of more than an adequate education for every child. A nondemocratic authority should then determine the democratic threshold. The threshold having been established, no political space would be left for discretionary democratic authority. (Judging from historical experience, it seems implausible that nondemocratic institutions are more reliable in establishing adequate education for every child than are democratic ones. The educational interests of disadvantaged minorities are often better protected by more centralized than by less centralized democratic bodies, but rarely by nondemocratic ones.)

Would any adequate threshold cost so much as to make discretionary democratic authority obsolete? Given how much federal, state, and local governments now spend on defense, criminal justice, social security, and other welfare goods, it is implausible to claim that if we provided an adequate education for every child, we would have no resources to spend on improving education above the threshold. We might, after democratic deliberation, collectively choose to spend more on missiles or medical care rather than to increase expenditures on schools. Such choices – even if mistaken – would be consistent with the democratic claims of the standard.

The policy implications of the democratic standard of distribution, therefore, are underdetermined in principle. What constitutes a just distribution of democratic education not only may vary among different democratic societies but also may change quite significantly over time in the same society. These changes may occur for two moral reasons, related to the two parts of the democratic standard. The authorization principle suggests that the priority and distribution of education above the threshold level should be open to democratic discretion. The threshold principle suggests that while the threshold itself is not similarly open, it is socially relative as it insists that schools provide all educable children with an education adequate to participate effectively in democratic processes.[17] The more educated most citizens are, the more education each citizen is likely to need to participate effectively in the democratic process. The democratic standard is consistent with the view that there is some absolute minimum of literacy below which no democratic society could be said to provide an adequate education to its citizens. But the standard demands more of democracies than supplying an absolute minimum; the threshold of an ability to participate effectively in democratic politics is likely to demand more and better education for all citizens as the average level and quality of education in our society increases.

The democratic interpretation avoids the counter-intuitive extremism of the standard interpretations of equal educational opportunity and improves upon intuitionism. It does, however, leave a crucial question (to which I return) unanswered: How do we determine the democratic threshold? To put the question more precisely: What kind and level of education is adequate to citizenship in our society today? While I cannot answer this question completely here, there is no reason to fall back on the conventional interpretations of equal educational opportunity that avoid uncertainty by embracing unacceptable ideals.

## Notes

1. For a popular statement and defense of this interpretation of the opportunity principle, see John W. Gardner, *Excellence: Can We Be Equal and Excellent*

*Too?* (New York: Harper and Brothers, 1961), esp. pp. 75 ff.

2. Gardner, *Excellence*, pp. 74–5.

3. Note that this liberal understanding does not identify the improvement of life chances simply with an increase of income, social status, or political power. Life chances include all opportunities to develop and exercise our human capacities.

4. A variant of maximization that avoids the problem of the moral ransom is what might be called "proportionality": educate every child to achieve the same proportion of his or her intellectual potential. Proportionality introduces new problems: (1) it offers no standard for setting the proportion; (2) if it did offer a standard, we still would not be able to judge what level of educational achievement represented that proportion of a child's potential; and (3) even if we could judge when achievement was proportional to potential, we would still wonder why some children should be denied enough education to become literate (say) just because they are intellectually less talented than other children.

5. See James S. Fishkin, *Justice, Equal Opportunity, and the Family* (New Haven, CT: Yale University Press, 1983), p. 32. Fishkin takes only native characteristics and not environment to be illegitimate correlates of life chances, although both are equally arbitrary from the moral point of view that he is characterizing.

6. Rawls, *A Theory of Justice* (Cambridge, MA: Harvard University Press, 1971), p. 74.

7. Ibid.

8. See Fishkin, *Justice, Equal Opportunity, and the Family*, pp. 51–67 and *passim*.

9. Ibid., pp. 10, 193.

10. Alternatively, equalization could be interpreted as minimizing the variance among educational attainments. The unattractiveness of this ideal is apparent when one imagines a policy that actively attempts to suppress intellectual achievement among some students to decrease the variance.

11. If we assume more than two levels of talent, the rule is to raise the educational accomplishment of the least talented to the level of the next least, and so on. On this assumption, even the average child might be deprived of any educational resources. Compare Jencks et al., *Inequality: A Reassessment of the Effect of Family and Schooling in America* (New York: Basic Book, 1972), p. 109.

12. Compare Onora A. O'Neill, "Opportunities, Equalities and Education," *Theory and Decision*, vol. 7 (1976): 290–1. O'Neill argues that our choice between equality of educational opportunity and equality of educational outcome depends on whether we view people as "socially produced" or as "autonomous choosers." My argument suggests that we can criticize the goal of equalizing educational outcomes quite independently of what O'Neill calls our "fundamental conceptions of the human condition."

13. See Robert Nozick's argument that "the foundations underlying desert needn't themselves be deserved, *all the way down*" (*Anarchy, State and Utopia* (New York: Basic Books, 1974), pp. 224–7). See also Sandel, *Liberalism and the Limits of Justice*, pp. 82–95. The concept of desert is complicated and the philosophical discussions correspondingly inconclusive. For the most complete conceptual analysis, see Joel Feinberg, *Doing and Deserving* (Princeton, NJ: Princeton University Press, 1970). See also Amy Gutmann, *Liberal Equality* (Cambridge: Cambridge University Press, 1980), pp. 160–7; and Alan Zaitchik, "On Deserving to Deserve," *Philosophy and Public Affairs*, vol. 6 (Summer 1977): 370–88.

14. For two different defenses of this conclusion, see Walzer, "Philosophy and Democracy," *Political Theory* 9:3 (August 1981), pp. 379–99; and Amy Gutmann, "How Liberal is Democracy," in Douglas MacLean and Claudia Mills (eds.), *Liberalism Reconsidered* (Totowa, NJ: Rowman and Allanheld, 1983), pp. 25–50.

15. Democratic decisions in the discretionary realm – allocating resources above the educational threshold – may indirectly define the threshold. What constitutes an adequate education for less advantaged children may be relative to the educational attainment of more advantaged children. This conception of an educational threshold can accommodate the phenomenon of relative deprivation.

16. 1875 Amendment to Article IV, sec. 7, para. 6 of the New Jersey Constitution of 1844: "The legislature shall provide for the maintenance and support of a thorough and efficient system of free public schools for the instruction of an children in this state between the ages of five and eighteen years."

17. Compare William Nelson "Equal Opportunity," *Social Theory and Practice*, vol. 10, no. 2 (Summer 1984): 157–84. Nelson defines equal opportunity on the basis of certain objective conditions of a good life that apply to any society independently of its social understandings (p. 168). Nelson's interpretation of equal opportunity is otherwise similar to mine, although he defends and develops it in a different way.

# 27

# Whom Must We Treat Equally for Educational Opportunity to be Equal?

## Christopher Jencks

Americans never argue about whether educational opportunity should be equal. Egalitarians say equal opportunity is not enough. Pragmatists say it is unattainable. But no significant group defends unequal opportunity, either in education or elsewhere.

Instead of arguing about the desirability of equal educational opportunity, we argue about its meaning. We all assume that equal opportunity is compatible with our vision of a good society. Since we disagree about what such a society should be like, we usually disagree about the meaning of equal educational opportunity as well.

Everyone's conception of equal educational opportunity requires that educational institutions "treat equals equally." But we have dramatically different views about *whom* educational institutions should treat equally and whom they can legitimately treat unequally. Indeed, the enduring popularity of equal educational opportunity probably derives from the fact that we can all define it in different ways without realizing how profound our differences really are.

This paper discusses five common ways of thinking about equal educational opportunity, each of which draws on a different tradition and each of which has different practical consequences.[1] To illustrate both the differences among these five conceptions of equal opportunity and also the different ways in which each of them can be interpreted, I will focus on a single concrete example: a third-grade reading class in a small town, taught by a teacher whom I will call Ms. Higgins. Like all of us, Ms. Higgins believes in equal opportunity. Her problem – and ours – is what her belief in equal opportunity implies about the distribution of the main educational resources at her disposal, namely her time and attention.

Two features of this example deserve comment. First, the unit of analysis is small – as small as I could make it. I believe, but will not try to prove, that all the *principled* claims about how Ms. Higgins ought to allocate her time among her pupils recur in essentially the same form when we argue about how school principals, boards of education, or legislatures ought to allocate scarce resources. I recognize, however, that the *practical* arguments for various possible distributions of Ms. Higgins's time are often quite different from those that come into play when a board of education or a legislature is allocating resources.

The second distinctive feature of my "case study" is that it focuses on *young* students. As students get

Previously published in *Ethics* 98 (April 1988), pp. 518–33. Reprinted by permission of the University of Chicago Press.

older, the case for paternalism grows weaker. As a result, both the principled and the practical arguments for certain courses of action grow weaker too. I focus on young children because I believe that their youth dramatizes certain ambiguities in our thinking about equal opportunity, but it may obscure others.

## Ms. Higgins's Choices

Before Ms. Higgins enters the classroom, she is likely to imagine that her commitment to equal opportunity implies that she should give every pupil equal time and attention. Once she starts teaching, however, she is likely to discover a number of principled reasons for deviating from this simple formula. Ms. Higgins's ruminations will, I think, eventually suggest at least five possibilities, to which I propose to attach the following labels:

1. *Democratic equality.* Democratic equality requires Ms. Higgins to give everyone equal time and attention, regardless of how well they read, how hard they try, how deprived they have been in the past, what they want, or how much they or others will benefit.

2. *Moralistic justice.* Moralistic justice requires Ms. Higgins to reward virtue and punish vice. In the classroom, virtue involves effort, and moralistic justice means rewarding those who make the most effort to learn whatever Ms. Higgins is trying to teach.

3. *Weak humane justice.* Since some students have gotten less than their proportionate share of advantages in the past, humane justice requires Ms. Higgins to compensate those students by giving them more than their proportionate share of her attention while they are in her classroom. But the "weak" variant of humane justice only requires Ms. Higgins to compensate those who have been shortchanged at home or in their earlier schooling, not those who have been shortchanged genetically.

4. *Strong humane justice.* This variant of humane justice requires Ms. Higgins to compensate those who have been shortchanged in *any* way in the past, including genetically. In practice, this means giving the most attention to the worst readers, regardless of the reasons for their illiteracy.

5. *Utilitarianism.* Most utilitarians assume that the best way to get individuals to do what we want is to make every activity, including education, a race

for unequal rewards. Equal opportunity means that such races must be open to all, run on a level field, and judged solely on the basis of performance. Thus, insofar as Ms. Higgins's attention is a prize, it should go to the best readers.

Equal opportunity can therefore imply either a meritocratic distribution of resources, a compensatory distribution of resources, or an equal distribution of resources. A meritocratic conception of equal opportunity can, in turn, favor either those who try hard or those who achieve a lot, while a compensatory conception of equal opportunity can favor either those who have suffered from some sort of handicap in the past or those whose current achievement is below average.

## Democratic Equality

If Ms. Higgins were a student teacher who had never thought carefully about teaching, and if we were to ask her what she thought equal opportunity implied about how she should distribute her time, she would probably answer that a commitment to equal opportunity meant giving all children equal time and attention. I refer to this view as "democratic" equality not because democracy has traditionally required it but because Americans habitually invoke the fact that they live in a democracy to justify it. We will say, for example, that our Constitution guarantees everyone "equal protection of the laws" and that this implies equal treatment. The idea of treating everyone in the same way, regardless of extenuating circumstances, certainly has a democratic ring to it.

Yet neither the Constitution of the United States nor democratic tradition requires either a board of education or Ms. Higgins to treat everyone in exactly the same way. School boards, for example, have never interpreted the democratic tradition as requiring them to spend equal sums on all pupils. They have set up programs of varying cost, especially at the secondary level, and have assumed that if they made these programs available on the basis of merit, past or current disadvantages, demand, or expected benefits, this was compatible with both equal opportunity and the equal protection clause of the Constitution.

As Ms. Higgins gains experience in the classroom she too is likely to feel dissatisfied with the idea that she must distribute her time in mathematically equal dollops to all children. Her first qualms about equal treatment are likely to arise when some of her pupils show more interest than others, and she finds herself responding to their interest with extra attention. This observation will lead her to think more seriously about moralistic justice.

## The Moralistic Theory of Justice

Moralistic theories of justice assert that we should all try to reward virtue and punish vice. When students make an effort to do what Ms. Higgins asks of them, moralistic justice allows her to respond not only with praise but with extra attention as well. When students make no effort to do what she asks of them, moralistic justice tells her she need not "waste her time" on them. While she might not put it this way, moralistic justice encourages her to think of her classroom as a moral community, held together by an unwritten contract which states that "I'll do my best if you'll do yours." Those who respect the contract reap its benefits. Those who do not respect it are subject to internal exile – to expulsion if they behave badly enough.

In principle, a moralistic view of the classroom should focus on intentions. This means that it should define virtue in terms of effort, not achievement. In practice, large institutions can seldom observe effort directly. All they can usually observe is actual achievement, which depends not only on current effort but also on ability and prior knowledge. Because large institutions habitually reward achievement rather than effort, Ms. Higgins may be tempted to do the same. But rewarding effortless achievement is not compatible with moralistic justice. Rather, it is a by-product of utilitarianism.

Moralistic justice is easy to reconcile with equal opportunity. One simply says that all students have an equal opportunity to make an effort and that all who make equal effort get equal treatment.

But moralistic justice is not likely to satisfy Ms. Higgins for long, because it treats third graders' motivation as fixed. If Ms. Higgins is at all perceptive, she will begin to ask why some children work harder than others and what she can do about this. Sooner or later such questions will force her to think about what I have called humane justice.

## Humane Theories of Justice

Instead of focusing on what we deserve because of our virtues and vices, "humane" theories of justice focus on what we deserve simply because we are members of the human species. Since we are all equally human, our claims as members of the species are all equal. Such claims, based on the mere fact of being human, are commonly labeled "rights." Since there is no general agreement about the nature of these rights, there are many versions of human justice. For convenience, I will try to array them on a spectrum running from strong to weak.

In its strongest variant, humane justice asserts that all individuals have an equal claim on all of society's resources, regardless of their virtues or vices. This version of humane justice demands equal outcomes rather than equal opportunity, however, so it need not concern us here.

What I will call here the strong variant of humane justice holds that society can make an adult's claim to resources conditional on various forms of socially useful behavior, but that society must offer all children an equal chance of meeting whatever requirements it sets. If some students need special help to develop the skills or character traits society values, society must give them whatever help they need. If, for example, some children need unusually good schooling to compensate for an unusually unfavorable home environment or unusual physical handicaps, society must make sure they get it.[2]

While advocates of this position do not insist explicitly on equal outcomes, it is hard to see how they can settle for less in the educational arena. If Johnny is a worse reader than Mary, Johnny must have had fewer advantages than Mary. Johnny's disadvantages may have been genetic, social, or educational, but whatever their origin strong humane justice demands that Ms. Higgins compensate Johnny by giving him extra attention (or by sending him to a remedial reading teacher who may give him extra attention in a less obtrusive way).

What I will call the weak variant of human justice has less stringent requirements. It holds only that all students have an equal lifetime claim on *educational* resources. Students have a claim to additional educational resources if they are currently disadvantaged because of some deficiency in their previous education but not if they are disadvantaged for non-educational reasons. If a student has had unusually bad schooling prior to entering Ms. Higgins's classroom, for example, she has an obligation to provide the student with extra help. If a student has incompetent parents, the case is more controversial, but since most advocates of humane justice see the home at least in part as an educational environment, most feel that Ms. Higgins owes children extra help if their parents are unable to do as much for them as a good parent should.

If students lack ability for genetic reasons, however, weak human justice does not require Ms. Higgins to give them extra help. In effect, the weak interpretation defines equal educational opportunity as "equal opportunity for the genetically equal and unequal opportunity for the genetically unequal." The aim of such an educational system would be to create a society in which success depended entirely on "native ability," just as it did in Michael Young's meritocracy.[3]

The logic behind the weak variant of humane justice seems to be that society is responsible for the environment in which children are raised but not for the genes they inherit. This view has always baffled me. I can understand the argument that society is not responsible either for children's genes or for their upbringing. I have never seen a coherent defense of the proposition that society is responsible for one but not the other.

The most common argument for compensating children who have been raised in unfavorable home environments is that these environments are a by-product of our collective commitment to unequal socioeconomic rewards for adults. Having committed ourselves to an economic system that produces a high level of inequality among adults, we acquire an obligation to neutralize the effects of such inequality on children. Since we do not appear to have a comparable commitment to perpetuating genetic inequality among adults, we have no comparable obligation to neutralize the effects of genetic inequality on children.

But if it can be said that we have "chosen" a high level of socioeconomic inequality among parents and have thus acquired a special obligation to its victims, can it not equally well be said that we have "chosen" not to limit the fertility of the genetically disadvantaged? Most people assume that restricting the right to have children is an unacceptable limit on adult liberty. As a result, many children are born into awful environments and many are born with unfavorable genes. Such a policy appears to create some societal obligation to the children on whom it imposes *either* genetic *or* environmental costs.

I suspect, however, that all these arguments are beside the point. The reason most of us want to limit society's responsibility for the genetically

disadvantaged is prudential, not ethical. Most of us assume that it is harder to offset the effects of genetic disadvantages than environmental disadvantages. Because our genes are essentially immutable, we assume that their consequences are immutable too. Because the environment is mutable, we assume its effects are equally mutable. But there is no necessary relationship between the mutability of causes and the mutability of their effects. Two examples should suffice to dramatize this point.

First, consider two children who are deaf, one because of an early childhood disease, the other because of a genetic defect. The fact that one child's deafness was a product of heredity while the other child's deafness was environmental in origin tells us nothing about the physical character of the problem or the likelihood that it has a medical remedy. If no remedy is available, both children face the same educational problems. Whether they will develop the skills and character traits required for a "normal" life depends on their parents, their schooling, and their other characteristics, not on the initial cause of their deafness. The cost of educating them also depends on these factors, not on the origin of their disorder.

Second, consider an eager but slow-witted girl who has great difficulty mastering reading. Assume her difficulty is genetic in origin and manifests itself in a generalized inability to master skills that require her to see analogies or remember large amounts of miscellaneous information for long periods. Compare her to another girl who also has great difficulty reading because she comes from a disorganized and abusive home, is always angry at her teachers and fellow students, and cannot concentrate on any task long enough to learn much. If we ask which of these children will benefit most from a minute of Ms. Higgins's time, the answer is far from obvious. If we ask experienced teachers, some will say they think it would be easier to teach the "slow" child, while others will say that they think it would be easier to teach the "disturbed" child. Such disagreement would probably persist if we stipulated that the slow child had been brought up in the wrong way, while the disturbed child had an inherited metabolic disorder.

For all these reasons the moral and empirical foundations of weak humane justice seem to me very shaky. Nonetheless, experience suggests that Ms. Higgins is more likely to endorse the weak interpretation of humane justice than the strong interpretation.

Another weak variant of humane justice, which I will call "moralistic humane justice," requires Ms. Higgins to pursue equal educational outcomes only when students make equal effort to do what she asks of them. Those who advocate this form of humane justice believe that society must provide all students with equal educational resources, including extra school resources to compensate for deficiencies in their home environments and perhaps even their genes, but not that society is responsible for an individual's values or character. They therefore reject the notion that Ms. Higgins must compensate children for the consequences of having the wrong values. If a parent fails to provide a child with books or gives the child very limited exposure to unusual words at home, Ms. Higgins has an obligation to provide compensatory help at school. But if a parent teaches a child that mastering unusual words is a waste of time, Ms. Higgins has no obligation to alter the child's values, even if these values will be socially and economically costly to the child in the long run.

There does not seem to be any principled reason why we should hold either Ms. Higgins or society as a whole responsible for giving all children equal educational resources but not for making sure that they learn to use these resources in ways that will promote their long-term self-interest. The argument for this view is once again strictly pragmatic. It asserts, correctly, that the only way to be sure that all children value learning equally is to make child rearing a collective rather than an individual responsibility, as the kibbutz does. This being politically unacceptable, making all children value learning equally is impractical. Equalizing access to educational resources requires less drastic institutional changes and is therefore more practical.

The argument that society is responsible for children's values also creates a "moral hazard" for the children. If children are not responsible for the consequences of their own choices, they have no incentive to make choices that are disagreeable in the short run but beneficial in the long run. If, for example, Ms. Higgins decides not to hold her working-class pupils personally responsible when they neglect their work, on the grounds that they come from homes where studying is not encouraged, their main incentive to study disappears.

While it is impossible to ensure that all children value learning equally, the way in which we organize schools can surely *reduce* the gap between students whose parents have taught them to value learning and students whose parents have not. Any theory that exonerates Ms. Higgins from all responsibility on this score is morally suspect, since it provides an excuse for doing nothing in circumstances where a lot can and should be done.

Unfortunately, it is philosophically difficult to find a middle ground between holding society completely responsible for children's values and holding children themselves completely responsible for their values. Most advocates of humane justice therefore choose to hold society responsible, at least in their public pronouncements and political arguments. But if society as a whole is responsible for an individual's preferences and values, the boundary between the individual and the larger society no longer has the moral significance that Europeans and Americans have traditionally assigned it. Indeed, the boundary almost disappears, and the notion that individuals are the proper units for moral accounting breaks down.

The assumption that society as a whole is responsible for children's values, and hence for their level of effort, inevitably changes the meaning of equal opportunity. Instead of asserting that opportunities are equal when the objective costs and benefits of various choices are equal in the eye of the average outside observer, this stance requires Ms. Higgins to take account of *all* the factors that influence an individual's choices, including subjective costs and benefits. If Johnny's parents do not praise him for reading as often as Mary's parents praise her, Johnny does not get the same subjective benefits from reading. Other things equal, Johnny will therefore make less effort to read. Most advocates of humane justice feel that under these circumstances Johnny has less opportunity to master reading than Mary has, even if he has the same books on his shelves at home and the same teacher at school.

This is not, of course, the way we usually use the term 'opportunity' in everyday language. If Johnny and Mary have the same access to books and are taught in the same way, we ordinarily say that they have the same opportunity to learn. If Mary's parents encourage her to take advantage of this opportunity, while Johnny's do not, we usually say that Mary has more incentive or motivation to learn, not that she has more opportunity to do so. But in the past twenty years many have argued that this traditional linguistic distinction is sociologically and ethically meaningless and that we should read equal opportunity more broadly.

## Humane Justice and Socioeconomic Inequality

American liberals and radicals have traditionally defined equal opportunity as requiring that children from different socioeconomic backgrounds have the same probability of learning to read competently, attending good colleges, getting good jobs, and enjoying a good life. If these probabilities vary, opportunity is unequal. This is almost always a matter of definition. No evidence regarding the reasons for the difference is ordinarily required.

Most liberals and radicals also seem to assume that children from different socioeconomic backgrounds are genetically indistinguishable. This assumption persists despite the fact that there are powerful logical and empirical arguments against it. We know, for example, that genes have some influence on academic achievement.[4] We also know that academic achievement has some effect on adults' socioeconomic position, independent of everything else we have been able to measure.[5] Logic therefore suggests that a child's genes must have some influence on his or her adult socioeconomic position. If that is so, adults in different socioeconomic positions must differ genetically. It follows that their children must also differ genetically. These differences may not be large, and they may not explain much of the achievement gap between children from different backgrounds, but they must exist.[6]

Nonetheless, few liberals or radicals will even entertain the possibility that genes contribute to achievement differences between socioeconomic groups. This position appears to be based on political expedience: people are more likely to believe that society should try to help the environmentally disadvantaged than the genetically disadvantaged. Thus even if you believe in your heart that poor children labor under genetic as well as environmental handicaps, you are likely to think it expedient to deemphasize this possibility when you are campaigning for programs to help such children.

Some advocates of humane justice also deny that middle-class children are unusually eager to master cognitive skills. Those who take this position typically insist that working-class children enter school eager to learn and are then "turned off" by large classes, authoritarian teachers, low expectations, and a curriculum that assumes knowledge or experience they do not have. There is certainly some truth in all this. Indeed, if we were to measure effort simply by looking at the number of minutes children spent doing schoolwork, we might not find much difference between middle-class and working-class children in the early grades. But effort also includes the games children choose to play (Scrabble versus basketball), the things they think about at breakfast (childish puns versus fast cars), and a multitude of other activities that contribute in subtle ways to cognitive development. If we define effort in this comprehensive way, the claim that middle-class children value cognitive skills more than working-class children is almost surely correct, though I know no hard evidence supporting it.

If children from different socioeconomic backgrounds are to have equal chances of doing well in school, Ms. Higgins must find ways to offset the effects of whatever genetic and motivational differences now distinguish them. If poor children labor under genetic disadvantages, she must give them extra attention. If their parents value cognitive skills less than middle-class parents, Ms. Higgins must reward poor children more than middle-class children who learn the same amount. Only in this way can she make the subjective value of learning equal for working-class and middle-class children. Some socialist societies have tried to achieve something like this by making bourgeois origins an explicit obstacle to advancement. Such policies hardly conform to American notions of equal opportunity, however.

These practical difficulties do not call into question the fundamental moral premise of humane justice, namely that educational resources should go disproportionately to the disadvantaged. The practical difficulties do, however, suggest that if equal opportunity means that children raised in different families must have equal probabilities of success, we can never fully achieve it. Since most of us think of rights as goals that *can* be achieved, we must either reject the argument that equal opportunity is a right, substituting the notion that it is an ideal, or else we must reject the conventional humane definition of equal opportunity.

If advocates of humane justice concede that equal probabilities of success are unattainable, they must face another difficulty. Their theory requires Ms. Higgins to spend more time with poor readers than with good readers. But *how much* more time? The logic of a deprivation-based theory of justice seems to imply that Ms. Higgins should devote *all* her time and attention to the worst reader in her class. If the worst reader moves ahead of the next worst, she shifts her attention to the next worst. She keeps doing this until everyone reads equally well. But if the worst reader *never* catches up, what principle (other than utilitarianism) can she use to justify not devoting her life to him?

## Moralistic versus Humane Justice

If a society can take concerted action to reward virtue and punish vice, it can usually enforce a high degree of conformity to its norms, whatever these may be. Moralistic justice has great appeal in such societies because it works. Such societies seldom have to carry out their threats.

In societies like our own, which have great difficulty taking concerted action against those who violate rules, violations are far more common. Paradoxically, as the likelihood that violations will be punished declines, the absolute amount of misery that society inflicts on those who violate its rules may well increase. When punishment is certain, violations are rare, so punishment is also rare. When punishment is less certain, violations become common, and punishment, while less likely in any individual case, may well be both more common and more severe in the society as a whole.

This paradoxical development often leads compassionate observers to discover reasons for rejecting moralistic justice. They are likely to argue that moralistic justice has "failed," without asking what would happen if we abandoned it altogether. Compassionate observers are also likely to argue that those who reject society's rules are simply reacting to the fact that society rejects them. Humane justice has considerable appeal in such societies, especially to the virtuous, who tend to assume that everyone would be as virtuous as they if everyone had the same advantages.

The tension between moralistic and humane justice is, of course, related to the old problem of free will versus determinism. The moralistic theory of justice assumes that children have free will. Parents should provide appropriate incentives for children to make the right choices, but if a child then makes a wrong choice, the child rather than the parent is expected to suffer for the mistake. The humane theory of justice assumes that the environments in which children find themselves determine their choices. As a result, those who create the environment are ultimately responsible for children's choices and are morally obligated to absorb the costs of foolish choices.

Both theories of justice are compatible with a "fair contest" theory of equal opportunity, but they assign Ms. Higgins different roles in this contest. Moralistic justice is a system for awarding prizes. It tells Ms. Higgins to act as a judge, giving different students what they deserve on the basis of their past academic effort. Humane justice focuses on preparing runners for the next contest. It tells Ms. Higgins to act as a coach, whose job is to ensure that all competitors get enough training.

Every moment in our lives is both an ending and a beginning. When we think of the moment as an ending, we apply the standards of moralistic justice. When we think of it as a beginning we apply the standards of humane justice. When we recognize that the moment is both, we find ourselves in a quandary. For this reason neither Ms. Higgins nor American society as a whole is likely to resolve the conflict between the two visions of equal opportunity that flow from these two theories of justice.

## Utilitarianism

Utilitarian theories of resource allocation try to maximize the average level of well-being in a society rather than trying to ensure just treatment of individuals. Maximizing the well-being of a population involves two distinct problems: (1) motivating individuals to do their best to promote the general welfare and (2) allocating scarce investment resources among competing claimants. Solving each problem requires resources. Utilitarians must therefore devise some formula for dividing resources between these two activities. In economics, this is usually seen as a problem of dividing output between consumption and investment. Claims on consumption goods are used as incentives for productive activity. Claims on investment capital are allocated on the basis of expected returns.

For Ms. Higgins, the problem is to what extent she should treat her time and attention as a reward for past performance and to what extent she should take student motivation as given and allocate her time on the basis of who will benefit most from it. Settling this question is critical because the "incentive model" and the "investment model" will lead Ms. Higgins to allocate her time very differently.

If Ms. Higgins wants her students to read well, for example, most utilitarians will tell her that she should reward her best readers with prizes of various kinds. These prizes may be high letter grades, gold stars, hugs, or attention, depending on what is most effective. But since attention is usually worth more to a third grader than grades, gold stars, or even hugs, utilitarian logic suggests that Ms. Higgins may do better if she uses attention as a prize than if she uses other things. This would mean giving more attention to her best readers. In contrast, when Ms. Higgins thinks of her time as an investment good and tries to distribute it among her students in such a way as to maximize their long-term contribution to the general welfare (including their own), she may well conclude that she should spend most of her time with her worst readers. Like the choice between moralistic and humane justice, Ms. Higgins's choice between an incentive strategy and an investment strategy depends on whether she views a given moment as an ending or as a beginning.

Viewing attention as a prize that motivates students leads naturally to the idea of equal opportunity. Utilitarians espouse equal opportunity because it sets rules for the distribution of prizes that appear likely to ensure maximum effort on the part of contestants. Three rules appear crucial. First, utilitarian equal opportunity requires that the competition be open to all. No one can be excluded for "irrelevant" reasons, such as race, sex, or family background. Second, utilitarian equal opportunity requires that prizes be distributed solely on the basis of performance, not on the basis of "irrelevant" criteria. Third, and most problematic, the utilitarian conception of equal opportunity requires that the rules of the contest be set so that as many people as possible have a reasonable chance of winning. This is desirable because it is the best way to maximize effort.

This utilitarian conception of a "fair contest" is akin to moralistic justice in that it focuses on motivating students to do their best and views Ms. Higgins's attention as a reward for past performance. But the utilitarian vision of equal opportunity differs from moralistic justice in that it rewards actual performance rather than effort. This difference is a matter of expedience rather than principle, however. If effort were easy to measure, utilitarians might well reward it instead.

The utilitarian conception of resources as an investment good is akin to humane justice in that it either ignores the problem of motivation or treats motivation as fixed. Utilitarian investment theories are also similar to what I have called strong humane justice in that both are preoccupied with producing a particular distribution of reading skills. But a utilitarian calculus focuses on maximizing the mean level of welfare whereas strong humane justice focuses on minimizing variation around the mean.

The utilitarian approach to investment also differs from humane justice in that it does not ordinarily invoke the ideal of equal opportunity. Nonetheless, it has important implications for equal opportunity, since it is the principle competing theory of resource allocation.

Investment-oriented utilitarianism requires Ms. Higgins to distribute her time so as to maximize society's long-term well-being. In order to do this she needs two kinds of information. First, she must know how much different sorts of students' reading skills will improve if the students get an extra minute of her time. Second, she must know how much raising students' reading skills will enhance their contribution to the general welfare. Each of these problems deserves brief discussion.

If Ms. Higgins simply asks herself whether her time will be of more value to good or bad readers, or to highly motivated or apathetic ones, she will be able to make a plausible a priori case for almost any conceivable answer. Like most utilitarian quandaries, this one demands empirical research. Unfortunately, if Ms. Higgins consults the research literature on this question, she will not find a clear-cut answer.

If Ms. Higgins asks how raising different kinds of students' reading scores will contribute to the general welfare, she will again be able to make a plausible case for almost any conceivable answer. If she looks at the research literature she will find that nobody has even asked the question, much less answered it convincingly. If she confines herself to adults' reports of their own happiness and has a computer handy, she will be able to discover that happiness increases as vocabulary scores increase and that this relationship is much stronger in the bottom half of the test score distribution than in the top half.[7] Thus, if she assumes that what is good for her students is good for the country, she will probably conclude that it is more useful to help move her worst readers up to the middle of the distribution than to move middling readers to the top.

But if Ms. Higgins is a good utilitarian she must ask herself not only what will make her own students happiest but also what will contribute most to the happiness of the species. If she asks this question, she may conclude that human happiness depends primarily on the way society is organized politically, socially, and technically and that her best hope of contributing to progress in these areas is to cultivate the talents of one or two outstanding students every year.

Because Ms. Higgins has no way of knowing with confidence how much her attention will boost any particular student's reading skills, much less how it will affect the student's long-term well-being or that of others in the society, the de facto effect of treating her attention as an investment good is to force her to make decisions whose consequences she cannot predict. This can have a variety of possible consequences.

1. Ms. Higgins may succumb to the claims of those who favor moralistic or humane justice, since such people almost always insist that their version of justice is also socially efficient. Those who are eager to reward effort and punish indolence, for example, will tell her that this is not only just but also the best way to maximize her students' long-run well-being. If she finds moralistic justice attractive on ethical grounds she may well accept such empirical claims without demanding hard evidence. Conversely, if she is eager to help students who have been shortchanged in the past, she will find plenty of writers who claim these students will benefit most from her attention, and she may well believe their claims.

2. Ms. Higgins may despair of calculating the long-run benefits of distributing her attention in different ways and may decide to focus exclusively on short-term costs. If she takes this view she is likely to conclude that the most efficient distribution of her attention is the one that leaves her with the most attention to distribute. If she finds working with slow learners tiring or frustrating, she will then conclude that the most efficient way to spend her time is with the gifted. If she finds working with slow learners raises her spirits, she will conclude that this is efficient.

3. Since Ms. Higgins does not know what will maximize social welfare in the long run, she may try to minimize the likely cost to society of her mistakes. Under plausible assumptions this will lead her to devote equal time and attention to everyone.[8]

## Equal Opportunity and the Burden of Proof

Given all the uncertainties that arise when Ms. Higgins tries to redefine equal opportunity so as to justify an unequal distribution of her attention, she may well begin to wonder whether any of the arguments for unequal treatment is really compelling. If her principal calls her on the carpet for favoring the talented, the diligent, the poor, or the incompetent, can she really defend herself?

The principles we use to distribute things vary with the nature of the things we are distributing. We try to distribute government jobs on the basis of virtue, public housing on the basis of disadvantages, and medical care on the basis of expected benefits. If the relative weight of these distributional principles depends on what we are distributing, none can claim to be universal. Indeed, in some cases they may all be irrelevant. Ms. Higgins must therefore ask whether any of these principles really applies to her classroom. Her arguments for ignoring all three principles would presumably go something like this:

*Virtue.* Virtue must be rewarded and vice punished in *some* way, but Ms. Higgins need not use her time and attention for this purpose. If judicious use of praise, blame, and grades ensures that most students do their best, Ms. Higgins can make her time equally available to everyone if she wishes.

*Disadvantages.* While Ms. Higgins can easily see that some of her students read better than others, she cannot usually tell whether these differences derive from differences in prior schooling, home advantages, genes, or motivation. If she rewards poor motivation with extra attention, she will undermine the implied moral contract between students and teachers, reducing students' future effort.

*Benefits.* While Ms. Higgins may want to take account of potential benefits when distributing her time, she may well conclude that in practice she has no way of knowing who benefits most from her time.

In the absence of any compelling argument for favoring one group over another, Ms. Higgins may conclude that her commitment to equal opportunity implies equal treatment for all. At a minimum, her commitment to equal opportunity requires her to give reasons for treating her students unequally. As we have seen, there is no general agreement about when Ms. Higgins can legitimately treat children unequally. In practice, therefore, demanding general acceptance of her reasons for distributing her time and attention unequally would force her to distribute them equally.

Ms. Higgins's reflections may, therefore, lead her full circle, back to what I initially called democratic equality. But in this incarnation, equal treatment no longer derives directly from democratic rhetoric. Instead, it derives from the fact that democracies typically put the burden of proof on those who favor unequal treatment, and in practice this burden is so heavy that the egalitarian "null hypothesis" can always carry the day.

## The Politics of Ambiguity

If equal opportunity can mean distributing resources either equally or unequally, if it can be compatible with inequalities that favor either the initially advantaged or the initially disadvantaged, and if the relative weight of these principles can vary from one situation to the next, it is small wonder that most Americans support the idea. A skeptic might wonder, however, whether an idea that can embrace so much means anything at all.

Because the ideal of equal opportunity seems to forbid behavior we want to minimize while blurring disagreement about what we want to maximize, it will undoubtedly continue to command broad support. It is an ideal consistent with almost every vision of a good society. For liberal lawyers intent on expanding the domain of rights, equal opportunity implies that citizens have a "right" to lots of things they want but cannot afford, ranging from better schools to wheelchair ramps in public places. For progressive social reformers who want to minimize misery, equal opportunity implies that we need new social programs to help those who labor under one or another kind of disadvantage. For conservative businessmen, equal opportunity implies that the prizes for unusual success should not be tampered with in a misguided effort to achieve equal results. For politicians of all persuasions equal opportunity is therefore a universal solvent, compatible with the dreams of almost every voter in a conflict-ridden constituency. This makes equal opportunity one of the few ideals a politician can safely invoke on all occasions.

Without common ideals of this sort, societies disintegrate. With them, conflict becomes a bit more muted. But the constant reiteration of such rhetoric also numbs the senses and rots the mind. This may be a price we have to pay for gluing together a complex society, but if so there is something to be said for smaller, more politically homogeneous societies, where the terms of discourse may not have to be quite so elastic. That is one reason we develop scholarly disciplines. It may also be one reason why scholars tend to prefer the political discourse of Sweden or Switzerland to that of America.

### Notes

1. Because this paper focuses on popular understanding of equal opportunity, I have not tried to tie my discussion to scholarly papers on the subject. Readers familiar with this literature will, however, find that it echoes many of the themes I discuss.

2. Advocates of humane justice often say they favor distributing resources on the basis of need, but the meaning of "need" is ambiguous in this context. When we say that Johnny needs a minute of Ms. Higgins's time more than Mary does, we can mean either that Johnny is a worse reader, and therefore "needs" to improve more, or that Johnny will *actually* improve more if he gets the time. The first use of "need" is analogous to its use in a phrase like "the 100 neediest cases." The second use is analogous to that in the statement "Adults need to eat more than children." Distributing resources on the basis of "need" can thus imply either humane justice or utilitarianism, depending on whether you equate need with prior deprivation or subsequent benefits. Because of this

ambiguity I will focus directly on disadvantages and benefits rather than on need.

3. Michael Young, *The Rise of the Meritocracy* (London: Thames & Hudson, 1958).

4. My colleagues and I summarized this evidence in Christopher Jencks et al., *Inequality* (New York: Basic Books, 1972). Subsequent work suggests that genes may have slightly more effect on test scores than *Inequality* found, but the differences are quite minor.

5. See, e.g., James Crouse, "The Effects of Test Scores," in Christopher Jencks et al., *Who Gets Ahead?* (New York: Basic Books, 1979).

6. For a review of empirical evidence on this point up to 1972, see Christopher Jencks et al., *Inequality*. For more recent evidence see Sandra Scarr and Richard Weinberg, "The Influence of 'Family Background' on Intellectual Attainment," *American Sociological Review* 43 (1978): 674–92.

7. The General Social Survey (GSS) is an annual survey of about 1500 adults conducted by the National

Opinion Research Center. In 1974, 1976, 1978, 1982, and 1984 it included a ten-item vocabulary test. It also included the following question: "Taken all together, how would you say things are these days – would you say that you are very happy, pretty happy, or not too happy?" The proportion who said they were "not too happy" averaged 26 percent among those with scores of 2 or 3, 14 percent among those with scores of 4 or 5, 10 percent among those with scores of 6 or 7,

8 percent among those with scores of 8 or 9, and 9 percent among those with scores of 10. For details on this survey, see James A. Davis and Tom W. Smith, *General Social Surveys, 1972–1984: Cumulative Codebook* (Storrs, CT: Roper Center, 1984).

8. If one error of two units costs more than two errors of one unit, and if nothing is known about the welfare function, equal treatment will maximize the expected value of the outcomes.

# Diversity and Nondiscrimination

# 28

# Culture, Subculture, Multiculturalism: Educational Options

## K. Anthony Appiah

[ . . . ]

### Question 1 Answered: The United States is Not a Society Because there is No Common Culture

What I have called the common culture is what a social group has socially in common: it is what people teach their children in order to make them members of their social group. By definition, a common culture is shared; it is the social bottom line. It includes language and table manners, religious ideas, moral values, theories of the workings of the natural and social worlds.[1] To have a common culture, to repeat the crucial point, is to have a common language and a common vocabulary of values and theories, even if some individuals or sub-groups are skeptical of the theories and reject the values. (It does not, thus, require shared commitment to the central values and theories of the natural and social world.)[2]

I associate cultures with social groups, not with nations, because I want to insist again that a group of persons living together in a common state, under common authorities, need not have a common culture. There is no single shared body of ideas and practices in India, or, to take another example, in most contemporary African states.

Thus, many, but by no means all, Ghanaians know (some) English. There is no language known to all (or even most) of us. There are Moslems and Christians and practitioners of the traditional religions of many ethnic groups. There are matrilineal and patrilineal conceptions of family; there are traditions of divine kingship and less hierarchical notions of politics. The modern constitutional order – the Presidency, the parliament, the courts – is not well understood by many and unknown to quite a few.[3]

Now I think it is fair to say that there is not now and there has never been a common culture in the United States, either. The reason is simple: the United States has always been multilingual, and has always had minorities who did not speak or understand English. It has always had a plurality of religious traditions; beginning with Native American religions and Puritans and Catholics and including

Previously published in Robert K. Fullinwider (ed.), *Public Education in a Multicultural Society* (Cambridge: Cambridge University Press, 1996), pp. 71–89. © 1996 Cambridge University Press. Reprinted by permission of the publisher and author.

now many varieties of Judaism, Islam, Buddhism, Jainism, Taoism, Bahai . . . and so on. And many of these religious traditions have been quite unknown to each other. More than this, Americans have also always differed significantly even among those who do speak English, from North to South and East to West, and from country to city, in customs of greeting, notions of civility, and a whole host of other ways.

To say this is not to deny that for significant parts of American history there has been a good deal of mutual knowledge across regional, religious, ethnic, and even linguistic barriers. My point is that the notion that what has held the United States together historically over its great geographical range is a common culture, like the common culture of a traditional society, is not sociologically plausible.

## National Culture versus National Common Culture

The notion that there is no American national culture will come as a surprise to many: observations about "American culture," taken as a whole, are common. It is, for example, held to be individualist, litigious, racially obsessed. I think each of these claims is actually true, because what I mean when I say there is no common culture of the United States is not what is denied by someone who says that there is an American culture.

Such a person is describing large-scale tendencies within American life that are not necessarily participated in by all Americans. I do not mean to deny that these exist. But for such a tendency to be part of what I am calling the common culture, they would have to derive from beliefs and values and practices (almost) universally shared and known to be so. And that they are not.

## Recognizing a Dominant Culture

At the same time, it has also always been true that there was a *dominant* culture in these United States. It was Christian, it spoke English, and it identified with the high cultural traditions of Europe and, more particularly, of England. And, until recently, when people spoke of American culture, this is what they meant.

This dominant culture included the common culture of the dominant classes – the government

and business and cultural elites – but it was familiar to many others who were subordinate to them. And it was not merely an effect but also an instrument of their domination. Because the dominant norms of language and behavior were those of a dominant class, their children, for example, were likely to have preferred access to the best educations – educations which themselves led to dominant positions in business, in government, and in the arts.

As public education has expanded in the United States, America's citizens, and especially those citizens educated in public elementary schools in this country, have come to share a body of historical knowledge, and an understanding – however tenuous – of the American political system. And it is increasingly true that whatever other languages children in this country speak, they speak and understand English, and they watch many of the same television programs and listen to much of the same music. Not only do they share these experiences, they know that they do; and so they can imagine themselves as a collectivity, the audience for mass culture. In that sense, most young Americans have a common culture based in a whole variety of kinds of English, but it is no longer that older, Christian, Anglo-Saxon tradition that used to be called American culture.

The outlines of this almost universal common culture, to which only very few Americans are external, are somewhat blurry. But it includes, for example, in its practices, baseball; in its ideas, democracy; in its religion, Christianity;[4] in its arts, rap music and music videos and many movies. This culture is to a large extent, as I have implied, the product of schools and of the media. But even those who share this common culture live in subcultures of language, religion, family organization, and political assumptions. And, more than this, most who are black and Hispanic have, irrespective of their incomes, radically different experiences and expectations of the state.

## Multiculturalism as an Alternative to Imposing the Dominant Culture

Now I take it that multiculturalism is meant to be the name of a response to these familiar facts: that it is meant to be an approach to education and to public culture that acknowledges the diversity of cultures and subcultures in the United States and that proposes to deal with that diversity in some other way than by imposing the values and ideas of the hitherto dominant Anglo-Saxon cultural tradition. That, I think, is the common core of all the things that have been called multiculturalism.

I think this common idea is a good one. It is a good idea for a number of reasons. It is a good idea, first, because the old practice of imposing Christian, Anglo–Saxon tradition was rooted in racism and anti-Semitism (and sexism and heterosexism . . . but that is another story). But it is a good idea, second, because making the culture of one subculture the official culture of a state privileges the members of that subculture – gives them advantages in public life – in ways that are profoundly anti-egalitarian and, thus, anti-democratic.

Yet agreeing to this idea does not tell you much about what you should do in schools and in public culture. It tells you that you mustn't impose certain practices and ideas, but it doesn't tell you what you should do affirmatively. I want to suggest that one affirmative strategy in this area is a bad idea for public education and that there are other strategies that are better. And then, in closing, I want to say something about why living together in a multicultural society is bound to turn out to be difficult.

## The Distinction between Cultures and Identities

There is one final piece of apparatus I need, however. I have been talking of "subcultures" and defining what I mean by this. And it would be natural to assume that the primary subgroups to which these subcultures are attached will be ethnic and racial groups (with religious denominations conceived of as a species of ethnic group). It would be natural, too, to think that the characteristic difficulties of a multicultural society arise largely from the cultural differences between ethnic groups. I think this easy assimilation of ethnic and racial subgroups to subcultures is to be resisted.

First of all, it needs to be argued, and not simply assumed, that black Americans, taken as a group, have a common culture: values and beliefs and practices that they share and that they do not share with others. This is equally true for, say, Chinese-Americans; and it is *a fortiori* true of white Americans. What seems clear enough is that being African-American or Asian-American or White is an important social identity in the United States. Whether these are important social

identities because these groups have shared common cultures is, on the other hand, quite doubtful; not least because it is doubtful whether they have common cultures at all.

With differing cultures, we might expect misunderstandings arising out of ignorance of each other's values, practices, and beliefs; we might even expect conflicts because of differing values or beliefs. The paradigms of difficulty in a society of many cultures are misunderstandings of a word or a gesture; conflicts over who should take custody of the children after a divorce; whether to go to the doctor or the priest for healing.

Once we move from talking of cultures to identities, whole new kinds of problems come into view. Racial and ethnic conflicts, for example, have to do with the ways in which some people think members of other races and ethnic groups should be treated, irrespective of their cultural accomplishments. It isn't because a black man won't understand his daughter, or because he will value her differently from a white man, or because he does not know some important facts, that Archie Bunker wouldn't want his daughter to marry one. Mr. Bunker's bigotry does not require him to differ culturally in any significant respect from black people. He would be as opposed to the marriage if the potential son-in-law had exactly the same beliefs and values (on non-race-related matters) as he had himself. Similarly, in Bosnia it is not so much that what Croats do makes them hateful to Serb bigots; or vice versa. It is rather that those things are hateful because Croats (or Serbs) do them.

These cases bring out the ways in which ethnic and racial identities are contrastive: it is central to being African-American that you are not Euro-American or Asian-American; *mutatis mutandis*, the same goes for being Euro-American or Asian-American. And these distinctions matter because (some) people think it appropriate to treat people differently depending on which of these categories they fall into; and these ways of treating people differently lead to patterns of domination and exploitation. Racial and ethnic identities are, in this way, like genders and sexualities. To be female is not to be male; to be gay is not to be straight; and these oppositions lead some to treat people differently according to their gender or sexuality, in asymmetrical ways that usually privilege men or straight people.

Now it is crucial to understanding gender and sexuality that women and men and gay and straight people grow up together in families, communities, denominations. Insofar as a common culture means common beliefs, values, and practices, gay people and straight people in most places have a common culture; and while there are societies in which the socialization of children is so structured by gender that women and men have seriously distinct cultures, this is not a feature of most "modern" societies.

I take the fact that questions about feminism (gender) and gay and lesbian identity (sexuality) come up often in thinking about multiculturalism (especially in the university) as an indication that what many people are thinking about is not the multiple subcultures of the nation but its multiple identities. All I want to insist on for now is that these are not the same thing.

## A Multicultural Nation's Problems with Public Education

I have been trying to explore the ways in which we are a multicultural nation, because, as I say, I want to say something about the consequences of this situation for public education.[6] But we should notice that it is not obvious what special problems the multicultural character of the American nation creates for the curriculum.

Once you have conceded what I claim is the key multiculturalist contention – that you should not use the public schools to impose the subculture of a dominant group – you might think you could proceed simply by asking what is worth teaching to American children and teaching that. This was, after all, the basis of the older curriculum; and if that curriculum confused what was worth teaching with what was valued in the subculture of the dominant class – the particular masquerading in a familiar way as the universal – the obvious correction would be to try to answer the question of what is worth teaching in a less (sub)culturally biased way.

The fact is that the older notion that we should instruct all children in "American culture" was, itself, a potentially democratic and egalitarian one. The advantages that the children of the dominant class gained by the fact that it was their home culture – their dialect of English, their table manners, the literature their parents read and admired – that was taught in schools and presupposed in public life, could be eradicated, if all children were given access to that culture through schooling. The multicultural critique might lead you to feel that it was

unfair to give the dominant class a head start in this way (a fact we could deal with, for example, by refraining from preferring their dialect in official speech). But I do not see that it would require you to do anything else to reflect the multicultural character of the nation in the curriculum.

Yet if we read the National Council for the Social Studies statement on multicultural education, it is clear that this influential group of educators take it for granted that much more is required. To begin with, they move freely (as I have urged we should not) from talk of multiculturalism to talk of ethnic identities. Though they agree that not every student cares much about an ethnic identity and that children should be free not to identify themselves ethnically,[7] they also insist that ethnicity should be an important factor in shaping educational policy:

1 Personal ethnic identity and knowledge of others' ethnic identity is essential to the sense of understanding and the feeling of personal well-being that promotes intergroup understanding. . . . (278)
2 Students cannot fully understand who they are . . . until they have a solid knowledge of the groups to which they belong. (282)[8]

In the background here are widespread assumptions about what is going wrong in our "multicultural" schools: that violence between children (which is plainly a barrier to learning) often grows out of intergroup misunderstandings; that minority students (especially African-Americans and Hispanics) underachieve because they and their cultures are not respected in the school. But if the conflict in the schools is a matter of contests between identities, there is no reason to think that teaching about various cultures will eradicate it. Understanding may not help with problems that do not arise from misunderstanding. What is required, very often, is not understanding of cultures but respect for identities; and a curriculum that takes the cultural works of African-Americans seriously may be helpful here, even if it does not communicate a deepened understanding of African-American culture.

And if the "solid knowledge" of my group is to be taught as a distinct body of beliefs and ideas, then it may actually lead me to be more culturally different from my peers of other races and ethnicities (who are taught different, though, no doubt, equally solid things about "their" tradition) and thus generate more possibilities for misunderstanding.

Passage (2) thus proposes a policy that increases the likelihood of the danger passage (1) seeks to avoid.

## Two Rationales for Separatism

Implicit in passage (2) is the thought that the way to deal with our many cultures in public education is to teach each child the culture of "its" group. This is the strategy of some (but by no means all) Afro-centrists and of some (but by no means all) of those who have favored bilingual education for Hispanics.

This is the strategy I oppose.

To explain my first basis for objection, I need to elicit a paradox in this approach, which we can do by considering the answer that this approach – I shall call it, tendentiously, Separatism – proposes to the question 'Why should we teach African-American children something different from what we teach other children?' The answer will come in two parts: the first part says that we should do so because they already come from a different culture; the second part says that we should do so because we should teach all people about the traditions from which they come.

It's the first answer that is paradoxical, at least if you think that the plurality of cultures is a problem. It is paradoxical because it proposes to solve the problems created by the fact that children have different cultures by emphasizing and entrenching those differences, not by trying to reduce them.

I should make it plain that I have no problem with the argument that children's home cultures need to be taken into account in deciding how to teach them: there's no point in giving kids information in languages or dialects they don't understand, or simply punishing them – rather than dealing with their parents or guardians – for behavior that they are being taught at home. But to admit that is to admit only that culture may sometimes make a difference as to how you should teach, not that it should make a difference as to what you should teach. And defending teaching children different histories (Afrocentric history) or different forms of speech or writing (Black English) on the grounds that this is already their culture simply begs the question; if we teach African-American children different histories from other children, then, indeed, it will become true that knowing that history and not knowing any other history will be part of the culture of African-Americans.

But the fact is that if we don't enforce cultural differences of this kind in the schools, surely they will largely disappear. And what that means is that the only serious argument for Separatism that survives is the second answer I considered earlier: the claim that we must teach each child the culture of "its" group because that is the right thing to do, because we should.

## Exploring the Second Rationale

That idea is much more powerful. It is presumably at the basis of the thought that many non-observant Jews share with observant Jews (who have other reasons for believing this), namely, that it is good to teach their children Jewish history and customs, because they are Jewish children. It is the argument – "we have Plato to our father" – that led to the sense of exclusion that many African-Americans felt when the history and culture of the United States were taught to them as the continuation of a white Western tradition; the argument against which so much Afrocentrism is a reaction.[9]

I myself am skeptical of all arguments of this form: my instinct is to believe that traditions are worth teaching in our public schools and colleges because they are beautiful and good and true – or, at least, interesting and important and useful – never because they are ours or yours, mine or thine. I was brought up a Protestant; but after my first seder, it struck me that this was a tradition worth knowing about for everybody, Jew or Gentile; and I have always valued the experience of family community among my Moslem cousins at Ramadan.[10]

It may be worth spending a little time reflecting on the unfashionableness of my instinctive view and insisting on some of its virtues, which may have been forgotten. I mentioned just now the "older view" that public education should teach an American culture. What was done in the name of that older view too often obscured the variety of the sources of America's cultures, as well as giving too rosy and unconflicted a view of the relations between America's various ethnic, racial, and religious subgroups. None of these mistakes needs resurrecting.

But this older view surely also held that what we should teach in public schools should be knowledge worth knowing, values worth respecting, practices useful in children's lives outside the school. Contemporary feminist, anti-racist and anti-ethnocentrist skepticisms lead us to ask, Worth knowing for whom? By whose standards? And these are fair questions. But in answering them we should take them seriously as questions about the curriculum as a practical business.

And this requires remembering some simple facts: the school curriculum contains, of necessity, an extremely small proportion of what is known; we read only the minutest sample of what has been written; and we have time to study only a fraction of the known history of the world, only the most basic scientific knowledge.

How, given these facts, can we pick from all these riches? To say we should favor truth over falsehood is to utter a truism worth holding on to; but it leaves vast decisions to be made. (It also neglects the fact that the whole truth is complicated, too complicated often to learn all at once, so that we teach children simplified versions of it, first of all – Newtonian half-truths before Einstein.) To say that in selecting what literature and art we should teach we should seek to transmit an appreciation of literary and aesthetic values is also fine enough; but to do this we need to read the mediocre and the near-great as well as the magnificent. More than this, while literary judgment can be reasoned about, it is also essentially contestable, so that part of what we need to teach is the idea that there are reasonable differences in matters of literary and artistic taste, differences that we cannot rely on argument or evidence to settle. Each of these complications makes the principle that we should teach the beautiful a poor instrument for discriminating among all the range of the arts those we should teach; and it offers little guidance as to how we should teach them.

Finally, of course, schools should teach the young what is good and evil: and also what is courageous and what foolhardy; what is compassion and what is sentimentality; where loyalty to family and friends ends and our responsibility to our fellow citizens, our fellow creatures, begins; and how to make all these moral discriminations. But there is here no easy consensus; there are too many hard cases, and we cannot expect that teaching young people to make these discriminations – which means helping them learn to think ethically – will be uncontroversial in a society where certain moral views are associated with particular group identities. For the schools will regularly be asked to recognize, say, religious identities by teaching their views.

I concede all these difficulties: indeed, thinking about them strikes me as a useful place to begin reflecting on the curriculum. But I repeat that I do not think it will help us in public education to add to our baggage of reasons for offering an element of a school curriculum to a child the thought: I teach you, this particular child, this thing because it is your tradition.

This is because I think this an inadmissible ground for the curriculum of a public school, not because I think that we should never hear such arguments. Indeed, they are among the most compelling arguments that a family or a church or temple or mosque can offer to a child. "In our family," I might tell my nephew, "we have done this for many generations. Your great-grand-uncle did it, in Asante, in the late nineteenth century; your grand-father did it when he was a boy in Kumasi." There are things and practices I value because we – my ancestors and I – have done them for generations, because I take pleasure in the sense of continuity with them as my ancestors.

If I had been to a Catholic or a Jewish or a Muslim school, I would have learned such traditions, too, not as my traditions but as somebody else's. I would have learned them not because the teachers and the school believed in them as traditions, but because they believed in them *tout court*. And because one can value them not just as traditions but as truths, I could decide to make them mine.

In the modern world many have sought to hold on to the profound pleasures of tradition even after they have left their faith behind. But, to repeat, in most Catholic or Jewish or Muslim schools, before the modern period, what was taught was taught as the truth about life, the universe, and conduct; and though people might have taken pleasure in thinking of it as a matter of the tradition of a family and a community, if they had not thought it true, they would have thought it worthless. For these schools one notion of the good and the true, a contested notion, attached to one identity, was a presupposition of the curriculum.

## An Alternative View

The public schools of a multicultural, multiethnic, religiously diverse society should not operate like these older religious schools: the public schools should not propagate one faith, support the traditions of one group, celebrate the heritage of one ethnicity. They should not teach particular traditions and religions; though, of course, they should teach *about* them.

The view I am articulating here is a view about the division between public and private spheres in the education of children: on such a view, ethnicity and religion are not to be transmitted by the organs of the state. Both, rather, are created and preserved outside the state by families, and by wider communities, including religious ones. Because there are many such cultures – and identities – created outside the state, in civil society, and because for many of us they are central to our conceptions of ourselves and of our lives, the school must acknowledge them. Because they have a great deal of impact on our relations, in communities and in the political life of the state, we are all better prepared for life in this nation if we know something of the cultures and identities of others and if we learn to engage in respectful discourse with them. Outside the school, children can be preached a specific religion; within it, they can hear about their own traditions, along with others, but they should not be proselytized, even on behalf of their families.

If there is any doubt about the stability of such a view, consider the alternative: a policy in which the public schools set out to teach children according to their identities and subcultures; that not only taught about collective identities but set out to reinforce and transmit them. If carried to its ultimate, this policy would require segregation into cultural and religious groups either within or between public schools, in ways that would be plainly unconstitutional in the United States since the *Brown* decision. For if we did have unsegregated classes teaching Jewish history, and African-American history, and Anglo history and Hispanic history and Chinese history in our schools, by what right would we forbid children from going to the "wrong" classes?

Of course there are things that we surely all believe that we should teach all American children: in particular, we should teach them something of the history of the American political system. And here is a reason why we cannot hope to teach each child only "its" cultural tradition: for understanding the American constitutional system and its history requires us to know about slavery and immigration, about the Civil War and Reconstruction, the Underground Railroad and Ellis Island. If there is a sense in which each of these belongs more to the history of some social groups than others, there is also a clear sense in which they belong to us all.

And it is *that* idea that motivates the approach to dealing with our multicultural society that I favor, that undergirds my multiculturalism. For it seems to me that what is ideal in a multicultural society, whose multicultural character is created outside the state in the sphere of civil society, is that the state should seek in its educational systems to make these multiple subcultures known to each other. A multicultural education, in my view, should be one that leaves you not only knowing and loving what is good in the traditions of your subculture but also understanding and appreciating the traditions of others (and, yes, critically rejecting the worst of all traditions).[11] This approach has its practical problems also: a curriculum filled with the history of Korean-Americans and African-Americans and Anglo-Americans and Jewish Americans and so on risks being a curriculum with a shallow appreciation of all of them. But the principle of selection is clear: we should try to teach about those many traditions from around the world that have come to be important at different stages of American history. This means that we begin with Native American and Protestant Dutch and English and African and Iberian cultures, adding voices to the story as they were added to the nation. Because different elements are important to different degrees in different places today, we can assume that the balance will be and should be differently struck in different places. (All of which presupposes a general improvement, I should add, in the quality of American elementary and secondary education.)

## A Final Objection to Separatism

I have a final argument against Separatism. It is that it is dangerous, for reasons that have to do with the final point I want to make, which is about the difficulty of managing multicultural – plural – societies.

I said earlier that no one is likely to be troubled by the variety of subcultures in high culture. Why is this? Because however important our participation in high culture is, it is unlikely to be at the heart of our ethnicity. High culture crosses ethnic boundaries to an extraordinary degree. (The boundaries that it crosses with less ease are those of class.) The result is that subdivisions of high culture are not so likely to become central to the organization of political life. The United States is not threatened by the cultural autonomy of the

American Philosophical Association or (even) the American Medical Association. In this respect the associations of high culture are like many elements of popular culture: the next New York mayoral election is not going to be between followers of the Mets and of the Yankees.

But differences in what I have called subcultures are rather different. We pass on our language to the next generation because we care to communicate with them; we pass on religion because we share its vision and endorse its values; we pass on our folkways because we value people with those folkways.

I have insisted that we should distinguish between cultures and identities, but ethnic identities are distinctive in having cultural distinctions as one of their primary marks. Ethnic identities are created in family and community life. These – along with mass-mediated culture, the school and the college – are, for most of us, the central sites of the social transmission of culture. Distinct practices, beliefs, norms go with each ethnicity in part because people want to be ethnically distinct: because many people want the sense of solidarity that comes from being unlike others. With ethnicity in modern society, it is often the distinct identity that comes first and the cultural distinction that is created and maintained because of it, not the other way around. The distinctive common cultures of ethnic and religious identities matter not simply because of their contents but also as markers of those identities.

Culture in this sense is the home of what we care about most. If other people organize their solidarity around cultures different from ours, this makes them, to that extent, different from us in ways that matter to us deeply. The result, of course, is not just that we have difficulty understanding across cultures – this is an inevitable result of cultural difference, for much of culture consists of language and other shared modes of understanding – but that we end up preferring our own kind; and if we prefer our own kind, it is easy enough to slip into preferring to vote for our own kind, to employ our own kind, and so on.

In sum: Cultural difference undergirds loyalties. As we have seen repeatedly in recent years, from South Africa to the Balkans, from Sri Lanka to Nigeria, from South Central Los Angeles to Crown Heights, once these loyalties matter they will be mobilized in politics and the public square, except to the extent that a civic culture can be created that explicitly seeks to exclude them. And that is why my multiculturalism is so necessary: it is the only

way to reduce the misunderstandings across sub-cultures, the only way to build bridges of loyalty across the ethnicities that have so often divided us. Multiculturalism of this sort – pluralism, to use an older word – is a way of making sure we care enough about people across ethnic divides to keep those ethnic divides from destroying us. And it must, I believe, be a central part of the function of our educational system to equip all of us to share the public space with people of multiple identities and distinct subcultures. I insisted early on the distinction between cultures and identities. It is especially important here. Teaching young people to respect those with other identities is not the same thing as teaching them some of the central practices and beliefs of a different subculture. When we teach Toni Morrison to children with serious attention, we are demonstrating respect for the cultural work of a black person in a culture where there is still pressure not to respect black people. We are showing that respect to black children; we are modelling that respect for other children. Each of these is something that a decent education can seek to do; neither is simply a matter of introducing people to a culture.

It seems to me that it will be important, too, to teach children to reflect critically on their identities, including their ethnic identities, if they care about them.

## Identity as an Important Part of Education

Locke famously argued that the trans-temporal unity of the self was created through memory. Contemporary work on this question has argued that this answer to the problem of identity is at best question-begging. For if I think I did something in the past and "remember" it from the perspective of a participant, that only shows that I am remembering what happened to me if that belief is true; and its being true, if it is a belief with a first-person perspective, requires not just that some person had such experiences but that I did. The role of "memory" in constituting the trans-temporal identity of a person should more appropriately, I think, be taken another way. To be a person is to have a sense of yourself as a creature with a history. Memory here is a route into the recalled experiences whose existence, if they are veridical, certifies the story I tell of myself. But the oft-suggested parallelism between memory and history should remind us that a history of a self is not just "one damn thing after another." Our personal histories are as narratively constructed as our collective stories. For most of us the history of myself is Whig history, with a telos, or more likely, a plurality of ends, with anticipations in childhood, intimations of what is to come. Part of the function of our collective identities, of the whole repertory of them that a culture makes available to its members, is to structure possible narratives of the self.

Across cultures, people care to give a certain narrative unity to their lives: each person wants to tell a story of his or her life that makes sense. The story – my story – should cohere in the way appropriate to a person of my culture. In telling that story, how it fits into the wider story of various collectivities is, for most of us, important. It is not just that, say, gender identities give shape (through rites of passage, for example) to one's life; it is also that ethnic and national identities fit that story into a larger narrative. And some of the most "individualist" of individuals value such things. Hobbes spoke of the desire for glory as one of the dominating impulses of human beings, one that was bound to make trouble for social life. But glory can consist in fitting and being seen to fit into a collective history; and so, in the name of glory, one can end up doing the most social things of all.

Once I consciously grasp (as opposed to merely presupposing) the significance and value of my identity for me, I can see what the significance and value of their collective identities would be for others. I will also learn, from history and from social studies, both that such identities are probably humanly inevitable and that the cost of conflicts between identities can be very high, as we see now in the Balkans and in Somalia. A reasonable response to this fact is to recognize the need to accommodate others within my state with different identities. Once ethnic identities cease to be unreflective, as such a line of thought is bound to make them, I will also come to see my identity as something that can be molded, if not individually then at least as part of a common political project, or indeed as something that can be put away altogether.

What is wrong with our collective identities is not that that is what they are; it is rather that we need to restrain the persistent urge for one identity to go on the rampage against others. To do this, we may have to reshape them. Because the same "facts" can fit into many different stories, this reshaping is

something we are indeed capable of. The picture I suggested earlier, in which public education simply acknowledges the ethnic identities created outside the state, is too simple. In reflecting on these identities we cannot but alter them; at least some of the children we teach about other cultures will not maintain the unreflective sense of the superiority of their own. To conceive of multicultural education in this way – as the teaching of cross-subcultural understanding and of respect for other identities – is to seek to constrain identities so that they may share a single society.

## Why not Simply Insist on a Single Culture?

Having argued that the school in our society should not simply leave everything ethnically where it is, the question of a single common culture is likely to resurface. Why not argue out democratically a common culture, making sure to learn the lesson of multiculturalism that this must not simply be the cover for a sectional interest?

My answer is, Because we do not have to do so. The question presupposes that what we really need is shared values, a common culture. I think this is a mistake. What I think we really need is provided in a conjunct of our original definition of a society, something so obvious that we soon left it behind. "Common institutions and a common culture," I said, but dropped talk of the common institutions almost immediately.

But to live together in a nation what is required is that we all share a commitment to the organization of the state – the institutions that provide the overarching order of our common life. This does not require that we have the same commitment to those institutions, in the sense that the institutions must carry the same meaning for all of us.

The First Amendment separates church and state. Some of us are committed to this because we are religious: we see it as the institutionalization of a Protestant insistence on freedom of conscience. Some of us are committed to it because we are Catholics or Jews or Moslems, who do not want to be pressed into conformity by a Protestant majority. Some of us are atheists who want to be left alone. We can live together with this arrangement provided we all are committed to it, for our different reasons.

There is a useful analogy here with much mass culture and other mass-produced goods. People in London and in Lagos, in New York and New Delhi, listen to Michael Jackson and drink Coca-Cola. They exist, in part, as an audience for his work, as consumers of that drink. But nobody thinks that what either of these products means in one place must be identical with what it means in every site of its consumption. Similarly, the institutions of democracy – the election, the public debate, the protection of minority rights – have different meanings to different subcultures. Once more, there is no reason to require that we all value them in the same way, for the same reasons. All that is required is that everybody is willing to "play the game."

A shared political life in a great modern nation is not like the life of a traditional society. It can encompass a great diversity of meanings. When we teach children democratic habits, through practice in public schools, what we are creating is a shared commitment to certain forms of social behavior.

We can call this a political culture, if we like. But the meanings citizens give to their lives, and to the political within their lives, in particular, will be shaped not only by the school, but by the family and church, by reading and by television, in their professional and recreational associations.

Maybe, in the end, there will be a richer American common culture; maybe it will lead to a consensus on the value of American institutions. Certainly cultural homogenization is proceeding apace. But it has not happened yet. And, so far as I can see, it doesn't have to happen in order for us to live together. Competing identities may be having a hard time living together in new democracies. But in this, the oldest democracy, so long as our institutions treat every significant identity with enough respect to gain its allegiance, we can muddle along in the meanwhile without a common culture. That, after all, is what we have been doing, lo, these many years.

## Notes

1. Not every society will distinguish between the natural and the social in the sort of way we do. So this formula is not meant to imply that every society has separable theories of what we call the natural and the social.

2. What I have been calling a subculture, then, consists of people who share specific practices, beliefs, and values that constitute the common culture of a subgroup of the nation.

3. Given that the constitution is about a year old as I write (it was promulgated in 1992 and came into full effect in 1993), this is not too surprising, I suppose. But much of the structure has been in place since independence with few changes.

4. This is not, remember, to claim that most Americans are Christians by belief. It is to say only that some of the central ideas and practices of Christianity are known to and understood by most Americans.

5. Men and women may have characteristically distinct experiences; but that doesn't, by itself, guarantee distinct cultures.

6. The arguments of this section are based on suggestions from Bob Fullinwider. I have taken up many suggestions he made in his helpful criticisms of my first draft. I accept full responsibility for these ideas, as I have expressed them, but I don't claim to have come to all of them myself.

7. National Council for the Social Studies, "Curriculum Guidelines for Multicultural Education," *Social Education* 55 (September 1992): 278.

8. Ibid.: "Multicultural education should stress the process of self-identification. . . ."

9. There is another problem with this way of thinking: it suggests that Western culture belongs to some American children more than others in virtue of their descent. This is doubly troubling: first, because the culture we teach in school belongs only to those who do the work to earn it; second, because it proposes to exclude certain children from certain educational experiences on what look like racial grounds.

10. Of course, I do not think – absurdly – that everyone should become both a Jew and a Moslem while holding on to Protestantism. The sort of participation in Jewish or Moslem celebrations that I am talking about is the participation of a guest, a visitor, a friend.

11. Postmodernism urges people to respond, "Worst by whose criteria?" My answer is, In the real world of intercultural moral conversation, nobody – except a postmodernist – defends his position by claiming that it follows simply from his criteria and leaves it at that. If we argue with those who practice clitoral excision and say it ought to be stopped, we need to tell those who practice it why. If we argue that it causes pain to girls and years of low-grade infections to women, and raises the risks of pregnancy; if we say that women who have not been circumcised are not, ipso facto, sexually insatiable; if we say that the practice deprives women of a source of pleasure; if we observe that the practice is not, in fact, recommended by the Koran:

nobody, except in a rhetorical moment of weakness, is going to defend the practice by saying that these facts – if such they are – are relevant only by our criteria. And when they suggest to us that "we" mutilate women – through cosmetic surgery; or that "we" practice male circumcision, which also reduces men's capacity for pleasure; or that an uncircumcised girl cannot get a husband: these facts – if such they are – do not strike us as relevant only by our criteria. (And, in any case, there are people here who are not so sure about the badness of the practice, and people there not so convinced of its goodness.) And this is in a hard case of intercultural disagreement. Most American subgroups share so many substantial ethical assumptions that the "Says who?" response is usually offered only by those who are losing an argument.

# 29

# The Promise of Racial Integration in a Multicultural Age

## Lawrence Blum

A social commitment to school integration beat a hasty retreat in the 1990s. In a series of legal decisions at the federal and federal district levels, states and school districts have been permitted to dismantle programs (such as busing and magnet schools) aimed at increasing racial diversity in their schools. The districts have been declared, in the key legal terminology, "unitary" – that is, whatever segregation currently exists is declared not to be a result or vestige of state-sponsored or state-created segregation. Not all school districts legally permitted to avoid or jettison desegregation actually go this route. Many sponsor initiatives to bring white students and racial minority students into the same schools.[1] All told, however, racial segregation in schools itself continues to increase, with Latinos increasingly segregated.[2]

Deliberate efforts to racially diversify school populations are losing public support as well, most strikingly among blacks, the group most strongly behind the decades-long push for integration. Justice Clarence Thomas, in his Supreme Court opinion in the *Missouri v. Jenkins* case of 1995, articulated an increasingly heard plaint. It is insulting and even racist, Thomas said, to assume that a black child has to sit next to a white child in class in order to learn. Thomas elaborates, "To presume that blacks must have a sufficient quota of whites in the classroom to learn is to presume that there is something inherently wrong with blacks."[3] Blacks are increasingly, or at least publicly, viewing efforts at integration as an *alternative* to energy put into enhancing the quality of schooling for black children.[4]

Defenses of desegregation – particularly of blacks or Latinos with whites – in the face of this opposition tends to focus on occupational benefits. Gary Orfield, a prominent researcher and advocate for school integration, replies directly to Thomas's argument by saying that integration works by providing "economically disadvantaged minority" students with greater life opportunities through "access to middle-class schools, and to the world beyond them."[5]

Many blacks still find the ideal of integration attractive but feel that given the current demographics of schools, the conditions for realizing important integrationist values are unlikely to

Previously published in Stephen Macedo and Yael Tamir (eds.), *Nomos XLIII; Moral and Political Education* (New York: New York University Press, 2002), pp. 383–403, 408–11, 412–21, 423–4. Reprinted by permission of the publisher.

materialize. Gloria Ladson-Billings articulates this sentiment well: "In a better world I would want to see schools integrated across racial, cultural, linguistic, and all other lines. But I am too much of a pragmatist to ignore the sentiment and motivation underlying the African American immersion school movement. African Americans already have separate schools. The African American immersion school movement is about *taking control* of those separate schools."[6]

The *mere* physical co-presence of children from distinct ethnoracial groups in the same school is not by itself a good.[7] Those who favor racial plurality in schools, and its intentional promotion, believe there to be vital goods to be secured in such schools not attainable, or much more difficult to attain, in schools composed entirely, or almost entirely, of one racial group. I argue in this paper that popular and to a large extent scholarly discussion of ethnoracial plurality in schools has lost sight of these goods, which are social, moral, and personal (to the individual student), as well as civic, the type of good to which I will devote most attention.

The neglect of these goods by both opponents and proponents of desegregation is connected with a public discourse that has tended to operate with an excessively narrow – consumerist, instrumentalist, and nondemocratic – conception of the appropriate goals and values of education itself. Recovering a richer conception of education will provide the foundation for a renewed concept of "racial integration" and its values.

I draw my conception of the value of racially mixed schools from the more general ideals of racial integration articulated by Martin Luther King, Jr. He said, "Integration is creative, and is therefore more profound and far-reaching than desegregation. Integration is the positive acceptance of desegregation and the welcomed participation of Negroes into the total range of human activities . . . [A] desegregated society that is not integrated . . . leads to 'physical proximity without spiritual affinity.' It gives us a society where men are physically desegregated and spiritually segregated, where elbows are together and hearts are apart."[8]

Randall Kennedy adds a more explicitly civic and democratic dimension to King's moral and spiritual vision. "Integrationists seek . . . to create a society in which the intimate and equal association for people of different races in all spheres of life . . . is *welcomed* as a normal part of a multiracial democracy."[9] We ignore King's and Kennedy's idealism at our peril

in education policy decisions. Unless we are aware of these ideals, and their associated range of social benefits, we cannot know what we are losing when we retreat from them, and whether the abandonment is worth the price.

The "ideal" nature of my argument – the recognition that it is only under certain conditions that various components of the integrationist ideal are realized – means that I am by no means advocating racial desegregation as an overriding policy objective. Under less than ideal conditions – including those currently obtaining in many classes, schools and districts – it may be reasonable to favor policies that do not press toward racially mixed schools, or even that facilitate certain kinds of single-race (or single-race-dominated) schools. At the same time, I will also argue that, despite the retreat from both the social ideal of integration, and the more minimal goal of racially plural schools, we actually know a good deal more than we did when King wrote those words about how to *realize* integrationist ideals in racially diverse schools.

## Integration and Assimilation

When King spoke of "desegregation," he meant a process by which schools that were monoracial (and generally created as such by the state) become deliberately racially mixed. ("Desegregation" can also be used to refer to the end-state created by that process.) In King's time, virtually the only schools that were racially mixed were ones that had been desegregated in this sense. Currently, however, racially mixed schools are frequently *not* a product of desegregation. While often called "desegregated," these schools draw a racially diverse group of students because of their location (schools in mixed neighborhoods, or located on the border of more than one monoracial neighborhood) or non-race-related features of the school (magnet schools), rather than by dint of race-based assignment or admissions policies.[10]

As King said, desegregation, or, more generally, the existence of a plurality of ethnoracial groups in a school, is a necessary step toward his conception of "integration," an embracing of that plurality and an attempt to establish humane, moral, and civic relationships among students of the different groups. Although schools have been in the process of becoming *less* racially mixed in the 1990s, reversing a trend prior to that point, a majority of students do attend schools that are racially plural in a meaningful sense. According to Orfield and Yun's findings, in 1996–7, the average urban black student attended a school with 35 percent blacks, 36.5 percent Latinos, and 15 percent whites. (To put this in some perspective, 35 percent of blacks as a whole attended schools that were 90–100 percent non-white.) In the suburbs the numbers for the average black student were 20 percent black, 30 percent Latino, and 40 percent white. In small cities, whites attended schools that were 14 percent black and 8.5 percent Latino; in the suburbs of large cities the percentages for the average white student were 6.8 percent black and 7.4 percent Latino.[11] If a racially plural school is defined as more than 10 percent of two groups (or more), the majority of Latino, black, Asian, and Native American children attend racially plural schools.[12] A not insubstantial minority of whites does so as well. (On average, whites attend schools with 81 percent white classmates.)[13]

The racial demography of a given school is quite relevant to its potential for attaining the personal, social, and civic goals I will address below. A minimal, critical mass of students of two or more groups is necessary for some of these goals, but the goals will be greatly facilitated if more than that number is present. Similarly a high percentage of one majority group poses greater challenges than a school with a lower percentage. And the ideal situation (present in very few schools) is one with no ethnoracial group in the majority. Beyond this, the ease of achieving some of the various aims is affected by the percentages of *whites* specifically. I am not able to comment further on the bearing of distinct ethnoracial demographic patterns on the forms of and possibilities for implementation of the goals I discuss below but want only to flag these demographics as important desiderata in achieving the goals of racial integration.

I will follow Dr. King and retain the language of "integration," at least some of the time. But I do want to enter a cautionary note regarding some of its associations. First, because of its history, "integration" has carried an implication that the groups involved are limited to blacks and whites. Latinos have fought their own battles for integrated schools and equal education,[14] but public recognition has been slow to incorporate that history. Given how irredeemably culturally plural the nation has become – with Latinos soon becoming as numerous as blacks, Asian-Americans the fastest-growing

panethnic group, and other groups not readily classified under the familiar categories – the association of the term "integration" with only white and black is unfortunate, and should be jettisoned.

A related, but more subtle, implication is that integration concerns only the mixing of students of color with whites. While many central issues concerning integration do indeed concern whites, the potential benefits of racial diversity of schools are not confined to interactions between whites and other groups. Seldom a matter for legal action, integration of distinct non-white groups is nevertheless starting to be a significant social and policy issue; the city of Pasadena for example has crafted a school integration policy that mixes Latinos and blacks.[15]

Finally, for many, the term "integration" carries assimilationist overtones – as if its meaning were that the minority group were being "integrated into" a structure and culture fully defined by the majority group. The minority group's own culture's integrity is not respected, nor its impact on the larger culture that includes it recognized and welcomed.[16] As the National Research Council stated in its magisterial 1989 study, *A Common Destiny: Blacks and American Society*, "[T]he preservation of black culture and group identity" is a condition "that many blacks' definition of 'integration' requires."[17] And power must be shared with racial minorities also.[18]

These assimilationist overtones are not surprising. When the great battles for school integration were waged in the 1950s and '60s, *cultural* differences among different groups were not sufficiently recognized, either in the legal argumentation or in the minds of the white educators attempting to implement integration.[19] Blacks were seen by whites as something like "whites with black skin." Moreover, assimilation had been the reigning social philosophy since the 1924 immigration restrictions, and before. Cultural pluralism had become a fringe philosophy after a minor flurry of support early in the century.[20]

Post-1965 immigration and the rise of the multicultural movement has placed issues of culture and group identity at the forefront both of education and of intergroup relations. Assimilation in its traditional meaning as conformity to a European-based American culture can no longer serve as a worthy social aim, and the ideal of integration must definitively break with it.

Integrated education must respect the cultural and racial identities of students, and recognize when cultural differences bear on the task of education. For example, students whose home languages are other than standard English – for example, Spanish, Vietnamese, or African-American Vernacular English (sometimes called "Ebonics") and for whom such languages are important to their cultural identity – should not be discouraged from using those languages in social interaction in school settings other than classrooms. Nor should the school devalue these languages or dialects and the cultural identities of which they are an integral part. This culture-respecting practice should, however, in no way diminish the emphasis on teaching standard English and its use as the language of instruction. The world of education's understanding of how to take account of cultural and identity differences among students has increased exponentially since the 1950s, and we are much better positioned to put in place a non-assimilationist ideal of integration than we were at that time.[21]

For all these reasons, the ideal I wish to elaborate and defend here might most accurately be described as "educational ethnoracial pluralism," incorporating what the current imprecise (and in some ways misleading) term "diversity" is generally taken to signify – the importance and value of recognizing ethnoracial group identity, culture, and distinctness. Yet that cumbersome phrase fails to carry "integration's" historic moral associations.

## *Brown* and the Genesis of the Ideal of Racial Integration in Schools

Any discussion of racial integration in schools must take account of the *Brown v. Board of Education of Topeka* decision, and I wish to place my own argument for integration in the context of those offered by the Court in that decision. The *Brown* ruling was a decisive moment in American legal and social history, striking a severe blow to the racial caste system in the South, and lending the highest official imprimatur to ideals of racial equality and integration. At the same time, the decision has been subject to much criticism for the insufficiency or misguidedness of its legal reasoning.[22]

The Court provided (at least) five rationales for ending segregation. These rationales occupy different levels of generality, and, in the decision, were not clearly laid out and separated from one another. They are:

1 White-dominated school districts could not be trusted to give black schools material and educational resources equal to white ones.
2 State-created segregated schools are premised on the inferiority of blacks to whites. Thus segregation implicitly conveys this constitutionally impermissible message, independent of the material resources of the two school systems.
3 This message of inferiority is inevitably damaging to black students' sense of worth, and has a negative impact on their motivation to learn. (Argument (2) did not depend on the actual psychological impact of the message of inferiority but only on the constitutional wrongness of its declaration by the state.)
4 Segregation is *inherently* unequal, hence wrong.
5 Equality of opportunity cannot be provided in separate schools.

The first argument still carries some force with desegregation advocates. By and large black-dominated school systems do receive fewer resources than white, and, perhaps more importantly, fewer than needed to secure equal educational opportunities for both groups. The large number of legal suits based on inequities in district funding within states (in some of which the courts have found in favor of the plaintiffs) testify to continuing inequity. (Many of these involve a racial dimension.) A pure resource equity argument is, however, less compelling now than it has been in the past. The gap in expenditures has certainly been greatly reduced since the 1950s. Apart from inequities in physical facilities and teacher salary, however, on the average, teachers in majority black and Latino schools are less well trained and have performed less well on tests designed to assess teacher knowledge and competence. Many blacks not otherwise attracted to the idea of sending their children to white-dominated schools feel that doing so is the only way to ensure that their children will receive adequate educational attention from the state.

The second argument is not applicable to current forms of segregation, since ("de facto") segregation in schools is no longer a matter of official state policy ("de jure"). The argument used in some cases subsequent to *Brown* that resulted in busing to achieve integration – that a certain district's segregated or insufficiently desegregated schools are a *legacy* from prior state-created segregation – objects to extant inequities and their genesis in earlier state-sanctioned segregation rather than to the official declaration of inferiority.[23]

The third argument, based on empirical connections between the declaration of inferiority, the children's sense of self-worth, and their resultant motivation to learn, is mooted by the same absence of state-declared inferiority just noted.[24] In any case, the empirical connections between segregation, self-worth, and academic motivation have never been well established and later desegregation cases seldom relied on them.[25]

The fourth argument, "inherent inequality," may come to no more than (2) – declaration of inferiority – in which case it is not a separate argument. However, Roy Brooks also points out that the *Brown* decision can be read as glossing "inherently unequal" as (3) – causing reduced self-esteem, motivation, and academic achievement (though he correctly notes the misleading character of that usage, since the language of "inherent" is generally understood to *contrast* with causal effects).[26] But the Court's statement "Separate educational facilities are inherently unequal" has often been understood more broadly, to condemn as unequal and wrong separate single-race or predominantly single-race schools in their own right, independent of how they are created or of specific effects those schools have on the children who attend them. The Court's language here lends itself to such a reading, though much of the rest of the decision does not dovetail with this "inherent inequality" idea. Much writing on racial integration draws at least partially on the idea that once a school has been shown to be segregated (by some measure), this renders it unequal and thus morally problematic, independent of other deficiencies in the school. This view has the virtue of retaining a strong morally critical edge to the idea of racial separation, but the conflation of separation and inequality makes it more difficult to pinpoint the basis of the moral ills involved. (I argue below that non-integrated schools *are* morally and civically problematic, but not necessarily because, or only because, they are *unequal.*)

The fifth and final notion is equality of opportunity. Argument (1), regarding equal educational resources, is one concretized form of that more general idea. The Court declared that "the opportunity of an education . . . where the state has undertaken to provide it, is a right which must be available to all on equal terms" and goes on to say that segregated schools "deprive the children of the minority group of equal educational opportunities."[27]

Yet the absence of a clear constitutional standing for the principle of equality of opportunity has made for some confusion. "Equal protection," the salient constitutional principle used in the *Brown* case to mandate equality, does not irrefutably supply a rationale for the more substantive principle of equality of opportunity, and the Court itself notes that the Fourteenth Amendment cannot be read as having intended to forbid segregated schools.[28] Yet the Court goes on to rely on the confused "inherent inequality" idea to bring school desegregation under the jurisdiction of "equal protection of the laws" in that Amendment.[29]

Nevertheless, whatever the weaknesses of its constitutional foundation, equality of opportunity has come to be the major argument, or family of arguments, used to support desegregation, and also constitutes a powerful idea in American political culture as a grounding for arguments in the domain of education. Let us look, then, at the relation between equality of opportunity and racial integration.

## Equality of Opportunity

By linking desegregation and equality so closely, the *Brown* Court initiated a confusion between the two ideas that continues in current thinking. In Jonathan Kozol's passionate and influential attack on racial inequalities in education, segregation and inequality routinely serve as proxies for one another.[30] Gary Orfield's series of extremely valuable empirical studies of desegregation are marred, from a normative point of view, by a tendency to assume both that racial separation can virtually never be anything other than inequality-producing, and also that inequality (of opportunity) is the *only* thing wrong with racially separated schools.[31] Both racial segregation and inequality of opportunity are indeed bad things, and empirical connections do exist between them. But they are bad for somewhat distinct reasons, and cannot serve as automatic proxies for one another.

Broadly speaking, there are two types of equality of opportunity relevant to schools – equality of educational opportunity, and equality of life chances or occupational opportunity. Equality of educational opportunity is quite a complex notion once one pushes on it a bit,[32] but our purposes will be served by the intuitive idea of equivalent educations, taking individual differences into account. (For example, a dyslexic child may require special tutoring to gain an education equivalent to that of a non-dyslexic child who does not receive tutoring.)

Educational opportunity was a major focus in many of the early desegregation legal and policy battles. Historically the African-American community has placed great value on education, both in its own right and as a means to occupational mobility. Robert Carter, a lawyer in the early desegregation cases, eloquently states the view prevailing at the time, of the link between desegregation and equality of educational opportunity:

> I believe I accurately speak for the lawyers [involved in the *Brown* cases] in saying that we believed that the surest way for minority children to obtain their constitutional right to equal educational opportunity was to require the removal of all racial barriers in the public school system, with black and white children attending the same schools, intermingled in the same classrooms, and together exposed to the same educational offerings. Integration was viewed as the means to our ultimate objective, not the objective itself.[33]

Carter mentions these beliefs in part to say that subsequent developments prevented the hoped-for desegregation, and its conversion into equality of opportunity, from taking place. Districts resisted integration by various means; extensive desegregation did not really begin in the South until after 1964. After (and before) that many whites left school districts in which their children would have gone to school with a substantial number of blacks (so-called "white flight"). Continuing housing segregation in the context of neighborhood districting helped prevent schools from becoming racially mixed. Blacks and other integration advocates underestimated white parents' resistance to their children attending schools with blacks. While originally desegregation was seen as a southern issue, when it moved north, blacks were disappointed to witness white reluctance and outright racism as well. Undoubtedly *part* of the recent black retreat from the "dream" of integration is black bitterness over white rejection, and a defensive retreat into the security and warmth of a community where they will not have to worry about acceptance.[34]

In addition, Robert Carter's assumptions about how desegregation would lead to equality of opportunity were faulty, or at least limited. Equal education requires not only the co-presence of different groups of students in schools and classes, and equal exposure to educational content. It also requires

teachers and schools to treat children of different racial groups equally, an assumption both Carter and the Court may have made but did not articulate.

Unfortunately the overwhelmingly white teaching force frequently failed, and still fails, to treat children of color and particularly black and Latino children, equally.[35] In their rich and comprehensive study of an ambitious desegregation program in St. Louis that buses urban black students to white-dominated suburban schools, Amy Stuart Wells and Robert Crain note that many of the white teachers do not believe in the black students' academic abilities, and hold various stereotypes and prejudices regarding them (for example, as unmotivated and disruptive).[36] Even independent of their distinct prejudices, the teachers often fail to understand the life situations and cultural backgrounds of their students, thus constraining their ability to deliver an equal education – to treat their students truly equally. (Earlier, I argued that schools had to recognize culturally distinct identities in service of a non-assimilationist, culture-respecting, integrationist ideal. Here, I am arguing that a related recognition is required for equality of educational opportunity.)

Wells and Crain contrast these teachers with a smaller number of what they call "visionary educators" whom the desegregation program has spurred to reevaluate their own pedagogies. "The visionary educators argue that showing students, especially African-American students, that white educators believe in them and support them is half the battle in trying to improve their academic achievement."[37] Thus there are racial, cultural, and class dimensions of what it would take for the largely white teaching force truly to provide equal education to students of color.[38] Doing so would be a significant achievement.

Apart from the behavior of teachers, a school can fail to provide equality of educational opportunity through a policy of tracking, defined here as assessing some measure of attainment (often thought of as "ability") in a cohort of students in the same grade, and then forming distinct classes according to results of that assessment. In desegregated schools, when (as is typical) the black and Latino children dominate the bottom track, with few in the top track, those children are almost inevitably deprived of equal educations.[39]

These complex forms of unequal treatment undermine equal educations. At the same time, a recognition of their character should be regarded as an important advance in our understanding of the range of factors involved in bringing about the ideal of equality of educational opportunity.

The unequal treatment of black students in urban or suburban, white-majority schools has persuaded some black parents to shun such schools. It is true that unless the equal treatment condition is met the equality of opportunity argument does not come fully into play as support for integrated schools. However, depending on the school's distance from this ideal, a black or Latino child might, all told, still be better off in a suburban school in which she was not treated fully equally than in an urban-majority black or Latino school with inferior educational resources. Many black parents send their children to such schools for precisely this reason.[40]

More recently, the focus on education as the domain of opportunity has been supplemented, and in some cases supplanted, by occupational or life chances opportunity, as the earlier quote from Gary Orfield suggests (above, p. 384). In the early years of desegregation, it might have been easier to believe that *educational* opportunity, and success, translated directly into *occupational* equality, and success. However, later research has indicated that occupational success functions partly independent of school success. Some researchers have shifted their focus to the longer-term issue of equal occupational opportunity as a distinct goal by which to assess desegregation, and have found that black students who attend racially integrated secondary schools do better in the world of work than their counterparts from monoracial schools.[41] If valid, this research provides not insubstantial support for racially mixed schools, especially a mixing of blacks and whites, though the argument is confined to middle-class whites.

I emphasize the distinguishing of equality of opportunity and racial integration primarily to *contrast* equality of opportunity arguments with other types of benefit of integrated education. While equality of opportunity (of either the educational or life chances variety) is indeed a vital goal by which to assess educational policy, racial integration included, it is nevertheless only one possible good and purpose of education, and of integrated education in particular.

In fact the notion of "equality of education" or "equality of educational opportunity" contains an ambiguity that has muddied the waters in this area. Equality of education is a good independent of the *quality* of education in question, as a matter of

justice. And *race-based* inequalities in education (as elsewhere) are particularly odious, even where the superior education received by whites is still relatively poor in quality.

Yet we must obviously be concerned about the quality of education received by all groups, and not only about its equal or unequal distribution among the groups. Perhaps ironically, the focus on equality of educational opportunity among both proponents and detractors of racial integration has had two confounding effects on the debate. First, it has tended to deflect a clear focus on the character and quality of the education received by the different groups. It has kept us from inquiring into the range of appropriate educational goals for a democratic and liberal society, goals that could then serve as standards by which to assess various forms of racial integration and separation. When the Thernstroms say (echoing Clarence Thomas's remark cited above, pp. 383–4), "[I]t is fortunate that there is no compelling evidence to support the belief that black students cannot learn, or cannot learn as well, when they attend schools with few white classmates," they seem to assume that we all agree what it is that these children are, or should be, learning.[42] The focus on the racial inequality issue encourages our failing to examine this assumption.

While the meaning of "education" in "equality of educational opportunity" can be neutral among conceptions of education, I believe that its general understanding in popular discourse, especially currently, tilts toward some conceptions of education and away from others. It tends to involve a consumerist, purely instrumental, and individualistic conception of education. The benefits of schooling are seen as accruing *only* to the individual student, rather than, for example, to the society or polity; it is individual students whose opportunities are at stake in "equality of opportunity."[43] What one student receives in the way of schooling is not seen as part of a larger picture in which other students are affected. Parents' search for good schools for their children has often become uncoupled from a sense that their child shares an educational fate with her cohort, that the education of one must be seen in the context of the education of others.

The educational benefits in the equality of opportunity framework also tend (again, not always, or necessarily) to be viewed in terms of cultural capital needed for the student to "get ahead" in the world, rather than in terms of their intrinsic educational, personal value. Schooling's social dimension

– social development that accompanies participating with fellow students in a learning community – also drops out of this picture. So the reigning understanding of equality of opportunity tacitly omits the moral, social, and civic dimensions of schooling, both as benefits to the society, and as non-individualistic or non-instrumental benefits to the student.

I will argue that these essential moral, social, civic, and personal dimensions of education can either be provided *only* in ethnoracially plural settings or that such settings are *much more likely* than monoracial ones to provide them. In virtually no case can the good be attained through mere ethnoracial co-presence alone; in that sense I agree with the criticisms of busing and other measures designed to increase ethnoracial plurality for its own sake that such measures lose sight of their relationship to the genuine goods of that plurality and to the several distinct factors needed to attain them. Those factors are manyfold, but I will focus on three – curriculum, pedagogy, and (a general catchall category) other school-based factors. (Thus I omit the vital factors related to the structural relations between ethnoracial groups in the larger society, which have a strong impact on relations among ethnoracial groups in schools.)

## Moral Goods in Integrated Education

While the civic, social, moral, and personal goods of integrated education are not entirely separable from one another, I will begin with moral goods, in part because Martin Luther King's paean to integration is cast in moral (and spiritual) terms, and also because this area has drawn extensive research. Moral growth among students regarding race involves at least the following goals: (1) reduction or elimination of racial prejudice, a goal that applies to all ethnoracial groups (because (ethno)racial prejudice has no racial boundaries),[44] and whose moral force derives in part from the more general moral principle of equal respect for all human beings;[45] (2) treating members of groups other than one's own as individuals (for example, by not stereotyping); (3) accepting members of groups other than one's own as co-equals in shared enterprises, and recognizing common interests with them in attaining superordinate goals; and (4) experiencing a sense of shared humanity with members of other groups, an exemplification of what Martin Luther King calls "a recognition of the solidarity of the human family."[46]

These goals have hardly been met in many ethnoracially plural schools. But at this point there is no excuse for accepting this unfortunate circumstance as an inevitable, or purely random, result of racial plurality. Largely spurred by court-mandated and voluntary efforts to desegregate schools, social scientists since the 1960s have engaged in extensive research on attaining these goals in ethnoracially plural settings. The language in which this research is couched is not always explicitly moral. For example, "improving intergroup relations" is a common formulation of a subject of research inquiry within social psychology, one that foregrounds a social, in contrast to a moral, aim. However, the moral aims are in fact presupposed. As a result of this research, we now know much about how racially mixed schools can reduce prejudice, increase mutual comfort and acceptance, weaken stereotyping, promote an appreciation of members of "racial outgroups" as individuals, promote a sense of shared attachment across ethnoracial boundaries to common goals and a consequent recognition of common interests, and, by implication at least, a recognition of common humanity. While many programs have not been fully tested, it is now clear that if teachers were appropriately trained and if school administrators would commit themselves to these goals, moral relationships between students of different races could be greatly improved, and the moral characters of students positively affected.[47] The education and education policy communities could make great strides toward King's vision of racial integration had they the will to do so.

All these moral/educational aims are extremely difficult to achieve in monoracial schools, of any race. Portions of some of them – aspects of multicultural curricula, or certain ways of teaching about stereotypes – could be accomplished in monoracial schools. But by and large the pedagogical programs and initiatives researched depend on the co-presence of students from different ethnoracial groups. They all concern ways to turn that presence into educationally and morally beneficial results.

## Civic Goods in Integrated Education

Racially integrated schooling plays, or can play, a vital *civic* role in a racially and ethnically plural democracy, a function not entirely distinct from the moral role just discussed. Civic education is increasingly recognized as an important component of schooling, as it was more explicitly in earlier historical eras, and a plethora of civic education programs have made their way into various schools, or have at least been crafted for this purpose. The *National Standards for Civics and Government* (created by the Center for Civic Education), and the esteemed California *History–Social Science Curriculum Framework* (which promotes a strong civic dimension in the study of history) are two prominent examples.[48]

Relations among ethnoracial groups are central to the requirements of civic education in the United States. Race has always been a central fault line in American life. Citizenship was formally limited to whites ("free white persons") in the 1790 Naturalization law, and racial restrictions on naturalization were not fully abandoned until 1952. Immigration policy was driven by racial considerations (not always acknowledged as such) until 1965, and initiatives to limit immigration in the mid-1990s (such as California's Proposition 187) are generally regarded as having a partly racist motivation as well.[49] While blacks were formally granted equal citizenship in the 13th, 14th, and 15th Amendments after the Civil War, their ongoing struggle for full status as equals in the American polity has suffered setbacks and reversals since that time, and has certainly not yet been completed.[50] The Supreme Court recognizes the deleterious yet historically central divisiveness of race by according laws containing racial distinctions the highest level of scrutiny among categories of social differentiation. While a staggering outpouring of major and/or popular general works on race in the United States in the 1990s disagreed on the extent and significance of improvement in the quality of lives of (primarily) blacks, there was much greater agreement on the large gulf of communication, perception, and social comity between the races.[51] This gulf is recognized by most to take its toll on the quality of civic cooperation and public interaction.

Yet, surprisingly, extant civic education programs give race very little attention. It is certainly not seen as a central civic concern. In general, the race-related civic goals such programs and guidelines propose consist in teaching that it is un-American to discriminate against people on the basis of race (as well as religion, creed, national origin, and the like).[52] These programs often also invoke a more general and vaguer idea of "equality" but without further elaboration of its implications for civic education regarding race.

Any attempt to spell out civic virtues is bound to be controversial. The burgeoning literature in this area within philosophy, political theory, and educational theory yields a wide range of qualities claimed as essential for citizens to sustain and reproduce the polity.[53] Differences stem from several sources – whether a minimalist or a more robust conception of civic education is sought; whether the liberal, democratic, market, republican, or other feature(s) of the society are particularly emphasized; how "moralized" the conception of citizenship; and others. Recognizing these controversies, I will offer a conception of citizenship specifically related to the domain of race that emphasizes the liberal, democratic, egalitarian, and participatory dimensions of our national traditions, and presupposes the recognition (1) of our history and continuing legacy of racial inequality and racialized understandings of (full) citizenship, (2) that ethnoracial differences constitute a particularly difficult and charged form of difference among our citizens, and (3) that, partly in consequence, ethnoracial differences mark significant lines of mutual ignorance and misunderstanding. Thus the model of civic education with which I operate goes beyond the minimal goal of cultivating those dispositions necessary to reproduce the current political order to encompass dispositions implied by ideals supposedly but not always actually embodied in current institutions and practices.

In this light I see at least four civic commitments, concerns, and abilities related specifically to the area of race that should be part of a civic education program. These incorporate but go beyond a commitment to non-discrimination just mentioned, and give substance to the idea of equality. One is a commitment to racial equity in the larger society, correcting the historical legacy of injustice. This involves, at least, a concern that the life chances of blacks and Latinos as groups be brought more in line with the life chances of whites, and, on the curricular level, presupposes students learning about the historical and current deficiencies of the American social order in the area of race.

This civic goal involves nurturing a general sense of social justice, directed specifically at racial inequities. That sense of racial justice is best promoted in a racially plural educational context, partly because students of color are more likely than white students to have had an experience of injustice and, especially in the case of blacks, Latinos, and Native Americans, to have been introduced by their families and communities to the idea of social justice as it bears on racial groups. Most (especially middle-class) white students, in the absence of direct educational exposure in this area, have little awareness or understanding of the experience of being racially discriminated against, being thought inferior, being an object of demeaning stereotyping, and the like. They have little understanding of how the world looks and feels to blacks, Mexicans, Puerto Ricans, or immigrants of color. They do not recognize the historical factors that have shaped the differing lives of distinct ethnoracial groups.[54]

White students' education in racial justice will thus be enhanced by exposure to the personal and familial experiences of students of color. Discussion of race and ethnicity-based experiences of injustice or insult personalizes the civic issues at hand, making them more compelling and accessible to white students than they would be through bare curricular study. (Explicit curricular study, however, must be a central part of this civic education, whether in racially plural or monoracial schools.) Even independent of the character of education and interaction in integrated schools, Orlando Patterson claims, "The sociological evidence is now overwhelming that Euro-Americans who went to school with Afro-Americans tend to be more tolerant and more in favor of greater educational and economic opportunities for Afro-Americans."[55]

A second, related but more general, aim is a broader sense of equal civic attachment and regard for members of all groups. As mentioned above, Smith has convincingly traced the historical sources of the deeply rooted failure of American society to regard its non-white members as full citizens. In addition, Thomas and Mary Edsall and others have convincingly argued that whites' failure to experience a sense of full civic attachment to blacks permeates many issues of public policy. Part of the opposition to government programs that has become a stable reference point in contemporary American politics stems, often on an entirely unacknowledged level, from a sense that people of color, and especially blacks, are the primary beneficiaries of such programs, whether this is true in any particular case or not.[56] For much of the white electorate, blacks and poorer Latinos are not experienced as fully part of the "we" whom they reflexively embrace in their view of the appropriate subjects of social policy. Equal civic attachment involves a sense of being bound up with those of other ethnoracial groups in a national, as well as local, community of shared fate,

accompanied by a conception of social good that embraces these other groups as well as one's own. That sense of shared fate frequently eludes members of many ethnoracial groups (not only whites) with regard to other groups, although its consequences are much more deleterious for the groups most in need of public attention and concern than they are for whites.

This sense of civic attachment can be promoted by ethnoracially plural education in a manner similar to the way the sense of racial justice can be promoted. Respectful classroom interchange that draws on differing experiences and perspectives of students of different groups tends to promote that sense of connection that can be expanded into a sense of civic attachment, while it still recognizes and validates the distinct ethnoracial identities that students bring to the classroom interchange.

Beyond this, schools can more directly promote civic attachment by explicitly constructing the school itself, its subunits, and to some extent its classes, as civic spaces. Being sensitive to promoting a sense of ownership of the school on the part of members of all groups by promoting participation in policy making and rule setting, in extracurricular activities, in community-affirming rituals, and the like, serves to encourage a sense of shared attachment among students, and shared responsibility for the school as a civic community.[57]

A third civic aim is to decrease social segregation and the social discomfort, strain, and absence of relation that so often currently exists among persons of different racial groups. This absence of social connection is, as a civic concern and a social phenomenon, distinct from social injustice and inequity (though they are sometimes conflated), and also distinct from equal civic attachment. This aim is civic in a broader sense. It concerns the quality of public life, not only engagement with processes related to the making of official policy.

The related educational task is for students to learn ways of being with members of other racial groups without perpetuating this sense of ethnoracial strain and disconnection. For this they need to learn to be interpersonally comfortable, including sharing public spaces in the school, with ethnoracial others. Students must learn to engage one another across these divides, and not be paralyzed by fear that what they say will offend someone of another group, yet be open to learning about what does offend, and able to discuss these matters further. None of this can be learned in monoracial schools. Stephan's work, mentioned earlier in connection with moral aims, is pertinent here.[58] Classes themselves must be mixed, and forms of cooperative education (including group projects with ethnoracially mixed groups) utilized that promote mutual respect.[59] Other venues for providing superordinate goals are drama, sports, and other extra-curricular activities, service and civic projects, and the like.

A fourth civic aim is the ability to communicate and engage with those of other distinct ethnoracial groups in the process of public deliberation, compromise, and shared institutional commitment necessary to the functioning of democratic institutions in a racially plural society. This cross-racial civic deliberation requires the more general civic skill of communicating honestly and fruitfully across the socially salient gulf of race difference about issues related to race. [ . . . ]

## Personal Benefits of Integrated Education

I have dwelt on the moral and especially the civic benefits of ethnoracially plural schooling because these are particularly striking lacunae in much dispute about integration and desegregation. But the individual student benefits in other ways, also not captured on the equality of opportunity model. The moral and civic virtues enable one to "live well," as Aristotle said. They provide richer and more meaningful forms of engagement with one's fellow citizens and human beings, and with the larger society.

Beyond this, learning about the experiences, outlook, and histories of ethnoracial groups other than her own is a vital part of a student's learning about the character of her own society and world. Any education with a plausible claim to being called "quality" must involve a deep understanding of the social reality of one's society. I mentioned earlier that, in an instrumental sense, children of color suffer more in the loss of social capital from an ignorance of their society. Whites can much *better* afford to be ignorant of the lives of non-whites than the reverse. Still, my point here is not this socially related cost but the intrinsic educational loss to the student of a lack of knowledge of other groups.

Of course some of this knowledge can be provided through a rich multiculturally sensitive curriculum, even in monoracial or near-monoracial schools. But, first, while some teachers in such schools may provide such a curriculum, the pressure and perceived need for it is likely to be much greater in ethnoracially plural schools.[60] Second, and more important, my argument has been that a school that draws on the experiences of students and their families in multiracial classroom settings will be the most felicitous setting for students of all groups to see the point, retain knowledge, and achieve a deeper understanding of the social realities of groups other than their own.

The second personal educational benefit is that knowledge of one's society involves a form of *self*-knowledge. In understanding the race-based experience of groups other than one's own, one comes to understand not only "the other" but also oneself. This is so on several levels. One is as an American. The plurality of ethnoracial groups is a deep part of the fiber of American life, so in understanding them one gains a deeper appreciation of one's Americanness as a social and cultural identity. In particular, all major ethnoracial groups have had an impact on the shape of popular and political culture that form the fabric of social existence for all Americans. Many whites recognize that certain styles of dress, modes of personal interaction, language, music, films, dance, and the like, originated with distinct non-white groups. Blacks are unquestionably the most prominent group in this regard; their cultural influence far outstrips their proportion of the population. But, especially in certain parts of the country, and increasingly everywhere, Latinos have had an impact on food, language, music, and the like. Fewer whites may recognize that cultural forms they think of as "white" or – more vaguely but still with an implication of whiteness – as "mainstream" have been decisively influenced by Latinos, blacks, Native Americans, and others.[61] Political culture and institutions too have been decisively shaped by the European encounters early in our history with Native Americans and Africans, and, later, especially with Mexicans. More recently, the Civil Rights movement has had a profound effect on public and legal understandings of equality and justice, American-style.

## Expanding the Horizons of White Students

Echoing the equality of opportunity argument, Orlando Patterson says, "Integration is about the acquisition of social and cultural capital [by

Afro-Americans]."[62] Yet all the benefits discussed in the previous sections accrue to whites as well as to students of color, or to the society as a whole. Segregated schooling and a segregated life are very constricting to white students.[63] These sheltered white students do not learn how to "read" the behavior of individuals in other ethnoracial groups. They do not get to know members of these groups as individuals. They cut off a large source of friendships and friendly acquaintanceships.

Sheltered white students fail to develop what some have called "multicultural and multiracial competence" – a recognition of and knowledge about cultural and racial differences that allows individuals to negotiate a culturally pluralistic world.[64] Lack of such competence will affect white students who will have to function in an increasingly culturally plural work environment. Janet Schofield cites a report commissioned by the U.S. Department of Labor, which concluded that "the ability to work effectively in a context of cultural diversity is one of the basic competencies which is required to perform effectively in the U.S. labor force."[65] An absence of integrated education could thus have a materially deleterious effect on whites. (As mentioned above, racial minorities are *more* harmed by lack of multicultural competence, a point integral to the occupational form of the equality of opportunity argument.)

In closing this discussion of the potential benefits of ethnoracial diversity in schools, let us note how it provides the answer to Clarence Thomas's oft-echoed show-stopper, "It is insulting to say that blacks need to sit next to whites in order to learn." The response given by proponents of the equality of opportunity argument, such as Orfield, and Wells and Crain, is "But for access to higher status knowledge and personal/occupational networks, blacks do need to sit next to whites." That answer is compelling as far as it goes, but its still-lingering sense of insult stems from a failure to recognize that white students have much to learn from black students also. Such mutual interchange among students of different ethnoracial background is of great value to blacks too, and to Latinos, Asian-Americans, whites, and so on. That benefit is to the individual student but also to the larger society.

## Conclusion

The retreat from a commitment to integrated education betokens a loss of faith in the democratic promise of schooling in a culturally pluralistic society. I have not explored whether that pessimism about schools is empirically justified. My argument has been more minimal. A range of vital personal and civic goods – communication, cooperation, understanding, civic attachment, commitment to racial justice, multiracial competence and personal comfort, social and self-understanding – is virtually unattainable without, or is greatly facilitated by, racial and cultural plurality in the student bodies of our schools. These goods have dropped out of sight in public discourse concerning both desegregation and school reform more generally.

[ . . . ]

The moral, civic, and personal sensitivities, concerns, and abilities must be deliberately taught; students do not acquire them through mere contact, in school, with members of other ethnoracial groups. Disappointingly, these goals are not given a central place even in most programs of civic and moral education, much less in teacher education more generally. Their full realization requires teachers and schools sensitive to cultural and life situation differences among students; who themselves believe that all students have contributions to make to the education of other students; who are committed to facilitating interracial understanding, conversation, and cooperation as an integral part of their educational goals; who have learned, or are in the process of learning, the pedagogical skills necessary to facilitate this goal. It also requires that teachers so described have the support of their institutions and its key administrators. The institution must not set the cultural identity of students against the school's own cultural norms but must manifest a culture of inclusion, respect, and faith in all children's ability to learn.

Is it asking too much that teachers learn to provide safe and trusting settings in which they can facilitate cross-racial connections, the frank expression and discussion of racial issues and experiences – in which they can teach racially oriented civic virtues? One hesitates to add new demands to teachers already grappling with new mandates of standardized tests and enhanced accountability. Nevertheless, racial and ethnic pluralism and the legacy of historical injustice will be with us for the foreseeable future, and will continue to play a large role in the real world of schools and classrooms. Teachers often conceive of their roles in narrow ways that prevent them from acknowledging the impact of these responsibilities – that it is not their place to deal with social development of students, that merely mixing students is sufficient to teach respect and acceptance, that they must totally ignore race and color in interaction with students.[66] But educators cannot really afford not to pay attention to racial matters, any more than they can afford not to deal with moral and civic issues generally.

While Martin Luther King, Jr.'s vision of deep moral and civic relationships across racial lines has lost its luster among all ethnoracial groups, a re-visioned conception – shorn of its assimilationist associations, and aware of the complexities or racial prejudice and division – remains as valid today as it was in King's time. The *Brown* Court was right to brand both educational inequality and racial separation as moral wrongs, even if its reasoning was not entirely adequate, and some of its specific arguments no longer applicable. Moreover, in the world of education, we now know better how to create the integrationist vision than we ever have known before. The future of the highest ideals of our democracy requires that we not abandon it.

## Notes

1. Examples in large metropolitan areas are Wilmington (Delaware), Louisville (Kentucky), and St. Louis. See Gary Orfield and John T. Yun, "Resegregation in American Schools," report of the Harvard University Civil Rights Project (1999), p. 18. J. S. Fuerst and Roy Petty in their 1992 study of school integration add: "[M]anaged integration – achieved largely through intelligent use of busing – is working in hundreds of small and medium-sized communities all across the country." "Quiet Success: Where Managed School Integration Works," *The American Prospect*, Summer 1992, p. 65.

2. Orfield and Yun. Gary Orfield and Susan Eaton, *Dismantling Desegregation: The Quiet Reversal of Brown v. Board of Education* (New York: New Press, 1996), ch. 3: "The Growth of Segregation."

3. *Missouri v. Jenkins*, 115 S. Ct. 2038 (1995).

4. See, for example, Glenn Loury, "Integration has had its day," *New York Times*, April 23, 1997. The lead article in the August 5, 1998, edition of *Education Week* begins, "African-American parents, by an overwhelming margin, want the public schools to focus on achievement rather than on racial diversity and integration, a survey released last week says." It goes on to say that white parents express anxiety about integration.

5. Orfield and Eaton, p. xv. David Shipler captures a related attitude among blacks, stated by Laura Washington, an editor and publisher: "My mother's not a real big fan of white people. But she said to me: 'You've got to live with them. If you're going to be professional and go out into the world you're going to have to work with them every day ... You need to learn how to understand how they think and how they live and the cultural differences, and you better learn it as early as you can. So go to an integrated high school.'" David Shipler, *A Country of Strangers: Blacks and Whites in America* (New York: Vintage, 1997), p. 102.

6. Gloria Ladson-Billings, *Dreamkeepers: Successful Teachers of African American Children* (San Francisco, CA: Jossey-Bass, 1994), p. 3.

7. I adopt David Hollinger's useful phrase "ethnoracial" group to emphasize the partly racial, partly panethnic/pancultural character of the five major such groups – African-Americans, Native Americans, Latinos, Asian-Americans, and Euro-Americans. Pluralism as an ideal must also be cognizant of distinct cultural groups within each of these ethnoracial groups (e.g. Haitian-Americans, Chicanos, Korean-Americans). David Hollinger, *PostEthnic America* (New York: Basic Books, 1995).

8. Martin Luther King, Jr., "The Ethical Demands for Integration," in James M. Washington (ed.), *A Testament of Hope: The Essential Writings and Speeches of Martin Luther King, Jr.* (San Francisco, CA: HarperCollins, 1986), p. 118.

9. Randall Kennedy, "In Praise of Racial 'Integration,'" in *IntellectualCapital.com*, July 24, 1997.

10. An argument could also be made that the term "desegregation" or "desegregated schools" should be completely abandoned except where it involves the process of altering racial demographics in a school previously intentionally created as racially segregated. Stephan and Abigail Thernstrom point out that the notion of "desegregation" (understood as a process rather than an end state) regnant in the 1970s – breaking up clusters of black students and placing them in majority white schools – is obsolete, if we confine ourselves to extant school district boundaries, for the cities to which desegregation orders of that era were applied no longer have white majority schools. Stephan and Abigail Thernstrom, *America in Black and White: One Nation Indivisible* (New York: Touchstone, 1997), pp. 337–8.

11. Orfield and Yun, pp. 25, 14. Since the authors' figures do not supply the percentage of actual schools with different racial demographics, one is unable to

determine the percentage of students sharing schools with students of particular percentages of ethnoracial groups other than their own.

12. As Fuerst and Petty note, "With little fanfare, integration has become a fact of life for the majority of African-American school children in the United States." ("Quiet Success," p. 65.)

13. Orfield and Yun, p. 15.

14. Antonia Darder, Rodolfo D. Torres, and Henry Gutierrez (eds.), *Latinos and Education: A Critical Reader* (New York: Routledge, 1997).

15. Peter Schmidt, "California district strives to mix blacks and Hispanics," *Education Week*, April 12, 1995, p. 3. See also Lynn Beck and Rebecca Newman, "Caring in One Urban High School: Thoughts on the Interplay among Race, Class, and Gender," in Deborah Eaker-Rich and Jane Van Galen (eds.), *Caring in an Unjust World: Negotiating Borders and Barriers in Schools* (Albany, NY: SUNY Press, 1996), concerning both tensions and positive relations among blacks and Latinos (mostly Central American immigrants) in a high school.

16. A black parent cited in an article about black disenchantment with integration makes this point about the reality, and whites' understanding, of integration: "Some blacks are rethinking integration for the simple reasoning that it never happened . . . We have extended the olive branch only to find that whites don't want integration, they want assimilation. People aren't willing to give up that much of their own identity for integration." Wil Haygood, "Race in American life: Ideals giving way to reality," *Boston Globe*, September 14, 1997, A1.

17. Cited in John Brenkman, "Race Publics," *Transition*, issue 66 (undated), p. 27.

18. David Shipler, *A Country of Strangers*, p. 34 and elsewhere, cites blacks making this point.

19. Many blacks were of course aware of the distinctness of black culture, which had been articulated in this period by Ralph Ellison, Langston Hughes, and others. Perhaps the black legal activists at the NAACP were equally aware that cultural differences might play a role in the success of integration. But such issues had no legal standing, and there was no reason to bring them into the desegregation arguments.

20. Horace Kallen, Randolph Bourne, Alain Locke, and W. E. B. DuBois were influential proponents of cultural pluralism in the first decades of the 20th century.

21. There exists a burgeoning literature on the importance of respect for and sensitivity to cultural and racial factors in providing effective, quality education to racial-minority children, and on methods for incorporating that respect into pedagogy. Some of the most important works are Sonia Nieto, *Affirming Diversity: The Sociopolitical Context of Multicultural Education*, 2nd edn (White Plains, NY: Longman, 1996); Gloria Ladson-Billings, *The Dreamkeepers*; Theresa Perry and Lisa Delpit, *The Real Ebonics Debate* (Boston, MA: Beacon Press, 1997); Ann Locke Davidson, *Making and Molding Identity in Schools: Student Narratives on Race, Gender, and Academic Engagement* (Albany, NY: SUNY Press, 1996); Lisa Delpit, *Other People's Children: Cultural Conflict in the Classroom* (New York: New Press, 1995); Rosina Lippi-Green, *English with an Accent: Language, Ideology, and Discrimination in the United States* (New York: Routledge, 1997); Sonia Nieto, *The Light in Their Eyes: Creating Multicultural Learning Communities* (New York: Teachers College Press, 1999).

22. For criticisms of the *Brown* Court's reasoning, see Andrew Kull, *The Color-Blind Constitution* (Cambridge, MA: Harvard University Press, 1992); Thernstrom and Thernstrom; David Armor, *Forced Justice: School Desegregation and the Law* (New York: Oxford University Press, 1995).

23. The important cases making explicit the legal standing of the legacy argument are *Green v. New Kent County* 430 U.S. 391 (1968) and *Swann v. Charlotte-Mecklenburg Board of Education* 402 U.S. 1 (1971).

24. A variation on this argument claims that in American society racial separation itself damages the self-worth of blacks. I argue elsewhere that *de facto* school segregation that results primarily from residential segregation partakes of something like the inferiority-declaring force of what was objectionable about *de jure* segregation. "'Racial Integration' Revisited," in Joram Graf Haber and Mark Halfon (eds.), *Norms and Values: Essays on the Work of Virginia Held* (Lanham, MD: Rowman & Littlefield, 1998), p. 211.

25. For an extended critique of the alleged empirical connections between segregation, self-worth, and academic motivation stated or implied in the *Brown* decision, see Roy Brooks, *Integration or Separation: A Strategy for Racial Equality* (Cambridge, MA: Harvard University Press, 1996), pp. 13–21. As Brooks points out (citing Walter Stephan) there are reasons for thinking that white-dominated schools in which blacks are a minority may well involve factors tending toward the *lowering* of black self-esteem – whites' racism against blacks, blacks' comparison of themselves to better-prepared white students, loss of power and status (compared to majority black schools) merely from being a minority (Brooks, p. 23).

26. Brooks, p. 12.

27. From text of Court's opinion, cited in Richard Kluger, *Simple Justice* (New York: Vintage, 1975), p. 781.

28. *Brown* in Kluger, p. 780.

29. *Brown* in Kluger, p. 782.

30. For example, the statement "In no school that I saw anywhere in the United States were nonwhite children in large numbers truly intermingled with white

children" is proffered early in the book in the context of a discussion of unequal education, as if it were barely conceivable that a group of black children could become educated in any significant sense in the absence of whites. Jonathan Kozol, *Savage Inequalities: Children in America's Schools* (New York: Harper Collins, 1991), p. 3.

31. Two of Orfield's studies are cited above (notes 1 and 2), and there have been many others over the past decades, with the Harvard University Civil Rights Project sponsoring them approximately every two years since the early 1990s.

32. See, for example, the issue of *Social Philosophy and Policy* devoted to "Equal Opportunity", vol. 5, issue 1, Autumn 1987; Kenneth Howe, *Understanding Equal Educational Opportunity* (New York: Teachers College Press, 1997); and Amy Gutmann, *Democratic Education* (with new preface and epilogue) (Princeton, NJ: Princeton University Press, 1999), pp. 128–39.

33. Robert Carter, "The Unending Struggle for Equal Educational Opportunity," *Teachers College Record*, vol. 96, no. 4, Summer 1995, p. 621.

34. Shipler, *A Country of Strangers*, 34 and elsewhere.

35. Nor are black teachers entirely immune from prejudice against especially poor black and Latino children.

36. Robert Crain and Amy Stuart Wells, *Stepping Across the Color Line: African-American Students in White Suburban Schools* (New Haven, CT: Yale University Press, 1997). Personalizing this general insight about unequal treatment, a black male student, interviewed by Sara Lightfoot in her study of "good high schools," speaks of white teachers in one school who seem repelled or afraid of darker-skinned black students, contrasting them with the school's principal, "who does not draw back from him." Sara Lawrence Lightfoot, *The Good High School: Portraits of Character and Culture* (New York: Basic Books, 1984).

37. Crain and Wells, p. 290.

38. Delpit, *Other People's Children*.

39. Wells and Crain describe a modification of a common three-tiered tracking system, namely a two-tiered one, used in some of the St. Louis schools they studied. The two tracks are "honors" and "everyone else." While the honors classes were often all-white, Wells and Crain plausibly claim that the presence of a strong racial mixture in the other track, and the absence of an almost-all-black bottom track, makes this form of tracking substantially superior for the black children to the three-track model. There are other lesser forms of tracking – for example, having permanent ability groups *within* a single desegregated classroom, but not creating the classes themselves by ability group sorting.

There is a good deal of literature on tracking debating its pros and cons, but a substantial body of research suggests that non-tracked schools are better for the "lower ability" students while not being detrimental to the "higher ability" ones. See Jeannie Oakes, *Keeping Track: How Schools Structure Inequality* (New Haven, CT: Yale University Press, 1985).

40. The METCO program in Boston, in which racial minority children can choose to attend suburban (generally overwhelmingly white) schools, at great inconvenience (long bus rides, culturally alien environments, difficulty of parental contact with school, and the like), has been a going concern for several decades.

41. Amy Stuart Wells and Robert Crain, "Perpetuation Theory and the Long-Term Effects of School Desegregation," *Review of Educational Research*, Winter 1994, vol. 64, no. 4, pp. 531–5. The relevant literature cites three factors that convert black attendance at white majority schools into enhanced occupational success, independent of student school achievement. The first comprises skills of interaction in a white world, which enhance the student's self-presentation in applying for jobs, and his or her subsequent ability to negotiate the cultural terrain of white-dominated workplaces, thus enhancing job performance. The second is access to information about colleges and jobs that would not be attained at schools serving a less-middle-class clientele, a climate of support for pursuing higher education, school counselors pushing and helping students to make application to colleges, and the like. The third is the school's reputation; in general, an employer, or college, is more likely to select a black graduate from the integrated than the segregated school. (Note that the first two aspects concern class factors as well as, or intertwined with, racial ones.) It is worth noting here that one of the important pre-*Brown* integration cases, *Sweatt v. Painter* 339 U.S. 629 (1950) – ruling against a segregated law school in Texas with facilities and expenditures comparable to the then-white-only University of Texas Law School – makes use of very similar arguments.

42. Thernstrom and Thernstrom, p. 342.

43. "Equality of opportunity" can also take a more group-based focus, where the groups in question are defined by race, class, or gender. While this conception is less individualistic, it still does not engage with the larger social good of education; moreover, some conceptions of this group-based good see the group as simply standing in for the interests of individuals within the group, rather than involving a good to the group in its own right. Such a conception is made explicit in Brooks, *Integration or Separation*.

44. The *consequences* of racial prejudice and their moral seriousness are not symmetrical across racial groups, however. For a discussion of this issue, see L. Blum, "Moral Asymmetries in Racism," in S. Babbitt and S. Campbell (eds.), *Racism and Philosophy* (Ithaca, NY: Cornell University Press, 1999).

45. Not all forms of departure from the principle of equal respect are equally objectionable. Among such forms, race-based discrimination is particularly invidious, because of the historic evils that have attended it.

46. King, "Ethical Demand for Integration," p. 121. Randall Kennedy speaks of seeing oneself and racial others as "neighbors united by ties that run deeper than those of racial kinship" and "not as members of separate racial tribes" ("In Praise of Racial 'Integration'"). This absolute prioritizing of common humanity over ethnoracial solidarity is not, I think, required by a true integrationist vision, including King's, and is not consistent with the pluralist version of integration that I advocate here. While in *some* sense our common humanity is deeper than our ethnoracial particularity, in other ways the solidarity of discriminated against racial groups is no less meaningful or valid than the common humanity.

47. Walter Stephan, *Reducing Prejudice and Stereotyping in Schools* (New York: Teachers College Press, 1999). A substantial body of literature in social psychology (summarized by Stephan, a major figure in the development of this literature) explores the conditions (in schools and classes) under which individual racial prejudice is reduced and interracial acceptance and liking promoted. Much of the literature operates within a paradigm deriving from Gordon Allport's 1954 work, *The Nature of Prejudice* (Reading, MA: Addison-Wesley, 1979 [1954]), known as the "contact hypothesis." That hypothesis asserts that contact between groups is more likely to lead to reduction in prejudice and greater acceptance when the contact is characterized by equal status; when it involves cooperative activity in the service of shared, superordinate goals; when it is supported by the authority of the surrounding institution(s); and when it involves the perception of common interests and common humanity between members of the two groups.

48. Center for Civic Education, *National Standards for Civics and Government*, 1994. *History–Social Science Framework* (for California Public Schools Kindergarten Through Grade Twelve) (adopted by California State Board of Education, 1987).

49. See Juan Perea, *Immigrants Out: The New Nativism and the Anti-Immigrant Impulse in the United States* (New York: New York University Press, 1997) and Rogers Smith (below, note 50).

50. In a recent exhaustively researched work on the history of American citizenship, Rogers M. Smith argues convincingly that the conception of American citizenship as inclusive of all who swear allegiance to (what are taken as) American values and institutions, independent of race, religion, and ethnicity, is seriously deficient, and that American laws and public understandings of citizenship have historically been bound up with racial (and other ascriptive) hierarchies. Only if we face up to the contamination of our understandings of citizenship by these racialist views can we fully achieve the liberal, democratic conception of citizenship that many wrongly regard as already triumphant. Rogers Smith, *Civic Ideals: Conflicting Visions of Citizenship in U.S. History* (New Haven, CT: Yale University Press, 1997). Matthew Frye Jacobson's *Whiteness of a Different Color: European Immigrants and the Alchemy of Race* (Cambridge, MA: Harvard University Press, 1998) argues that notions of "whiteness" have been and are deeply intertwined with ideas about "Americanness."

51. A small sample of major popular or scholarly works on race in this period: Cornel West, *Race Matters* (Boston, MA: Beacon Press, 1997); Jennifer Hochschild, *Facing Up to the American Dream: Race, Class, and the Soul of the Nation* (Princeton, NJ: Princeton University Press, 1995); Andrew Hacker, *Two Nations: Black and White, Separate, Hostile, and Unequal*; Patricia Williams, *The Alchemy of Race and Rights* (Cambridge, MA: Harvard University Press, 1991). Other works mentioned herein: Thernstrom and Thernstrom, Sniderman and Piazza, Shipler, Tatum, Patterson.

52. It is the burden of books like Smith and Jacobson to argue that racial discrimination is only partly, and ambiguously, "un-American."

53. A good summary of some of the most influential trends in recent citizenship theory is Will Kymlicka and Wayne Norman, "Return of the Citizen: a Survey of Recent Work on Citizenship Theory," *Ethics*, 104 (January 1994), pp. 352–81.

54. Conversely, school may well be the one setting in which blacks, Latinos and other people of color can learn how the world looks to white people. It is sometimes said (in contrast to the converse) that racial minorities do understand whites, since they must learn something about the white world in order to make their way in it. The truth in this insight can be greatly overstated. Racially isolated blacks and Latinos often carry around extremely oversimplified and overgeneralized views of whites; and the knowledge necessary to navigate a white-dominated society may remain at a surface level. In addition, the different groups of color themselves may well be isolated from one another socially, and school may provide the best, or the only, venue in which they can learn about one another as well.

55. Orlando Patterson, *The Ordeal of Integration: Progress and Resentment in America's "Racial" Crisis* (Washington, DC: Civitas, 1997), p. 191.

56. Thomas and Mary Edsall, *Chain Reaction: The Impact of Race, Rights, and Taxes on American Politics* (New York: W. W. Norton, 1992). See also Donald Kinder and Lynn Sanders, *Divided by Color: Racial Politics and Democratic Ideals* (Chicago: University of Chicago Press, 1996). Paul M. Sniderman and Thomas Piazza, *The Scar of Race* (Cambridge, MA:

Harvard University Press, Belknap Press, 1993). While Sniderman and Piazza are concerned to demonstrate that far from all opposition to government programs benefitting blacks stems from racial prejudice, their findings nevertheless support the idea that *some* of the opposition lies in this source and that there is still a good deal of racial prejudice among whites, even if (as I agree) many social analysts misleadingly overstate both the degree of white racism and its impact on stances on policy issues.

57. Lawrence Kohlberg, better known for his paradigm-creating work in moral development theory, also did pioneering work in creating democratic communities in schools. See F. Clark Power, Ann Higgins, and Lawrence Kohlberg's misleadingly titled *Lawrence Kohlberg's Approach to Moral Education* (New York: Columbia University Press, 1989).

58. See note 47.

59. "Cooperative learning," which brings groups of racially heterogeneous students together in working groups, with a common task, and scope for all to make distinctive and recognizable contributions to the group effort, is generally regarded as facilitating more positive intergroup relations. See the summary by two of the leading researchers in this area, David W. Johnson and Roger T. Johnson, "Social Interdependence: Cooperative Learning in Education," in Barbara Benedict Bunker and Jeffrey Z. Rubin (eds.), *Conflict, Cooperation, and Justice: Essays Inspired by the Work of Morton Deutsch* (San Francisco, CA: Jossey-Bass, 1995).

60. This is a purely pragmatic argument. On my view, the need for a rich multicultural curriculum is not dependent on the ethnoracial demographic of a school (though the details of it may be – for example, a district with a large Laotian immigrant population has reason to give more attention to Laotian culture, history, and experience than a district that does not).

61. Almost all forms of what most whites think of as distinctively "American" music for example (even including country and western music) have been shaped, often decisively, by the black presence in America.

62. Patterson, *Ordeal of Integration*, p. 191. Patterson does not entirely believe that this is the *only* value of integration since, as noted earlier, he cites the increase in tolerance and concern for justice for Afro-Americans on the part of whites as an important effect of integration.

63. To note one pointed example, a middle-class white girl who attended a mixed school reported how acquaintances of hers who attended all-white schools rolled up the windows of their cars when a car of black kids pulled up alongside them. H. Andrew Sagar and Janet Ward Schofield, "Integrating the Desegregated School," in *Advances in Motivation and Achievement*, volume I (New York: JAI Press), 230.

64. This argument does not distinguish between racial groups and ethnocultural groups. These are by no means the same. First generation Haitian-Americans have cultural norms distinct from African-Americans, though both are "black" and may be subject to similar racism. There are important cultural differences among different "white" groups. Every so-called "racial" group in the United States – that is, groups thought of racially even when a geographical term like "Asian" or "Latino" is used to designate them – contains myriad cultural groups within it. Nevertheless, the way that cultural and racial group identity are so intertwined in the United States makes the above argument applicable to both.

65. Janet Ward Schofield, "Review of Research on School Desegregation's Impact on Elementary and Secondary School Students," in Kofi Lomotey and Charles Teddlie (eds.), *Readings in Equal Education*, vol. 13 (New York: AMS Press, 1996), p. 92.

66. Janet Ward Schofield, *Black and White in School: Trust, Tension, or Tolerance* (New York: Teachers College Press, 1989), a superb study of the effects of desegregation in a middle school, masterfully articulates attitudes held by teachers (both white and black, though somewhat less by the latter group) that stand in the way of their being proactive in civic education in the area of race. See especially chapter 2: "The Teachers' Ideology."

# 30

# "Getting Religion": Religion, Diversity, and Community in Public and Private Schools

## Meira Levinson and Sanford Levinson

### The Diversity Argument Elaborated: The Importance of "Mingling"

Since their founding in America, "public" or "common" schools (as they were originally designated) have been justified by reference to the social goods that were and are thought to be produced by the process of bringing together children of different backgrounds in a single setting. As Horace Bushnell wrote in 1853 of the "great institution . . . of common schools," "There needs to be some place where, in early childhood, [individuals] may be brought together and made acquainted with each other; thus to wear away the sense of distance, otherwise certain to become an established animosity of orders; to form friendships; to be exercised together on a common footing of ingenuous rivalry. . . . Without this he can never be a fully qualified citizen, or prepared to act his part wisely as a citizen."[1] Similarly, Theodore Roosevelt commented some half-century later, "We stand unalterably in favor of the public school system in its entirety," because when "Americans of every origin and faith [are] brought up in them,"

they "inevitably in after-life have kindlier feelings toward their old schoolfellows of different creeds, and look at them with a wiser and manlier charity, than could possibly be the case had they never had the chance to mingle together in their youth."[2] These high ideals carry into contemporary times. As Stephen Macedo has recently written, "The whole point of the common school is to be a primary arena where children from the different normative perspectives that compose our polity encounter one another in a respectful setting, learn about one another, and discover that their differences do not preclude cooperation and mutual respect as participants in a shared political order."[3] One might be tempted to ask, with a suitably rhetorical flourish: If "common" does not mean this, then what *does* it mean?

All three of these men agree that a diverse student body is essential for educating citizens. It is generally agreed that citizenship in a liberal democracy requires that one tolerate and even respect people who are different from oneself, who hold different beliefs, and engage in actions or life practices that are unfamiliar, discomfiting, or even

Previously published in Alan Wolfe (ed.), *School Choice: The Moral Debate* (Princeton, NJ: Princeton University Press, 2003), pp. 110–18, 123–4, 305–6. © 2003 Princeton University Press. Reprinted with permission of Princeton University Press.

repugnant. The reason is eminently practical: In a contemporary society consisting of many different groups with quite conflicting ways of understanding the world, a Hobbesian world of endless conflict can be avoided only if individual citizens develop at least enough respect for one another to resist the temptation to suppress those they disagree with or, equally important, to escape the constant anxiety that one will herself be the target of suppression if other groups come to power. (The existence of legal "parchment barriers" against such suppression will scarcely suffice to control the manifold forms of hostility or oppression that can result from antagonistic views of the Other.) In order for people to come to tolerate and respect others, it is generally thought that they need to interact with these "others" in close, meaningful ways that enable them to see the commonalities among them (that are therefore respect-worthy) and at least to understand the reasons for the differences that remain between them.[4] It is also useful if these interactions occur at an early age, before prejudices have the chance to harden and block the development of mutual understanding. Schools are thus seen as being essential, possibly unique, institutions for bringing diverse individuals together under these conditions. As a result, diverse schools are lauded for their service in promoting toleration and civic virtue.

This is no small point. Both of us attribute great – and positive – significance to our experiences growing up in Southern communities with a group of close friends drawn from a variety of Christian religious denominations, ranging from Roman Catholic to Southern Baptist.[5] Not only did we (separately) spend a lot of time discussing and debating fundamental questions of religion, but we also learned to tolerate the different answers that were given. Sanford Levinson has written about his experiences in Hendersonville, North Carolina, and the importance of ensuing friendships: "We too often automatically sneer at the phrase 'some of my best friends are Jewish (or any other religion or race),' but, surely, it would be a profound social good if all of us could in fact say, with conviction, that some of our best friends are from groups other than those with which we most centrally identify."[6] It is hard to believe that societies as heterogeneous as our own can flourish (or perhaps even survive) if the particular intimacies of friendship are limited to those who are exactly like oneself.[7]

We see this same process playing out in schools today. In the eighth-grade Boston classroom where

Meira Levinson teaches, it has been striking to observe how the presence of even one student from a minority group can over time alter other students' attitudes toward that group. In one notable discussion, students' diatribes against the house calls made by Jehovah's Witnesses were brought to a screeching halt when they discovered that one of the most popular boys in the class is a Jehovah's Witness. Although the initial change in the tenor of the discussion was undoubtedly due to students' feeling the need to *show* respect rather than their actually *feeling* more respect, students also then started paying attention to an explanation about *why* Jehovah's Witnesses proselytized door-to-door – an explanation which they had totally ignored (although it had been brought up by the teacher) earlier in the conversation. Increases in mutual respect have also been brought about by critical confrontation in the classroom. For example, in another class, a Haitian student commented that the Chinese ate rats,[8] and turned to the sole Asian student in the classroom for confirmation. When informed that she was Vietnamese, not Chinese, he responded, "Vietnamese, Chinese, whatever" – but was none too pleased a second later to hear the teacher comment, "Yeah, Dominican, Haitian, Puerto Rican, whatever." This led to a series of discussions about history (Asian, American, Caribbean, Latin American), stereotypes, prejudice, cultural differences, and (of course) eating habits, among other topics, and noticeably increased some students' toleration of and understanding of each other, although there is still a long way to go. Furthermore, it has been blindingly clear that this author's students in a highly integrated Boston middle school are much more worldly and tolerant than her students were in an all–African American middle school in Atlanta, largely because of the relative limitedness of the latter's experience with Others.

Such anecdotal offerings are bolstered by some social scientists, such as those relied on by both the University of Michigan, and in turn the federal district court that ruled in favor of the university, when they defended the university's racial- and ethnic-preference programs against Fourteenth Amendment attack. Patricia Y. Gurin, a professor of psychology at the university, prepared a report that found that "students . . . are better prepared to become active participants in our pluralistic, democratic society once they leave" what the court described as "a racially and ethnically diverse student body."[9] The judge also quoted Professor

Gurin's finding that such students were also "better able to appreciate the common values and integrative forces that harness differences in pursuit of common ground."[10]

In addition to diversity's civic accomplishments, student (and sometimes teacher) diversity is also lauded for enabling individual students to develop their capacities for autonomy. This is an educational goal distinct from students' development of civic toleration and respect – although as many people have pointed out (including each of us in other contexts), probably not a distinct pedagogical process; while the goals may be logically separable, their achievement or failure seem not to be separable in practice.[11] The aim of helping students develop their autonomy, however, is a distinct justification for maintaining diverse, "common" schools. As children encounter peers and teachers who do and believe different things from what they do and believe, and as they discuss, compare, and debate their own ways of life with others, children necessarily move from accepting their lives simply as unexamined givens to some version of an examined life. Indeed, in explaining his own intellectual development (including developing into a highly self-conscious intellectual), Sanford Levinson gives far greater weight to his friends and their intense discussions than to the formal courses he took at Hendersonville High School. And this is not meant as a particular knock at that particular high school; one suspects that many persons could offer similar autobiographical anecdotes even if they attended far more urbane institutions of secondary education.

The material offered by Professor Gurin (and the University of Michigan) is relevant to this strand of the argument as well. She reports that multiple sources of data demonstrate that "students who experienced the most racial and ethnic diversity in classroom settings and in informal interactions with peers showed the greatest engagement in active thinking processes, growth in intellectual engagement and motivation, and growth in intellectual and academic skills." They are also described as especially able to "understand and consider multiple perspectives [and] deal with the conflicts that different perspectives sometimes create."[12] Diversity thus seems an altogether winning policy, insofar as it led Gurin to conclude that "on average, students who attend more diverse institutions" exhibit a greater "intellectual engagement and motivation index" and a greater "citizenship engagement index."[13] In addition, an amicus brief

by the United States cited "a study by Alexander Astin, Director of the Higher Education Research Institute at the University of California, in which Astin associates diversity with increased satisfaction in most areas of the college experience and an increased commitment to promoting racial understanding and participation in cultural activities, leadership, and citizenship."[14] There are, no doubt, many empirical studies of primary and secondary schools that reach similar conclusions, though, equally without doubt, one could raise all sorts of methodological questions about the ways that one could actually test with confidence for the qualities allegedly causally linked with diversity.

In sum, diversity in schools is thought (and was historically thought) to be both civic promoting and autonomy promoting. Schools with diverse student bodies serve both the community, by promoting the civic virtues of toleration and respect for others, and the individual, by enabling students' development of autonomy through interaction with students who are different. As a result, for both toleration-promoting (civic) and autonomy-promoting (individualistic) reasons, "common schools" with diverse student bodies should be maintained, protected, and further developed, and school diversity should be taken into consideration when examining and evaluating school voucher programs or other school-assignment options.

To say that diversity matters, of course, is to leave many questions unanswered. The most obvious is, what kinds of diversity matter? The importance of racial and ethnic diversity is what is defended in the Michigan (and earlier University of Texas Law School) case, just as gender diversity is assumed insofar as in America (although, notably, not in Great Britain and many other countries), virtually all public schools are coeducational. For both civic- and autonomy-promoting reasons, however, it would seem that religious diversity would be at least as highly desirable. [ . . . ]

## "Getting Religion"

Should our measurement of student diversity include religious diversity? On civic-toleration grounds, the answer *must* be yes. In the United States, there is considerable mutual suspicion between and among conservative Christians, secularist cosmopolitans, liberal and Orthodox Jews,[15] atheists, Muslims, Mormons, Wiccans, members of the Nation of

Islam, and Scientologists, to name only a few of the relevant groups. Whether or not it is accurate to describe Americans as involved in a "culture war,"[16] it is hard to believe that sustained, respectful interaction among members of different religious groups would not be beneficial to American society. In order to promote the development of a mutually tolerant and respectful civil society, therefore, it would seem that schools should have a student body that is religiously diverse (as well as diverse along other dimensions). Indeed, immediately after university presidents Bowen and Bok speak of the importance of "greater 'cultural awareness across racial lines . . .' and stronger commitments to improving racial understandings," they go on to write as well of the "importance of differences in religion."[17] If schools are successful in their efforts to "get religion" in the sense of encouraging attendance by religious students, then their classmates might be considerably more likely to "get religion" at least in the sense of realizing that people holding even exceedingly odd religious views are nonetheless members of the same overarching community.

On autonomy-promoting grounds, it would also seem obvious that children would be well served by going to school with other children from a variety of religious backgrounds and genuinely engaging with them in respectful discussion about the ways and reasons their lives are different. Although cultural-coherence arguments have some play here – we should not rock a child's foundations before those foundations are even in place – certainly by middle school students should be exposed to practitioners of a variety of religious beliefs if the aim is to help them both to recognize the reasonableness of other beliefs and ways of life and to critically examine their own beliefs and practices in service of developing their autonomy. This seems to be especially true for religious diversity, because religion is explicitly about belief (at least for most religions), unlike race, social class, gender, and the like. While racial diversity, for example, clearly serves civic-toleration ends, it less obviously directly promotes autonomy, insofar as white students cannot chose to become black, for example; even the questioning of one's assumptions, which is the hallmark of autonomy, would depend in this case on the questionable assumption itself that racial diversity necessarily implies belief diversity. Religious diversity thus not only promotes children's development of autonomy, but may be superior to other types of diversity in doing so.

This assumption that students' interaction with others will lead to engagement with others (and Otherness) is buttressed in a recent article by University of Chicago law professor Emily Buss. As she notes (and as any parent or, indeed, middle-school teacher knows without needing to read academic tomes), adolescents often withdraw in one measure or another from the intensity of the domestic setting and develop close friendships with peers, who are often those they meet at school. Citing a great deal of evidence from the literature of child development, Buss views such relationships as central to the formation by adolescents of what will, in time, become their mature adult identity. "It is largely through these relationships that [adolescents] pursue the difficult and important task of identity formation – the sorting and selecting of values, beliefs, and tastes that will define their adult selves. Who those peers are and, particularly, the diversity of their convictions and attitudes, will have a significant effect on the course of that development."[18]

As a practical matter, this means that some religious children will be likely to be lured away from "home truths" because of the impact of their more secular classmates; it also means, though, that the opposite may occur as well, that a Jewish child will in fact be persuaded that salvation requires acceptance of Jesus as her Savior or simply that a secular child raised in a relentlessly rationalistic household will develop a more "spiritual" posture toward the world than the parents might prefer. So what? It is hard to see how a liberal society can prefer, as an abstract matter, a shift from religious to secular identities, whatever might be the preferences of most people who call themselves liberals. And the fact that the various parents of the respective children might be unhappy about their "straying" from the parents' preferences is not an interest that a liberal society can regard as particularly significant. The primary goals of any such society are the reproduction of its basic commitments (i.e., to a defensible form of liberalism) in future generations and, at the same time, production of the conditions by which students can themselves become autonomous selves and not the mere reflections of their parents' desires as to how they should live their lives.[19]

If religious diversity in schools is important for promoting both civic virtue and individual autonomy, then adherents of either goal (liberal civic education or the development of an autonomous self) would have a strong incentive to oppose public vouchers for religious schools if it is true that they would serve both to increase the number of homogeneous schools and at the same time decrease the amount of religious diversity in public schools. (Indeed, strong proponents of these goals should also oppose even private financing of religious schools, as one of us has demonstrated elsewhere,[20] but this is obviously a very controversial position. And, thanks to *Pierce v. Society of Sisters*,[21] it would also certainly violate currently accepted constitutional norms. [ . . . ]

It is to be expected that most religious schools explicitly promote religious segregation. To take the easiest case, a Seventh-Day Adventist or fundamentalist school that is run by and uses curricula supplied by the parent church or like-minded co-religionists is unlikely, as an empirical matter, to attract students from different religious backgrounds, even assuming that the schools in fact have space remaining after serving their primary constituency of fellow members of the given church. The same is true for a yeshiva or, indeed, a Jewish Day School. [ . . . ] Catholic schools, interestingly enough, seem quite receptive to non-Catholic students, though it would also be surprising if there were no significant selection biases with regard to parents who choose to send their children to such schools. (How often do atheist or even agnostic parents choose a Catholic education for their children?)

In addition to religiously segregating students who choose to attend such a school, religious schools also function to promote religious segregation in the public and nonsectarian private schools they leave behind. [ . . . ] As religious students make use of school vouchers to attend religious schools, fewer religious students will remain back in the public schools, thus reducing religious diversity in these public schools. (Presumably some students using already-available vouchers at nonsectarian private schools would also choose to switch to religious schools once vouchers became available, so the argument would apply to some extent to private schools as well.) This assumes, of course, that a greater proportion of religious students than non-religious students would choose to avail themselves of vouchers to attend religious schools, but this assumption does not seem unreasonable. This is therefore an additional diversity-based (and ultimately civic- and autonomy-based) argument against religious-school vouchers.

The same grounds that initially seem to mandate against religious-school vouchers, however, also mandate in favor of new, positive, religious-diversity-promotion policies in the public schools. Religious diversity should be taken into account along with racial, ethnic, socioeconomic, and gender diversity. A heavy-handed program would be to assign students to schools in a way that promotes religious diversity, via altering catchment areas and bus routes.[22] But a less heavy-handed and more realistic policy could establish schools that act as religious "magnets" to draw religious minorities voluntarily into otherwise religiously homogeneous schools. One "magnet" draw could be an adjusted school schedule that satisfies local board requirements but has longer days on Mondays through Thursdays and halfdays on Fridays, or plays only Thursday-night football games, or takes off Rosh Hashanah, Eid Fitr, Epiphany, and Chinese New Year as official school holidays in exchange for extending the term slightly longer into the summer. Another approach would be to have a vegetarian cafeteria that is compliant with Jewish, Muslim, Buddhist, Jain, or Hindu dietary practices. Both of these strategies are entirely structural and would have no appreciable effect on the curriculum, but could significantly increase the religious diversity of the student body. This could be true as well of a third accommodation, which would be to allow "moments of silent reflection" or the installation of chapels into which, for example, Muslim students could go to say those of their five daily prayers which occur during school hours.[23] These would, presumably, alleviate at least some expressed concerns that schools are hostile to even the most minimal expression of religious commitments.[24]

A fourth strategy that does have curricular implications, but ones that seem quite minor, would be to broaden or change foreign-language offerings at the middle- or high-school level to include Hebrew, Arabic, Japanese, or Hindi, and the like, depending on the local population. This approach again might attract a number of families who would otherwise either stay in a neighborhood school within a minority-religious enclave or seek out private religious schools for their children. All of these strategies would have the instrumental goal of encouraging religious diversity on the grounds that it is at least as valuable in pursuing traditional liberal goals as racial and ethnic diversity, at least insofar as the grounds for that pursuit rest on civic-education or individual-autonomy justifications. [ . . . ]

What [ . . . ] the civic and personal goals that diversity is supposed to help satisfy may suggest, then, is that receipt of public funds – in the form of direct funding of public schools or vouchers for private schools – should be contingent either on satisfying certain diversity criteria or on adopting strategies to increase diversity at the school. In the case of public schools, therefore, schools and districts might adopt the religious "magnet" programs discussed above as a way of increasing their religious diversity, while also continuing – or, more accurately, reviving – the pursuit of racial, ethnic, socioeconomic, and other forms of diversity. Private – both religious and nonsectarian – schools that wished to receive public vouchers would need to prove they were either already sufficiently diverse (and the meaning of this would obviously need to be debated and clarified in practice) or that they were taking practical, measurable steps to make themselves more so. Some schools would choose to comply; others would not, and therefore would not receive vouchers. And interestingly, [ . . . ] some religious schools are more likely to be in compliance than some nonsectarian private schools are.

It is worth noting that these arguments strongly weigh against any support of home schooling. Almost by definition, home schooling works against the kinds of diversity that we, with many others, deem important. It is, obviously, not at all the case that specific home schooling parents might not be extremely sensitive to the kinds of concerns we are emphasizing and would, therefore, make special efforts to introduce their children to a wide array of people. But we are, to put it mildly, wary either of believing that there will be many such parents or, more importantly, of accepting as desirable a mode of education that limits the amount of contact that children will have with others during the "schooling" process itself. As several of our earlier anecdotes suggested, the presence of other children can be vital to appreciation of the dangers of facile stereotyping. It may be, for libertarian reasons, that parents should retain, legally, the right to home school their children. But any such decisions should receive no affirmative public support that might, indeed, serve as an incentive for yet other parents to choose that path.

Note well, though, that the major reason to reject public subsidies for home schooling must be the acceptance of some version of our argument about the desirability of diversity and its importance with regard both to civic education and development of an autonomous self. If education were merely instrumental – dealing, say, with the acquisition of certain knowledge capable of being tested for on standard examinations – then it is altogether possible that many home schooled children could do just fine. Indeed, supporters of home schooling point, with justifiable pride, to the academic success of many homeschooled children, though we have no good evidence about how representative these children are of the entire universe of home-schooled students.

## Notes

1. Horace Bushnell in Rush Welter (ed.), *American Writing on Popular Education: The Nineteenth Century* (New York: Bobbs-Merrill, 1971), p. 182.
2. Quoted in Stephen Macedo, *Diversity and Distrust: Civic Education in a Multicultural Democracy* (Cambridge, MA: Harvard University Press, 2000), p. 93.
3. Macedo, *Diversity and Distrust*, p. 194.
4. We put it this way because it might be too heroic an aspiration that everyone accept the substantive "reasonableness" of the views – and, even more so, the behavior – of others. One need not believe, for example, that it is truly "reasonable" not to mix milk and meat in order to respect the reasons that lead observant (and even some non-Orthodox) Jews to maintain adherence to this tradition of kashruth.
5. See Sanford Levinson, "Some Reflections on Multiculturalism, 'Equal Concern and Respect,' and the Establishment Clause of the First Amendment," *University of Richmond Law Review* 27 (1993), p. 989

(noting also the costs of growing up in a segregated society that meant that all of these friends were white).
6. Levinson, "Some Reflections on Multiculturalism," pp. 995–6.
7. This means, among other things, that (liberal) society as a whole almost certainly benefits from the "intermarriages" that are often bewailed by leaders of particular groups. To take what some would consider an extreme example, every marriage of an Israeli Jew with an Israeli Arab, whether Christian or Muslim, would be a cause for rejoicing on the part of any liberal.
8. Which is, in fact, true of at least some Chinese; see, e.g., Peter Hessler, "A Rat in My Soup," *New Yorker*, July 24, 2000, pp. 38–41. However, the student's assertion was not made by way of pointing to the remarkable culinary differences among cultures but, rather, as a sign of the true Otherness of all Chinese.

9. *Gratz v. Bollinger*, 122 F. Supp. 2d 811, 822 (2000), citing the "Gurin Report," p. 3. It should be obvious that this decision patently conflicts with Judge Friedman's decision several months later in *Grutter v. Bollinger*, 137 F. Supp. 2d 821 (2001). Presumably, the Sixth Circuit Court of Appeals will choose between them (and then, inevitably, the Supreme Court will be given an opportunity to weigh in).

10. *Gratz v. Bollinger*, at 822, quoting the Gurin Report at p. 5.

11. Meira Levinson, *The Demands of Liberal Education* (Oxford: Oxford University Press, 1999), pp. 101–6; Amy Gutmann, "Civic Education and Social Diversity," *Ethics* 105 (April 1995), pp. 516–34; Harry Brighouse, "Is there Any Such Thing as Political Liberalism?" *Pacific Philosophical Quarterly* 75 (1994), pp. 318–32; Eamonn Callan, *Creating Citizens* (Oxford: Oxford University Press, 1997), ch. 1, esp. pp. 39–42.

12. *Gratz v. Bollinger*, at 822, citing the Gurin Report, p. 5.

13. *Gratz v. Bollinger*, at 822, citing the Gurin Report, p. 5.

14. *Gratz v. Bollinger*, at 822, citing Brief for the United States, pp. 20–1.

15. Whose suspicions of each other is, one suspects, as easily as great as any suspicion directed at Jews from outside these communities.

16. Compare, for example, James Davidson Hunter, *Culture Wars* (New York: Basic Books, 1991); and James Davidson Hunter, *Before the Shooting Begins: Searching for Democracy in America's Culture War* (New York: Free Press, 1994), with Alan Wolfe's considerably more optimistic assessment in *One Nation after All: What Middle-Class Americans Really Think about God, Country, Family, Racism, Welfare, Immigration, Homosexuality, Work, the Right, the Left, and Each Other* (New York: Viking, 1998).

17. Bowen and Bok, *The Shape of the River: Long-term Consequences of Considering Race in College and University Admissions* (Princeton, NJ: Princeton University Press, 1998), p. 228.

18. Emily Buss, "The Adolescent's Stake in the Allocation of Educational Control between Parent and State," *University of Chicago Law Review* 67 (2000), p. 1233.

19. These arguments are spelled out in Levinson, *The Demands of Liberal Education*, chs. 1 and 2.

20. Levinson, *The Demands of Liberal Education*, pp. 144–5; Levinson, "Some Reflections on Multiculturalism," p. 1011.

21. 268 U.S. 510 (1925).

22. One might also be tempted to describe it as not only heavy-handed, but unconstitutional. If, though, racial preferences, which are presumptively unconstitutional, can nonetheless be justified because of the "compelling interest" of diversity, as many of their proponents allege, then it would seem that an identical argument would legitimize the otherwise prohibited taking into account of religion when designing catchment areas. See Sanford Levinson, "Diversity," *University of Pennsylvania Journal of Constitutional Law* 2 (2000), pp. 602–5; Eugene Volokh, "Diversity, Race as Proxy, and Religion as Proxy," *UCLA Law Review* 43 (1996), pp. 2059, 2070–6.

23. See Jodi Wilgoren, "On Campus and on Knees, Facing Mecca," *New York Times*, February 13, 2001, which describes efforts that MIT has made with regard to the increasing number of Muslims on its campus. Indeed, it turns out that the University of Texas Law School, unlike MIT a decidedly state institution, has reserved a room within its library that serves as a chapel for students who wish to make use of it.

24. They also need not be seen as coercing other students into religion. In Meira Levinson's experience in teaching in Atlanta, at least, where Georgia law mandates forty seconds (!) of daily silent reflection, middle schoolers often stopped for silent reflection in the most absurd physical posture possible (in midstep, for example, balanced on one foot, or perched precariously on a desk) as teachers snapped repeatedly, "Quiet! Close your mouths! Silent reflection!" In what at other times felt like an emphatically religious (Christian) setting, especially for a public school, "silent reflection" never seemed to acquire any religious overtones.

# Impairment, Disability, and Excellence

# 31

# The Myths of Learning Disabilities

## G. E. Zuriff

If the reports are to be believed, our children are in the grip of a cognitive epidemic. Nearly two-and-a-half million U.S. school children are currently diagnosed with learning disabilities (LD), an increase of roughly 150% in fifteen years. In Massachusetts, for example, 17% of schoolchildren have LD. Between 1988 and 1994, the number of students entering college with LD increased 142%. Of all disabled children, 52% are LD, up from 24% in 1976. My purposes in this paper are to: (1) provide an historical understanding of the LD concept; (2) raise serious objections to the conceptual and empirical bases of the LD concept; and (3) show that LD is a socially constructed disorder (i.e. one created to serve social needs) rather than a medically or scientifically based one.

The LD concept was introduced in the 60s to describe children of normal cognitive capacity who nevertheless had trouble learning in school because of assumed neurological dysfunctions. These LD children were thought to have problems in the *psychological processes* needed for academic success, not in their basic intelligence. They therefore could be helped by instruction in the deficient psychological processes.

Educators and parents of LD children soon founded several national organizations to inform the public and advocate for the learning disabled. The Learning Disabilities Association of America, the largest, now has over 60,000 members in 775 chapters. In addition, a new industry emerged to diagnose, treat, and lobby for LD persons and to consult to businesses, colleges, and government.

Eventually this LD lobby brought pressure to bear on state and Federal governments. Their major victory came in 1975 with the signing of a Federal law mandating that all children, regardless of disability, are entitled to a free and appropriate public education. To support this entitlement, the Federal government provides funds to local educational programs based on the number of participating students. Now known as the Individuals with Disabilities Education Act (IDEA), this act mandates that schools must provide all disabled students, including LD students, free services, diagnosis, an individualized education plan, and special education specifically designed for their disability.

Congress also passed Section 504 of the Rehabilitation Act of 1973 and the Americans with Disabilities Act of 1990 (ADA). These laws protect the

Previously published in *Public Affairs Quarterly* 10(4) (October 1996), pp. 395–405. Reprinted with permission of Public Affairs Quarterly.

civil rights of individuals with disabilities in employment, public accommodations, transportation, and government services. Under these laws, LD is considered on a par with physical disabilities. Not only is discrimination outlawed, but businesses, public facilities, and universities must make "reasonable" accommodations for persons with disabilities. For example, colleges are required to modify any degree requirement, examination format, or admission standard that discriminates against LD students. Similarly, for employers of a LD individual, these accommodations may include special computers, aides to read material to the employee, or reassignment of certain tasks to other employees.

Thus, a diagnosis of LD carries profound implications throughout life. But along with the LD child (let us call her Jennifer), there are other students having academic problems. Labelled "slow learners" rather than LD, they are seen as possessing low intelligence, and their poor performance is therefore to be expected. The slow learner (call him Scott) is not considered disabled and is thus ineligible for the benefits and protections afforded Jennifer. The difference between Jennifer and Scott is supposedly best captured in the fact that Scott does poorly in nearly all his classes, as would be expected of someone with low cognitive ability, while Jennifer does quite well in many classes, and fails only a few, suggesting that she is basically intelligent and would excel in school but for her specific brain dysfunction.

One might assume that with the billions spent under IDEA and ADA, and with the millions of Americans deeply affected by these laws, there is a clear definition of LD and good reasons why Jennifer is said to have it but not Scott. Yet a careful conceptual examination of LD shows that many of our commonly held assumptions are only myths and that the LD concept is seriously flawed.

The first myth of LD is that Jennifer and Scott must be treated differently because Jennifer, but not Scott, is known to have a brain dysfunction. Contrary to this widely held belief, however, of all the millions diagnosed with LD, few have had a brain examination showing anything wrong. In nearly all LD cases, the diagnosis is based on observations of academic work and performance on psychological tests. Brain dysfunction is inferred by a process of elimination – if no other cause for Jennifer's unexpected school performance is discovered, the conclusion is that a neurological condition must be responsible. In Scott's case, however,

because he is merely a slow learner and his poor performance is expected, there is nothing to explain and no brain dysfunction need be inferred. Nevertheless, the fact remains that we still do not know the biological basis for either Jennifer's or Scott's school difficulties.

To understand this myth's hold on the LD movement, we must understand its history. In pioneering research at the end of the 19th century, early neurologists studied the often strange symptoms of individuals who survived traumatic head injuries. In some cases, the patients returned to near cognitive normalcy with a few peculiar exceptions in language. For example, a brain-damaged patient might speak and understand English quite well but have lost the capacity to read. These patients could see and hear the letters; their problem was that they could not make sense of specific language information.

Eventually, similarities were noted between these patients and uninjured school children who were normal in nearly every respect but who had specific deficits in language skills. Some showed good intelligence in many subjects but had serious difficulties in reading, writing, or verbal expression. From these observations, early neurologists constructed a critical but deeply flawed syllogism: If people with known brain damage (i.e. head injured patients) show certain cognitive symptoms (i.e. specific language deficits) but are otherwise normal, then children who show the same cognitive symptoms and are also otherwise normal, must have similar brain damage from other causes.

Thus began a long and tortuous history of attempts to find the specific brain dysfunction responsible for LD. As each theory has proven wrong, others have arisen to take its place. The belief in a neurological cause has proven irresistible and remains a central tenet of the LD movement.

To see the weakness of the syllogism, consider another analogy. One morning my car does not start. My neighbor tells me that when his car failed to start, he discovered worn spark plugs. I then reason: His car and mine have similar symptoms (i.e. problems starting); since the reason for his car's symptoms is worn spark plugs, my car also must have worn spark plugs. We immediately recognize the logical flaws. My car might not be starting for a variety of reasons (e.g., no gas, weak battery); a similarity of symptoms does not necessarily entail a similarity of causes. In the same way, the children and the brain-injured patients may have similar symptoms for very different reasons. Furthermore, in the case of my car, we have ample evidence that with increased use, plugs do get worn and fail to start the car. With children, we have no evidence whatsoever that the kind of brain damage caused by a head injury can also occur in a child with no head injuries.

Besides its tenuous logic, the brain dysfunction myth is questionable on other grounds. It assumes that LD children suffer with a brain dysfunction, but slow learners do not. According to the myth, Scott's brain is normal; it is just functioning inefficiently – there are fast normal brains and slow normal brains. Why should we accept this myth? When it comes to math and reading, Scott and Jennifer both function very poorly. We have no evidence that in these subjects, their brains are operating differently. Even if we do someday find differences in functioning, if neither brain is doing well in these areas, why call one brain "dysfunctional" and the other just "slow?" After all, cognitive capacities are all based somewhere in the nervous system, and both Jennifer's and Scott's problems are ultimately to be traced to the brain.

To be sure, modern neuroscientists using anatomical techniques and magnetic resonance imaging scans have found abnormalities in the brains of a very small number of dyslexic children. However, the brains of these LD children are judged abnormal only in comparison to those of normal children. No study to date has compared the brains of LD children to those of slow learners. Were such comparisons to be made, we may well find that Scott and Jennifer share common abnormalities in the brain areas associated with math and reading but they differ markedly in other areas. Or we may find that Jennifer and Scott exhibit no brain similarities, and that their brains differ from normal brains in different ways. In this latter case, we still have no rationale for considering only the deviations in Jennifer's brain to be "dysfunctions."

The only known difference between Jennifer and Scott is that Scott has difficulties in all his subjects while Jennifer has difficulties in only some. Clearly, we should reject the myth of brain dysfunction and either admit that Scott's consistently poor academic performance is equally the result of brain dysfunctions, or admit that Jennifer's uneven school performance is the result of normal variations among normal brains.

If Jennifer and Scott are not distinguished by brain examination, how is LD identified for Federal grants and special accommodations? According to a 1976 U.S. Office of Education definition, LD involves a "severe discrepancy between achievement and intellectual ability" in one or more of 8 specified areas, including listening and reading comprehension, and mathematical calculation. Although this formulation was later dropped by the Office, it was adopted by many states to interpret the vague language of IDEA. This definition fits the image of Jennifer as a bright child whose brain disorder manifests itself in the discrepancy between how well she should be performing based on her intelligence and her actual poor achievement. Scott on the other hand, is not LD because he shows no discrepancy; as a slow learner, his low performance is appropriate to his overall low intelligence.

Diagnosis is thus a two-step procedure. Children are given I.Q. tests to measure intelligence as well as a series of standardized achievement tests to assess academic achievement. Any student showing at least a normal score on the I.Q. test but a significantly lower score on one of the achievement tests is diagnosed with LD. For example, Jennifer may score an I.Q. of 103, indicating that she is of above average intelligence, while Scott may have scored only a below-average 89. Yet, both may score a poor 85 on reading achievement. Because only Jennifer shows a "severe discrepancy," she alone is diagnosed as LD.

Plainly, every discrepancy definition must specify "normal intelligence." For some states the cut-off point is an I.Q. of 90 and for others, 85. Thus, in some states, Scott would not qualify for LD benefits, regardless of how low his achievement scores are because they would be considered the expected result of his below normal intelligence. He also is not eligible for special education as mentally retarded because mental retardation requires an even lower I.Q., as low as 70 in many states. He remains stuck in the grey area of "slow learner" – an I.Q too high for mental retardation status, but too low for LD.

That children identified as LD through these discrepancy definitions are qualitatively different from slow learners is a second myth of LD. Discrepancy definitions are riddled by problems. First, although I.Q. tests have proven to be good predictors of a variety of adult achievements, they do not measure the full range of intellectual potential. There are many kinds of intelligences, and I.Q. measures only a narrow range of these, particularly those dealing with abstraction and analysis.

A second problem is that, whether or not I.Q. tests are biased, the fact is that African-Americans have an average I.Q. test score of 85, 15 points below the average score of whites. This means that if a LD definition specifies 85 as the lower limit for normal intelligence, then half the African-American population will automatically be excluded from qualifying for LD benefits, regardless of their academic difficulties, as compared to only 15% of whites. This use of I.Q. tests in LD diagnosis probably accounts for the fact that although under IDEA, whites and blacks receive special education at comparable rates, only 44% of those blacks qualify as LD as compared to 52% of the whites.

Problems with achievement tests are even more serious. Although the number of achievement tests generated by educators has proliferated, among the nearly 100 tests currently available, very few have been rigorously studied and proven their validity. Even fewer are scaled adequately for adults and for college level skills.

Another questionable assumption of the discrepancy model is that performance in school should be consistent with I.Q. score, and discrepancies therefore reflect something amiss. Yet, we all know of scientific whizzes in math and physics who are not very good at writing; as well as brilliant literary critics who are lost when they see mathematical symbols. The fact is that we lack good data on how frequently discrepancies occur within our population. Indications are that discrepancies are normally distributed, just as cognitive abilities are. An unusually large discrepancy is thus no more a symptom of a disorder than is an unusually low achievement unaccompanied by a discrepancy.

The discrepancy model also assumes that I.Q. and achievement tests, although correlated, measure different things. This is why Jennifer can be viewed as having high intelligence but low math achievement. However, it is well known that achievement problems, especially deficiencies in reading and language listening, can depress I.Q. scores, and this depressing effect increases with grade level. Ironically, because of his reading problems, Scott will thus have an increasingly difficult time scoring in the "normal range" of I.Q. to qualify as LD. The alleged independence of I.Q. and achievement tests is further undermined by the fact that thinking or reasoning is often included among the achievement skills included in LD definitions. Yet, reasoning and thinking are the very core of intellectual aptitude, and it seems philosophically odd that there can be a severe discrepancy between intelligence and reasoning.

The discrepancy model further assumes that the low intelligence of slow learners fully accounts for their academic failings. However, recent research has shown that many children with low I.Q.s may do quite well in reading. In fact, among children with reading problems, I.Q. score is not a good predictor of the degree of reading impairment. This research thus overturns the assumption that Scott's reading deficiencies are a direct result of his low I.Q.

Because of these problems with the discrepancy model, many researchers recommend abandoning it. However, because of the discrepancy myth's strong hold, they have replaced the aptitude/achievement discrepancy formula with yet another discrepancy formulation. This new discrepancy is not between aptitude and achievement, but among the achievements themselves. This "intra-skill definition" still works against Scott. Since his performance is consistently low in all academic skills and not "specific," he does not show the required intra-skill discrepancy, and he still will not qualify as LD. To be sure, this newer definition avoids the objections to I.Q. tests, but it leaves all the problems associated with invalid achievement tests, the vagueness and arbitrariness of a cut-off point for a "significant discrepancy," the high probability of "false positives" due to multiple testing, and inconsistencies in diagnostic criteria.

These problems suggest a third myth – that LD is a well defined disorder. In a 1985 survey of leaders in the study of LD, 59% reported that the most critical problem facing the field was in finding an accepted definition for LD. In 1991, an entire issue of *Learning Disability Quarterly* was devoted to articles on defining LD. The confusion continues today. Although the 1977 Department of Education definitions are regarded as obsolete and unscientific, they still determine eligibility for Federal funds, and are therefore the most widely used. Because they are vague, they have been differently interpreted by the various states. In addition, many states have their own definitions for state laws. Complicating matters more, researchers, educators, administrators, and organizations have their own, sometimes contradictory, definitions. At the bottom of this chain of abstraction are the specialists who ultimately decide which students receive special education for LD. Studies have shown that their decisions are often not only inconsistent with one another but also inconsistent with the diagnostic criteria they think they are following.

Under ADA, the situation is yet more confusing. The law does not specify assessment methods, diagnostic criteria, or who is authorized to diagnose LD. For example, the University of Georgia found that 54% of applicants claiming LD did not meet the University's eligibility criteria, and similarly, the New York State Board of Law Examiners disqualifies most applicants for special accommodations on the bar exam. Yet, in both situations, most applicants provided documentation supporting their claims and had previously been granted special accommodations for LD. The myth that LD is a well defined psychological disorder is thus undermined by controversy and uncertainty over diagnostic criteria.

A disturbing illustration of how LD diagnosis can spin out of control occurred at the prestigious Dalton School in Manhattan. In 1984, Emily Fisher Landau donated more than $2 million to establish a learning disability program there. With 14 learning specialists for only 400 children, LD diagnosis ran amok. Within one three-year period, 36% of all 5-year-olds were being given remedial help. By 1992, half of Dalton's students entering fourth grade had already received remedial help – all this occurring at a highly selective school, where the mean I.Q. is above 130 and 40% of the graduates enter Ivy League colleges. Fortunately, in 1992, the program was dismantled when the teachers revolted, refusing to administer the diagnostic tests, and the number of LD pupils at Dalton plummeted back to earlier levels.

Even if discrepancy definitions can be made precise and conceptually coherent, it is yet only another myth that they distinguish among low achieving students in any meaningful way. One popular myth is that LD students have trouble hearing, seeing, or "processing" verbal materials. For example, they supposedly see letters out of sequence or reversed. Our mythical picture is that Jennifer can read perfectly well, but when she looks at a page, the letters are distorted, making reading difficult. Accordingly, in the 70s, treatment for LD students was not specialized instruction in the skills troublesome to them but rather "off-task process training," that is, training to improve their presumed perceptual/ motor deficiencies. LD students trained on exercise mats, trampolines, and other non-academic skills.

Eventually, however, research showed that process training does not improve cognitive skills, academic performance, or even the processes they were designed to improve. Yet, the myth stubbornly

refuses to die. For example, among individuals requesting special accommodations on the New York State Bar Exam on the basis of LD, the most commonly cited supporting clinical evidence is some sort of visual processing deficit.

Too often, a diagnosis of a problem in "processing" information is misunderstood to mean that the individual has a sensory problem. In fact, the term "processing," borrowed from computer jargon, is simply a technical sounding word referring to any cognitive activity such as understanding, learning, and interpreting. To say that someone has a deficit in processing a specific kind of information is to say merely that person has problems learning, understanding, remembering, or using that kind of information. In those cases in which LD individuals are shown to have processing deficits, for example, in phonological processing (i.e. the ability to hear sounds precisely and associate them with written letters), these deficits are no different from those of slow learners having comparable academic problems. Reversals do not occur more often in dyslexics than in slow learners having comparable reading problems, nor do reversals account for most of the reading problems in dyslexics. In numerous studies comparing children with discrepancies to children having comparable school problems but with no discrepancies (i.e. "slow learners"), it is nearly always found that the two groups are virtually indistinguishable in the nature of their learning problems.

The most pernicious myth of LD is that individuals diagnosed with LD on the basis of a discrepancy require special kinds of education while slow learners do not. Yet, careful research shows that both LD students and slow learners benefit from the very same kind of special education and have the same prognosis. In fact, many of the instructional techniques now recommended for LD children were first used successfully with slow learners. This instruction focuses, not surprisingly, directly on the academic skills troubling the pupil rather than on some assumed perceptual process deficit. Direct instruction is self-paced and intensive, with the child moving on to the next level of difficulty only after the prerequisite level is highly mastered. Although both Scott and Jennifer will benefit from this special education, only Jennifer will receive it because only she has the discrepancy requisite for the LD label and funding.

The remedy for this unconscionable situation is simple enough and has been advocated by several leading researchers for years. *All* students having serious trouble in school are learning disabled in certain ways and should be given appropriate remedial instruction, regardless of whether they show discrepancies. All the dollars spent each year on LD diagnoses can be better spent on improving the education of all children failing in school. Determining which children are in need of remedial instruction can most simply and efficiently be carried out by the regular teacher. An additional assessment by an educational specialist could screen for emotional problems, inadequate prior instruction, or sensory impairments and map each child's particular problem areas. Most importantly, we can skip the costly step of determining if the student is LD or simply a slow learner, and immediately provide the appropriate remedial instruction.

Why has this solution been resisted for so long? The more fundamental question is why is the field of learning disabilities in such a conceptual mess? With the passage of IDEA and the Rehabilitation Act, LD became an entitlement, and a LD diagnosis became the admission ticket to that entitlement. With a LD diagnosis, a parent can guarantee a child improved educational opportunities through high school, Federal funds to support that education, special accommodations in college and employment, and Supplemental Security Income, if needed.

Once a LD diagnosis became an entitlement ticket, its definition ceased to be a matter of objective research. Instead, definitions were subject to the forces of politics, court decisions, ideology, government regulations, racial conflicts, special interest lobbying, and school budgets. Although many serious scholars in the LD field have long rejected discrepancy formulae for defining LD, their opinions have little effect compared to these societal currents. LD has become a socially constructed disorder, formulated largely by political and social interests.

For parents, the clear incentive is to acquire the entitlement ticket. Those with money and skills in operating the system can use their resources to maneuver through the bureaucracy to obtain the ticket. Educators fear that wealthy parents worried about getting their children into good colleges are seeking the LD designation to give their children an advantage. For example, the number of graduating high school students who request an untimed Scholastic Assessment Test on the basis of LD has more than doubled in five years. Many of these students had never before claimed LD. In the words of one anonymous special education

director quoted in the *Boston Globe*, "It's been hard to stem the tide of people wanting untimed testing. If you have the money, you can go to any hospital in Boston and find a disability."

The incentives for public schools are not different. For every child the school identifies as LD, it receives government money. Schools and teachers can blame neurological dysfunctions, rather than school programs, for school failures. Every child moved out of the regular classroom and into special education means a smaller class for the teacher, a higher average score for the school on standardized tests, and one fewer problem child for the teacher. Conversely, for the nearly 100,000 LD special education teachers funded under IDEA, every LD student assigned to them represents further job security. Similarly, for the legions of LD test producers, evaluators, and consultants, the more LD candidates, the more they can sell their goods and services.

Colleges face similar incentives. For the past decade, colleges, especially those heavily dependent on tuition revenues, have faced the serious problem of a dwindling source of students. Many schools have responded by recruiting non-traditional students, for example older students and foreigners. Another source of non-traditional students is the more than 65,000 LD students graduating from high school annually. Good support services and accommodations for LD students thus become effective marketing tools targeting a rapidly growing clientele. Twenty years ago these students could not have met college admission standards, often set by faculty. Today however, as required by law, colleges can bypass traditional admission standards and take into account an applicant's LD.

With this powerful convergence of interests to expand LD entitlement eligibility, it is not surprising that the number of persons diagnosed with LD has exploded. In recent years, the annual increases in the number of disabled students under IDEA is almost totally attributable to the growth in the number of LD children. The Office of Special Education Programs is currently investigating the causes for this continued growth, but given the incentives operating, the causes should not be hard to find.

Why then not simply drop discrepancy diagnoses and give all children educational programs matched to their strengths and weaknesses? Again, the answer seems to be political. Under the status quo, local, state, and Federal governments must provide extra money for LD special education only for those who somehow manage to obtain a LD diagnosis, while slow learners, above the level of mental retardation, remain in the less expensive regular classroom. Were special education to be made available to all who could benefit, costs would skyrocket. Any suggestion to expand LD eligibility is therefore resisted by the fiscal pressures operating on politicians. In fact, the Federal government, already struggling with the growth in LD numbers under current definitions, has imposed a cap of 12% on the percentage of the public school population in each state that it will fund.

Ironically, another source of resistance against expansion of LD eligibility consists of LD organizations. These groups correctly recognize that were slow learners to be provided LD special education, it is unlikely that funding will increase in proportion to the resulting dramatic increase in eligibility. Consequently, the quality of services now available to LD students would have to be diluted, a result they oppose. This lifeboat attitude says, in effect, that for fear of jeopardizing our own benefits, we oppose adding others to the boat, even though they will benefit and even though we boarded in questionable ways.

The alternative, of course, is to advocate for *all* children experiencing school problems. Of all our national goals, an optimal education for all children must surely be of high priority. LD will not cease to exist with an expansion of eligibility. There will still be children with severe academic problems, but not all of them will show discrepancies. Yet, all of them will benefit from the same special education, and all deserve it. Until further research shows otherwise, we should drop the myths of LD, and meet the individual needs of each child.

# 32

# A Capability Perspective on Impairment, Disability, and Special Needs

## Lorella Terzi

## Introduction

What disability is and how it can be defined in relation to human diversity and personal heterogeneities more generally is a theme common to several disciplines. In particular, recent perspectives in socio-medicine, disability studies and political philosophy have all engaged the topic of disability, outlining some of its dimensions with reference to their own internal debates. Socio-medical approaches and disability studies have mainly concentrated their analyses on the definition of disability and on its causal factors, and have provided contrasting understandings of what disability is and how it relates to human diversity and social and political matters. In their political struggle for equal consideration and equal entitlements, and against any reduction of disability to a biological notion of abnormality, disabled people's movements advocate the 'celebration of difference', or a positive recognition of disability as part of the inescapable human diversity that so enriches our life experience and our society (Corker, 1999; Morris, 1991; Shakespeare, 1997; Thomas, 1999; Wendell, 1996). In this context, the concept of disability is articulated in terms of differences to be positively recognized, rather than stigmatized and discriminated against.

Conversely, the concept of human diversity plays a crucial role in contemporary theories of social justice. These theories engage with the questions of what traits constitute personal advantages or disadvantages, whether these are naturally or socially determined, and how and why diverse personal traits do or do not have to be taken into account in determining what is just. A disability is usually referred to as an individual disadvantage and considered as a further 'complexity' in the already complex framework of a just distribution of benefits and burdens, however defined. Aspects of this debate have also addressed the causal factors of disability, whether natural or social, mainly in connection with interpersonal comparisons of disadvantage and a concern for social justice (Dworkin, 2000; Nagel, 2002; Rawls, 1971, 2001; Sen, 1992). What is a cause of celebration for disability scholars and disabled people's movements has become an object of inquiry for political philosophers, particularly liberal egalitarians.

Notwithstanding this diversity of approaches, the debate raises three interrelated questions that are

Previously published in *Theory and Research in Education* 3(2) (2005), pp. 197–223. © 2005 Sage Publications. Reprinted with permission of Sage Publications Ltd.

important both to disability studies and to political theories of social justice: 'What is disability and how can we think of it within a concept of human diversity?' 'What relevance do the causal factors of disability have for a theory of justice?' and 'How ought disability to be evaluated and considered in the design of equitable and inclusive social and political arrangements?' In addressing these questions, the debate operates on two distinct but interlocking levels: a theoretical level, concerned with definitional and causal issues, and a political level, where theoretical understandings of disability and ideals of social inclusion are translated into matters of equal rights and entitlements for disabled people. The three questions, and their respective answers, form a fundamental framework for addressing impairment, disability, and different abilities or special needs in education.

In the first section that follows, I shall address how current models of disability present an unsatisfactory understanding of impairment and disability, at both the theoretical and political levels of analysis. I shall then, in the second section, outline how the capability approach advances the theorization of impairment and disability at both of these levels. Finally, in the third section, I shall apply the capability perspective on impairment and disability to related educational issues.

## Human Diversity and 'Models' of Disability

The current debate on disability is mainly characterized by two contrasting conceptions, or 'models' of disability, each with its own definition of disability in relation to human diversity and its own view on the design of inclusive social arrangements and policies.[1] Biomedical and socio-medical approaches to disability underpin the definitions of the International Classification of Impairments, Disability and Handicaps (WHO, ICIDH, 1980) proposed by the World Health Organization (WHO). This Classification, based on the distinction between *impairment, disability* and *handicap,* defines *impairment* as an 'abnormality in the structure or the functioning of the body' whether due to disease or trauma, *disability* as the 'restriction in the ability to perform tasks' due to impairment, and *handicap* as the 'social disadvantage' that could be associated with impairment, disability, or both (Bury, 1996: 22).

This classification implies a causal relation between individual impairments, seen as departures from human normality, and disabilities, seen as restrictions in abilities to perform tasks. According to it, therefore, disabilities are attributable primarily to individual biological conditions that depart from normal human functionings and cause handicaps to be experienced as disadvantages. These definitions promote an understanding of disability and the disadvantage associated with it as primarily an individual condition arising from natural causes – hence the labelling of this view as the 'individual model' of disability by disabled people's movements.

Consider as an illustration of this view, the case of congenital blindness. According to this model, a visual impairment, being a departure from standard human repertoire, determines a restriction of activity and, consequently, causes disability, which may then result in handicap. While being a clear departure from human average functioning, this condition determines a restriction in some activities, in that visually impaired people are, for instance, unable to drive, and this inability constitutes a disability, which, in turn, produces a social disadvantage. The disabilities take the form of inability to perform certain tasks, from everyday ones, like driving the children to school on a given day, to broader ones, like choosing an occupation that involves driving.

The set of definitions presented by the WHO classification involves a distinction between *normality*, or normal average human functioning, and *abnormality* as divergence from this standard. Moreover, normality as a functional concept carries a wider connotation of natural superiority. Within this view, in fact, disability is referred to as caused by an individual 'abnormality', linked to certain inabilities to perform tasks and, therefore, to disadvantages. Here, the relational aspect of disability, its relation to individual impairment and to handicap, is fundamentally grounded in the causal link established between natural impairment and disability, and the resulting disadvantage is attributed primarily to a specific individual condition. Consequently, as disability scholars have repeatedly asserted (Finkelstein, 1980; Oliver, 1990; Shakespeare, 1997), disability is considered mainly a target of treatment and rehabilitation intended to achieve as much as possible an approximation to normality.

This view of disability as divergence from normal average functioning has major implications for theory and social policy alike. The diagnostic application of the WHO classification appears useful and unproblematic in both medical and social policy settings, yet further analysis reveals that this approach suffers from at least three theoretical limitations. First, in individualizing disability, this view downplays social factors. Whether an inability to perform certain tasks becomes a disability and, in turn, a handicap, does also depend upon the social structure and the environment in which people find themselves. Thus, the visually impaired person of my previous example would be badly disadvantaged in social arrangements where driving is paramount to achieving other goals and no alternatives are available. She would be unable to take her children to school and would either have to rely on the help and assistance of others or find an alternative arrangement. On the other hand, the same person would not be as disadvantaged if alternative provisions were made available, such as accessible and reliable public transportation or a specifically designed service. Furthermore, she would not be disadvantaged with respect to driving in a hypothetical society consisting entirely of non-drivers. Second, the concept of human diversity implied by this set of definitions in effect assumes away wider consideration of diversity in terms of age, sex, general intellectual and physical abilities, social circumstances, and climatic differences (Sen, 1992: 28), and leads to a monolithic assumption of disability as abnormality or deviation from a normal condition. The multidimensionality of human diversity is thereby understated. Third, as sociologists and educationists have suggested, this view may lead to or be used to justify a stark and exclusionary separation between normal individuals and those defined as abnormal.

In light of many such considerations, the WHO has recently revised the Classification and provided a more circumstantial perspective on *Functioning, Disability and Health* (WHO, ICFDH, 2001). However, since the original classification has had a considerable impact and is still widely referred to by disability scholars, the analysis I offer here is based on the original Classification.

Opposed to this conception is the 'social model of disability', which has emerged from the political activism of disabled people's movements and the reflection of disabled scholars on their own experience. Mainly developed by Michael Oliver, the social model plays a major role in Disability Studies and is fundamental to the theoretical positions of disabled

people's movements. In Oliver's account, the social model 'does not deny the problem of disability but locates it squarely within society' (Oliver, 1996: 32). Basically, Oliver sees disability, by contrast with impairment, as something imposed on disabled people by oppressive and discriminating social and institutional structures. Thus, according to the social model, *impairment* is 'lacking part or all of a limb, or having a defective limb, organ or mechanism of the body', and *disability* is

> the disadvantage or restriction of activity caused by a contemporary social organization which takes no or little account of people with impairments and thus excludes them from participation in the mainstream of social activities. (Oliver, 1996: 22)

Disability, therefore, 'is all that imposes restrictions on disabled people', and, as such, 'disablement is nothing to do with the body', (Oliver, 1996: 35), but is instead caused by the oppression of social and economic structures bearing on impaired individuals.

The aim of the social model of disability is to redress both sources and causes of disability – both individual, natural differences and social arrangements – and to deny any theoretical legitimacy to the notions of normality and abnormality. According to this view, disability is caused by social structures, which, like the concept of human average functioning, take no account of impaired people. A disability is seen as an imposed restriction added by society to existing impairments, and normality, in Oliver's words, 'is a construct imposed on a reality where there is only difference' (Oliver, 1996: 88). Social model theorists oppose any idea of normality, which they consider ideologically constructed with the aim of controlling and excluding disabled people from the mainstream of social institutions.

Consider visual impairment as it is understood by the social model: the visually impaired person experiences disability arising from the restrictions imposed by economic and social structures, which, in providing only for sighted people, exclude visually impaired people from the mainstream of social activities. Thus, according to this understanding, the disability experienced by the visually impaired person would be caused by the fact that society is designed on the basis of an average – consequently restricted – idea of normal human functioning.

This idea of normal functioning does not provide for visually impaired people, preventing them from undertaking a wide range of activities.

The social model of disability has developed into a multifaceted, critical analysis of the concepts of human diversity and disability, and defined the terms of debate in Disability Studies. Recent works by disability scholars (Morris, 1991; Thomas, 1999; Wendell, 1996) have described disability in terms of difference, and have promoted the celebration of disability as difference or an aspect of human diversity. Feminist disability scholars such as Wendell and Morris, while acknowledging the cultural and social aspects of ideas of normality and abnormality, nevertheless reintroduce considerations related to the individual condition of impairment, with its biological dimension and restrictions of activity, pain, and illness. Thus, Wendell 'appears to accept that there are some biological differences which really do set some bodies apart from others' (Thomas, 1999: 105), and Morris argues,

> [w]e are different. We reject the meanings that the non-disabled world attaches to disability but we do not reject the differences that are such an important part of our identities. (Morris, 1991: 17)

These and other authors (Corker, 1999; French, 1993) assert the value of disability as a part of human experience, and advocate an inclusive society with no social, economic, or cultural barriers to participation (Terzi, 2004: 154).

This view of disability as difference has the political force and legitimacy that comes with voicing disabled people's own experience, reflection, and political aims. However, beyond the political appeal and the constant reminder of the moral importance of this debate, the social model of disability has evident shortcomings. First, there is an aspect of over-socialization of sources and causes of disability. In stating that disability is a restriction of activity caused by discriminatory economic and social structures, the model over-socializes the reality of disability. It is difficult to see, in fact, how the inability of a blind person to read non-verbal cues can be ascribed to a social condition. Second, in so doing the model overlooks the complex dimensions of impairment and its effects on activities and abilities, hence disabilities. There are aspects of pain, fatigue, and sometimes illness related to certain impairments, and these play roles in the lives of disabled people, which are not accounted for by the social model. Finally, the social model reaches untenable conclusions. If we reject the idea of normality as a guiding concept, how would we evaluate impairment and disability? Would any possible functioning or non-functioning be considered equally in a social model of disability? And in that case, what would then constitute impairment and what disability? Moreover, in promoting the celebration of difference in the absence of a clear definition of what difference means and how it has to be evaluated, the social model loses sight of what is specific to impairment and disability. Consequently, the social model fails to address disability in a theoretically coherent way and in a politically feasible manner (Terzi, 2004: 155).

It appears therefore evident that both the individual and social models of disability have theoretical deficiencies that limit their value as a basis for policy. The individual model of disability understates the relational and social character of disability, overlooks more complex dimensions of human diversity, suggests social policies that overemphasize the adjustment of the individual person and underemphasize social changes, and may lead to policies unilaterally informed by concepts of assistance rather than principles of equal entitlement. Conversely, the social model ends up over-socializing causes and misplacing responsibility for impairment and disablement; in proposing disability as an aspect of difference within human diversity, it under-specifies what difference is and yields a proposal that is more rhetorical than substantial. Both models, in defining disability as generic restriction of activity, fail to provide a definition of disability that can adequately inform the design of inclusive institutional and social schemes.

These considerations point to the need for a different approach to conceptualizing impairment and disability, an approach which considers disability as a specific variable of human diversity and evaluates its impact on the positions of individuals within institutional and social arrangements. The capability approach, developed by Amartya Sen and Martha Nussbaum, is such a framework, and it is well suited to assessing the relevance of impairment and disability in designing just and inclusive institutional and social arrangements. I shall consider what the capability approach can contribute to our understanding of impairment and disability in the section that follows.

# A Capability Perspective on Impairment and Disability

## Sen's Capability Approach: Human Diversity and Disability

Sen's priority in developing the capability approach has been to provide a more adequate framework for the conceptualization of human development and for the analysis and assessment of poverty. The frameworks commonly used in welfare economics are too narrowly based on income generation or income distribution, he contends. In examining poverty, inequality, and their relation to social arrangements, Sen's work also critically engages with the philosophical debate on equality and distributive justice, and develops a complex and compelling form of egalitarianism (Sen, 1992). I shall argue that Sen's capability approach offers new and important resources for redefining impairment and disability, and designing inclusive social policies. I begin with some key concepts: the space of capability, the informational basis of the metric used in interpersonal comparisons of equality, and the democratic decision process entailed by the approach.

Sen maintains that closely linked to the central question of what it is that social arrangements should aim to equalize, are two fundamental issues: first, the choice of the 'evaluative space' in which to assess equality, and second, the metric that should be used in comparing people's relative advantages and disadvantages. He identifies the evaluative space for the assessment of inequality and, conversely, for determining what equality we should seek, in the space of the freedoms to achieve valuable objectives that people have, that is, in the space of *capability*. Rather than aiming to equalize resources or welfare, Sen argues that equality should be defined and aimed at in terms of the capability each individual has to pursue and to achieve well-being, i.e. to pursue and enjoy states and objectives constitutive of her or his well-being. Thus, the capability approach delimitates a space for the assessment of individual well-being and the freedom to achieve it.

Within this space, Sen distinguishes *functionings* and *capabilities*. Functionings are defined as 'beings and doings constitutive of a person's being', such as being adequately nourished, being in good health, being happy and having self-respect, or taking part in the life of the community (Sen, 1992: 39).

Achieved functionings are the specific functionings that a person has accomplished and realized at any given time (Alkire, 2002: 6). Since functionings are constitutive of a person's being, according to Sen, 'an evaluation of a person's well-being has to take the form of an assessment of these constitutive elements' (Sen, 1992: 39).

Capabilities, on the other hand, are capabilities to function, and they represent a person's freedoms to achieve valuable functionings. In other words, they represent:

> Various combinations of functionings (beings and doings) that the person can achieve. Capability is, thus, a set of vectors of functionings, reflecting the person's freedom to lead one type of life or another. (Sen, 1992: 40)

Capabilities amount to the substantive freedoms a person has, or the 'real alternatives' available to the person herself to achieve well-being. In that respect, capability is related to well-being both instrumentally, as a basis for judgements about the relative advantage a person has and her place in society, and intrinsically, since achieved well-being itself depends on the capability to function, and the exercise of choice has value of its own as part of our living (Sen, 1992: 41, 62).

The capability approach endorses equality of capabilities as a policy objective and asserts the fundamental importance of capabilities and functionings as value-objects for the assessment of individual well-being (Sen, 1992: 46). With this in mind, it is important to address the basis for interpersonal comparisons implied by the space of capability.

The 'evaluative space' of capability encompasses the use of a 'metric' (Pogge, 2003) to evaluate people's relative advantages and disadvantages. In other words, the capability approach theorizes a space where consideration of the 'basic heterogeneities of human beings' or 'empirical fact' of human diversity is crucial in assessing the demands of equality (Sen, 1992: 1). In Sen's words, 'Human diversity is no secondary complication (to be ignored, or to be introduced "later on"); it is a fundamental aspect of our interest in equality' (Sen, 1992: xi). According to his view, human beings are diverse in four fundamental ways. First, they are different with respect to their personal, internal characteristics, such as gender, age, physical and mental abilities, talents, proneness to illness, and so forth. Second, different individuals are different with respect to external circumstances, such as inherited wealth and assets, environmental factors, including climatic differences and social and cultural arrangements (Sen, 1992: 1, 20, 27–8). Third, a further and important form of diversity, defined as *interindividual variation*, pertains to differences in the conversion of resources into freedoms or, in other words, to different individual abilities to convert commodities and resources in order to achieve valued objectives (Sen, 1992: 85). To illustrate this last point, Sen provides the example of a lactating woman, who, due to her specific condition, needs a higher intake of food for her functionings than a similar but non-lactating woman. A fourth, fundamental way in which human beings are diverse is that they have different conceptions of the good, and therefore aim at different ends or objectives. Sen calls this *inter-end variation*, and the recognition of it leads him to envisage capabilities as the overall freedoms that people have 'to achieve actual livings that one can have a reason to value' (Sen, 1992: 85; 1999: 18), without specifying what ends there is reason to value or (hence) specifying a definitive list of capabilities.

Within this view of human diversity as central, the capability approach holds that it makes a difference whether someone is a man or a woman, has physical and mental prowess or weaknesses, lives in a temperate physical environment or in a more adverse climatic zone, and lives in certain social and cultural arrangements rather than in others. The differences entailed by these variations have to be accounted for when addressing the demands of equality. The actual differences in conversion factors and conceptions of valuable ends and objectives that people have must be considered too. Thus, ultimately, the metric used to make interpersonal comparisons includes the four central aspects of human diversity pertaining to personal characteristics, external circumstances, inter-individual variations in conversion factors, and inter-end variations related to the plurality of conceptions of the good.

An example taken directly from Sen's work may help to illustrate the use of this metric, and to introduce considerations pertaining to disability that will be expanded later on.

Consider two persons 1 and 2, with 2 disadvantaged in some respect (e.g. physical disability, mental handicap, greater disease proneness). They do not have the same ends or objectives, or the same conception of the good. Person 1 values A more than B, while 2 has the opposite valuation. Each values 2A more than A and 2B more than B. With the given set of primary goods (resources and opportunities) person 1 can achieve 2A or 2B, also – though there may be no great merit in this – A or B. On the other hand, given 2's disadvantage . . . she can achieve only A and B. (Sen, 1992: 83)

It is evident here that person 2 finds herself in a situation of inequality owing to her personal characteristics and how she converts resources into functionings, despite having the same amount of resources or opportunities. Her disability, which is regarded for the purposes of this example as an inherent disadvantage, must be taken into account in evaluating equality.[2]

It is this set of considerations regarding human diversity and its centrality in the metric used to compare individual advantages and disadvantages that has ultimately led Sen to conceptualize the space of capabilities and functionings as the relevant space for equality. He identifies the capability approach as a framework of thought, a general approach to the assessment of individual advantage or disadvantage in social schemes, while declining, in light of the variability of human ends, to specify a definitive list of capabilities or functionings. He leaves these details to the processes of public choice, reasoning, and democratic procedure that are themselves the most freedom-preserving means by which social policy can be determined. Hence, the deliberately under-specified character of the capability approach (Sen, 1999: 78; Robeyns, 2003: 6). Capabilities are context-sensitive, or sensitive to social and cultural arrangements, and their selection should be the result of a democratic process involving public consultation, Sen argues. This implies that, in considering a person's capability set, attention should be given to individual conceptions of well-being, and to their interplay with political, social and cultural settings, thus, ultimately, with conditions that may influence choice and reasoning. Some authors (Alkire, 2002; Robeyns, 2003) have expanded this aspect of the capability approach, envisaging different perspectives on what forms this process of social deliberation and democratic participation may take with regard to such things as the analysis of gender inequality or with the operationalizing of capability in poverty reduction.

What does the capability approach contribute to our understanding of impairment and disability and to our moral quest for an inclusive society? In what follows I shall outline how aspects of the capability approach can provide a new framework for thinking of impairment and disability as multi-dimensional and relational, and how this framework can inform issues of distributive justice and policies of inclusion.

A superficial reading of Sen's work suggests that it treats the identification of disability with personal disadvantage as non-problematic. For instance, in addressing personal heterogeneities, Sen maintains that:

> People have disparate physical characteristics connected with disability, illness, age or gender, and these make their needs diverse. For example, a disabled person may need some prosthesis, an older person more support and help, a pregnant woman more nutritional intake, and so on. The 'compensation' needed for disadvantages will vary, and furthermore some disadvantages may not be fully 'correctable' even with income transfer. (Sen, 1999: 70)

Similarly:

> Equal income can still leave much inequality in our ability to do what we would value doing. A disabled person cannot function in the way an able-bodied person can, even if both have exactly the same income. (Sen, 1992: 20)

And finally:

> The extent of comparative deprivation of a physically handicapped person vis-à-vis others cannot be adequately judged by looking at his or her income, since the person may be greatly disadvantaged in converting income into the achievements he or she would value. (Sen, 1992: 28)

These examples suggest how disability, defined as an individual condition, influences individual functionings, as these are correlated with various personal characteristics and diverse individual conversion factors. Disability is equated with an individual disadvantage that should be taken into consideration in interpersonal comparisons. However, it would be an oversimplification of Sen's approach to read this as an endorsement of the WHO's definition of disability as individual limitation causally linked to biological impairment.

A more sensitive reading yields two important contributions that Sen's capability approach makes to our understanding of impairment and disability and their assessment in interpersonal comparisons aiming at equal consideration and freedoms for disabled people. The first insight relates to how we can think of impairment and disability as aspects of human diversity, and more specifically to Sen's understanding of personal heterogeneities and their role in the metric for assessing equality. The second insight concerns democratic participation and the active participation of disabled people and disabled people's movements in the process of identifying relevant capabilities and evaluating how social policies should be designed when aiming at inclusion. Both require some explanation.

The first reason for considering the capability approach as innovative with respect to current understandings and models of impairment and disability relates both to the centrality of human diversity in assessing equality in the space of capability and to the specific understanding of human diversity proposed by Sen. First, in repositioning human diversity as central to the evaluation of individual advantages and disadvantages, Sen's capability approach promotes an egalitarian perspective that differs from others in dealing at its core with the complexities of disability. Second, Sen's concept of human diversity, in encompassing personal and external factors as well as an individual conversion factor, implies an interrelation between individual and circumstantial aspects of human diversity. This enables disability theory to overcome current understandings of impairment and disability as unilaterally biologically determined,[3] because disability can be regarded as one of the aspects of individuals emerging from this interlocking of personal and external factors. Moreover, the capability approach provides an egalitarian framework in which entitlement does not depend upon the causal origin of disability. It does not matter, in capability terms, whether a disability is biologically or socially caused as such; what matters is the scope of the full set of capabilities a person can choose from and the role impairment plays in this set of freedoms. Furthermore, the capability framework opens the way to considerations of impairment and disability as multidimensional and relational, a conception that will be discussed further on, in that it sees disability as one aspect of the complexity of human heterogeneities, and therefore as one aspect of the complexity of individuals in their interaction with their physical, economic, social, and cultural environment. In this respect, the capability approach goes also in the direction of promoting a conception of disability as one aspect of human diversity, comparable to age and gender, without suggesting monolithic and direct notions of diversity as abnormality. This appears to be fundamental in overcoming the discrimination and oppression denounced by disabled people's movements as inherent in current notions of normality, abnormality, and diversity.

An example may be useful at this stage. Walking is a functioning, and so is moving about from one space to another, and it is a functioning that enables other functionings, such as taking one's children to school, or going to work, or serving as a head of state. In this sense moving about may be seen as a basic functioning enabling more complex functionings to take place. Now consider an impaired person who uses a wheelchair. In determining the full set of capabilities that a wheelchair user has to achieve her valued ends, the capability approach looks at how this specific physical activity (moving about by wheelchair) interacts with circumstantial factors, such as the physical environment where the person lives and the presence of wheelchair accesses to buildings, and how it interacts with personal conversion factors, such as general strength, health, and aspects of attitude. The approach also considers the interplay between wheelchair use and the person's most valuable ends, one of which could be, for example, having an interest in politics and aspiring to serve as a head of state. The capability approach allows us to say that being a wheelchair user may be considered a disadvantage when the wheelchair is not provided or the physical environment is not designed appropriately. In the same way many persons would be disadvantaged would stairs or lift not be fitted between flights in buildings, since very few people would be able to move from floor to floor (Perry et al., 1999: 2). The provision of a wheelchair and wheelchair accessibility is a matter of justice on the capability approach, because these contribute to the equalization of the capability to pursue and achieve well-being.

Let's continue with this example and consider the achievement of more complex functionings, such as serving as a head of state. Let us suppose that acting in her political capacity is fundamental to the achievement of well-being for the physically impaired person considered in this example. And let us also assume that the physical environment is designed so as to prevent her from moving about, thus ultimately preventing her from the achievement of some basic functionings. This person, although potentially able to exercise her political role, is prevented from achieving her valued end by the interaction of some of her personal features with some of the characteristics of her physical environment. In this case, well-being freedom appears to be restricted in some fundamental ways, hence the full set of capabilities available to this person is diminished.

The capability approach's second main contribution to disability theory pertains to democratic participation in determining relevant capabilities. Here the approach is compatible with the demands of disabled people's movements on the one hand, and with questions of the design of social schemes and policies on the other. Disabled people's organizations have long denounced their *de facto* marginalization from active participation in society and have reclaimed their role in society as a matter of right. The capability approach, through its reconsideration of human diversity, and by assigning itself the role of 'neutral observer', seems to provide a substantive framework to fulfill disabled people's demands. In promoting some forms of public consultations on the choice of relevant capabilities, it commends a participatory democratic process that avoids exclusion and discrimination as a matter of principle.

The role accorded to democratic decision, however, if extremely relevant to the democratic empowerment of disabled people, is problematic in failing to provide sufficient normative guidance for adjudicating the demands of disabled people vis-à-vis the demands of others. Choices concerning which capabilities to protect are to be made through democratic processes, but the capabilities essential to democratic participation would themselves need to be protected as a matter of prior constitutional principle, in order to ensure just outcomes.[4]

These considerations provide the basis for a multidimensional and relational concept of impairment and disability that will be outlined in the next section. In the remainder of this section I consider Martha Nussbaum's approach to capabilities, which goes beyond Sen's in its understanding of justice as a fundamental dimension of the issues surrounding impairment and disability.

## Nussbaum's Capability Approach, Disability and Justice

Nussbaum has presented her own account of the capabilities approach through a philosophical perspective on issues of international development aimed specifically at reconsidering and addressing the unjust conditions of women in developing countries (Nussbaum, 2000). In her book *Frontiers of Justice: Disability, Nationality, Species Membership* (Nussbaum, 2005),[5] she has extended her account of the capabilities approach in connection with previously unexplored issues of justice, including justice for mentally disabled citizens. She endorses Sen's concept of capability as the space for comparisons of freedom and quality of life, but refines the approach in some important ways. In particular, she gives it a universal and normative dimension by stipulating a list of central human capabilities and a threshold of adequacy in the universal possession of these capabilities. These elements form the basis for constitutional principles to be adopted by all nations (Nussbaum, 2000: 12).

The central human capabilities listed and endorsed by Nussbaum include 'life', 'bodily health', 'bodily integrity', 'senses, imagination and thought', 'emotions', 'practical reason' and 'affiliation', as well as 'play' and 'other species', and 'control over the environment', understood as both political and material control. She identifies these and the other items listed as 'combined capabilities', or 'internal capabilities combined with suitable external conditions for the exercise of functioning' (Nussbaum, 2000: 84). Further, she distinguishes basic capabilities, generally intended as the basic innate equipment of individuals, from internal capabilities, seen as 'developed states of the person that are sufficient conditions for the exercise of the requisite function' (Nussbaum, 2000: 84). Each capability on the list is therefore some combination of innate and internal capabilities and external conditions. Among these, practical reason and affiliation are particularly important capabilities, because they make it possible for other capabilities to be pursued in ways that are genuinely human. Practical reason, intended in its Aristotelian sense of being able to form one's conception of the good and to engage in the planning of one's life, and affiliation, or being able to engage in meaningful relationships and having the social bases of self-respect and dignity, are fundamental capabilities without which a life loses its characteristically human features (Nussbaum, 2000: 82).

Nussbaum's focus on central human capabilities subsumes and is related to the intuitive idea of the moral worth and the dignity of each and every human being (Nussbaum, 2000: 5). She maintains

that when we ask the question central to the capabilities approach, 'What is this person actually able to do and to be?', we imply a set of considerations related to evaluating the position of the person in interpersonal comparisons while, at the same time, referring to some core human capabilities, the absence of which would preclude the possibility of leading a truly human life (Nussbaum, 2000: 71). In posing that central question, we are evaluating what this individual person, considered as an end in herself, is actually in a position to be and to do, what her liberties and opportunities are, and how the resources she can use allow her to function in a human way (Nussbaum, 2000: 71, 74). Nussbaum thus defines a universal set of capabilities, which should be secured for every person at least up to the threshold below which any life loses its dignity or humanness.

The universality of the list of capabilities provided by Nussbaum's approach is justified not only by the idea of respect for human dignity, but through a political concept of overlapping consensus. The political justification is grounded on the recognition that the items on the list can be considered crucial to human functioning by people who otherwise endorse very different conceptions of the good. In other words, the normative universality of central human capabilities could be politically endorsed – as the 'underpinnings of basic political principles that can be embodied in constitutional guarantees' (Nussbaum, 2000: 74) – through an overlapping consensus, by people of different religions, beliefs, cultures and understandings of what constitutes a good life. Nussbaum's political justification through an overlapping consensus intersects here with her appeal to the moral worth and dignity of persons, through the idea that the central human capabilities 'can [be] convincingly argued to be of central importance in any human life, whatever else the person pursues or chooses' (Nussbaum, 2000: 74). She maintains that by providing a list of central human capabilities and by setting a threshold level below which a life cannot be deemed truly human, the capabilities approach sets the basis for a decent social minimum that governments have to deliver (Nussbaum, 2000: 71). Capabilities cannot be directly distributed, but governments are to provide the social bases for central human capabilities. Governments 'cannot make all women emotionally healthy', for instance, but they 'can do quite a lot to influence emotional health through suitable policies' (Nussbaum, 2000: 82).

Nussbaum further articulates her position on the normative aspect of capabilities by relating them to human rights, understood both as political and civil liberties and as economic and social rights (Nussbaum, 2000: 97). She maintains that the political dimension of capabilities provides the philosophical underpinning for basic constitutional principles, and in that way plays a role similar to that of human rights. But she maintains, furthermore, that the capabilities approach in some ways goes further than the language of rights, and that for two reasons. First, 'thinking in terms of capability gives us a benchmark as we think about what it is to secure a right to someone' (Nussbaum, 2000: 98). Second, as a capabilities analysis considers what people are actually able to be and to do, how they are enabled to live,

> Analyzing economic and material rights in terms of capabilities thus enables us to set forth clearly a rationale we have for spending unequal amounts of money on the disadvantaged, or creating special programmes to assist their transition to full capabilities. (Nussbaum, 2000: 99)

For these reasons, the political dimension of the capabilities approach has ramifications for equality with respect to both political liberties and resource distribution. For instance, from a capabilities perspective, acts of (invidious) discrimination entail a 'failure of associational capability, a type of indignity or humiliation' (Nussbaum, 2000: 86), and the demands associated with the delivery of the threshold level of capabilities imply policies entailing redistribution of resources. Consequently, even if the capabilities approach does not constitute a theory of justice, it does provide elements for a framework in which justice has a central and fundamental role.

Having outlined these features of Nussbaum's approach, I suggest that it advances the analysis of the political and normative dimensions of impairment and disability in three main ways. First, the universality of its conception of human capabilities makes it applicable to all individuals, irrespective of differences due to impairments. Second, it can precisely inform and guide interpersonal comparisons involving impairment and disability, pursuant to evaluating the respective positions of individuals in social arrangements. Finally, it allows us to frame matters of justice for people with disabilities in the language of basic constitutional guarantees, or inescapable demands on governments for their inter-

vention in securing the social bases of capabilities. These claims require some elaboration.

First, the universality of central human capabilities and their being sought for each and every person implies not only including all individuals under this framework, irrespective of their differences and the causes of their differences, but entails also a regard for the dignity of each person as an underlying principle. This makes the capabilities approach developed by Nussbaum an appealing basis for a principled political project of inclusion. The definition of a threshold of adequate capability to be aimed at leaves open the question of what is mandated when the health and bodily integrity of impaired people does not allow them to reach the threshold level (Kittay, 2003), but Nussbaum evidently does not intend that their condition would disqualify them from moral concern. Her *Frontiers of Justice: Disability, Nationality, Species Membership* (2005) introduces as a fundamental dimension of justice the care and love of others that are the response of a decent society to our condition of humanity; a decent society would provide care and respect for our needs in times of dependency and would provide this care and respect to mentally impaired people, doing so for love of justice.

Second, the merit of considering each person's capabilities in the evaluation of their respective positions in social arrangements seems intuitively evident, and the application of this to impairment and disability is clear. Asking 'What is this person able to be and to do?' and thinking of the person as physically or mentally impaired allows for a reconsideration of the actual condition of impairment and disability and their effects and consequences. The approach thereby allows these factors to be fully recognized and assessed in evaluating each person's capabilities.

Finally, the third contribution that Nussbaum's capabilities approach makes to the analysis of disability is a normative and political framework that is fully compatible with disabled people's movements' efforts to overcome the discrimination and oppression of disabled people in society and secure the recognition of their entitlements as citizens. Nussbaum's approach, in identifying the central human capabilities as having a role similar to that of human rights, and grounding government policy standards in the resulting normative concepts, provides a framework that accords the legitimate demands of disabled people full constitutional recognition.

## A Capability Perspective on Impairment and Disability

Having summarized the aspects of Sen's and Nussbaum's versions of capability theory that seem most useful for the construction of a multi-dimensional and relational view of impairment and disability, a view concerned with issues of definition as well as justice, I shall now on this foundation attempt to construct such a view. In doing this, I shall also draw on accounts of the relational aspect of disability developed by Allen Buchanan (Buchanan, 2000), John Perry and others (Perry et al., 1996, 1999).

I begin with matters of definition. It is important to distinguish impairment from disability, and to see how and why disability is inherently relational and circumstantial, or, in other words, a phenomenon of the interface between personal characteristics of the individual and the specific design of the social and physical environment that the individual inhabits. *Impairment*, either physical or mental, relates to the loss of some aspect of functioning. For instance, a lesion of the spinal cord that results in restricted movements – whether caused by a genetic condition or trauma – is an impairment of average movement functioning (Buchanan, 2000: 285). Perry defines impairment in this sense as 'a physiological disorder or injury' (Perry, 1996: 3). Disability, on the other hand, is the inability to perform some significant class of functionings that individuals in some reference group (e.g. children or adults) are on average and ordinarily able to do under favourable conditions, or 'where the inability is not due to simple and easily corrigible ignorance or to a lack of the tools or means ordinarily available for performing such a task' (Buchanan, 2000: 286).

In defining a disability we are thus referring to a reference group, according to Buchanan, and where no members of the reference group are actually able to function in a specific way, we do not speak of disability. Consequently, 'because no infants are able to drive cars, we do not say that any infant is disabled in this regard' (Buchanan, 2000: 286).[6] Buchanan's definition also suggests that disabilities are inabilities that cannot be overcome by simply supplying relevant information or tools. For instance, if one is unable to play Monopoly because one does not know the rules of the game or because one lacks the game board and pieces, one's inability does not constitute a disability. On

the other hand, if someone cannot perform certain functionings that, on average, people in the reference group are able to, and if this is connected to an identifiable impairment, then the person is disabled with respect to that specific functioning. Thus, for example, if a blind adult person is unable to drive, whereas on average and under favourable conditions an adult is able to do so, then the blind person is disabled with respect to driving.

Disability, so defined, is distinct from impairment, and impairment does not always result in disability. Buchanan provides a very convincing example to illustrate this. He suggests the case of a hearing impaired person who has lost the hearing function with regard to a range of sound frequencies that is detected on average by persons. If the range of sounds undetectable by the impaired person is irrelevant to the functionings in her social environment, then she is not disabled (Buchanan, 2000: 287). Consequently, whether impairment does or does not result in disability depends on the design of the physical and social setting and on whether or not it is possible to overcome the impairment. For example, if the means existed to provide cars whose operation did not require sight – the functions associated with sight being played by computerized monitoring devices, say – then a blind adult might be able to overcome her inability to drive, hence, her disability with respect to that functioning. Thus, disability can be seen as inherently relational, or arising from the interplay between impairment and social arrangements. The relation between impairment and disability does not appear to be one of straightforward causality.

Disability involves impairment, but a full understanding of it requires recognition of its other dimensions. Disability can involve impairment of multiple functionings, arising from different impairment effects. Certain traumas, illnesses, or the pain and fatigue associated with back injuries and arthritis, may impair not only physical functionings, such as walking, for instance, but also aspects of health or other functioning. Disability also has a temporal dimension, as the inability to function in a certain way can be temporary, such as after an eye operation, or more permanent, such as in the event of blindness resulting from a permanent loss of optic nerve function, occurring in conditions that do not allow the inability to be overcome. There is, finally, a dimension of dependency, either on tools or on other people, to help with carrying out functions that, on average, are done more or less independently by people in the reference group. So, for instance, a quadriplegic person or a severely cognitively impaired child may require a personal assistant or support not needed by an average individual of the relevant reference group in order to achieve certain basic functionings.

As we have seen, the design of physical infrastructures and social schemes plays a substantial role in the relation between impairment and disability. Circumstantial elements such as wheelchair accessible buildings and public transportation, as well as the provision of different tools, all provide interfacing between the individual and her environment, and the greater the interfacing is, the less possibility there is that impairment will result in disability. So, for instance, blindness becomes a disability with respect to reading text messages on computer screens to obtain information, when, and if, no use of Braille displays and speech-output screen readers is provided (Perry, 1996: 4). Moreover, society's attitude and dispositions towards severely cognitively impaired people, although more difficult to assess, have a considerable influence on the extent to which their impairments result in disability. An illustration of this is provided by Eva Feder Kittay's description of how people's indifference to her daughter Sesha's attempts to communicate narrowed the range of interactions she could enjoy and amplified her disability (Kittay, 2003).

In a capability perspective, impairment may restrict functionings, and thus yield a disability, through the complex interrelation between the individual's characteristics, her conversion factors, and her environment. When the whole capability of the person in achieving her valued ends is thereby compromised, impairment and disability become matters of justice. It is in this way that disability and justice are related to one another in the capability approach. The capability framework allows us to think of disability as inherently relational and multidimensional, as one aspect of human diversity that has to be considered when evaluating the reciprocal positions of individuals and the distribution of benefits and burdens in social arrangements. In identifying disability as an aspect of individuals emerging from the interlocking of personal and external factors, the capability approach sets aside the debate over whether the causes of disability are natural or social, and promotes a direct concern with functionings and with providing the social bases of adequate capability to pursue valued ends. The

capability approach thereby provides a criterion of justice that is sensitive to disabled people's interests. The definitional aspect of the perspective seems to have some similarity with the revised WHO classification of Functioning, Disability and Health (WHO, ICFDH, 2001) and with its circumstantial elements. Nevertheless, the capability perspective on impairment and disability provides us with a framework informed by considerations of justice and equal entitlements for impaired and disabled people, which is something the WHO classification does not do. Two elements appear crucial in positioning a capability perspective on disability with respect to dimensions of justice: the place of disability in the metric chosen in evaluating people's reciprocal positions in social arrangements, and the choice of design of the social framework.

The capability approach invokes a metric of interpersonal comparison in which the personal characteristics that regulate the conversion of resources and goods into valuable ends should define individual shares. Thus, according to capability theorists, physical and mental impairments should receive attention under a just institutional order and the distribution of resources and goods should be correlated with the distribution of natural features. Thus, for instance, the interest of a wheelchair user has to be accounted for in comparisons made in the space of capabilities and, consequently, a wheelchair provided as a matter of justice. Moreover, consideration should be given to the full set of capabilities available to the person using the wheelchair, and when environmental or social barriers hinder her capabilities these should be removed as a matter of justice too.

Seeking equality in the space of capability implies using a metric in which disability, considered as one aspect of human diversity and as a limitation on relevant capability, has to be addressed within the distributive pattern of functionings and capabilities. This implies extra provision for disabled people as a matter of justice, and such provision does not appear to be a straightforward 'compensation' for some natural individual deficits, since social frameworks are as fundamental to the relational nature of disability as individual traits are.

The fundamental element of a capability perspective on disability relates the criterion of social justice to the design of social arrangements. If we agree that the design of the dominant social framework substantially determines who is competent and who is incompetent (Buchanan, 2000: 290), who is included and who is excluded, and whether impairment becomes disability, hence a limitation of capability, then the burdens of justice must be discharged largely through the choice of appropriate social arrangements.

Buchanan defines the dominant cooperative framework as the 'institutional infrastructure of social interaction' (Buchanan, 2000: 288) and describes the framework of most advanced industrialized societies as extremely complex, and involving institutional structures as well as economic ones, highly specified symbolic languages, and the dominance of competitive markets in the private sectors. The demands on individuals in this society are very high and determine a correspondingly high threshold of competence, involving complex arrays of skills and abilities. In placing these demands on individuals, this dominant social framework already implies who is excluded and who is included. The choice of dominant social framework is, according to Buchanan, like choosing which game a group of people is going to play. If the game chosen is, say, bridge, then young children will be necessarily excluded from the game. Conversely, if the game chosen is 'family', then participation by children is certainly possible. The point is that the choice of the framework determines the level of inclusion, and involves competing interests, namely the interest of those able to efficiently participate in the scheme and those excluded from it. The design and choice of a dominant cooperative social framework is consequently a matter of justice, and one that should be guided by a criterion of social justice that balances the interests of impaired persons with those of the unimpaired. Thus, the slogan of the disabled people's movement, 'change society, not the individual', needs to be evaluated with respect to these considerations, too.

There are, however, two compelling reasons for inclusion, hence for a criterion of social justice that aims at promoting capability with respect to disability. The first relates to the devastating consequences of exclusion on the lives and well-being of those excluded, and the second relates to the balancing of interests that such a criterion can aspire to. With regard to the first reason, if the choice of the dominant social scheme is in itself a matter of justice, and if one of the requirements of justice is people's entitlement to equal respect in light of their equal moral worth, then it seems plausible to argue that efforts should be made to ensure that all individuals are full participants in society (Buchanan,

2000: 295). Thus exclusion, with its consequences on the lives of individuals, appears morally untenable in that it evidently breeches the entitlement to equal respect of some individuals, namely those who are excluded. However, as Buchanan clearly outlines, the moral 'priority' of inclusion in relation to disability does not imply overriding the interests of non-disabled people (Buchanan, 2000: 296). A balancing of interests in the distribution of advantages and disadvantages might allow for certain individuals to be more advantaged within a specific cooperative scheme, since, and perhaps providing that, these advantages could overall benefit the situation of those least advantaged by the same choice of scheme.

The capability perspective on disability can inform such a criterion for social justice in evaluating the demands of disability within the space of capability, in considering disability as having a specific place in the metric used to assess individual shares, and in reinstating the importance of the social framework both in influencing disability and in determining inclusion. Furthermore, conceptualizing disability within a capability framework has important implications in the context of education. I consider some of these implications in the concluding section.

## The Capability Perspective on Disability, Special Needs and Education

A number of educationists have recently explored the potentially fruitful application of the capability approach to education, and the education of children in particular (Saito, 2003; Unterhalter, 2003). I shall draw on these previous explorations in briefly outlining some implications of the capability perspective for education, then outline the lessons of this perspective for special and inclusive education. I argue that the capability perspective on disability provides a promising starting point for reconsidering the educational entitlements of disabled children and children with special needs.

I shall start by exploring two central aspects of the relationship between the capability approach and education, the first pertaining to the value of education and the second pertaining to the expansion of capability (Saito, 2003: 18). With respect to the value of education, the role Sen ascribes to capability relates to both the intrinsic and the instrumental value of education in promoting personal well-being (Brighouse, 2000; Saito, 2003; Unterhalter, 2003). Education is instrumentally good in that it yields other benefits, like better life prospects and career opportunities. In this sense being educated improves one's opportunities in life. On the other hand, education is good in itself, in that being educated, other things being equal, enhances the prospects of engaging in a wide range of activities and fully participating in social life. Thus, being educated contributes to a more fulfilling life. Therefore, according to Unterhalter:

> The capabilities approach helps us understand the nature of the intrinsic good of education, because it helps distinguish those aspects of education that are linked to schooling and intertwined with achieved functionings, for example skills to undertake a certain kind of work . . . and those aspects of education that are part of a wider concern with substantive freedoms. (Unterhalter, 2003: 8)

The capability approach, more than other perspectives, highlights both the intrinsic and instrumental value of education, and places a specific emphasis on its intrinsic value, Unterhalter argues.

This first aspect of the relationship between education and capability relates substantially to the second and more relevant one, that is, to the role education plays in expanding capabilities. Education expands the capability sets available to individuals by expanding both ability and opportunity (Saito, 2003: 27). For example, learning mathematics not only expands individuals' various capacities connected to mathematical reasoning and problem solving, but also widens the individuals' set of opportunities and capabilities with respect to choices of such things as occupation. Furthermore, the broadening of capability produced by education extends to complex capabilities. In fact, while promoting reflection, understanding, information and awareness of one's capacity, education promotes at the same time one's capacity to formulate exactly the valued beings and doings one has reasons to value.

Education enhances both well-being freedom and well-being achievements, and the capability approach captures the importance of providing the conditions for the development of capability in both of these senses. It alerts us to the importance of educational provision for children and adults alike. As Unterhalter writes:

> This seems to indicate the importance of attending to the aspect of developing freedoms in relation to curriculum content and pedagogies and the resources that support these. (Unterhalter, 2003: 7)

This is particularly important with regard to children's education, but at the same time more problematic, given the particular status of children, which requires adults to protect their interests and meet their needs, but does not permit full agency freedom or the exercise of autonomous choices (Shapiro, 2003). Sen has emphasized the importance of concentrating not on the freedom the child has, but on the freedom she will have in the future. Thus, writes Sen,

> I think the main argument for compulsory education is that it will give the child when grown up much more freedom and, therefore, the educational argument is a very future oriented argument. (Sen, quoted in Saito, 2003: 27)

Consequently, while expanding capabilities, education plays a very important role in promoting the future freedoms children will have to choose their valued beings and doings. Saito has plausibly argued that in order for education to promote future freedom it must have certain characteristics; it must promote autonomy, or, in other words, the capacity to make informed choices on the kind of life one has reason to value (Saito, 2003: 28).

These central aspects of the relationship between the capability approach and children's education form a possible background for reconsidering some of the issues related to the education of disabled children and children with special needs. Two sets of questions arise. The first relates to the difference such an approach makes with respect to the conditions for developing capabilities, and the second is connected to the difference it makes with respect to the distribution of resources and opportunities.

In other words, in thinking about the provision of education for disabled children and children with special needs, the choice of the educational structure or system of schooling, and the choice of its funding system or scheme of resource distribution, are fundamental. Recall that the choice and the design of social and environmental arrangements play a substantial role in determining levels of inclusion. In the same way, the choice and the design of school systems and the ways in which they are funded are central to inclusion. I have addressed elsewhere in this article the relevance of inclusion in thinking of justice and my contention here is broadly that the same arguments apply to education. Considering that 'inclusion is in general a necessary condition for protecting a person's most basic interests – in well-being, in having a wide range of opportunities, and in self-esteem' (Buchanan, 2000: 291) – it seems plausible that an inclusive education system promotes children's interests in developing capabilities. Yet one may want to question why we should promote an inclusive system and not a special, separate one for disabled children and children with special needs. The argument for this view might be that a special system could better promote children's future freedoms, for instance in creating an environment more conducive to the achievement of certain levels of functionings, which are specific to the children's situations. Indeed, much of the current educational debate in the UK, for instance, focuses on this question. What answer does the capability perspective on disability suggest? It alerts us to two sets of considerations. First, it acknowledges the importance of the reasons for inclusion, making us reconsider the consequences of exclusion on the overall well-being of those excluded. Second, and more importantly, it alerts us to the relevance of the full promotion of all capabilities and of exercising certain functionings in childhood in order to develop the relevant mature capability (Nussbaum, 2000: 90). It seems at least questionable that separate settings would in fact provide children with conditions and opportunities for the full development of their capabilities to communicate, to relate to others, to respect and tolerate individual differences. Rather, special settings would more likely deprive all children, not only disabled ones, of the opportunities to exercise these functionings and develop the relevant capabilities. Further, in focusing on equality in the space of capabilities, this approach considers how providing special settings would bear on equality. Disabled people who were educated in special schools speak of the substantial 'deprivation' of 'normal' opportunities they suffered

and the negative consequences on their lives as a whole (Barnes et al., 1999).

Furthermore, in considering personal differences as central to issues of distributive justice, the capability perspective on disability justifies a funding system sensitive to the need for additional resources for disabled children and children with special needs. It does this because it treats the resources needed to equalize capabilities as a condition of equality. However, there are complexities and difficulties that remain to be resolved in order to provide a principled framework for a just distributional scheme informed by the capability approach. An obvious goal for future work in developing the approach is to devise such a scheme.

One final remark concerning the content of education is in order. When thinking of expanding capabilities for disabled children and children with special needs, the choice of curricular content and pedagogical practices, as well as of the 'educational environment' supporting these, appears fundamental. Recall here the relational aspects of disability. Designing curricula implies promoting certain functionings and the related capabilities, so choosing a highly 'academic' oriented curriculum would have implications for levels of achievement and successful participation. Similarly, pedagogical practices involving cooperation and mutual support would likely promote full participation, by contrast with practices promoting competition and putting 'children against all children in a battle for success' (McDermott, 1993: 293). With regard to such matters, the capability perspective on disability draws our attention to the important interface between children's learning and the design of curriculum and pedagogical practices.

This is only the beginning of the insights that a capability perspective on disability might bring to the issues surrounding education for disabled children and children with special needs. Much work remains to be done, most importantly toward developing a principled framework for a just distribution of educational resources and opportunities aimed at inclusion.

## Notes

1. I have critically analysed the social model of disability in Terzi (2004).
2. I address below the relationship between disability and disadvantage in Sen's view.
3. I owe this observation to discussions with Harry Brighouse.
4. I owe this insight to discussions with Eamonn Callan.
5. I am deeply grateful to Martha Nussbaum for providing me with the book manuscript in advance of publication and giving permission to cite it.
6. I leave for another occasion the issues surrounding the choice of reference class.

# References

Alkire, S. (2002) *Valuing Freedoms: Sen's Capability Approach and Poverty Reduction* (Oxford: Oxford University Press).

Barnes, C., Mercer, G. and Shakespeare, T. (1999) *Exploring Disability: A Sociological Introduction* (Cambridge: Polity Press).

Brighouse, H. (2000) *School Choice and Social Justice* (Oxford: Oxford University Press) .

Buchanan, A. (2000) 'Genetic intervention and the morality of inclusion', in A. Buchanan, D. W. Brock, N. Daniels and D. Wikler (eds.) *From Chance to Choice: Genetics and Justice* (Cambridge: Cambridge University Press), pp. 258–303.

Bury, M. (1996) 'Defining and researching disability: challenges and responses', in C. Barnes and G. Mercer (eds.) *Exploring the Divide: Illness and Disability* (Leeds: The Disability Press), pp. 17–38.

Corker, M. (1999) 'Differences, conflations and foundations: the limits to 'accurate' theoretical representation of disabled people's experience?' *Disability and Society* 14(5): 627–42.

Dworkin, R. (2000) *Sovereign Virtue: The Theory and Practice of Equality* (Cambridge, MA: Harvard University Press).

Finkelstein, V. (1980) *Attitudes and Disabled People: Issues for Discussion* (New York: World Rehabilitation Fund).

French, S. (1993) 'Disability, impairment or something in between?', in J. Swain, V. Finkelstein. S. French and M. Oliver (eds.) *Disabling Barriers – Enabling Environments* (London: SAGE), pp. 17–25.

Kittay, E. F. (2003) 'A response to Martha Nussabaum's Tanner lecture on Justice for Mentally Disabled Citizens' (unpublished manuscript).

McDermott, R. P. (1993) 'The acquisition of a child by a learning disability', in S. Chaiklin and J. Lave (eds.), *Understanding Practice: Perspectives on Activity and context* (Cambridge: Cambridge University Press), pp. 269–303.

Morris, J. (1991) *Pride Against Prejudice: Transforming Attitudes to Disability* (London: Women Press).

Nussbaum, M. C. (2000) *Women and Human Development: The Capabilities Approach* (Cambridge: Cambridge University Press).

Nussbaum, M. C. (2005) *Frontiers of Justice: Disability, Nationality, Species Membership* (Cambridge, MA: Harvard University Press).

Nagel, T. (2002) *Concealment and Exposure* (Oxford: Oxford University Press).

Oliver, M. (1990) *The Politics of Disablement* (London: Macmillan Press).

Oliver, M. (1996) *Understanding Disability: From Theory to Practice* (Basingstoke; Palgrave).

Perry, J., Macken, E., Scott, N. and McKinley, J. (1996) 'Disability, inability and cyberspace', in B. Friedman (ed.), *Designing Computers for People: Human Values and the Design of Computer Technology* (Stanford, CA: CSLI Publications).

Perry, J., Macken, E. and Israel, D. (1999) 'Prolegomena to a theory of disability, inability and handicap', in L. Moss, J. Ginzburg, J. and M. De Rijke (eds.), *Logic, Language and Computation*, vol. 2 (Stanford, CA: CSLI Publications).

Pogge, T. W. (2003) 'Can the capability approach be justified?' Available at http://aran.univ_pau.fr/ee/index.html (accessed June 2003).

Rawls, J. (1971) *A Theory of Justice* (Oxford: Oxford University Press).

Rawls, J. (2001) *Justice as Fairness: A Restatement* (Cambridge, MA: Harvard University Press).

Robeyns, I. (2003) 'Sen's capability approach and gender inequality: selecting relevant capabilities', forthcoming in *Feminist Economics*, no. 2. Available at: www.ingridrobeyins.nl (accessed June 2003).

Saito, M. (2003) 'Amartya Sen's capability approach to education: a critical exploration', *Journal of Philosophy of Education* 37(1): 17–34.

Sen, A. (1992) *Inequality Reexamined* (Oxford: Oxford University Press).

Sen, A. (1999) *Development as Freedom* (Oxford: Oxford University Press).

Shakespeare, T. (1997) 'Cultural representation of disabled people: dustbins of disavowal?', in L. Barton and M. Oliver (eds.), *Disability Studies: Past, Present and Future* (Leeds: Disability Press).

Shapiro, T. (2003) 'Childhood and personhood' (unpublished manuscript).

Terzi, L. (2004) 'The social model of disability: a philosophical critique', *Journal of Applied Philosophy* 21(2): 141–57.

Thomas, C. (1999) *Female Forms: Experiencing and Understanding Disability* (Buckingham: Open University Press).

Unterhalter, E. (2003) 'Education, capabilities and social justice', *UNESCO EFA Monitoring Report* (UNESCO), in press.

Wendell, S. (1996) *The Rejected Body: Feminist Philosophical Reflections on Disability* (London: Routledge).

WHO (ICFDH) (2001) *International Classification of Functioning, Disability and Health* (Geneva: World Health Organization).

WHO (ICIDH) (1980) *International Classification of Impairments, Disability and Handicap* (Geneva: World Health Organization).

# 33

# Educating Gifted Children

# Laura Purdy

## Introduction

Deciding how to educate so-called "exceptional" students is both a moral and an educational question. Yet there is relatively little literature attempting to take both kinds of considerations into account.[1]

It is generally agreed that weak students unable to cope with the regular curriculum should have extra help. But there is no such agreement about bright children, and programs attempting to provide such help are often controversial.

How might one go about arguing such a case? As we are all too aware, there are many moral theories and many interpretations of those theories; none is without serious objections, and rarely does theory produce an irrefutable answer to a particular problem. One might react by withdrawing from practical ethics, or by giving up on theory. Most of us are, I think, muddling through, choosing the theory whose costs we are most willing to pay, but also noticing that attempting to resolve concrete problems brings us nose to nose with problems for which standard theories have no wisdom. My approach is eclectic, a sort of feminist consequentialism that

allows me to take proper account of the facts – without which good intentions will lead to unforeseen and perhaps undesirable results – without falling into some relativistic morass.

What then is the case for special education for bright students? The basic consequentialist argument is clear: children become bored or rebellious if they are not challenged. They may then turn away from intellectual pursuits, often disrupting classes as they do so.[2] If these children then go on to choose occupations below their potential, both they and society lose out. They lose because life satisfaction depends in part on using one's capacities. Society loses because it needs all the competent, imaginative people it can get to solve its problems. Since these problems are a source of misery and suffering, wasting talent is immoral.

In response, many would assert that democracy requires a common education for all children. Special education for weak students is defended on the grounds that it reduces inequality. But if universalizability – the principle that morally relevant differences can justify different treatment – supports appropriate education for these weak students, then can universalizability support unusually strong

Previously published in Randall Curren (ed.), *Philosophy of Education 1999* (Urbana, IL: Philosophy of Education Society, 2000), pp. 192–9.

students? Does the failure to develop their potential (and the concomitant disruption to others) justify the support for appropriate education? The main objection seems to be that it is unfair to use scarce resources to further improve the position of those already better off because of their intelligence. However, there is evidence that intelligent children not given special help can be left worse off than average children to whom the school is geared. It could be argued that these children are still no worse off than those with environmental or genetic strikes against them. But no one holds that *those* children should be abandoned. Furthermore, one need not concede that the only (or even the best) way to achieve a more egalitarian world is by deliberately failing to develop human potential. It would be far preferable to aim at developing all children's potential, to change oppressive social institutions that promote inequality, and to reduce the hugely unequal social rewards created by current social arrangements.

Definitive conclusions about justice must await answers about the best educational strategies, however. Many approaches to educating intellectually able children have been suggested, from radical reorganization of the curriculum to doing nothing.[3] The two basic – and most feasible – approaches are enrichment and acceleration.

## Enrichment and Acceleration

### Enrichment

Enrichment attempts to provide greater depth and breadth of material than is usually available within the existing twelve-year sequence. The posited advantage is that children stay with their age-mates, and thus spend the usual number of years in school.[4]

These alleged advantages do not stand up to careful scrutiny. Even if enrichment does enable children to stay with their age-mates, contrary to popular opinion, social maturity correlates more strongly with mental age than chronological age.[5] And why is it desirable for every child to spend twelve years in school? Since children develop mentally, socially and even physically at different rates, it would be plausible to believe that years of schooling should be flexible. For educators focused on "attention to the whole child" reluctance to take this possibility seriously is contradictory and betrays unwarranted reliance on rigid developmental theories.

It has also been argued that enrichment leads to superior academic performance. Research results have been mixed. William K. Durr comments that one of the most thorough studies compiled revealed no changes because of "concentrated enrichment." Objective measures of achievement, social adjustment, or attitudes of individuals toward themselves showed no meaningful improvement, despite subjective reports to the contrary by those involved. Some other studies do show significant results, however. For example, graduates of Cleveland's Major Work Classes did better in "leadership, reading activities, sense of social responsibility, and development of individual attitudes" than members of control groups.[6] One difficulty with both implementing and studying enrichment may be its diverse forms, as well as the potential for programs that sound better than they are. This problem is not imaginary: Dorothy A. Sisk reports that "much of the so-called enrichment of many programs for the gifted and talented is being found to exist only on paper."[7]

Sisk also points out that educators are also finding that although enrichment does increase breadth of information, it often fails to provide occasions for depth.[8] This raises the question whether a good enrichment program is in such sharp contrast with acceleration as has been assumed. This is indeed plausible: how much English, math, or science can one teach without impinging on concepts and techniques usually studied later? Thus "enriched" Algebra I becomes Algebra II. If one does encroach on the more advanced curriculum without giving students credit for what they have learned, then boredom is merely deferred. Problems of repetition are likely to be aggravated by changes in curriculum over time, and diversity of curriculum in different systems, since many families move often. If the concepts or techniques are not studied later, one must wonder how significant they are. The case for many enrichment models is therefore somewhat weaker than it appears: their alleged social advantages are dubious, and their academic value cannot be taken for granted.

### Acceleration

Acceleration, allowing children to progress faster than usual through the educational system, can be accomplished via one or more of the following: early entrance to grade school, grade-skipping, fast-paced classes, AP courses, credit by examination, or part-time college work.

Both educators and parents seem haunted by the fear that acceleration causes social and emotional maladjustment. However, there seems to be no evidence for it. Cautions about the evils of acceleration abound, unsupported by footnotes.[9] Study after study shows not only that accelerated individuals suffer no harm, but also that in most cases they benefit socially and emotionally from accelerative measures. Daurio provides a thorough review of this literature.[10] Durr summarizes some of these results.[11] Studies done in the thirties and forties showed that grade school accelerates were superior in adjustment, and that secondary school accelerates were as popular and socially active as nonaccelerates. The results of grade skipping appear to be equally reassuring, and students in special fast-paced classes showed no ill effects.[12]

Given this kind of evidence, it is hard to see why resistance to acceleration is so widespread. Perhaps the studies are mistaken in principle or marred by methodological problems that invalidate them. But there appear to be no attempts to argue for such claims. Perhaps it is assumed that they are biased, since one of the well-known hazards of research is for the expectations of the researcher to bias the results. But then the unanimity of the research results is doubly surprising. One is forced to the conclusion that either no opponents of acceleration have done research, or that if they have, the results changed their minds. Perhaps all the research is outdated and no longer relevant to current circumstances. On the contrary, there is a steady stream of studies and some of the more contemporary ones support the most radical strategies. Some of the most radically accelerated individuals are delighted with the opportunity to satisfy their desire for challenging material and forge ahead academically.[13] The Study of Mathematically Precocious Youth (SMPY) longitudinal studies continue to demonstrate long-term benefit.[14]

Perhaps we are witnessing the power of anecdotal evidence about such well-known educational disasters as William James Sidis, an intellectual prodigy who eventually withdrew from the intellectual arena to live in obscurity. But Sidis's undistinguished record could be a consequence of any number of factors, most plausibly, severe parental pressure.[15]

Also common are anecdotal reports of unhappiness on the part of accelerated individuals. But it is well known that anecdotal evidence provides only weak evidence. First, is there reason to believe that a larger percentage of accelerates than average individuals show evidence of having been unusually unhappy? And second, even if accelerates were unhappy, it remains to be shown that acceleration was the cause of their unhappiness, given that intelligence is not always an unmixed blessing. The relevant question is how unhappy they were compared to individuals of similar intelligence not accelerated. Hence the worry that acceleration causes social or emotional maladjustment appears to be unsubstantiated.

It is also argued that accelerated children will be at a disadvantage in sports because of their small size. But children develop physically at different rates and younger children can be bigger or stronger than older ones. Furthermore, not all children care about sports, and those who do can be encouraged to take up sports emphasizing primarily skill or intelligence. Or arrangements could be made for children to have gym or play on teams with younger children. If promoting learning is the central goal of education, children should not be held back to secure the lesser goal of promoting sports.

This concern about sports may well arise from a deeper underlying worry that children of very different sizes should not be spending their school hours together. But a "normal" classroom contains children who vary in age up to a year, and who therefore would be different sizes even if all children were the same size at the same age – which, naturally, they are not. A demand for limited variation in student size seems in any case inappropriate for educators who extol the virtues of the heterogeneous classroom in the course of their arguments for enrichment. If other students make fun of a child, teachers should discipline them.

Some have argued against acceleration on the grounds that children should not have to work too hard. But bright children pursuing the usual curriculum work much less than average children, so it can hardly be regarded as unfair to give them more advanced work. The objection that an accelerated child must work too hard also makes sense only if one is more concerned about having everyone cover a given amount of material, rather than helping each individual realize his or her potential. Last, this worry fails to take account of the fact that for many people, both children and adults, congenial and challenging "work" is often perceived as pleasurable.

These arguments exhaust the principal non-academic objections to acceleration. Let us therefore now turn to the academic ones.

One objection to acceleration is that it does not make sense to accelerate individuals when their talents may lie in only one or two areas. But research shows that talented individuals often excel in many areas.[16] Camilla P. Benbow suggests that if otherwise able children are weak in one area, they can be given individual help.[17] This is at least as plausible as keeping a student at a lower level to accommodate the weaker area.

Another objection, aimed primarily at grade skipping, is that acceleration causes gaps in students' knowledge. Since this method of acceleration is one of the most convenient, it is important to determine whether such gaps are a problem. But research shows this worry to be unsubstantiated; even for the most radically accelerated students in the SMPY program, gaps do not seem to hinder progress; perhaps one reason is that there is a great deal of review and repetition built into the curriculum in most school systems.[18]

It is also argued that accelerated students grasp only superficially the material they cover. Thus Gibb asserts that accelerates have superficial mathematical understandings, but she provides no support for her view, and S. P. Daurio found no evidence for it.[19]

What about other areas where superficiality would be still harder to demonstrate? The charge of superficiality would in any case apply only to classes that attempt to cover material faster than usual. It is not relevant to early entrance or grade skipping, in which cases material is covered by the accelerated student at the same pace and therefore at least as thoroughly as by average students. However, the objection depends upon the dubious thesis that to learn something quickly is to learn it only superficially, and ignores the obvious fact that individuals learn at different rates, and the fact that the more interested one is in a subject the better one tends to learn it.

Hence it is clear that none of the alleged disadvantages of acceleration stand up to scrutiny.[20] One might nevertheless ask what positive reasons there might be for using it.

Some such reasons have already emerged in the foregoing discussion: many studies show that acceleration is significantly beneficial. SMPY studies show, for example, that "accelerated youths who reason extremely well mathematically will tend to go much further educationally, in more difficult fields, and at more demanding universities, than if they were left age-in-grade."[21] Moreover, such opportunities may well lead to greater social adjustment.[22] One study showed, for example, that a group of students who entered college early had higher grade point averages, got more scholarships, won more academic awards, held more class offices and took part in more activities, including athletics.[23] This researcher found that those who showed greatest evidence of maladjustment were bright individuals who had not been accelerated, and average ones who had been accelerated. And not only do accelerated students do better than nonaccelerated ones, but Frederick Tuttle concludes that positive harm may come of failure to accelerate.

Clearly, accelerated bright children forge ahead academically. But why do they succeed better socially? The most plausible answer is provided by the aforementioned evidence that social development is more strongly correlated with mental age than chronological age, and that people tend to have the most satisfying friendships with those who understand the world at a similar level of complexity.

A further advantage of acceleration is that individuals can squeeze more education into less time, so accelerated students typically have more schooling than others do. Perhaps part of the explanation is that boredom extinguishes interest in learning and challenge reinforces it.

Faster progress also readies individuals for work earlier. This has obvious financial advantages, if society can offer them jobs. Having more productive years has special significance for the research professions. Harvey C. Lehman's studies show that the most productive years in many professions are the early thirties; scientific discoveries peak even earlier, with much brilliant work being done by individuals in their twenties or even their teens.[24] So helping more children advance faster means more new discoveries.

In sum, the arguments in favor of enrichment are weaker than one might think and the objections to acceleration are far less substantial than they are often taken to be, and the arguments for it more compelling. Thus, in the absence of more radical ideas (such as providing every student with much more individual attention), it is clear that on both academic and social grounds, the backbone of measures for superior students should be acceleration.

## Moral Conclusions

Broader moral considerations reinforce this position. One is simply the cost-benefit analysis. Enrichment programs tend to be quite expensive, requiring extra teachers and facilities, whereas acceleration tends to save money. Jackson has elaborated some of these financial advantages of acceleration for individuals and for society. Just entering college with a year of AP credit could save a year of study, reducing economic strain on families and students, as well as providing state and federal governments with substantial tax revenues. If appropriately extended across society, social and personal outlays on education would be significantly reduced, individuals could earn additional billions of dollars a year, and tax collections would rise significantly.[25]

Such financial considerations may sound crass, but it should not be necessary to point out that money spent one place is lost to other needs. Since expenditures on defense seem untouchable, social welfare expenditures play off against each other in a zero sum game. So it is immoral, other things being equal, to spend money pursuing objectives that could be achieved more cheaply. The same argument holds within the field of education, for we are not providing everything average and disadvantaged students need, and changing this situation will not be cheap. If there are proven strategies that allow us to help better students while liberating resources for others, it is immoral not to prefer those strategies.

Other moral reasons for choosing acceleration rather than enrichment are connected with smaller scope, but still important, moral issues: problems in identifying appropriate participants in special programs, and the development of snobbery among the chosen, together with lack of self-confidence among those not chosen. Labeling some children "gifted" may create undesirable feelings of superiority in those so designated, and feelings of inferiority in those failing to qualify. Worse still, such labels may be artificial and self-fulfilling prophecies based on inadequate criteria.

Although we do not have good information about the first issue, it seems reasonable to believe that the worst offenders are likely to be programs separating students for frequent short periods, and those providing cultural enrichment that might be desirable for all children. It also appears reasonable to believe that acceleration is less likely to cause unnecessarily painful emotions. Acceleration can be done discreetly; accelerates have no special privileges except those conferred by being in a higher grade, and their old classmates do not have to witness their constant comings and goings.

Because of the potentially undesirable consequences of sorting pupils into different categories, it is crucially important that the sorting criteria be reliable. IQ has been one of the most widely used, yet IQ tests have been the subject of enough justifiable criticism to warrant considerable skepticism about their worth. This problem is aggravated by the general problem of somewhat arbitrary cut-off points. The same problem arises, to a lesser extent, with acceleration, and the solution, it seems to me, is the same in each case. Decisions about students' programs ought to pay at least as much attention to motivation, achievement and multiple-ability tests such as the DAT and SAT, as to IQ.[26] The force of this point is multiplied by evidence that achievement has a good deal to do with self-confidence. Furthermore, the role of expectation in eliciting good performance is still unclear. Perhaps ability is not fixed, but can be increased to some extent even at relatively late ages. This raises questions about programs that do assume it to be fixed, and which can be offered only to a small percentage of the population because of limited resources. This is not a problem for acceleration: students can be accelerated any time their performance justifies it, and there is in principle no limit to the number of students who can finish school early.

These questions assume special importance because of the association of race, class, and income with selection into gifted programs. If even part of mental capacity is due to the environment, then this finding raises overwhelming questions about justice. If any motivated student can try acceleration (quietly dropping back if unsuccessful), that would help counteract such discrimination.

In conclusion, there is a strong case for special treatment of superior students, although it does not follow that any given program is defensible. As there is evidence that the results of acceleration are more favorable to individuals, their families, and to society than enrichment, it should be the main way of accommodating the needs of bright students.

# Notes

1. An appealing exception is Renzulli's work, as in, for example, Joseph S. Renzulli and Sally M. Reis, "The Enrichment Triad/Revolving Door Model: A Schoolwide Plan for the Development of Creative Potential," in *Systems and Models for Developing Programs for the Gifted and Talented*, ed. Joseph S. Renzulli (Mansfield Center, CT: Creative Learning Press, 1986), pp. 217–68.

2. Kevin G. Bartkovich and W. C. George, *Teaching the Gifted and Talented in the Mathematics Classroom* (Washington, DC: National Education Association, 1980).

3. See Renzulli (ed.), *Systems and Models*, for a variety of models for recognizing and developing talent. Unfortunately, despite this array of models, "doing nothing" still appears to be a popular option to judge by a survey by Karen L. Westberg and Francis X. Archambault, Jr. Whether it happens out of conviction that there is something wrong with special attention to bright children or whether teachers are still generally expected to provide it in the context of the regular classroom remains to be shown. Certainly, adapting teaching to accommodate individual differences is challenging, because it requires special training and more work. See Karen L. Westberg and Francis X. Archambault, Jr., "Multi-Site Case Study of Successful Classroom Practices for High Ability Students," *Gifted Child Quarterly* 41, no. 1 (Winter 1997): 21–32.

4. See D. A. Worcester, "Enrichment," *Educating the Gifted: Acceleration and Enrichment* (revised and expanded proceedings of the ninth annual Hyman Blumberg symposium on research in early childhood education), ed. W. C. George, S. J. Cohn, and J. C. Stanley (Baltimore, MD: Johns Hopkins University Press, 1979), pp. 98–104.

5. For further discussion, see M. C. Reynolds, J. W. Birch, and A. A. Tuseth, "Research on Early Admissions," in *The Intellectually Gifted: An Overview*, ed. W. Dennis and M. W. Dennis (New York: Grune and Stratton, 1976).

6. S. P. Daurio, "Educational Enrichment versus Acceleration: a Review of the Literature," in George, Cohn, and Stanley, *Educating the Gifted*, p. 23.

7. See Dorothy A. Sisk, "Acceleration versus Enrichment: a Position Paper," in George, Cohn, and Stanley, *Educating the Gifted*, pp. 236–8. Gary A. Davis and Sylvia B. Rimm repeat this concern in *Education of the Gifted and Talented* (Englewood Cliffs, NJ: Prentice-Hall, 1985), p. 121.

8. Sisk, "Acceleration versus Enrichment," pp. 236–8.

9. See, for example, Gibb, "Educational Acceleration of Intellectually Talented Youths," in George, Cohn, and Stanley, *Educating the Gifted*, pp. 220–1.

10. Daurio, "Educational Enrichment versus Acceleration," pp. 24–53.

11. W. K. Durr, *The Gifted Student* (Oxford: Oxford University Press, 1964), chap. 6.

12. J. R. Hobson, "High School Performance of Underage Pupils Initially Admitted to Kindergarten on the Basis of Physical and Psychological Examinations," in George, Cohn, and Stanley, *Educating the Gifted*, pp. 165–7.

13. See, for example, Colin, in Camilla Persson Benbow, "SMPY's Model for Teaching Mathematically Precocious Students," in Renzulli (ed.), *Systems and Models*, p. 21.

14. Ibid., p. 19.

15. See K. Montour, "William James Sidis, the Broken Twig," *American Psychologist* 32 (1977): 265–79.

16. Davis and Rimm, *Education of the Gifted and Talented*, pp. 128–9.

17. Benbow, "SMPY's Model," pp. 12–18.

18. Davis and Rimm, *Education of the Gifted and Talented*, pp. 99–101.

19. Gibb, "Educational Acceleration of Intellectually Talented Youths," pp. 220–1, and Daurio, "Educational Enrichment versus Acceleration."

20. See Davis and Rimm, *Education of the Gifted and Talented*, chap. 5.

21. Benbow, "SMPY's Model," p. 23.

22. Reynolds, Birch, and Tuseth, "Research on Early Admissions."

23. Frederick Tuttle, *Gifted and Talented Students* (Washington, DC: The National Education Association, 1978), pp. 16–19.

24. Harvey Lehman, *Age and Achievement* (Princeton, NJ: Princeton University Press, 1953), chap. 1.

25. D. M. Jackson, "A Possible Economic Correlation of Acceleration for the Individual and for Society," in George, Cohn, and Stanley (eds.), *Educating the Gifted*, pp. 204–5.

26. Renzulli and Reis emphasize this point in "The Enrichment Triad/Revolving Door Model," pp. 216–64.

# 34

# Perfectionism and Educational Policy

## Joel Kupperman

In this paper I will characterize what seems to me a plausible form of what has been called "perfectionism." I then will argue that it offers an acceptable account of how some societal resources should be distributed. Finally, I will discuss some implications of this for educational policy.

## I

The term "perfectionism" seems to have been invented by John Rawls who, in *A Theory of Justice*, identified perfectionism as a teleological doctrine, directed toward "the realization of human excellence in the various forms of culture," and rejected it.[1] Aristotle and Nietzsche were spoken of as having held the rejected view. Some writers since, apparently drawing on Rawls, have referred to perfectionism in terms appropriate to an unwholesomely elitist way of organizing society.[2] The suggestion was that perfectionism was morally as well as philosophically unacceptable.

Because of this background it seems important to begin by explaining the limits of the perfectionism to be endorsed. Despite widespread Aristotelian-baiting, the reader should understand that perfectionists need not endorse slavery or extreme social inequality. The perfectionism to be defended is Aristotelian in holding that human excellence is a compound of intellectual virtues (I would want to give weight also to qualities involved in creation and appreciation of what is aesthetically of a high order) and virtues exhibited in the manner of our relations with others; it is to some degree non-elitist, in that many of these virtues can be shared by the vast majority of members of a society in ways that it is important to promote; and it is limited in a respect that I will now explain.

Let us distinguish between decisions that call for moral judgment and decisions that do not. A distinguishing feature is this: we treat a decision as falling within the purview of morality if and only if we would term at least some of the courses of action that are open as "morally wrong" or "immoral."[3] Inadvisable choices that lie outside the bounds of morality are frequently referred to by terms such as "unwise", "not nice", "tacky," "tasteless," etc.; these are characteristic terms of non-moral evaluation, although some are occasionally applied to what is considered immoral. I will make

Previously published in *Public Affairs Quarterly* 1 (January 1987), pp. 111–19. Reprinted with permission of Public Affairs Quarterly.

the following assumptions about what is morally wrong. (1) It is morally wrong to treat another person in the ways forbidden by the core of traditional morality: i.e. to murder, torture, steal, etc. (2) It is also morally wrong for a society to leave some of its members without enough to eat, adequate clothing and shelter, or adequate education and medical care if the society has the resources to provide all of these things for its members.[4] (3) If a member of society has enough to eat, adequate clothing, shelter, education and medical care, but is not as well off as Rawls' theory would call for, the latter does not by itself imply that this person has been morally wronged.[5]

The perfectionism to be defended does not allow perfectionist considerations to be used to justify treating someone in a way that is morally wrong. This means, among other things, that we must give priority to seeing that everyone has enough to eat, etc., if this is possible. What the perfectionism does claim is that in some cases in which we are to choose among social arrangements none of which morally wrongs anyone, we should give some weight (not necessarily all the weight) to "the realization of human excellence in the various forms of culture." Given the third assumption about moral wrongness, we can see that there are cases in which a government, a hospital, or a university can make decisions about allocation of resources which are such that, even if they obliquely affect the fortunes of one of the worst-off members of society, do not fall within the purview of morality. A transfer of resources from one program to another of a university, hospital, or government can be unwise and undesirable without necessarily being immoral. My thesis is that perfectionist considerations should have weight in some decisions of this sort.

## II

The case for the limited perfectionism that has been outlined rests on one further normative judgment, which concerns the unacceptability of what I will call Tepid New World. Tepid New World is somewhat modeled on Aldous Huxley's Brave New World, but lacks both its social stratification and its totalitarian political structure. Huxley's novel functions in part as a thought experiment that refutes hedonistic utilitarianism; Brave New World is designed to maximize happiness. I mean Tepid New World as a thought experiment designed to undermine anti-perfectionism.

We are to suppose that the society of Tepid New World is democratic; everyone has equal liberty. People are entirely free to denounce the character of their society and its prevailing tastes and mores, although it is not likely that many will listen to them. There is a considerable degree of social and economic equality to the point at which we are to suppose that Tepid New World meets the standards for a just society laid down in *A Theory of Justice*. Finally, we are to suppose that Tepid New World is like Brave New World in that enormous skill and technology have been devoted to instant gratification of people's desires for pleasure. The inhabitants of Tepid New World are like those of Brave New World in that almost all of them live simply for a round of pleasures, and are very satisfied with their world. As in Brave New World, the arts (and, one assumes, the impractical sciences) are at an exceedingly low point. There is very little encouragement of artistic or intellectual creativity, and both standards and accomplishments in these domains are virtually non-existent.

It might be said that Tepid New World, like Huxley's original, is purely a fantasy, something that could not exist. This objection is difficult to sustain *a priori*; human nature has throughout history taken many bizarre forms. Most human conduct appears to be governed by what has been called the "Aristotelian Principle," which involves a taste for complexity and challenge; but, as Rawls remarks, this "formulates a tendency and not an invariable principle of choice, and like all tendencies it may be overridden."[6] Also the taste for complexity and challenge could come to be entirely focused on such activities as video games and surfboard riding. In any event, there is no apparent reason why Tepid New World cannot constitute a test for any set of principles of social choice.

My suggestion is that the cultural deficiencies that make Tepid New World distinctive are socially undesirable to the degree they occur, and that as an extreme case Tepid New World is an unacceptable social outcome, even if its inhabitants are on the whole very pleased with it. Tepid New World is less acceptable than a society which has vigorous cultural activities of a high quality and in which the worst-off members are less prosperous than in Tepid New World but still have enough to eat, adequate clothing and shelter, and decent education and medical care.

Some undoubtedly will reply that in an "original position" in which people do not know what their place in society will be *or* what their conception of the good is, Tepid New World will be preferred to a less egalitarian but culturally more robust society. But is this a fair test? It seems artificial to deny a conception of the good to people who are, in effect, trying to arrive at a conception of a good society.[7] Admittedly, if a group of people in the "original position" do know their conceptions of the good, they are much less likely to arrive at a unanimous decision, but is this an objection to allowing them such knowledge? If they know what liberty is, and what money (whose distribution they must consider) is, why can they not know their conception of the good?

The remainder of the argument for a limited perfectionism can be outlined as follows. We have seen that the unacceptability of Tepid New World is based on its cultural deficiencies; it would be improved if it was marked by more intellectual and artistic vigor. It is debatable whether there ever has been a society of which this was not true; is it ever possible to have too much of these qualities? Leaving this to the side, we can say that there is no society now in the world, and none imaginable that is much like the one we live in, that is in danger of having too much intellectual and artistic vigor. Any society that we are at all likely to make real decisions about could benefit from a heightened cultural life.

The next step is to claim that, all things equal or nearly equal, we should promote increased intellectual and artistic vigor. One does not have to be a consequentialist to take this particular step from what is good to what should be done. Even Kant would have agreed that, if (*ex hypothesi*) there is no moral reason against doing what is required to promote greater intellectual and artistic vigor in a society, then there is reason to do it. Further, the actions that are called for are not only a matter of individual effort in personal life, but also of political and social choice. It seems fair to assume that major factors that contribute to, or detract from, cultural vigor are determined by societal arrangements: e.g. the treatment of intellectual and artistic matters in the educational system, commissions to artists that are paid for out of public funds, government funding of scientific equipment, etc. Thus the imperative to promote intellectual and artistic vigor is, at least in part, an imperative that governs political choices.

It is important to re-emphasize at this stage both the limitations on, and the complexity of, the perfectionism argued for. The claim is that we should promote intellectual and artistic vigor in a society; this perfectionist imperative though is inoperative if someone would be morally wronged by our doing what is required, and even if there is no moral reason against doing what is required to promote intellectual and artistic vigor, the possibility is left open that there might be reasons of economy, convenience, or whatever, that in the particular case at hand outweigh the possible gains in intellectual and artistic vigor. A further complexity is that the perfectionism argued for gives weight to the virtues displayed in human relationships as well as to intellectual and aesthetic virtues; there may be societal choices whose primary effect is to promote the former virtues, and there may be cases in which we have to choose which virtues are in greatest need of societal resources. There is no room in this brief paper though to explore these complexities, and I will continue to concentrate on the intellectual and aesthetic virtues, partly because there is a clearer connection in some cases between the promotion of these and the expenditure of money.

A strong case can be made for example for the proposition that the money spent by the National Endowment for the Arts and the National Endowment for the Humanities, and by comparable bodies in the United Kingdom, contributes greatly to cultural vigor within the two countries. The strongest case though can be made with regard to such organizations as the National Science Foundation, partly because these days most work of high quality in the sciences requires expensive equipment, and partly because there may be slightly greater consensus about the standards for who deserves the aid of the NSF than there is about, say, the standards for who deserves the aid of the NEA.

James P. Sterba, in a recent review essay, has remarked that perfectionist views of justice either have not been developed to the stage at which they support practical recommendations, or support much the same practical recommendations that are endorsed by rival views.[8] The foregoing suggests that this must be qualified. The limited perfectionism for which I have been arguing supports a view of funding for, say, the NSF sharply different from that suggested by John Rawls. His view is that "the social resources necessary to support associations dedicated to advancing the arts and sciences and culture generally are to be won as a fair return for services rendered, or from such voluntary contributions as citizens wish to make . . ."[9] The fate of the National Science Foundation if Rawls' voluntaristic proposal were adopted would not be a happy one. My argument has shown, I think, that the reasons that make Tepid New World an unacceptable society support societal expenditure for organizations, such as the NSF, that promote the realization of human excellence.

## III

It is very tempting, but surely mistaken, to regard the differences between perfectionist and anti-perfectionist approaches to educational policy as centering simply on expenditures of money. One anti-perfectionist line of thought is clearly marked: Rawls has suggested that "greater resources might be spent on the less rather than the more intelligent, at least over a certain time of life, say the earlier years of school."[10] A perfectionist is bound to disagree with this. But this does not mean either that a perfectionist would have to support greater expenditure in the early years on those who seem likely to be highly intelligent than on those who seem likely to be fairly unintelligent, nor must a perfectionist reject the idea of compensatory heavy spending for groups of students some of whom may not have above average intelligence.

One reason why the issues do not concern simply money is that much of what is crucial in the education of those who are most likely to make contributions to the arts and sciences does not necessarily require increased public expenditure. One major desideratum is that teachers be able to make their subjects intellectually challenging. The recent publication *What Works* puts the point nicely in relation to homework: "Assignments that require students to think, and are therefore more interesting, foster their desire to learn both in and out of school."[11] This is common sense, but is also backed by research. We might suppose that teachers who themselves had had a good liberal education would be more likely to be successful in stimulating exceptionally promising students to think, both in the classroom and in homework assignments. Such people though often appear unwilling to go through the programs of education schools that lead to certification. Thus a policy, such as that recently initiated by the State of New Jersey, that allows someone who is not the

product of a school of education to launch a career as a public school teacher might well contribute to the perfectionist goal of improving the intellectual and cultural prospects of promising students. Yet such a policy essentially costs nothing. Conversely special school programs for "gifted students," that do require special public expenditure, may turn out to be useless or worse than useless from a perfectionist point of view. My recent observations suggest that this is usually the case: a common fault is an emphasis on "creative" activities that seem cute to adults and are boring to children, and a lack of intellectual stimulation.

The bulk of the literature on equality in education does not deal with the issues of this paper, but rather with the question of compensatory education for disadvantaged groups; much of it centers on the Coleman Report of 1966.[12] Without entering this debate I can say that support of such compensatory education, and of the expenditure necessary for it, is consistent with the kind of perfectionist position that has been outlined. There would be a conflict only if compensatory education for disadvantaged groups required a less than average commitment (of the sort Rawls advocated for the early years) to students (of whatever racial group, etc.) who seem especially promising; but there is no reason to think that this is so. The differences between the rationale for compensatory education of disadvantaged groups, and the rationale for compensatory education of those judged to be of less than average intelligence, are worth noting. The fact of past injustices (such that some people regard compensatory education as, literally, compensation) marks one difference. To my mind, a clearer and more powerful justification of compensatory education for disadvantaged groups is based on the fact that very many people seem to identify with members of their own racial or religious group to the extent of being discouraged when there are few representatives of the group in positions of power and importance; conversely they become heartened when the number of representatives in enviable positions becomes larger. Thus there is a sense in which one must bring groups, and not just individuals, into the mainstream and the rewards of the life of our society. There is no corresponding group identification on the part of people of average or below average intelligence, and no corresponding need for increasing successes within the group. It is true that during the Nixon administration one senator urged that mediocre people deserved a representative on the Supreme Court, but the way that was received shows a good deal about the difference between the two cases.

The implication of perfectionism for educational policy is that, whether or not we spend additional money on the education of students who seem likely (on the basis of our limited knowledge of developmental curves) to make contributions in the arts and sciences, we should view the education of such students with especial concern. Anti-perfectionists are right to worry about the dangers of "elitism"; a democratic society does not want to be dominated by elites whose members' sense of identity centers on the image of themselves as members of the elite, and certainly no one should view it as a point in favor of an educational system that it produced snobs. But the dangers of elitism are matched by the dangers of anti-elitism. A student who comes to feel that no achievement is likely to get adequate recognition is at risk of lowered self-esteem; and in many American schools these risks exist across every area of achievement except athletics. If very many promising students find their educations unchallenging and boring, or if many of them become deficient in self-esteem, then our society has taken several steps in the direction of Tepid New World. The realization of human excellence in the various forms of culture is an important social goal, and work on it must begin in our educational system.[13]

## Notes

1. John Rawls, *A Theory of Justice* (Cambridge, MA: Harvard University Press, 1971), p. 25.
2. See, for example, Alan Donagan, *The Theory of Morality* (Chicago, IL: University of Chicago Press, 1977), pp. 25–6; Tom Regan, *The Case for Animal Rights* (Berkeley and Los Angeles, CA: University of California Press, 1983), p. 234. Regan characterizes perfectionism as "morally pernicious."
3. This is a very brief and over-simple treatment of a complicated subject. See John Stuart Mill, *Utilitarianism*, Chap. V, para. 14; and also Joel Kupperman, *The Foundations of Morality* (London: George Allen & Unwin, 1983), Chap. 1.
4. It should be emphasized that this brief paper does not attempt to arrive at a precise formulation of the acceptable kind of perfectionism: the argument is that *some* kind of perfectionism that is Aristotelian, to some degree non-elitist, and limited is correct. No one should take phrases like "adequate shelter" to be highly precise. There is room for those who agree with the argument of the paper to disagree about what counts as adequate shelter.
5. The main reason for not accepting this assumption would be of course Rawls' theory itself, with its image of a just society arrived at in the "original position." I will give reason later in the paper, though, to think Rawls' design of the thought experiment of the "original position" misconceived.
6. Op. cit., p. 429.
7. Ibid., p. 142.
8. James P. Sterba, "Recent Work on Alternative Conceptions of Justice," *American Philosophical Quarterly*, vol. 23 (1986), p. 18.
9. Op. cit., p. 329.
10. Ibid., p. 101.
11. *What Works. Research about Teaching and Learning* (Washington, DC: US Department of Education, 1986), p. 42.
12. See, for example, Harvard Educational Review, *Equal Educational Opportunity* (Cambridge, MA: Harvard University Press, 1969); Andrew Kopan and Herbert Walberg (eds.), *Rethinking Educational Equality* (Berkeley, CA: McCutcheon, 1974).
13. Conversations on the topic with John Troyer and with Thomas Hill, Jr. helped me in work on this paper. Neither should be assumed to agree with the position taken. I was helped also by comments made at the London School of Economics, where I gave a first version in June 1985, and by James Griffin.

# PART IV

# Teaching and Learning

# Introduction to Part IV

The *manner* in which we educate is as important as the content we aim to teach, the ends and responsibilities we have in view, and the authority with which we act. *How* we educate makes a world of difference. Teaching is the heart of the matter, and many of the questions that pertain to teaching are deeply ethical. How should a teacher perceive her relationship with a student? Is it a professional–client relationship, a caretaker–beneficiary relationship, or a master–apprentice relationship? Or is it a liberator–peer relationship as suggested by Freire (see Part I)? Is teaching best thought of as a profession, a craft, or a calling? What are the qualities that characterize good teaching? What are the personal qualities that make for a good teacher? In what ways can *teacher education* best contribute to good teaching? What are the roles of *skills* and *good judgment* in good teaching? When it comes to *managing* a classroom, how should teachers go about creating and maintaining a productive and safe learning environment? How can they best respond to undesirable forms of student conduct, such as sexual harassment? These are the concerns of the first two sub-sections, "Teaching" and "Discipline and Care." The next two sections, "Inquiry, Understanding, and Constructivism" and "Critical Thinking and Reasoning," concern the specifically pedagogical issues of how teachers may best enable students to *understand* and *think* for themselves.

A sensible teacher wants her students to *understand* what she teaches them, but how can she bring it about that they do understand? To what extent does it suffice to *explain* things to students? To what extent must they *see* or *experience* things for themselves? How may teachers best encourage students to engage in *inquiry* and think things through for themselves? A long tradition going back to St. Augustine holds that understanding is a mental act or experience of "illumination" or grasping the nature of something, which is non-transferable in the sense that its occurrence in the learner's mind may be occasioned by a teacher's words, but is *not transmitted* along with the words (see St. Augustine, 1995; on St. Augustine's debt to Plato, see Matthews, 1998). Opposed to the *transmission model* (the assumption that teachers can transmit knowledge to students) is a long tradition of support for the idea – now known as *constructivism* – that students must discover, think through, or "construct" knowledge for themselves. Others agree that inquiry, critical thinking, and active learning are essential to meaningful learning, but argue that many forms of inquiry and critical thinking require initiation into established traditions of disciplinary knowledge or inquiry. How can one engage in meaningful inquiry in physical science without some command of mathematics, for instance? How can one engage in meaningful historical inquiry without some prior knowledge of history and the nature of historical evidence? On the other hand, if we can teach mathematics as a tool of inquiry and subject in its own right, might we not also teach *critical thinking* or *reasoning* as a tool of inquiry in its own right? To what extent should teachers *reason* with students and promote critical thinking? Is instruction in critical thinking a good way to promote active learning?

The final sub-section in Part IV is the role of grading and testing in teaching and educational assessment. Student evaluation by teachers plays a complex role in schooling, serving both to motivate students and to inform them of their progress, but also as a basis for advancement and credentials. There are significant ethical issues at stake, including ones about the extent to which different forms of evaluation support sound pedagogy. The use of standardized tests by external agencies raises related ethical questions, but also a largely distinct set of questions about test design and the foundations of *psychometrics* (the science and enterprise of using tests to "measure" mental attributes). To what extent can tests be successful in measuring meaningful learning?

## Teaching

We are all well acquainted with the activity we call "teaching," so there is an obvious sense in which we know what it is. It is harder to say or *define* what it is with any precision or much certainty of being right. Is there any point in trying? Many philosophers have thought there is. They have thought that by defining "teaching" we can become more aware of the nature of teaching – and therefore what is *not* teaching and to be avoided (such as indoctrinating). Philip W. Jackson disputes this in "Real Teaching" (no. 35), a chapter from his book *The Practice of Teaching* (1986). He begins by arguing that teaching cannot be defined behaviorally, and that the specific *skills* a teacher might employ are not "the heart of the matter." Rather, a teacher needs to be "at home within a particular instructional milieu," and be able "to see and react in a certain spirit or manner" to what occurs. She requires a "pedagogical outlook." Jackson goes on to survey and dispense with three definitions of teaching that were introduced in the 1960s. The two proposed by Thomas Green and Israel Scheffler are alike in holding that teaching (or teaching in the "standard" sense) is in its nature

respectful of truth, evidence, and the student's right to receive and judge reasons. Jackson argues that such attempts to define "genuine" teaching are flawed; they reflect ideals that provide legitimate critical perspectives for judging the *quality* of teaching, but illicitly smuggle those ideals into the concept of teaching itself. Is it better to think about what characterizes *good* teaching, and leave it at that? How do we begin to think about that? Does making good use of pedagogical opportunities require attunement to both the subject and the students?

R. S. Peters conceived of education as initiation into public traditions and *forms of knowledge* (see reading no. 7), and Kenneth A. Strike's paper in Part II (no. 20) develops a related image of teachers as practitioners of *intellectual disciplines*. In order to be a practitioner of an intellectual discipline who can initiate others into its practice, one must achieve a kind of mastery of the discipline. As Israel Scheffler says in an extract reprinted here as "The Teacher's Grasp of Subject-Matter" (no. 36), the teacher requires a "reflective grasp of the 'forms of thought' a field embodies," and "a capacity to formulate and explain its workings" to the uninitiated. Scheffler argues that the study of *philosophy* can help prepare the teacher for this, because the task of philosophy is to "articulate and analyze the forms [of thought] themselves." His example is the teaching of science, and the ways in which the philosophy of science can attune teachers to the structures of scientific thinking and guide them in course preparation.

The teacher's attunement to students is the subject of David T. Hansen's paper, "Understanding Students" (no. 37). Understanding "what is distinctive about individual students" is "the heart of the practice" of teaching, and essential to the teacher's core commitment to "serve students' intellectual and moral growth," writes Hansen. A good teacher is attentive to the intellectual and moral development of each student, and mindful of her own "regard for and treatment of" each student. She is attentive to how students are developing in relation to the subject and attentive to the kinds of persons they are becoming. What kind of relationship should a teacher have with her students? A relationship in which the teacher's care, concern, and assistance are pedagogically focused on the student's intellectual and moral development, writes Hansen.

In the reading "Beyond the Reflective Teacher" (no. 38), Terence H. McLaughlin evaluates the model of the teacher as a "reflective practitioner."

The language of "reflection" is intended to connote professional "thoughtfulness, judgment, and autonomy," and in so doing to stand as a bulwark against the narrowing of teacher education and accountability measures to a focus on useful skills or "competences" (see reading no. 20 in Part II). There is, however, a great deal of indeterminacy in the notion of "reflection." McLaughlin considers several possible conceptions of the nature of the reflection involved, and presses questions about the *value* of reflection and the range of objects teachers are supposed to reflect upon. "An invitation to simply 'reflect' without attention to the ways in which adequacy in reflection can be secured is idle," he writes. So how should adequacy in reflection be understood and promoted? Is effective reflection grounded in knowledge of educational foundation disciplines or "general principles of professional practice"? McLaughlin leaves some important questions open for further investigation, but suggests that a teacher's practical judgment might be understood on the model of Aristotelian *phronesis* or practical wisdom (see reading no. 55 in Part V). As a starting point, McLaughlin argues that a teacher's good pedagogical judgment would arise, at least in part, from her personal qualities or virtues, her experience, and her "broad and rich grasp of the values of the educational enterprise."

## Discipline and Care

In "Social Control" (39), John Dewey contrasts the harsh and "autocratic" discipline of the "traditional" school with the more "humane" but lax atmosphere of the "progressive" school (see no. 7 in Part I and no. 21 in Part II). Although they are opposed in their methods, he rejects aspects of both and argues that they share a common error. In both, the teacher "acts largely from the outside" of the students' social world, in the "traditional" school through imposition of personal commands, and in the "progressive" school on the premise that it is wrong to impose order through personal commands. Dewey proposes that the teacher act instead from *within* the students' social world, as a leader who orchestrates group activities designed to provide all students with opportunities to make valued contributions. When the capacities of students are exercised and developed through such activities, "it is not the will or desire of any one person which establishes order." Control is "social," and

grounded in willing participation in activities that have their own internal rules or requirements.

Systems of classroom management are generally focused on establishing routines and articulating and enforcing rules, sometimes with students' help. Students are sometimes enlisted in formulating the rules, and it is not uncommon for teachers to involve students in enforcing the rules through such devices as honor codes and forms of collective responsibility. An important question about such systems of management is whether they can be fair and effective if children are not able to satisfy their *basic psychological needs* within the structures that the school and the teacher aim to establish. If children need to experience their own developing competence, then Dewey's idea that classroom activities should be tailored to provide *all* students with opportunities to make contributions is highly salient. If children need to experience connection and belonging, and are disposed to embrace the norms of communities that promote their well-being and accept them as respected members on fair terms, is it not also highly desirable that schools be constituted as caring communities? Nel Noddings describes the teacher as entering into a caring relation with each student, and argues that schools should be redesigned to facilitate this, in "The One-Caring as Teacher" (no. 40), a section from her book *Caring* (1984). She notes the relevance of school size and curriculum specialization to how well teachers are able to connect meaningfully with students. In evaluating her proposals, it is worth noting that larger schools, and schools in which teachers have less time with each student, tend to have worse problems with violence and vandalism.

Elizabeth Chamberlain and Barbara Houston examine the limitations of a legalistic or rule enforcement model for managing a specific behavioral problem, in their paper, "School Sexual Harassment Policies: The Need for Both Justice and Care" (no. 41). Sexual harassment seems to be prevalent in middle schools, and it is associated with a range of serious problems that many girls experience in early adolescence. Chamberlain and Houston point out that, while "legally oriented school policies make a strong positive contribution to the mitigation of sexual harassment," the mere announcement and enforcement of these policies does not seem to reduce the incidence of harassment of girls by boys. The reasons for this are documented in vivid detail in their reading. Staff and students alike have trouble distinguishing harassment from "normal" heterosexual behavior in a social world saturated with male dominance, and victims are reluctant to bring complaints that would endanger their place in the social world of the school. The ethic of care that Chamberlain and Houston bring to bear on this problem incorporates the idea that, as a matter of both effectiveness and justice, the imposition of a rule must be predicated on *teaching* what those who must obey it need to know in order to understand why it is reasonable to accept the rule as legitimate. The authors conclude that in solving social and behavioral problems in schools, primacy must be accorded to moral education that makes the policies to be imposed part of "the subject matter of educational study."

## Inquiry, Understanding, and Constructivism

The reading "Learning by Discovery" (no. 42) is composed of extracts from Books II and III of Jean-Jacques Rousseau's *Emile*. The material from Book II introduces the idea that children, like cats, have a strong exploratory urge that motivates spontaneous learning through the senses. Rousseau writes that the exercise of the senses provides a basis of *ideas* and sensory judgment that culminates in the emergence of *intellectual reason* or "the act of comparing ideas." Since *knowledge* is the intellectual perception of a relation between ideas, it is the *distinctness* and *clarity* of that perception that "constitutes the accuracy of the mind," he says. Book III follows the boy, Emile, through a course of learning by discovery that includes geometry, astronomy, and physics. A lesson in magnetism doubles as a natural lesson in morality and the perils of pride, and Rousseau hints that Emile's explorations of nature will eventually lead him to infer the existence of a God responsible for both natural and moral order in the world.[1] The limits of Rousseau's own understanding of science are evident in some of his examples. Contrary to his suggestion, there are no conceivable observations a child could make that would let him infer the superiority of a Copernican, heliocentric model of the solar system over a Ptolemaic, geocentric one. Without rejecting the value of student inquiry and self-directed learning, then, one must ask which specific steps of reasoning and discovery children can plausibly take on their own. Is scientific reasoning the same as "natural" or intuitive reasoning? How much of

science is discoverable through simple empirical (observational) methods, and how much depends upon *invented* forms of reasoning such as idealized mathematical modeling of natural phenomena?

D. C. Phillips's reading, "The Good, the Bad, and the Ugly: The Many Faces of Constructivism" (no. 43), provides an introduction to the *constructivist* theories of learning, knowledge, and pedagogy that have dominated pedagogical thinking in recent years. "There is a very broad and loose sense in which all of us these days are constructivists," Phillips writes; we all agree that "human knowledge – whether it be the bodies of public knowledge known as the various disciplines, or the cognitive structures of individual knowers or learners – is *constructed*." But there are many forms of constructivism, and Phillips's aim is to catalog them according to the major disagreements that divide them. Some constructivists are concerned with individual cognition, others with the development of public bodies of knowledge. Constructivists differ in the degree to which they regard knowledge as purely an invention of individuals or groups. They also differ with regard to the nature of the mechanisms of knowledge construction. Phillips's assessment is that what is "good" in these views is the recognition that learning requires the *active participation* of the learner, what is "bad" is a tendency to ignore or misrepresent the role of justification or evidence in knowledge, and what is "ugly" is the quasi-religious or ideological quality of many defenses of constructivism.

Richard E. Grandy offers a different but equally illuminating set of distinctions in "Constructivisms and Objectivity: Disentangling Metaphysics from Pedagogy" (no. 44). *Cognitive constructivism* holds that individual knowers *understand* the world through the representations they have constructed of it. *Metaphysical constructivism* is the very different view that the things we have knowledge of are themselves constructed by us in cognition, the sun no less than a sundial. Grandy argues that although many constructivists perceive a link between the two views, metaphysical constructivism is generally irrelevant to pedagogy. Cognitive constructivism has "strong empirical support," and, he suggests, it has useful ways to improve science instruction. *Epistemic constructivism* is "the view that knowledge is constructed by us rather than directly imbibed from the environment." But does "us" mean each of us independently of one another, or "us" collectively and through some kind of group process?

Grandy sees the "dynamic interaction between groups and individuals as critical," and infers that students must "develop the skills to participate in the epistemic interchanges that take place in scientific communities." To facilitate this, classroom communities "must have the appropriate features of an objective scientific community."

Philosophers agree that having knowledge involves believing a proposition that is true, and doing so on the basis of appropriate evidence, or with justification, or through a mechanism or method that reliably yields true beliefs. Catherine Z. Elgin expresses this by saying that knowledge requires "tethered" true belief. In her reading "Education and the Advancement of Understanding" (no. 45), she argues that if teaching requires possessing and conveying knowledge then "teaching looks to be well nigh impossible." Because adequate theories provide much of the grounds for believing many claims in the sciences and other fields, teachers don't actually *know* a lot of what they teach, and they don't convey to students enough of the grounds for believing what they teach to convey *knowledge*. Is teaching impossible, then? Elgin argues that we should hold onto the idea that teaching is possible, and should reject the idea that "you cannot teach what you do not know." The view she defends is that *understanding* is a more important educational goal than conveying facts, and teachers can advance a student's understanding of a subject without possessing or conveying knowledge in the strict sense. Elgin observes that "much education proceeds by a series of approximations," and she elaborates on the idea that understanding can be conveyed by theories or systems of thought that are reasonable but imperfect. She concludes that: "What makes for a good Fourth Grade education is not the set of facts the Fourth Grader knows, but the level of understanding she has achieved and the resources she can deploy to advance that understanding." Elgin assumes that student inquiry plays an important role in learning, but suggests that the methods, conceptual resources, and standards and background assumed in inquiry will shape the quality of understanding achieved.

## Critical Thinking and Reasoning

John Locke asserted famously that children understand reasoning "as early as they do language." As a physician, tutor to the 1st Earl of Shaftesbury's son and grandchildren, and a committed empiricist, he presumably had some observational basis for this claim. In the brief extract included here under the title "Reasoning with Children" (reading no. 46) we find him insisting that children should be treated as "rational creatures" and dealt with through reasoning as much as possible, using reasons they can understand (for the ethical rationale for this, see the Introduction to Part I). In "Against Reasoning with Children" (no. 47), a brief extract from *Emile*, Rousseau responds that reasoning with children doesn't seem to work, that reason develops much later than Locke contends, and that to reason with children in order to encourage them to be rational "is to begin with the end, to want to make the product the instrument." Children are not yet reasonable in the sense of being moved by considerations of duty or what is right as such, says Rousseau, so how can efforts to persuade them not degenerate into exercises in "flattery and promises"? If a person is not yet reasonable, how can reasoning with him make him so? "Use force with children, and reason with men," Rousseau advises.

Our contemporary selections on critical thinking and reasoning with children begin with "Education for Critical Thinking" (no. 48), an extract from Matthew Lipman's book *Thinking in Education*. Lipman identifies *good judgment* as the outcome and chief characteristic of critical thinking, and emphasizes the importance of good judgment in life, in the professions, and as a central goal of education (cf. no. 9 in Part I). He defines critical thinking as "*thinking that* (1) *facilitates judgment because it* (2) *relies on criteria*, (3) *is self-correcting, and* (4) *is sensitive to context*." In the course of explaining these defining traits, Lipman illustrates his methods for converting classrooms into *communities of inquiry* in which children become self-correcting critical thinkers. He argues that instruction in critical thinking empowers students to be active learners, and can improve education by increasing "the quantity and quality of meaning that students derive from what they read and perceive and that they express in what they write and say." The selection concludes with the recommendation that all courses at all levels be taught in a manner that encourages critical thinking, and that critical thinking also be included in the curriculum as a subject in its own right, ideally as a course in philosophy, "the narrative philosophy that emphasizes dialogue, deliberation, and the strengthening of judgment and community."

"The Reasons Conception of Critical Thinking" (no. 49) is a chapter from Harvey Siegel's book *Educating Reason: Rationality, Critical Thinking and Education* (1988). In it he elaborates the view that "a critical thinker is one who is *appropriately moved by reasons*," or who believes and acts on the basis of reasons. There is a *reason assessment component* to this and a *critical spirit component*. The critical thinker must understand and be able to use the principles that govern the assessment of reasons, and must also *respect* reason and be *disposed* to engage in reason assessment and act accordingly. In developing the details of this analysis, Siegel addresses the views of Robert Ennis, who identifies *subject-neutral* principles and proficiencies of reason assessment (Ennis, 1962), and also the views of John McPeck, who argues that the only significant principles and proficiencies of reason assessment are *subject-specific* (McPeck, 1981). Siegel defends the importance of principles and proficiencies of both kinds, and holds that critical thinkers require a "theoretical grasp of the nature of reasons, warrant, and justification," or in other words an understanding of *epistemology*. He describes critical thinking as an *educational ideal* that has implications for both the content and manner of instruction. Citing Scheffler, he recognizes a student as having a right "to question and demand reasons," and a teacher as having an obligation "to provide reasons whenever demanded" and "submit her reasons to the independent evaluation of the student."

Are there limits to how far the educational ideal of critical thinking or reason should be pursued? If respect for others requires that we deal with them through honest and reasoned persuasion, does that mean that it is never right to ignore a request for reasons or fail to acknowledge the force of a reason someone has put forward? Emily Robertson's 1999 Presidential Address to the Philosophy of Education Society, "The Value of Reason: Why Not a Sardine Can Opener?" (no. 50), offers a strong but qualified defense of rational persuasion as a social practice or stance toward others. The practice of reasoning together embodies a *moral ideal* and a conviction that generally speaking there is no alternative to relying on reason in pursuing truth, success in action, and living well. Robertson catalogs some alternatives to the stance of rational persuasion, in order to clarify both what is distinctive about it and what motivates certain criticisms of reason. What is really at issue in these criticisms, she suggests, is what kind of human relationships

are appropriate. She argues that, while the ideal of reasoning with others in good faith is generally appropriate, circumstances may sometimes justify the limited adoption of other stances. The personal and social benefits of solidarity and diplomacy may sometimes outweigh the benefits of establishing the truth, and the unfairness of ground rules or the uncooperativeness of others may sometimes justify a stance that is oppositional and not receptive to persuasion.

## Grading and Testing

The subject of grading "is terribly confused," writes Robert Paul Wolff, in "A Discourse on Grading" (reading no. 51), a chapter from his book *The Ideal of the University* (1969). "Even teachers, for whom grading is one of the principal activities of their professional life, frequently have very little idea why they give grades at all," he says. To promote a better understanding of grades and their relationship to teaching and education, Wolff distinguishes between *criticism*, *evaluation*, and *ranking*. *Criticism* analyzes a product or performance in the light of standards that students must use as points of reference in order to learn, and its contributions to learning place it "at the very heart of education." *Evaluation* issues judgments of absolute merit based on independent standards of excellence, whereas *ranking* yields a linear ordering based on comparative judgments of the performances of different students. Wolff argues that evaluation and ranking are external to education as such, and have rationales that are professional and economic. Grades convey criticism in only the most summary way, and seem most useful (if also troublesome) as instruments of evaluation and ranking.

The reading "Coercion and the Ethics of Grading and Testing" (no. 52) is a study in educational ethics focused on the matter of respecting the student's right to intellectual self-determination. When grades are used as intended, are they *coercive*? Are they *intellectually coercive*? The question seems significant when one considers the extent to which schools determine what students believe and think about, and it is answered through a purely student-centered moral framework that takes rights of intellectual self-determination seriously. That framework seems to have substantial implications for the *ways* we test and grade students, and the reading outlines those implications and concludes that efforts to develop new ways of testing and grading student performances are called for. The use of *process measures* of student achievement is defended as an acceptable middle way between the condemnation of all grading and testing and the acceptance of the *status quo* that has prevailed. *Process measures* would focus on processes of thought, the development of judgment, and the understanding of inquiry in its various forms.

Stephen P. Norris and his co-authors Jacqueline P. Leighton and Linda M. Phillips consider the enterprise of high stakes testing and the psychometric theory that underlies it, in the reading "What is at Stake in Knowing the Content and Capabilities of Children's Minds? A Case for Basing High Stakes Tests on Cognitive Models" (no. 53). The authors take it as given that high stakes tests should aim to assess the most meaningful kinds of learning, and they set about showing how far we have to go in being able to do that. They argue that psychometric theory continues to rely on a faulty *behaviorist* model, and that conventional methods of test development are deficient in failing to make use of information about how children actually think. They recommend basing tests on *cognitive* models that understand the quality of children's thinking in terms of *metacognition*, reasoning strategies, and principles of sound thinking. These aspects of children's thinking and the authors' methods of studying them are illustrated in some detail through examples drawn from tests of critical thinking, mathematics, and reading.

## Note

1. This provides a clue as to how Rousseau envisions a convergence between a natural education of a man "for himself" and a civic education of a citizen "for others." A natural education will preserve individual freedom, but yield sentiments of "natural religion" that direct the will toward the collective good. See the introduction to Part I.

## References

Augustine, St. 1995: *Against the Academicians* and *The Teacher*, trans. P. King (Indianapolis, IN: Hackett).

Ennis, R. 1962: "A Concept of Critical Thinking." *Harvard Educational Review* 32(1): 81–111.

Matthews, G. 1998: "The Socratic Augustine." *Metaphilosophy* 29(3): 196–208.

McPeck, J. 1981: *Critical Thinking and Education* (New York: St. Martin's Press).

# Teaching

## 35

# Real Teaching

## Philip W. Jackson

There used to be a game show on television some years back whose format was as simple and straightforward as it was entertaining. The show's panelists – four "TV personalities" as they are usually called – were introduced to successive trios of strangers, each made up of one person who worked at some unusual occupation, such as taming lions or cutting diamonds, plus two others of the same sex and supposedly the same name who claimed to be similarly employed but were actually imposters. The point of the game was to identify the honest member of each trio by asking all three of them questions about the line of work in which they claimed to be engaged. When the time limit for questions had been reached and each of the contestants had made a guess as to which of the three was telling the truth, the show's announcer would call upon the *real* Mister or Miss So-and-So to stand and be identified. Cries of surprise, followed by laughter and applause, crowned the departure of each trio of contestants.

That once popular show, called "To Tell the Truth," invariably comes to mind whenever my thoughts turn to the question of what teaching is like as an occupation and how it might be defined. It does so because the show's format reminds me

of an experience I had some time ago as a newly appointed principal of a nursery school. That experience is itself worth describing in some detail, for it introduces in a rather dramatic if lighthearted way the questions to be examined in this chapter.

I was a newcomer to both school administration and nursery schools at the time. Consequently, in order to familiarize myself with the institution and how its teachers behaved I spent as much time as I could during my first few weeks on the job poking about the school as a complete stranger might, watching what was going on and trying to get a feel for the place. The teachers, who wanted to get to know me as much as I did them, warmly welcomed me to their classrooms. Their doing so made the experience as enjoyable as it was informative.

As the days wore on I slowly became aware of certain things the teachers did that distinguished them from the kinds of teachers I had spent most time with in the past – those with much older pupils. For example, I noticed that when nursery school teachers spoke to individual children or listened to what they had to say they first descended to the child's height by bending at the knees until their faces were on a level with the child's own. At the

Previously published in *The Practice of Teaching* (New York: Teachers College Press, 1986), pp. 75–8, 79–83, 84, 86–97.

same time, I was bemused to note, when I myself spoke or listened to a child I tended to bend at the *waist* rather than the knees. As a result, I hovered above the tyke like some huge crane, causing him or her to gaze skyward and, if out of doors on a bright day, to shade the eyes while doing so.

I noticed also that when reading to pupils the nursery school teachers did something else both odd and amusing. They propped the books they were reading on their laps with the open pages facing the students. The reason for doing so was obviously to allow the children to see the book's illustrations. But what made such a natural thing so amusing to me was that it required the teachers to develop the knack of reading upside down!

These and other examples of what seemed to me to be characteristic behavior of nursery school teachers so intrigued me that I decided to share my discoveries with the teachers themselves. I thought it possible they might add to my store of examples. I also expected them to be mildly amused by my report on the outcome of my observations.

Broaching the topic over lunch one day, I rather casually announced that it seemed as though my observations around school were beginning to pay off. "I think I'm beginning to catch on to a few of the tricks of your trade," I began. "For example, I've noticed that when you teachers . . ." and then I described a few of the things I had seen, mimicking postures and gestures in a somewhat exaggerated way, just to add to the fun. I concluded by claiming that should the chance ever occur to pass myself off as a nursery school teacher, I now thought I knew enough to be easily mistaken for the real McCoy.

My mimicking of their behavior amused the teachers, as I had thought it would, and so did my boast at the end. But the latter, rather surprisingly, turned out to be more than simply amusing. It triggered a discussion that went on far past lunch, one that we returned to on several occasions in the ensuing months. The focus of that recurrent discussion was whether I or anyone else could indeed get away with impersonating a teacher without ever being found out and what it would mean, insofar as teaching is concerned, if that were to happen.

The teachers could easily imagine a person getting away with such a pretense for quite some time. They even conceded that I might succeed in doing it myself for a while. But the notion of someone pretending to be a nursery school teacher and *never* getting caught, was a condition they found puzzling.

For if the person were never found out, they reasoned, shouldn't we at some point stop thinking of him or her as an imposter, even though this knowledge remains his or her own secret? Indeed, should the 'teacher' not at some point stop thinking of himself or herself that way? In short, when does the successful imposter actually become the real McCoy, or does that never happen? If not, why not?

A closely related question that we also discussed was whether the imposter had only to *behave* like a nursery school teacher in order to carry off the deception or whether there was more to it than that. Some of the teachers thought it would be necessary for the imposter to *think* like a nursery school teacher in order to *behave* like one. But that introduced the question of what it meant to think like a teacher. How does a nursery school teacher think?

The teachers and I went round and round in our discussions of these and other questions about teaching, all stimulated by my casual and, as I thought at the time, humorous observation that it might be possible to get by as a nursery school teacher without any formal training whatsoever. From that starting point, we soon discovered, the paths of speculation fan out in many directions. Can one determine whether a teacher is genuine or a fake (or good rather than bad) simply by watching her or him? Can teaching be defined behaviorally? What does it mean to say that teaching in general or good teaching in particular can be defined in any way at all? Where might such a definition come from? Is it something discovered or decided upon? If the former, how is that accomplished? If the latter, who does the deciding? And so on.

As could be guessed, the teachers and I never did succeed in answering most of the questions we so enthusiastically and, I fear, naively wrestled with back then. Nor have I yet done so. But both individually and collectively we did develop some tentative notions about the directions in which a few of the answers might lie. For me at least, several of those tentative notions have since become convictions.

What are they? Insofar as they relate to the topic of this chapter, my convictions are three in number. The first says there is no such thing as a behavioral definition of teaching and there never can be. We can never simply watch a person in action and be sure that something called teaching is going on. The second, closely related to the first, says that our attempt to say when a person is or is not teaching is always an act of interpretation. We are forever "readers" of human action, seeking to determine which "reading" is correct from among those possible. The third conviction, one that follows on the heels of the first two, denies the possibility of our ever arriving upon an enduring definition of what it means to teach. In the remainder of this chapter each of those propositions will be treated in turn.

# I

To begin, let's return to my early days as a nursery school principal, wandering from class to class in order to learn what nursery school teaching was all about. Picture my going about that task. Do you imagine I was very puzzled about when a teacher was or was not teaching? I assure you I was not.

As I moved from one room to another I *saw* with my own eyes teachers teaching and I did not for a moment doubt my judgment. [ . . . ]

The notion that teaching is what teachers can be seen doing seems sensible enough as an observational guide. There are limits to such a principle, of course, but everyone seems to know what they are. For example, if the teacher stops to tie his shoes or take off his jacket, or if he steps out in the hall for a drink of water, most people would not think of describing such actions as instances of teaching behavior. Thus it is tacitly assumed by most observers that not *everything* a teacher does while on the job is classifiable as teaching, though *most* of it probably will be. Many of the actions to be excluded are easily agreed upon.

A somewhat more difficult distinction is called for by the teacher who is standing in front of the class with his or her arms folded, waiting for the noise to abate. Is she or he at that instant teaching or merely getting ready to teach? And what about the teacher who is monitoring seatwork or marking papers? Should those activities be counted as part of teaching as well?

Judgments about such matters seem to depend, in part, on why the teacher in question is being observed in the first place. A supervisor of student teachers, for example, might find it very important to comment on the way a trainee prepared the class for instruction. From his or her point of view, standing in front of the class with arms folded is very much part of a teacher's repertoire of attention-getting devices and therefore is definitely an aspect of teaching worthy of comment.

Contrast that situation with someone doing research on teaching via an observational device

focusing exclusively on teacher–pupil interaction. Under those circumstances, coding would begin when instruction was actually underway. Until then, from the researcher's point of view, teaching had not yet begun.

These examples point to a well-known truth, that some of a teacher's actions are easier to classify as instances of teaching than are others. When a teacher is explaining something to students or demonstrating a skill that is later to be imitated, who can doubt that at that instant teaching is underway? Similarly, when teachers are listening to students or watching what they do, there seems little or no ambiguity about whether or not they are actually teaching.

It is when the interactions between teachers and students do not obviously bear upon what is to be learned that the greatest uncertainty arises. But even these ambiguous instances are often resolvable once the observer's purposes are known. What aspects of a teacher's behavior are to be counted as instances of teaching is a question whose answer depends on prior considerations having to do with the circumstances under which the question is raised in the first place.

An additional distinction related to how to talk about teaching introduces an argument with an interesting history in education and in philosophy as well. It has to do with whether we should keep separate the idea of teaching as an accomplishment from that of teaching as an effort, an attempt to do something.[1]

One way of managing this dispute would be to limit the use of the term "teaching" to its sense as something that has been accomplished. This would require that we insist on evidence that learning has occurred before we can acknowledge that teaching has occurred. John Dewey, for one, seems to have something like this in mind when he tells his readers that,

> Teaching may be compared to selling commodities. No one can sell unless someone else buys. We should ridicule a merchant who said that he had sold a great many of goods although no one had bought any. But perhaps there are teachers who think that they have done a good day's teaching irrespective of what pupils have learned. There is the same exact equation between teaching and learning that there is between selling and buying.[2]

Were we to take Dewey seriously on this point, it would affect the way we discussed what we saw when we observed teachers in action. The discovery that the students we had observed had learned nothing from their teacher would force us to acknowledge that the teacher had not been teaching, no matter what she might have appeared to be doing when we observed her. She may have been *trying* to teach, we might readily admit, but she wasn't actually teaching.

Under certain circumstances it makes good sense to restrict the use of the term in this way. It does so when it comes to what we would like to say about the activity, especially when we speak of teaching in the past tense. To say that Jones taught Smith how to swim but Smith learned nothing whatsoever about the sport does sound a bit peculiar, if not downright contradictory. It makes us want to counter with, "Well then, Jones didn't *really* teach Smith how to swim."

But note that if we insist upon this necessary connection between teaching and learning we then find it impossible to say with certainty that a person is teaching until after the fact – until evidence that learning has occurred is in hand. Lacking such evidence, all we can say as we watch teachers in action is that they *look* as though they are teaching, or perhaps, "They are definitely trying to teach." To put the matter somewhat differently, by too strict an insistence on the teaching-learning con-nection we automatically rule out the possibility of unsuccessful teaching.

To qualify as an instance of teaching, if a teacher's actions *must* result in learning, then we are left with the question of what to call the same set of actions when such a result is not forthcoming. They can't be called instances of teaching that didn't work, for we have just ruled out that possibility. Treating them as "tries," rather than "successes," allows us to declare that the teacher has tried to teach, which may be quite enough to say in many circumstances. Indeed, it could be that in everyday affairs that's what most people mean when they use the term. When we say, "Look, there's a person teaching," what we mean is, "There's a person trying to teach." The "trying to" is understood. Its omission is simply a kind of verbal shorthand.

To short-circuit an argument that seems to get more and more picayune as it goes along, most people would probably be content to have the phrase "trying to" tacked on to their descriptions of teachers in action wherever the word "teaching" appears. The cost of such a grammatical change seems a small price to pay for avoiding what could be an interminable debate. But note that by

inserting such a qualifier in our speech we do not manage to sidestep the problem entirely. Indeed, we simply carry it with us. We may no longer face the question of how we know when a person is teaching, but we now must ask how we know when a person is *trying* to teach.

## II

We can answer that question with confidence, it would seem, in only one of two ways. Either we must have some prior knowledge of what trying to teach looks like, or we must trust the testimony of the person who says that is what he or she is doing. Let's look at the first possibility a little more carefully.

How did I know that the teachers I witnessed in the nursery school were trying to teach? Perhaps I possessed at the time some idea of what "trying to teach" looks like in general. The rest is simply a matter of matching the teachers observed with that prior conception. In other words, because those teachers were behaving in ways I recognized as being "teacherly," I confidently concluded that they were trying to teach. Is that the way my sense of recognition worked?

Something like that process must surely have been in operation, no doubt, but is it sufficient to explain my feeling of confidence? I think not. To understand why, consider the following situation.

A visitor to a school peeks through the window of a classroom door and sees a woman with chalk in hand standing before a group of approximately twenty-five young people seated at desks. The woman is gesturing toward a mathematical formula written on the blackboard. The visitor naturally concludes that he is witnessing a class in session; he is corrected by the principal, who happens by with the news that what is going on in that room is not a class at all but rather a rehearsal of a scene from the play *The Prime of Miss Jean Brodie*, which the local drama society is putting on in a few days.

What does such an unlikely turn of events tell us about the problem of identifying an instance of someone trying to teach? Obviously, the observer who thinks he knows an act of teaching when he sees it can be fooled. People can pretend to teach. The whole scene can be make-believe. That rarely happens, of course, but it *could* happen and that's the important point. In other words, the identification of teaching can never be made on visual evidence alone. Something else is required, something having to do with the genuineness of the total situation.

Recall that when the hypothetical questioner asked why I was so confident in my judgment, I began by saying that I knew this was a school and these were classrooms and those people teachers and those students. I was confident, in other words, that I was not walking around a movie set, witnessing the filming of *Up the Down Staircase* or something like that.

There was even a touch of impatience in my answer, for my imaginary interrogator seemed to question the obvious. But my answer showed that my sense of confidence very much depended on a host of half-buried assumptions, beginning with the few I have mentioned and including many others as well.

Not only did I know what schools and classrooms and teachers were like, being able to recognize them on sight, and trusting my conviction that I was witnessing the real McCoy, but I also knew a reasonable amount about the ends those objects were designed to serve (or prepared to fulfill, as we would say of teachers themselves). I further knew something about their historical development, their political and social significance, and so on. In other words, the events I was witnessing were embedded within a cultural and historical context of which I was only partially conscious at the time, but one that infused them with meaning, all the same. That gave me confidence that I was witnessing an instance of teaching and not something else. Without that background of tacit understanding my feeling of confidence could never have arisen.

[ . . . ]

The point to be noted is that teaching, like most other human actions, is not so much "seen" as it is "read." In other words, though we may feel that what we are witnessing in classrooms is as plain as the nose on our face (as I did during my wanderings about the nursery school), we feel that way thanks to the largely unconscious operation of a vast apparatus of understanding that we seldom bother to bring to the surface of awareness for close scrutiny.[3]

[ . . . ] is there anything like a pedagogical outlook on things, a "teacherly" way of viewing the world?[4]

When we recognize the great variety of teachers the world over, it is hard to imagine that such a diverse group might be bound together by any single perspective on their work, an outlook that would characterize them all. At the same time, by staying at a rather low level of generalization and by focusing on perception alone, we can observe distinctions between the ways "experts" and "laymen" look at things that would seem to hold true for the difference between teachers and nonteachers as well.

For example, other things being equal, we might expect the expert's view to be more differentiated than that of the layman. We would expect him or her to have a "finer" than ordinary perception of the object of his expertise, to see it in greater detail. We would also expect such a person to have a "quicker" vision as well, to be able to take in a lot of information at a glance, homing in quickly on features worthy of special attention. We would expect the expert to have an eye for irregularities and trouble spots. We would also expect him to see opportunities missed by others. He or she would be expected to be more "future-oriented," to see possibilities where others see none.

We would also expect the expert to see things in perspective, to know, for example, whether to treat something with alarm or more routinely. In other words, we would not expect the expert to get "rattled" by the unexpected quite as easily as might the layman. In sum, we normally expect the expert to be more thoughtful than the nonexpert about things, not in the sense of thinking *more*, but rather in the sense of thinking *differently*. Moreover, this thoughtfulness can be reflected in a variety of ways.

As applied to teachers and teaching, this set of expectations yields an image of the seasoned teacher that distinguishes him or her, at least in principle, from laymen in general and possibly even from novice teachers. Expert teachers "see more" than do nonexperts. They are alive to the latent pedagogical possibilities in the events they witness. Within a classroom setting, they anticipate what is going to happen. They can spot an inattentive student a mile off. They can detect signs of incipient difficulty. Their senses are fully tuned to what is going on around them. They are not easily rattled. As younger students sometimes swear is true, they behave as though they had eyes in the back of their heads.

Is this image of expert teaching accurate? Are all seasoned teachers really like that? Are any of them? In short, are we talking about what is or what ought to be?

The quick sketch given here admittedly comes closer to the "ought" than the "is" of teachers and teaching. At the same time, it is not entirely a fiction.

It reminds me sufficiently of teachers I have known that I will defend it as a model realizable in the here and now.

But even more important than whether many or most teachers come to resemble our hypothetical expert, how does such a perspective on teaching address the array of questions treated in this chapter? Of special interest is what it seems to say about the relationship between what a teacher *does* and what he or she *thinks*.

I now return for a final time to the rather light-hearted discussions that took place in the nursery school, and readily admit, though it should be abundantly obvious, that I knew all along a person could not become a nursery school teacher simply by learning how to hold a book while reading a story to children or by bending this way or that while talking or listening to a small child. The teachers knew that as well, of course, which explains their willingness to go along with the fun. They knew, and I knew, that to be a real nursery school teacher one had to see and to react in a certain spirit or manner to a special portion of the world – rooms full of three- and four-year-olds. Specific skills, such as knowing how to make playdough or how to bandage a cut knee, had an important place in that world, as we might expect them to, but to mistake such skills for the heart of the matter, as my lunchtime boast seemed to do, was – well, just laughable, that's all.

Is the situation drastically different with other types of teaching? My own experience in colleges and universities leads me to say no. There too the difference between the novice (who for rhetorical purposes has been likened to an imposter) and his or her more experienced colleagues turns out to be less a matter of skill than one of feeling and acting at home within a particular instructional milieu.

This sense of "being at home" in the classroom is hard to specify, I admit, but as a psychological state it is quite genuine all the same. One of the nursery school teachers nearly referred to it directly when she said, "Well, even if the imposter never gives himself away, *he* knows he doesn't belong there."

## III

The final question to be raised in this chapter is the one toward which my discussion with the nursery school teachers pointed but never reached: Is there some ultimate, non-modifiable definition of teaching (*true* teaching, let's call it) that we can discover through empirical and/or logical maneuvering?

We need first to acknowledge that the question is academic, in the sense that teachers themselves seem not to worry about it very much. Except when prodded by one of their instructors while in training or by a school administrator with nothing better to do, most teachers I have known seldom wonder aloud about the *true* meaning of teaching. Like other kinds of practitioners the world over, they usually are too busy doing what they have to do to worry about formal definitions of their practice.

Yet here are groups of people – educational philosophers among them – who do have time for such matters and who look upon it as part of their professional responsibility to answer the definitional question, whether practicing teachers are interested or not. Moreover, the answers they offer are more than academic exercises. These answers appear in textbooks and other "official" documents where they may potentially influence how teachers and others think about teaching.

This is hardly the place to examine all such efforts in detail. However, I would like to touch upon three different approaches to the task of determining once and for all what teaching is or should be. In my judgment, each of the three is seriously flawed, yet each builds from a foundational premise that in certain respects is quite appealing. Each strikes me as contributing to an understanding of why the search for a final, logically airtight definition of teaching is not only a futile undertaking but may even be harmful if allowed to legislate what teachers themselves must believe about their work.

I will call these three approaches to the definition of teaching the, *generic*, the *epistemic*, and the *consensual*. The meaning of those terms will become clear in the exposition to follow.

What I call a *generic* approach to the definition of teaching works like this: It begins by insisting that there be an important difference between a definition of teaching, on the one hand, and the performance of teaching on the other. This distinction is important, for it divides the labor of speaking authoritatively about teaching between two groups of professionals – educational philosophers and educational researchers. From this point of view it is the job of the philosophers to propose a definition of teaching that is sufficiently general to cover whatever future research might discover about the right *way* to teach. The job of researchers, in turn, is to discover answers to questions about how teaching should proceed. The result of the former effort will be singular and universal; that of the latter, plural and particular. Here is the way one well-known educational philosopher, B. O. Smith, poses the problem and then goes on to solve it.

> "The way in which teaching is or can be performed," Smith tells us, is mistaken for teaching itself. In its generic sense, teaching is a system of actions intended to induce learning. So defined, teaching is everywhere the same, irrespective of the cultural context in which it occurs. But these actions may be performed differently from culture to culture or from one individual to another within the same culture, depending on the state of knowledge about teaching and the teacher's pedagogical knowledge and skill. Didactics, or the science and art of teaching, are not the same as the actions which they treat. A definition of teaching as such, which packs a set of biases about how these actions are to be conducted, confuses teaching with its science and its art."[5]

This approach has a degree of common sense about it that must be acknowledged at the start. Teaching may be variably performed, that much is certainly true. Thus it makes good sense to seek a definition of teaching that is flexible but not so broad that it embraces everything under the rubric of "teaching." The question is whether Smith's definition of teaching as a system of actions intended to induce learning fits the bill. I fear it does not.

Consider, for instance, the giving of medicine to a hyperactive child in order to calm him or her down so that she or he might benefit from instruction. This certainly must be acknowledged as a system of actions intended to induce learning, must it not? But is it an instance of teaching? I suspect few would be willing to consider it so.

And what of the work of school administrators? Much of what they do would certainly conform to Smith's generic definition of teaching. But, again, who would want to call most principals or superintendents teachers? I for one would not, and once again, I suspect most people would agree.

So Smith's generic definition of teaching, if I understand it correctly, is far too broad to be of much use. All of teaching fits within it, sure enough, but so do many other activities that we do not want to confuse with teaching.

And even if the definition could be tightened to exclude those activities we do not want,[6] it is still hard to imagine that such a definition might be useful in practice. Suppose we could define teaching generically – that is, say nothing about how teaching should be done but differentiate between teaching and all other activities. What would we do with such a definition once we had it? What questions of consequence would it help to answer? That I can think of none may reflect nothing more than my lack of imagination, but it is enough to leave me dubious about the promise of a *generic* approach to the definition of teaching.

An *epistemic*, as contrasted with a *generic*, definition of teaching links the activity to the concept of knowledge propounded by most modern epistemologists. In this view, knowledge is understood to be "evidentially supported belief." If we add to that understanding the corollary that teaching is primarily concerned with the transmission of such knowledge, we can begin to see that it *logically entails* certain kinds of actions and not others.

For example, it obliges teachers to provide grounds or reasons for the beliefs they seek to inculcate in their students. It requires them to be respectful of the truth and to be prepared at all times to reevaluate their own beliefs in the light of new evidence and in the face of fresh argument. It also demands that they seek to develop in each student his or her own capacity to test the worthiness of everything taught.

These obligations have nothing to do with personal choice or preference. Like a geometer's proof, they flow naturally from the starting premises of the argument, which say that teaching has to do with the spread of knowledge as contemporaneously defined and with the conditions conducive to that end.

From those same premises there follows a list of "don'ts" as well as "dos." Teachers committed to viewing knowledge as "evidentially supported belief" are also obliged not to intimidate, or threaten, or lie, or propagandize. They are sworn to avoid at all costs anything known to be inimical to the conduct of human inquiry and to the motivational spirit which animates it. Should they violate either set of these obligations, the positive or the negative, they step beyond the parameters of teaching as circumscribed by an epistemic definition.

This approach to a definition of teaching is attractive in several ways. To begin with, it is more philosophically sophisticated than is the generic approach. It does not so readily embrace features that teaching shares with many other activities. Instead, it tries to identify what is unique to teaching, what distinguishes it from all or almost all other activities. Also, it speaks out on behalf of a conception of teaching that has many supporters, both within the profession and outside of it. The teacher as a purveyor of knowledge, in the sense explicated, is an ancient and honored image of what teachers and teaching are all about.

At the same time, the epistemic view is not without difficulties of its own. For one thing, it does not address educational goals that are only indirectly associated with the transmission of knowledge. It may well be that the development of attitudes, interests, values, and the like can be reduced to knowledge of one sort or another, but I doubt that many teachers regard those goals in that way.

Finally, the epistemic approach to a definition of teaching leaves us in an awkward position with respect to teachers, past and present, who did and do indeed indoctrinate, intimidate, propagandize, and goodness knows what else, thinking it quite proper to do so.[7] What shall we say of them? Here is an answer given by Thomas Green, another educational philosopher, who is at the same time a strong advocate of an epistemic approach to the definition of teaching.

> Lying, propagandizing, slander and threat of physical violence are not teaching activities, although they may be ways of influencing persons' beliefs or shaping their behavior. We know *in fact* that these activities are excluded from the concept of teaching with as much certainty as we know that training and instruction are included.   [Emphasis added][8]

> It is a matter of no consequence that there have been societies which have extended the concept of teaching . . . [to include such practices] . . . That propaganda, lies, threats, and intimidation have been used as methods of education is not doubted. But the conclusion warranted by this fact is not that teaching includes such practices, but that education may. Propaganda, lies, threats are more or less effective means of influencing and shaping beliefs and patterns of behavior. It follows that teaching is not the only method of education. It does not follow that the use of propaganda, lies and threats are methods of teaching.[9]

We can treat undesirable actions on the part of teachers as instances of nonteaching, but one wonders what we gain by such a move. What it does, so far as I can tell, is sweep an interesting question under the rug, that question being: Why might teachers, past and present, have put such tactics to use in the first place? To imply that they did so out of ignorance, that they lacked knowledge of the true

meaning of teaching, seems a bit condescending, to say the least. It also begs the question of how or whether we can have a "true" definition of the term.

The third approach (I call it *consensual*) to the question of how to define teaching is close in spirit to the second, but more accommodating in tone and less rigidly tied to epistemological claims. It allows for many ways of teaching, but it seeks to distinguish between those that are *standard* and those that are *nonstandard*. Israel Scheffler, yet another educational philosopher, is an articulate spokesman for this point of view. "Teaching may, to be sure, proceed by various methods," Scheffler begins,

> but some ways of getting people to do things are excluded from the *standard range* of the term 'teaching.' To teach, *in the standard sense*, is at some points at least to subject oneself to the understanding and independent judgment of the pupil, to his demand for reasons, to his sense of what constitutes an adequate explanation. To teach someone that such and such is the case is not merely to try to get him to believe it: deception for example, is not a method or mode of teaching . . . To teach is thus, *in the standard use of the term*, to acknowledge the 'reason' of the pupil, i.e. his demand for and judgment of reasons, even though such demands are not uniformly appropriate at every phase of the teaching interval.   [Emphasis added][10]

In what kind of society would Scheffler's version of teaching flourish? "It would be a place," he tells us,

> where the culture itself institutionalizes reasoned procedures in its basic spheres, where it welcomes the exercise of criticism and judgment, where, that is to say, it is a democratic culture in the strongest sense. To support the widest diffusion of teaching as a model of cultural renewal is, in effect, to support something peculiarly consonant with the democratization of culture and something that poses a threat to cultures whose basic social norms are institutionally protected from criticism.[11]

So in the final analysis it is only in a democratic society, or one in the process of becoming so, that teaching in Scheffler's sense of the term can be carried on. His standard use of the term is consensual in the dictionary sense of "existing or made by mutual consent without the intervention of any act of writing." But the consenting parties, in Scheffler's view, must be like-minded in broad political terms.

The notion that teaching in its "truest" sense can be carried on only in a democratic society may be comforting to those of us who believe we live in such a society. But how fair is it to restrict by definition the idea of teaching to a particular political context? Is there not something a trifle chauvinistic about such a move?

Of course we should feel free to criticize the way teaching is carried out in societies other than our own, just as we should here at home. But I fail to see how it helps to approach this job of criticism armed with a definition that to start with rules out the possibility of our calling what goes on in non-democratic countries "teaching." Scheffler dodges this question, at least in part, by his willingness to speak of *non-standard* teaching. Yet, reading his words carefully, I must conclude that what he means by the *non-standard* form of the activity is almost not teaching at all.[12]

There is much to be said for both the epistemic and the consensual approaches to the definition of teaching, as this brief exposition sought to make clear. Each rests on a premise that many of today's teachers are almost certain to find attractive. It makes good sense to think that teaching is centrally concerned with the transmission of knowledge, as the epistemic approach insists we do. It is also appealing to think that teaching is a kind of emancipatory activity, either sustaining a democratic society or paving the way for its emergence, as the consensual approach requires.

But in the final analysis both views turn out to be more limiting than edifying. We must ask, why should teaching be perceived solely in terms of its contribution to the transmission of knowledge? And why must it be confined to the kind of teaching that typifies democratic societies (if any kind actually does)? But if we reject such limitations are we not forced back to a generic definition of the kind Smith proposed, one so general as to be useless? Not necessarily.

There is, I would suggest, a fourth approach to the question of how teaching is defined, an approach that I call *evolutionary*. The term comes from Stephen Toulmin, who describe such a view in the following way.

> A properly evolutionary way of dealing with experience obliges us to recognize that no event or process has any single unambiguous description: we describe any event in different terms, and view it as an element in a different network of relations, depending on the standpoint from which – and the purposes for which – we are considering it.[13]

What would be the consequences of looking upon teaching in this way? We begin by conceding that there is no unequivocal definition of teaching that holds for all time and all places. What we accept as a satisfactory view of the process today within our society may not be the definition agreed upon in another time or another culture. But that does not mean that everyone holding different views, whether in the past or the present, can now be called wrong. What such an evolutionary view commits us to is neither the truth nor the falsity of any single definition; rather, it is an attempt to locate teaching within what Toulmin calls "a network of relations." Its place within that network is its ultimate source of meaning and significance.

Lest this sound far too abstract to be of practical help, let us move closer to the everyday world of teaching to see what the possible consequences of such a view might be. First of all, it would put to rest all ontological questions of the kind I discussed with teachers during my early days as a nursery school principal – questions of who is real and who is fake, whether one is really teaching as opposed to doing something else that might resemble teaching but is not the genuine article, and so forth.

This does not mean that people could no longer lie about their teaching abilities or falsify their credentials to make people believe they have had training when they have not. In short, it does not eliminate the possibility of frauds and fakes within the ranks of teachers. It does help us see that what is fraudulent in such situations is not teaching *per se* but the claim to competence.

To put the argument in a nutshell, there is no such thing as "genuine" teaching. There is only an activity that people call teaching, which can be viewed from a variety of critical perspectives. Sometimes the criticism that teaching can undergo leads us to conclude that the person performing the activity, or claiming to be able to perform it, has deceived us in some way. Such deceptions are rare, we would hope, but they have been known to happen.

Of far more practical importance than anything involving "genuine" teaching are questions of "good" and "poor" teaching. What does an "evolutionary" view of the process enable us to say about that? It leads to the understanding that we can make few if any judgments about the quality of teaching without reference to the context in which the action takes place; "context" is understood to cover far more than the physical setting of the action. The phrase "cultural context" comes closer to the meaning being sought here. It includes the awarenesses, presuppositions, expectations, and everything else that impinges upon the action or that contributes to its interpretation by the actors themselves and by outsiders as well.

Consider this example. Teachers of approximately a hundred years ago routinely applied hickory sticks to the backsides of recalcitrant or misbehaving students, or so we are told. What shall we, today, make of that fact? Shall we think of our colleagues of years ago as having been poor teachers for behaving as they did?

I find that too hasty and harsh a judgment. Moreover, I see nothing to be gained by it. To learn something from the past it seems to me far more fruitful to ask why that particular practice (and others like it) have gradually died out. Such a question is also much more in keeping with what I am calling an "evolutionary" point of view. An understanding of the demise of the hickory stick yields a correlative understanding of why many related practices have disappeared as well.

But what about contemporary practice? Does an evolutionary and contextual outlook leave us powerless to criticize what goes on today? Does it get stalled at the level of "mere understanding," leaving the tough job of being critical and of taking a stand on issues to someone else?

Not at all. There is no incompatibility between understanding an activity and either approving or disapproving it. Here an example might help. Suppose we learn of a teacher who seeks to win a student over to his or her own point of view through deception of one kind or another. Does not such a practice surpass understanding and call for immediate censure? Scheffler, for one, would say so, for he explicitly tells us that "deception . . . is not a method or mode of teaching." But what if we learn that the teacher in question is none other than Jean-Jacques Rousseau and the student his famous fictional creation, Emile?[14]

In such an instance would we not be better advised to try to understand what Rousseau was up to and why he did what he did *before* we conclude that censure is in order? What applies to fiction holds in real life as well. Confronted with any instance of teaching we might either praise or blame, we must always ask: What are the circumstances of the case? Why were these actions undertaken?[15]

Our answers to such questions no more prevent us from censuring any particular teacher (or a whole nation full of them, if need be) than does an investigation of an alleged crime prevent us from punishing the criminal. Indeed, the process of deliberating on such matters resembles that of case law more closely than it does that of establishing proof of a theorem in geometry or mathematics. [ . . . ]

Who are real teachers and what is real teaching? There are no such things, says the person who has adopted an evolutionary point of view. There are interpretations of events, including those in which teachers are the central actors. There are arguments that can be made on behalf of this or that teaching practice. Some arguments are better than others. Doubtless there are some practices that most of us teaching today would defend. Part of our professional responsibility is to get on with that defense. If we are lucky, as I was during my fledgling days as a nursery school principal, the task of deciding who is and who is not a teacher, though serious enough in the long run will have its lighter moments as well.

## Notes

1. The distinction between words that describe our trying to do something and words covering our success in having done it was brought to the fore within philosophical circles by Gilbert Ryle in his influential book *The Concept of Mind* (New York: Barnes and Noble, 1949). In that work Ryle distinguished between what he called "task verbs" and "achievement verbs." The former refer to things one is trying to do, the latter to things one has done. For example, "kicking" is a task verb, "scoring" an achievement verb. A similar distinction holds between treating and healing, hunting and finding, listening and hearing, and so forth. Teaching, as luck would have it, has come to be used in both senses, as something tried and as something accomplished, hence the confusion that plagues our understanding when it is not clear which of these senses applies.

2. John Dewey, *How We Think* (Lexington, MA: D. C. Heath, 1933), pp. 34–5.

3. A process similar to the one described here is treated in some detail by Michael Polanyi in his book *Personal Knowledge* (Chicago, IL: University of Chicago Press, 1958). Polanyi referred to these unarticulated forms of knowing as "tacit knowledge."

4. This question is treated in an intriguing manner in J. M. Stephens, *The Process of Schooling: A Psychological Examination* (New York: Holt, Rinehart & Winston, 1967). Stephens hypothesizes that people with certain proclivities and impulses, such as the proclivity to detect errors and the impulse to correct them, are naturally drawn to teaching.

5. B. Othanel Smith, "A concept of teaching," in B. Othanel Smith and Robert H. Ennis (eds.), *Language and Concepts in Education* (Chicago, IL: Rand McNally, 1961), pp. 87–8.

6. One way to do so would be to restrict the meaning of the verb "induce" to that of "moving by persuasion or influence." But even this narrowing of normal usage seems to leave the definitional door too far ajar.

7. For a powerful statement on behalf of teachers as indoctrinators and propagandizers, see George C. Counts, *Dare the Schools Build a New Social Order?* (New York: John Day, 1932).

8. Thomas F. Green, "A typology of the teaching concept," in C. J. B. Macmillan and T. W. Nelson (eds.), *Concepts of Teaching: Philosophical Essays* (Chicago, IL: Rand McNally, 1968), pp. 36–7 (italics added).

9. Ibid., p. 37.

10. Israel Scheffler, *The Language of Teaching* (Springfield, IL: Charles C. Thomas, 1960), pp. 57–8 (italics added).

11. Ibid., p. 59.

12. There is a real question whether it is possible to define teaching ontologically – in a way that speaks of its true meaning or essence – without also getting entangled with a definition that is axiological – one that involves the meaning of "good" teaching. For a discussion of this issue see W. A. Hart, "Is teaching what the philosophers understand by it?" *British Journal of Educational Studies* 24: 2 (June 1976), pp. 155–70.

13. Stephen Toulmin, "The charm of the scout," *New York Review of Books*, April 3, 1980, p. 38.

14. *Emile* is full of instances in which the teacher seeks to deceive his pupil in some way, to achieve what he alleges to be a pedagogical end.

15. For an interesting discussion of how the case study point of view has moved from medicine to ethical theory and has rejuvenated the latter, see Stephen Toulmin, "How medicine saved the life of ethics," *Perspectives in Biology and Medicine* 25: 4 (Summer 1982), pp. 736–50.

# 36

# The Teacher's Grasp of Subject-Matter

## Israel Scheffler

I have above referred to general conceptions and selective principles required in teaching, and this is perhaps the central point in seeing the potential contribution of philosophies-of to teacher training. To appreciate the point, we may first examine the particular example of philosophy of science, and notice its complex relations with scientific practice. The time is now long past in which philosophers could pretend to a vantage point of superior certitude to that offered by the sciences themselves. They no longer construe themselves as legislating, from such a vantage point, to the scientific practitioner or as taking sides in scientific controversies, at least in their professional capacity. Their philosophical work, in so far as it is addressed to science, takes its initial departure from scientific practice itself, striving to describe and codify it, and to understand and criticize it from a general epistemological standpoint that is, however, shared by scientists as well. Philosophy of science thus springs from scientific practice, but its descriptive and explanatory effort, like all second-order reflection on practice, has the potentiality of closing the circle, of feeding back into practice and altering it. That it springs from practice does not prevent it from exercising a critical and reformative function; that it exercises such a function does not, on the other hand, mean that it is an indispensable starting point for practice. One can, and regularly does, acquire competence within a field of scientific inquiry without preliminary grounding in philosophy of science. Even the strongest proponents of the value of the latter field of study would not, I believe, wish to argue that every scientist requires prior sophistication in this field in order to do his own job ideally well. It is enough that the field itself exists and is cultivated in such a way that communication with practice is possible.

Contrast this situation now with that of the teaching of science. The teacher of science is, of course, also a practitioner, but his practice is of a critically different sort from that of the scientist himself. He needs to have a conception of the field of science as a whole, of its aims, methods, and standards; he needs to have principles for selecting materials and experiences suitable for inducting novices into the field, and he needs to be able to communicate both with novices and with scientific sophisticates.

Editor's title. Originally published as "Philosophies-of and the Curriculum," in James F. Doyle (ed.), *Educational Judgments: Papers in Philosophy of Education* (London: Routledge & Kegan Paul, 1973), pp. 212–14, 214–18. © Israel Scheffler. Reprinted with kind permission of the author.

Whereas the particular scientific investigator need have no overall conception of science but requires only sophistication in his special subject-matter, the science teacher's subject-matter embraces scientific thought itself; his professional purpose, that is to say, can be articulated only in terms of some inclusive conception of scientific activity which it is his object to foster. Whereas the scientific researcher need not at all concern himself with the process of training others for research, the science teacher needs to reflect on the proper selection and organization of scientific materials for educational purposes, and so to presuppose a general perspective on those materials. Whereas, finally, the scientific worker requires only sophistication in the special jargon of his intellectual colleagues, the teacher requires something more – the ability to step out of the inner circle of specialists and to make their jargon intelligible to novices aspiring to sophistication. The teacher requires, in other words, a general conceptual grasp of science and a capacity to formulate and explain its workings to the outsider. But the scope of this requirement is, I suggest, virtually indistinguishable from that of the philosophy of science. No matter what additional resources the teacher may draw on, he needs at least to assume the standpoint of philosophy in performing his work.

The philosophy of science is thus related to two forms of practice, that of scientific investigation and that of science teaching. But these forms of practice are themselves diverse in level. If philosophy of science is a second-order reflective approach to scientific inquiry, science teaching itself incorporates such a second-order reflective approach as well. The science teacher needs to do other things than reflect on science, to be sure, but whatever he does is likely to be qualified by his second-order reflections on the field of science. Unlike the researcher, he cannot isolate himself within the protective walls of some scientific speciality; he functions willy-nilly as a philosopher in critical aspects of his role. And his training is, correspondingly, likely to profit from the special contributions that philosophy of science offers.

Analogous considerations apply, I believe, to the other teaching subjects as well; for example, to mathematics, to history, to art, to literature, and so forth. [ . . . ]

It is perhaps worthwhile at this point to attempt a more specific characterization of the contributions that philosophies-of might be expected to make. I have already suggested that the educator, like the philosopher, seeks a general account of those fields represented by teaching subjects, that he requires some reflective grasp of the 'forms of thought' they might be said to embody. To speak of 'forms of thought' is of course a simplification, for what is in question relates not only to inference but also to categorization, perception, evaluation, decision, attitude, and expectation, as crystallized in historical traditions of a variety of sorts. The simplification nevertheless serves to illuminate a critical point, for forms may be embodied as well as articulated. And the successive embodiment of forms of thought, which constitutes their perpetuation, does not itself require an articulate grasp of their general features. To acquire the traditional mental habits of the scientist, that is to say, requires only that one learn how to deal scientifically with some range of problems, and to treat critically of the materials bearing upon them. The philosopher, on the other hand, takes these very mental habits as his object, rather than the scientific problems to which they are, or may be, applied. His task, in short, is to articulate and analyze the forms themselves, and to try to understand their point. He wants to achieve such comprehensive analytical understanding not for some ulterior practical motive, but for its own sake, although he does not, of course, deny that understanding may affect practice.

The educator, by contrast with the philosopher, is concerned with the deliberate processes through which forms of thought may be handed on; he strives not only to understand these processes but to institute or facilitate them, so that the mental habits in question may in fact be properly acquired. Although an articulate grasp of these habits is *not* required for their acquisition, it *is* involved in the task of understanding and facilitating such acquisition. To make his own objectives intelligible, the educator needs to be able to analyze and describe those habits which it is his purpose to hand on to the next generation. An articulate grasp of such habits does not, in general, itself figure as part of the content he transmits to students; it does not therefore follow that it is of no use to the educator. A parent's sophisticated understanding of sexuality is of the utmost usefulness in helping him to discuss the issue with his children, though he would generally be ill-advised simply to recount such understanding to them.

If the philosophy-of a given subject is, thus, directed toward the analysis and understanding of the form of thought embodied by the subject, it is of potential use to the educator in clarifying his own objectives. The educator is not, to be sure, necessarily concerned with such understanding for its own sake – he needs it in order to facilitate the acquisition of the mental habits in question. Certainly, for this larger practical goal, he needs more than simply a clarity of objectives. Equally, however, no amount of educational experimentation or psychological information can substitute for such clarity of objectives.

In so far as the analytical understanding of a form of thought is the task of the philosophy-of that form, it has, then, a contribution to make to education. But such contribution does not exhaust its role. Understanding merges with criticism and evaluation, with issues of justification and appraisal. The philosophy of science, for example, is traditionally concerned not only to define inductive methods, but to evaluate their epistemological warrant, not only to describe forms of probabilistic inference, but to inquire into their justification. Analogously, questions of aesthetic value, of mathematical certainty, of the reliability of historical reasoning, of the function of literature, all relate closely to the question of defining correlated forms and fall within the philosophies-of those forms.

For the educator, surely, such questions are inescapable. He cannot define his role simply as it is given by received traditions; he must be prepared to justify his perpetuation or alteration of them as a consequence of his efforts. This means that the process of clarifying his objectives has a critical and normative aspect to it. He needs, of course, to strive for a clear grasp of the form of thought embodied in the tradition to which he is heir. But in taking on the responsibility of educational transmission, he assumes the obligation of evaluating whatever it is in that tradition he elects to perpetuate. At the risk of oversimplification, we may say that he requires not only a descriptive but a critical clarification of the forms of thought represented by his subject. It goes without saying that philosophies-of do not provide the educator with firmly established views of justification; on the contrary, they present him rather with an array of controversial positions. But this array, although it does not fix his direction, liberates him from the dogmatisms of ignorance, gives him a realistic apprehension of alternatives, and outlines relevant considerations that have been elaborated in the history of the problem.

The analytical understanding and critical appraisal of the form of thought which the educator takes as his objective provide him with some help in curriculum formation. With a general notion of the form in question, he has some idea of exemplifications in concrete materials to be employed in teaching. To complete his task, he certainly needs to call upon elements outside philosophy; he needs independent acquaintance with materials, and information or hypotheses as to the educational effectiveness of various selections and sequences. But the latter alone are also, in themselves, insufficient. For he is concerned to hand on materials, not just as materials, but as embodiments or exemplifications of form, that is to say, of method, style, aim, approach, and standards. Having a general view of the latter, and an independent knowledge of received materials, he can strive to select, shape, and order exemplifications so as to satisfy the further demands of educational efficiency and comprehensiveness.

In the very process of shaping, philosophies-of make a further contribution that may be illustrated by the philosophy of science. For it is clearly a mistake to suppose that the latter field is limited to general accounts of scientific method, or of inductive reasoning, etc. On the contrary, it embraces also the analytical description of historical cases or systematic branches of scientific endeavor in such a way as to bring out their methodological or inferential characteristics. Such analytical description typically proceeds in two phases: first, a refined articulation of the content of the historical inquiry or branch of science in question, and second, a systematic account of the elements of the articulation and their relations, designed primarily to exhibit their methodological or epistemological linkages. Philosophy of science is thus capable of aiding the educator not only in formulating a general conception of scientific method, but also in processing scientific materials so as to display them as embodiments of that method.

Philosophers have traditionally undertaken a further task of significance to education: the tracing of connections between specialized exemplifications of forms of thought and commonsense conceptions. They have, that is to say, been concerned to interpret, translate, or explicate the content of such exemplifications in terms that are intelligible to the non-specialist. To make science generally understandable, they have, for example, tried not only to specify the forms of reasoning implicit in scientific argumentation, but also to translate or reduce particular scientific concepts and theories to those familiar or at least accessible to common sense.

Assuming the common-sense or outsider's point of view as a basis, they have attempted to explain the specialized or insider's conceptions in terms of it. Although their construals of common sense have varied radically, the function fulfilled by their efforts is nevertheless, I believe, of great significance from an educational point of view. For the educator is constantly in the position, not only of representing and advancing specialized exemplifications of thought, but also of explaining and interpreting such exemplifications to the outsider, that is, the novice. In this translational or explanatory role, he has in the philosopher an experienced ally.

To summarize, I have outlined four main efforts through which philosophies-of might contribute to education: (1) the analytical description of forms of thought represented by teaching subjects, (2) the evaluation and criticism of such forms of thought, (3) the analysis of specific materials so as to systematize and exhibit them as exemplifications

of forms of thought, and (4) the interpretation of particular exemplifications in terms accessible to the novice.

My suggestion has been that philosophies-of constitute a desirable additional input in teacher preparation, beyond subject-matter competence, practice in teaching, and educational methodology. Nor do I wish to suggest, by any means, that the matter concerns simply the organization of teacher training. On the contrary, if the contributions of philosophies-of for teacher training are to be made practically available, thought needs to be given to the general process of relating such philosophies to education, and I believe that this effort may provide an important focus for educational philosophy. A rich body of materials relative to each teaching subject lies ready for such effort, structured in such a way as to make it naturally amenable to educational interests, and inviting philosophical analysis pointed toward teaching practice.

# 37

## Understanding Students

## David T. Hansen

[ ... ]

Thinking about what it means to understand students can be valuable to teachers. It can help them address a related, and perhaps more visceral, concern that some bring to their work, namely: What kind of relationship should I form with students? Will I like and respect them, and will they like and respect me? Many teachers wonder how close or how distant they should be with students, whether and to what extent they should be friends with them, how much of their personal lives they and their students should disclose, and more. These pertinent and often deeply felt questions attest to teachers' appreciation for the human dimensions of pedagogy that many educators have articulated and embraced during the last two centuries. At the same time, however, such concerns are difficult to address without an awareness of the distinctive aims of teaching – aims that, among other things, distinguish the work from other social endeavors such as doctoring, parenting, counseling, and nursing. Such aims characterize teaching as a unique practice with its own recognizable activities and obligations.

The process of understanding students brings teachers into the heart of the practice. At teaching's core is the commitment to serve students' intellectual and moral growth. That purpose helps give teachers their overall bearings. It provides a vantage point, a place to stand, in determining how to perceive and teach students. [ ... ]

At the center of understanding students is learning how to be intellectually and morally attentive as a teacher. My interest in these forms of attentiveness, and in the larger process of understanding students that these forms serve, derives in part from a study in which I sought to understand the views and practices of four highly regarded teachers who work in an urban setting.[1] I found that the language of calling, or vocation, helped capture their underlying motivations and conceptions of teaching better than the contemporary languages of profession, occupation, or job. The language of calling illuminates the sustained and deep regard the teachers have for their students, a quality perhaps shared by dedicated practitioners everywhere. Moreover, that quality appears to be more educationally promising than what is suggested by terms like personal relationship.

[ ... ]

Previously published in *Journal of Curriculum and Supervision* 14(2) (Winter 1999), pp. 171–85. Reproduced by permission of ASCD (Association for Supervision and Curriculum Development), Alexandria.

## Intellectual Attentiveness in Teaching

The question "What are the purposes of teaching?" is obviously too big to come to grips with here. Nevertheless, it must be asked in order to make sense of the idea of understanding students. The brief and admittedly cursory response that follows paves the way for examining the notion of being intellectually attentive as a teacher. The second half of the article addresses its closely related partner, moral attentiveness.

Teaching exists in a distinctive space of questions and concerns about the meaning of becoming human.[2] Teachers do not invent either the questions or the concerns. Posed differently, teachers do not invent the terms of the practice. Rather, they take on these terms; they embrace them, they enact them. For example, teaching entails leading or guiding others to know what they did not know before – the course of historical events or the structure of the solar system. It means helping students to articulate or apprehend what they did not know they knew – for example, elements of logical and persuasive argument that they may have learned unawares through years of talking and playing with friends. Teaching means assisting or coaching others in how to do things they could not do before – for instance, how to prepare a science experiment or how to play a musical instrument. Teaching involves promoting or encouraging attitudes students did not embody before – for example, to enjoy reading or to enjoy discussion with peers rather than just looking for "the answer." Still another term or aspect of teaching is spurring students to reconsider old beliefs in favor of potentially better ones – for example, that they can think for themselves and that they can accomplish things through their own initiative and effort.

These purposes share a common element. They involve drawing or guiding students into new intellectual and moral terrain. Serving as such a guide – Sockett considers teachers to be "guides through difficulty"[3] – obliges the teacher to be intellectually attentive to students. This attentiveness involves teachers becoming as close to students as they possibly can. However, the kind of "closeness" teachers seek with students differs from what they might cultivate with a colleague, a spouse, a son or daughter, a parent, a doctor, a counselor, a pastor, and so forth. Furthermore, this stance does not constitute a middle ground between the intimacies of friendship, on the one hand, and the distances

sometimes associated with professionalism, on the other hand.[4] Intellectual attentiveness takes its meaning from the distinctive ground that teachers occupy. That ground renders their work into something other than "helping" young people. Barcena and colleagues argue that it is not enough to define the educational relationship as an assistance-based one. The important thing is not merely to be of assistance, but to be of pedagogical assistance. This is what distinguishes an educational relationship from other forms of assistance or help, such as psychological or therapeutic.[5]

Adults can be helpful in many roles – for example, as parents, ministers, nurses, or counselors. But neither parenting, ministering, nursing, nor counseling places both intellectual and moral development at its center in the uniquely formal and public ways that teaching does. In the usual course of events, parents, ministers, nurses, and counselors are not formally responsible for educating other peoples' children. Teachers are. Moreover, because parents or social workers may have achieved success in their respective endeavors does not automatically imply that they would be successful teachers. Teaching has its own characteristic set of responsibilities and obligations.[6] Consequently, teachers' understanding of students has dimensions of meaning that are different from, although not necessarily antithetical to, the ways in which parents, friends, or counselors might understand those students.

The kind of closeness embedded in the idea of intellectual attentiveness centers around factors that in educational practice are virtually indistinguishable: the subject matter, the classroom setting, and the persons students are becoming. Being intellectually attentive means getting as close to students' responses to subject matter as time and opportunity afford. Those responses can pertain to mathematical understanding, historical or literary interpretation, scientific experiment, artistic creation, or athletic development. Intellectual attentiveness also involves teachers' being alert to aspects of student conduct that influence students' engagement with subject matter. Such aspects include those that enable and support students in using their minds – concentration, signs of emerging confidence, and persistence. Other aspects of student conduct discourage their use of mind – for instance, interrupting others, not taking their time or their energy seriously, and giving way to excessive self-doubt. In short, being intellectually attentive means focusing as closely as the teacher can on what students know, feel, and think about the subject at hand, all with an eye toward their building both knowledge of the world and a sense for how to continue learning about the world.

This process, furthermore, is moral. It entails teachers' care and concern for students in their relation to the subject, not to the teacher per se, and whether or not that relationship is productive and meaningful. The process is intellectual because it presumes the teacher's familiarity with the subject, including its logic and structure. It presupposes a sense of the values that inhere in subject matter. For example, teaching and learning mathematics involve developing qualities of imagination and curiosity.[7] Studying literature includes cultivating disciplined respect for language and for choice of words.[8] Teaching and learning history involve appreciating critically what different people have found important in life.[9] To be intellectually attentive means being alert to the emergence of such qualities of mind in students. This process entails more than teachers' checking whether students have ingested a particular group of facts. It means appreciating that facts are pedagogically relevant in light of students' development of their intellectual capacity and perspective.

At this point, another factor in intellectual attentiveness comes into play: awareness of the persons students are becoming. To understand students, the teacher seeks closeness not solely to the persons they are now, but also to the persons they are becoming and are capable of becoming – for example, individuals who can read and write critically, think and act independently, relate efficaciously with others, develop and pursue interests, and more. This awareness does not necessarily mean that teachers must anticipate what students may be like as adults, although that prospect could be relevant, especially with adolescents. To be intellectually attentive means considering the persons students may be becoming in the very next moment. It means being on the lookout for signs of students' incipient interests, strengths, and capacities. It means not just noting such signs but seizing upon them in order to help guide students into new terrain – to come to grips with subject matter and with issues of personal conduct as they bear on learning in social settings like the classroom. This intellectual attentiveness, or closeness, takes its identity not from thinking about issues of personal relationship, but rather from the larger purposes of teaching touched on previously.

Educators have amply documented the knowledge and background teachers need to serve those purposes. In addition to their knowledge of subject matter, teachers' intellectual attentiveness draws on their mindfulness and understanding of psychological, cognitive, cultural, and social aspects of their students' learning. Depending upon the situation, a teacher's lens may be cultural ("I wonder if Rachel seems tense because she's not comfortable with our classroom procedures"), or emotional-developmental ("Now I appreciate our counselor's take on why Alex has such a short fuse"), or cognitive ("Shawn may be struggling simply because she's never been asked to think in the ways these questions lead us to"). More typically, the great variety of pedagogical situations oblige teachers to be open to an always shifting combination of such lenses.

Concern for appropriate "lenses" attests to the fact that what I have been calling intellectual attentiveness involves perception. To attend as closely as one can to students' responses to subject matter literally means being alert and watchful as students tackle various challenges. It means, for example, noting frowns of doubt and confusion, smiles of curiosity and delight, and gestures of resignation or determination. It involves awareness of how students respond to and treat one another, especially with regard to one another's ideas and endeavors. What scholars have called the "enacted curriculum" becomes much richer and deeper as teachers attend to student responses to subject matter.[10] Teachers' perceptions of what students are about and of what is unfolding in the classroom are central to the task of intellectual attentiveness.

## Moral Attentiveness in Teaching

These remarks about the importance of perception provide a bridge to a second, closely connected concept: moral attentiveness. It bears emphasizing that everything said about intellectual attentiveness thus far has moral overtones, with moral understood to pertain to what it is good for human beings to do and to be. The purposes of teaching outlined previously are themselves moral as well as intellectual. They are moral because they presuppose that human development is a good thing. They presuppose that a person's life will be better rather than worse for learning the kinds of things teachers are charged with teaching: for example, thoughtful reading, writing, numerating, thinking, and problem solving.

Moreover, the qualities of intellectual attentiveness examined above – identifying students' responses to subject matter, seeing what they can and cannot do, and discerning what they think and feel about ideas and activities – all presume a crucial moral disposition on the part of the teacher: the willingness to attend closely to students in the first place. That process can be time consuming ("Robert is so quiet, I still haven't figured out what he's grasping"), fraught with uncertainty ("Am I right to conclude that Diane is an adequate writer given her age and experience?"), and often frustrating ("John acts so confidently, and yet his work is not up to par; I wish I knew how to deal with this"). Because of these facts, being intellectually attentive to students presumes a certain moral tenacity on the part of the teacher, which translates into not giving up on or prejudging young people.

It also presupposes what I want to call moral attentiveness, a term with roots in contemporary moral philosophy and in educational scholarship. Some philosophers have argued that the moral life is more a matter of paying attention to particular contexts and persons than it is a matter of articulating and applying general ethical principles or rules of conduct.[11] Without dismissing the value of considering such principles, these thinkers argue that virtues such as patience, respectfulness, humility, and so forth are more dynamic and decisive in the everyday business of dwelling morally with other human beings. Some educational scholars have recently argued that what they call "moral perception" or "situational appreciation" is crucial to the enactment of morally and intellectually sound teaching.[12] The terms they employ highlight the teacher's capacity and willingness to pay fine-grained attention to classroom contexts and student individuality. Contemplation, discernment, disposition, orientation, sensibility: this is the language such scholars suggest is indispensable for helping us to understand what serious-minded teachers do.

What does being "morally attentive" to students mean, and why is this concept relevant to teaching? Being morally attentive to students does not entail articulating and then applying a moral theory to one's work in the classroom. Nor does it mean articulating and then applying a set of moral or ethical principles of conduct. At first glance, these claims may seem dubious or discordant. Who can doubt the value of pondering and employing ethical principles when one is genuinely unsure about how to handle a difficult situation? In such circumstances, it can surely be helpful to weigh in a detached fashion principles such as truth-telling and fairness with the likely consequences of choices of action. A number of scholars have demonstrated how this is so when teachers are faced with thorny dilemmas in which every course of action seems to have negative aspects.[13] According to the literature, ethical principles and standards can help a teacher survey his or her choices more comprehensively and intelligently, all with an eye on the desired aim of helping rather than harming students.

However, moral attentiveness pertains not to resolving dramatic classroom or school dilemmas, the kind that both scholars and teachers often emphasize and that seem to invite talk of decontextualized principles. Rather, like its close partner intellectual attentiveness, moral attentiveness takes its meaning from the everyday work of teaching and learning. Most teachers do not confront eight hours a day of nonstop crisis. Even in challenging institutional settings, the bulk of their classroom time is given over to the ordinary and familiar business of teaching and learning. That business is infinitely complex and demanding in its own right, and here moral attentiveness comes into play. Teachers' moral attentiveness has two components: alertness to the development of their students' character, and awareness of their own regard for and treatment of students. These components are so thoroughly intertwined in actual practice that I will examine them together.

[ . . . ]

Students are the persons who stand before the teacher. In one way or another, each is a unique and unprecedented human being. Each student has witnessed, heard, and learned things nobody else has. Each incarnates a distinctive and evolving set of capacities, inclinations, dispositions, and attitudes.

Being morally attentive to students means taking seriously these familiar if perhaps easily overlooked realities. Such a stance differs from sentimentalism, which represents a non- or even anti-intellectual orientation toward teaching. That posture is not what Rousseau had in mind in urging educators to take children seriously. However, to echo Rousseau again, nor does such a stance presume that the teacher must be alert for what is morally "lacking" in students. It does not mean measuring students' individual character against some preset standard of what respectfulness, for instance, entails as a factor in learning. Like other virtues such as patience, persistence, openmindedness, honesty, and courage, respectfulness can be enacted in many different ways that depend heavily on the particular context. In a school where tardiness is the norm, for example, it may be a sign of respect for learning when students show up promptly to class. In another setting, respect may manifest itself more relevantly, at the moment, in the seriousness with which students take each other's ideas. Moreover, the meaning of these and other virtues can evolve as students grow and change. For example, it may have been an act of courage in September when young Yvonne spoke up in discussion for the very first time. In March, courage for Yvonne now means attempting to give her first formal presentation to the whole class. For another student in the same group, Andrew, courage might mean volunteering for the first time in November, and in March serving as a note taker rather than public speaker. For teachers, being morally attentive means being mindful that all the young Yvonnes and Andrews in the classroom are becoming persons of one kind or another, and they are doing so before teachers' very eyes. This implies that teachers need to develop eyes for such matters. [ . . . ]

The virtues also accompany intellectual growth, which is why intellectual and moral attentiveness can be treated separately only for heuristic purposes. For example, patience as an aspect of learning does not exist in an intellectual vacuum. It takes its meaning in contexts such as waiting one's turn to speak, not overlooking crucial steps in an experiment in one's excitement to learn the results, and practicing chords so one can play a guitar piece. But all of those activities, each intellectual in its own right, also do not take place in a vacuum, in this case a moral one. They can only materialize with the enactment of patience. That moral quality accompanies the intellectual process, or there will be no such process, period.[14]

Earlier I suggested that intellectual attentiveness means focusing on students' conduct as it facilitates or undermines their learning. In light of the present remarks, such a focus clearly entails moral attentiveness as well. A student who acts impatiently may be thwarting his or her opportunities for new educational experience both in the immediate moment and possibly in future ones as well.

## Understanding Students and Growing as a Teacher

[ . . . ]

Both forms of attentiveness are demanding and difficult to learn, and consequently relate directly to teachers' own development. Intellectual attentiveness draws on teachers' knowledge of subject matter, including knowledge of its logic and structure as well as its relevant facts, and knowledge of psychology, culture, cognition, emotional development, and more. It calls on teachers to be attentive to students' subtle as well as overt responses to subject matter and, more broadly, to the process of learning itself. Moral attentiveness is perhaps even more demanding because it involves pondering and treating students in a larger frame of individuality than the intellectual. Put differently, it calls on teachers to move beyond categories of knowledge bequeathed to them by their education and their formal preparation as teachers. It means attending precisely to what is distinctive about individual students, which means that which lies beyond all such categories (although not divorced from them).

In this light, moral attentiveness helps contextualize and humanize teachers' knowledge. It gives teachers a focus for how to make use of their knowledge. Reciprocally, as I have suggested, intellectual attentiveness helps orient teachers' moral sensibilities. It helps them move beyond concerns of personal relationship considered in isolation from educational practice.

## Notes

1. David T. Hansen, *The Call to Teach* (New York: Teachers College Press, 1995).
2. Charles Taylor, *Sources of the Self: The Making of the Modern Identity* (Cambridge, MA: Harvard University Press, 1989), pp. 29, 51.
3. Hugh Sockett, "Education and Will: Aspects of Personal Capability," *American Journal of Education* 96 (February 1988), pp. 195–214.
4. For a helpful perspective on this continuum, see Margret Buchmann and Robert E. Floden, *Detachment*

and Concern: Conversations in the Philosophy of Teaching and Teacher Education (New York: Teachers College Press, 1993).

5. Fernando Barcena, Fernando Gil, and Gonzalo Jover, "The Ethical Dimension of Teaching: a Review and a Proposal," Journal of Moral Education 22 (Fall 1993), p. 246.

6. C. J. B. Macmillan and Thomas W. Nelson (eds.), Concepts of Teaching: Philosophical Essays (Chicago, IL: Rand McNally, 1968); Thomas F. Green, The Activities of Teaching (New York: McGraw-Hill, 1971).

7. Brent Davis, Teaching Mathematics: Toward a Sound Alternative (Hamden, CT: Garland); Magdalene Lampert, "When the Problem is Not the Question and the Solution is Not the Answer: Mathematical Knowing and Teaching," American Educational Research Journal 27 (Spring 1990), pp. 29–63.

8. Italo Calvino, Six Memos for the Next Millennium (Cambridge, MA: Harvard University Press, 1988); Sandra Stotsky, Connecting Civic Education and Language Education (New York: Teachers College Press, 1991).

9. R. G. Collingwood, The Idea of History (London: Oxford University Press, 1956 [original work published in 1946]); D. Z. Philips, "Is Moral Education Really Necessary?" British Journal of Educational Studies 27 (February 1979), pp. 42–56.

10. Anne M. Bussis, Edward A. Chittenden, and Marianne Amarel, Beyond Surface Curriculum: An Interview Study of Teachers' Understandings (Boulder, CO: Westview Press, 1976); John I. Goodlad and M. Frances Klein, Behind the Classroom Door (Worthington, OH: Charles A. Jones, 1970); Rebecca K. Hawthorne, Curriculum in the Making: Teacher Choice and the Classroom Experience (New York: Teachers College Press, 1992); Cynthia Paris, Teacher Agency and Curriculum Making in Classrooms (New York: Teachers College Press, 1993); Jon Snyder, Frances Bolin, and Karen Zumwalt,

"Curriculum Implementation," in The Handbook of Research on Curriculum, ed. Philip W. Jackson (New York: Macmillan, 1992), pp. 402–35.

11. See, for example, Lawrence A. Blum, Moral Perception and Particularity (Cambridge: Cambridge University Press, 1994); Iris Murdoch, The Sovereignty of Good (London: Ark, 1985 [original work published in 1970]); and Martha Nussbaum, Love's Knowledge: Essays on Philosophy and Literature (New York: Oxford University Press, 1990).

12. Margret Buchmann, "The Careful Vision: How Practical is Contemplation in Teaching?" American Journal of Education 98 (November 1989), pp. 35–61; David C. Bricker, "Character and Moral Reasoning: an Aristotelian Perspective," in Ethics for Professionals in Education, ed. Kenneth A. Strike and P. Lance Ternasky (New York: Teachers College Press, 1993), pp. 13–26; James Garrison, Dewey and Eros: Wisdom and Desire in the Art of Teaching (New York: Teachers College Press, 1997); Shirley Pendlebury, "Practical Arguments and Situational Appreciation in Teaching," Educational Theory 40 (Spring 1990), pp. 171–9.

13. Gary D. Fenstermacher, "The Concepts of Method and Manner in Teaching," in Effective and Responsible Teaching: The New Synthesis, ed. Fritz K. Oser, Andreas Dick, and Jean-Luc Patry (San Francisco, CA: Jossey-Bass, 1992), pp. 95–108; Gary D. Fenstermacher and Virginia Richardson, "The Elicitation and Reconstruction of Practical Arguments in Teaching," Journal of Curriculum Studies 25 (March–April 1993), pp. 101–14; Karl D. Hostetler, Ethical Judgment in Teaching (Boston, MA: Allyn and Bacon, 1997); Kenneth A. Strike and Jonas F. Soltis, The Ethics of Teaching (New York: Teachers College Press, 1985); Kenneth A. Strike and P. Lance Ternasky (eds.), Ethics for Professionals in Education (New York: Teachers College Press, 1993).

14. People can certainly be bullied into doing things, but that is not an "intellectual process" as understood here.

# 38

# Beyond the Reflective Teacher

## Terence H. McLaughlin

In its recent survey of initial teacher training courses in England and Wales, the Modes of Teacher Education Project investigated whether courses were based upon an 'agreed model of the teacher' as part of their 'underlying philosophy'. Of the course leaders who answered 'yes' to this question, the vast majority across all phases and courses described this model as that of the 'reflective practitioner' (Whitty et al., 1992, pp. 297–9). This finding should not surprise us, for the concept of the 'reflective practitioner' – and more generally 'the reflective teacher' – is not only currently widely fashionable, but also has a strong intuitive appeal.

This appeal is easy to understand. Who, after all, would want to champion the *unreflective* practitioner? However, for some time it has been widely recognised that, in common with other educational nostrums, 'the reflective practitioner' is often used as a vague slogan rather than as a concept whose meaning and implications are well thought through and worked out. Such slogans are not without their educational and political value (on the use of the language of 'the reflective practitioner' as a rallying cry to oppose a number of recent developments and trends in the reform of teacher training see Furlong,

1992, pp. 176–7). But, given our current ambition to achieve a much more precise understanding of the concepts and processes involved in teaching and teacher training, the notion of 'the reflective practitioner' cannot escape careful analysis.

In this article I shall suggest that we need to move 'beyond the reflective teacher' in two ways. First, we need to move beyond the slogan of the reflective teacher to explore in more detail what the concept involves and the extent of its adequacy as an account both of teaching and of the demands of teacher training. Second, we need to go beyond the concept itself to acknowledge its incompleteness and its need to be supplemented by, and situated within, a richer account of the nature and requirements of teaching and teacher training. The article has three sections. In the first section I outline briefly the nature of the appeal of the notion of the 'reflective practitioner'. In the second, I pose and explore some critical questions relating to the notion. These concern the nature of reflection, the grounds on which reflection might be thought to be valuable in teaching and the extent to which developmental considerations relating to it can be discerned. In the final section I address the question

Previously published in *Educational Philosophy and Theory* 31(1) (1999), pp. 9–18, 19–25. Reprinted by permission of Blackwell Publishing Ltd and the author.

of the respects in which we need to go beyond the concept of 'reflection' in our understanding of teaching and teacher training.

## The Appeal of 'the Reflective Practitioner'

The wide popularity and appeal of the concept of 'the reflective practitioner' is not best explained in terms of a subscription to the details of any specific and well-worked out model of the notion, such as that famously offered by Donald Schön (Schön, 1983, 1987). A number of competing models and conceptions of 'the reflective practitioner' exist, varying in the meaning which they give to the terminology they use and in the nature of the theoretical articulation of the notion which they offer (on this see, for example, Calderhead, 1989; Zeichner, 1994). The preoccupation with 'reflection' in the wide-ranging research tradition into teacher thinking and action, for example, involves a number of varying conceptions of how 'reflective practice' is to be understood (for recent collections of papers on these matters see Tabachnich and Zeichner, 1991; Russell and Munby 1992; Calderhead and Gates 1993; Carlgren et al., 1994). Zeichner comments 'Underlying the apparent similarity among those who embrace the slogans of reflective practice are vast differences in perspectives about teaching, learning, schooling and the social order . . . Everyone, no matter what his or her ideological orientation, has jumped on the bandwagon . . . furthering some version of reflective teaching practice' (Zeichner, 1994, pp. 9–10).

The intuitive general appeal of 'the reflective practitioner' to teachers and teacher educators is two-fold. First, in stressing the significance of 'reflection', the notion captures an aversion to, or suspicion of, a range of attitudes, arguments and policies which seek in different ways to diminish the importance, scope and sophistication of professional thoughtfulness, judgement and autonomy. The targets aimed at here are varied. They include the various narrow and minimalist accounts of teaching and teacher training which have emerged in contemporary debates from the pens of populist writers, certain provisions of policy in the recent reform of teacher training which may reduce opportunities for students to develop critical capacity and perspective, and the perceived threat to the reflective practice of teaching arising from an emphasis on 'skills' and 'competences' (on skills see, for example, Smith,

1987, and on competences, Elliott, 1991; Furlong and Maynard, 1995, ch. 2). The second appealing feature of the notion of 'the reflective practitioner' is the vagueness and elasticity of what is meant by 'reflection'. This enables the slogan to be invoked without involving commitment to any particular view of, or theory about, many underlying and related questions. Thus, for example, those who appear to disagree quite extensively about significant aspects of teacher training make a common appeal to the importance of 'reflection' (see, for example, Elliott, 1993; Hargreaves, 1993). In an area where there is much uncertainty, and a good deal of conceptual and empirical research still to be done, a general inclusive concept with which many can identify has its virtues. However, if progress is to be made in achieving a fuller understanding of the nature and requirements of teaching and teacher training we should heed Zeichner's call for us to pass beyond 'the uncritical celebration' of teacher reflection 'We need to focus our attention on what kind of reflection teachers are engaging in, on what it is teachers are reflecting about and on how they are going about it' (Zeichner, 1994, p. 18).

## 'The Reflective Practitioner': Some Critical Questions

The kinds of question invited by the concept of 'the reflective practitioner' (understood henceforth as 'the reflective teacher') are complex and varied.

First, there are questions about how 'reflection' is to be understood. These include queries about the nature of reflection (e.g. how explicit and systematic it is or should be, and how it is related to action) and about its scope and objects (e.g. the matters on which teachers are invited to reflect about).

Second, there are questions about the value of reflection. One way of putting the central question here is to ask whether 'reflection' is valued as an end in itself or as a means to other ends. Given the complexity of means/end relationships in education, however, this way of posing the issue needs to be regarded with caution. It is better put in the following form: is reflection valued simply as a process, or in terms of the quality of the judgements – and possibly action – to which it leads? If reflection is valued because of the quality of judgements achieved or aimed at, attention focuses upon the 'content' of reflection. This raises the question of the criteria that can be invoked for adequate reflective judgement.

If reflection is valued because of the action to which it leads, a number of questions arise: does being reflective mean merely thinking about one's teaching or doing something about it? Is a reflective teacher *ipso facto* a good teacher? How, for example, is a weak reflective teacher different from a strong unreflective teacher?

Third, questions arise about the development of reflection. How does an observer recognize a reflective teacher? To what extent can developmental principles for teacher reflection be discerned which can serve to illuminate programmes of teacher training?

This large range of questions (which overlap with, and are partly drawn from, some questions raised by Russell, 1993, p. 144) cannot be addressed fully here. I shall, however, offer some remarks on each of them.

## The nature of reflection

Teaching involves a complex amalgam of inter-related kinds of achievement. In general terms, the teacher must have knowledge and understanding of wide-ranging sorts, the ability in the light of that knowledge and understanding to make rational practical judgements about what to do in particular circumstances, skills to carry out what is decided and dispositions (motives and tendencies) to actually do what is judged appropriate (Hirst, 1979). Whilst these kinds of achievement can be isolated in this way for purposes of formal analysis, their essential interrelatedness both practically and logically is obvious. Knowledge and understanding, for example, are involved in practical judgements, skills and dispositions, and are particularly significant in the case of teaching. In specific terms, the sorts of practical tasks and activities in which these kinds of achievement are exercised are extensive and many faceted, as revealed in the many empirical studies of the nature of teaching (e.g. Brown and McIntyre, 1993).

It is frequently claimed or implied that teachers should be *reflective* across all these elements of achievement, task and activity. As suggested earlier, the opposing claim – that teachers should be unreflective about these matters – sounds unappealing. Indeed, the notion of a wholly unreflective teacher is somewhat incoherent. Human agency of any kind involves thought, much of which is tacit and unexamined. The significance of implicit and intuitive elements in human action generally is illuminated by the telling remark of Martin Hollis that if 'rational man' is defined as one who chooses each action by reflecting consciously on what to do next, he would never be able to get to his own front door, immobilised by the decision about which sock to put on first. Given a society of such people, continues Hollis, 'civilization would collapse into paralysis, like some giant centipede told to put its best foot forward first' (Hollis, 1977, p. 62).

However, it is hard to conceive of human agency which does not require reflective thought of any kind. At the very least we encounter practical obstacles and challenges of various sorts to our plans and assumptions, which require us to reflect (at least in some sense and to some extent) on them. If this is true of human agency itself, it is still more true in the case of teaching. Forms of reflection arise naturally from the activity of teaching, even if they are confined to lower-level matters of (say) strategy and tactics. Practical judgements requiring reflection (again, in some sense and to some extent) are inescapable in teaching. The positive claim that teachers should be reflective, however, goes beyond these basic points and arises from an acknowledgement of the practical and evaluative complexities inherent in the work of the teacher' (McLaughlin, 1994, pp. 152–3) which underscore the need for the sorts of professional thoughtfulness, judgement and autonomy referred to earlier.

However, in what sense should 'reflection' be understood here? On one interpretation, 'reflection' means simply 'thinking'. More specifically, it conjures up notions such as 'pondering', 'considering', 'deliberating', 'meditating' and the like, together with 'critical assessment'. More detailed accounts of the notion take a number of forms. It is helpful to approach these by reference to two continuums along which conceptions of the notion of 'reflection' are located.

The first continuum refers to the *nature* of reflection. Expressed roughly, at one end of this continuum are views of reflection which stress the explicit and the systematic and, at the other end, views which lay emphasis upon the implicit and the intuitive. The matters to which the explicit/systematic or implicit/intuitive are taken to refer to here are both the nature of the reasoning involved and the extent to which it involves a 'standing back' from action.

At the explicit and systematic end of this continuum is a view of reflection which involves 'technical reason'. 'Technical reason' is exhibited in

Aristotle's notion of *techne*, an activity of making or production (*poesis*), aimed at a pre-specifiable and durable outcome (a product or state of affairs) which constitutes its purpose (*telos*). Inherent in this activity is 'technical knowledge' which gives the 'expert maker' 'a clear conception of the why and wherefore, the how and with-what of the making process and enables him, through the capacity to offer a rational account of it, to preside over his activity with secure mastery' (Dunne, 1993, p. 9). The limitations of 'technical rationality' as a form of reflection to govern the professional practice of teaching through the application of 'scientific' theory and technique in an instrumental way to solve the problems of practice are widely acknowledged (see, for example, Schön, 1983, ch. 2; Carr and Kemmis, 1986 ch. 2). At the heart of these difficulties is the inappropriateness of conceiving of teaching as a *techne*. Educational ends are neither clear, fixed, unitary nor evaluatively straightforward, and are not achieved (primarily) through technical means/end processes which can be mastered through scientific or technical knowledge and skill.

Also at the explicit and systematic end of this continuum are views of reflection which, whilst not necessarily invoking the notion of 'technical reason', are 'rationalist' in a broader sense, laying a similar stress on the need for reflection to involve the application of theory (in particular the resources and conclusions of the foundation disciplines of education) to the demands and realities of practice. The inadequacy of this account of reflection arises from its faulty conceptualisation of the relationship between rational action and theoretical knowledge. One aspect of this faulty conceptualisation is that the essentially abstract and general character of theoretical knowledge renders impossible its fruitful application to the details of practice in a direct and straightforward way (Hirst, 1983).

The conception of reflective thinking outlined by John Dewey can also be described as 'explicit' and 'systematic' in character. For Dewey, reflection is 'turning a subject over in the mind and giving it serious and consecutive consideration' (Dewey, 1933, p. 3); 'Active, persistent, and careful consideration of any belief or supposed form of knowledge in the light of the grounds that support it and the further conclusions to which it tends' (ibid., p. 9). For Dewey, reflective thinking originates in a state of doubt or perplexity about a given matter, seeks through enquiry to resolve the perplexity, and invites in the process criticism, examination

and test (ibid., pp. 12–16). Dewey places a strong emphasis upon scientific modes of thinking and reasoning in his conception of reflectiveness, as seen by his remarks on inference and testing (ibid., ch. 6), and on the structure of reflective thinking with its five phases or aspects, culminating in hypothesis testing (ibid., ch. 7; see also, for example, ch. 11 on systematic method). A number of the features of Dewey's account of reflective thinking invite doubt about its adequacy as a comprehensive account of teacher reflection. Is the sort of reflection engaged in by teachers always so explicit and systematic? Do 'problem solving' and scientific forms of thought have the salience in teacher reflection which Dewey suggests? (on general limitations in Dewey's stress on problem solving in education see Peters, 1977, esp. pp. 112–13).

There are some affinities between Dewey's account of reflective thinking and accounts which stress 'technical reason', although, given the richness and complexity of Dewey's thought, these affinities should not be pushed too far. Nor should Dewey be interpreted as denying the significance of the implicit and the intuitive in human action. (For an overall perspective on Dewey see, for example, Tiles, 1988. For similarities between Dewey's view and that of Schön, cf. Schön, 1987, pp. 26–31.)

At the implicit and intuitive end of the continuum concerning the nature of reflection we encounter Donald Schön, whose arguments about the nature of professional knowledge are by now well known. Schön's rejection of the adequacy of 'technical rationality' as an account of professional knowledge is emphatic. Professional decisions often involve not merely the 'solving' of problems which are already 'given' and well formed, but a process of wrestling with 'messy, indeterminate situations' (Schön, 1987, p. 4) requiring the 'setting', 'framing', 'construction' (or interpretative determination) of 'problems' in forms of judgement which go beyond the technical. Professionals in these matters are 'world makers' (ibid., p. 36). In addition, the cases and situations confronting the practitioner often involve uniqueness, uncertainty and value-conflict, and therefore cannot be dealt with by the application of routinisable and pre-specifiable procedures and strategies. For Schön, it is in these 'indeterminate zones of practice' that the distinctiveness and importance of professional competence is to be found.

In giving his own account of professional competence in these matters, Schön is wary of using terms such as 'wisdom' and 'intuition', which are in his view apt to be used as 'junk categories' attaching names to phenomena that elude conventional strategies of explanation' (ibid., p. 13). As is well known, his approach is to analyse carefully the 'core of artistry' which is inherent in professional practice. Artistry is an exercise of intelligence and a kind of knowing, revealed in arts such as problem framing, implementation and improvisation. Much of this artistry, along with our everyday competences of recognition, judgement and skill is tacit in character '[it does] . . . not depend on our being able to describe what we know how to do or even to entertain in conscious thought the knowledge our actions reveal' (ibid., p. 22). What is involved is 'knowledge in action', contained in, and revealed by, intelligent action itself.

Schön notes that it is possible through observation and reflection on our actions to attempt a description of our tacit knowledge (ibid., pp. 25–6). He takes such reflection to be occasioned by situations of surprise, when our knowing-in-action is insufficient for the unexpected (although Schön does not want to be tied to too restrictive an account of what may stimulate reflection: ibid., p. 29). Schön distinguishes between reflection on action (which is retrospective in character, whether it takes place immediately after the action or much later) and reflection in action, where the reflection can make a difference to what we are doing and therefore has immediate significance for practice. 'Reflection in action' takes a professional form in the shape of 'reflection in practice'. Central to Schön's account of professional competence, it has the crucial function of questioning the 'assumptional structure' of knowing in action (ibid., p. 28) but is often tacit and closely integrated into smooth performance, as in Schön's examples of the cellist sight-reading an unfamiliar piece and the jazz musicians improvising together (ibid., pp. 29–30). At the heart of matters here is a 'reflective conversation with the materials of a situation' (ibid., p. 31). Further stages of reflection involve reflection upon our reflection-in-action so as to produce a verbal description of it, and then reflection upon the description which emerges (ibid., p. 31), so as to facilitate a reflective grasp of practice which is ever widening.

Although the details of Schön's account cannot be pursued further at this point (see, for example, Schön, 1983, chs 5, 6, 9), it is important to note its similarity – at least in some respects – to the activity which Aristotle contrasted with *techne: praxis*. *Praxis* involves the engagement of persons in activity with others which is non-instrumental in that it is not intended to realise goods 'external' to the persons involved but rather excellences characteristic of a worthwhile form of life. Joseph Dunne's helpful illumination of this notion also brings into focus elements of it on which Schön is silent:

> As an activity that both involved one with other people and at the same time was a realisation of one's self, *praxis* engaged one more intimately, or afforded one less detachment, than the *poesis* over which one exercised an uncompromised sovereignty. And for this reason – that is, e.g., brought one's emotions so much more into play and both formed and revealed one's character – as well as because of its bringing one into situations that were very much more heterogeneous and contingent than the reliably circumscribed situations of *poesis*, praxis required for its regulation a kind of knowledge that was more personal and experiential, more supple and less formulable, than the knowledge conferred by *techne*. (Dunne, 1993, p. 10)

This knowledge is described by Aristotle as *phronesis* (or practical wisdom), a major 'ordering agency' in our lives more generally. On a view such as this the sort of reflective thinking that is appropriate for teachers is that harmonious with, and arising out of, *phronesis*, and appropriate for the person who possesses it – the *phronimos*. Whilst Schön's discussion of the nature of professional knowledge resonates with the sort of knowledge characteristic of 'phronesis', his account stops short of a full discussion of the qualities of character and 'personhood' which arise in the Aristotelian perspective. This perspective, and the extent to which it can be appealed to as the basis for a fuller understanding of the nature of teacher reflection, will be returned to later.

Different views of reflection emerging along the continuum we have been considering are associated with different views both of the theory/practice relationship (in general and as it bears upon the promotion of reflection) and of the proper demands of teacher training and development. With regard to the relationship between theory and practice, 'technical rationality' and 'Rationalist' approaches can lend support to crude 'theory into practice' accounts of this relationship, with reflection seen as served by exposure to theory appropriate for 'application'. In contrast, a view such as that of Schön illuminates, and lends support to, accounts which see the role of theory as implicit within, and contributing in different ways to the reflective critique of, the common sense or practical knowledge of teachers (Hirst, 1983, 1990a; Griffiths and Tann, 1992). The Aristotelian account is associated with a complex and well-articulated account of the theory/practice relationship (on this see, for example, Carr, 1995a, ch. 4 and Dunne, 1993, esp. pt 2). With regard to the demands of teacher training, views at the implicit and intuitive end of the continuum underscore the importance of practical experience and training in the preparation of teachers. Crucial for Schön is the notion of a 'reflective practicum' (ibid., pp. 36–40, chs. 7, and 10, pt 4) in which the artistry needed to function in the 'indeterminate zones of practice', and, in particular, proficiency in reflection-in-action is developed. Schön's substantial examples of reflective practice in the two books referred to do not include teaching, and the analogies and disanalogies between the examples he does give and teaching are instructive (for an application of Schön's theories to teacher training see, for example, Furlong et al., 1988, esp. ch. 4). Different views of reflection are also related to differing conception of the extent to which teachers should be properly seen as 'researchers' (on this general matter see, for example, Rudduck and Hopkins, 1985; Schön, 1983, pp. 307–25. On action research see, for example, Carr, 1995a, ch. 7. For a critique of the concept of 'the teacher as researcher' see Kemmis, 1995).

The second continuum along which views of reflection can be located refers to the *scope* and *objects* of reflection: the matters on which teachers are invited to, or expected to, reflect about. Schön points out that the objects of reflection of a practitioner can be very wide, including 'the tacit norms and appreciations which underlie a judgement . . . the strategies and theories implicit in a pattern of behaviour . . . the feeling for a situation which has led to a particular course of action . . . the way in which he has framed the problem he is trying to solve . . . the role he has constructed for himself within a larger institutional context' (Schön, 1983, p. 62). One way of describing the continuum on which the scope and objects of reflection are located is in terms of a concern at one end of the continuum for specific and proximate matters and a concern at the other for matters which are general and contextual.

At the specific and proximate end of the continuum are objects of reflection which relate in a close way to the 'present and particular' concerns of the teacher, especially within the classroom. Included here are the myriad interactions and judgements in the classroom in all their complexity, which relate in a concrete way to the various forms of achievement being aimed at for pupils and to the ways in which they can be realised. At the general and contextual end of the continuum are reflections about matters relating to the educational enterprise viewed from a broader and less immediate perspective. Matters for consideration here include the overall aims and purposes of the educational enterprise, the nature of 'ability', the functions and effects of processes of teaching and schooling and the significance of wider influences on the educational system as a whole, which in turn involve questions of a philosophical, psychological, social and political kind. Schön draws attention to the dangers arising from reflection which is limited in scope (Schön, 1983, ch. 9), and brings out the value of, and need for, research into matters (such as 'frames', 'overarching theories' and the like) which help to illuminate these broader matters (Schön, 1983, pp. 307–25). A concern that teacher reflection should range over the full range of this continuum, and not be confined to the specific and proximate is expressed in the various accounts which have emerged of 'levels' of reflection (e.g. McIntyre, 1993, pp. 44–7; Griffiths and Tann, 1992, pp. 76–80; for a related discussion on 'levels of training' see Furlong et al., 1988, pp. 129–32). The extent to which students in initial training for teaching can, and should, engage in reflection at the general and contextual end of the continuum is a matter of significance.

The two continua which have been identified, the first concerning the nature of reflection and the second, its scope and objects, are related to each other in a complex way. Differing objects of reflection invite differing forms of reflection. Attention is needed to these differences. Discussions of the ideal of 'the reflective teacher' often equate 'reflection' with 'reflection on one's own experience of practice' (e.g. Griffiths and Tann, 1992, p. 71; McIntyre, 1993, pp. 42–3). [ . . . ]

The concept of 'reflection' in teaching therefore involves a wide range of conceptions of the nature of reflection and of its scope and objects. These conceptions are not necessarily in opposition to each other but emphasise different aspects of the nature of reflection. Often an appeal to the notion of the 'reflective teacher' as the underlying rationale of a course of teacher training can silence debate by achieving a ready consensus. Far from closing down such a debate, however, such an appeal, properly understood, should open it up – across a wide range of relevant matters.

## The value of reflection

Discussions of 'reflection' (of whatever sort) in teaching often seem to suggest that reflection is *per se* a good thing. But is this the case, and, if so, why?

One question which arises is whether a reflective teacher is *ipso facto* a good teacher. What counts as 'good teaching' is, of course, not a straightforward matter (on this see, for example, Brown and McIntyre, 1993, chs. 2 and 3). However, on any view of what 'good teaching' amounts to, reflection is not a sufficient condition of it. Teaching involves more than reflection. We would think little of a teacher who was rich in the capacity to reflect (in whatever sense) but who was unable to establish appropriate relationships with pupils, or was disinclined to invite them to engage in any work. Whether reflection is a necessary ingredient in good teaching depends in part upon the sort of reflection that is being referred to and in part on how 'good teaching' is being understood. As mentioned earlier, reflection in some minimal sense is inescapable in teaching. Some of the forms of reflection discussed by Schön seem to be partially constitutive of good teaching in any recognisable sense of the term. Reflection-in-action, for example, is very tightly related to anything that might be regarded as effective classroom performance. And since *phronesis* is understood precisely as uniting good judgement and action, it also seems to be partially constitutive of good teaching. Whether reflection on matters at the general and contextual end of the continuum identified earlier is necessary for good teaching is a more complex matter. It is certainly possible to conceive of teachers who are capable of performing at a certain level of competence without being in possession of a broader perspective on their work arising from reflection on the sort of general and contextual matters we have been referring to. One way of making a strong connection between such wider reflective understanding and good teaching is to *define* a good teacher as one who possesses it. Another is to claim that such wider understandings are implicit in adequate reflection-in-action and in *phronesis*.

Empirical researchers may be tempted to investigate whether such wider understandings do, for the most part, enhance practice, especially when specific attempts are made to achieve such an enhancement. The difficulties in researching such a matter are, however, extensive. They include problems in establishing the nature and extent of the understanding possessed by a given individual, as well as the multifarious problems involved in judging its impact on practice. These arise not least from the fact that many of the influences on pupils arising from teachers with an expanded outlook of the sort in question are very subtle in nature, and involve aspects of the personhood of the teacher.

Discussion of the value of teacher reflection involves the question of the quality of reflection. [ . . . ]

The recognition that the adequacy of reflection requires assessment is exhibited by a number of writers. For Dewey, the adequacy of reflection is crucial. Reflection commences, claims Dewey, 'when we begin to inquire into the reliability, the worth, of any particular indication; when we try to test its value and see what guarantee there is that the existing data really point to the idea that is suggested in such as way as to justify acceptance of the latter' (Dewey, 1933, p. 11). For Dewey reflection implies belief on evidence (ibid., pp. 11–12). Hirst lays particular emphasis on the significance of critical assessment and justification. Despite his continuing critique of 'rationalism' (Hirst, 1993), Hirst retains his belief that educational theory is 'primarily the domain which seeks to develop rational principles for educational practice' (Hirst, 1983, p. 5), albeit principles which are 'practical' in character. For Hirst a crucial question is whether the 'theory' implicit in human action and in teaching is 'any good'. 'Are its concepts adequate to capture the complexities of the situations concerned? Is what is believed about these situations true? Are the judgements that are made justifiable on rational grounds?' (Hirst, 1990a, p. 74). For Hirst, the notion of a domain of rationally developing general principles of professional practice is necessary to the intelligibility of the notions of professionalism and professional development (Hirst, 1990b, p. 156. For his related criticisms of the Oxford Internship scheme for its inattention to the significance of justified principles and of what is required for students to be helped to make adequate reflective judgements see pp. 151–9). From such a point of view, an invitation to simply 'reflect' without attention to the ways in which adequacy in reflection can be secured is idle and, indeed, damaging to educational practice. The notion of an appropriate form of criticism is also inherent within the notion of the Aristotelian notion of '*phronesis*' (see Carr, 1995a, ch. 4) and forms part of the grounds on which Carr insists that interpretative research cannot rest content with merely describing what practitioners say about their practice (Carr, 1995a, chs. 5 and 8).

If the importance of the critique of reflective judgement is insisted upon, however, crucial questions arise about the basis on which criteria can be specified relevant to judgements of adequacy. What is to count as 'adequate' reflection and on what grounds? The inherent difficulty of such questions is amplified by the heterogeneous character of 'reflection'. [ . . . ]

Difficulties of this kind are exacerbated by the phenomenon of postmodernism, with its own form of radical questioning of the very possibility of general standards of judgement. Margaret Wilkin, for example, argues that a postmodern perspective renders highly problematic the project of rationally criticising and enriching the practical judgements of student teachers. What could such a project mean in the absence of even the possibility of general standards or norms in relation to which the relevant judgements can be made? (Wilkin, 1993).

Such questions raise fundamental philosophical issues about the evaluative basis of education itself. This debate cannot be pursued here (on an attempt to render compatible an acceptance of certain theses of postmodernism with enlightenment ideals see, for example, Carr, 1995a, esp. ch. 9, 1995b). For the present discussion, however, it is important to note that teacher trainers cannot sidestep this debate by invoking the concept of 'the reflective teacher' and seeking to deflect questions about the adequacy of reflective judgement by appealing to reflection as a 'process'.

[ . . . ]

## Beyond Reflection

As we have seen, the difficulties involved in giving a clear account of what is involved in the notion of 'the reflective teacher' are extensive, and the agenda of issues and problems which have emerged require attention if the notion is to function in a meaningful way in relation to teaching and teacher training.

In the final section of this paper, I shall focus attention beyond the notion of reflection to the broader moral, intellectual and personal qualities – qualities of mind and dispositions of character and personhood – that should characterise the teacher. The suggestion here is that we need to recognise the significance of the teacher as a certain sort of person, and that this should be acknowledged in the demands of teacher training. This is important not only in relation to resolving some of the issues which have emerged in relation to 'reflection' but as a worthy emphasis in its own right.

Discussions of the concept of 'the reflective teacher' are apt to treat the notion in a way which abstracts 'reflection' from the broader personal qualities of the teacher. Certainly, reflection involves a number of related attitudes and virtues (see, for example, Dewey, 1933, pp. 28–34). But attention needs to be focused on more wide-ranging human qualities.

The sorts of qualities needed by teachers in the task of teaching as a whole are illustrated by William Hare's discussion of the need for teachers to possess appropriate forms of humility, courage, impartiality, open-mindedness, empathy, enthusiasm, judgement and imagination (Hare, 1993). These particular qualities are not presented by Hare as exhaustive, and we can readily envisage additions to them, such as patience, self-knowledge, warmth and humour (see also John Wilson's attempt to outline 'the qualities of an educator'; Wilson, 1993, ch. 5 esp. pp. 130–42). It is important to note the respects in which teaching involves these broader aspects of personhood. Smith and Alred, for example, insist that, in relation to pupils, the teacher is one who brings his or her whole being as a person to bear (Smith and Alred, 1993, p. 106), and whose qualities are rooted in the kind of person he or she is rather than in abilities which are possessed (ibid., p. 112). This point is related to the insistence by Michael Oakeshott that certain forms of learning can only be brought about by the example of the teacher (see, for example Oakeshott, 1989, esp. 60–2).

Central to the qualities of a teacher is the form of practical wisdom or *phronesis*, discussed earlier, which contains *inter alia* a broad and rich grasp of the values of the educational enterprise. Dunne comments that practical knowledge is 'a fruit which can grow only in the soil of a person's experience and character' (Dunne, 1993, p. 358). Dunne continues: 'In exposing oneself to the kind of experience and acquiring the kind of character that will yield the requisite knowledge . . . [one] . . . is at the same time a feeling, expressing, and acting person, and one's knowledge is inseparable from one as such' (ibid., p. 358). Wilfred Carr describes *phronesis* as 'a comprehensive moral capacity which combines practical knowledge of the good with sound judgement about what, in a particular situation, would constitute an appropriate expression of this' (Carr, 1995a, p. 71). *Phronesis* is an attractive concept with respect to a number of the difficulties which emerged earlier concerning 'reflection'. It offers the prospect of a unified concept of reflection, with practical judgement playing a role in deciding the nature and extent of forms of reflection necessary for particular purposes. It also offers a context for the resolution of the questions of the adequacy of reflective judgement mentioned earlier. Practical wisdom is seen at the heart of the matter, rather than the justification of principles (of whatever kind). Further, the character of *phronesis* is such that it constitutes a fruitful concept which will enable the scope of teacher training to be extended to embrace the sorts of wider human qualities just mentioned.

The suggestion that Aristotelian *phronesis* offers a richer unifying ideal for teaching and teacher training – embracing the attractive features of 'reflection' but remedying its indeterminacy and rootlessness – is worthy of sustained attention. It is worth noting, however, some of the difficulties which the suggestion must address. The central difficulty, to use some words of Dunne is 'the complicity of *phronesis* with an established way of life' (Dunne, 1993, p. 373). *Phronesis* seems to demand established and relatively stable 'communities of practice' (Pendlebury, 1990, 1994). It might be argued that we no longer have the stable communities of educational practice that *phronesis* demands. We no longer, for example, have a stable and rooted sense of the sort of person that a teacher should be and the sort of practice that education is. Another (related) difficulty is the perception that, given the well grounded differences of view about education which are characteristic of modernity and postmodernity, *phronesis* possesses neither a sufficiently robust and sceptical form of reflection to do justice to the genuine demands of fundamental query and criticism nor the resources to defend itself against sceptical and relativist accusations that it is itself only one conception competing against others.

The tension between the demands of 'rootedness' and 'criticism' present in these difficulties are already widely acknowledged in relation to schooling, where it is resolved to some extent by acknowledging the demands of a plurality of different kinds of school, some offering education in the context of a distinctive 'community of commitment' and others in a 'common school'. One outcome of increased attention to the wider human formation for the teacher implied by Aristotelian *phronesis* may be to open up discussion of the value of a plurality of different forms of teacher training, in some of which the relevant Aristotelian 'communities of practice' can be formed and nourished.

In conclusion, it seems clear that we have no choice but to go beyond 'the reflective teacher' as a slogan. Whether we should go beyond 'the reflective teacher' as a concept, either in the Aristotelian direction I have indicated or another, is a matter deserving much future debate.

## References

Bkown, S. and McIntyre, D. (1993) *Making Sense of Teaching* (Buckingham: Open University Press).

Calderhead, J. (1989) Reflective teaching and teacher education. *Teaching and Teacher Education* 5(1): pp. 43–51.

Calderhead, J. and Gates, P. (eds.) (1993) *Conceptualizing Reflection in Teacher Development* (London: Falmer Press).

Carlgren, I., Handal, G. and Vaage, S. (eds.) (1994) *Teachers' Minds and Actions: Research on Teachers' Thinking and Practice* (London: Falmer Press).

Carr, W. (1995a) *For Education: Towards Critical Educational Inquiry* (Buckingham: Open University Press).

Carr, W. (1995b) Education and democracy: confronting the postmodernist challenge. *Journal of Philosophy of Education* 29(1): pp. 75–91.

Carr, W. and Kemmis, S. (1986) *Becoming Critical: Education, Knowledge and Action Research* (London: Falmer Press).

Dewey, J. (1993) *How We Think: A Restatement of the Relation of Reflective Thinking to the Educative Process* (New York: D. C. Heath).

Dunne, J. (1993) *Back to the Rough Ground: 'Phronesis' and 'Techne' in Modern Philosophy and in Aristotle* (Notre Dame, IN: University of Notre Dame Press).

Elliott, J. (1991) Competency-based training and the education of the professions: is a happy marriage possible?, in J. Elliott (ed.), *Action Research for Educational Change* (Milton Keynes: Open University Press).

Elliott, J. (1933) Three perspectives on coherence and continuity in teacher education, in J. Elliott (ed.),

*Reconstructing Teacher Education: Teacher Development* (London: Falmer Press).

Furlong, J. (1992) Reconstructing professionalism: ideological struggle in initial teacher education, in M. Arnot and L. Barton (eds.), *Voicing Concerns: Sociological Perspectives on Contemporary Education Reforms* (Wallingford: Triangle Books).

Furlong, J. and Maynard, T. (1995) *Mentoring Student Teachers: The Growth of Professional Knowledge* (London: Routledge).

Furlong, V. J., Hirst, P. H., Pocklington, K. and Miles, S. (1998) *Initial Teacher Training and the Role of the School* (Milton Keynes: Open University Press).

Griffiths, M. and Tann, S. (1992) Using reflective practice to link personal and public theories, *Journal of Education for Teaching*, 18(1): pp. 69–84.

Hare, W. (1993) *What Makes a Good Teacher: Reflections on Some Characteristics Central to the Educational Enterprise* (London, Ontario: The Althouse Press).

Hargreaves, D. H. (1993) A common-sense model of the professional development of teachers, in J. Elliott (ed.), *Reconstructing Teacher Education: Teacher Development* (London: Falmer Press).

Hirst, P. H. (1979) Professional studies in initial teacher education, in R. Alexander and E. Wormald (eds.), *Professional Studies for Teaching* (Guildford: Society for Research in Higher Education).

Hirst, P. H. (1983) Educational theory, in P. H. Hirst (ed.), *Educational Theory and its Foundation Disciplines* (London: Routledge & Kegan Paul).

Hirst, P. H. (1990a) The theory-practice relationship in teacher training, in: M. Booth, J. Furlong and M. Wilkin (eds.), *Partnership in Initial Teacher Training* (London: Cassell).

Hirst, P. H. (1990b) Internship: a view from outside, in P. Benton (ed.), *The Oxford Internship Scheme: Integration and Partnership in Initial Teacher Education* (London: Calouste Gulbenkian Foundation).

Hirst, P. H. (1993) Education, knowledge and practices, in R. Barrow and P. White (eds.), *Beyond Liberal Education: Essays in honour of Paul H. Hirst* (London: Routledge).

Hollis, M. (1977) The self in action, in R. S. Peters (ed.), *John Dewey Reconsidered* (London: Routledge & Kegan Paul).

Kemmis, S. (1995) Some ambiguities in Stenhouse's notion of 'the teacher as researcher': towards a new resolution, in J. Rudduck (ed.), *An Education That Empowers: A Collection of Lectures in Memory of Lawrence Stenhouse* (Clevedon: Multilingual Matters).

McIntyre, D. (1993) Theory, theorizing and reflection in initial teacher education, in J. Calderhead and P. Gates (eds.), *Conceptualizing Reflection in Teacher Development* (London: Falmer Press).

McLaughlin, T. H. (1994) Mentoring and the demands of reflection, in M. Wilkin and D. Sankey (eds.), *Collaboration and Transition in Initial Teacher Training* (London: Kogan Page).

Oakeshott, M. (1989) Learning and teaching, in T. Fuller (ed.), *The Voice of Liberal Learning: Michael Oakeshott on Education* (New Haven, CT: Yale University Press).

Pendlebury, S. (1990) Practical reasoning and situational appreciation in teaching, *Educational Theory* 40, pp. 171–9.

Pendlebury, S. (1994) Striking a balance: practical wisdom and agency stances in teaching. Paper presented to the Cambridge Branch of the Philosophy of Education Society of Great Britain.

Peters, R. S. (1997) John Dewey's philosophy of education, in R. S. Peters (ed.), *John Dewey Reconsidered* (London: Routledge & Kegan Paul).

Rudduck, J. and Hopkins, D. (eds.) (1985), *Research as a Basis for Teaching: Readings from the work of Lawrence Stenhouse* (London: Heinemann).

Russell, T. (1993) Critical attributes of a reflective teacher: is agreement possible? in J. Calderhead and P. Gates (eds.), *Conceptualizing Reflection in Teacher Development* (London: Falmer Press).

Russell, T. and Munby, H. (eds.) (1992) *Teachers and Teaching: From Classroom to Reflection* (London: Falmer Press).

Schön, D. (1983) *The Reflective Practitioner: How Professionals Think in Action* (New York: Basic Books).

Schön, D. (1987) *Educating the Reflective Practitioner* (San Francisco, CA: Jossey-Bass).

Smith, R. (1987) Teaching on stilts: a critique of classroom skills, in M. Holt (ed.), *Skills and Vocationalism: The Easy Answer* (Milton Keynes: Open University Press).

Smith, R. and Alred, G. (1993) The impersonation of wisdom, in D. McIntyre, H. Hagger and M. Wilkin (eds.), *Mentoring: Perspectives on School-Based Teacher Education* (London: Kogan Page).

Tabachnich, B. R. and Zeichner, K. (eds.) (1991) *Issues and Practices in Inquiry-Oriented Teacher Education* (London: Falmer Press).

Tiles, J. E. (1988) *Dewey* (London: Routledge).

Whitty G., Barrett, E., Barton, L., Furlong, J., Galvin, C. and Miles, S. (1992) Initial teacher education in England and Wales: a survey of current practices and concerns, *Cambridge Journal of Education*, 22(3): pp. 293–306.

Wilkin, M. (1993) Initial training as a case of postmodern development: some implications for mentoring, in: D. McIntyre, H. Hagger and M. Wilkin (eds.), *Mentoring: Perspectives on School-Based Teacher Education* (London: Kogan Page).

Wilson, J. (1993) *Reflection and Practice: Teacher education and the teaching profession* (London, Ontario: Althouse Press).

Zeichner, K. (1994) Research on teacher thinking and different views of reflective practice in teaching and teacher education, in I. Carlgren, G. Handal and S. Vaage (eds.) (1994), *Teachers' Minds and Actions: Research on Teachers' Thinking and Practice* (London: Falmer Press).

# Discipline and Care

# 39

# Social Control

## John Dewey

I have said that educational plans and projects, seeing education in terms of life-experience, are thereby committed to framing and adopting an intelligent theory or, if you please, philosophy of experience. Otherwise they are at the mercy of every intellectual breeze that happens to blow. I have tried to illustrate the need for such a theory by calling attention to two principles which are fundamental in the constitution of experience: the principles of interaction and of continuity. If, then, I am asked why I have spent so much time on expounding a rather abstract philosophy, it is because practical attempts to develop schools based upon the idea that education is found in life-experience are bound to exhibit inconsistencies and confusions unless they are guided by some conception of what experience is, and what marks off educative experience from non-educative and mis-educative experience. I now come to a group of actual educational questions the discussion of which will, I hope, provide topics and material that are more concrete than the discussion up to this point.

The two principles of continuity and interaction as criteria of the value of experience are so intimately connected that it is not easy to tell just what special educational problem to take up first. Even the convenient division into problems of subject-matter or studies and of methods of teaching and learning is likely to fail us in selection and organization of topics to discuss. Consequently, the beginning and sequence of topics is somewhat arbitrary. I shall commence, however, with the old question of individual freedom and social control and pass on to the questions that grow naturally out of it.

It is often well in considering educational problems to get a start by temporarily ignoring the school and thinking of other human situations. I take it that no one would deny that the ordinary good citizen is as a matter of fact subject to a great deal of social control and that a considerable part of this control is not felt to involve restriction of personal freedom. Even the theoretical anarchist, whose philosophy commits him to the idea that state or government control is an unmitigated evil, believes that with abolition of the political state other forms of social control would operate: indeed, his opposition to governmental regulation springs from his belief that other and to him more normal modes of control would operate with abolition of the state.

Previously published in *Experience and Education* (New York: Touchstone, 1997), pp. 51–60. © 1938 by Kappa Delta Pi. Reprinted with the kind permission of Kappa Delta Pi, International Honor Society in Education.

Without taking up this extreme position, let us note some examples of social control that operate in everyday life, and then look for the principle underlying them. Let us begin with the young people themselves. Children at recess or after school play games, from tag and one-old-cat to baseball and football. The games involve rules, and these rules order their conduct. The games do not go on haphazardly or by a succession of improvisations. Without rules there is no game. If disputes arise there is an umpire to appeal to, or discussion and a kind of arbitration are means to a decision; otherwise the game is broken up and comes to an end.

There are certain fairly obvious controlling features of such situations to which I want to call attention. The first is that the rules are a part of the game. They are not outside of it. No rules, then no game; different rules, then a different game. As long as the game goes on with a reasonable smoothness, the players do not feel that they are submitting to external imposition but that they are playing the game. In the second place an individual may at times feel that a decision isn't fair and he may even get angry. But he is not objecting to a rule but to what he claims is a violation of it, to some one-sided and unfair action. In the third place, the rules, and hence the conduct of the game, are fairly standardized. There are recognized ways of counting out, of selection of sides, as well as for positions to be taken, movements to be made, etc. These rules have the sanction of tradition and precedent. Those playing the game have seen, perhaps, professional matches and they want to emulate their elders. An element that is conventional is pretty strong. Usually, a group of youngsters change the rules by which they play only when the adult group to which they look for models have themselves made a change in the rules, while the change made by the elders is at least supposed to conduce to making the game more skillful or more interesting to spectators.

Now, the general conclusion I would draw is that control of individual actions is effected by the whole situation in which individuals are involved, in which they share and of which they are co-operative or interacting parts. For even in a competitive game there is a certain kind of participation, of sharing in a common experience. Stated the other way around, those who take part do not feel that they are bossed by an individual person or are being subjected to the will of some outside superior person. When violent disputes do arise, it is usually on the alleged ground that the umpire or some person on the other side is being unfair; in other words, that in such cases some individual is trying to impose his individual will on someone else.

It may seem to be putting too heavy a load upon a single case to argue that this instance illustrates the general principle of social control of individuals without the violation of freedom. But if the matter were followed out through a number of cases, I think the conclusion that this particular instance does illustrate a general principle would be justified. Games are generally competitive. If we took instances of co-operative activities in which all members of a group take part, as for example in well-ordered family life in which there is mutual confidence, the point would be even clearer. In all such cases it is not the will or desire of any one person which establishes order but the moving spirit of the whole group. The control is social, but individuals are parts of a community, not outside of it.

I do not mean by this that there are no occasions upon which the authority of, say, the parent does not have to intervene and exercise fairly direct control. But I do say that, in the first place, the number of these occasions is slight in comparison with the number of those in which the control is exercised by situations in which all take part. And what is even more important, the authority in question when exercised in a well-regulated household or other community group is not a manifestation of merely personal will; the parent or teacher exercises it as the representative and agent of the interests of the group as a whole. With respect to the first point, in a well-ordered school the main reliance for control of this and that individual is upon the activities carried on and upon the situations in which these activities are maintained. The teacher reduces to a minimum the occasions in which he or she has to exercise authority in a personal way. When it is necessary, in the second place, to speak and act firmly, it is done in behalf of the interest of the group, not as an exhibition of personal power. This makes the difference between action which is arbitrary and that which is just and fair.

Moreover, it is not necessary that the difference should be formulated in words, by either teacher or the young, in order to be felt in experience. The number of children who do not feel the difference (even if they cannot articulate it and reduce it to an intellectual principle) between action that is motivated by personal power and desire to dictate and action that is fair, because in the interest of all, is small. I should even be willing to say that upon the whole children are more sensitive to the signs and symptoms of this difference than are adults. Children learn the difference when playing with one another. They are willing, often too willing if anything, to take suggestions from one child and let him be a leader if his conduct adds to the experienced value of what they are doing, while they resent the attempt at dictation. Then they often withdraw and when asked why, say that it is because so-and-so "is too bossy."

I do not wish to refer to the traditional school in ways which set up a caricature in lieu of a picture. But I think it is fair to say that one reason the personal commands of the teacher so often played an undue role and a reason why the order which existed was so much a matter of sheer obedience to the will of an adult was because the situation almost forced it upon the teacher. The school was not a group or community held together by participation in common activities. Consequently, the normal, proper conditions of control were lacking. Their absence was made up for, and to a considerable extent had to be made up for, by the direct intervention of the teacher, who, as the saying went, "*kept* order." He kept it because order was in the teacher's keeping, instead of residing in the shared work being done.

The conclusion is that in what are called the new schools, the primary source of social control resides in the very nature of the work done as a social enterprise in which all individuals have an opportunity to contribute and to which all feel a responsibility. Most children are naturally "sociable." Isolation is even more irksome to them than to adults. A genuine community life has its ground in this natural sociability. But community life does not organize itself in an enduring way purely spontaneously. It requires thought and planning ahead. The educator is responsible for a knowledge of individuals and for a knowledge of subject-matter that will enable activities to be selected which lend themselves to social organization, an organization in which all individuals have an opportunity to contribute something, and in which the activities in which all participate are the chief carrier of control.

I am not romantic enough about the young to suppose that every pupil will respond or that any child of normally strong impulses will respond on every occasion. There are likely to be some who, when they come to school, are already victims of injurious conditions outside of the school and who have become so passive and unduly docile that they fail to contribute. There will be others who, because of previous experience, are bumptious and unruly and perhaps downright rebellious. But it is certain that the general principle of social control cannot be predicated upon such cases. It is also true that no general rule can be laid down for dealing with such cases. The teacher has to deal with them individually. They fall into general classes, but no two are exactly alike. The educator has to discover as best he or she can the causes for the recalcitrant attitudes. He or she cannot, if the educational process is to go on, make it a question of pitting one will against another in order to see which is strongest, nor yet allow the unruly and non-participating pupils to stand permanently in the way of the educative activities of others. Exclusion perhaps is the only available measure at a given juncture, but it is no solution. For it may strengthen the very causes which have brought about the undesirable anti-social attitude, such as desire for attention or to show off.

Exceptions rarely prove a rule or give a clue to what the rule should be. I would not, therefore, attach too much importance to these exceptional cases, although it is true at present that progressive schools are likely often to have more than their fair share of these cases, since parents may send children to such schools as a last resort. I do not think weakness in control when it is found in progressive schools arises in any event from these exceptional cases. It is much more likely to arise from failure to arrange in advance for the kind of work (by which I mean all kinds of activities engaged in) which will create situations that of themselves tend to exercise control over what this, that, and the other pupil does and how he does it. This failure most often goes back to lack of sufficiently thoughtful planning in advance. The causes for such lack are varied. The one which is peculiarly important to mention in this connection is the idea that such advance planning is unnecessary and even that it is inherently hostile to the legitimate freedom of those being instructed.

Now, of course, it is quite possible to have preparatory planning by the teacher done in such a rigid and intellectually inflexible fashion that it does result in adult imposition, which is none the less external because executed with tact and the semblance of respect for individual freedom. But this kind of planning does not follow inherently from the principle involved. I do not know what the greater maturity of the teacher and the teacher's greater knowledge of the world, of subject-matters and of individuals, is for unless the teacher can arrange conditions that are conducive to community activity and to organization which exercises control over individual impulses by the mere fact that all are engaged in communal projects. Because the kind of advance planning heretofore engaged in has been so routine as to leave little room for the free play of individual thinking or for contributions due to distinctive individual experience, it does not follow that all planning must be rejected. On the contrary, there is incumbent upon the educator the duty of instituting a much more intelligent, and consequently more difficult, kind of planning. He must survey the capacities and needs of the particular set of individuals with whom he is dealing and must at the same time arrange the conditions which provide the subject-matter or content for experiences that satisfy these needs and develop these capacities. The planning must be flexible enough to permit free play for individuality of experience and yet firm enough to give direction towards continuous development of power.

The present occasion is a suitable one to say something about the province and office of the teacher. The principle that development of experience comes about through interaction means that education is essentially a social process. This quality is realized in the degree in which individuals form a community group. It is absurd to exclude the teacher from membership in the group. As the most mature member of the group he has a peculiar responsibility for the conduct of the interactions and intercommunications which are the very life of the group as a community. That children are individuals whose freedom should be respected while the more mature person should have no freedom as an individual is an idea too absurd to require refutation. The tendency to exclude the teacher from a positive and leading share in the direction of the activities of the community of which he is a member is another instance of reaction from one extreme to another. When pupils were a class rather than a social group, the teacher necessarily acted largely from the outside, not as a director of processes of exchange in which all had a share. When education is based upon experience and educative experience is seen to be a social process, the situation changes radically. The teacher loses the position of external boss or dictator but takes on that of leader of group activities.

In discussing the conduct of games as an example of normal social control, reference was made to the presence of a standardized conventional factor. The counterpart of this factor in school life is found in the question of manners, especially of good manners in the manifestations of politeness and courtesy. The more we know about customs in different parts of the world at different times in the history of mankind, the more we learn how much manners differ from place to place and time to time. This fact proves that there is a large conventional factor involved. But there is no group at any time or place which does not have some code of manners as, for example, with respect to proper ways of greeting other persons. The particular form a convention takes has nothing fixed and absolute about it. But the existence of some form of convention is not itself a convention. It is a uniform attendant of all social relationships. At the very least, it is the oil which prevents or reduces friction.

It is possible, of course, for these social forms to become, as we say, "mere formalities." They may become merely outward show with no meaning behind them. But the avoidance of empty ritualistic forms of social intercourse does not mean the rejection of every formal element. It rather indicates the need for development of forms of intercourse that are inherently appropriate to social situations. Visitors to some progressive schools are shocked by the lack of manners they come across. One who knows the situation better is aware that to some extent their absence is due to the eager interest of children to go on with what they are doing. In their eagerness they may, for example, bump into each other and into visitors with no word of apology. One might say that this condition is better than a display of merely external punctilio accompanying intellectual and emotional lack of interest in school work. But it also represents a failure in education, a failure to learn one of the most important lessons of life, that of mutual accommodation and adaptation. Education is going on in a one-sided way, for attitudes and habits are in process of formation that stand in the way of the future learning that springs from easy and ready contact and communication with others.

# 40

# The One-Caring as Teacher

## Nel Noddings

Whatever I do in life, whomever I meet, I am first and always one-caring or one cared-for. I do not "assume roles" unless I become an actor. "Mother" is not a role; "teacher" is not a role.[1] When I became a mother, I entered a very special relation – possibly the prototypical caring relation. When I became a teacher, I also entered a very special – and more specialized – caring relation. No enterprise or special function I am called upon to serve can relieve me of my responsibilities as one-caring. Indeed, if an enterprise precludes my meeting the other in a caring relation, I must refuse to participate in that enterprise. Now, of course, an enterprise by its very nature may require me to care for a problem or set of problems. If I am a bus driver, or airline pilot, or air traffic controller, or surgeon, I may properly "care" for the problems and tasks presented. My major responsibilities focus on the other as physical entity and not as whole person. Indeed, as traffic controller, I do not even meet the other whose safety I am employed to protect. In such enterprises I behave responsibly toward others through proficient practice of my craft. But, even in such enterprises, when encounter occurs, I must meet the other as one-caring. It is encounter that is reduced and not my obligation to care. Clearly, in professions where encounter is frequent and where the ethical ideal of the other is necessarily involved, I am first and foremost one-caring and, second, enactor of specialized functions. As teacher, I am, first, one-caring.

The one-caring is engrossed in the cared-for and undergoes a motivational displacement toward the projects of the cared-for. This does not, as we have seen, imply romantic love or the sort of pervasive and compulsive "thinking of the other" that characterizes infatuation. It means, rather, that one-caring receives the other, for the interval of caring, completely and nonselectively. She is present to the other and places her motive power in his service. Now, of course, she does not abandon her own ethical ideal in doing this, but she starts from a position of respect or regard for the projects of the other. In the language of Martin Buber, the cared-for is encountered as "Thou," a subject, and not as "It," an object of analysis. During the encounter, which may be singular and brief or recurrent and prolonged, the cared-for "is Thou and fills the firmament."

Previously published in *Caring: A Feminine Approach to Ethics and Moral Education* (Berkeley, CA: University of California Press, 1984), pp. 175–82, 210–11. © 2003 The Regents of the University of California. Permission via Copyright Clearance Center.

When a teacher asks a question in class and a student responds, she receives not just the "response" but the student. What he says matters, whether it is right or wrong, and she probes gently for clarification, interpretation, contribution. She is not seeking the answer but the involvement of the cared-for. For the brief interval of dialogue that grows around the question, the cared-for indeed "fills the firmament." The student is infinitely more important than the subject matter.

The one-caring as teacher is not necessarily permissive. She does not abstain, as Neill might have, from leading the student, or persuading him, or coaxing him toward an examination of school subjects. But she recognizes that, in the long run, he will learn what he pleases. We may force him to respond in specified ways, but what he will make his own and eventually apply effectively is that which he finds significant for his own life. This recognition does not reduce either the teacher's power or her responsibility. As we saw in our earlier discussion of the cared-for, the teacher may indeed coerce the student into choosing against himself. He may be led to diminish his ethical ideal in the pursuit of achievement goals. The teacher's power is, thus, awesome. It is she who presents the "effective world" to the student.[2] In doing this, she realizes that the student, as ethical agent, will make his own selection from the presented possibilities and so, in a very important sense, she is prepared to put her motive energy in the service of his projects. She has already had a hand in selecting those projects and will continue to guide and inform them, but the objectives themselves must be embraced by the student.

Buber suggests that the role of the teacher is just this: to influence. He says:

> For if the educator of our day has to act consciously he must nevertheless do it "as though he did not." That raising of the finger, that questioning glance, are his genuine doing. Through him the selection of the effective world reaches the pupil. He fails the recipient when he presents this selection to him with a gesture of interference. It must be concentrated in him; and doing out of concentration has the appearance of rest. Interference divides the soul in his care into an obedient part and a rebellious part. But a hidden influence proceeding from his integrity has an integrating force.[3]

When, out of intrinsic interest or trust and admiration for the teacher, the student does embrace an objective, he may need help in attaining it. The teacher, as one-caring, meets the student directly but not equally. Buber says that the teacher is capable of "inclusion," and this term seems to describe accurately what the one-caring does in trying to teach the cared-for. Milton Mayeroff, for example, in his discussion of caring, emphasizes this duality in the one-caring:[4] the "feeling with" that leads the one-caring to act as though for herself, but in the projects of the other and the accompanying realization that this other is independent, a subject. In "inclusion," the teacher receives the student and becomes in effect a duality. This sounds mystical, but it is not. The teacher receives and accepts the student's feeling toward the subject matter; she looks at it and listens to it through his eyes and ears. How else can she interpret the subject matter for him? As she exercises this inclusion, she accepts *his* motives, reaches toward what *he* intends, so long as these motives and intentions do not force an abandonment of her own ethic. Inclusion as practiced by the teacher is a vital gift. As we saw earlier, the student's attempts at inclusion may result in a deterioration of the learning process.

The special gift of the teacher, then, is to receive the student, to look at the subject matter with him. Her commitment is to him, the cared-for, and he is – through that commitment – set free to pursue his legitimate projects.

Again I want to emphasize that this view is not romantic but practical. The teacher works with the student. He becomes her apprentice and gradually assumes greater responsibility in the tasks they undertake. This working together, which produces both joy in the relation and increasing competence in the cared-for, was advocated, we may recall, by Urie Bronfenbrenner in his discussion of cooperative engagement in tasks, and it was also implied by Robert White's discussion of competence as the desired end of "effectance motivation." The child wants to attain competence in his own world of experience. He needs the cooperative guidance of a fully caring adult to accomplish this. The one-caring as teacher, then, has two major tasks: to stretch the student's world by presenting an effective selection of that world with which she is in contact, and to work cooperatively with the student in his struggle toward competence in that world. But her task as one-caring has higher priority than either of these. First and foremost, she must nurture the student's ethical ideal.

The teacher bears a special responsibility for the enhancement of the ethical ideal. She is often in contact with the ideal as it is being initially constructed and, even with the adult student, she has unique power in contributing to its enhancement or destruction. In dialogue, she can underscore his subjectness – encourage him to stand personally related to what he says and does. He is not just part of the lesson, a response to be recorded as "move 15" or whatever. He is a human being responsible for his words and acts, and the one-caring as teacher meets him thus. Why he thinks what he thinks is as important as what. The domain to which he refers for justification is significant. How he relates to others as he does all this is important.

Besides engaging the student in dialogue, the teacher also provides a model. To support her students as ones-caring, she must show them herself as one-caring. Hence she is not content to enforce rules – and may even refuse occasionally to do so – but she continually refers the rules to their ground in caring. If she confronts a student who is cheating, she may begin by saying, *I know you want to do well*, or, *I know you want to help your friend.* She begins by attributing the best possible motive to him, and she then proceeds to explain – fully, with many of her own reservations expressed freely – why she cannot allow him to cheat. She does not need to resort to punishment, because the rules are not sacred to her. What matters is the student, the cared-for, and how he will approach ethical problems as a result of his relation to her. Will he refer his ethical decisions to an ethic of caring or to rules and the likelihood of apprehension and punishment? Will he ask what his act means in terms of the feelings, needs, and projects of others, or will he be content with a catalog of rules-of-the-game?

A teacher cannot "talk" this ethic. She must live it, and that implies establishing a relation with the student. Besides talking to him and showing him how one cares, she engages in cooperative practice with him. He is learning not just mathematics or social studies; he is also learning how to be one-caring. By conducting education morally, the teacher hopes to induce an enhanced moral sense in the student. This view was held, also, by John Dewey. Sidney Hook describes the relation in Dewey's thinking:

> How, then, does Dewey achieve the transition from what we have called the morality of the task to the task of morality? His answer – original for his time and still largely disregarded – is to teach *all* subjects in such a way as to bring out and make focal their social and personal aspects, stressing how human beings are affected by them, pointing up the responsibilities that flow from their inter-relatedness.[5]

Everything we do, then, as teachers, has moral overtones. Through dialogue, modeling, the provision of practice, and the attribution of best motive, the one-caring as teacher nurtures the ethical ideal. She cannot nurture the student intellectually without regard for the ethical ideal unless she is willing to risk producing a monster, and she cannot nurture the ethical ideal without considering the whole self-image of which it is a part. For how he feels about himself in general – as student, as physical being, as friend – contributes to the enhancement or diminution of the ethical ideal. What the teacher reflects to him continually is the best possible picture consonant with reality. She does not reflect fantasy nor conjure up "expectations" as strategies. She meets him as he is and finds something admirable and, as a result, he may find the strength to become even more admirable. He is confirmed.

The sort of relatedness and caring I have been discussing is often dismissed as impossible because of constraints of number, time, and purpose. Richard Hult, in his discussion of "pedagogical caring," notes that such requirements seem to require in turn close personal relationships of the I-Thou sort. He says: "While these may sometimes occur and may be desirable, most pedagogical contexts make such relationships implausible if not undesirable."[6] He concludes that caring as Mayeroff has described it, and as I have described it, "cannot be the kind of caring demanded of teachers." I insist that it is exactly the kind of caring ideally required of teachers.

I think that Hult and others who take this position misunderstand the requirement that Buber has described as an I-Thou encounter; that Marcel has described in terms of "disposability"; that Mayeroff has described as identification-with-recognition-of-independence; that I have described as engrossment and displacement of motivation. I do not need to establish a deep, lasting, time-consuming personal relationship with every student. What I must do is to be totally and nonselectively present to the student – to each student – as he addresses me. The time interval may be brief but the encounter is total.

Further, there are ways to extend contact so that deeper relationships may develop. If I know how my student typically reacts to certain topics and tasks, I am in a better position to guide him both sensitively and economically. Why can we not opt for smaller schools, for teachers and students working together for three years rather than one, for teachers teaching more than one subject? We are limited in our thinking by too great a deference to what is, and what is today is not very attractive. Our alternative is to change the structure of schools and teaching so that caring can flourish, and the hope is that by doing this we may attain both a higher level of cognitive achievement and a more caring, ethical society.

When we begin our educational planning, we may start with schools as they are, identify their primary functions, and ask how they may best be organized to serve their functions. Or we may start with our picture of caring and education and ask what sort of organization might be compatible with this picture. When James Conant made his influential recommendations concerning the organization of secondary education,[7] he began with the intellectual function of schools and, assuming a national need for high-powered curricula in mathematics and science, suggested that larger schools were required to support such programs. I have begun by identifying the maintenance and enhancement of the ethical ideal as the primary function of any educational community, and so I shall be interested first not in the establishment of programs but in the establishment and evaluation of chains and circles of caring. To establish such chains and circles, we may need to consider smaller schools.

I shall say more about how schools might be organized to support caring and, in particular, we should discuss, in the context of teaching, dialogue, practice, and confirmation. We should remind ourselves, before we leave this initial discussion on the one-caring as teacher, that there is another in the caring relation. The student also contributes to caring. The one form of mutuality that is excluded from the teacher-student relation is an attempt at inclusion on the part of the student. A focus of student attention on the teacher's instructional strategies is fatal to the relationship – and to the student's learning. The student may, however, care for the teacher as a person. He may be fascinated by her and hold her in the highest regard. He may be willing to help her with physical tasks and, indeed, to assist her in teaching other students. Nothing in our discussion was meant to preclude the possibility of the student's caring but, within the teacher-student relation, his caring is different from that of the teacher.

The student has his greatest effect on the relationship as the one cared-for. If he perceives the teacher's caring and responds to it, he is giving the teacher what she needs most to continue to care. As the infant rewards his caring mother with smiles and wriggles, the student rewards his teacher with responsiveness: with questions, effort, comment, and cooperation. There is some initiative required of the cared-for. Just as the one-caring is free to accept or reject the internal "I must" of caring, so the cared-for is free to accept or reject the attitude of caring when he perceives it. If the cared-for perceives the attitude and denies it, then he is in an internal state of untruth.

Many of our schools are in what might be called a crisis of caring. Both students and teachers are brutally attacked verbally and physically. Clearly, the schools are not often places where caring is fulfilled, but it is not always the failure of teachers that causes the lapse in caring. Many urban teachers are suffering symptoms of battle fatigue and "burn-out." No matter what they do, it seems, their efforts are not perceived as caring. They themselves are perceived, instead, as the enemy, as natural targets for resistance.

The cared-for is essential to the relation. What the cared-for contributes to the relation is a responsiveness that completes the caring. This responsiveness need not take the form of gratitude or even of direct acknowledgment. Rather, the cared-for shows either in direct response to the one-caring or in spontaneous delight and happy growth before her eyes that the caring has been received. The caring is completed when the cared-for receives the caring. He may respond by free, vigorous, and happy immersion in his own projects (toward which the one-caring has directed her own energy also), and the one-caring, seeing this, knows that the relation has been completed in the cared-for.

We see another cogent reason for insisting on relation and caring in teaching. Where is the teacher to get the strength to go on giving except from the student? In situations where the student rarely responds, is negative, denies the effort at caring, the teacher's caring quite predictably deteriorates to "cares and burdens." She becomes the needy target of her own caring. In such cases, we should supply special support to maintain the teacher as one-caring. Communities are just barely awakened to this need. But no indirect caring can fully compensate for the natural reward of teaching. This is always found in the responsiveness of the student.

What am I recommending? That students should be more responsive to their teachers? Can we command them to respond? This approach seems wrong, although parents might reasonably talk to their children about the difficulties of teaching and ways in which students can support and encourage their teachers simply by exhibiting a spontaneous enthusiasm for their own growth. But, realistically, such a recommendation seems unlikely to be productive. What I am recommending is that schools and teaching be redesigned so that caring has a chance to be initiated in the one-caring and completed in the cared-for. Sacrifices in economies of scale and even in programs might be called for. These would be minor if we could unlock our doors and disarm our security guards. Schools as institutions cannot care directly. A school cannot be engrossed in anyone or anything. But a school can be deliberately designed to support caring and caring individuals, and this is what an ethic of caring suggests should be done.

## Notes

1. For the opposite view, see Jessie Bernard, *The Future of Motherhood* (New York: Penguin Books, 1974).
2. Martin Buber discusses the teacher's "selection of the effective world" in "Education," in *Between Man and Man* (New York: Macmillan, 1965), pp. 83–103.
3. Ibid., p. 90.
4. Milton Mayeroff, *On Caring* (New York: Harper and Row, 1971), pp. 3, 5, 10, and passim.
5. Sidney Hook, Preface to John Dewey, *Moral Principles in Education* (Carbondale: Southern Illinois University Press, 1975), p. xi.
6. Richard E. Hult, Jr., "On Pedagogical Caring," *Educational Theory* (1979), p. 239.
7. See James B. Conant, *The American High School Today* (New York: McGraw-Hill, 1959); also, *The Comprehensive High School* (New York: McGraw-Hill, 1967).

# 41

# School Sexual Harassment Policies: The Need for Both Justice and Care

## Elizabeth Chamberlain and Barbara Houston

*Sexual harassment in school is the worst. . . .*
*As a girl you can't be accepted unless you*
*wear big clothes. Then it's like, "Oh, a girl," not*
*like, "Oh, a body."*

(Orenstein, 1994, p. 262)

We are all familiar with the fact, if only from our own experience, that a certain level of sexual teasing happens in school. But we may not be aware that it characterizes the daily lives of some students. We may not know the extent of sexual bullying and humiliation that occurs, nor the serious harm associated with it.

There is now ample evidence that student-to-student harassment exists, and that it adversely affects students educationally, socially, and emotionally (Larkin, 1994; Sherer, 1994; Shoop and Edwards, 1994; Stein and Sjostrom, 1994; J. Strauss, 1993; S. Strauss, 1992). In 1993, the American Association of University Women (AAUW) sponsored a large-scale survey of students in grades 8 to 11 in which 85 percent of the girls and 76 percent of the boys reported having been sexually harassed at school, with most students reporting the first

instance of sexual harassment having happened between grades 6 and 9. In this same survey girls overwhelmingly reported that they subsequently experienced serious consequences from being sexually harassed, including a reluctance to attend school, more frequent absences, a decision to remain silent in classes, difficulty in paying attention, studying, or working on projects at school, and a change of educational plans and vocational aspirations to avoid other likely occasions of harassment (AAUW, 1993).

The law has addressed sexual harassment both in the workplace and in schools. Legally oriented policies which define and prohibit sexual harassment are in place in public schools. Still, student-to-student sexual harassment remains ubiquitous (Shoop and Edwards, 1994; Stein and Sjostrom, 1994; Streitmatter, 1994). The policies seem not to work. Girls do not use them and do not trust them (Stein, 1993; S. Strauss, 1992). The question is why?

It is our view that the policies do not work because schools treat sexual harassment as a legal issue rather than as an educational issue which has

Previously published in Michael Katz, Nel Noddings, and Kenneth A. Strike (eds.), *Justice and Caring: The Search for Common Ground in Education* (New York: Teachers College Press, 1999), pp. 146–66. © 1999 by Teachers College, Columbia University. All rights reserved. Reprinted with permission of the publisher.

legal components. Court cases have been useful in making schools aware of student-to-student sexual harassment, but they have also led schools to frame the problem almost exclusively as a legal issue, to be handled bureaucratically, not as an educational issue that demands pedagogical attention.

In this chapter we briefly trace the development of legally oriented school sexual harassment policies and note their shortcomings. We call the school policies on sexual harassment legally oriented because they reflect case law, they use legal terms and definitions in their formulation, and the primary impetus for writing the policies has often been to avoid legal liability. Such policies are thought to operationalize justice in the school setting by focusing on rights and procedures. They grant students both the power to name sexual harassment as a wrong, and the right to claim redress. We contend that such an approach, while helpful, is by itself inadequate. We argue that an effective student-to-student sexual harassment policy must acknowledge the developmental level of students to whom the policy applies; the complex social system in which students function; the local cultural norms which tend to override the legal dictates; and the unequal social standing among students. We go on to develop the view that policies more appropriate to schools which aim to provide a framework for education and growth, and not merely for restriction and punitive controls, will require a deliberate education oriented meshing of a justice/rights framework with that of the ethics of care.

For several reasons we focus our discussion on male-to-female student harassment in public coeducational middle schools. (Although we have chosen to use the terms *middle school* and *middle school students*, we mean to include all those who might be called "middle level students," i.e., students who attend either or both middle school and junior high school.) First, a lot of student-to-student sexual harassment happens in these venues. The middle school is the site of the marked escalation of sexual harassment within the public educational system (Stein, 1993). Second, along with other researchers and educators, we are concerned with an array of "symptoms" that show up among early adolescent women: a silencing of their voices (Gilligan, Lyons, and Hammer, 1990), a drop in self-esteem (AAUW, 1993; Orenstein, 1994), a loss of academic achievement, and a diminished sense of personal direction (AAUW, 1993; Fine, 1993), along with the onslaught of problems such as eating disorders,

depression, and self-mutilation (Pipher, 1994). These are precisely the reactions female adolescents report as their response to their experiences of chronic pervasive sexual harassment, especially in middle school settings (Larkin, 1994; Stein and Sjostrom, 1994; S. Strauss, 1992). Our third reason for focusing on the middle school is that we have an obvious ethical responsibility to serve as models, protectors, guides, and advisors to these students, and they have ethical potential to make use of that guidance. Students at this age are for the most part open to ethical reflection about sexual harassment and still anticipate that adults will provide boundaries and guidelines for them. In order to satisfy that responsibility, however, we need to be sure which policies will best express our values.

Two preliminary observations: first, it is common to call student-to-student sexual harassment "peer harassment," but for reasons which will become evident later, we find the latter term misleading and prefer the former. Second, it seems to us that the voices and stories of students are most effective in illuminating the situations students experience. Consequently, we use examples drawn from published ethnographies as well as representative composites from contributor Elizabeth Chamberlain's 20 years of experience in middle schools.

## The Law and School Sexual Harassment Policies

There is no doubt that the legal recognition and definition of sexual harassment has been the impetus for educators to grapple with the phenomena in public school settings. Explicit legal procedures and clarification of key terms have raised the awareness of both students and staff to the seriousness of the matter.

In response to legal developments, various manuals, guides, and publications have been written, designed to assist school administrators and faculty in formulating policies which will be legally viable. The definition of sexual harassment typically echoes the languages and policies established in adult workplaces. For example, one current student handbook version reads:

> Sexual harassment means unwanted sexual advances, requests for sexual favors, and other inappropriate verbal, written, or physical conduct of a sexual nature. Such behavior can interfere with performance and can

create an intimidating or offensive environment. Some examples of sexual harassment include: subtle pressure for sexual activity; unwelcome touching or other physical contact (inappropriate intimacy, grabbing/touching/shoving/groping/rubbing-up-against/cornering); spreading sexual rumors, including graffiti; sexist remarks about an individual's clothing, ability, body, or sexual activity; teasing about bodily functions, stage of physical development, or one's sex in general; gestures, jokes, pictures, leers. (Oyster River Cooperative School District Policy, 1994, p. 6)

These legally oriented school policies make a strong positive contribution to the mitigation of sexual harassment in two important ways. First, by naming, providing definitions, and making legally actionable many insidious behaviors which have hitherto been discomforting, embarrassing, and offensive, yet not legally identifiable, they give validation and importance to the perceptions of those who have endured such behaviors and they make available a sanctioned platform from which to discuss them. Second, legally oriented policies have made it clear that the power to determine that an action is discomforting or unwanted rests with the one receiving the action, regardless of the actor's tacit or stated intentions. For vulnerable persons, this is a significant shift in determining who controls access to one's person. Regardless of whether the objectionable action is a verbal comment, a gesture, a look, or a touch, the receiver of the action determines its acceptability.

Most significant, the legal characterization of sexual harassment confers rights on those targeted in sexual harassment: the right to define and defend one's own personal space, the right to limit access to one's body and clothing, the right to proclaim one's feelings of violation, and the right to defend one's reputation against sexual rumors or graffiti – in short, the right to be treated with respect, not as a sexual object.

Obviously, legally oriented policies are not insignificant. As Catharine MacKinnon (1987) observes, "The law is not everything – but it is not nothing, either" (p. 116). Useful as it is to see legally oriented sexual harassment policies as rights granting, it is important to avoid two implausible reductionistic tendencies – to equate legal policy with justice, and to interpret justice solely in terms of the assertion and reinforcement of rights. It would be a mistake to reject or undervalue legally oriented policies; it would, however, also be a mistake to think that such policies are enough. In our view they are from an educational perspective insufficient, and from an ethical perspective unsatisfactory.

## The Shortcomings of Legally Oriented Policies

While legally oriented sexual harassment policies may conceivably protect a school district from liability, there is little if any evidence that such policies prevent or even interrupt the incidence of student-to-student sexual harassment in public schools. In fact, reports indicate not only that has student-to-student harassment continued unabated, but that students distrust the policies and are reluctant to use them (J. Strauss, 1993; Stein, 1993). This leads us to ask exactly why these policies fail to alter the patterns of sexual harassment in middle schools. What prevents girls from accessing the procedures that are in place to empower them to both name the offense and claim their rights?

One serious substantive shortcoming of the policies, from our point of view, is the mismatch between the legal categories of sexual harassment and its occurrence in the middle school milieu. Two specific problems emerge when the legal categories of sexual harassment defined by the court, either "quid pro quo" or "hostile environment," are employed in sexual harassment policies for middle schools. First, the categories fail to cover what, from an educational point of view, we would regard as significant harm; and second, this dichotomous characterization of sexual harassment leaves student-to-student harassment covered by the more ambiguous category, "hostile environment." The latter category is confusing for administrators, teachers, and students, and it also requires too high a threshold of harm before intervention is warranted.

Of the two forms of sexual harassment the law recognizes, "quid pro quo" and "hostile environment," the former means literally "something for something." It applies only in instances where one person is in a formally recognized position of power or authority over another and (1) uses that position to exert pressure for sexual favors or (2) engages in sexual conversations, gestures, or comments to someone who has formally less authority, or alternatively, (3) retaliates for the latter's refusal of sexual advances. While it would appear that this category might adequately cover teacher-to-student sexual harassment, there are only certain losses the court recognizes – for example, diminishment of a grade, or poor letters of reference. It will not cover such losses as lowering of self-esteem, or diminishment of comfort level, social status, or emotional well-being which the receiver of sexual harassment may experience and which, from an educational point of view, can be potentially devastating and cause developmental harms.

The court's dichotomous characterization of sexual harassment means that by default all student-to-student harassment falls into the "hostile environment" category because students are considered peers (i.e., of equal formal standing within the school). However, as Shoop and Edwards (1994) point out, the determination of "hostile environment" is confusing for educators because the behavior can occur over a period of time and include a large variety of incidents and possibly a large number of actors. In cases of "hostile environment," a plethora of comments, activities, insinuations, and practice may combine to create a general atmosphere which does not respect females as a gender, yet no one specific actor is easily seen to be accountable for the continuation or creation of that "hostile environment." And it may not be clear to any of the actors or officials that such behavior exceeds the norm and alters conditions to the point where they can be deemed "hostile." Thus this category too fails to cover straightforwardly behavior that makes students feel insulted or uneasy (and causing them to report, "I never go down that hallway" or "I don't eat lunch at noon because they're there" or "I won't take classes if he's going to be in them").

We suggest that the legal categories and legally oriented policies are too blunt to be the sole or primary instrument used to deal with student-to-student harassment in educational settings. In particular, with student-to-student harassment, when the legal template is applied, too much of what we need to attend to falls outside its jurisdiction. And unfortunately, once a school has a legally oriented policy in place, the tendency is to think that only behavior which clearly satisfies the standard of proof required by law is worthy of educators' attention.

But the far more serious difficulty with the current legally oriented approach is the assumption of school policy makers that information about its illegality and the available enforcement of rights are sufficient to reduce the incidence of sexual harassment.

The alarming and disheartening finding is that these policies do very little to reduce student-to-student sexual harassment because (1) administrators, teachers, and students do not recognize student-to-student sexual harassment when it occurs (i.e., they can't name it as such); and (2) even when they do recognize it, research tells us that many who suffer it are reluctant to claim redress (Larkin, 1994; Mann, 1994; Stein and Sjostrom, 1994; J. Strauss, 1993).

Rather than blaming administrators for their ineptness in applying the policy or students for their hesitancy to use the policy and their mistrust of it, we think we can get further by investigating the assumptions of those who are content to rely solely on legally oriented policies. In particular, we need to examine two assumptions: (1) the Reconfiguration Presupposition – the assumption that students and staff will have no difficulty in naming "normal" patterns of behavior as inappropriate, wrong, or illegal; and (2) the Equality Presumption – that all student actors, male or female, have equal standing within social relationships (i.e., that all students have both the agency to act in their own behalf and community permission to do so). Sadly, both presumptions are highly questionable in middle school settings.

### The Reconfiguration Presupposition: Naming the Offense

The assumption that legal definitions and lists of examples of forbidden behaviors are sufficient to allow staff and students to identify and eliminate sexual harassment in their schools takes for granted that there is a cultural consensus on naming what is "sexual," "offensive," and "unwelcome." But when we are dealing with sexual harassment among early adolescents in a middle school setting, the single most significant obstacle remarked on repeatedly by researchers is the difficulty staff and students have in distinguishing offensive behaviors such as those covered by sexual harassment policies from "normal heterosexual behavior" (Larkin, 1994; Shoop and Edwards, 1994; Stein and Sjostrom, 1994; J. Strauss, 1993).

The behaviors addressed by sexual harassment policies are inseparable from the entire web of social customs and enculturated beliefs which define us as male and female. Much of the behavior which policies make "illegal" and wrong is often seen as normalized heterosexual behavior in the eyes of students and staff.

Middle school students and their teachers and parents are immersed in a larger culture in which sexual innuendo and sexualized comments are embedded in nearly all forms of media. Advertisements, television programs, music, video games, and even T-shirts present sexual images and messages in direct opposition to attitudes of mutual regard and respect between genders.

Socially insecure and with limited repertoires of behavior to use during courtship rituals of adolescence, both boys and girls may resort to crude or inept attempts to gain the attention of one another. Donna Eder (1995) in her ethnographic study of middle schools records numerous conversations between groups of girls and boys where the agenda was for a girl and a boy to establish that they are interested in "going with" one another. (It is a peculiar norm that such conversations among middle-level students generally do take place in groups, not individually.) Eder records examples of such group conversations disintegrating from awkward to vulgar in a matter of minutes.

Another source of confusion for many middle school students is the tendency to rely on an intention analysis when assessing one's own behavior, a practice not unknown to adults. In instances of sexually harassing behavior, people are apt to define or categorize their own behavior in terms of intention rather than the content or the consequences of the behavior. In daily social interactions intent does matter. One reacts differently to an inadvertent contact in a crowded elevator than to a purposeful shove. Yet a person's intent is difficult to document and not always relevant. In cases of sexual harassment, the intention of "being funny" or "having fun" on the part of the offender does not prevent a comment or action from being received as hurtful, offensive, intrusive, intimidating, or assaultive.

Individual interpretations influenced in large part by the surrounding cultural practices may vary greatly from the explicit legal definitions of proscribed behaviors which appear on a list in a policy statement. And the cultural normalization may be so widely accepted that no one within the cultural setting will be inclined to question or challenge local interpretation. To illustrate this point we offer the following example.

Bra snapping appears on nearly every list of prohibited behaviors in published sexual harassment policies, yet it remains nearly ubiquitous in middle school settings (AAUW, 1993; Stein, 1993; S. Strauss, 1992). One author has discussed this behavior with scores of young men and their parents, who appear to be at a loss to understand why anyone would classify what they perceive to be a harmless,

playful "greeting" gesture as objectionable. Their confusion stems not from a lack of understanding about what bra snapping is, but from the context in which it is prohibited. Both students and parents know, for example, that it is not an acceptable greeting for a grandmother, an adult staff member, or a stranger at the shopping mall. Yet their interpretation of it as a way to say "Hi" or gain the momentary attention of a female classmate remains firm. Fathers often shake their heads and echo the students' viewpoint, saying, "I remember doing it at this age–everyone does." Mothers recall being subjected to it and also tend to accept it as a middle school phenomenon, one which may be classified as a mild annoyance or even as a positive sign of male interest.

The adult school staff may contribute to the confusion between the naming of an action and the cultural meaning that becomes ascribed to it. When teachers in a faculty training session on sexual harassment discussed bra snapping, there was consensus about what the behavior was and that it constituted violation of the person. Still, several staff indicated that if or when they witnessed it during the course of a class, they might not intercede (1) if the girl did not appear to object, or (2) if dealing with the action would create a major interruption of the class in progress.

Without entering a full discussion about consent, suffice it to note that a student may appear to be consenting to an action when she is not. The teacher's assessment based on a quick observation is insufficient to assess the quality or depth of consent. And when a girl knows that a teacher has witnessed an action such as bra snapping and does not intervene, the girl will have no confidence that her perception of being violated will be validated, and she may therefore continue to give passive obedience to the custom, assuming that her own perception of being unjustly discomforted is inaccurate. If a girl does protest under such circumstances, she may be cited for creating a class disruption (Eder, 1995; Larkin, 1994) or be ostracized by her peers for faulty social skills and an inability to interpret a male gesture accurately (Larkin, 1994). In short, the offended girl has no way to access the official sexual harassment policy without accepting negative consequences for herself. If, after a period of time, this student does complain that a specific male classmate has repeatedly snapped her bra and refused to stop after being requested to do so, and in effect, begins the legal process of filing a grievance, she is likely to be asked what took her so long to complain and come under suspicion herself as a co-contributor to the problem.

The point is that the definitions and procedures outlined in a sexual harassment policy are not only open to interpretations mediated by individuals' and groups' understanding of specific intentions and circumstances, they are also in direct opposition to the norms, values, and beliefs of a cultural setting when they define as offensive and objectionable the same behaviors that have been ritualized and condoned by local social practices. If students, and teachers, are successfully to reconfigure "normal" behavior as sexual harassment, we shall need to have recourse to a more complex and more subtle pedagogy than a statement of legal definitions accompanied by a listing of prohibited behaviors.

### The Equality Presumption: Claiming Redress

The equality presumption is the name we give to the fact that legalistic policies are designed as a one-size-fits-all policy. Such policies ignore differences between adults in a workplace setting and youngsters in school settings; they also ignore the differences in social standing between females and males within the wider culture and within the middle school culture.

Unlike workplaces, schools are contexts we create for the explicit purpose of helping youngsters who are still growing to learn, change, and develop socially and emotionally as well as intellectually. Legally oriented sexual harassment policies fail to take into account the social developmental patterns we know occur with adolescents. For example, one of these developmental tasks is to test rules and explore boundaries established by adults. Whether discovering ingenious ways to chew gum in science class without detection or to insult a peer sexually, thus gaining a momentary feeling of power, the adolescent is busy playing what educators at this level dub the "stump-the-adult game."

Barrie Thorne (1994) and Donna Eder (1995), in their ethnographic studies of middle level schools, have documented many of the "games" in which young adolescents engage. Males, in particular, engage in contests among themselves. These demonstrations of "toughness" may include spitting contests, belching fests, or insult competitions. Eder points out that the boys were expected to demonstrate their masculinity by controlling their emotions during insult exchanges and that "keeping cool"

during sexual insults posed the biggest challenge. The girls in Eder's study, however, did not engage in such insult games, and when they became targets of the boys' games, they had neither the practice to keep their cool nor the repertoire of insults to "play the game." The boys' comments to the girls clearly implied that they were viewing the girls as sexual objects and as convenient practice targets. The following scene happened in a lunchroom setting:

> Cindy came over to the table and wanted to know who was throwing stuff. She addressed herself to Eric. Eric grabbed her arms when she got close. Joe told her that he wanted to eat her and grabbed her waist. She told him to let go. Joe said he changed his mind and walked away. Eric started pulling her down on his lap and told her, "Just a little more. I can almost see down your shirt." She got away, and before she attacked Eric, Bobby called her over and started talking to her. She calmed down immediately.   (Eder, 1995, p. 88)

As obvious as the sexual harassment is in this scene, neither Cindy nor the boys viewed it as such. They believed they were engaged in game behavior; Cindy did not enjoy the encounter, but she still accepted it as a game.

The point here is that one of the accepted differences between adults and youngsters is that the latter are still acquiring knowledge about what it means to show respect for persons and what counts as a violation of that respect. We can't assume they have that knowledge.

Ironically, the most important single virtue of a legally oriented policy is also its most significant defect: it assumes that students are peers and equals: each can be violated, and if violated, each can claim redress. This fails to acknowledge the prevailing power imbalance that exists between males and females, a fact which has a bearing both upon the ability to name sexual harassment as such, and, perhaps more significant, upon the ability to claim redress.

Any school policy which realistically hopes to address student-to-student harassment must acknowledge that the conventional norms of acceptable male sexual overtures or expressions reflect a system of male dominance that gives males unquestioned right of access to females (Frye, 1983; Rich, 1979). Rituals of courtship in the larger culture are characterized by male initiatives, including aggression, and assume that females both seek and desire such initiatives. Additionally, females are held accountable for dual and often conflicting duties of both attracting male attention and setting limits upon male behavior.

Student surveys on sexual harassment reported by Susan Strauss (1992) are revealing: from a group of males, "It's a man thing. When a girl has on something revealing, you have to say something about it. . . . If a girl doesn't tell us we're sexually harassing her, we're going to continue to do it" (pp. 15–17).

Another consequence of the fact that sexual harassment is part of a larger framework that constructs gender as a dominant-subordinate relation between boys and girls, men and women, is that the very notion of "victim" is problematic. While being acknowledged as a victim is supposed to be helpful in having others recognize that the target of sexual harassment did not cause, and is not responsible for, the rude actions of others and places legal responsibility on the actor who violated the rules, the target person still needs to develop a sense of her own agency to respond, to access the policy procedure for justice, and to claim her rights. But as Susan Wendell (1990) notes, "Victims can and frequently do take the perspective of the oppressor. The victim with this perspective usually feels guilty for her or his victimization and takes all or most of the responsibility for it" (p. 24).

In cases of sexual harassment, it has been our experience that all the parties affected – parents, staff, and other students – join the "victim" in continuing this stance of her accepting responsibility. "You shouldn't have worn that dress," "You shouldn't have teased him first," "You were obviously flaunting yourself in front of those guys," "What were you doing there?" and other similar pronouncements of the victim's culpability abound.

It can be especially hurtful when other students echo the blame-the-victim reaction. A girl reported to Orenstein (1994) that while managing the boys' basketball team, she had been grabbed:

> And this boy Fred walked up during practice and he just reached out [she extended both arms] and he grabbed both of my tits. And this other boy standing there said, "Did he just touch you?" I said, "Yeah," and he said, "Fred, you shouldn't do that." Fred said, "I didn't do anything!" and walked away. Then this guy turns to me and says, "Next time, you really should watch yourself." Like it was my fault!   (p. 262)

Such judgments create an environment where it becomes unlikely that the target of harassment will feel justified and supported in claiming her rights. She will not feel empowered to effect a change or develop a plan to change the prevailing customs of harassment: the only option which presents itself is for her to restrict *her own* movements, dress, and interactions.

In one of the middle schools Peggy Orenstein studied, a guidance counselor, hearing that sexual harassment was a problem for girls, convened a group to discuss what was happening. At first the girls were most reluctant to give specifics about behaviors directed at them or the names of the boys involved. Orenstein reports the full transcript of the meeting, and midway through the time allocated for the meeting she notes:

> The girls are loosening up now, and a tone of exasperation is replacing their initial reluctance. They begin recounting boys' remarks in detail: they talk about boys who say, "Suck my fat Peter, you slut," who call them "shank" and "ho" (a variation on "whore" popularized by male rap artists). They talk about boys who pinch their bottoms in the hallways or grab their breasts and shout, "Let me tune in Tokyo!" They insist it isn't just "bad" boys who badger them: it's boys with good grades, boys who are athletes, boys who are paragons of the school. *And they all agree, their fear of reprisal is much too acute to allow them to confront their harassers.* (1994, p. 120; emphasis added)

## No Means for Reconciliation

Social relationships are the essential purpose of life for most middle school students. Their reasons for attending school have less to do with compulsory attendance laws or educational aspirations than for making and maintaining their social relationships. Legally oriented policies on sexual harassment do not recognize the crucial importance of the maintenance of the social network which precedes, follows, and surrounds an occasion of sexual harassment. Most sexual harassment in schools occurs among classmates and friends. If, or when, a "victim" does claim her rights, she must manage to do so while maintaining daily relationships with the "perpetrator" and his friends, for unlike the circumstances in a case of being mugged by a stranger on the street, the target of an attack in school cannot avoid returning to the "scene of the crime." The need to maintain friendships, to be accepted by peers, and not to be labeled a snitch, a rat, or "the girl who got Bobby in trouble" often overrides the wish to defend oneself or one's rights.

Both the strain one experiences for snitching and the struggle to maintain relationships in spite of conflict surrounding a sexual harassment incident is apparent in this typical note sent by a girl to her "best friend," who had complained about a popular boy touching her (picture this written in fuchsia marker, covering two full pages):

> Hey, Bitch – I don't know why you got Bobby in trouble. He is a really good kid. Now he's mad and is really going to beat your butt. I don't know why you did that – he's wicked cute. You better tell Ms. Chamberlain you made it up or we'll tell everyone that your[sic] a ho and what you did with Steve. Smarten up, bitch.
>
> [signed,] your best friend 4eva[sic] (please write back), Sally.
>
> P.S. Want to go to the mall after school? [with small boxes to be checked yes or no].

A female who resists or challenges the male's de facto right to embarrass, touch, or tease her risks rupturing relationships not only with the male(s) charged with harassment, but also with other females who are struggling to maintain heterosexual relationships.

One of us was poignantly reminded of this fact at the end of a counseling session with a group of girls who had had complaints about the way boys were treating them. The girls had been able to identify the sorts of actions that made them uncomfortable and had devised viable ways to confront harassers and strategies for resistance. At the end of the group session one of the girls commented: "In here, we're so strong – so sure of ourselves. But when we get back to class, we don't *do* the things we *plan* in here." Another student responded, "Yeah, because, you know, you have to be careful. I mean, you still have to have somebody to dance with."

## School Sexual Harassment Policies, Justice, and Care

Let us be clear. We are not claiming that the afore-mentioned difficulties of sexual harassment policies are difficulties of the law. Rather, the mistake, we have argued, is to think that sole reliance on legally oriented policies can be educationally sufficient. From an ethical perspective, it may be accurate to say that justice and rights are *implicit* in legally oriented sexual harassment policies, but they are difficult to activate.

From an educational perspective, students' confusions about rights range widely. Some express bewilderment even about how to conduct conversations with one another when they have become conscious of respecting rights. One boy who had been disciplined for sexually harassing a female classmate expressed his confusion about what to him were new and strange rules. He told Peggy Orenstein (1994), "I'll just wait until high school, and talk to girls then" (p. 128). At the other, more dangerous extreme, Michelle Fine and Pat Macpherson (1992) report that some adolescent women, in order to conform to the prevailing social order, accepted constriction on their person rights, including the right to be free of sexual assault from their boyfriends. They were aware of the existence of their rights in the abstract but could not envision a heterosexual relationship that would, or could, accommodate the enactment of their rights.

Such difficulties should not dissuade us from having justice and rights be a goal, something we pursue, but we do need to recognize that we can hit a barrier when the social nexus, the relationships presupposed by rights, does not support the stated policy. What is genuinely problematic is not the adoption of policies which acknowledge rights but rather the absence of what Minow (1990) calls "the only precondition" for the exercise of one's rights, namely, "that the community be willing for the individual to make claims and to participate in the defining and redefining of personal and social boundaries" (p. 301).

### An Ethics of Care Perspective

One way to deal with this barrier is to bring in another ethical perspective, one that focuses on relationships as does the ethics of care (Gilligan, 1982; Noddings, 1984, 1992), whose fundamental imperative instructs us to maintain and enhance caring relations – that is, relations marked by "a commitment to receptive attention and a willingness to respond helpfully to legitimate needs" (Noddings, 1996, p. 265.) There are several ways in which the introduction of a care perspective can assist us in developing more ethically satisfying and education-ally effective sexual harassment policies.

First, the ethics of care would have us pay greater attention to the *particularities* of the persons and situations for which school sexual harassment policies are designed: more attention to *what* we are trying to accomplish, and *how*, for *whom*, in what *setting*, and with what *attitude*. It would prompt us to notice that we are dealing with youngsters who are in the midst of their social development, who are still learning how to be with others, how to establish relationships with others. Further, it would have us pay attention to the fact that we are discussing policies for adolescents in *schools*; that is, in a context in which one expects mistakes and subsequent learning from them, in social institutions which are or ought to be committed to educating students even about caring relations. This means that coercion may not be ruled out, but we will want to make sure that any coercion we invoke is not exercised in a manner that contradicts caring (Noddings, 1990).

Second, the ethics of care better explains some of the students' difficulties with sexual harassment policies. When girls resist using the formal procedures available to them to name a wrong and seek redress, when they are hesitant to exercise their rights because they "don't want to make trouble for him," or because they still want to "have someone to dance with," they may well be caught in what from the ethics of care perspective we can recognize as an *ethical* dilemma. On one hand, they want to care for themselves and resist their violation, on the other, they feel the obligations of friendship and do not want to rupture valued relationships with peers. If we fully appreciate their dilemma as an ethical one, involving competing moral values, we are more likely to be moved to change the conditions that place them in conflict rather than construe the situation as one in which female students simply lack the interest, skill, or courage needed to assert their rights.

Once we take seriously the ethics of care's imperative to maintain and enhance caring relations, and we see how we might foster more caring as well as just relations among students, we can appreciate that the ethics of care has one great advantage over an approach that focuses only on justice and rights: it affords us a way to begin the work of reconciliation among the students, when appropriate. The practice of care can help us to differentiate cases – between those offenders who say, "If I had known it would have such bad consequences for her, I wouldn't have done it," and those visible offenders who are well-known, defiant repeaters. For the latter, coercion and the full demands of justice, along with re-education efforts, are needed to ensure the safety of the school community. For the former, we can begin to see their "crimes" as conflicts between students, an impairment of their relations that more appropriately might call for reconciliation

rather than punishment and retribution (Knopp, 1991). Understanding the conflict within the larger communal context of the classroom and the school community, we can begin to look at how we can establish, or reestablish, trust and trustworthiness, and restore mutual caring relations. A care perspective might encourage what we could call "restorative justice" (Knopp, 1991, p. 183).

Another consequence of introducing an ethics of care perspective into our discussion of school sexual harassment policies is that we can gain a different perspective upon rights. The ethics of care has us recognize that rights are grounded in the process of communication and meaning making rather than in some abstract legal foundation. A relational perspective will have us remember that as "tools of communal dialogue," rights can be viewed as "a vocabulary used by community members to interpret and reinterpret their relationships with one another" (Minow, 1987, pp. 1890–1).

Furthermore rights are not the only critical tool we can use to challenge abuses within relationships of unequal power. The ethics of care, we shall argue, can also serve this function. But first we must consider what the critics claim are obstacles to its doing so.

## Are Justice and Care Enough?

Just as there are barriers with rights, some claim that there are also barriers we can encounter with a care perspective. One central worry is the ethics of care's alleged inability to focus on social structures, and its consequent limited scope of moral critique. Jaggar (1995) and others such as Card (1990) and Hoagland (1990) see care's attention to a situation's specificity and particularity as sometimes a "significant liability." For example, in cases of sexual harassment, focusing on particular female students and what they experience may well help us to see the effects insensitive and bullying behavior can have on them, but "it can also divert moral attention away from the social structures of privilege that legitimate such behavior" (Jaggar, 1995, p. 195).

Alison Jaggar considers both justice, which condemns sexual harassment as a violation of individual rights, as well as care, inadequate. Her point is that

> neither care nor justice reasoning as ordinarily construed constitute[s] the kind of hermeneutical moral thinking capable of questioning conventional definitions

of assault as well as of exploring the complex assumptions about sexuality, aggression, and gender that make . . . [sexual harassment] not only thinkable but predictable and even normal.   (p. 198)

Because we have observed the powerful normalizing role of social conventions, we concur with Jaggar's insistence on the need to keep a focus on structural problems, but we are less pessimistic than she about the ethics of care and justice, for we see elements in both that can help.

One of these elements is the publicity criterion in contractarian theories of justice. For example, John Rawls (1971) contends that contractarian theories of justice must establish *public* systems of rules such that "everyone engaged in it knows what he [or she] would know if these rules and his [or her] participation in the activity they define were the result of an agreement" (p. 56). And it is clear that "A person taking part in a [just] institution knows what the rules demand of him [or her] and of others. He [or she] also knows that the others know this and that they know that he [or she] knows this" (p. 56).

We can note that the spirit of justice, on Rawls's conception, would seem to support the idea that persons should not be subject to rules about sexual harassment without knowing "what [they] would know if these rules and [their] participation in the activity they define were the result of an agreement." Not surprisingly, Kurt Baier (1958), whom Rawls follows on this point, calls his condition of publicity the "teachability" criterion. Attempting to design school sexual harassment policies so as to meet an approximate version of Rawls's publicity condition or Baier's teachability criterion leads us to ask: what would students need to know if these rules and their participation in these sexual harassment policies were to be Rawls's "result of an agreement"? This is one of the central questions we would take from a justice perspective to put at the forefront in shaping school sexual harassment policies.

The ethics of care also has its own educational answer to the worry critics raise about how to reveal and resist the entrenched power of structural inequalities. The answer briefly stated, is to give primacy to moral education. The task, as Noddings (1996) says, "is to study, both philosophically and empirically, why we harm or refuse to harm one another and why we care or refuse to care for one another as we satisfy our deeply felt desire to belong" (p. 266).

Jane Roland Martin (1992), another proponent of revising education so as to emphasize the three Cs of care, concern, and connection, answers Jaggar's worry more directly. Martin argues that we need to introduce a gender-sensitive approach to studying care which makes the questionable social patterns of behavior an object of explicit study.

Student-to-student sexual harassment, as we have noted, occurs as part of a pattern in which students are caught in social circumstances that they themselves need to understand. It makes sense, therefore, to bring students into the conversation. In her book *The Schoolhome* (1992), Martin gives us some clear examples. In one imagined classroom she depicts a girl and boy having just performed the scene about the sun and moon from Act IV of Shakespeare's *The Taming of the Shrew* in which Petruchio insists that Kate say the sun is the moon.

> The teacher asks them why Petruchio forces Kate to say what is patently untrue. One of the onlookers in the class mutters, "No problem. He's a practical joker." But the boy who is going to play Petruchio in another scene of the play says, "I am not. I'm trying to get her to obey me." "You're right," one of the girls interjects. "Petruchio says, I will be master of my own. She is my goods, my chattels," the students recite in unison. Then the teacher asks, "What happens to people if you are constantly telling them that what they see isn't really there?" "They think they are crazy," a girls says; "My father does it to my mother all the time." "When this happens to someone," the teacher asks, "can she speak her mind?" "She doesn't even know her mind," the girl answers.   (p. 114)

Martin then points out that "The ensuing silence has more meaning for the students than any words [might have]" (p. 114).

The students discuss how to do the final scene with Kate's long submission speech. Will they do it straight, or with irony?

> They have a long conversation about how Kate's submission, whether genuine or not, is achieved. Is Petruchio by any chance brainwashing Kate? They discuss what effects male dominance has on the two parties. Does he drive her crazy or simply underground, turning her into a wily manipulator? Is he a joker or is he practicing a form of domestic battery? They ask what gives him the right to call her his goods, his chattels. Before her marriage was she her own person or her father's? And whose person is Petruchio? (pp. 114–15)

Martin notes that

> In [the] safe atmosphere where students can talk about the domestic violence in the play's action and the misogyny in its language, sense Petruchio's sadism and Kate's pain, *Taming* . . . [is] an especially effective educational vehicle. . . . Like other Shakespeare plays it illuminates some of those big questions that all of us must confront. Its special virtue is that it raises questions that girls and boys in our culture face here and now: . . . What happens to women who speak out? . . . Can boys and girls, men and women live and work together without the one sex being dominant and the other submissive? (pp. 115–16)

The ethics of care's revisioning of education includes just such dialogue.

## Conclusion

We cannot hope to develop effective school sexual harassment policies without making them the subject matter of educational study, which in turn entails acknowledging, discussing, and ultimately challenging the norms that support sexual harassment. Sexual equality needs to be enacted so that the norms, beliefs, values, and practices of equality are embodied throughout the entire school culture. In short, the policy is *performed*, not merely articulated. We have argued that the values of both care and justice are required to underwrite such educative revisions. Students, teachers, and staff can then develop the skills, knowledge, and discernment needed to act in accord with existing legal policies, but more important, they can cultivate relationships in which such policies would in large measure become superfluous.

## References

American Association of University Women Educational Forum (1993) *Hostile Hallways: The AAUW Survey on Sexual Harassment in America's Schools* (Washington, DC: Nan Stein).

Baier, Kurt (1958) *The Moral Point of View* (Ithaca, NY: Cornell University Press).

Card, Claudia (1990) Caring and evil. *Hypatia*, 5(1): 101–8.

Eder, Donna (1995) *School Talk: Gender and Adolescent Culture* (New Brunswick, NJ: Rutgers University Press).

Fine, Michelle (ed.) (1992) *Disruptive Voices: The Possibilities of Feminist Research* (Ann Arbor, MI: University of Michigan Press).

Fine, Michelle (1993) Sexuality, schooling, and adolescent females: The missing discourse of desire. In Lois Weiss and Michelle Fine (eds.), *Beyond Silenced Voices: Class, Race, and Gender in United States Schools* (Albany: State University of New York Press), pp. 75–100.

Fine, Michelle and Macpherson, Pat (1992) Over dinner: Femininism and adolescent female bodies. In Michelle Fine (ed.), *Disruptive Voices: The Possibilities of Feminist Research*. (pp. 175–204) (Ann Arbor: University of Michigan Press), pp. 175–204.

Frye, Marilyn (1983) *The Politics of Reality* (Trumansburg, NY: Crossing Press).

Gilligan, Carol (1982) *In a Different Voice* (Cambridge, MA: Harvard University Press).

Gilligan, Carol, Lyons, Nona, and Hammer, Trudy (eds.) (1990) *Women, Girls and Psychotherapy: Reframing Resistance* (New York: Harrington Park Press).

Hoagland, Sarah (1990) Some concerns about Nel Noddings' caring. *Hypatia*, 5(1): 109–14.

Jaggar, Alison (1995) Caring as a feminist practice of moral reason. In Virginia Held (ed.), *Justice and Care: Essential Readings in Feminist Ethics* (Boulder, CO: Westview Press), pp. 179–202.

Knopp, Fay (1991) Community solutions to sexual violence. In Harold Pepinsky and Richard Quinney (eds.), *Criminology as Peace Making* (Bloomington: Indiana University Press), pp. 183–92.

Larkin, June (1994) *Sexual Harassment: High School Girls Speak Out* (Toronto: Second Story Press).

Lewis, John, and Hastings, Susan (1994) *Sexual Harassment in Education* (Topeka, KS: National Organization on Legal Problems in Education).

MacKinnon, Catharine (1979) *Sexual Harassment of Working Women* (New Haven, CT: Yale University Press).

MacKinnon, Catharine (1987) *Feminism Unmodified: Discourses on Life and Law* (Cambridge, MA: Harvard University Press).

Mann, Judith (1994) *The Difference: Discovering the Hidden Ways we Silence Girls: Finding Alternatives That Can Give them a Voice* (New York: Warner Books).

Martin, Jane Roland (1992) *The Schoolhome: Rethinking Schools for Changing Families* (Cambridge, MA: Harvard University Press).

Minow, Martha (1987) Interpreting rights: An essay for Robert Cover. *The Yale Law Journal*, 96(8): 1860–915.

Minow, Martha (1990) *Making all the Difference: Inclusion, Exclusion, and American Law* (Ithaca, NY: Cornell University Press).

Noddings, Nel (1984) *Caring: A Feminine Approach to Ethics and Moral Education* (Berkeley: University of California Press).

Noddings, Nel (1987) Do we really want to produce good people? *Journal of Moral Education, 16*(3): 177–88.

Noddings, Nel (1990) Ethics from the standpoint of women. In Deborah Rhode (ed.), *Theoretical Perspectives on Sexual Difference* (New Haven, CT: Yale University Press), pp. 160–73.

Noddings, Nel (1992) *The Challenge to Care in Schools: An Alternative Approach to Education* (New York: Teachers College Press).

Noddings, Nel (1996) On community. *Educational Theory, 46*(3): 245–67.

Orenstein, Peggy (1994) *Schoolgirls: Young Women, Self-esteem, and the Confidence Gap* (New York: Doubleday).

Oyster River Cooperative School District Sexual Harassment and Policy Guidelines. April 1994.

Pipher, Mary (1994) *Reviving Ophelia: Saving the Lives of Adolescent Girls* (New York: Ballantine Books).

Rawls, John (1971) *A Theory of Justice* (Cambridge, MA: Harvard University Press).

Rich, Adrienne (1979) *On Lies, Secrets, and Silence: Selected Prose, 1966–1978* (New York: Norton).

Ruddick, Sara (1995) Injustice in families: Assault and domination. In Virginia Held (ed.), *Justice and Care: Essential Readings in Feminist Ethics* (Boulder, CO: Westview Press), pp. 203–23.

Sherer, M. L. (1994) No longer just child's play: School liability under Title IX for peer sexual harassment. *University of Pennsylvania Law Review, 141*: 2119–68.

Shoop, Robert, and Edwards, Debra (1994) *How to Stop Sexual Harassment in our Schools: A Handbook and Curriculum Guide for Administrators and Teachers* (Boston, MA: Allyn and Bacon).

Stein, Nan (1993) It happens here, too: Sexual harassment and child sexual abuse in elementary and secondary schools. In S. K. Pollard and D. Pollard (eds.), *Gender and Education* (Chicago: University of Chicago Press), pp. 191–203.

Stein, Nan (1995, June) Is it sexually charged, sexually hostile, or the constitution? Sexual harassment in K-12 schools. *Education Law Reporter, 98*: 621–31.

Stein, Nan and Sjostrom, Lisa (1994) *Flirting or Hurting? A Teacher's Guide on Student to Student Sexual Harassment in Schools* (Washington, DC: National Education Association).

Strauss, Joanne (1993) Peer sexual harassment of high school students: A reasonable student standard and an affirmative duty imposed on educational institutions. *Law and Inequality, 10*: 163–86.

Strauss, Susan (1992) *Sexual Harassment and Teens* (Minneapolis, MN: Free Spirit).

Streitmatter, Jean (1994) *Toward Gender Equity in the Classroom: Everyday Teachers' Beliefs and Practices* (Albany: State University of New York Press).

Thorne, Barrie (1994) *Gender Play: Girls and Boys in School* (New Brunswick, NJ: Rutgers University Press).

Wendell, Susan (1990) Oppression and victimization; choice and responsibility. *Hypatia, 5*(3): 15–43.

# Inquiry, Understanding, and Constructivism

# 42

# Learning by Discovery

## Jean-Jacques Rousseau

### *Emile*: Book II

Look at a cat entering a room for the first time. He inspects, he looks around, he sniffs, he does not relax for a moment, he trusts nothing before he has examined everything, come to know everything. This is just what is done by a child who is beginning to walk and entering, so to speak, in the room of the world. The whole difference is that, in addition to the vision which is common to both child and cat, the former has the hands that nature gave him to aid in observation, and the latter is endowed by nature with a subtle sense of smell. Whether this disposition is well or ill cultivated is what makes children adroit or clumsy, dull or alert, giddy or prudent.

Since man's first natural movements are, therefore, to measure himself against everything surrounding him and to experience in each object he perceives all the qualities which can be sensed and relate to him, his first study is a sort of experimental physics relative to his own preservation, from which he is diverted by speculative studies before he has recognized his place here on earth. While his delicate and flexible organs can adjust themselves to the bodies on which they must act, while his still pure senses are exempt from illusions, it is the time to exercise both in their proper functions, it is the time to teach the knowledge of the sensible relations which things have with us. Since everything which enters into the human understanding comes there through the senses, man's first reason is a reason of the senses; this sensual reason serves as the basis of intellectual reason. Our first masters of philosophy are our feet, our hands, our eyes. To substitute books for all that is not to teach us to reason. It is to teach us to use the reason of others. It is to teach us to believe much and never to know anything.

[ . . . ]

To exercise the senses is not only to make use of them, it is to learn to judge well with them. It is to learn, so to speak, to sense; for we know how to touch, see, and hear only as we have learned.

[ . . . ] [Do] not exercise only strength; exercise all the senses which direct it. Get from each of them all that they can do. Then verify the impression of one by the other. Measure, count, weigh, compare. Use strength only after having estimated resistance.

Editor's title. Originally published as Books II and III of *"Emile", or On Education*, trans. Allan Bloom (New York: Basic Books/HarperCollins, 1979), pp. 125, 132–3, 140–1, 157–8, 167, 168–70, 171, 172–7. Reprinted by permission of the Perseus Books Group.

Always arrange it so that the estimate of the effect precedes the use of the means. Interest the child in never making insufficient or superfluous efforts. If you accustom him to foresee thus the effect of all his movements and to set his mistakes right by experience, is it not clear that the more he acts, the more judicious he will become?

Is there a mass to lift? If he takes too long a lever, he will waste motion. If he takes too short a one, he will not have enough strength. Experience can teach him to choose precisely the stick he needs. This wisdom is, hence, not beyond his age. Is there a load to carry? If he wants to take one as heavy as he can carry and not try any he cannot lift, will he not be forced to estimate its weight by sight? Does he know how to compare masses of the same matter and of different size? Let him choose between masses of the same size and different matters. He will have to set himself to comparing their specific weights. I have seen a very well-raised young man who, only after putting it to the test, was willing to believe that a container full of big pieces of oak was less heavy than the same container filled with water.

[ . . . ]

Anything which gives movement to the body without constraining it is always easy to obtain from children. There are countless means of interesting them in measuring, knowing, and estimating distances. Here is a very tall cherry tree. How shall we go about picking the cherries? Will the barn ladder do for that? Here is quite a large stream. How shall we cross it? Will one of the planks from the courtyard reach both banks? We would like to fish from our windows in the mansion's ponds. How many spans ought our line to have? I would like to hang a swing between these two trees: will a rope two fathoms long be enough for us? I am told that in the other house our room will be twenty-five square feet. Do you believe that it will suit us? Will it be larger than this one? We are very hungry. There are two villages. At which of the two will we arrive sooner for dinner? Et cetera.

[ . . . ]

It remains for me to speak in the following books of the cultivation of a sort of sixth sense called *common sense*, less because it is common to all men than because it results from the well-regulated use of the other senses, and because it instructs us about the nature of things by the conjunction of all their appearances. This sixth sense has consequently no special organ. It resides only in the brain, and its sensations, purely internal, are called *perceptions*

or *ideas*. It is by the number of these ideas that the extent of our knowledge is measured. It is their distinctness, their clarity which constitutes the accuracy of the mind. It is the art of comparing them among themselves that is called *human reason*. Thus what I would call *sensual* or *childish* reason consists in forming simple ideas by the conjunction of several sensations, and what I call *intellectual* or *human reason* consists in forming complex ideas by the conjunction of several simple ideas.

Supposing, then, that my method is that of nature, and that I did not make mistakes in its application, we have led our pupil through the land of sensations up to the boundaries of childish reason. [ . . . ]

## Book III

[ . . . ]

The child's progress in geometry can serve you as a test and a certain measure of the development of his intelligence. But as soon as he can discern what is useful and what is not, it is important to use much tact and art to lead him to speculative studies. Do you, for example, want him to look for a proportional mean between two lines? Begin by arranging it so that he has to find a square equal to a given rectangle. If the problem has to do with two proportional means, you would first have to interest him in the problem of doubling a cube, etc. See how we gradually approach moral notions which distinguish good and bad! Up to now we have known no law other than that of necessity. Now we are dealing with what is useful. We shall soon get to what is suitable and good.

The same instinct animates man's diverse faculties. To the activity of the body which seeks development succeeds the activity of the mind which seeks instruction. At first children are only restless; then they are curious; and that curiosity, well directed, is the motive of the age we have now reached. Let us always distinguish between the inclinations which come from nature and those which come from opinion. There is an ardor to know which is founded only on the desire to be esteemed as learned; there is another ardor which is born of a curiosity natural to man concerning all that might have a connection, close or distant, with his interests. The innate desire for well-being and the impossibility of fully satisfying this desire make him constantly seek for new means of contributing to it. This is the first principle of curiosity, a principle natural to the human heart, but one which develops only in proportion to our passions and our enlightenment. [ . . . ]

Make your pupil attentive to the phenomena of nature. Soon you will make him curious. But to feed his curiosity, never hurry to satisfy it. Put the questions within his reach and leave them to him to resolve. Let him know something not because you told it to him but because he has understood it himself. Let him not learn science but discover it. If ever you substitute in his mind authority for reason, he will no longer reason. He will be nothing more than the plaything of others' opinion.

You want to teach geography to this child, and you go and get globes, cosmic spheres, and maps for him. So many devices! Why all these representations? Why do you not begin by showing him the object itself, so that he will at least know what you are talking to him about?

One fine evening we go for a walk in a suitable place where a broad, open horizon permits the setting sun to be fully seen, and we observe the objects which make recognizable the location of its setting. The next day, to get some fresh air, we return to the same place before the sun rises. We see it announcing itself from afar by the fiery arrows it launches ahead of it. The blaze grows; the east appears to be wholly in flames. By their glow one expects the star for a long time before it reveals itself. At every instant one believes that he sees it appear. Finally one sees it. A shining point shoots out like lightning and immediately fills all of space. The veil of darkness is drawn back and falls. Man recognizes his habitat and finds it embellished. The verdure has gained a new vigor during the night. The nascent day which illuminates it, the first rays which gild it, show it covered by a shining web of dew which reflects the light and the colors to the eye. The birds in chorus join together in concert to greet the father of life. At that moment not a single one keeps quiet. Their chirping, still weak, is slower and sweeter than during the rest of the day; it has the feel of the languor of a peaceful awakening. The conjunction of these objects brings to the senses an impression of freshness which seems to penetrate to the soul. There is here a half-hour of enchantment which no man can resist. So great, so fair, so delicious a spectacle leaves no one cold.

Full of the enthusiasm he feels, the master wants to communicate it to the child. He believes he moves the child by making him attentive to the sensations by which he, the master, is himself moved. Pure stupidity! It is in man's heart that the life of nature's spectacle exists. To see it, one must feel it. The child perceives the objects, but he cannot perceive the relations linking them; he cannot hear the sweet harmony of their concord. For that is needed experience he has not acquired; in order to sense the complex impression that results all at once from all these sensations, he needs sentiments he has not had. If he has not long roamed arid plains, if burning sands have not scorched his feet, if the suffocating reflections of stones struck by the sun have never oppressed him, how will he enjoy the cool air of a fine morning? How will the fragrances of the flowers, the charm of the verdure, the humid vapors of the dew, and the soft and gentle touch of the grass underfoot enchant his senses? How will the song of the birds cause a voluptuous emotion in him, if the accents of love and pleasure are still unknown to him? With what transports will he see so fair a day dawning, if his imagination does not know how to paint for him those transports with which it can be filled? Finally, how can he be touched by the beauty of nature's spectacle, if he does not know the hand responsible for adorning it?

Do not make speeches to the child which he cannot understand. No descriptions, no eloquence, no figures, no poetry. It is not now a question of sentiment or taste. Continue to be clear, simple, and cold. The time for adopting another kind of language will come only too soon.

Raised in the spirit of our maxims, accustomed to draw all his instruments out of himself and never to have recourse to another person before he has himself recognized his insufficiency, he examines each new object he sees for a long time without saying anything. He is pensive, and not a questioner. Be satisfied, therefore, with presenting him with objects opportunely. Then, when you see his curiosity sufficiently involved, put to him some laconic question which sets him on the way to answering it.

On this occasion, after having contemplated the rising sun with him, after having made him notice the mountains and the other neighboring objects in that direction, after having let him chat about it at his ease, keep quiet for a few moments like a man who dreams, and then say to him, "I was thinking that yesterday evening the sun set here and that this morning it rose there. How is that possible?" Add nothing more. If he asks you questions, do not respond to them. Talk about something else. Leave him to himself, and be sure that he will think about it.

For a child to get accustomed to being attentive and for him to be strongly impressed by some truth involving objects of sense, he has to worry over it for a few days before he discovers it. If he does not conceive of this one adequately in this way, there is a means of making it even more evident to his senses; and that means is to turn the question around. If he does not know how the sun gets from its setting to its rising, he knows at least how it gets from its rising to its setting. His eyes alone teach him that. Clarify, therefore, the former question by the latter. Either your pupil is absolutely stupid, or the analogy is too clear to be able to escape him. This is his first lesson in cosmography.[1]

Since we always proceed slowly from one idea based on the senses to another, we familiarize ourselves with one for a long time before going on to another, and, finally, we never force our pupil to be attentive; it is a long way from this first lesson to knowledge of the path of the sun and the shape of the earth. But since all the apparent movements of the celestial bodies depend on the same principle and the first observation leads to all the others, less effort, although more time, is needed to get from a diurnal revolution to the calculation of eclipses than is needed to understand day and night well.

Since the sun turns around the earth, it describes a circle, and every circle must have a center. We already know that. This center cannot be seen, for it is at the heart of the earth. But one can mark on its surface two points which correspond to it. A spike passing through the three points and lengthened up to the heavens on both sides will be the axis of the earth and of the sun's daily movement. A round top turning on its tip represents the heavens turning on their axis; the top's two tips are the two poles. The child will be delighted to know one of them. I show it to him on the tail of the Little Bear. This is our entertainment for the night. Little by little he gains familiarity with the stars, and from there is born the first taste for knowing the planets and observing the constellations.

We have seen the sun rising on Midsummer Day. We also go to see it rising on Christmas Day or some other fair winter day, for you know that we are not lazy and that we make a game of braving the cold. I am careful to make this second observation in the same place where we made the first; and, provided that some skill has been used in preparing the observation, one or the other will not fail to cry out, "Oh, oh! Here is something funny! The sun does not rise anymore in the same place. Here are our old markers, and now it is rising over there, etc. . . . there is, then, a summer east and a winter east, etc. . . ." Young master, you are now on your way. These examples ought to suffice for you to teach the celestial sphere very clearly while taking the earth as the earth and the sun as the sun.

In general, never substitute the sign for the thing except when it is impossible for you to show the latter, for the sign absorbs the child's attention and makes him forget the thing represented.

[ . . . ]

Remember always that the spirit of my education consists not in teaching the child many things, but in never letting anything but accurate and clear ideas enter his brain. Were he to know nothing, it would be of little importance to me provided he made no mistakes. [ . . . ] The issue is not to teach him the sciences but to give him the taste for loving them and methods for learning them when this taste is better developed. This is very certainly a fundamental principle of every good education.

[ . . . ]

There is a chain of general truths by which all the sciences are connected with common principles out of which they develop successively. This chain is the method of philosophers. We are not dealing with it here. There is another entirely different chain by which each particular object attracts another and always shows the one that follows. This order, which fosters by means of constant curiosity the attention that they all demand, is the one most men follow and, in particular, is the one required for children. In orienting ourselves to draw our maps, we had to draw meridians. Two points of intersection between the equal shadows of morning and evening provide an excellent meridian for an astronomer of thirteen.[2] But these meridians disappear. Time is needed to draw them. They subject one to working always in the same place. So much care, so much constraint would end by boring him. We foresaw it. We provide for it in advance.

Here I am once again in my lengthy and minute details. Reader, I hear your grumbling, and I brave it. I do not want to sacrifice the most useful part of this book to your impatience. Make your decision about my delays, for I have made mine about your complaints.

A long time ago my pupil and I had noticed that amber, glass, wax, and various other bodies when rubbed attracted straws and that others did not attract them. By chance we find one which has a still more singular virtue, that of attracting at some distance – without being rubbed – shavings and other bits of iron. How long this quality entertains us without our being able to see anything more in it! Finally, we find that the iron itself acquires this quality from the lodestone when drawn across it in any single direction. One day we go to the fair;[3] a magician attracts a wax duck floating in a tub of water with a piece of bread. Although we are quite surprised, we nevertheless do not say, "He is a sorcerer," for we do not know what a sorcerer is. Constantly struck by effects whose causes we do not know, we are in no hurry to make any judgments, and we remain at rest in our ignorance until we happen to find the occasion to escape it.

After returning home, by dint of talking about the duck at the fair, we get it into our heads to imitate it. We take a good, well-magnetized needle; we surround it with white wax that we do our best to shape in the form of a duck, with the needle going through the body and its point constituting the bill. We put the duck in the water, we bring the top part of a key close to the bill, and we see with a joy easy to understand that our duck follows the key exactly as the one at the fair followed the piece of bread. To observe the direction the duck faces when left at rest in the water is something we can do another time. As for now, busy with our plan, we do not want more.

The very same evening we return to the fair with bread ready in our pockets, and as soon as the magician does his trick, my little doctor, who was hardly able to contain himself, says to him that this trick is not difficult and that he himself will do as much. He is taken at his word. Immediately he pulls the bread with the piece of iron hidden in it from his pocket. On approaching the table, his heart thumps. Practically quaking, he holds out the bread. The duck comes and follows him. The child cries out and shivers with delight. At the crowd's clapping and acclamation he gets dizzy; he is beside himself. The mountebank, confounded, comes nevertheless and embraces him, congratulates him, and begs the child to honor him again by his presence the next day, adding that he will make an effort to gather a still larger crowd to applaud his skill. My proud little naturalist wants to chatter. But I immediately shut him up and take him away covered with praise.

The child counts the minutes till the next day with a ridiculous excitement. He invites everyone he meets; he would want the whole of humankind to be witness to his glory. He hardly can wait for the hour. He is ahead of time; we fly to the appointment. The hall is already full. On entering, his young heart swells. Other games are going to be first. The magician surpasses himself and does surprising things. The child sees nothing of all that. He is agitated; he sweats; he is hardly able to breathe. He spends his time handling the piece of bread in his pocket with a hand trembling with impatience. Finally his time comes. The master announces him to the public with pomp. He comes forward with a bit of shame; he takes out his bread and . . . new vicissitude of things human! The duck, so responsive the day before, has turned wild today. Instead of offering its bill, it turns tail and flees. It avoids the bread and the hand offering it with as much care as it followed them previously. After countless useless attempts and constantly being jeered at, the child complains, says that he is being deceived, that another duck has been substituted for the first one; he defies the magician to attract this one.

The magician, without responding, takes a piece of bread and offers it to the duck. Immediately the duck follows the bread and comes toward the retreating hand. The child takes the same piece of bread, but far from succeeding better than before, he sees the duck make fun of him and do pirouettes all around the tub. He finally steps back in confusion and no longer dares to expose himself to the jeers.

Then the magician takes the piece of bread the child has brought and uses it with as much success as his own. He pulls the iron out of it in front of everyone. Another laugh at our expense. Then, with the bread thus emptied, he attracts the duck as before. He does the same thing with another piece cut in front of everyone by another's hand. He does the same with his glove, the tip of his finger. Finally he moves away to the middle of the room and in the emphatic tone peculiar to such people, declaring that his duck will obey his voice no less than his gesture, he speaks to it, and the duck obeys. He tells it to go right and it goes right, to return and it returns, to turn and it turns. The movement is as prompt as the order. The redoubled applause is that much more of an affront to us. We escape unnoticed and shut ourselves up in our room without going to recount our successes to everyone as we had planned.

The next morning there is a knock at our door. I open it, and there is the magician. Modestly he complains of our conduct. What did he do to us to make us want to discredit his games and take away his livelihood? What is so wonderful about the art of attracting a wax duck to make it worth purchasing this honor at the expense of an honest man's subsistence? "My faith, messieurs, if I had some other talent by which to live, I would hardly glorify myself with this one. You should have believed that a man who has spent his life practicing this paltry trickery knows more about it than do you who have devoted only a few moments to it. If I did not show you my master strokes right off, it is because one ought not to be in a hurry to show off giddily what one knows. I am always careful to keep my best tricks for the proper occasion; and after this one I have still others to stop tactless young men. Finally, messieurs, I come out of the goodness of my heart to teach you the secret that perplexed you so. I beg you not to abuse it to my hurt and to be more restrained the next time."

Then he shows us his device, and we see with the greatest surprise that it consists only of a strong lodestone, well encased in soft iron, which a child hidden under the table moved without being noticed.

The man puts his device away, and, after giving him our thanks and apologies, we wish to make him a present. He refuses it. "No, messieurs, I am not pleased enough with you to accept your gifts. I leave you obliged to me in spite of yourselves. It is my only vengeance. Learn that there is generosity in every station. I get paid for my tricks and not my lessons."

In leaving, he addresses a reprimand to me explicitly and out loud. "I willingly excuse," he says to me, "this child. He has sinned only from ignorance. But you, monsieur, who ought to know his mistake, why did you let him make it? Since you live together, as the elder you owe him your care and your counsel; your experience is the authority which ought to guide him. In reproaching himself for the wrongs of his youth when he is grown up, he will doubtless reproach you for those against which you did not warn him."

He departs, leaving us both very embarrassed. I blame myself for my soft easygoingness. I promise the child to sacrifice it to his interest the next time and to warn him of his mistakes before he makes them; for the time is approaching when our relations are going to change, when the master's severity must succeed the comrade's compliance. This change ought to take place gradually. Everything must be foreseen, and everything must be foreseen very far ahead of time.

The next day we return to the fair to see again the trick whose secret we have learned. We approach our magician-Socrates with profound respect. Hardly do we dare to raise our eyes to him. He covers us with attentions and gives us a place of distinction, which humiliates us again. He does his tricks as usual, but he entertains and indulges himself for a long time with the duck trick while looking often at us with quite a proud air. We know everything, and we do not breathe a word. If my pupil dared so much as to open his mouth, he would deserve to be annihilated.

Each detail of this example is more important than it seems. How many lessons in one! How many mortifying consequences are attracted by the first movement of vanity! Young master, spy out this first movement with care. If you know thus how to make humiliation and disgrace arise from it, be sure that a second movement will not come for a long time. "So much preparation!" you will say. I agree – and all for the sake of making ourselves a compass to take the place of a meridian.

Having learned that the magnet acts through other bodies, we have nothing more pressing to do than to make a device like the one we have seen. A table hollowed out, a very flat tub fitted into the table and filled with a few inches of water, a duck made with a bit more care, etc. Often busy around the tub, we finally notice that the duck at rest always points in pretty nearly the same direction. We follow up this experience; we examine this direction; we find that it is from south to north. Nothing more is needed; our compass is found, or as good as found. Now we are into physics.

There are various climates on the earth and various temperatures in these climates. One feels the variation of the seasons more as one approaches the pole. All bodies contract with cold and expand with heat. This effect is more measurable in liquids and more accessible to the senses in spirituous liquids: hence the thermometer. Wind strikes the face; air is, therefore, a body, a fluid; one feels it although one has no means of seeing it. Turn a glass upside down in water; the water will not fill it unless you allow the air a way out; air is, therefore, capable of resistance. Push the glass farther down; the water will make headway in the airspace without being able to fill that space completely; air is, therefore, capable of compression up to a certain point. A ball filled with compressed air bounces better than any other matter; air is, therefore, an elastic body. When you are stretched out in the bath, lift your arm horizontally out of the water; you will feel that it is loaded with a terrible weight; air is, therefore, a heavy body.

By putting air in equilibrium with other fluids, its weight can be measured; this is the source of the barometer, the siphon, the air gun, and the pneumatic pump. All the laws of statics and hydrostatics are to be found by experiments just as crude. I do not want to go into an experimental physics laboratory for any of this. This whole apparatus of instruments and machines displeases me. The scientific atmosphere kills science. Either all these machines frighten a child, or their appearance divides and steals the attention he ought to pay to their effects.

I want us to make all our machines ourselves, and I do not want to begin by making the instrument prior to the experiment. But I do want us, after having caught a glimpse, as it were by chance, of the experiment to be performed, to invent little by little the instrument for verification. I prefer that our instruments be less perfect and accurate and that we have more distinct ideas about what they ought to be and the operations which ought to result from them. For my first lesson in statics, instead of going to look for scales, I put a stick across the back of a chair, and I measure the length of the two parts of the stick in balance. I add weights to both sides, sometimes equal, sometimes unequal, and, pushing and pulling as much as is necessary, I finally find that balance is the result of a reciprocal proportion between the quantity of the weights and the length of the levers. Now my little physicist is already capable of rectifying scales before seeing one.

Without question, one gets far clearer and far surer notions of the things one learns in this way by oneself than of those one gets from another's teachings. One's reason does not get accustomed to a servile submission to authority; furthermore, we make ourselves more ingenious at finding relations, connecting ideas, and inventing instruments than we do when, accepting all of these things as they are given to us, we let our minds slump into indifference – like the body of a man who, always clothed, shod, and waited on by his servants and drawn by his horses, finally loses the strength and use of his limbs. Boileau boasted of having taught Racine to have difficulty in rhyming. Among so many admirable methods for abridging the study of the sciences we greatly need someone to provide us with a method for learning them with effort.

The most palpable advantage of these slow and laborious researches is that they keep the body active and the limbs supple during speculative studies and continuously form the hands for the work and the practices useful to man. All the instruments invented to guide us in our experiments and to take the place of accuracy of the senses cause the senses to be neglected. The graphometer frees us from having to estimate the size of angles. The eye, which used to measure distances with precision, relies on the chain which measures them for it. The balance frees me from judging by hand the weight I know by means of the balance. The more ingenious are our tools, the cruder and more maladroit our organs become. By dint of gathering machines around us, we no longer find any in ourselves.

But when we put the skill which used to take the place of these machines into manufacturing them, when we use the sagacity which was required to do without them for making them, we gain without losing anything, we add art to nature, and we become more ingenious without becoming less adroit. If, instead of glueing a child to books, I bury him in a workshop, his hands work for the profit of his mind; he becomes a philosopher and believes he is only a laborer. Finally, this exercise has other uses of which I shall speak hereafter, and it will be seen how from the games of philosophy one can rise to the true functions of man.

I have already said that purely speculative knowledge is hardly suitable for children, even those nearing adolescence. But without making them go very far in systematic physics, nonetheless arrange that all their experiments are connected with one another by some sort of deduction, in order that with the aid of this chain they can order them in their minds and recall them when needed; for it is quite difficult for isolated facts and even reasonings to stick in the memory if one lacks some connection by which to recall them.

In the quest for the laws of nature, always begin with the phenomena most common and most accessible to the senses, and accustom your pupil to take these phenomena not for reasons but for facts. I take a stone and feign placing it in the air. I open my hand; the stone falls. I look at Emile, who is attentive to what I am doing, and I say to him, "Why did this stone fall?"

What child will stop short at this question? None, not even Emile, if I have not made a great effort to prepare him not to know how to respond. All will say that the stone falls because it is heavy. And what is heavy? That is what falls. The stone falls, therefore, because it falls? Here my little philosopher is really stumped. This is his first lesson in systematic physics, and, whether it profits him in this study or not, it will still be a lesson in good sense.

**Notes**

1. Emile learns Ptolemaic astronomy because it is the observation of common sense. Copernican astronomy will follow when he himself makes the observations which lead to it.

2. A meridian here is simply a north-south line. In the northern hemisphere, the sun is due south at high noon, so that a shadow cast by a stake points due north. Shadows of equal length are cast by a stake in the morning and evening at times equally distant from noon; and the north-south line (as also the shadow at noon) bisects the angle formed by any such pair of shadows. There are several ways of obtaining this bisector; what Rousseau has in mind here is the construction of a rhombus where one morning shadow and two evening shadows of the same length as the first form the sides. The fourth side can be easily supplied. The diagonal at right angles to the course of the sun is the meridian.

3. Rousseau added a note for the next edition in response to a man who had written an *Anti-Emile*. "I could not keep from laughing in reading a subtle critique of this little tale by M. de Formey. 'This magician,' he says, 'who prides himself on his emulation with a child and gravely sermonizes his teacher is an individual of the world of Emiles.' The clever M. de Formey was unable to suppose that this little scene was arranged and that the magician had been instructed about the role he had to play; for, indeed, I did not say so. But on the other hand, how many times have I declared that I did not write for people who have to be told everything?"

# 43

# The Good, the Bad, and the Ugly: The Many Faces of Constructivism

## D. C. Phillips

Across the broad fields of educational theory and research, constructivism has become something akin to a secular religion. In her book *Evolution as a Religion* (1985), Mary Midgley wrote that the theory of evolution "is not just an inert piece of theoretical science. It is, and cannot help being, also a powerful folk-tale about human origins. Any such narrative must have symbolic force" (1985, p. 1). She might well have written the same about constructivism, which is, whatever else it may be, a "powerful folk-tale" about the origins of human knowledge. As in all living religions, constructivism has many sects – each of which harbors some distrust of its rivals. This descent into sectarianism, and the accompanying growth in distrust of non-believers, is probably the fate of all large-scale movements inspired by interesting ideas; and it is the ideological or ugly side of the present scene, which is reflected in my article's title.

The educational literature on constructivism is enormous, and growing rapidly; a significant indicator is that the 1993 AERA Annual Meeting Program contained more than a score of sessions explicitly on this topic. Even as interesting a symposium as that which recently appeared in the *Educational Researcher* (vol. 23: 7, 1994) was able to give only an inadequate hint of the many varieties of constructivism that presently exist. It is part of my purpose in this essay to complicate matters even more by pointing to relevant discussions in other literatures that are rarely, if ever, mentioned by those embroiled in the educational debates. In particular, I will try to show that in the fields of epistemology and philosophy of science, in the relatively young discipline of science studies (an interdisciplinary philosophical, sociological, and historical field), and in the rapidly burgeoning feminist literature, there is much of relevance and interest to be found. The term *constructivism* does not occur with great frequency in these other bodies of literature – for example, the recent encyclopedic volume edited by Dancy and Sosa (1992), *A Companion to Epistemology*, gives it only three passing references – but nevertheless closely related ideas are the subject of vigorous debate.

To compensate for introducing these new complexities, however, I also will offer a way of viewing the various forms of constructivism that, I claim, will produce some order and clarity – I will argue that the main constructivist writers can be located

Originally published in *Educational Researcher* 24(7) (1995), pp. 5–12. © 1995 American Educational Research Association. Reproduced with permission of the publisher.

along each of three different dimensions or axes, and this highlights the relationships and differences between them. Given the volume of literature, to make good even on this promise is such a daunting task that almost all of my discussion will have to remain descriptive and clarificatory in orientation – to venture into criticisms (of which, I must admit, I have a number that I regard as quite serious) would require more space than even a tolerant editor of *ER* can make available. Besides which, informed critique must be based on a clear understanding of the position (or range of positions) being examined, and it is this necessary and preliminary task that will occupy me in the present article. My critical and evaluative discussion will be held over to a longer work that is in preparation. None of this, however, should be interpreted as meaning that I find all constructivist views unattractive – I hold that there is a very broad and loose sense in which all of us these days are constructivists, but, as usual, "God is in the details."

To turn, then, to the descriptive task in hand: The rampant sectarianism, coupled with the array of other literatures that contain pertinent material, makes it difficult to give even a cursory introductory account of constructivism, for members of the various sects will object that their own views are nothing like this! But to get the discussion underway, this oversimple gloss should convey the general idea (a more precise account of the issues at stake shall emerge as the discussion progresses): These days we do not believe that individuals come into the world with their "cognitive data banks" already prestocked with empirical knowledge, or with pre-embedded epistemological criteria or methodological rules. Nor do we believe that most of our knowledge is acquired, ready-formed, by some sort of direct perception or absorption. Undoubtedly humans are born with *some* cognitive or epistemological equipment or potentialities (the nature and degree of which the experts in developmental psychology still dispute – witness, for example, the well-known argument between Piaget and Chomsky about innateness and genetic programming), but by and large human knowledge, and the criteria and methods we use in our inquiries, are all *constructed*. Furthermore, the bodies of knowledge available to the growing learner are themselves human constructs – physics, biology, sociology, and even philosophy are not disciplines the content of which was handed down, ready formed, from on high; scholars have labored mightily over the generations to construct the content of these fields, and no doubt "internal politics" has played some role. Thus, in sum, human knowledge – whether it be the bodies of public knowledge known as the various disciplines, or the cognitive structures of individual knowers or learners – is *constructed*. And here, then, is the source of an initial confusion: Some constructivist sects focus their attention on the cognitive contents of the minds of individual learners, others focus on the growth of the "public" subject-matter domains, while a few brave groups tackle both – thus doubling the amount of quicksand that has to be negotiated. The problem is that readers of the constructivist literature are usually left to figure out for themselves which of these programs is being pursued. (For an argument that these different domains must not be conflated, see Phillips, 1987, ch. 12.)

## The Range of Constructivist Authors

Even on the basis of so preliminary and sketchy an account, it should be clear that potentially there is an enormous number of authors, spanning a broad philosophical or theoretical spectrum, who can be considered as being in some sense constructivist. The following nonexhaustive list is indicative of the range, complexity, and "symbolic force" of constructivist ideas:

1. Ernst von Glasersfeld, who has had very great influence in the contemporary international science and mathematics education communities, quotes with some approval the words of Ludwig Fleck (1929), a precursor of Thomas Kuhn – "The content of our knowledge must be considered the free creation of our culture. It resembles a traditional myth" (von Glasersfeld, 1991a, p. 118). Elsewhere he writes that from

> the naive commonsense perspective, the elements that form this complex environment belong to a *real* world of unquestionable objects, as *real* as the student, and these objects have an existence of their own, independent not only of the student but also of the teacher. Radical Constructivism is a theory of *knowing* which, for reasons that had nothing to do with teaching mathematics or education, does not accept this commonsense perspective. . . . Superficial or emotionally distracted readers of the constructivist literature have frequently interpreted this stance as a denial of "reality." (von Glasersfeld, 1991b, p. xv).

2. The complex epistemology of Immanuel Kant was quintessentially constructivist. The human cognitive apparatus (in particular our "category-governed modes of synthesis" in the case of natural science, as one commentator put it) was responsible for shaping our experience, and giving it causal, temporal, and spatial features. As Kant wrote at the beginning of his *Critique of Pure Reason*,

> But though all our knowledge *begins* with experience, it does not follow that it all arises *out of* experience. For it may well be that even our empirical knowledge is made up of what we receive through impressions *and of what our own faculty of knowledge* . . . supplies from itself. If our faculty of knowledge makes any such addition, it may be that we are not in a position to distinguish it from the raw material. (Kant, 1959, p. 25)

3. In the introductory section of their edited volume *Feminist Epistemologies* (1993), Linda Alcoff and Elizabeth Potter focus upon the sociopolitical processes by which our public bodies of knowledge are constructed. They write that the

> philosophical myth, like the myth of natural science, is that politics may motivate a philosopher to undertake philosophical work and that work may be put to better or worse political uses, but that a philosopher's work is good to the extent that its substantive, technical content is free of political influence. . . . The work presented here supports the hypothesis that politics intersect traditional epistemology. . . . [These essays] raise a question about the adequacy of any account of knowledge that ignores the politics involved in knowledge. These essays show . . . that to be *adequate*, an epistemology must attend to the complex ways in which social values influence knowledge. (p. 13)

4. The work of Thomas S. Kuhn on scientific revolutions and paradigms has been a major influence on several of the constructivist sects; for he stressed the active role of scientific communities in knowledge-construction. He wrote near the end of *The Structure of Scientific Revolutions*:

> The very existence of science depends upon vesting the power to choose between paradigms in the members of a special kind of community. Just how special that community must be if science is to survive and grow may be indicated by the very tenuousness of humanity's hold on the scientific enterprise. . . . The bulk of scientific knowledge is a product of Europe in the last four centuries. No other place and time has supported the very special communities from which scientific productivity comes. (Kuhn, 1962, pp. 166–7)

5. Jean Piaget is also generally regarded as a foundational figure by many constructivists. The following is clear enough:

> Fifty years of experience have taught us that knowledge does not result from a mere recording of observations without a structuring activity on the part of the subject. Nor do any a priori or innate cognitive structures exist in man; the functioning of intelligence alone is hereditary and creates structures only through an organization of successive actions performed on objects. Consequently, an epistemology conforming to the data of psychogenesis could be neither empiricist nor preformationist, but could consist only of a constructivism. (Piaget, 1980, p. 23)

6. John Dewey, influenced here by William James, wrote that all the difficulties connected with the problem of knowledge spring

> from a single root. They spring from the assumption that the true and valid object of knowledge is that which has being prior to and independent of the operations of knowing. They spring from the doctrine that knowledge is a grasp or beholding of reality without anything being done to modify its antecedent state – the doctrine which is the source of the separation of knowledge from practical activity. If we see that knowing is not the act of an outside spectator but of a participator inside the natural and social scene, then the true object of knowledge resides in the consequences of directed action. (Dewey, 1960, p. 196)

An expanded list could be generated very easily, with the addition of Jurgen Habermas, Giambattista Vico, sociologists of knowledge such as David Bloor or Barry Barnes or Steve Fuller, and a string of mainstream cognitive scientists who have interests in learning (Donald Norman would be a good example). If we were to move into mainstream educational writing, the list would become intolerably long.

As can be seen from even only the six views that have been quoted, constructivism can be developed in interesting psychological, epistemological, sociological, and historical directions. But because there are so many versions of constructivism, with important overlaps but also with major differences, it is difficult to see the forest for the trees – it is a matter of pressing concern to find some way of categorizing them so that the overall picture does not get lost.

## A Framework for Comparing Constructivisms

Each of the various forms of constructivism are complex; they are not "single issue" positions, but (explicitly or implicitly) they address a number of deep problems. To take merely one example from the six figures cited earlier, Ernst von Glasersfeld is not simply putting forward a view about the teaching of mathematics and science; it is clear that he is also advancing an epistemology, a psychology, and his own interpretation of the history of science and philosophy. But Piaget, Dewey, Kuhn, and the feminist epistemologists are no less complicated. As a result of their complexity, then, the various forms or sects of constructivism can be spread out along several different dimensions or continua or axes (each of which represents one key issue); forms that are close along one axis (i.e., are close on one issue) may be far apart on another.

1. The first axis or dimension requires relatively little discussion, as it was pretty obvious in the examples cited earlier. For convenience it can be given the label "individual psychology versus public discipline." Some constructivists – Piaget and Vygotsky would be quintessential figures here – have been concerned with how the individual learner goes about the construction of knowledge in his or her own cognitive apparatus; for other constructivists, however, the individual learner is of little interest, and what is the focus of concern is the construction of human knowledge in general. Many recent feminist epistemologists belong to this second group. In the middle of this first continuum, however, are a number of constructivists who have an interest in *both* poles, and who believe that their theories throw light on both the question of how individuals build up bodies of knowledge and how human communities have constructed the public bodies of knowledge known as the various disciplines. Occasionally von Glasersfeld seems to be in this middle camp; certainly Immanuel Kant and Karl Popper are also to be found there.

It needs to be stressed that constructivists who have the same general interest – for example in how individuals learn or construct knowledge – may differ markedly with respect to the mechanisms they see at work. Piaget and Vygotsky, for example, gave quite different accounts of this matter; one stressed the biological/psychological mechanisms to be found in the individual learner, whereas the other focussed on the social factors that influenced learning.

2. The second dimension or axis along which the various versions of constructivism can be spread is, arguably, the most crucial one (although it is also the most complex) – for it is the dimension that, in essence, allows us to define a thinker as being *constructivist*. For there is a point somewhere along this dimension where one ceases to *be* a constructivist. This dimension or continuum can be characterized crudely in terms of the label "humans the creators versus nature the instructor." The issue is as follows: When knowledge is constructed (whether it is in the mind or cognitive apparatus of the individual learner, or whether it is a public discipline), is the process one that is influenced chiefly by the minds or creative intelligence of the knower or knowers, together perhaps with the "sociopolitical" factors that are present when knowers interact in a community? Or, at the other extreme, is the knowledge "imposed" from the outside; does nature serve as an "instructor" or as a sort of template that the knowing subject or subjects (or community of knowledge builders) merely copy or absorb in a relatively passive fashion? In short, is new knowledge – whether it be individual knowledge, or public discipline – *made* or *discovered*?

It is arguable that theorists who occupy the "outer" or "external nature" or "discovery" end of the axis – like, for example, the late-17th-century British empiricist philosopher John Locke – are at best only minimally constructivist in orientation, or are not constructivist at all, for in their theories the contribution of human activity to knowledge construction is relatively insignificant. But "true-blue" constructivists are spread out along the continuum, with some of them being nearer than others to the "outer" or "nature as instructor" pole of the continuum.

It will be instructive to pursue the case of the empiricist John Locke a little further. In his work, and that of his associationist descendants, nature external to the knower is the source of the sensations that produce "simple ideas" fairly mechanically or automatically (although it is important to remember that for Locke other types of simple ideas come from reflection or inner experience); and from these simple units the more complex armamentarium of ideas is built up by various inborn combinatorial processes (or faculties). The mind (or "the understanding") is described in Locke's writings in very passive terms – the mind is a receptacle (an empty cabinet, a wax tablet, a piece of blotting paper) for storing whatever ideas come from experience. The mind is not able to produce simple ideas of its own, so that, for example, if the knower has not had experience of a particular color, he or she – no matter how clever – cannot invent the simple idea of that color. Thus Locke writes, using the example of a snowball:

> The power to produce any idea in our mind, I call "quality" of the subject wherein that power is. Thus a snowball having the power to produce in us the ideas of white, cold and round, the powers to produce those ideas in us as they are in the snowball, I call "qualities." (Locke, 1947, p. 45)

In short, it is the object in the external realm of nature – the snowball – which is causally responsible (via experience) for producing our knowledge; the snowball's qualities have "the power to produce in us" the ideas of whiteness and so on.

The position just described hardly warrants the label "constructivist" at all. What makes Locke's case more complex to assess is his insistence that once the "understanding" is "furnished" with a number of (externally produced) simple ideas, the mind can operate on these to construct something new:

> In this faculty of repeating and joining together its ideas, the mind has greater power in varying and multiplying the objects of its thoughts . . . It can, by its own power, put together those ideas it has, and make new complex ones. (Locke, 1947, p. 65)

Our simple ideas may be mere reflections of nature, but complex ideas are produced (constructed) by the human mind.

Unfortunately there is another complexity: Though statements like this seem to place Locke over the border and into the constructivist camp, the picture is muddied again by the fact that in some places (although not in all) Locke suggests that these combinatorial powers or faculties (that produce the complex ideas) are not only "wired in" before birth but also function virtually automatically. (This is certainly the way the faculties are depicted in the "mental chemistry" of Locke's 19th-century followers; and it should be noticed that there is a parallel issue here for our contemporaries who are enamored of computational theories of the mind – such theories sometimes are forced to assume the existence of an inner "homunculus," to leave some room for human creativity. See Searle, 1992, ch. 9). The only thing that it seems safe to say, then, is that Locke is close to the "outside/instruction by nature/discovery" end of the dimension under discussion here, and he also is close to the outer perimeter of constructivism – which side of the border he actually is on is a difficult judgement call.

We do not have to look far for examples of theorists at the other, "humans the creators" pole, of this second constructivist continuum or dimension. Most varieties of late 20th-century constructivism have as a major tenet the claim that knowledge is produced by humans, in processes that are unconstrained – or minimally constrained – by inputs or instruction from nature. But at this end of the continuum there is a great deal of confusion, for (as we saw earlier) some constructivists are focusing upon how developing individuals learn, whereas others are looking at how the "public" disciplines originate. There is further bifurcation even than this, for some hold that knowledge production comes about solely from intellectual or cognitive processes internal to each individual knower, whereas for others the processes are regarded as sociopolitical (and therefore in a sense public) and not simply or solely "inner," mental or intellectual in nature. These various views are combined in several different ways,

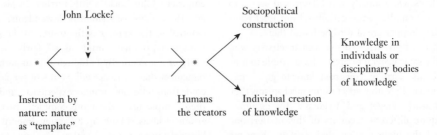

**Figure 43.1** Complexities of the second constructivist dimension

as will become evident later. On the principle that one picture is worth a thousand words, the accompanying diagram displays the complexities of this second constructivist dimension. Several examples will illustrate some of the possibilities at the "humans the creators" end of this second dimension.

(*a*) Members of the "strong program" in sociology of knowledge (such as Barnes, 1974, Collins, 1985, and perhaps even Fuller, 1988) – who are working on the origin of the public bodies of knowledge known as the disciplines, especially the sciences – can be read as being far from the "nature as template" view, but also as being far from the "individual creation of knowledge" view; when in their least compromising mood, they hold the view that sociopolitical processes can account *fully* for the form taken by the bodies of knowledge codified as the various disciplines.

(*b*) Perhaps the clearest example of a theorist who also is far from the "nature as instructor" end of the continuum, but who is not a social constructivist but instead stresses that knowledge construction is an individual matter, is Ernst von Glasersfeld. He provides the following striking rejection of the "nature as template" view, and affirms that it is the cognitive effort of the individual that results in the construction of knowledge:

> The notion that knowledge is the result of a learner's activity rather than that of the passive reception of information or instruction, goes back to Socrates and is today embraced by all who call themselves "constructivists." However, the authors whose work is collected here, constitute the radical wing of the constructivist front. . . . This attitude is characterized by the deliberate redefinition of the concept of knowledge as an *adaptive function*. In simple words, this means that the results of our cognitive efforts have the purpose of helping us cope in the world of experience, rather than the traditional goal of furnishing an "objective" representation of a world as it might "exist" apart from us and our experience. (von Glasersfeld, 1991b, pp. xiv–xv)

Von Glasersfeld acknowledges a significant debt to Piaget, which may explain why he focuses on the individual knower, and pays scant attention to the social processes in knowledge construction. (Von Glasersfeld's admirers may have their hackles raised by this last remark, for his educational concerns of course lead him to address the role of the teacher. But he faces severe problems of consistency here: it is clear that in much of his writing von Glasersfeld problematizes the notion of a "reality" external to the cognitive apparatus of the individual knower/learner. But as a result, it is difficult to see how he can consistently allow that social influences exist. After all, teachers and parents and siblings and so forth – no less than the atoms and molecules and forces of the external physical universe – are part of the realm external to the knower that von Glasersfeld is so skeptical about.)

Karl Popper is a philosopher who is situated at about the middle of the "humans the creators versus nature the instructor" continuum, for his theory of the development of knowledge can be summarized as "man proposes, nature disposes" – a view that nicely involves both poles of the continuum. Popper's view offers both an account of the growth of public bodies of knowledge (especially the sciences), but it can also be interpreted in such a way as to throw light on the psychology and epistemology of individual learning (Berkson and Wettersten, 1984). Popper was fond of expounding his view in terms of a crude flow diagram:

> problem → tentative theory → error elimination → new problem

The tentative theory is a creation of the human intellect; the error elimination (via testing) is done by nature.

3. The third dimension for comparing types of constructivism was touched on earlier: The construction of knowledge is an *active* process, but the activity can be described in terms of individual cognition or else in terms of social and political processes (or, of course, in terms of both). Furthermore, this activity can either be physical or mental, or again both. If a theorist were to argue that knowledge construction is carried out automatically, by the following of some predetermined inflexible routine or by some mechanical process, then his or her work would not count as constructivist; we saw in the case of John Locke that insofar as he postulated that simple ideas were built into complex knowledge by "prewired" cognitive processes (to use contemporary idiom rather than Locke's terminology), he could not be regarded as being situated within the general constructivist camp – for

although there is a place for mental activity in his model, it is not always clear that it is conscious or deliberate activity *of the knower*.

A nice contrast with Locke is Jean Piaget (closely followed here by von Glasersfeld); Piaget is as individualistic as Locke with respect to how knowledge is constructed (his voluminous writings only make scant reference to the role of the social environment, and Piaget typically depicts the developing child as a lone, inventive young scientist, struggling to make independent sense of the surrounding world). But Piaget does place enormous stress on the fact that the young knower is both mentally and physically active; indeed, knowledge growth is described by Piaget in terms of the dynamic processes of assimilation, accommodation, and equilibration, and the construction and internalization of action schemas (see Phillips, 1987, ch. 13, for further discussion).

Another important example of active constructivism is provided by the work of John Dewey and William James. Both these pragmatists (together with latter-day admirers such as Richard Rorty; see Kulp, 1992) vigorously attack what they call the "spectator theory of knowledge." In the late 19th century James had written a critique of Herbert Spencer's theory of mind, in which he said that mind was not a spectator, but rather "the knower is an actor" (James, 1920, p. 67) – a view that James elsewhere argued was underwritten by evolutionary theory (see for example his *Talks to Teachers on Psychology*). Dewey picked up on all this, and consistently expounded his own constructivist view of knowledge in contrast to the errors of the "spectator theory." (See, for example, Dewey's *The Quest for Certainty*, 1960.)

The spectator theory, as Dewey interpreted it, can be explicated by means of an analogy with football. According to the spectator theory, the way a knower obtains knowledge is analogous to the way a person can learn about football. He or she can learn by watching, by being a spectator; while learning, the spectator remains passive, and does not affect the course of the game. In contrast, in the theory held by James and Dewey the knower is an organic part of the same situation as the material to be known. To return to the football analogy, the person learning about football would be playing in the game; he or she would be affecting the game and, in the process, obtaining knowledge about it – the knower would be learning by participating or acting. (It is interesting to note, as an aside, that the spectator theory of knowledge has been largely ignored in the epistemological literature of the last few decades; Kulp (1992) has produced the only lengthy discussion of it, and although recognizing that it has some strengths, he reaches a generally negative conclusion. See also Phillips, 1971.) Lest all this make Dewey seem unduly individualistic, it is important to note that he also stressed the social nature of knowledge construction, both in individual learners and also with respect to the development of the public bodies of knowledge codified in the various disciplines; but the social activity he depicted was always harmonious and co-operative – unlike many social constructivists in the late 20th century he did not pay much attention to the internal politics of knowledge producing communities, or the effects of power differentials on the types of knowledge produced.

To turn to the other end or pole of this particular dimension, Lynn Hankinson Nelson stresses that knowledge construction is an active process – even a struggle – carried out by groups or communities, not by individuals. In an interesting passage, she writes:

> In suggesting that it is communities that construct and acquire knowledge, I do not mean (or "merely" mean) that what comes to be recognized or "certified" as knowledge is the result of collaboration between, consensus achieved by, political struggles engaged in, negotiations undertaken among, or other activities engaged in by individuals who, *as individuals, know* in some logically or empirically "prior" sense. . . . The change I am proposing involves what we should construe as the *agents* of these activities. My arguments suggest that the collaborators, the consensus achievers, and, in more general terms, the agents who generate knowledge are communities and subcommunities, not individuals. (Nelson, 1993, p. 124)

Examining the range of contemporary constructivist writers who see the development of knowledge as essentially social in nature, it turns out that most hold that knowledge construction is "rational" in that it proceeds deliberately according to methodological rules and criteria that are consciously held within a sociocultural group. But – importantly – they stress that these rules and criteria were constructed by social processes, and thus were influenced by power relations, partisan interests, and so forth. Many feminist epistemologists hold variants of this position. Other forms of constructivism – most notably the so-called "strong program" in sociology of knowledge associated with Barnes, Collins, and others (Barnes, 1974; Collins, 1985) – go somewhat further, and would put the explanatory burden even more firmly on sociological factors rather than rational or quasirational considerations. As Martin Hollis puts it, the strong program "distinguishes sharply between intellectual systems and social systems, and tries to explain the former as an effect of the latter" (Hollis, 1992, p. 77) To use an analogy, it is as if the strong program would have us explain what happened in, say, one of the world championship chess games between the Russian Kasparov and the British player Short in 1993, entirely in sociopolitical terms with no reference being made to the rules and theories and strategy of chess! (It is of more than passing interest that Thomas S. Kuhn has recently stated that "I am among those who have found the claims of the strong program absurd: an example of deconstruction gone mad." See Kuhn, 1992, p. 9.)

A contrasting and more conservative position would be the one held by the philosopher of science Imre Lakatos: Knowledge is actively built up over time within a research program that progresses as it responds to intellectual considerations (including data obtained from nature); and sociopolitical factors only enter the story when there is need to explain why the scientists involved in that particular research program lapsed into error or deviated from what would have been rationally optimal for them to believe, given the data available to them at the time (Lakatos, 1978).

This gradation within the ranks of social constructivists is nicely captured by the sociologist and historian of science who is one of the central figures in contemporary "science studies," Bruno Latour:

> "Radical," "progressivist," "conservative," "reactionary," "golden mean". . . . A radical is someone who claims that scientific knowledge is entirely constructed "out of" social relations; a progressivist is someone who would say that it is "partially" constructed out of social relations but that nature somehow "leaks in" at the end. At the other side of this tug-of-war, a reactionary is someone who would claim science becomes really scientific only when it finally sheds any trace of social construction; while a conservative would say that although science escapes from society there are still factors from society that "leak in" and influence its development. In the middle, would be the marsh of wishy-washy scholars who add a little bit of nature to a little bit of society and shun the two extremes. (Latour, 1992, p. 276)

The groundbreaking figure in the social-constructivist tradition, of course, is Thomas S. Kuhn; but the philosopher Helen Longino is representative of much interesting work being done by contemporary feminist philosophers (insofar as any one person can represent such a diversified field). Her position falls somewhere between those of the "strong program" and Imre Lakatos. In her book *Science as Social Knowledge* (1990), and in a number of essays, she attacks the assumption made within traditional individualistic epistemology that a knower can be conceived validly as being an isolated individual, stripped of interests, motives, biases, and other socially determined traits. Longino goes on to stress that a knower must be able to subject assumptions and knowledge-claims to critical scrutiny, which cannot be done in genuine isolation from a community (and without using communal standards). Thus, she argues, knowledge must be viewed as being actively "constructed not by individuals but by an interactive dialogic community" (Longino, 1993, p. 112). In social science jargon, she is suggesting a change of the "unit of analysis" in epistemology. Earlier we met Nelson's rather similar views.

## Epistemological versus Sociopolitical and Educational Concerns

The three dimensions along which, I have argued, the various forms or sects of constructivism can be located are all, to a greater or lesser degree, *epistemically related* dimensions. Clearly, all forms of constructivism take a stand on epistemological issues, but we will form a distorted picture of all of them if we let matters rest here. I believe it is important to recognize that the constructivist sects also differ with respect to the intensity with which they harbor various educational and sociopolitical concerns. For it is apparent that although some constructivists have epistemological enemies whom they are anxious to defeat, most have pressing social and political concerns that motivate their work. It should not come as a surprise, of course, that in the late 20th century many of those who hold a position that is extremely sensitive to the fact that knowledge is produced should also have heightened sensitivity to the sociopolitical conditions under which this production takes place. What I am suggesting here is that it would be a mistake to think that when the philosophical concerns of the constructivists have been identified (and examined), our work is over – the concerns run deeper than this.

Consider several obvious examples: von Glasersfeld, Dewey, and the feminist epistemologists. All of these make epistemological points of varying degrees of sophistication (as has been sketched in the earlier discussion); but all of them also have important educational or social concerns, each of which has a degree of credibility that is independent of the fate of the respective epistemologies. It even could be argued that for many constructivists the latter concerns are more central. (And, of course, a reader can be sympathetic to the educational or social concerns without being a fellow-traveller with regard to the epistemology, or vice versa.)

Thus, von Glasersfeld's epistemology, which I have claimed elsewhere is developed in a flawed way (Phillips, 1992; see also Matthews, 1992; 1994, ch. 7), is an important springboard from which he and the radical constructivists have launched an important educational movement (see Noddings, 1990, for a somewhat similar assessment). His individualism and subjectivism in epistemology leads him (or perhaps was accepted because it allows him) to argue that each individual science and mathematics student is responsible for building his or her own set of understandings of these disciplines; teachers cannot assume that all students have the same set of understandings, or that their own ways of understanding are shared by their students. Moreover, it is clear from von Glasersfeld's perspective that everyone studying a field like science has his or her own set of conceptions and preconceptions that influence the course of subsequent learning; teachers should drop the fashionable but misleading talk of student "misconceptions," for this implies that there is a standard set of "correct" conceptions that all learners should have. One result of all this is to highlight the need for individual attention to students, and the need to give guidance about how bodies of understanding are built up. *It could be argued here that a weak or at least a controversial epistemology has become the basis for a strong pedagogic policy.* Here is how one prominent researcher in the domains of science and mathematics education summarizes the beneficial influence of radical constructivism:

> When one applies constructivism to the issue of teaching, one must reject the assumption that one can simply pass on information to a set of learners and expect that understanding will result. Communication is a far more complex process than this. When teaching

concepts, as a form of communication, the teacher must form an adequate model of the student's ways of viewing an idea and s/he then must assist the student in restructuring those views to be more adequate from the student's and from the teacher's perspective. Constructivism not only emphasizes the essential role of the constructive process, it also allows one to emphasize that we are at least partially able to be aware of those constructions and then to modify them through our conscious reflection on that constructive process. (Confrey, 1990, p. 109)

In the case of John Dewey, constructivist epistemology also leads directly to social and pedagogic policies. (In his *Democracy and Education* Dewey specifically claimed that philosophy *is* the theory of education.) As he saw it, the pedagogical and social ramifications of his epistemological opposition to the spectator theory of knowledge were quite broad. Starting from the constructivist position that the knower is an "actor" rather than a "spectator," Dewey staunchly advocated the use of activity methods in the schoolroom – for students are potential knowers, yet traditional schooling forces students into the mold of passive receptacles waiting to have information instilled, instead of allowing them to move about, discuss, experiment, work on communal projects, pursue research outdoors in the fields and indoors in the library and laboratory, and so forth. Consider this wonderful description of the traditional schoolroom, where his negative attitude to the passivity of the spectator theory is crystal clear:

> Just as the biologist can take a bone or two and reconstruct the whole animal, so, if we put before the mind's eye the ordinary schoolroom, with its rows of ugly desks placed in geometrical order, crowded together so that there shall be as little moving room as possible . . . and add a table, some chairs, the bare walls, and possibly a few pictures, we can reconstruct the only educational activity that can possibly go on in such a place. It is all made "for listening." (Dewey, 1899/1969, p. 31)

The general idea should now be clear enough; the interested reader can try his or her own hand at constructing an analysis of the broader concerns that are tied in with Piaget's and Habermas's views on the construction of knowledge (to mention only two of the other most obvious examples). But a third example is worth pursuing here, for it leads in quite a different sociopolitical direction.

Feminist epistemologists such as Sandra Harding and Helen Longino clearly have social concerns that reinforce their commitment to their respective social-constructivist epistemologies (the two have philosophies that are similar but by no means identical). In stressing that the knower cannot be conceived as being an artificially objectified and solitary individual isolated from a historical and socio-cultural setting (this rival view, as we saw earlier, is close to that held by von Glasersfeld), they wish to highlight the degree to which these previously neglected social and political factors play an epistemological role. Harding stresses that in a society that is stratified "by race, ethnicity, class, gender, sexuality, or some other such politics," the activities of those at the top "both organize and set limits on what persons who perform such activities can understand about themselves and the world around them" (Harding, 1993, p. 54). Such activities, of course, include those in the epistemological arena; and necessarily the knowledge generated by such people is going to be deficient. However, the activities of marginalized people "at the bottom of such social hierarchies" can provide a sounder starting point for epistemological inquiry (p. 54). Harding's contention is that people at the bottom can generate more critical questions to guide inquiry, for their position is less "limiting" (p. 55). In short, for Harding constructivist epistemological considerations (no matter how contentious) lead directly to the important issue of social empowerment.

Helen Longino, after citing the influence of Kuhn, Feyerabend, and others, goes on to stress the ways in which science is a communal rather than an individual endeavor; scientific knowledge "is constructed . . . by individuals in interaction with one another in ways that modify their observations, theories and hypotheses, and patterns of reasoning" (Longino, 1993, p. 111). She then discusses four criteria that must be satisfied if "transformative critical discourse" is to be achieved – there must be publicly recognized forums; the community must not only tolerate dissent but its beliefs must actually change over time; there must be publicly recognized standards of evaluation of theories, observations,

and so on; and communities must be "characterized by equality of intellectual authority" (pp. 112–13). Perhaps Longino's overriding concern – which is both epistemological and social – is that "no segment of the community, whether powerful or powerless, can claim epistemic privilege" (p. 118).

## Concluding Remarks

I opened the present discussion by identifying the quasi-religious or ideological aspects of constructivism as being *ugly*. The *good*, as I hope I have made clear, is the emphasis that various constructivist sects place on the necessity for active participation by the learner, together with the recognition (by most of them) of the social nature of learning; it seems clear that, with respect to their stance on education, most types of constructivism are modern forms of progressivism. Constructivism also deserves praise for bringing epistemological issues to the fore in the discussion of learning and the curriculum; while I do not agree with some (or even many) of their specific philosophical points, the level of sophistication of the debates in education journals is much improved as a result of their presence. The *bad*, which I have not been able to document adequately in the present discussion, is the tendency within many forms of constructivist epistemology (despite occasional protestations to the contrary) towards relativism, or towards treating the justification of our knowledge as being entirely a matter of sociopolitical processes or consensus, or toward the jettisoning of any substantial rational justification or warrant at all (as is arguably the case with the radical constructivists). My own view is that any defensible epistemology must recognize – and not just pay lip service to – the fact that nature exerts considerable constraint over our knowledge-constructing activities, and allows us to detect (and eject) our errors about it. This still leaves plenty of room for us to improve the nature and operation of our knowledge-constructing communities, to make them more inclusionary and to empower long-silenced voices.[1]

## Note

1. It is relevant to note that the philosopher Alvin Goldman has a promising research program in this area (see Goldman, 1992).

## References

Alcoff, L. and Potter, E. (eds.) (1993) *Feminist Epistemologies* (New York: Routledge).

Barnes, B. (1974) *Scientific Knowledge and Sociological Theory* (London: Routledge).

Bereiter, C. (1994) Constructivism, socioculturalism, and Popper's World 3. *Educational Researcher*, 23(7): 21–3.

Berkson, W. and Wettersten, L. (1984) *Learning from Error: Karl Popper's Psychology of Learning* (LaSalle, IL: Open Court).

Bredo, E. (1994) Reconstructing educational psychology: Situated cognition and Deweyian pragmatism. *Educational Psychologist*, 29(1): 23–35.

Chomsky, N. (1979) *Language and Responsibility* (New York: Pantheon).

Collins, H. (1985) *Changing Order* (London: Sage).

Confrey, J. (1990) What constructivism implies for teaching. In R. B. Davis, C. A. Maher, and N. Noddings (eds.), *Constructivist Views on the Teaching and Learning of Mathematics, Journal for Research in Mathematics Education Monograph*, 4: pp. 107–22.

Dancy, J. and Sosa, E. (1992) (eds.) *A Companion to Epistemology* (Oxford: Blackwell).

Dewey, J. (1917) The need for a recovery of philosophy. In *Creative Intelligence* (New York: Holt).

Dewey, J. (1960) *The Quest for Certainty* (New York: Capricorn).

Dewey, J. (1969) *The School and Society* (reprinted as a joint edition with *The Child and the Curriculum*) (Chicago: University of Chicago Press).

Fuller, S. (1988) *Social Epistemology* (Bloomington and Indianapolis: Indiana University Press).

Goldman, A. (1992) *Liaisons* (Cambridge, MA: MIT Press/Bradford Books).

Habermas, J. (1971) *Knowledge and Human Interests* (Boston, MA: Beacon Press).

Harding, S. (1993) Rethinking standpoint epistemology: "What is Strong Objectivity?" In L. Alcoff and E. Potter (eds.), *Feminist Epistemologies* (New York: Routledge), pp. 49–82.

Hollis, M. (1992) Social thought and social action. In E. McMullin (ed.), *The Social Dimensions of Science* (Notre Dame, IN: University of Note Dame Press), pp. 68–84.

James, W. (1920) Remarks on Spencer's definition of mind as correspondence. In W. James, *Collected Essays and Reviews* (London: Longman).

Kant, I. (1959) *Critique of Pure Reason* (London: Dent/Everyman).

Kuhn, T. S. (1962) *The Structure of Scientific Revolutions* (Chicago: University of Chicago Press).

Kuhn, T. S. (1992) *The Trouble with the Historical Philosophy of Science*. The Robert and Maurine Rothschild Distinguished Lecture (Cambridge, MA: Harvard University Department of the History of Science).

Kulp, C. B. (1992) *The End of Epistemology* (Westport, CT: Greenwood Press).

Lakatos, I. (1970) Falsification and the methodology of scientific research programs. In I. Lakatos and A. Musgrave (eds.), *Criticism and the Growth of Knowledge* (Cambridge: Cambridge University Press), pp. 91–6.

Lakatos, I. (1978) History of science and its rational reconstructions. In I. Lakatos, *The Methodology of Scientific Research Programs* (Cambridge: Cambridge University Press), pp. 102–38.

Latour, B. (1992) One more turn after the social turn. In E. McMullin (ed.), *The Social Dimensions of Science* (Notre Dame, IN: University of Notre Dame Press), pp. 272–94.

Locke, J. (1947) *An Essay Concerning Human Understanding* (London: Dent/Everyman).

Longino, H. (1990) *Science as Social Knowledge* (Princeton, NJ: Princeton University Press).

Longino, H. (1993) Subjects, power and knowledge: Description and prescription in feminist philosophies of science. In L. Alcoff and E. Potter (eds.), *Feminist Epistemologies* (New York: Routledge), pp. 101–20.

Matthews, M. R. (1992) Old wine in new bottles: A problem with constructivist epistemology. In H. Alexander (ed.), *Philosophy of Education 1992*, Proceedings of the Forty-Eighth Annual Meeting of the Philosophy of Education Society (Urbana, IL: Philosophy of Education Society, University of Illinois), pp. 303–11.

Matthews, M. R. (1994) *Science Teaching: The Role of History and Philosophy of Science* (New York: Routledge).

Midgley, M. (1985) *Evolution as a Religion* (London: Methuen).

Nelson, L. H. (1993) Epistemological communities. In L. Alcoff and E. Potter (eds.), *Feminist Epistemologies* (New York: Routledge), pp. 121–59.

Noddings, N. (1990) Constructivism in mathematics education. In R. B. Davis, C. A. Maher, and N. Noddings (eds.), *Constructivist Views on the Teaching and Learning of Mathematics, Journal for Research in Mathematics Education Monograph*, 4: pp. 7–18.

Norman, D. (1980) What goes on in the mind of the learner. In W. McKeachie (ed.), *Learning Cognition, and College Teaching* (San Francisco: Jossey-Bass), pp. 37–49.

Phillips, D. C. (1971) John Dewey and the organismic archetype. In R. I. W. Selleck (ed.), *Melbourne Studies in Education 1971* (Melbourne: Melbourne University Press), pp. 232–71.

Phillips, D. C. (1984) Was William James telling the truth after all? *The Monist*, 67(3): 419–34.

Phillips, D. C. (1987) *Philosophy, Science, and Social Inquiry* (Oxford: Pergamon Press).

Phillips, D. C. (1992) On castigating constructivists. In H. Alexander (ed.), *Philosophy of Education 1992*, Proceedings of the Forty-Eighth Annual Meeting of the Philosophy of Education Society (Urbana, IL:

Philosophy of Education Society, University of Illinois), pp. 312–15.

Piaget, J. (1980) The psychogenesis of knowledge and its epistemological significance. In M. Piattelli-Palmarini (ed.), *Language and Learning* (Cambridge, MA: Harvard University Press).

Searle, J. (1992) *The Rediscovery of Mind* (Cambridge, MA: Bradford/MIT).

Vico, G. (1982) *Vico: Selected Writings*, ed. L. Pompa (Cambridge: Cambridge University Press).

von Glasersfeld, E. (1984) An introduction to radical constructivism. In P. Watzlawick (ed.), *The Invented Reality* (New York: W.W. Norton), pp. 17–40.

von Glasersfeld, E. (1990) An exposition of constructivism: Why some like it radical. In R. B. Davis, C. A. Maher, and N. Noddings (eds.), *Constructivist Views on the Teaching and Learning of Mathematics, Journal for Research in Mathematics Education Monograph*, 4: pp. 19–29.

von Glasersfeld, E. (1991a) Cognition construction of knowledge, and teaching. In M. R. Matthews (ed.), *History, Philosophy, and Science Teaching* (New York: Teachers College Press), pp. 117–32.

von Glasersfeld, E. (1991b) Introduction. In E. von Glasersfeld (ed.), *Radical Constructivism in Mathematics Education* (Dordrecht, The Netherlands: Kluwer), pp. xiii–xx.

# 44

# Constructivisms and Objectivity: Disentangling Metaphysics from Pedagogy

## Richard E. Grandy

### Introduction

This chapter is an attempt to construct a philosophical background and underpinnings of the SEPIA project. SEPIA stands for Science Education Portfolio Instruction and Assessment, and was an NSF-funded research effort carried out in Pittsburgh area middle schools jointly by researchers from the University of Pittsburgh and ETS. Some of the applied pedagogy and implementation of the project can be found in Duschl and Feather (1995). In the best spirit of rational reconstruction, however, this is not a philosophical prologemenon which existed in articulated form before the project but rather emerged through discussion and modifications. Moreover, agreement in details is not to be expected among the various participants.

### Constructivisms: Cognitive, Epistemic, and Metaphysical

Since constructivisms are a dominant topic these years (Fosnot 1993; Giannetto 1992; Glasson et al. 1992; Goldin 1990; Matthews and Davson-Galle

1992; Matthews 1994; O'Loughlin 1992, 1993; Von Glasersfeld 1992), and since SEPIA incorporates a number of constructivist principles, it will be helpful to delineate those principles and to distinguish them from some other principles which are not included. This may be a more generally useful exercise, of course, since it seems to me that there is not sufficient clarity about the variations on constructivism, let alone their relations and implications. I also believe that an understanding of the various elements and kinds of constructivism will be helpful in evaluating what is required of teachers in implementing SEPIA or any other curriculum that incorporates these important elements of constructivism.

There are a wide range of terms, and I am sure I will offend some authors by using the following distinctions rather than theirs. I distinguish cognitive constructivism, epistemic constructivism, and metaphysical constructivism.

*Cognitive constructivism* is the view that individual cognitive agents understand the world and make their way around in it by using mental representations that they have constructed. What they could in principle construct at a given time

Previously published in Michael R. Matthews (ed.), *Constructivism in Science Education* (Dordrecht: Kluwer Academic Publishers, 1998), pp. 113–23. © 1998 Kluwer Academic Publishers. Reprinted with permission of Springer Verlag.

depends on the conceptual, linguistic, and other notational resources, e.g., mathematics and graphing, at their disposal and on their current representations of the world that they have constructed through their personal history. What they actually construct depends also on their motivations and on the resources of time and energy available to devote to this particular task.

By *metaphysical constructivism* I mean the (collection of) views that the furniture of the world is constructed by us. This view can be subdivided into the individualistic, which postulates individual constructions of individual worlds, and the social, which postulates social constructions of shared worlds. This view typically contrasts with metaphysical realism, the view that (much of) the furniture of the world exists independently of minds and thoughts. There are some obvious issues for the social sciences that I will not explore here, since social institutions are clearly human creations; the implications for geography or psychology or human biology are unclear and will also not be explored here.

Metaphysical realism itself comes in a range of positions on the optimism/pessimism scale with regard to the knowability of the structure. Optimistic metaphysical realism holds that not only does the universe have an intrinsic structure, that God used a blueprint if you like, but that the structure is knowable in principle by humans – we could understand the blueprint. Less optimistic, though still guardedly hopeful, versions would be that we can develop representations which are approximately correct descriptions of some aspects of the universe. How either of these positions is justified philosophically is a matter we will not linger over here, for my main point is that these issues are irrelevant for science education once we understand fully the implications of cognitive constructivism.

A metaphysical realist who accepts cognitive constructivism must recognize that whatever knowledge is attained or even attainable about the ultimate structure of the universe must be represented in the constructions of the cognizer. While accepting cognitive constructivism has very important consequences for the teacher, which I will elaborate on shortly, once you have embraced cognitive constructivism it makes very little difference what attitude one has toward the metaphysical realist issues. However independent of us the structure of the universe may be, what we can achieve by way of producing more knowledgeable students depends on the representations they can construct. This

seems to me of great importance because if Constructivism is presented as a package which includes both cognitive constructivism and metaphysical anti-realism then teachers who have long-standing philosophical inclinations toward realism will find the package unpalatable. Cognitive constructivism is a relatively empirical theory which has strong evidential support from psychology, artificial intelligence and education; metaphysical realism is a venerable philosophical doctrine supported by philosophical arguments, and subject to equally venerable philosophical objections.

Accepting cognitive constructivism has very significant consequences for understanding the tasks, and the demands of the tasks, required of the science teacher (Bloom 1992). All science teachers have, and must necessarily always have had, a philosophy of science – a set of beliefs about the nature of scientific inquiry, of scientific progress, of scientific reasoning, of scientific data, theories, and so on. Often this has been at least somewhat unconscious and implicit, often acquired unreflectively along with the content knowledge in science classes. And often, in the past at least, this philosophy of science incorporated beliefs in the continuous linear progress of science, of the empiricist inductive scientific method, in the immutability of scientific facts, in scientific realism, perhaps even metaphysical realism, and so on. It has often included the philosophy of science education which is described as direct teaching (Duschl 1990), or, as I think of it, the modified Dragnet theory of teaching. Unlike the old Dragnet show we don't just give them the facts, but on that model we do just give them the facts, definitions and theories, and nothing but the facts, definitions and theories.

Whatever the remainder of one's philosophy of science, to accept cognitive constructivism means recognizing that each student constructs a representation based on their experience, including but by no means limited to teachers' verbal input. The teacher must assess the extent to which the student's representation is isomorphic to the teacher's, but of course cognitive constructivism applies reflexively and the teachers have no direct infallible access to the students' representations but instead construct their own representations of the students' representations. Since one of the typical student's motivations, for better or worse, is to please the teacher it may also be valuable for the teacher to construct a representation of the student's representation of the teacher's representation.

The practical issues of this process can be discussed under the heading of assessment (Duschl and Feather 1995), but I want to make some general more philosophical points about the process. Teachers are necessarily pursuing this process under time constraints and must repeatedly balance the potential value of further exploring the student's representation in all of its detailed uniqueness against categorizing the student's representation as sufficiently similar to others seen in the past to allow a particular course of further instruction to be developed without further investigation.

Of course that is only part of the task, for the teacher may well need to understand also why the student has constructed that particular representation. The divergence from the desired kind of representation may result from lack of the tools to construct an alternative, lack of accepted evidence that the current representation is insufficient or lack of motivation to construct an alternative (Ames 1990). The next step to bringing about desired change will likely depend on which of these factors is prevalent, and this implies that the teacher must have an understanding of motivational psychology, of the evidence the student accepts, what the student counts as evidence, and what conceptual tools the student can make use of. If this is correct, then the conceptual change movement was in the right direction, but the process of instigating conceptual change in the student is more complicated than was probably initially recognized.

## Objectivity and Change

Some science educators are unwilling to pronounce any student representation a 'misconception'. The reasons for this reluctance are important to analyze and understand. There is a very important positive aspect to this taboo which stems from the insight that the students produce the best representations that they are capable of producing at the time given their information, conceptual and motivational constraints. The student is not to be faulted. But if we are unwilling to evaluate representations, unwilling to judge some representations and understandings as more accurate, more general, more consistent than others, then there is no reason to teach 'science'. Why spend our time on such a frustrating activity if we do not think that the student is in principle capable of a representation which is in some important sense an improvement?

If the representations of the teachers or of the scientific community are not in some judgmental way better than those of neophyte students then there is nothing to teach and time would be better spent on spelling.

Having said that, and emphasizing the difference between judging the representation and judging the student, we should note that the fact that the teacher sees room for improvement does not mean that the best way to proceed is by directly criticizing the student's representation. One important aspect of the cognitive constructivist view is that the student's repertoire typically includes more than one way of representing a situation. Just as we can draw various maps representing various aspects of the world – highways, rainfall, elevation, population – the cognitive agent represents any situation in sundry ways. We recognize now that it is not just a matter of enabling the student to construct a Newtonian representation of a situation, but that there is the further project of ensuring that the Newtonian representation, rather than the intuitive physics representation, is applied. There is nothing wrong with having multiple theories or representations – the best-known examples are the use of Newtonian physics for large slow objects, and relativity or quantum mechanics for the very fast or very small. This use of multiple representations is probably ubiquitous in the sciences – Cartwright (1983) cites a number of such cases, including six competing mathematical treatments of quantum damping (see p. 78) as part of her argument for the ontological priority of causes over laws. But there is an important and somewhat elusive element of expertise in knowing what representation to deploy. And, most importantly, there is abundant evidence that students continue to deploy intuitive versions of Aristotelian physics after training at the college level in Newtonian mechanics (Bruer 1993, p. 130).

It will be helpful to distinguish, using Megill's terms, absolute from disciplinary objectivity. Absolute objectivity was the goal of some of the mathematical explorations of inductive logic during the heyday of logical positivism, and has long been a philosophical Holy Grail. Like metaphysical realism, it is irrelevant, in my view, to the process of science pedagogy since absolute objectivity is at best an ideal and in the classroom we are but beginning the process of developing a sense of objectivity. Absolute objectivity requires criteria of validity which are invariant over time or culture or discipline. In contrast, it seems to me that a very worthwhile, and manageable goal, is to develop and nurture disciplinary objectivity.

> Disciplinary objectivity emphasizes not universal criteria of validity but particular, yet still authoritative, disciplinary criteria. It emphasizes not the eventual convergence of all inquirers of good will but the proximate convergence of accredited inquirers within a given field. (Megill 1991, p. 305)

Megill qualifies his adjective 'disciplinary' with a footnote saying that many of the criteria tend to be even more specific than disciplinary, i.e., originating from subdisciplines. This is important for the culture of the classroom, for the discipline we hope students will construct is not professional biology or geology, but an age appropriate variant of that, which is also limited by the constraints on time, equipment and other resources. The goal is to create in the classroom a subculture which is in some appropriate ways related to the discipline under study.

## Epistemic Constructivism: Social or Individual?

In my presentation of constructivisms and their relations in the first section I ignored *epistemic constructivism*, the view that knowledge is constructed by us rather than directly imbibed from the environment. This seems to me a reasonable consequence of cognitive constructionism, though a thorough defense would require a detailed discussion of the various possible analyses of knowledge. Rather than engage in that enterprise, I would like to flag an important aspect of the use of the term 'construction' that has, I think, been insufficiently remarked on. The use of the term 'constructivism' is arguably a metaphor extending to the abstract a notion that makes good physical sense – we construct dams, buildings, airplanes.

What I want to note is that in the case of physical construction there are always important constraints on the construction process if we are constructing for some useful purpose and not simply to expend time and energy. Some methods of construction are more efficient than others, some are faster, some are slower and more expensive but produce a more enduring product. Many shoddy methods of construction produce nothing of value. Surprisingly, little discussion has been expended on the issue of the methods and materials of construction that go into constructing representations of scientific objects, data and theories.

Accepting that knowledge is constructed, a natural metaphysical question that arises at this point is whether one sees the scientific group or the individual as the basic unit of analysis and explanation of knowledge. Two fairly representative but divergent positions are the following which are, or were, held by two distinguished philosophers of science from the University of Minnesota:

> What I propose . . . is a much more thorough going contextualism than the one which urges us to remember that scientific inquiry occurs in a social context, or even that scientists are social actors whose interests drive their scientific work. What I urge is a contextualism which understands the cognitive processes of scientific inquiry not as opposed to the social, but as themselves social. This means that normativity, if it is possible at all, must be imposed on social processes and interactions, that is, that the rules or norms of justification that distinguish knowledge (or justified hypothesis-acceptance) from opinion must operate at the level of social as opposed to individual cognitive processes. (Longino 1992)

In contrast

> The conclusion is simple. The most promising approach to a general theory of science is one that takes individual scientists as the basic units of analysis. It follows that we must look to the cognitive sciences for our most basic models, for it is these sciences that currently produce the best causal models of the cognitive activities of individual human agents. (Giere 1989)

The view I am advocating accepts neither model, but sees the continuing dynamic interaction between group and individuals as critical (cf. Cobb 1994a,b; Driver et al. 1994, for related arguments). 'Although learning science involves social interactions, . . . we have argued that individuals have to make personal sense of newly introduced ways of viewing the world' (Driver et al. 1994, p. 11). Objective knowledge is the result of an interactive process between individuals and community. It is essential to see that although a group is in an obvious sense constituted at a given time by a set of individuals, as a group changes over time members are attracted to the group or become part of it because of the properties of the group as a whole. The group, and the perception of the group, shape the cognitive behavior of those who join it. Moreover, epistemic evaluation seems appropriate for both individual and group processes, although the units and the measure of evaluation differ.

At the professional level of science education, there is a tension between ensuring that everyone who is given the formal credentials of the discipline share the fundamental values and concepts so that the coherence of the discipline is preserved, and ensuring that innovative thinkers who may question even fundamental values and concepts are not excluded so that the possibility of creative innovation is preserved. In other words, both the group, as a group, and the individuals who constitute it must have appropriate characteristics in order for there to be a significant cognitive activity worth calling knowledge. One analysis of the role of the group is that of Longino (1994).

She lists four conditions for a community to meet in order for a consensus to qualify as knowledge:

1  There must be publicly recognized forums for the criticism of evidence, of methods, and assumptions and reasoning.
2  There must be uptake of criticism. The community must not merely tolerate dissent; its beliefs and theories must change over time in response to the critical discourse taking place within it.
3  There must be publicly recognized standards by reference to which theories, hypotheses, and observational practices are evaluated and by appeal to which criticism is made relevant to the goals of the inquiring community . . .
4  Finally, communities must be characterized by equality of intellectual authority. What consensus exists must be the result not of the exercise of political or economic power, or of the exclusion of dissenting perspectives, but a result of critical dialogue in which all relevant perspectives are represented. This criterion is meant to impose duties of inclusion; it does not require that each individual, no matter what her or his past record or state of training, should be granted equal authority . . . (Longino 1994, pp. 144–5)

These requirements were written with the professional community, not the classroom in mind, but I think they are a reasonable set of guidelines for the classroom scientific community as well. There are a number of crucial and vague terms, but while these can be fleshed out in somewhat more detail,

the exact details will have to be developed and negotiated separately in each individual case.

## Individual, Society and History

For either individual or social construction of science more is needed than theories, data and instruments. What is missing are the epistemic connections that relate theories to supporting data, to conflicting theories, to anomalous data, to equivocal data. The concept of a data domain, as developed by Ackermann (1985) and of the importance of anomalous data (Chinn and Brewer 1993) within that domain needs to be emphasized. While the individual has some freedom to argue against the grain of the scientific community, to a large extent what can be taken as data and what is disqualified, what is strong evidence and what is weak evidence, is always judged against the background provided by the community's experience with the theories, the data domain and the instruments in question. The data domain may be very refined, as in the case of professional level well-established sciences, or much more in flux, as it will be in the classroom scientific community, but the demarcation between what counts and what does not, however fluctuating it may be over time, is critical to the ongoing enterprise. And initiation into the process of constructing data, evaluating data, citing data and contesting data are all part of the individual's skills in the social setting.

The role of history of science in science teaching has received much attention (e.g., Aikenhead 1992; Gil-Perez 1992; Niedderer 1992; Matthews 1994, and further references there) and I cannot resist adding a few sentences on how the conception above relates to the use of history. The history of the development of a particular scientific theory or conception – the Copernican system, plate tectonics, Darwinian evolution – is one or more routes by which reasonable inquirers arrived at a conclusion. The starting point for late-twentieth century students is not the same as for the historical inquirers. The most obvious example being that most students 'know' that the earth goes around the sun when they come to science class, even though they are frequently unable to develop the appropriate conclusions from that knowledge. The reasons are complex, but they include in most cases the fact that they bring to bear a version of intuitive physics. This latter bears many resemblances to the sophisticated neo-Aristotelian physics of the sixteenth century, but it would be a mistake to treat them as identical. And the motivations of sixteenth and seventeenth century intellectuals were different in many very important respects than those of our current students.

On my view, knowing the history of a scientific development provides the teacher with a set of arguments and experiments and an epistemic route from one cognitive locus to another. This is often an important part of the tool kit that can be used to assist learners in constructing their own representations more satisfactorily. But as I have outlined above, the history of science by itself is far from sufficient for the teacher confronted with a very complex set of tasks. I see the extent of the utility of history of science as being subject to possible empirical study. A second point is that independent of issues of bringing the students' constructions to a different state by calling on the same arguments and experiments that were historically used, reflection on the history of science itself can provide important fodder for the epistemic learning mill. The concepts of data, anomalous data, questionable data and so on can be illustrated in the history of science as well as in the classroom productions. This is another step in forging the cultural links between the classroom inquiry and the larger scientific process.

## Conclusion

I have argued that we can distinguish the claims of cognitive constructivism from those of metaphysical constructivism. Cognitive constructivism has strong empirical support and indicates some important directions for changing science instruction. It implies that teachers need to be cognizant of representational, motivational and epistemic dimensions which can restrict or promote student learning. Metaphysical issues are irrelevant to the pedagogical enterprise except when explicit philosophical issues arise. The resulting set of tasks for a science teacher are considerably larger and more complex than the older more traditional conception, but the resources of cognitive sciences and the history of science can provide important parts of the teacher's intellectual tool kit.

A critical part of this conception of science education as informed by cognitive constructivism is that the students must develop the skills to participate in the epistemic interchanges that take place in scientific communities. They must be provided opportunities and materials to develop those skills and the classroom community must have the appropriate features of an objective epistemic community.

## References

Ackermann, R. J. (1985) *Data, Instruments, and Theory: A Dialectical Approach to Understanding Science* (Princeton, NJ: Princeton University Press).

Aikenhead, G. (1992) 'How to Teach the Epistemology and Sociology of Science in a Historical Context', in S. Hills (ed.), *Second International HPS&ST Proceedings* (Kingston: University of Kingston), pp. 23–34.

Ames, C. A. (1990) 'Motivation: What Teachers Need to Know', *Teachers College Record* 91: 409–21.

Bloom, J. (1992) 'Contextual Flexibility: Learning and Change from Cognitive, Sociocultural, and Physical Context Perspectives', in S. Hills (ed.), *Second International HPS&ST Proceedings* (Kingston: University of Kingston), pp. 115–26.

Bruer, J. T. (1993) *Schools for Thought: A Science of Learning in the Classroom* (Cambridge, MA: MIT Press).

Cartwright, N. (1983) *How the Laws of Physics Lie* (Oxford: Clarendon Press).

Chinn, C. and Brewer, W. (1993) 'The Role of Anomalous Data in Knowledge Acquisition: A Theoretical Framework and Implications for Science Instruction', *Review of Educational Research* 63: 1–50.

Cobb, P. (1994a) 'Constructivism in Mathematics and Science Education', *Educational Researcher* 23: 4.

Cobb, P. (1994b) 'Where is the Mind? Constructivist and Sociocultural Perspectives on Mathematical Development', *Educational Researcher* 23: 13–23.

Driver, R. et al. (1994) 'Constructing Scientific Knowledge in the Classroom', *Educational Researcher* 23: 5–12.

Duschl, R. A. (1990) *Restructuring Science Education: The Importance of Theories and Their Development* (New York: Columbia University Press).

Duschl, R. A. and Feather, R. (1995) 'Developing and Nurturing Objectivity in Science Classrooms', in *Proceedings of the Third International Conference on History and Philosophy of Science and Science Teaching* (Minneapolis, MN: University of Minnesota Press), vol. 1, pp. 314–25.

Fosnot, C. (1993) 'Rethinking Science Education: A Defense of Piagetian Constructivism', *Journal of Research in Science Teaching*, 30(9): 1189–1201.

Giannetto, E. (1992) 'The Relations Between Epistemology, History of Science and Science Teaching from the Point of View of the Research on Mental Representations', in S. Hills (ed.), *Second International HPS&ST Proceedings* (Kingston: University of Kingston), 359–74.

Giere, R. (1989) 'The Units of Analysis in Science Studies', in S. Fuller et al. (eds.), *The Cognitive Turn* (Dordrecht: Kluwer Academic), pp. 3–11.

Giere, R. (1988) *Explaining Science: A Cognitive Approach* (Chicago, IL: University of Chicago Press).

Gil-Perez, D. (1992) 'Approaching Pupil's Learning to Scientific Construction of Knowledge: Some Implications of the History and Philosophy of Science in Science Teaching', in S. Hills (ed.), *Second International HPS&ST Proceedings* (Kingston: University of Kingston), pp. 375–90.

Glasson, G. et al. (1992) 'Social Constructivism in Science Learning: Toward a Mind-World Synthesis', in S. Hills (ed.), *Second International HPS&ST Proceedings* (Kingston: University of Kingston), pp. 399–406.

Goldin, G. (1990) 'Epistemology, Constructivism, and Discovery Learning in Mathematics', in R. B. Davis, C. Maher and N. Noddings (eds.), *Constructivist Views on the Teaching and Learning of Mathematics* (NCTM), pp. 31–47.

Longino, H. (1992) 'Essential Tensions – Phase Two: Feminist, Philosophical and Social Studies of Science', in E. McMullin (ed.), *The Social Dimensions of Science* (Notre Dame, IN: University of Dame Press), pp. 198–216.

Longino, H. (1994) 'The Fate of Knowledge in Social Theories of Science', in F. F. Schmitt (ed.), *Socializing Epistemology: The Social Dimensions of Knowledge* (Lanham, MD: Rowman & Littlefield), pp. 135–57.

Matthews, M. and Davson-Galle, P. (1992) 'Constructivism and Science Education: Some Cautions and Comments', in S. Hills (ed.), *Second International HPS&ST Proceedings* (Kingston: University of Kingston), pp. 135–44.

Matthews, M. (1994) *Science Teaching: The Role of History and Philosophy of Science* (New York: Routledge).

Megill, A. (1991) 'Four Senses of Objectivity', *Annals of Scholarship* 8: 301–20.

Niedderer, H. (1992) 'Science Philosophy, Science History and the Teaching of Physics', in S. Hills (ed.), *Second International HPS&ST Proceedings* (Kingston: University of Kingston), pp. 201–14.

O'Loughlin, M. (1992) 'Rethinking Science Education: Beyond Piagetian Constructivism Toward a Sociocultural Model of Teaching and Learning', *Journal of Research in Science Teaching* 29(8): 791–820.

O'Loughlin, M. (1993) 'Some Further Questions for Piagetian Constructivists: a Reply to Fosnot', *Journal of Research in Science Teaching* 30(9): 1203–1207.

Von Glasersfeld, E. (1992) 'A Constructivist Approach to Experimental Foundations of Mathematical Concepts', in S. Hills (ed.), *Second International HPS&ST Proceedings* (Kingston: University of Kingston), pp. 553–72.

# 45

# Education and the Advancement of Understanding

## Catherine Z. Elgin

Plato's *Meno* ends on a disheartening note. Virtue cannot be taught, Socrates concludes, because there are no teachers of virtue. And there are no teachers of virtue because no one – not even those who are virtuous themselves – knows what virtue is.[1] The background assumption is that you cannot teach what you do not know. Let us call this Plato's Teaching Assumption (PTA for short). At first glance, PTA seems plausible. I cannot hope to teach you the atomic number of gold if I do not know what it is. Even if I happen to guess the correct answer and impart my opinion to you, we would hardly dignify my accomplishment by calling it 'teaching'. 'Teaching' is a success term, and mere inculcation of opinions does not qualify as the right sort of success. But the implications of accepting Plato's teaching assumption are bleak. For Socrates' conclusion generalizes far beyond the ethical realm. If one cannot teach what one does not know, it is not just virtue that cannot be taught. Neither can (much of) anything else. The requirements on knowing and teaching are too high.

Plato maintains that knowledge differs from (mere) right opinion through having a tether – something to secure it or hold it fast.[2] This seems right. Although epistemologists disagree vociferously about the nature and strength of the requisite tether, they generally agree that some sort of tether is needed to confer a right to be sure, and without such a right, one does not know. Although lucky guesses turn out to be correct, we have no right to be sure of them. Hence they do not qualify as knowledge. Epistemologists differ over whether knowledge is contextual or acontextual, whether it rests on justification or reliable mechanisms, whether an internalist or an externalist stance is appropriate. The common denominator is that knowledge requires tethered true belief. So, if you can teach only what you know, you can teach only what you have tethered true beliefs about. And if teaching is conveying knowledge, then when you teach, you convey tethered true beliefs to your students.

Even if we manage to evade global skepticism, we must concede that we don't actually *know* much of what we and our colleagues purport to teach. I won't embarrass you by asking how much philosophy you actually know. (Are your views true? Are they adequately justified or reliably produced? Are they so much as mutually consistent?) Even the 'mature sciences' rarely yield knowledge, strictly so-called.

Previously published in David Steiner (ed.), *Proceedings of the 20th World Congress of Philosophy*, vol. 3 (Charlottesville, VA: Philosophy Documentation Center, 1999), pp. 131–40. Reprinted with permission of the publisher.

Anomalies, discrepancies, and outstanding problems challenge the adequacy of our most strongly supported theories. So long as it lacks the resources to answer such challenges, a scientific theory is insecurely tethered, hence is not a repository of knowledge. Nor are the models it generates. Since they involve idealizations, approximations, and simplifying assumptions, they neither are nor purport to be true representations of the phenomena they concern. If PTA is correct, no more than virtue can philosophy or science be taught.

At the cutting edge of inquiry, where cognitive advances take place, matters are controversial, truth is elusive, and any tether is bound to be fairly loose. The latest findings in a field do not immediately merit the status of knowledge. They have to stand the test of time and become enmeshed in accepted, confirmed theories before we consider them adequately grounded. But if the latest findings do not qualify as knowledge, then according to PTA they cannot be taught. This means that in graduate seminars that focus on recent work in a field, teaching does not occur. That may be right. Advanced seminars at their best are collaborative exchanges, not conduits of already established knowledge. As we back away from the cutting edge, we retreat to seemingly more solidly grounded conclusions. So perhaps it is in less advanced courses that knowledge is conveyed. This accords with our words. We lead seminars, we say. But we teach introductory ethics, astronomy, metallurgy, or whatever.

There are at least two problems with this proposal. One has to do with systematicity, the other with accessibility. The worry about systematicity is that there is no effective way of isolating antecedently established results from what is going on at the cutting edge. New discoveries can unsettle findings we consider firmly established and shift the grounds we take to establish them. It's not just the permanent possibility of scientific revolution that causes difficulties. We might feel fairly safe in considering steel a metal and fairly safe in believing that future inquiry is unlikely to lead scientists to conclude otherwise. So we might think the fact that steel is a metal is a bit of knowledge that can be taught in an introductory metallurgy class. But even if we are sanguine about the fact that steel is a metal, we may be (and probably should be) more circumspect in our assessment of our grounds. Further investigation may result in the refinement of the criteria for classifying something as a metal. Even if the newly sanctioned criteria didn't require us to revise our classification

of steel, they might constitute a revision in the grounds for classifying it. In that case, our previous claim to knowledge is undercut. If we used to think that something is a metal because it has a particular lattice structure $L$ and metallurgists conclude that it is not $L$ but related structure $L^*$ that makes something a metal, then our previous reason for counting steel as a metal was incorrect. That being so, our earlier conviction that steel is a metal was not adequately tethered. We believed the right thing for the wrong reason. Current investigations are designed to elaborate, extend, and/or challenge accepted theories. The continued acceptability of those theories and the statements of fact they generate depends on how the investigations turn out.

So does the interpretation of those statements. What we understand when we understand the statement 'Steel is a metal' depends on and derives from an understanding of the theory or system of thought that generates it. For it is that theory that spells out the implications and implicatures of the statement. As the theory is extended, revised, and/or deepened, the interpretation of the statement evolves as well.

Holism pulls against knowledge. If, as Quine says, statements face the tribunal of experience as a corporate body,[3] we can't know individual facts. To know the fact that steel is a metal, we need to know a good deal of metallurgy. For we need to know what it means to claim that steel is a metal, what such a claim commits us to, what sort of evidence supports that claim, and what makes that evidence adequate. To the extent that the theory is vulnerable, so is our claim to know the fact. If PTA is correct, then if the theory is vulnerable, so is our competence to teach that fact.

The other worry concerns accessibility. If we are to convey knowledge to our students, we need to impart both content and grounds. But the more basic the course, the less prepared students are to understand the complexities of the subject. Perhaps there are adequately tethered truths about, say, magnetism. Perhaps the instructor knows those truths. Still, according to PTA, to teach them, to impart knowledge of them, requires conveying both the truths and the tether. And to impart the tether is to convey to the students in a way that they can grasp both the grounds for believing them and the reasons for considering those grounds adequate. This may seem unproblematic. We're not, after all, trying to teach the complexities of electromagnetism in a Fourth Grade science class. The truths imparted in elementary courses tend to be more general and less nuanced than the ones more advanced students and professionals grapple with. Hence, one might think, they and their grounds are more easily taught. But the complexities that emerge at higher levels are integral to the content and grounds for the generalizations we seek to impart. If a particular alignment of atoms is what makes something magnetic, then to know what is being claimed in saying that a material is magnetic requires appreciating the significance of that alignment. If teaching is imparting knowledge, we cannot teach magnetism to students who lack the resources to understand what that alignment is and why it matters.

Maybe the worry about accessibility is misguided. Granted, the instructor can't convey to novices the full content and grounds for the facts she imparts. But, one might argue, if those facts are secured by an adequate theory, and the instructor knows as much, then in imparting the facts to her students, she teaches them. This is not wholly implausible. We purport to know a variety of more or less free floating facts – the atomic number of gold, the main product of Bolivia, the causes of the Franco-Prussian War, and so on. Often these bits of information are products of educational encounters. Why shouldn't we say that we were taught such facts, we learned them, so now we know them? But if a parrot were trained to recite on demand the causes of the Franco-Prussian War or the atomic numbers of the elements, we wouldn't say that it knew them, for it wouldn't understand its own words. Even if *we* can provide its utterances with content and grounds, it cannot. So it does not know. No more should we claim that a student who memorizes such matters by rote knows them. For he, like the parrot, knows not whereof it speaks. To understand an assertion requires an appreciation of what its acceptance would commit one to, and what would count as reason to accept it. Neither the parrot nor the rote memorizer has such an appreciation.

Teaching looks to be well nigh impossible. PTA insists that we can teach only what we know. Given the stringent demands on knowledge and the systematic interdependence of seemingly established and tentative findings, we know very little. Moreover, since 'teaching' is a success term, and attempts to teach are successful only if students learn, we can teach only what our students are capable of learning. If teaching is a matter of conveying knowledge, then unless the students can grasp the entire theory (or a suitably extended, isolable fragment of it that provides a statement of fact with its content and grounds), they cannot learn, and so we cannot teach them, that fact.

Rather than abandoning hope of teaching, I suggest that we reject PTA. Even if we concede (as we should) that imparting one's lucky guesses is not the same as teaching, and that competence with the subject matter is a requirement on teaching, it does not follow that teaching consists in imparting knowledge, or that you can teach only what you know. Rather, I suggest, teaching consists in advancing understanding. How does this help?

First, understanding, unlike knowledge, does not require truth. An approximation, idealization or sketch, although not true, reveals some understanding of a subject. If I have a rough understanding of the workings of the spleen, I may be able to convey it to my students, thus advancing their even more rudimentary understanding of physiology. And if my mechanic has a deep understanding of the workings of the carburetor, he may be able to convey to me at least a superficial understanding of it. Even if I acquire no truths about how the carburetor works (the details required for truth in this area being beyond my ken), I may now have at least some idea what is going on under the hood. And investigators who recognize that their current best theories are not precisely true may nevertheless have something to teach. Despite the anomalies, tensions, and outstanding problems at the forefront of physics, if we concede that physics provides an understanding of its subject-matter, physics can be taught. Indeed, to understand physics requires recognizing the existence and appreciating the significance of the anomalies, tensions, and problems that remain. Teaching a subject involves conveying the limits as well as the established findings of the field. If I'm right, philosophy can be taught too. Granted, we don't have anything like the progress of the physical sciences to brag about. Still, we can reasonably claim to have achieved some understanding of the problems we study. We can, in principle, convey that understanding to our students.

Second, understanding admits of degrees. A rough approximation exhibits some understanding of its subject-matter, a close approximation, greater understanding. PTA needs to assume that education is a matter of moving from easily learned truths to more difficult truths. For knowledge requires truth. But much education proceeds by a series of approximations. We begin with a crude outline, and elaborate, extend, and emend it as we go. Although Newtonian theory isn't strictly true, it is an excellent first approximation. Hence, teaching about physical interactions as though they conformed to Newtonian laws is a good way to begin to teach physics.

Third, understanding is not restricted to facts. We understand rules and reasons, objectives and obstacles, actions and passions, techniques and tools, forms, functions, and feelings, as well as facts. If the objective of teaching is the advancement of understanding, then the scope of teaching is wider than PTA assumes. Understanding need not be couched in literally true sentences. It may be located in apt terminology, insightful metaphors, useful fictions, penetrating questions, effective non-verbal symbols, intelligent behavior. We've got to grasp a lot more than the established facts to understand a subject. And we've got to convey a lot more than established facts to teach a subject. To teach science, for example, requires conveying an understanding of the scientific method. It also requires conveying an appreciation of the role of anomalies and outstanding problems, the significance of evidence, the power of the idealizations, and the importance of the requirement that results be replicable. Merely to impart a list of facts that scientists have discovered (that $e = mc^2$; that vitamin C prevents scurvy; that hydrogen is lighter than oxygen, etc.), would not be to teach science. To teach philosophy requires enabling students to understand and assess the significance of the arguments that constitute a philosophical position and to contrive arguments of their own. Merely to impart a list of positions philosophers have held (Thales believed that everything is water; Descartes believed that mind and body are distinct; Quine believes that whatever is, is physical, etc.) or a list of the philosophical propositions the professor believes to be true . . . would not be to teach philosophy. To teach a subject – philosophy or physics or auto-mechanics – is to teach how its various commitments interweave to provide an understanding of the items in the domain.

The question is: what constitutes understanding? Truth, I said, is not required. Nevertheless, there must be some standard that distinguishes understanding from mere opinion. If we say (as we should) that there are no absolutely secure propositions on which to build our theories, and no failsafe rules of reasoning, how do we decide what belongs in a good theory or system of thought? In *Considered Judgment* I argue that we understand a subject when our relevant commitments constitute a system of thought in reflective equilibrium.[4] Understanding advances when a system in reflective equilibrium is extended, elaborated, or supplanted by a better system.

Whether or not we are justified, we accept some sentences, stances, and methods without reservation. Being our current best guesses about the matter at hand and the appropriate ways of dealing with it, these function as our working hypotheses. We do not contend that they are surely right or to be held true come what may. But because they are our best guesses, they have some claim on our epistemic allegiance. We need a reason to give them up.

To be sure, reasons are often all too readily available. Our working hypotheses may be mutually incompatible, jointly untenable, or otherwise at odds with each other. Our methods may yield inconsistent answers or provide no answers to questions we consider both relevant and significant for the subject at hand. Our standards of acceptability may endorse too many, or too few, or intuitively wrong answers. And so on. For any number of reasons, available resources may be inadequate to achieve our cognitive and practical objectives. To arrive at an acceptable theory or system of thought, we typically need to revise, extend, and correct the judgments, methods, and approaches we started with. A process of delicate adjustments occurs, its goal being a system of mutually supportive, independently supported commitments. Such a system, I maintain, is in reflective equilibrium. To achieve reflective equilibrium may require drawing new evaluative and descriptive distinctions or erasing previously drawn lines, reordering priorities or imposing new ones, reconceiving the relevant facts and values or recognizing new ones as relevant. To test the system for accuracy, we see whether it reflects (closely enough) the commitments we began with; to test it for adequacy, we see whether it realizes our cognitive and practical ends. Reflecting closely enough does not require and is not ensured by exact replication of the commitments we began with. We realize that those commitments are incomplete and suspect that they are flawed; we recognize that our initial conception of our objectives is vague and perhaps inconsistent. We do not expect our working hypotheses to be precisely right. Nonetheless, being our current best guesses, they function as guides to research.

A system of thought is in reflective equilibrium just in case its components are reasonable in light of one another, and the system as a whole is as reasonable as any available alternative in light of our relevant antecedent commitments. Such a system is one that on reflection we can endorse. It is tethered, not to epistemological absolutes, but to our prior understanding of the matter at hand. It does not purport to yield irrevocable truths or permanently tenable epistemic commitments. New evidence and further refinements can upset the balance. But the commitments that constitute such a system are reasonable in the epistemic circumstances. Because they hang together to constitute a creditable system, they provide an understanding of the subject at hand. They admit of elaboration and refinement, as well as revision or rejection in light of further investigation. So the understanding the system yields can be broadened, deepened, and corrected. But being our new constellation of working hypotheses, the system provides a springboard for further inquiry. The commitments that comprise it become our current best guesses about the matter at hand.

Understanding, as I construe it, is holistic. It is a matter of how commitments mesh to form a mutually supportive, independently supported system of thought. It is advanced by bootstrapping. We start with what we think we know and build from there. This makes education continuous with what goes on at the cutting edge of inquiry. Physicists take the scientific community's consensus about electromagnetism as their working hypotheses. Fourth Graders start with what they take themselves to know about magnets, or metals, or whatever else seems relevant. Both groups build from what they already accept, extending, revising, reconceiving as necessary to advance their understanding of the phenomena. Methods, standards, categories, and stances are as important as facts. The understanding that a scientist or a Fourth Grader obtains from her inquiries is inseparably linked to the methods she uses, the standards she takes her investigations to be subject to, the assumptions she takes to be the uncontroversial background to her work, and the conceptual resources she has to work with. So something like E. D. Hirsch's list of facts every Fourth Grader should know is slightly silly. At least, knowledge of those facts would not make a child an educated Fourth Grader. What makes for a good Fourth Grade education is not the set of facts the Fourth Grader knows, but the level of understanding she has achieved and the resources she can deploy to advance that understanding. Facts are part of the story, but so are fictions, methods, standards,

and categories. A major part of understanding is recognizing what problems remain to be solved.

Literal truth is not privileged. Non-verbal symbols, non-factual symbols, non-true symbols may belong to systems in reflective equilibrium. So may methods, perspectives, values, and standards. To evaluate them requires asking what we can do with them. In studying literature, for example, the question arises how the insights gleaned from a work export to other areas. How can we make sense of other things in light of the insights a fiction affords? This is a question that arises whether the work in question is *Ulysses* or *Horton Hatches the Egg*. The same question arises for factual treatises. We need to ask how our findings export from the lab as well. If we can't answer that adequately, we don't know what to make of them. They are cognitively inert.

Holism undermines PTA because the content of a claim derives from and depends on the system of thought it belongs to. What it means to say that iron is magnetic turns on what such a claim commits us to. Since, according to PTA, the children who haven't mastered electromagnetic theory don't know what their words commit them to, they don't know what they are saying. My account is not vulnerable to this difficulty because it contends that understanding a claim, like understanding the facts it pertains to, is a matter of degree. Since the children's system of thought is sparser and cruder than the physicist's, it is reasonable to think that the physicist has a deeper, more sophisticated, more accurate conception of a magnet than the children have. She consequently draws on a richer network of presuppositions and background assumptions and her use of the term commits her to a more complex constellation of implications and implicatures. But it does not follow that the children's words are vacuous. They, too, draw on a network of commitments in reflective equilibrium. That network supplies them with an understanding of their words and their objects. Their network is sparser than the scientist's. So the children's conception of a magnet is comparatively impoverished. This is as it should be. But there is enough agreement between the two conceptions that we can (sometimes with a dollop of the principle of charity) recognize them as conceptions of the same thing. This agreement affords a basis for communication and a platform for teaching. Scientists and science teachers, having a greater understanding of the subject, can raise questions and introduce considerations that push the children to broaden and deepen their understanding.

If we look back at the *Meno*, we see an example of this. Socrates insists (what no one has ever believed) that he is not teaching the slave geometry.[5] True, he is not imparting geometric truths to the boy. But he is asking leading questions that guide the slave toward a better understanding of the relation between the length and area of a square. Socrates began the exercise with a better understanding of geometry than the slave had. But there is no reason to think that he either understood or needed to understand the truth, the whole truth, and nothing but the truth to teach effectively.

Should we say then that you can teach only what you understand? Maybe. But if we do, we should recognize that the principle is more a terminological stipulation than an insight about education. If I understand enough about a matter to successfully direct your efforts to advance your understanding, as Socrates directed Meno's slave, we call what I do teaching and what you do learning. If we're pretty much on a par, grappling with the material, puzzling it out together, we call what we do collaborative investigation. It is a difference in degree, not in kind. And often it may be unclear which description is appropriate.

## Notes

1. Plato, *Meno*, trans. G. M. A Grube (Indianapolis, IN: Hackett, 1976), 89d–96d.
2. Plato, *Meno*, 98a.
3. W. V. Quine, 'Two Dogmas of Empiricism,' *From a Logical Point of View* (New York: Harper Torchbooks, 1961), p. 41.
4. Catherine Z. Elgin, *Considered Judgment* (Princeton, NJ: Princeton University Press, 1997).
5. Plato, *Meno*, 82e.

# Critical Thinking and Reasoning

# Reasoning with Children

## John Locke

§81. It will perhaps be wondered that I mention *reasoning* with children: and yet I cannot but think that the true way of dealing with them. They understand it as early as they do language; and, if I misobserve not, they love to be treated as rational creatures sooner than is imagined. 'Tis a pride should be cherished in them and, as much as can be, made the great instrument to turn them by.

But when I talk of *reasoning* I do not intend any other but such as is suited to the child's capacity and apprehension. Nobody can think a boy of three or seven years old should be argued with as a grown man. Long discourses and philosophical reasonings at best amaze and confound, but do not instruct children. When I say therefore that they must be *treated as rational creatures* I mean that you should make them sensible by the mildness of your carriage and the composure even in your correction of them that what you do is reasonable in you and useful and necessary for them and that it is not out of *caprichio*,* passion, or fancy that you command or forbid them anything. This they are capable of understanding; and there is no virtue they should be excited to nor fault they should be kept from which I do not think they may be convinced of, but it must be by such *reasons* as their age and understanding are capable of and those proposed always in very *few and plain words*. The foundations on which several duties are built and the fountains of right and wrong from which they spring are not perhaps easily to be let into the minds of grown men not used to abstract their thoughts from common received opinions. Much less are children capable of *reasonings* from remote principles. They cannot conceive the force of long deductions: the *reasons* that move them must be *obvious* and level to their thoughts, and such as may (if I may so say) be felt and touched. But yet, if their age, temper, and inclinations be considered, there will never want such motives as may be sufficient to convince them. If there be no other more particular, yet these will always be intelligible and of force to deter them from any fault fit to be taken notice of in them, viz. that it will be a discredit and disgrace to them, and displease you.

Editor's title. Previously published in *Some Thoughts Concerning Education*, from Ruth W. Grant and Nathan Tarcov (eds.), *"Some Thoughts Concerning Education" and "Of the Conduct of the Understanding"* (Indianapolis, IN: Hackett, 1996), Section 81, p. 58. Reprinted with permission of Hackett Publishing Company Inc. All rights reserved.

* Caprice.

# Against Reasoning with Children

## Jean-Jacques Rousseau

### *Emile*: Book II

To reason with children was Locke's great maxim. It is the one most in vogue today. Its success, however, does not appear to me such as to establish its reputation; and, as for me, I see nothing more stupid than these children who have been reasoned with so much. Of all the faculties of man, reason, which is, so to speak, only a composite of all the others, is the one that develops with the most difficulty and latest. And it is this one which they want to use in order to develop the first faculties! The masterpiece of a good education is to make a reasonable man, and they claim they raise a child by reason! This is to begin with the end, to want to make the product the instrument. If children understood reason, they would not need to be raised. But by speaking to them from an early age a language which they do not understand, one accustoms them to show off with words, to control all that is said to them, to believe themselves as wise as their masters, to become disputatious and rebellious; and everything that is thought to be gotten from them out of reasonable motives is never obtained other than out of motives of covetousness or fear or vanity which are always perforce joined to the others.

This is the formula to which all the lessons in morality that are given, and can be given, to children can just about be reduced:

MASTER: You must not do that.

CHILD: And why must I not do it?

MASTER: Because it is bad to do.

CHILD: Bad to do! What is bad to do?

MASTER: What you are forbidden to do.

CHILD: What is bad about doing what I am forbidden to do?

MASTER: You are punished for having disobeyed.

CHILD: I shall fix it so that nothing is known about it.

MASTER: You will be spied on.

CHILD: I shall hide.

MASTER: You will be questioned.

CHILD: I shall lie.

MASTER: You must not lie.

CHILD: Why must I not lie?

MASTER: Because it is bad to do, etc.

This is the inevitable circle. Get out of it, and the child does not understand you any longer. Is this not

Editor's title. Originally published as *"Emile," or On Education* trans. Allan Bloom (New York: Basic Books/HarperCollins, 1979), Book II, pp. 89–91. Reprinted with permission of the Perseus Books Group.

most useful instruction? I would be quite curious to know what could be put in the place of this dialogue. Locke himself would certainly have been very much at a loss. To know good and bad, to sense the reason for man's duties, is not a child's affair.

Nature wants children to be children before being men. If we want to pervert this order, we shall produce precocious fruits which will be immature and insipid and will not be long in rotting. We shall have young doctors[1] and old children. Childhood has its ways of seeing, thinking, and feeling which are proper to it. Nothing is less sensible than to want to substitute ours for theirs, and I would like as little to insist that a ten-year-old be five feet tall as that he possess judgment. Actually, what would reason do for him at that age? It is the bridle of strength, and the child does not need this bridle.

In trying to persuade your pupils of the duty of obedience, you join to this alleged persuasion force and threats or, what is worse, flattery and promises. In this way, therefore, lured by profit or constrained by force, they pretend to be convinced by reason. They see quite well that obedience is advantageous to them and rebellion harmful when you notice either. But since everything you insist on is unpleasant and, further, it is always irksome to do another's will, they arrange to do their own will covertly. They are persuaded that what they do is right if their disobedience is unknown, but are ready on being caught – in order to avoid a worse evil – to admit that what they do is wrong. Since the reason for duty cannot be grasped at their age, there is not a man in the world who could succeed in giving duty a truly palpable sense for them. But the fear of punishment, the hope of pardon, importunity, awkwardness in answering, wrest all the confessions from them that are demanded; and it is believed that they have been convinced when they have only been pestered or intimidated.

What results from this? Firstly, by imposing on them a duty they do not feel, you set them against your tyranny and turn them away from loving you. Secondly, you teach them to become dissemblers, fakers, and liars in order to extort rewards or escape punishments. Finally, by accustoming them always to cover a secret motive with an apparent motive, you yourselves give them the means of deceiving you ceaselessly, of depriving you of the knowledge of their true character, and of fobbing you and others off with vain words when the occasion serves. Laws, you will say, although they obligate conscience, nevertheless also use constraint with grown men. I admit it, but what are these men if not children spoiled by education? This is precisely what must be prevented. Use force with children, and reason with men. Such is the natural order.

**Note**

1. In the original sense of *learned* man.

# 48

# Education for Critical Thinking

## Matthew Lipman

Wherever knowledge and experience are not merely possessed but *applied to practice*, we are likely to see clear instances of judgment. Architects, lawyers, and doctors are professionals whose work constantly involves the making of judgments. The same is true of composers, painters, and poets. It is true of teachers and farmers and theoretical physicists as well; all of them have to make judgments as part of the practice of their occupations and their lives. It is again true of any of us when we are in moral situations: We have to make moral judgments. There are practical, productive, and theoretical judgments, as Aristotle would have put it. Insofar as we consistently make such judgments well, we can be said to behave wisely.

Good professionals make good judgments about their own practice as well as about the subject matter of their practice. A good doctor not only makes good diagnoses of patients and prescribes well for them but also makes good judgments about medicine and his or her ability to practice it. Good judgment takes everything relevant into account, including itself.

A judgment, then, is a determination – of thinking, of speech, of action, or of creation. A gesture,

such as the wave of a hand, can be a judgment; a metaphor like "John is a worm" is a judgment; an equation like $e = mc^2$ is a judgment. They are likely to be *good* judgments if they are the products of *skillfully performed* acts guided or facilitated by appropriate instruments and procedures.

Critical thinking is applied thinking. Therefore, it is not just process – it seeks to develop a product. This involves more than attaining understanding: It means producing something, said, made, or done. It involves using knowledge to bring about reasonable change. Minimally, the product is a judgment; maximally, it is putting that judgment into practice.

There is another sense in which critical thinking develops a product. Critical thinking is involved in all responsible interpretation (the production of meaning) and in all responsible translation (the preservation of meaning). Just as book, film, and music reviews are products about products, judgments about judgments, all instances of critical thinking are thinking about thinking, rather than thinking about some mute subject matter. A critical paleontologist thinks about life forms of the past and about *how* people have thought about life forms of the past. A critical geologist considers, in

Previously published in *Thinking in Education*, 2nd edn. (Cambridge: Cambridge University Press, 2003), pp. 210–15, 218–30. © 2003 Matthew Lipman, published by Cambridge University Press. Reprinted with permission of the publisher and author.

addition to rocks, the assumptions people have made in their thinking about rocks. In this fashion, the critical thinking that accompanies every discipline helps refine the end products – the meanings – that that discipline produces. If we now look at the process of critical thinking and identify its essential characteristics, we will be in a better position to understand its relationship to judgment. I will argue that critical thinking is *thinking that* (1) *facilitates judgment because it* (2) *relies on criteria*,[1] (3) *is self-correcting, and* (4) *is sensitive to context*.

## Critical Thinking Relies on Criteria

We suspect an association between the terms "critical" and "criteria" because they resemble each other and have a common ancestry. Also, we are all familiar with book, music, and film critics, and it is not uncommon to assume that those among them whose criticism is considered excellent are those who employ reliable criteria.

We are also aware of a relationship between criteria and judgments, for a *criterion* is often defined as "a rule or principle utilized in the making of judgments." It seems reasonable to conclude, therefore, that there is some sort of logical connection between critical thinking and criteria and judgment. The connection, of course, is to be found in the fact that critical thinking is reliable thinking, and skills themselves cannot be defined without criteria by means of which allegedly skillful performances can be evaluated. So critical thinking is reliable thinking that both employs criteria and can be assessed by appeal to criteria.

Furthermore, it might be profitable to consider what uncritical thinking might be. Surely uncritical thinking suggests thinking that is flabby, amorphous, arbitrary, specious, haphazard, and unstructured. The fact that critical thinking can rely upon criteria suggests that it is well-founded, structured, and reliable thinking. It seems to be defensible and convincing. How does this happen?

Whenever we make a claim or utter an opinion, we are vulnerable unless we can somehow back it up. We should therefore ask ourselves questions such as these: "When our opinions come under fire, to what do we appeal?" "When our claims are contested, what do we invoke?" "When our assertions are not convincing, what do we cite to strengthen them?" In attempting to answer questions like these, we are led to see that claims and opinions must be supported by reasons. What is the connection between reasons and criteria?

Criteria *are* reasons; they are one kind of reason, a particularly *reliable* kind. When we have to sort things out descriptively or evaluationally – and these are two very important tasks – we have to use the most reliable reasons we can find, and these are classificatory and evaluational criteria. Criteria may or may not have a high level of public acceptance, but they have a high level of acceptance and respect in the community of expert inquirers. The competent use of such respected reasons is a way of establishing the objectivity of our prescriptive, descriptive, and evaluative judgments. Thus, architects will judge a building by employing such criteria as *utility*, *safety*, and *beauty*; magistrates make judgments with the aid of such criteria as *legality* and *illegality*; and critical thinkers rely upon such time-tested criteria as *validity*, *evidential warrant*, and *consistency*. Any area of practice – like the examples just given of architectural practice, judicial practice, and cognitive practice – should be able to cite the criteria by which that practice is guided.

The intellectual domiciles we inhabit are often of flimsy construction; we can strengthen them by learning to reason more logically. But this will help little if the grounds or foundations upon which they rest are spongy. We need to rest our claims and opinions, as well as the rest of our thinking, upon a footing as firm as possible.

Here, then is a brief list of the sorts of things we invoke or appeal to and that therefore represent specific kinds of criteria:

- standards
- laws, bylaws, rules, regulations, charters, canons, ordinances, guidelines, directions
- precepts, requirements, specifications, gauges, stipulations, boundaries, limits, conditions, parameters
- conventions, norms, regularities, uniformities, covering generalizations
- principles, assumptions, presuppositions, definitions
- ideals, purposes, goals, aims, objectives, intuitions, insights
- tests, credentials, factual evidence, experimental findings, observations
- methods, procedures, policies, measures

All of these are instruments that can be employed in the making of judgments. They are part of the apparatus of rationality. Isolated in categories in a taxonomy, as they are here, they appear inert and sterile. But when they are at work in the process of inquiry, they can function dynamically – and critically.

It has already been noted that by means of logic we can validly *extend* our thinking; by means of reasons such as criteria, we can justify and *defend* it. The improvement of student thinking depends heavily on students' ability to identify and cite good reasons for the opinions they utter. Students can be brought to realize that for a reason to be called good it must be *relevant* to the opinion in question and *stronger* (in the sense of being more readily accepted or assumed to be true) than the opinion in question.

Since the school or college is a locus of inquiry, procedures employed therein must be defensible, just as job applicants are provided with specifications for hiring or promotion. When assigning grades to students, teachers must be prepared to justify such grades by citing the reasons – that is, the criteria – that were employed in arriving at the judgments at issue. It will hardly do for the teacher to claim that a judgment was arrived at intuitively or to say that criteria were unnecessary and irrelevant. Critical thinking is *cognitive accountability*.[2] When teachers openly state the criteria they employ, they encourage students to do likewise. By providing models of *intellectual responsibility*, teachers invite students to assume responsibility for their own thinking and, in a larger sense, for their own education.

This does not mean that all aspects of our lives are always and necessarily occasions for inquiry. There are things we prize that we may not care to appraise; there are people we esteem whom we may not want to estimate. Where the harm done to intimacy and privacy outweighs the benefits to be derived from such evaluations, the call for criteria and standards may well be ignored. In any event, if there are matters about which we do not care to reflect publicly, the drawing of such boundary lines should be as far as possible of our own choosing.

[ . . . ]

## Critical Thinking is Self-corrective

Much of our thinking moves along uncritically. Our thought unrolls impressionistically, from association to association, with little concern for either truth or validity and with even less concern for the possibility that it might be erroneous.

Among the many things we may reflect upon is our own thinking. We can think about our own thinking, but we can do so in a way that is still quite uncritical. And so, granted that "metacognition" is thinking about thinking, it need not be equivalent to critical thinking.

The most characteristic feature of inquiry, according to C. S. Peirce, is that it aims to discover its own weaknesses and rectify what is at fault in its own procedures. Inquiry, then, is *self-correcting*.[3]

One of the most important advantages of converting the classroom into a community of inquiry (in addition to the undoubted improvement of moral climate it brings about) is that the members of the community begin looking for and correcting each other's methods and procedures. Consequently, insofar as each participant is able to internalize the methodology of the community as a whole, each is able to become self-correcting in his or her own thinking.

## Critical Thinking Displays Sensitivity to Context

An astute copyeditor going over an essay prior to publication will make innumerable corrections that can be justified by appeals to recognized canons of grammar and spelling. Idiosyncratic spellings are rejected in favor of uniformity, as are grammatical irregularities. But stylistic idiosyncrasies on the author's part may be treated with considerably greater tolerance and sensitivity. This is because the editor knows that the style is not a matter of writing mechanics; it has to do with the context of what is being written as well as with the person of the author. At the same time, thinking that is sensitive to context involves recognition of:

1  *Exceptional or irregular circumstances.* For example, we normally examine statements for truth or falsity independent of the character of the speaker. But in a court trial, the character of a witness may become a relevant consideration.
2  *Special limitations, contingencies, or constraints wherein normally acceptable reasoning might find itself prohibited.* An example is the rejection of certain Euclidean theorems, such as that parallel lines never meet, in non-Euclidean geometries.
3  *Overall configurations.* A remark taken out of context may seem to be flagrantly in error, but

in the light of the discourse taken as a whole it can appear valid and proper, or vice versa. Critical thinking in this sense is a descendent of Aristotle's awareness that individual situations need to be examined on their own terms and not forced into some Procrustean bed of general rules and regulations: "For when the thing is indefinite the rule also is indefinite, like the lead rule used in making the Lesbian moulding; the rule adapts itself to the shape of the stone and is not rigid, and so too the decree is adapted to the facts."[4]

Critical thinking is thinking that is sensitive to particularities and uniqueness. It is the very opposite of that kind of casuistry that forces general rules upon individual cases, whether such rules are appropriate or not. It follows that critical thinking is hostile to all stereotyping; and since such stereotyping is the mechanism through which biased thinking operates, to all prejudice. There is a close alliance between critical thinking and informal logic, inasmuch as the latter deals with inferential reasoning that does not have certain conclusions but merely probable ones and does not claim the universality that is claimed by, say, deduction. The informal logician strives to identify the many fallacies to which thinking is prone, and to identify as well those individual cases that are not fallacious. The informal logician will examine the many varieties of inductive and analogical reasoning but will also give thought to the logical basis of figurative language, as for instance in simile and metaphor.

4  *The possibility that evidence is atypical.* An example is a case of overgeneralizing about national voter preferences based on a tiny regional sample of ethnically and occupationally homogeneous individuals.

5  *The possibility that some meanings do not translate from one context or domain to another.* There are terms and expressions for which there are no precise equivalents in other languages and whose meanings are therefore wholly context-specific.

With regard to *thinking with criteria* and *sensitivity to context*, a suitable illustration might be an exercise or assignment that involves the application of a particular criterion to a set of fictional situations. Suppose the criterion in question is *fairness*, which is itself a way of construing the still broader criterion of justice. One form that fairness assumes is *taking*

## Taking Turns: Exercise from *Wondering at the World*

There are times when people engage in sharing. For example, they go to a movie and share the pleasure of looking at the movie together. Or they can share a piece of cake by each taking half.

In other cases, however, simultaneous sharing is not so easily accomplished. If two people ride a horse, someone has to ride in front. They can take turns riding in front, but they can't ride in front at the same time. Children understand this very well. They recognize that certain procedures must be followed in certain ways.

For example, ask your students to discuss the number of ways they "take turns" in the classroom during the ordinary day. They take turns washing the blackboard, going to the bathroom, going to the cloakroom, and passing out the papers. On the playground, they take turns at bat, they take turns lining up for basketball, and they take turns at the high bar.

Ask your students what they think the connection is between "taking turns" and "being fair." The resulting discussion should throw light on the fact that sometimes being fair involves the way children are to be treated simultaneously, while at other times it involves the way they are to be treated sequentially. For example, if it is one child's birthday and there is going to be a party with cupcakes, there should be at least one cupcake for every child. This is being fair simultaneously. Later, if you want to play "Pin the Tail on the Donkey," children should sequentially take turns in order to be fair. (The prospect of everyone *simultaneously* being blindfolded and searching about with a pin boggles the mind.)

turns. Look at an exercise taken from *Wondering at the World*,[5] the instructional manual to accompany *Kio and Gus*,[6] a Philosophy for Children program for children nine to ten years old.

The students performing this exercise are applying the criterion of *turn taking* (that is, *reciprocity* or *fair play* or *justice*) to half a dozen specific situations requiring sensitivity to context. Classroom discussion should be able to distinguish between those situations in which the procedure of turn taking is appropriate and those in which it is dubious. When exercises like these are employed in a community of inquiry setting, the stage is set for critical thinking in the classroom. It is not the only way to accomplish this, needless to say. But it is one way.

---

## Exercise: The appropriate or inappropriate interpretation of "taking turns."

|  | Appropriate | Not Appropriate | ? |
|---|---|---|---|
| 1 Pam: "Louise, let's take turns riding your bike. I'll ride it Mondays, Wednesdays, and Fridays, and you ride it Tuesdays, Thursdays, and Saturdays." | ☐ | ☐ | ☐ |
| 2 Gary: "Burt, let's take turns taking Louise to the movies. I'll take her the first and third Saturday of every month, and you take her the second and fourth Saturday." | ☐ | ☐ | ☐ |
| 3 Jack: "Louise, let's take turns doing the dishes. You wash and I'll dry." | ☐ | ☐ | ☐ |
| 4 Chris: "Okay, Louise, let's take turns with the TV. You choose a half-hour program, then I'll choose one." | ☐ | ☐ | ☐ |
| 5 Melissa: "Louise, what do you say we take turns doing our homework? Tonight I'll do yours and mine, and tomorrow you can do mine and yours." | ☐ | ☐ | ☐ |
| 6 Hank: "Louise, I hate to see you struggle to school each day, carrying those heavy books! Let me carry yours and mine today, and you can carry yours and mine tomorrow." | ☐ | ☐ | ☐ |

---

## Practical Reasoning Behaviors that Signify Closure

The question most frequently asked by teachers expected to teach for critical thinking is "How can I tell when I am teaching for critical thinking and when I am not?" Revealingly, the question is itself a demand for criteria.

The definition I have offered is a kind of bridge over four supporting piers: self-correction, sensitivity to context, criteria, and judgment. What a teacher would like to know is what classroom behaviors are associated with each of these categories.[7] And even if the teacher does observe these behaviors separately, does it follow that he or she is applying the definition?

We can take up the supporting concepts one by one:

### Self-correction
*Examples of associated behaviors*:

(a) students point out errors in each other's thinking

(b) students acknowledge errors in their own thinking

(c) students disentangle ambiguous expressions in texts

(d) students clarify vague expressions in texts

(e) students demand reasons and criteria where none have been provided

(f) students contend that it is wrong to take some matters for granted

(g) students identify inconsistencies in discussions

(h) students point out fallacious assumptions or invalid inferences in texts

(i) students identify the commission of fallacies in formal or informal reasoning

(j) students question whether inquiry procedures have been correctly applied

### *Acquiring sensitivity to context*
*Examples of associated behaviors*:

(a) students differentiate among nuances of meaning stemming from cultural differences

(b) students differentiate among nuances of meaning stemming from differences in personal perspectives or points of view

(c) students recognize differences due to language differences, disciplinary differences, and differences of frames of reference

(d) students contend to establish authenticity and integrity of interpretations of texts

(e) students contest accuracy of translations

(f) students point out how definitional meanings are modified by contextual circumstances

(g) students note changes in meaning due to alterations of emphasis

(h) students recognize changes in meaning resulting from shifts in speakers' intentions or purposes

(i) students note discrepancies between present situation and seemingly similar past situations

(j) students search for differences between seemingly similar situations whose consequences are different

### Being guided (and goaded) by criteria
*Examples displayed by students, who invoke*:

(a) shared values, such as ideals, purposes, goals, aims, and objectives

(b) conventions, such as norms, regularities, uniformities, and precedents or traditions

(c) common bases of comparison, such as shared respects, properties, or characteristics

(d) requirements, such as precepts, specifications, stipulations, and limitations

(e) perspectives, including areas of concern, frames of reference, and points of view

(f) principles, including assumptions, presuppositions, and theoretical or conceptual relationships

(g) rules, including laws, bylaws, regulations, charters, canons, ordinances, and directions

(h) standards: criteria for determining the degree of satisfaction needed to satisfy a criterion

(i) definitions: assemblages of criteria that together have the same meaning as the word to be defined

(j) facts: what there is, as expressed in warranted assertions

(k) tests: probes or interventions for the purpose of eliciting empirical findings

### Judgment
*Examples displayed by students, who seek*:

(a) settlements of deliberations

(b) verdicts of trials or inquests

(c) decisions, as by administrators, executives, parents, teachers, etc.

(d) determinations: conclusive findings of investigative proceedings

(e) solutions to actual or theoretical problems

(f) classifications or categorizations

(g) evaluations of performances, services, objects, products, etc.; assessments

(h) distinctions, in the form of negative predications

(i) connections, in the form of affirmative predications

(j) deliberate, intentional makings, sayings, or doings

## Professional Education and the Cultivation of Judgment

It should be evident now why law and medicine were cited earlier as likely places to look for exemplary instances of critical thinking. Medicine and law both involve the flexible application of principles (criteria) to practice (judgment), extreme sensitivity to the uniqueness of particular cases (context sensitivity), refusal to allow either principles or facts to become Procrustean beds to which the other is to be fitted, and a commitment to tentative, hypothetical, self-correcting procedures as befits a species of inquiry (self-correction). Both judges and doctors recognize the importance of being judicious: of making good judgments in the carrying out of their practice. Law and medicine at their best illustrate what critical thinking can be and ought to be. It remains for educators to design appropriate courses in critical thinking and to help teachers and professors recognize the critical thinking elements in their present practice that need to be strengthened.

What, then, is the relevance of critical thinking to the enhancement of elementary school, secondary school, and college education? Why are so many educators convinced that critical thinking is the key to educational reform? A good part of the answer lies in the fact that we want students who can do more than merely think; it is equally important that students exercise good judgment. It is good judgment that characterizes the sound interpretation of a written text, the well-balanced and coherent composition, the lucid comprehension of what we listen to, and the persuasive argument. It is good judgment that enables us to weigh and grasp what a statement or passage states, assumes, implies, or suggests. And this good judgment cannot be operative unless it rests upon proficient reasoning skills that can assure competency in inference as well as upon proficient inquiry, concept-formation, and communication and translation skills. If critical thinking can produce an improvement in education, it will be because it increases the quantity and quality of meaning that students derive from what they read and perceive and that they express in what they write and say.

The infusion of critical thinking into the curriculum carries with it the promise of the academic empowerment of the student. Once this is recognized, it will be necessary to come to grips with the question of the best way to bring about such infusion. In the meantime, it will be well to keep in mind that students who are not taught to use criteria in a way that is both sensitive to context and self-corrective are not being taught to think critically.

Last, a word about the employment of criteria in critical thinking to facilitate good judgment. Critical thinking, as we have seen, is skillful thinking, and skills are proficient performances that satisfy relevant criteria. Without these skills, we would be unable to draw meaning from a written text or from a conversation, nor could we impart meaning to a conversation or to what we write. But just as in an orchestra there are such families as the woodwinds, the brasses, and the strings, so there are these different families of thinking skills, And just as within an orchestral family there are individual instruments – oboes and clarinets and bassoons, each with its own standard of proficient performance – so there are families of thinking skills, like induction, questioning, and analogical reasoning, that represent particular kinds of proficient performances in accordance with relevant criteria. We are all familiar with the fact that an otherwise splendid musical performance can be ruined if so much as a single instrumentalist performs below acceptable standards. Likewise, the mobilization and perfection of the thinking skills that go to make up critical thinking cannot neglect any of these skills without jeopardizing the process as a whole.

This is why we cannot be content to give students practice in a handful of cognitive skills while neglecting all the others that are needed for the competency in inquiry, in language, and in thought that is the hallmark of proficient critical thinkers. Instead of selecting and polishing a few skills that we think will do the trick, we must begin with the raw subject matter of communication and inquiry – with reading, listening, speaking, writing, and reasoning – and we must cultivate whatever skills the mastery of each process entails. When we do this, we come to realize that only philosophy can provide the logical and epistemological criteria that are now lacking in the curriculum.[8] This is far from saying that these are the only skills and criteria that are lacking, but they do represent a significant proportion of what is needed to make student thinking more responsible.

At the same time, it should be evident that, just as individual skills are not enough, the orchestration of skills is not enough either. Critical thinking is a normative enterprise in that it insists upon standards and criteria by means of which critical thinking can be distinguished from uncritical thinking. Shoddy work may be due less to a lack of skill than to the worker's having low standards, an insufficient commitment to quality, or a lack of judgment.[9]

Of course, psychologically oriented studies of critical thinking are often considered normative in the sense that the behavior of the "most successful" thinkers is described and recommended as a model for the way one ought to think. But this is a narrow and precarious base on which to set criteria and standards. Consider how much more broadly based in human experience are the logical criteria that guide our reasonings. Or consider the standards that prevail in the arts, crafts, and professions in contrast to the questionable implications of successful problem solving in this or that experiment. If critical thinking is to be insisted upon in education, it will have to develop conventions and traditions of cognitive work and accountability that teachers will readily recommend to their students. It is not enough to initiate students into heuristic and algorithmic procedures; they must also be initiated into the logic of good reasons, the logic of inference, and the logic of judgment.

Even if the claims I have been making on behalf of critical thinking up to this point are conceded to be true, much has been omitted, just as a witness may manage to tell the truth but not the whole truth. What I have in mind in particular is that critical thinking alone should not be considered the only dimension of thinking to be cultivated in order to improve thinking in the schools. Although it represents a component that contributes a great deal to such cognitive improvement, critical thinking skills are complemented by creative and caring thinking.

Any empirical instance of thinking is likely to involve aspects of all three modes, for no thinking is purely critical or purely creative or purely caring, and certainly excellent thinking will be strongly represented in all three categories. Determining the generic traits of creative and caring thinking may be more difficult than defining the specification of such traits in critical thinking. But there can be little doubt that, to improve thinking, the creative and the caring complement the critical. An education that nurtures uninventive thinking is no better than one that nourishes uncritical thinking. And how can we meaningfully address issues that involve, say, children, embryos, animals, or the environment if at the same time we care nothing for these things? What sort of architect would it be who cared nothing about the houses she designed and the people who were to inhabit them?

Finally, there is the question of the role of critical thinking in education. I have already suggested that all courses, whether in primary, secondary, or tertiary education, need to be taught in such a way as to encourage critical thinking in those subjects. Indeed, this opinion is so common in such areas as the social sciences as to be fairly uncontroversial. What I would add, however, is that critical thinking should be added to the curriculum as an independent course. Without an independent course that teaches the generic aspects of critical thinking, it will be difficult for the teachers in the particular disciplines to convey to their students why critical thinking is important.

It cannot be sufficiently emphasized, however, that there is nothing in the practice of critical thinking that does not already exist in some form or other in the practice of philosophy, even if there is an enormous amount in philosophy that is not in critical thinking. Educators would do well to try to understand the relationship between the two. My own opinion is that there is no better way of involving students in an independent course in critical thinking than by making it a course in philosophy. Not the traditional, academic philosophy of the university tradition, but the narrative philosophy that emphasizes dialogue, deliberation, and the strengthening of judgment and community. Such redesigned philosophy has existed now for a quarter of a century and has repeatedly demonstrated its viability. It would be a pity if it were overlooked in favor of glib commercial approaches that have only a glimmer of academic merit.

## Notes

1. Useful discussions of the nature of criteria are to be found in Michael Anthony Slote, "The Theory of Important Criteria," *Journal of Philosophy* 63:8 (April 1966), pp. 221–4, and. Michael Scriven, "The Logic of Criteria," *Journal of Philosophy* 56 (October 1959), pp. 857–68.

2. I see no inconsistency between urging "cognitive accountability" (i.e., feeling an obligation to supply reasons for stated opinions) and urging the development of intellectual autonomy among students. If providing students with cognitive skills is a form of empowerment, such increased powers entail increased responsibilities, especially to and for oneself. There are times when we cannot let other people do our thinking for us, and we must think for ourselves. And we must learn to think for ourselves by thinking for ourselves; other people cannot instruct us in how to do it, although they can put us in a community of inquiry where it becomes a relatively easy thing to do. The point is that students must be encouraged to become reasonable for their own good (i.e., as a step toward their own autonomy) and not just for our good (i.e., because the growing rationalization of the society requires it).

3. C. S. Peirce, in "Ideals of Conduct," *Collected Papers of Charles Sanders Peirce*, ed. Charles Hartshorne and Paul Weiss (Cambridge, MA: Harvard University Press, 1931–5), vol. 1, discusses the connection between self-correcting inquiry, self-criticism, and self-control.

4. *Nichomachean Ethics*, 1138 3 1.

5. Matthew Lipman and Ann Margaret Sharp, *Wondering at the World* (Upper Montclair, NJ: IAPC, 1986), pp. 226–99.

6. Matthew Lipman, *Kio and Gus* (Upper Montclair, NJ: IAPC, 1982).

7. A number of instruments are available to evaluate the thinking of elementary school children. Although there appear to be none that effectively evaluate children's judgment, there are some that concentrate more or less successfully on children's reasoning. I would cite here the *New Jersey Test of Reasoning Skills* (Upper Montclair, NJ: IAPC, 1983). For an instrument to evaluate possible changes in teacher attitudes toward students' cognitive potentials, there seems to be very little available other than the *Cognitive Behavior Checklist* (Upper Montclair, NJ: IAPC, 1990).

8. An earlier version of the preceding portion of this chapter appeared in *Educational Leadership* 16:1 (September 1988), pp. 38–43, under the title "Critical Thinking – What can it Be?"

9. This point has been well made by Mark Selman in "Another Way of Talking about Critical Thinking," *Proceeding of the Forty-third Annual Meeting of the Philosophy of Education Society*, 1987 (Normal, IL: 1988), pp. 169–78.

# 49

# The Reasons Conception

## Harvey Siegel

*At its core, rationality . . . consists in doing (or believing) things because we have good reasons for doing so . . . if we are going to determine whether a given action or belief is (or was) rational, we must ask whether there are (or were) sound reasons for it.*[1]

*Rationality . . . is a matter of* reasons, *and to take it as a fundamental educational ideal is to make as pervasive as possible the free and critical quest for reasons, in all realms of study.*[2]

*Applying [the skills and understandings necessary for autonomous education] . . . involves a* disposition *to do so, an attitude of "critical-mindedness", and a willingness to challenge prevailing norms. This disposition is almost never fostered in our public schools, which is one of our greatest* educational *failings.*[3]

In chapter 1 I introduced the "reasons" conception of critical thinking, according to which a critical thinker is one who is *appropriately moved by reasons.* In this chapter I shall attempt to amplify and clarify this conception. I begin by exploring the connection between critical thinking and rationality, after

which are examined the "reason assessment" component of critical thinking and the "critical attitude" component. The educational significance of the reasons conception, according to which critical thinking constitutes a fundamental educational ideal, is considered as well.

## 1 Critical Thinking, Rationality, and Reasons

To be a critical thinker is to be appropriately moved by reasons. To be a rational person is to believe and act on the basis of reasons. There is then a deep conceptual connection, by way of the notion of reasons, between critical thinkers and rational persons. Critical thinking is best conceived, consequently, as the *educational cognate* of rationality: critical thinking involves bringing to bear all matters relevant to the rationality of belief and action; and education aimed at the promulgation of critical thinking is nothing less than education aimed at the fostering of rationality and the development of rational persons.

Rationality, in its turn, is to be understood as being "coextensive with the relevance of reasons."[4]

Originally published in *Educating Reason* (New York: Routledge, 1988), pp. 32–47, 149–54. © 1988 Harvey Siegel. Reprinted with kind permission of the author.

A critical thinker is one who appreciates and accepts the importance, and convicting force, of reasons.[5] When assessing claims, making judgments, evaluating procedures, or contemplating alternative actions, the critical thinker seeks reasons on which to base her assessments, judgments, and actions. To seek reasons, moreover, is to recognize and commit oneself to *principles*, for, as R. S. Peters puts it, "principles are needed to determine the relevance [and strength] of reasons."[6] Israel Scheffler describes the relationship between reasons and principles in this way:

> reason is always a matter of abiding by general rules or principles . . . reason is always a matter of treating equal reasons equally, and of judging the issues in the light of general principles to which one has bound oneself . . . if I could judge reasons differently when they bear on my interests, or disregard my principles when they conflict with my own advantage, I should have no principles at all. The concepts of *principles, reasons* and *consistency* thus go together. . . . In fact, they define a general concept of rationality. A rational man is one who is consistent in thought and in action, abiding by impartial and generalizable principles freely chosen as binding upon himself.[7]

To illustrate the connection between reasons, principles, and consistency: suppose that Johnny's teacher keeps him after class one day as punishment for throwing spitballs. When asked by his parents why Johnny was kept after class, his teacher replies: "Johnny was kept after class because (i.e. for the reason that) he was disrupting the class." The teacher's *reason* for keeping him after class is that his behavior was disruptive. For this properly to count as a reason, the teacher must be committed to some *principle* which licenses or backs that reason, i.e. establishes it as a bona fide reason, e.g. "All disruptive behavior warrants keeping students after class" (or "This sort of behavior warrants keeping students after class"), which must be consistently applied to cases. If the teacher is not committed to some such principle, then her putative reason for keeping Johnny after class does not constitute a genuine reason; Johnny or his parents would be perfectly entitled to challenge the teacher, for example by noting that Mary, who also threw spitballs, was not kept after class. Johnny might well say: "Since you don't apply any relevant principle consistently, you have no reason to keep me after class. If throwing spitballs is not a reason for detaining Mary, it cannot be a reason for detaining me either." Of course there may be mitigating

circumstances; Mary may be a first time offender and Johnny a repeater, etc. Nevertheless, the point remains that the teacher's putative reason is rightly regarded as a reason, which warrants or justifies her behavior, only if it is backed by some principle which (can itself be justified and) is consistently applied in relevantly similar cases. To take a final example: if having a grade point average of 0.6 is a reason for having Mary repeat grade 10 (in light of the principle that a grade point average of 0.6 in grade 10 is insufficient for promotion to grade 11, or some similar principle), it is a reason for having Johnny repeat it as well. Here we see the connection between reasons, principles and consistency. In general, $p$ is a reason for $q$ only if some principle $r$ renders $p$ a reason for $q$, and would equally render $p'$ a reason for $q'$ if $p$ and $p'$, and $q$ and $q'$, are relevantly similar.

Because of this connection between reasons and principles, critical thinking is principled thinking; because principles involve consistency, critical thinking is impartial, consistent, and non-arbitrary, and the critical thinker both thinks and acts in accordance with, and values, consistency, fairness, and impartiality of judgment and action.[8] Principled, critical judgment, in its rejection of arbitrariness, inconsistency, and partiality, thus presupposes a recognition of the binding force of standards, taken to be universal and objective, in accordance with which judgments are to be made.[9] In the first instance, such standards involve criteria by which judgments can be made regarding the acceptability of various beliefs, claims, and actions – that is, they involve criteria which allow the evaluation of the strength and force of the reasons which may be offered in support of alternative beliefs, claims and actions. This leads us naturally into consideration of the reason assessment component of the reasons conception of critical thinking.

## 2   The Reason Assessment Component

The basic idea here is simple enough: a critical thinker must be able to assess reasons and their ability to warrant beliefs, claims and actions properly. This means that the critical thinker must have a good understanding of, and the ability to utilize, principles governing the assessment of reasons.

There are at least two types of such principles: subject-specific principles which govern the assessment of particular sorts of reasons in particular contexts; and subject-neutral, general principles which apply across a wide variety of contexts and types of reason. Subject-neutral principles include all those principles typically regarded as "logical," both informal and formal. So, for example, principles regarding proper inductive inference, avoiding fallacies, proper deductive inference – in fact, virtually all that is usually included in informal logic texts, and virtually all of Ennis's list of proficiencies – count as subject-neutral logical principles. On the other hand, principles which apply only to specific subjects or areas of inquiry – e.g. principles governing the proper interpretation of bubble chamber photographs in particle physics, or those governing proper assessment of works of art, or novels, or historical documents, or the design of bathroom plumbing fixtures – are (as McPeck insists), though not general, nevertheless of central importance for critical thinking. There is no *a priori* reason for regarding either of these types of principles as more basic (or irrelevant) to critical thinking than the other; nor is there, at least to my knowledge, any significant empirical evidence to that effect. Similarly, there is no reason for regarding the skills associated with one sort of principle (e.g. the skill or ability to read a bubble chamber photo, a subject-specific skill) as more or less fundamental to critical thinking than the skills associated with the other sort (e.g. the skill or ability to reason well inductively, or assess the merits of observations, or recognize and avoid the fallacy of begging the question – all these being subject-neutral, logical skills).

This latter point is sufficient, I think, to establish that, from the educational point of view, the important question is not "Is there a generalized skill (or set of skills) of critical thinking?" but rather "How does critical thinking manifest itself?" The answer to this latter question is: "In both subject-specific and subject-neutral ways, for reasons, and the principles relevant to their assessment, are both subject-specific and subject-neutral." The McPeck-inspired debate over the first question, which has greatly preoccupied many members of the Informal Logic Movement of late, is thus in an important sense beside the point. There is no *a priori* reason for regarding either sort of principle or skill as more basic to critical thinking than the other; nor is there compelling empirical evidence to support such a judgment.[10]

Earlier I claimed that the reason assessment component of critical thinking requires that the student be able to assess reasons and their warranting force properly, and that this in turn requires that the student have a good grasp of the principles governing such assessment. A full account of the reason assessment component involves more than this, however. In addition to the ability to assess reasons and their warranting force (and a grasp of the related governing principles), critical thinkers need also to have a theoretical grasp of the nature of reasons, warrant, and justification, and so some understanding of why a given putative reason is to be assessed as it is. That is, the reason assessment component involves *epistemology*.

Perhaps the best way to get at this point is through a look at McPeck's discussion of the relation between critical thinking and epistemology. McPeck calls his approach to critical thinking the "epistemological approach," and he too argues that epistemology is central to critical thinking.[11] But McPeck's discussion of the relation between critical thinking and epistemology is problematic. For McPeck, the "epistemological approach" involves striving for an understanding of the constitution of good reasons for beliefs, so that:

> A student would learn not only what is thought to be the case in a given field (that is, the "facts") but also why it is so regarded. With this kind of understanding . . . a person is then in a position to make the kinds of judgment required of a critical thinker.[12]

On this view, the student is a critical thinker in some content area, e.g. science, if the student understands the criteria of evaluation and justification of scientific beliefs. To have this understanding is to have an understanding of the epistemology of science. McPeck is quite explicit that good reasons, and so epistemology, are in his view subject-specific – not just reasons, but criteria for assessing the goodness of reasons are subject-specific; epistemology is to be replaced by a series of epistemologies, one for each "field of human endeavor":

> In chapter 2 it was argued that epistemology is, in effect, the analysis of good reasons for belief, including their specific character and foundation. Also, because collective human experience has discovered that different kinds of beliefs often have different kinds of good reason supporting them, it follows that there will be many different epistemologies corresponding to different fields of human endeavor. A corollary of this is that logic itself is parasitic upon epistemology, since logic is merely the formalization of good reasons once they have been discovered. Thus epistemology, and to

some extent logic, have intra-field validity but not necessarily inter-field validity. . . . (Most programmes for critical thinking effectively deny this proposition, hence my disagreement with them.)[13]

There is a confusion here in McPeck's use of "epistemology." Epistemology is the *general* study of reasons, warrant, and justification, and a student striving to be a critical thinker in (e.g.) science does not study "the epistemology of science," understood to be distinct from "the epistemology" of other subject areas. Rather, the student strives to understand the specific principles and criteria by which scientific reasons are assessed, supplemented by a deeper understanding of the nature of reasons, warrant and justification generally. McPeck uses "epistemology" to refer both to subject-specific criteria of reason assessment, and to the general account of what it is to be a reason, to offer warrant for a belief, and to be justified. Once this conflation is noted, McPeck's claim that epistemology has "intra-field validity but not necessarily inter-field validity" collapses.[14] McPeck is surely right that students should come to learn why reasons for given claims in particular fields are rightly regarded as strong, powerful, compelling, weak, trivial, and so on according to the criteria for assessing reasons in those fields. But such an "epistemology of the subject" is only a part of epistemology as it is usually (and properly) understood. For the student who is to be a critical thinker must come to understand not only the criteria of reason assessment in specific fields, but also the nature of reasons generally and the fact that good reasons in different fields, singled out as good by different field-specific criteria, nevertheless stand in the same relation to the beliefs they support despite their being singled out by disparate criteria. If not, the student will have only the most shallow understanding of "the epistemology of the subject" – "*here* we regard *this* sort of thing as a good reason" – without understanding why this sort of thing should count as a reason here, but another sort of thing as a reason there. In short, McPeck's call for an epistemological approach to critical thinking stops short of a fully epistemological approach, for it fails to recognize that epistemology conceived as inquiry into the nature of reasons, warrant, and justification speaks to, and backs, the particular criteria of reason assessment McPeck refers to as "the epistemology of the subject."

It is perhaps worth noting that McPeck's own discussion belies his construal of epistemology as field- or subject-specific. For consider McPeck's claim that epistemology has intra-field but not necessarily inter-field validity, and the reasons he offers in support of that claim. Are those reasons, or the criteria which sanction them, field-specific? If so, to what field? To raise these questions is to realize that epistemology, understood as McPeck does as the analysis of good reasons, cannot be conceived of as subject- or field-specific. For:

1  many reasons and beliefs are not subject-specific, and so fall under no subject-specific set of reason-assessment criteria; and, more importantly,

2  critical thinking requires not simply a grasp of field-specific criteria of reason assessment, but also a general understanding of the nature of reasons, warrant and justification as these notions function across fields.[15]

To summarize: I have suggested thus far that a central component of critical thinking is the reason assessment component. The critical thinker must be able to assess reasons and their ability to warrant beliefs, claims and actions properly. Therefore, the critical thinker must have a good understanding of, and the ability to utilize, both subject-specific and subject-neutral (logical) principles governing the assessment of reasons. (This ability involves the "sub-ability" of determining which principle(s), and which sort of principle, are appropriate for the assessment of the putative reasons at hand.) A critical thinker is a person who can act, assess claims, and make judgments on the basis of reasons, and who understands and conforms to principles governing the evaluation of the force of those reasons. The account offered highlights the close conceptual connections between critical thinking and reasons, and between reasons and principles. The fact that there are (at least) two general types of principles of reason assessment – subject-specific and subject-neutral – suggests that much recent debate between various members of the Informal Logic Movement and McPeck concerning the generalizability of critical thinking skills is misconceived and irrelevant to the theory of critical thinking. McPeck and those members of the Movement are both right; both subject-specific, non-generalizable, and subject-neutral, generalizable skills, principles and information are highly relevant to reason assessment and so to critical thinking. Neither can be ruled out on *a priori* grounds; nor can either be ruled out – at least at present – on empirical grounds. (How central each is to the proper teaching of critical thinking is a matter to be resolved by further empirical study.) Finally, epistemology is also a crucially important component of a proper conception of critical thinking, for the critical thinker must have a good grasp of the nature of reasons, warrant and justification generally, as these notions function across fields, in order both to carry out and to understand the activity of reason assessment.[16]

Suppose that a student masters the reason assessment component of critical thinking, and is able to assess reasons, and to understand the nature of reasons and their assessment, in the ways articulated above. Has such a student earned the title "critical thinker"? So far, she has not, though she is undeniably well along the way to doing so. For, as we saw in the previous chapter, being able to assess reasons is not sufficient for being a critical thinker, though it is necessary. Equally necessary is that our student have an appropriate *attitude* toward the activity of critical thinking. This brings us naturally to the second component of critical thinking to be considered: the "critical attitude," or "critical spirit" component.

## 3   The critical spirit

In order to be a critical thinker, a person must have, in addition to what has been said thus far, certain attitudes, dispositions, habits of mind, and character traits, which together may be labelled the "critical attitude" or "critical spirit." Most generally, a critical thinker must not only be *able* to assess reasons properly, in accordance with the reason assessment component, she must be *disposed* to do so as well; that is, a critical thinker must have a well-developed disposition to engage in reason assessment. A critical thinker must have a *willingness* to conform judgment and action to principle, not simply an ability to so conform. One who has the critical attitude has a certain *character*[17] as well as certain skills: a character which is inclined to seek, and to base judgment and action upon, reasons; which rejects partiality and arbitrariness; which is committed to the objective evaluation of relevant evidence; and which values such aspects of critical thinking as intellectual honesty, justice to evidence, sympathetic and impartial consideration of interests, objectivity, and impartiality. A critical attitude demands not simply an ability to seek reasons, but a commitment

to do so; not simply an ability to judge impartially, but a willingness and desire to do so, even when impartial judgment runs counter to self-interest.[18] A possessor of the critical attitude is inclined to seek reasons and evidence; to demand justification; to query and investigate unsubstantiated claims. Moreover, a person who possesses the critical attitude has habits of mind consonant with the just-mentioned considerations. Such a person habitually seeks evidence and reasons, and is predisposed to so seek – and to base belief and action on the results of such seeking. She applies the skills and abilities of reason assessment in all appropriate contexts, including those contexts in which her own beliefs and actions are challenged. For the possessor of the critical attitude, nothing is immune from criticism, not even one's most deeply-held convictions. Most fundamentally, the critical attitude involves a deep commitment to and respect for reasons – indeed, as Binkley puts it, a *love of reason*:

> the attitudes we seek to foster in the critical reasoning course might be summed up under the label "love of reason." We not only want our students to be *able* to reason well; we want them actually to do it, and so we want them to be eager to do it and to enjoy it – to think it important. We want it to assume an important place in their lives.[19]

This is, we want our students to *value* good reasoning, and to be disposed to believe and act on its basis. This is the heart of the critical attitude.[20]

Such a view as this, which includes attitudes, dispositions, habits of mind, and traits of character in a conception of critical thinking, seems to violate the time-honored distinction between cognition and affect (or thinking and feeling, or thought and value, or reason and emotion).[21] This violation, however, is as it should be. For the idea that reasons and emotions are unconnected, and the related idea that the exercise of reason requires complete independence from the emotions,[22] must both be rejected. As many recent writers have suggested, the "life of reason" – that is, the life of the critical thinker, who bases belief, attitude and action upon appropriate reasons and evidence – must have appropriate attitudes, passions, and interests as well as sufficient skills of reason assessment.[23] The conceptions of the reasonable person as one without emotion, and as one who "turns off" her emotions while engaging in reason, are untenable. Rather, the reasonable person has integrated with her reason assessment skills a host of *rational passions*, which together constitute and instantiate the critical attitude. Such a person actively seeks reasons and evidence on which to base judgments; such an attitude involves:

> a love of truth and a contempt of lying, a concern for accuracy in observation and inference, and a corresponding repugnance of error in logic or fact. It demands revulsion at distortion, disgust at evasion, admiration of theoretical achievement, respect for the considered arguments of others.[24]

As Paul puts it, the rational passions include:

> A passionate drive for *clarity*, accuracy, and fairmindedness, a fervor for getting to the bottom of things . . . for listening sympathetically to opposition points of view, a compelling drive to seek out evidence, an intense aversion to contradiction, sloppy thinking, inconsistent application of standards, a devotion to truth as against self-interest – [which are] essential components of the rational person.[25]

The critical thinker, finally, must *care* about reason and its use and point. She "must care about finding out how things are, about getting things right, about tracking down what is the case,"[26] and must have "the feeling of humility which is necessary to the whole-hearted acceptance of the possibility that one may be in error."[27] In sum, the image of the critical thinker/rational person as a "bloodless reasoning machine" will not do.[28] The critical thinker has a rich emotional make-up of dispositions, habits of mind, values, character traits, and emotions which may be collectively referred to as the critical attitude. This attitude is a fundamental feature of the critical thinker, and a crucially important component of the reasons conception of critical thinking.

As Peters puts it, "the use of reason is a passionate business."[29] The reasons conception reflects this fact, and rejects the commonly-drawn distinction between cognition and affect. Besides the emotional and attitudinal dimensions of critical thinking already considered, a person who is to be a critical thinker must be, to the greatest extent possible, emotionally secure, self-confident, and capable of distinguishing between having faulty beliefs and having a faulty character. A positive self-image, and traditionally conceived psychological health, are important features of the psychology of the critical thinker, for their absence may well present practical obstacles to the execution of critical thinking.[30]

All of this suggests that education aimed at the development of critical thinking is a complex business, which must seek to foster a host of attitudes, emotions, dispositions, habits and character traits as well as a wide variety of reasoning skills. Since this cluster of traits to be fostered are traits of persons, not acts of thinking, the present discussion raises again the distinction between an account of critical think*ing* and an account of the critical think*er*. I would like to close out the present section by briefly returning to that distinction.

On the reasons conception, critical thinking involves actions which are not just acts of thinking.[31] For the critical thinker is appropriately *moved* by reasons; she acts in accordance with the force of relevant reasons. Thus the critical thinker is, importantly, a rational actor.[32] As important to critical thinking as rational action is, however, it is crucial to see that critical thinking far outstrips rational action. For a critical thinker is not simply a person who acts rationally (and who has well-developed skills of reason assessment). A critical thinker not only *acts* in certain ways. A critical thinker *is*, in addition, a certain sort of person.[33] Dispositions, inclinations, habits of mind, character traits – these features of the critical thinker are present, and definitive of the critical thinker, even when they are not being utilized or acted upon. Just as sugar has the disposition to dissolve in water while still in the sugar bowl, so does the critical thinker have the dispositions, habits of mind and character traits we have considered while not engaged in reason assessment or (other) rational action. The conception of critical thinking being offered here is as much a conception of a certain sort of person as it is a conception of a certain set of activities and skills. When we take it upon ourselves to educate students so as to foster critical thinking, we are committing ourselves to nothing less than the development of a certain sort of person. The reasons conception is a conception, not only of critical thinking, but of the critical thinker as well.[34]

These last remarks call attention to a matter that has been neglected for the last several pages. So far in this chapter I have endeavoured to articulate the reasons conception: to motivate it in terms of the relations between critical thinking, reasons, and rationality; to consider the detailed aspects of its two components, the reason assessment component and the critical spirit component; and to draw attention to the fact that the reasons conception – as any fully-developed conception of critical thinking must be – is a conception not only of a certain sort of activity, but of a certain sort of person. It remains to consider the way in which critical thinking, and in particular the reasons conception, functions as an educational notion and impacts on our educational ideas. We must, that is, consider the relation between critical thinking and education.

## 4 The Relevance of Critical thinking to Education

### Critical thinking and the ethics of education

A striking feature of critical thinking (understood, from now on, as the reasons conception) is its impressive generality and wide-ranging relevance to education. Critical thinking is relevant to, and has implications for, the ethics of education as well as the epistemology of education. It touches the manner as well as the content of education. It will be worthwhile to spell out in some detail this wide-ranging relevance and generality.

Critical thinking is relevant to the *ethics* of education in at least two ways. First, ethical considerations arise in educational contexts in that how we teach – our *manner* of teaching – has an ethical as well as an instrumental side. We want to teach effectively, so that learners stand a good chance of learning; however, our methods of instruction must meet certain moral standards if they are to be acceptable. For instance, instructional methods which call for physical or psychological abuse of the learner are morally objectionable, no matter how effective. The way in which critical thinking is tied up with the manner of teaching will be dealt with below; this is the first way in which critical thinking is linked with the ethics of education.

The second way concerns the learner's moral education. Educators are bound, both morally and practically, to contribute to the moral education of the learner. Exactly how moral education is to proceed is a matter of some dispute, but it is clear that the learner's moral education should include, at least, instruction aimed at the inculcation in the student of certain intellectual habits, dispositions, and reasoning skills necessary for the learner to reach moral maturity. For example, moral education must seek to develop in the student a willingness and an ability to face moral situations impartially rather than on the basis of self-interest, for adequate moral behavior demands such impartiality. Hand in hand with impartiality is empathy, for the mature moral agent must be able to put herself in the position of others, and grasp their perspective and feelings, if they are to take seriously into consideration the interests of others; the development of empathy as a moral sentiment is thus equally a part of adequate moral education. Likewise, a morally mature person must recognize the centrality and force of moral reasons in moral deliberation, and moral education must strive to foster that recognition. Such "rational virtues" as impartiality of judgment, ability to view matters from a variety of non–self-interested perspectives, and recognition of the force of reasons, to name just three such virtues, are indispensable to moral education. They are also, we have seen, central aspects of critical thinking. Here, then, is the second way in which critical thinking is relevant to the ethics of education.[35]

### Critical thinking and the epistemology of education

Equally informed by critical thinking is the *epistemology* of education. A learner is, if she is successfully educated, expected to come to know many things. The "items of knowledge" a learner is expected to come to know are tremendously diverse, from simple "facts" to complex theories. Such facts and theories, moreover, are to be understood as well as known. It is not enough simply to know (in the sense of being able to repeat) the axioms of Euclidean geometry, for example; the learner is expected to understand them as well (as evidenced by, for example, the ability to utilize them correctly in formulating proofs of theorems). Such knowledge and understanding demands, among other things, a proper understanding of the relevance of reasons and rules of inference and evidence. Without understanding the way in which (for example) the parallel line axiom offers a reason for taking the angle-side-angle theorem to be true, the learner cannot be said to understand fully either the axiom or the theorem. Moreover, the principles governing the correct assessment of inference and evidence are themselves important features of the curriculum. That is to say, a learner may profitably study canons of argument and evidence appraisal in their own right as objects of study, as well as master them in order to understand other items of knowledge whose understanding depends on such mastery. Such items of the curriculum, then, are central to the education of the learner; to grasp the connection between premise and conclusion or evidence and conclusion is to understand the way in which premises and evidence constitute or provide reasons for conclusions. To understand the role of reasons in judgment is to open the door to the possibility of understanding conclusions and knowledge-claims generally. And, as we have seen, the ability to recognize the importance of and properly assess reasons is a central feature of critical thinking. Here, then, is the way that critical thinking is relevant to the epistemology of education.

## Critical thinking and the content of education

Intertwined with aspects of the ethics and epistemology of education are the content and manner of education. We can usefully divide the realm of education into two distinct parts: the *content* of education, which includes all that educators seek to impart to their students; and the *manner* of education, which includes the ways in which educators try to impart that content. Critical thinking has ramifications for both of these domains. We can see in another way the generality of critical thinking by spelling out the ramifications of critical thinking for both domains.

Critical thinking is highly relevant to the *content* of education. Accepting Ryle's distinction between knowledge how and knowledge that,[36] educational content includes both the development of skills and specific abilities (knowledge how), and propositional information (knowledge that). Critical thinking is relevant to both these types of educational content.

Critical thinking includes an important set of skills and abilities which education seeks to foster. As such, it is part of the "knowledge how" of educational content. We want students to be critical thinkers, and we seek to develop in them skills to that end, much as we seek to develop their reading, spelling, and computational skills. (These skills have of course been considered under the "reason assessment" component of critical thinking.) Similarly, we try to inculcate in students attitudes, dispositions, and habits likely to improve both their ability to think critically, and their inclination to do so. That is to say, we seek to instill in students the critical spirit, in that we try to impart to them the dispositions, habits of mind, and character traits which constitute that spirit. Since these skills and habits fall under the general heading of "knowledge how," we may say that critical thinking is part of the "how" of our educational content.

Critical thinking also falls under the "knowledge that" portion of educational content. We want to get students to be able to think critically, and that means, in part, getting them to understand what the rules of assessment and criteria of evaluation of claims are. We want our students to learn, for example, the evidential criteria underlying our judgments that some piece of evidence supports claim $X$, but that another piece does not support claim $Y$. We want students to learn *how* to apply such criteria. This, we have seen, is part of the way in which critical thinking concerns the "knowledge how" portion of educational content. But we also want students to be able to *reflect* on these criteria, and to endeavor to improve them.[37] In addition, we want students not simply to apply criteria blindly, but to understand their point, the justification of claims that they offer, and the higher-order justifications of them as legitimate criteria of assessment and evaluation that we can offer in their behalf. All this is part of our educational content of the "knowledge that" sort. So, critical thinking is an important part of the content of education, touching both the "knowledge how" and "knowledge that" portions of that content.

## Critical thinking and the manner of education

Perhaps most significant of all the connections between critical thinking and education are those between critical thinking and the manner of teaching – the *critical manner*. The critical manner is that manner of teaching that models and reinforces the critical spirit. A teacher who utilizes the critical manner seeks to encourage in his or her students the skills, habits and dispositions necessary for the development of the critical spirit. This means, first, that the teacher always recognizes the right of the student to question and demand reasons; and consequently recognizes an obligation to provide reasons whenever demanded. The critical manner thus demands of a teacher a willingness to subject all beliefs and practices to scrutiny, and so to allow students the genuine opportunity to understand the role reasons play in the justification of thought and action. The critical manner also demands honesty of a teacher; reasons presented by a teacher must be genuine reasons, and the teacher must honestly appraise the power of those reasons. In addition, the teacher must submit her reasons to the independent evaluation of the student:

> To teach . . . is at some points at least to submit oneself to the understanding and independent judgment of the pupil, to his demand for reasons, to his sense

of what constitutes an adequate explanation. To teach someone that such and such is the case is not merely to try to get him to believe it: deception, for example, is not a method or a mode of teaching. Teaching involves further that, if we try to get the student to believe that such and such is the case, we try also to get him to believe it for reasons that, within the limits of his capacity to grasp, are *our* reasons. Teaching, in this way, requires us to reveal our reasons to the student and, by so doing, to submit them to his evaluation and criticism. . . . To teach is thus . . . to acknowledge the "reason" of the pupil, i.e. his demand for and judgment of reasons.[38]

Teaching in the critical manner is thus teaching so as to develop in students the skills and attitudes consonant with critical thinking. It is, as Scheffler puts it, an attempt to initiate students "into the rational life, a life in which the critical quest for reasons is a dominant and integrating motive."[39] Here reasons, rationality, and teaching come together in the critical manner. Teaching in the critical manner is thus perhaps the clearest way in which critical thinking appropriately guides educational practice.[40]

## 5 Critical Thinking as an Educational Ideal

We have seen thus far that critical thinking has ramifications for both the ethics and the epistemology, and both the content and the manner, of education. These ramifications are numerous, varied, and wideranging. They demonstrate the impressive generality of critical thinking as an educational notion. But what sort of notion is it? How should we conceive of the *educational* notion of critical thinking?

We should, I think, conceive of it as an educational *ideal*. Critical thinking, at least in the way it has been conceptualized in the present chapter, speaks to virtually all of our educational endeavors. It provides both important goals for our educational efforts, and direction for the achievement of those goals. It is highly relevant to the determination of what we should teach, how we should teach, how we should organize educational activities, what the points of many of those activities are, how we should treat students and others in the educational setting, and so on. Perhaps most importantly, it provides a conception of the sort of person we are trying, through our educational efforts, to create, and the sort of character to be fostered in such a person. Critical thinking provides an underlying rationale for

educational activities, a criterion for evaluating those activities, and a guiding principle for the organization and conduct of those activities. Surely such a broad-gauged notion is properly thought of as an ideal.

In fact, I should like to suggest, critical thinking is best thought of as a *regulative* ideal. It defines regulative standards of excellence which can be used to adjudicate between rival educational methods, policies, and practices. We have spelled out some of the features of critical thinking: certain skills, attitudes, habits, dispositions and character traits of the learner; certain sorts of practices, qualities and attitudes of the teacher; certain sorts of content of the curriculum; and certain sorts of properties, both contentual and organizational, of educational activities. To say that critical thinking is a regulative educational ideal is to say that the notion of critical thinking, or its constituent components, can and should be used as a basis by which to judge the desirability and justifiability of various features of or proposals for the educational enterprise. For example, according to the regulative ideal of critical thinking, whichever of two rival teaching methods conforms more closely to the manner of teaching described above as the critical manner is *prima facie* more desirable and ought to be utilized. Similarly, of two educational practices, whichever tends to develop in students those skills, habits, dispositions and character traits central to critical thinking is *prima facie* more desirable and ought to be chosen. In general, our guiding question in assessing educational activities should be: does this manifest, and foster, critical thinking? To the extent that we take this as our guiding evaluative question, we take critical thinking to be a fundamental educational ideal. In this way, critical thinking regulates our judgments and provides standards of excellence on which to base evaluations of educational practices, and so is usefully called a *regulative* ideal. It aids us in evaluating, and choosing between, alternative curricula, teaching methods, theories, policies, and practices.[41]

It should be clear that taking critical thinking to be an educational ideal is a highly significant move, with potentially far-reaching, even revolutionary, consequences. Hence it is far from clear that we should take it as such. The aim of this chapter has been simply to set out a conception of the ideal. The task of justifying the ideal, that is of providing reasons for granting the notion of critical thinking the prestige, force and power to guide education that I have just suggested it ought to be granted, is the topic of the next chapter.

# Notes

1. L. Laudan, *Progress and its Problems*, p. 123.
2. I. Scheffler, *Reason and Teaching*, p. 62, emphasis in original. Cf. also Popper's remarks on the "attitude of reasonableness," in *The Open Society and its Enemies*, vol. 2, p. 225.
3. N. C. Burbules, "A Theory of Power in Education," p. 113, emphasis in original.
4. I. Scheffler, *Conditions of Knowledge*, p. 107. Cf. also Scheffler, *Reason and Teaching*, pp. 62–3. It should already be apparent, though it will become even more so as we proceed, that the theory of critical thinking thus rests ultimately on the theory of rationality.
5. Throughout I should be taken to mean that the critical thinker accepts the convicting force of *good* reasons, i.e. of reasons which actually have convicting force and which warrant conviction. I have not added "good" before each occurrence of "reason," because I take it to be implied by "appropriate" in "appropriately moved by reasons." To be *appropriately* moved is to be moved to just the extent that the reasons in question warrant. I am grateful to several correspondents, especially Emily Robertson, for suggesting this clarification.
6. R. S. Peters, "Reason and Habit: The Paradox of Moral Education," p. 248, bracketed phrase added. Cf. also Peters, *Reason and Compassion*.
7. I. Scheffler, "Philosophical Models of Teaching," p. 76, emphasis in original. I would add to this conception of the rational person only that the principles freely chosen themselves admit of rational justification. Cf. op. cit., p. 79.
8. As Peters says, "Reason . . . is the antithesis of arbitrariness" (*Reason and Compassion*, p. 77); as Scheffler puts it, "Reason stands always in contrast with inconsistency and with expediency" ("Philosophical Models of Teaching," p. 76).
9. Any view which rejects such standards is thus incompatible with critical thinking. Articulating and justifying the standards are tasks for the theory of rationality. The point now being argued in the text is simply that critical thinking and rationality require, and so presuppose, such standards; this requirement in turn helps to delineate what is to count as critical and/or rational thinking.
10. Of course it may be the case that one sort *is* more important educationally, either because one sort is more utilized in the life of a critical thinker, or is more difficult to master, and so on. Here it seems clear that the matter can be settled only empirically.
11. J. E. McPeck, *Critical Thinking and Education*, for example, pp. 22–4 and 155–7.
12. Op. cit., p. 157.
13. Op. cit., p. 155.
14. Ibid. I suspect that the problem McPeck faces here stems in part from his view that the goodness of reasons is "discovered" by "collective human experience" (ibid.), as if justification is a "natural fact" about the world, rather than something established by epistemological argument. But I cannot pursue the point here. Critical discussion of "naturalized epistemology" may be found in my "Justification, Discovery and the Naturalizing of Epistemology," and my "Empirical Psychology, Naturalized Epistemology, and First Philosophy."
15. It is worth noting that these difficulties with McPeck's discussion of "the epistemology of the subject" stem, at least in part, from his uncritical acceptance of Stephen Toulmin's views on field-dependence. McPeck cites Toulmin (*Human Understanding*, pp. 32–3, 79–80) to the effect that criteria of argument assessment are intra-, not inter-field; but fails to consider the obvious self-reflexive question regarding the generality or field-specificity of the criteria by which Toulmin's claim is itself to be evaluated. I believe that McPeck is far too uncritical of Toulmin's views on logic, rationality, and epistemology. For critical discussion of McPeck's appeal to Toulmin, cf. Govier's review of McPeck's book, pp. 171–2; for critical discussion of Toulmin's most recent foray into the area of critical thinking/informal logic, cf. Ralph Johnson's thorough review, "Toulmin's Bold Experiment"; for consideration of Toulmin's views on rationality and epistemology, cf. my "Truth, Problem Solving and the Rationality of Science." I am grateful to Dennis Rohatyn for discussion of McPeck's use of Toulmin.

    The sort of generality which I am here arguing is necessary for a satisfactory account of the relationship between epistemology and critical thinking is analogous to Walton's and Woods' demands for generality in the theory of fallacy. Cf. Blair and Johnson's "Introduction," in their *Informal Logic: The First International Symposium*, regarding Walton's and Woods' papers.
16. It should be clear that I am not here attempting to formulate specific principles of reason assessment. Many philosophers, informal logicians, and critical thinking theorists have done a far better job of articulating such principles than I could hope to do. My aim has rather been to say something about the place of such principles in a general conception of critical thinking.
17. On the relation between rationality and character, cf. Scheffler, *Reason and Teaching*, pp. 28, 64, and *passim*; also Scheffler, "In Praise of the Cognitive Emotions," p. 142 and *passim*.
18. I am assuming here that it is possible that reasons and self-interest might conflict, and so that a thoroughgoing rational egoism is impossible – that is, that acting immorally is contrary to reason. The question

of the relation between rationality and morality is an old and deep one.

19. R. W. Binkley, "Can the Ability to Reason Well Be Taught?" p. 83. Further insightful discussion of critical spirit may be found in Passmore, "On Teaching to be Critical"; also in Paul, "Critical Thinking: Fundamental to Education for a Free Society."

Scheffler notes, in *The Language of Education*, chapter 5, a systematic failure to distinguish, in curricular contexts, between what he calls "norm-acquisition" and "skill-acquisition," which results in a failure to recognize that we often want our students to develop, not just skills and abilities, but dispositions and habits of mind and action:

> we talk of "citizenship" as if it were a set of skills, whereas our educational aim is, in fact, not merely to teach people *how* to be good citizens but, in particular, to *be* good citizens, not merely *how* to go about voting, but *to* vote. We talk about giving them "the skills required for democratic living," when actually we are concerned that they acquire democratic habits, norms, propensities. To take another example, *we talk of giving pupils the "ability to think critically" when what we really want is for them to acquire the habits and norms of critical thought.* (pp. 98–9, last emphasis added)

Here, in a nutshell, is why it is necessary to incorporate a critical spirit component (along with a reason assessment component) into a full conception of critical thinking. We want students to *be*, and be *disposed* to be – not just be *able* to be – critical thinkers.

20. Notice that the attitudes, dispositions, habits of mind, and character traits constitutive of the critical spirit are general and subject-neutral. The disposition to demand reasons, for example, is the same whether one is demanding reasons for a claim in physics, photography or philosophy. Thus the critical spirit offers a variety of characteristics of critical thinking which are general, and so stand as counter-examples to McPeck's claim that features of critical thinking are uniformly subject-specific. I am grateful to Robert Floden for pointing this out to me.

21. Another time-honored distinction which needs to be exploded is that between critical and creative thinking. The relationship between critical thinking and creativity is a complex one, but it is not one of mutual exclusion. The critical thinker, for example, needs to be creative in developing reasons, arguments, examples, etc., as well as critical in assessing those creations. While I cannot argue the point in any detail here, I would suggest that critical thinking involves creativity, and that creative thinking involves criticality. The distinction between boring, automatic critical thinking and wild, unconstrained, undisciplined creative thinking is untenable, and assumes an inde-

fensible conception of creativity. For fine discussions of the weaknesses of the standard view of creativity, and an argument for the indispensability of disciplined, principled critical thinking to an adequate conception of creativity, cf. S. Bailin, "Creativity and Quality," and Bailin, *Achieving Extraordinary Ends: An Essay on Creativity*. On the interconnectedness of critical and creative thinking, cf. Passmore, "On Teaching to be Critical"; also Ennis, "A Conception of Critical Thinking – with Some Curriculum Suggestions," pp. 14–15. I want to emphasize that nothing about the reasons conception of critical thinking forces a sharp split between critical and creative thinking, or the view that creativity, properly conceived, is not part of the repertoire of the critical thinker. I am grateful to Francis Schrag, Edward Mooney, and especially Sharon Bailin for correspondence/conversation concerning this point.

22. As Denis Phillips reminds me, what is usually meant here is that certain emotions (e.g. hatred, envy, anger, etc.) ought not to interfere with or inappropriately override the exercise of reasoned judgment. This is of course correct. The point in the text is simply that a wholesale bifurcation between reason and emotion is untenable.

23. Cf. Scheffler, "In Praise of the Cognitive Emotions"; Peters, "Reason and Passion" and *Reason and Compassion*, especially Lecture Three; and Paul, "Critical Thought Essential to the Acquisition of Rational Knowledge and Passions."

24. Scheffler, "In Praise of the Cognitive Emotions," p. 141.

25. Paul, "Critical Thought," p. 23, emphasis in original.

26. Peters, *Reason and Compassion*, p. 75. For a provocative attempt to connect care with critical thinking in a different way, cf. H. Alderman, "Dialectic as Philosophical Care," who suggests that care for argument is related in a more direct way with care for persons. Popper (*The Open Society*, p. 236) notes that Socrates also made this link.

27. Peters, *Reason and Compassion*, p. 79.

28. Although, as noted in note 22 above, it goes without saying that critical thinking requires the monitoring of certain emotions, and the prevention of particular emotions from overriding the proper exercise of reasoned judgment. One must care enough about truth, for example, to have one's concern for truth outweigh and nullify any feeling (e.g. of envy or hatred) which might tend to distort one's judgment about the truth of some claim.

29. Peters, *Reason and Compassion*, p. 101.

30. A related point is made by Scheffler, in *Conditions of Knowledge*, p. 90. Cf. also T. F. Green's related remarks about "psychic freedom," in his "Indoctrination and Beliefs," pp. 38–9. This psychological make-up is something to be striven for, and developed to varying degrees, over time, not

something to be accomplished once and for all. I am grateful here for discussion with Robert Floden and Dennis Rohatyn.

31. Assuming here that acts of thinking are acts, the present point is simply that acts of thinking are not the only sort of acts there are.

32. In the philosophy of action a distinction is frequently drawn between what are called the "internalist" and "externalist" perspectives. The rationality of an action can be appraised externally, by inquiring as to whether there are (were) good reasons for performing the action; or internally, by inquiring as to whether the agent has (had) good reasons for performing the action, and acts (acted) for those reasons. Full consideration of this matter would take us far afield. It is clear, however, that critical thinking is to be understood in an internalist way, in so far as the critical thinker acts in accordance with reasons she has. An excellent and thorough discussion of the internalist/externalist literature and its relevance to education may be found in E. E. Robertson's "Practical Reasons, Authority, and Education." I am grateful to Robertson for correspondence and conversation on these and related matters.

33. Cf. Passmore, op. cit., pp. 195ff.

34. Of course achieving the ideal – *being* a critical thinker – is a matter of degree. Taking critical thinking as an ideal means fostering the features of critical thinking to the greatest extent possible. But there is no magic point or threshold at which the non-critical thinker turns into a critical thinker. Presumably most people have the capacity to be at least minimally critical, and presumably no one is perfectly critical. Critical thinking must be taken as an ideal which we strive for, and approximate to to varying degrees. I am thankful for discussion with Robert Floden, Emily Robertson, and Dennis Rohatyn on this point.

35. These points are developed more fully in Israel Scheffler, "Moral Education and the Democratic Ideal." Cf. also Scheffler, *The Language of Education*, chapter 5, esp. pp. 94–5.

36. Gilbert Ryle, *The Concept of Mind*.

37. For it is, of course, not the case that we have the "ultimate" or final criteria in our pockets. The refinement and improvement of criteria is an ongoing part of rational inquiry. Cf. Scheffler, *Reason and Teaching*, pp. 78–80, regarding the improvability of principles and criteria of reason assessment.

38. Scheffler, *The Language of Education*, p. 57, emphasis in original.

39. Scheffler, *Conditions of Knowledge*, p. 107. Further discussion of the critical manner of teaching as initiating the student into the rational life can be found on pp. 11, 90, and 106–7; also in Scheffler, *Reason and Teaching*, pp. 1–3 and 76–80. Similar points, in a different context, concerning the manner of teaching are made by L. J. Waks, "Knowledge and Understanding as Educational Aims," pp. 109–10. Cf. also Passmore, "On Teaching to be Critical," pp. 198ff.

40. C. J. B. Macmillan suggests ("Love and Logic in 1984") that there are limits to the relationship between teaching and rationality which render problematic the deep connection between the two suggested here. But I think that the limits Macmillan points to are themselves problematic, and reflect too uncritical an acceptance of Wittgensteinian assumptions.

There is clearly much more to say concerning the relationship between critical thinking and teaching, teacher education and teacher evaluation. I regret that space – and competence – prevent my saying more here. I hope that the present work will encourage others to join me in exploring the enormous ramifications that critical thinking, taken as an educational ideal, has for our conception of teaching and for our institutional education and treatment of teachers.

41. For a useful discussion of the analogous role of regulative ideals in science, cf. Kordig, *The Justification of Scientific Change*, pp. 111–13.

## Bibliography

Alderman, H., "Dialectic as Philosophical Care," *Man and World*, 6, no. 2 (May 1973), pp. 206–20.

Bailin, S., "Creativity and Quality," in E. E. Robertson (ed.), *Philosophy of Education 1984: Proceedings of the Fortieth Annual Meeting of the Philosophy of Education Society* (Normal, IL: The Philosophy of Education Society, 1985), pp. 313–21.

Bailin, S., *Achieving Extraordinary Ends: An Essay on Creativity* (Dordrecht: Martinus Nijhoff, 1987).

Binkley, R. W., "Can the Ability to Reason Well Be Taught?" in Blair and Johnson (eds.), pp. 79–92.

Blair, J. A. and Johnson, R. (eds.), *Informal Logic: The First International Symposium* (Inverness, CA: Edgepress, 1980).

Burbules, N. C., "A Theory of Power in Education," *Educational Theory*, 36, no. 2 (Spring, 1986), pp. 95–114.

Ennis, R. H., "A Conception of Critical Thinking – with Some Curriculum Suggestions," in J. Hoagland (ed.), *Conference '85 on Critical Thinking: Proceedings of the April 11–12 Conference on Critical Thinking at Christopher Newport College* (Newport News, VA: Christopher Newport College Press, 1986), pp. 13–40.

Govier, T., Review of John E. McPeck, *Critical Thinking and Education, Dialogue*, 22 (1983), pp. 170–5.

Green, T. F., "Indoctrination and Beliefs," in Snook (ed.), *Concepts of Indoctrination*, pp. 25–46.

Johnson, R., "Toulmin's Bold Experiment," *Informal Logic Newsletter*, 3, no. 2 (1981), pp. 16–27, and 3, no. 3, pp. 13–19.

Kordig, C. R., *The Justification of Scientific Change* (Dordrecht: D. Reidel, 1971).

Laudan, L., *Progress and its Problems* (Berkeley, CA: University of California Press, 1977).

Macmillan, C. J. B., "Love and Logic in 1984," in E. E. Robertson (ed.), *Philosophy of Education 1984: Proceedings of the Fortieth Annual Meeting of the Philosophy of Education Society* (Normal, IL: Philosophy of Education Society, 1985), pp. 3–16.

McPeck, J. E., *Critical Thinking and Education* (New York: St Martin's Press, 1981).

Passmore, J., "On Teaching to be Critical," in R. S. Peters (ed.), *The Concept of Education* (London: Routledge & Kegan Paul, 1967), pp. 192–211.

Paul, R. W., "Critical Thinking: Fundamental to Education for a Free Society," *Educational Leadership*, September 1984, pp. 4–14.

Paul, R. W., "Critical Thought Essential to the Acquisition of Rational Knowledge and Passions," paper presented at the Connecticut Conference on Thinking, sponsored by the Connecticut State Department of Education, 1984.

Peters, R. S., "Reason and Habit: The Paradox of Moral Education," in I. Scheffler (ed.), *Philosophy and Education*, pp. 245–62.

Peters, R. S., "Reason and Passion," in G. Vesey (ed.), *The Proper Study*, Royal Institute of Philosophy Lectures, vol. 4 (London: Macmillan, 1971).

Peters, R. S., *Reason and Compassion* (London: Routledge & Kegan Paul, 1973).

Popper, K. R., *The Open Society and its Enemies*, vol. 2 (Princeton, NJ: Princeton University Press, 1962).

Robertson, E. E., "Practical Reasons, Authority, and Education," in R. E. Roemer (ed.), *Philosophy of Education 1983: Proceedings of the Thirty-Ninth Annual Meeting of the Philosophy of Education Society* (Normal, IL: Philosophy of Education Society, 1984), pp. 61–75.

Ryle, G., *The Concept of Mind* (New York: Barnes & Noble, 1949).

Scheffler, I., *The Language of Education* (Springfield, IL: Charles C. Thomas, 1960).

Scheffler, I. *Conditions of Knowledge* (Chicago, IL: Scott Foresman, 1965).

Scheffler, I. (ed.), *Philosophy and Education*, second edition (Boston, MA: Allyn & Bacon, 1966).

Scheffler, I., *Reason and Teaching* (New York: Bobbs-Merrill, 1973). First published in 1973 by Routledge & Kegan Paul.

Scheffler, I., "Philosophical Models of Teaching," in Scheffler, *Reason and Teaching*, pp. 67–81.

Scheffler, I., "Moral Education and the Democratic Ideal," in Scheffler, *Reason and Teaching*, pp. 136–45.

Scheffler, I., "In Praise of the Cognitive Emotions," reprinted as Appendix B in Scheffler, *Science and Subjectivity*, pp. 139–57. Originally published in *Teachers College Record*, vol. 1977, pp. 171–86.

Siegel, H., "Is it Irrational to be Immoral? A Response to Freeman," *Educational Philosophy and Theory*, 10, no. 2 (October 1978), pp. 51–61.

Siegel, H., "Justification, Discovery and the Naturalizing of Epistemology," *Philosophy of Science*, 47, no. 2 (1980), pp. 297–321.

Siegel, H., "Rationality, Morality, and Rational Moral Education: Further Response to Freeman," *Educational Philosophy and Theory*, 12, no. 1 (March 1980), pp. 37–47.

Siegel, H., "Truth, Problem Solving and the Rationality of Science," *Studies in History and Philosophy of Science*, 14, no. 2 (1983), pp. 89–112.

Siegel, H., "Empirical Psychology, Naturalized Epistemology, and First Philosophy," *Philosophy of Science*, 51, no. 4 (1984), pp. 667–76.

Toulmin, S., *Human Understanding*, vol. I (Princeton, NJ: Princeton University Press, 1972).

Waks, L. J., "Knowledge and Understanding as Educational Aims," *Monist*, 52 (1968), pp. 105–19.

# 50

# The Value of Reason: Why Not a Sardine Can Opener?

Emily Robertson

## Introduction

In his *Travels in Hyper-Reality*, Umberto Eco ponders the alleged crisis of reason and asks what we are supposed to use in reason's place: "feeling, delirium, poetry, mystical silence, a sardine can opener, the high jump, sex, intravenous injections of sympathetic ink?"[1] Eco is puzzled by what Richard Bernstein has famously called "the rage against reason."[2] From the perspective of reason's critics, those who insist on the vocabulary of rationality, truth, objectivity, to name a few, are at best "lovably old-fashioned prigs" and at worst authoritarian personalities unable to respect difference and complicitous with racism, sexism, and other forms of oppression.[3] Faced with such claims, defenders of rationality are perplexed by a demand to defend what they think is obvious. "That we should care about rationality goes without saying," wrote Paul Horwich in a recent review.[4] Attempts to deny rationality, truth, and so forth, are held to be self-contradictory. For example, Susan Haack writes, "One could not discover by honest inquiry that there is no such thing as honest inquiry, that it could not be really-and-truly true that 'truth' is no more than

ideological humbug."[5] Or, more colorfully, from Eco again: "What I continue to consider irrational is somebody's insistence that, for instance, Desire always wins out over the *modus ponens* . . . but then . . . to confute my confutation, he tries to catch me in contradiction by using the *modus ponens* . . . I feel a Desire to bash him one."[6] And so the "debate" continues with about as much openness to mutual persuasion as the Republicans and Democrats showed in the recent impeachment hearings.

I take this debate seriously and count myself among reason's defenders, as those of you who have heard me read other papers before this Society know. I agree with Jim McClellan's remark that "[p]hilosophically speaking, like turtles, it is reason all the way down."[7] Yet I have increasingly had the feeling that these debates are not quite scratching where it itches. And so instead of engaging the debate directly by defending theories of rationality against their critics, I want to take a different approach. I would like to shift the focus from the distinctively philosophical issues of metaphysics and epistemology to the social practices of rational persuasion. I see the practices of rational persuasion as the social ground in which the normative concept

Previously published in Randall Curren (ed.), *Philosophy of Education 1999* (Urbana, IL: Philosophy of Education Society, 2000), pp. 1–14. © 2000 Philosophy of Education Society.

of rationality is rooted. Further, I am less interested in analyzing the language game of rational persuasion, in describing "the ideal speech situation," than I am in depicting the attitudes and perspective, the phenomenological stance, as I will call it, of those who see themselves as participants in this language game. My focus is on the attitudes that underpin the practices of rational persuasion. I agree with Ronald de Sousa that rationality is "a teleological concept."[8] On the teleological conception, rational belief aims at truth, rational action at success, rational desire at the good, and so on, however these end states are defined.[9] I see the practices of rational persuasion as conversation oriented toward truth or another appropriate end state of rational inquiry. For the purposes of this essay, I have limited the focus to truth, but I think parallel arguments could be made for other goals of reason.

I am going to develop a phenomenology of participants in the practices of rational persuasion *negatively* by surveying some practices that strike me as alternatives to it. Physical force, for example, is an obvious alternative to rational persuasion, but there are discursive alternatives as well. While I will develop a catalog of such alternatives as part of my exposition, the usual caveats apply; I do not assume these alternatives exhaust the territory. The point of the survey is to discover what might be distinctive about the practices of rational persuasion in order to consider why one might value those features and the stance that embodies them. I agree with Eco that "the problem [the alleged crisis of reason] affects us not only at the level of learned debate, but also in daily behavior and political life."[10] In short, it matters whether the practices of rational persuasion are fostered, practiced, and sustained. And insofar as the current intellectual zeitgeist obscures their significance, philosophical arguments directed against it have significant work to do.

I am not claiming – and this is an important point – that the alternatives I will propose to the practices of rational persuasion are necessarily *irrational*. They are forms of action that may well be rational in some circumstances. In this way, I am hoping to relocate the debate about reason from the all-or-nothing choice described in the opening paragraphs to a debate about what choice of human relationship it is rational (sorry, I do not know how to avoid the word) to make on particular occasions. I have become persuaded that this may be what the debate is really about. I am hoping that my approach

will generate conclusions that have validity whatever one's stand on a number of vexed metaphysical and epistemological issues, but I am not going to argue for that hope in this paper. But it is this hope that leads me to believe I can say something to those who genuinely ask "Why care?" without begging any questions or "waxing transcendental."

## Alternatives to the Stance of Rational Persuasion

### Interest Group Politics

The first alternative, which I call "interest group politics," is based on an experience I had that first led me to consider rationality from the perspective of the presuppositions of rational persuasion as a form of social interaction. The example also helps to illuminate what I take to be a fundamental characteristic of the phenomenological stance of those involved in these practices. In a faculty meeting where we were discussing which graduate students would get assistantships, one faculty member persisted in arguing for a student no one else supported. Finally another faculty member asked him, "Are you saying that $X$ should get an assistantship because you believe it or because you want to be able to tell her that you did your best for her?" The jolt I felt when that question was asked, my quite visceral reaction that were he behaving that way it would be wrong, and that despite my colleague's apparent acceptance of such a strategy, made me analyze the phenomenology of my own stance in that situation. I, too, had students I worked with and wanted to support. But I was open to the possibility that someone else was more deserving, better qualified. In a phrase borrowed from Andrew Oldenquist, I was open to the possibility that I might be "obligated to lose." In a well-known paper on loyalty, Oldenquist writes: "We have every reason to try to find a basis for dialogue with the competitor, the Spartan, or the andromedan, for it supplements the possibility of winning by force or trickery with the possibility of winning (or cutting losses) by reasoning and persuasion. But it also adds the possibility of being obligated to lose."[11] I was open to the possibility that I might lose, not because I was not powerful enough to have my way, but because I might be shown wrong; someone else's reasons might be better.

I thought when the incident happened, and still do, that it would have been unethical in that context to take the stance my colleague implied. But I have to acknowledge that I do not always find it as problematic. We are not unfamiliar with the member of Congress whose speech on the House floor is really aimed at the folks back home. And I myself as a department chair was unwilling to risk incurring an obligation to lose in a discussion in the Dean's Cabinet with other chairs when the topic was whose program should be cut. To reiterate an earlier point, I am not claiming that interest group politics is irrational. I am claiming that the phenomenological stance of a participant in such political negotiations is different from the stance of a participant in the social practices of rational persuasion. The jolt I felt on hearing my colleague's remark made me conscious of my own understandings, and aware that they were possibly not shared, that I might not have understood what was going on. In general, participants in interest group politics are unwilling, on the key issues at least, to risk incurring an obligation to lose. On those points, they are not open to rational persuasion.

What does it mean to say that one might possibly be *obligated* to lose? The notion of "obligation" emphasizes the normative and social content of rationality. Persons who recognize that they might be obliged to lose have accepted communal norms for determining what it is permissible to rationally believe in the situation.[12] They are open to the possibility of being shown wrong in light of those norms. They hold their beliefs "evidentially" in the sense developed by Thomas Green.[13] More fundamentally, to accept the possibility of being obligated to lose is to believe that "truth" is an intelligible concept and that truth is independent of at least one's own beliefs. That is why it makes sense to suppose that you might discover you were wrong, might be obligated to lose.

There is a second feature of the contrast in attitudes between interest group politics and rational persuasion. Rational persuasion requires treating others as participants rather than as things to be managed or manipulated. There is a difference between using other's words as signs of their states of mind or clues to how they can be brought to share your views and treating them as staking their own "claim[s] to truth," to use Gadamer's expression. In contrast, the attitude toward other parties to the conversation of one whose interests do not permit risking the obligation to lose is akin to what Strawson called the "objective attitude":

> To adopt the objective attitude to another human being is to see him . . . as a subject for what . . . might be called treatment; as something certainly to be taken account, perhaps precautionary account, of; to be managed or handled . . . But it cannot include the range of reactive feelings and attitudes which belong to involvement or participation with others in interpersonal human relationships. . . . If your attitude towards someone is wholly objective, then though you may fight him, you cannot quarrel with him, and though you may talk to him, even negotiate with him, you cannot reason with him. You can at most pretend to quarrel, or to reason, with him.[14]

Rational persuasion requires treating others as participants.

*Mediation and diplomacy*

A second example of a social practice alternative to rational persuasion grew out of another experience of having my assumptions about what was happening disrupted. A few years ago, for the first time in twelve years of schooling, my husband and I found ourselves invited to a conference in the principal's office to discuss a dispute between our daughter and one of her teachers. I will not bore you with the details except to make absolutely plain that it was not our daughter Rachel's fault! At any rate, at an early point in the discussion when Rachel began to dispute her teacher's account of what had happened, the principal said, "We're not here to decide the truth, we're here to learn each other's perceptions." In that moment I had to decide what I wanted from the meeting: uncovering the truth about what had happened (that is, seeing Rachel vindicated from every flaw) *or*, what I immediately understood the principal to be aiming at, namely, figuring out a way that Rachel and her teacher could continue their relationship. I imagine that high level diplomacy can be a lot like that, that it is not devoted to rationally persuading each other of the truth of the matter, but to figuring out a way to go on, to live with each other in some semblance of peace and harmony.

Perhaps, it has occurred to me, some disputes between the supporters of rationality and its critics involve their taking these different stances. For example, Anne Seller writes from a feminist perspective on the political implications of a commitment to realism or relativism. She says:

Knowledge tells us how to make sense of the world, how to adapt to it, what demands realistically to make of it. It tells us what is there. Politics too is trying to make sense, to live with, adapt to . . . But . . . the knowledge of what peace and equality are [is not] something that can be bumped into by an individual with a map and compass . . . What peace and equality are discovered to be will depend on the decisions that various communities have taken. Through our decisions with a community, we decide how we want to belong to the world, how we want to set about understanding it, living in it and changing it. We have nothing else to rely upon except each other in taking those decisions.[15]

Unlike interest group politics, mediation does not involve covert rejection of the possibility of being shown wrong, but it does accord the search for truth a lesser role in the exchange. The alternative of mediation points out that while truth is a good, it is not necessarily one that trumps all other goods in all circumstances. As my colleague Tom Green sometimes puts it, if it really is true that the heavens may fall from our pursuit of truth, maybe we should reconsider. So there is a question about when truth matters and why it matters. To choose the stance of rational persuasion in a specific context is to accord greater weight to truth in those circumstances than to other competing goods.[16]

## Disruption

Disruption as a stance was exhibited in a fascinating recent article by Jeffery Rosen in *The New Yorker* about the increasing frequency of hung juries. One woman hung a jury in what appeared to be an open and shut case. An off-duty policeman was a witness to a shooting incident between rival gangs. He arrested the shooter and recovered the weapon. The policeman, the defendant, and half the jury were African-American. The lone holdout was a young black woman studying to be a law librarian. Her cousin had been killed by the police, she said. She found herself unable to pass judgment. She said God told her that He had forgiven the defendant. The other members of the jury angrily confronted her, but she would not yield. Although this woman's action seemed more like a visceral response than a calculated strategy, Rosen notes that Paul Butler, an African-American legal scholar, recommends that "black jurors . . . free guilty black defendants as a form of political protest and of black self-help." In cases where long sentences would be imposed on young black men for non-violent drug possession, juries are more frequently taking his advice.[17]

I have argued that being willing to run the risk that one might be obligated to lose involves an attitude of acceptance of communal norms that determine what is rationally permitted in the circumstances. Disruption is the stance of someone who refuses to endorse the local norms of rationality. One who takes this stance refuses to be a participant in a game one believes is rigged. Disruption can be both a practical and a theoretical stance. For example, Elizabeth Gross writes: "feminist theory . . . is not a true discourse . . . It could be appropriately seen, rather, as a *strategy* . . . [an] intervention with definite political . . . aims . . . intellectual guerilla warfare."[18] Hence adopting the stance of rational persuasion involves implicit acceptance of the communal norms as prima facie fair.

For the reasons I have suggested, I am focusing my analysis on alternative stances rooted in ordinary life. However, it may be worth mentioning here a form of disruption that grows out of postmodern theoretical stances because it reveals another dimension of the stance of rational persuasion. I am thinking of Lyotard's "paralogy" and Rorty's "irony" or "edification."[19] What is the point of these practices? Discussing the practice of edification, Rorty points to "a contest between an entrenched vocabulary which has become a nuisance and a half-formed new vocabulary which vaguely promises great things."[20] Understood as creating new moves, edification and related practices could be understood as compatible with the stance of rational persuasion, as creating new theories or criticizing traditional methods and standards, as consistent with the constant effort to improve the standards of rationality themselves. But Rorty suggests another possibility: "playfulness." "The ironic, playful intellectual is a desirable character-type," he says.[21] Understood in this way, the practice seems to be a form of disruption, but not necessarily with resistance to injustice as its aim. Perhaps the point is to keep us off balance, to make us less sure of the course we have taken, to keep the options open.

I leave open the question of whether this form of disruption is simply a game some intellectuals play or whether it is (or can be) embodied in ordinary life practices. What does its possibility reveal about the practices of rational persuasion? One possibility is that those who fixate on rational persuasion are rigid personalities, useful if you want to solve a problem, but not much fun at a party. But one need not be fixated to defend the desirability of rational persuasion in at least some contexts. However, I do think that adopting the stance of rational persuasion reveals a certain seriousness, an engagement in the situation, rather than the detached stance of the ironist.

## Love, loyalty, and identity politics

As Jim Macmillan acknowledged in his slogan, there is love as well as logic.[22] More generally, there are the Gemeinshaft bonds of shared history, racial and ethnic identity, nationality, and religion. There are many accounts of the differences between these forms of relationship and what I am calling the stance of rational persuasion. As traditionally conceived, they are misfits to the list I am constructing because they are in Tonnies's vocabulary, "found" not "willed."[23] Traditionally, they are not a self-consciously chosen "stance" in the way in which interest group politics or mediation might be. Nor are they primarily *discursive* alternatives of the sort I have been considering. But leaving them out would be clearly short-sighted, since the postmodern reappropriation of these markers of identity through the politics of recognition *is* such a stance and initiates a discursive alternative. For example, K. Anthony Appiah says of pan-African identity that it must be acknowledged that "race and history and metaphysics do not enforce an identity . . . we must choose, within broad limits set by ecological, political, and economic realities, what it will mean to be African in the coming years."[24]

For Appiah, the challenge to rational persuasion and truth-telling that identity construction presents concerns whether the crafting of politically potent alliances requires the "noble lie." He argues, for example, that theoretical arguments establishing the nonexistence of race as a biological category are not sufficient for political purposes. One would need to show as well "that they are useless falsehoods at best or dangerous ones at worst: that another set of stories will build us identities through which we can make more productive alliances." Further, such group identities work best when they are taken to be real or natural, he believes. A full recognition of their invented character seems to work against taking them seriously. Hence one "cannot build alliances without mystifications and mythologies."

While in this particular case, Appiah thinks, happily, that one does not have to choose between the truth (that is, that race has no biological reality) and political utility, the possibility of conflict remains a live one. This means, Appiah thinks, that "there is . . . no large place for reason in the construction . . . of identities. One temptation, then, for those who see the centrality of these fictions in our lives, is to leave reason behind: to celebrate and endorse those identities that seem at the moment to offer the best hope of advancing our other goals, and to keep silence about the lies and the myths."[25]

The Enlightenment valorization of reason required rational justification of particularist sentiments such as patriotism, religion, and racial and ethnic identity. Enlightenment rationalism came to be identified with a commitment to the possibility of universal truth and norms of impartiality and objectivity. Relationships of love and loyalty as potential sources of bias and partiality were thus thought hostile to the rational pursuit of truth.[26] It is not clear to me, however, to what extent these Enlightenment commitments are necessary features of the stance of rational persuasion that we have been considering. In a particular conversation in which the participants take the stance of rational persuasion, the norms of rationality appealed to could be local, as in theological debate about what it is right for those of our faith to acknowledge. And in such debates, religious commitments, far from being eliminable as a source of bias, are a necessary condition of the debate's having point. So phenomenologically, what *is* the difference between regarding oneself as in a discussion oriented toward truth and foregrounding the thought that this is one's beloved (or one's brother or sister in either a literal or extended sense)?

Once, in the midst of my attempt at rational persuasion, a former partner shouted at me "you are the most rational person I know." It was not a compliment. The comment initiated a phenomenological change in me. I suddenly realized that what he wanted from me in that moment was my attention, my support, my endorsement of his belief that he had been wronged – in short, my solidarity with him. The truth and a rational plan of action could wait.

Richard Rorty describes solidarity as a way people have of making sense of their lives by "telling the story of their contribution to a community."[27] He contrasts the desire for solidarity with the desire for objectivity, understood as the pursuit of Truth, with a capital "T," but the tradition of truth-seeking he refers to carries more metaphysical baggage than the homey stance of rational persuasion we are considering. Nevertheless, there is some commitment to objectivity involved in rational persuasion; if the truth were not something taken to be independent of one's own belief, what meaning could be given to the thought that one might have an obligation to lose? Solidarity is based on the perception of shared bonds with others, whether these bonds are taken as given and natural or constructed for the occasion. Rational persuasion aims at assent to an outcome because, based on the available reasons and the relevant norms of rationality, it is the outcome most likely to be true or good or beautiful, not because it is necessarily our way of doing things or that it is the most politically effective course given our interests or that it celebrates and affirms the bonds of our relationship. (The commitment of rational persuasion to objectivity and the conversational pressures to agreement that rational persuasion exerts are made clearer in the discussion of our final alternative.)[28]

*Retreat.* The last alternative I will consider is the "just say no" alternative of retreat. In her well-known essay "The Problem of Speaking for Others," Linda Alcoff discusses Joyce Trebilcot's renunciation of the practice of speaking for others in the lesbian feminist community. Trebilcot says that she " 'will not try to get other wimmin to accept my beliefs in place of their own' on the grounds that to do so would be to practice a kind of discursive coercion and even a violence."[29] Alcoff argues that this kind of retreat is not a possible stance. Alcoff notes that "when I speak for myself, I am constructing a possible self, a way to be in the world, and, whether I intend to or not, I am offering that to others, as one possible way to be."[30]

Rational persuasion involves willingness to be responsible for making changes in others and a knowing acceptance of that responsibility. While even an "offering" runs the risk of changing others if Alcoff is correct, the stance of rational persuasion makes such changes intentional. Allan Gibbard argues that to call a belief "rational" is to make "a conversational demand . . . that the audience accept what . . . [one] says, that it share the state of mind [one] expresses."[31] I assume that it was the making of such demands that Trebilcot regarded as a form of violence and thus sought to avoid. While leading one's own life or stating one's own beliefs may lead others to entertain those actions or beliefs as

*possibilities* for themselves, it does not necessarily seem to make a *demand* on them in the way that an attempt at rational persuasion does. So is Trebilcot right after all? Does rational persuasion involve making coercive conversational demands?

I agree that there is a normative element in the stance of rational persuasion, but I do not think that prescriptive demands are the best way to capture that element. Recall that the stance of rational persuasion requires each participant to be similarly open to rational persuasion from the other participants. This is another way of noting that those taking the stance of rational persuasion must acknowledge that they might be obligated to lose. The demand is thus not an interpersonal demand but one that stems from the reasons and norms that are judged relevant to the case at hand. The "demand" stems from the objectivity claimed for the judgment in question, not from personal "browbeating."[32] Only if the norms and reasons invoked are arbitrary and unrelated to the issue at hand might they properly be regarded as coercive constraints. That was the possibility we considered in the discussion of disruption. Absent those circumstances, while one taking the stance of rational persuasion does aim at getting others to accept his or her beliefs "in place of their own," they do so because they believe these are the beliefs best supported by the evidence not in order to exercise personal power.

## Why Care?

What have we learned about the dispositions at the root of the social practices of rational persuasion from canvassing the alternatives? (1) First there's the openness to the possibility of being *obligated* to lose. The notion of "obligation" emphasizes the normative content of rationality. Persons who recognize that they might be obliged to lose have accepted communal norms for determining what it is permissible to believe in the situation. They are open to the possibility of being shown wrong in light of those norms. They hold their beliefs "evidentially." (2) To enter such discussions is to have a concern for truth and, in the particular context, to value truth more highly than competing goods, such as harmony or solidarity. (3) Rational persuasion requires treating others as participants rather than as things to be managed, or manipulated. (4) It is a stance that requires accepting the fairness of relevant norms of rationality. (5) It is an engaged attitude of seriousness, not one of ironic detachment. (6) It involves a commitment to truth as independent of one's individual belief; in this sense, it expresses a commitment to the belief's objectivity. (7) It involves accepting responsibility for making changes in others through efforts to persuade them to share one's beliefs.

The possibilities we have canvassed also remind us that there are local alternatives to the stance of rational persuasion. While I would argue that there is no possibility of wholesale rejection of rationality, there are choices in particular environments. The global arguments, then, seem to me sometimes futile. We might be better served by asking what the right stance is to take here and now. Are the rules fair, or reasonably so, or is the game rigged? Is knowing the truth in this context more important than obtaining other competing goods? And, of course, part of the paradox is that these questions must be rationally entertained. This is why there is no global alternative, no possibility of substituting "sardine can openers" for reason. But the stance of rational persuasion would not be the issue it is if there were not the possibility of adopting alternative stances in particular cases. Those who endorse rationality as an educational ideal may have sometimes given the impression that every instance of adopting alternative practices is a failure. But I have argued that at a practical level, this cannot be right. The serious arguments, rationally conducted I hope, are about when adopting the stance of rational persuasion makes sense.

Some of you may suspect that in making my case I have helped myself to a set of distinctions the critics deny. For example, Rorty sees no distinction between aiming at truth and the attempt to arrive at agreement.[33] If so, there would be no difference between negotiation or mediation and discourse oriented toward truth. So have I smuggled in philosophical content here?

I think my account of the differences in our subjective attitudes among these stances shows there is a distinction in ordinary life between the stance of rational persuasion and the alternatives. I have presented my account as a phenomenology of everyday life practices in the hope that all of us could recognize ourselves in my discovery that when I was engaged in rational debate others had other ends in mind. I do not suppose that this phenomenology constitutes an epistemic or metaphysical argument. But I do think it shows that concepts of reason, truth, objectivity, have a basis in ordinary life practices.

Perhaps these everyday attitudes are based on an illusion, a naive realism, for example, that Derrida claims is the metaphysics of the West. Thus the academic engagement of questions of metaphysics and epistemology have a point. Nevertheless, the critics owe us an account of how we could modify our form of life so as to incorporate their insights. Really to adopt as a global perspective the stances that various critics of reason recommend, if it could be done, would be to alter the human world in far-reaching ways.

Why value the stance of rational persuasion? Does it appeal only to us "lovably old-fashioned prigs?" If we understand rationality, as I proposed at the beginning of this essay, as a teleological concept, then to abandon rationality entirely would require either rejection of the goals of rationality (truth, strategic success of action, a good life) or extreme skepticism about the claims of any forms of judgment (any traditions of reason) to be better ways of reaching these goals, than, say, flipping a coin. (Of course we can criticize particular traditions of how to achieve rationality in belief, desire, or action, but that requires commitment to rational thought rather than its abandonment.) Total abandonment does not seem like a live option – can we replace reason with a sardine can opener and still achieve our goals? But it is not the epistemic merits of rationality that I have focused on here. I have been concerned to reveal the phenomenological stance of those engaged in the practices of rational persuasion when compared with alternative stances. I think this stance embodies a moral ideal. It involves opening one's own beliefs to the independent evaluation and judgment of another. It means revealing the reasons for one's beliefs and inviting others to share them. The idea that the truth of the matter at hand may be independent of the beliefs of any of the parties to the conversation poses the possibility of converging on the truth with whatever resources we have. This idea transforms the debate into joint inquiry rather than the imposition of one will on another. So the practices of rational persuasion are worth caring for if these forms of human relationship are worth caring for and if truth matters.

Some who might not disagree that the stance of rational persuasion is possible still doubt its effectiveness and desirability, however. Audrey Thompson, for example, with tongue in cheek but also with some seriousness, I think, suggests that those like us with a taste for argument are hopelessly out of touch: the "devotion to argumentation . . . is . . . an embarrassingly *passé* sartorial taste that makes *you* feel comfortable and maybe even classy but from which everyone else averts their eyes and ears."[34] She points to the phenomenon I suspect we have all experienced when in a college committee meeting you say exactly the right thing, complete with sound supporting arguments, but everyone just stares at you for a moment and proceeds with the discussion as if you had never spoken. On my analysis, this response means we have not understood what stance the participants are taking; some other game is being played.

But Thompson has a stronger challenge. She writes:

> Rational argumentation works for intellectuals in a way that it doesn't and can't for everyone else because it specifically leaves behind – claiming to supersede – everything associated with passion, bodies, desire, interest, investment, and contingency (meaning things like people's actual lives). . . . It works insofar as it is elite, rarefied, specialized, and transcendent. In a sense, argumentation is a counter-discourse . . . for those who want to rise above the errors and messy human involvements of relationships, popular culture, and popular politics. Yet if you strip ideas of their investments and passions, you strip them of their interest and significance; and if you claim universality for them, instead of acknowledging their investments, you lie about them. (It's striking how regularly rational arguments are used to not-listen, to perform sleights of hand, to deny privilege, and to lie.)[35]

Does my analysis offer any resources for responding to this challenge? I doubt whether "offering a rational argument" always involves taking the stance of rational persuasion. I do not doubt that arguments can be used as weapons to fend off the opposition rather than risking incurring an obligation to lose. And I agree that nothing in the stance of rational persuasion itself somehow guarantees that participants will be free of bias, not self-deluded, somehow liberated from competing motivations. But I am not clear why Thompson thinks (if she does) that we cannot try to persuade each other rationally about the things that matter in our lives. For example, while resistance to racism is not simply a matter of truth-telling, truth-telling can be helpful. As Appiah says, "We cannot change the world simply by evidence and reasoning, but we surely cannot change it without them either."[36]

For me, the stance of rational persuasion is at the core of what universities are about. It is not that we cannot recognize that there are other values. I do not deny the need for negotiation, disruption, even, under extreme conditions, guerrilla warfare. The choices are hard and context dependent. But I believe that as university faculty we are particularly entrusted with passing on, with exemplifying, the stance of rational persuasion. The criticism of particular traditions of reason in reason's name, the unmasking of political interests masquerading as objective truth is an extremely valuable contribution to our common enterprise. But from my perspective to reject the form of life that this unmasking is in the interest of is to destroy our special reason for being. Some have suggested that this interest in argument is just the peculiar interest of some Western intellectuals. I have tried to show that the interest is rooted in ordinary life, that it's rejection, if at all possible (and I think it's not) would require substantial alteration in how we interact with each other, would require the demise of a way of being that, setting aside its instrumental cognitive value, embodies a moral ideal that has rightly inspired many. Of course, nothing I have done here today shows that these social practices do not rest on mistaken philosophical assumptions. And so the philosophical labor invested in the analysis of these assumptions has value. But the debates about rationality are not simply "learned debates" but also have meaning in "daily behavior and political life."[37] They involve fundamental choices about the character of human relationships in particular circumstances.

This essay has been in many ways a personal statement, rather unlike the papers I have typically read before this society. (But, hey, if you cannot seize the bully pulpit when you are president, then when?) Once long ago I underwent a series of tests as part of an opportunity to explore various career options. The psychologist who wrote the final report said of me: "You try always to state the exact truth as you see it; thus you are likely to be misunderstood by most people for whom truth is only one aspect of reality." In this essay I have tried to consider what some of the other aspects are and to understand why they might be chosen as alternatives to the pursuit of truth on particular occasions. But most of all I have been concerned to understand and defend the value of the form of life involved in attempts at rational persuasion. Thus I end where I began with Eco by joining in solidarity with him to offer a "limited *viva* for *modus ponens*."[38]

## Notes

1. Umberto Eco, *Travels in Hyper-Reality*, trans. W. Weaver (London: Picador, 1987), p. 125.
2. Richard Bernstein, "The Rage Against Reason," in *Construction and Constraint: The Shaping of Scientific Rationality*, ed. Ernan McMullin (Notre Dame, IN: University of Notre Dame Press, 1988), p. 216.
3. The quotation is from Richard Rorty, *Essays on Heidegger and Others* (Cambridge: Cambridge University Press, 1991), p. 86. As quoted in Susan Haack, *Manifesto of a Passionate Moderate* (Chicago, IL: University of Chicago Press, 1998), p. 7.
4. Paul Horwich, "Gibbard's Theory of Norms," *Philosophy and Public Affairs* 22, (1993), p. 67.
5. Haack, *Manifesto of a Passionate Moderate*, p. 147.
6. Eco, *Travels in Hyper-Reality*, p. 131.
7. James E. McClellan, Jr., "Margonis's Challenge," in *Philosophy of Education 1997*, ed. Susan Laird (Urbana, IL: Philosophy of Education Society, 1998), p. 375.
8. Ronald de Sousa, *The Rationality of Emotion* (Cambridge, MA: MIT Press, 1987), p. 163.
9. Embedded in the concept of rational judgment is the assumption that some ways of forming beliefs or deciding how to act or what ends to seek are more likely to meet with success than are others. The modes of judgment and the reasons they provide are not properly thought of as *merely* instrumental means to their ends, however, but must recommend the belief or action in question: rationality is a normative concept. See Roderick Firth, "Epistemic Merit, Intrinsic and Instrumental." in *Proceedings and Addresses of the American Philosophical Society* 55 (1981), pp. 5–23. See also J. David Velleman, *Practical Reflection* (Princeton, NJ: Princeton University Press, 1989), especially chap. 7.
10. Eco, *Travels in Hyper-Reality*, pp. 131–2.
11. Andrew Oldenquist, "Loyalties," *The Journal of Philosophy* 79 (April 1982), p. 183.
12. Allan Gibbard, *Wise Choices, Apt Feelings* (Cambridge, MA: Harvard University Press, 1990), p. 7.
13. See Thomas F. Green, *Activities of Teaching* (New York: McGraw-Hill, 1971), chap. 3.
14. P. F. Strawson, *Freedom and Resentment and Other Essays* (London: Methuen, 1974), p. 9.
15. Anne Seller, "Realism versus Relativism" in *Feminist Perspectives in Philosophy*, ed. Morwenna Griffiths and Margaret Whitford (Bloomington: Indiana University Press, 1988), p. 180. I do not think Seller is exactly right here. There may be things we need to know about the world in order to work out relations of peace and equality. I am enough of a Deweyan to think that even ethical concepts need to be modified in light of the experiences produced by living under them; it is not simply a matter of our "social constructions." The questions here can be extremely difficult. For example, after a brutal and repressive regime has ended, do we need to know who committed what crimes even if we decide not to punish the offenders?
16. Interest group politics and mediation can be viewed as aspects of participation in a democratic form of political life. While consideration of the stance of democratic participation does not appear to reveal new aspects of the stance of rational persuasion, it does raise questions about the role of the latter with respect to the former. Both reason's friends and reason's foes claim their epistemological/metaphysical position is friendly to democracy. Dewey, famously, saw affinities between rational inquiry as modeled by the scientific community and democratic social relations. But Rorty, while championing solidarity over objectivity, finds his own brand of pragmatism especially hospitable to democracy. He writes: "We pragmatists commend our antiessentialism and antilogocentrism on the ground of its harmony with the practices and aims of a democratic society." See Richard Rorty, *Essays on Heidegger and Others* (Cambridge: Cambridge University Press, 1991), p. 135. What role should rational persuasion play in maintaining democratic traditions? Certainly there is a difference between being outvoted and being wrong, between losing in a fair, democratic decision-making process and discovering one has an obligation to lose. It's the difference between the stance of rational persuasion and the alternatives that is the focus of this analysis. When the stance of rational persuasion should be adopted is a difficult pragmatic question.
17. Jeffrey Rosen, "Annals of Justice: One Angry Woman," *The New Yorker*, 24 February and 3 March 1997, pp. 54–64.
18. Elizabeth Gross [now Grosz], "What is Feminist Theory?" in *Feminist Challenges*, ed. Carole Pateman and Elizabeth Gross (London: Allen and Unwin, 1986), p. 177.
19. See Jean-François Lyotard, *The Postmodern Condition: A Report on Knowledge*, trans. Geoff Bennington and Brian Massumi (Minneapolis: University of Minnesota Press, 1984); See Richard Rorty, *Contingency, Irony, and Solidarity* (Cambridge: Cambridge University Press, 1989).
20. Rorty, *Contingency, Irony, and Solidarity*, p. 9.
21. Richard Rorty, "Freud and Moral Reflection," in *Pragmatism's Freud*, ed. J. H. Smith and W. Kerrigan (Baltimore, MD: Johns Hopkins University Press, 1986), p. 15.
22. C. J. B. Macmillan, "Love and Logic in 1984," in *Philosophy of Education 1984*, ed. Emily E. Robertson (Normal, IL: Philosophy of Education Society, 1985), pp. 3–16.
23. See Robert A. Nisbet, *The Sociological Tradition* (New York: Basic Books, 1966), chap. 3.

24. K. Anthony Appiah, "The Limits of Pluralism," in *Multiculturalism and American Democracy*, ed. Arthur M. Melzer et al. (Lawrence: University of Kansas Press, 1998), p. 41.

25. Ibid., pp. 40, 44.

26. See Andrew Oldenquist, "Loyalties." See also Charles Taylor, "The Politics of Recognition," in *Multiculturalism: Examining the Politics of Recognition*, ed. Amy Gutmann (Princeton, NJ: Princeton University Press, 1994), pp. 25–73.

27. Richard Rorty, "Solidarity or Objectivity?" in *From Modernism to Postmodernism: An Anthology*, ed. Lawrence Cahoone (Oxford: Blackwell, 1996), p. 573. (Originally published in Richard Rorty, *Objectivity, Relativism, and Truth* (Cambridge: Cambridge University Press, 1991), pp. 21–34.)

28. We might connect the stance of loyalty with our earlier discussion of interest group politics. In the section on interest group politics, I considered the relationship between a representative of the relevant group and those regarded as outsiders. In that case, no openness to losing was possible on the key issues. Loyalty becomes like interest group politics when considering conversation outside the group. In this section, I have been considering what the in-group relationship is like. Here I think the possibilities are more complex. In-group conversation can be a form of rational persuasion in which the features that bind the group together are given substantial weight. (My earlier reference to theological debate within a religious group is an example.) Here the loyalty lies in establishing what counts as a reason. Or it may be that membership in the group is made a requirement of participation in the conversation because only with those who are "one of us" is it possible to have a fully open debate. But there is also the mode of relationship, the stance, in which it is the fact of the bond itself which takes priority. It is here that the contrast with the stance of rational persuasion is clearest.

29. Joyce Trebilcot, "Dyke Methods," in *Lesbian Philosophies and Culture*, ed. Jeffner Allen (Albany: State University of New York Press, 1990), pp. 15–29. As quoted in Linda Alcoff, "The Problem of Speaking for Others," in *Feminist Nightmares: Women at Odds*, ed. Susan Weisser and Jennifer Fleischner (New York: NYU Press, 1994), p. 186.

30. Alcoff, "The Problem of Speaking for Others," p. 186.

31. Allan Gibbard, *Wise Choices, Apt Feelings*, p. 172.

32. Ibid., p. 193.

33. See Rorty, "Solidarity or Objectivity?"

34. Audrey Thompson, "A Modest Proposal for Preventing Philosophers of Education from Being a Burden to their Students or Their Country; and for Making Them Beneficial to Their Publick," *Educational Foundations* 12, no. 3 (1998), p. 68. See also Scott H. Bilow, "Rationality Overrated?" in *Philosophy of Education 1997*, ed. Susan Laird (Urbana, IL: Philosophy of Education Society, 1998), pp. 486–90.

35. Ibid., p. 70.

36. Appiah, "The Limits of Pluralism," p. 45.

37. Eco, *Travels in Hyper-Reality*, pp. 131–2.

38. Ibid., p. 132.

# Grading and Testing

# 51

# A Discourse on Grading

## Robert Paul Wolff

For most American students, the dominant educational fact for the first eighteen years of schooling – if they last that long – is the *Grade*. From those first simple report cards which the first-grader carries home, through the quiz grades, paper grades, test grades, aptitude scores, and college boards, to the course grades, honors thesis grades, and Law School Aps or Graduate Record scores, the American student lives, breathes, grows, and defines himself in a world of grades. To some, grades are merely a harassment; to others, they are a mild incentive. But in many young people, the brightest and most promising among them, a fixation on grades develops. Rather like misers, who begin by craving wealth and end by craving its symbol, these students develop a pathological anxiety over the grades themselves, quite independently of their usefulness or significance. The fetishism of commodities gives way to a fetishism of marks, and as the pathological consumer will window-shop even when he has no money, merely to be near commodities and draw comfort from them, so the grade lover (or "achievement-oriented" student, as it is fashionable to call him) soothes himself with recollections of near-perfect test scores and straight-A semesters,

"He had 800's on his College Boards!" expresses the same intensity of libidinal cathexis as do the numbers "38–24–38" in a somewhat different context. Despite the concentration of attention on the activity of grading, the subject is terribly confused. Even teachers, for whom grading is one of the principal activities of their professional life, frequently have very little idea why they give grades at all and what the conditions would be under which they could dispense with grading.

There are three different activities which commonly go under the name of "grading." Before we can determine the role of grading in the ideal university, we must sort out the several kinds of grading and consider their relationship to the process of education. The three species of grading are *criticism*, *evaluation*, and *ranking*.

*Criticism* is the analysis of a product or performance for the purpose of identifying and correcting its faults or reinforcing its excellences. Thus a teacher will correct a spelling error or incorrect sentence construction, show a student where he has gone wrong in a geometry proof, or pronounce correctly the French phrase which the pupil has garbled. So too, at a more advanced level, a professor will

Previously published in *The Ideal of the University* (Boston, MA: Beacon Press, 1969), pp. 58–68. © 1969 Robert Paul Wolff.

point out an incoherence in the development of an argument, or call attention to significant data which have been ignored. At the elementary level of spelling and syntax (which even the writers of doctoral dissertations must attend to, alas), there is not a great deal of disagreement over what is correct and what is not. When more complex matters of style, argument, and evidence are at stake, however, criticism becomes inextricably bound up with intellectual norms which themselves may be matters of dispute. A teacher who criticizes a student's work for concentrating upon unimportant issues, or for using terms which are unclear, or for ignoring certain kinds of evidence, inevitably expresses his own normative commitments. Hence, at the most advanced levels of education, both teacher and student must be aware of the possibility that they simply are wrong for one another and might better discontinue their relationship.

*Evaluation* is the measuring of a product or performance against an independent and objective standard of excellence. It issues characteristically in some sort of *grade* which expresses the teacher's judgment of the absolute merit of the student's performance. For example, a teacher may have some idea in mind of what constitutes an acceptable performance in arithmetic. Any student who surpasses that level receives a pass-grade; the others are failed. Sometimes the teacher will measure performance against a linear scale, permitting grades of "excellent, good, pass, and fail," or "A, B, C, D, and F," or even – where fine discrimination among performances are possible – a continuous range of grades from zero to one hundred.

The whole subject of scales of measurement is rather more complicated than it appears on the surface. It is quite possible for a grading system to discriminate between unacceptable and acceptable performances, and yet fail to provide a linear scale of grades along which the various performances can be located. Thus, a connoisseur of violin playing may feel quite confident in judging some performances as excellent and others not, without however having any way of deciding among excellent performances by Heifetz, Milstein, and Oistrakh. The problem is not that they play "equally well," but that beyond a certain level of technical skill and interpretative finesse a choice among them becomes a matter of taste. *But* – and this is a very important point not often appreciated by students – the difference between a great violinist and a bad fiddler *is* a matter of objective evaluation, even though

only taste can guide us in choosing among great violinists. Doctoral candidates in philosophy, for example, frequently imagine that faculty disagreements over dissertations stem from doctrinal differences which only taste can resolve; whereas in fact the dispute is usually over whether the dissertation meets those minimal standards on which partisans of every ideology can agree.

Some sort of evaluative standard is usually implicit in acts of criticism, although there is no necessary connection between the two. When Pablo Casals conducts a master class in the cello, he may of course merely correct wrong fingerings or phrasings and suggest differences in interpretation, but he is likely as well to say "that was very good" after a particularly lovely bit of playing. This suggests that he has in mind a conception of the *right* way to play the piece, against which he measures the performances of his pupils.

In many intellectual activities, reality itself provides at least a partial scale of objective evaluation. If the historian seeks to discover what happened in some past time, then the primary measure of his success is the truth of what he asserts, not its wit or charm or the felicity of his expression. The most delightful false account is bad history; its literary worth cannot make up for gross errors of fact, as Thomas Carlyle's famous work on the French Revolution shows. But truth is not enough either in history or in the sciences. As someone once said of sociology, the problem is not to say something true, but to say something important. Generally speaking, one can get very wide agreement in the arts and sciences about what constitutes a *bad* performance, but very little agreement on the criteria of *good* or *excellent* performances. Even in the professions, this generalization seems to hold. Doctors will agree that $X$ is a bad doctor, and lawyers that $Y$ is an incompetent lawyer. But ask them who are the great doctors and lawyers, and opinions may vary as widely as the criteria of importance and significance to which the several practitioners owe their allegiance.

Where an objective linear scale of excellence is perceived by the evaluator, the choice of the grading system will be determined by two factors: the number of discrete levels of performance which can be distinguished with any certainty, and the needs of the institution in which the grading is done. The simplest system is pass-fail, or acceptable-unacceptable. To this may be added the grade of distinction; then the grades excellent and good; until finally we arrive at the familiar five-step grading systems used in many college and graduate courses: "A, B, C, D, and F."[1] The move to a numerical system involves no new assumptions about the process of grading, and the widespread suspicion of numerical grades on the part of those who are quite content with "A"s and "B"s is a mere superstition. The virtue of numbers, of course, is that they can be aggregated and averaged, making possible a comparative ranking of students who have been evaluated in a number of performances.

*Ranking* is the grading activity which produces the greatest anxiety and provokes the most opposition. It is a relative comparison of the performances of a number of students, for the purpose of determining a linear ordering of comparative excellence. The simplest ranking is the sort which mathematicians call "ordinal" – that is to say, *best, second best, third best*, and so on down to *worst*. Such a ranking says nothing about *how much* better one student is than another. In a class of twenty students, the difference between the first and the last may be so small that it taxes the ability of the teacher to distinguish among their performances. Sometimes the difference is enormous, a fact which creates very great teaching problems. My own experience is that in the classes I have taught at Harvard, Chicago, Wellesley, and Columbia, there is a huge gap in excellence of performance between the "A" students and the "B" students, a marginal gap between the low "B" and high "C" students, and another very large gap between the solid "C" students and those who are marginal or actually failing. The difference between the best and the worst is likely to be so great that calling them all students in the same course is more an act of faith than a statement of fact. My criticisms of the work of the best deal with nuances of style and subtleties of argumentation. Those at the other end of the scale are still struggling to master the syntactical structure of English sufficiently to make elementary logical distinctions.

The difference between evaluation and ranking is captured in that anxious question so often on the lips of students, "Is this course graded on a curve?" Evaluation establishes a relationship between each student and an objective scale of measurement. Since in general the performances of students do not affect one another, it is perfectly possible for every student in a class to rank high on the scale, or for every student to fail. Some teachers however set the grade levels only *after* the students have been evaluated, so that a certain distribution of grades is

guaranteed. Typically, they want a small number of failing grades and distinctions and a large number of low and high passes. The resulting distribution can be plotted on a graph in a familiar bell shape known as "the curve." Grading on a curve assures that the class will be sorted out along a scale of relative excellence, but of course it provides no clue to the level of performance signified by a particular grade. When I was a freshman, I took an extremely difficult physics course intended for prospective concentrators. The very best students in the class regularly scored more than 100 on examinations (there were bonus questions). The worst had negative grades (one was penalized so many points for each mistake). The mean was roughly 40. When the final grades were computed, my 38 earned me a "C+," but after looking over the distribution of grades the professor decided that there were not enough honor grades – the "curve was lowered," and I got my "B–." So it is that I can honestly say I did honor work in physics in college!

Criticism, evaluation, and ranking serve three entirely distinct functions in the process and institutions of education. *Criticism* lies at the very heart of education. To learn is to submit oneself to the discipline of a standard, *even if the standard is self-created and self-imposed*. The mathematician submits himself to standards of consistency and simplicity, the scientist to the standards of truth and explanatory power. The social scientist measures his work by its relevance to human concerns as well as by the scientist's standard of truth. The artist strives for beauty. The only way to become a mathematician, a physicist, a historian, or a poet is to put one's whole self into each attempt and then submit the result to criticism. Painful as criticism is, even from those one loves best or respects most, there is no other way to learn.

The most dangerous heresy of pedagogy is the popular belief that subjective feeling is the criterion of success in education. Repelled by the perverse and sadistic view that "it only helps if it hurts," countless educational rebels have proclaimed the doctrine that what counts is how the performance *feels* to the student himself. If he "feels good" about his poem or his philosophical argument, then nothing else matters. Education must liberate the student's libidinal energies and shun the stultifying criticism which seeks to shape those energies in ways dictated by the teacher.

There is, of course, a truth hidden in this heresy. When education has been reduced to repression, and learning to rote, the spontaneous energies of the student may over a time be so dampened that some extreme therapy is needed to re-evoke them. A totally free environment may be necessary, in which any response is welcomed, and expression cheered. But, sooner or later, criticism must re-enter the process if the energies are to be focused effectively and the expression acquire style. Unfortunately, some students suffer a deadening education for so long that they lose the courage to sustain their spontaneity in the face of even the mildest criticism. At the first word of correction, they retreat into sullen obedience and produce mechanically the performances they think are wanted from them. I have seen such students among the ranks of the ablest undergraduates at our best colleges, and it all but tears my heart out. Ghetto schools are populated by them, if Jonathan Kozol, Herbert Kohl, and others are to be believed.

Evaluation, unlike criticism, is external to education properly so-called. Once a teacher has shown a student how he can state an argument more cogently, express an insight with greater felicity of phrasing, or muster evidence more persuasively for a conclusion, nothing is gained educationally by adding the words "good" or "bad." Where an objective standard of success is intrinsic to the activity, as in the case of a geometry proof which either is or is not valid, or a poem which is or is not a true sonnet, it is of course educationally valuable for the teacher to tell the student whether the standard has been met. But such additions to the act of criticism fall far short of what is usually called "giving a grade."

The true rationale of evaluation is not educational but professional. When a candidate seeks admission to a profession on the basis of some performance, the judges must ascertain whether he has *qualified*. For prospective professors, lawyers, or doctors, "*pass*" means admission to the profession with the legal right to practice and make a living thereby; "fail" means exclusion, and if second chances have been exhausted, the necessity of looking for some other career.

Since the first, or bachelor's, degree is not in itself a qualifying degree for any profession, it would seem that colleges could dispense with the practice of grading their preprofessional undergraduates. As far as any educational considerations are concerned, this is perfectly true. But for a long time now, the professional schools and programs have burdened undergraduate education with a major part of their admissions problem. By requiring a bachelor's degree as a prerequisite for work toward "higher" degrees, the professional schools force the colleges to take on a grading task which is irrelevant to education and sometimes positively harmful. The college becomes obsessed with ensuring that students "satisfy the requirements for the degree," independently of whether or not they are fruitfully involved in the educational life of the community. Imagine two students in Columbia College. John is deeply committed to the study of American history, but he "fails" a number of courses in mathematics, languages, and literature. After making every allowance that a wise and generous administrator can permit himself, the Dean reluctantly informs John that he may not continue his education at Columbia. No one denies that he has been fruitfully engaged in his historical studies, but after all, a student who fails most of his courses cannot be permitted to keep enrolling for more work! William, by contrast, is a thoroughly uninspired student who maintains himself in good academic standing by distributing his energies prudently, if dispassionately, among his several courses. No professor or fellow student would for a moment pretend that William has ever had a genuine educational experience at Columbia, but in due course he is awarded the Bachelor of Arts degree and welcomed to the company of Columbia alumni. Everything in the organization and conduct of Columbia College (or virtually any other American liberal arts college) conspires to persuade John that he is a failure and William that he is a success. And yet the sole justification for such a lamentable state of affairs is the necessity of ensuring that "Columbia graduates" are qualified for whatever further educational or professional endeavors they may undertake. Would anyone deny that a genuine, lasting, disciplined commitment to a single field of inquiry results in a more successful education than a continuous but impersonal fulfillment of an appropriate set of degree requirements? And yet, how many professors and deans – or students, for that matter – can be found who will argue for giving John a degree as well as William?

Ranking, as distinguished from evaluation and criticism, performs a function which is neither professional nor educational, but merely – in the broad sense – economic. The purpose of comparative ranking is to facilitate the fair allocation of scarce resources and utilities. Education is not in itself a scarce commodity (though opportunities for education may very well be). The Ideas, as Plato would have put it, can be embodied in any number of examples; the Pythagorean theorem does not flicker and grow dim as more and more minds embrace it. So far as the development of disciplined intelligence is concerned, it hardly matters who is first, second, or third. Nor does professional qualification intrinsically demand a ranking of the successful candidates. There are no national quotas of doctors or lawyers or architects;[2] qualification requires only a simple pass or fail, in or out.

Ranking only becomes necessary when more people want something than the available supply can satisfy. It is not admission to college which demands a ranking of high school graduates – for each Fall there are more places in freshman classes across the land than qualified students to fill them – but admission to the small number of highly *desired* colleges.[3] Similarly, if there were scholarships for all who needed them, no elaborate system of nationwide tests would be necessary; but there is a shortage of money, so naturally the applicants must be *ranked*.

It is really rather startling to reflect that the *sole* justification for all that frenzied, anxious test-taking and grade-grubbing which absorbs millions of American teenagers is the differential allocation of high school seniors to colleges in varying degrees of demand! No other intellectual, cultural, social, spiritual, psychological, or educational purpose is served by it. If places in colleges were assigned at random to all students meeting certain minimal standards of qualification, there would not be a single good reason for a secondary school student to worry about whether his grades placed him first in the nation or just barely above the cutoff point.

The same is true, of course, for college ranking and admission to the favored graduate and professional schools. Up to a point, as I have noted, professional schools use college grades as evidence of minimal qualification; but those schools with more applicants than places rely upon relative rankings, together with such ranking devices as objective tests and letters of recommendation, to establish an order of priority among the candidates. Here again, no other purpose is served by cumulative grade averages, class rank, and all the other devices for the making of efficient invidious comparisons among students.

It would be pleasant to think that the repeated ranking ceases on admission to a graduate or professional program, but of course that is not so.

Beyond graduate school lies the world, and there again favored places must be assigned to top-ranking candidates. The choice residency, the junior partnership in Wall Street firms, the assistant professorship at the Ivy League university, all such places are for the best-qualified, not for the merely qualified. I think it is fair to say that the first title or degree conferred without differential ranking in the academic world is professor emeritus!

So ranking serves to apportion a scarce supply of *desired* places. Are those places also *desirable*, or is the endless competition a struggle for illusory rewards? I wish I could honestly say that the battle is a sham, but alas, the rewards are real enough for those few who make it to the top. The desired colleges really do offer a better education than those whose freshman classes are perpetually under-manned. The students are brighter, the faculty more exciting, the physical surroundings more pleasant, the cultural life richer. Harvard, Yale, Princeton, Columbia, Swarthmore, Amherst, and the rest are truly better schools. To be sure, a bright and eager student can find an exciting education at a hundred other schools across the country; but even those hundred are the best of the more than two thousand colleges and universities. As for graduate and professional schools, the difference between the favored and the forgotten is, if anything, even greater. There are three dozen American universities, at most, where one can study philosophy profitably. The student who does not win admission to one of those departments is probably better off reading philosophy on his own.

I need hardly elaborate on the differential distribution of rewards available to candidates who have actually entered into professional practice. An income of two hundred thousand dollars a year and the power that goes with a senior partnership in a Wall Street law firm bears little relationship to the lower-middle-class existence of the courthouse hack who battens on the machine bosses and picks up a living from defending clients accused of petty larceny. The victory may not be worth the battle, but there can be no question that in the American educational system today, the spoils belong to the victor.

It should be obvious that there is no easy way to disentangle education from the essentially extraneous processes of evaluation and ranking. So long as some colleges and professional schools really offer better educational opportunities and a competitive edge in the struggle for wealth, power, and status in American society, there will be more applicants than places at every stage in the educational system from kindergarten to graduate school. It is a bitter irony that the competition is merely intensified by the painstaking efforts of administrators to make the selection process more just.

The evil inheres in the scarcity of desired places and the dependence of social rewards on educational accomplishment, not in any particular system of grading. Nothing is to be gained, for example, by substituting written evaluations for numerical grades. Letters of recommendation degenerate into discursive rankings when many candidates seek few places. As with all of the most intractable social evils, this destructive competition is the product of a social *virtue*, namely, the effective implementation of the principle of equality of opportunity.

Later on, I shall suggest some ways in which evaluation and ranking might be at least partially separated from education itself, but there are no clever reforms or institutional tricks which will effect a total separation. Only a social revolution of the most far-reaching sort could free education from the twin curses of evaluation and ranking.

## Notes

1. Harvard, with admirable consistency, refuses to be beguiled by the accident that "F" is the initial letter of "fail." It uses a grading system of "A, B, C, D, and E."
2. Not officially, at any rate. I am not concerned here with the current attempts of the medical and some other professions to restrict artificially the numbers admitted to their ranks, in the interest of keeping incomes high.
3. I use this awkward locution in order to leave open the question whether everything which is *desired* is also *desirable*. Needless to say, the two are not always identical.

# 52

# Coercion and the Ethics of Grading and Testing

## Randall Curren

Two distinct but related issues in the ethics of grading and testing will concern me in this paper. The first of these is the charge, associated in the past two decades with libertarian educational theory, that the common practice of grading students' work is intrinsically coercive.[1] The second is the larger national debate about "authentic" assessment, educational standards, and standardized measures of educational outcomes. With respect to the latter issue, my particular concern is the moral grounds that can be adduced in support of new measures of educational achievement or progress. There are important connections between these issues, and one I shall pursue here is that in developing an account of the ethics of grading rich enough to generate a satisfactory response to the charge of coercion, one also uncovers moral grounds for preferring some of the newer forms of standardized measures over the kind of multiple-choice examinations that have prevailed in recent decades. In essence, I will argue that there are morally preferable forms of measures, adaptable to both classroom and standardized uses, which constitute an acceptable middle way between a condemnation of all grading and testing and an acceptance of the status quo that has prevailed.

I will begin, in what follows, with the complaint that grading is intrinsically coercive, a complaint I shall refer to as the "Coercion Argument." I will then review some conventional answers to this argument, and will conclude that they suffice to show that the normal uses of testing and grading are not "strongly coercive," that is, not wrongful *violations* of students' rights.[2] Yet I will also conclude that these answers are not wholly satisfactory, because even "weak" intellectual coercion that involves an infringement justified by other interests of the child is a matter of serious concern. I will then present a response to this problem of "weak" coercion, and in doing so will rely on the moral framework deployed by Allen Buchanan and Dan Brock in their book *Deciding for Others*.[3] The object of their inquiry is responsible surrogate decisionmaking in a health care context, and I might well have chosen to offer an analysis similar to theirs without reference to anything beyond the educational domain; but the structural similarities between the two domains make their framework a convenient and illuminating one to use.

With the analysis developed in response to the problem of "weak" coercion in hand, I will then

Previously published in *Educational Theory* 45(4) (Fall 1995), pp. 425–41. © 1995 Board of Trustees, University of Illinois. Reprinted with permission of Blackwell Publishing Ltd.

consider the implications of this analysis for the kinds of measures of student progress we must develop and use if we are to respect properly students' rights of intellectual self-determination. Concluding that in the primary and secondary years the burden of respecting students' rights of intellectual self-determination is seldom met in practice, I will argue that measures of the sort I shall call "process measures" are morally preferable to those most commonly used. In closing, I will outline the challenges involved in developing and making wider use of these "process measures."

## The Coercion Argument and its Libertarian Origins

Libertarian views on children and education typically rely on some notion of equal rights for children and adults, and are opposed as much to compulsory schooling and curricula as to compulsory testing and evaluation.[4] They deny, in one way or another, that there are morally relevant differences between adults and children which could justify compelling children to attend school, study what no adult is compelled to study, or submit to examinations of how and what they think in order that others may more effectively change their minds. If it is wrong and obnoxious to judge, criticize, and compare adults (in the absence of special consensually based circumstances or understandings), then the logic of their position compels one to hold that the same is true in the case of children. Libertarians generally accept the legitimacy of freely negotiated contracts between adults, however, so they tend also to concede that evaluation may be acceptable on the basis of a freely negotiated contract encompassing the terms of attendance and instruction generally, or in instances in which the child's desire to be assisted in the pursuit of some autonomous intellectual pursuit is clear.[5] This is to hold, in effect, that a child may elect to solicit evaluations as an aid to her intellectual endeavors, but that in the absence of such an invitation the use of evaluations and grades would amount to wrongful and coercive impositions on the child's intellectual autonomy.

The picture we get here is that even in their central function as measures of achievement of course or unit objectives or measures of competence in some unit of an academic subject domain, good grades generally constitute rewards for intellectual conformity, and bad or mediocre grades constitute threatened and sometimes devastating penalties for nonconformity.[6] This assumes that many, if not all, children do care about what grades they get, or that they are at least vulnerable to the disapproval and the threat to their future interests implicit in bad grades.[7] The threats of disapproval and reduced life prospects are, on this picture, comparable to other threats that are wrongfully coercive inasmuch as they engender fear of an unjustified loss in order to produce compliance with some demand. To the extent that poor grades embody or signify unjustified penalties of these kinds, they would constitute, according to this view, coercion in a strong sense and hence a violation of the child's right of intellectual autonomy.

## Conventional Responses to the Libertarian Argument

One fairly obvious response to the Coercion Argument begins by separating the two forms of threats said to be at work in grades, the threat of disapproval and the threat of reduced life prospects, and holds that the latter is a spurious ground for finding grades coercive. Coercion involves the threat of an unjustified loss of something one has or will have a legitimate claim to, but it is hard to see how the difference that grades might make to a child's future prospects can qualify as such a loss. It might be that a given child's prospects would be better with good grades than with bad ones, *supposing some children continue to get worse grades*, but a child could have no just claim to a bright future secured through grades better than others' unless those superior grades were deserved.[8] Dropping the supposition that others will continue to get poor grades amounts to imagining a system in which all students always get good grades as a matter of policy, and that is a system scarcely distinguishable from one without any grades. So to ask what a child's prospects would be in the absence of the threats inherent in grades can only be to ask what those prospects would be in an educational, social, and economic system without any grades at all. There is no sure way to determine what a child's life would have been like in a world without academic grades. The idea that in getting bad grades a child's prospects are reduced from what they otherwise would have been, or from what they rightfully should be, is thus highly speculative at best.

To this, the defender of the Coercion Argument might respond that it is nevertheless true that in some cases there might be reasons to think that there is a clear loss of future prospects. The rejoinder to this would then be that even in those cases there remains the question of whether the child has any legitimate claim to the more promising future she might have had in a system without academic grades. The issue becomes at this point one of distributive justice, and to advance their position any further the defenders of the Coercion Argument would have to argue that, whatever benefits there may be to hiring on the basis of qualifications, and using grades as indicators of those qualifications, the distribution of goods that results is unjust. The commitments inherent in the general libertarian position make this a very difficult line of argument to pursue, however, so this leg of the libertarian argument appears quite unpromising.

This leaves us with the suggestion that it is the threat of disapproval inherent in grades that is intellectually coercive, and I will turn now to some of the standard arguments in the literature of grading and children's rights that provide responses to it.

One promising response may be found in James Terwilliger's "Assigning Grades," though the defense of grading offered there is intended as a reply not to the Coercion Argument per se, but to what Terwilliger calls the "humanistic" perspective on teaching and grading, a perspective sharing the libertarian concern with children's freedom.[9] Terwilliger's "pragmatist" response to this "humanistic" perspective is that students need to make practical choices about how much to study, what assistance with their studies they should obtain, and what courses of study to pursue; and that they are more, not less, free in being able to make those choices in light of the information provided by grades. This relies on the idea that in being able to make better choices one is *more free*, and also on the idea that for children in school the better choices are the ones that will enable them to obtain a good education: to learn what they need and are expected to learn, and, where their school offers them choices, to pursue studies beyond the required core which are appropriate to their abilities and aspirations.

There is much good sense in this "pragmatist" view, but there is a weakness inherent in its reliance on the idea that grades provide students with information that is useful in deciding how best to act in pursuit of their studies. Specifically, free and informed action is one thing, and freedom of thought quite another. For all that has been said, a

loss of freedom of thought might be quite compatible with a gain in freedom of action. So even if this argument could establish that the student who is informed of her progress through grades is more free on balance, which it does not in its present form attempt to do, it would still not show that the student does not suffer a loss of freedom of thought. It might with proper amendment serve to justify the practice of grading, showing thereby that it cannot be coercive in a sense entailing a violation of freedom of thought, but as I will argue below this would still leave us with a residual problem of whether children's intellectual freedom is being adequately respected.

Laura Purdy provides what is probably the best and most thorough refutation of the libertarian view of children's rights and education.[10] In the context of a discussion of the moral role of the school, she observes that

> Even quite thoughtful people sometimes talk as if there is something sacred about individuals' values so that it is wrong to attempt to persuade people to alter them. . . . It seems that what is taken to be vital about such beliefs is that they are taken to be *ours*. Underlying this view is some concept of "pure," uninfluenced choice.[11]

Questioning the coherence of this idea of uninfluenced choice, and noting that even without schooling children will be bombarded by a nearly "limitless array of ideas and positions," Purdy argues quite persuasively that the important question to be addressed is "whether [children] *learn to make better judgments* if left entirely to their own devices or whether they should be exposed to teaching about important matters."[12] Purdy relies here, much as Terwilliger does, on the idea that it is more important to children's interests that their choices be good, than that their choices be uninfluenced by the adults in their schools. Her argument goes well beyond his, however, in emphasizing the role of *judgment* in choice, and in identifying a class of judgments much broader than those implicit in the class of choices he has in mind, namely all those which may have practical significance, sooner or later, in the child's life. And what she argues is that the facts bear out the conclusion that "teaching children how to test claims will do a great deal more for their welfare than abandoning them, unfortified by information and skills, to hard experience."[13]

On this view, the development of skills in "critical thinking" becomes a central task of education:

> The goal is to help individuals reason constructively. This task involves, among other things, stressing the importance of justifying beliefs and teaching what counts as justification. . . . Such teaching doesn't necessarily imply a single, clear standard for every knowledge claim, but rather a variety of strategies and tests that would enable one to judge the relative reliability of claims. It does imply that every significant claim to knowledge would be accompanied by discussion of the warrants for its belief.[14]

I am quite sympathetic to this general line of argument, and also to Purdy's insistence that "respect for individuals is compatible with attempting to influence them [provided we use the right methods]."[15] Applied to the use of grades as measures of student progress in developing good judgment as a foundation for wise choices, it supports a reasonable justification of the use of grades to report students' progress to them.

Construed as an answer to the Coercion Argument, however, there are two problems with this line of argument. The first is a problem of insufficient scope. For though it is a reasonable defense of using grades in the way described, it is doubtful whether the entire standard curriculum, even imbued through and through with critical thinking, can be described as contributing to practical judgment in so substantial a way that the gain would justify the cost in intellectual regimentation. One cannot assume that skills and habits of "test[ing] claims" will transfer easily from domains such as biology and geometry to the sphere of practical judgment in everyday living. Furthermore, even if one could make that assumption, it would still not be clear that expecting such critical thinking to transfer from all of the various parts of the standard curriculum would be an efficient way of cultivating good practical judgment.

The second problem is that this argument shares the same weakness as Terwilliger's argument, because they both assume that the improved quality of practical choices will justify efforts to shape children's minds. However much weight we assign to the child's interest in practical self-determination and the right corresponding to it, we are left, as before, with the question of whether the intellectual freedom of children is being sacrificed to competing interests. This residue of

possible "weak" coercion is a problem worth taking seriously, because an infringement of a right is something unfortunate and regrettable in itself, even if it occurs in the context of a course of action that is acceptable, all things considered. There are dilemmas in public and private life alike in which we are faced with no better choice than to sacrifice a lesser good to one that is greater. The appropriate moral attitude in such instances includes regret and remains vigilant to the prospect of avoiding the loss that occasions it, whenever possible. If it were true that we can only prepare children adequately for the demands of practical life at the cost of their intellectual freedom, we would be faced with such a dilemma, and I think that the course of action we would feel compelled to follow would be one we should seriously regret.

This dilemma is avoidable, however, and I will turn now to the elaboration of a moral framework that will make this clear.

## The Moral Framework

Let us conceive of grading as a form of *substituted judgment*, or an act in which the judgment of one person is imposed on, and on behalf of, another person who is found to be unable to judge competently and decide some matter for herself. In practical contexts, the judgments imposed concern alternative courses of action and what it is best to do. The decisions are ones about what the person of impaired or immature competence is to do, be assisted in doing, or what will be done on her behalf. In an academic context, such judgments and corresponding decisions concern what is true and what to assert, what strategy to adopt in pursuit of an answer or in assessing a claim, and so on. When students show that they are not yet able to make these judgments and decisions well on their own, teachers intervene by "correcting" the judgments expressed in students' performances. Viewing a graded assignment as an intellectual performance, every correction amounts to a substitution of the teacher's judgment for the student's.[16]

Among the practical contexts in which substituted judgment is an issue, the domain of health care is noteworthy for the degree to which the standards governing substituted judgment have been thought through by ethicists. None have been more thorough or careful in this regard than Allen Buchanan and Dan Brock, and their account will prove helpful to us here, even though the health care and educational domains are different in some important ways. The two basic standards we will consider are the *substituted judgment standard* and *the best interest principle*,[17] and I will argue in what follows that they are both important to justifying evaluation and grading, and that they apply to different aspects of these educational practices.

At the foundation of Buchanan and Brock's account is the idea that the value and moral force of rights of self-determination vary with the competence of their possessor, in such a way that imposing substituted judgments may be justified when a lack of competence can be properly demonstrated. The capacities requisite to self-determination, when they are intact and reasonably well-developed, enable an agent to identify and satisfy her desires with enough success that a regard for her well-being and a respect for her claim to be self-determining converge, by and large. Regard for well-being and respect for claims of self-determination begin to pull in different directions, however, when the capacities required for competent self-determination are not fully present. These capacities are essentially those required for rational judgment and choice, and include abilities to perceive, comprehend, think things through, imagine and rationally project future courses of events, evaluate alternatives in light of a sound appreciation of one's own dominant interests and preferences, and so on.

Even though it is likely that every adult will at least occasionally lack the competence to make some *specific* complex decision that she will face, it is nevertheless true that adults can usually make decisions well enough that there is in their case no acceptable alternative to the policy of a general presumption of global decisional competence (in other words, competence to make all the decisions they face). As Buchanan and Brock point out, the alternatives are decidedly less attractive, those being "a general presumption of incompetence . . . or . . . having no general presumption and so having to settle the competence of each instance of decision-making case by case."[18] The substance of this presumption, as they say, is that

> it is presumed of any adult that he or she has sufficient decision-making capacities to make . . . decisions for him- or her-self and to warrant these decisions being respected by others. . . . even if others view the decisions as less than optimal, foolish, or not the decisions those others would make in similar circumstances.[19]

This presumption may be overcome in particular cases when it can be demonstrated that the capacities needed for competent decision-making are substantially lacking, but in the absence of such a demonstration any attempt to impose a different choice would be morally intolerable. Their view is that the lack of the capacity for rational decision need only be *substantial* for intervention to be warranted, since even a partial lack of competence may undercut the value of making one's own decisions enough for that value to be outweighed in particular instances by the damage done to one's interests by poorly made decisions. It is also important to Buchanan and Brock's view that, when faced with an individual whom there is good reason (or "probable cause") to regard as not globally competent, and whose competence to make specific decisions must therefore be determined, competence should be determined relative to the demands of the specific decisions to be made. They argue that this determination should take into account not only the cognitive demands imposed by the decision, but also the importance of the interests at stake, and the degree to which those interests are threatened. One of the most important interests that may be at stake is, of course, the interest in self-determination itself, since a person's choices can profoundly affect her interest in self-determination through the difference they make to the development or preservation of her capacity for competent judgment and choice.

Since competence is to be determined relative to the demands of the specific decisions to be made, a decision-relative standard of competence must be relied upon. A question of special importance for the present inquiry is what form this standard of competence should take. The alternatives that Buchanan and Brock consider are a *minimal competence standard*, an *outcome standard*, and a *process standard*, the process standard being the best choice of the three, since it affords the best protection of self-determination consistent with the patient's well-being.[20] Minimal standards, such as the condition that the patient "merely be able to express a preference," are not really standards of *competence* at all, and so afford no protection to the patient's well-being. They are insufficiently sensitive to competence-based limitations on the scope of rights of self-determination, and would preclude beneficial intervention even when there would be no moral barrier to doing so. Outcome standards look only to the content or outcome of the patient's deliberations, and regard her as competent to make a decision only if that outcome is judged to be objectively reasonable. This kind of standard inevitably involves a judgment about the rationality of a decision with respect to aims and preferences that are presumed to be normal or objectively desirable; such a standard can therefore make little allowance for differences in judgment arising from legitimate differences of aim or preference. This kind of standard thus makes the opposite kind of error from the first, and accords no independent value to self-determination. By contrast with both of these, a process standard focuses on the quality of the understanding and processes of reasoning leading up to the patient's decision. In doing this, it makes room for the legitimate variability of human ends and preferences. Just as important, it can strike a reasonable balance between regard for well-being and regard for self-determination, and limit authorized substitutions of judgment to those compatible with the patient's rights of self-determination.

All of this pertains so far to the question of *when* it is appropriate for a duly authorized person to substitute her judgment for another's, and brings us now to the question of the standards that govern the judgments themselves when it *is* acceptable to make and impose them. The two standards to which I have already referred are the *substituted judgment standard* and the *best interests principle*.[21] The first of these takes priority in any case in which it is applicable, and holds that the authorized surrogate should choose "as the incompetent individual would choose in the circumstances were he or she competent."[22] In any case where differences of aim or preference might come into play, this requires a prior knowledge of the patient's aims and preferences, and so also a patient of enough maturity to *have* fairly stable aims and preferences. Where these requirements cannot be met, the principle that applies is the *best interests principle*, which directs the surrogate to choose the course of action "with the greatest net benefit to the patient."[23]

Turning now to children, what separates them from adults is that the capacities required for competent choice are generally not well enough developed to ensure that their well-being or future capacity for competent self-determination will be served by their choices. With respect to health care decisions, Buchanan and Brock take the developmental evidence to suggest that the capacities needed for competence have usually developed to adult-like levels by fourteen or fifteen years old. On the strength of that conclusion they recommend that

the legally and socially recognized general presumption of incompetence for children be reversed for those fifteen or older, but that it be retained for those fourteen and below. For those between nine and fourteen they recommend the creation of suitable mechanisms through which this presumption of incompetence could be rebutted on a case-by-case, decision-by-decision basis. The more complex the decision, the greater the demonstrable decision-making capacity would have to be to overcome this presumption. The more serious the peril to the child's well-being, the higher the standard of evidence that would have to be met in establishing the presence of that capacity.

Buchanan and Brock identify two further and associated differences between adults and children. First, the well-being of children is more linked to developmental needs, and less to their relatively unstable expressed aims and preferences, than is the well-being of adults. Second, and similarly,

an important part of children's and adolescents' interest in self-determination is not their interest *qua* children in making decisions for themselves, but their interest in developing the capacities to be self-determining adults.[24]

This would be true of anyone who lacked, but still had the potential to acquire, normal competence; no matter what a person values (short of wishing above all to be irrational), the value to a person of making decisions for herself is determined in part by how competently she can make those decisions. Accordingly, if the point of rights of self-determination is to protect personal interests in self-determination, then we must regard those who have the potential to acquire normal competence as owed a form of prospective, or forward-looking, respect. This is a form of respect assignable as an unqualified duty not to impede the development of the capacities that contribute to competent self-determination, together with a qualified duty to take positive steps to promote that development.[25] The latter duty falls most obviously on those with some responsibility for the bearer of the rights in question.

Regarding the content of that duty, the development of competence requires the exercise of the requisite emerging capacities, but also coaching, instruction, and sometimes intervention to prevent choices that could be expected to threaten substantially the continuation of that development.

Such efforts in the cause of the child's developmental interests, and in the face of present incompetence to make choices consistent with those interests, would be no infringement of the interests in self-determination thereby promoted. Respect for the child's right of self-determination would *demand* such intervention by those with responsibility for the child, given the relative values to the child of making authoritative use of her present capacities, compared with acquiring the competence to judge and choose more wisely in the future.

Buchanan and Brock are concerned with practical self-determination, but there are no obvious grounds for supposing intellectual self-determination to be any less important, or significantly different in its logic from what they suggest. To the foregoing we need only add in connection with intellectual self-determination that promoting intellectual competence in those who lack it, in the right circumstances and in the right manner, would seem obligatory on the part of those charged with their care. Since it is obligatory it is surely permissible, and since it is justified not by extraneous interests, but by the interest in intellectual self-determination itself, it cannot be an infringement of the right of intellectual self-determination.

## The Legitimacy of Evaluation

With this moral framework in hand, my suggestion is that the evaluation and grading of students is best regarded as combining in one process both a determination of competence and the imposition of substituted judgments in just those instances where the student's lack of competence to make the judgment in question is demonstrated. As we have seen, a process of this sort can be not only morally legitimate, but quite free of any infringement of the student's right of intellectual self-determination, if (1) it rests on either a legitimate presumption of incompetence or specific grounds for making an individual determination of competence; (2) it relies on an acceptable standard of competence; (3) the judgment that is substituted for the student's satisfies the appropriate standard; and (4) the student's prospective rights of intellectual self-determination are adequately respected. A final condition, discussed at length by Buchanan and Brock but so far unmentioned here, is that (5) the judgments of competence and substituted judgments must be made on proper authority and subject to appropriate

institutional safeguards. In this section I shall develop the account of the ethics of evaluation and grading implied by this characterization, and show that these five conditions can be met. I will thus conclude that, with some adjustment of evaluation practices, the challenge to evaluation and grading posed by the Coercion Argument can be fully met.

The first point to be addressed in establishing the moral legitimacy of "correcting" students' judgments through adverse assessments is the reliance on a general presumption of a lack of competence to make judgments of the kinds that those who have mastered an academic subject can make. It is reasonable to think that a presumption of subject-specific noncompetence for all students does need to be established, since they are routinely subjected to evaluations without any individualized showing of "probable cause" to suspect that they lack the competence to make sound judgments in the subject-matter domains in question. In the absence of a showing of probable cause or of the legitimacy of an initial presumption of noncompetence one could reasonably regard the whole act of subjecting students to evaluations as unwarranted interference. So we must ask what the basis for an initial presumption of subject-specific noncompetence might be.

With regard to required courses of study, this presumption would have to be established on the strength of evidence about the general timing and patterns of cognitive development. One would need to be able to say on reasonable empirical evidence that people at the age of those required to undertake the various courses of study would generally not have prior competence to make the kinds of judgments at stake in those studies. It seems to me that we are already in a fairly good position to say this, but that efforts at curriculum development should probably be focused more on deficiencies of judgment and the development of good judgment in subject-domains, and less on what students do not and should know.

This leaves the matter of elective courses of study. In connection with these, one would have to regard a presumption of subject-matter specific incompetence as arising by contract or mutual understanding, subject to the proviso that curricula not be structured in such a way as to leave students only with optional courses of study in which they would generally already be competent. This proviso is not hard to satisfy, and so long as it is it would be quite reasonable to rely on students to sign up for studies in which they are not already expert.

(Of course, if a student's prior mastery is known from the outset, she is best directed to an alternative course of study which would be more fruitful.) In these conditions, the student's act of signing up for the course could be understood to entail an admission of subject-specific and level-specific noncompetence, or an acceptance of a presumption of such noncompetence as a condition of instruction. This understanding can be regarded with some reason as implicit in current practice, and to the extent that it is this is morally unproblematic. It thus seems generally reasonable for teachers and examiners to rely on a rebuttable presumption that students are generally not competent to judge what is true and false, cogent and spurious, and so on, at their present level of study in the domains of study they undertake in school. That presumption provides a component of the moral grounds for evaluating students' progress toward full competence in those domains of study.

The second requirement for the moral soundness of evaluation and grading is that they rely on an acceptable standard for determining students' competence, and here problems with traditional practice do begin to emerge. As we have seen, Buchanan and Brock advocate the use of a process standard of competence in a health care setting; I believe this is also the most appropriate kind of standard to use in evaluation and grading, though for reasons that are only partly the same. Part of the argument for using a process standard in domains of practice is that it allows for legitimate variations in human aims and preferences that may make a difference to what choices are rational for a given person. The judgments at stake in evaluation and grading are not ones about what to do, however, but simply about what to believe, on what evidence to believe it, how to investigate what one does not know, and the like. The fundamental, universal interest at stake in all of this is the development of intellectual powers, good judgment, and an accurate appreciation of the nature of things. This is an interest that all agents, all human beings, share, whatever else they care about, even though children and many adults may give little thought to it. What concerns us, in other words, is epistemic rationality, and variations in ends and preferences do not enter into it in the way they enter into practical rationality. So part of the argument for a process standard of competence does not apply in the academic context. Nevertheless, it is clearly the right standard to use, because it is a direct measure of the quality of reasoning and thought that constitute good judgment. An outcome measure, which detects nothing more than conclusory statements, cannot possibly provide an adequate measure of the competence of judgment. As a basis for making inferences about competence of judgment, any measure of this sort will inevitably be subject to both false positives and false negatives: the former in any instance in which an acceptable answer is produced without independent judgment (as for instance from simple memory), and the latter in any instance in which an unacceptable answer masks judgment that is largely competent but flawed or unanticipated. Evaluations of students typically do rely heavily on such outcome measures, measures that look simply at the correctness of conclusory statements, and little if any on the basis for making them. The analysis developed here suggests that this is morally problematic. Any time an outcome measure produces a false negative assessment of competence that a feasible process measure would have avoided, it would be reasonable to say that some form of interference with a student's interest in intellectual self-determination has occurred.

The third requirement is that the judgment that is substituted for the student's must satisfy the appropriate standard for substituted judgment. This is strongly linked in the present context to the determination of competence or its absence: the standards of rationality and good judgment that the process measures of competence rely on will be no different from the standards that guide the content of the substituted judgment. The appropriate standard here is the *substituted judgment standard*, because it takes priority over the best interests principle in any case in which it applies. It does apply here, even in the absence of any knowledge of individual student aims and preferences, since these have no pertinent bearing on epistemic rationality. Indeed, this principle may be applied even to children who still lack settled preferences, since it requires in this context simply that the teacher judge as the child would, were she, the child, competent to make the kinds of academic judgments at issue. The upshot of this is simply that the teacher or grader is warranted, first, in overturning any judgment that the student would not make were she competent in the forms of judgment belonging to the current level of study in the subject domain in question. Second, she is warranted in substituting the judgment the student would make if competent, or giving some indication of the range of judgments that would be competent. One implication of this is that if there is no uniquely competent judgment to be made, the teacher or grader should be sensitive to that. One possibility that may arise, though with what frequency it would be difficult to know, is that with respect to some forms of judgments, cultural differences might incline students toward different judgments from among those that are competent. Contingencies of this sort would demand a kind of sensitivity that requires not only an awareness of the different but reasonable premises that students may rely on, but also more attention and sensitivity to the quality of student inference, inquiry, and judgment than the training of many teachers may prepare them for.

The fourth condition for the moral soundness of evaluation and grading is the requirement that the student's prospective rights of intellectual self-determination be respected. The presumption underlying this condition is that children lack the competence to make many sorts of judgments that they need to be able to make in order to be intellectually autonomous or self-determining. The standard to be followed is the best interest principle, applied not with respect to the child's general interests, but rather with respect to her interest in intellectual development and autonomy.[26] This is not to say that the child's general interests will not be taken into account, for they should be in designing courses of study and many other aspects of schooling, but rather to add an additional requirement beyond respect for the child's general interests: to recognize the significance of the interest in intellectual self-determination as something distinct from an interest in being intellectually prepared to meet the practical challenges of life. Students only become intellectually self-determining by developing the capacities of thought and judgment this requires, so the development of such capacities must guide pedagogy, the curriculum, and evaluation itself, if the enterprise of evaluation and grading are to satisfy the moral requirements arising from students' rights of intellectual autonomy. This would require the adoption of a "thinking" curriculum and the reform of evaluation practices to support more effectively efforts to promote development of competent thinking and judgment. With respect to the latter, process measures will again be preferable for their superior capacity to monitor and encourage quality of thought and judgment.

This provides us with an answer to the Coercion Argument that avoids the problem, noted in Purdy's response to the libertarians, of relying entirely on the idea of preparing students to make good practical judgments. For while it takes the development of good practical judgment to be an important goal of education, it assigns independent importance to intellectual freedom itself, and shows that freedom is not infringed, but rather promoted, by proper instruction and evaluation. The content and character of academic studies and evaluation must serve the student's developmental interests as they are related to her general future well-being, as Purdy insists, but they must also be designed to promote intellectual self-determination. It is only if they are that the restrictions of intellectual freedom they involve will be justified by the interest in intellectual freedom itself, which is what is required if we are to avoid infringing the right of intellectual self-determination.

This answer also avoids the other problem we saw in Purdy's account, which was that it seemed to apply to only that part of the curriculum that could be justified for its contribution to the development of practical judgment. The account I am suggesting here applies to any part of the curriculum to which the Coercion Argument might apply: any in which students are expected to make statements that might be challenged. My point is that all those parts of the curriculum that call upon students to say what is true are ones in which their intellectual self-determination can and should be served by promoting their capacity to think and judge for themselves.

The final requirement that I have identified calls upon teachers to be skilled in the forms of judgment they are teaching and monitoring, and calls upon schools and school districts, who authorize teachers to evaluate and grade students, to take reasonable measures to ensure that teachers have those skills. It also demands that some institutional safeguards exist, including mechanisms of appeal and oversight. Among the latter, one might include the use of standardized tests and assessments to provide models and accountability to a "thinking" curriculum and system of evaluation.

Moreover, even if state and national standards and the measures through which they are maintained are not officially used as mechanisms of accountability, they will inevitably influence the goals and style of teaching and learning, shaping both the uses of classroom time and the character of classroom evaluations of students. It is thus quite important that they satisfy the moral demands enumerated here, even if (as seems likely) it would take a great deal more than the reform of standards and standardized measures to bring classroom practice into conformity with the requirements outlined here.

To summarize the results of this section, I have held that grading is a form of substituted judgment, which when carried out properly is a process of sorting the judgments that students produce into those that are competent and those that are not. It amounts to a procedure through which an initial presumption of subject- and level-specific incompetence can be rebutted on a decision-by-decision basis, and through which the epistemic decisions that can be competently made by the student (when they *are* competently made) are recognized and allowed to stand. It is thus, ideally, only judgments that a student is reasonably found not competent to make that are penalized or overridden. Provided the finding that competence is lacking is properly authorized and based on reasonable criteria, then, there is no infringement of the student's rights of intellectual self-determination. There is no infringement because the most reasonable view of these rights is that in the absence of intellectual competence the interest in acquiring that competence outweighs the interest in having the current judgments or choices of that incompletely developed capacity be authoritative.

It is important to emphasize that this analysis provides only part of a full investigation of the moral status of testing and grading practices. It does not answer every moral objection to testing and grading. Nor does it show that grades, as we know them, are the best vehicle for imparting the kinds of judgments defended here as necessary to promoting students' intellectual autonomy. For all I have said, a system of written evaluative comments might serve this purpose better, and be more desirable on other grounds as well.

## The Need for Reform

To summarize: while a minimal *standard* of competence would require teachers to let incompetent academic judgments stand, an *outcome standard* would also be seriously defective in allowing teachers to focus only on the rightness or wrongness of conclusory statements and to ignore the processes of thought and judgment that yield those statements. Even when "objective" test items have been successfully constructed in such a way as to eliminate all reasonable grounds for giving answers other than the designated right answer (which is less often than one might hope), an objectively incorrect answer may mask a quality of thought and judgment that should be acknowledged and cultivated.[27] Worse still, even correct outcomes may indicate little about the processes that yield them; and all too often they reveal nothing more than the ability to recall fragmentary facts.[28] Outcome measures are for this reason a poor vehicle for promoting epistemic competence and thereby respecting the student's interest in intellectual self-determination. A *process standard*, which provides the best guide for how to respect self-determination, would dictate continued reform of evaluation practices to focus less on recall of specific subject matter content and more on processes of thought, the development of judgment, and deeper forms of understanding of the various domains of inquiry. This does not mean that all use of "objective" test items is morally suspect, for the development of good judgment and mastery of different modes of inquiry does require, among other things, that one learn a great number of facts. There may yet be a place for well-crafted multiple-choice items that demand thinking rather than recall; but it means that the balance between process and content items should shift dramatically.[29]

The enactment of such reform will require efforts to develop techniques for designing prompts that elicit thinking and judgment, and related techniques for scoring responses so as to reveal the quality of thought and judgment elicited. The prompts will have to identify and elicit forms of response, whether written, oral, or performed, that will display thought in ways that make its quality observable, such as by demanding that an answer be justified or requesting an evaluation of an argument, a problem solution, or the design of an experiment or investigation. Explanatory thinking, which is as important to many domains of inquiry as their modes of inquiry and confirmation, should also be a focus of teaching and evaluation, and can be elicited and effectively assessed by prompts that call for multiple possible explanations of unfamiliar phenomena or critiques of proposed explanations.

It will take some work to identify the most productive forms of prompts suitable to each subject area at each grade level. This work, and the development of scoring guides and training for teachers and others who will set and score exams, must be grounded in an adequate conception of the nature of the thinking and judgments proper to each subject domain. Even the most progressive curriculum frameworks in use in the United States still lack this. They acknowledge the importance of observing, classifying, measuring, inferring, and the like (the so-called "basic process skills"), but do not adequately identify and direct teachers' and examiners' efforts toward the larger structures of "higher order" thinking. The past few years have seen some efforts in the right direction, however, at the National Assessment of Educational Progress, the Educational Testing Service, the New Standards Project, nationally, and in a number of states as well.

In California, for example, a framework for the construction and scoring of essay items as process measures in standardized biology testing, based upon a division of biological thinking into explanatory, investigative, and confirmatory types, has proven successful in field trials, and might prove a useful point of departure for other subject domains as well.[30] The challenges entailed by this agenda are in any case quite substantial, and not unrelated to those involved in the design and implementation of the "thinking curriculum" that evaluation of this sort would need to be linked to. If the foregoing analysis is correct, they are challenges that a proper moral regard for children's rights of intellectual self-determination compels us to accept.

## Notes

1. Reports of grade inflation at the college level suggest that some university faculty have come to regard grading as coercive because they have lost their faith in reason. See John Leo, "'A' for Effort: Or for Showing Up," *US News and World Report*, 18 October 1993, p. 22. I am not aware of any serious attempts to develop such an argument, however, and will confine my attention to the libertarian argument.

2. See Judith Jarvis Thomson, *Rights, Restitution and Risk* (Cambridge, MA: Harvard University Press, 1986), pp. 40, 51–5, on the distinction between an "infringement" of a right, which is justified by the overriding value or importance of competing interests, and a "violation" of a right, which cannot be so justified and which is therefore wrongful all things considered.

3. Allen Buchanan and Dan Brock, *Deciding for Others* (Cambridge: Cambridge University Press, 1989).

4. See, for example, William Rickenbacker (ed.), *The Twelve Year Sentence: Radical Views of Compulsory Schooling* (La Salle, IL: Open Court Publishing, 1974); Beatrice Gross and Ronald Gross (eds.), *The Children's Rights Movement: Overcoming the Oppression of Young People* (New York: Anchor/ Doubleday, 1977); Ann Swidler, *Organization without Authority: Dilemmas of Social Control in Free Schools* (Cambridge, MA: Harvard University Press, 1979); William Aiken and Hugh LaFollette (eds.), *Whose Child?: Children's Rights, Parental Authority, and State Power* (Totowa, NJ: Rowman and Allenheld, 1980); Howard Cohen, *Equal Rights for Children* (Totowa, NJ: Littlefield, Adams, 1980); Michael Smith, *The Libertarians and Education* (London: George Allen and Unwin, 1983); and Geoffrey Scarre, *Children, Parents, and Politics* (Cambridge: Cambridge University Press, 1989).

5. See, for example, Swidler, *Organization without Authority*, chap. 1; Garth Boomer (ed.), *Negotiating the Curriculum* (Sydney: Ashton Scholastic, 1982); and Smith, *Libertarians and Education*, pp. 83–97.

6. While recognizing that the character of the judgments expressed by grades is neither this simple, nor uniform across all educational contexts (see R. J. Stiggins, "Inside High School Grading Practices: Building a Research Agenda," *Educational Measurement* 8 [1989], pp. 5–14), I will assume in what follows that we are concerned with grades as simple measures of achievement of course or unit objectives or competence in some part of an academic subject domain. To the extent that this is not how grades are used, they will require a different justification from the one I will propose. Some uses of grades may be more difficult or impossible to justify, but that is a topic best left for another occasion.

7. See Smith, *Libertarians and Education*, pp. 64, 66–7.

8. A student who gained an advantage through undeserved superior grades would be, in economic or rational-choice theoretic terms, a "free-rider," or one who enjoys goods (whatever they are) secured through the compliance of others with a cooperative scheme whose terms she herself defies.

9. James Terwilliger, "Assigning Grades – Philosophical Issues and Practical Recommendations," *Journal of Research and Development in Education* 10 (1977), pp. 21–39, 24–7.

10. Laura Purdy, *In Their Best Interest? The Case Against Equal Rights For Children* (Ithaca, NY: Cornell University Press, 1992).

11. Ibid., p. 158.

12. Ibid., pp. 160, 159 (emphasis added). Rosemary Chamberlin makes a similar argument, in *Free*

*Children and Democratic Schools* (New York: The Falmer Press, 1989), pp. 100–2.

13. Purdy, *In Their Best Interest?*, p. 162.

14. Ibid., p. 165.

15. Ibid., p. 158.

16. It is, of course, true that most corrections are supposed to be substitutions of right answers for wrong ones, but if this is the whole of the matter it is difficult to see how an adequate response to the Coercion Argument might be framed. One could argue that the possession of truth and knowledge is more conducive to intellectual autonomy than falsehood and ignorance, and that correcting students' work corrects their false beliefs and gives them knowledge, but this is not a wholly satisfactory answer. Unless corrections include or link up with evidence or justifications, it is doubtful that they do lead students to new knowledge. Even if they did, there are enough other dimensions of epistemic agency unaccounted for that one could scarcely judge whether the net result for the student is a gain in intellectual autonomy or a loss.

17. See Buchanan and Brock, *Deciding for Others*, pp. 112 and 122 ff.

18. Ibid., p. 2l.

19. Ibid.

20. Ibid., pp. 48–51.

21. I should note here that there is a third – but for our purposes completely inapplicable – principle that takes the highest priority in Buchanan and Brock's hierarchy of standards. In general, their account is considerably more detailed and sophisticated than it is possible or necessary to make clear here.

22. Buchanan and Brock, *Deciding for Others*, p. 112.

23. Ibid., p. 123.

24. Ibid., p. 231.

25. The language and principles here are essentially Kantian, except that the two forms of duties are typically rendered in translation from the German as "perfect" and "imperfect" duties.

26. One could argue that this application of the *best interest standard* would necessarily coincide with a similar application of the *substituted judgment standard*, but the former captures better the character of the decision to be made. The point is not, as in grading itself, to suggest or impose the judgments that the student would make were she competent, but to make decisions that will promote the student's best interests.

27. I thus agree with Grant Wiggins when he insists, in "A True Test: Toward More Authentic and Equitable Assessment," *Phi Delta Kappan* 71 (1989), p. 708, that the reasons that test-takers have for their answers are not irrelevant, but on very different grounds from his. His suggestion, that there is inherent inequity in a test that "is unable to encompass the inevitable idiosyncratic cases for which we ought always to make exceptions to the rule," has significance only for those answers whose merits may be misjudged by the dominant kinds of measures, whereas the concern I have raised applies more pervasively.

28. Elliot Eisner offers grounds for concern about this lack of information about processes of thought and quality of reasoning when he notes that it leaves us in a poor position to further "the development of problem-solving skills"; see Elliot W. Eisner, "Reshaping Assessment in Education: Some Criteria in Search of Practice," *Journal of Curriculum Studies* 25 (1993), p. 227. This is an important point, but different from the one I am making here. Problem-solving skills may play a role in thinking effectively and exercising independent and well-considered judgment, but they are not all there is to it, and the reasons for wanting students to be good problem-solvers might be quite different from the reasons for respecting their claims to self-determination.

29. One *can* evaluate content knowledge using process measures, such as essays that call for thinking and judgment but also require that the student rely upon an understanding of content knowledge, but this is not an efficient way to evaluate how completely a student has mastered the knowledge base of a subject domain.

30. This work, conducted by R. Darrell Bock, Randall Curren, Megan Martin, and Michele Zimowski, in cooperation with the Golden State Examinations Program of the California Assessment, is reported elsewhere [see R. Curren (2004) "Educational measurement and knowledge of other minds," *Theory and Research in Education* 2(3), pp. 235–53, 247–51 – Editor].

# 53

# What is at Stake in Knowing the Content and Capabilities of Children's Minds?

## A Case for Basing High Stakes Tests on Cognitive Models

Stephen P. Norris, Jacqueline P. Leighton, and Linda M. Phillips

## Introduction

Randall Curren argues that it is possible to design tests that enable us to know the content and capabilities of children's minds. He dismisses many of the views of Davis (1998), who contends that in principle it is impossible to acquire this sort of knowledge. Curren refers to a body of empirical research demonstrating test designs that provide the information on children's minds that many educators seek and want. 'Through patient empirical research, guided by adequate conceptions of the kinds of understanding and thinking we are trying to evaluate' (Curren, 2004: 251), we will learn to do even better, he predicts.

We concur. Nevertheless, there are many significant changes in perspective that have to take place before efforts to learn the content and capabilities of children's minds can hold much sway in educational testing. Despite several decades of theoretical prompting, educational testing has not broken once and for all from its behaviorist legacy. It might seem astonishing, but in pointing to *mind* as the focus for testing, Curren is quite at odds with

much of the educational testing establishment. The language of testing, especially of high stakes testing, remains firmly in the realm of 'behaviors', 'performance', and 'competency' defined in terms of behaviors, test items, or observations. The validation models for high stakes tests frequently are founded on the concept of sampling from a population of behaviors or performances and, through statistical generalization, making inferences about what individuals can do. Furthermore, the construction of these models usually begins and ends within the perspective of experts in subject matter content and technical testing experts, not within the perspective of students – the ones being tested. That is, what is on children's minds is not taken into account as integral to the test design and interpretation process. It therefore should be no surprise if the resulting tests reveal little about the quality of children's thinking.

In this article, we argue that behaviorist-based validation models are ill-founded. A major problem is their reliance on a statistical generalization model for test validation. The problem is a mismatch between the sampling units (test items, behaviors,

Previously published in *Theory and Research in Education* 2(3) (2004): 283–307. © Sage Publications 2004. Reprinted by permission of Sage Publications Ltd.

or observations) and the generalizations reached, which go beyond populations of those units. Generalizations typically are made to abilities and competencies, which, we shall argue, cannot be defined in terms of populations of test items, behaviors, or observations, but must be defined as mental powers with infinite implications. In the place of the behaviorist and statistical validation model, we shall propose basing tests on cognitive models that theorize the content and capabilities of children's minds in terms of such features as meta-cognition, reasoning strategies, and principles of sound thinking. The use of such models encourages the validation of tests on the basis of data more directly indicative of cognition than test performance itself – for instance, on verbal reports of reasoning and verbal protocol analysis. This approach is the one most likely to yield the construct validity for tests long endorsed by some testing theorists.

We shall argue also that a shift to cognitive models for basing educational tests would have more than scientific implications. There is an ironic risk in creating testing instruments that provide more convincing evidence of what children are thinking. Better instruments will yield results that are more difficult to dispute and more binding once obtained. Are we prepared for this in education? There can be a perverse comfort in something done poorly, because no matter how the results turn out, no matter whose desires they contravene, the results can be disputed and overturned. What happens when that is more difficult to do?

Three sections will follow. In the first, we demonstrate the inadequacies of the testing model employed for one high stakes test used in a large Canadian jurisdiction, the Alberta High School Diploma Examination. We know from experience that the Alberta examination is fairly typical of many high stakes tests in purpose and use (e.g. the SAT in the USA). In the second section, we provide our prescription of how high stakes and other educational tests can be based upon cognitive models. In the final section, we explore some of the implications of filling and taking our prescription, some of which might be upsetting to many current practices.

## Inadequacy of the High Stakes Model of Competency and Inference from Scores

The Alberta High School Diploma Examination (from here on called the Diploma Exam) is a high stakes paper-and-pencil test that was introduced in the province of Alberta in 1984. Its purpose is to satisfy three objectives: (a) to certify individual student achievement in core academic courses at the Grade 12 level; (b) to ensure that academic standards in these courses are maintained across the province; and (c) to report individual and group standings. It is the first two objectives that produce the high stakes: the first for students and their teachers; and the second for teachers, schools and school districts.

The design of each Diploma Exam is based on the curricular objectives of its corresponding core academic course. A consortium of classroom teachers, school authorities, representatives from post-secondary institutions, officials from the Learning Assessment and Curriculum branches of Alberta Learning (the Ministry of Education) and the French Language Services Branch of the Alberta Government take part in developing the Diploma Exam, a process that takes 18 months to complete. The first stage involves preparing an interim blueprint for the Diploma Exam based on the expectations for students within each knowledge domain of the curriculum. Classroom teachers and examination developers use the blueprint to generate test questions that meet curricular as well as technical (statistical) standards.

We shall confine our comments and conclusions to the approximately 65 percent of the items that are objectively scored, that is, for which there are predetermined right or best answers and students' reasoning leading to their answers is not captured as part of the testing. Preliminary test questions are screened, edited, and revised according to the blueprint specifications and technical standards. Test questions are field-tested with a sample of approximately 250 students. Each field-tested question is reviewed for problems and modified accordingly. For instance, if an item has problematic statistical properties (e.g. it does not exhibit any differences in performance among students) or ambiguities (e.g. instructions are judged unclear by teachers), it is revised and submitted for additional field tests.

According to Alberta Learning, validity and reliability are first considered at the planning (or blueprint) stage: 'To ensure that each examination is a fair and equitable measure of students' accomplishments in the course, and to ensure that results will be meaningful and reliable, examination developers incorporate curricular as well as statistical standards into the examination design'

(Alberta Learning, 2003, Planning section: para. 4). After the questions are developed, validity and reliability concerns are again considered during the field-testing of questions. It is during this phase that teachers may comment on the appropriateness of questions. Also, during field-testing, statistical analyses of the questions are conducted to reveal whether questions written to be easy or difficult are indeed easy or difficult for students to answer as indicated by the proportions of students who answer them correctly.

There are two theoretical presuppositions underlying the Diploma Exam that are common to many high stakes tests, and that we wish to examine and challenge: (a) adults' judgments about an item's curricular integrity and difficulty, based only upon their own reading of the item, are sufficient for ensuring the validity and reliability of the Diploma Exam; and (b) students' competencies can be conceptualized adequately without attention to the explanatory roles of competencies, and in instrumental and operational terms as the proportion of a set of test items they answer correctly.

*Adult Inferences about Item Quality*

Although the Diploma Exam is intended for students, students' thinking about the items does not play a direct and explicit role in its development. Items are developed and vetted by teachers and subject experts, and, even when the items are tried with samples of students, only students' answers, and not the thinking that led to their answers, form the data that are used for revision. We wish to illustrate the serious issues for the validity of the examination that arise because of this approach, by describing one significant problem that often leaves test developers in a quandary – namely, differential item functioning (DIF).

DIF occurs when groups of students with presumed similar levels of ability have different probabilities of answering a test question correctly. For example, imagine a group of boys and a group of girls. The group of girls is found to outperform the group of boys on a specific test question designed to measure hypothesis testing. One reason the girls outperform the boys on this question might be that they know more about hypothesis testing than boys. However, another possibility is that there is something about the context of the test question that, although irrelevant to hypothesis testing, favored the girls' performance nonetheless. Test questions are biased when they contain sources of difficulty (or of ease) that are irrelevant to the construct being measured and that affect the test performance of different groups differently. The upshot of such irrelevant sources of variance is that they lead to (a) systematic errors that misrepresent test performance for members of particular groups, and (b) incorrect inferences about the knowledge and skills of different groups. In our example, the test question might be measuring boys' hypothesis testing skills in novel domains, but measuring girls' heuristic skills in familiar domains. In either case, the test question is suspect of measuring different constructs in different groups of students and thus of compromising inferences made from the test.

DIF is a constant concern on large-scale achievement tests, especially tests that tend to show gender differences (e.g. mathematics) (Bielinski and Davison, 2001) and language-group differences (Gierl and Khaliq, 2001). This concern is exacerbated by the fact that statistical analyses can identify suspect test questions (those showing DIF), but not whether these questions are really behaving poorly. Perhaps more perniciously, statistical analyses are not useful for identifying items that *ought* to display DIF but do not – that is, cases where the presumption of similar levels of ability between groups is in error. So, we need to know more fully than revealed by item performance alone *why* students perform the way they do. To address the explanatory question, the approach used in the Diploma Exam involves consulting subject experts and compiling judgmental review panels. Unfortunately, this approach yields adult inferences about what students are thinking and has proven not as successful as was once anticipated (Camilli and Shepard, 1994; Engelhard et al., 1990; Gierl and Khaliq, 2001). In fact, little progress has been made in understanding the underlying causes of DIF (American Educational Research Association et al., 1999; Roussos and Stout, 1996) and in identifying where DIF ought to be expected but is not found.

It is our contention that the question of the underlying causes of student performance cannot be formulated sensibly under the model of competencies used in the construction of the Diploma Exam and many other high stakes tests. The reason is that according to the competency model on which the examination is based – a model we discuss in the following section – the meaning of performance on the test items is supposed to be built into the meanings of the items themselves. Simply put, on the competency model employed, if one group outscores another, there is but one explanation: the first group has more competency than the second. This explanation follows because getting an item right or wrong is what it means to have or not to have a competency. The question of what explains DIF therefore cannot fruitfully arise, because the answer is predetermined by the test construction.

As will become clear in the following section, although the fact of DIF could be recognized as an interesting issue under the competency model employed in high stakes tests (that is, it might be considered interesting that, say, girls outperform boys on an item), one cannot in that model formulate the thought that groups of boys and girls who perform differently on an item might be employing different underlying psychological constructs, or the thought that groups who perform the same on an item might do so as a result of entirely different underlying causes. From a scientific, and also from an educational perspective, it is knowing the underlying causes of performance that is of central importance. We now turn to problems in the conceptualization of competency that underlie high stakes testing.

## The High Stakes Testing Model of Competency

In high stakes testing, student competency is viewed instrumentally and operationally. Concepts such as ability, knowledge, and educational goals are defined in terms of classes of behaviors. According to the strongest and most influential versions of this view, competency can be completely specified by and reduced to observable behaviors, and competency does not exist independently of those observable behaviors. The logic of high stakes testing is fundamentally dependent upon this conception of competency. Inferences from scores on high stakes tests are based upon a statistical generalization model. In statistical generalization, elements are sampled (at random for most robust generalizations) from a population, domain, or universe of elements. These elements are then examined for a property, and an inference is made about the presence of the property in the population based upon its presence in the sample.

High stakes tests often begin with the construction of a population, the elements of which might be test items, behaviors, or observations. The idea is that a test contains a sample of these elements, and the inferences from scores on the test are statistical generalizations based on properties of the elements sampled. This inference model is fatally flawed for a variety of reasons. We shall briefly document some of these flaws here, but refer the reader to Tomko (1981) for a fuller treatment.

The first flaw is that the elements sampled by high stakes tests cannot support the type of inferences desired. Based on the tests, educators want to say something about children's competencies, about what they can and cannot do. However, there is no clear sense in which the tests sample competencies or abilities. The sampled elements are behaviors, tests items, or observations. It is a requirement of statistical generalization that the concepts used to name the elements sampled and the properties of those elements be the same concepts used in the generalized conclusion. For example, a percentage of red-colored balls in the sample must generalize to a percentage of red-colored balls in the population. Using a statistical generalization model of inference, it is not legitimate to make inferences from properties of behaviors, test items, or observations to children's competencies or abilities.

The second flaw is that the competency model of high stakes tests forces upon us conclusions we should not wish to accept. In the previous example of DIF between groups of boys and girls, we have no alternative but to say that the girls are more competent. The question of DIF needing to be explained disappears as a serious research question, because *by definition* competency is defined as the proportion of test items answered correctly. Once items are designed according to the model and procedures we have described, there is no such issue as *why* the questions are answered differently by boys and girls; no such speculation that they could be doing so because their performance is governed by different psychological processes; no such possibility that they could have the same competency yet perform differently on the test item; and no such possibility that they could have different competencies yet perform the same on the item.

The third flaw has to do with the availability of the elements of the populations for sampling. The soundest statistical generalizations are made when elements are sampled randomly from the population. A requirement of random selection is that all elements have an equal and non-zero chance of being selected. For example, in an opinion survey, it is most desirable that the choice of whom to interview be based on a random selection of individuals each of whom has exactly the same chance of being chosen. Anything less than this (and practice rarely reaches as high as this ideal) compromises the generalization reached on the basis of the sample. Can test items, behaviors, and observations be made available for selection such that each has an equal and non-zero chance of selection?

Let us focus first on test items. The statistical generalization would have to proceed as follows. A population of test items is made available, and a sample (preferably random) is selected. The test items are examined for a property, presumably for whether they were answered correctly by some individual to whom the items were administered. One then generalizes from the proportion of sampled test items that have this property to the proportion in the population that has it. There are several glitches.

The first glitch is that we can infer from properties that the sampled items have, only to properties that the population items *would* have, not the properties they *do* have. The items in the population cannot have the property that they were answered correctly or incorrectly by the individual, because the individual has not even tried most of them. The best it seems we can do is to infer the properties the items would have, if the examinee were to answer them. This is not a trivial problem, because the conclusion is to properties held by items in the future. Since they are in the future, the items with suitable properties cannot be available for selection now, and this is required by the statistical generalization model. Since it is a possible future, and not necessarily an actual one, the items are doubly removed. All elements of the population have to be available for selection at the time the data are collected to make the inference valid, and elements from possible futures cannot be available.

The second glitch has to do with whether the test items are conceived as item-tokens or item-types. An item-token is a specific example of an item, say this one: $3 + 4 = ?$. This item-token is a member of a number of classes of items, $3 + 4 = ?$ on all occasions of its use, $x + y = ?$, which are called item-types. When students take tests, they answer item-tokens. However, the question arises how the item-tokens are selected from the item-types. Without further restrictions, the item-type, $x + y = ?$, is unbounded because it is an infinite class. It is not possible to select randomly from an infinite class, because it is not possible to make all members of the class available for selection. The class can be limited, say by stipulating that $-10$ $< x < 10$ and that $-20 < y < 20$, but in doing this we seriously limit the educational interest in the test, because the significance of the conclusions is severely diminished.

Generally, we want to be able to say, when we say that children can add, that they can add any numbers. At least, we want to be able to say this once they have reached a certain point in their arithmetic learning. The statistical generalization model seems not to be able to lead to a conclusion of this scope. Even with the context of seemingly limited classes, the same problem arises. All we have to do is add the element of occasion to the writing of an item. Generally, when we say that children can solve $3 + 4 = ?$, we mean that they can do it any time. Since we cannot sample randomly from the infinite number of occasions that we would wish our inference to cover, the statistical generalization model collapses once more.

The third glitch is that the second glitch is compounded by the fact that, for any given test, we are usually interested in classes of classes of items. Staying with arithmetic, but recognizing that the conclusion is more general, we are usually interested in whether children can do problems of a related nature: $x + y = ?$, $x - y = ?$, $x + y - z = ?$, and so forth. To make a test, we would first have to sample from the classes themselves, that is, sample the item-types, and then, for each item-type sample item-tokens from it. Notwithstanding the seemingly overwhelming problem of sampling randomly from infinite populations, we have the additional complication of a two-stage sampling procedure. The ordinary statistical generalization model is not able to deal with this complication.

Our analysis for test items applies *mutatis mutandis* if the elements of the population are conceived as behaviors or observations. Moreover, for both behaviors and for observations, educators definitely wish to infer to behavioral and observational events in the future. That is, we wish to infer from the behavior that a child exhibits on a testing occasion, or from an observation that we make of a child on a testing occasion, to behaviors and observations that are likely to occur in the future. Clearly, future behaviors and observations cannot be made available for sampling. Again, the statistical generalization model faces an insurmountable obstacle. For all of the reasons presented in this section, the statistical generalization model is unsuitable for making inferences from scores on high stakes tests.

## An Alternative Model of Competency and Inference from Scores

The model of competency adopted by high stakes testing has been adopted in the name of science. Ironically, the quest to be scientific has crippled the item selection methodology and the ability to make inferences of the desired type from test scores. We say 'ironically', because natural science unabashedly posits unobservable entities that underwrite what we perceive as concrete. The model is also beguiling, because it leads to conclusions we wish to accept in some instances. It seems sensible, for example, to infer from performance on a broad sampling of arithmetic items what arithmetic operations students know how to perform. The problems occur when performance catches us by surprise, such as in instances of DIF. In those situations, the high stakes testing model provides us no alternative but to repeat what was done in developing the test in the first place – namely, to consult subject experts. What would happen to our theorizing about high stakes tests if we were to give up on competencies as classes of behaviors and to adopt a model of competencies as underlying explanatory constructs? What would happen to our practices?

### Competencies as Underlying Explanatory Constructs

According to the model we propose in this section, competencies are real, yet unobservable, powers that people possess in virtue of their natures. Magnetism can serve as a useful analogue from the natural sciences; it is a power certain materials possess in virtue of their natures. If we focus on the strongest form of magnetism, ferromagnetism, then it is a power only five elements possess (cobalt, dysprosium, gadolinium, iron, nickel). The power can exist to varying degrees, and much is known of the internal constitution of these elements that gives rise to magnetism. It is known, for example, that magnetic power arises from moving charges of electricity. At the atomic level, moving electrons within all atoms induce magnetic fields. In the ferromagnetic elements, because of their internal structure, many of these magnetic fields are able to align along a single direction and to produce a cumulative effect and thus a stronger field.

This elementary introduction to the theory of magnetic power allows us to highlight a number of features that are instructive to examine from the point of view of a theory of human competence. First, the theory models the underlying structures and the processes that give rise to magnetism and its effects. Human competency can be seen as arising from mental structures, such as knowledge, repertoires of strategies, and principles of thinking. Second, with magnetism, there is a loose relationship among structures and processes and observable behaviors. Magnetism is not associated with any unique observable behavior or class of behaviors. Magnetic power is not associated with a unique structure, there being five elements and many alloys that can exhibit magnetism. The power of magnetism to attract and repel objects creates observable manifestations, but these are not uniquely associated with magnetism, as electrically charged objects also are able to attract and repel and all objects with mass exhibit gravitational attraction. Analogously, there is no necessity for particular human competencies to arise from one and only one structure and process. There is no theoretical need to assume that there is a delimitable set of observable behaviors that any particular competency enables a person to produce. In fact, it is perfectly reasonable to assume that a competency could give rise to an infinity of behaviors, given the time.

The analogy to magnetism requires supplementation. The most important addition from our point of view is that competencies have an irreducible normative element that cannot be captured or modeled purely descriptively. Thus, for example, the mere fact that students might use particular strategies or principles in their thinking says absolutely nothing about whether that use is appropriate or correct. Normative judgments must be made outside the descriptive account of competencies, unlike the case of physicalist accounts of natural phenomena such as magnetism. This model of competencies leads to an alternative approach to that of statistical generalization for making inferences from test scores.

### Inference to the Best Explanation

In inference to the best explanation, a set of statements is supported to the extent that they provide the best explanation of something (Ennis, 1969). In the case of high stakes testing, an examinee's performance would be explained by the examinee possessing a certain competency or level of competency. The explanation would be fleshed out by providing detail on the underlying cause of the performance in terms of knowledge, cognitive strategies and principles the examinee employed, and a normative appraisal of the appropriateness of the examinee's thinking. The explanation would provide a cognitive model whereby we could see how the performance arose and why it was or was not successful. Detailing such models would require different sorts of validation data than those described for the Diploma Exam. One of the primary sources of data, and the one to be illustrated in this article, is verbal reports of cognitive processing.

## Verbal Reports of Cognitive Processing

Verbal reports of thinking are often thought to provide the most direct evidence possible on the knowledge, strategies, and principles that examinees use to answer items on tests (Ericsson and Simon, 1993; Pressley and Afflerbach, 1995). Such evidence is relevant to the construct validity of those tests, because of the inferences it can support about the content and capabilities of children's minds. In the context of test use, a test could inherit the weight of this direct evidence gathered in the design context, even though in the use context no further direct evidence might be gained on the causes of performance, if, for example, the items were multiple-choice. Eliciting verbal reports of examinees' thinking on tests, comparing the information in the verbal reports to examinees' choices of answers, and using these comparisons systematically to weigh and balance the evidence for the quality of items, seems a valuable approach for developing and validating tests. In particular, it is a way to satisfy two competing desires: the desire to use multiple-choice tests because they provide a convenient and efficient way to gather information on students' competencies, and the desire to have information on the process as well as the products of students' thought.

Verbal reporting also has particular relevance for addressing questions of DIF. Using verbal report methods, investigators could catalogue systematic differences in the ways particular groups of students solve test questions, including the sources of difficulty (or ease) that are extraneous to the construct being measured. Although this approach is not currently used to investigate DIF, some educational researchers (Baxter and Glaser, 1998; Hamilton et al., 1997; Katz et al., 2000) have investigated students' cognitive processing on achievement test questions. Interestingly, some of the findings indicate that students sometimes misinterpret what adults

consider clear question objectives. For example, Hamilton et al. (1997) found that many students, including successful ones, were confused by phrases used in some of the science test questions from the tenth grade National Education Longitudinal Study (NELS) of 1988. The investigators noted 'how use of the small-scale interview procedure provided insights into students' cognitive processes that were not apparent to [the investigators] from reading the items' (Hamilton et al., 1997: 188). In addition, Hamilton et al. (1997) discovered that some items (e.g. Basic Knowledge and Reasoning items) placed greater and unexpected demands on students' reasoning abilities in comparison to other items (Quantitative Science items).

With this introduction, we shall provide some examples from our own research of the use of verbal reports of cognitive processing in developing best explanations of performance on test items. The items, including one on critical thinking, one on mathematical reasoning, and one on reading comprehension, are examples of items that could appear on high stakes tests such as the Diploma Exam.

### Example from a critical thinking test

First, consider an example taken from a study of the design and validation of a critical thinking test of observation appraisal (Norris, 1992). Here is Item 3 from Part A of the test, which is set in the context of a traffic accident:

> A policewoman has been asking Mr. Wang and Ms. Vernon questions. She asks Mr. Wang, who was one of the people involved in the accident, whether he had used his signal.
>
> Mr. Wang answers, '*Yes, I did use my signal.*'
>
> Ms. Vernon had been driving a car which was not involved in the accident. She tells the officer, '*Mr. Wang did not use his signal.* But this didn't cause the accident'.

Examinees were to choose which, if either, of the italicized statements is more credible. To reason through this question correctly, an examinee first needs to derive from the text the relevant information about Wang's and Vernon's involvement. The text is simple enough that most high school students should have no difficulty with this aspect of the task. Second, an examinee must retrieve from background knowledge the relevant facts that not using a turn signal can cause an accident and that being held responsible for an accident can cause trouble with the law. Again, high school students would have such common knowledge. Finally, an examinee has to infer that, because a person knows that admitting to not using a signal could be interpreted as causing an accident, Wang is in a conflict of interest that reduces his credibility with respect to Vernon.

In order to determine whether students who chose the keyed answer, that Ms Vernon was more credible, reasoned well and those who chose another answer did not, we asked students to think aloud on the item. Here are the verbatim transcriptions of the verbal reports of two students:

STUDENT A: . . . ah . . . ah, Mr. Wang, like he probably didn't, like you know, it was just, he probably thought he used his signal, but really didn't. And Miss Vernon, she was watching, so she'd be able to tell from back if he was using it or not. Right? Being the case, so, I'd tend to believe Vernon.

STUDENT B: I would say that he did use his signal because anybody who's in the car . . . coming up to an intersection or anything . . . he, he usually knows what he's doing. So I'd be more inclined to believe the first.

Student A chose the keyed response and Student B an unkeyed one. Neither student thought critically on the item, however. Student A's reasoning that Wang just 'thought he used his signal', but Vernon would 'be able to tell from back' because 'she was watching' is arbitrary. There is no information in the item to justify the claims about either Wang or Vernon. It is used to rationalize a choice of answer rather than to justify it. Given the information in the item, it is just as reasonable to say that Wang would 'be able to tell from inside that he used his signal' and that Vernon just 'thought he did not use his signal'. Student B reasoned just this way and failed to distinguish between Wang's knowing what he had done and his reporting accurately what he had done, and failed to allow that someone in another car can know what another driver is doing.

From these verbal reports we can conclude that Student A thought poorly but chose the correct answer nevertheless, and that Student B thought poorly and chose the incorrect answer. The evidence from Student A tells against the quality of the item; the evidence from Student B speaks to the quality of the item. Evidence such as this, accumulated across many students from the population for which the test is designed and across all the items on the test, can support general conclusions about what the test is or is not measuring.

*Example from a mathematics test*

Second, consider an example taken from a study on the design and validation of objectively scored math items (Leighton et al., 1999). One item involved the following scenario:

> Suppose that you are going to have a party and that you have decided to ride your bike to the store to buy some cans of pop. On the back of your bike is a carrier with a box in which you will carry the cans. This box is 32 cm long, 19 cm wide and 27 cm high. It has a flat lid. Each can of pop is 12.5 cm high, has a 6 cm diameter, and has a volume of 355 ml. If the cans are stacked in one direction (all vertically or all horizontally) on top of one another, what is the maximum number of cans you can carry in the box?

Students were given the opportunity to rate four fictitious student-generated solutions on a 5-point scale extending from 'very good' to 'very bad'. The first student-generated solution involved stacking the cans vertically in the box for a final answer of 30 cans. The second solution involved finding the volume of the box and then dividing the volume of the box by the volume of each can for a final answer of 46. The third solution was very similar to the first, except it involved stacking the cans horizontally for a final answer of 24 cans. The fourth solution involved stacking the cans horizontally and generating an answer of 24, followed by stacking the cans vertically and generating an answer of 30, and then deciding on the vertical stacking. After students rated the four solutions, they were asked to select the best solution from among the four. The fourth solution was keyed the best because it involves exploring both methods of stacking and then comparing the numbers resulting from each method. The second solution was considered the weakest because it neglects the physical properties of the cans.

Consider the thoughts of Crystal, a student with a 93 percent average in mathematics, on solution four (the keyed solution):

CRYSTAL: I like student 4's work because they are calculating both options . . . standing the cans vertically and horizontally. And they explain what they mean . . . like each step. They show a lot of work which is a good thing . . . but I wouldn't have written it all in sentences, I would've just shown my work.

INTERVIEWER: OK.

CRYSTAL: And that's good because they show how many you can fit for both options once again. And their answer is really good because it shows how they got to both solutions and then they decided which one would be better for the party and to answer the question.

INTERVIEWER: Which one was the best solution?

CRYSTAL: Out of the four students, student four had the best solution because he or she explained everything in depth . . . like they considered both possibilities to the solution.

From this report, it appears that Crystal was on track. She acknowledged the advantage of comparing the number of cans generated from each method of stacking. However, there is an aspect of Crystal's thinking that is confusing: although she endorsed the fourth solution, including the benefits of stacking the cans in both directions and then deciding that this is the best solution, she previously had rated solution two (the weakest solution) very highly. Therefore, the interviewer engaged her in further questioning with the expectation of understanding some of her beliefs about the ratings and final choice.

INTERVIEWER: Let's go back to the ratings so I can ask you some more questions. Let's go back to student two . . . you said you would have done it this way.

CRYSTAL: Yeah.

INTERVIEWER: Can I ask you why?

CRYSTAL: I guess because for me . . . formulas make more sense than trying to think geometrically . . . like well . . . this can is this tall it fits better this way . . . I think better using formulas and all that.

INTERVIEWER: OK. If we could go back to student two for a minute . . . you gave student two a completely right for the final answer and also you gave student four a completely right. Do you think both answers are completely right?

CRYSTAL: Well . . . student two's was really good and it could have been really close 'cause I didn't know the answer to this problem . . . And . . . But it was better than right but it wasn't completely right and student four's . . . after looking at it . . . is completely right . . . like it would be the right answer. Student two's is closer to the answer than the other ones because of the work she showed and whatever, but it is not completely right . . . it's not 100 percent . . . it would be about 98 percent maybe if I didn't know the right answer. And student four's would have to be about 100 percent.

Although Crystal chose solution four as the best answer, she is only slightly less enthusiastic about solution two (recall that there is a large discrepancy in the solutions, 46 cans versus 30 cans). Her approval of solution two raises the question whether Crystal endorsed solution four for the right reasons. It is possible that she understands the benefits of trying more than one method of solving a problem (such as stacking the cans in two directions) but fails to understand, more fundamentally, the constraints on the solution to this task – that the stacking involves solids within a box and not liquids within a container. What kind of inference can be made about Crystal's performance? If we knew only that she selected solution four as the best answer, we might be tempted to infer that she engaged in sound spatial thinking. But this inference would be wrong. With the verbal report information, we have raised many questions about Crystal's reasoning compared to the definitive answers suggested by the performance on the multiple-choice aspect of the task.

*Example from a reading test*

Consider an example from a pilot version of *The Test of Inference Ability in Reading Comprehension* (TIA) (Phillips, 1989; Phillips and Patterson, 1987), which consists of three full-length stories representative of the three kinds of text at the middle grade levels: narration, exposition and description. 'UFOs' is an exposition about unusual phenomena, telling of different UFO reports, offering plausible explanations for some of the reports, and suggesting that with improved technology we may be able to explain UFOs. The first paragraph of the UFO story and the test item to be discussed follow.

> Thousands of people around the world believe that they have seen weird, unidentified flying objects. Anything in the sky that people do not understand may be called a UFO. People sometimes call UFOs 'flying saucers', 'spaceships from other planets' and 'extraterrestrial space mobiles'. Stories have been told that UFOs light up an area with many colored lights and that creatures of different sizes and colors have been seen in them. Another story was that UFOs drain power from any electrical sources in the area. UFO stories may be very different.

> Question 2. Anything unidentified in the sky might be called a UFO because:

> A. that is the term used when you do not know what it is.

B.  that is something which nobody has ever seen.
C.  that is what people call it when they jump to conclusions.
D.  that is the shape of whatever it is in the sky overhead.

Selection A was deemed to be the best answer. Stephanie, a grade six student, chose B. However, the use of verbal reporting revealed that she relied upon good reasoning. When asked why she chose B, Stephanie replied:

STEPHANIE:  Well, it says in the story that many people have seen weird things so they don't really know what they have seen. Not everyone has seen the same things, which makes me wonder what they have seen, or if they have seen anything at all.

INTERVIEWER:  I'm not sure I follow you, can you tell me more about why you chose B?

STEPHANIE:  I think that it's called a UFO because no one knows what it is, maybe no one has ever seen anything like it before, so we don't know what it is or where it came from, it's unidentified, it's a UFO.

The vexing problem is that given Stephanie's explanation, it is evident she understands why unidentified objects in the sky are called UFOs, yet she has selected an answer not keyed correct. Indeed, her reasoning suggests she should have chosen A. Therefore, we cannot assume that when a student has given a wrong answer that the student does not understand.

Pat, a grade seven student, selected the correct answer A. However, hearing his explanation, it would appear that he gave the correct answer for poor reasons. When asked why he chose A, Pat replied:

PAT:  Well, we call anything that we are unsure of what it is unidentified. I can think of lots of things that are unidentified like life forms in the ocean, cars that are unfamiliar to us, strangers we don't know, you know all sorts of things can be UFOs.

INTERVIEWER:  I'm not sure I follow you. Can you tell me more about why you chose A?

PAT:  It's simple. Stuff that we don't know what they are, we can't identify them. So they are called UFOs.

The interviewer queried whether all unidentified stuff would be called UFOs and Pat replied 'Oh yah, that's what it means.' Therefore, we cannot assume that when a student has selected the keyed answer that the student has selected it for the right reasons.

## Cognitive models and tests

Cognitive models of performance tend to cover features of thought such as: patterns of attention (Leighton and Dawson, 2001; Norris and Phillips, 1994; Phillips and Norris, 1999); patterns of dependence, overdependence, underdependence on various sources of information (Phillips, 2002); completeness and incompleteness of thinking (Leighton and Bisanz, 2003; Norris and Phillips, 1987); reference to and reliance upon norms and principles of thinking (Norris and Phillips, 1987); strategy use and meta-cognition (Norris et al., 2003; Phillips, 1988); the generality of thinking; and knowledge structures (Leighton and Bisanz, 2003; Leighton and Sternberg, 2003). The verbal reports of students' thinking that we have illustrated can support the development of cognitive models of test taking by revealing a number of these features. We shall illustrate each by reference to the verbal reports.

## Patterns of attention

The features of test items to which students attend can reveal much about their thinking. For example, in the critical thinking example, Student A focused on possible facts about the driver and the witness that were not introduced in the item, and limited the possibilities explored to just one conjecture about each person. Student B focused on a possible fact only about the driver and said nothing about the witness. Neither student attended to possible alternative interpretations. In the mathematics example, Crystal's evaluation of solution two focused on the formula for volume without attention to the actual goal of the task to indicate the number of cans that fit in the box. Crystal's evaluation of solution four focused on the use of two methods for solving the problem. She also focused on the amount of work shown, which is not an indicator of the correctness of the solution at all. In the reading example, Pat focused on the word 'unidentified' and did not make effective use of the definition of UFO provided in the specific context of sightings in the sky. Stephanie's initial focus was on weird things that people were not really sure they had seen. Responding to the interviewer's query for clarification, she was very clear and precise about why she thinks anything unidentified in the sky might be called an unidentified flying object – even though she has selected an incorrect response.

*Patterns of dependence, overdependence, underdependence*

In the critical thinking example, both Students A and B showed too much dependence for their decisions on possible facts concerning the driver and witness drawn from their background knowledge and did not depend enough upon the information provided in the text of the item. In the mathematics example, Crystal showed an overdependence on formulas as illustrated by her comments on solution two and also overdependence on amount of work illustrated as an indicator of good mathematical thinking. In contrast, Crystal showed an underdependence on the information describing the task objectives. In the reading example, Pat showed an overdependence on the single word 'unidentified' and on his background knowledge. His choice of answer depended little on the context of the sightings in the sky. Stephanie demonstrated a balanced dependence upon both relevant text information and background knowledge.

*Completeness and incompleteness of thinking*

In the critical thinking example, both Students A and B showed incompleteness of thinking in their over-reliance on certain possibilities they drew from their background knowledge, in their under-reliance on other possibilities that they could have considered from their background knowledge, and from their lack of attention to the details that the text provided. Furthermore, both students failed to compare the driver and witness on equal grounds, and Student B did not seem really to consider one of the people at the accident scene. In the mathematics example, Crystal showed completeness of thinking when expressing her thoughts on the value of using multiple methods to solve a problem and then deciding on the best solution. However, in the end, she exposed incomplete thinking by failing to grasp that solution two does not meet the goal of the task. In so doing, she raised serious doubts about whether she has understood the problem at all. In the reading example, Pat showed incompleteness of thinking and failed to question his interpretation even when the interviewer questioned him. Pat displayed a confidence unwarranted by the examples he cited. Stephanie showed greater completeness of thinking than Pat even though she chose an unkeyed answer.

*Reference to and reliance upon norms and principles of thinking*

In the critical thinking example, neither Student A nor Student B recognized the relevance of conflict of interest in reducing the reliability of testimony. Student A seemed to use a norm comparing the reliability of opinion versus observation, but did not use the norm in a balanced way. Student B seemed to rely upon a norm associated with the reliability of first-hand knowledge, but did not set it against the countervailing norm of conflict of interest. In the mathematics example, Crystal revealed reliance on such criteria as the importance of showing your work and the supremacy of formulaic approaches to solving mathematical problems. In addition, she seemed to have a probabilistic scale on which to evaluate solutions to mathematical tasks. This is evidenced when she assigned a 98 percent correct to solution two and a 100 percent correct to solution four. She also demonstrated the general desirability of searching for multiple solutions and comparing the solutions in order to choose the best one. In the reading example, Pat was concerned to construct a response that provided what he considered to be analogous examples to support his interpretation. However, he did not analyze the available text information and depended upon one word (unidentified) out of three (unidentified flying objects) rather than seeing the necessity of synthesizing the information from all three. He made use of partial text information. Stephanie demonstrated an analysis and synthesis of relevant text information and background knowledge to construct a consistent and complete inference.

*Strategy use and meta-cognition*

In the critical thinking example, neither Student A nor Student B explicitly considered alternatives, but seemed to focus on a single point. Also, neither student appeared to assess the importance of the information provided in the item for answering it. The approach of both students seemed to involve deciding whom to believe and then trying to justify the choice, rather than coming to a decision as the result of a process of reasoning. There was no evidence that either Student A or Student B wondered whether his or her response was adequate given the nature of the task. In the mathematics example, Crystal failed to realize that use of the formula for volume is inappropriate when the goal of the task is to determine the number of cans that can be stacked in one direction. In her representation of the problem, she neglected to earmark the physical properties of the objects, which compromised the conclusions she reached about solution two. In the reading example, Pat failed to question his default assumption that the word 'unidentified' could be applied to anything unknown. He continued to confirm his partial use of available text information by citing examples from his background knowledge to the exclusion of available and relevant text information. Stephanie selected a response that was inconsistent with her interpretation. It appears she confused 'never seen' with 'unidentified' in her choice of answer, though her thinking showed that she understood the concept of unidentified flying objects.

*The generality of thinking*

In the critical thinking example, neither Student A nor Student B seemed to look for an overarching principle to ground a choice among answers. Both focused on particularities that were mere unsupported conjectures, and there was no evidence of abstraction to general forms of sound thinking. In the mathematics example, Crystal appeared to recognize a host of possible solutions, but seemed to suggest the best solution is a matter of personal interest. She did demonstrate the general desirability of searching for multiple solutions and comparing the solutions in order to choose the best one. In the reading example, Pat's thinking about the inferential task demonstrated that he is not strategic and that he is unprincipled in his interpretation. His response made sense to him but he was not concerned with general issues of acceptable thinking. Stephanie's thinking about the inferential task tended to be consistent and complete, but she could have been more systematic in her answer selection by adopting the general strategy of adjudicating each one prior to making a choice.

*Knowledge structures*

In the critical thinking example, both Student A and Student B appealed to everyday knowledge about people's psychology, such as the difference between knowing and thinking, observing and opining. Neither student appealed to other features from everyday psychology, such as the distinction between knowing what is the case and telling the truth about what is the case, the effect of fear of getting in trouble with the law, and the effect of speaking from an objective position. In the mathematics example, Crystal demonstrated her knowledge of mathematics by recognizing the formula for volume, and demonstrated her knowledge of searching for multiple solutions. In the reading example, Pat demonstrated that he can identify the words, construct partial inferences, and call upon partially relevant background knowledge. However, he was not guided by the principle to seek a complete and consistent interpretation of the text information. Stephanie could identify the words, and construct consistent and complete inferences by attending to and monitoring for relevant text and background knowledge information.

# Implications and Conclusions

According to Alberta Learning, those who develop the Diploma Exam consider validity and reliability both at the planning and at the field-testing stages of the development process. However, the assumption that these stages by themselves adequately address validity and reliability might be too optimistic. At both of these stages, adults – albeit subject experts – make inferences about what students' interpretations of and reactions to test questions will be, without any evidence of how students actually think. These adult inferences are speculative, and potentially camouflage poorly behaving test questions that lead to either inflated or deflated estimates of students' competence. Implicit in this process appears to be a belief something like the following: if you wish to generalize to future performance on test items (particularly of the objectively scored type commonly used on high stakes tests), then it does not matter what students' reasons are for the answers they choose. It is our view that this belief is false: In order to infer from present to future performance of students, we must be able to point to some strategy or consistent method of reflection that they have used or failed to use. The Diploma Exam, like many other high stakes exams, could strengthen its claims to validity and reliability by investigating students' cognitive processing of test questions. If the intention is to project future performance outside of testing, then performance on tests cannot be understood solely from features of the test items themselves.

The verbal reports of students' thinking offered us a vision of the content and capabilities of their minds that their chosen answers to the items alone could not. From the verbal reports we see how students sometimes chose keyed answers on the basis of poor reasoning and unkeyed answers on the basis of good reasoning. This evidence alone demonstrates that we cannot generalize solely from responses to multiple-choice items, without at least some evidence of how students reason about them. That evidence can come either from the students whose performance we wish to generalize or from students just like them who have been asked to provide their reasoning on the items. Without such evidence we cannot generalize, because we see in the verbal reports that a good deal of the students' reasoning was arbitrary. Given that fact, it is most reasonable to assume that it would *not* be replicated on future occasions, and thus reasonable to assume that students' answer choices would differ also.

So what is the value of using verbal reports of thinking to learn about the content and capabilities of students' minds? What inferences can such data support that additional performance data on more objectively scored items cannot? Verbal reports address in specific detail the question of why students answer test items the way that they do. Although verbal reports provide no window into the brain, they are revelatory of thinking at a much deeper level than objectively scored test items alone. Also, because the information gained is indicative of causal processes and can support the development of causal models of test performance, they are projective of future performance to a degree that objectively scored high stakes tests themselves cannot be.

We maintain that verbal reports such as those we documented here can help improve high stakes tests in a number of ways. First, the detail they provide on the errors of students' thinking can be used to develop response options that simulate or replicate those types of errors. Having accomplished this, students' answer choices would be able to support more specific and secure inferences about their thinking and would consequently be much more valuable for diagnosis and remediation. Second, the information from verbal reports would enable test developers to design items that target different aspects of the cognitive model that the reports imply, such as patterns of attention and dependence on various sources of information, completeness of thinking, reliance upon norms and principles of thought, strategy use and meta-cognition and knowledge structures used. Third, tests developed in this manner would lead to greater understanding of students' thinking compared to tests that are developed entirely from adults' perspectives. Finally, there are enormous implications for construct validity, including helping to decipher occurrences of DIF, defining more precisely the limits of constructs underlying the test, enabling more exact representation of what tests are measuring, and learning more about what we mean by the psychological constructs we use and attempt to measure.

Returning to our title: 'What is at Stake in Knowing the Content and Capabilities of Children's Minds?', the challenge occurs once it is realized that better tests yield results that are more difficult to dispute. As we have shown, current tests can be disputed on the basis of the wealth of evidence that students can choose answers keyed correct yet think poorly and answers keyed incorrect yet think well. However, what would happen if those deficiencies in tests were addressed using the approach to cognitive modeling that we have described? Tests based upon cognitive models would set a higher standard for students, because right answers would be rewarded only when conjoined with sound reasoning. If students cannot rise to those standards, and clear deficiencies in their reasoning can be seen as the cause, then what might be revealed also are deficiencies in teaching and in the way that educators conceive the goals of schooling and education. Perhaps in rewarding correct answers without attention to the reasoning that underlies them, the education system rewards the types of poor thinking found in our examples: thinking that pays little attention to the logical requirements of a task, but that pays much attention to irrelevant aspects of the situation; thinking that values opinion supporting pre-determined answers and ignores the principled application of criteria to the contested sides of an issue; thinking that settles on the first thought that makes sense and that fails to consider obvious alternative considerations; and, generally, thinking that is not turned upon itself as a check against bias, prejudice, and credulity. What is at stake in knowing the content and capabilities of children's minds is the quality of the education system that is charged with the development of mind in our youngest citizens.

# References

Alberta Learning (2003) *Diploma Examination Development Process*, brochure, Learner Assessment Branch, Government of Alberta, Canada: Alberta Learning.

American Educational Research Association, American Psychological Association, National Council on Measurement in Education (1999) *Standards for Educational and Psychological Testing* (Washington, DC: American Educational Research Association).

Baxter, G. P. and Glaser, R. (1998) 'Investigating the cognitive complexity of science assessments', *Educational Measurement: Issues and Practice*, 17: 37–45.

Bielinski, J. and Davison, M. L. (2001) 'A sex difference by item difficulty interaction in multiple choice mathematics items administered to national probability samples', *Journal of Educational Measurement*, 38: 51–77.

Camilli, G., and Shepard, L. (1994) *Methods for Identifying Biased Test Items* (Newbury Park, CA: Sage).

Curren, R. R. (2004) 'Educational measurement and knowledge of other minds', *Theory and Research in Education* 2(3): 235–53.

Davis, A. (1998) *The Limits of Educational Assessment* (Oxford: Blackwell).

Engelhard, G., Hansche, L. and Rutledge, K. E. (1990) 'Accuracy of bias review judges in identifying differential item functioning on teacher certification tests', *Applied Measurement in Education*, 3: 346–60.

Ennis, R. H. (1969) *Logic in Teaching* (Englewood Cliffs, NJ: Prentice-Hall).

Ericsson, K. A. and Simon, H. A. (1993) *Protocol Analysis* (Cambridge, MA: MIT Press).

Gierl, M. J. and Khaliq, S. N. (2001) 'Identifying sources of differential item and bundle functioning on translated achievement tests', *Journal of Educational Measurement*, 38: 164–87.

Hamilton, L. S., Nussbaum, E. M. and Snow, R. E. (1997) 'Interview procedures for validating science assessments', *Applied Measurement in Education*, 10: 181–200.

Katz, I. R., Bennett, E. and Berger, A. E. (2000) 'Effects of response format on difficulty of SAT-Mathematics items: It's not the strategy', *Journal of Educational Measurement*, 37: 39–57.

Leighton, J. P. and Bisanz, G. L. (2003) 'Children's and adults' knowledge and models of reasoning about the ozone layer and its depletion', *International Journal of Science Education*, 25: 117–39.

Leighton, J. P. and Dawson, M. R. W. (2001) 'A parallel processing model of Wason's card selection task', *Cognitive Systems Research*, 2–3: 207–31.

Leighton, J. P., Rogers, W. T. and Maguire, T. O. (1999) 'Assessment of student problem solving on ill-defined tasks', *Alberta Journal of Educational Research*, 45: 409–27.

Leighton, J. P. and Sternberg, R. J. (2003) 'Reasoning and problem solving', in A. F. Healy and R. W. Proctor (eds.), *Experimental Psychology* (New York: John Wiley), pp. 623–48.

Norris, S. P. (1992) 'A demonstration of the use of verbal reports of thinking in multiple-choice critical thinking test design', *Alberta Journal of Educational Research*, 38: 155–76.

Norris, S. P. and Phillips, L. M. (1987) 'Explanations of reading comprehension: Schema theory and critical thinking theory', *Teachers College Record*, 89: 281–306.

Norris, S. P. and Phillips. L. M. (1994) 'The relevance of a reader's knowledge within a perspectival view of reading', *Journal of Reading Behavior*, 26: 391–412.

Norris, S. P., Phillips, L. M. and Korpan, C. A. (2003) 'University students' interpretation of media reports of science and its relationship to background knowledge, interest, and reading difficulty', *Journal for the Public Understanding of Science*, 12: 123–45.

Phillips, L. M. (1988) 'Young readers' inference strategies in reading comprehension', *Cognition and Instruction*, 5: 193–222.

Phillips, L. M. (1989) 'Developing and validating assessments of inference ability in reading comprehension', *Technical Report no. 452* (Champaign, IL: Centre for the Study of Reading, University of Illinois, ERIC Document Reproduction Service Number ED 303 767).

Phillips, L. M. (2002) 'Making new or making do: Epistemological, normative, and pragmatic bases of literacy', in J. Brockmeier, M. Wang and D. R. Olson (eds.), *Literacy, Narrative and Culture* (Surrey, UK: Curzon Press), pp. 283–300.

Phillips, L. M. and Norris, S. P. (1999) 'Interpreting popular reports of science: What happens when the reader's world meets the world on paper?', *International Journal of Science Education*, 21: 317–27.

Phillips, L. M. and Patterson, C. C. (1987) *Phillips–Patterson Test of Inference Ability in Reading Comprehension (Multiple-Choice Format)* (St John's, NL: Institute for Educational Research and Development, Memorial University of Newfoundland).

Pressley, M. and Afflerbach, P. (1995) *Verbal Protocols of Reading: The Nature of Constructively Responsive Reading* (Hillsdale, NJ: Erlbaum).

Roussos, L. and Stout, W. (1996) 'A multidimensionality-based DIF analysis paradigm', *Applied Psychological Measurement*, 20: 355–71.

Tomko, T. N. (1981) 'The Logic of Criterion-Referenced Testing', unpublished doctoral dissertation (Champaign, IL: University of Illinois at Urbana-Champaign).

# PART V

# Curriculum and the Content of Schooling

# Introduction to Part V

If we could have a general theory of the curriculum, what kind of theory would it be? It might be *descriptive* or *diagnostic*, and grounded in social theory. It might be *prescriptive* and grounded in theories of learning and development, as some forms of *constructivism* aspire to be. It might be *prescriptive* and grounded in philosophical theories of human flourishing or knowledge. Some theoretical work bearing on curriculum does not aim to articulate a general theory, however, but to establish more limited conclusions about specific parts of the curriculum or the enterprise of curriculum design and planning. There are also questions concerning the content of what is communicated or learned in schools that do not pertain to the curriculum as such, or do not pertain *only* to the curriculum. Questions about moral and civic education fall under the latter category.

As we saw in Part I, a major focus of philosophical concern with the curriculum has been the idea of a *liberal* education or education in the *liberal arts*. One contemporary response to this, evident in Appiah's paper in Part III (see reading no. 28) and in the lecture by Maxine Greene (no. 60), has been to contest the "canon" or traditional textual basis of liberal studies. How *multicultural* should curricula be, and on what principles should they be designed? Another contemporary response, represented in Part I by the reading by Freire (no. 8), has been to impute to schools the function of reproducing inequality (see the introduction to Part III), and to identify a "hidden curriculum" (expressed by the social organization of the school) or theorize a hidden aspect of the curriculum. An influential theory of the latter variety holds that school curricula are systems of exclusionary knowledge codes that mediate the transmission of privilege (see Feinberg, 1983). A third contemporary response to the liberal arts model argues that the curriculum should be based not on the diverse forms of disciplinary knowledge but on diverse human developmental potentials and diverse "centers of care" or objects of potential interest and attachment (Noddings, 1992).

The readings that follow will focus on moral education, which has been a major focus of philosophical concern with the content of schooling, and controversies drawn from each of four major areas of the curriculum: the social sciences, natural sciences, humanities, and "health" or what was once called "life adjustment" studies. More specifically, we will consider the teaching of history and patriotism, the evolution *v.* creationism controversy, sex education, and the endangered arts.

## Moral Education

Many philosophically significant questions arise in connection with moral education, and some of those questions are evident in other parts of this anthology in the writings of Plato, Rousseau, Dewey, Callan, Brighouse, Appiah, Blum, Levinson and Levinson, Hansen, Noddings, Chamberlain and Houston, and Lipman. Our concern here is with some central ideas about the nature of moral learning and the content and structure of moral education. One important focus of debate since the 1960s has been the *cognitive-developmental theory* of moral development and education, developed by Lawrence Kohlberg. According to this theory, human beings develop morally by progressing through a fixed sequence of six stages of increasingly other-regarding or "universal" moral reasoning, in which the final stage corresponds to a genuinely moral commitment to *universalizable* rules of action. Kohlberg originally advocated a moral education consisting of discussion of moral dilemmas in order to encourage progress through these stages and across diverse domains of decision-making, though he later advocated a *just community approach* that incorporated elements of Dewey's democratic progressivism and equal voices for students in formulating school rules (see Dewey, 1975; Power et al., 1989). Since the 1980s, a second important focus of debate has been virtue-centered or neo-Aristotelian approaches, which defend roles for both habituation and critical reason in moral education, and hold that emotion, perception, and judgment are developmentally interrelated. Like Kohlberg's just community approach, these neo-Aristotelian approaches have sought to overcome a perceived theoretical neglect of moral *motivation* and commitment. A third focus of recent work has been *identity formation* and its relationship to moral development and motivation.

In the reading "Moral Conventions and Moral Lessons" (no. 54), Robert K. Fullinwider begins by asking how the school's curriculum may contribute to the development of children's moral judgment, imagination, and reasoning. The essence of learning morality, he says, is "learning how to apply moral concepts and make discriminations among different cases," first through doing it and then through initiation into a "tradition of discourse and criticism." A moral education is *case-based* and it "is first and foremost an education in literature, history, drama, and art," since it is through these subjects that we can "vicariously live the moral lives of other people" and extend and deepen our grasp of moral language, complexity, and the values underlying moral precepts. Fullinwider illustrates these ideas, then turns to Kohlberg's theory and the opposition it posits

between *conventional* thought and mature *moral* thought. Fullinwider notes the philosophical origins of Kohlberg's conception of mature moral judgment, and argues that the sequence of stages in the latter's theory rests on the "very basic error" of confusing the universal and the general. The theory misidentifies the nature of real moral judgments and wrongly equates "our conventions" (which include traditions of criticism) with "majority public sentiment," Fullinwider concludes.

Aristotle is widely understood to hold that the work of moral education is to encourage *good habits*, because good habits are the source of *good character*. There is much truth in this, but the aim of my "Cultivating the Moral and Intellectual Virtues" (no. 55) is to provide a more complete exploration of Aristotle's conception of moral education. According to Aristotle, habit does not create *true* or *complete* virtue, because the moral and intellectual virtues form an interdependent *unity*. True virtue is not blind but *judicious*. It involves *good judgment* (*phronêsis*), and it is arguably the proper aim of moral education. It follows that moral education must cultivate both the dispositions of desire and perception that Aristotle calls moral virtues *and* the powers of understanding, judgment, and reasoning that he calls intellectual virtues. Kohlberg was not alone in perceiving an opposition between the inculcation of community values and the encouragement of critical thinking, however, and this suggests there are at least *prima facie* tensions in the instructional synthesis implied by Aristotle's conception of true virtue. An examination of these tensions yields a *paradox of progressive morality*, and the reading concludes with a survey of four possible solutions to this paradox.

J. David Velleman's reading "Motivation by Ideal" (no. 56) is about moral motivation, and it offers an unusually revealing examination of the relationships between motivation, identity, and the narratives that structure our initiation into practices and express the ideals we emulate and sometimes come to embody. Its three-part thesis is that "[moral motivation] often depends on the force of an ideal; an ideal gains motivational force when we identify with it; and acting out of identification with an ideal is like a game of make-believe, in which we pretend to be that with which we identify." The main "game of make-believe" or form of learning that Velleman examines is Tae Kwon Do. "A martial art typically relies on a . . . story-within-a-story," he writes, an "inner" story of combat, and an "outer" story, "which is usually a fiction only for beginning students and then only briefly, . . . that they are devotees of a venerable tradition, transmitted to them by a revered master and shared with others in a spirit of humility and mutual self-restraint." There is an obvious tension between the two stories, and Velleman probes that tension in order to explore the interaction between moral motivation and other motives. We enact self-images and narratives that we make up but make true through the enactment, and in doing that we come to be motivated by ideals, he says. The emulation of many moral ideals requires make-believe, but the emulation of Immanuel Kant's ideal image of a *moral will* may not require make-believe; "to do the moral thing by emulating a moral person really is to be moral, since enacting a moral image of oneself is what being a moral person consists in," Velleman concludes.

## Curricular Controversies

Nationalistic sentiments in times of war tend to be reflected in greater efforts to inculcate patriotism in the schools. This may reinforce the sense of solidarity a nation needs to persevere through the rigors of war, but it may also contribute to the persecution of suspect minorities, a stifling of healthy public debate, and acquiescence in bad government policies (see Ben-Porath, 2006). Should schools teach patriotism, but counterbalance that with forms of education that might strengthen democratic values? Should schools promote cosmopolitan values instead of patriotic ones and treat national sovereignty as "provisional," as Dewey recommended (in reading no. 6)? In the reading "Should We Teach Patriotic History?" (no. 57), Harry Brighouse argues that we should be "deeply suspicious of teaching patriotism in schools" and should regard history as a "particularly inappropriate" vehicle for teaching it. He surveys four principled justifications of patriotism, and responds with several objections: Patriotism is generally "tainted by xenophobia and jingoism." Inculcation of it in government schools undermines unencumbered consent to the state and thereby the state's legitimacy. Its inculcation interferes with spontaneous cultural formation and is too easily used as a weapon against movements for justice. It does not "help us carry out our duties to those with whom we share a scheme of social cooperation" in a world in which those schemes are increasingly global. Turning to the teaching of history, Brighouse advocates

a "warts and all" approach that aims to: (1) convey the truth about history; (2) enable students to discern the social processes that shape history; and (3) enable students to understand and think critically about the institutions that shape their society and world. He argues that these legitimate purposes are jeopardized by attempts to promote a national identity, because "in practice it is so hard to pursue the patriotic purposes while respecting the truth."

Is the teaching of biological evolution controversial in any First World country besides the United States? It may not be, but Robert T. Pennock's reading "Should Creationism be Taught in the Public Schools?" (no. 58) frames a response to the creation *v.* evolution debate that suggests principles of curriculum choice which are applicable anywhere. Pennock recounts the history of the exclusion of the theory of evolution from American public school curricula, which ended with the overturning of anti-evolution laws in 1968, and subsequent attempts by foes of evolution to dilute or reverse that legal defeat. Pennock surveys the varieties of anti-evolutionary views and movements, as well as their arguments from fairness, parental rights, academic freedom, epistemological viewpoint diversity, and religious protection. It is not unfair "to teach what is true even though many people don't want to hear it," writes Pennock. He responds to these diverse arguments, leaving for last an argument of Alvin Plantinga's that challenges the teaching of evolution on the basis of a parent's alleged basic right "not to have comprehensive beliefs taught to her children that contradict her own comprehensive beliefs." Pennock argues that a rational social contract would not include any such right, since it could result in schools being "forced to omit even basic scientific facts," and would leave children hostage to the dictates of parents who may be bigots, ideologues, narrow-minded, or ignorant. A rational social contract would preclude public institutions from teaching views based on "private epistemologies" and require that they teach "public knowledge."

Disagreements about sex education abound, and Michael J. Reiss provides an illuminating framework for sorting them out in "Conflicting Philosophies of School Sex Education" (no. 59). The basis for his paper is a content survey of sex education instructional materials in the UK. Relying on that, he identifies the "main philosophical frameworks within which sex education in the United Kingdom is presented." These hold that sex education should not occur in schools; that its aim should be to promote physical health; that it should promote personal auto-nomy; that it should promote responsible sexual behavior; that it should take place within a religious framework. Reiss provides a balanced assessment of the advantages and disadvantages of each of these proposed approaches, and in doing that lays the groundwork for "a possible way forward." A "valid" sex education program for schools "promotes per-sonal autonomy, requires pupils to consider the needs and wishes of others, and takes place within a moral framework." Because there is no fully settled moral framework governing sexual conduct in a pluralistic society such as the UK, Reiss holds that "schools need to enable pupils to appreciate the diversity of views that may validly be held about controversial issues related to sexuality."

Why are the arts "treated as frivolities and thrust . . . quite aside in our schools"? Why is it important that they not be treated this way? In Maxine Greene's 1993 lecture "The Artistic–Aesthetic Curriculum"

(no. 60), she speaks directly to teachers gathered at the Lincoln Center Institute, evoking many of the recurrent themes in her decades of work on behalf of education in the arts: the capacity of the arts to "release" our imagination and perception; the way this enables us "to look at things as if they could be otherwise" and take action to transform them; the "initiation into something grand and lustrous" that combats boredom and banality and moves students to reach beyond themselves and the everyday; the location of artistic meaning in the audience's participatory involvement in making connections to its own lived experience; the role of the arts in promoting "active learning" and the creation of school communities; the presumption that all cultures have "something important to say," and can move us toward a multicultural "fusion of horizons." As teachers of the arts, "We all have a world to make, in a larger world that does not always understand," writes Greene.

## References

Ben-Porath, S. 2006: *Citizenship under Fire: Democratic Education in Times of Conflict* (Princeton, NJ: Princeton University Press).

Dewey, J. 1975: *Moral Principles in Education* (Carbondale, IL: Southern Illinois University Press).

Feinberg, W. 1983: *Understanding Education* (Cambridge: Cambridge University Press).

Noddings, N. 1992: *The Challenge to Care in Schools* (New York: Teachers College Press).

Power, F. C., Higgins, A., and Kohlberg, L. 1989: *Lawrence Kohlberg's Approach to Moral Education* (New York: Columbia University Press).

# Moral Education

# 54

# Moral Conventions and Moral Lessons

## Robert K. Fullinwider

### I

In 1684 John Locke began writing a series of letters to his friend Edward Clarke, who wanted advice on how to educate his child. Locke, the physician and bachelor, offered copious suggestions on every topic, from diet to clothing to good habits for the bowels. But his main interest centered on how to produce good character. " 'Tis Vertue," he wrote, "which is the hard and valuable part to be aimed at in Education. . . . All other Considerations and Accomplishments should give way and be postpon'd to this."[1] And as to the best circumstances for education in virtue, Locke had this advice. Asked by Clarke whether it was better to send his child to school or to educate him at home, Locke recommended the latter:

> [H]e that lays the Foundation of his Son's Fortune in Vertue, advised Locke, takes the only sure and warrantable way. And 'tis not the Waggeries or Cheats practised amongst School-boys, 'tis not their Rough-ness one to another, nor the well laid Plots of Robbing an Orchard together, that make an able Man; But the Principles of Justice, Generosity and Sobriety, joyn'd with Observation and Industry, Qualities, which I judge School-boys do not learn much from one another.

Locke went on to say, "He that considers how diametrically opposite the Skill of living well, and managing, as a Man should do, his affairs in the World, is to that malapertness, tricking, or violence learnt amongst Schoolboys, will think the Faults of Privater Education infinitely to be preferr'd."[2]

We, of course, don't do as Clarke did and educate our children at home; we send them to school. And Locke's observations suggest one important reason – as valid now as then – why our schools must attend to moral education. Having brought boys and girls together in a school, where they are bound to learn from each other, we cannot avoid the responsibility to make sure that their learning is appropriately corrected and guided. We cannot disclaim responsibility for their moral development once we have set them at hazard to influences that may be corrupting, harmful, misleading, or dangerous.

Not everything children learn from one another is corrupting, harmful, and misleading; children are not always up to waggery and orchard-robbing. In fact, contrary to Locke, it is principally from their interactions with one another – in their games and play and social life – that children do learn the rudiments of justice and generosity and other

Previously published in *Social Theory and Practice* 15(3) (Fall 1989), pp. 321–38. © 1989 *Social Theory and Practice*. Reprinted with permission of *Social Theory and Practice*.

virtues, though Locke was probably right about sobriety. Children develop from their interchange with one another a vocabulary of moral criticism and response. They learn how to classify snitches and cowards and bullies and double-crossers and stuck-ups and cheats; and they know these chaps don't deserve admiration or acceptance, in contrast to true friends, good sports, and loyal confederates, who merit respect and emulation. They learn about stinginess and generosity and sharing and selfishness, and how to apply these concepts. It is not stinginess, for example, to refuse to share with someone trying to exploit or take advantage of you; and it is not generosity to give with an ulterior motive to put another in your debt; and children soon learn to make these distinctions.

And they argue. "Susie is stuck-up," accuses one. "She thinks she's too good to take part in our games." "No she doesn't," responds the second. "She's just shy; that's all." "No, it's more than shy; she always has that snooty look on her face." "It isn't a snooty look; it's a squint. Her eyesight is bad." "Well, she always gets good grades!" "It isn't stuck-up to get good grades." Back and forth, the disputants assert or contest the application of a concept, referring to different features of Susie that ought or ought not to weigh in assessing her attitude toward others.

Behind the argument lies a common understanding that being stuck-up reflects an unwarranted sense of superiority. Asked to explain why this sense is unwarranted, the two disputants might fall back on principles like "everybody is as good as anybody else," or "we're all equal in the sight of God." They may not be very articulate about these principles or how the principles play a role, if at all, in the assessment of Susie, but they will nevertheless commit themselves to judgments that presuppose some view about the superiority and inferiority of people. If they are reflective, they may be led to explore directly their broader views and how they cohere with their other beliefs about goodness and badness.

An entire moral education transpires in the intercourse of children and adolescents with each other in school and out. In their life with one another, children experience the pain of betrayal and the sting of ingratitude and the anxiety of guilt and the humiliation of punctured vanity. They obtain the satisfactions of confidences kept and esteem given and love returned and fair dealing honored. They learn to judge morally and to argue about their judging.

Our unwillingness to leave the moral education of children to the influence of what Locke called "Company," and our insistence that family, church, and school must take a deliberate hand, reflects our view – fully justified – that the education children provide one another is too parochial and crude. Moral judgment needs to be refined, moral imagination enlarged, moral argument made more sophisticated. How do we do this? What is the contribution of the school's curriculum? Those are the crucial questions.

## II

Learning morality, as we see clearly when looking at children in "Company," is learning a *social practice*. It is learning how to apply moral concepts and make discriminations among different cases, and this acquired capacity is intuitive rather than technical. Learning morality is like learning how to write, not like learning geography or mathematics.[3] Learning to write consists in learning a few elementary concepts and rules and then *doing it*, that is, writing over and over and over, with the advice and corrections of those who already do it well. And it also consists in reading – reading exemplary writing that inspires emulation.

Moral learning is the same. The young child begins with a few rudimentary concepts and rules such as "take turns," "don't hit people," and "don't call them names," and comes to feel shame and regret at bad behavior, appreciation for benefits, and resentment at wrongs. With this foundation, moral learning is set in motion: it is simply, as Aristotle says, learning by doing. There is not a science of moral judgment any more than there is a science of writing. Instead, in both cases, children get better through increased experience and practice, which enables them to make finer and sharper discriminations, and to argue from a greater range of cases. They develop the capacity as writers to *see* a sentence or a paragraph as clumsy, graceless, plain, clear, or needed, and as moral judgers to *see* an action as ungrateful, cowardly, generous, or obligatory.

The process of deliberate educational refinement, enlargement, and sophistication proceeds in the same way as the initial learning, but less through the direct moral experience of the schoolyard and playground than through the indirect experiencing of the moral lives of real and fictional people. That is why a moral education is first and foremost an education in literature, history, drama, and art.[4]

Through these subjects we vicariously live the moral lives of other people, and, as it were, try out for size their virtues, commitments, ideals, decisions, excuses, and self-assessments. But because we are not really the characters involved, we can also distance ourselves from them to make assessments that diverge from their own self-evaluations and to see more clearly than we can in our own cases the pulls of envy, passion, timidity, and pride in producing self-deception and distorted judgment. Through such experience we gain a greater command of moral language, a greater appreciation of complexity, and a more balanced sense of right and wrong; and we more directly discern the deeper values that lie behind and are expressed through ordinary moral precepts and conventional forms.

We thus become better moral reasoners because moral reasoning is largely taxonomic.[5] It is a matter of classifying cases under the right moral descriptions. Is this a case of *guilelessness* or *naïveté*? *Plainspokeness* or *insensitivity*? *Frankness* or *impudence*? Was that killing an *assassination*, *execution*, *euthanasia*, *tyrannicide*, *thuggee*, *self-defense*, or *plain murder*? Was this misrepresentation a *fib*, *tall story*, *exaggeration*, *equivocation*, *forgery*, or *lie*? Getting the situation well-described is half the battle, since the appropriate moral response – abhorrence, resentment, anger, amusement, or mere disgust – generally follows straightaway. We don't first describe something as *betrayal*, *duplicity*, *double-cross*, *bad faith*, or *fraud* and then go looking for a moral reason to tell us if it's a bad thing or not.

Of course, moral life is complicated and sometimes we want to redescribe a situation more to our own favor: yes, I did double-cross him, but he deserved it because he had cheated me earlier; yes, I did offer a fraudulent account, but it was done to protect myself from her effort to do me harm; yes, I was duplicitous, but he was unable to handle the truth at the time. I attempt to make the dominant description of the case one of *retribution* or *self-defense* or *paternalism*, a description that puts my conduct in a better light.[6]

Moral argument arises over appropriate classifications and reclassifications and it proceeds by analogy. "This case is like that one," I claim. "No it isn't," you counter. And as in the example about Susie being stuck-up, we end up contesting about the relevant features of the present case, so that we can finally come to agreement, if we can, on which paradigm case determines the issue. That paradigm will settle the correct classification, and the classification will often enough settle the moral argument. Consequently, the more paradigms we share, and the richer our common moral vocabulary, the more likely we are to be able to reach a nuanced description of the present case that will ultimately satisfy us both. The wider the range of our actual or vicarious moral experience, the more discriminating we can be in our classifications.

Moral education, thus, is case-based. It is from a background of richly described exemplary cases, situations, and characters that we structure our moral reactions and the criticisms and revisions we make of them. Even Kant, the arch-formalist in morality, recommends educating children by a "catechism of right" that would "contain, in popular form, cases of conduct which are met with in ordinary life, and which naturally call up the question whether something is or is not right." Kant gives an example of what his proposed catechism might say. "If, for instance," he writes, "someone, who ought to pay his creditors today, is touched at the sight of a needy person and gives him the sum which he is owing and should now pay – is that right? No! It is wrong; for I must be free before I can be generous."[7] This example is typical of Kant's rigorism about duty, but nevertheless it teaches an important elementary lesson about obligation: having obligated myself to you for a certain sum, that money is, so to speak, encumbered. It is not available to me to use freely. My giving it to a needy person is little different than my giving away money that I only happen to be transporting for you. That the money is used for good does not change the fact that I'm not free to use it.

Now, for Kant this fact ends the matter about right and wrong in the case; but we might concede the distinction he wishes to draw while imagining variations on the case in which my giving the money away, even though it is not strictly mine, might nevertheless be justified. Further elaborations of the case may make us sensitive to yet other distinctions and complexities that the simple case leaves out or brushes over. Similarly, such elaborations can make us better able to see when the money may be yet actually mine to give, though appearances suggest otherwise. Thus, consider Uncle Glegg's response to Tom Tulliver's decision in *The Mill on the Floss* to nullify his poor aunt's debt to his comatose and financially ruined father before creditors can acquire the note for the debt and call it in:

"Well," said Mr. Glegg, who had been meditating after Tom's words, "we shouldn't be doing any wrong by the creditors, supposing your father *was* bankrupt. I've been thinking o' that, for I've been a creditor myself and seen no end o' cheating. If he meant to give your aunt the money before he ever got into this sad work o' lawing, it's the same as if he'd made away with the note himself, for he'd made up his mind to be that much poorer. But there's a deal o' things to be considered, young man," Mr. Glegg added, looking admonishingly at Tom, "when you come to money business, and you may be taking one man's dinner away to make another man's breakfast. You don't understand that, I doubt?"

"Yes, I do," said Tom decidedly. "I know if I owe money to one man, I've no right to give it to another. But if my father had made up his mind to give my aunt the money before he was in debt, he had a right to do it."

"Well done, young man! I didn't think you'd been so sharp," said Uncle Glegg with much candor.[8]

Moral education means understanding through a variety of cases both the core concept of obligation – its constraint on liberty of action – and the complications in real life that modify the reach and weight of a particular obligation. A discriminating moral sense can appreciate the force and relevance of the considerations advanced by Tom and Uncle Glegg, and our own moral judgment here may echo Uncle Glegg's: "Well done, young man!"[9]

A school's curriculum in literature, drama, and history can build on and refine the rudimentary moral knowledge children have already acquired in "Company." For example, part of their knowledge – as we've seen – is about "being stuck-up." This notion is a member of a very important family of concepts having to do with pride, conceit, arrogance, and humility that a good liberal arts curriculum can exemplify and illustrate. Foolish pride and false pride and excessive pride can all be shown in their various forms, as well as proper pride and pride that gives way to the needs of love and justice.

How we value ourselves is intimately connected to how we value other people; and lessons about conceitedness, boastfulness, vanity, arrogance, and being stuck-up are amongst the most important elements of a good moral education. How we are to put a proper value on our persons without exalting ourselves over others is something we can learn only from seeing how this achievement is exemplified in people, and how its failure produces something that is ridiculous if not palpably ugly and offensive.

An instructive caution, for example, is provided by Mr. Bounderby, that wonderfully self-infatuated character in Charles Dickens' novel *Hard Times*, who is an unforgettable model of excessively dwelling on one's achievements while overestimating their worth and marking superiority in them as superiority in all things. Discovering that we are behaving like a Bounderby can chasten our inclinations toward self-promotion.[10]

This educational process of refining moral sense should aim to leave children with a rich vocabulary, a trained imagination, a store of examples and paradigms, and an inclination to reflect about the larger values revealed in their moral experience.

Now, what I have said about moral learning may seem entirely obvious. Even so, educators and academics don't always believe the obvious. My argument suggests that moral knowledge emerges from encountering, mastering, and reflecting on a tradition of discourse – a tradition that is the source of common terms and their appropriate applications. This view seems on its face repudiated by the dominant academic theory of moral learning, Lawrence Kohlberg's theory of moral development, which explicitly opposes mature moral thought to conventional thought.

## III

Kohlberg's theory is extremely influential among both academics and educators, and a virtual academic industry has grown up around it. It is also a theory with serious defects. In the remainder of this essay I describe the theory, explain its assumptions, and show how it goes wrong about convention.

The theory postulates several stages and levels of moral development from early childhood to adulthood. The first two stages constitute the preconventional level of moral thinking: children respond in terms of obedience and avoidance of punishment (stage 1) or in terms of getting their desires satisfied (stage 2). At the conventional level, persons find their standards in the approval of others (stage 3) or in the laws and conventions of society (stage 4). The postconventional level is the level of "principled" morality: individuals judge right and wrong in terms of a supposed social contract (stage 5) or in terms of "self-chosen ethical principles appealing to logical comprehensiveness, universality, and consistency" (stage 6).[11] According to Kohlberg, each of these stages has two features. Each higher stage is reached only after passing through the preceding stage or stages; and each higher stage is "better" or "superior" to its lower stages.

The aim of moral education according to Kohlberg is to move students to higher stages than they presently occupy.[12] It might seem an unrealistic goal to seek to move them to the two highest stages in light of the fact that most adults, according to Kohlberg, reason only at stages 3 and 4; philosophers and Supreme Court justices and five percent of the population reason at stages 5 and 6.[13] Yet Kohlberg insists that "the aim of the developmental educator is . . . the eventual adult attainment of the highest stage."[14]

This aim defines an educational regimen different from what Kohlberg calls the "bag of virtues" or "Boy Scout" approach, which, in his words, "indoctrinates" students into conventional morality.[15] Kohlberg directly connects the "Boy Scout" or virtue approach, which he rejects, to Aristotle's dictum that moral learning is learning by doing.[16]

What is it that leads Kohlberg to repudiate the idea that moral education is inculcation into a tradition of discourse and criticism? For one thing, it is his taking over from philosophers the idea that adequate moral judgments are *universalizable* and *reversible prescriptions*, and his believing that only the so-called "principled" judgments made in stages 5 and 6 fully meet this condition.[17]

Kohlberg associates universalizability with the test imposed by Kant's Categorical Imperative. The test works like this: suppose I can avoid a financial loss by telling a lie, and I wonder if this is morally permissible. I must ask myself if I am willing to accept that everyone who wanted to lie to avoid financial loss could do so. If I cannot accept this universal permission, then I cannot morally give myself personal permission. Thus, to universalize a prescription or permission is to extend it to others in the same situation.[18] Universalizability prevents me from making an exception of myself. Reversibility, on the other hand, is a Golden Rule procedure: I imagine myself in the shoes of other people and judge from their perspective.[19] Kohlberg also refers to reversibility as role-taking and "moral musical chairs."[20] Now, why does Kohlberg think that the principled judgments of stages 5 and 6 meet these two tests better than conventional morality?

Kohlberg's thinking is illustrated in his treatment of capital punishment. He describes a stage 4 conventional thinker as defending capital punishment by appeal to the prescription, "Act in accordance with [my] society's norms and rules," a prescription that Kohlberg says cannot be universalized.[21] However, a conventional believer in capital punishment, though his norms may be conventional in the sense of being derived from and standardly held in his community, nevertheless judges by some *specific* precept such as "All who wantonly murder deserve to die" or "Those who murder forfeit their right to life." And these precepts are perfectly universal.

Neither is there any bar to the conventional believer applying these precepts consistently to himself and conceding that he ought to be executed should he wantonly murder. Moreover, even if the conventional believer claims his precepts are sound just because they are his community's, he can still meet a universalizability test by proposing not that each community should act by *his* community's norms but that each should act by *its* own norms. The conventional believer's stage 4 norms need not be defectively universal.

Reversibility, properly understood, fares no better in distinguishing stages 3–4 from stages 5–6. Morality requires not that judgment be acceptable to every point of view but that it be acceptable from a disinterested point of view.[22] Putting ourselves in the shoes of other people is not a formal consistency requirement on judgment but a heuristic to help us fully understand and weigh other's needs and desires as we judge from a moral point of view. Suitably disinterested points of view (e.g., "the point of view of society's good") are available to those who resolve conventions in favor of capital punishment.

Kohlberg's lack of success at indicting conventional moral reasoning with logical inferiority stems from a very basic error, namely, conflating universality and generality. The difference among the following three sentences, (i) "All husbands should respect their wives," (ii) "All individuals should respect their spouses," and (iii) "All persons should respect all other persons," is not one of increasing universality but increasing generality. Each sentence is fully universal (i.e., possesses the universal quantifier "all"), but the second and third apply to more people, both as subject and object. The latter two are more general.

Similarly, it is increased generality, not increased universality, that really differentiates higher from lower level principles in the Kohlbergian stages. The principles in the highest stages, says Kohlberg, are "free from culturally defined content."[23] They don't refer to institutions, roles, historical situations, or social conventions. Instead, they are principles commanding a respect for the "dignity of human beings as individuals," or a "reciprocity and equality of human rights," or other similarly general content referring only to persons as such. Generality of content is not a condition of logical consistency though in may be desirable in basic moral principles.

Precisely because the principles at stages 5 and 6 are fully general and lack social content, making use of them does *not* allow us to avoid conventionalism in any interesting sense, nor does it obviate Aristotle's claim that moral learning is learning by doing. In the first place, the formal properties of moral principles upon which Kohlberg puts so much emphasis – that they be universalizable, reversible, and so on – give us no basis at all for drawing any moral conclusions about anything. They no more restrain the range of possible moral views we can adopt than the principle of logical consistency restrains the range of possible true statements we can say. Likewise, the substantive but completely general principles of respect and equality of rights characteristic of the last two stages possess too little content to underwrite any interesting moral judgments. Real judgment requires social content, not the absence of it.

Kohlberg's preferred principle at stage 6 is "universal respect for fundamental human rights and for human personality." This respect, he says, "provides a moral guide defining the way in which any human should act."[24] But respect, characterized in this completely general and abstract way, is no guide at all. The principle of respect for persons is not a substitute for convention; on the contrary, it requires conventional form to give it concrete meaning. Let's ask what counts as respect for persons in our place and time and how a child can come to learn it? Here is some of the social knowledge we possess about respecting the person of another: (i) that it is not a violation of another's person to look her directly in the face when you speak to her; (ii) that strangers who demonstrate to you their bonhomie by slapping you on the back and emphasize their wittiness by poking you in the arm are ill-mannered and boorish in failing to keep a proper distance; (iii) that people who against your will stroke or fondle your body sexually commit assault, a serious violation of your person. This social knowledge is *conventional*, arising from our understanding of various norms of and customary expectations about intimacy and physical distance,

norms and expectations that may not obtain everywhere. A child in our society will learn how to respect the persons of others by doing and observing the sorts of things that count as respect – by mastering the conventional forms of distance, deference, familiarity, intimacy, and equality.

Abstract general principles like respect for human dignity – the philosopher's stock in trade – have some use as themes for unifying or organizing together into a pattern the myriad dimensions of our moral knowledge. They help us see why quite disparate forms of moral conduct or moral feeling might be related to one another. Moral theories invoking these principles try to show that our best understood and most defensible customs maximize human happiness, or reflect the elements of natural reason, or would be chosen from some hypothetical contractual situation, or give content to the injunction to respect people equally. These theories exhibit moral life as manifesting general tendencies that seem rationally respectable. But the theories and their abstract principles are no substitute for the underlying structure of moral practice upon which they are parasitic and which they try to explain. Moral knowledge is knowledge of practice, not knowledge of theory.

This is what Aristotle meant by saying that moral learning is learning by doing. Consider a virtue like courage, one that Aristotle often talks about. How can we know what courage is? We can specify the concept of courage as the "duty to defend or pursue what is important to us in the face of obstacles that make this difficult or dangerous, although neither futile nor suicidal," to use a recent definition.[25] But this doesn't tell us very much. No rule can make the application of this definition mechanical. No rule can tell us when our commitments are important or how important, how long and intense our defense or pursuit of them must be to be appropriate, and what actions in the circumstance will be most effective. These all require *judgment*, judgment that emerges from the experience of doing courageous things or observing others doing courageous things, not from a glib command of very general principles.[26] And so it is likewise for all the virtues and values of moral life. What we owe our children is not deflection into theoretical generalities but the best possible acquaintance with our moral conventions.

Kohlberg's anticonventionalism rests in part on his confusion of the universal and the general, but also in part on a frequently tendentious characterization of convention. This latter point is well illustrated in his treatment of an event familiar to his readers in the 1970s, the My Lai massacre during the Vietnam War, in which American soldiers herded into a ditch and shot to death more than several hundred women and children. Now, we might be inclined, observes Kohlberg, to think that in America killing innocent civilians in war is considered morally wrong, but "[w]hat the My Lai massacre and the public opinion polls about it prove," he claims, "is that American conventional morality finds such a massacre right under many circumstances. . . ." He goes on to say that the "one enlisted man who clearly resisted engaging in the massacre was at a principled level, rather than adhering strongly to conventional American values."[27]

Kohlberg here equates conventional belief with majority public sentiment, no matter how ephemeral or shallow or badly grounded. The momentary and emotional upwelling of American public opinion against punishing Lt. William Calley, the lead perpetrator of the massacre, is made by Kohlberg to count as "our conventional morality" whereas our public law, our solemn treaty obligations, our prosecution of the Nuremburg war criminals, and our religious traditions – all of which condemn murder of innocents in wartime – count for nothing. But this is clearly a facile and worthless conception of "our moral conventions." Moreover, it is an entirely gratuitous claim by Kohlberg that the enlisted man who refused to participate in the massacre resisted rather than acted on American traditions. He was in fact an ordinary foot soldier like the others but one who was able in the pressures of the moment to adhere to the views of right and wrong he had been taught – very conventional views.[28]

Although in ordinary speech "being conventional" can just mean being unreflective and unimaginative, going along with the crowd, accepting at face value every parochial norm, and obeying every order, this facile sense of "conventional" is not the one needed accurately to describe the Kohlberg stages, where the contrast between conventional and postconventional turns on the presence or absence of specific social content in the stage principles or rules.[29] Stage 4 cannot be characterized as the uncritical and unimaginative use of rules with specific social content; otherwise there would be a stage – involving critical and imaginative use of rules with specific social content – intermediate between it and stages 5 and 6, whose own principles lack such content. In order for stage 4 to be a type of moral reasoning, and not just the inferior instance

of a type, "convention" must refer to the set of socially rich precepts, legal paradigms, historically embodied ideals, and interpretive materials that a thoughtful and informed member of society would invoke in a moral argument.[30]

There are, of course, conventions and conventions. There may, indeed, arise and flourish local customs and practices that license bad behavior. Army units in Vietnam, for example, were under great pressure to produce high body counts, and command supervision of the rules of engagement – which explicitly protected noncombatants – was lax. A "culture" arose on the battlefield making civilians fair targets. But that "culture" stood then and stands today condemned by other, broader conventions, embodied in our history, law, and political thought, as well as our philosophical and religious traditions. No person can read Prosecutor Robert Jackson's address to the Nuremburg court, no person can read Francis Lieber's General Order no. 100 establishing military law for the Union Army in the Civil War, no person, indeed, can read General Sherman's correspondence with General J. B. Hood over the evacuation of Atlanta, without recognizing a standard – a convention – that provides plenty of critical bite against massacres and abuses of civilians in war, no matter how frequently our military actions fail to live up to it.

Kohlberg and others like him think that teaching children conventional morality means teaching them to be uncritical, conservative, and acquiescent to public opinion. Nothing could be further from the truth, on any useful understanding of "our moral conventions." It is precisely by giving children the richest possible acquaintance with our conventions – and the legal, historical and literary models and examples that embody them best – that we arm them with critical standards against the winds of fashion, public opinion, parochial customs, and vulgar passions. The ready inference made by Kohlberg and others from "conventional" to "uncritical" betrays not only a confusion about conceiving the stages of conventional and postconventional development but also a failure to appreciate the abundance in our culture of conventions for appraising and criticising other conventions. Mastering conventional forms does not render us socially and morally blind nor lock us into defense of the status quo.

Criticism and convention go together. The power and force of social criticism generally resides precisely in its imaginative application and extension of well-known precepts or paradigm cases or familiar critical practices. Criticism that cuts itself loose from convention tends to be publicly opaque and recondite.

Kohlberg's stages are not really stages in moral learning and moral knowledge at all; they are stages in theoretical sophistication. That, after all, explains the otherwise preposterous finding that philosophers are typically stage 6 thinkers. Of course! They are trained theoreticians. But they are no better at moral knowledge and moral judgment and lead no better moral lives than any other educated person.[31] The typical stage 5 and 6 principles are the materials out of which political and moral theorists ply their

trade. It does no real harm to students to encourage their own theorizing in these terms. It is good to be inquisitive about the deeper values that might be thought to organize and systematize our moral knowledge. But that knowledge itself is rooted in practice. Facility in the language of theory is no substitute for command of moral conventions.

Where schools fail to ground students in our culture's moral conventions, moral education still takes place, but it is the moral education that Locke worried about: school will be where the children learn principally from one another and little from anyone else.

## Notes

1. James L. Axtell (ed.), *The Educational Writings of John Locke* (Cambridge: Cambridge University Press, 1968), p. 170.

2. Ibid., pp. 166, 169. One recent writer who emphasizes the influence of students on one another is Kevin Ryan, "Our Educational Reform and the Moral Education of Our Children," *The World & I* 3 (March 1988), pp. 594–5.

3. The next few paragraphs borrow from my essay "Learning Morality," *QQ: Report from the Institute for Philosophy and Public Policy* 8 (Spring 1988), pp. 12–15. My Aristotelian account of moral learning leans heavily on Martha C. Nussbaum, *The Fragility of Goodness* (Cambridge: Cambridge University Press, 1986), Chapter 10; and M. F. Burnyeat, "Aristotle on Learning to Be Good," in *Essays on Aristotle's Ethics*, ed. Amelie Oksenberg Rorty (Berkeley, CA: University of California Press, 1980).

4. "But the most essential and fundamental aspect of culture is the study of literature, since this is an education in how to picture and understand human situations" (Iris Murdoch, *The Sovereignty of the Good* [New York: Schocken Books, 1971], p. 34). Murdoch likewise emphasizes moral judgment as a kind of "seeing."

5. Albert R. Jonsen and Stephen Toulmin, in *The Abuse of Casuistry* (Berkeley, CA: University of California Press, 1988), emphasize the taxonomic nature of moral reasoning (see pp. 14, 69, and elsewhere).

6. We also revise our descriptions of others. Consider M's reclassification of D's attributes in *The Sovereignty of the Good*: D came to be seen by M as "not vulgar but refreshingly simple, not undignified but spontaneous, not noisy but gay, not tiresomely juvenile but delightfully youthful" (pp. 17–18).

7. *The Educational Theory of Immanuel Kant*, trans. and ed. Edward Franklin Buchner (Philadelphia, PA: J. B. Lippincott, 1904), pp. 205–6.

8. George Eliot, *The Mill on the Floss* (New York: New American Library, 1981), pp. 233–4.

9. And so might Kant's own judgment concur. Tom's and Uncle Glegg's arguments suggest not that it is just to override an obligation to creditors but that, having already implicitly reserved his sister's debt from being encumbered by any debt of his own, so that his sister's note would not fall within the range of his assets obligated to creditors, Tom's father retained the freedom to dispose of the note as he would. Alternatively, readers may be inclined to see the implicit reservation as too fine a thread upon which to secure the father's retained freedom, but feel that, though there is an obligation to the creditors that encompasses the sister's debt, it is just nevertheless to favor the sister at the creditors' expense. This is a judgment Kant could not endorse.

10. The discussion of pride here draws from Gabriele Taylor, *Pride, Shame, and Guilt: Emotions of Self-Assessment* (Oxford: Clarendon Press, 1985).

11. Lawrence Kohlberg, "The Moral Atmosphere of the School," in David Purpel and Kevin Ryan (eds.), *Moral Education . . . It Comes with the Territory* (Berkeley, CA: McCutcheon, 1976), p. 216.

12. Lawrence Kohlberg, *Essays on Moral Development*, vol. 1: *The Philosophy of Moral Development* (New York: Harper & Row, 1981), p. 58.

13. Ibid., pp. xxxiii, 88.

14. Ibid., p. 91.

15. Ibid., pp. 2, 31, and elsewhere.

16. Ibid., p. 31.

17. Ibid., p. xxxii: "Judgments to be moral should rest on certain principles, on those principles that are universalizable. Each higher moral stage comes closer to this principled form."

18. Ibid., pp. 198, 274.

19. Ibid., pp. 197, 202, and elsewhere.

20. Ibid., p. xxxiii.

21. Ibid., p. 275.

22. Ibid., p. 280: "a reversible ... resolution is one whereby everyone whose interests are at stake is 'given his due' according to some principle that everyone judges to be morally valid, given that each person is *not egoistic* but is willing to take a moral point of view; that is, to consider his own claims impartially and to put himself in the shoes of the others" (emphasis added). What does this description of reversibility mean in practice? The ideas of "non-egoistic reversibility" and "the moral point of view" become very muddled tools when Kohlberg applies them to the issue of capital punishment. Stage 6 reversibility, according to Kohlberg, involves choosing a rule of punishment from behind a "veil of ignorance" (an idea borrowed from John Rawls). From this choice position, says Kohlberg, "it would never be rational to prefer one's prospects under capital punishment to one's prospects under an alternative system" (p. 286), a conclusion generated by adopting in turn the *self-interested* perspectives of the "rational capital offender" and the "rational ordinary citizen" (p. 284), and choosing to embrace the punitive policy with the least bad outcome should one be either party (p. 287). Of course, by *this* line of reasoning, we would reject life sentences, too, and any other harsh punishment. This is because in Kohlberg's thought-experiment the "rational capital offender" is *a determinate representative position* (whose probability of getting [or deserving] *some* sentence is 100%) while the "rational ordinary citizen" is an *average or composite representative position* (whose probability of being murdered is extremely small no matter what punishment policy prevails). Kohlberg's confusions about universalizability, reversibility, and the moral stages are so tangled and intertwined that it is impossible here and in the text to do more than gesture in the direction of the main problems.

23. Ibid., p. 69.

24. Kohlberg, "The Moral Atmosphere of the School," p. 209.

25. Charles Larmore, *Patterns of Moral Complexity* (Cambridge: Cambridge University Press, 1987), p. 6.

26. These points are made by Larmore.

27. Kohlberg, *Essays on Moral Development*, vol. 1, p. 127.

28. Kohlberg evidently is referring to PFC James Dursi, who ignored a direct order from Lt. Calley to fire into a ditch filled with Vietnamese civilians. See Joseph Goldstein et al., *The My Lai Massacre and its Cover-Up: Beyond the Reach of Law* (New York: Free Press, 1976), p. 502; and Arthur Everett, Kathryn Johnson, and Harry Rosenthal, *Calley* (New York: Dell, 1971), p. 162.

29. See note 23 and accompanying text.

30. Convention seems difficult for moral psychologists to grasp properly; see the introduction and articles in Jerome Kagan and Sharon Lamb (eds.), *The Emergence of Morality in Young Children* (Chicago: University of Chicago Press, 1987), where convention sometimes refers to a source of motivation, sometimes to a source of authority, and sometimes to a source of feeling (pp. xiii, xvii, 3, 26, 35).

31. See, e.g., James Rest, "An Interdisciplinary Approach to Moral Education," in Marvin Berkowitz and Fritz Oser (eds.), *Moral Education: Theory and Application* (Hillsdale, NJ: Lawrence Erlbaum Associates, 1985), p. 17, who observes completely without irony that philosophy graduate students score highest on Kohlberg scales and that "this makes sense if we regard moral philosophers as experts in moral reasoning." The "moral reasoning" at which philosophers are expert has nothing to do with moral maturity.

# 55

# Cultivating the Moral and Intellectual Virtues

# Randall Curren

One of the most familiar aspects of Aristotle's account of virtue is the distinction he draws between the intellectual and moral virtues at the end of Book I of the *Nicomachean Ethics*:

> some kinds of virtue are said to be intellectual and others moral, contemplative wisdom (*sophia*) and understanding (*sunesis*) and practical wisdom (*phronêsis*) being intellectual, generosity (*eleutherio tês*) and temperance (*sôphrosunê*) moral.  (I.13 1103a5–7)

This division of the virtues follows the pattern of his division of the soul or psyche. "By human virtue (*anthropine aretê*) we mean not that of the body, but that of the soul:" he says (I.13 1102a16). Understanding the soul to be the source and cause of growth and movement, he divides it into rational and irrational elements, and divides the irrational part itself into the desiring part responsible for initiating movement and the nutritive part responsible for growth. Setting aside the nutritive part of the soul, and having implicitly identified the rational and desiring elements as the parts of the soul that contribute to action, Aristotle then says that "virtue is distinguished into kinds in accordance with" the difference between the rational and desiring parts of the soul (I.13 1103a4). That is to say, he identifies the moral virtues as states of the desiring part of the soul, and intellectual virtues as states of the rational part of the soul. Moral virtues thus come to be defined as dispositions to feel and be moved by our various desires or emotions neither too weakly nor too strongly, but in a way that moves us to choose and act as reason would dictate and allows us to take pleasure in doing so (II.5–6). Intellectual virtues are later defined as capacities or powers of understanding, judgment, and reasoning which enable the rational parts of the soul to attain truth (VI.2 1139b11–13), the attainment of truth being the function of the calculative or practical part no less than the scientific or contemplative one.

Having drawn this distinction between the intellectual and moral virtues at the end of Book I, Aristotle opens Book II with a remark about the origins and development of virtue that contrasts these forms of virtue in a way that would seem quite significant for the enterprise of moral education:

> Virtue, then, being of two kinds, intellectual and moral, intellectual virtue in the main owes both its birth and

Previously published in *Aristotle on the Necessity of Public Education* (Lanham, MD: Rowman & Littlefield, 2000), pp. 201–12, 253–4. © 2000 Rowman & Littlefield Publishers, Inc. Reprinted with permission of Rowman & Littlefield Publishing Corporation.

its growth to teaching . . . while moral virtue comes about as a result of habit, . . . none of the moral virtues arises in us by nature . . .   (I.1 1103a14–20)

The obvious implication of this for the moral upbringing and education of children is that moral virtue is not something that can be taught or engendered through verbal instruction alone, but is rather something that can only be brought about by ensuring that children consistently act in the right ways. The development of habit presumably requires consistency of conduct, or conduct that is consistently shaped in all its details toward what is desirable, and Aristotle's claim here is that habit is the proximate origin of moral virtue. The development of good habits is thus the target at which moral instruction should aim:

> by doing the acts that we do in our transactions with other men we become just or unjust, and by doing the acts that we do in the presence of danger, and being habituated to feel fear or confidence, we become brave or cowardly. The same is true of appetites and feelings of anger. . . . Thus, in one word, states arise out of like activities. . . . It makes no small difference, then, whether we form habits of one kind or of another from our very youth; it makes a very great difference, or rather *all* the difference.   (II.1 1103b17–25)

As interest in Aristotle has spread beyond the universities to the larger educational community, what has received the most attention is this idea that moral learning is properly concerned with developing virtues of character and requires supervised practice of the right kinds.[1] Yet Aristotle's account of the development of moral virtue is not as simple as it may appear to be from these opening passages. Although he distinguishes the moral and intellectual virtues, he also holds that no one is fully virtuous or has true moral virtue without having the intellectual virtue of practical wisdom (VI.13 1144b7–17, 1144b30–2), and that no one can become practically wise without first possessing natural or habitual moral virtue (VI.12 1144a29–37, VII.13 1144b20). These interdependencies are grounded in the premise that humans are a union of intellect and desire (VI.2 1139a32–b5). They are explained more specifically by a conception of goodness or virtue as not merely a form of moral innocence, but rather what enables its possessor to achieve outward success in pursuing the proper ends of action (I.12 1101b2–3,[2] II.9 1109a24–9), and by the view that although it is the function of thought to identify the

proper ends of action, its capacity to do so is limited by the fact that people tend to regard what they are accustomed to taking pleasure in as good (III.4, VI.5 1140b7–19). Since virtue is what enables one to perform actions that *successfully* pursue good ends, it will require success in the intellectual tasks of discerning what is salient in the circumstances of action and thinking through what it is best to do. Good habits formed under the guidance of *others'* good judgment will not fully equip one to face life's complexities. On the other hand, to the extent that one's conception of the proper ends of action and perception of the circumstances of action are formed and limited by one's emotional dispositions, one can only have the intellectual virtue of practical wisdom or *phronêsis* if one is morally virtuous.

These interdependencies between the intellectual and moral virtues are exceedingly important to Aristotle's theory of virtue and the human good, and my purpose will be to explore their significance for moral education. I shall begin by saying a few words about their role in Aristotle's ethical theory, and then shift my attention to their bearing on current curricular developments. Aristotle's account of the relationships between the moral and intellectual virtues suggests the importance of integrating what is now promoted under the rubrics of character education and instruction in critical thinking, and it provides a useful starting point for thinking about how to succeed in integrating these pedagogical enterprises. If his account is correct, then neither can be complete without the other, although they are popularly perceived to be in conflict and little theoretical consideration has been devoted toward a synthesis.[3] I shall devote much of my attention here to examining some philosophical obstacles which seem to stand in the way of a synthesis, and I shall do so in a way that sets the issues on a larger historical stage, in order to see better what is at stake and to appreciate better what is distinctive in the Aristotelian view.

Aristotle distinguishes the moral and intellectual virtues but he also asserts the double-edged thesis that practical wisdom both presupposes and completes moral virtue. In taking this position he follows Plato in rejecting the moral intellectualism of Socrates, while also preserving the doctrine of the unity of virtue. Virtue "in the strict sense" involves practical wisdom, and this explains, he says, why

> some say that all the virtues are forms of practical wisdom, and why Socrates in one respect was on the

right track while in another he went astray; in thinking that all the virtues were forms of practical wisdom he was wrong, but in saying they implied practical wisdom he was right. . . . [I]t is . . . the state that implies the *presence* of right reason, that is virtue; and practical wisdom is right reason about such matters. Socrates, then, thought the virtues were forms of reason (for he thought they were, all of them, forms of knowledge), while we think they *involve* reason.

It is clear, then, . . . that it is not possible to be good in the strict sense without practical wisdom, nor practically wise without moral virtue. But in this way we may also refute the dialectical argument whereby it might be contended that the virtues exist in separation from each other; the same man, it might be said, is not best equipped by nature for all the virtues, so that he will have already acquired one when he has not yet acquired another. This is possible in respect of the natural virtues, but not in respect of those in respect of which a man is called without qualification good; for with the presence of the one quality, practical wisdom, will be given all the virtues. (VI.13 1144b16–45a2)

Practical wisdom entails the presence of all the virtues because although one may have some natural or habituated virtues in some degree without having them all, if one lacks the perceptions associated with even one form of virtue, then one's perception of moral particulars, conception of the proper ends of action, and deliberations about what to do will all be corrupted in at least that one respect. There will be situations in which the emotions associated with the missing form of virtue will be felt too strongly or weakly and will lead one astray. It is in this way that practical wisdom entails the presence of all the virtues, and since true virtue requires practical wisdom this implies that one cannot have any one virtue fully without having all the others.

This unity of virtue thesis is a centerpiece of Aristotle's ethical theory inasmuch as it grounds his central thesis about the essential place of virtue in a happy life. [ . . . ] He holds that happy lives involve activity of the rational soul "in accordance with the highest virtue," namely *sophia* or contemplative wisdom, and it follows from his views on the unity of virtue that such activity is impossible without moral virtue (Kraut 1989; Korsgaard 1986; cf. *Laws* I 631c).

For our purposes, however, what has most immediate importance is Aristotle's distinction between habituated virtue and full or true virtue, and his conception of the consummation of virtue in *phronêsis* (practical wisdom, good judgment, or

practical intelligence). There are several reasons to accept the idea that true virtue is the proper object of moral instruction.

## Why "True" Virtue?

First, only a true virtue is good without qualification, and it is surely better for people to acquire traits that are good without qualification than ones that are not. On the one hand, supposing that it is possible to have moral knowledge without having a settled disposition to do what one knows is right, it is not unreasonable for us to prefer that our fellow human beings acquire not only the knowledge but the disposition to act on it. On the other hand, a moral disposition that is not guided by understanding and good judgment can have bad consequences for both its possessor and others. Loyalty *in due measure* is a good and fine thing, for instance, but conceived as a disposition that is not accompanied by good judgment it exposes its possessors to risks of manipulation and betrayal, and may induce them to inflict wrongful harm in the service of their affiliations.[4] The disadvantages of blind loyalty are significant enough that one may reasonably doubt whether it is a good thing to inculcate it, but the same cannot be said of loyalty that is judicious.

A second reason for regarding true virtue as the appropriate object of moral instruction is that justice [ . . . ] requires that we morally educate children, and respect for human beings as rational creatures requires that we do this in a way that is conducive to the emergence of autonomous moral judgment and understanding, which is to say genuine, and not just habitual, virtue.[5]

A third related reason is that justice requires that the conditions be created for rational consent to the laws, existing and proposed, in the manner appropriate to a citizen, which is to say in a manner arising from a desire to do the right thing, and guided by autonomous good judgment.[6] Rational consent is only possible to the extent that justice is *transparent*. That is, it is only possible to the extent that laws and institutions are open to inspection, and citizens have been educated in both the powers of inspection and judgment and the cooperative virtues on which the very enterprise of collective deliberation and consent depends. True, and not just habitual, virtue is demanded both in the giving of rational consent and in a citizen's manner of compliance with law.

Finally, quite apart from any consideration of law and governments, a moral community is by all rights an enterprise whose functions, such as guidance and correction, are more or less universally distributed among its members. There are no reasons why this should not include exercises of moral judgment which may create pressure toward modifications and progress, and if it does include these, then a moral order is an enterprise which demands widely distributed moral intelligence and autonomous judgment, not just obedience. It demands true virtue.

## The Paradox of Progressive Morality

Let us suppose, then, that it is clear that true virtue in Aristotle's sense is the appropriate aim of moral instruction, and that this entails cultivation of both the moral and intellectual virtues. The popular perception of an opposition between inculcation of "community values" and encouragement of critical thinking suggests there are at least prima facie tensions in this project of instructional synthesis, arising from the objections that may be lodged against each side of this instructional divide by the other. It will be useful to enumerate these objections, identify the tensions which this enumeration yields, and take stock of the moral tradition's attempts to grapple with them.

The objections or problems which I shall survey here I shall call: (1) the problem of indoctrination; (2) the problem of foreclosed options; (3) the problem of force; (4) the problem of skepticism; (5) the problem of local variation, and (6) the problem of free-riding. The problems of indoctrination and free-riding together give rise to a bind, or paradox, which I shall call the *paradox of progressive morality*.

1. *Indoctrination*. A common fear about moral education is that it will inevitably be indoctrinating, in the sense that it will establish beliefs which are not all evidently true, and will do so in such a way that those beliefs are not easily dislodged at any later time. The dimly perceived specter of Plato's *Republic* looms in the background of this fear, and Aristotle's moral psychology inherits some of the *Republic*'s fundamental assumptions. It is commonly assumed now, as then, that the powers of reason take time to develop in children, and that until those powers have developed, their beliefs remain vulnerable to manipulation. Another Aristotelian

and Platonic assumption with broad contemporary currency is that what we have been habituated to in our youth tends to exercise an *enduring* influence on what we desire and perceive to be good. A third assumption, also evident in Aristotle's thought and derived from Plato's, is that children become neither good nor responsive to reason without an upbringing that surrounds them with good models and guides them toward good habits. On these assumptions, moral habituation may be supposed both a prerequisite for critical thought, as Aristotle held, *and* an obstacle to its unfettered employment. Is it not generally true that one is not in a good position to judge the conception of the good one has been raised in, since one will tend to see what one has grown accustomed to as good?

2. *Foreclosed options*. A second and related objection is that in suppressing alternative conceptions the good, moral habituation restricts life options. The child's so-called "right to an open future" is breached.

3. *Force*. A third objection is that moral habituation necessarily involves *force*, and is thus morally suspect, particularly in government schools. If moral habits must be cultivated without the benefit of children being antecedently reasonable, then a substantial reliance on force may seem inevitable. Peter Simpson's work on Aristotelian educational theory exemplifies exactly this line of thinking, in insisting that in the Aristotelian account of becoming good, habits of good conduct can only be established by force, since they cannot be established by rational persuasion (Simpson 1990, n. 13).

4. *Skepticism*. Coming at this from the other side, one might worry that children are all too easily initiated into the deadly game of logic, that once immersed in its culture of criticism, they can all too effectively wash themselves and each other in a "cynical acid"[7] which eats away even the sturdiest moral fibers, denuding them of the sheltering fabric of culture, community, and tradition. One need only imagine that the attitude of the critical thinker is to believe just what there is adequate reason to believe, and that there are no rational foundations for morality, or none that can be easily discovered.

5. *Local variation*. A fifth problem is that even if there are rational foundations for morality *generally*, there will almost certainly be legitimate local

variations, since some problems of social coordination will have no single best solution. Different interests may be balanced somewhat differently, leaving the members of each of the various moral communities pained in one way here, in another way there. What is local in this way appears, and is in some sense, arbitrary. This renders it vulnerable to critical scrutiny, however valuable and irreplaceable it may be.

6. *Free-riding.* Even if there were easily discernible foundational arguments for morality generally, and for any merely local rules, one might fear that instruction in critical thinking will embolden children in their embrace of self-interested arguments to free-ride on public morality, to take advantage of the self-restraint of those who accept the demands of morality. The idea of morality as a system of conduct-guiding norms is that it provides reasons for action that take precedence over all others. Its norms are solutions to problems of social coordination which yield mutual advantage when complied with, and this mutual advantage provides us all with reasons of prudence to prefer life in a community constrained by such norms. Some people may understand how this provides a rational foundation for morality, but not fully accept what it demands, namely that we all accept the reasons of morality as compelling reasons, even when the reasons of prudence counsel a different course. The price of morality's benefits is accepting *limits on our liberty to govern ourselves by our own reason*, but how rational will this seem to one who is encouraged by instruction in critical thinking to think for herself?

The situation in which "everyone is governed by his own reason" is inevitably "a condition of war," says Hobbes (1651, xvi.4), but the "fool," without denying the existence of a social covenant, "questioneth whether injustice . . . may not sometimes stand with that reason which dictateth to every man his own good. [He questions whether] it be not against reason [to violate the covenant]" (xv.4). "The force of words being . . . too weak to hold men to the performance of their covenants," and virtue being too rare, we must authorize a sovereign to establish moral law by force of arms and the suppression of academic freedom, says Hobbes (xiv.31, xviii.9, xlvi.23 OL). If we are to find some principled grounds on which to resist the repugnantly illiberal aspects of this Hobbesian solution, we need to show either that habits of virtue, and the

sentiments, perceptions, and inclinations of which they are composed, are robust and resistant to any corrupting influence that critical reason might have, or that critical reason can be counted on to counsel fair play and adherence to moral norms.

Surveying this list, we find three forms of the concern that moral training compromises individual freedom and three forms of the concern that the liberating capacity of critical reason undermines fidelity to common morality. At least four of these concerns were on the philosophical agenda at its outset, and have been perennially at the heart of philosophical concern with education, the problems of *local variation* and *foreclosed options* being the exceptions. I will set these exceptions aside in what follows, and begin my discussion of the others with some brief remarks on their place in the philosophical tradition.

Thrasymachus argues in Book I of Plato's *Republic* that laws aim at the advantage of the rulers alone, while those who have made the laws "declare what they have made – what is to their own advantage – to be just for their subjects" (338e). His argument confronts Socrates with a problem of indoctrination which the Socratic elenchus cannot answer, but which Plato hopes to.[8] The elenchus offers no hope of arriving at a consistent set of *true* beliefs unless one has begun with beliefs which are weighted toward the truth to begin with. In the face of systematic error, which could arise from systematic deception, it is powerless, and this points up the desirability of having some basis for judging a society which is independent of what is taught in it.

Thrasymachus's consistent disdain for conventional morality may also be considered an expression of moral skepticism, to be answered by Plato's theory of moral knowledge, while the challenge from Glaucon that follows in Book II shows how the free-rider problem arises even among those who accept the rationality of entering into a social covenant to create and enforce a common morality. It is in hopes of answering this free-rider problem that Plato spends the better part of Books II–IX trying to show that virtue is not simply an instrumental good, related to happiness only unreliably through external sanctions, but an internal good of the psyche without which no one can have any prospect of happiness. It is, at least in part, in hopes of answering this problem that Rousseau later undertakes to convince us that Emile can *without benefit of instruction* discover the natural laws of morality and physics, and from the latter the existence of God and the afterlife (thus, the essential elements of "natural religion").[9]

Thrasymachus represents the problem of force, no less than the problem of indoctrination, and Plato affirms in response that in the best kind of city children are educated by "persuasion" embodied in music and poetry, and not by "force," as they are in deficient cities (III 401b–402a, VIII 548c). In the *Republic* (III 401b–402a, VIII 548c, IX 590c–d) as in the works of Locke (1693, §31–85), the resistance to using force in education rests in the idea that reliance on force tends to undermine the development of responsiveness to reason, and the idea that force need be used only sparingly, since children are quite ready to imitate those who are praised and admired, and quite inclined to adopt the standards and way of life of those who take care of them.

What this brief historical introduction begins to reveal is that the problems of indoctrination and free-riding are the most challenging. The problem of force depends upon failing to recognize the ways in which children are drawn to the good without force or rationally compelling argument. Plato, Aristotle, and Locke all had a reasonably good understanding of how this occurs. On Aristotle's account, what is lacking in most children without moral training is specifically an attachment to what is admirable (*kalon*) or appropriate (*prepon*) (*NE* X.9 1179b4–26), and argument alone will not engender such an attachment; but this does not mean that children are without other motives that can be relied upon to persuade them, often without force, to engage in conduct that will allow them to develop a taste for what is admirable or appropriate, and a devotion to it for its own sake.[10] They thereby become responsive to reasons of a distinctively moral kind, which Aristotle regards as practical reasons of the highest order.

By contrast, what may seem the obvious adequate response to the problem of indoctrination is not adequate. That response would note the reference, in my statement of the problem of indoctrination, to establishing "beliefs which are not all evidently true" and hold that there is no problem if we take care to inculcate only beliefs which are evidently true. I think there is a lot of good sense in this response, and that public school districts in the United States typically do attempt to exercise such care when they pursue initiatives in character education. Non-violence and mutual respect are on

the list, but beliefs about sexual orientation, gender roles, and what constitutes a family are not. When the various constituencies in a district are brought to the table, their initial apprehensions about "whose values" are to be taught give way to a consensus that is remarkably stable across districts.

As gratifying as such success may be, however, we have to make some allowance for our collective fallibility. Recognizing our fallibility, and making allowance for the possibility of moral progress, should lead us to embrace the ideal of a moral community that is held together by norms that are open to public evaluation and revision, a community that chooses fundamental law for itself and makes moral progress by revising it over time. Even if we take care to find common ground in what we teach, if we teach it in a way that precludes any possibility of thinking beyond it, then the ideal of a progressive common morality is compromised, and a form of the problem of indoctrination remains.

The problem of skepticism is also an easier one than the free-rider problem. Although it is periodically fashionable to profess moral skepticism, the contractarian view that it is mutually advantageous and therefore rational to impose on ourselves duties of mutual respect, or at least self-restraint, is not only an attractive fall-back position in theory, but is easily grasped as self-evident in practice. Although there may be specific provisions of particular moral codes that may not be mutually advantageous, the general proposition that moral order is mutually advantageous seems true. On the other hand, the free-rider problem would remain unsolved even if the problem of skepticism *were* solved.

Taken together, the problems of indoctrination and free-riding create something of a bind or dilemma, a *paradox of progressive morality*, if you will:

1  Either one's capacity to critically evaluate the morality one is habituated into is limited by the perceptions and sentiments one acquires in that habituation, or it is not.
2  If it is limited in this way, then no consistent system of morality is open to internal public scrutiny, and no one brought up in that system has any rational assurance that it is not deficient.
3  If one's critical capacity is not limited in this way, then the perceptions and sentiments which incline one to give the reasons of morality priority can be undermined by critical thinking, resulting in moral free-riding.

The problem, in short, is how morality can both command our fidelity and be open to effective public scrutiny and appropriate revision. It would seem that it can only have one of these properties at the expense of the other.

The classical and modern traditions share a common aspiration to solve the free-rider problem by means of a theoretical demonstration that it is rational to be moral, but divide on the questions of whether the requisite moral knowledge can be *easily* acquired and whether it can be acquired *independently* of one's prior moral beliefs. To the extent that it can be acquired *easily* and *independently* of one's prior moral beliefs and perceptions, a solution to our paradox may be found in the possibility of us all having moral knowledge.

As we have seen, the Platonic and Aristotelian view is that moral habituation and the true moral beliefs it engenders provide an essential foundation for becoming reasonable and acquiring moral insight, and that such insight is difficult to achieve. When a person who has been properly cared for and trained acquires the ability to reason, reason will confirm the sound perceptions established by that training and care (*Rep.* 402a). Belief must precede knowledge, as it were. But in the circumstances that prevail in most cities, most people will never acquire that knowledge, and the preservation of their incomplete virtue will require some modest enforcement of laws which embody natural moral law (*NE* X.9 1180a1–4). Though the texts are less clear on this point, the view of Aristotle and the later Plato may be that even the moral insight of people of considerable practical wisdom may not obviate the need for some form of external assistance.[11]

By contrast, the view that emerges in the early modern period is that faith and reason converge, but may do so independently of one another. According to the doctrines of *natural reason* and *natural religion*, human beings possess as a gift of nature a faculty of reason by which they can easily discover within themselves a knowledge of God, moral law, and the afterlife. Such knowledge of the moral law and its divine enforcement would provide us all with assurance that virtue pays and provide an independent measure of human laws and customs. It is this doctrine that provides Rousseau with a solution to the tension he sees between domestic and public education, between education in the interests of the child and education in the interests of society. On a proper understanding of natural law, which the child will allegedly discover for himself, these interests coincide.

I am not sanguine about the prospects for making good on the idea that there is easily, and thus widely, attainable moral knowledge which not only provides an independent measure of the soundness of whatever moral code one has grown up with, but also a compelling motive to be moral. The Aristotelian account of virtue and reason seems more plausible in this respect. If such knowledge is not widely attainable, however, what possibilities for escaping the *paradox of progressive morality* remain? I can think of four which may warrant some consideration.

First, one might hypothesize that reason can outstrip the sentiments, that what one rationally judges to be best will not always be possible for one emotionally. If this is true, then critical reason may be able to provide evaluations of one's moral mother tongue sufficient for moral progress, even as it remains the language of one's heart. Progress would be intergenerational, not intragenerational, and the sentiments of each generation would bind its actions, if not its tongue. A difficulty with this suggestion is that if the advances in moral judgment are not put into practice in any way, it is not clear how intergenerational progress can proceed. Inconsistencies between speech and conduct are as likely to engender cynicism as progress, especially on Aristotelian assumptions about how moral virtues are cultivated.

Second, one might argue that allowance for fallibility in our identification of fundamental moral principles is misplaced, that what we think of as moral progress is progress in the consistency and sensitivity of application of the same fundamental principles which have been transmitted already through many generations. On this line of argument, there is no harm in people being forever bound in their sentiments, conduct, and perception of the good by the correct fundamental morality they are brought up in. That will prevent them from exploiting opportunities to free-ride, while a training in critical thinking and moral case analysis will develop their capacity for advancing moral progress through sensitive and creative application of the fundamental principles they have learned. This is a solution quite consistent with the moral finality of Plato's *Republic* and *Laws*, but not obviously compatible with Aristotle's conception of *phronêsis*. The idea that moral insight is tied up with the discernment of particulars and is aggregative (Sherman 1989:

13–55) does not lend itself to this suggested partitioning of principle and application.

Third, a suggestion which is more authentically Aristotelian than either of the preceding is that, as a body of citizens reaches better collective judgments about matters of moral concern, it can and should bind itself under new laws, thereby creating for itself the motivation to act in a more enlightened way. This is possible, by Aristotle's lights, even if people who have been brought up well, and have acquired a conception of what is admirable (*kalon*) or appropriate (*prepon*) and a seriousness about doing what is admirable or appropriate, remain in some danger of backsliding. Given the advancement of moral insight and judgment which such people can attain when they bring their somewhat different perspectives together in conversation, they will at least be in a position to advance enlightened legal reform, and will wish to, and they will thereby bind themselves under morally progressive laws, while both instructing and binding those who have not achieved the same progress of understanding. Aristotle stakes a great deal of his political theory on the idea that legal reform can be an effective instrument of moral progress, provided the instructional and motivating force of law is not undermined by changing it too much or too frequently (*Pol.* I.2 1253a30–9, II.8 1269a14–23).

A final possibility is that if children are initiated into habitual practices of giving and taking reasons, including moral reasons, they will become both morally serious and committed critical thinkers, motivated by conceptions of themselves as both moral and devoted to the truth. Being motivated in this way will preclude free-riding, since selfishness and making an exception of oneself will be incompatible with a desire to be moral; but if thoughtfulness about what counts as a reason has been

cultivated, it is hard to see how the perceptions and sentiments formed by such an upbringing would preclude an examination of fundamental morality and a potential for moral progress. On this alternative, one pictures the intellectual virtues as themselves originating in training or habituation in accordance with norms of reason, as much as in teaching, and one pictures training in the habits of virtue as also including a training in the practice of giving adequate reasons for what one does and respecting the adequate reasons that others give. This is not a straightforwardly Aristotelian view to the extent that it rejects the idea that reason emerges late, identifies a stage of habituation in norms of reason, and sees habits of giving and taking reasons as part of the habituation of ethical virtue. In these ways it is a more obviously Lockean view than Aristotelian, but the differences may be more apparent than real. Locke regards children as able to grasp reasons, though not the deepest reasons, and he thinks it a good thing to initiate children from the earliest possible age in the practices of reason giving. I am not sure that Aristotle's conception of moral habituation precludes any of this, since it must surely promote the development of rational and self-critical capacities if it is to promote true virtue (Sherman 1989: 157–99). What *is* precluded on Aristotle's account is the view that children are responsive to reason in the sense of grasping and being moved by appeals to what is good, admirable, or appropriate; but this is not to say that they are incapable of reasoning or unresponsive to other kinds of reasons.

This final solution is in some ways the most attractive, but a great deal remains to be examined. This must suffice, however, as an indication of the agenda for the theory and practice of moral education entailed by Aristotle's view of the relation between the moral and intellectual virtues.

## Notes

1. Two examples of the use being made of the Aristotelian dictum that we learn justice and lyre-playing alike "by doing" (1103a31–b2) are the arguments currently being given for public service requirements for high school graduation in the United States ("service learning") and a recent variant of "control theory." Harris Woffard, former director of the Peace Corps and current director of the Corporation for National Service, has recently cited Aristotle in defense of service learning requirements in a speech given at the White House/Congressional Conference on "Character Building" (Washington, DC, 7 June 1996). He argues that if children are to become generous or benevolent they must devote some of their energies to helping others. Gregory Bodenhamer, a former juvenile probation officer who now trains parents, teachers, and school administrators in techniques for managing difficult adolescents, has developed a self-consciously Aristotelian account of parenting (Bodenhamer 1995). One illustration

of his Aristotelianism is his insistence that children should not be told that it is their choice to do the right thing or something else, with a reminder of the consequences of bad choices. Many children will care more about doing what they want to do at the moment than about future consequences, and will soon grow accustomed to choosing the worse over the better. The better and more Aristotelian approach is to insist on acceptable conduct and provide supervision sufficient to induce it.

2. Rackham (1934) translates *NE* I.12 1101b2–3, "praise belongs to goodness, since it is this which makes men capable of accomplishing noble deeds," which captures better than the alternatives the background notion, pervasive in Aristotelian ethics, that virtue is what enables a person or thing to do well what is appropriate to it.

3. The idea that there is a direct opposition between inculcation of morality and instruction in critical thinking is evident, among other places, in the criticisms leveled at the US courts for endorsing the view that state and local authorities have a legitimate interest in inculcating "community values" through the public schools. See, e.g., van Geel 1983 and Roe 1991. It is also evident in Julia Annas's observation, in her commentary on Plato's *Republic*, that some educationalists "think that a child's intellectual autonomy is destroyed by too thorough a training in accepting group values at an early age," a problem faced by Plato "in an especially acute form" (Annas 1981: 87). A rare effort toward synthesis is Pritchard 1996.

4. It was for such reasons, offered by a community representative who had served in the Vietnam War, that loyalty and patriotism were recently struck from a tentative list of "core values" to be taught in a public school district in New York State. Courage and honesty remained on the list, although similar objections could be made to them. This inconsistency could be attributed to a failure to consistently consider the traits under discussion as entailing the good judgment needed to "hit the mean" between different kinds of error. My observations from the trenches of the character education movement suggest that unrecognized vacillations between true and merely habitual virtue are common.

5. [*Editor's note*: The claim that *justice requires* that we morally educate children rests on an *argument from a rule of law*, developed at length in earlier chapters, that education is foundational to a just and enforceable rule of law. Establishing a rule of law is necessarily a largely educative process, and the burden of ensuring the adequacy of the education involved falls upon the public or government that claims a right to impose and enforce the laws in question.]

6. [*Editor's note*: This claim relies on a specific *consent version* of the *argument from a rule of law*, which holds

that coercive force cannot legitimately be used to secure compliance with law in the absence of *care to ensure conditions favorable to* free, informed, and rational consent to the laws, including the universal provision of education for democratic citizenship.]

7. The phrase is Oliver Wendell Holmes's.

8. [*Editor's note*: The Socratic elenchus is the form of questioning that Socrates is depicted as using in Plato's Socratic dialogues, the ones commonly thought to depict the historical Socrates very much as he was. The aim of such questioning is to demonstrate the inconsistency of a person's beliefs by deriving a contradiction from beliefs he will admit to having, and in that way to enable him to examine and set aside mistaken beliefs. Socrates may have thought that in principle this could eventually enable a person to arrive at a completely consistent and true set of beliefs. In the first book of the *Republic*, Plato seems to illustrate the fact that this method could not be expected to rectify the beliefs of someone whose views are thoroughly or consistently *mistaken*.]

9. See Rousseau (1762): 98–9 (on the child's discovery of property rights), 168–77 (on astronomical, kinematic, and other scientific discoveries), and 313–14 (on the discovery of God through the design argument).

10. Note Aristotle's references to children being moved by affection (*NE* X.9 1180b4–7) and by love and respect for elders (*Pol.* I.12 1259b11–12), and to social instincts which create some natural tendency to cooperation (*Pol.* I.2 1253a30). Simpson's suggestion that there is no middle ground between being moved by reason and being moved by force (Simpson 1990, n. 13) rests on a misunderstanding of the context of Aristotle's remark about the form of the rule of the soul over the body at *Pol.* I.5 1254b2–31 in Aristotle's discussion of natural slavery. See Simpson (1990: 153).

11. See, e.g., *Rh.* II.3; *Laws* 653c–d, where Plato describes the religious festivals of a city as restoring the virtue which people tend to lose over the course of their lives; and Lord 1982, which argues that Aristotle develops a similar view through the idea that public performances of tragedies induce a cathartic purging of emotions that tend to accumulate and corrupt practical wisdom. Commentators commonly attribute to Aristotle the assumption that "wisdom must be so solid and steady an understanding of the truth that its knowledge can never be dislodged" (Cooper 1998: 266), but it is hard to find grounds for attributing to him the view that a person who is once wise is thereby permanently wise. In general he seems to hold the view that life is a struggle against death and that the preservation of the virtues that depend upon life is also a struggle that we are bound to lose eventually (Gill 1989: 230–4).

## References

Aristotle:

NE   *Nicomachean Ethics*
Pol.  *Politics*
Rh.   *Rhetoric*

all in Jonathan Barnes (ed.), *The Complete Works of Aristotle: The Revised Oxford Translation*, 2 vols (Princeton, NJ: Princeton University Press, 1984).

Annas, J. (1981) *An Introduction to Plato's Republic* (Oxford: Clarendon Press).

Bodenhamer, G. (1995) *Parent in Control* (New York: Simon & Schuster).

Cooper, J. (1998) "The Unity of Virtue." *Social Philosophy & Policy* 15: 1, pp. 233–74.

Gill, M. L. (1989) *Aristotle on Substance* (Princeton, NJ: Princeton University Press).

Hobbes, T. (1651) *Leviathan, Or the Matter, Form, and Power of a Commonwealth Ecclesiastical and Civil*, ed. E. Curley (Indianapolis: Hackett, 1994).

Korsgaard, C. (1986) "Aristotle on Function and Virtue," *History of Philosophy Quarterly* 3: 3, 259–79.

Kraut, R. (1989) *Aristotle on the Human Good* (Princeton, NJ: Princeton University Press).

Locke, J. (1693) *Some Thoughts Concerning Education*, in *Some Thoughts Concerning Education and Of the Conduct of the Understanding*, ed. R. W. Grant and N. Tarcov (Indianapolis: Hackett, 1996).

Lord, C. (1982) *Education and Culture in the Political Thought of Aristotle* (Ithaca, NY: Cornell University Press).

Plato, *Republic*, in John Cooper (ed.), *Plato: Complete Works* (Indianapolis: Hackett, 1997).

Pritchard, M. (1996) *Reasonable Children* (Lawrence: University Press of Kansas).

Rackham, H. (1934) *Aristotle: The Nicomachean Ethics* (Cambridge, MA: Harvard University Press).

Roe, R. (1991) "Valuing Student Speech: the Work of Schools as Cognition and Conceptual Development," *California Law Review* 79: 4, pp. 1269–1345.

Rousseau, J.-J. (1762) *Emile*, trans. A. Bloom (New York: Basic Books, 1979).

Sherman, N. (1989) *The Fabric of Character: Aristotle's Theory of Virtue* (Oxford: Clarendon Press).

Simpson, P. (1990) "Making the City Good: Aristotle's City and its Contemporary Relevance," *The Philosophical Forum* 22: 2, pp. 149–66.

van Geel, T. (1983) "The Search for Constitutional Limits on Governmental Authority to Inculcate Youth," *Texas Law Review* 62: 2, pp. 197–297.

# 56

# Motivation by Ideal

## J. David Velleman

When philosophers discuss our motive for acting morally, they tend to assume that it serves as one contributor to the broad conflux of motives that jointly determine most of our behavior. Although philosophers recognize the possibility of our being divided into mutually isolated motivational currents of the sort posited, at the extreme, to explain phenomena such as multiple personality, they assume that our moral motive must not be thus divided from our other motives, lest its manifestations in our behavior turn out to be irrational and, at the extreme, insane. Their assumption is that the actions flowing from our moral motive must in fact flow from a unified stream of all our motives, augmented by a moral tributary.

This assumption influences which questions are asked about moral motivation and which answers are considered plausible. The assumption encourages philosophers to ask, for example, how to identify our moral motive among the impulses that pass under the eye of ordinary deliberative reflection, and how that motive can possibly prevail against the impulses that so conspicuously favor immorality.

I am going to argue that the motive behind moral actions can become isolated from our other motives, generating behavior that is irrational in some respects though rational in others. In my view, moral action performed from moral motives can be less than fully rational precisely because of the division in its motivation. The reason why moral motivation can become isolated from our other motives, I shall argue, is that it often depends on the force of an ideal; an ideal, gains motivational force when we identify with it; and acting out of identification with an ideal is like a game of make-believe, in which we pretend to be that with which we identify. My argument will begin, then, with a consideration of adult make-believe.

For many years, I regularly kicked my wife in the head. We were studying Tae Kwon Do, and we often found ourselves paired together in drills or sparring. There we stood, high-school sweethearts from the sixties, each apparently trying to knock the other's block off.

What is the motivational explanation for such behavior? The motives most obviously actuating me in the circumstances were my desires to enhance my cardiovascular fitness and to have some fun in the process. But surely there would be something

Previously published in *Philosophical Explorations* V(2) (May 2002), pp. 90–2, 93–103. Reprinted with permission of Taylor & Francis; www.tandf.co.uk

odd about saying that I kicked my wife in the head in order to lower my cholesterol or just for fun. Of course. I knew – or, at least, hoped – that my wife would suffer no harm. She was wearing a foam helmet, I was wearing padded footgear, and I didn't strike with all of my strength. You might think, in fact, that I didn't so much kick her in the head as do something else that was only superficially similar, such as tap her on the temple with my toe. Such a tap could indeed have been produced by many motives of mine, including affection. Yet to say that I was trying to deliver a tap would misrepresent the encounter: a pulled punch or kick may feel like a tap to the recipient, but it is in fact quite dissimilar, since it is thrown with full force and "pulled" only in the sense of being aimed to fall short.

What calls for further explanation is not so much the fact that I kicked my wife on these occasions as the spirit in which I did so. For one thing, the effort behind my kicks was disproportionate to the motives that led me to the activity of sparring. The desires and beliefs that militated for kicking my wife may well have been stronger than the desires and beliefs that militated against, but not by enough of a margin to account for the zeal with which I went at her. Shouldn't effort be proportionate to motivation?

Then there is the manner of my kicks, which also seems to require further explanation. One and the same gross movement can evince different motives through subtle differences of posture, timing, muscle tension, and body english. The kicks that I aimed at my wife did not have the inflection of calisthenics or soccer or dance; they had the inflection of combat.

The key to explaining these aspects of my behavior, I think, is that Tae Kwon Do had helped me to solve a familiar motivational problem. The effort that one must expend in order to stay fit tends to require more motivation than can be supplied by one's desire for fitness: that's why so many exercise programs fail. If one wants to stay fit, one needs to find some additional source of motivation to draw on. Some forms of exercise give one access to competitiveness as an additional motive, others to team spirit, a love of nature, or musical inspiration. My additional source of motivation in Tae Kwon Do was aggression, and aggression is what accounted for the energy and inflection of my kicks.

Reflection on this case convinces me that there must be some truth in Freud's theory of the drives. What's true in that theory, I think, is the postulation

of highly labile psychic energies, which have only a vague direction in themselves but can be invested in specific activities.[1]

In studying Tae Kwon Do, I discovered that I had a fund of aggression to spend on kicks and punches, whether they were aimed at a leather bag, a handheld target, or a person's head. This aggression is not best characterized in terms of desire and belief. I did not enter the *do jang* wanting to smash something and looking for something to smash: rough contact with medium-sized objects was not something I desired at all. But it was something for which I found a considerable reserve of energy, in the form of aggression; and that aggression could be turned on virtually any solid object, including any person who happened to be my assigned opponent.

I am similarly inclined to believe in a drive corresponding roughly to the Freudian libido. We sometimes describe a person as having a lot of love to give but nowhere to give it. Such a person has a fund of tenderness that could potentially be spent on a lover, a child, a cat, even a garden or a scrapbook. In this case, unspent energy may be experienced as frustration, and so the person may develop a desire for someone or something to love. But such a desire need not develop; and even when it does, it remains distinct from the fund of energy whose disbursement it seeks. The person's desire for someone or something to love is a contingent reaction to his unspent tenderness, not an essential constituent of it.

[ . . . ]

Another idea that I want to borrow from Freud is that drives can take on a specific direction by "leaning" on some other, more specific motive. According to Freud, the infantile libido leans on and takes direction from the motive of hunger, with the result that the nutritive activity of sucking becomes a source of sensual pleasure, and the breast becomes a sexual object. Similarly, I think, aggression can take direction from more specific motives, such as professional ambition or athletic competitiveness. Aggressive energy is then invested in professional or athletic pursuits, which in turn take on an aggressive character.

The spirit of my kicks in Tae Kwon Do can thus be explained by the aggression from which they drew some of their motivation. Yet the explanation can hardly end here. The aggressiveness of my kicks was not like the aggressiveness of my driving, for example, which emerges, without my knowledge and even despite my efforts to contain it. The aggressiveness of my kicks was knowing and intentional because I was engaged in a fight. And yet I had no motives for, and many motives against, literally fighting my opponents. I was behaving aggressively in this case because I was engaged in fictional aggression, and so an explanation of my behavior requires an account of the operative fiction.

A martial art typically relies on a story – indeed, on a story-within-a-story, especially for students in the West. The "inner" story is a story of combat. At the founding of the discipline, this story may have been about combat on the battlefield, but in the modern *do jang* it is often about being attacked on the proverbial street. Some students have actually lived through a version of this story, especially women who seek out the martial arts after surviving rape or domestic abuse. But even these students train under a fiction, insofar as they are not really being attacked by their fellow students.

The "outer" story of a martial art, which is usually a fiction only for beginning students and then only briefly, is that they are devotees of a venerable tradition, transmitted to them by a revered master and shared with others in a spirit of humility and mutual self-restraint. The beginning student acts out this story before it can possibly be true of him, by bowing to his instructor and fellow students, calling them "Sir" and "Ma'am," wearing ritual garments and reciting ritual phrases, all from the first moment of the first class. For some students this story always remains a fiction, in the sense that they are never more than playing at participation in the tradition; but for most it soon becomes a true story, and the phrases of Korean or Japanese that were at first only mouthed come to be sincerely meant.

The inner and outer stories of a martial art are in direct conflict. The ferocity with which one tries to disable or kill an attacker, according to the inner story, is the very opposite of the humble deference that, according to the outer story, one owes to the instructor who may be playing the attacker's role. This conflict is vividly demonstrated when someone is injured in competitive sparring. The competitor responsible for the injury, who a moment ago seemed intent on bloody murder, suddenly kneels with his back to his opponent, in a posture of passivity and penitence, because he has drawn a single drop of blood. The fiction of combat is instantly dispelled, leaving only the outer story of deferential self-restraint.

This scene illustrates two further claims that I want to make about motivation, in addition to my prior claim on behalf of drives. The first of these further claims is that our motives are often manifested in our behavior under the guidance of a story: how we act on them is determined by the story that we are enacting.

The most ambitious version of this claim, which I have defended elsewhere, is that all of our autonomous actions are the enactments of stories, most of which are true but all of which are made up.[2] At any particular time we have motives for taking various actions, and the action we take is usually the one whose story we have in mind to enact. We are therefore in a position to make up the story of our behavior as we go, in the assurance that we'll behave accordingly, provided that we confine ourselves to stories whose enactment could be fueled by motives that we actually have. And the story that we make up is true, not only in that we proceed to enact it, but also in that it represents our action as its own enactment – as the action that we are hereby setting ourselves to take.

My view is that this process depends on a motive that is almost always in the background, and rarely in the foreground, of our autonomous actions: the desire to make sense of what we're doing. This desire moves us to take actions that make sense to us, and the actions that make sense are the ones about which we have a story to tell. Thus, although we ultimately do what is favored by the overall balance of our motives, that balance has often been tipped by the inclusion of our motive for doing things that make sense to us – a motive that is purely formal and does not appear in our conscious story of what we're doing. That story may tell of other motives, in light of which the action makes sense to us; but we perform the action not only out of those narrated motives but also out of our motive for making sense, which is enlisted by the availability of the narrative itself.

When a story renders an action intelligible to us, it becomes a *rationale* for the action. And when we are thereby led to perform the action, as the intelligible thing to do, we act on the basis of the story in its capacity as *rationale*. In other words, we act for a reason.

Thus, when I entered the *do jang* on a particular evening, I thought of myself as continuing my martial arts training, which I thought of myself as pursuing for the sake of cardiovascular fitness and fun. These thoughts were not just an idle commentary on my behavior; they constituted a story that I was in the process of enacting, with actions that I would not have taken in the absence of a story to tell about them. That I was seeking to continue my training out of desires for fitness and fun – that story was the *rationale* under which I entered the *do jang*. It was my reason for walking in the door.

Yet when I kicked an opponent in Tae Kwon Do, the story I enacted wasn't true, since it was a story of fending off a mortal attack. My behavior was therefore an enactment in the thespian sense – or, if you like, a game of make-believe.

I have argued elsewhere that the term 'make-believe' means "mock-belief," because it refers to a fantasy or imagining that stands in for a belief by playing its motivational role.[3] My examples on that occasion were primarily imaginings that play the role of ordinary instrumental beliefs – such as the belief that I can communicate with someone by speaking to him, which is ordinarily one of the motives behind my verbal behavior. When I address remarks to other drivers on the road, however, or to the referees of a sporting event on television, I am not moved by the belief that I can thereby communicate with them; I'm moved instead by imagining that I can. Because imagining here plays the motivational role of a belief, it qualifies as "mock-belief," and I can be described as making believe. I'm making believe that I can communicate with these people, because I am acting on a mock-belief to that effect.

In the present context, I want to consider imaginings that substitute for beliefs in a slightly different motivational role. If I really believed myself to be under attack, that belief would serve as a narrative premise under which some courses of action would make sense and others would not, and I would be guided accordingly as I improvised my part in the encounter. Strictly speaking, this belief would be functioning as an instrumental motive, since it would influence me by causing some steps but not others to appear intelligible and hence conducive to making sense of what I do, which is a desired outcome. But this outcome is not an end-in-view – not, that is, an end-in-the-story, something whose pursuit I would enact. It's just something that I want, conduciveness to which makes actions attractive to me. And what it makes attractive to me, in particular, are actions about which I have a story to tell.

I think that fantasy and imagining can play this motivational role as well. When I imagined that I was facing an attack in Tae Kwon Do, I was thereby led to imagine some steps as making sense and others as making none, and I was guided accordingly as I improvised my part in the ensuing fights – make-believe fights, guided by a mock-belief. I then enacted a story that was fictional in every sense, since it was not only made up but also untrue.

Part of the story, of course, was that I fought out of a desire to disable or kill my opponent, and in reality I didn't have any such desire to draw on. What I drew on instead, I have argued, is a labile fund of aggression, which leaned in this case, not on any desire to harm my opponent, but on the motivational force lent to the story itself by my inclination to do what made sense in light of that story. I may actually have imagined the felt thrust of aggression to be a desire to harm my opponent, much as I was obliged, in self-defense drills, to imagine wooden batons to be knives. (In that case, my aggression served as a "prop," in the sense defined by Kendall L. Walton.)[4] In reality, however, my aggression's being focused upon my opponent was due to my conceiving of it as a desire to harm him, rather than the other way around. That is, imagining it as a desire to harm my opponent lent intelligibility to the act of kicking, thus giving me a motive for kicking, on which my aggression could lean.

The game of make-believe was thus fueled by two elements – a drive and an imagining – and the game would fail if either element was missing. Some students of the martial arts don't have much aggression to draw on, and they consequently aren't fully equipped to play the game. Merely imagining that they are under attack isn't enough to make them fight, in the absence of a drive that could supply the force of their imagined desires with respect to an attacker. So their threatening yells always sound like peeps, and their blows really are no more than taps. Other students seem to have sufficient aggression but to be inhibited from entering into the requisite make-believe, at least in some circumstances. For example, some men simply can't bring themselves to imagine that they are trying to kill or disable a woman. Though capable of fighting other opponents aggressively, they can't muster the imagining that would bring their aggression to bear on these opponents, and so they merely go through the motions.

Of course, none of us actually tried to kill or disable an opponent. We were restrained by our sense of mutual respect and deference. But I do not think that the motive of deference simply combined with aggression to yield an intermediate vector-sum – a deferential aggression, or aggressive deference, or whatever. To pull a punch is not simply to strike at half-strength, out of some lukewarm mixture of hot and cold motives. This is the second of my further claims about motivation.

In making this claim, I do not mean to reject the principle that a person's behavior flows from the combined force of his motives; I mean only to point out that, because of the motivational force exerted by an agent's self-conception, there are two distinct ways in which his other motives can combine.

One way requires the agent to think of himself as acting on both motives at once and hence to be guided, not only by their combined forces, but also by his conception of how those forces combine. In this case, the agent is consciously engaged in a mixed activity – restrained hostilities, or perhaps hostile self-restraint. The agent's behavior is determined partly by the combined forces of his motives and partly by his conception of what would make sense for him to do in light of their combination, his story of how he is acting on both at once.

Another way for motives to combine is for the agent to conceive of himself as acting on only one of them, while the other tacitly modifies this activity. Thus, for example, an agent's desire to avoid bodily harm steers him away from obstacles even when he is single-mindedly engaged in vigorous activity and not consciously exercising caution. What makes for the difference between these two ways of mixing motives is the motivational role of the agent's self-conception, which is not epiphenomenal on his behavior, not just an idle commentary. In one case, the agent deliberately acts on both motives, by enacting a story of both; in the other case, the agent enacts the story of one motive, while this enactment is subject to unheralded modification by the other.

When we think about the mixing of motives, we usually have the former process in mind, because we assume that people are simultaneously aware of the various motives vying for control of their behavior. We may therefore assume that if students of the martial arts are both mutually deferential and mutually hostile, they must conceive of themselves in both terms at the same time. But such a conflicted self-conception would result in sparring that could only be described as half-assed. In fact,

students imagine themselves entirely as hostile opponents while they are sparring, but this role is externally constrained by their deferential motives as colleagues.

Consider what happens when a participant in make-believe gets "carried away". Sometimes students do get carried away in sparring, especially new students who haven't yet learned how to manage the conflicting stories that they are supposed to enact. The reason why it's possible to get carried away, I think, is that a participant in make-believe puts his real identity and his real relations to other participants temporarily out of mind. In order to enact his fictional identity and his fictional relations to others, he must devote his mind to the fiction. In doing so, however, he trusts that the motives he has put out of mind will nevertheless hold him back from excesses, or will pull him up short if things get out of hand. His knowledge of who the participants really are, and his inclinations toward those real people, are motives that stand by and supervise, as it were, either by setting boundaries to the game of make-believe, within which they are not in view, or by forcing their way into view and breaking up the game, if it goes too far. The agent gets carried away when this external supervision fails and the game proceeds headlong, without either restraint or interruption.

Getting carried away often leads to irrational action. When someone gets carried away in a philosophical debate, for example, he presses his point at the expense of other people's feelings and his own reputation for collegiality, both of which he cares about, on balance, more than the question under dispute. In some cases, of course, intellectual enthusiasm may have blinded the agent to the undesirable consequences of his behavior; but in others, he sees those consequences yet presses on with the argument regardless.

From the agent's point-of-view, his motives may appear to wax and wane as circumstances change. In the heat of the argument, the prospect of securing his point consumes all of his attention and interest; whereas in a cooler moment, the philosophical point may seem unimportant. But this introspectable change need not be a change in the agent's desires themselves; it may instead be a change as to which desire is reinforced by the agent's conception of what he is doing. In the heat of the argument, the agent thinks of himself exclusively as pressing his point, and this self-conception provides reinforcement exclusively to his motives for doing so. Even if the agent notices the annoyance of his interlocutor, he doesn't think of it as something that he currently wants to avoid or to mitigate. Managing his relations with colleagues is not something toward which he thinks of himself as currently motivated, and so his potential motives for that activity are not bolstered by his interest in self-understanding.

These motives are nevertheless present, and as I have suggested, they have two chances to prevent him from getting carried away, corresponding to the two ways in which motives can combine. First, the desire for good relations with colleagues can leave the agent's pursuit of the argument uninterrupted while restraining it from the outside, in the same way as the desire to avoid bodily harm restrains his physical activities even when he isn't deliberately being cautious. And then, if unreflective restraint fails, the agent's desire for good relations with colleagues can obtrude itself on his attention, so that his concentration on the argument is broken and he comes to think of himself, under the circumstances, as having more than one end at stake.

These modes of restraint look quite different, both from the agent's perspective and from the perspective of observers. Some philosophers can throw themselves into an argument without fear of giving offense, because they will be unreflectively restrained from going too far. These philosophers are said to trust themselves in the heat of an argument, where the "selves" they trust are not reflective selves who might be trusted to make the right choice in deliberation but rather motives that can be trusted to restrain them without reflection or deliberation. Other philosophers never fully commit themselves to the point they're trying to make, because they are busy monitoring the expressions of their listeners and interjecting polite qualifications. Because they can't rely on their collegial motives for implicit restraint, they must explicitly adopt self-restraint as an additional activity whenever they get into an argument.

The same contrast applies to participants in the martial arts. If a student can't trust himself in sparring, he must consciously ride two horses at once, both his aggression and his self-restraint. If a student can trust himself, then he can ride his aggression wholeheartedly and count on his self-restraint to run alongside on its own. If the latter strategy fails, the student may be forced to adopt the former – not exactly to switch horses in mid-

stream but to shift part of his weight onto the second horse. And part of what he counted on from his self-restraint, at the outset, was that it would force itself into his activity in this manner if it failed to steer him adequately from the outside.

Both forms of restraint are exemplified in an agent's behavior most of the time. Because moments of true single-mindedness are rare, an agent is often consciously multi-tasking, and yet he is also influenced by additional motives that remain out of view. Bustling down the street on several errands at once, he implicitly trusts himself not to step into potholes or bowl over fellow pedestrians – which is to say, he knows that various latent motives of his will either restrain his conscious pursuits or interrupt them if tacit restraint should fail.

An agent's self-conception thus separates his motives into two groups. One group comprises motives that the agent manifests in the process of consciously enacting them; the other comprises motives that manifest themselves primarily by externally modifying such enactments. The former are the motivational horses that the agent is riding, as I have put it, and the latter are relegated to the role of hemming him in or cutting him off as necessary.

The process becomes further complicated if the agent imagines himself to have motives that he doesn't actually have. The agent may be moved to enact this imaginative self-conception, especially if he has motivational resources that can mimic the force of the imagined motives, such as aggression that can be focused onto a particular person by being conceived as a desire to kill or disable him. The agent's actual motives are then divided into those on which he is acting under a mistaken or imaginary guise, and those which are relegated to hemming in or cutting off that game of make-believe.

[ . . . ]

As we have seen, this division in an agent's motives can lead to action that is irrational in relation to the totality of his desires and interests, as when it lets him get carried away in a debate, to his subsequent regret. But I think that the temporary irrationality of getting carried away can sometimes be exploited for more permanent gains in rationality. For an agent can get carried away with the better of his motives as well as the worse.

A colleague who studies rational choice tells me that he could never have quit smoking without indulging in some irrationality.[5] Although the long-run costs of smoking outweighed the long-run benefits, he says, the costs of smoking the next cigarette never outweighed the benefits of smoking that one cigarette, since he could always decide to quit after the next cigarette rather than before. In order to stop smoking in the long run, of course, he had to forego the next cigarette at some point, at an obvious sacrifice of utility. The only way for him to stop was thus to do something irrational. How did he manage to do it?

The answer, he tells me, was *not to think of himself as a smoker*. At the beginning, of course, not to think of himself as a smoker was incorrect, since he was still addicted to smoking, both physically and psychologically. I suggest, then, that he resorted to make-believe. He imagined that he was not addicted – that he didn't like the taste of cigarettes, wasn't in the habit of smoking them, had no craving for them – and he then enacted what he was imagining, pretending to be the non-smoker that he wanted to be. And I suggest that this make-believe succeeded because it excluded the smoker's tastes, habits, and cravings from the story that he was enacting. That story lacked the narrative background that would have made it intelligible for him to buy, light, or smoke the next cigarette.

I suggest, further, that my colleague got carried away with this make-believe, and that getting carried away was essential to his success at kicking the habit. His motives for smoking were relegated to externally constraining his enactment of a non-smoker's story. Those motives had proved irresistible when they were available at center-stage to motivate the next episode in the story; but when they were written out of the plot and left to operate, as it were, *ex machina*, they were unable to deflect the story from its natural conclusion.

I suggest, finally, that when my colleague got carried away with enacting an image of himself as a non-smoker, he was being motivated by an ideal. That's what an ideal is: the image of another person, or a currently untrue image of oneself, that one can get carried away with enacting.[6] To imagine oneself in that image, and to act accordingly, is to identify with and emulate the ideal.

An alternative to my conception of ideals would be to think of them as descriptions or images that motivate by way of one's desire to satisfy them and one's realistic beliefs about how to do so. According to this alternative conception, taking another person as one's ideal entails wanting to resemble him, which

directly motivates behavior like his, conceived as a constitutive means to the desired resemblance. I doubt whether the motivational force of an ideal flows directly from such a desire in most cases.[7]

Suppose that one idealizes a person for his generosity and wants to resemble him in this respect.[8] Insofar as this desire directly moves one to do generous things, those acts will not in fact be motivated by generosity, after all, and so one's attempted imitation of the ideal will be an obvious failure. Indeed, one would be unlikely to acquire or to learn generosity through acts motivated in this way. The desire to mold oneself in the image of a generous person will meet with better success if it moves one first to imagine being a generous person and then to enact this self-image, making believe that one is generous and using as props whatever motives one has that can be cast in the role of generosity. (Such props might be drawn from that fund of tenderness that Freud calls the libido.) Emulating generosity in this fashion, one comes closer to being and to feeling generous, and one has a better chance of becoming really generous, by gradually working one's way into the role. One can thus gradually adopt or assume the motive of generosity in a way that one never could by imitating it from the outside.

The desire to resemble an ideal can initiate this process only by motivating a deliberate turn toward make-believe; but other attitudes can initiate it directly, because they already engage the imagination. In the former case, the desire to resemble an ideal depends for its motivational force on an assessment of how one falls short of the ideal and what one must do to close the gap. The desire may ultimately favor a process of conjuring up and enacting an idealized self-image, but only on the basis of a realistic calculation that the process will be conducive to a resemblance not yet attained. Now consider an attitude like respect or admiration for the ideal. Precisely because these attitudes are not goal-oriented motives, they tend to favor wishful thinking over purposeful activity. Admiring someone isn't a motive for bringing about anything in particular, and so it doesn't call for an instrumental calculation of the steps required to bring anything about. But admiring someone can naturally motivate wishfully picturing oneself in his image. Emulation therefore flows directly out of admiration.

When a smoker draws on an ideal for motivation to quit, his behavior is in some respects irrational.

He ignores various facts that would be relevant to fair-minded deliberation: the fact that he would enjoy the taste of a cigarette, that he is in the habit of smoking, that he is even now craving a smoke, and so on. And he acts instead on various considerations that are figments of his imagination: that he feels fine without a cigarette, that he wouldn't enjoy one, that lighting up would be an uncharacteristic thing for him to do.

Yet his make-believe world is a world of make-believe reasons. His imaginative considerations guide him in the manner of reasons for acting, just as the facts would guide him if he acted on realistic grounds. These imaginative considerations serve as narrative premises in light of which only some actions make sense as the continuation of his story. And when an agent does what makes sense in light of a narrative premise, or *rationale*, he is acting for a reason, albeit one that isn't true.

What's more, this make-believe reasoning enables the agent to become more rational in the long run. For by pretending to be a non-smoker, he actually becomes a non-smoker, which is a more rational sort of person to be. As a smoker, he was deeply conflicted: his reasons for smoking were at odds with all of his other reasons for acting, although they were strong enough to prevail in a review of what he had reason to do next. He therefore chose to smoke, but always at the sacrifice of the many countervailing reasons that had been outweighed. In kicking the habit, he lost his reasons for smoking, leaving the field to his countervailing reasons, which can now guide his actions unopposed. Because his actual reasons have become less conflicted, he sacrifices less in doing what he actually has most reason to do.[9]

Indeed, the agent may have had sufficient reason to identify with a non-smoking ideal, even when he lacked sufficient reason to forego his next cigarette. Foregoing his next cigarette in his story as a smoker would have left the resulting discomforts and inconveniences at center-stage, as salient repercussions to be faced. The second act of this story would have been "The Smoker Copes with Withdrawal" – an episode that's difficult to improvise without ending up in a third act entitled "The Smoker's Relapse." The difficulty of charting an intelligible course through the story of quitting as a smoker is what made for the rationality of continuing to smoke instead. The point of identifying with the ideal of a non-smoker was precisely to gain access to a different story, presenting a different set of reasons. That alternative story entailed not smoking the next cigarette,

of course, but not smoking that cigarette was a different option for a non-smoker than it was for a smoker. For a smoker, not smoking that cigarette was a matter of changing course and facing the consequences; for a non-smoker, it was a matter of going on as usual. To be sure, the non-smoker in this case would be a merely make-believe non-smoker, who would experience twinges and shakes of what was in reality nicotine withdrawal. But those discomforts would not be expected repercussions to be faced and overcome; they would be inexplicable irritations to be ignored, if possible. And the smoker who wants to quit has good reason to prefer facing the consequent discomforts under the guise of irritations to be ignored rather than expected repercussions to be faced. Hence he had good reason for undertaking the pretense of being a non-smoker.

The smoker who wants to quit is like other agents who have reason to make themselves temporarily irrational – warriors who have reason to work themselves into a frenzy in order to frighten the enemy, or negotiators who have reason to become obstinate in order to win concessions. Unlike the warrior or the negotiator, however, the smoker does not have reason to arrange for something to interfere with his faculty for practical reasoning. On the contrary, the irrationality that the smoker has reason to cultivate requires the exercise of an intact deliberative faculty; it merely requires that faculty to operate on input from the agent's imagination rather than on his knowledge of the facts. When the agent's deliberative faculty operates in this way, he becomes insensitive to considerations that are genuine reasons for him to act, and so he becomes dispositionally irrational. And because he thereby neglects reasons against the action that he performs, he may end up performing an irrational action.

I have now argued, on the one hand, that it was rational for the smoker to undertake the activity of pretending to be a non-smoker, that this activity involved an exercise of an intact rational faculty, and that it resulted in the smoker's becoming a more rational agent. On the other hand, I have argued that the activity of pretending to be a non-smoker was irrational in the sense that it made the smoker insensitive to some of the reasons that actually applied to him, and consequently led him to do something that wasn't supported by the balance of actual reasons.

I think that such irrationality is often involved when an agent is motivated by a personal ideal

– including the overarching ideals that embody Hume's general perspective or the Aristotelian virtues.[10] Whether one is emulating an impartial observer or a virtuous human being, one may be engaged in make-believe and hence in an activity that's irrational in the respects described above.

Note, however, that I have not included Kant's Categorical Imperative in the list of moral ideals whose emulation tends to require make-believe.[11] The reason is that, in my view, Kantian moral theory manages to kick away that particular ladder.

The Categorical Imperative is an ideal image of the will, as acting on only those maxims which it can simultaneously will to be universal laws. But what moves this ideal will to act only on universalizable maxims? The answer is that it is restrained from acting on other maxims by respect for the law. And respect for the law is just respect for the Categorical Imperative, which is an ideal image of the will as acting only on universalizable maxims. To act out of respect for this ideal is therefore to emulate a will that acts out of respect for the very same ideal.

In the case of the Kantian ideal, then, emulation tends to rise to the level of attainment. What is ideal about the person we emulate is precisely that he is moved by an ideal, and indeed the same ideal by which we are moved. Hence to emulate him is already and really to resemble him, and so it is

unlike emulating him with respect to a motive that doesn't rely on emulation. To do generous things by emulating a generous person is not yet to be generous, though it may be a means of learning generosity. But to do the moral thing by emulating a moral person really is to be moral, since enacting a moral image of oneself is what being a moral person consists in.

So we are not enacting a false conception of ourselves in emulating the Categorical Imperative, because we are making that conception true just by emulating it. Of course, we could get carried away with enacting that self-conception, by losing sight of our countervailing motives, so that they lapse into abeyance for want of reinforcement from our self-conception. Wouldn't we then be acting on a false self-conception and hence irrationally? Not necessarily. After all, the Categorical Imperative could be – come to think of it, I'm sure that it is – the image of a will that gets carried away with enacting that very self-image. The motivational division that underlies make-believe – the division between enacted motives and motives that externally modify such enactments – remains essential to our acting on the Categorical Imperative; but what gets enacted is not a false self-conception.

Insofar as we are Kantian moral agents, then, we are not just pretending. When we dream of our morally better selves, our dreams really can come true.

## Notes

1. Let me emphasize that I am borrowing only some elements of Freudian drive theory. I am not borrowing the model of stimulus reduction, for example, but only the notion of indeterminate motivational forces. Indeed, my conception of their indeterminacy is different from Freud's. Freud described drives as having determinate aims but being readily redirected toward other aims instead. I prefer to think of drives as having only inchoate aims.

2. Of course, the "stories" enacted in our autonomous actions are not the stuff of novels: they can be as trivial as the story that goes "My leg itches, so I'm scratching it." For this view of autonomy, see Velleman (1989): Velleman (2000a), Chapters 1, 2, 7, and 9; Velleman (2000b). My view of agency bears similarities to: Hollis (1977), Harré (1979), and Anscombe (2000).

3. "On the Aim of Belief", in Velleman (2000a), pp. 244–81.

4. Walton (1993).

5. Thanks to Jim Joyce for this example.

6. By "an untrue image of oneself", I mean a self-image that would not be true even if one enacted it. Of course, my colleague eventually became a non-smoker by pretending to be one, but at the outset his pretense was false.

7. For background to this section, see "On the Aim of Belief", in Velleman (2000a), pp. 256–72.

8. See Aristotle's discussion at *Nicomachean Ethics*, 1105a ff.

9. I discuss these issues further in "Willing the Law."

10. [Editor's note: The perspective of David Hume (1711–76) to which the author refers is the theory that moral judgment expresses evaluative reactions experienced by a person who has adopted the point of view of an ideal observer, an observer who is impartial (or benevolent) and has an accurate understanding of the act and its circumstances.]

11. For my interpretation of the Categorical Imperative, see Velleman (1998, 1999).

## References

Anscombe, E. (2000) *Intention* (Cambridge, MA: Harvard University Press).

Brakel, L. (2002) "Phantasy and Wish: A Proper Function Account for Human A-Rational Primary Process Mediated Mentation," *Australasian Journal of Philosophy* 80, pp. 1–16.

Harré, R. (1979) *Social Being* (Oxford: Basil Blackwell).

Hollis, M. (1977) *Models of Man* (Cambridge: Cambridge University Press).

Velleman, J. D. (1989) *Practical Reflection* (Princeton, NJ: Princeton University Press).

Velleman, J. D. (1998) "The Voice of Conscience," *Proceedings of the Aristotelian Society*, November 1998, pp. 57–76.

Velleman, J. D. (1999) "A Rational Superego," *Philosophical Review* 108, pp. 529–58.

Velleman, J. D. (2000a) *The Possibility of Practical Reason* (Oxford: Oxford University Press).

Velleman, J. D. (2000b) "From Self-Psychology to Moral Philosophy," *Philosophical Perspectives* 14, pp. 349–77.

Velleman, J. D. (forthcoming) "Willing the Law," in *Practical Conflicts*, ed. Monika Betzler and Peter Baumann (Cambridge: Cambridge University Press).

Walton, K. (1993) *Mimesis as Make-Believe: On the Foundations of the Representational Arts* (Cambridge, MA: Harvard University Press).

# Curricular Controversies

# 57

## Should We Teach Patriotic History?

## Harry Brighouse

Cosmopolitan liberals often deny the propriety of public education reinforcing in children the particularistic ties they learn in their families and communities. The role of public education should be to expand children's horizons, to teach them that they are part of a larger moral community than that in which they were raised, and that their life options should not be limited to those endorsed by their parents and communities. Thus the cosmopolitan aims both to liberate children from their roots, and to induce proper moral concern with the rest of humanity.

But cosmopolitans also often assume, or in some cases argue, that this project justifies encouraging patriotic identification with the liberal democratic state. This state, after all, embodies universalistic values, and identification with it is liable to distance people appropriately from their more parochial concerns. Arthur Schlesinger Jr's much discussed *The Disuniting of America*, for example, has two central themes. First he criticises multiculturalists who want to use "history as a weapon" to sustain or even create separate ethnic identities in America. Consciously echoing Edward Said, he says that

"History as a weapon is an abuse of history. The high purpose of history is not the presentation of self nor the vindication of identity, but the recognition of complexity and the search for knowledge"[1] and later that "history as therapy means the corruption of history as history . . . honest history calls for the unexpurgated record."[2] On the other hand he criticizes the same multiculturalists for promoting a history and pedagogy which may lead to the "decomposition of America": the breaking of the bonds of identity which unite an ethnically and culturally diverse population in loyalty to a single nation state: "Above all, history can give a sense of national identity. We do not have to believe that our values are absolutely better than the next fellow's or the next country's, but we have no doubt they are better for us, reared as we are – and are worth living by and dying for. For our values are not matters of whim or happenstance. History has given them to us."[3]

In this chapter I cast doubt on the desirability of using schooling to encourage loyalty to, or identification with, the nation state, and criticize the arguments for it. I want to address the particular

Previously published in Kevin McDonough and Walter Feinberg (eds.), *Education and Citizenship in Liberal-Democratic Societies* (Oxford: Oxford University Press, 2003), pp. 157–75. © Harry Brighouse 2003. Reprinted with kind permission of the author.

question of whether it is permissible for patriotism to be taught to children in schools; and whether, if it should, the teaching of history is the right vehicle for teaching patriotism. I argue that there are good reasons for being deeply suspicious of teaching patriotism in schools: there are additional reasons for thinking that even if it should be taught, history is a particularly inappropriate discipline with which to convey it.

This goes against the grain of the thought of just about everyone concerned with teaching history in the United States today. Open any US high school American History text book, and you will find it imbued with a sense of identification with the country whose history it relates. Uses of "we", "our", and cognates abound, identifying the reader and author with their, in many cases long dead, compatriots. So, in many books, do identifications of "America" or "the nation" as an intentional agent. So, finally, do moralizing commentaries on the motives and characters of individual agents in history. Here are some examples from a bestselling textbook, Daniel Boorstin and Brooks Mather Kelley's *A History of the United States since 1861* (all emphases are mine):

Explaining the entry of the US into the First World War: "Most Americans, including the President, were drawn by powerful unseen forces toward the British cause. *We* spoke the English language . . . *our* laws and customs were built on English foundations. *We* had fought the American revolution to preserve *our* rights as Englishmen."[4]

Concerning the Red Scare: "The mania of these times would last even after the war. The *virus* of witch-hunting and super-patriotism was not so easy to cure."[5] General Douglas MacArthur was "*a true American hero*" but, in his dispute with Truman over Korea "more and more Americans came to see that Truman was talking sense."[6]

Rosa Parks was a "tired black seamstress;" Martin Luther King: "a natural leader, *American to the core*"; in response to segregation he was "indignant and saddened but not angry. He was a *thoughtful* man and a Christian."[7]

A section called "Why we were in Vietnam" contains the following:

A third reason for going into Vietnam was to protect *our* reputation. *We* wanted other free countries to believe that *we* would stand by them if they were attacked by

Communists. This was called *our* "credibility." If *we* did not protect South Vietnam, *we* feared other nations would not believe *we* would help them. Then *our whole worldwide system* of defense and deterrence against the Communists might collapse.[8]

Different textbooks moralize in different ways, emphasize different virtues and faults; and disagree about both the significance and moral content of events. But the consensus favoring such commentary on, and identification with, the past is striking.[9] This may seem surprising given the apparent place of history in America's so-called culture wars, and the charges that the authors of history standards are unpatriotic and unconcerned with their students' identification with the nation. In fact, there is no disagreement. Gary Nash, himself a prolific author of high school texts, comments: "the argument is in fact between two visions of patriotic history. On one side are those who believe that young people will love and defend the United States if they see it as superior to other nations and regard its occasional falls from grace as short pauses or detours in the continuous flowering of freedom, capitalism, and opportunity. . . . On the other side are historians who believe that *amor patriae* is nurtured by looking squarely at the past, warts and all. Only this clear-sightedness will obviate the cynicism that sugar-coated history produces when youngsters get older and recognize 'the lies my teacher told me.'"[10]

The chapter proceeds as follows. In Section 1, I discuss briefly the justifications of patriotism and the further arguments that patriotism is something that should be taught to children in school, and in particular that history is an appropriate vehicle for teaching it. Section 2 casts doubt on the arguments for patriotism and even more doubt on the idea that it should be taught. In Section 3, I argue that history is a discipline particularly inappropriate for conveying patriotic feeling.

## 1 Why Patriotism?

What is patriotism? For the most part I shall mean a special sense of identification with one's state and one's compatriots, which inclines one sometimes to give them prior consideration to non-compatriots. One's compatriots are normally the citizens of the state of which one is a citizen, though there may be exceptions (e.g. people who have been unjustly stripped of citizenship, and others who actively want but are unjustly denied citizenship).[11] On some accounts patriotism involves distinctive obligations to compatriots. But on others it just involves a special sense of attachment or fellow feeling: John White writes of the sentiment involved when he contemplates "the relative flatness of the landscape and the rainy weather after returning from a week in Maderia; hearing about the knife attack on George Harrison by a fellow Liverpudlian, two women waiting for the 184 bus and wondering why it was late; the New Year's Honours list."[12] I understand patriotism narrowly, as including just the sense of fellow feeling, though it will be vital to discuss the stronger sense of patriotism since the idea that we have distinctive patriotic obligations is a major motivation for thinking that we should encourage fellow feeling for them. I shall restrict my attention to views which are, broadly, compatible with a liberal democratic outlook. Historically patriotism and its justifications have stood apart from the liberal democratic tradition, but since no set of social arrangements could be just or legitimate unless it was liberal and democratic, justifications of patriotism which are incompatible with this outlook are non-starters. Liberal democratic justifications of patriotism are simply the best available, so it is on them that I want to cast doubt.

There are four broadly liberal justifications of patriotism.

First is the claim that we have particularistic obligations to our compatriots which we do not have toward non-citizens, by virtue of sharing their nationality. These are not the only obligations we have, and they are sometimes overridden by universalistic obligations. The model is usually that of the family: it is an accepted part of common sense morality that we have duties to our family members that we do not have toward non-family members, and it is hard to reconcile these special duties with an exclusively universalistic approach to morality.[13]

Second is the claim that the character of political institutions, and the relationships that hold within them, mean that the universal obligation of respect for persons yields a duty of partial concern toward compatriots. Richard Miller argues that the mere fact of sharing a state with someone else gives us a reason to prioritize their interests over those of foreigners because our political choices will result in laws which they are bound to obey. "Equal respect for all is incompatible with supporting the coercive enforcement of terms of self-advancement

under which some are seriously burdened, regardless of their choices, in ways that could be alleviated at relatively little cost to the advantaged."[14]

A third argument avoids describing patriotism as a duty, but still asserts that it is, or at least can be, a very good thing. This is the argument that patriotism facilitates the stability of the (just) liberal state. Trust is a practical necessity for stability: since citizens will make conflicting demands on the polity and will do so based on different judgments about what is the right or best thing for the state to do, it is vital for the stability of the liberal state that citizens be able to interpret their disagreements as due to the burdens of judgment rather than the self-seeking behavior or unreasonableness of their opponents. Since the burdens of judgment are heavy, and the amount of disagreement they permit is great, citizens need to be able to trust those with whom they conflict in order confidently to attribute their error to the burdens of judgment rather than unreasonableness. Patriotism facilitates this trust, and according to Eamonn Callan it is "only through initiation into a just polity, and coming to care about the people and the particular institutions it encompasses" that we "come to draw on that reservoir of trust" that is achieved over time by the work of other citizens.[15]

Finally, it is often argued that patriotism is instrumental for distributive justice. The idea is that the fellow feeling engendered by patriotism helps citizens with correct views about distributive justice to act justly, since their motivation from duty is buttressed by their motive of association. Patriotic ties can direct our attention toward our duties to fellow citizens, and provide a sort of backup motivation for action in accordance with justice when the motive of principle, for whatever reason, fails, thus helping to secure justice. Principle and association are distinct, but in a liberal state complementary, sources of motivation.

It never follows immediately from the fact that some trait or kind of behavior is good that it should be taught to children. There are many goods, and some can be instilled in people only at the expense of others. Many goods are consciously neglected by schools, on the assumption that they, or noncompatible alternative goods, will be taught to children elsewhere.

The first two cases for patriotism mentioned above are those that most naturally lend themselves to supporting a policy of universal teaching of patriotism. Both justifications claim that we have direct duties to our compatriots that we do not have to others, and if it is true that we have these duties it is incumbent on us to carry them out, in so far as doing so does not conflict with other, more stringent, duties. If a correct theory of justice must observe a standard of publicity – that is, if its principles must not only be fulfilled but must also be transparently known, and known to be fulfilled, by citizens, as if as a matter of common agreement, then it is important that the duties be known by citizens.[16] Teaching them in school is not the only way of carrying this out, but it is a convenient and natural way of doing so.

The case from instrumentality for some other good to teaching patriotism is more complex. Three further conditions are needed to justify promoting patriotism. It must be claimed: first, that no alternative good is instrumental for stability or justice which can be as readily taught with as few opportunity costs; second, that the good for which patriotism is claimed to be instrumental is important enough to justify whatever opportunity costs are involved in teaching patriotism; and third, that teaching patriotism *universally* is needed in order to ensure the threshold level of uptake required in order to secure the good for which patriotism is supposed to be instrumental; or that, if it is not, there is some independent reason for teaching it universally given that one is teaching it at all. These are instances of general conditions on justifying state action to provide or secure something which is either merely a public good or is merely instrumental (but not necessary) for some other good which is necessary as a matter of justice.

With respect to the second necessary claim, I must admit that justice and stability are extremely important goods, and it is hard to see what opportunity costs could be claimed that would justify not contributing to their security, if their security were in doubt absent the presence of a high level of patriotism. But I shall cast doubt on the first and third claims as well as on the instrumentality claim itself.

## 2 Problems with Teaching Patriotism

The first problem is that the instrumental justifications all assume an extremely benign version of patriotism. David Miller, in an early article on the subject, cites the peculiarly English insularity of the Water Rat in *Wind in the Willows*:

Beyond the Wild Wood comes the Wild World. And that's something that doesn't matter, either to you or me. I've never been there, and I'm never going, nor you either if you've got any sense at all. Don't ever refer to it again, please.[17]

Nationalism is not, he says, necessarily illiberal, as evidenced by the Rat's non-imperialistic parochialism. While "it is descriptively true in many historical cases" that "national identities are . . . biased in favor of the dominant cultural group, the group that has historically dominated the politics of the state", it is not integral to national identities that they should be loaded in this way.[18] Eamonn Callan similarly assumes that patriotism need not be illiberal and would not endorse teaching an illiberal patriotism. Patriotism need not have the spillover effect of turning children into jingoists.

In this Miller and Callan are examples of a recent trend of emphasizing nationalism's kinder and gentler face.[19] But the mere compatibility of patriotism with liberalism is not greatly reassuring. Callan remarks of induction into the role of citizen that individuals do not become attached to schemes of cooperation in general, but to "this scheme of just cooperation . . . *these* fellow citizens."[20] Similarly, one does not learn patriotism in general, but *this* particular version of patriotism – the patriotism of this country. Even the most benign actual patriotisms of existing countries are tainted by xenophobia and jingoism: certainly, the Water Rat's patriotism is by no means representative of the British (or English) patriotism we should expect to be taught in schools, whether through the hidden or the open curriculum. The mere possibility that nationality or patriotism can be inoffensive tells us nothing about the likelihood that the versions of patriotism promoted by real states will be inoffensive in the appropriate way.

National identities vary from nation to nation. Within many national identities *is* a sense of superiority that justifies overriding the legitimate interests of non-nationals (as well as some just claims of co-nationals). Callan may be right that patriotism can lend a supporting hand to justice, or to stability, in a long-lived liberal polity whose national identity has already been tamed. But in many actual liberal countries, even those with relatively inoffensive national identities, patriotism all too often cuts against justice: the attachments and precepts it involves pull citizens in the opposite direction, and help to obscure the actual working of social and political processes. This is never truer than in times of national crisis. Given the *actual* content of British national identity, I believe that the handful who protested against the British war against Argentina in 1982 were indeed (as accused by the press) traitors, not to the state, but to the prevailing ideal of Englishness or Britishness.

National identities also, of course, vary from person to person. And here lies a second problem. Friends of patriotism, or national identification, like to claim that there are coercive and non-coercive ways in which the state can promote a sense of attachment. Andrew Mason, for example, draws this distinction with regard to assimilationist policies:

"*Coercive* measures might include laws which prohibit members of a cultural community from engaging in their customs and practices. . . . *Non-coercive* measures, in contrast, might include giving the customs and symbols of the dominant culture public status and respect (giving public holidays for festivals recognized by the dominant culture but not others); employing the language of the dominant culture in public affairs; requiring that state schools teach in that language and educate children in the history, geography, and literature of the dominant culture; subsidizing the dominant culture in various ways or giving tax cuts to those who participate in it."[21]

David Miller also draws the distinction, giving the example of protecting national culture through "inducements rather than by coercion: farmers can be given incentives to preserve their hedgerows; the domestic film industry can be subsidized out of cinema revenues; important works of art can be purchased for national collections; and so forth."[22] But each of Mason's and Miller's mechanisms *is* coercive. Miller's examples coerce the cinemagoer and the taxpayer, who are forced to pay for something they would not choose to pay for voluntarily, and in the name of a culture which the coerced person has shown no interest in when making cultural choices. The inducements they are forced to provide must be inducements to do *something*, and the content of that something depends on some fixed idea about the proper content of the national culture. In the case of cinema it is that the culture is more truly British (or French, or German, or whatever) if the movies people watch are made in the native country by (largely) native production companies. In the case of the farmer the view is that hedgerows are more important to British culture than less expensive and more efficiently produced

foods. Similarly with Mason's purported examples of non-coercion. National holidays restrict the options of those workers and employers who would rather not observe them; state schools are funded through coercively acquired taxation and (usually) are the only realistic option for most children to get an education.

Of course, dissenters are likely to prefer the purportedly "non-coercive" strategies which merely force them to subsidize other peoples cultural practices over the more determinedly coercive strategies which prevent them from engaging in their own. But the strategies are, nonetheless, coercive. Miller says of his preferred strategies that they can "provide an environment in which the culture can develop spontaneously."[23] But if subsidies are to be provided to maintain and develop a "national" culture, those subsidies have to be provided by a granting authority. That authority, if it is responsible, does not distribute the subsidies randomly – instead it has in mind some set of criteria which projects have to meet in order to qualify. Those criteria must be explicit, and they will guide the development of the culture. The development of the culture will not be spontaneously based on the diverse and fluid cultural interests of the population, but will be guided by the non-spontaneous criteria of a cultural elite (since members of this, rather than some randomly selected group of citizens, will most likely comprise the granting authority).

These problems with state promotion of national attachments are especially telling against teaching them to children. Children are uniquely vulnerable and capable of developing full-fledged views of their own about the good life. If their own views of the good life and of the place of their loyalty to country within it are to be truly their own, and not merely explainable by the inculcating activity of the state, it is important that they be encouraged to reflect critically on the character of their national identity. This could be done while they are taught to be patriotic, but it could just as easily not be done. Furthermore if the national culture, and hence the content of the nation's "patriotism," is to be a function of the spontaneous activity and critical reflection of engaged citizens, it is at least dangerous to give the state the authority to determine the content of the patriotism that will be instilled in children, even when that state is democratic. Just as with the trajectory of a national culture, if the state directs teachers and schools to imbue a sense of identification with and loyalty to the state and nation in schools, it must have some guidelines both on how to do it and on what the character is of the state and nation toward which the children's attachment is to be directed. That will guide the future direction of people's senses of what it is to be "British" or "American" or "Italian." The development over time of the national identity is not spontaneous and based on the fluid and diverse interests of individuals, but is shaped in part by the state's sense of the proper content of the patriotic idea.

It is familiar now that, with respect to the circumstances in which they develop their conceptions of the good life and stance toward the state, children must be subject to *some* coercive authority, and that, as long as the family is taken for granted, that authority must be either that of the parents or some agent of the state. Children cannot develop their views authentically without any paternalistic influence. Elsewhere I argue that with respect to some aspects of the child's moral development it is important for the state to have coercive authority. Does not this mitigate the objection that teaching patriotism coerces children?

No. The objection here is not that the state does a wrong to children by *coercing* them. It does two wrongs. It wrongs the child by conditioning his or her consent to the state, thus jeopardizing his or her ability to give the freely offered consent that is the marker of liberal legitimacy. And it wrongs the whole of society by distorting the process of cultural formation and reformation, and in particular by distorting the development of the national idea. There is a strong case for depriving the state of authority with respect to the stance the child develops toward the state: not because this allows the child to develop its views without the influence of any authority, but because granting parents authority will more reliably reproduce a diversity of stances toward the state which constitute the patriotism of conationals who are free and equal.

A further problem with teaching patriotism is that patriotic attachments may interfere with other loyalties and attachments which are instrumental for justice (if not necessarily for stability). Consider the case of Britain. The gradual move toward a more distributively just state over the course of the hundred years beginning around 1870 was driven mainly by two motors: the universalistic idealism of the liberal and latterly the socialist traditions, and the class loyalties and self-interested activity of the labor movement. Patriotism has interfered with these developments – it has been a weapon of the

conservative class, wielded with too much success, though less than they would have liked. Some historians see the successful promulgation of the American national loyalty as a key explanation of the failure of the United States, unique among advanced industrial countries, to develop an effective and politically powerful working-class movement. In other countries which have approached egalitarian ideals of distributive justice, class loyalties have played a far greater role than national loyalties, and again, patriotic loyalties have served more to disrupt than to propel the movements toward justice.

It is instructive here to turn to consider Richard Rorty's discussion of the reformist left in *Achieving Our Country*.[24] His main thesis in the book is that the contemporary academic, or "cultural," left in the United States has been misled by theorists like Lasch that America is irredeemably corrupt, and by theorists like Lacan and Foucault that human agency is ineffectual. The reformist left of the first half of the last century, by contrast, loved America, and this love enhanced their effectiveness: "Few of the people who wrote for leftist periodicals, either those aimed at workers or those aimed at bourgeois intellectuals like my parents, had any doubt that America was a great, noble, progressive country, in which justice would eventually triumph."[25]

His characterization of this left as one which never doubted that there was greatness in America is correct (broadly speaking), as is his description of the optimism about the reformability of social institutions. But it is not at all clear that this left was patriotic in his sense, or that, if it was, its patriotism contributed to its effectiveness. The reformist left, unlike Rorty, and unlike the culturalist left that he criticizes, believed in universal values, such as equality, liberty, and democracy. It believed, at least officially, that working class Americans had more in common, both in their experience and their interests, with working class Europeans and Asians than with ruling class Americans, and it believed that the commonalities of class either were, or should be made, more motivationally efficacious than the ties of nationality. Even after its "Americanization" the Communist Party remained slavishly devoted to the leadership in Moscow. Class (albeit, in the Communist Party's case, a grotesque notion of it) was the fundamental loyalty, not nation. Socialists, even more than liberals, have distrusted patriotism and national loyalties. In addition to the reason they share with liberals, the fear that national loyalties lead to unacceptable disregard for the universal obligations owed to all persons, socialists have feared, reasonably, that national loyalties and ties disrupt class loyalties which socialists have seen (not without reason) as the primary motor of moves toward justice. Nor is the fear that workers will fail to unite across the world, but that ties to the members of their own domestic bourgeoisie will inhibit their ability to unite with other members of their domestic working class.

Need Eamonn Callan be troubled by all this? Maybe not. Once a fully just liberal society has been established, and that society's sense of what it is is conditioned by justice, patriotism may play a role much more like the one that Callan assigns to it. This may be true, and the objection I have presented above does not imply that it is impermissible to teach it in such circumstances. But I do want to emphasize that we cannot read off from the propriety of teaching patriotism within a well-ordered Rawlsian just society whether it would be appropriate in the societies we actually inhabit.

But there is another problem which Callan cannot shrug off so easily. His argument for the instrumentality of patriotism for stability and justice assumes (*à la* Rawls) that the purpose of morality of association is to shore up whatever tendency individuals have to treat justly others within their scheme of social cooperation. This is all very well if the boundaries of the state coincide with those of a scheme of social cooperation. But it is almost never the case that the boundaries of a state coincide with those of a scheme of social cooperation. Although it is now a cliché to talk about the globalization of the economy, it has been the case ever since the discovery of the New World that many of us interact in morally important ways with distant strangers even in peacetime. My car was made in Japan; my employer licenses sportswear that is made in Indonesia and sold all over the world; I drink tea grown in India, blended in England, and sold in Wisconsin; I pay taxes to a government which uses them to sue the European Union for favoring Caribbean over South American banana growers.

Neither Rawls nor Callan says much about the identity conditions of schemes of social cooperation (I say this not to fault them). But once a certain level of economic interaction has been established, it must be the case that the boundaries between schemes of cooperation have been breached, and that then the polity includes only a small part of the scheme of social cooperation. Patriotism will not help us to carry out our duties to those with whom we share a scheme of social cooperation. Richard Miller's invocation of the special character of political interactions does not help to counter this objection, at least in the real world.[26] For our interactions with foreigners are governed by collective coercive institutions: there are tax treaties, trade agreements, military alliances and enmities, immigration and emigration laws. Organizations such as the WTO, the IMF, the World Bank, and the various agencies of the UN, all rely for their functioning on coercively raised funds, and operate through the authorization of participating governments. They formalize the coercive character of international interactions, and demonstrate the international character of schemes of social cooperation.

## 3   Why History is an Especially Inappropriate Vehicle for Teaching Patriotism

In Section 2, I have cast a good deal of doubt on the propriety of teaching patriotism to children, at least in schools. In this section I want to set those doubts aside (though they may creep back in), and assume for the sake of argument that there could be some place for teaching patriotism in the school curriculum. Here, instead, I want to argue that that place should not be within the history curriculum. There are particular problems with teaching patriotism through history.

First consider an argument that *fails* to establish that patriotism should not be taught through history. This is that the *telos*, or the distinctive aim, of history is to access the truth about the past. There are two problems with this view. First, history has a number of legitimate aims – truth is not the only one. Second, we may properly have different aims in teaching history than we do in practising it. This is true of many activities: the practitioner of a sport may aim at excellence in the sport; but someone teaching the sport may properly aim merely to ensure that his students enjoy themselves playing sport, whether or not they achieve excellence. The practitioner of Spanish aims to communicate with other Spanish speakers; but the teacher of Spanish may aim to give the student a full appreciation of the ways in which different natural languages can have different grammars and structures. The responsible teacher of philosophy does not seek to instill true beliefs in her students, though approaching the truth is a major motivation in her practice of the subject.

I want to show that teaching patriotism would conflict with other purposes which clearly are legitimate, and in my view are central. If a positive argument could be given for the legitimacy of teaching patriotism as a purpose of teaching history, and that doing so is more important than the other purportedly legitimate purposes with which it conflicts, I would be proven wrong. The previous section, I hope, shows that such an argument will be very difficult to make. But my aim here is to shift the burden of proof – to show that a positive argument is needed and cannot be assumed.

Here are three legitimate purposes for teaching history:

1   Truth: it is legitimate to try to convey the truth about history to children; to teach them what actually happened, insofar as we know. It is legitimate to teach children that Europeans came to the Americas in the fifteenth century; that the British colonies rebelled late in the eighteenth century and established an independent federation of States; that Prince Metternich's diplomacy was motivated by the desire to delay the collapse of the old order in Europe for as long as possible; that Henry Kissinger was a biographer of Metternich; that there were revolutions throughout Europe in 1848; that Henry VIII established a church of England; and so on.

2   A second purpose is to teach them how to discern causal connections in social processes and, perhaps, more importantly, to teach them what difficulties are involved in discerning such connections. It is legitimate to teach them that there are disagreements about the causal processes which led to the invasion of England in 1066; to the First and Second World Wars, and the Civil War in the United States; about the fall of the Roman Empire and the rise of the English industrial working class. It is legitimate to teach them what kinds of evidence scholars consider to count in favor of and against such causal claims.

3   It is legitimate to teach them the history of the particular institutions they can be expected to inhabit, so that they can more effectively and knowledgeably negotiate those institutions. In the American context this would involve teaching about the development of the two-party system; the evolution of the constitution and changes in constitutional interpretation, and the kind of reasoning which is accepted as legitimate in public debate and judicial review; the development of the New Deal and Great Society programs and the paths not taken; the ways that political power has been sought by different movements and interest groups. It is legitimate both to teach this so that children can come to understand the institutions they will operate within, and to think critically about those institutions themselves, so that their endorsement or rejection of the institutions is reasoned and informed.

There is no deductive argument that encouraging patriotism through the teaching of history will conflict with these other legitimate purposes. Some examples will help illustrate the difficulties.

Take the first aim. A good deal of what actually happened makes any country distinctly unlovable to someone possessed of an effective sense of justice. I suspect the conservative patriots are right to want anti-Communism, Hiroshima, Watergate, the secret war on Cambodia, and slavery to be glossed over rather quickly. The persistence of poverty in the midst of the American Dream and the lengths to which the state has gone at various times to inhibit the success of movements for social justice is quite impressive, and cannot reflect well on the nation itself. Britain's history is similarly flawed. While the empire may have been relatively benign, British imperialism is distinctly unlovable – and the manifest willingness of less advantaged Britons to partake in the benefits of imperialism makes it hard to think of imperialism as incidental to the history of the "true" nation.

Of course, in the history of both countries, from the perspective of justice, there is a great deal to admire: Roman rule; the Peasants revolt; the Diggers and Levellers; the War of Independence; the First Amendment; the Chartists; the antislavery campaign; the underground railroad; the early Labour Party; the suffragettes; the rise of the CIO; the Labour Landslide of 1945 and some of what that government did; the civil rights movement. But even within these episodes there is much of which to be critical: the Pankhursts' autocratic and elitist practice; Labour's support for World War One; Martin Luther King's personal failings; John L. Lewis's manipulation of the Communist Party; and the Communist Party's support for Stalin. Teaching the truth about these episodes not only involves one in teaching children that the agents of social justice have usually been deeply and widely hated by many of their compatriots, but also in teaching them of the flaws and problems with even those whose actions pushed history in the direction of justice. Will the warts and all approach to history (which must surely include a warts and all approach to the beauty spots) enhance love of country, as Nash and the new textbook writers think it will? There are good reasons for doubting so, at least for many children.

Take the second aim. An educator aiming to instill love of country will have difficulties teaching about the causal processes which led up to the Civil War in the United States, especially given the preconceptions her children are likely to have. Take three radically different interpretations. The war was about protecting states' rights from the encroachments of an increasingly powerful federal government; it was about preserving the union and abolishing slavery; it was about creating flexible labor markets and liberalizing trade. Only one of these explanations reflects well on the moral character of the war; while it is not the least plausible, it is not the most plausible, and the others all have some plausibility. Given the second purpose, the pedagogue's aim must be to encourage reflection in the light of the best evidence she can present, and discourage that any of that reflection be distorted either by her desire or that of any of her students to present the events in a favorable light. Patriotic concerns when teaching the Civil War are also likely to inhibit the third aim. It continues to have a central place in the moral story Americans tell themselves about their country. One cannot understand contemporary American political institutions without an accurate picture of the Civil War; yet teaching the complexity of motives on both sides (many of which were morally obnoxious) is unlikely to contribute to love of country.

Consider again how the presentation of Rosa Parks in the Boorstin textbook distorts learning about social processes. What he says about her is true: she was a tired black seamstress. But what is conveyed is that she just finally snapped, and thought something to the effect of "I am not going to take this any more"; and that her spontaneous refusal prompted a spontaneous protest movement. Read Gary Nash's own textbook covering the issue and we find a different, more revealing story: "Protests like Parks's were not new, but hers was the kind of case community leaders had been waiting for. Parks was dignified, soft-spoken, well-liked. She was a former secretary of the local NAACP chapter and was active in her church.

The previous summer she had attended an interracial workshop at the Highlander Folk School in Tennessee. Now, local civil rights leaders asked if she would be willing to fight her case for as long as it took to win."[27] The impression left by the Boorstin textbook risks obscuring the role of non-spontaneous organization in promoting social change in this case.

It might seem from my approving quote from Nash's textbook that my position is just his position in disguise, but I do not think that is true. Nash claims that the truth – warts and all – will serve the development of patriotic attachment and that this aim is a proper aim of teaching history. My position is that patriotic purposes have no legitimate role in the teaching of history: so I would endorse the "warts and all" pedagogy, but entirely without regard to whether it serves the development of patriotic attachments. If it did not, that would not in any way count against the pedagogy, as, for Nash, it presumably would (though maybe not decisively – since he does not investigate the possibility of conflict there is no way of discerning whether truth or patriotism is more important to him).

There is, I think, a third position which lies between Nash's and mine: that while patriotic purposes may be permissible in the teaching of history, their pursuit is strictly constrained by truthfulness and other legitimate purposes I have identified. However, at the level of textbook composition, the three positions may be very similar, because in practice it is so hard to pursue the patriotic purposes while respecting the truth. Certainly, when searching for turns of phrase or modes of presentation that are inimical to my own view, I was unable to find any offenders in Nash's own textbooks. At the level of classroom teaching, there may be a difference: the non-patriotic educator would disregard the effects of her questions and the direction of classroom discussion on the attachments of her students, and may be more willing than the patriotic educator to delve into the moral significance of the private failings of historically important figures whose public lives are liable to inspire attachment to country. For example, let us assume that Martin Luther King's multiple infidelities and plagiarism are not historically significant. Then the warts and all patriot and the non-patriot will concur on omitting mention of them from textbook treatments. They will also concur (I presume) that they should not be denied if a child raises questions about them in class. Nevertheless the warts and all patriot may, believing that dwelling on them could have the misleading effect of diminishing the greatness of King's leadership in the minds of her students, wish to move on promptly from the question. The non-patriot, unconcerned with that possible effect, although she believes the private behavior was not historically significant, may be more willing to entertain *discussion* of their historical significance (with children of an appropriate age), and may even raise the issues herself for the purpose of having that discussion.

## 4 Concluding Comments

How, then, should history textbooks be written? Any book, after all, has to be written from *some* point of view. If they may not be written from a patriotic point of view, is it permissible for them to promote class loyalty (and if so, which class), or identification with one's cultural group (or the cultural group of another)?

I shall answer this question very briefly, but first I want to clarify the conclusion of my argument. Although I have focused on textbook writing, my real concern is with the way history is *taught*. The Boorstin book could quite well be used in conjunction with other materials by a sensitive teacher to perform the legitimate functions of teaching history and to avoid the illegitimate. The teacher could introduce source materials concerning the Selma bus boycott and the Red Scare showing what actually happened and how, and could point out and encourage discussion about the many attempts by Boorstin to get his audience to identify with "America." Or the teacher could counter the Boorstin text with something like Howard Zinn's *A People's*

*History of the United States*, a book which, although patriotic in something like Rorty's sense, clearly aims to expose the warts of America's history in order to stimulate criticism of America's leaders and to encourage a deeply critical identification with the nation. From the conclusion that history should not be used to teach patriotism we cannot conclude that history books, even history textbooks, may not be written from a patriotic perspective.

While I cannot vindicate this claim here, my belief is that using history to promote the other kinds of loyalties mentioned would encounter many difficulties similar to those I have raised with promoting patriotism. One view is that African-American children should be taught history in a way that affirms and encourages their identities as African-Americans; in the 1930s a series of textbooks were written presenting history for working-class children to encourage their identification as working class. I suspect that whatever the identity being promoted, its promotion jeopardizes the required functions of teaching history, and risks indoctrinating children so that their affirmations of the identity will lack authenticity. But presenting children with a variety of texts, all constrained by the truth, while presenting a variety of viewpoints might be an adequate way of stimulating them to reflect on the loyalties the authors hold and are trying to promote. It seems reasonable to use textbooks that are written from an angle as it were, so long as children read a variety of such books and their teachers can help the students negotiate the complexity of the views. However, the primary attention of liberal authors of textbooks should not be on directly encouraging identities in, or teaching values to, readers, but on teaching them what happened and teaching them the skills essential to figuring out why.

## Notes

1. Arthur Schlesinger, *The Disuniting of America* (New York: W. W. Norton, 1992), p. 72.
2. Ibid., p. 93.
3. Ibid., p. 137. Schlesinger never explicitly advocates using history teaching to promote national identity, but it does seem to be a subtext of his book; albeit that any teaching of history must, in his view, be constrained by the truth and the "unexpurgated record" (I discuss this possible position in Section 4). An excellent discussion of Schlesinger can be found in Robert Fullinwider, "Patriotic History," in Robert Fullinwider (ed.), *Multiculturalism and Public Education*

(Cambridge: Cambridge University Press, 1996). Fullinwider's essay was a major stimulus to my own thinking on this issue, and the present essay is an attempt to circumvent Fullinwider's defence of patriotic history.
4. Daniel Boorstin and Brooks Mather Kelley, *A History of the United States since 1861* (Needham, MA: Prentice Hall, 1990), p. 208.
5. Ibid., p. 221.
6. Ibid., p. 366.
7. Ibid., p. 379.
8. Ibid., p. 441.

9. There are exceptions: some Africanist educators, for example, writing primarily for Black students, emphasize identification not with America but with the experience of African-Americans in the past. However, they share the idea that students should be offered a "usable past," one which encourages their identification with some appropriate group.

10. Gary Nash, Charlotte Crabtree, and Ross E. Dunn, *History on Trial* (New York: Alfred A. Knopf, 1999), p. 15.

11. In the first case I think of Americans who have been stripped of citizenship because of their engagement with communist regimes; in the second I think of Turkish adults who have been born and raised in Germany.

12. John White, "Patriotism without Obligation" (unpublished), p. 4.

13. David Miller, *On Nationality* (Oxford: Oxford University Press, 1995), p. 50.

14. Richard Miller, "Cosmopolitan Respect and Patriotic Concern," *Philosophy and Public Affairs*, 27 (1998), pp. 202–24 at 215.

15. Eamonn Callan, *Creating Citizens* (Oxford: Oxford University Press, 1997), p. 88.

16. See John Rawls, *A Theory of Justice* (Cambridge, MA: Harvard University Press, 1971), esp. pp. 55–6, and Andrew Williams, "Incentives, Inequality, and Publicity," *Philosophy and Public Affairs*, 27 (1998), pp. 225–47 for useful discussions.

17. "In Defence of Nationality," *Journal of Applied Philosophy*, 10 (1993), pp. 3–16 at 3.

18. D. Miller, "In Defence of Nationality," p. 11.

19. See, for example, Yael Tamir, *Liberal Nationalism* (Princeton, NJ: Princeton University Press, 1995), several contributions to Robert McKim and Jefferson McMahan, *The Morality of Nationalism* (Oxford: Oxford University Press, 1998), several contributions to Kai Nielsen, Jocelyn Couture, and Michel Seymour (eds.), *Rethinking Nationalism* (*Canadian Journal of Philosophy* Supplementary volume 22, 1996), and the other works referred to in this article.

20. Callan, *Creating Citizens*, p. 93.

21. Andrew Mason, "Political Community, Liberal-Nationalism, and the Ethics of Assimilation", *Ethics*, 109 (1999), pp. 261–86 at 268 (emphasis in original).

22. David Miller, *On Nationality*, pp. 87–8.

23. Ibid., p. 88.

24. Richard Rorty, *Achieving our Country* (Princeton, NJ: Princeton University Press, 1998).

25. Ibid., p. 59.

26. "Cosmopolitan Respect and Patriotic Concern." See also Thomas Hurka's contribution to *The Morality of Nationalism*.

27. Gary Nash, *American Odyssey: The United States in the Twentieth Century* (New York: McGraw Hill, 1999), pp. 674–5.

# 58

# Should Creationism be Taught in the Public Schools?

## Robert T. Pennock

### The Question

Should creationism be taught in the public schools? The full range of issues for educational philosophy and policy that are the subject of debate in the creation/evolution controversy are too numerous to be covered in any one article, so in this first section I begin by analyzing the question so that we might better focus our discussion. I will use this opportunity to point out related questions that have so far not been considered in the debate, but that deserve the attention of philosophers of education. In subsequent sections I will discuss, in turn, [ . . . ] creationists' extra-legal arguments, epistemological arguments, religious protection arguments and arguments from educational philosophy and justice that are relevant to our specific question. Because creationism is primarily an American phenomenon, some of the considerations will be specific to the circumstances in the United States, but many of the arguments are generally applicable.

(a) *The Public Schools*. The controversies about educational policies concerning creationism have almost exclusively involved the teaching of evolution in the public schools, so this is a natural locus from which to consider the problem. However, several key elements of the controversy would be quite different if we looked at the issue in other educational settings, such as private and parochial schools, home schooling, and in higher education.

There has been very little consideration of the issues for private rather than public schools, no doubt because the governance of the former is not subject to public control and review in the same way. However, there is still a measure of external oversight in that private schools must meet certain standards in order to get and maintain accreditation. It is a reasonable question to ask whether a school deserves to be accredited if it teaches creationism rather than evolution in its science classes. Given that accreditation implies that a school meets professional standards in the appropriate subject matter, a school that teaches creationism in science classes does not meet the standard, since evolution is at the core of basic scientific knowledge. Moreover, as we shall see, creationism rejects not only evolution, but other well-established scientific facts from across the sciences. In general, however, we tend to take for granted that private schools, if they do not receive public funds or certification, are not subject to

Previously published in *Science & Education* 11 (2002), pp. 111–18, 119–33. © 2002 Kluwer Academic Publishers. Reprinted with permission of Springer Verlag.

public standards and may teach whatever private, esoteric doctrines they choose.

For parochial schools, we fully expect that religious views will be taught. This is the most natural setting for creationist views, and it is primarily here that we find creationism taught in science classes. This is not to say, of course, that all or even most parochial schools teach creationism. For instance, based on an informal assessment of my undergraduate students, those who studied at Catholic high schools typically have had the best education on evolution, often better than their public school counterparts. Fundamentalist and evangelical 'Bible schools', on the other hand, often cite the creationist orientation of their science curriculum as a major selling point to their clientele. As they see it, all true knowledge has a biblical basis. Gil Hansen, head of the Fairfax Baptist Temple school, explains his school's educational philosophy, which seems to be representative on this point: 'What we do here is base everything on the Bible. This becomes really the foundation, the word of God is the foundation from which all academics really spring' (Duvall 1995). How does the school teach evolutionary theory? Hansen is clear about the school's position on this as well: 'We expose it as a false model'.

Unless the government begins to significantly fund parochial schools with tax dollars, such as through a voucher program or through religious charter schools, parochial schools can probably expect to remain free to teach creationism or whatever religious doctrines they choose. Moreover, fundamentalist and evangelical schools often choose to forego secular educational accreditation, and may be accredited only within their own independent system. Nevertheless, I would still argue that there are serious issues of educational philosophy to consider even in this setting. Is it right to teach children that something known to be true is false? Is it not bad faith to misrepresent the findings of science in what is purported to be a science class? If the basis for knowledge is taken to be biblical revelation, is it not intellectually dishonest to put such revelations forward as science? Important moral questions are at issue here; religious schools that teach creationism as science are violating basic norms of honesty.

Most of these same considerations apply if we move to consideration of home schooling. There have always been parents who, for one reason or other, chose to teach their own children at home rather than send them to school, but currently the vast majority of home schoolers consists of religious conservatives who do not want their children to be exposed to what they take to be the evils of the public schools, be it sex education or evolution. Home schooling raises some unique policy issues, since basic education is compulsory and parents must demonstrate that they are providing their children with an education that meets state standards. Oversight of parents who teach their own children is inconsistent, and it seems to be fairly common that fundamentalist home schoolers teach the bare minimum of what they have to of subjects they object to, and then regularly supplement the required curriculum with the religious education – in Bible study, creationism, and so on – that they desire. Are parents doing an educational disservice to their children in teaching them creationism on the sly? One might ask whether stricter oversight is necessary in such cases.

Examining the issue in the setting of higher education overlaps some of the previous considerations, but with some relevant differences. One of the most important is the age and maturity of the students. Most undergraduates are at a more advanced developmental stage than they were in high school, so some new educational goals begin to apply. Certainly one of the most significant is that we expect undergraduates to begin to hone their critical and evaluative thinking skills, and to develop disciplined independence of mind. At this stage, it can be quite appropriate and instructive to discuss creationist views, so that students can learn to see what is wrong with them. Of course, there are any number of other topics that could also serve the same end, but a professor might legitimately choose to dissect creationism in the same way that one might choose to have students dissect a snake rather than a frog in anatomy class. One question we will have to address is whether this might not be a reasonable educational goal in secondary school public education as well.

For the most part, we will leave consideration of these other venues aside, and focus on the public schools, which historically have been (and for the most part remain) the central locus of the controversy. The general causes of the creationism controversy – perceived conflicts between evolution and some Christian views about Creation – have remained fairly constant over the decades, but these have manifested themselves differently in different periods. In the early decades of the public school system in the United States, few textbooks incorporated evolution, and once they did begin to do so many states responded by passing legislation that banned the teaching of evolution altogether. In 1925, the antievolutionary Butler Act in Tennessee led to the first legal battle over creation and evolution in the schools – the famous *Scopes* trial. Such anti-evolutionary laws remained in effect until they were finally overturned by the US Supreme Court in 1968. Creationists countered at first by passing state laws in the early 1970s to give 'equal emphasis' to the Biblical account. Since these and similar state laws were struck down in the 1980s, creationist activists have turned to other tactics and venues, getting laws passed that require, for example, 'disclaimers' to be read before biology classes in which evolution would be covered. Alabama public school students, for example,[1] find a disclaimer pasted in their biology textbooks that begins:

> This textbook discusses evolution, a controversial theory some scientists present as a scientific explanation for the origin of living things, such as plants, animals and humans. No human was present when life first appeared on earth. Therefore, any statement about life's origins should be considered as theory, not fact.

In other states, creationist 'stealth candidates' on local school boards and State boards of education speak publicly at first only of a 'back to basics' education policy, but then work to change science curriculum standards to include creationism or to gut any evolution component, even though evolution is basic to biological science. A few go further and require that 'evidence against evolution' or 'alternative analyses of evidence' be presented. Some teachers simply ignore the law and go ahead and teach their creationist views, for instance about 'intelligent design', in their individual classrooms. These and other examples of creationist activism in the public schools keep this venue at the center of the controversy.

(b) *Kinds of creationism.* The next element of the question before us that we need to examine is the notion of creationism itself. If creationism were to be taught, what would that include? In general, creationism is the rejection of evolution in favor of special creation of some form, but we must recognize that there are a wide variety of different, competing views that fall under this concept.

The most common form of 'creation-science' is what is known as 'young-earth creationism' (YEC). In the law they got passed in 1982 in Arkansas,

creationists proposed the following outline of what they wanted to have taught.

> (1) Sudden creation of the universe, energy, and life from nothing; (2) the insufficiency of mutation and natural selection in bringing about the development of all living kinds from a single organism; (3) Changes only within fixed limits of originally created kinds of plants and animals; (4) Separate ancestry of humans and apes; (5) Explanation of the earth's geology by catastrophism, including the occurrence of a worldwide flood; and (6) A relatively recent inception of the earth and living kinds. (La Follette 1983, p. 16)

A more complete outline of the young-earth 'Creation model' may be found in (Aubrey 1998 [1980]). It is also important to understand that creationism does not end with its rejection of biological evolution, though this is the main thesis that so far has been at issue in the public controversy. As we see in the list above, and as I have shown in detail elsewhere (Pennock 1999, ch. 1), creationism also rejects scientific conclusions of anthropology, archeology, astronomy, chemistry, geology, linguistics, physics, psychology, optics, and so on. For instance, when creationists on the Kansas State Board of Education removed references to evolution from the state's science curriculum standards in 1999, they also took out plate tectonics, the geological chronology, Big Bang cosmology, and any mention of the ancient age of the earth.

We must also be aware that there is now considerable factionalism among creationists. Disagreements about the details of Christian theology, partial acceptance of scientific views, and different political strategies have given rise to splinter groups that question one or another of the standard views. Old-earth creationists, for example, do not insist that the world is only six to ten thousand years old and accept something closer to the scientific chronology. A few creationists doubt that there was a single, catastrophic worldwide flood, and hold that the Noachian Deluge may have been local to the Mediterranean, or, if global, then 'tranquil' rather than catastrophic. Adherents of the YEC view far outnumber members of other factions, but it is important that we recognize that creationism is not a monolithic view and is split by deep divisions.

Though the traditional creationists remain the most active in their political and educational work, there was a significant evolution of creationism in the 1990s, beginning with the publication of *Darwin on Trial*, by Berkeley law professor Phillip Johnson.

Johnson neither endorses nor denies the young-earth view, and argues that we should understand creationism as belief in the process of creation in a more general sense. People are creationists, according to Johnson's definition, 'if they believe that a supernatural Creator not only initiated this process but in some meaningful sense *controls* it in furtherance of a purpose' (Johnson 1991, p. 4). Rather than speaking of 'creation-science,' Johnson and others among these new creationists call their view 'intelligent-design theory' and advocate a 'theistic science'. Intelligent-design creationists include both young-earth and old-earth creationists, but for the most part they keep their specific commitments hidden and speak only of the generic thesis of 'mere creation'. As do other creationists, they oppose accommodation to evolution and take it to be fundamentally incompatible with Christian theism. In another way, however, they go further than creation-science does; they reject scientific methodology itself, arguing that scientific naturalism itself must be tossed out and replaced by their theistic science (though they are never clear about what its distinctive methods might be).

Although it has been fundamentalist and evangelical Christian creationists, especially the YECs, who have been the most active in opposing the teaching of evolution in the schools and pressing for inclusion of their view of Creation, we cannot fairly evaluate the question without also taking into account non-Christian creationist views. For the most part, adherents of these views have not been as politically active in the United States, so these have not reached the public attention to the same degree. It is impossible to even begin to canvas these numerous views, but I will mention by way of example, two recent cases that have made the news.

In Kennewick, Washington, the 1996 discovery of a fossil human skeleton led to a very public legal battle between science and religion. The 9000 plus year old bones were claimed by a coalition of Northwest Indians who wanted to immediately bury them. However, features of the skull seemed to be more Caucasian than Indian, and scientists questioned whether it was really a tribal ancestor and suggested that further analysis could help reveal something of early human history in the area. Armand Minthorn, of Oregon's Umatilla Tribe said his people were not interested in the scientists' views: 'We already know our history. It is passed on to us through our elders and through our religious practices.' Their history says that their God created

them first in that place. Many Amerindian tribes have origin stories that, on their face, are antithetical to evolutionary theory and other scientific findings. (In parts of northern Canada, an alliance of Native Indians and Christian creationists has formed to oppose teaching evolution in the schools. It is an uneasy union, of course, because the groups differ sharply in what story of Creation they would put in its stead.) The controversy over the Kennewick skeleton also involves another religious group, the Asatru Folk Assembly, an Old Norse pagan group. The members of this pre-Christian faith revere Viking-era Scandinavian gods and goddesses, and believe that their ancestors were the first inhabitants of the region. They expect that scientific study of the skull would support their claim of priority, though their other religious beliefs would certainly put them at odds with other aspects of the scientific picture.

Another religious anti-evolutionary view became newsworthy in 1995, when NBC broadcast a program entitled *Mysterious Origins of Man*, that purported to reveal scientific evidence that human beings had lived tens of millions of years ago. Creationists were at first elated by this primetime repudiation of evolution, but quickly withdrew their endorsement when they learned that the program was based on the 1993 book *Forbidden Archeology* (Cremo and Thompson 1993), which advances purportedly scientific evidence for a position that mirrors a Hindu view of creation and reincarnation.

Finally, let me mention one more type of view that is relevant to the controversy. The Raëlian Movement, which had its start in France in the 1970s, calls itself a 'scientific religion'. Raëlians reject evolution and believe that life on earth is the result of purposeful, intelligent design, but they also reject creationism, in the sense that they believe that the creator was not supernatural. Instead, they believe that life on earth was genetically engineered from scratch by extraterrestrials. The founder of the Raëlian Movement, Claude Vorilhon, claims that he knows this because the truth was revealed to him by an extraterrestrial, who anointed him as the Guide of Guides for our age. Some 70,000 adherents worldwide, many in the US and Canada, share this faith.

In considering whether creationism should be taught in the public schools, we must always keep in mind that all these (and many more) anti-evolutionary views would have to be included as 'alternative theories' to the scientific conclusions.

(c) *Taught How?* The third element of the question that requires preliminary discussion involves the *kind* of academic course in which, and the *way* in which creationism might be taught.

The issues change dramatically, for instance, if the different forms of creationism were to be taught in a comparative religion class. The Constitution is not taken to bar discussion of religion in a course of this sort. One could imagine a course that surveyed the splendid variety of views of creation of different religions, and could make a good case that such a course might serve a useful educational purpose in fostering an appreciation of American and global cultural diversity. Many opponents of teaching creationism in the schools would be willing to compromise if the topic were to be introduced in such a course. The controversy arises mostly because creationists insist that their view be included as part of the science curriculum, and that it replace or be given equal weight to evolution.

Moreover, creationists want evolution to be revealed as a false model. Creationist textbooks that are used in fundamentalist schools often go further and teach that it is an evil view as well, promoted by atheist scientists who want to lure people away from God. Textbooks that they have promoted for use in public schools, however, keep the sermonizing about evolutionary evils to a minimum. The most common creationist proposals have followed what is known as the 'dual model' approach, whereby 'the two theories' are presented and contrasted. The Arkansas 'Balanced Treatment' Act specified that the schools should give equal consideration to 'creation-science' and 'evolution-science'. Since all such legislation has been found unconstitutional, creationists now try to argue that science classes should simply present 'alternative theories' besides the scientific view. In practice, however, the proposals are essentially unchanged. For example, the textbook *Of Pandas and People* (Davis and Kenyon 1993), which presents intelligent-design creationism and is by far the most carefully crafted creationist offering to date, follows the same misleading framework of presenting the views of those who hold 'the two' theories of biological origins, natural evolution and intelligent design, neglecting the variety of other views. The terms may have changed, but the dubious strategy it adopts is the same: evolutionary theory is claimed to be riddled with holes, with creationism left as the only alternative. Students are told that the textbook will allow them to do what no other does, namely, let them decide for themselves which theory is true. Of course, the deck is stacked so that evolution appears to lose on every point.

One cannot, however, judge simply from such creationist textbooks how creationism would likely be taught were it allowed in the classroom, since these are currently written more for political than for pedagogical purposes, to present an innocent face and get a foot in the door. (*Pandas*, for example, which is offered as a biology text, contains a long section that gives philosophical arguments for why intelligent-design should not be disqualified as a scientific hypothesis, and why it purportedly does not violate the court rulings that have found teaching creationism in the public schools to be unconstitutional. This is hardly standard fare for secondary school textbooks.) One can get a more realistic sense of what might happen in classrooms by looking at cases in which teachers have gone ahead and taught creationism despite the laws prohibiting it. To give just one representative instance, in a middle school in Harrah, Oklahoma, a suburb of Oklahoma City, a teacher took away students' textbooks and distributed creationist material, teaching the students that a person who believes in evolution cannot believe in God (RNCSE 1998, vol. 18, no. 2, p. 5).

Finally, let me suggest one further way that creationism might be taught that has not been considered in the literature: Creationist views could be taught as illustrations of how *not* to do science. Specific creationist tenets could be presented and then the evidence reviewed, showing how scientists came to see that they were false. If not carried to extremes, this might turn out to be a useful educational exercise, in that examination of some of the many errors of so-called 'creation-science' or 'intelligent design' could help teach students how real science is done. As John Dewey pointed out, science education is a failure if it consists of nothing more than the recitation and memorization scientific facts (Dewey 1964 [1910]; 1964 [1938], p. 19). To teach science well is to teach the methods of scientific reasoning, and a critical examination of creationism could serve very well for this purpose. If the courts were to permit the teaching of creation in public school classrooms, this critical approach could become a common educational exercise in many science classrooms. Indeed, this is the only intellectually responsible way that it could be taught in a science class.

I will return to some of these issues shortly, but having delimited the focus of our discussion, let me now turn to the relevant arguments.

[ . . . ]

## Creationist Extra-Legal Arguments

In pressing for the reintroduction of their views into the schools, creationists most often argue that the legal rulings are themselves unjust in one or another way, appealing to a handful of arguments from fairness, majority rule, parental rights, academic freedom, and censorship. Here I'll briefly review and then respond to these as they have been put forward by creationist lawyer Wendell Bird in a video that creationists air on public access television stations. It was Bird who laid out the legal strategy in the early 1980s of promoting creationism as though it were a science. Bird argued the creationist side in the *Edwards v. Aguillard* case in which the Supreme Court overturned laws that had been based on that strategy. Since that defeat, Bird rarely speaks of 'creation-science' and instead uses the term 'abrupt appearance theory'. Bird's arguments here are representative of the main creationist arguments, but they are not unique to him. Indeed, most of these arguments were previously made by Great Commoner, William Jennings Bryan, in his antievolution crusade that led up to the *Scopes* trial.

By far the most common argument creationists make is to say that it is *unfair* for the law to exclude their view from the public school science classroom. Isn't it biased and one-sided, they challenge, to teach evolution to the exclusion of creationism? Bird argues that 'The only fair approach is to let the children hear all the scientific information and make up their own minds'. Phillip Johnson makes the argument in stronger terms, claiming that excluding creationism amounts to 'viewpoint discrimination' (Johnson 1995, pp. 33–4). Bird tries to bolster the argument by appealing to *majority rule*, saying 'The fact is that, contrary to all of the smoke, the great majority of the American public feels that it is unfair to teach just the theory of evolution'. He cites polls indicating that a large percentage of Americans believe that 'the scientific theory of Creation' should be taught alongside evolution in the schools.[2] This majoritarian argument was the main plank of Bryan's position, and he too cited figures about Americans' beliefs. As Bryan saw it, 'The hand that writes the pay check rules the schools' (Larson 1997, p. 44). A related argument involves claimed *parental rights* to determine what one's children will study in the public schools. If it is granted that parents have such a right, then a creationist parent should be able to insist that creationism be taught or evolution excluded.

Creationists also appeal to what is properly taken to be a prime educational value, *academic freedom*. Bird says:

> To me the basic issue is academic freedom, because no one is trying to exclude evolution from public schools while teaching a theory of creation. Instead, the evolutionists are trying to exclude alternatives, while, in general, defending the exclusive teaching of evolutionism.

This way of putting the argument is somewhat disingenuous, since creationists have indeed tried to exclude evolution from the public schools, and were very successful in keeping it out until just the past few decades. Moreover, they have subsequently tried to exclude it unless it were taught in conjunction with their view, and they continue to work to diminish or undermine its place in the science curriculum in whatever way they can. Bird is correct, however, that science educators do now usually defend the exclusive teaching of the scientific view, and this leads to his final objection. Mentioning organizations that oppose teaching creationism, he concludes that what they are doing amounts to *censorship*:

> They have a very specific desire to preserve the exclusive teaching of evolution and to exclude any teaching of a scientific theory of creation or a scientific theory of abrupt appearance. That's censorship in my view.

We should agree that, at first glance at least, some of these charges exert a powerful emotional pull upon us. No one wants to be seen as engaging in censorship or in unfair, discriminatory exclusion of a popular viewpoint. It is certainly incumbent upon professionals to take such charges seriously, and to examine them carefully to see whether they have merit. When we do this, however, we find that the charges do not apply or are irrelevant to the issue before us.

The notion of parental rights to determine what one's children are to be taught may sound attractive at first, but parents typically have no special expertise about specific subject matter, and they certainly do not have a right to demand that teachers teach what is demonstrably false. A recent poll showed that 44% believe the creationist view that 'Humans were created pretty much in their present form about 10,000 years ago', but it is not relevant that a large number of Americans reject the scientific findings and do not believe that evolution occurred.[3] It does not matter what the poll figures are because matters of empirical fact are not appropriately decided by majority rule. Nor is it 'unfair' to teach what is true even though many people don't want to hear it. Neither are the schools 'censoring' creationism; they are simply and properly leaving out what does not belong in the curriculum.

The charge that such a policy violates academic freedom is not so easily dismissed. One might reasonably dispute about whether academic freedom applies in the public elementary and secondary schools in the same *way* that it does in higher education, but prima facie there seems to be no good reason to think that this important protection should be afforded to university professors and not to others of the teaching profession who serve in other educational settings. However, academic freedom is not a license to teach whatever one wants. Along with that professional freedom comes special professional responsibilities, especially of objectivity and intellectual honesty. Neither 'creation-science' nor 'intelligent-design' (nor any of the latest euphemisms) is an actual or viable competitor in the scientific field, and it would be irresponsible and intellectually dishonest to teach them as though they were.[4]

In the previous century, the situation in science with regard to the question of the origin of species was quite different, but it cannot now be fairly said that the basic theses of evolution are scientifically controversial. There are currently no 'alternative theories' to evolution that scientists take seriously, since the evidence has gone against previous contenders (including the forms of creationism held by 19th-century scientists) and continues to accrue in favor of evolutionary theory, Evolution is in no sense 'a theory in crisis', as creationists purport. This is not to say that there are not interesting, problems that remain to be solved, but that is true of every science, and such issues are of sufficient complexity that they are properly reserved for consideration at professional meetings, in the primary literature, and in graduate programs. Unresolved issues at the cutting-edge of science are well above the level that would be likely to be included in secondary school textbooks. What is included at the lower levels that concern us here is well confirmed and scientifically uncontroversial.

## Epistemological Arguments

Creationists of course refuse to accept the evidence that supports the various hypotheses of evolutionary theory. As they see it, one must look to revelation to determine what is absolutely true, rather than believing the 'mere theories' of science. The basic issue, as they see it, is whose truths are to be taught. God help us, they say, if we fail to teach our children God's Truth. Phillip Johnson has outlined a new legal strategy for reintroducing creationism into the public schools, arguing that excluding the religious perspective amounts to 'viewpoint discrimination'. Citing the 1993 *Lamb's Chapel* case, in which the court found that a school could not bar an evangelical Christian perspective in a class that discussed the subject of family relationships, Johnson claims that it is similarly improper to bar consideration of intelligent design when the topic of biological origins is discussed in science class.

One major problematic assumption behind this kind of argument is thinking that questions about empirical fact are simply a matter of one's peculiar point of view, so that excluding one or another is 'discrimination', in the sense of subjective prejudice rather than the sense of objective assessment of differences. But there is a real difference between what is true and what is false, what is well-confirmed and what is disconfirmed, and surely it is a good thing for science to discriminate the true empirical hypotheses from the false by empirical tests that can tell which is which. Creationists also are interested in truth, but they believe that they already know what the truths are – indeed, as Johnson puts it, with what the truths 'with a capital "T"' are. However, one cannot ascertain truths except by appropriate methods, and creationists are typically unwilling to say even what their special methods are, let alone show that they are reliable.

A second major questionable assumption is that it makes sense to talk about 'the religious' or even 'the creationist' viewpoint. Professor Plantinga recognizes that truths must be ascertained by a justifiable method, but he argues that different epistemological assumptions may be taken to be properly basic. On that ground, he argues for what he calls an 'Augustinian science', in which scientists pursue their research along parallel epistemological tracks. Christians, he tells us, should do their science starting with 'what Christians know' (Plantinga 1997). The problem with this is that there is little that Christians can say univocally that they know.

Christians disagree, sometimes violently, about what it is they supposedly know. With the exception perhaps of Roman Catholicism, fundamentalist Christianity actually provides perhaps the broadest general consensus to be found, since it traces its roots to a series of publications at the beginning of the 20th century; the explicit purpose of which was to try to distill just 'the fundamentals' of the faith. But even our brief view of the factions among creationists reveals the splinters that nevertheless form among even fundamentalists over disagreements about the smallest points of theology. (Intelligent-design creationists try to paper over this problem by remaining silent about the details and promoting the minimal positive thesis that God creates for a purpose. Though even this vaguely stated view may resonate with religious meaning, it is devoid of empirical content – it certainly neither opposes nor supports any particular view about the truth of evolutionary theory – and provides no method of investigation.) The problems increase exponentially once we look beyond Christianity, and bring Hindu, Pagan, Amerindian and other creationist viewpoints into the classroom, taking into account what these other religions take to be properly basic beliefs. If these theologically perspectival epistemologies are taken to stand on a par with ordinary natural science, then what we will be left with is a Balkanized science where specific private revelations that one or another group professes to 'know' and take as given will vie with one another with no hope of public resolution.

The knowledge that we should impart in public schools is not this private esoteric 'knowledge', but rather public knowledge – knowledge that we acquire by customary, natural means. The methodological constraints that science puts upon itself serve to provide just this sort of knowledge, and thus it is scientific knowledge that is appropriate to teach in the public schools.[5]

## Religious Protection Arguments

It is in part because the esoteric knowledge claims of religions are of a different sort than the conclusions of scientific investigation, that we need the special Constitutional protection of freedom of religion. This leads to several additional arguments for excluding creationism from the public schools.

The main reason typically offered against the teaching of creationism is that it improperly promotes one religious view over others. We need not dig into the theological soils in which creationism is rooted to see that this is so. In their literature, creationists write as though they are defending the

Christian faith and that the enemy consists solely of godless evolutionists, but in reality it is the religious who are more often in the forefront of the opposition to seeing creationism taught in the schools. The plaintiffs opposing the 'Balanced Treatment' Act in the Arkansas case included Episcopal, Methodist, A.M.E., Presbyterian, Roman Catholic, and Southern Baptist officials, and national Jewish organizations. Though creationists attempt to portray their views as purely scientific and non-sectarian, other religious groups are not taken in by the disguise, and quite understandably argue that to sanction the teaching of creationism would indeed be to privilege one religious viewpoint over others.

One might argue that this unfair singling out of one view could be avoided by allowing *all* religious views into the science class. So should we then, following the creationists' pedagogic philosophy, teach them all and let the children decide which is the true one? This is hardly a wise course of action, in that it would make the classroom a theological battleground where different religions were inevitably pitted against one another.

Creationists and other conservative Christians often take issue with the Court's interpretation of the Constitution that set up the 'wall of separation' between Church and State in the 1947 *Everson v. Board of Education* case. However, the idea of tossing all religions into the science classroom to see which wins, would violate what some take to be the original intent of the establishment clause of the First Amendment. The influential 19th-century. Supreme Court Justice Joseph Story wrote that its main object was not just to prevent the exclusive patronage of some particular religion that would result from any national ecclesiastical establishment, but also 'to exclude all rivalry among Christian sects' (Larson 1989, p. 93). Religious rivalry and outright persecution was all too common in the American colonies when theocracy was the norm, and it seems reasonable to thank the secularization of the government and the Constitutional policy of religious neutrality in large measure for the fact that the United States has been relatively free of the sectarian violence that continues in other parts of the world. In a comparative religion class, religious differences could be respectfully described and studied, but in the setting of a science class, where the point is to seek the truth by submitting differences to the rigors of crucial tests, it is hard to see how conflict could be avoided.

Creationist law professor Phillip Johnson argues that this rationale of neutrality is 'wearing thin' (1995, p. 28) in that teaching evolution is tantamount to governmental endorsement of naturalism, which he says is the 'established religion' (1995, p. 35) of the West. Here he is giving a variation of a complaint that creationists have made over the decades, that 'evolutionism' is a religion, but this argument has already been tested in court, and evolution has been properly found not to be a religion. Neither is scientific naturalism religious.[6] Scientific organizations might be tempted to get the religious tax exemptions if the court were to rule otherwise, but they could not in good conscience accept them.

Let me mention one further reason to oppose the introduction of creationism into the schools under this heading that I have not seen discussed before, and that some religious people might find to be compelling, namely, that introducing creationism in the science classroom would necessarily place their religious beliefs under critical scrutiny. Creationists typically teach that Christianity stands or falls with the truth or falsity of each and every specific claim in the Bible interpreted literally, or at least 'robustly'. Fundamentalist and evangelical Christian parents who are familiar only with creationist literature (which invariably describes evolution as 'merely a theory', and seen to be obviously false to anyone not 'blinded' by 'naturalistic biases'), do not have any idea of how vast is the amount of evidence that supports evolutionary theory, and how weak are the specific claims of creationists. They also do not recognize that a few of what one might call 'missionary atheists' are as eager as creationists to have the 'Creation hypothesis' included in the public school curriculum, being confident that a side-by-side examination of the claims and evidence would destroy any student's naïve beliefs in the religious view. In my experience, science teachers who teach evolution currently go out of their way to be respectful of their students' religious views and not to challenge them. However, should the curriculum change so that they had to discuss the various 'Creation' or 'design' hypotheses – the Hindu, Amerindian, Pagan, and Raëlian versions, as well as the multiple Christian ones – as though these were simply 'alternative theories', they could not avoid a direct confrontation.[7] Given that we expect the government to neither help nor hinder religion, it would not be a wise policy to open the door to having children's religious beliefs explicitly analyzed and rebutted in the public schools in this way.

## Educational Arguments

In this section, let us set the above considerations aside and simply ask whether it would be a good educational policy to teach creationism if there were no other factors to consider. To answer the question put this way we must turn our attention to philosophy of education more generally.

The choice of what to teach in the public schools must be made in light of the goals of public education. I take it for granted that one of the basic goals of education is to provide students a realistic picture of the natural world we share. Another is to develop the skills and instill the civic virtues that they will require to function in society in harmony. While there are several common purposes of this kind towards which all public education aims, the more specific goals, of course, will vary depending upon, among other things, the age of the student. It makes little sense, for example, to confront students with material that is beyond their developmental level. We also need to ask what is to be included when one teaches a discipline. What should be taught under the particular subject heading of *Science*? In particular, does creationism belong within that subject area?

If we think of science in terms of its set of conclusions, then it is clear that creationism does not belong. That creationism and science both have things to say about 'the subject of origins' is not sufficient to say that the views of the former are a part of the subject matter we ought to teach. The specific hypotheses of creation-science have been rejected by science as the evidence accumulated against them, and the general thesis that 'God creates' is not a hypothesis that science considers or can treat at all. Some scientists do discuss their theological musings – some theistic, some atheistic – in their popular writings, but research on the questions of the existence, or possible activities and purposes of a Creator simply is not to be found in the primary scientific literature. The only proper way to treat the specific empirical claims of creation-science in a science textbook is, thus, as an interesting historical footnote about hypotheses that have been long overturned.

But now let me return to Dewey's important contention that to teach science properly is to teach not a collection of facts but a way of thought. Science education that focuses only on scientific conclusions, and omits teaching scientific methods, misrepresents the nature of scientific inquiry and fails in its basic mission of preparing students with the best skills to function in the natural world. 'Theistic science', despite its name, rejects science's methodology and therefore does not belong within the subject. 'Creation-science', 'abrupt appearance theory', 'intelligent-design theory' and so on are the creationists' cuckoo eggs that they hope will pass unnoticed, enabling them to garner the resources (and cultural prestige) of science and the forum of the science classroom for their own religious ends.

We should not haggle over mere terminology, but it remains the case that neither the conclusions nor the methods of creationism are properly described as 'science'. Disciplinary boundaries may not be sharply defined, nor should we expect them to be, but they are generally distinguished by a characteristic order. It is because practitioners must adhere to constraints – be they the precedents of (tentatively) accepted conclusions or the procedures of inquiry themselves – that the notion of a 'discipline' makes sense at all.

Could creationism be taught under a different heading, rather than as a science? If 'theistic science' were to prove its value as an independent discipline, then educators might have to consider whether it would be worthwhile in relation to the educational goals of the public schools to include in the curriculum. Historically, theistic science had many centuries to prove itself, but in the end scientists concluded that they had no need of that hypothesis, and contemporary creationists have nothing to show for their attempts to revive the view that theology is the queen of the sciences. Intelligent-design creationists plead that they are only beginning their researches and plead for patience when asked for concrete results of their approach, and at present there is no sign that they will succeed in developing a fruitful discipline. It does not make sense to create a separate class to teach a discipline that does not exist.

The fact that intelligent-design and other versions of creationism have nothing positive to offer accounts for the pattern that we find in all creationist literature and in proposed texts such as *Of Pandas and People*, namely, that they consist almost exclusively of pointing out purported explanatory gaps in evolutionary theory. The 'Creation theory' or the 'design hypothesis' is supposed to win by default. As we have seen, this dual model strategy has appeared in various forms, but the current favorite is in the creationist proposals to teach their view under the heading of 'critical thinking'.

As mentioned above, there is some merit in the idea of considering the creation/evolution controversy as a case study to develop critical thinking. At the university level this can work, but there are several practical obstacles to implementing it at lower levels. The main problem is simply the sheer quantity of material that would have to be covered. It takes a semester-long college course just to give undergraduates an introduction to evolutionary theory, and one needs at least that much background to be able to begin to judge the evidence for oneself. It is also questionable whether high school students have developed cognitively to the degree that would make such an exercise worthwhile. Even some honors level college freshman are not sufficiently mature intellectually to begin that sort of evaluative project.

But there is a more important reason for not following the creationists' proposal to teach critical thinking by criticizing evolutionary theory in the way they desire. Creationists are ideologues who 'know' in advance what is the 'absolutely true' answer to the question of origins, and they want the critical tools to be used against evolutionary theory rather than turned upon their own views. But it is simply not intellectually honest or professionally responsible to teach as though scientific conclusions were simply a matter of opinion, or that the creationist views of the origin of species are on a par with the findings of evolutionary theory.

Consider what the effect would be if we were to buy into the curricular framework that creationists propose; it would not be only evolutionary biology that would have to be put under critical scrutiny. Take, for instance, the subject of world history. There are any number of advocacy groups that, for religious, political or other ideological reasons, advance some idiosyncratic version of history that is at odds with the findings of historians. If we accept the creationists' proposals regarding evolution, we should also be sure to present alternative theories, attach disclaimers to the standard accounts, and give equal time to the 'evidence against' the conclusions of historical research so that the students can judge for themselves. In studying the assassination of President Kennedy, for example, we might begin by screening Oliver Stone's movie *JFK*, and then go on to consider the other theories, such as that Vice President Johnson masterminded his death, or that the CIA was behind it, or the Mafia. When studying the landing of American astronauts on the moon, we should probably issue a disclaimer and respectfully consider the views of those who believe that the whole event was filmed by the government in a secret Hollywood studio as part of an elaborate charade. When teaching about World War II we would need to give balanced treatment to those who hold that the Holocaust never happened and was just a Zionist propaganda ploy to gain sympathy for Jews.[8] But such a notion of 'fairness' and 'balance' is absurd. It is certainly not sound educational philosophy.

We should be no less diligent in teaching the results of careful investigation of the history of life on earth as we are in teaching the history of our nation and the other nations of the world. Critical thinking does not mean indiscriminate thinking, but thinking governed by the rules of reason and evidence.

## Plantinga's Rawlsian Argument

In this final main section, I turn to a new argument put forward by Alvin Plantinga in a paper he titled 'Evolution and Creation: A Modest Proposal'.[9] Rather than directly address the question of whether creationism should be taught in the public schools, Plantinga turns the table and asks whether *evolution* should be taught. His central rebuttal against the arguments I gave above overlaps the earlier creationists' arguments claiming 'unfairness' and 'parental rights'. He links these by appealing to a Rawlsian notion of justice, claiming that every party to the social contract has a basic right (BR), 'not to have comprehensive beliefs taught to her children that contradict her own comprehensive beliefs' (Plantinga 1998). When Jonathan Swift made his own 'modest proposal' that the Irish might solve the problem of starvation during the potato famine by devouring children, it was clear that he was being satirical. It seems, however, that Plantinga means for us to take (BR) seriously, even though its effects upon children's education would be much the same as Swift's. My contention is not, as Plantinga supposes in his paper, that science overrides (BR). I would not accept (BR) in the first place, nor should anyone who is concerned with justice.

Plantinga argues for (BR) as follows: 'The teacher can't teach all or even more than one of . . . conflicting sets of beliefs as the truth; therefore it would be unfair to select any particular one and teach *that* one as the truth' (Plantinga 1998). But this argument is seriously flawed; even if there is no way for everyone to eat the whole pie, it does not follow that

there is no fair way to divide it or even to pick just one person who will get it. Plantinga appeals to the Rawlsian analysis of justice, but does not describe the reasons that he thinks would lead free and equal people in Rawls's Original Position to agree to such a basic right. We need to see this reasoning before we can evaluate the justice of the proposal from a Rawlsian perspective.[10] Perhaps he thinks that it would go something like this: One knows that people are likely to disagree about 'comprehensive beliefs' such as those profound religious beliefs about God and God's methods of Creation, but under the veil of ignorance one does not know what one's own view will be on such matters or whether, say, one would be in a position see to it that only those beliefs were taught in the schools. Plantinga must think that under such conditions rational persons would agree to institute (BR) as a defensive safeguard – since no one could be sure that their own preferred view would be taught, they all would want at least the right to see to it that another view that opposes it not be taught either. In other words, I supposedly would reason as follows: since I might be a creationist whose epistemology tells me that true knowledge comes only from the Bible and that evolution is contrary to God's Truth, I would want the right to exclude evolution from the schools to protect my children from what I would take to be its evil influence. But this reasoning is surely mistaken. Rational agents would never agree to such a gag rule as a basic right for a variety of reasons.

First, to do so would be to gut the curriculum, for even the most well-established facts may threaten some element of some person's comprehensive beliefs. As we saw, creationists' comprehensive beliefs put them at odds with not just the facts of evolutionary biology, but also with the findings of most other sciences. Furthermore, because of the interconnections among scientific theories, opposition to what might appear to be just a single finding, necessarily involves opposition to many other ones as well. Nor are creationists the only ones that would make use of (BR); there are thousands of special interests groups that would use such a right to prohibit the teaching of specific facts or even whole subjects they objected to. One does not have to look far to find parents who would object to teaching about racial equality, the facts of reproductive health, or that even that the earth is round.[11] Only the utterly trivial could have a chance of escaping the gag of (BR). No rational person would agree to such a policy.

Plantinga tries to avoid this conclusion by suggesting that we could teach things hypothetically. That is, while we could teach no account of creation as fact, we could teach them all conditional upon their specific epistemic base (EB). On this proposal, presumably a teacher would have to include a list of hypotheticals, along the lines that 'If one starts with EB-YEC then God created the world and human beings 10,000 years old'; 'If one starts with EB-Raël, then extra-terrestrials created human beings by genetic engineering hundreds of thousands of years ago' and so on. But this has similar problems. Though more people might accept this kind of hypothetical teaching, no doubt there would remain a significant number who would still object to having their children exposed to such ideas even hypothetically. On the other hand, even if we supposed that no parent would exert BR, rational agents would still reject the proposal in that it would have the complementary problem – rather than gut the curriculum, it would balloon it to absurd proportions in that teachers would have to present a huge series of antecedent comprehensive beliefs (potentially every parents' specific EB), followed by the relevant consequents for each, again for all but the most trivial issue.

Second, under the veil of ignorance one should not limit one's deliberations to the scenario in which one was a parent with a comprehensive belief that he or she did not want challenged. The rational person would also have to think about being a child growing up in the household of such a parent. Sadly, we all know parents who are bigots or ideologues and others who are simply narrow-minded or ignorant. A good education may be a child's only window to a clear picture of the world and to an open future. To agree to (BR) would be to close that window. This would be a serious harm for the children of such parents. It would harm other children as well, all of whom could be deprived of a decent education, because the public schools could be forced to omit even basic scientific facts, simply because *some* parent found them offensive to his or her private religious beliefs. Indeed, it is difficult to think of any substantive fact that could pass unchallenged, if we grant with Plantinga that each person may appeal to (BR) from the warrant of her personal 'epistemic base' (EB$_p$). Judging the question after considering the points of view of both parents and children, rational persons in Rawls's Original Position would reject (BR). Thus, a school policy that ignores (BR) is not unjust, for (BR) itself is unjust.

So, what *would* rational agents agree to? They would assent, I believe, to something very similar to our current system, along the lines I mentioned above – a separation of the public and the private. They would require that public institutions, like the public schools, not teach views based upon 'private epistemologies' such as special revelation, because one cannot rationally adjudicate among beliefs that different persons purport 'to know' simply 'as a Christian' or a Hindu, a Raëlian, a Pagan, or whatever. Rational agents would agree to a basic right to hold such beliefs privately, but as a defensive measure, would not want the government to support beliefs of this sort even 'conditionally', as in Plantinga's proposal, since it would be impossible for schools to teach the myriad of private views without favoring some over others. Instead they would require that public institutions be constrained to public knowledge. In teaching about the empirical world, this means that the schools should limit their science curriculum to scientific findings – testable conclusions that we can rationally draw on the basis of observational evidence and the methodological assumption of natural law.

Although for such reasons I am afraid we cannot stomach the main entrée that Plantinga offers, perhaps we may still at least break bread together in another way. While we cannot agree that we should teach creationism even conditionally, we can agree that we should not teach science (including evolutionary theory) dogmatically. Scientific truths are never more than approximate, and always come attached with some greater or lesser degree of likelihood that depends upon their evidential support. While it may be reasonable to teach well-confirmed findings as 'sober' truths, scientists must always remain cognizant that even these might have to be revised should new evidence appear that undermines their support; even 'settled' truths may not legitimately be put forward as being absolute. The good science teacher will point this out. This is not the same as teaching science 'conditionally', as though its epistemic base were no better or worse than any private epistemology; rather it is just a straightforward acknowledgment of some features of its methodology. Knowing the rational limits of science, the rational person would agree not to have it portrayed as something it is not. It is not a religion and should not be taught as one. Its findings are trustworthy, but they are not dogma.[12] Teaching science simply as a set of facts to be memorized can make it seem like a catechism, but teach science properly, by also teaching its methods of investigation, and dogmatism will not be an issue. Creationists and others who hold to some private epistemology may still teach in their homes and churches that man does not live by bread alone, but surely the reasonable and just compromise is to agree that in the public schools we should content ourselves with sharing science's simple, basic fare.

## The Answer

In reviewing the arguments, we find many good reasons for excluding creationism from the schools, and few good reasons for not doing so. On balance, it seems clear that the wiser course is not to allow the conflict into the classroom. Should creationism be taught in the public schools? The answer is that it should not.

## Notes

1. As I revise this paper now in December 1999, evolution disclaimers are making national news again, as the Oklahoma State Textbook Committee, whose appointed membership is heavy with religious conservatives, has just mandated that publishers wishing to do business with the state include the same disclaimer that is used in Alabama in any textbook that includes evolution.

2. Such a poll question is misleading and biased, however, in that it assumes what is false, namely, that there is just *one* theory of Creation, and that it is a science.

3. The 44% figure comes from a November 1997 poll. There has been no statistically significant change in the percentage of Americans who accept this creationist view since 1982 (45%), when the Gallup poll began to track beliefs about human origins. The social, political and demographic breakdown of the poll figures showed that 'those most likely to believe in the *creationist version* were older Americans, the less well-educated, southerners, political conservatives (the New Religious Right?), biblical literalists, and Protestants, particularly in fundamentalist denominations such as Baptists' (Bishop 1998).

4. It should be obvious, but let me nevertheless state explicitly that in making these arguments I am taking it for granted that evolutionary theory is true. I mean this, of course, in the standard scientific sense of approximate, revisable truth; no one thinks that evolutionary theory is complete or that one or another of its specific elements might not have to be modified should new, countervailing evidence be found. Creationism is false in the basic sense that, whatever its specific positive commitments, it by definition rejects evolution. Most of creationists' specific claims about the processes of the origins of cosmological, geological, and biological phenomena (among others) have been shown to be false as well, provided that we are able to judge these by ordinary scientific means and standards. Note, however, that I do not assume that this means that God does not exist; the larger question of whether a supernatural designer created the world is not answerable simply by appeal to scientific methods. I have discussed some of the evidence for these conclusions elsewhere (Pennock 1999, chapters 2–3), and will not review them here.

5. I previously developed this position in a paper 'Creationism in the Science Classroom: Private Faith vs. Public Knowledge' delivered at the 1995 Conference on Value Inquiry, the proceedings of which have yet to be published. I expand the argument in Pennock (1999, chapter 8), and so will not rehearse it here.

6. I have previously rebutted Johnson's claims about scientific naturalism, and shown how it is a methodological and not a dogmatic view in Pennock (1996), and elaborated that argument in Pennock (1999, chapters 4 and 6).

7. Creationists want to include only their own view, of course. In 1973, they convinced the Tennessee legislature to pass a law that would require public school textbooks to give equal emphasis to the Genesis view and to explicitly identify the evolutionary view of human origins as 'merely a theory' and not a scientific fact, and attached an amendment so that the Bible did not also have to carry that disclaimer, and another amendment to expressly exclude the 'teaching of all occult or satanic beliefs of human origins.' In the 1975 *Daniel v. Waters* case Federal Court of Appeals immediately struck down the law as 'patently unconstitutional', holding that claims to the contrary would be 'obviously frivolous' and did not merit review, citing the amendments in particular and noting that no law could give such preferential treatment to the Biblical view of creation over 'occult' ones (Larson 1989, p. 136).

8. I mention such examples of conspiracy theories intentionally. As one reads creationist literature, from Morris to Johnson and beyond, one is struck by the regularity with which creationists describe scientists as being engaged in a deliberate conspiracy to deceive everyone into accepting evolution so that they might maintain their cultural authority, promote atheism, and spread immorality.

9. As noted earlier, Professor Plantinga's paper was a commentary upon mine and was also read at the December 1998 Association for Philosophy of

Education meeting. All the quotations in this section are from the written version of that paper, which Professor Plantinga kindly provided me so I could write my reply.

10. According to John Rawls's influential view, justice in a pluralistic democracy is a function of fairness, with fairness understood in terms of fair procedures (Rawls 1971). The 'Original Position' is an abstraction of such a procedure in which we are to imagine ourselves as rational persons who are contracting to form what will be the basic social institutions, while under a 'veil of ignorance' that prevents our knowing in advance what position we will hold in that society once it is constituted.

11. On biblical authority, schools in Zion, Illinois around the time of the *Scopes* trial not only rejected evolution, but also 'Modern Astronomy' and its 'infidel theories' of a moving, round earth. See Schadewald (1989) for a description of how the flat-earth view persisted in Zion schools until the mid-1930s, and continues to have a few adherents even today.

12. See Siegel (1984, pp. 359–62) for a rebuttal of the creationist claim that teaching evolution amounts to indoctrination.

# References

Aubrey, Frank (1998) [1980] 'Yes, Virginia, There is a Creation Model', *Reports of the National Center for Science Education* **18**(1), p. 6.

Bishop, George (1998) 'What Americans Believe about Evolution and Religion: A Cross-National Perspective', paper read at 53rd Annual conference of the *American Association for Public Opinion Research*, at St. Louis, Missouri.

Cremo, Michael A. and Thompson, Richard L. (1993) *Forbidden Archeology: The Hidden History of the Human Race* (Alachua, FL: Govardhan Hill Publishing).

Davis, Percival and Kenyon, Dean H. (1993) *Of Pandas and People* (Dallas, TX: Haughton Publishing).

Dewey, John (1964) [1910] 'Science as Subject Matter and as Method', in R. D. Archambault (ed.), *John Dewey on Education: Selected Writings* (Chicago: University of Chicago Press).

Dewey, John (1964) [1938] 'The Relation of Science and Philosophy as a Basis of Education', in R. D. Archambault (ed.), *John Dewey on Education: Selected Writings* (Chicago: University of Chicago Press).

Duvall, J. (ed.) (1995) 'School Board Tackles Creationism Debate', *CNN Interactive (WWW)*, November 5.

Johnson, Phillip E. (1991) *Darwin on Trial*, 1st edn (Washington, DC: Regnery Gateway).

Johnson, Phillip E. (1995) *Reason in the Balance: The Case Against Naturalism in Science, Law & Education* (Downers Grove, IL: InterVarsity Press).

Kitcher, Phillip (1982) *Abusing Science: The Case Against Creationism* (Cambridge: MIT Press).

La Follette, Marcel Chotkowski (ed.) (1983) *Creationism, Science, and the Law: The Arkansas Case* (Cambridge, MA: MIT Press).

Larson, Edward J. (1989) *Trial and Error: The American Controversy over Creation and Evolution*, updated edition (Oxford: Oxford University Press).

Larson, Edward J. (1997) *Summer for the Gods: The Scopes Trial and America's Continuing Debate over Science and Religion* (New York: Basic Books).

Pennock, Robert T. (1996) 'Naturalism, Evidence and Creationism: the Case of Phillip Johnson', *Biology and Philosophy* **11**(4), pp. 543–59.

Pennock, Robert T. (1999) *Tower of Babel: The Evidence against the New Creationism* (Cambridge, MA: MIT Press).

Plantinga, Alvin (1997) 'Methodological Naturalism?', *Perspectives on Science and Christian Faith* **49**(3), pp. 143–54.

Plantinga, Alvin (1998) 'Creation and Evolution: a Modest Proposal', unpublished conference paper.

Rawls, John (1971) *A Theory of Justice* (Cambridge, MA: The Belknap Press of Harvard University Press).

Reisch, George A. (1998) 'Pluralism, Logical Empiricism, and the Problem of Pseudoscience', *Philosophy of Science* **65**, pp. 333–48.

RNCSE (Reports of the National Center for Science Education) (1998), vol. 18, no. 2.

Ruse, Michael (ed.) (1988) *But is It Science? The Philosophical Question in the Creation/Evolution Controversy* (Buffalo, NY: Prometheus Books).

Schadewald, Robert (1989) 'The Earth was Flat in Zion', *Fate*, May, pp. 70–9.

Siegel, Harvey (1984) 'The Response to Creationism', *Educational Studies* **15**(4), pp. 349–64.

Smith, Mike U., Harvey Siegel and Joseph D. McInerney (1995) 'Foundational Issues in Evolution Education', *Science & Education* **4**, pp. 23–40.

# 59

# Conflicting Philosophies of School Sex Education

## Michael J. Reiss

Almost everyone – including parents, students, pupils, professional educators and politicians – agrees that sex education is an important issue. However, there still exists widespread disagreement as to what its aims should be, how these should be realised, and indeed whether sex education should be taught in schools at all. To some extent these disagreements result from unstated assumptions about the content, methodology and aims of sex education. In addition, a consensus does not exist as to whether teachers of sex education should adopt a particular moral framework in this area.

In a recent survey of the aims of sex education in Europe and the USA, I concluded that these have broadened over the years (Reiss, 1993). Before the Second World War, what sex education took place was seen as a way of reducing illegitimacy and decreasing the extent of sexually transmitted diseases. In a modified form these aims remain today. Most educators would hold that sex education should reduce teenage pregnancy and help prevent transmission of HIV and other causes of sexually transmitted diseases.

Other aims of sex education have been added over time, often because any one aim (e.g. appropriate knowledge about contraception) has been found to be pointless unless accompanied by other aims (e.g. ability to be assertive). Most of today's programmes of sex education seek to provide knowledge to do with human development and reproduction while at the same time attempting to reduce embarrassment and enabling students to think for themselves about their sexuality and sexual behaviour. Many programmes also seek to develop decision-making skills or assertiveness, while some encourage a feminist perspective on sexuality.

Although philosophers have written quite extensively about sex, surprisingly little has been written from a philosophical perspective about sex education. In an early and important piece of writing, Harris (1971) concluded that sex education should promote rational sexual autonomy. More recently, Jones (1989) agreed with this, but added two further desired outcomes:

> One of these is working towards minimizing the unhappiness felt on account of sexual matters and helping people to achieve as much sexual satisfaction and pleasure as possible. The other is the fostering of enquiry into, and critical reflection on, sexual issues, i.e. encouraging disinterested enquiry in this area. (Jones, 1989, p. 57)

Previously published in *Journal of Moral Education* 24(4) (1995), pp. 371–82. © 1995 The Norham Foundation. Reprinted with permission of Taylor & Francis and the author.

The aim of this paper is to describe and assess critically the main philosophical frameworks within which sex education in the United Kingdom is presented through published materials used in schools. Ideally, a philosophical framework for sex education would articulate fully its assumptions and make closely argued links to the philosophical and health education literatures. The term "philosophical framework", however, is used here more loosely. A framework is identified as philosophical if it attempts to address in a sustained and coherent way questions of meaning and justification relating to its presuppositions and recommendations.

## Methodology

Relevant sex-education materials were read or watched. The materials encompassed books, articles, Local Education Authority guidelines, sex education policies produced by individual schools, pamphlets, computer programmes and videos. Most of the materials had been collected by myself over the last 10 years; many are out of print although still used in schools and departments of education. I suspect that the philosophical frameworks identified below are found in many other countries outside the United Kingdom, but the difficulty of obtaining literature in this field, much of which is produced locally or is ephemeral, precluded a less parochial survey.

I am, of course, well aware that the sex education that children receive in schools (the implemented curriculum) may differ significantly from the intended curricula reviewed here, and that what children learn (the attained curriculum) may differ significantly from either or both of these. However, these distinctions do not negate the importance of studying the intended messages presented by those who put together school sex education materials.

A final preliminary point. The aim of this paper is not to criticise specific sex education materials. Obviously I have my own subjective views about the validity and worth of these materials. However, the aim is rather to identify the various philosophical positions which are adopted in this field. In some cases a piece of sex education material adopts more than one of the positions I have identified. Whether or not this is educationally helpful generally depends on the clarity with which the two, or more, positions are identified and related to one another. However, this does mean that any extract I cite should not be

taken as necessarily representative of the whole of the material from which it is taken.

Having examined the various materials, I identified a total of five main philosophical positions or frameworks. It is difficult, objectively, to defend my identification of these five positions but I hope those familiar with the principles and practice of school sex education will find that they are broadly consonant with their own perceptions. In each of the five sections that follow I describe one of these positions and then attempt to identify its strengths and weaknesses. It is not, of course, the case that these five positions are mutually exclusive. It is perfectly possible that a school could adopt elements from more than one of them. In the final section of this paper I attempt to suggest what, in practice, schools might do in this area.

Two other points: first, I have not attempted to comment on the age-specific suitability of the various philosophical positions identified here. Most sex educators believe that school sex education should take place across the whole of the 5–16/19-year age range. If the reader wishes to keep a particular age range in mind, a 12–14-year-old may be imagined. Secondly, no especial significance should be attached to the order in which I treat the five identified philosophical positions on school sex education, beyond the fact that they are ordered so as to make it easiest, I hope, for the reader to see the relationships between them.

## Five Philosophical Positions

### School Sex Education Should Not Occur

Perhaps the most straightforward philosophical position to adopt in respect to school sex education is to assert that it should not take place. For example, an article in *Family Matters*, the newsletter of the Conservative Family Campaign, states that:

> Under the banner of education, teachers have become seducers – corrupters of innocence who usher young people into forbidden sexual experiences that lead to teen pregnancy, abortion, sexual diseases, and mental and emotional problems. (Masters, 1992)

To some, such a quote, and by association the more general argument that schools should keep out of sex education, may appear extreme. However, the main point made by those who believe that school sex education should not occur is that sex education is the responsibility of parents. Schools do not have the right to deal with such matters, nor do they have the abilities. All too often, it is maintained, schools adopt an amoral, or even an immoral, approach. It is sometimes argued that childhood is a time of innocence and that that time should not be shortened through a premature exposure to the world of adults. Further, teachers may lack the skills and abilities needed to teach sex education. Perhaps even more importantly, teachers may hold very different beliefs and values from those held by parents.

A strength of this approach is that it places the onus for sex education firmly on parents. It therefore prevents parents shrugging their shoulders and leaving schools to "deal with it". Further, interviews with ex-pupils often show that schools provide little or no effective sex education (e.g. Allen, 1987).

There are, however, a number of difficulties with this approach. An immediate difficulty is that, in one sense, a school cannot avoid sex education occurring. It is impossible, for instance, to teach almost any piece of literature without transgressing onto the field of sex education. Consider, for instance, Shakespeare's *Romeo and Juliet*, Hardy's *Tess of the D'Urbervilles* and Laurie Lee's *Cider with Rosie*. Each of these has relationships between men and women at its heart. Similarly, imagine biology without human reproduction, geography without population studies, history without the suffragette movement, or religious education without a consideration of the roles of men and women. Each of these subjects would be emasculated (if that is not too sexist a term) by the exclusion of such matters.

Further, school sex education is not simply a matter of scattering particular topics across the time-tabled curriculum. Sexuality and gender issues are built into the very structure and ethos of the school. Anyone who has sat on an equal opportunities working party knows how every aspect of school life gives messages to pupils about what it is to be male or female.

Another problem with the suggestion that schools should avoid sex education is that surveys consistently show this is the opposite of what young people and their parents want. In her 1985 survey of 14–16-year-olds and their parents in three cities in England, Isobel Allen found that 96% of the parents and 95% of the teenagers felt that schools should provide sex education (Allen, 1987). Much the same had been reported earlier by Christine Farrell, who found in 1974 that 96% of parents interviewed thought that sex education should be provided at secondary school (Farrell, 1978).

A further difficulty with this philosophical framework is that it cannot safely be assumed that parents are always more suited than schools to deliver sex education. Think of a child who has been sexually abused by his or her father. Of course, sexual abuse can, and sometimes does, occur in schools, but it is surely the case that effective sex education in such schools would reduce the incidence of school-based child abuse, or at any rate not cause it to increase.

## School Sex Education Should Promote Physical Health

On the presumption that school sex education should take place, perhaps the simplest philosophical position to take is that a school should do what is necessary to promote the physical health of its pupils. Traditionally, this has been taken to mean that schools should teach pupils about puberty, pregnancy, contraception and sexually transmitted diseases. Indeed, the Royal College of Obstetricians and Gynaecologists, in its 1991 Report on "Unplanned Pregnancy", put sex education in schools top of its list of recommendations in the belief that school sex education was the most important factor in helping to reduce unplanned and unwanted pregnancies (RCOG, 1991).

It is often argued that sex education in general, and teaching about contraception in particular, leads to an increase in under-age sexual activity (e.g. White, n.d.). In fact the most recent and thorough reviews of the literature, sponsored by the World Health Organization, strongly conclude that, if anything, the opposite is the case:

> In summary, the overwhelming majority of articles reviewed here, despite the variety of methodologies, countries under investigation and year of publication, find no support for the contention that sex education encourages sexual experimentation or increased activity. If any effect is observed, almost without exception, it is in the direction of postponed initiation of sexual intercourse and/or effective use of contraceptives. (Grunseit and Kippax, 1993, p. 10)

It has proved more difficult to evaluate the effectiveness of school sex education in reducing the incidence of sexually transmitted diseases.

It might be thought that the promotion by a school of the physical health of its pupils/students is a relatively uncontroversial matter. As we have seen, there is a certain amount of disagreement as to whether sex education actually achieves its aim in this area. Let us assume, however, that school sex education either has no effect on the rates of sexual intercourse and conceptions, nor on the transmission of sexually transmitted diseases, or actually reduces one or more of them. Let us further make the reasonable assumption that, among under-16-year-olds/teenagers, this enhances physical health. Despite the granting of these assumptions it is not, however, the case that this means that this aim of sex education is necessarily right. To presume this is to assume the ends (less under-age sexual intercourse, fewer under-age pregnancies and lower rates of sexually transmitted diseases) justify the means that achieve them.

Suppose, for instance, that sex education reduces teenage pregnancy rates through the wider use of contraceptives, but at the same time increases the incidence of sexual activity – a possible result, some would argue, of an HIV-induced "condom culture". Some people will conclude that this is a desirable state of affairs; others – for example because premarital or under-age sexual intercourse is deemed wrong – the contrary. Even if a sex education programme reduced the extent of under-age sexual intercourse and led to lower rates both of pregnancy and sexually transmitted diseases, it could still be the case that this might be an undesirable state of affairs. This would be so if the teaching methods were unacceptable, for instance if pupils were given untruthful or misleading information (e.g. if the health risks of under-age conception were exaggerated). In other words, sex education cannot be solely about the promotion of physical health.

On the other hand, the belief that sex education should promote physical health may have surprising implications. There is good evidence that gay and lesbian pupils are several times more likely to commit suicide than their heterosexual counterparts (Khayatt, 1994). It seems likely that certain types of sex education could reduce this incidence. In other words, the wholehearted adoption of a sex education specifically geared towards the promotion of physical health might lead to some radical and controversial programmes.

## School Sex Education Should Promote Personal Autonomy

As has already been mentioned, Harris (1971) and Jones (1989), each writing from a philosophical perspective, agree that sex education should promote rational sexual autonomy. This position is adopted in a number of Local Education Authority and school policies on sex education. For example, Hampshire's guidelines for sex education state that one of the aims of sex education is that it should "promote the ability to make informed decisions" (Hampshire Education, n.d., p. 4). Similarly, Surrey's curriculum guidelines for sex education present three main aims of sex education, one concerned with knowledge, one with attitudes and one with behaviour. The behaviour aim states:

> The acquisition of skills for decision-making, communicating, personal relationships, parenting, and coping strategies. Many different skills are involved in these broad headings and they would include negotiating, asserting, managing feelings and dealing with stress, threat, enticement and prejudice.
>
> To help young people to deal with their own circumstances and where appropriate, to change both themselves and their environment. (Surrey Inspectorate, 1987, p. 3)

The concept of rational personal autonomy is, of course, an ancient one, informed by Plato and other Ancient Greek philosophers and developed further by philosophers with such different presumptions as Kant and Mill. It is generally held that rational personal autonomy is displayed by individuals who act intentionally, with understanding and without external controlling influences that determine their actions (for a fuller discussion see Haworth, 1986). However, each of these three criteria is problematic, especially when young people are considered. Is it realistic to expect actions, particularly sexual actions, to be undertaken intentionally, with understanding and without external controlling influences?

Three responses need to be made. First, these criteria, especially the latter two, can be met to various degrees. A successful sex education can therefore be envisaged as one that significantly enhances them. Secondly, and more substantively, the notion of "understanding" is itself not a trivial one. People are deeply divided about the "facts" of such relevant issues as masturbation, homosexuality and lifetime monogamy. Thirdly it is, obviously, naive to equate "without external controlling influences that determine their actions" with "without being affected in any way by what others think, say or do". No man is an Island, entire of itself, and that is especially true with regard to our sexuality and sexual mores.

Sex educators have increasingly recognised that sex education is not and cannot be value-free. The 1994 Department for Education Circular on sex education requires that "school programmes of sex education should therefore aim to present facts in an objective, balanced and sensitive manner, set within a clear framework of values and an awareness of the law on sexual behaviour" (GBDFE, 1994, p. 6). It is salutary to note that this requirement, which I suspect five years ago would have been greeted by many sex educators with considerable suspicion, was in 1994 received quite positively, in my experience, in the United Kingdom by independent sex educators and organisations such as the Sex Education Forum and Family Planning Association. The belief that morality can be excluded from sex education is becoming less prevalent.

The question then shifts towards the framework of values within which rational sexual autonomy might be pursued. Broadly speaking, three main frameworks can be envisaged: first, a self-centred one; secondly, one that promotes responsible sexual behaviour towards others; thirdly, one within a religious set of values. Although the first of these is not actively advocated by almost anyone who has thought about, or written on, the issue, it can result from the sort of sex education that all too often takes place in many schools. This is the type of sex education that confines itself to, at most, a narrow, biological treatment of puberty, pregnancy and contraception. Although technically amoral, this sort of sex education can be construed by pupils as "do what you want". By analogy, consider the Family Planning Association's statement in its Charter for Sexual Health and Family Planning that "The FPA supports a woman's right to choose abortion rather than continue with an unwanted pregnancy" (FPA, 1990, p. 1). This begs the question of an unborn child's rights. Similarly, much school sex education can omit a consideration of the interests of others, and so present the message "do what's best for you".

### School Sex Education Should Promote Responsible Sexual Behaviour

I take it for granted here that religious perspectives on school sex education include the promotion of responsible sexual behaviour (see the next section in connection with this). Here, rather, I am looking at what a secular philosophy might have to offer beyond the promotion of a rational sexual autonomy.

We can begin by noting that there is, of course, a diversity of secular perspectives on morality. Indeed, the very question as to whether there exists an absolute set of moral values is a source of contention among those who reject a religious set of shared values (Mackie, 1977; White, 1990). However, examination of sex education materials that exclude a religious dimension shows considerable agreement about the sorts of responsible sexual behaviour that should be promoted. For example, three widely cited and influential sex education publications present the following among their aims of good sex education:

> To promote responsible behaviour. To increase individual responsibility for sexual behaviour so that neither one's own, nor one's partner's body or feelings are hurt. This includes not passing on sexually transmitted diseases, initiating unwanted pregnancies, nor forcing unwanted sexual activity on other people. (Went, 1985, p. 19)

> We believe that moral stands such as the elimination of racism, sexism, exploitation and oppression, should be propounded in all work with young people.
> The things we value and strive towards are caring, non-exploitative relationships, the opportunity to learn and grow personally, educational processes that enhance self-esteem, and the chance to share and communicate equally with the women and men in our private and working lives. (Clarity Collective, 1989, Introduction)

> • it encourages awareness and respect of self and others
> • it encourages reflection and responsibility. (Massey, 1991, p. 9)

By avoiding a particular religious slant, a secular approach may appear to avoid charges of bias or indoctrination successfully. In reality, however, a secular approach runs much the same risks of succumbing to these dangers as does a religious approach. One strength of a secular approach is that a teacher adopting it may be less likely than one adopting a religious approach simply to present pupils with the "right answer" to any particular question concerned with sexuality. On the other hand, children in the United Kingdom exist in what is in many ways a secular, certainly a multicultural, society. Because of this, in my experience, many sex educators working in schools with a particular religious affiliation are sensitive to, and experienced at, dealing with issues where a uniform framework of moral values and beliefs cannot be presumed. Of course, this does not mean that only those who teach in a school with a particular religious affiliation can deal with such issues.

A more fundamental question which needs to be addressed by those who advocate a secular approach to school sex education is the extent to which a school should dictate what is right and what is wrong and the grounds on which it does so. An increasing number of sex education materials, for instance, present masturbation as acceptable, even desirable, mainly on the basis that it is widespread and does not do you any physical harm. Now it is indeed the case that masturbation is widespread and does not do you any physical harm, but that is not, of course, a sufficient reason for deeming it to be desirable or even acceptable. Similarly, few of the sex education materials written within a secular framework grapple with the issue of sexual fidelity and whether this is desirable or not: is lifetime monogamy best, or serial monogamy, or promiscuity, or multiple partners, or are there no answers?

### School Sex Education Should Take Place within a Religious Framework

All the major religions have something to say about human sexuality. What they have to say generally derives from their scriptures (e.g. the Torah in Judaism, the Qur'an in Islam) as interpreted by religious leaders (e.g. the Sangha in Buddhism, the Magisterium in Roman Catholicism) in relation to the ongoing worshipful life of believers (e.g. the umma' in Islam, the Church in Christianity).

The first significant attempt in the United Kingdom to agree on a religious perspective on sex education resulted in an agreed statement by members of six major UK religions (Islamic Academy, 1991). This statement described perceived deficiencies in contemporary sex education, listed principles which it was felt ought to govern sex education and provided a moral framework for sex education. The moral framework in question "Enjoins chastity and virginity before marriage and faithfulness and loyalty within marriage and prohibits extramarital sex and homosexual acts", "Upholds the responsibilities and values of parenthood", "Acknowledges that we owe a duty of respect and obedience to parents and have a responsibility to care for them in their old age and infirmity" and "Affirms that the married relationship involves respect and love" (Islamic Academy, 1991, p. 8).

More recently, a Family Planning Association/ Health Education Authority Working Group, of which I was one of 20 members belonging to the various major religions represented in the United Kingdom, produced, *inter alia*, 10 agreed statements on sex education. These were presented under the following headings: Cohabitation, Secular and divine law, Male and female equality, Teachers and sex education, Celibacy, Relationships and marriages, Homosexuality, Disability and sexuality, Faith and changes in society and Respect and differences. These statements were more tentative than those of Islamic Academy (1991). For example, the statement on cohabitation stated:

> The increasing frequency of cohabitation outside marriage has increased dilemmas for some of our faiths. For some, cohabitation outside marriage devalues marriage as it does not fulfil some of the conditions required for a marriage to be valid. For others cohabitation may nowadays sometimes be seen as a possible stage on the journey towards marriage. (Lenderyou and Porter, 1994, p. 42)

A different approach has been taken by the Sex Education Forum which produced a pack with seven religious perspectives on sex, sexuality and sex education, in addition to a secular perspective (Thompson, 1993). This approach chose, therefore, to present a range of views, rather than attempting to reach a consensus.

As anyone familiar with any religious tradition knows, it may be impossible to achieve a consensus about almost any topic concerned with sexuality within that tradition, let alone across distinct religions. For example, within just the Church of England, almost every conceivable spectrum of belief exists on the topic of homosexuality (e.g. Reiss, 1990; Vickerman, 1992; Brown, 1993). For this reason, agreed statements by members of inter-faith working parties may tell one more about the criteria used to identify the members of the working party than about the shared values of the various religions from which they come.

The obvious strengths of any programme of sex education that roots itself firmly within the traditions and understanding of one particular denomination or religion are also its weaknesses. By identifying a distinctive perspective on sexuality such a programme can bring the full riches of that faith's understanding to bear. At the same time, such a programme risks alienating those for whom such a perspective is foreign and indoctrinating even those who may find such a perspective conducive. How sex education within a religious framework can attempt to avoid these twin dangers is a question to which I shall return in the following, final section of this paper.

## A Possible Way Forward

In the United Kingdom we live, as do people in most countries in the world, in a pluralist society in which no single set of shared moral values holds sway. This should not necessarily be seen as a disaster either by those with a religious faith or by those who have a secular perspective. However, it does mean that it is all the more important for schools to construct a moral framework capable of dealing with this diversity of moral views, both in schools and in society generally.

One way forward is for a school with a particular religious or denominational affiliation to adopt a religious framework on sex education. This does not, of course, disqualify such a school from the need for it to prepare its pupils for life in a wider society which fails universally to hold these particular views. Nevertheless, it has been argued that a school that adopts a particular religious framework for its moral ethos can still embrace such liberal educational values as the development of independence and autonomy in its pupils (McLaughlin, 1992). However, it can be objected that the existence of different educational goals and approaches in different schools sits uneasily with the notion of children's rights; from such a viewpoint is the existence of such educational diversity desirable?

What of the bulk of schools that do not commit themselves to a single, shared set of religious values? Such schools may still be able to adopt a common set of values. As outlined in a recent National Curriculum Council discussion paper, all schools can, and should, promote moral development *sensu*:

- The will to behave morally as a point of principle
- Knowledge of the codes and conventions of conduct agreed by society
- Knowledge and understanding of the criteria put forward as a basis for making responsible judgements on moral issues
- The ability to make judgements on moral issues. (NCC, 1993, p. 4)

What is needed is for schools and teachers of sex education to acknowledge that the choice, or identification, of the moral framework within which sex education is taught – recognising that an absence of an explicit, articulated moral framework is itself a moral framework – is a matter of controversy. This, I hope relatively uncontroversial, proposal is worth insisting on precisely because what characterises so many sex education materials is their stridency and the apparent certainty with which their own particular moral stance is posited, nay, promulgated.

From a psychological point of view this may well be because we find issues concerned with sexuality deeply personal and sensitive – as indeed they are and should be. But the personal and sensitive nature of thses issues may mean that we find it threatening to us as individuals when someone disagrees with our views, especially if the views are relatively unexamined and unanalysed.

Fortunately, there is a coherent and quite well established body of educational theory and practice about how to teach controversial issues (Dearden, 1984; Bridges, 1986). With regard to sex education, I suspect a blend of affirmative and procedural neutrality may be best. In this a teacher would elicit information and different points of view about the controversy from pupils and present to them as many sides of the controversy as possible without indicating which she/he personally supports or, if this is unrealistic, without asserting her/his own views too strongly. Such an approach does not, of course, mean that a teacher accepts any comments as valid. Certain attitudes, opinions or behaviours would still be considered unacceptable. (For a detailed discussion about the practical consequences of using these approaches in the teaching of controversial issues see Stradling, Noctor and Baines, 1984.)

To give a specific example, in facilitating a discussion on homosexuality a teacher might enable her/his students to appreciate that a diversity of views on this matter exists; specifically that some people feel that homosexuality (both the state and the expression of that state in sexual behaviours) is natural/normal/good/right, while other people feel that homosexuality is unnatural/abnormal/bad/wrong. A teacher might manage the discussion in such a way that heterosexual students would realise the extent of discrimination and harassment experienced by many gays and lesbians, explore the consequences for all of us of living in a heterosexist culture and would have their ignorance lessened, while any homosexual students would feel acknowledged, not discriminated against and able, if they so chose, to put their points of view without fear of subsequent recriminations.

In conclusion, a pupil receives some sex education in a school even if that school has no formal programme of sex education or if that pupil is withdrawn from timetabled sex education lessons. Valid sex education in schools promotes personal autonomy, requires pupils to consider the needs and wishes of others, and takes place within a moral framework. Genuine dispute exists as to the desired nature of this framework and, because of this, schools need to enable pupils to appreciate the diversity of views that may validly be held about controversial issues related to sexuality.

## References

Allen, I. (1987) *Education in Sex and Personal Relationships: Research Report no. 665* (London: Policy Studies Institute).

Bridges, D. (1986) Dealing with controversy in the curriculum: a philosophical perspective, in: J. J. Wellington (ed.), *Controversial Issues in the Curriculum* (Oxford: Basil Blackwell), pp. 19–38.

Brown, A. (1993) *Sex Education: Guidelines for Church School Governors* (London: The National Society (Church of England) for Promoting Religious Education).

Clarity Collective (1989) *Taught Not Caught: Strategies for Sex Education*, 2nd edn (Wisbech: LDA).

Dearden, R. F. (1984) *Theory and Practice in Education* (London: Routledge & Kegan Paul).

Family Planning Association (FPA) (1990) *Manifesto for Sexual Health and Family Planning* (London: FPA).

Farrell, C. (1978) *My Mother, Said . . . The Way Young People Learned about Sex and Birth Control* (London: Routledge & Kegan Paul).

Great Britain: Department For Education (GBDFE) (1994) *Circular number 5/94 – Education Act 1993: Sex Education in Schools* (London: DFE).

Grunseit, A. and Kippax, S. (1993) *Effects of Sex Education on Young People's Sexual Behaviour* (Geneva: Youth and General Public Unit Office of Intervention Development and Support Global Program on AIDS, World Health Organization).

Hampshire Education (n.d.) *Guidelines: Sex Education in Hampshire schools* (Winchester: Winchester Health Promotion Department).

Harris, A. (1971) What does 'sex education' mean?, *Journal of Moral Education*, 1, pp. 7–11.

Haworth, L. (1986) *Autonomy: An Essay in Philosophical Psychology and Ethics* (New Haven, CT: Yale University Press).

Islamic Academy (1991) *Sex Education in the School Curriculum: The Religious Perspective – An Agreed Statement* (Cambridge: Islamic Academy).

Jones, R. (1989) Sex education in personal and social education, in P. White (ed.), *Personal and Social Education: Philosophical Perspectives* (London: Kogan Page), pp. 54–7.

Khayatt, D. (1994) Surviving school as a lesbian student, *Gender and Education*, 6, pp. 47–61.

Lenderyou, G. and Porter, M. (1994) *Sex Education, Values and Morality* (London: Health Education Authority).

Mackie, J. L. (1977) *Ethics: Inventing Right and Wrong* (London: Penguin).

Massey, D. (1991) *School Sex Education: Why, What and How – A Guide for Teachers*, 2nd edn (London: Family Planning Association).

Masters, R. (1992) Sexual overload: the effects of graphic sex education on innocent minds, *Family Matters*, November 1992, no page numbers.

McLaughlin, T. H. (1992) The ethics of separate schools, in M. Leicester and M. J. Taylor (eds), *Ethics, Ethnicity and Education* (London: Kogan Page), pp. 114–36.

National Curriculum Council (NCC) (1993) *Spiritual and Moral Development – A Discussion Paper* (York: NCC).

Reiss, M. J. (1990) Homosexuality – sense and sensibility, *Crucible*, 29, pp. 66–74.

Reiss, M. J. (1993) What are the aims of school sex education? *Cambridge Journal of Education*, 23, pp. 125–36.

Royal College of Obstetricians and Gynaecologists (RCOG) (1991) *Report of the RCOG Working Party on Unplanned Pregnancy* (London: RCOG).

Stradling, R., Noctor, M. and Baines B. (eds) (1984) An overview, in: *Teaching Controversial Issues* (London: Edward Arnold), pp. 103–21.

Surrey Inspectorate (1987) *Curriculum Guidelines: Sex Education – Primary and Secondary* (Woking: Surrey County Council).

Thompson, R. (ed.) (1993) *Religion, Ethnicity and Sex Education: Exploring the Issues* (London: National Children's Bureau).

Vickerman, S. (1992) *Christianity and Homosexuality* (London: Lesbian and Gay Christian Movement).

Went, D. (1985) *Sex Education: Some Guidelines for Teachers* (London: Bell & Hyman).

White, J. (1990) *Education and the Good Life: Beyond the National Curriculum* (London: Kogan Page).

White, M. (n.d.) [1994] *Children and Contraception – Time to Change? A Critical Appraisal of Government Policy on Teenage Sexual Activity* (London: Order of Christian Unity).

# 60

# The Artistic-Aesthetic Curriculum

## Maxine Greene

You have undoubtedly heard me, over the years, exploring some of the meaning of "art," of "aesthetic education," and you are as aware as I that the search can never be complete. There are at hand copies of the two lectures I gave this summer to both new and returning participants; you will find there a continuing effort to communicate a sense of what informed encounters with the several arts can make possible for people young and old, whoever they are. You will notice that I started with an account of the photography exhibition at the Metropolitan Museum of Art, "The Waking Dream." Part of what I said was, as always, an account of my personal response to what I saw on the several occasions I visited the exhibition. Part of it was an attempt to use the show and the experiences it provoked as a kind of metaphor for the awakenings, the unexpected disclosures, the new vistas made possible by what happens and what can happen during the days spent at Lincoln Center Institute. And, yes, I used it all as a lead-in to a discussion of imagination (which I should like to pursue a little further today), the cognitive capacity which has been so overlooked or ignored or denied by both the political leaders and the educational leaders working to define "Goals 2000" and the various "outcomes" considered necessary for this country's economic and technological growth.

Precisely what is that capacity? Why do so-called "postmodern" thinkers give the imagination a centrality when they talk about the ways in which we become involved with our worlds? Why is it overlooked, either deliberately or unthinkingly, by those expressing interest in the "active learner," in enhanced literacy on every level? Is there not some sense in which the inventiveness, the innovativeness presumably sought in a technological society are related to imagination? Why is the activation of imagination (*your* imagination, your colleagues', your students') so crucial in the realization of works of art? If it is indeed the case that an aesthetic experience requires aware participation on the part of the perceiver, the listener, the reader, how can there be such participation without the ability to bring an "as-if" into being, to look through the windows of the actual to what might be and what ought to be?

Always obsessive to some degree about the importance of both imagination and perception, I have perhaps relied too much upon the poets and

Previously published in *Variations on a Blue Guitar* (New York: Teachers College Press, 2001), pp. 177–85, 227–30. © 2001 by Teachers College, Columbia University. All rights reserved. Reprinted with permission of the publisher.

writers I have loved particularly in the course of my life: Stevens writing about the "blue guitar" and about those rationalists donning sombreros, once they took the risk of looking at "the ellipse of the half-moon"; Bishop writing about inventing the new day, the new year; Woolf yearning for shocks of awareness, for the "moments of being" that depended on disentangling herself from the life of habit, "the cotton wool of daily life"; Walker Percy's "moviegoer" talking about freeing himself from immersion in everydayness and embarking on a "search," a search for new possibilities – about being "on to something," saying that not to be on to something meant being in despair. Always, there is the linking of imagination to the opening of possibility. I have quoted Emily Dickinson: "The Possible's slow fuse is lit / By the Imagination" (1960, p. 689). Can there be any teacher, especially in these days, who can read that without summoning up the faces of apathetic young people, hopeless young people, boys and girls afflicted with a feeling of futility that may well be the worst enemy of education today?

To speak of imagination in relation to encounters with the arts is not to talk of fantasy or castles in the air or false hopes. As I view it (and I know you may not see it in the same way), imagination is what enables us to enter into the created world of, yes, *Charlotte's Web* and *Winnie the Pooh* and *Don Juan*, and Toni Morrison's *The Bluest Eye*, and Shakespeare's *Much Ado About Nothing*, and George Eliot's *Middlemarch*, and Marquez's *Love in the Time of Cholera*, and Puig's *Kiss of the Spider Woman* as novel, film, or musical play. Doing so, we find ourselves creating new patterns, finding new connections in our experience. I quoted Dewey a few days ago on the ways in which art clarifies and concentrates the meanings of things ordinarily dumb and inchoate, and the ways in which works of art can keep alive "the power to experience the common world in its fullness." This would not happen, I am sure, if it were not for the ability to pull aside the curtains of habit, automatism, banality, so that alternative possibilities can be perceived. And it is imagination that makes this kind of experience attainable for people – this break with literalism, this summoning up of the "as-if," the "not yet," the "might be." I think back in my own history and try to recapture what all this has meant and still means for me: the problem of alienation and emancipation in some manner enhanced by my lending Hawthorne's Hester Prynne my life;

the matter of the "soul's slavery" generating all sorts of questions after reading *The Awakening*; the new experiences created by those scenes in the Hebrides in *To the Lighthouse*; the startling and renewed vision of Stravinsky's *The Firebird* in the Harlem Dance Theater's production of the ballet; the peculiar realization made palpable by Pecola's wanting to look like Shirley Temple in *The Bluest Eye* and the remembered girl-child wanting the same thing in Tillie Olsen's "I Stand Here Ironing"; the ideas of invisibility and nobodiness etched in my consciousness by James Baldwin and Ralph Ellison; the alternatives to my standard views of time and history discovered in *A Hundred Years of Solitude*. I could go on and on trying to recapture the ways in which encounters with art forms opened windows in experience for a little girl from Brooklyn, and then for a bigger girl continually (although indirectly) taught to accept things as they were and make the best of them. Indeed, I am not sure even now that thinking of that sort may partially explain why the arts are treated as frivolities and thrust, as they so frequently are these days, quite aside in our schools.

In any case, I want to urge you to go back in your own life narratives and try to recover those moments when imagination, released through certain encounters with the arts, opened worlds for you, disclosed new vistas (not always pleasant ones, I grant), helped you look at things as if they could be otherwise. And, yes, helped you play somehow with language, with the thought of carnival, with having (as James Joyce once said) "two thinks at a time." Then, I believe, you might ask yourself how you actually understand what "art" is and what "aesthetic" means. There is no final, authoritative definition of either, I would remind you; but it remains important, if you are to make your own enthusiasm and your own understanding contagious, for you to be as self-reflective here as you are asked to be with regard to other disciplines. Again, do you cherish the arts because they seem to you to bring you in touch with something transcendent, even some universal value, something that moves you to aspire, to strain upwards, beyond yourself? (When I say that, I think of *King Lear*, of Beethoven's Ninth Symphony, of Verdi's *Requiem*, of Martha Graham's *Night Journey*, of the Sistine Chapel, of certain spirituals.) Is this what you hope for for your students – why you wish to initiate them into something grand and lustrous, beyond the everyday? Or do you value art forms because they express (or embody) the feelings and perceptions of certain peculiarly sensitive and observant women and men – Wordsworth, say, Mary Cassatt, Toni Morrison, Nikki Giovanni, Emily Dickinson, Tennessee Williams, Vincent Van Gogh – who saw and heard more, felt more acutely, were more in touch than ordinary folks like thee and me? Or is it the marvelous perfection of certain magically wrought forms – a Mozart symphony, a Yeats poem, a Joyce novel, Flaubert's *Madame Bovary*, T. S. Eliot's *Four Quartets*, Mark Rothko's mysterious washes opening to unimaginable depths?

Or do you value the art experiences you have had here and in other places because of what they have signified for your own sense of the world around, your own pursuits of meaning? Do you take what we think of as a "participatory" approach to the arts, one based on the belief that the active participation of the perceiver or reader or listener is required for the completion of the artistic process, and that this completion is essential for the aesthetic effect? When you, for example, encounter a work as presumably remote in space and time as Molière's *Don Juan*, according to this view, you will not be likely to have a full experience with it if you take a disinterested, distanced view. Here, too, connections have to be found, can be found, to your own lived experience and your own choices and your own activities. This view (sometimes called "pragmatic") is closely related to what is called the "reader response" theory in the study of literature. The emphasis here is on the qualities of the play and on the lived experience of those who attend to it and work to make it, in its enactment, an object of their experience – something to be grasped in its detail and its fullness. And grasped by the total person, not by a particular subjective cast of mind. As you have seen or will soon see, it is difficult to watch Don Juan in what would seem a total amorality without being moved to ponder your own moral choices and the standards governing them, especially at a time when there appear to be no objective standards recognized and acknowledged by all. Our feelings about class and power cannot but be affected, as must our feelings about fidelity and purity and "the war between men and women." In my own case (and I am sure in some of yours), I cannot quite set aside the Mozart opera, nor the Shaw play about Don Juan, the same Don Juan, "in hell." Nor can I set aside the philosopher Kierkegaard writing about the first stage of development being best represented by Don Juan, with his constant flitting, his constant sampling, his refusal to commit himself. He never reaches the "ethical stage," said Kierkegaard, because he cannot gain the "courage to be" (1940). I know this is the Molière version and not Mozart or da Ponte or Shaw or any of the many who rendered noncommittal, irresponsible behavior; but all the other things I have read and heard and seen play into the lived experience I have with this Don Juan, as I work to make it – physically, dialogically, imaginatively, conceptually – an event in the life I live with others. The meaning of the play is not hidden somewhere in the work; it is not predetermined. According to this view, it emerges more and more clearly in the audience involvement or by means of that involvement, and diverse persons achieve what they look upon as meaningful through their particular attentiveness, their willingness to look through the various perspectives the play presents, and against their own lived worlds.

Now there is no requirement for you to take this view of how to render a work of art open to yourself and, in time, to others. You may well think an appreciation has no "right" to appropriate a work in this fashion. You may think that to focus on experience this way is to lose sight of the work of art, glowing there in its own peculiar space, free of the mundane world. You may think that, for all the talk of context, this approach sacrifices the wonder, the glory, even the "sacred" character of the arts. Or that too little is done to bring the appreciator in touch with the creative impulse that burns like a candle in the artist, a candle that may help those coming close to light their own. In the last analysis, it is a choice you have to make as individual and as teacher, struggling to be true to what you know and have encountered in your life, trying at once to communicate to others in a manner that allows them to reach out freely and make Molière's work and Mozart's and Morrison's and, yes, Madonna's authentically and reflectively and critically their own.

One of the reasons for trying to make this clear in your own terms and in accord with your philosophy is that only then will you be able to communicate to colleagues or administrators or school boards the relevance of what we call aesthetic education or its significance for school restructuring and school reform. And, indeed, this may be one of our central responsibilities: to clarify for ourselves and others how what we do here does relate and might relate to what is commonly described as "active learning" and to the emergence of communities in school. Last time, I quoted Dewey on the ways in which works of art that are widely enjoyed in a community are, he said, "marvelous aids in the creation of such a life" (1980). Naturally, we hope (as you yourselves do) that – in your own encounters with others in your schools – you can enable people to recognize that.

All you need to do is picture your life in workshops in previous years and how, through your mutual participation in learning the languages of the various arts and bringing particular works alive, you did indeed bring a community into being. Not only was it one that brought you together with other people, very often very different people, in shared learning and shared creating; it may well have been a community that enabled you to recover a lost spontaneity in yourself – to feel yourself in the process of shaping a more distinctive identity for yourself because of your being among and in the presence of others. I have seen this over and over, as participant teachers here have sung in ensembles they created, orchestrated their diverse verses in spirituals or other forms, brought a dramatic scene into existence out of what seemed a discordant variety of voices and improvised gestures, discovered not only how dance movement carves out different designs in space, but how a plurality of movements can be ordered into new patterns – sometimes symmetrical, sometimes not – new relations in space and time.

How, on the various levels at which you teach, can you create the kinds of situations where involvement with the arts not only enables you and your students to combat boredom and banality, but develops among all of you the sense of agency that is most apparent (or so it seems to me) in encounters with the arts? This takes me back, of course, to the participatory approach or to the "reader response" approach. I have in mind the notion that works of art can never be realized by a merely passive attention. There has to be an active, energetic reaching out – so that the noticing we have so often described will take place, so that diverse perspectives can be looked through when it comes to a poem or painting or play, and diverse frequencies can be attended to when it comes to a musical piece. It is with this in mind, of course, that we attach so much importance to the work done with teaching artists – to the moving, and sounding, and rendering that engage you with the actual languages of the arts, with the perceptual landscapes out of which they grow, and with the

meanings that can be sedimented upon those perceptual landscapes, the landscapes of pattern and shape and color and sound where our lives began. How can we think of this in connection with the teaching of history, of social studies, or of the interdisciplinary humanities courses we begin to see in the so-called "coalition" schools? How can we show the connection between our attentiveness to the concrete particularities of things in the domains of the arts and the posing of investigative, curious, sometimes impassioned questions that lead to the general descriptions, the overarching explanations of the sciences? How can the problem-solving of the choreographer, of the painter, of any of those who deal with relation, with design, with the shifting shapes of organization, be at once appreciated, participated in, and connect with what it is to "do" math? How can involvement with Hudson River landscapes, and Tuscan landscapes, and British Midlands landscapes, and French impressionist landscapes release visual imagination – and at once provoke questions that lead to doing geography? How can we in public schools play our part in the "blurring of the disciplines," so that aesthetic education becomes resource and provocation, so that the arts become centrally significant even as they open spaces on the "margin" where moments of freedom and presence occur? Here is where your inventiveness – along with that of your teaching artists – comes in. We all have a world to make, in a larger world that does not always understand.

Last time I spoke, I tried to argue for the connection between what we do here and what might happen as we deal with multiculturalism and its multiple demands. I will not repeat again the powerful arguments for paying heed to works thrust consciously or thoughtlessly outside the range of our attention over the years – some of them now regarded as some of the finest human creations in history. I always think of South American literatures, about which I knew so little for so long, about Mexican art over the centuries, about Cambodian dance in its enormous intricacy and symbolic power, about the sculptures of Benin. I could go on; so could any one of you. It seems to me that, if we are to do justice to the works now being brought to our attention, we ought not simply add them to curricula in a kind of categorical way, or with a kind of affirmative action attitude. There is no question that the enrichment and enlargement of the works at hand are necessary and important: children, in so many ways feeling themselves to be strangers, clearly benefit if they find books and plays and other works of art that have to do with people who look like them and act as their families do. But there is more: there is, again, the importance of doing justice to the works from other cultures, of enlarging the experiences of people within our own culture, of making it possible for them to participate well enough in a variety of art forms so as to lend them (as they do more familiar works) their lives. How do we choose? How do we avoid the presumption that all the different art forms of another culture are equally valuable – and, in doing so, imposing another kind of stereotype? The philosopher Charles Taylor addresses "the politics of recognition" in the following passage:

> Indeed, for a culture sufficiently different from our own, we may have only the foggiest idea . . . of in what its valuable contribution might consist. Because, for a sufficiently different culture, the very understanding of what it is to be of worth will be strange and unfamiliar to us. To approach, say, a raga with the presumptions of value implicit in the well-tempered clavier would be forever to miss the point. What has to happen is . . . a "fusion of horizons." We learn to move in a broader horizon, within which what we have formerly taken for granted as the background to valuation can be situated as one possibility alongside the different background of the formerly unfamiliar culture. The "fusion of horizons" operates through our developing new vocabularies of comparison. (1992, p. 67)

Taylor concludes by saying that we do indeed owe all cultures the presumption that each has something important to say; but, at once we have to try to understand how other cultures make their judgments of worth.

We have to attend to the members of other cultures – to see how they read the materials of their own cultures, and how they interpret the materials of ours. I find myself extraordinarily taken by the African novelist Achebe's reading of Joseph Conrad's *Heart of Darkness*, because he sees things I never saw. Similarly, Edward Said's reading of Albert Camus' *The Plague* emphasizes the fact that the Arabs who died of plague are, compared with the Europeans in the book, all nameless and faceless. Achebe does not say, however, that we ought not to read Conrad. His reading, like Said's reading of Camus, extends the range of imaginative possibility beyond what we were capable of seeing for ourselves. I admire enormously – and gain

inordinately from – Toni Morrison's reading of *Moby-Dick* and of Willa Cather's *Sapphira and the Slave Girl* and of certain Hemingway short stories. Such readings remind us that our canon, our standards, take up a relatively small place in the world; such readings offer us expansion as well as inclusion.

I am reminded of this expansiveness on occasions when a rich dialogue takes place in my classroom after people have read a novel from a participatory or "reader response" point of view, when they have – against the background of their own lived lives – looked through the diverse perspectives the book provides and achieved it as meaningful for themselves. Speaking with their own voices, perceiving from their own locations, they are very likely to articulate a range of meanings. When it is over, the work in question (*The Great Gatsby, Invisible Man, The Bluest Eye*, "Bartleby the Scrivener") is richer, more suggestive, full of more possibilities than it was in my own reading, despite the number of critics I called upon to help me. If we can teach people to notice what is there to be noticed, if we can enable them to reflect upon the medium in use (the language, the paint and canvas, the clay), if we can move them to release their imaginations and break with literal expectations, we are more likely to do justice to a range of works of art, even if we can make no final judgments about their quality.

With what we have said here about expansion and new perspectives and experiential possibilities, we can only welcome the challenges of multiculturalism. Multiplicity means a new opening, after all, in an often monological world. And we are learning that we cannot cover everything that comes to our attention: we can only make them exist as possibility for our students. If our students are attentive, if they are authentic, if they are aware of the fact that all the works they encounter belong to diverse contexts that on some level must be understood, our teaching can be the kind of teaching that moves all kinds of persons to take their own initiatives as they learn how to learn. Perhaps, as they move toward the "fusion of horizons," they can make their own judgments in collaboration with others. They can, at once, attend to the judgments made by members of other cultures – not only of what is valuable in their worlds but of what demands confrontation in our own. Yes, we want our students, in the expanding communities in which they will live their lives, to attend to particulars, to engage, to move in the spaces opened by works of art, each of which (we may discover) makes its own distinctive demands. We need to hold in mind somehow that many works of art (wherever they come from) address themselves to human freedom – meaning the capacity to choose and (we would hope) the power to act in a changing world. We want our students to choose themselves and to be strengthened in their choosing by art experiences that open doors, that allow them to realize how wide and various and enticing the contemporary world can be. I have been trying to say throughout that we are all in process, we who are teachers along with those we teach. And in a pluralist world, with newcomers appearing every day, we somehow have to realize that no one of them is fixed forever, identified forever by a culture, a religion, a class, an ethnic identity. Like ourselves, they may be aware of their roots, of their beginnings, but like ourselves, they need to use their imaginations "to light the slow fuse of possibility." Feeling our own new beginnings, we have been learning here – as the seasons give way to new seasons, as things change and change again – what it means to break with anchorage, what it means to move with others, to care for others, to reach beyond where we are.

## References

Dewey, J. (1980) *Art as Experience* (New York: Perigee Books).

Dickinson, E. (1960) *The Complete Poems of Emily Dickinson*, ed. T. H. Johnson (Boston, MA: Little, Brown).

Kierkegaard, S. (1940) Stages on life's way. In R. Bretall (ed. and trans.), *Kierkegaard* (Princeton, NJ: Princeton University Press).

Taylor, C. (1992) *Multiculturalism and "the Politics of Recognition"* (Princeton, NJ: Princeton University Press).

# Index

# Index